SPECIALIZED ADMINISTRATIVE LAW
OF THE EUROPEAN UNION

Specialized Administrative Law of the European Union

A Sectoral Review

Edited by

HERWIG C. H. HOFMANN

*Professor of European and Transnational Public Law,
University of Luxembourg*

GERARD C. ROWE

*Professor emeritus of Public Law,
Viadrina European University Frankfurt (Oder)*

ALEXANDER H. TÜRK

Professor of Law, King's College London

OXFORD
UNIVERSITY PRESS

OXFORD
UNIVERSITY PRESS

Great Clarendon Street, Oxford, OX2 6DP,
United Kingdom

Oxford University Press is a department of the University of Oxford.
It furthers the University's objective of excellence in research, scholarship,
and education by publishing worldwide. Oxford is a registered trade mark of
Oxford University Press in the UK and in certain other countries

Published in the United States of America by Oxford University Press
198 Madison Avenue, New York, NY 10016, United States of America

British Library Cataloguing in Publication Data
Data available

Library of Congress Control Number: 2018948335

ISBN 978–0–19–878743–3

Printed and bound by
CPI Group (UK) Ltd, Croydon, CR0 4YY

Editors' Preface

This edited collection aims to provide a deepened understanding of the administrative implementation of European Union public policy through a treatment of EU sectoral administrative law, across a wide range of policy fields. This is intended, inter alia, to demonstrate how sector-specific administrative structures, bodies, competences, procedures, forms of action, and controls in the numerous and diverse policy areas of the Union are influenced by, and themselves influence, the generally applicable EU administrative law. In doing so, the work seeks to amplify and deepen the coverage provided by *Administrative Law and Policy of the European Union* (Hofmann, Rowe, and Türk, OUP 2011; second revised edition forthcoming), where we explored the *general* legal framework for administrative action in the European Union. Much of the law discussed there has, though, itself emanated from policy-specific settings. A detailed treatment of special EU administrative law is necessary because, despite there being a substantial body of general administrative law, the bulk of the Union's administrative law is indeed particular to such policy-specific settings. A presentation of the Union's general administrative law cannot do justice to that diversity and variation. The key aim, therefore, of the present volume is to meet that need. This book is thus intended as a companion and complement to, and an expansion of, our treatment of general administrative law.

In order to achieve this goal, we seek to illuminate further the roles and interactions of Union and Member State institutions and bodies, as well as those of private parties, international organizations, and third countries. Also, our intention is to illustrate the application and relevance of general principles and approaches in specific policy settings. Moreover, the present work offers the opportunity for comparisons across sectors and, where matters are duplicated, provides indications of where a more comprehensive general approach could be advantageous for the Union. In addition, we point to policy areas which have proven to be fertile testing grounds for approaches sometimes adopted later in other areas.

It should be noted here that not all possible sectoral fields of Union law and policy are covered in this work. The aim of the present collection is to provide at least an indicative illustration of distinguishing sectoral elements and characteristics, through chapters which cut across virtually all the possible sub-categories of Union sectoral policy, noting the diversity, divergences and convergences, and overlaps. If nothing else, this survey should stimulate thinking, and further work, on the issues identified, as well as offering practical guidance for those active in one or more of the sectors addressed, or in comparable sectors.

The need for a deeper understanding of the administrative law of the European Union should not be underestimated. Political discourse and media treatment often reflect misunderstandings of the way in which the European Union operates on a day-to-day basis, misunderstandings which may feed misconceptions—and indeed distortions—of the very nature of the Union. The unifying aim of the editors and the contributors, is therefore, to offer a deeper and more exact understanding of the administrative operation of the Union. This, in turn, is intended to highlight the unique character of the public administration which takes place within it, while at the same time offering criticisms which might lead to the improved functioning and healthy evolution of Union law, which is, in our view, the legal foundation of one of the most impressive and successful attempts in the supranational exercise of public power anywhere in the world.

We, the editors, thank the many authors in this work, and congratulate them on their valuable contribution to that larger goal.

H.C.H.H, G.C.R, A.H.T.
Luxembourg and London
Spring 2018

Summary Table of Contents

Detailed Table of Contents

PART I INTRODUCTION

PART II FOREIGN RELATIONS AND AFFAIRS

PART III SECURITY AND JUSTICE

PART VII DISTRIBUTIVE POLICY

Chronological Table of Cases of the Court of Justice of the European Union

DECISIONS OF THE COURT OF JUSTICE

OPINIONS OF THE COURT OF JUSTICE

DECISIONS OF THE GENERAL COURT

DECISIONS OF THE CIVIL SERVICE TRIBUNAL

Table of Other Cases

Table of Legal Acts of the European Union

REGULATIONS

DIRECTIVES

DECISIONS

COMMISSION DIRECTIVES

Table of International Treaties and Conventions

List of Abbreviations

AAP	annual action programme
ACER	EU Agency for the Cooperation of Energy Regulators
ACER Regulation	Regulation (EC) No 713/ 2009 of the European Parliament and of the Council establishing an Agency for the Cooperation of Energy Regulators OJ 2009 211/ 1
ACP	African, Caribbean and Pacific countries
ACTA	Anti-Counterfeiting Trade Agreement
AD Regulation	Regulation 2016/1036 on protection against dumped imports from countries not members of the European Union
ADA	WTO Anti-Dumping Agreement
AETR	European Agreement on Road Transport (*Accord Européen sur les Transports Routiers*)
AFET	Foreign Affairs Committee
AFSJ	Area of Freedom, Security and Justice
AG	Advocate General
AGP	Agreement on Government Procurement
AML	anti-money laundering
AP	Action plan
ARO	Asset Recovery Office
AS Regulation	Regulation 2016/1037 on protection against subsidized imports from countries not members of the European Union
ATM	Air Traffic Management
Birds Directive	Directive 2009/147/EC of the European Parliament and of the Council of 30 November 2009 on the conservation of wild birds, OJ 2010 L 20/7–25 (Birds Protection Directive)
BIT	Bilateral Investment Treaty
BOI	Binding Origin Information
BTI	Binding Tariff Information
CA	Contracting Authority
CAP	Common Agricultural Policy
CBHC	Cross-Border Health Care
CCIP	Customs Code Implementing Provisions
CCNR	Central Commission for the Navigation of the Rhine
CCP	Common Commercial Policy
CCT	Common Customs Tariff
CEAS	Common European Asylum System
CEE/CEEC	central and eastern European countries
CEN	European Committee for Standardisation (*Comité Européen de Normalisation*)
CENELEC	European Committee for Electrotechnical Standardization (*Comité Européen de Normalisation Électrotechnique*)
CEOS	Conditions of Employment of Other Servants
CEPOL	European Union Agency for Law Enforcement Training

CEPT	European Conference of Postal and Telecommunications Administrations (*Conférence européenne des administrations des postes et des télécommunications*)
CER	Community of European Railways
CESNI	European Committee for Drawing up Standards in the field of Inland Navigation
CETA	EU-Canada Comprehensive Economic Trade Agreement
CF	Cohesion Fund
CFI	Court of First Instance
CFR	Charter of Fundamental Rights of the European Union
CFSP	Common Foreign and Security Policy
CHAFEA	Consumers, Health and Food Executive Agency
CIS	Common Information System
CIS	Customs Information System
CIS	Common Implementation Strategy
CIS-WFD	Common Implementation Strategy for the Water Framework Directive
CJEU	Court of Justice of the European Union
CMPHU	Committee for Medicinal Products for Human Use
CMPVU	Committee for Medicinal Products for Veterinary Use
CMS	Case Management System
CNU	CEPOL National Unit
COELA	Working Party on Enlargement and Countries Negotiating Accession to the EU
COM	Commission policy document or proposal for EU legislation
Comitology Regulation	Regulation 182/2011 laying down the rules and general principles concerning mechanisms for control by Member States of the Commission's exercise of implementing powers
COMP	Committee on Orphan Medicinal Products
CoR	European Committee of the Regions
CORDIS	Community Research and Development Information Service (European Commission)
Coreper	Committee of Permanent Representatives to the EU (*Comité de représentants permanents*) (strictly Coreper I and Coreper II)
Corr	Corrected
COSI	Standing Committee on Internal Security
COSS	Committee on Safe Seas and the Prevention of Pollution from Ships
COTER	Committee for Territorial Cohesion Policy and EU Budget
CPA	Classification of Products by Activity
CPV	Common Procurement Vocabulary
CSR	country specific recommendations
CTC	Counter-terrorism Coordinator/Centre
CVM	Cooperation and verification mechanism
DAS	Statement of Assurance (*Déclaration d'assurance*)
DCFT	Deep and Comprehensive Free Trade
DCFTA	Deep and Comprehensive Free Trade Area
DCI	Development Cooperation Instrument

DG	Directorate-General
DG BUDG	Directorate-General for Budget (European Commission)
DG ECHO	Directorate-General for European Civil Protection and Humanitarian Aid Operations (European Commission) (formerly the European Community Humanitarian Aid Office)
DG ELARG	Directorate General Enlargement (European Commission)
DG ENER	Directorate General for Energy (European Commission)
DG ENV	Directorate General for the Environment (European Commission)
DG MOVE	Directorate General for Mobility and Transport (European Commission)
DG NEAR	Directorate General for Neighbourhood and Enlargement Negotiations (European Commission)
DG RELEX	Directorate General for External Relations (European Commission)
DG SANTE	Directorate General for Health and Food Safety (European Commission)
DPIA	Data Protection Impact Assessment
DPLEA Directive	Directive 2016/680 on data protection in the law-enforcement sector
DPO	Data Protection Officer
DSB	Dispute Settlement Body
DSU	WTO Understanding on Rules and Procedures Governing the Settlement of Disputes (Dispute Settlement Understanding)
EAAS	European External Action Service
EAEC	European Atomic Energy Community (EURATOM)
EAFRD	European Agricultural Fund for Rural Development
EAGF	European Agricultural Guarantee Fund
EAGGF	European Agricultural Guidance and Guarantee Fund
EAHC	Executive Agency for Health and Consumers
EASA	European Aviation Safety Agency
EASO	European Asylum Support Office
E-Auctions	Electronic Auctions
EBA	European Banking Authority
EBCC	European Bird Census Council
EBCG	European Border and Coast Guard
EC	European Community
EC	European Community Treaty
EC Treaty	European Community Treaty
ECA	European Court of Auditors
ECAA	European common aviation area
ECB	European Central Bank
ECDC	European Centre for Disease Prevention and Control
ECHA	European Chemicals Agency
ECHO	see DG ECHO
ECHR	European Convention on Human Rights
ECI	European Citizens' Initiative
ECJ	European Court of Justice (i.e., the Court of Justice as the higher of the two courts comprising the CJEU), the lower court being the General Court (GC))
ECLI	European Case-Law Identifier

ECNS	Eurojust National Coordination Systems
ECR	European Court Reports
ECRIS	European Criminal Records Information System
ECSA	European Community Shipowner Association
ECT	Energy Community Treaty
ECtHR	European Court of Human Rights
EDES	Early Detection and Exclusion System
EDF	European Development Fund
EDP	European Delegated Prosecutor
EDP	excessive deficit procedure
EDPB	European Data Protection Board
EDPS	European Data Protection Supervisor
EEA	European Environment Agency
EEAS	European External Action Service
EEB	European Environmental Bureau
EEC	European Economic Community
EFFIS	European Forest Fire Information Service
EFSF	European Financial Stability Facility
EFSM	European Financial Stabilisation Mechanism
EIA	environmental impact assessment
EIB	European Investment Bank
EIC	European Intelligent Transport Systems Committee
EIDHR	European Instrument for Democracy and Human Rights
EIEM	European Information Exchange Model
EIONET	European Environment Information and Observation Network
EIOPA	European Insurance and Occupational Pensions Authority
EIS	European Information System
EJN	European Judicial Network
EMA	European Medicines Agency
EMAS	Eco-Management and Audit Scheme
EMFF	European Maritime and Fisheries Fund
EMSA	European Maritime Safety Agency
EMU	Economic and Monetary Union
ENI	European Neighbourhood Instrument
ENI Regulation	European Neighbourhood Instrument Regulation -Regulation (EU) No 232/2014 of the European Parliament and of the Council of 11 March 2014 establishing a European Neighbourhood Instrument, OJ 2014 L 77/ 27–43
ENISA	European Network and Information Security Agency
ENP	European Neighbourhood Policy
ENTSO	European Networks of Transmission System Operator
ENTSO-E	ENTSO responsible for electricity transmission infrastructures
ENTSO-G	ENTSO responsible for natural gas infrastructures
ENVI	Committee on the Environment, Public Health and Food Safety (European Parliament)
EORI	Economic Operator Registration Information
EP	European Parliament
EPC	European Patent Court

EPP	Euro Plus Pact
EPPO	European Public Prosecutor's Office
E-Procurement	Electronic Procurement
EPSO	European Personnel Selection Office
ERA	European Railway Agency
ERDF	European Regional Development Fund
ERGEG	European Regulators' Group for Electricity and Gas (now replaced by ACER)
ERN	European Reference Networks
ESCB	European System of Central Banks
ESF	European Social Fund
ESF	European Structural Funds mechanism
ESIF/ESI Funds	European Structural and Investment Funds
ESM	European Stability Mechanism
ESMA	European Securities and Markets Authority
ESS	European Statistical System Committee
ESSF	European Sustainable Shipping Forum
ETC	European Topic Centre
ETC-NPB	European Topic Centre on Nature Protection and Biodiversity
ETS	Emissions Trading Scheme
ETSI	European Telecommunications Standards Institute
EU ETS	EU Emissions Trading Scheme
EU Funds	European Union Funds
EU	European Union
Eu-LISA	European Agency for the Operational Management of Large-scale IT Systems in the Area of Freedom, Security and Justice
EURATOM	European Atomic Energy Community (EAEC)
EURODAC	European Asylum Dactyloscopy Database (EU fingerprint database for identifying asylum seekers and irregular border-crossers)
Eurojust	European Union Judicial Cooperation Unit (*Unité de coopération judiciaire de l'Union européenne*)
EUSFTA	EU–Singapore Free Trade Agreement
EWC	European Waste Catalogue
EWRS	Early Warning and Response System
EWS	Early Warning System
Export Regulation	Regulation 2015/479 on common rules for exports
FCT	Fiscal Compact (officially called Treaty on Stability, Coordination and Governance in the Economic and Monetary Union—TSCG)
FCTC	Framework Convention on Tobacco Control
FIDE	File Customs Identification Database
Financial Regulation	Regulation (EU, Euratom) No 966/2012 of the European Parliament and of the Council of 25 October 2012 on the financial rules applicable to the general budget of the Union, OJ 2012 L 298/1–96
FIU	Financial Information Unit
FRA	Fundamental Rights Agency of the European Union
Frontex	European Border and Coast Guard Agency

FRS	Fundamental Rights Strategy
FYR of Macedonia	Former Yugoslav Republic of Macedonia
GATS	General Agreement on Trade in Services
GATT 1947	General Agreement on Tariffs and Trade 1947
GATT	General Agreement on Trade and Tariffs
GC	General Court
GCCA/GCCA+	Global Climate Change Alliance
GDP	gross domestic product
GDPR	General Data Protection Regulation
GEAR	High Level Group on the Future of the Automotive Sector
GIPs	General Implementing Provisions
GMO	genetically modified organisms
GNI	Gross National Income
GNSS	Global Navigation Satellite System
GPA	Government Procurement Agreement
GSP	Generalised System of Preferences
Habitat Directive	Council Directive 92/43/EEC of 21 May 1992 on the conservation of natural habitats and of wild fauna and flora, OJ 1992 L 206/7–50
HABITAT/Habitat Committee	Committee (C13400) on the conservation of natural habitats and of wild fauna and flora, under the Habitat Directive
HIP	humanitarian implementation plan
HLEG	High Level Expert Group
HLG	High Level Group of Scientific Advisors
HMPC	Committee on Herbal Medicinal Products
HR	High Representative of the Union for Foreign Affairs and Security Policy
HTA	Health Technology Assessment
HWC	Hazardous Waste Catalogue
ICS	Investment Court System
IDOC	Investigation and Disciplinary Office
IGC	Intergovernmental conference
IIA	Inter-Institutional Agreement
IMF	International Monetary Fund
Import Regulation	Regulation 2015/478 on common rules for imports
IMS	Information Management Strategy
INEA	Innovation and Networks Executive Agency
INSPIRE	Committee (C33600) on Infrastructure for Spatial Information in the European Community
INTA	Committee on International Trade
INTCEN	European Union Intelligence and Situation Centre
IPA/IPA-II	Instrument for Pre-Accession Assistance
ISA	Independent Supervisory Authority
ISDS	Investor-State Dispute Settlement
ISS	Internal Security Strategy
IST	Intelligent Transport System
IUCN	International Union for the Conservation of Nature

IWT	Inland Waterway Transport
JHA	Justice and Home Affairs
JIT	Joint Investigation Team
JMC	joint monitoring committee
JPSG	Joint Parliamentary Scrutiny Group
JSB	Joint Supervisory Body
LCC	Life Cycle Costing
LDCs	least developed countries
LGBT	lesbian, gay, bisexual, and transsexual
LIFE	Programme for the Environment and Climate Action
LIFE+	Financial Instrument for the Environment
MEAT	Most Economically Advantageous Tender
MEP	Member of the European Parliament
MFA	macro-financial assistance
MFF	Multiannual Financial Framework
MIP	multiannual indicative programme (European semester macroeconomic imbalances procedure)
MoU	memorandum of understanding
MSFD	Marine Strategy Framework Directive – Directive 2008/56/EC of the European Parliament and of the Council of 17 June 2008 establishing a framework for community action in the field of marine environmental policy, OJ 2008 L 164/19–40
NACE	Statistical Classification of Economic Activities in the European Community (*Nomenclature statistique des activités économiques dans la Communauté européenne*)
NAP	National allocation plan under the EU ETS
NCB	National Central Bank
NFP	National Focal Point
NGO	non-governmental organization
NME	non-market economy
NPAA	National Programme for Adoption of the *Acquis*
NRC	National Reference Centre
OCM	OLAF Content Management
ODA	Official Development Assistance
OJ/OJEU	Official Journal of the European Union (or of the European Communities, as appropriate)
OLAF	European Anti-Fraud Office (*Office européen de lutte antifraude*) (European Commission)
OMC	Open Method of Coordination
OMT	Open-market transaction
ORNIS/Ornis-Committee	Committee (C11800) for the adaptation to scientific and technical progress of the directive on conservation of wild bird, under the Birds Directive
PCE	principle of coherence and efficiency
PCP	Primary Contact Point
PECBMS	Pan-European Common Bird Monitoring Scheme
PIN	Prior Information Notice
PIU	Passenger Information Unit
PJC	Police and Judicial Cooperation

PNR	Passenger Name Record
PRM	Persons with Reduced Mobility
QMV	Qualified Majority Voting
RAB	Rapid Alert system for Blood and Blood Components
RAG	Regional Aid Guideline (European Commission)
RAP	Rules of Application (of the Financial Regulation)
RASFF	Rapid Alert System for Food and Feed
RATC	Rapid Alert platform for human Tissues and Cells
REACH Regulation	Regulation (EC) No 1907/2006 of the European Parliament and of the Council of 18 December 2006 concerning the Registration, Evaluation, Authorisation and Restriction of Chemicals (REACH), establishing a European Chemicals Agency, OJ 2006 L 396/1–849
REMIT Regulation	Regulation (EU) No 1227/ 2011 on wholesale energy market integrity and transparency
REX	UCC Registered Exporter System
SAA	Stabilization and Association Agreement
SAC	Special Area of Conservation
SAFE Framework	SAFE Framework of Standards to Secure and Facilitate Global Trade
SAM	Scientific Advice Mechanism
SAM	State Aid Modernisation
SCA	Special Committee on Agriculture
SCENIHR	Scientific Committee on Emerging and Newly Identified Health Risks
SCHEER	Scientific Committee on Health, Environmental and Emerging Risks
SCI	Site of Community Importance
SCMA	WTO Agreement on Subsidies and Countervailing Measures
SDF	Standard Data Form
SEIS	Shared Environmental Information System
SESAR	Single European Sky ATM Research Program
SGEIs	Services of General Economic Interest
SIDS	small island developing States
SIRENE	Supplementary Information Request at the National Entries
SIS	Schengen Information System
SITCEN	Situational Centre
SME	Small and Medium Enterprise
SOE	state of environment
SPA	Special Protection Area
SPC	Summary of Product Characteristics
SPP	Strategic Planning and Programming cycle
SSM	Single Supervisory Mechanism
STOA	Office for Scientific and Technological Option Assessment (European Parliament)
STRIA	Strategic Research and Innovation Agenda
SWG	scientific working group
TAP	Telematic Applications for Passengers Committee
TBR	Trade Barriers Regulation
TBT Agreement	Agreement on Technical Barriers to Trade

TCMV	Technical Committee – Motor Vehicles
TCN	Third-Country National
TDIs	Trade Defence Instruments
TDMs	Trade Defence Measures
TEC	Treaty establishing the European Community
TEN	Transport, Energy, Infrastructure and Information Society (Section of the European Economic and Social Committee (EESC))
TEN-E Regulation	Regulation 347/ 2013 on guidelines for trans- European energy infrastructures.
TEN-T	Trans-European Transport Network (European Commission)
TE-SAT	Terrorism Situation and Trend
TEU	Treaty on the European Union
TFEU	Treaty on the Functioning of the European Union
TIR	Transport International Routier
TOR	traditional own resources
TRIPs	Agreement on Trade-Related Aspects of Intellectual Property Rights
TSCG	Treaty on Stability, Coordination and Governance in the Economic and Monetary Union (also known as the Fiscal Compact, FCT)
TSI	Technical Specification for Interoperability
TSO	Transmission System Operators
TTIP	Transatlantic Trade and Investment Partnership
UCC	Uniform Customs Code
UCC-DA	Uniform Customs Code Delegated Act
UCC-IA	Uniform Customs Code Implementing Act
UCC-TDA	Uniform Customs Code Transitional Delegated Act
UCLAF	Anti-Fraud Coordination Unit (*Unité de coordination de la lutte antifraude*)
UK	United Kingdom
UN	United Nations
UNECE	United Nations Economic Commission for Europe
UNHCR	United Nations High Commissioner for Refugees
VAT	Value Added Tax
VFM	value for money
VIS	Visa Information System
Water Framework Directive	Directive 2000/60/EC of the European Parliament and of the Council of 23 October 2000 establishing a framework for Community action in the field of water policy, OJ 2000 L 327/1–73
WCO	World Customs Organization
WEEE	waste electrical and electronic equipment
WFD	Water Framework Directive
WISE	Water Information System for Europe
WTO	World Trade Organization
WWF	World Wildlife Fund

Notes on Contributors

Catherine Barnard   Professor in European Union Law and Employment Law, and Senior Tutor and Fellow, Trinity College, University of Cambridge. Senior Fellow, ESRC 'UK in a Changing Europe' Project. Formerly, Government Adviser, Balance of Competence Review. Research in EU institutions, employment law; migrant workers' access to benefits in the UK. Active in FullFact, a non-partisan, fact-checking charity, related to claims about the EU.

Roland Bieber   Professor Emeritus, Jean Monnet Chair of European Law, and former Director, Center of Comparative, European, and International Law, Faculty of Law, University of Lausanne. Former visiting and part-time Professor, recently Research Fellow, Department of Law, European University Institute, Florence. Former Legal Adviser, European Parliament, Luxembourg.

Christopher H Bovis   Professor of International and European Business, University of Hull. Specialist in public procurement, public-private partnerships, and public sector management. Adviser to national governments in public sector reforms. Has acted on behalf of both the public sector and industry on project work.

Kieran Bradley   Special Adviser to the EU Court of Justice on Brexit and staff matters. Formerly, judge, and president of chamber, EU Civil Service Tribunal, and a Director, European Parliament Legal Service. Adjunct Professor, School of Law, Trinity College Dublin. Fellow, Robert Schuman Institute at the University of Luxembourg. Deputy Chair, Appeal Board, European Centre for Medium-Range Weather Forecasts. For the present contribution, acting in a purely personal capacity; views expressed may not be attributed to any institution or body with which he is or was associated. Thanks go to Roberto Schiano and Giulia Predonzani for comments on the text; full responsibility remains with the author.

Richard Crowe   Member, Legal Service of the European Parliament, in the Unit for Institutional and Budgetary Law. Formerly at the Legal Service of the European Court of Auditors and the Academy of European Law (ERA), Trier, as Head of the European Public Law Section. Graduate, University of Limerick, the Honorable Society of King's Inns, Dublin, and the College of Europe, Bruges.

Philipp Dann   Professor of Public and Comparative Law, Humboldt University, Berlin. Works in the area of European and international law, with a special focus on development issues.

Diana Dimitrova   FIZ Karlsruhe–Leibniz Institute for Information Infrastructure. Formerly, Law Faculty, University of Leuven, Belgium. Research focusing on data protection in the Area of Freedom, Security and Justice, with special interest in border control and migration, as well as police cooperation.

Laurence W Gormley   Professor of European Law & Jean Monnet Professor, University of Groningen, Faculty of Law, where he leads the Jean Monnet Centre of Excellence and is Head of the Department of Business Law, European Law and Tax

Law. Barrister (Middle Temple). Professor, College of Europe, Bruges. Past President of the European Law Faculties Association (ELFA).

Elspeth Guild Jean Monnet Professor *ad personam*, Queen Mary University of London. Professor of European Immigration Law, Radboud University Nijmegen. Senior Research Fellow, Centre for European Policy Studies, Brussels. Partner, London law firm Kingsley Napley. Expert on the EU's Common European Asylum System and adviser to EU institutions on it.

Herwig C H Hofmann Professor of European and Transnational Public Law at the University of Luxembourg and founding director of its Robert Schuman Institute of European Affairs. Co-founder and coordinator, Research Network of EU Administrative Law (ReNEUAL).

Marcus Klamert Member, Legal Service of the Federal Chancellery of Austria. Senior Lecturer, Vienna University of Business and Economics. The chapter benefitted from work at DG SANCO (2012–2013), Unit Tobacco Control and Substances of Human Origin, under the lead of Dominik Schnichels, who commented on an earlier version. All views expressed are personal.

Nicola Kountouris Professor in Labour Law and European Law, Faculty of Laws, University College London. Research in employment law and EU law, especially regulation of personal work relations from a comparative and supranational perspective. Has acted as an independent expert for the ILO and the ETUC on regulation of the employment relationship and the 'gig-economy'.

André M Latour Professor of Public Law, including Energy, Environmental and Public Business Law, Westphalian University of Applied Sciences, Department of Business Law. Member, Westphalian Energy Institute.

Isidora Maletić Fellow, Centre of European Law, King's College London. All views expressed are personal.

Joseph A McMahon Professor of Commercial Law, UCD Sutherland School of Law, University College Dublin, Ireland. The author thanks his colleague, Professor Michael Cardwell, for helpful comments on an earlier draft of the chapter.

Claire Micheau Policy Officer, DG Competition, European Commission. Associate Professor, University of Helsinki. Formerly lecturer in law, Trinity College Dublin and Paris 1 Panthéon-Sorbonne. Any opinions expressed are strictly personal and do not reflect the views of any institution or organization.

Valsamis Mitsilegas Professor of European Criminal Law and Global Security, Academic Lead for Internationalisation and, since 2012, Head, Department of Law, Queen Mary, University of London (QMUL). Formerly Dean (Research), Humanities and Social Sciences, and Inaugural Director, Queen Mary Institute for the Humanities and Social Sciences (IHSS); Director, Queen Mary Criminal Justice Centre; Legal adviser, House of Lords European Union Committee. Research in European criminal law; migration, asylum and borders; security and human rights, including mass surveillance and privacy; transnational crime, including organized crime and money laundering.

Andrea Ott   Professor of EU External Relations Law and Jean Monnet Chair in EU law, Faculty of Law, Maastricht University, Netherlands.

Katerina Pantzatou   Associate Professor in Tax Law at the University of Luxembourg's Faculty of Law, Economics and Finance. Formerly a Post-doctoral FNR/Marie Curie researcher at the University of Luxembourg and PhD student at the European University Institute.

Gerard C Rowe   Professor emeritus of Public, Administrative, Environmental and Local Government Law, Comparative Law and Economic Analysis of Law, and Chair, Academic Board, Master of International Human Rights and Humanitarian Law, Europa-Universität Viadrina, Frankfurt (Oder). Professeur associé, University of Luxembourg. Fellow, Robert Schuman Institute of European Affairs, University of Luxembourg. Formerly at Faculty of Law, University of New South Wales, Sydney; Research Fellow, Research Group on 'Rational Environmental Law and Policy', Centre for Interdisciplinary Research (ZiF), University of Bielefeld.

Jens-Peter Schneider   Professor of Public Law including European Administrative, Information, and Environmental law, University of Freiburg, Germany. Co-founder, Research Network of EU Administrative Law (ReNEUAL). Member, Academic Expert Group for Regulatory Issues of the German (Federal) Network Agency for Electricity, Gas, Telecommunications, Post and Railways. The author thanks his assistant, Gustav Ollinger, for his support in finalizing the chapter.

Jörg Philipp Terhechte   Professor of Public Law, European and International Law, and of Regulation and Cartel Law, Leuphana Law School; Vice-President; Head, Professional School; Head, Centre for Gaming Law & Culture; and Director, Competition & Regulation Institute: Leuphana Universität Lüneburg. Honorary Professor of Law, University of Glasgow. The author thanks Judith Crämer and Evin Dalkilic for their excellent advice and support in drafting the chapter.

Alexandros Tsadiras   Associate Professor of European Union Law, Department of Law, European University Cyprus. Research in administrative law, EU law, European litigation, and extra-judicial protection. Currently active in projects on multilevel governance in EU policies and on the principle of good administration as a fundamental human right. Has acted as a national expert for Greece and Cyprus on European Commission projects. Adviser to consultancy firms.

Alexander H Türk   Professor of Law, Dickson Poon School of Law, King's College London. Director of Programmes, Centre of European Law. Special interests in EU constitutional and administrative law.

Niovi Vavoula   Post-doctoral Research Assistant, Queen Mary, University of London (QMUL). Part-time teacher, London School of Economics and Political Science. Research in EU immigration law, EU criminal law and privacy and data protection law.

Ilaria Vianello   Senior Research Fellow for the Afghanistan Projects, Max Planck Foundation for International Peace and the Rule of Law, Heidelberg, working on administrative law reforms in Afghanistan.

Martin Wortmann Lawyer in Private Practice. Formerly, Research Fellow, University of Giessen. Specialized in comparative constitutional law and worked extensively on human rights in international economic law.

PART I
INTRODUCTION

1

A Conceptual Understanding of EU Sectoral Administrative Law

Herwig C H Hofmann, Gerard C Rowe, and Alexander H Türk

Any attempt to survey the sectoral administrative law of the European Union begs a number of fundamental questions. First, how do we understand 'administrative law', especially in relation to a supranational structure and system, such as that of the Union? Secondly, what exactly might we understand by 'sectoral' or 'specialized' administrative law, again especially in the context of the EU? Thirdly, just what is the difference between European Union law as such, and its *administrative* law. These distinctions, and the definitions attempted, are not addressed here just as scholarly abstractions. We take the view that understanding them and differentiating between these terms will make clear from the outset what this book attempts to cover, especially with respect to the concepts of both *general* EU administrative law and *specialized* EU administrative law employed here (which may or may not be similar to conceptualizations found in national contexts where these terms are employed).

A The Concept of 'Administrative' Law

The conceptual understanding of *administrative* law of the European Union used in this book arises from a combination of *functional, organizational,* and *procedural* perspectives of the exercise of powers to implement EU public policy.[1] Although the distinction between the substance of policy, on the one hand, and the administrative organization, methods, and procedures for its implementation, on the other hand, is not always completely sharp, nevertheless it is one which provides guidance for present purposes. It allows one to distinguish to a certain degree between *ends* (substantive policy and its law) and *means* (administrative achievement,[2] including principles, organization, powers, obligations, procedures, and rights, both generally and in individual policy fields).

---

[1] H C H Hofmann, G C Rowe, and A Türk, *Administrative Law and Policy of the European Union* (OUP 2011) 3–19.

[2] Separating sectoral policy substance from the sectoral administration which is charged with the implementation of that substance. Admittedly, however, this distinction is not sufficient for locating the 'public administration' as one of the structural components of democratic public governance (the 'state'), and specifically within the separation of powers. After all, the legislature and the judiciary are, within that broad construct of governance, also *means* for the achievement of policy substance. The concern of the discussion in the text does not stand in contradiction to that conclusion, but merely rather to delineate the subject matter of administration and administrative law from the substance of public policy, so as to indicate, as clearly as possible, the focus in the present work.

Although procedural law is of great importance within administrative law, it is by no means the only concern, especially in view of the obligation of public law to provide for the principled framework of administrative action, for the identification and protection of rights, and for the orgnizational structure of administrative activity. The disciplines of public administration and administrative law deal, then, with very many matters. These include at least all of the following:

- general *constitutional principles* of particular relevance to the activity of the public administration;
- the *allocation*—often *delegation*—of *tasks* and *powers* to, and competences upon, public officials (including powers of enforcement);
- the imposition of *obligations* on such officials as part of, or restrictions upon, the exercise of such powers;
- the institutional and organizational *structure* within which such officials operate, exercise power, or satisfy duties and obligations;
- the allocation of financial and other *resources* to such institutions and actors;
- the *legal principles* which *specifically* underlie the activities of the public administration as such;
- the law and practice of *information management* for, and within, the public administration;
- the catalogue of *acts and measures* available to public administrators to perform their duties and exercise their powers, including abstract-general measures, single-case measures, and (public) contracts, including, *inter alia*, powers of inspection and investigation in the context of enforcement;
- the detailed rules governing—framing and limiting—the exercise of *discretion* and the making of *decisions* (and possibly taking other action) by public officials;
- the *procedures* which are applicable to the adoption of measures and acts (which may include obligations of participation of the public or persons particularly affected), and to the performance of related tasks, including enforcement procedures;
- the role of *private actors* in the performance of public administrative tasks and the legal framework for this;
- the means and institutions of *supervision* and control over public officials; and
- the law relating to the *employment of public servants* and employment within the public sector.

Taking all such matters into account, one comes back to the fundamental concept that administrative law is law about the *framework* of administrative action in a comprehensive sense. Therefore, when speaking of administrative law, we are not referring only to (the law of administrative) *procedure(s)*[3] but include many organizational and

---

[3] We need to make this observation very explicitly: it appears to us that conceptions of public administration and administrative law often tend to be reduced to this, at least in name (see eg classic administrative law codifications, such as the US Administrative *Procedures* Act, or the German

other elements which bear upon procedures, including ensuring the protection of individual rights in the process.

B 'Sectoral' Administrative Law

We have relied on the above understanding of public administration and its law in our earlier work on general administrative law (mentioned above).[4] The present work turns attention to the special, policy-specific elements of EU administrative law. By way of clarification, the notion of *general* administrative law covers all of that body of *administrative* law (in the sense set out above) which—more or less—is applicable to, and across, *all* substantive policy sectors or fields. This does not just relate to procedures standardized across all sectors—to underscore the point made above—but rather includes all (guiding, organizational, structural, procedural, enabling, restrictive, and supervisory) elements which are common, or very similar, to the administration of the various policy fields. So, for example, a constitutional principle such as the rule of law, or a specific principle like that of good administration, or the obligation to hear the representations of affected parties, or to observe obligations associated with data protection, will be of general applicability across the different fields of action of the public administration.

Also, for our purposes and understanding, *administrative* law is not to be confused with the law which embodies the substance of a specific public policy (such as, in the EU, agriculture, environment, energy, Union enlargement, foreign aid, budget, transport, etc.). This point has particular relevance when one undertakes a consideration of *specialized* or *sectoral* administrative law, as we do here. Accordingly, the focus of the individual chapters is not to provide a detailed account of the legal substance of any given policy area and, as such, this volume is also not to be read as a compendium of European Union law as a whole, or even of the sectors addressed. The individual sectoral chapters do not seek to address the substantive Union law of each of the sectors touched upon (except where some attention to substantive law cannot be divorced from the law of its administration). The chapters on the administrative law of the EU agriculture sector or the EU environmental sector in this volume, for example, are not essays on 'EU agriculture law' or 'EU environmental law'. They are just treatments of the administration and the associated administrative law of those policy sectors, but *sector-specific* to the extent that their focus does not fall within the 'general part' of public administration and administrative law as described above. Each chapter concerns, as far as possible, only the law which relates genuinely to the *administration* of each sectoral field since, for the purposes of this book, we do not want to conflate substantive (regulatory) law with administrative law (in our sense of the term).[5]

Verwaltungsverfahrensgesetz [Administrative *Procedures* Law]: to a not inconsiderable extent these titles are misnomers).

  [4] Hofmann, Rowe, and Türk (n 1).
  [5] This is the case, for example, in Germany or Austria with the category of '*besonderes Verwaltungsrecht*' [special administrative law]. There, within each of the fields of special administrative law (eg planning

The different fields of *sectoral* administrative law across a large array of policy sectors of the Union are proof of the fact that much, and rather varied, administrative law is specific to each of the many different policy sectors of the Union. The sectoral diversity relates to all the matters which we listed above as falling within the compass of administrative law. Institutional structures, procedures, types of measures, powers, supervisory structures, and much more besides, vary across and among the sectoral divisions. The challenge is not just to record these variations, but rather to make sense of the sectoral diversity and density in EU administrative law, and to assess it in the light of questions such as:

- Can we, despite the diversity, identify characteristics common to all sectors, or at least to groups of sectors?
- What are the major differences in the administrative diversity which emerge from a sector-by-sector consideration?
- Are such differences especially pronounced with respect to certain elements of administrative law; in other words, are the differences between policy areas greater in regard, say, to organizational structure, but less varied in regard, say, to supervision?
- Are there characteristics of specific policy sectors (or groups of sectors), which in fact demand their own specific administrative law (insofar as such specificity has been identified in the present contributions)?
- Alternatively, would it be possible to arrive at a greater degree of commonality, i.e., to rein in some of the diversity of administrative-legal arrangements under the umbrella of the general part of administrative law?

and finally,

- What, if any, are the distinguishing features of *European* administrative law which emerge from this consideration; in other words, are there characteristics which differ from those of national systems of public administration, and, if so, what do such characteristics tell us about the EU itself, and about the nature of the European project?

All of these questions seem to us both interesting and important, especially as at least some of the answers may inform and enlighten us in relation to important administrative policy issues. Put another way, the administrative (law) method used successfully in one sector may inform the practice in another sector, and even suggest solutions to problems apparent there. Nevertheless, we have no illusions: the present work does not provide comprehensive answers to all such questions. It will become clear that, even within each of the essays here on individual sectors, it is rarely possible to canvass the whole of the administrative law within a given policy field, nor to achieve a full understanding of the administrative activity there.

---

and building law, environmental law, water law, energy law, media law, health law, roads law, and various fields of economic regulation, etc) that label applies to *all* the law, both substantive and administrative, within each of the fields concerned.

C Overall Coverage and Organization of Contributions

The order and grouping of the contributions, as presented in this work, represents a broad attempt to identify coherent categories of sectors of Union policy and action. This attempt is, however, merely offered as a very broad, and indeed rather tentative, aid to orientation. Alternative orderings might have tried to reflect the way in which topics are organized in the treaties, or perhaps the degree of administrative integration in a given sector. Such alternatives, although plausible in their own right, were not adopted, as we preferred to try to trace commonalities in policy area matters in the approach followed.

The chosen ordering arguably does allow—at least broadly—some distinction to be observed between, on the one hand, sectoral fields of Union policy which have something of a constitutive character (e.g., enlargement, or neighbourhood policy), and those with a substantive regulatory focus (e.g., the single market in goods, environment, energy, competition). Other sub-groupings can also be identified by noting that fields such as the civil service and budget (in Part VII) are hardly 'policy sectors' in their own right at all, having what might be called an 'infra-administrative' character. There, the administrative tasks and associated administrative law are, of their nature, different from those in many of the other sectoral sub-groupings. Such an infra-administrative character could also correctly be associated with the topic of data protection (which is also not a sector as such). However, we have placed the chapter dealing with that topic in Part III 'Security and Justice', because it specifically concerns data protection in the sphere of police and justice, thus having a keenly sector-specific focus.

Broadly, the book has attempted to achieve a relatively uniform, reiterated approach to the administrative law of each of the sectors considered, and thus of each of the present chapters. It will be readily apparent, though, that, while a certain uniformity of presentation has been achieved across many of the contributions, sectoral variations and associated perceptions of the administrative law pertinent to each sector have meant that there is some variation in the way matters are dealt with. Some chapters do, in fact, depart from a standardized approach, which was in any case not intended as a straightjacket for individual contributions.

Some of the differences in the administrative law and practice in the various sectors reflect real (and often necessary) differences in content, method, procedure, and outcomes. Strict uniformity in the approach taken in each chapter would clearly be counter-productive were it to suppress the expression of such specificities. On the contrary, as editors, we take the view that it is precisely against the background of a *broadly uniform approach* in the presentation that the differences of substance and function in the various sectors will best emerge. In particular, this should allow a clear differentiation between sectoral divergences, which are necessary (and functionally grounded), and sectoral variations in administration, which are merely fortuitous.

The common structure, to which the chapters of this book generally adhere, allows broadly that comparable matters and subjects are dealt with at the same place, or at least under a relatively similar heading, in each chapter. The common structure of sections and headings is maintained in the chapters, except where specific headings or topics simply have no key relevance to the sector concerned, or where the author's own perception of the subject cuts across such a sub-division. Given this broadly common approach throughout the book, readers should, relatively readily, be able to draw comparisons across sectors, and to note contrasts and differences such as exist.

The largely standardized shape of most contributions echoes, perhaps unsurprisingly, the chapter structure of the editors' own *Administrative Law and Policy of the European Union*, referred to above. There is indeed, a considerable convergence between the structure of that book on general administrative law, and the structure of many of the individual contributions on sectoral administrative law here. The key elements of that standardized structure (apart from an introductory overview of the sector and sketch of EU competence, policy, and legal background in the field concerned) are:

- administrative *tasks* within the sector concerned;

- *sources* of (administrative) law in the sector concerned, including primary (general) sources of law (e.g., the Treaties, Charter, European Convention on Human Rights (ECHR), general principles), secondary EU law (directives and regulations of the Council and the European Parliament), and tertiary EU law (e.g., Commission regulations), including measures of general application (e.g., the Financial Regulation), where they are specifically relevant to the sector addressed;

- underlying *general legal principles*, for example those touching the relationship between the Union and the Member States (e.g., limited attribution of competences, subsidiarity, sincere cooperation) or of broader constitutional character (e.g. democracy, fundamental rights, proportionality, transparency, legitimate expectations, good administration, rights of defence)—but only insofar as specifically sectorally relevant;

- particular *sector-specific principles* (e.g., in the environmental sector, principles such as sustainability, integrated protection, or user-pays);

- sectoral *organization*, institutions and structures, including: the key administrative actors within the sector on both supranational (Union) and national level; structural interaction between actors; administrative networks and cooperative arrangements; agencies; comitology and other committees; and special organizational arrangements for the management of programmes and/or budget implementation;

- administrative *procedures* within the sector, including: direct administration; comitology procedures; composite procedures (typically joint ones involving actors on different levels); and those for information management, programme management, and budget implementation;

- legal rules governing the substance of sector-specific *decision-making* (on whatever level), especially in regard to discretions, or to the standards applicable to non-discretionary decision-making;

- *abstract-general administrative acts* and measures available, including: agenda setting and framework measures; subordinate legislation; administrative rulemaking, both as (formally) non-binding, unilateral administrative rules (recommendations, opinions, interpretive guidance, notices, codes of practice, etc), and as rules negotiated between Union institutions and/or between Member States; rule-making by private parties; co-regulation (especially for standard-setting); self-regulation; and (where applicable) the role of social partners;

- *single-case administrative acts* and measures used, including: individual administrative decisions by both Union and Member State decision-makers (with coverage of issues such as legal basis, competences, form, validity, legal effect; revocation, modification, conditions); administrative agreements; and factual conduct (typically actions which involve no formal, binding, or ultimate decision, but possibly affecting individual rights).

- *administrative enforcement* of sectoral law, specifically the enforcement of EU law vis-à-vis parties external to the Union and Member State administrations (to be distinguished from the supervision over the EU administration on all its levels and in all its forms, as noted in the following);

- ex ante and ex post *supervision* and control of (sectoral) administration, including: administrative supervision, i.e., within the administration itself (either through specialist sectoral structures, e.g., in agencies, in D-Gs, comitology and other specialized committees, or through general, not sector-specific bodies, e.g., the Court of Auditors, OLAF, the Human Rights Agency, the EDPS, etc.); political supervision (e.g., through the European Parliament and especially parliamentary committees, or through the European Ombudsman); and judicial review through the CJEU of actions by the sectoral administration.

Many—perhaps most—of these foci of attention are addressed in each of the sector-specific chapters, but, as can be seen, these different elements get more or less coverage depending on the characteristics of the sector concerned, and on the perception of the individual authors.

PART II

FOREIGN RELATIONS AND AFFAIRS

2

Enlargement Policy

Andrea Ott

A Introduction

The EU enlargement policy was labelled in 2003—shortly before the 'big bang' enlargement of 2004—the most successful EU external relations policy.[1] Due to that success, the European Neighbourhood Policy (ENP) has, since 2003, copied certain characteristics of the policy and instruments.[2] However, after the 2004 accession of twelve new Member States and the subsequent accession of Romania and Bulgaria in 2007 and finally of Croatia in 2013, a general enlargement fatigue can be diagnosed among the existing EU Member States.[3] EU Member States have become wary of further accession in times of recurring crises of the European Union project and in light of the challenge of post-accession integration of new Member States, especially of Bulgaria and Romania, as an ongoing project. At the same time they are not willing to abandon such an effective tool for influencing and aligning third countries' policies to EU law and for stimulating reforms in national administrative and legal orders of neighbouring countries in anticipation of accession.[4] Montenegro, Serbia, and Turkey have started accession negotiations, Albania and the Former Yugoslav Republic of Macedonia secured a recognized candidate status, while Bosnia-Herzegovina and Kosovo are being viewed as potential candidates.[5] While the enlargement policy is still in place, and consistently updated and reassessed, the European Commission under Commission President Juncker indicated in 2014 that no further enlargement would take place in the following five years.[6] This 'downgrading' of enlargement is also visible in the merging of the Directorate Generals of ENP and Enlargement into

---

[1] See the former Dutch Prime Minister Wim Kok in his report to the European Commission, 'Enlarging the European Union' 2003 EUI Robert Schuman Centre for Advanced Studies. For a good summary on EU enlargement see F Emmert and S Petrovi, 'The Past, Present, and the Future of EU Enlargement' (2014) 37 *Fordham International Law Journal* 1348.

[2] On the background of the ENP see M Cremona, 'The European Neighbourhood Policy' in A Ott and E Vos (eds), *Fifty Years of European Integration: Foundations and Perspectives* (TMC Asser Press 2009) 221–41.

[3] J O'Brennan, 'On the Slow Train to Nowhere? The European Union, "Enlargement Fatigue" and the Western Balkans' (2014) *European Foreign Affairs Review* 221.

[4] 'Key policy': see Council Conclusions on Enlargement and Stabilisation and Association Process as adopted by the Council on 15 December 2015, Brussels, 15 December 2015 15356/15 and the General EU Position and negotiating framework with principles governing the negotiations on opening the IGC on the Accession of Serbia to the European Union (Brussels, 21 January 2014).

[5] Iceland applied for membership in 2009 but withdrew its application in 2015.

[6] Jean-Claude Juncker in a European Parliament hearing on 15 July 2014 and mission letter of Juncker to the Commissioner Johannes Hahn (10 September 2014) https://ec.europa.eu/commission/sites/cwt/files/commissioner_mission_letters/hahn-mission_en.pdf.

DG NEAR since 2015. The seeds of discontent among and between Member States with regard to the future path of enlargement policy are increasingly difficult to hide. For the first time, in December 2016 no consensus on yearly Council Conclusions on Enlargement and Stabilisation and Association Process, laying down the main aims and objectives of this policy, was able to be established between EU Member States.[7]

When looking at this EU policy from the perspective of policy design, the legal instruments employed, and the institutions involved, the enlargement policy stands out as both unique and hybrid in comparison with other EU internal and external relations policies. The enlargement policy can be characterized as a hybrid considering its inter-governmental and supranational features and in the light of its instruments, and the bodies and competences involved. It is a peculiar EU policy because it sets out to reform third countries' national administrative and constitutional systems, an area in which the EU has no internal competence.[8] This occurs through the conditions of eligibility, the Copenhagen criteria.[9] In three European Council meetings (Copenhagen 1993, Essen 1994, and Madrid 1995), the accession conditions were fine-tuned and fleshed out. These conditions can be categorized as: political (stability of institutions, guarantee of democracy, rule of law, human rights, respect for and protection of minorities, and good neighbourliness); economic (existence of a functioning market economy and capacity to cope with competitive pressure and market forces within the Union); legal (ability to adopt the *acquis*); administrative (actual administrative capacity to apply the *acquis communautaire*); and institutional (the capacity of the Union to absorb and integrate).[10] Especially the so-called Madrid criterion on administrative capacity extends the reach of the European Administrative Space beyond the EU borders.[11] It provides the standard for evaluating both the concrete ability of a third country to apply the *acquis* and the administrative structures in light of benchmarks and criteria which the candidate has to satisfy in order to become eligible for accession. Internally, once a country joins, the EU has no competence to evaluate its administrative capacity, as Article 6 TFEU on supporting competences demonstrates. Since the accession of Romania and Bulgaria the Union has aimed to bridge this discrepancy in the reach of EU conditionality with a new transitional post-accession conditionality. This takes the form of the mechanism for cooperation and verification involving a concrete review of certain benchmarks with regard to the freedom, security, and justice *acquis*, built into the accession treaty.[12]

---

[7] See Council, Brussels, 13 December 2016, 15370/1/16: 'The presidency notes the absence of a consensus allowing the adoption of Council conclusions'.

[8] See Art 6 TFEU indicating a supporting competence for administrative cooperation.

[9] Presidency Conclusions, Copenhagen European Council, 21–22 June 1993, Bulletin of the European Communities, No 6/1993, 7.

[10] See generally A Tatham, 'Don't Mention Divorce at the Wedding, Darling!': EU Accession and Withdrawal after Lisbon' in A Biondi, P Eeckhout, and S Ripley (eds), *EU Law after Lisbon* (Oxford University Press 2012) 128–254 at 131; on the evolution of the criteria, K Inglis, *Evolving Practice in EU Enlargement with Case Studies in Agri-Food and Environment Law* (Martinus Nijhoff 2010) 57–59.

[11] Presidency Conclusions, Madrid, 15 and 16 December 1995; see further D Kochenov, *The Failure of Conditionality* (Kluwer Law International 2008) 174.

[12] See generally M Spernbauer, 'Benchmarking, Safeguard Clauses and Verification Mechanisms—What's in a Name? Recent Developments in Pre- and Post-Accession Conditionality and Compliance with EU Law' (2007) 3 *Croatian Yearbook of European Law and Policy* 273.

The decisive steps in the enlargement process are conducted under the guidance of the European Council and an intergovernmental conference (IGC). The EU Commission has taken a central administrative role in managing accession, but no accession is possible without the ratification of the accession treaty by all EU Member States. The IGC has an important function in the revision of founding Treaties,[13] and legal changes are approved through international agreement between the incoming and the existing EU Member States. The IGC is characterized as a decision-making procedure but has, in fact, over time become an institutionalized forum attended by the Member States, while also having representatives of the Commission, the European Parliament, and even candidate countries as observers should revision of the Treaties be at issue, as in the 2003 revision process.[14] Within a given accession process it is configured as the IGC on the accession of the candidate country,[15] it opens negotiation chapters with that country, and the EU delegation consists of the ministerial representative of the current EU presidency, and a Commission representative, which is the EU Commissioner for ENP and Enlargement.[16] More frequent meetings occur on the ambassador level through the Working Party on Enlargement and Countries Negotiating Accession to the EU (COELA).

The peculiar nature of the enlargement policy is also demonstrated by the competences and subject matters covered by primary law. Enlargement policy is not comparable with, for example, the exclusive competence in trade or parallel competences in development policy. No separate chapter in the Treaties is devoted to enlargement policy, although the enlargement policy involves the core principles and values of the Union. According to the Article 21(1) TEU, the 'Union's action on the international scene shall be guided by the principle of its own creation, development and enlargement'.

B Sources of Law and the Definition of Administrative Tasks in the Enlargement Policy

As highlighted above, the enlargement policy is not a separate policy field addressed in the external relations provisions of the EU Treaties. The primary law provision of Article 49 TEU covers only the rudimentary structure of the accession process and procedure. This rule addresses the first phase, namely the formal application, and applies when the last step of concluding an accession treaty between the incoming and existing Member States has been reached. It does not mention all the stages which have to be passed through once a state applies for accession to the Union and which have

---

[13] See Art 48 TEU for the ordinary revision procedure.

[14] See on this the intergovernmental conference of the European Union—setting up the Finnish delegation for negotiations http://formin.finland.fi/public/?contentid=60012&contentlan=2&culture=en-US.

[15] First Accession Conference with Serbia Opening statement by Serbia, including the general EU position http://register.consilium.europa.eu/doc/srv?l=EN&t=PDF&gc=true&sc=false&f=AD%201%20 2014%20INIT;   http://www.seio.gov.rs/upload/documents/pristupni_pregovori/the_opening_state-ment_of_the_republic_of_serbia.pdf.

[16] See eg Second meeting of the Accession Conference with Serbia at Ministerial level—First two chapters opened, Brussels, 14 December 2015.

come to constitute the substantial core of EU enlargement policy over many years. In addition, that Treaty provision has evolved in the course of several treaty reforms by linking the application for accession to respect for values under Article 2 TEU. The Lisbon Treaty added to Article 49 TEU that 'the conditions of eligibility agreed upon by the European Council shall be taken into account,[17] whereby reference was made in primary EU law to the so-called Copenhagen criteria, which are considered the politically binding framework rules for accession.

The main steps in the accession process can be divided into 5 phases. The first phase of official application is covered by Article 49 TEU. The Council informs the European Parliament, the Commission and national parliaments of any such application. Through country reports the Commission evaluates progress on a yearly basis, by reference to the benchmarks of the Copenhagen criteria and the so-called European standards inspired by the structure of the association agreement between the EU and the candidate country. Once negotiations have started, the content of these progress reports is influenced by the structure of the so-called negotiating chapters.[18] Then, following a favourable opinion by the Commission[19] and consent of the European Parliament, an applicant state will be accorded candidate status by the European Council. Accession negotiations are opened after a unanimous decision by the European Council and a favourable recommendation by the Parliament. Negotiation takes place in an intergovernmental setting in form of the above-mentioned accession conferences between the candidate country and the EU Member States in which the *acquis* is split up into negotiation chapters, currently thirty-five, each addressed separately. In parallel, the Commission starts a screening process with the applicant country, in order to verify whether individual items of the *acquis* listed in a given chapter have been transposed into the country's national law. Only when the country shows that it has already implemented a chapter of the *acquis*, or that it will implement it by the date of accession, can the chapter be provisionally closed. Exceptionally, a candidate country may agree to special arrangements with respect to a part of the *acquis*. The Commission informs the Council and the European Parliament throughout the process, in particular by means of already mentioned annual progress reports. The candidate country also draws up annual national programmes in which it assesses its own progress in implementing the different chapters of the *acquis*, the National Programmes for the Adoption of the *Acquis* (NPAA). Transitional arrangements, especially those for temporary derogations from part of the *acquis*, may also apply.[20] The negotiating parties may also discuss whether (and how) some rules might be introduced gradually to allow the new members to adapt.

---

[17] Inglis, *Evolving Practice in EU Enlargement with Case Studies in Agri-Food and Environment Law* (n 10) 46–47.

[18] These documents are published as Commission staff working documents; see for Kosovo http://ec.europa.eu/enlargement/pdf/key_documents/2015/20151110_report_kosovo.pdf.

[19] Communication from the Commission to the European Parliament and the Council, Commission Opinion on Serbia's application for membership of the European Union, COM(2011) 668 final.

[20] K Inglis, 'The Accession Treaty and Its Transitional Arrangements: A Twilight Zone for the New Members of the Union' in C Hillion (ed), *EU Enlargement* (Hart Publishing 2004) 77–109.

The final stage is reached with the Accession Treaty, ratified by all existing Member States and the applicant state. EU accession law determining the conditions for entry consists of a very short accession treaty[21] together with the adjustments to the existing treaties accompanied by more detailed conditions fleshed out in the act of accession and provisions on implementation contained in technical detailed annexes.[22] Accession treaties, acts of accession, and their annexes are characterized by their hybrid legal nature. They constitute on the one hand international agreements among the contracting parties but belong on the other hand, once ratified, also to primary EU law, amending and derogating from the *acquis communautaire*.[23]

A further legal basis governing the relations between incoming and existing Member States and the European Union as such, both preceding and existing parallel to the enlargement process, is constituted by Article 217 TFEU covering a relationship of association involving reciprocal rights and obligations, common actions and special procedures. In the past, the association practice has contained both accession association agreements (which pave the way for a prospective accession) and so-called development association agreements (which aim to support third countries, such as Chile, or country groups, such as the ACP countries, in their development). The difference between these two is that the accession association agreements as such refer in their preambles expressly to an accession perspective.[24] With the exception of Portugal and Spain,[25] all acceding countries after the northern enlargement in 1973 signed an association agreement with the EC/EU.[26] In addition, Article 8 TEU, in the primary law as a result of the Lisbon Treaty, covers the special relationship with neighbouring countries, aimed at establishing an area of prosperity and good neighbourliness. There is common agreement in literature and practice that this provision is designed for countries belonging to the ENP with no concrete accession perspective.[27]

---

[21] In the case of the Treaty of Accession with Croatia, it contains four articles.

[22] In the act of accession of Croatia, it contains fifty-five articles. See further on this Inglis, *Evolving Practice in EU Enlargement with Case Studies in Agri-Food and Environment Law* (n 10) 147–52.

[23] See on this CJEU Joined Cases 31 and 35/86 *LAISA v Council* [1988] ECLI:EU:C:1988:211, para 12; A Ott, 'Unity in Diversity? Differentiation in EU Law and Policy in an Enlarged European Union' Natolin Paper 14 (2004) http://www.natolin.edu.pl/pdf7zeszyty/NatolinZeszytl5_Ott.pdf (last accessed 3 October 2015); C Hillion, 'EU Enlargement' in P Craig and G de Búrca (eds), *The Evolution of EU Law* (2nd edn, Oxford University Press 2011) 212.

[24] See eg the Association Agreement with Turkey ('recognizing that the support given by the European Economic Community to the efforts of the Turkish people to improve their standard of living will facilitate the accession of Turkey to the Community at a later date'), the Association Agreement with Poland ('recognizing the fact that the final objective of Poland is to become a member of the Community and that this association, in the view of the Parties, will help to achieve this objective'); AA with Croatia ('recalling the European Union's readiness to integrate to the fullest possible extent Croatia into the political and economic mainstream of Europe and its Status as a Potential candidate for EU membership on the basis of the Treaty on European Union and fulfilment of the criteria defined by the European Council in June 1993, subject to the successful implementation of this Agreement, notably candidate for EU membership on the basis of the Treaty on European Union and fulfilment of the criteria defined by the European Council in June 1993, subject to the successful implementation of this Agreement, notably regarding regional cooperation').

[25] For political reasons at the time of the 1970ties no association agreements were concluded and instead with Portugal and Spain in 1972 and 1970 respectively a FTA; see eg for Spain [1970] OJ L182/2.

[26] See in this regard Greece, Malta, Cyprus, the former Europe Agreements with CEE, and the SAA with the Western Balkan states.

[27] See further I Vianello, 'European Neighbourhood Policy' Chapter 3 in this volume.

C Legal Rules and Administrative Acts Governing Enlargement Policy

In its institutional construction the enlargement policy is recognizable in the major political decisions taken by the Council and, more especially, those by the European Council on an extra, intergovernmental layer. The daily practical administration of EU enlargement is in the hands of the European Commission. In retrospect, it has been argued that enlargement moved from being an intergovernmental procedure to a Community- and Commission-led policy but that, after 2004, a renationalization of enlargement has taken place.[28] Although this might be a valid view for the overall picture in the last ten years, the general set-up and the clear divide between the intergovernmental tasks on the one hand and administrative tasks on the other hand has not fundamentally changed since the first enlargements of the European Union. The pre-accession strategy engineered by the Commission has governed the administrative procedure since 1994 and has been continuously revised, first by the enhanced pre-accession strategy since 1997[29] and finally through the renewed consensus on enlargement in 2006.[30] The policy is distinguished by its well documented administrative practice, relying on soft and hard law tools. The renewed consensus on enlargement is based on the experience regarding the accession of Romania and Bulgaria and has been transformed by a focus on important rule-of-law issues. Negotiations opened after 2006, following the renewed consensus on enlargement, had to start at an early stage with the difficult chapters on administrative and judicial reform, combating corruption and the rule of law.[31] Progress was then to be measured by opening and closing benchmarks[32] of the individual negotiation chapters. In the case of Serbia, the European Council requested the Council in June 2013 to adopt a general negotiating framework in line with this renewed consensus.[33]

The negotiating framework lays out, then, the principles governing negotiations. These principles concern the institutional division of tasks, and the general rules and procedures applicable. The Council acts by unanimity on a proposal of the Commission to lay down benchmarks for the opening and the provisional closure of chapters.[34] Such benchmarks refer to the legislative alignment with the *acquis*, but can also include the fulfilment of commitments under a stabilization and association agreement (SAA) the extent that these mirror commitments under the *acquis*. In the

---

[28] See with this argument Hillion, 'EU Enlargement' (n 23) 187, 200.

[29] See on this K Inglis, 'The Pre-accession Strategy and the Accession Partnerships in A Ott and K Inglis, *Handbook on European Enlargement* (TMC Asser Press 2002) 103–11.

[30] European Council Conclusions, Brussels, 12 February 2007, 16879/1/06 REV 1, based on a Commission communication Enlargement Strategy and Main Challenges 2006–2007, including annexed special report on the EU's capacity to integrate new members COM(2006) 649.

[31] Communication from the Commission to the European Parliament and the Council, Enlargement Strategy and main challenges 2006–2007 COM(2006) 649.

[32] See also M V Keketija and A Lazowski, 'The Seventh EU Enlargement and Beyond: Pre-accession Policy vis-à-vis the Western Balkans Revisited' (2014) 10 *Croatian Yearbook of European Law and Policy* 1.

[33] Conference on accession to the EU—Serbia, General EU position, Brussels, 9 January 2014, para 9 http://www.seio.gov.rs/upload/documents/pristupni_pregovori/neg_frame.PDF.

[34] Conference on accession to the EU—Serbia, General EU position, Brussels, 9 January 2014, para 42.

case of Serbia, these concern the concrete benchmarks for improvement in relations with Kosovo and are addressed under the special Chapter 35.[35]

The reason for this transparent approach, which gained in importance in the run-up to the 2004 enlargement, is to engender public support in all countries, both candidate states and existing Member States, but also to create predictability and procedural certainty for the candidate country being judged on its performance as an insider, although institutionally still an outsider.[36]

1 The toolbox of enlargement administration

The enlargement policy stands out with its 80% reliance on soft law tools, while legally binding instruments are in fact limited in number. Focussing only on those which are mutually binding, a handful of instruments can be identified, the most prominent being the 'Association Agreement' and the 'Accession Treaty'. Under the umbrella of the pre-accession strategy, hard and soft law instruments are structured into political, financial, and programming tools, but can be further differentiated into bilaterally or unilaterally binding and non-binding measures. The EU has chosen, under the umbrella of the pre-accession strategy, to employ soft law measures or unilaterally legally binding instruments in form of 'Accession Partnerships' (for the Western Balkan states called European Partnerships)[37] and 'Financial Regulations'. The renewed consensus in the pre-accession strategy following 2006 emphasizes that difficult issues such as administrative and judicial reforms and the fight against corruption will be addressed at an early stage of negotiations and that a more systematic use of benchmarks are to apply using concrete criteria for the opening and closing of individual negotiation chapters.[38]

The extensive use of non-binding or soft-law tools has two main explanations. Firstly, enlargement policy extends the reach of EU law to third countries and cannot, therefore, directly employ the classical secondary European legislative instruments (regulations and directives) for them. Secondly, the enlargement process is time-consuming and/or 'open-ended'.[39] It requires a certain flexibility to adapt quickly, for which complex bilateral international agreements are not suited. In addition, conditionality ensures that such soft law measures achieve a quasi-binding effect on these third countries in line with the final aim of joining the European Union.

The primary instruments, legally binding for both sides, are (at the beginning of the process) an 'Accession Association Agreement' between the EU, the Member States and the third country and (at the end) the 'Accession Treaty' between the Member

---

[35] Conference on accession to the EU—Serbia (n 33) Annex 11–12.

[36] The EU uses the term of credibility, Council Conclusions, Brussels, 15 December 2015 (OR. en) 15356/15.

[37] See further S Blockmans, *Tough Love: The European Union's Relations with the Western Balkans* (TMC Asser Press 2007) 277.

[38] Communication from the Commission to the European Parliament and the Council, Enlargement Strategy and Main Challenges 2006–2007COM(2006) 649.

[39] See eg the EU Negotiating Framework for Serbia, point 20 ('negotiations are an open-ended process whose outcome cannot be guaranteed beforehand'); Conference on accession to the European Union—Serbia—Brussels, 9 January 2014.

States and the acceding country. Both types of instruments require, as international agreements, ratification by all involved parties, and can be delayed where national interest appear to require this.[40] They are, in their nature, also inflexible instruments which cannot quickly be put into force or changed, providing a snapshot of the relations between the parties at the moment of negotiations or, more particularly, their completion. In the light of these characteristics, they are accompanied by a panoply of other legal and policy instruments. The overall policy strategy is shaped by 'European Partnerships' updated yearly and by Commission progress reports, with monitoring priorities laid down in the 'Accession Partnerships'. These elements are complemented by financial and participatory instruments and by political instruments. One of the aims, that of familiarizing candidate countries as much as possible, before accession, with the Union's institutional and policy structures, is accomplished by enabling the participation (as it were, in advance), in EU programmes, policies, and sub-institutions (specifically EU agencies).[41] Such cooperation can also extend to intergovernmental Common Foreign and Defence Policy missions in crisis areas, as Turkish participation in the European Union Police Mission in the former Yugoslav Republic of Macedonia shows.[42] Another approach to achieve both alignment and familiarization is demonstrated by replicating successful supranational initiatives in, for example, the field of aviation and energy safety within the Energy Community and the European Common Aviation Area.[43]

Such legally binding instruments as Association Agreements or European Partnerships are interwoven with non-binding ones, such as Council conclusions, Commission opinions or Commission progress reports. Hard law instruments of a political nature frame the beginning and end of the important phases of pre-accession and accession. These steps are marked by the signing and ratification of association agreements, accession treaties, and readmission and visa facilitation agreements,

[40] See the example of Italy and the ratification of the Slovenian Europe Agreement, which was delayed by Italy owing to a border dispute with Slovenia and the Slovenian condition with regard to ratifying the accession treaty with Croatia only if an agreement could be reached to handle the debt of Slovenian bank Ljubljanska Bank towards Croatian customers.

[41] For this purpose, for instance, the EC and Turkey concluded in 2002 a framework agreement on the participation of Turkey in Community/Union programmes Framework Agreement between the European Community and the Republic of Turkey on the general principles for the participation of the Republic of Turkey in Community programmes; Commission Communication to the Council, Participation of candidate countries in Community programmes, agencies and committees COM(99) 710 final.

[42] Agreement between the European Union and the Republic of Turkey establishing a framework for the participation of the Republic of Turkey in the European Union crisis management operations, Agreement between the European Union and the Republic of Turkey on the participation of the Republic of Turkey in the European Union Police Mission (EUPOL Proxima) in the former Yugoslav Republic of Macedonia. Agreement between the European Union and the Republic of Turkey on the participation of the Republic of Turkey in the European Union-led Forces (EUF) in the Former Yugoslav Republic of Macedonia. Agreement between the European Union and the Republic of Turkey on the participation of the Republic of Turkey in the European Union Police Mission (EUPM) in Bosnia and Herzegovina (BiH). See further S Blockmans, Participation of Turkey in the EU's Common Security and Defence Policy: Kingmaker or Trojan Horse?' in H Kabaalioglu, A Ott, and A Tatham (eds), *EU and Turkey: Bridging the Differences* (Economic Development Foundation 2011) 143.

[43] S D Hofer, 'Neo-functionalism reloaded: The Energy Community with Southeast Europe' (2007) http://www.hks.harvard.edu/kokkalis/GSW9/Hofer_paper.pdf; S Gstöhl, 'Political dimension of an externalization of the EU's Internal market', *EU Diplomacy Papers* 3/2007, 17.

binding bilaterally among the contracting parties. Binding financing tools comprise financial regulations in form of the Instrument for Pre-Accession Assistance (IPA), bilateral financial framework agreements. Finally, programming tools are constituted by bilateral framework agreements and unilateral Accession or European Partnerships. If any of these are adopted by the EU by way of a regulation they are not formally binding on the candidate countries. The unilateral accession partnerships have, in the SAA pre-accession process, been renamed the European Partnerships, as mentioned above, and link static bilateral SAAs to the subsequent accession process.[44] The Council decides through a decision, following a proposal by the Commission, on the principles, priorities, and conditions to be contained in the European Partnership with a given country. Annexes to these Council decisions list very detailed key priorities, divided into short-term and medium-term priorities. In the case of Serbia, for example, this includes: ensuring full cooperation with the International Criminal Tribunal for the former Yugoslavia; constructive cooperation on matters relating to Kosovo; continuing efforts to implement reform of the public administration, including establishment of a civil service pay system which ensures transparent recruitment and promotion, as well as professionalism and accountability; strengthening of European integration structures; and improved coordination throughout the public administration and parliament giving particular attention to policy coordination.[45]

2 International agreements

The only legally binding bilateral instruments for all participants involved, namely the Union as such, Member States, and the candidate country, are the Association Agreements. The signing and ratification by all the EU Member States and the applicant country typically takes three years because these instruments have to be ratified as mixed agreements, not just in accordance with Article 217 TFEU and adopted by the Council under Article 218 TFEU but also by all the Member States according their respective constitutional requirements.[46] The Council alone has, as an interim solution relied upon since the 1990s, concluded 'interim agreements' with the applicant countries on free trade and trade-related matters falling within the EU exclusive competence on trade.[47] The only exception (to that exception) has been the first Accession Association agreement concluded post-Lisbon with Kosovo in 2016; there the EU concluded a SAA, without ratification by the Member States.[48] This was, however, not

---

[44] Council Regulation 533/2004 of 22 March 2004 on the establishment of partnerships in the framework of the stabilisation and association process [2004] OJ L86/1.

[45] Council Decision of 18 February 2008 on the principles and conditions contained in the European Partnership with Serbia including Kosovo as defined by UN Security Council Resolution 1244 of 1 June 1999 and repealing Decision 2006/56/EC [2008] OJ L80/46.

[46] This is with the exception of the association agreement with Kosovo, which could not be concluded a mixed agreement because some Member States do not recognize Kosovo as an independent state.

[47] See eg for Latvia [1994] OJ L374/1 or for a more recent example: the Interim Agreement on Trade and trade-related matters with Albania, OJ; L.E Ramsey, The implications of the Europe Agreements for an expanded European Union, ICLQ Vol.44 (1995) 164–71.

[48] Council Decision (EU) 2ß16/342 of 12 February 2016 on the conclusion, on behalf of the Union, of the Stabilisation and Association Agreement between the European Union and the European Atomic Energy Community, of the one part, and Kosovo of the other part, [2016] OJ L71/1.

the result of Lisbon Treaty revisions resulting in association agreements' becoming an exclusive EU competence. On the contrary, this was triggered by the fact that five Member States (Slovak Republic, Greece, Cyprus, Romania, and Spain) currently do not recognize Kosovo and consequently are not be able to ratify an international agreement with it.

Binding international agreements are concluded by the Council, or the Commission on behalf of the Union. These can enable participation in the EU policy fields of migration,[49] air transport,[50] and CFSP missions,[51] in EU programmes,[52] and even in EU agencies before accession.[53] Additional examples comprise visa facilitation agreements,[54] framework agreements on participation in EU programmes, and financing agreements.[55] Competence for such delegated treaty-making by the Commission in conferred by the Council and the European Parliament in an international agreement or in secondary legislation. The Commission is provided with the clearly defined power to conclude such financial framework agreements under Article 8 of the IPA II Regulation[56] on the implementation of the assistance for the candidate countries.[57]

---

[49] Agreement between the European Community and the former Yugoslav Republic of Macedonia on the readmission of persons residing without authorisation, [2007] OJ L334/7–24.

[50] Agreement between the EC and Council of Ministers of the Republic of Albania on certain aspects of air services, Council Decision of 24 June 2010 on the conclusion of the Agreement between the European Community and the Council of Ministers of the Republic of Albania on certain aspects of air services, [2010] OJ L166/16.

[51] Agreement between the EU and the Republic of Albania on the participation of the Republic of Albania in the EU military operation in the Republic of Chad and the Central African Republic.

[52] Framework Agreement between the European Community and Serbia and Montenegro on the general principles for the participation of Serbia and Montenegro in Community programmes [2005] OJ L192/29.

[53] Turkey is currently a member in two regulatory agencies, the European Environmental Agency since 2001 and the European Monitoring Centre for Drugs and Drug Addiction since 2007. This is enabled by an international agreement which also regulates full participation with the exception that Turkey has no right to vote in the Management Board. Agreement between the European Community and the Republic of Turkey concerning the participation of the Republic of Turkey in the European Environment Agency and the European Environment Information and Observation Network, [2001] OJ L213/112–119 Agreement between the European Community and the Republic of Turkey on the participation of the Republic of Turkey in the work of the European Monitoring Centre for Drugs and Drug Addiction, [2007] OJ L323/24–33.

[54] Agreement between the European Community and the Republic of Albania on the facilitation of the issuance of visas—Declarations, [2007] OJ L334/85–95; Agreement between the European Community and the republic of Serbia on the facilitation of the issuance of visas, OJ [2007] L334/137–147. See also the Agreement between the EU and the Republic of Albania establishing a framework for the participation of the Republic of Albania in the European Union crisis management operations, [2012] OI L169/2.

[55] Financing Agreement between the government of Montenegro and the European Commission concerning the cross-border programme Serbia-Montenegro under the instrument for pre-accession for the year 2011 (15 July 2013) http://www.mvpei.gov.me/ResourceManager/FileDownload. aspx?rId=158301&rType=2; Financing Agreement between Turkey and the European Commission http:// www.ab.gov.tr/files/ardb/evt/2_turkiye_ab_iliskileri/2_2_adaylik_sureci/2_2_7_turkiye_ab_mali_ isbirligi/2_2_7_1_ipa/2_2_7_1_1_ipai_finansman_antlasmalari/2010_fa_ipa_i_merkezi_projeler_ 03_02_2011_kisim_3.pdf; Financing agreement between Turkey and the Commission concerning the multi-annual operation programme 'Transport' for community assistance from the instrument of pre-accession assistance under the 'regional development' component in Turkey.

[56] Regulation (EU) No 231/2014 of the European Parliament and of the Council establishing an Instrument for Pre-accession assistance (IPA II) [2014] OJ L77/11.

[57] Framework agreement between Serbia and Commission on IPA II http/www.evropa.gov.rs/ Documents/Home/DACU/12/104/105/106/246/FWA%20Serbia.pdf; Framework agreement between the Republic of Albania, represented by the government of the Republic of Albania and the European

Another mandate can be found in Article 5 of the Framework Agreements between the EU and Serbia or Albania on participation in EU programmes to conclude memoranda of understanding (MoUs) or agreements on the specific participation in EU programmes.[58] Participation of candidate countries in EU agencies as observers can be provided for through bilateral 'Association Council Decisions'.[59] In addition, ministries or government agencies of candidate states cooperate with EU agencies through working arrangements[60] and, exceptionally, through binding international agreements.[61]

In this context, the double track policy of the Union in achieving harmonization with candidate countries also needs to be mentioned. The first track seeks to ensure achievement of the harmonization aims through the association and pre-accession process. The second track focuses on EU policy fields of external importance, namely the common aviation area and the common energy market.

The EU targets the Western Balkan states, Turkey, and also some ENP countries, for participation in the Energy Community and the European Common Aviation Area. The Energy Community Treaty (ECT) was concluded in 2006 and currently has—in addition to the 28 EU Member States—Albania, Bosnia and Herzegovina, FYR of Macedonia, Moldova, Montenegro, Serbia, Kosovo, and Ukraine as participants.[62] It endeavours to achieve a single energy market through the adaptation of the *acquis* in the field of energy, environment, and competition law and, according to the European Commission, is modelled on the European Coal and Steal Community of the 1950s. Harmonization aimed at an internal energy market among the participating countries is reinforced by an external energy trade policy and the mutual assistance principle. The European Common Aviation Area was established on the basis of an agreement (ECAA), signed in 2006 and provisionally applied, between the EU,

Commission on the arrangements for Implementation of Union financial assistance to the Republic of Albania under the instruments for pre-accession assistance (IPA II) http://www.integrimi.gov.al/f1les/pages_Files/Framework_Agreement_-__English.pdf.

[58] Council Decision of 22 November 2004 concerning the signing of a Framework Agreement between the European Community and the Republic of Albania on the general principles for the participation of the Republic of Albania in Community programmes Framework Agreement between the European Community and the Republic of Albania on the general principles for the participation of the Republic of Albania in Community programmes [2005] OJ L192/1 (Art 5: 'The specific terms and conditions regarding the participation of Albania in each particular programme, in particular the financial contribution payable, will be determined by agreement, in the form of a Memorandum of Understanding, between the Commission, acting on behalf of the Community, and the Government of Albania'; Commission Decision of 10 April 2013, approving, on behalf of the EU, a MoU on the participation of the Republic of Albania in the action programme in the field of lifelong learning (2007–2013), Brussels, 10 April 2013; MoU between the EC and the Republic of Albania on the participation of the Republic of Albania in the programme 'Europe for Citizens' (2 February 2009) http://ec.europa.eu/citizenship/pdf/doc760_en.pdf.

[59] See eg Decision 1/2010 of the EU Croatia SAA of 25 May 2010 on the participation of Croatia as an observer in the FRA and the respective modalities thereof [2010] OJ L279/68.

[60] See eg Serbian Ministry of Interior Working Arrangement establishing operational cooperation with Frontex http://frontex.europa.eu/assets/Partners/Third_countries/WA_with_Serbia.pdf.

[61] This is the case for instance with Europol, Under the Europol Decision, Europol was mandated to conclude agreement with third countries and international organization, in the 2017 Europol Regulation this is limited to non-binding working arrangements.

[62] Council Decision of 29 May 2006 on the conclusion by the European Community of the Energy Community Treaty, [2006] OJ L198/15–17.

its Member States and neighbouring countries. It aims to create a common aviation area based on free market access, freedom of establishment, equal conditions of competition, and common rules in the fields of safety, security, air traffic management, social aspects, and the environment.[63] In order to create effective rules in both such cases, the wording of the fundamental freedoms is repeated in identical terms (see Articles 7 and 41 ECT and Articles 6 and 7 ECAA). In addition, intergovernmental bodies are created and certain elements of judicial protection of the EU Treaties are incorporated, reinforcing the parallelism with homogeneity clauses and a sincere co-operation clause (Article 6 ECT and Article 4 ECAA). In the case of the ECT, the EU Treaty infringement procedure is copied in such that a party, regulatory body or private body can bring a complaint to the attention of the secretariat, which can take it up, and ultimately on to the ministerial council in case of non-compliance (Articles 89–92 ECT).

3 EU legislation

An important organising role in the political and financial steering process is assigned to the EU and its Member States through regulations establishing both the Accession Partnerships and the European Partnership with the Western Balkans states, as high-lighted above. The details of priorities are provided in individual Council decisions on the European Partnerships. The stabilization and association process of the Western Balkan states, established through a static international agreement, is thus linked with a more flexible instrument and with financial programming under a specific financial regulation for candidate countries. The currently applicable IPA II Regulation is in force for the period 2014–2020.[64] Support within this framework falls mainly into: (a) the categories of reforms in anticipation of Union membership and the related institution and capacity building; (b) socio-economic and regional development; (c) employment, social policies, education, promotion of gender equality, and human resources development; (d) agriculture and rural development; and (e) regional and territorial cooperation.

4 Forms of non-binding acts

The overwhelming majority of the tools employed are soft law measures of the Commission to steer the political and financing process. Such instruments are exemplified by the IPA multi-annual indicative planning documents,[65] strategy papers, various

---

[63] Multilateral agreement between the European Community and its Member States, the Republic of Albania, Bosnia and Herzegovina, the Republic of Bulgaria, the Republic of Croatia, the former Yugoslav Republic of Macedonia, the Republic of Iceland, the Republic of Montenegro, the Kingdom of Norway, Romania, the Republic of Serbia and the United Nations Interim Administration Mission in Kosovo (1) on the establishment of a European Common Aviation Area, [2006] OJ L285/3.

[64] IPA II Regulation (n 56) 95–108.

[65] Multi-annual indicative planning document (MIPD) 2011–2013 Bosnia and Herzegovina, ec.europa. eu references

progress or country reports[66] (for example, the progress reports on the Cooperation and Verification Mechanism for Bulgaria and Romania[67]), the Commission's opinion on an application for membership the European Union.[68] In addition, the Council and the European Council issue non-legal—but politically binding—acts in the form of 'Conclusions'.[69] The tools can be categorized according to author and aim. They can also be subdivided into unilateral and bilateral instruments, as indicated above for hard law tools.

(a) Unilateral soft law tools

These instruments are adopted by the European Council, the Council, the Commission and the candidate country itself for political, financing, and programming purposes. The European Council adopts political conclusions the importance of which can be highlighted through the Copenhagen Criteria of 1993[70] and the renewed consensus of 2006.[71] Council conclusions are relevant for political steering.[72] The Commission's instruments are papers and progress reports,[73] action plans, the IPA multi-annual planning document,[74] and progress reports (e.g., on the Cooperation and Verification Mechanism for Bulgaria and Romania).[75] The Commission's tools are characterized by their aims with regard to programming and administrative review. The candidate country publishes NPAAs[76] and action plans.[77]

(b) Bilateral soft law tools

In pursuance of the enlargement policy, the Commission primarily employs soft law instruments of a unilateral nature. Bilateral soft law tools in the form of administrative arrangements, political MoUs, joint declarations or exchanges of letters are not used to the same extent as in relations to other third countries or international

[66] For instance, Report from the Commission to the Council and the European Parliament on Albania's progress in the fight against corruption and organized crime and in the judicial reform, Brussels, 4 June 2014 (COM 2014)331final.

[67] Report from the Commission to the European Parliament and the Council on the Progress in Bulgaria under the Cooperation and Verification Mechanism, Brussels, 27 January 2016 COM(2016) 40 final.

[68] Communication from the Commission, Opinion on Croatia's application for membership of the European Union COM(2004) 0257 final.

[69] K Lenaerts and P van Nuffel, *European Union Law* (3rd edn, Sweet & Maxwell 2011) para 22-104.

[70] Presidency Conclusions, European Council, Copenhagen, 21–22 June 1993.

[71] Presidency Conclusions, European Council, 14–15 December 2006 http://www.consilium.europa. eu/ueDocs/cms_Data/docs/pressData/en/ec/92202.pdf (last visited on 23 October 2016).

[72] Council conclusions on Albania, Luxembourg, 24 June 2014, granting Albania candidate status.

[73] Commission staff working document Turkey 2015, report accompanying the document Communication from the Commission to the European Parliament, the Council, European Economic and Social Committee and the Committee of the regions, EU enlargement strategy, COM(2015) 611 final http://ec.europa.eu/enlargement/pdf/key_documents/2015/20151110_report_turkey.pdf.

[74] Multi-annual Indicative Planning Document MIPD, Republic of Serbia, 2011–2013.

[75] Commission Progress Report Romania COM(2016) 41.

[76] See eg the Turkish National action plan for EU accession Phase-II (June 2015–June 2019) http://www.ab.gov.tr/index.php?p=42260&l=2. http://www.ab.gov.tr/files/pub/nap-ii-en.pdf.

[77] For instance: Serbia First action plan, 2014–2015.

organizations.[78] Examples of bilateral working arrangements of a non-binding nature, however, exist in the cooperation between EU regulatory agencies and accession candidates.[79] Agencies with an external dimension thus carry out the important function of familiarizing candidate countries with the task of implementation of EU policy.[80] This is achieved in particular by providing candidate countries with observer status (i.e., without voting rights) in these agencies and by agreeing on political—but legally non-binding—working arrangements for establishing cooperation, as in the case of Serbia, Turkey, or Albania.[81]

D Administrative Procedures within Enlargement Policy

The mix of administrative procedures in the form of both direct administration and composite procedures becomes visible in financial programming and implementation. The IPA II Regulation 2014 laid down the general framework and specific objectives (Article 1). The programming is to be implemented directly, indirectly, or in shared management, in line with Regulation 236/2014 laying down common rules and procedures for the implementation of the Union's instruments for financing external action.[82] For example, in the Framework Agreement on financial support for Serbia, four different methods of implementation are mentioned: (1) direct management by Commission departments, including its staff in Union delegations, and/or through executive agencies, under Financial Regulation Article 58(1)(a); (2) indirect management, whereby the Commission entrusts budget implementation tasks of certain programmes or actions to the IPA II beneficiary, under Financial Regulation Article 58(1)(c)(i), while retaining overall final responsibility for general budget implementation in accordance with Financial Regulation Article 58(2); (3) indirect management with entities other than IPA II beneficiaries, as laid down in Financial Regulation Article 58(1)(c)(ii), (iii), and (v)–(vii); and (4) shared management with Member States for cross-border cooperation programmes involving Member States of the European Union, implemented in accordance with the IPA II Implementing Regulation, in accordance with Financial Regulation Article 58(1)(b).[83]

---

[78] See eg S Bartelt and A Ott, 'Die Verwaltungszusammenarbeit der Europäischen Kommission mit Drittstaaten und internationalen Organisationen: Kategorisierung und rechtliche Einordnung' in J P Terhechte, *Internationale Dimensionen des europäischen Verwaltungsrechts* (Europarecht Beiheft 1/2016) 141–70.

[79] See eg working arrangement establishing operational cooperation between Frontex and the Ministry of the Interior of the Republic of Serbia or the working arrangement with Albania, see http://frontex. europa.eu/assets/Partners/Third_countries/WA_with_Albania.pdf (last accessed 19 October 2016).

[80] See for the EASA for instance the working arrangement between the EASA and the Civil Aviation Directorate of the Republic of Serbia on collection and exchange of information on the safety of aircraft using EU airports and airports of non-EU states that participate in the EU SAFA Programme, including airports of the Republic of Serbia https://www.easa.europa.eu/system/files/dfu/53188_PKY_ M.Zivanovic_SAFA%20WA%20ATT.PDF.

[81] The working arrangements indicate that they are not binding under international law; see eg para 16 of the MoU between Frontex and the Ministry of Foreign Affairs of the Republic of Turkey from 28 May 2012.

[82] Regulation No 236/2014 [2014] OJ L77/95.

[83] Art 7 of the Framework Agreement between the European Commission and Serbia,http://www. evropa.gov.rs/Documents/Home/DACU/12/104/105/106/246/FWA%20Serbia.pdf. See for an example of (4) the Interreg-IPA CBC Hungary-Serbia http://www.interreg-ipa-husrb.com/en/file/163/.

The Commission adopts annual action programmes and multi-annual action programmes and concludes framework agreements and sectoral agreements with the IPA II beneficiary (Article 5 Commission Implementing Regulation 231/2014). All these measures are adopted on the Union side through Commission decisions. The framework agreement between the Commission and a candidate country, benefiting under IPA II, forms a binding international agreement, setting out specific arrangements for the management, control, supervision, monitoring, evaluation, reporting, and audit of the IPA II assistance.[84] Conditions for indirect management applicable to IPA II beneficiaries are set out in Article 4(4) of the IPA II Regulation and in Articles 7–12 Commission Implementing Regulation 447/2014, specifying the structures needed for management, control, supervision, monitoring, evaluation, reporting, and internal audit. The IPA II beneficiary appoints a National IPA Coordinator as the main counterpart of the Commission in the overall process of strategic planning, coordination of programming, monitoring of implementation, evaluation, and reporting of IPA II assistance (Article 4 Commission Implementing Regulation). The rules also foresee cross-border cooperation between one or more EU Member States and one or more IPA II beneficiary, or between two or more IPA II beneficiaries, or cooperation between IPA II beneficiaries and countries falling under ENP instruments.[85] Such cross-border cooperation can be implemented through an international agreement, denoted in Article 8(2) IPA II Regulation as subsidiary agreements of the implementing authorities.

From the Union side, in order to conclude such an administrative agreement outside the framework of Article 218 TFEU, the Commission derives its mandate from the power delegated under Article 216 TFEU in combination with Article 8(1) IPA II Regulation, further details being stipulated in Article 5 Commission Implementing Regulation. Cross-border cooperation programmes are to be implemented under shared management (Article 36 Implementing Commission Regulation) and, as such, Member States and the Commission are to be responsible for the management and control of the programmes according to Regulation 966/2012 and Delegated Regulation 1268/2012. The participating countries designate a single managing and audit authority (Article 36 Implementing Commission Regulation). Under such a cooperation programme, a joint monitoring committee (JMC) between EU Member State and participating candidate country must also be set up (Article 38 Implementing Commission Regulation 447/2014). The Commission participates in this JMC in an advisory capacity (Article 38(4) Implementing Commission Regulation). Together with the managing authority, the JMC carries out monitoring of the cross-border cooperation programme.

This financial framework also provides for the protection of the financial interests of the Union (Article 7 Regulation 236/2014) with regard to which OLAF may carry out investigations. In order to extend this to third-country partners, Article

---

[84] See eg Framework Agreement between Serbia and EU Commission on the arrangements for implementation of the Union financial assistance to the Republic of Serbia under the instrument for pre-accession assistance (IPA II).

[85] See eg the Interreg-IPA Cross-border programme Hungary–Serbia approved on 15 December 2015.

7(4) Regulation 236/2014 stipulates that cooperation measures with third countries and with international organizations, contracts, grant agreements, and grant decisions shall contain provisions expressly empowering the Commission, the Court of Auditors, and OLAF to conduct audits, on-the-spot checks, and inspections according to the respective competences of these bodies. The Commission also engages in dialogue with the IPA II beneficiary on public financial management and assesses the level of compliance of the IPA II beneficiary's administration with the principles of an open and orderly public financial management system. When the candidate countries administration shows deficiencies in this regard, appropriate measures need to be taken (Article 4(3) Implementing Commission Regulation).

Moreover, agencies with an external dimension, such as the European Aviation Safety Agency (EASA),[86] Frontex, Europol, and the European Police College (CEPOL),[87] cooperate with accession countries. Such cooperation is established either through working arrangements or, especially concerning Europol in the past, through international agreements. For example, the 'working arrangement' establishing operational cooperation between the European Agency for the Management of Operational Cooperation at the External Borders of the Member States of the European Union (Frontex) and the Ministry of the Interior of Republic of Serbia,[88] states that it is, as regards legal status, not to be considered as an international treaty (Point 7). Practical implementation of its contents is not to be regarded as the fulfilment of international obligations by the European Community and its institutions. So, for the majority of agencies, non-binding arrangements for cooperation are concluded, though in the case of Europol the mandate applicable until March 2017 allowed for the conclusion of international agreements (as with Eurojust and CEPOL). International agreements on cooperation and 'strategic planning' have in fact been concluded by all candidate countries—except Turkey—with Europol. Under the new Europol Regulation (from 2017) only non-binding working arrangements will emerge.

E Organization and Legal Principles Specific to Enlargement

Administrative management of the enlargement policy in the three recent enlargement waves was in the hands of DG Enlargement (DG ELARG). Since 1 January 2015, as a result of organizational restructuring, DG ELARG merged with the administration of the ENP to form the Directorate-General for Neighbourhood and Enlargement Negotiations (DG NEAR), while other administrative sub-units moved to DG REGIO.[89]

---

[86] Working arrangement with Serbia http://www.easa.europa.eu/system/files/dfu/Serbia.pdf; the one with Albania is labelled a cooperation agreement: 'CEPOL's Governing Board approved the text of the Cooperation Agreement between the European Police College (CEPOL) and the Police Training Centre of the Albanian State Police by written procedure on 26 July 2012' http://www.parlament.gv.at/PAKT/EU/XXIV/EU/09/29/EU_92931/imfname_10376951.pdf.

[87] https://www.cepol.europa.eu/sites/default/files/13-2015-GB.pdf.

[88] http://frontex.europa.eu/assets/Partners/Third_countries/WA_with_Serbia.pdf.

[89] ELARG.D.l, 'Task Force Turkish Cypriot Community' transferred to DG REGIO and the Directorate DEVCO.F, 'Neighbourhood', containing one head of unit level function in Delegation, from DG DEVCO and Integration of the Directorate as NEAR.B, 'Neighbourhood South'. The units

As explained above, any pre-accession strategy is focussed on familiarising candidate countries with EU programmes and policies. With regard to agencies, two distinct situations have to be separated. The participation of third countries in the work of EU agencies, such as those under the EEA or accession candidates, is enabled through a special observer status. Independently of such a status, international relations between the governments of the candidate states and the agencies are channelled through working arrangements. EU regulatory agencies having an external dimension, such as Europol, Frontex, and EASA, have concluded such cooperative arrangements with all accession candidates. Albania, Macedonia, Montenegro, and Serbia have concluded a strategic and operational agreement on cooperation with Europol, aimed at preventing and combating organized crime, terrorism, and other forms of international crimes such as illegal immigrant smuggling or corruption.[90] However, it should be noted that the interaction between EU agencies and the Commission is not coordinated so as to assess and/or improve progress in the enlargement process.

The overarching principles dominating the enlargement process are *differentiation* and *conditionality*. Every country is assessed according to its own merits. While each particular accession process has until now, with the exception of Norway, resulted in accession in fact, the Union has decided to speak—since it accorded a concrete accession perspective to Turkey—of an 'open process', suggesting a more differentiated or selective approach. The most important principle is conditionality, which should be divided into pre-accession conditionality and post-accession conditionality.[91] This principle points to the fact that the EU sets out certain conditions and benchmarks which, if not met, can result in various countermeasures, such as the suspension of financial aid or even the suspension of accession talks as a whole. In the renewed enlargement strategy, the principles of *consolidation* and *communication* are also stressed. Conditions and benchmarks often relate to administrative and judicial reforms and the fight against corruption; such difficult issues will typically be addressed at an early stage in the process. Furthermore, the outcomes of political and economic dialogue will feed into accession negotiations. The pace of any accession process will depend on the level and pace of reforms in the candidate country, each candidate being assessed in the light of its own progress. The Union refrains from setting any target dates for accession until the negotiations are close to completion,[92] in other words until the conditions which have been set down are at least broadly met.

In Article 5 IPA II Regulation *compliance*, *coherence*, and *complementarity* in respect of financing rules and practice are highlighted. Financial assistance and its management has to be consistent with Union policies, must comply with international

---

DEVCO.F. 1, 'Geographical Coordination Neighbourhood East' and DEVC0.F.3, 'Regional Programmes Neighbourhood East' integrated as NEAR.C. l, 'Geographical Coordination Neighbourhood East' and NEA R C.2, 'Regional Programmes Neighbourhood East').

[90] In the case of Turkey, only a cooperation agreement has been concluded https://www.n.europa.eu/agreements/turkey.

[91] K Inglis, 'Accession Treaties: Differentiation Versus Conditionality' in A Ott and E Vos, *Fifty Years of European Integration: Foundations and Perspectives* (TMC Asser Press 2009) 139–56; K Inglis, 'EU Enlargement: Membership Conditions Applied to Future and Potential Member States' in S Blockmans and A Lazowski (eds), *The European Union and its Neighbours* (TMC Asser Press 2008) 61–92.

[92] Brussels European Council 14–15 December 2006, Presidency Conclusions, 14–15 December 2006.

agreements concluded between the Union and beneficiary countries, and, finally, satisfy Union commitments under multilateral agreements. With regard to this, the Commission and the Member States also commit themselves to increased transparency and accountability in assistance delivery, including public disclosure of information on the volume and allocation of assistance, ensuring that data is internationally comparable and can be easily assessed, shared, and published. For this purpose, Commission, Member States and the EIB cooperate for coherence and avoidance of duplication of assistance. Apart from aiming for effectiveness and efficiency, the Commission and the Member States are expected to adopt the steps necessary to ensure better coordination and complementarity with multilateral and regional organizations and entities (such as international financial institutions, UN agencies, funds, programmes, and non-Union donors). Article 4 Commission Implementing Regulation stresses the principle of 'ownership', in the sense that the programming and implementation of IPA II assistance lies primarily in the hands of the beneficiary states.

As explained above, the enlargement policy stands out—next to the ENP policy— with its extensive use of soft law tools. Such tools, owing to the conditionality principle, effectively impose on candidate countries obligations lying outside formal legal requirements. Most such tools fall within the broad policy, financing and programming framework of both the European Commission and EU agencies as administrative actors. These soft law instruments are important both for shaping public opinion and for creating a manageable framework for applicant countries, they are accessible, and they fulfil general standards of *transparency* and *good governance*. However, it is undeniable that management of each accession application is an open-ended process influenced by its political setting of ambivalence and unpredictability. Recently, the Commission has referred to the need for a 'credible' process which works for both parties.[93]

F Administrative Enforcement of EU Enlargement Policy

In the context of EU enlargement, the need for, and the extent of, administrative enforcement in relation to third parties is more limited than in most other EU policy fields. As explained above, this particular policy field is dominated by non-binding instruments, and the few binding instruments can be split up according to their pre- and post-accession relevance. In the pre-accession phase, the prospect of enlargement has direct and indirect implications for third parties such as the applicant countries' businesses and individual parties, but the enforcement of the relevant rules is achieved nationally in the enforcement of EU measures by way of approximation. However, conjointly with political instruments, mainly financial instruments are employed and for these instruments the enforcement mechanisms are the same as those generally applicable with regard to financial measures. Such enforcement against a 'third country'

---

[93] Communication from the Commission to the European Parliament, the Council, the ECOSOC and Committee of Regions, 2016 Communication on EU Enlargement Policy, Brussels, 9 November 2016 COM(2016) 715 final.

(here, an applicant state) occurs as it is a beneficiary of IPA funding. In order to establish liability and to enforce budgetary rules, the Commission concludes an international framework agreement with the country concerned. Article 8 IPA II Regulation, in combination with Article 5 IPA II Commission Implementing Regulation, confers competence on the Commission to conclude such a framework agreement 'setting out specific arrangements for the management, control, supervision, monitoring, evaluation, reporting and audit of IPA II assistance committing the IPA II beneficiary to transpose into its legal order the relevant Union regulatory requirements'.[94] Article 6 IPA II Commission Implementing Regulation further lays down that financing agreements shall provide, inter alia, the terms on which IPA II assistance shall be managed, including the applicable methods of implementation, aid intensities, implementation deadlines, and rules on the eligibility of expenditure.[95] For instance, Article 50 of the Financing Agreement between Albania and the Commission covers supervision, control, and audit (all performed by the Commission), also involving OLAF and auditing by the European Court of Auditors. In regard to indirect management by the IPA II beneficiary, the Commission and the Union delegation in Albania can carry out ex-ante verification of tendering and contracting, and undertake ex-post controls of tendering, contracting, contract execution together with supervision of the functioning of the management. The IPA II beneficiary is required to designate a national body to facilitate effective cooperation and exchange of information, including information of an operational nature, with OLAF. This designated body also performs tasks on behalf of the Union, and shall prevent, detect, and correct irregularities and fraud when executing those tasks. To this end, the IPA II beneficiary must carry out, in accordance with the principle of proportionality, ex ante and ex post controls including on-the-spot checks on representative and/or risk-based samples of transactions, so as to ensure that the actions financed from the EU budget are carried out effectively and implemented correctly. The IPA II beneficiary must also recover funds unduly paid, and bring legal proceedings where necessary in this regard. The majority of cases analysed by, pre-dating accession, relate to the abuse of pre-accession funding in Bulgaria and Romania.[96]

The role of the European Ombudsman in review of administrative action in relation to enlargement is limited. It can, though, be highlighted by reference to a few decisions. such as where the European Commission refused to allow access to its comments on draft Serbian legislation, or where a team leader in a EU pre-accession programme in Turkey was dismissed.[97] In both of these cases, no maladministration was found by the Ombudsman. Scrutiny by the European Court of Auditors of EU pre-accession and post-accession funding have been more elaborate and critical. Special reports have assessed both the general instruments and the use of pre-accession

---

[94] IPA II Regulation (n 56).
[95] Commission Implementing Regulation (EU) No 447/2014 of 2 May 2014 on the specific rules for implementing Regulation (EU) No 231/2014 of the European Parliament and of the Council establishing an Instrument for Pre-accession assistance (IPA II).
[96] Especially SAPARD funding, see the OLAF annual report 2015, 26.
[97] Decision in case OI/7/2015/ANA, 2 September 2016. Decision 2477/2005/GG on 14 August 2008.

funding by the individual candidate country and led to recommendations directed to the Commission.[98]

G Supervision and Control of Enlargement Policy

1 Administrative and political supervision of enlargement policy

The classic administrative procedure for compliance control in the EU is the infringement procedure which is, however, cumbersome and time-consuming. Owing to the conditionality applying in the enlargement process, several more effective compliance mechanisms have been created by the Union for use vis-à-vis a candidate country. Since establishing the negotiating framework for Turkey, an extra layer of compliance control in the accession progress has been introduced. Negotiations can be suspended in case of a serious and persistent breach of the values of the Union. Taking the Serbian negotiating mandate as an example, negotiations were opened on the basis that Serbia respects, and is committed to promoting, the values on which the Union is founded namely the respect for human dignity, freedom, democracy, equality, the rule of law, and respect for human rights, including the rights of persons belonging to minorities (Article 2 TEU). This suspension mechanism can, following a Commission recommendation, be triggered by a qualified majority of the Council, in this example, after having heard Serbia. The Member States take action then in the IGC, in accordance with the Council decision, and the European Parliament is informed.[99] The parallel procedure (once a country as become Member State), suspension under Article 7(2) TEU, requires a higher voting majority (unanimity of the European Council) and consent of the EP, where it has been established that there is a clear risk of a serious breach by a Member State of the values expressed in Article 2 TEU.

A further compliance mechanism, relating also to conditionality, is the setting of benchmarks unanimously by the Council following a Commission proposal. In the implementation of the renewed consensus, the Council lays down such benchmarks for the provisional closure and, where appropriate, for the opening of each chapter. Interim benchmarks for the chapters 'Judiciary and fundamental rights' and 'Justice, freedom and security' are set according to the same procedure.[100]

After 2004, further compliance control mechanisms were introduced in acts of accession, i.e., once the candidate country has acceded. These are safeguard clauses relating to the internal market and to justice and home affairs. Avoiding the cumbersome

---

[98] Special report No 21/2016: EU pre-accession assistance for strengthening administrative capacity in the Western Balkans: A meta-audit http://www.eca.europa.eu/en/Pages/DocItem.aspx?did=37609; Special Report No 19 2014, EU Pre-accession Assistance to Serbia http://www.eca.europa.eu/Lists/ECADocuments/SR14_19/QJAB14019ENN.pdf.

[99] General EU Position, Ministerial meeting opening the IGC on accession of Serbia to the EU (Brussels, 21 January 2014), Brussels, 9 January 2014, AD 1/14, para 22.

[100] Paragraph 42: 'The Union will communicate such benchmarks to Serbia. Depending on the chapter, precise benchmarks will refer in particular to legislative alignment with the *acquis* and to a satisfactory track record in the implementation of key elements of the *acquis* demonstrating the existence of an adequate administrative and judicial capacity. Where relevant, benchmarks will also include the fulfilment of commitments under the Stabilisation and Association Agreement, in particular those that mirror requirements under the *acquis*'.

formal infringement procedure, the Commission is able to react to failure to fulfil commitments undertaken during the accession negotiations, where these create an imminent risk to, or a serious breach of, the functioning of the internal market, or serious shortcomings or risks during the transposition, implementation or application of the *acquis* in the area of freedom security and justice (Article 38 or 39 of the Croatian Act of Accession, respectively).[101] Also, in the case of Croatia, an accession postponement clause (Article 39) was introduced together with a pre-accession monitoring clause (Article 36). The wording of the safeguard provisions leaves open what measures may be appropriate; Article 38 of the Croatian Act of Accession establishes that the proportionality principle must be applied. Despite the possible threat to use the safeguard clauses against Poland,[102] Romania, and Bulgaria during the first three years, the only example in practice until now was the case of Bulgaria between 2006 and 2008. There, the Commission invoked the internal market safeguard clause concerning the Bulgarian aviation sector by not recognising airworthiness and maintenance certificates issued by the Bulgarian authorities and did not qualify Bulgarian air carriers as Community air carriers.[103]

In addition, in response to specific shortcomings of Romania and Bulgaria in the areas of judicial reform, the fight against corruption and organized crime, a new cooperation and verification mechanism (CVM) was launched in December 2006 to monitor progress according to individual benchmarks set for these countries.[104] While the other safeguard measures in the previous accession treaties extend post-accession conditionality to the fields of internal market and justice and home affairs (JHA) only to a maximum of three years after accession, this CVM is applied as long as these benchmarks are not met. The legal basis for the application of the CVM can be found in two Commission Decisions laying down the specific benchmarks,[105] requiring more transparent, and efficient judicial process or professional, non-partisan investigations into allegations of high-level corruption.[106] It has been argued that the Commission Decision, as a legally binding document specifying aims in fields in which the EU has

---

[101] See further A Ott, 'Differentiation Through Accession Law: Free Movement Rights in an Enlarged European Union' in B de Witte, A Ott, and E Vos (eds), *Between Flexibility and Disintegration* (Edgar Elgar Publishing 2017) 146–78.

[102] In the case of Poland, the threat had already been used in March 2003. See Ott (n 101) 152.

[103] Commission Regulation [1962/2006] OJ L408/8 and Commission Regulation 875/2008 [2008] OJ L240/3; Spernbauer, 'Benchmarking, Safeguard Clauses and Verification Mechanisms—What's in a Name? (n 12) 286; and Inglis, *Evolving Practice in EU Enlargement with Case Studies in Agri-Food and Environment Law*, (fn. 10), p.192.

[104] See 2016 reports http://ec.europa.eu/cvm/progress reports_en.htm#thirteen.

[105] Commission Decision of 13/XII/2006 establishing a mechanism for cooperation and verification of progress in Bulgaria to address specific benchmarks in the areas of judicial reform and the fight against corruption and organized crime http://ec.europa.eu/enlargement/pdf/bulgaria/bg_accompanying_measures_1206_en.pdf; Commission Decision C of 13/XII/2006 establishing a mechanism for cooperation and verification of progress in Romania to address specific benchmarks in the areas of judicial reform and the fight against corruption http://ec.europa.eu/enlargement/pdf/romania/ro accompanying_measures_1206_en.pdf; OJ L354 of 14 December 2006, 58–60; [2007] OJ L142M of 5 June 2007, 827–29 (MT).

[106] Annex of Commission Decision of 13/XII/2006 establishing a mechanism for cooperation and verification of progress in Bulgaria to address specific benchmarks in the areas of judicial reform and the fight against corruption and organized crime, Brussels, 13 December 2006, C(2006) 6570 final.

	2004 enlargement	2007 enlargement	2013 enlargement
2 + 3 + 2 years	Temporary provisions: - market access - labour market	Temporary provisions: - market access - labour market	Temporary provisions: - market access - labour market
Up to 3 years after accession	Economic safeguard clause (Art. 37)	Economic safeguard clause (Art. 36)	Economic safeguard clause (Art. 37)
	Internal market safeguard clause (Art. 38)	Internal market safeguard clause (Art. 37)	Internal market safeguard clause (Art. 38)
	JHA safeguard clause (Art. 39)	JHA safeguard clause (Art. 38)	JHA safeguard clause (Art. 39)
	Transitional measures for CAP (Art. 41)	Transitional measures for CAP (Art. 41)	Transitional measures for CAP (Art. 41)
	Transitional measures for veterinary, phytosanitary and food safety rules, (Art. 42)	Transitional measures for veterinary, phytosanitary and food safety rules, (Art. 42)	Transitional measures for veterinary, phytosanitary and food safety rules, (Art. 42)
Special clauses		Accession postponement clause (Art. 39): one year	Pre-accession monitoring clause, (Art. 36)

Figure 2.1 Accession Treaty and Act of Accession Provisions inducing flexibility[a]

[a]The table is reproduced from Ott, Differentiation Through Accession Law (n 101) 153.

no competences, would violate the principle of subsidiarity.[107] If this claim were correct, the attribution of powers may also be violated. However, the legal basis for this Commission Decision is found in Articles 37 and 38 of the Act of Accession with Bulgaria and Romania. According to those provisions, where the countries do not fulfil commitments undertaken in the accession negotiations or fall short in the implementation in the field of the JHA *acquis*, the Commission may take appropriate measures in the form of European regulations and decisions, so long as the shortcomings persist. Those primary law provisions are the legal bases for action, and consequently of the same rank in the legal hierarchy as other primary law, and thus cannot be considered a breach of any principles of the same rank, in accordance with the hierarchy of norms.

The nature of administrative supervision depends on which part of pre-accession aid is covered and resorts to classical supervision methods employed with regard to EU funding when it comes to pre-accession financial assistance. In other fields supervisory review is more restricted as far as political steering instruments are involved. In the run-up to accession, the Parliament has a limited (political supervisory) role,

[107] R Carp, 'The Struggle for the Rule of Law in Romania as an EU Member State: The Role of the Cooperation and Verification Mechanism' (2014) 10 *Utrecht Law Review* 8.

dependent on its being informed of any Council and Commission decision. The Parliament also has an indirect supervisory role, influencing the political process through EP resolutions, published annually with regard to candidate and potential-candidate countries and otherwise reacting to changes in EU enlargement policy.

2 Judicial review of EU enlargement policy

The nature and extent of ex ante (typically administrative or political) supervision depends on whether the instruments used in the enlargement process are employed at intergovernmental or supranational level. As regards supranational measures, especially financial tools, the classical control mechanisms are applicable as for other financial instruments under EU law. Legal review ex post is more complicated as measures defining the enlargement process are (as already noted), in the majority, soft law tools, with a limited number of legally binding tools such as the accession treaty, acts, or protocols on accession conditions together with their respective annexes, having the status of EU primary law. In addition, we need again to distinguish between pre-accession, accession, and post-accession phases, and between the associated states as such, and the natural and juristic persons from these states.

The soft law measures which are employed in the pre-accession phase to manage and steer both policy (especially goals and standards) and implementation (especially process and organization) cannot be brought before the European courts. This is not so much because they are soft law measures, because the Court has confirmed the availability of judicial review of soft law measures through the annulment procedure, where actions have concern for the institutional balance and for the division and allocation of competences between EU institutions.[108] The absence of judicial review results rather from that fact that soft law measures extending the administrative reach of the Union have no legal implications for existing Member States or Union institutions and their relationship with one another. Instead, any implications are those for a third country which has, in principle, no legal standing (see also below) under the annulment procedure. Exceptionally, association agreements have provided in the past that the Court of Justice can rule on conflicts of interpretation between the EU and the associated states. For instance, this is stipulated in the Ankara Agreement, which in Article 25(2) foresees that if the Association Council cannot settle the conflict, the question can be submitted to the Court of Justice.[109] The practical use of such judicial competence is, however, non-existent. It is for sovereignty reasons not an attractive option for a third country and the Court of Justice has made it obligatory that such a reference is binding on the parties once a matter has referred to the Court.[110]

---

[108] Case C-233/02 *France v Commission* ECLI:EU:C:2004:173; Case C-660/13 *Council v Commission* (*MOU Switzerland* case) ECLI:EU:C:2016:616.

[109] EEC–Turkey Association Agreement [1963] OJ 217 of 29 December 1964.

[110] EEA Agreement Opinion, Opinion 1/91 ECLI:EU:C:1991:490. See for this Art 20(3) ECAA [2006] OJ L285/3–46: 'If the Joint Committee after four months from the date when the matter was brought before it has not succeeded to take a decision resolving the dispute, the parties to the dispute may refer it to the Court of Justice whose decision shall be final and binding'). Another exception of exclusive jurisdiction by the ECJ in case of an international agreement and decisions under this agreement by

The predominantly soft law measures adopted in the enlargement policy are typically unilateral, addressing the candidate countries and cannot be brought before the ECJ under the annulment procedure (Article 263 TFEU). However, an accession treaty and the act of accession have been the subject matter of disputes, as well as provisions of accession association agreements, such as the Europe Agreement, within the EU legal order. The distinction we make in the enlargement process between the pre-accession, accession, and post-accession is also relevant for the availability of judicial review. The ECJ has regularly reviewed the legal impact and direct effect of accession association agreements, enabling third country nationals from CEE to rely under certain circumstances on Europe Agreement provisions to their advantage within EU Member States.[111] Also, an accession treaty of which the act or protocol of accession forms an integral part, have already been the substance of disputes before the Union courts. However, as explained above, these rules have the status of primary law and thus cannot be claimed to be null and void through the annulment procedure; instead they can be changed only in accordance with revision procedures foreseen in the TEU.[112] Nevertheless, these primary rules are still considered relevant points of reference for interpretation where they are infringed by secondary EU law[113] or national law, with issues of detail depending on the procedure and applicant involved.[114] The transitional measures applied in the Greek, Spanish and, and Portuguese accession provisions have been subject of judicial scrutiny, the Court coming to the conclusion that the transitional regime applied to workers from the states concerned, and that national derogations by existing Member States needed to be applied in a restrictive manner.[115] In another case, the ECJ accorded the Commission a wide margin of discretion, restricting judicial review to manifest errors of assessment in the application of the economic safeguard clauses established in act or protocols of accession.[116] Another question has been the extent to which the legal status of candidate countries can be protected in various stages between the signing of an accession treaty, its ratification and the ultimate accession of a new Member State, especially concerning the *acquis* adopted and published before accession but enforceable against the new Member State only from the date of accession.[117] In these different stages, which may last up to two

the Commission concerning the third state is Art 20 of the EU–Switzerland bilateral agreement on air transport, [2002] OJ L114/73.

[111] See eg the following case law: Case C-162/00 *Pokrzeptowicz-Meyer* ECLI:EU:C:2002:57; Case C-18/90 *Kziber* ECLI:EU:C:1991:36; Case C-265/03 *Simutenkov* ECLI:EU:C:2005:213; and Case C-438/00 *Kolpak* ECLI:EU:C:2003:255.

[112] Joined Cases 311 and 35/86 *Laisa* ECLI:EU:C:1988:211; Case C-445/00 *Austria v Council* ECLI:EU:C:2003:445.

[113] The Act of Accession provides for specific legal bases to adopt legislation see Art 51 of the Croatian Act of Accession; see on this A Lazowski, 'European Union Do Not Worry, Croatia Is behind You: A Commentary on the Seventh Accession Treaty' (2012) *Croatian Yearbook of European Law and Policy* 1, 7.

[114] See eg the following case law: Case C-233/97 *KappAhl Oy* ECLI:EU:C:1998:585; Case C-589/13 *Martin Meat* ECLI:EU:C:2015:405; see with further references A Ott, 'Grundfreiheiten' in F Merli and S Huster (eds), Die Verträge zur EU-Osterweiterung' (Berliner Wissenschaftsverlag 2008) paras 80–81.

[115] See ECJ Case 77/82 *Peskeloglu* ECLI:EU:C:1983:92; Case 305/87 *Commission v Greece* ECLI:EU:C:1989:218; Case C-539/13 *Merck* ECLI:EU:C:2015:87.

[116] Case 11/82 *Piraiki-Patraiki* ECLI:EU:C:1985:18.

[117] See on this further AG Cruz Villalón in Case C-336/09 P *Poland v Commission* ECLI:EU:C:2011:860, paras 28–30.

years, there will have been new EU secondary law adopted which must also be implemented by the incoming Member State. According, for example, to Article 2 of the Act of Accession of Poland such secondary law emerging in that interim period is binding upon the new Member States and are applicable to it from the moment of formal and completed accession. However, where such a measure is adopted between signing the accession treaty and its entry into force, the time-limit on admissibility (two months of publication of the legislative act, Article 263(5) TFEU) is applicable, thus not allowing an incoming Member State to challenge secondary law passed before accession.

Given the strict time limit of two months, the question has arisen as to the exact point from which the time period starts to run. Specifically, this was raised in regard to adaptations to the Common Agricultural Policy which, according to Article 23 of the Act of Accession Poland could be modified, if necessary, before the date of accession. The Court, however, sidestepped this issue, instead denying the Polish pleas on matters of substance.[118] In another case some years later, again involving Poland, the Court (on appeal) did address the issue of the time-limit, ruling that the action was admissible. The Court reasoned that, since the EU is based on the rule of law, its institutions were subject to review of the conformity of their acts with the Treaty and general principles of law. Compliance with these principles meant that both new and old Member States have to be treated equally. Consequently, a new Member State has to have the opportunity to raise the question of validity within the annulment procedure. Consequently, the two-month period began to run only from the day of accession, and not from the date of publication of the measure at hand.[119]

Another question has concerned the extent to which the *acquis communautaire*, in the form of regulations and directives, is applicable to individuals from the date of accession despite the fact, owing to a backlog in translation into the new official languages, these EU instruments had not yet been published in the *Official Journal* in the language of the incoming Member State. This was the situation in *Skoma-Lux*, involving a Czech wine importer who argued that an EU regulation which the company breached had not been published in Czech in the OJ. The Court, referring to the wording of Article 297(1) 3rd sentence TFEU stipulating that such a regulation is be published in the *Official Journal*. Relying on the principles of legal certainty and equal treatment (comparing the position of individuals in old and new Member States), obligations on the individuals concerned could not be imposed under the circumstances of the case.[120] Hence, in the context of ex post review and concerning the position of accession countries, once the status of the new Member States is confirmed by the signing of the accession treaty, the principle of the rule of law played a decisive role in evaluating the procedural rights of privileged and non-privileged applicants.

---

[118] Case C-273/04 *Poland v Council* ECLI:EU:C:2007:622; Lazowski (n 114) 7 argues that standing was implicitly acknowledged.

[119] Case C-336/09P *Poland v European Commission* ECLI:EU:C:2012:386.

[120] Case C-161/06 *Skoma-Lux* ECLI:EU:C:2007:773, paras 36–42; confirmed by Case C-146/11 *AS Pimix* ECLI:EU:C:2012:450.

H Conclusion

The field of Union enlargement stands out among the other fields of EU external relations policy for several reasons. Union action within this field is responsible for reforming constitutional, legislative, and administrative legal orders of the accession candidate through the application of the conditionality principle, even in areas in which the Union as such has no internal competence. This area of Union policy employs a panoply of legally and politically binding and non-binding instruments, assembled under the umbrella of the pre-accession policy and divisible into political, financing, and programming tools. As mostly soft law tools, they are applied to non-EU Member States under the conditionality principle with the aim of effective preparation for the intended EU accession. As a result, this generates a rather sharp differentiation between a strict conditionality prior to accession, and a weaker compliance-control once the candidate country has become a full and formal member of the Union.[121] Such strict antecedent conditions and benchmarks can, under certain conditions, be extended for some years into the post-accession phase through transitional arrangements, safeguard clauses in the Accession Treaty, and certain other specific provisions. Once this extended period of time elapses, however, no adequate, effective, or politically palatable tools exist to ensure that the standards embodied in the *acquis* and related Union goals are met or enforced, as recent and continuing rule of law and democracy issues in Hungary and Poland demonstrate. Article 7 TEU requires a serious breach of Union values, such as the rule of law, for decisive action to result, and no practice of its use exists. Also, the cumbersome and more static infringement procedure is triggered only by breaches of substantive EU law. Consequently, much attention has been devoted to stem the 'backsliding of the rule of law'[122] in the post-accession period, and to confronting the difficulties of enforcing EU fundamental values, in particular the rule of law and the principle of democracy, in post-accession EU Member States, by establishing an assessment process which can apply ahead of the extreme option of Article 7 TEU, and as an alternative to the infringement procedure. According to the now developed Rule of Law Framework, the Commission will initiate at an early stage a dialogue with the Member State concerned to prevent any systemic threat to the rule of law.[123]

---

[121] On this discrepancy between pre- and post-accession review of the rule of law see C Hillion, 'Overseeing the Rule of Law in the EU' in C Closas and D Kochenov, *Reinforcing Rule of Law Oversight in the European Union* (Cambridge University Press 2016) 58; and D Kochenov, 'Busting the Myths Nuclear: A Commentary on Article 7 TEU' EUI Working Papers, Law 2017/10.

[122] D Kochenov and L Pech, quoting Commissioner F Timmermans in D Kochenov and L Pech, 'Better Late than Never? On the European Commission's Rule of Law Framework and Its First Activation' (2016) 54 *Journal of Common Market Studies* 1062.

[123] Communication from the Commission of 11 March 2014, 'A New EU Framework to Strengthen the Rule of Law' COM(2014) 158 final. This resulted in the Commission Recommendation (EU) 2018/103 of 20 December 2017 regarding the rule of law in Poland complementary to Recommendations (EU) 2016/1374, (EU) 2017/146, and (EU) 2017/1520 to the Council to initiate an Art 7(2) TEU procedure, [2018] OJ L 17/50.

In addition, the field of the enlargement policy is characterized by its well documented administrative practice. This reaches beyond the boundaries of EU law and
its application within the framework of formal membership, to third countries, thus
extending the reach of the European Administrative Space. Such an extension comprises transparency, coupled with recourse to numerous soft law instruments, an approach located in the necessity to gain public support in the countries concerned with
impending or intended enlargement, and to create predictability and procedural certainty for the candidate country. Predictability is, however, in tension with the flexibility needed in an evolutionary process where Member States and Commission, as the
main administrative actors, will adapt and tailor the conditions of accession as they go
along. This takes place in a dynamic political setting: it has, for example, been argued
that EU's ability to influence the Western Balkan states has diminished in comparison
with what was achieved in anticipation of the Eastern Enlargement process. This is
mainly related to the fact that the aim—or prospect—of accession has become more
uncertain for current candidates. The Union has sharpened its Copenhagen conditions over time, and a further—politically very labile and unpredictable—condition in
the form of the criterion of the capacity for absorption or integration has been introduced. Throughout the 1990s, enlargement required the Union to be prepared for new
Member States only institutionally. This was slowly transformed by adding financial
sustainability (since 2004) and, at the time of the renewed consensus in 2006, the need
for a broad and sustained public support[124] has ultimately become an erratic admission criterion.[125]

So, despite its past success as arguably the most successful limb of the Union's external relations policy, reforming third countries' administrative and political systems
and aligning them to the EU values, institutions, and policies, the enlargement field
has been weakened in its impact and effectiveness. In direct comparison with the—
failed—grand design of the 2003 ENP, the enlargement policy has fared better, but
it is in need of offering credible incentives for candidate countries with no realistic
perspective of joining in fact. An ambivalent approach of conducting the EU pre-
accession process without a predictable (successful) outcome for a candidate country
threatens the credibility of the Union,[126] and therefore its capacity for positively influencing third countries. Hence, the enlargement policy, depending as it does on a
strong consensus among EU Member States, can be said to be at the crossroads of either remaining a separate and effective key policy thread, or being downgraded into
merely a 'neighbourhood policy deluxe'.

---

[124] Brussels European Council, 14–15 December 2006, Presidency conclusions, Brussels, 12 February
2007, 16879/1/06; see also in the same vein Hillion, 'EU Enlargement' (n 23) 204.
[125] See on this criterion F Amtenbrink, 'On the European Union's Institutional Capacity to Cope with
Further Enlargement' in S Blockmans and S Prechal (eds), *Reconciling Deepening and Widening of the
European Union* (TMC Asser Press 2007) 111–31.
[126] For the Commission this term works both ways, namely that the existing Member States only
recommend a candidate for 'membership once it is fully prepared' and 'candidate countries' credibility
rests in their genuine commitment to EU-related reforms'; see S Füle, Understanding Enlargement 2011.
Credibility is also mentioned in this context by the Global Strategy for the EU's Foreign and Security
Policy, 2015, High Representative; and Bishop speaks about a principled pragmatism: see S Bishop, 'The
EU Global Strategy, Realpolitik with European Characteristics' Security Policy Brief, No 75 June 2016.

3

European Neighbourhood Policy

Ilaria Vianello

A Introduction

The European Union officially launched the European Neighbourhood Policy (ENP) in 2003,[1] even if its roots can be traced back to 1997 when the central eastern European enlargement began to gather momentum.[2] Arguably, the policy goes back even further to the EU's response to the break-up of the former Soviet Union in the early 1990s. At that time, the EU started negotiating the partnership and cooperation agreements with the newly independent states and launched the Barcelona Process with Mediterranean countries in 1995.[3] The Commission dealt separately with the different groups of neighbours (the Eastern and the Southern) until 2002 when, in a strategy paper, it specifically identified the need to establish a new, more coherent approach for all countries concerned.[4] A Commission communication on the new 'Wider Europe' policy was published in 2003 and was endorsed by the Council in Thessaloniki in the same year. The Council summarized the overall goal of this new policy as being:

> [t]o work with partners to reduce poverty and create an area of shared prosperity and values based on free trade, deeper economic integration, intensified political and cultural relations, enhanced cross-border co-operation and shared responsibility for conflict prevention between the EU and its neighbours; [and to] anchor the EU's offer of concrete benefits and preferential relations ... to progress made by the partner countries in different areas, in particular political and economic reform as well as in the field of JHA [Justice and Home Affairs].[5]

Subsequently, in June 2007, the Council set out what it called the 'key principles' of the ENP:

- a strategy based on joint ownership to promote modernization and reform

---

[1] Communication from the Commission to the Council and the European Parliament of 11 March 2003, 'Wider Europe:Neighbourhood: A New Framework for Relations with our Eastern and South Neighbours' COM(2003) 104.

[2] The Commission, in its 2001 Strategy Paper, started to develop the concept of 'proximity policy' towards the new neighbours, with references to an expanded range of common interests, including economic reforms, alignment to the regulatory framework of the internal market, migration and border management. Commission Strategy Paper of 13 November 2001, 'Making a Success of Enlargement', at 7.

[3] For a more comprehensive analysis on the origins of the policy see Marise Cremona, 'The European Neighbourhood Policy: More than a Partnership?' in Marise Cremona (ed), *Developments in EU External Relations Law* (Oxford University Press 2008) 245–300, at 246.

[4] Commission Strategy Paper of 9 October 2002, 'Towards the Enlarged Union', at 6–7.

[5] Communication from the Commission to the Council and the European Parliament of 11 March 2003, 'Wider Europe: Neighbourhood' (n 1).

- a single, inclusive, balanced, and coherent policy framework
- a performance-driven differentiation and tailor-made assistance and
- a policy distinct from the question of EU membership which, however, did not prejudice possible future developments.[6]

Once the core of the policy was established, the Commission, together with the High Representative of the Union for Foreign Affairs and Security Policy (HR) and the European External Action Service (EEAS),[7] continued to modify some aspects of the ENP with the aim of adapting it to the changing circumstances. For example, in 2011 after the eruption of the Arab Spring, the Commission and the EEAS adopted a Joint Communication 'A New Response to a Changing Neighbourhood', according to which more support was to be provided to partner countries building deep and sustainable democracies.[8] Another more recent and radical example is the 2015 Commission and HR Consultation Paper calling for a more profound revision of the neighbourhood policy.[9] Such a revision would be aimed at challenging 'the assumption on which the policy is based, as well as its scope, and how instruments should be used'.[10] The perceived need for policy revision finds its roots in the recent inability of the Union to offer adequate responses to rapid developments in, and the shifting aspirations of, its neighbours. In November 2015 the Commission and the HR then adopted a Joint Communication, elaborating a review of the ENP in light of the responses obtained from the joint consultation.[11] Despite the raised expectations, the Commission Communication on the new ENP did not manage really to break through its structural limitations.[12] However, it tried to take a more pragmatic and focused approach, in particular by identifying specifically all the policy objectives upon which relations between the Union and the neighbours should be based.

In order to achieve all the goals set forth by the ENP, the EU has so far, together with its external partners, developed what has been defined as a 'governance mode of foreign policy'.[13] Through this the Union aims at creating stable, long-term,

---

[6] GAER Council conclusions on European Neighbourhood Policy of 18 June 2007.

[7] The European external action service is foreseen by the Treaty of Lisbon (Art 27(3) TEU) and was created after its entrance into force. Council Decision 2010/427/EU of 26 July 2010 establishing the organization and functioning of the European External Action Service [2010] OJ L201/30.

[8] The renewed ENP put at the forefront political association and economic integration, the mobility of people, more EU financial assistance, a stronger partnership with civil society and better cooperation on specific sector policies. Joint Communication from the Commission and the High Representative of the European Union for Foreign Affairs and Security Policy of 25 May 2011, 'A New Response to a Changing Neighbourhood' COM(2011) 303.

[9] Joint Consultation Paper of the Commission and the High Representative of the European Union for Foreign Affairs and Security Policy of 4 March 2015, 'Towards a New European Neighbourhood Policy' JOIN(2015) 6.

[10] ibid 3.

[11] Joint Communication of the Commission and the High Representative of the European Union for Foreign Affairs and Security Policy of 18 November 2015, 'Review of the European Neighbourhood Policy' JOIN(2015).

[12] This view is also shared by Hrant Kostanyan, 'The European Neighbourhood Policy reviewed: Will pragmatism trump normative values' *CEPS European Neighbourhood Watch*, Issue 121, December 2015.

[13] Gráinne de Búrca, 'EU External Relations: The Governance Mode of Foreign Policy' in Bart Van Vooren, Stevens Blockmans, and Jan Wouters (eds), *The EU's Role in Global Governance: The Legal Dimension* (Oxford University Press 2013) 39–58, at 42; Cremona (ed), *Developments in EU External Relations Law* (n 3) 1, at 9.

institutionalized relationships within regulatory frameworks—normally inter-national agreements—which often themselves foresee the creation of other policy-making, norm-generating, coordinating, and monitoring institutions, resembling the regulatory frameworks which have developed internally within the EU. Within this external 'governance mode', a pivotal role is played by the Union adminis-tration. The Commission and the EEAS are charged with administering the com-plex, multi-layered, and sectoral relations between the Union and its neighbouring states. The increasing use of administrative instruments in the Union external action raises various questions as to why—and how—EU administrative principles and standards can and should be applicable to this policy field.[14] It is against this background that this chapter seeks to explain the relevance of administrative law for Union action in its neighbourhood; and to highlight some specificities and nuances which the external ENP domain introduces into the EU administrative system. As this chapter does not cover the European enlargement policy (for this, see Chapter 2 in this volume), the terms 'neighbour' and 'neighbouring countries' are used here only with regard to countries taking part in the ENP as such.[15] It should also be noted that this chapter addresses the ENP in its current form and makes only few references to the latest ENP revision since as yet this has not led to significant changes in the administrative tools used by the Union to implement this policy.

B Administrative Tasks within the ENP

Administrative tasks specific to the ENP are found nowhere as such in the Treaties. However, they can generally be located within the general tasks of the Commission listed under Article 17(1) of the Treaty of the European Union (TEU)[16] and of the High Representative under Articles 18(4) and 27 TEU. The policy-specific adminis-trative tasks were developed by the administration itself, which over the years has evolved in the wake of changing circumstances, ad-hoc solutions to face the chal-lenges posed by the external geopolitical context, and the political realities internal to the EU. For example, the 2004 Central Eastern European 'Big Bang enlarge-ment' saw the need to address both the relations between the EU and its new neigh-bours (i.e., Ukraine, Belarus, etc.), as well as the situation of the staff of Directorate General Enlargement (DG ELARG) which found itself 'task-less' from one day to the next. Against this background, in 2003 the 'Wider Europe' taskforce was formed within Directorate General for External Relations (DG RELEX), staffed by DG ELARG civil servants with the goal of addressing the challenges posed by the new

---

[14] Ilaria Vianello, 'EU External Action and the Administrative Rule of Law: A Long-Overdue Encounter' (Ph D Thesis, European University Institute, defended on 13 December 2016, cadmus.eui. eu); document on file.

[15] The countries covered by the ENP are Armenia, Azerbaijan, Egypt, Georgia, Israel, Jordan, Lebanon, Moldova, Morocco, Palestine, Tunisia, Ukraine, and Algeria. Belarus, Libya, and Syria remain outside most of the ENP structures.

[16] Treaty of the European Union of 30 March 2010 [2010] OJ C83/01.

geopolitical position of an enlarged EU.[17] This transfer of human resources from DG ELARG to DG RELEX explains the many similarities between the ENP and the content of pre-accession instruments.[18] In fact, this transfer led to some direct, mechanical borrowing of instruments and strategies from the successful enlargement experience for the newly established ENP.[19] The 2015 consultation on the need for a fundamental revision of the ENP represents another example of how it was the administration itself which pushed for the establishment of clear and defined administrative tasks. Various queries were raised by the Commission and the EEAS specifically in reference to the use of their powers in relation to perceived tasks.[20]

The creation of ad-hoc solutions has crystallized over the years to form a broad array of both administrative tasks and procedures aimed at implementing the ENP. This evolutionary process was the result of a steady dialogue between the Commission and the Council, where the latter welcomed suggestions made in the Commission Communications with subsequent Council Conclusions. The main tasks, then, of the administration in the ENP can be identified as: planning and agenda setting; monitoring; issuing recommendations and opinions; and handling the disbursement of funds. For example, the Commission—and more recently the EEAS—are charged with the duty of establishing overarching strategic policy targets between the EU and each neighbouring state through action plans; and of monitoring the progress made in their implementation for each ENP country.[21] Next to monitoring and planning, the Commission and the EEAS are responsible for programming the establishment and implementation of funds.[22]

C Sources of Administrative Law in the ENP Sector

Until the entrance into force of the Treaty of Lisbon, there was no specific reference in primary law to the ENP; therefore, Article 8 TEU is a new neighbourhood-specific provision. Article 8 TEU does not refer to the ENP as such. However, it was drafted with

---

[17] Elsa Tulmets, 'Experimentalist Governance in EU External Relations: Enlargement and the European Neighbourhood Policy' in C F Sabel and J Zeitlin (eds), *Experimentalist Governance in the European Union Towards a New Architecture* (Oxford University Press 2010) 297, 315.

[18] Cremona, 'The European Neighbourhood Policy' (n 3) 245, 265; Narine Ghazaryan, *The European Neighbourhood Policy and the Democratic Values of the EU: A Legal Analysis* (Hart Publishing 2014) 74; Tulmets, 'Experimentalist Governance in EU External Relations' (n 17) 315.

[19] Judith Kelly, 'New Wine in Old Wineskins: Promoting Political Reforms through the New European Neighbourhood Policy' (2006) 44 *Journal of Common Market Studies* 29, 31–32.

[20] See eg 'Are the ENP Action Plans the right tool to deepen our partnerships? Are they too broad for some partners? Would the EU, would partners, benefit from a narrower focus and greater prioritisation?'; or 'Can EU and/or partner interests be served by a lighter reporting mechanism? Should the reporting be modulated according to the level of engagement of the ENP partner concerned?' Joint Consultation Paper of the Commission and the High Representative of the European Union for Foreign Affairs and Security Policy of 4 March 2015, 'Towards a New European Neighbourhood Policy' (n 9).

[21] Communication from the Commission to the Council and the European Parliament of 11 March 2003, 'Wider Europe:Neighbourhood' (n 1) 12.

[22] ENP strategy papers and annual programming documents—even if they are formally adopted as Commission implementing decisions—are Commission and EEAS documents. See eg Single Support Framework for EU support to Lebanon (2014–2016) https://ec.europa.eu/europeaid/sites/devco/files/ssf-lebanon-2014-2016_en_0.pdf (last accessed 23 May 2017).

the latter in mind, giving grounds for it to be considered as a 'constitutionalisation' of the ENP.[23] Article 8(1) sets out the ultimate objectives of the policy (i.e., to 'develop a special relationship with neighbouring countries, aiming to establish an area of prosperity and good neighbourliness, founded on the values of the Union'), whereas paragraph (2) establishes that the Union—in order to achieve those objectives—may conclude specific agreements with neighbouring states. Despite the introduction of this neighbourhood-specific provision in the Treaties, Article 8 has so far been relied upon only in the preamble of the European Neighbourhood Instrument Regulation (ENI Regulation).[24] The reasons for this are ultimately to be found in the presence in the Treaties of other already detailed provisions on the conclusion of association agreements (Article 217 of the Treaty on the Functioning of the European Union (TFEU))[25] and on the adoption of regulations providing financial assistance to third countries (Articles 209(1) and 212(2) TFEU).

In addition to Article 8 TEU, there are other two groups of legal sources that apply to two specific aspects of the administrative action of the Union in the context of neighbourhood policy: financial assistance regulations and agreements concluded by the EU with the ENP states. The ENI Regulation, together with the regulation laying down common rules and procedures for the implementation of the Union's instruments for financing external action,[26] indicate to the administration the principles and the procedures that need to be respected when programming and implementing funds in the ENP context. Even though outside the scope of this chapter to provide a detailed analysis of the administrative activities specifically aimed at implementing the agreements concluded by the Union with the ENP states,[27] it ought not be forgotten that the bilateral agreements can provide indications for the administration of the content of the ENP-specific instruments. Other than under the enlargement policy, countries participating in the ENP are not offered an EU-membership perspective. Therefore, where the administration in the setting of enlargement policy knows that the final aim is accession and has the aim of supporting a third country to achieve this goal, the same cannot be said for administrative action within the ENP. The administration within the ENP—not having a clear and concrete *finalité*—makes use of agreements as indicators against which to modulate its conduct.

---

[23] Peter Van Elsuwege and Roman Petrov, 'Article 8 TEU: Towards a New Generation of Agreements with the Neighbouring Countries of the European Union?' (2011) 36 *European Law Review* 688, 690.

[24] Regulation (EU) 232/2014 of 11 March 2014 of the European Parliament and of the Council establishing a European Neighbourhood Instrument (ENI) [2014] OJ L77/30.

[25] Treaty on the Functioning of the European Union of 30 March 2010 (n 16).

[26] Regulation (EU) 236/2014 of 11 March 2014 of the European Parliament and of the Council laying down common rules and procedures for the implementation of the Union's instruments for financing external action [2014] OJ L77/95.

[27] Each agreement concluded by the Union (and its Member States) with each neighbouring state establish an Association Council ('Partnership and Cooperation Council' or 'Association Council' depending on the type of agreement) composed of members of the Council of the European Union and of the European Commission, on the one hand; and of members of the government of the neighbouring state, on the other. Association Councils have the power to take decisions within the scope of the agreements in the cases provided for therein.

D Underlying Sector-specific Principles within the Administration of the ENP

Two overarching principles seem to characterize and influence administrative action in the ENP: joint ownership and differentiation. How binding on the administration these two are very much depends on the legal nature of the instruments adopted by it. For non-legally binding instruments, for example progress reports, the principles can be conceived of as 'values' which the administration is encouraged to uphold in its interaction with ENP states.[28] Such values are also reflected in the internal administrative procedures that lead to the adoption of, e.g., action plans and the progress reports themselves. The EEAS guideline on the drafting action plans indicates the importance of respecting joint ownership by taking into account the partner country's own plan for reform.[29] In the case of legally binging measures, such as strategy papers and programming documents, the overarching precepts become instead sector-specific legal principles as such, mandated by secondary law. The ENI Regulation itself clearly states that Union support needs to be incentive-based and differentiated, meaning that greater financial assistance is to be granted to ENP countries that show particular willingness to respect the Union's funding values.[30] Moreover, Union support is to be aligned with any corresponding national or local strategy (thus guaranteeing ownership).[31]

E Sectoral Organization, Institution, and Structures

The Commission, together with the EEAS, are the main bodies responsible for conducting the plethora of administrative activities which implement the ENP. The division of competences between the EEAS and the Commission is based on internal arrangements; nevertheless, this distribution does not always have sharp contours.[32] The Commission and the EEAS staff working on the ENP are located in headquarters in Brussels and at the Union Delegations in third countries. The Commission has established a Directorate General (DG NEAR) devoted to carrying the ENP forward, conducting enlargement negotiations and handling relations with EEA–EFTA

---

[28] Values compared to principles have a more indeterminate configuration and can be seen as part of the cultural patrimony or common heritage of Europe; whereas legal principles possess a more defined structure which makes them more suitable for the creation of legal rules. Laurent Pech, 'A Union Founded on the Rule of Law: Meaning and Reality of the Rule of Law as a Constitutional Principle of EU Law' (2010) 6(3) *European Constitutional Law Review* 359, 366.

[29] EEAS, *Non-Paper: Guidelines for Future ENP Action Plan*, Access to Documents request SG1—Corporate Board Secretariat.

[30] Article 4(1) Regulation (EU) 232/2014 (n 24).   [31] ibid Art 4(5).

[32] Both an official from the EEAS and an official from the Commission working in Brussels on the ENP shared the view that despite internal arrangements on the division of tasks, their everyday work did not strictly follow the division of competences envisaged. Interviews conducted on 18 November 2013 and 19 November 2013, Brussels. The same can be said to hold true also for the delegations on the ground. During two interviews at the delegation in Sarajevo it was clear that the staff of the delegation itself did not clearly know who was EEAS staff and who Commission staff. Interviews were conducted on 16 July 2013, Sarajevo.

countries. DG NEAR—beside the EEAS—works closely with related DGs in charge of thematic priorities (e.g. DG REGIO, DG EMPL, DG AGRI, etc.). The EEAS is a *sui generis* organ, neither legislative nor judicial in nature; as such, it represents a novel kind of administrative body. It is not a fully-fledged EU institution, but at the same time it is more than an agency or mere advisory body.[33] The EEAS does not work in isolation: rather, it is closely tied to the work of the High Representative, is placed under her authority,[34] and assists her in her various functions.[35]

Alongside the Commission and the EEAS staff, there are other actors providing inputs to the drafting of the different administrative acts and measures implementing the ENP. The 'unbounded administration'[36] taking part in the ENP decision-making process ranges across third country governments, international organizations, civil society, and non-governmental organizations (both international and local). All these actors are required—either by positive law or in accordance with self-imposed administrative guidelines[37]—to participate at different stages and to different extents in the development and implementation of the ENP administrative acts and measures. The involvement of these actors is, however, not always proceduralized, nor harmonized. The Union administration establishes information networks with these—or some of these—actors. The existence of this 'unbounded administration' raises some important questions as to the formal position of third countries in the decision-making process,[38] and as to the role granted to civil society and international organizations. In other words: who is invited, and to what extent is their view taken into consideration?

Finally, it is important to point out how international organizations such as the United Nations (and its agencies), the World Bank, the International Monetary Fund, the Organisation for Security and Cooperation in Europe, and certain international non-governmental organizations (NGOs) are, on the one hand, external to the institutional setup of the Union but, on the other hand, formally associated therewith by reason of their common specific interests in the ENP countries.[39] Alongside institutionalized forms of interaction, officials both in Brussels and in the EU delegations to third countries tend to create with these international actors epistemic communities which seek to go beyond their formal professional role as a particular group or entity. As a consequence, they are often able to determine common agendas—which are then reflected in the Union's external administrative activities—with the aim of persuading decision-makers in third countries to change their policy goals.[40]

---

[33] Art 1(2) Council Decision 2010/427/EU (n 7). For more detailed analysis see Joris Larik, 'The EU on the Global Stage after the Lisbon Treaty: External Action and the External Action Service' in Sabino Cassese, Bruno Carotti, Luca Casini, Eleonora Cavalieri, and Euan MacDonald (eds), *Global Administrative Law: The Case Book* (Institute for International Law and Justice 2012) 21.

[34] Art 1(3) Council Decision 2010/427/EU (n 7).   [35] ibid Art 2(1).

[36] Curtin defines these actors as 'administration unbounded', ie 'the practice of actors other than the administration as such being included in a process of reaching decisions'. Deirdre Curtin, *Executive Power of the European Union: Law, Practice, and Living Constitution* (Oxford University Press 2009) 19.

[37] See eg Art 4(5) Regulation (EU) 232/2014 (n 24); and EEAS, *Guidance Note ENP Package 2014* (section on sources, inputs, and consultations), Access to Documents request GESTDEM reference 2013/5084.

[38] Marc Maresceau, 'Pre-accession' in Marise Cremona (ed), *The Enlargement of the European Union* (Oxford University Press 2003) 9–42, at 33.

[39] See eg Art 5(4) Regulation (EU) 232/2014 (n 24); and EEAS, *Guidance Note ENP Package 2014* (n 37).

[40] Mai'a K Davis Cross, 'Rethinking Epistemic Communities Twenty Years Later' (2013) 39 *Review of International Studies* 137, 147.

F Sector-specific Forms of Acts and Measures within the ENP

Two groups of administrative activities can be identified within the ENP. The first group includes joint Commission and EEAS Communications, progress reports, action plans, and Memoranda of Understanding. The second group includes acts and measures linked to the programming and disbursement of financial assistance. The peculiarity of these instruments is their ability not only to inform, regulate, and implement internal EU decision-making, but also to indicate to third countries what they need to do in order to intensify relations with the Union. The fact that these instruments do not (necessarily) have a particular third country as clear addressee should not mislead us. The instruments—even if addressed, e.g., to the Council—(implicitly) have as their main addressee a third country which should (in effect, is invited to) follow the suggestion made in the document; adopt the standards indicated in the latter; and address gaps identified, unless they wish to risk the trigging of negative sanctions or to renounce (potential) benefits.[41] This section analyses the most relevant ENP acts and measures, in order to highlight their sector-specific relevance.

1 Measures of the first group: setting the agenda for action

Action plans (APs) lay down the strategic objectives of the cooperation between each ENP country and the EU. Their implementation helps fulfil the provisions of the agreements concluded by the Union with each neighbouring state, build ties in new areas of cooperation, and encourage and support the ENP country's objective of further integration into European economic and social structures.[42] Action plans are adopted within the joint bodies established by the agreements concluded by the Union and each ENP country. Externally, APs do not have a legally binding effect on third countries; they are political or policy documents whose implementation is not subject to prior formal ratification by the parties.

For some eastern neighbours, APs have been succeeded by 'association agendas'. Compared to APs, these were envisaged with the aim of broadening the areas of cooperation between the EU and the ENP states, including in their texts explicit reference to the *acquis* and seeking to reflect more fully the partner country's own reform agenda.[43] The Commission proposed that these new documents promote preparation for the implementation of the new agreements.[44] Now, after the entry into force of the latest association agreements with some of the eastern neighbours, the

---

[41] See section H on administrative enforcement.

[42] European Neighbourhood Policy, 'ENP action plans' http://eeas.europa.eu/enp/documents/action-plans/index_en.htm (last accessed 23 May 2017).

[43] Commission Non-Paper on 'the successor documents to current ENP Action Plans' expanding on the proposal of the Commission Communication of 3 April 2008 on the 'Implementation of the European Neighbourhood Policy 2007' COM(2008) 164 final.

[44] Prior to the adoption of the latest association agreements, association agendas aimed at clearly identifying on a sector-by-sector basis the priorities which required urgent action in anticipating the entry into force of the new agreements.

association agendas have been updated to prepare and facilitate the implementation of those agreement themselves.[45] Despite such changes, association agendas are comparable with APs.[46] The adoption of the association agendas has not, however, taken a linear path. Interestingly enough, a new EU–Morocco Action Plan was adopted in December 2013[47]—instead of an association agenda—although the Union had started negotiations for a Deep and Comprehensive Free Trade Area (DCFTA) initiative with Morocco and despite the existence already of an Association Agreement with Morocco.[48]

Progress reports are joint staff working documents of the Commission and the EEAS addressed to the Council, the European Parliament, the European Economic and Social Committee, and the Committee of the Regions. Their aim is to record and assess the progress made in the implementation, by each ENP country, of the priorities listed in their respective AP or association agenda. The November 2015 review of the ENP suggested, however, abandoning regular progress reports in favour of a 'new style of assessment, focusing specifically on meeting the goals agreed with partners'.[49] How this type of assessment would differ from the old progress reports remains unclear. However, an important difference would be that these reports would be timed to provide the basis for a political exchange of views in the relevant high-level meetings with partner countries, such as the Association and Cooperation Councils. In addition to the country-specific reporting, the new ENP revision or reporting process foresees regular transversal reports which track developments in the EU neighbourhood.

Memoranda of understanding (MoUs) implementing the ENP are examples of international agreements of not legally binding nature. They reflect political agreement between the Union and one or more third states, but with the express intention of not becoming bound in a legal sense. The fields covered by these instruments are numerous, encompassing a wide range of topics, such as energy,[50] political priorities for cooperation,[51] conditions of loans and terms of repayment,[52] and many others.

---

[45] See Guillaume Van der Loo, *The EU–Ukraine Association Agreement and the Deep Comprehensive Free Trade Area* (Brill Nijhoff, 2016) 93–95.

[46] See association agenda between the EU and Ukraine http://eeas.europa.eu/enp/pdf/pdf/action_plans/2010_eu_ukraine_association_agenda_en.pdf (last accessed 23 May 2017).

[47] The EU–Morocco action plan was formally adopted in December 2013 http://eeas.europa.eu/enp/pdf/pdf/action_plans/morocco_enp_ap_final_en.pdf (last accessed 23 May 2017).

[48] European Commission Service Position Paper on the trade sustainability impact assessment in support of negotiations of a deep and comprehensive free trade agreement between the European Union and Morocco http://trade.ec.europa.eu/doclib/docs/2015/april/tradoc_153336.pdf (last accessed 23 May 2017).

[49] Joint Communication of the Commission and the High Representative of the European Union for Foreign Affairs and Security Policy of 18 November 2015, 'Review of the European Neighbourhood Policy' (n 11) 5.

[50] See eg Memorandum of Understanding on Strategic Partnership on Energy between the European Union and Azerbaijan http://www.europarl.europa.eu/meetdocs/2009_2014/documents/dsca/dv/dsca_20130321_14/dsca_20130321_14en.pdf (last accessed 25 May 2017).

[51] See eg EU–Jordan Memorandum of Understanding on further cooperation http://europa.eu/rapid/press-release_STATEMENT-14-316_en.htm (last accessed 25 May 2017).

[52] See eg EU–Ukraine Memorandum of Understanding establishing conditions of loans and the terms of repayment. Commission implementing decision C(2015) 3444 Final of 18 May 2015 approving the Memorandum of Understanding between the European Union and Ukraine related to macro-financial assistance to Ukraine.

The function of the MoUs is very much dependent on the fields they address, varying from being purely exploratory arrangements through to establishing administrative action.[53]

The instruments just described have, as already mentioned, both internal and external functions and effects. Internally they can be—to different degrees—preparatory, steering, and interpretative: of preparatory character, in being employed as reference documents for further collaborative projects and actions between the Union and its neighbouring countries;[54] steering, because they lay down guidelines and priorities for the EU's engagement with its neighbours;[55] and interpretative, in fleshing out the scope and substance of international agreements.[56] As instruments of external character, they may have preparatory, rule-making, and interpretative functions. The preparatory elements emerges here insofar an instrument may guide a third country in the transformation of a general *telos* (i.e., partnership) towards more concrete individual acts applicable to single case situations. The key function of such instruments is to assist the addressee in evaluating a situation or circumstance and in taking appropriate action. The action suggested can be regarded by a third countries as constituting an invitation to follow certain steps leading to, for example, the adoption of legislation or to the changing of a political agenda.[57] Progress reports and action plans, for instance, indicate quite clearly and in a detailed manner what the third state needs to do in order to intensify its relations with the Union.[58] As such, these instruments—and the consequential actions—may well constitute an initial step towards the realization or implementation of legally binding measures in the third state concerned.[59] When they give rise to such legally binging measures, we can easily perceive this also as a

[53] Bart Van Vooren and Ramses A Wessel, *EU External Relations Law: Text, Cases and Materials* (Cambridge University Press 2014) 54.

[54] Examples of this type would be the Galileo agreement with Ukraine on access to satellite navigation, signed in December 2005. Cremona, 'The European Neighbourhood Policy' (n 3) 276.

[55] See eg progress reports and action plans are used in order to legitimize the Commission's choices in the distribution of financial assistance. The ENI financial regulation makes a clear reference in its text to the ENP instruments as being sources for guiding the programming of financial assistance. Art 3 Regulation (EU) 232/2014 (n 24) .

[56] Van Vooren in his articles carries out a detailed analysis of how action plans fulfil an interpretative function. Bart Van Vooren, 'A Case-study of Soft Law in EU External Relations: The European Neighbourhood Policy' (2009) 34 *European Law Review* 698.

[57] See eg the Georgia National Action Plan for the Implementation of the EU–Georgia Association Agenda (Decree No 59 of the Government of Georgia 26 January 2015) indicates to transpose in national legislations the standards identified in the association agenda http://www.eu-nato.gov.ge/en/eu/association-agreement (last accessed 25 May 2017).

[58] See eg the Action Plan with Jordan, which requires the latter (among others):

- To sign a Memorandum of Understanding with the Monitoring and Information Centre (MIC) of the Community Civil Protection Mechanism;
- To review all legislation concerning children to ensure compliance with the UN Convention on the Rights of the Child (CRC) and other relevant international human rights instruments and standards.
- To continue working on the full implementation of the WTO agreement on the application of the sanitary and phytosanitary measures and actively participate in relevant international bodies (OIE, IPPC, and Codex Alimentarius).

[59] This definition of preparatory acts is shaped around the meaning given by Hofmann, Rowe, and Türk with regard of internal preparatory acts. Herwig C H Hofmann, Gerard C Rowe, and Alexander H Türk, *Administrative Law and Policy of the European Union* (Oxford University Press 2013) 546.

form of extra territorial-rule-making. Finally, also in the external dimension, such instruments might acquire an interpretative function where the third country's courts rely on them in interpreting obligations enshrined in a (binding) agreement between the EU and the country concerned. Courts in EU neighbourhood states have also relied upon action plans in justifying their reference to the EU *acquis* when interpreting legal concepts and provisions transplanted from EU legislation.[60]

2 Measures of the second group: financing the agenda for action

Union financial support under the ENI Regulation aims at moving closer to the achievement of the overall *finalité* of the ENP (i.e., the creation of 'an area of shared prosperity and good neighbourliness') and in particular at implementing existing and future agreements between the Union and neighbouring countries as well as agreed action plans or equivalent documents.[61] The measures described above (in the first group) serve as key reference points for setting the Union's priorities for support under the ENI Regulation and for assessing progress.[62] Under the ENI Regulation, the Commission is empowered to adopt delegated and implementing acts.

The implementing powers granted to Commission enable it to adopt strategy papers, programming documents and specific rules establishing the uniform conditions for the implementation the ENI Regulation. Strategy papers and programming documents set out the objectives and priorities for Union support.[63] While seemingly purely technical activities, these implementing instruments have a clear policy-orientation character (expressly acknowledged in the preamble of the Regulation).[64] Strategy papers and programming documents allow the Commission to identify areas needing support: lesbian, gay, bisexual, and trans (LGBT) support, promotion of reconciliation, capacity-building measures for improving law enforcement, to name just a few. Finally, the Commission can adopt delegated acts in order to amend Annex II of the ENI Regulation itself,[65] comprising a long list of priorities in the Union's support for neighbouring countries.

G Administrative Procedures within the Sector

The procedures and procedural rules governing the administrative measures of the first group identified above are not always clearly defined. Some are in fact solely regulated by self-imposed administrative rules appreciable only by making a request for EU documents. The strictness with which such self-imposed rules are applied is a matter of choice of the Commission and the EEAS, as distinct from requirements which may be externally imposed. Procedures for the adoption of acts belonging to the second group of measures are laid down in secondary legislation and are thus binding.

---

[60] Anna Khvorostiankina, 'Legislative Approximation and Application of EU Law in Moldova' in Petrov Romanov and Peter Van Elsuwege (eds), *Legislative Approximation and Application of EU Law in the Eastern Neighbourhood of the European Union* (Routledge 2014) 159–77, at 174.
[61] Art 1 Regulation (EU) 232/2014 (n 24). [62] ibid Arts 3(2) and 4(2). [63] ibid Art 7.
[64] ibid Recital (28). [65] ibid Arts 13 and 14.

1 Procedures for agenda-setting (measures of the first group)

The elaboration of action plans and association agendas is in the hands of the Commission and the EEAS. Theoretically, action plans and association agendas should be drafted through collaboration between the EU and each ENP state.[66] Indeed, it is the joint body set up by the agreements concluded by the EU with each ENP country that endorses these instruments as recommendations. However, to what extent the drafting of the action plans and association agendas is in fact done collaboratively with the third country concerned is very case specific. With some countries there are genuine reciprocal negotiations. With certain other states this option is not available, since they do not have the technical expertise necessary for collaborative negotiation. In such a case, the EU team can shape action plans and association agendas depending to a large extent on its willingness, political drive, and appetite for effecting change.[67] Internally to the EU, action plans and association agendas—before endorsement by the joint bodies—have been typically presented by the Commission to the Council for swift adoption as Council Decisions on the policy stance to be taken by the Union and the Member States. However, since 2009 the Council has refused to continue the pre-Lisbon practice, asserting that action plans and association agendas are political documents to be adopted (merely) as recommendations. Nevertheless, with the adoption of the ENI Regulation—where it is clear and undeniable that action plans and association agendas do produce legal effects—the Council has been in effect requested to change its approach and procedure once again.[68] As at the time of writing, the consensus is more or less that Council Decisions will be adopted relying upon Article 218(9) TFEU as procedural legal basis and upon Article 217 TFEU (or Articles 209 and 207 TFEU together) as the substantive legal basis (leaving aside legal bases relating to the Common Foreign and Security Policy (CFSP)).[69] With that another important question has emerged as to who will be responsible for drafting action plans and association agendas in the future: can the proposal be joint (Commission and High Representative), if there is no substantive CFSP legal basis?

The procedures applicable to the drafting and the adoption of progress reports are entirely regulated by self-imposed administrative rules.[70] Progress reports are written in close cooperation with the EU delegations in third countries, which are also responsible for preparing the first draft.[71] Progress reports, however, undergo numerous reviews before they are made public, to the extent that EEAS and Commission officials in the delegations are barely able recognize their first draft in the published

---

[66] EEAS, *Non-Paper: Guidelines for Future ENP Action Plan* (n 29); EEAS, *Guidance Note ENP Package 2014* (n 37).

[67] Interview with Commission official from the Legal Service, 24 April 2015, email exchange.

[68] 'The key points of reference for setting the priorities for Union support under this Regulation and for the assessment of progress as outlined in article 2(3) shall be: action plans or other equivalent documents such as the association agendas …'. Art 3(2), Regulation (EU) 232/2014 (n 24).

[69] Interview with Commission official from the Legal Service, 24 April 2015, email exchange.

[70] EEAS, *Non-Paper: Guidelines for Future ENP Action Plan* (n 29); EEAS, *Guidance Note ENP Package 2014* (n 37).

[71] EEAS, *Non-Paper: Guidelines for Future ENP Action Plan* (n 29); EEAS, *Guidance Note ENP Package 2014* (n 37).

version.[72] During the drafting of progress reports numerous stakeholders provide input at different stages in the process. Such stakeholders include partner countries, local NGOs, the Council of Europe, international financial institutions (such as the IMF, the WB, the EBRD, etc.), and international organization like the ILO, WHO, UNICEF, and others.[73] Progress reports can be viewed as the result of ingenious work by the Commission and the EEAS which often find themselves in the position of giving content to criteria that they themselves are required to monitor (e.g., the rule of law, democracy, etc).[74] This leaves open the question as to the appropriate choice of instrument—and the associated procedure followed—for the purpose of monitoring compliance.

The procedures for the conclusion of memoranda of understanding should in principle not differ substantially from the conclusion of international agreements. In *France v Commission* the Court of Justice made clear that the non-binding nature of an act cannot be utilized in order to avoid satisfying the principle of conferred power or institutional balance.[75] The Court in *Council v Commission* confirmed this approach.[76] The Court is of the view that the initial Council decision authorizing negotiations for a MoU does not extinguish the Council's power under Article 16(1) TEU to decide whether or not the Union should become a party to the instrument after negotiations. This is so, even if the content of the non-binding agreement negotiated by the Commission with a third country corresponds to the negotiating mandate given by the Council.[77] However, in practice the procedure has not always been clear nor reflected this principle. Looking closely at the examples of MoUs within the wider neighbourhood context, it is not always clear who was involved in the negotiations, who were the signatories to the documents, and for which subject areas the measures could be used.[78] The most recent MoUs have been adopted internally as Commission implementing decisions. For example, the recent MoU on macro-financial assistance concluded with Ukraine has been adopted as a Commission implementing decision,[79] relying on the European Parliament and Council decisions on macro-financial

---

[72] Interviews with EEAS and Commission officials at the European Delegation in Sarajevo, 16 July 2013, Sarajevo.

[73] EEAS, *Guidance Note ENP Package 2014* (n 37).

[74] Tulmets, 'Experimentalist Governance in EU External Relations' (n 17) 312.

[75] Case C-233/02 *France v Commission* EU:C:2004:173, para 40.

[76] Case C-660/13 *Council v Commission* EU:C:2016:616.   [77] ibid para 46.

[78] A MoU on a strategic partnership on energy was concluded by the Union with Egypt with the aim of gradually integrating Egypt's energy market with that of the EU. The MoU was signed by the Commissioner for External Relations and European Neighbourhood Policy, the Commissioner for Energy, and the Minister for Foreign Affairs of Egypt. The signature of the Presidency of the Council of the European Union was foreseen but not made. Differently, a very similar MoU on a strategic partnership in the field of energy between the EU and Azerbaijan was eventually signed by the Presidency of the European Council, the President of the Commission and the President of the Republic of Azerbaijan. Memorandum of Understanding on Strategic Partnership on Energy between the European Union and the Arab Republic of Egypt http://eeas.europa.eu/egypt/docs/mou_energy_eu-egypt_en.pdf (last accessed 25 May 2017); Memorandum of Understanding on Strategic Partnership on Energy between the European Union and Azerbaijan http://www.europarl.europa.eu/meetdocs/2009_2014/documents/dsca/dv/dsca_20130321_14/dsca_20130321_14en.pdf (last accessed 25 May 2017).

[79] Commission implementing decision C(2015) 3444 Final (n 52).

support as the legal basis.[80] Likewise, a similar procedure was used with regard to Tunisia.[81] A further example is the MoU concluded by the Union with Belarus on a Mobility Partnership, adopted as a Commission Decision using as the legal basis Articles 49 TFEU and 17 TEU.[82] This more recent practice does not appear to fit comfortably with the Court's decision in *Council v Commission*: is the comitology examination procedure enough to guarantee Council supervision? What is the place of the European Parliament? Should it not also have the obligation—and role—of checking whether the Commission respected relevant constraints on the final deal?[83]

2 Procedures for financing agenda-action (measures of the second group)

As established by the ENI Regulation,[84] strategy papers and programming documents are Commission implementing acts. They are, therefore, adopted in accordance with the comitology examination procedure.[85]

H Administrative Enforcement of EU Sectoral Law

When discussing the enforcement of EU law in the ENP a distinction needs to be made: one issue is enforcement internally, i.e., against Member States; the other is enforcement against third counties, i.e., the indirect addressees of EU measures. Moreover, before embarking on this analysis, a caution is necessary: the likelihood enforcement measures will be used is in fact very low. The politically sensitive nature of such instruments, blended with the generalized lack of clarity as to the exact legal obligations burdening Member States, prevents the application of enforcement mechanisms in fact.

An interesting example of the internal enforcement situation is offered by action plans. If these are non-binding acts between the EU and a third country under international law, this does not imply that their adoption is without legal effect within the EU legal order itself. As discussed previously, action plans—before being endorsed by the joint councils established under the agreements concluded with third countries—are adopted internally as Council Decisions on the policy stance to be taken by the Union and the Member States in the joint councils. Such a Council Decision constitutes

---

[80] Art 3(1) of Decision (EU) 2015/601 of 15 April 2015 of the European Parliament and of the Council providing macro-financial assistance to Ukraine [2015] OJ L100/1.

[81] Art 3(1) of Decision (EU) 534/2014 of 15 May 2014 of the European Parliament and of the Council providing macro-financial assistance to the Republic of Tunisia [2015] OJ L151/9. Commission implementing decision C(2014) 5176/ Final of 16 July 2014 approving the Memorandum of Understanding between the European Union and Tunisia related to macro-financial assistance to Tunisia.

[82] Commission Decision C(2015) 3955 Final of 15 June 2015 on Joint Declaration establishing a Mobility Partnership between the Republic of Belarus and the European Union and its participating Member States.

[83] Vianello, 'EU External Action and the Administrative Rule of Law' (n 14).

[84] Arts 7, 9, and 12 of Regulation (EU) 232/2014 (n 24).

[85] Art 5 of Regulation (EU) 182/2011 of 16 February 2011 of the European Parliament and the Council laying down the rules and the general principles concerning mechanisms for control by Member States of the Commission's exercise of implementing powers [2011] OJ L55/15.

an agreement between the Union and the Member states on how their relations with a third country are to be conducted. Therefore, to the extent that this type of Decision can be interpreted as a measure aimed at achieving Union tasks established in the Treaties, the duty of loyal cooperation could be a source of legal effect on Member States. With regard to the external relations of the Union, Member States have, under that duty, both positive and negative obligations. Positively they are required to act as 'trustees of the Union interest'[86] by taking any measure appropriate to ensure fulfilment of the obligations arising from acts of EU institutions. The negative side of the same duty requires that Member States remain silent where not to do so could jeopardize the attainment of EU objectives.[87]

The aim of the ENP instruments is ultimately to support reforms in the countries to which they are addressed, in order to promote democracy, human rights protection, market liberalization, approximation of third country laws with EU legislation, and so on. Therefore, in order to increase the effectiveness of such instruments, the Union attaches to their fulfilment by recipient states incentives or sanctions. Positive conditionality has been, for example, spelled out in the latest Association Agreement concluded by the Union with Ukraine. That agreement is based on an explicit 'market access' conditionality, implying that Ukraine will be granted additional access to a section of the EU Internal Market only if the Union decides, after strict monitoring, that Ukraine has successfully implemented its commitments to legislative approximation.[88] Negative conditionality is mainly focused on the protection of human rights, democracy, and the rule of law. Agreements concluded by the Union with neighbouring countries include standard conditionality clauses. In general, an 'essential element clause', defining the core common values of the relationship (normally human rights, democracy, and the rule of law), is combined with a 'suspension clause' which allows for the agreement to be suspended where one of the parties violates any such essential element.[89] The current ENI Regulation—in contrast to its predecessor ENPI[90]—does not in fact contain such a clause since the European Parliament and the Council could not reach agreement to whether the Parliament would necessarily be involved in decision-making process leading to the suspension of financial assistance. However, even in the absence of an express stipulation, suspension is not excluded in the case of violations of, e.g., human rights. The only issue to be resolved would be whether the European Parliament would have a claim to be involved in that decision.[91]

---

[86] Marise Cremona, 'Member States as Trustees of the Union Interest: Participating in International Agreements on Behalf of the European Union' in Anthony Arnull and others (eds), *Constitutional Order of States: Essays in EU Law in Honour of Alan Dashwood* (Hart Publishing 2011) 435–57.

[87] Andres Delgado Casteleiro and Joris Larik, 'The Duty to Remain Silent: Limitless Loyalty in EU External Relations?' (2011) 36(4) *European Law Review* 524, 522–39.

[88] See Arts 475 and 476 of the Association Agreement between the European Union and its Member States, of the one part, and Ukraine, of the other part [2014] OJ L161/3.

[89] For more information see Lorand Bartels, *Human Rights Conditionality in the EU's International Agreements* (Oxford University Press 2005).

[90] Arts 1 and 28 of Regulation 1638/2006 of 24 October 2006 of the European Parliament and of the Council laying down general provisions establishing a European Neighbourhood and Partnership Instrument (ENI) OJ 2006 L310/1.

[91] Statement by the European Parliament on the suspension of assistance granted under the financial instruments in Regulation (EU) 236/2014 (n 26).

I Supervision and Control of, and within, the ENP Sector

The external relations character of the ENP sector does not exclude administrative activities implementing the policy area from being subject to various modes of supervision. However, very little oversight is expressly foreseen, despite the significant impact of such activities both in shaping the Union strategic action in the neighbourhood as well as in influencing third countries' political and legal agenda. This section will consider in turn administrative, political and external (rarely, judicial) supervision of ENP administrative action.

1 Administrative supervision

Ex-ante administrative supervision of the instruments belonging to the first group of measures (progress reports, action plans, etc.) very much rests on the hierarchical pyramid of the EEAS and that of DG NEAR. Progress reports and action plans before being adopted are reviewed and re-worked by the directors and the managing directors within the EEAS and DG NEAR.[92] In regard to the most recent examples of MoUs, supervision has been conducted ex ante within specialist structures, specifically comitology. For the instruments of the second group (strategy papers, programming documents implementing financial support), supervision is also conducted ex ante within comitology[93] and ex post by a mixture of the Commission's own reporting and of independent external evaluators.[94]

2 Political supervision

The instruments of the first group are normally presented every year as a package (the 'ENP package') by the Commissioner responsible for the ENP and for enlargement negotiations to the Foreign Affairs Committee (AFET) of the European Parliament. Normally, at the centre of the discussion are the state of play of the policy and the ENP progress reports, being the only documents which are produced yearly.[95] As the presentation and discussion occurs after the ENP progress reports have been in fact adopted, it is a form of *ex post* political supervision. The European Parliament tries, however, to influence the implementing activity of the Commission in the ENP *ex ante* by adopting resolutions inviting the Commission to focus on certain aspects of the process of policy development.[96]

---

[92] *Guidance Note ENP Package 2014 Progress Reports* (section on time line and definition of roles), Access to Documents request GESTDEM reference 2013/5084.

[93] Art 7(2)(4)(5) Regulation (EU) 232/2014 (n 24).   [94] ibid Arts 12 and 13.

[95] See eg the 31 March and 1 April 2014 agenda of the AFET Parliamentary Committee http://www.europarl.europa.eu/sides/getDoc.do?pubRef=-//EP//TEXT+COMPARL+AFET-OJ-20140331-1+01+DOC+XML+V0//EN (last accessed 30 July 2018).

[96] Some examples of European Parliament resolutions are: 'European Parliament Resolution on the European Neighbourhood Policy' P6_TA (2006) 0028; 'European Parliament resolution of 15 November 2007 on Strengthening the European Neighbourhood Policy' 2007/2088(INI); 'European Parliament Report on the Review of the European Neighbourhood and Partnership Instrument' 2008/2236(INI).

The European Parliament also exercises some form of *ex post* political supervision in respect of the Commission's powers in implementing financial assistance. The Commission's own reporting, and possible external evaluators' reports on progress in implementing objectives and in delivering results of Union external financial assistance, are also to be submitted to the Parliament.[97] The Commission shall also take into due account any European Parliament proposals for hiring independent external evaluators for monitoring the impact and effectiveness of the Commission's policies, actions, and programming.[98] Furthermore, as already mentioned, express provision allowing for suspension of financial assistance is not to be found in the ENI Regulation, but has been replaced by an EP statement which affirms that 'as co-legislator and co-branch of the budgetary authority'[99] the Parliament has to be entitled to exercise its prerogatives fully if a suspension decision is to be taken. With this move the European Parliament makes clear its claim to exercise a supervisory role over the Commission's and Council's exercise of powers in implementing the ENP.

A final interesting, sector-specific type of supervision is carried out by NGOs, think-tanks and associations active across all the neighbourhood states, one of the aims of which is the review of the various EU progress reports and action plans. Such organizations produce proper shadow progress reports and action plans maintaining the same structure and format of those compiled by the Commission and the EEAS. For example, an NGO from Israel every year monitors and evaluates EU progress reports on ENP implementation in Israel.[100] Such reports and related documentation are also used by the EEAS in Brussels, in order to review the information gathered by Union delegations in third countries.[101] Moreover, these same organizations also suggest policy strategies to the Commission and the EEAS with the aim of, for example, better involving civil society in the adoption of ENP measures. The Commission has in the past welcomed such suggestions and implemented them in its actions.[102] Although one can acknowledge a clear difference between the political supervision carried out by the European Parliament and that performed by actors external to the EU legal order, it is striking the use that the Commission and the EEAS makes of these instruments from non-institutional sources.

---

[97] Arts 12 and 13 Regulation (EU) 236/2014 (n 26).   [98] ibid Art 12.

[99] Statement by the European Parliament on the suspension of assistance granted under the financial instruments in Regulation (EU) 236/2014 (n 26).

[100] Report http://www.ngo-monitor.org/article/analysis_of_the_eu_s_report_implementation_of_the_european_neighborhood_policy_in_israel_progress_in_and_recommendations_for_actions_ (last accessed 25 May 2017).

[101] Interview with an EEAS civil servant working on the ENP, 18 November 2013, Brussels.

[102] For example, the Balkan Civil Society Development Network was very vocal in respect of how the Commission supported the development of civil society in the Balkans. The network developed a report titled 'The Successes and Failures of the EU Pre-accession Policy in the Balkans: Support to Civil Society' and wrote a letter to the Commission urging the latter to better include local civil society organisations in the programming and implementation of the pre-accession financial assistance instrument. The action of the network was effective enough to push the Commission to adopt guidelines for EU support to civil society in enlargement countries for the years 2014–2020.

3 External review of ENP administration

The Court of Justice has so far never reviewed administrative acts and measures aimed at implementing the ENP. Despite their politically sensitive nature, the reasons are rather straightforward. First, some of these measures are non-binding acts and in particular lack binding force vis-à-vis third parties, and are therefore broadly non-justiciable. Second, it is extremely difficult for non-privileged applicants to show direct and individual concern in applications for annulment of Union acts under Article 263(4) TFEU. Nevertheless, a few cases have reached the Court in which individuals from third countries challenged the inaction of the Commission.[103] The Court in these cases recognized the wide margin of discretion that the Commission enjoyed in the management of the Union's external relations in so far as that management involves complex political and economic assessments.[104] Where an action was brought for damages under Article 340 TFEU, the main challenge for the individuals was to determine how the Commission had manifestly and gravely disregarded the limits of its discretion in the absence of transparent and clear rules limiting and guiding the exercise of the Commission's power. The reviewing of Commission implementing decisions by the CJEU is less problematic: besides being legally binding, for strategy papers and programming documents the ENI Regulation and the Financial Regulation are quite detailed as to the boundaries of the Commission's discretion.

The European Ombudsman, thanks to its mandate and its ability to go beyond the rights of complainants, was able in some instances to offer guidance as to the boundaries of administrative power when acting externally—even in the absence of legally binding rules.[105] In these cases the Ombudsman, in assessing whether the administration was in breach of the principle of legality (Article 4 European Code of Good Administrative Behaviour) took into consideration the following points: whether the administration had the responsibility to exercise a specific power; whether it complied with a list of sources (not limited to primary and secondary law); and whether the administration had to follow certain procedures (whether explicitly laid down or implied). In other words, the Ombudsman was able to review the Commission's external administrative action against the net of internal self-regulatory guidelines of the Commission, as well as against the values contained in the external policies themselves. Complaints launched by individuals that are neither EU nationals nor EU residents (nor having their registered office in a Member State) should, formally, be rejected as inadmissible. Nevertheless, over the years the Ombudsman started to

---

[103] See Case T-367/03 *Yedaş Tarim ve Otomotiv Sanayi ve Ticaret AŞ v Council of the European Union and Commission of the European Communities* EU:T:2006:96; Case T-346/03 *Krikorian v European Parliament, Council and Commission* EU:T:2003:348; Case T-2/04 *Korkmaz v Commission* EU:T:2006:97; Case T-292/09 *Mugraby v Council and Commission* EU:T:2011:418; Case C-581/11 P *Mugraby v Council and Commission* EU:C:2012:466.

[104] Case T-292/09 *Mugraby v Council and Commission* EU:T:2011:418, para 60.

[105] Decision on 26 October 2000 of the European Ombudsman on complaint 530/98/JMA against the European Commission, external relations, breach of article 4 ECGAB; Decision on 28 June 2005 of the European Ombudsman on complaint 933/2004/JMA against the European Commission, external relations, breach of article 4 ECGAB; Draft Recommendation on 26 March 2015 of the European Ombudsman on complaint 1409/2014/JN against the European Commission.

consider cases lodged by individuals from third countries since they were seen as raising important issues.[106]

Finally, all actions financed under the ENI Regulation in accordance with financial strategy papers and programming documents are supervised *ex-post* by the Commission's anti-fraud office (OLAF) and by the European Court of Auditors. The type of supervision carried out by these two organs aims at establishing whether there has been fraud, corruption, or any other illegal activity affecting the financial interests of the Union in connection with grant agreements, grant decision, contractors, and subcontractors who have received Union funds.[107] Furthermore, they might also assess whether the Commission's management of funds was effective in achieving its goal.[108]

J Conclusions

The mode of foreign 'governance'—influence, encouragement, and pressure—that the Union establishes with its neighbours clearly foresees the active involvement of the administration. Over the years the administrative actors involved have developed ad-hoc solutions aimed at addressing the changing needs of an evolving Union determined to pursue long term and stable relations with its new neighbours. The administration—finding itself in a general vacuum of norms—has created new instruments and measures aimed at implementing the Union's primary political choice: establishing an area of prosperity and good neighbourliness founded on the values of the Union. Consequently, not only has the ENP increasingly been coordinated through the use of a great diversity of tools but it has also moved away from its core political nature to a more technocratic-driven, administrative setting. In particular, the instruments of the first group discussed above have gained more and more legal significance both internally (by indicating which priorities shall receive financial assistance) and externally as standard-setting instruments for third countries.

Despite the attempts made to structure, organize, and proceduralize administrative action in the ENP, these new forms of measures have however started to provoke signs of tensions as to how the administrative power is exercised and controlled. The power here is exercised in a non-linear manner, in the sense that administrative action does not always find its origin in a clear legal base and is often exercised without having a clear negotiation mandate. Administrative power is sometimes exercised here in a discretionary fashion, for example, in determining which stakeholders should be consulted and whose suggestions should be accepted.[109] Such discretion granted to

---

[106] For example, see complainants: Decision on 26 February 2016 of the European Ombudsman on complaint 1409/2014/JN against the European Commission, external relations, breach of article 4 ECGAB, Duty of care; Decision on 2 September 2016 of the European Ombudsman on complaint OI/7/2015/ANA against the European Commission, external relations, breach of article 23 ECGAB.

[107] Art 7 Regulation (EU) 236/2014(n 26).

[108] See eg Special report 21/2016: EU pre-accession assistance for strengthening the administrative capacity in the Western Balkans: A meta-audit, 13 September 2016.

[109] A substantial administrative discretion with important political implications is concealed behind these evaluations, which should be subjected to the controls of administrative law. Carol Harlow, 'Global Administrative Law: The Quest for Principles and Values' (2006) 17 *European Journal of International Law* 187, 202.

the Commission in implementing the ENP should not be perceived as bad per se, but it does needs to operate within a framework of rules and principles to guide its action. Finally, the powers of the administration here also exercised in an informal manner. However, administrative activities that are not published and, that are not conducted according to clear rules of procedures, become legally invisible. The fact that the power is exercised in an unregulated manner may lead to a lack of transparency, predictability, intelligibility, and trust in EU administrative and regulatory procedures and their outcomes.[110]

The challenges on the way towards integrating the proliferation of these new forms of administrative action and their—partly potential—regulatory framework into a coherent system of administrative law and principles are numerous. Most importantly, it ought not be forgotten that the realm of the ENP, of its nature, requires the transference and transformation of the more traditional decisional forms of EU action (by the EU and the Member States) into new ones that would meet the needs of decision-making performed in an essentially different setting, that of the relations between the EU and third countries.[111]

---

[110] Herwig C H Hofmann, Jens-Peter Schneider, and Jacques Ziller, 'Administrative Procedures and the Implementation of EU Law and Policies' *Law Working Paper Series Université du Luxembourg Faculty Law Economic and Finance* 2014-09.

[111] For an attempt at integrating the EU external administrative activities into a coherent system of administrative law see Vianello, 'EU External Action and the Administrative Rule of Law' (n 14).

4

Common Commercial Policy and External Trade

Jörg Philipp Terhechte

A Introduction: External Dimensions of the European Administrative Space

As a supranational community of states with an internal market, the European Economic Community (EEC) was always designated to administer the external trade relations of its Member States.[1] According to this, the EEC contained special provisions on the Common Commercial Policy (CCP) and other rules governing external trade, which were, after an initial period, continuously enforced.[2] Against this historic background, the administrative dimensions of CCP and other EU rules governing external trade constitute a field in which the European institutions and the Member States have gained 'administrative experience' for more than fifty years.[3] For this reason, it is not surprising that this part of EU law also played an important role in the emergence of 'European administrative law' in the late 1980s.[4] The rules governing the CCP and other facets of external trade are still of major interest when it comes to the analysis of the administrative structures of the European policy sectors.[5]

Nowadays, the CCP, together with some other policy fields, such as the customs rules and the Common Foreign and Security Policy (CFSP), constitute the 'external dimension' of the European administrative space.[6] It is also an important field of reference when it comes to the interaction between European administrative law and

---

[1] See Ulrich Everling, 'Article 113 EEC Treaty' in Ernst Wohlfarth, Ulrich Everling, Hans Joachim Glaesner, and Rudolf Sprung (eds), *Die Europäische Wirtschaftsgemeinschaft. Kommentar zum Vertrag* (Verlag Franz Vahlen 1960) 338 ff.

[2] The CCP is (today) laid down in Art 206 ff TFEU. Other 'external trade instruments' are for example customs (Arts 28(1), 31 TFEU) and economic sanctions (Art 215 TFEU).

[3] See in general on EU external trade and customs law Christoph Herrmann and Marian Niestedt, 'Einleitung zum EU-Außenwirtschafts- und Zollrecht' in Horst Günter Krenzler, Christoph Herrmann, and Marian Niestedt (eds), *EU-Außenwirtschafts- und Zollrecht* (C H Beck 2017).

[4] See eg Jürgen Schwarze, *Europäisches Verwaltungsrecht* (Nomos 1988) 28 ff, 375 ff, 785 ff.

[5] See Chapter 1, this volume.

[6] See on the concept of the European administrative space Johan Olsen, 'Towards a European Administrative Space?' (2010) 10 *Journal of European Public Policy* 506; Armin von Bogdandy, 'Verwaltungsrecht im europäischen Rechtsraum—Perspektiven einer Disziplin' in Armin von Bogdandy, Sabino Cassese, and Michael Huber (eds), *Handbuch Ius Publicum Europaeum Band IV: Verwaltungsrecht in Europa: Wissenschaft* (C F Müller 2011) § 57(1); Jörg Philipp Terhechte 'Einführung: Das Verwaltungsrecht der Europäischen Union als Gegenstand rechtswissenschaftlicher Forschung— Entwicklungslinien, Prinzipien und Perspektiven' in Jörg Philipp Terhechte (ed), *Verwaltungsrecht der Europäischen Union* (Nomos 2011) 49 § 1(7).

international law.[7] There are only a few areas of EU law in which international law, especially the law of the World Trade Organization (WTO), plays such a pervasive role as it does in the CCP and other European rules on external trade. This also applies to the EU customs rules, which find their origin mainly in the standards of the World Customs Organization (WCO) and the WTO. In addition, the conclusion of trade agreements has tremendous influence upon the administrative dimension of the CCP.

Due to the importance of the CCP it is remarkable that some common features of European administrative law were not reflected upon, or given particular attention, in its development. This field of Union law may, therefore, be characterized as a 'latecomer' when it comes to the evolution of the core principles of European administrative law (such as transparency, accountability, or good administration), as well as of judicial review and the role of human rights. The Court of Justice of the European Union (CJEU) very early on held that the institutions enjoy wide discretion when it comes to the administration of the Union's external trade policy, and, thus, exercised judicial review only to a limited extent. Recently, however, trade policy seems to more and more be curbed by human rights considerations.[8] It remains to be seen whether this trend will play an overarching role in the CCP. Finally, the role of the European Parliament within the context of the CCP has been and (still) is subject to criticism, even though the Lisbon Treaty led to an appreciable 'democratic promotion' and politicization of the CCP.[9] The latest reforms and the new initiatives of the European Commission in the field of the CCP could be characterized as a 'new wave of constitutionalisation', aiming as they do to strengthen the role of constitutional principles of EU law.[10]

---

[7] On this see Jörg Philipp Terhechte, 'Internationale Dimensionen des europäischen Verwaltungsrechts' in Jörg Philipp Terhechte (ed), *Internationale Dimensionen des europäischen Verwaltungsrechts* (2016) 1 *EuR-Beiheft* 9.

[8] See eg Joined Cases C-402/05 P and C-415/05 P *Kadi and Al-Barakaat International Foundation v Council and Commission* ECLI:EU:C:2008:461; Joined Cases C-584/10 P, C-593/10 P, and C-595/10 P *Commission and Others v Kadi* ECLI:EU:C:2013:518; Case C-362/14 *Schrems* ECLI:EU:C:2015:650.

[9] See Marise Cremona, 'A Quiet Revolution: The Changing Nature of the EU's Common Commercial Policy' in Marc Bungenberg and others (eds), *European Yearbook of International Economic Law 2017* (Springer 2017) 3–34, 26 ff; Markus Krajewski, 'New Functions and New Powers for the European Parliament: Assessing the Changes of the Common Commercial Policy from the Perspective of Democratic Legitimacy' in Marc Bungenberg and Christoph Herrmann (eds), *European Yearbook of International Economic Law—Special Issue: Common Commercial Policy after Lisbon* (Springer 2013) 67 ff; David Kleimann, 'Taking Stock: EU Common Commercial Policy in the Lisbon Era' (2011) *CEPS Working Document* No 345 https://www.ceps.eu/publications/taking-stock-eu-common-commercial-policy-lisbon-era (last accessed 7 April 2018); Marika Armanoviča and Roberto Bendini, 'The Role of the European Parliament in Shaping the EU's Trade Policy after the Entry into Force of the Treaty of Lisbon' (July 2014) DG EXPO/B/PolDep/Note/2014_54.

[10] Stephen Woolcock, 'The Treaty of Lisbon and the European Union as an Actor in International Trade' (2010) *ECIPE Working Paper* No 1 http://ecipe.org//app/uploads/2014/12/the-treaty-of-lisbon-and-the-european-union-as-an-actor-in-international-trade.pdf (last accessed 7 April 2018); Christoph Herrmann, 'The Treaty of Lisbon Expands the EU's External Trade and Investment Powers' (2010) 14 *ASIL Insights* 29 https://www.asil.org/insights/volume/14/issue/29/treaty-lisbon-expands-eu%E2%80%99s-external-trade-and-investment-powers (last accessed 7 April 2018); Youri Devuyst, 'The European Union's Competence in International Trade after the Treaty of Lisbon' (2011) 39 *Georgia Journal of International and Comparative Law* 639; Anna de Luca, 'New Developments on the Scope of the EU Common Commercial Policy under the Treaty of Lisbon' in Karl P Sauvant (ed), *Yearbook On International Investment Law and Policy 2010-2011* (Oxford University Press 2012) 165–215; Markus Krajewski, 'The Reform of the Common Commercial Policy' in Andrea Biondi, Piet Eeckhout, and Stefanie Ripely (eds),

The following remarks are focused on the administrative dimension of the CCP. Other fields of external trade, such as the special provisions on the customs union, international trade agreements, or economic sanctions under Article 215 TFEU will be analysed in the context of the CCP only. This approach is taken due to the fact that, in the fields of both trade agreements and sanctions, administrative action does not play the same role as within the CCP. Nevertheless, these policy fields have very substantial influence on the administration of the CCP.

This chapter concentrates first, in Section B, on the foundations of the CCP and external trade policy, especially the evolution of the autonomous trade instruments, the scope of the CCP as defined by the CJEU over the years, and recent developments such as the reform of the CCP (which, inter alia, aims to strengthen the role of core administrative principles like transparency and due process). Following this, the (legal) sources of the CCP and other external trade instruments are examined (Section C). Subsequently, the underlying legal principles will be analysed, in particular the principles of transparency and due process, as well as the overall goals of the Treaty on the European Union[11] (Article 3 TEU and Article 206 TFEU[12]) (Section D). In a next step, the organization, institutions and structures of the CCP and other external trade instruments (Section E) as well as the relevant administrative procedures (Section F) are addressed. After this, the legal rules governing decision-making (Section G), the role of abstract-general and single-case administrative acts and measures (Section H), and the forms of administrative enforcement Section (I) are examined. Finally, the structures of political supervision and judicial review will be addressed (Section J) before some concluding remarks (Section K).

B Foundations of the Common Commercial Policy

1 Evolution

The evolution of the CCP and the rules governing external trade cannot be separated from the creation of the internal market,[13] as well as international developments through the conclusion of multilateral trade agreements. The internal market (now Article 3(3) TEU and Article 26 TFEU) was never seen as a solely 'internal' endeavour but was always intended to be complemented by an external dimension.[14] However, the scope of Article 113 of the Treaty of Rome reflected the international perspective

---

EU Law After Lisbon (Oxford University Press 2012) 292–311; Markus Krajewski, 'External Trade Law and the Constitutional Treaty: Towards a Federal and More Democratic Common Commercial Policy?' (2005) 42 *Common Market Law Review* 91; Gonzalo Villalta Puig and Bader Al-Haddab, 'The Common Commercial Policy after Lisbon: An Analysis of the Reforms' (2011) 36(2) *European Law Review* 289; Sieglinde Gstöhl, 'The European Union's Trade Policy' (2013) 11 *Ritsumeikan International Affairs* 1.

[11] Consolidated Version of the Treaty on the European Union (TEU) [2016] OJ C202/13.

[12] Consolidated Version of the Treaty on the Functioning of the European Union (TFEU) [2016] OJ C202/47.

[13] As the CJEU put it: 'a commercial policy is in fact made up by the combination and interaction of internal and external measures, without priority being taken by one over the others'. Opinion 1/75 *Re Understanding on a Local Cost Standard* ECLI:EU:C:1975:145, 1363.

[14] Manfred Elsig, *The EU's Common Commercial Policy: Institutions, Interests and Ideas* (Routledge 2002) 12.

on trade at that time—primarily concerned with trade liberalization in relation to goods—and thus was confined to trade in goods. Although there had been negotiations and plans for the establishment of an international trade organization[15] as early as the 1940s, such an institution did not come into being at that time. Merely the General Agreement on Tariffs and Trade (GATT 1947), that was intended to become part of the organizational regime for international trade, entered into force, and became a de facto institution for almost fifty years.[16] On the level of the EEC, preparations for the introduction of a customs union led to the implementation of a work programme in 1962, which inter alia required Member States to hold consultations before the introduction of trade instruments.[17] In 1968, the common customs tariff (CCT)[18] as well as a regulation on dumped imports[19] entered into force. The introduction of the CCT brought about rules on common procedures regarding the importation of goods into the territory of the customs union.[20] This can be seen as the birth of administrative procedures directing the external dimension of the internal market.

In the following years, the CCP further evolved in correspondence with international rules. This worked quite smoothly, despite the occasional frictions between Member States and the Commission regarding questions of competence, and an ever-growing number of legal bases for the conclusion of international trade agreements.[21] The Uruguay Round negotiations that led to the creation of the World Trade Organization, however, notably disrupted the existing regime on the European level, since the multilateral negotiations included topics such as trade in services (in form of the General Agreement on Trade in Services (GATS)) and intellectual property rights (in the form of the Agreement on Trade-Related Aspects of Intellectual Property Rights (TRIPs)).[22] Today, the Union's CCP, including its administrative aspects, is

---

[15] See on the international trade organization negotiations John Odell and Barry Eichengreen, 'The United States, the ITO, and the WTO: Exit Options, Agent Slack, and Presidential Leadership' in Anne O Krueger (ed), *The WTO as an International Organization* (University of Chicago Press 1998) 181, 184 ff; on the ITO Charter George Bronz, 'The International Trade Organization Charter', (1949) 62 *Harvard Law Review* 7, 1089–125.

[16] Petros C Mavroidis, 'The Genesis of the GATT Summary' in Henrik Horn, Petros C Mavroidis (eds), *Legal and Economic Principles of World Trade Law* (Cambridge University Press 2013) 1, 3.

[17] See Council Decision on a programme of action in matters of common commercial policy, OJ 1962 P 90/2353, para A.3(b).

[18] Règlement (CEE) No 950/68 du Conseil, du 28 juin 1968, relatif au tarif douanier commun [1968] OJ L172/1 (no English version available containing the annex); see also Règlement du Conseil (CEE) No 2041/68 du 10 Décembre 1968 portant établissement d'une liste commune de libération des importations dans la Communauté à l'égard des pays tiers [1968] OJ L303/1, (no English version available); see also Regulation (ECC) No 1496/68 of 27 September 1968 on the Definition of the Customs Territory of the Community; Regulation (EEC) No 803/68 of 27 June 1968 on the Valuation of Goods for Customs Purposes; Regulation (EEC) No 802/68 of 27 June 1968 on the Common Definition of the Concept of the Origin of Goods.

[19] Council Regulation (EEC) No 459/68 of 5 April 1968 on protection against dumping or the granting of bounties or subsidies by countries which are not members of the European Economic Community [1968] OJ L93/1.

[20] See eg Règlement du Conseil (CEE) No 2043/68 du 10 décembre 1968 portant établissement graduel d'une procédure commune de gestion des contingents quantitatifs à l'importation dans la Communauté [1968] OJ L303/42 (no English version available); on the development of the customs union see Kathrin Limbach, *Uniformity of Customs Administration in the European Union* (Bloomsbury Publishing 2015) 11 ff.

[21] See Cremona, 'A Quiet Revolution' (n 9) 4; see references below under section B(ii).

[22] See on this below under section B(ii).

largely shaped by WTO obligations. Bilateral or other trade agreements, which have also been concluded in considerable number, do not really have an effect on this, since they tend to be aligned with the multilateral obligations as well.

2 Scope of the CCP

In the past, the scope of the CCP has been especially subject to discussion. Although the CCP embodies an integral part of the EEC Treaty, the exact definition of what is covered by the relevant provisions has always been complicated. The harmonization of the external trade relations of the Member States has at all times been subject to tensions that needed (and still need) to be resolved and kept in balanced.[23] On the one hand, the creation of a common commercial policy inevitably requires the transfer of competences from the national to the supranational level, if the corresponding tasks are to be exercised effectively. On the other hand, external relations in general constitute a classical *domaine réservé* under international law. More specifically, external trade relations involve sensitive policy concerns and diplomacy, which states prefer to keep within their own sphere of competence. Determining the scope of the CCP, its precise definition (with a non-exhaustive list of measures in Article 113(1) EEC Treaty), and thus the extent of Union competences, has consequently been the topic of much debate, leading to extensive jurisprudence of the CJEU.

Early on the Court made clear that the CCP was to enjoy a broad compass. In *Opinion 1/75*,[24] it acknowledged the shift of trade competence from the Member States to the EEC. According to the Court, the CCP had the same content as the commercial policy of an individual state.[25] In *Opinion 1/78*,[26] the CJEU further underlined the broad and dynamic character of the CCP which allowed the EEC to adapt to changes and developments in international trade flexibly, as well as to prevent an incoherent application of that policy.[27] However, the story does not end here. As so often, Member States soon became afraid of empowering the Union too much, prompting the Court

---

[23] For this purpose, Art 113(3) EEC Treaty foresaw the creation of a special committee (the so-called Article 113 Committee) which was appointed by the Council and should assist the Commission and act within the framework of such directives as the Council may issue to it when the Commission would negotiate agreements with third countries in the field of the CCP; see on that Arne Niemann, 'Beyond Problem-Solving and Bargaining: Genuine Debate in EU External Trade Negotiations' (2006) 11 *International Negotiation* 467, 477 ff.

[24] Opinion 1/75 *Re Understanding on a Local Cost Standard* ECLI:EU:C:1975:145.

[25] ibid para 2.

[26] Opinion 1/78 *Re International Agreement on National Rubber* ECLI:EU:C:1979:224.

[27] ibid para 45:
'Article 113 empowers the community to formulate a commercial 'policy', based on 'uniform principles' thus showing that the question of external trade must be governed from a wide point of view and not only having regard to the administration of precise systems such as customs and quantitative restrictions. The same conclusion may be deduced from the fact that the enumeration in Article 113 of the subjects covered by commercial policy (changes in tariff rates, the conclusion of tariff and trade agreements, the achievement of uniformity in measures of liberalization, export policy and measures to protect trade) is conceived as a non-exhaustive enumeration which must not, as such, close the door to the application in a Community context of any other process intended to regulate external trade. A restrictive interpretation of the concept of common commercial policy would risk causing disturbances in intra-community trade by reason of the disparities which would then exist in certain sectors of economic relations with non-member countries.'

to render its infamous ruling in *Opinion 1/94*[28] on the WTO agreements. In brief, the Court decided to limit the Union's exclusive competence in the CCP to trade in goods, cross-border trade in services, and measures prohibiting the free circulation of counterfeit goods in the Community.[29] Therefore, the GATS as well as the TRIPs had to be concluded as mixed agreements.[30]

Nevertheless, the Commission did not give up in its relentless efforts to further broaden the scope of the CCP and ensure its uniform application. With the overhaul of the EEC Treaty through the Treaty of Amsterdam in 1997,[31] the Treaty of Nice in 2001,[32] and, ultimately, the Constitutional Treaty,[33] the Commission laid the groundwork for the extensive—yet, from a pro-European integration perspective, not overly extensive—reform of the CCP by the Treaty of Lisbon. Through the Treaty of Amsterdam, the new Article 133(5) of the Treaty Establishing the European Community (TEC; ex Article 113 EEC Treaty) merely provided the Council with the theoretical possibility of extending, by a unanimous vote, the application of the CCP to the negotiation and conclusion of international agreements on services and intellectual property. Similarly, the Treaty of Nice[34] fell short of a substantive revision, since it foresaw only the application of the institutional provisions of the CCP to the negotiation and conclusion of agreements in services and intellectual property, while agreements relating to trade in cultural and audiovisual services, educational services, and social and human health services remained within the shared competence of the Union and its Member States. Agreements on transport services would continue to remain outside the scope of the CCP. The Constitutional Treaty finally ought to have brought about the changes desperately needed, and hoped for, by providing for qualified majority voting (QMV) for all parts of the CCP, as well as extending its scope to cover trade in services, commercial aspects of intellectual property and foreign direct investment. Yet, as is well-known, the Constitutional Treaty was never to be adopted.

However, the drafters of the Lisbon Treaty retained most of the provisions of the Constitutional Treaty—thus finally achieving the substantive overhaul of the CCP. New Articles 206 and 207 TFEU now provide for a broad exclusive competence of the Union including, next to goods, also trade in services, commercial aspects of intellectual property, and foreign direct investment. While one would expect that, after one treaty proposal had failed, its successor would have been more carefully negotiated

[28] Opinion 1/94 *Re Competence of the Community to Conclude International Agreements Concerning Services and the Protection of Intellectual Property* ECLI:EU:C:1994:384.

[29] Devuyst, 'The European Union's Competence in International Trade after the Treaty of Lisbon' (n 10) 649.

[30] Eva Steinberger, 'The WTO Treaty as a Mixed Agreement: Problems with the EC's and the EC Member States' Membership of the WTO' (2006) 17 *European Journal of International Law* 837; Piet Eeckhout *EU External Relations Law* (2nd edn, Oxford University Press 2011) 212 ff; Christophe Hillion and Panos Koutrakos (eds), *Mixed Agreements Revisited: The EU and its Member States in the World* (Hart Publishing 2010).

[31] Treaty of Amsterdam Amending the Treaty on European Union, the Treaties Establishing the European Communities and Certain Related Acts [1997] OJ C340/1.

[32] Treaty of Nice Amending the Treaty on European Union, the Treaties Establishing the European Communities and Certain Related Acts [2001] OJ C80/1.

[33] Treaty Establishing a Constitution for Europe [2004] OJ C310/1.

[34] Christoph Herrmann, 'Common Commercial Policy after Nice: Sisyphus Would Have Done a Better Job' (2002) 39 *Common Market Law Review* 7.

and written so as not to alarm the Member States, *Opinion 2/15*[35] tells in some ways a different story. It is true that *Opinion 2/15* has paved the way for the conclusion of comprehensive trade agreements by the Union alone, without the involvement of the national parliaments. Yet, once more, it has dissatisfied the aspirations of the Commission, which had hoped to conclude deep and comprehensive trade and investment agreements with third states, in order to remain competitive and join the 'mega-regionals' trend. In the foreseeable future, and as evidenced by the 'CETA-Saga', it seems unlikely that such broad agreements will easily be concluded. This is because the Court has made clear that many aspects, typically those pertaining to investment agreements, in fact fall within the shared competence of the Union and its Member States. In the case of the EU–Singapore Free Trade Agreement (EUSFTA), the CJEU came to the conclusion that this meant it had to be concluded as a mixed agreement, which amounts to the introduction of a duty of shared competence (mixity), thereby giving Member States a de facto veto of any agreement going beyond trade.

3 Administrative dimensions of the Common Commercial Policy and external trade

Administrative proceedings are always a tool for guaranteeing and enhancing legitimacy, and the CCP is no exception in this regard. In the European Union's CCP and external trade policy, administrative procedures are most pronounced when it comes to trade defence measures (TDMs), that is, anti-dumping measures, measures for countervailing subsidies, and safeguard measures in the form of additional tariffs.[36] The reason for this stems from the EU legal order itself as well as its international obligations. Regarding the latter, it is particularly the WTO Agreements, but also other free trade agreements concluded by the Union, which require members to follow certain administrative procedures when they wish to implement trade defence measures. Apart from that, trade defence measures entail economic burdens which can have an existential impact on importers and exporters. It is, therefore, necessary to ensure transparency in such procedures and respect for due process principles with regard to the individuals concerned. In this context, the jurisprudence of the Court on the relevance of human rights, when it comes to economic sanctions under Article 215 TFEU, could serve as an inspiration for the CCP.[37]

4 Recent developments

The Commission had been working on a modernization of the EU's trade defence instruments regarding anti-dumping measures and countervailing duties for years and made a first proposal in 2013.[38] In particular, the modernization of trade defence

---

[35] Opinion 2/15 *Re Conclusion of the Free Trade Agreement between the European Union and the Republic of Singapore* ECLI:EU:C:2017:376.

[36] On TDMs in general see Ivo Van Bael and Jean-François Bellis, *EU Anti-dumping and Other Trade Defence Instruments* (Kluwer Law International 2011).

[37] See section D(iv).

[38] Proposal for a Regulation of the European Parliament and of the Council amending Council Regulation (EC) No 1225/2009 on protection against dumped imports from countries not members of the

instruments was to increase transparency, introduce the possibility of *ex officio* investigations, and improve the enforcement and effectiveness of trade defence instruments (TDIs).[39] The relevant basic regulations required an overhaul due to the entry into force of the new Comitology Regulation in 2011.[40] The new basic regulations on antidumping and countervailing measures, embodying the new comitology rules, entered into force in 2016. However, these were not the only revisions undertaken by the EU, other changes have followed and just recently been completed.

In addition, in the field of anti-dumping, efforts were made to revise the methodology for calculating anti-dumping duties. The Commission presented a proposal relating to this in November 2016[41] and the Committee of the Permanent Representatives of the Governments of the Member States to the European Union (COREPER) agreed to the Council's proposal in December 2016.[42] The need for action has become all the more pressing following China's initiation of proceedings before the Dispute Settlement Body (DSB) of the WTO in March 2017, challenging the Union's method of calculating the normal value for 'non-market economy' (NME) countries in antidumping proceedings involving China.[43] This is especially relevant in light of the fact that section 15(a)(ii) of China's WTO Accession Protocol[44] has expired. Based upon that protocol, the NME methodology was used for the calculation of anti-dumping duties against China. Now, the EU may apply the regular anti-dumping regime to China, which means that duties will most likely be higher—an outcome which China obviously opposes.

European Community and Council Regulation (EC) No 597/2009 on protection against subsidised imports from countries not members of the European Community, COM(2013) 192 final; on the issue of modernization in general see Frank Hoffmeister, 'Modernising the EU's Trade Defence Instruments: Mission Impossible?' in Christoph Herrmann, Bruno Simma, and Rudolf Streinz (eds), *European Yearbook of International Economic Law—Special Issue: Trade Policy between Law, Diplomacy and Scholarship* (Springer 2015)365 ff; Wolfgang Müller, 'The EU's Trade Defence Instruments: Recent Judicial and Policy Developments' in Marc Bungenberg and others (eds), *European Yearbook of International Economic Law'* (Springer 2017) 205–26, 212 ff.

[39] See on that the contributions in the Workshop on the Modernisation of the EU's Trade Defence Instruments (TDI) April 2014 EXPO/B/INTA/FWC/2009-01/Lot7/40.

[40] European Parliament and Council Regulation (EU) No 182/2011 laying down the rules and general principles concerning mechanisms for control by Member States of the Commission's exercise of implementing powers [2011] OJ L55/13; see further Claudio Dordi and Antonella Forganni, 'The Comitology Reform in the EU: Potential Effects on Trade Defence Instruments' (2013) 47 *Journal of World Trade* 259.

[41] Commission Proposal for a Regulation of the European Parliament and of the Council amending Regulation (EU) 2016/1036 on protection against dumped imports from countries not members of the European Union and Regulation (EU) 2016/1037 on protection against subsidised imports from countries not members of the European Union COM(2016) 721 final; see for an overview of the proposed changes the press release of the Commission, 'Commission proposes changes to the EU's anti-dumping and anti-subsidy legislation' IP/16/3604 (9 November 2016) http://europa.eu/rapid/press-release_IP-16-3604_en.htm) (last accessed 19 February 2018).

[42] See press release of the Council, 'Trade defence instruments: Council agrees negotiating position' 740/16 (13 December 2016) http://www.consilium.europa.eu/en/press/press-releases/2016/12/13-trade-defence-instruments-general-approach/ (last accessed 1 February 2018).

[43] WTO European Union—Measures Related to Price Comparison Methodologies WT/DS516; a panel was established in July 2017; see also Sophia Müller, *The Use of Alternative Benchmarks in Anti-Subsidy Law—A Study on the WTO, the EU and China* (Springer 2018).

[44] WTO, 'Accession of the People's Republic of China', 10 November 2001, WT/L/432; see also Andrei Suse, 'Old Wine in a New Bottle: The EU's Response to the Expiry of Section 15(A)(Ii) of China's WTO Protocol of Accession' (2017) *Leuven Centre for Global Governance Studies Working Paper* No 186 https://ghum.kuleuven.be/ggs/publications/working_papers/2017/186suse (last accessed 20 March 2018).

In October 2017 the European Parliament and the Council finally agreed on the Commission proposal from 2016[45] with regard to the *new anti-dumping methodology*, and the respective regulation entered into force in December 2017.[46] In broad terms, it provides for a new calculation of dumping in anti-dumping investigations, focusing on the distortion of prices and costs based on state intervention. Existing TDMs are subject to transitional arrangements. In addition, the way in which subsidies are investigated was adjusted.[47]

Apart from that, the Council, the European Parliament and the Commission also came to a political agreement on the general modernization of TDIs. The resulting *negotiated proposal* of December 2017[48] was approved by the European Parliament on 23 January 2018.[49] The Council, then, adopted its position on the proposed regulation in its first reading in April 2018[50] and the text was finally approved by the European Parliament in May 2018.[51] Ultimately, Regulation 2018/825 entered into force on 8 June 2018, meaning that any new investigations of dumping or subsidization initiated on or after this date will have to conform to the new rules.[52] These rules

[45] European Commission, 'Commission welcomes agreement on new anti-dumping methodology' (3 October 2017) http://trade.ec.europa.eu/doclib/press/index.cfm?id=1735&title=Commission-welcomes-agreement-on-new-anti-dumping-methodology (last accessed 3 October 2017).

[46] European Parliament and Council Regulation (EU) No 2017/2321 amending Regulation (EU) 2016/1036 on protection against dumped imports from countries not members of the European Union and Regulation (EU) 2016/1037 on protection against subsidised imports from countries not members of the European Union [2017] OJ L338/1.

[47] See European Commission, 'The EU is changing its anti-dumping and anti-subsidy legislation to address state induced market distortions' MEMO/17/3703 http://europa.eu/rapid/press-release_MEMO-17-3703_en.htm (last accessed 19 February 2018).

[48] See press release of the European Commission, 'Commission welcomes landmark deal modernising the EU's trade defence', IP/17/5136 (5 December 2017) http://europa.eu/rapid/press-release_IP-17-5136_en.htm (last accessed 19 February 2018).

[49] European Commission, 'Commission welcomes progress in approval of the modernised EU's trade defence rules' (23 January 2018) http://trade.ec.europa.eu/doclib/press/index.cfm?id=1788&title=Commission-welcomes-progress-in-approval-of-the-modernised-EUs-trade-defence-rules (last accessed 23 January 2018); European Commission 'EU modernises its trade defence instruments' MEMO/18/396 (23 January 2018) http://europa.eu/rapid/press-release_MEMO-18-396_en.htm (last accessed 19 February 2018).

[50] Position of the Council at first reading with a view to the adoption of a Regulation of the European Parliament and of the Council amending Regulation (EU) 2016/1036 on protection against dumped imports from countries not members of the European Union and Regulation (EU) 2016/1037 on protection against subsidised imports from countries not members of the European Union, Document No 5700/18, 3 April 2018; see further Position of the Council at first reading with a view to the adoption of a Regulation of the European Parliament and of the Council amending Regulation (EU) 2016/1036 on protection against dumped imports from countries not members of the European Union and Regulation (EU) 2016/1037 on protection against subsidised imports from countries not members of the European Union— Draft Statement of the Council's reasons, Document No 5700/18, 4 April 2018; Council of the European Union, 'Council adopts its position on a new legal framework against unfair trade competition (16 April 2018) http://www.consilium.europa.eu/en/press/press-releases/2018/04/16/council-adopts-its-position-on-a-new-legal-framework-against-unfair-trade-competition/ (last accessed 11 July 2018).

[51] Gisela Grieger, 'Modernising trade defence instruments' (July 2018) *European Parliament Briefing*, 1 & 11 http://www.europarl.europa.eu/RegData/etudes/BRIE/2018/621884/EPRS_BRI(2018)621884_EN.pdf (last accessed 11 July 2018).

[52] European Parliament and Council Regulation (EU) No 2018/825 amending Regulation (EU) 2016/1036 on protection against dumped imports from countries not members of the European Union and Regulation (EU) 2016/1037 on protection against subsidised imports from countries not members of the European Union [2018] OJ L143/1; European Commission, 'EU trade defence: stronger and more

provide for a number of changes aimed at the better protection of European companies and workers, as well as at improving procedures and transparency, further underlining the relevance of co-administrative principles in the CCP and external trade.[53] The changes include: a shortening of the investigation period for the imposition of provisional measures from nine to seven months (maximally eight months); the introduction of an early warning system for the imposition of provisional duties, informing companies at least three weeks in advance of it as well as more support for small and medium-sized companies (SMEs) through the establishment of a 'SME-helpdesk' run by the Commission providing them with general information on procedures, how to submit a claim and any other queries they may have. Furthermore, the regulation also adapts the way in which duties are calculated. For one, the 'lesser duty rule' will no longer apply in all cases, thus, allowing the EU to impose higher duties, especially where imports of products using raw materials and imports of energy at an artificially low price are concerned. Furthermore, the Commission will take account of compliance with European social and environmental legislation of a violating company in the calculation of duties. However, the Commission has stressed that it will no longer accept price undertakings from countries that do not abide by the standards of the ILO or other environmental agreements in the enforcement of anti-dumping or anti-subsidy measures.[54]

Apart from these rather technical changes, in its strategy paper, 'Trade for all'[55] the EU has made clear that it wishes to introduce more procedural transparency in anti-dumping and anti-subsidy investigations. Since May 2016, the Commission, therefore, publishes executive summaries of the notices of initiation and requests for reviews of anti-dumping and anti-subsidy proceedings on its website, the new online platform 'TRON' (from 'TRade ONline').[56] Apart from that, the Commission has published a fact-sheet,[57] which aims to simplify the communication between parties and the Commission in trade defence investigations.

C Administrative Law Sources in EU Common Commercial Policy and External Trade

1 International law

The sources of administrative law of the European Union's Common Commercial Policy and external trade law are determined not only by EU law itself. Rather, the Union is required by international law to adhere to certain procedural requirements,

effective rules enter into force' http://trade.ec.europa.eu/doclib/press/index.cfm?id=1859 (last accessed 11 July 2018).

[53] ibid.   [54] ibid.

[55] European Commission Communication, 'Trade for all—Towards a more responsible trade and investment policy' COM(2015) 497 final, 19.

[56] European Commission, 'Trade Defence: Investigations' http://trade.ec.europa.eu/tdi/ (last accessed 7 April 2018); European Commission, 'Trade Defence: Notices' http://trade.ec.europa.eu/tdi/ (last accessed 7 April 2018).

[57] European Commission, 'Correspondence with the European Commission in Trade Defence Cases' http://trade.ec.europa.eu/doclib/docs/2011/june/tradoc_148003.pdf (last accessed 19 March 2018).

in particular by the rules of the WTO, when it comes to the importation of goods or the application of trade defence measures. As a consequence, European rules in the field of the CCP and external trade largely reflect WTO rules and corresponding WTO case law. They should, therefore, be viewed against that background, in order to ensure compliance of the CCP and EU external trade administrative law with the rules of international law.[58]

2 European Union law

In the EU legal order itself, sources of administrative law in the CCP and external trade law are to be found in primary and secondary law, as well as tertiary law in the form of delegating and implementing acts (Articles 290 and 291 TFEU).[59]

The customs union as well as the CCP belong to the EU's exclusive competence pursuant to Article 3(1)(a) and (e) and Articles 206 and 207 TFEU. This competence includes the adoption of legally binding legislative acts (Article 2(1) TFEU) as well as the conclusion of international agreements (Articles 3(2) in conjunction with 216 TFEU). Article 207(2) makes clear that '[t]he European Parliament and the Council, acting by means of regulations in accordance with the ordinary legislative procedure, shall adopt the measures defining the framework for implementing the common commercial policy'. Thereby, 'the common commercial policy shall be based on uniform principles' (Article 207(1)), which is especially relevant in the context of TDIs. Thus, Member States can take regulatory action in this field 'themselves only if so empowered by the Union or for the implementation of Union acts' (Article 2(1) TFEU). For instance, Article 10 Regulation 2015/479 allows Member States to adopt or apply

> quantitative restrictions on exports on grounds of public morality, public policy or public security, or of protection of health and life of humans, animals and plants, of national treasures possessing artistic, historic or archaeological value, or of industrial and commercial property.

Thus, the relevant legislation for TDMs is unilaterally adopted by the Union in the form of regulations (Article 288 TFEU) and in accordance with the ordinary legislative procedure (Article 289 TFEU), requiring qualified majority voting, as well as the involvement of the European Parliament as co-legislator.

Together with this, the EU may also make use of soft-law instruments with no legal but practical effects, for example, rules of conduct, etc. Apart from that, the relevance of Council conclusions and Commission communications should not be underestimated, given that these determine the direction in which the EU intends to go. Article 22(1) TEU provides that the Council 'shall identify the strategic interests and objectives of the Union' for its external action.

---

[58] See eg European Parliament and Council Regulation (EU) No 2015/1843 laying down Union procedures in the field of the common commercial policy in order to ensure the exercise of the Union's rights under international trade rules, in particular those established under the auspices of the World Trade Organization [2015] OJ L272/1 Art 11(5).

[59] See further on the Comitology Regulation below under section G(ii); see also Paul Craig, 'Delegated Acts, Implementing Acts and the New Comitology Regulation' (2011) 36 *European Law Review* 671.

In their external action, Union institutions have to respect the principle of conferral, pursuant to which 'each institution shall act within the limits of the powers conferred on it in the Treaties, and in conformity with the procedures, conditions and objectives set out in them' (Article 13(2) TFEU). Along with not acting beyond their competences, the Union and the Member State are also required to work together in sincere cooperation and 'in full mutual respect, assist each other in carrying out tasks which flow from the Treaties' (Article 4(3) TEU). Even prior to the Treaty of Lisbon, the institutions cooperated with one another, specifically by concluding inter-institutional agreements, now explicitly required by Article 295 TFEU.[60]

Legislative acts define the framework for the implementation of the CCP. Correspondingly, EU trade defence instruments have been amended in 2015 and 2016 respectively. Revision became necessary because of the new comitology procedures introduced in 2011.[61] Hitherto, the Commission had been working on the modernization of the Union's trade defence instruments for years (see above). The legal framework governing the CCP and EU external trade thus consists of a number of regulations adopted by the European Parliament and the Council.

Regulation 2016/1036 on protection against dumped imports from countries not members of the European Union (Anti-Dumping (AD) Regulation)[62] and Regulation 2016/1037 on protection against subsidized imports from countries not members of the European Union (Anti-Subsidy (AS) Regulation)[63] provide the basic framework for the adoption of measures that should offset trade imbalances due to allegedly unfair trade practices. A product is considered to be dumped when 'its export price to the Union is less than a comparable price for a like product, in the ordinary course of trade, as established for the exporting country'.[64] Hence, the AD Regulation aims to protect (European) national producers of like products from competition of third state produces. A subsidy, on the other hand,

> shall be deemed to exist if there is a financial contribution by a government in the country of origin or export, there is any form of income or price support within the meaning of Article XVI of the GATT 1994 and a benefit is thereby conferred. Furthermore, this subsidy has to be specific to an enterprise or industry or group of enterprises or industries.[65]

Thus, the AS Regulation allows for the introduction of countervailing measures designed to offset the unfair advantage obtained through a subsidy.

Further secondary law in this field includes Regulation 2015/478 on common rules for imports (Import Regulation),[66] which lays down the basic principle of the free

---

[60] See latest Framework Agreement on relations between the European Parliament and the European Commission [2010] OJ L304/47.

[61] European Parliament and Council Regulation (EU) No 182/2011 (n 40).

[62] European Parliament and Council Regulation (EU) No 2016/1036 on protection against dumped imports from countries not members of the European Union [2016] OJ L176/21.

[63] Council Regulation (EU) No 2016/37 on protection against subsidised imports from countries not members of the European Union [2016] OJ L176/55.

[64] Art 1(2) of AD Regulation.   [65] Arts 3 and 4 of AS Regulation.

[66] Regulation (EU) No 2015/478 on common rules for imports [2015] OJ L83/16; see also Evin Dalkilic and Jörg Philip Terhechte, 'Verordnung (EU) 2015/478 über eine gemeinsame Einfuhrregelung' in Horst

importation of goods from third countries.[67] Furthermore, it contains the applicable procedures for the imposition of safeguard measures. This type of measure—foreseen in, and derived from, the WTO Agreements[68]—is not aimed at counterbalancing unfair trade practices. Rather, it provides states with the possibility to restrict the importation of a particular product when the corresponding domestic industry faces the threat of or an actual serious injury. Correspondingly, Regulation 2015/479 on common rules for exports (Export Regulation)[69] stipulates the free exportation of goods, subject to certain exceptions '[i]n order to prevent a critical situation from arising on account of a shortage of essential products, or to remedy such a situation'.[70] In such a case, the Commission may take protective measures, to prevent such shortage or at least limit it. Finally, Regulation 2015/1843 lays down the procedures in the field of the common commercial policy to ensure the exercise of the Union's rights under international trade rules, in particular those established under the auspices of the WTO[71] (Trade Barriers Regulation (TBR)).[72] Specifically, it provides individuals with a means of obtaining access to WTO dispute settlement mechanisms.[73]

The Lisbon Treaty has introduced what may be termed tertiary EU law, in the form of delegating (Article 290 TFEU) and implementing acts (Article 291 TFEU), which means that subordinate legislative powers are conferred upon the Commission and, under certain specified circumstances, upon the Council. Essentially, tertiary EU law is derived from secondary EU law. Usually, the relevant (secondary) regulations and directives in a particular policy field of the Union, such as trade defence, will foresee the possibility of the adoption of tertiary EU law. While delegated acts are more legislative in nature, implementing acts—especially in the context of external trade—are often executive in nature.[74] Thus, in the field of the CCP and external trade, the Commission is traditionally charged with the execution of trade defence measures and, in order to so, will resort to implementing acts. For instance, on the basis of the AD Regulation, the Commission will usually enact implementing regulations for the imposition of anti-dumping duties.[75]

Günter Krenzler, Christoph Herrmann, and Marian Niestedt, *EU-Außenwirtschafts- und Zollrecht* (C H Beck 2015).

[67] Exceptions apply to textile products and products originating in certain third countries, see ibid Art 1(1)(a) and (b), see further Regulation (EU) No 2015/936 on common rules for imports of textile products from certain third countries not covered by bilateral agreements, protocols or other arrangements, or by other specific Union import rules [2015] OJ L160/1; Regulation (EU) No 2015/755 on common rules for imports from certain third countries [2015] OJ L123/33.

[68] See ArtXIX General Agreement on Tariffs and Trade (GATT), 15 April 1994, 1867 UNTS 187 and the WTO Agreement on Safeguards (ASG), 15 April 1994, 1869 UNTS 15.

[69] Council Regulation (EU) No 2015/479 on common rules for exports [2015] OJ L83/34.

[70] ibid Art 5(1).   [71] European Parliament and Council Regulation (EU) No 2015/1843 (n 58).

[72] See Robert Macdonald MacLean *EU Trade Barrier Regulation: Tackling Unfair Foreign Trade Practices* (2nd edn, Sweet & Maxwell 2006).

[73] See section J(iii) below.

[74] Paul Craig and Gráinne de Búrca, *EU Law: Text, Cases and Materials* (6th edn, Oxford University Press 2015) 114 ff.

[75] For example, Commission Implementing Regulation (EU) No 2018/554 amending Council Implementing Regulation (EU) No 412/2013 imposing a definitive anti-dumping duty and collecting definitively the provisional duty imposed on imports of ceramic tableware and kitchenware, originating in the People's Republic of China [2018] OJ L92/4.

D Administrative Tasks in EU Common Commercial Policy and External Trade

1 General

The CCP has traditionally been a field of exclusive Union competence, which throughout the years has considerably broadened in scope, including with respect to administrative tasks. Many important issues pertaining to the CCP require a considerable amount of administration, for example, customs processing. Thus, it is a policy field which has always required a lot of executive-administrative activity. Therefore, the administrative tasks in the context of the CCP and Union external trade lie primarily with the Commission, the executive organ of the Union. Procedures in these fields are highly formalized, as they tend to be very invasive for affected (economic) actors. This is particularly true for the application of trade defence instruments. In addition, the conclusion of free trade agreements with third countries may also have an impact upon economic actors. The implementation of trade defence measures requires a prior investigation, in order to determine whether the respective prerequisites are met. The administrative tasks in this respect primarily consist of the gathering of information. Generally, such information refers to economic data that the Commission will obtain from businesses (importers/exporters and Union industries and producers). In this process, the Commission frequently relies on the cooperation of the Member States. Furthermore, the Commission's administrative tasks include the observance of procedural rights of the economic actors involved, for example, the proper conduct of hearings of the relevant stakeholders, including the opportunity for all parties involved to present their position to the Commission.

2 Factual background—administrative action within the CCP

In the field of the CCP and external trade law, trade defence measures play a significant role and proceedings take place more or less continuously. Figure 4.1 illustrates new investigations on anti-dumping and anti-subsidy measures between 2014 and the first five months of 2018.[76] It demonstrates the continuous efforts of the Commission to stop any kind of distorting behaviour of third country exporters, in order to secure a fair trade environment, especially for European businesses. On average, the Commission initiates 14 new investigations per year (even though in 2017 there were only eleven). Despite this, it seems that prior 'violators' tend to fall into old habits, otherwise there would scarcely be a need for the Commission to reopen nine anti-dumping and/or anti-subsidy cases in 2016; in 2017, though, there were only two re-openings. On the other hand, it seems that the Commission has been becoming more stringent in the imposition of definitive

---

[76] European Commission, 'Trade Defence Statistics: Anti-Dumping, Anti-Subsidy, Safeguard Statistics Covering the First 6 Months of 2018' (June 2018) p 5 http://trade.ec.europa.eu/doclib/docs/2018/august/tradoc_157236.pdf (last accessed 12 September 2018).

Comparison Tables
Anti-Dumping and Anti-subsidy
New investigations[2]

	2014	2015	2016	2017	2018
Investigators initiated during the period	16	14	15	11	3
Reopenings since 2016	X	X	9	2	3
Investigations concluded:					
- imposition of definitive duty or acceptance of undertakings	3	12	7	12	2
- terminations[3]	4	3	8	2	3
Provisional measures imposed during the period	2	10	9	2	1
Measures which expired automatically after their 5-year impostion	2	4	5	5	-

Figure 4.1 Comparison Tables Anti-Dumping and Anti-Subsidy

duties, with twelve such cases in 2015 and 2017 respectively. Such statistics should be read carefully as they could also indicate that foreign exporters have been cooperating with the EU and have undertaken to end their anti-competitive behaviour. It also appears that the Commission is very judicious in imposing provisional measures: in 2014 and 2017 there were only two, whereas in 2015 and 2016 there were ten and nine respectively, presumably reflecting the graveness of the alleged dumping or subsidization in the cases concerned. Apart from that, it appears that the number of measures which automatically expire after five years is continuously rising, perhaps further testimony to the fact that the Commission overall is doing a rather good job in protecting European businesses, and in enforcing the international and European trading rules.

3 Influencing the trade policy agenda

While this section does not provide a comprehensive overview how the European policy agenda is set, it offers pointed examples of some of the means the European institutions possess in order to set—but especially influence—the CCP and external trade agenda. Generally, the overall direction of Union policy is set by the European Council, which 'shall provide the Union with the necessary impetus for its development and shall define the general political directions and priorities thereof' (Article 15(1) TEU). Therefore, it regularly adopts a long-term position, such as the 'Strategic agenda for the union in times of change',[77] which foresees, for example, the completion of negotiations on international trade agreements, as well as engaging of global partners in regard to respect for human rights.[78] Beyond this, and similar to the Council of the EU,

---

[77] See Annex I to the Council Conclusions (26–27 June 2014) EUCO 79/14, 14.
[78] ibid 17, 20, and 21.

the European Council may set the Union's external trade agenda through its conclusions, which identify specific policy issues of concern and provide an outline of measures or actions to be taken and goals to be reached.[79] While they do not have the force of law, European Council conclusions have strong political weight (concluded, as they are, by the heads of government) and provide the framework within which the other institutions discuss policy and legislative strategies.

Parallel to this, the Commission, as 'motor of European integration', is responsible for the setting of objectives and priorities for the political action of the Union (Article 17(1) TEU). One of the instruments preferably used by the Commission are communications, aimed at articulating its own thinking on highly topical issues and influencing policy development, decision-making, and, ultimately, legislative initiatives. An example was provided above,[80] the Commission's 'Trade for all' strategy. In the respective communication, the Commission urged greater transparency for anti-dumping and anti-subsidy proceedings, and thus requirements on the publication of information on TDIs were introduced. Therefore, agenda-setting and -influencing by merely making opinions known can indeed be said to have an impact upon administrative practice in the Union.

Apart from that, also the European Parliament, as guardian of the civic concerns of society at large (which may often be forgotten both in the technical—indeed, technocratic—and EU-driven approach of the Commission and in the Member State-centric pragmatism of the Council) has considerable influence on the Union agenda-setting in the CCP.[81] The preferred soft-instruments of the European Parliament to exert influence are declarations[82] and resolutions directed at the decision-making of other institutions. An example is offered by its resolution on the EU-China bilateral investment treaty (BIT),[83] where it urged the inclusion of environmental, social, and workplace standards, as well as the principles of sustainable development and human rights. Again, in its resolution on the EU–Japan free trade agreement,[84] it asked the Council to delay negotiations until it had the possibility to express its opinion.[85] It seems in fact that the resolution-approach of the Parliament is becoming a new regular practice in the context of agenda setting, because a similar resolution was also adopted in regard to the Transatlantic Trade and Investment Partnership (TTIP).[86]

---

[79] European Council, 'Setting the EU's political agenda' http://www.consilium.europa.eu/en/european-council/role-setting-eu-political-agenda/ (last accessed 17 November 2017).

[80] See section B3 above.

[81] In the context of democratic legitimacy and the role of the European Parliament see section E(iii) and section F(iii) below.

[82] See section F(iii) on ACTA.

[83] European Parliament Resolution on the EU-China Bilateral Negotiations for a Bilateral Investment Treaty, 9 October 2013, 2013/2674 RSP.

[84] European Parliament Resolution on EU Trade Negotiations with Japan, 25 October 2012, 2012/2711 RSP.

[85] ibid para 13.

[86] European Parliament Resolution containing the European Parliament's recommendations to the European Commission on the negotiations for the Transatlantic Trade and Investment Partnership (TTIP), 8 July 2015, 2014/2228(INI).

E Underlying Legal Principles
and Individual Rights in the Sector

1 Relevance

Overall, underlying legal principles play a significant role when it comes to the administration of the Union's CCP and external trade. This is, inter alia, because measures taken in the field of the CCP and external trade are frequently very invasive with respect to the economic interests of the individuals concerned, possibly even to the point where they endanger people's livelihood. Such principles and the attention to individual rights in this field aim to ensure the observance of transparent procedures and adherence to due process. These principles draw on the Treaties' general aims (2 below) which are reflected in considerations of democratic legitimacy (3) and, from a perspective of individual guarantees, human rights (4). They find more specific expression in the principles of transparency (5) and those that are gathered under the right to good administration (6).

2 Role of the general aims of the Treaties

Apart from those principles that serve to ensure the rights of individuals, the CCP and the Union's external trade policy is shaped by general, overarching principles spelt out in the Treaties.[87] Trade and human rights, for example, were long treated as distinct matters.[88] In case of the European Union, the inclusion of non-trade objectives in trade agreements with third countries was further complicated by a lack of clarity of the distribution of competences.[89] The Lisbon Treaty, however, brought about a fundamental change in that regard. Pursuant to Article 3(5) TEU, the EU shall '[i]n its relations with the wider world ... uphold and promote its values and interests' and 'contribute to ... free and fair trade'. According to Article 21(2) TEU, the EU's external policies and actions shall

(d) foster the sustainable economic, social and environmental development of developing countries, with the primary aim of eradicating poverty [and]
(e) encourage the integration of all countries into the world economy, including through the progressive abolition of restrictions on international trade.

Pursuant to Article 206 TFEU, by establishing a customs union 'the Union shall contribute, in the common interest, to the harmonious development of world trade, the progressive abolition of restrictions on international trade and on foreign direct

---

[87] For a detailed overview see Christoph Vedder, 'Linkage of the Common Commercial Policy to the General Objectives for the Union's External Action' in Marc Bungenberg, Christoph Herrmann (eds), *Common Commercial Policy after Lisbon* (Springer 2013) 115.

[88] Somewhat notorious in that regard is the WTO Singapore Ministerial Declaration from 1996 in which the Ministerial Conference effectively shifts the responsibility for dealing with core labour rights to the International Labour Organization (ILO); see Singapore Ministerial Declaration (adopted on 13 December 1996), WT/MIN(96)/DEC, para 4.

[89] See Angelos Dimopoulos, 'The Effects of the Lisbon Treaty on the Principles and Objectives of the Common Commercial Policy' (2010) 15 *European Foreign Affairs Review* 153, 157 ff.

investment, and the lowering of customs and other barriers'. Ultimately, it is the goal of the Union to become 'a highly competitive social market economy' (Article 3(3) TEU). To bridge the gap between social and economic objectives it seems only logical and consequent that the EU has to 'ensure consistency between the different areas of its external action and between these and its other policies' (Article 21(3) TEU). Means available seeking to ensure that the European Union will in fact be guided by those principles in the conduct of the CCP and external trade include the conduct of sustainability impact assessments,[90] as well as the inclusion of human rights clauses[91] as 'essential elements'[92] in free trade agreements.

The legal nature of these guiding principles is not entirely clear and has been discussed extensively.[93] Suffice it to say, European institutions not only enjoy a considerable degree of discretion when it comes to the Union's external policies,[94] but the principles and values to be taken into account in the Union's external policy may also be in conflict with each other.[95] Nonetheless, a few points can be made for clarification. First, the CJEU recognized in *Opinion 2/15*[96] that 'the objective of sustainable development ... forms an integral part of the common commercial policy'. Thus, the CCP is not only refined by, and bound to, such non-economic principles, but similarly those principles now also serve as a legal basis to further extend the CCP in a more social direction. Secondly, as regards the potential conflict between economic and social principles, it should be noted that the institutions enjoy rather broad discretion in the assessment of such contradictions. The recent case-law of the Court may provide some guidance on the matter. In *Front Polisario v Council*,[97] the General Court (GC) held that the EU–Morocco Association Agreement—primarily aimed at trade liberalization—was in breach of fundamental human rights due to the Moroccan

---

[90] With respect to recent developments regarding human rights impact assessments see Elisabeth Bürgi Bonanomi, 'Measuring Human Rights Impacts of Trade Agreements—Ideas for Improving the Methodology: Comparing the European Union's Sustainability Impact Assessment Practice and Methodology with Human Rights Impact Assessment Methodology' (2017) 9 *Journal of Human Rights Practice* 481.

[91] On that see Tobias Dolle, 'Human Rights Clauses in EU Trade Agreements: The New European Strategy in Free Trade Agreement Negotiations Focuses on Human Rights—Advantages and Disadvantages' in Norman Weiß and Jean-Marc Thouvenin (eds), *The Influence of Human Rights on International Law* (Springer 2015) 213–28.

[92] That is, the breach of human rights obligations can entail the suspension of the agreement in question, see Karel de Gucht 'EU Trade Policy as a Means to Influence Globalization' (May 2014) Speech at Humboldt-Universität zu Berlin 3 http://trade.ec.europa.eu/doclib/docs/2014/may/tradoc_152514.pdf (last accessed 8 April 2018).

[93] For a detailed overview of the discussion see Thomas Cottier and Lorena Trinberg, 'Article 206 TFEU' in Hans von der Groeben, Jürgen Schwarze, and Armin Hatje (eds), *Europäisches Unionsrecht* (7th edn, Nomos 2015) paras 29 ff; Angelos Dimopoulos, 'The Effects of the Lisbon Treaty on the Principles and Objectives of the Common Commercial Policy' (2012) 15 *European Foreign Affairs Review* 153. Krajewski, 'The Reform of the Common Commercial Policy' (n 10) 292; Alessandra Asteriti, 'Article 21 TEU and the EU's Common Commercial Policy: A Test of Coherence' in Marc Bungenberg and others (eds), *European Yearbook of International Economic Law* (Springer 2017) 111.

[94] See Case T-292/09 *Mugraby v Council and Commission* ECLI:EU:T:2011:418, para 60.

[95] See on that Vedder, 'Linkage of the Common Commercial Policy to the General Objectives for the Union's External Action' (n 87) 142 ff; Asteriti (n 93) 111.

[96] Opinion 2/15 *Re Conclusion of the Free Trade Agreement between the European Union and the Republic of Singapore* ECLI:EU:C:2017:376, para 147.

[97] Case T-512/12 *Front Polisario v Council* ECLI:EU:T:2015:953.

occupation of Western Sahara, and the denial of the right of self-determination to the people living in Western Sahara. Therefore, the agreement should not be concluded, since the conflict between the general external objectives and the trade principles was simply too great. The Court of Justice, however, rejected the conclusions of the GC.[98] Having said that, the Court did not base its judgment on a thorough discussion of a conflict between the Treaty objectives, but rather relied on international law, according to which the territorial scope of application of the agreement did not apply to Western Sahara.

3 Democratic legitimacy

While the role of the European Parliament—the only democratically elected body of the EU—has exponentially increased with the entry into force of the Lisbon Treaty, it is particularly in the Union's autonomous trade policy that the Commission still takes on the leading role. It is true, though, that the European Parliament is now the fully accepted co-legislator of the Council when adopting secondary law necessary for laying down the framework within which the EU's autonomous trade policy is to be conducted (see Articles 207(2) and 289 TFEU). To this extent, the autonomous trade policy of the Union has most definitely become more democratic and more political, given that previously the European Parliament was not involved at all.[99] Yet, the adoption of TDMs is exclusively up to the Commission,[100] which, from a technical perspective, is logical, but, from a perspective of legitimacy, at least open to debate. This is further underlined by the wording of Article 207(2) TFEU which provides that the Parliament and the Council 'shall adopt the measures defining the framework for implementing the common commercial policy'. Thus, specific measures, or rather individual decisions such as TDMs, are most certainly not what is meant by this provision. As mentioned throughout this text, these measures are adopted on the basis of the relevant basic regulations, by way of implementing acts of the Commission. Here, the Parliament's involvement is limited to laying down general rules and principles for the Member States, which they need to pay attention to when considering the Commission's implementing acts within the comitology procedure.

Along with this, one should also consider the enhanced role of the Parliament's Committee on International Trade (INTA), now accepted as a legislative committee and thus largely involved in the law-making process.[101] The committee plays an important role in making the EU's external trade policy more transparent, usually meeting in public and thus allowing the position of the members of the European Parliament (MEPs) to be known from the start. Yet, this does not mean that the positions of the other actors involved are made public as well—these instead are subject

---

[98] Case C-104/16 P *Council v Front Polisario* ECLI:EU:C:2016:973; this was confirmed in Case C-266/16 *Western Sahara Campaign UK* ECLI:EU:C:2018:118.

[99] Krajewski, 'New Functions and New Powers for the European Parliament' (n 9) 69.

[100] Christoph Herrmann, 'Das Verwaltungsrecht der handelspolitischen Schutzinstrumente' in Jörg Philipp Terhechte (ed), *Verwaltungsrecht der Europäischen Union* (2nd edn, Nomos 2018/2019) § 30(50).

[101] Krajewski, 'New Functions and New Powers for the European Parliament' (n 9) 69.

to confidentiality[102] and are discussed in *in camera* sessions, to the exclusion of the public. Thus, discussions might be more transparent, and therefore 'political' from a parliamentarian perspective, but a great deal of business is still done behind closed doors.[103]

Another tool that was introduced by the Lisbon Treaty in order to strengthen democratic legitimacy and participation is the European citizens' initiative (ECI, Articles 11(4) TEU, 24(1) TFEU, and Regulation 211/2011[104])[105] which has already come to a test in the field of the CCP. In 2014, an ECI was launched to prevent both the free trade agreements negotiated by the EU with Canada (Comprehensive Economic and Trade Agreement (CETA)) and the United States of America (TTIP), reportedly involving the collection of more than 3 million signatures within a year.[106] More concretely, the initiative asked that the Commission recommend to the Council the cancellation of the negotiating mandate for TTIP, and that it should not conclude CETA. Initially, the Commission refused to register the initiative. Regarding TTIP, the Commission argued that only legal acts, the effects of which go beyond the relations between Union institutions, can be covered by an ECI. Accordingly, a Council decision cancelling the Commission's negotiating mandate was a purely preparatory legal act, outside the scope of Articles 2(1) and 4(2)(b) Regulation 211/2011. With respect to the request not to conclude CETA, the Commission held that asking it to *refrain* from acting was equally outside the ECI scope, as Article 10(1)(c) Regulation 211/2011 speaks of 'action'. Apart from that, a requirement for a communication in consequence to that legal provision, announcing that the Commission did not intend to propose a corresponding legal measure, would unduly restrict its right of initiative. The GC did not follow the Commission's line of argumentation and made clear that,

far from amounting to an interference in an ongoing legislative procedure, ECI proposals constitute an expression of the effective participation of citizens of the European Union in the democratic life thereof, without undermining the institutional balance intended by the Treaties.[107]

Overall, the EU's external trade policy has most definitely become more transparent, and more political, because at the legislative stage the European Parliament may now give forceful expression to its views, and even veto legislation (or international agreements), when it feels that the public interest has not sufficiently been taken account of. While the Union is still criticized for remaining non-transparent and lacking democratic legitimacy, it should be remembered that, especially in the

---

[102] Framework Agreement on relations between the European Parliament and the European Commission [2010] OJ L304/47, Annex II.

[103] Krajewski, 'New Functions and New Powers for the European Parliament' (n 9) 69.

[104] Regulation (EU) No 211/2011 of the European Parliament and of the Council of 16 February 2011 on the citizens' initiative [2011] OJ L65/1.

[105] In detail on the ECI see Dorota Szeligowska and Elitsa Mincheva, 'The European Citizens' Initiative—Empowering European Citizens within the Institutional Triangle: A Political and Legal Analysis' (2012) 13 *European Politics and Society* 270; see also the other contributions in that issue.

[106] The initiative is called *STOP TTIP*; for more information see https://stop-ttip.org/about-stop-ttip/?noredirect=en_GB (last accessed 11 April 2018).

[107] Case T-754/14 *Efler and Others v Commission* ECLI:EU:T:2017:323, para 47.

context of international agreements, the public at large in the 1990s had really little idea what was negotiated, nor did the European Parliament have a legislative veto. The fact that full democratization is still not achieved is based on the construct called the European Union. Originally founded as an international organization, it is facing the same problems regarding democratic legitimacy as any other such body.[108] It has, however, quickly grown beyond that in the scope of its activity and competence, but the political process of democratic integration has not kept up with these developments. So far, however, there have been continuous—albeit gradual—improvements, and it is certainly fair to say that the European Union performs a lot better in this regard than other international organizations.[109]

4 Human rights

Human rights play an increasingly important role in the context of the CCP and, especially in the adoption of restrictive measures pursuant to Article 215 TFEU. Whereas the debate within the CCP seems to be limited to the outer dimensions of human rights (e.g. human rights clauses in EU trade agreements and human rights criteria in the EU's Generalised System of Preferences (GSP)),[110] it is obvious that external measures taken by the Union in relation to trade can directly affect the (human) rights of individuals, in particular in the case of targeted (or so-called smart) sanctions. This tool, employed under Chapter VII of the Charter of the United Nations, has gained particular popularity in the aftermath of 9/11. Such a sanction is directed to individuals, companies or organizations. Their implementation on the Union level finds its legal basis in the CFSP and Article 215(2) TFEU. The human rights implications of targeted sanctions have gained widespread attention as a result of the Court's *Kadi* judgments.[111] Mr Kadi was subject to targeted sanctions as determined pursuant to Chapter VII of the UN Charter and implemented by the Council and the Commission. On the UN level no mechanisms existed that would have put Mr Kadi in a position to have the decision reviewed. His complaint against the EU regulation implementing the UN decision was dismissed by the GC which held that the Union organs had no discretion in the implementation, and that judicial scrutiny was thus limited. The CJEU, however, annulled the implementation of UN sanctions by the Union as far as they related to Mr Kadi, since they violated his procedural rights.[112] Subsequently, another

---

[108] See on that eg Robert A Dahl, 'Can International Organizations Be Democratic? A Sceptic's View' in Ian Shapiro and Casiano Hacker-Cordón (eds), *Democracy's Edges* (Cambridge University Press 1999) 19–36.

[109] On the role of the European Parliament see further section F(iii) below.

[110] See Samantha Velluti, 'The Promotion and Integration of Human Rights in EU External Trade Relations' (2016) 32 *Utrecht Journal of International and European Law* 41; Lachlan Mckenzie and Katharina L Meissner, 'Human Rights Conditionality in the European Union Trade Negotiations: The Case of the EU–Singapore FTA' (2017) 55 *Journal of Common Market Studies* 832.

[111] Joined Cases C-402/05 P and C-415/05 *Kadi and Al-Barakaat International Foundation v Council and Commission* (n 8).

[112] ibid para 369. The case also addressed the claim of a violation of Mr Kadi's property rights, which was eventually found to be not justified because the regulation in question did not enable him 'to put his case to the competent authorities, in a situation in which the restriction of his property rights must be regarded as significant'; of the numerous literature on both judgments see Juliane Kokott and Christoph Sobotta, 'The *Kadi* Case: Constitutional Core Values and International Law—Finding the Balance? (2012) 23 *European Journal of International Law* 1015.

regulation with sanctions targeted at, inter alia, Mr Kadi was implemented, but again both the GC and the Court found a violation of Mr Kadi's procedural rights.[113] In its recent jurisprudence, the CJEU has demonstrated its willingness and capacity to give meaning and effect to the Union's commitments with respect to human rights.[114] In particular the entry into force of the Charter of Fundamental Rights of the European Union (CFR) in 2000 and the acknowledgement of its status as primary law through the Treaty of Lisbon (Article 6 TEU) have contributed to this development.

5 Transparency

In primary law, the principle of transparency is laid down in Article 1(2) TEU and Article 15 TFEU.[115] It is also reflected in EU secondary law shaping the CCP and Union external trade actions (see, e.g., Recital (5) and Article 9(4) TBR). On the other hand, persons involved in the proceedings may have a legitimate interest in keeping certain information confidential. Thus, a balance has to be struck between those two principles (see, e.g., Recital (28) and Article 5(11) of the AD Regulation), as the information gathered by the Commission may involve sensitive business and commercial data. When commercial confidentiality prevents the release of information, the Commission may be obliged to provide a non-confidential summary (see, e.g., Article 6(3) AD Regulation and Article 11(3) AS Regulation). It comes as no surprise that national authorities providing the Commission with the relevant information are required to review the accuracy of the information. Therefore, not only the Commission but also the Member States may conduct so-called on-spot investigations in the territory of other WTO members (Articles 6(4) and 16(2) AD Regulation and Articles 11(4) and 26(2) AS Regulation).

6 Good administration

As mentioned before, the European courts' level of scrutiny in the field of external (trade) relations is somewhat restrained due to the inseparable political considerations involved. This restraint, however, does not refer to the administrative proceedings leading to the adoption of a given measure. Procedural rights are now codified in the right to good administration in Article 41 CFR. For the purpose of the administrative dimension of the CCP and external trade, the right to be heard,[116] the right of every person to have access to his or her file, while respecting the legitimate interests

---

[113] See Case T-85/09 *Kadi v Commission* ECLI:EU:T:2010:418; Joined Cases C-584/10 P, C-593/10 P and C-595/10 P *Commission and Others v Kadi* (n 8); of the numerous literature see Armin Cuyvers, '"Give me one good reason": the unified standard of review for sanctions after Kadi II' (2014) 51 *Common Market Law Review* 1759.

[114] See also eg the *Schrems* judgment of the CJEU, Case C-362/14 *Schrems* (n 8). While not a measure taken under the European Union's CCP or external trade, the safe harbour principles were negotiated in order to enable trade with the US by means of the free flow of data.

[115] See also Stefan Kadelbach, 'Case C-349/99P et al.' (2001) 38 *Common Market Law Review* 179.

[116] See Joined Cases C-402/05 P and C-415/05 *Kadi and Al-Barakaat International Foundation v Council and Commission* (n 8), paras 333 ff.

of confidentiality and of professional and business secrecy,[117] as well as the obligation of the administration to give reasons for its decisions (Article 41(2) CFR)[118] are of particular importance. The right to be heard, for example, finds expression in Article 9(5) of the TBR, which foresees that the Commission shall hear the parties concerned 'if they have, within the period prescribed in the notice published in the Official Journal of the European Union, made a written request for a hearing showing that they are a party primarily concerned by the result of the procedure'. The Court clarified the importance of this principle even before individual measures are taken.[119] Furthermore, the principle of due process requires that the regulations in question prescribe that there be a written procedure (Article 6(6) AD Regulation and Articles 11(6) and 30 AS Regulation).

F Organization and Structures in Common Commercial Policy and External Trade

1 Commission as key actor

Even though Article 207(2) TFEU gives an enhanced role to the European Parliament in matters of the CCP, this does not extend to the implementation of particular trade defence measures.[120] The key administrative actor in this field is the Commission (Article 17 TEU).[121] It initiates the necessary investigations (Article 6 AD Regulation, Article 11 AS Regulation, and Article 5 Import Regulation), subsequently conducts them, and terminates them if necessary (Article 9(1) and (2) AD Regulation, Article 14(1)–(3) of the AS Regulation, and Article 6(2) Import Regulation). The implementing regulations were formerly adopted by the Council, acting on a proposal from the Commission, unless the Council decided by a simple majority to reject the proposal within a month of its submission.[122] The current procedure, however, provides that the Commission can impose provisional or definitive measures by adopting implementing regulations (Articles 9(2), (4), and 7(6) AD Regulation, Articles 14(2), 15(1), and 24(4) AS Regulation and Articles 6(3), 7, and 15 Import Regulation). In the adoption of such measures, the Commission works closely with the Member States in the sense that it must take account of their interests and viewpoints as articulated in the comitology committees. While the Commission has a 'soft obligation' to take 'the utmost account of the conclusions drawn from the discussions within the committee and of the opinion delivered'(Article 4 Comitology Regulation) in the context

---

[117] Joined Cases C-584/10 P, C-593/10 P, and C-595/10 P *Commission and Others v Kadi* (n 8), paras 111, 116.

[118] ibid para 116.

[119] In *Interpipe Niko Tube ZAT*, for example, it held that 'respect for the rights of the defence is of crucial importance in anti-dumping investigations.', Joined Cases C-191/09 P and 200/09 P *Interpipe Niko Tube ZA* ECLI:EU:C:2012:78, para 77.

[120] Herrmann, 'Das Verwaltungsrecht der handelspolitischen Schutzinstrumente' (n 100) 1067 § 30(41).

[121] See in general on the role of the Commission as executive organ of the EU Craig and de Búrca *EU Law: Text, Cases and Materials* (n 74) 31 ff.

[122] See Art 9(4) Council Regulation (EC) No 1225/2009 (n 38).

of the advisory procedure, in the examination procedure a Commission proposal for implementing legislation may be blocked by the committee through a qualified majority vote. In such a case, the Commission still has the possibility of referring the matter to the appeal committee (Article 6 Comitology Regulation). The comitology procedure and its application in EU external trade policy will be explained and explored further below.

2 Sector-specific committees

Other actors involved are the sector-specific committees (see the list of the relevant committees in the appendix) as part of the process prescribed by the Comitology Regulation[123] in conjunction with the respective basic regulations.

The most important committee most certainly is the Trade Defence Instruments Committee. It is the loyal companion of, and at times troublemaker for, the Commission in the exercise of its implementing powers in TDIs, by giving opinions on draft implementing measures. The committee is composed of Member State representatives and chaired by the Commission. In the context of the advisory or examination procedure, it provides guidance and, at times, a clear legal direction for the Commission on matters such as the imposition of provisional or definitive measures, the initiation of expiry review proceedings, as well as amendments and extensions of existing TDMs (see above, Articles 4 and 5 Comitology Regulation).[124]

3 The European Parliament

As mentioned above in relation to the issue of the democratic legitimacy of the Union's common commercial and external trade policy, the European Parliament has enjoyed a significant increase in status. Thus, it may now exert considerable influence in the context of the conclusion of international agreements and, to a lesser degree, in trade defence, which may lead—as hoped by many and feared by some—to a politicization of EU external trade policy. Next to being the co-legislator of the Council, when adopting the basic regulations for the exercise of EU competence in trade defence, it is now also actively involved in the negotiation and conclusion of international trade and investment agreements since it can now exercise a veto right (see Articles 207(2) and (3), and 218 TFEU).[125]

Especially in the context of trade negotiations, the augmentation of the European Parliament's powers has become quite apparent. For one, the practice of informal information exchanges between the institutions has been explicitly recognized in the Treaties (Article 218(10) TFEU) to ensure that the Parliament can indeed make its voice heard on trade negotiations and make its concerns known. Secondly, the

---

[123] European Parliament and Council Regulation (EU) No 182/2011 (n 40).

[124] European Commission, 'Trade Defence Instruments Committee' http://trade.ec.europa.eu/doclib/docs/2013/april/tradoc_151013.pdf (last accessed 7 April 2018).

[125] See Lore van den Putte, Ferdi de Ville, and Jan Orbie, 'The European Parliament's New Role in Trade Policy: Turning power into impact, *CEPS Special Report* No 89, May 2014 http://aei.pitt.edu/51025/1/CEPS_SR_89_EP_New_Role_in_EU_Trade_Policy.pdf (last accessed 9 April 2018).

Parliament is not afraid to use its veto power, as evidenced by its rejection of the Anti-Counterfeiting Trade Agreement (ACTA).[126] This is an example of the Parliament's attempt to strengthen the place of human rights protection in the context of the CCP and external trade. Already prior to the final rejection of ACTA, the Parliament had made use of informal, but agenda-influencing means by issuing a declaration condemning ACTA for a lack of transparency, and by voicing strong concerns with respect to its weak protection of fundamental rights.[127]

The rather extensive treaty-making powers of the Parliament stand in stark contrast to its powers with regard to TDMs. It is true that, as co-legislator, the Parliament has managed to influence the contents of envisaged regulations considerably. For instance, in the context of the modernization of the Generalized Scheme of Preference (GSP),[128] the Parliament ensured inter alia that the system was more transparent and subject to its scrutiny, and that tougher tariffs for social dumping were applied.[129] When it comes to the implementation of trade defence instruments, the European Parliament's influence is very limited. As explained, this is where the Commission simply takes over, due to its technical expertise and the executive nature of the implementing acts, as well as because of the need to act fast which is per se excluded in the context of the ordinary legislative procedure. Thus, the only way for the EP to influence trade defence 'decisions' is by laying down general principles, on the basis of its right to scrutiny in the comitology procedures.

4 The role of the Member States

The Member States also play an important role in the structure of the CCP and external trade administrative framework. For one thing, national customs authorities are charged with the implementation of trade measures taken by the Union. These actions are obviously of a purely administrative nature and concern only the execution of the decisions taken on the European Union level. Apart from that, Member States may play a part in the initiation of an investigation. In the case of anti-dumping, for example, 'any natural or legal person, or any association not having legal personality, acting on behalf of the Union industry' (Article 5(1) AD Regulation) may submit a written complaint to the Commission, so that the latter may initiate an investigation. Such a complaint, however, may also be submitted to a Member State, which is in turn obliged to forward it to the Commission. Furthermore, Member States are required to inform the Commission if they have sufficient evidence of dumping, even when no complaint has been made (Article 5(1) AD Regulation). During a given investigation, the Commission cooperates with,[130] and frequently relies upon, the Member States when it comes to the collection of

---

[126] European Parliament Recommendation on the draft Council decision on the conclusion of the Anti- Counterfeiting Trade Agreement, 22 June 2012, A7-0204/2012.

[127] Declaration of the European Parliament on the lack of a transparent process for the Anti-Counterfeiting Trade Agreement (ACTA) and potentially objectionable content, [2011] OJ CE 308/88.

[128] In essence, the GSP provides developing countries and least developed countries with reductions in tariffs.

[129] See van den Putte, de Ville, and Orbie (n 125) 4.   [130] See Art 6 (1) AD Regulation.

necessary information.[131] Besides, interaction between the Commission and the Member States is marked by obligations of the Commission to provide information to the Member States.[132]

G Administrative Procedures in EU Common Commercial Policy and External Trade

1 Direct administration

The initiation of administrative procedures is generally the task of the Commission, mostly in response to requests by a Member State, a Union industry, or one or more European companies (see Article 3, 4, and 6 Trade Barriers Regulation (TBR),[133] Articles 4 and 5 AD Regulation, and Articles 9 and 10 AS Regulation).

In the context of trade barriers, initiation is dependent upon whether there is sufficient evidence of the existence of a trade barrier, and of the resulting injury or adverse effects on trade (see Articles 5(3) and 9(1) TBR). The illustrative list in Article 11 TBR lays down the factors for determining the quality of the evidence received.

In anti-dumping cases, an investigation is initiated upon written complaint, or on behalf, of a Union industry (Article 5(1) AD Regulation) or the Commission itself (Article 5(6) AD Regulation). In a next step, the Commission will collect the necessary information through requesting Member States, Union industries, and known exporters and importers to provide evidence to it (Article 6(3) AD Regulation). Where the requested parties do not cooperate, the Commission will use only the 'facts available', which corresponds to publicly available information (Article 18 AD Regulation). For obvious reason this will often be to the detriment of the foreign exporter. Nevertheless, also here initiation is dependent on whether the quality of the evidence is sufficient to demonstrate dumping, injury, and a causal link between the allegedly dumped imports and the alleged injury (Article 5(2) AD Regulation).

The procedure in anti-subsidy investigations is the same. First, the Commission will initiate an investigation upon a written complaint, or on behalf, of a Union industry (Articles 10(1) AS Regulation) or itself (Article 10(8) AS Regulation). Then, it will attempt to gather the necessary evidence from the parties involved (Article 11 AS Regulation) and, in case of their non-cooperation, use facts otherwise available (Article 28 AS Regulation). Clearly, also here the evidence has to be sufficient to warrant an investigation.

2 Role of comitology

Measures taken in the CCP and EU external trade administration are subject to the new comitology procedures laid down in Regulation 182/2011.[134] In general, decisions

---

[131] See eg Art 6(4) AD Regulation: 'The Commission may request Member States to carry out all necessary checks and inspections, particularly amongst importers, traders and Union producers, and to carry out investigations in third countries …'.

[132] See eg AD Regulation, Arts 2(7)(c), 5(1), and 8(9); AS Regulation, Arts 10(8) and 13(9).

[133] Regulation (EU) No 2015/1843 (n 58).

[134] Regulation (EU) No 182/2011 (n 40); see on the Comitology Regulation Craig, 'Delegated Acts, Implementing Acts and the New Comitology Regulation' (n 59).

on the adoption of measures are subject to the examination procedure, provided for in Article 5 of the Regulation. The advisory procedure is normally required when decisions on the review of measures or the termination of investigations are concerned. Furthermore, there is also a procedure for urgent cases, which require immediate implementation, as with provisional anti-dumping or anti-subsidy measures (Article 8 Comitology Regulation).

Thus, the Commission's exercise of its implementing powers is controlled using a revised system of comitology. As mentioned above, the restructured comitology system involves two different procedures. On the one hand, there is the examination procedure which applies to implementing acts of general scope (Article 2(2)(a) Comitology Regulation) and other implementing acts relating to programmes with substantial implications, the common agricultural and common fisheries policies, the environment, health, security and safety of humans, animals or plants, the CCP, and taxation (Article 2(2)(b)(i)–(v) Comitology Regulation). On the other hand, the advisory procedure is a sort of default procedure which applies to all other implementing acts (Article 2(3) Comitology Regulation), for example, acts of individual character rather than general scope.

Under both procedures, the Commission submits a draft of the implementing act to a committee composed of representatives of the Member States, such as the Trade Defence Instruments Committee. The respective committee will then deliver a positive or a negative opinion on the Commission's proposal. In the advisory procedure, the committee's opinion is not legally binding; at least it may be regarded as persuasive since the Commission is to take 'the utmost account' of it (Article 4(2) Comitology Regulation). In the examination procedure, the adoption of the draft implementing act depends on the opinion of the committee, since it is binding to the effect that a negative opinion generally precludes adoption (Article 5(3) Comitology Regulation).

Comitology allows Member States to exercise ex ante control of proposed implementing acts and thereby make their concerns known early on during the drafting stage. The other Union institutions, specifically the European Parliament and the Council, are granted only rights of scrutiny and access to information under the Comitology Regulation, but they do not play a direct role in the primary control mechanism: the committees! This effectual shift of supervisory powers from the institutions to the Member States may be explained by the fact that implementing acts have the potential of impeding the exclusive Member State prerogatives.[135] Figure 4.2 provides an overview of these procedures.

3 Information management

Information management in the field of the CCP and Union external trade is of considerable significance. This is due to procedural requirements that need to be observed when the Commission investigates the existence of dumping, subsidization, etc. The information gathered involves a broad spectrum, ranging from general economic data on the global, European, or Member State level, through to specific, perhaps sensitive business data. Naturally, the latter requires responsible management in order to

---

[135] See also Craig and de Búrca *EU Law: Text, Cases and Materials* (n 74) 142 ff.

	AD Regulation	AS Regulation	Regulation on Common Rules for Imports	Regulation on Common Rules for Exports	TBR
Advisory procedure	Decision on the initiation of review, Article 11(6); suspension of measures, Article 14(4); reinstatement of measures, Article 14(4) subpara. 2	Acceptance of satisfactory voluntary undertakings offers Article 13(1);	Termination of safeguard investigation or surveillance, Article 6(2); imposition of surveillance, Article 10(2); decision on initiation of review, Article 22(2)		Suspension of procedure, Article 12(2) and (3)
Examination procedure	Termination of investigation regarding accepted undertakings, Article 8(5); termination of investigation, Article 9(2); adoption of definitive measure, Article 9(4); amendment of measures, Article 12(3); extension of measures, Article 13(3);	Termination of investigation regarding accepted undertakings, Article 13(5); termination of investigation, Article 14(2); adoption of definitive measure, Article 15(1)	Imposition of safeguard measure, Articles 15(6), 16; revocation or amendment of safeguard measure or surveillance, Article 20(2); repeal, maintenance or amendment of safeguard measure, Article 22(3); extension of safeguard measures, Article 23(4)	Implementation of protective export measures, Articles 5(1), 6(1); revocation or amendment of protective measures, Article 7(1)	Termination of procedure, Article 12(1)
Immediately applicable implementing acts (Article 8 Comitology Regulation)	Adoption of provisional measures, Article 7(4), in conjunction with the advisory procedure	Adoption of provisional measures, Article 12(3), in conjunction with the advisory procedure	Imposition of safeguard measure, Articles 15(6), 16	Implementation of protective export measures, Articles 5(1), 6(1)	
Determination of Union interest	'The views expressed in the committee should be taken into account by the Commission under the conditions provided for in Regulation (EU) No 182/2011', Article 31(5)	'The views expressed in the committee should be taken into account by the Commission under the conditions provided for in Regulation (EU) No 182/2011', Article 21(5)			

Figure 4.2 Overview: Comitology Procedures in TDIs

safeguard the legitimate interests of businesses. Undertakings involved in proceedings regarding anti-dumping or subsidization are especially vulnerable, as any investigation concerns them directly. Consequently, both the Anti-Dumping Regulation and the Regulation on Countervailing Measures contain a provision on confidentiality (Article 19 AD Regulation; Article 29 of the Regulation on Countervailing Measures). These provisions require inter alia that the Commission and the Member States not reveal any information received for which confidential treatment has been requested by its supplier, unless specific permission has been granted from that supplier, nor to divulge information exchanged between the Commission and the Member States, and, finally, to limit the use of received information to the purpose for which it was requested.

4 Indirect administration

The foundation of the administration of the EU's CCP and external trade policy is mainly derived from customs law, or rather the administration of the customs rules enacted by the EU. From the early days of the European Union the enforcement of customs law was decentralized, since there was never the intention to create a central European customs authority, which anyway would not have been very sensible because customs rules need to be enforced where goods from third countries cross national borders.[136] Still, a certain degree of interaction is always necessary, especially between the Commission and the national customs authorities, in order to ensure the uniform application of Union law and especially customs law as required by the WTO.[137] Thus, in the EU's CCP and external trade it is the Member States which are charged with the administrative enforcement of Union measures.

Before any enforcement action may be taken, Member States are first and foremost obliged 'to adopt all measures of national law necessary to implement legally binding Union acts' (Article 291(1) TFEU). As mentioned above, in the enforcement of the different trade defence regulations, utmost importance is placed on their uniform application. Nonetheless, Member States are still given some room for their own action, because the principle of procedural autonomy allows them to decide independently which authorities are competent, what their internal structure is, and which procedural norms are applicable to implement and enforce EU law.

Despite this, the customs authorities of the Member States apply uniform EU-wide customs rules, even as regards procedural rules. Union law often already contains clear instructions on the procedures to be followed, and national administrative and procedural law is only regarded as a supplementary category of legal norms in order to fill gaps left by the EU legal measures. Decisions of the national custom authorities are usually subject to review by the national administrative or tax courts. In the national proceedings, the CJEU may be consulted only if questions of EU law arise in national proceedings (Article 267 TFEU). Yet, the (the enforcement proceeding) competence

---

[136] Heike Jochum 'Europäisches Zollverwaltungsrecht' in Jörg Philipp Terhechte (ed), *Verwaltungsrecht der Europäischen Union* (Nomos 2011) 1031 § 29.

[137] On the problem of a uniform application of EU customs rules Timothy Lyons, 'The Interaction of Customs and Non-tariff Barriers' in Christoph Herrmann, Markus Krajewski, and Jörg Philipp Terhechte (eds), *European Yearbook of International Economic Law 2015* (Springer 2015) 19–42, 25 ff.

for the adoption of trade defence measure ultimately rests with the Union pursuant to the principle of conferral and the EU's exclusive competence for the CCP (Articles 3(1) (a) and (e), 206, and 207 TFEU).

Where the Union has adopted a decision in the context of trade barriers, anti-dumping or anti subsidy cases, such decision may, at the stage of enforcement, no longer be reviewed by the national administrative authorities. Also here, the Court is the only body that could intervene if asked for a preliminary ruling (Article 267 TFEU) or through the initiation of an action for annulment (Article 263 TFEU). Member States may become ultimately involved in the decision-making process only through participation in the respective committees in the comitology procedure (Articles 4 and 5 Comitology Regulation) outlined above.

H Legal Rules Governing Common Commercial Policy Decision-making

1 General aims

Traditionally, the EU's CCP and Union external trade policy was not committed to non-trade concerns, but rather limited to trade liberalization.[138] Thus, Article 113 EEC Treaty did not really contain a clear objective, except for that of trade liberalization. This changed noticeably with the Lisbon Treaty, and resulted in an accumulation of different economic and non-economic objectives (Article 21 TEU, Article 205 TFEU, and Article 206 and 207(1) TFEU). Such commitments are now provided for in the Treaties not once, but three times.[139] In addition, the Union has to observe the cross-sectoral clauses of Articles 7 ff TFEU as provisions of general application. Thus, administrative action in the field of the CCP, as well as in other fields of external trade, have to take into account the complex matrix of Union aims.

2 The Union interest

As the key administrative actor in the field of the CCP and external trade, the Commission enjoys a considerable degree of discretion when it comes to the adoption of specific measures. This discretion is reflected in the criterion of 'Union interest', found in all the basic regulations governing the CCP[140] and confirmed by the Court of Justice and the GC.[141] For example, Article 21 of the Anti-Dumping Regulation and

---

[138] It was precisely this silence in the treaties on non-trade matters that frequently gave rise to disputes between Member States and the Commission with respect to the Commission's competences in the negotiation and conclusion of international agreements (see section B(ii) above).

[139] See on the general aims section E(ii) above.

[140] See Art 31 AS Regulation; Art 21 AD Regulation; Arts 10(1), 15(1), 16 and 22 Import Regulation; Arts 5(1) and 6(1) Export Regulation; Arts 5(2), 9(1), 12(1), and13(1) TBR; on the concept of 'Union interest' see further Balázs Horváthy, 'The Concept of "Union Interest" in EU External Trade Law' (2014) 55 *Acta Juridica Hungarica* 261.

[141] Case C-191/82 *Fediol I* ECLI:EU:C:1983:259, para 26, where the ECJ makes clear that the Commission enjoys broad political discretion when assessing the Union interest; see also Case T-162/94 *NMB France and Others v Commission* ECLI:EU:T:1996:71, para 72; Case T-97/95 *Sinochem v Council* ECLI:EU:T:1998:9, para 51; Case T-118/96 *Thai Bicycle v Council* ECLI:EU:T:1998:184, para 32.

Article 31 of the Regulation on Countervailing Measures list the information that the Commission needs to take into consideration as a basis for its final decision. It also requires the Commission to appreciate 'all the various interests taken as a whole, including the interests of the domestic industry and users and consumers'. Eventually, the decision will balance economic and political considerations, since the adoption of measures always entails the danger of being considered as a provocation by the affected state, which may respond with restrictive measures. In its decision, the Commission is merely limited by an obligation not to adopt any measures 'where the authorities, on the basis of all the information submitted, can clearly conclude that it is not in the Union's interest to apply such measures'.

3 Political background

Especially in the field of external (trade) relations, legal and political considerations are intertwined. From a political perspective, therefore, the decision to impose trade defence measures has classically been determined by political concerns, instead of purely hard evidence. There have been continuous efforts in the past to depoliticize decisions as far as possible by instituting clear legal procedures. However, the tide is turning, as may be seen in the emerging trade war initiated by the United States in early 2018. Such political determinations to adopt TDMs make it all the more difficult to review such decisions from a judicial point of view, and is the reason that the courts tend to show a considerable degree of restraint in that respect.[142]

I Abstract-general and Single-case Acts and Measures in the Sector

1 Abstract-general rules

In view of the fact that the CCP pertains to the exclusive competence of the Union, and that Member States no longer possess any significant regulatory powers going beyond the sphere of enforcement, it is particular in this field of Union law that abstract-general rules have become the norm. This is further evidenced by the fact that the instruments to be used to adopt such rules are regulations which, unlike directives, are directly applicable in the national legal orders, and do not require an act of implementation such as directives (Article 288 TFEU). The basic regulations governing the framework of the Union's CCP and external trade confer the right on the Commission to adopt subordinate legislation, that is, implementing regulations (Article 291(2) TFEU). These particularly concern the implementation of trade defence measures. Through Article 291 TFEU, and the powers thus conferred onto the Commission, it is ensured that TDMs are implemented in a uniform manner, since Member States are generally free as to the form and method when implementing Union law. Article 291(2) TFEU provides that 'where uniform conditions for implementing legally

---

[142] See Case T-73/12 *Einhell Germany and Others v Commission* ECLI:EU:T:2015:865, para 56 with further references; see also section J(ii) below.

binding Union acts are needed, those acts shall confer implementing powers on the Commission, or … on the Council'. In taking executive measures, the Commission is permitted to take measures only where this is necessary, that is, where implementation cannot be sufficiently achieved through actions at the Member State level (principle of subsidiarity, Article 5(3) TEU). As established above, such action will only be taken in the space confined by the general rules laid down by the European Parliament and the Council, in conjunction with the Member States' committees in the context of the comitology procedures, even though the Court has given the word 'implementation' a broad meaning. In *Parliament v Commission*[143] it held that 'the Commission is authorised to adopt all the measures which are necessary or appropriate for the implementation of the basic legislation, provided that they are not contrary to it'.

2 Single-case acts (decisions)

Anti-dumping and countervailing measures, such as additional tariffs, can generally be considered as single-case administrative acts as they relate to specific enterprises, as in the case of the imposition of duties and additional tariffs or the introduction of quantitative restrictions on products from third countries if they are dumped on the European market, or by obtaining an unfair advantage through subsidies.[144] Safeguard or protective export measures, on the other hand, concern a specific product or product category, thus being of an abstract-general nature. Also, in the field of EU customs law, single-case acts constitute the norm, the difference being that here it is often the national customs authorities which take such decisions, for example as regards the classification of goods, or decisions on the binding information as to the origin of goods.[145] Another form of single administrative act comprises economic sanctions and embargos, which may be addressed directly to states, but also to non-state entities as well as individuals (e.g. persons presumed to be terrorists).[146]

---

[143] Case C-403/05 *Parliament v Commission* ECLI:EU:C:2007:624, para 51.
[144] See eg Art 1(2) of Commission Implementing Regulation (EU) 2016/1246 of 28 July 2016 imposing a definitive anti-dumping duty on imports of high fatigue performance steel concrete reinforcement bars originating in the People's Republic of China [2016] OJ L204/70; Commission Implementing Regulation (EU) 2016/1159 of 15 July 2016 imposing a definitive anti-dumping duty on imports of sodium cyclamate originating in the People's Republic of China and produced by Fang Da Food Additive (Shen Zhen) Limited and Fang Da Food Additive (Yang Quan) Limited [2016] OJ L192/23; Art 1(2) of Commission Implementing Regulation (EU) 2017/1187 of 3 July 2017 imposing a definitive countervailing duty on imports of certain coated fine paper originating in the People's Republic of China following an expiry review pursuant to Art 18 of the Regulation (EU) 2016/1037 of the European Parliament and of the Council [2016] OJ L171/134; Art 1(2) of Commission Implementing Regulation (EU) 2017/1141 of 27 June 2017 imposing a definitive countervailing duty on imports of certain stainless steel bars and rods originating in India following an expiry review under Art 18 of Regulation (EU) 2016/1037 of the European Parliament and the Council [2017] OJ L165/2.
[145] European Commission, Guidance on Binding Origin Information, 1 July 2017 https://ec.europa.eu/taxation_customs/sites/taxation/files/guidance_boi_en.pdf (last accessed 9 April 2018); European Commission, Customs Decisions Business User Guide, 4 August 2017 https://ec.europa.eu/taxation_customs/sites/taxation/files/1_customs_decisions_business_user_guide_en.pdf (last accessed 9 April 2018).
[146] For an overview of the sanctions currently in force see European Commission, Restrictive measures (sanctions) in force, 4 April 2017 http://ec.europa.eu/dgs/fpi/documents/Restrictive_measures-2017-08-04-clean_en.pdf (last accessed 9 April 2018).

3 Soft Law

In the context of the external trade policy of the Union, soft law does not really play role similar to that in, for instance, competition law.[147] The reason for this is the rather invasive nature of this field of Union law, especially for economic actors. To offset this invasiveness, it is thus necessary to provide for highly formalized rules which are clearly understandable and which do not require further interpretation through soft law. As mentioned above, this is also the reason why the legislative instruments used in this exclusive area of Union law are regulations, and not directives.[148] The only sources of soft law with marginal impact upon the rules governing the CCP and external trade law—rather, however, at the outskirts than in the hard core of trade provisions—which come to mind, are, for example, the standards of the WCO (e.g., the SAFE Framework of Standards to Secure and Facilitate Global Trade (SAFE Framework)[149]), general corporate governance standards,[150] or, for example, the Commission's reflection paper on globalization from 2017.[151]

J Supervision and Control of Common Commercial Policy Administration

1 Political and administrative supervision

Political oversight in the context of EU external trade policy is important because many economically, politically and socially relevant decisions and choices are made. Their effect can extend beyond the purely internal sphere of the territory of the European Union and can, thus, influence the process of globalization. That process in turn greatly impacts upon internal developments within the Union and its Member States. Therefore, it is all the more important to have structures, competences, and procedures which can ensure a certain degree of supervision over the making of such decisions.

Administrative supervision is ensured by the required comitology procedures. Apart from that, Article 11 of the Comitology Regulation grants the European Parliament or the Council the right to indicate to the Commission that, in their view, a draft implementing act exceeds the implementing powers provided for in the basic

---

[147] See in general on soft law Linda Senden, *Soft Law in European Community Law* (Hart Publishing 2004); Jürgen Schwarze, 'Soft Law im Recht der Europäischen Union' (2011) 1 *Zeitschrift Europarecht* 3.

[148] It may be observed, however, that the global trend of politicizing and socializing ancillary fields of trade law, in the sense that these fields do not provide for the hard-core trading rules, are nowadays viewed in light of international standards such as eg in the field of raw materials and the goal of a sustainable use of them. See Winfried Huck, 'Die Integration der Sustainable Development Goals (SDGs) in den Rohstoffsektor' (2018) 7 *Europäische Zeitschrift für Wirtschaftsrecht* 266.

[149] See website of the WCO, WCO SAFE Package http://www.wcoomd.org/en/topics/facilitation/instrument-and-tools/tools/safe_package.aspx (last accessed 12 April 2018).

[150] See eg Commission Communication, 'Action Plan: European company law and corporate governance—a modern legal framework for more engaged shareholders and sustainable companies' COM(2012) 740 final.

[151] COM(2017) 240 final.

act.[152] The Commission will then be required to review the draft implementing act and notify the Parliament and the Council whether it intends to maintain, amend, or withdraw the draft act. By February 2016, the Parliament had made use of this right four times.[153] While the Commission enjoys broad discretion with respect to the adoption of implementing acts, such a power is not unlimited as the Parliament and the Council may lay down general rules and principles in advance, with the purpose of providing Member States with a mechanism, as well as a benchmark, for better control over the Commission in the exercise of its implementing powers (Article 291(3) TFEU).

2 Jurisdiction of the CJEU

As mentioned above, EU law in the field of the CCP and external trade builds largely on existing international obligations, notably those under WTO Agreements. In the field of trade defence, the Council and the Commission enjoy a notable degree of discretion so that

> the review of the exercise of that discretion by the European Union Courts must be confined to ascertaining whether the relevant procedural rules have been complied with, whether the facts on which the contested choice is based have been accurately stated and whether there has been a manifest error of assessment of the facts or a misuse of powers.[154]

Apart from that, the question thus arises what role international rules play when European regulations, for example, implementing trade defence measures are challenged before the Union courts. Article 13 WTO Anti-Dumping Agreement (ADA) as well as Article 23 of the WTO Agreement on Subsidies and Countervailing Measures (SCMA) require members to provide for independent judicial, arbitral or administrative review of their measures. In the EU, the General Court is the competent court for individuals, as well as for Member States, who challenge regulations implementing trade defence measures (Articles 256(1) TFEU and 51(a) second indent CJEU Statute).

---

[152] Critically on this Constantin Fabricius, 'Das Kontrollrecht von Rat und Parlament nach der Komitologie-Durchführungsverordnung' (2014) *Europäische Zeitschrift für Wirtschaftsrecht* 453, who argues that Art 11 Comitology Regulation violates EU primary law.

[153] European Parliament Resolution on Commission Implementing Regulation (EU) No 1337/2013 laying down rules for the application of Regulation (EU) No 1169/2011 as regards the indication of the country of origin or place of provenance for fresh, chilled and frozen meat of swine, sheep, goats and poultry, 6 February 2014, P7_TA(2014)0096; European Parliament Resolution on draft Commission Implementing Decision XXX granting an authorisation for uses of bis(2-ethylhexhyl) phthalate (DEHP) under Regulation (EC) No 1907/2006, 25 November 2015, P8_TA(2015)0409; European Parliament Resolution on Commission Implementing Decision (EU) 2015/2279 authorising the placing on the market of products containing, consisting of, or produced from genetically modified maize NK603 × T25 (MON-ØØ6Ø3-6 × ACS-ZMØØ3-2) pursuant to Regulation (EC) No 1829/2003, 16 December 2015, P8_TA-PROV(2015)0456 and European Parliament Resolution on the draft Commission implementing regulation adopting a list of invasive alien species of Union concern pursuant to Regulation (EU) No 1143/2014, 16 December 2015, P8_TA-PROV(2015)0455; see also Report from the Commission to the European Parliament and the Council on the implementation of Regulation (EU) No 182/2011 (n 40).

[154] Case T-73/12 *Einhell Germany and Others v Commission* (n 137) para 56, with further references.

Union institutions are bound by international agreements concluded by the EU (Article 216(2) TFEU), since they form an integral part of its legal order.[155] These agreements prevail over acts of the EU, with the consequence that the validity of internal Union acts or legislation may be reviewed in light of international obligations, and may lead to the setting aside of internal Union measures, as in the *Open Skies* case.[156] It is further acknowledged that international agreements are in general directly applicable,[157] without requiring an act of transformation.[158] Regarding GATT/WTO Agreements, however, the Court has early on taken a different position, that is, that Union acts are not reviewable in the light of the provisions of those international measures.[159] For individuals or Member States challenging Union acts, this means that they cannot successfully claim non-compliance of a given EU regulation with Union obligations arising from the WTO Agreements. Even though, then, not the case for the WTO Agreements, because of the Court's denial of direct effect[160] (confirmed for the GATT 1947 in *International Fruit Company and Others*),[161] in principle all international agreements can have direct effect. On the basis of the supremacy of EU law, Member States may thus be required to set aside incompatible national legislation if its provisions are unconditional and sufficiently precise.[162] Secondary EU law may also be annulled if it is incompatible with an international agreement.[163]

---

[155] Case C-181/73 *Haegemann* ECLI:EU:C:1974:41, para 5; Case C-12/86 *Demirel* ECLI:EU:C:1987:400, para 7.

[156] See Case C-366/10 *Air Transport Association of America and Others* ECLI:EU:C:2011:864, para 50, with further references.

[157] Peter Hilpold, *Die EU im WTO/GATT-System* (2nd edn, Peter Lang-Verlag 2000) 303 ff; see in detail F Martines, 'Direct Effect of International Agreements of the European Union' (2014) 25 *European Journal of International Law* 129.

[158] Martines, 'Direct Effect of International Agreements of the European Union' (n 157) 134.

[159] See eg Case C-21/72 *International Fruit Company and Others* ECLI:EU:C:1972:115, rejecting the applicability on the grounds that Art XI GATT does not confer rights on EC citizens, paras 19 ff; see also Case C-120/06 P *FIAMM and Others* ECLI:EU:C:2008:476, para 111; and Case C-21/14 P *Commission v Rusal Armenal* ECLI:EU:C:2015:494, para 38, more broadly referring to the 'nature and purpose' of the WTO Agreements (both with further references); see in detail also Pieter Jan Kuijper/Marco Bronckers, 'WTO Law in the European Court of Justice' (2005) 42(5) *Common Market Law Review* 1313; Michelle Q Zang, 'Shall We Talk? Judicial Communication between the CJEU and WTO Dispute Settlement' (2017) 28 *European Journal of International Law* 273, 276.

[160] Case C-149/96 *Portuguese Republic v Council* ECLI:EU:C:1999:574, paras 34–46. In a later judgment, the CJEU confirmed this and held in Case C-377/02 *Van Parys v BIRB* ECLI:EU:C:2005:121 that to accept that the Community Courts have the direct responsibility for ensuring that Community law complies with the WTO rules would deprive the Community's legislative or executive bodies of the discretion which the equivalent bodies of the Community's commercial partners enjoy. It is not in dispute that some of the contracting parties, which are amongst the most important commercial partners of the Community, have concluded from the subject-matter and purpose of the WTO agreements that they are not among the rules applicable by their courts when reviewing the legality of their rules of domestic law. Such lack of reciprocity, if admitted, would risk introducing an anomaly in the application of the WTO rules.

Thus, direct effect of the WTO Agreements has been denied on the basis of reciprocity, because third states which are parties to the WTO Agreements as well may exclude such effect in their domestic legal systems.

[161] Joined Cases C-21–24/72 *International Fruit Company and Others* ECLI:EU:C:1972:115, paras 20 ff.

[162] Case C-344/04 *IATA and ELFAA* ECLI:EU:C:2006:10, para 39; Case C-308/06 *Intertanko and Others* ECLI:EU:C:2008:312, para 45.

[163] Case C-104/81 *Kupferberg* ECLI:EU:C:1982:362, para 10 ff; see Martines, 'Direct Effect of International Agreements of the European Union' (n 157) 132 ff.

The CJEU has, however, developed two exceptions to this principle.[164] In *Fediol v Commission* the Court affirmed that economic agents are entitled to rely on GATT provisions before the Court when the Union act expressly and specifically refers to them.[165] In *Nakajima v Council* the Court reviewed the then basic anti-dumping regulation in light of the Anti-Dumping Code, as the basic regulation had been 'adopted in order to comply with the international obligations of the Community'.[166] Although both of these judgments related to the GATT, the Court later confirmed them with regard to the WTO Agreements, even while favouring a rather restrictive position with respect to those exceptions.[167] In that regard, the Court does not always appear to be very coherent in its jurisprudence, particularly related to the long-running debate on the direct effect of the WTO Agreements, thereby making the matter all the more contentious.

Next to this, it is similarly possible to extend indirect effect to the WTO Agreements. In *Commission v Germany*,[168] the Court held that 'the primacy of international agreements concluded by the Community over provisions of secondary Community legislation means that such provisions must, so far as is possible, be interpreted in a manner that is consistent with those agreements'. This finding was specifically confirmed for the GATT in *Werner*[169] and, with respect to the WTO Agreements, specifically the TRIPS, in *Hermès International*.[170]

Apart from that, Regulation 2015/476[171] determines the applicability of WTO rulings in the context of anti-dumping and anti-subsidy measures taken by the EU. Yet, WTO rulings too are not directly effective.[172] Nevertheless, similar to the Member State principle of the harmonious interpretation of national law in light of Union law, the Commission has to take account of WTO rulings when it adopts anti-dumping and anti-subsidy measures to ensure their conformity with WTO law (Articles 1 and 2 Regulation 2015/476).

Member States, too, can seek judicial review of Union acts in the field of the CCP. Germany was the first Member State to challenge a Union act on the ground of its alleged violation of WTO law. The measure in question concerned the common organization of the market in bananas,[173] already twice previously declared WTO-inconsistent by GATT panels.[174] Challenges by Member States, however, ought not to

---

[164] See Hélène Ruiz Fabri, 'Is There a Case – Legally and Politically – for Direct Effect of WTO Obligations?' (2014) 25 *European Journal of International Law* 1, 151–73.

[165] Case C-70/87 *Fediol v Commission* ECLI:EU:C:1989:254, paras 19–22.

[166] Case C-69/89 *Nakajima v Council* ECLI:EU:C:1991:186, para 31.

[167] Case C-149/96 *Portugal v Council* ECLI:EU:C:1999:574, para 49; most recently see Case C-21/14 P *Commission v Rusal Armenal* ECLI:EU:C:2015:494, para 41.

[168] Case C-61/94 *Commission v Germany* ECLI:EU:C:1996:313, para 52.

[169] Case C-70/94 *Werner* ECLI:EU:C:1995:328, para 23.

[170] Case C-53/96 *Hermès International* ECLI:EU:C:1998:292, para 34 ff.

[171] European Parliament and Council Regulation (EU) No 2015/476 on the measures that the Union may take following a report adopted by the WTO Dispute Settlement Body concerning anti-dumping and anti-subsidy matters [2015] OJ L83/6.

[172] Case C-93/02 P *Biret* ECLI:EU:C:2003:517, paras 51 ff.

[173] Council Regulation (EEC) No 404/93 on the common organization of the market in bananas [1993] OJ L047/1.

[174] See GATT Panel Reports, EEC (Member States)—Bananas I, DS 32/R and EEC—Bananas II, DS 38/R.

be too frequent, as they can influence decision-making during the comitology proceedings (see above).

The extent of the Court's jurisdiction will generally be limited to reviewing whether
procedural requirements have been complied with, or whether the Commission manifestly erred in its assessment.[175] This follows from the fact that the Commission enjoys
a certain degree of discretion when it comes to the implementation of trade defence
measures.[176]

Another point to be made with respect to judicial review—even though it is only
marginally related to administration in the context of the CCP and external trade
law—is the pressing issue of the concurrent competences of the CJEU and other international courts or arbitral tribunals, emerging to a greater or lesser degree from the
possibility (directly or indirectly) of rulings on Union law. At present it is particularly
the compatibility of investor-state dispute settlement (ISDS) which is the focus of discussion. The common denominator of judicial review in the context of EU trade defence measures is the vesting of individuals or businesses with a means of enforcing
their rights and having actions of the host state reviewed. Without ISDS, foreign investors would not have the possibility of directly enforcing their rights against a host
state, but could only rely on the diplomatic protection through their own home state.
Unlike trade defence, there exist, however, no rules, such as the TBR, which simplify
the reliance on diplomatic protection, leaving it entirely to the home state to decide
whether to act or not. Therefore, ISDS is an essential feature of rules governing the
protection of foreign investments. The Commission has taken it upon itself the reform of ISDS in order to make it more acceptable to Member States, as well as to the
Court, by proposing the establishment of a public 'investment court system' (ICS)[177]
as part of its 'trade-for-all' strategy (which had already indicated the need for such
a system).[178] Whether such a proposal will in fact materialize is still uncertain, and
will greatly depend on the opinion of the Court with regard to the compatibility of
an ICS with Union law, a question upon which it has been asked to rule by Belgium
in the aftermath of the 'CETA-Saga'.[179] As evinced in the context of EU accession to
the European Convention on Human Rights (ECHR),[180] as well as in regard to the

---

[175] Natasa Rados, 'Art. 5 Anti-Dumping Grundverordnung' in Horst Günter Krenzler, Christoph
Herrmann, and Marian Niestedt (eds), *EU-Außenwirtschafts- und Zollrecht* (C H Beck 2015) para 16;
Thomas Cottier and Lorena Trinberg, 'Art. 207 AEUV' in Hans von der Groeben, Jürgen Schwarze, and
Armin Hatje (eds), *Europäisches Unionsrecht* (7th edn, Nomos 2015) para 78.

[176] See eg Art 16 Regulation on Common Rules for Imports, Art 21 Anti-Dumping Regulation, and
Art 31 Anti-Subsidy Regulation, according to which a determination shall be made by the Commission
as to whether the Union's interest calls for intervention.

[177] The idea of the Commission to establish a multilateral investment court (MIC) was already developed during the negotiations of the Transatlantic Trade and Investment Partnership (TTIP)—currently
on hold due to the Trump administration—with the aim of being used in multiple agreements. European
Commission, 'Concept Paper: Investment in TTIP and beyond: the path for reform' (2015) http://trade.
ec.europa.eu/doclib/press/index.cfm?id=1608 (last accessed 11 April 2018).

[178] European Commission Communication, 'Trade for all—Towards a more responsible trade and investment policy' (n 55) 21.

[179] Belgian request for an opinion from the European Court of Justice https://diplomatie.belgium.be/
sites/default/files/downloads/ceta_summary.pdf (last accessed 11 April 2018).

[180] Opinion 2/13 *Re Accession of the European Union to the European Convention for the Protection of
Human Rights and Fundamental Freedoms* ECLI:EU:C:2014:2454.

European Patent Court (EPC),[181] the CJEU is rather reluctant to allow other courts potentially to straddle its own jurisdiction. The main reason of this is that the Union legal order is one autonomous of any other, and that the CJEU is the only judicial body with the power to interpret EU law, a position not to be undercut by any other body.

3 Trade Barriers Regulation

The Trade Barriers Regulation (TBR) sits somewhere between the dispute settlement mechanisms under the auspices of the WTO and the possibility for individuals to have anti-dumping and anti-subsidy measures reviewed before the European courts.[182] Specifically, the TBR regulates the procedure for a given Union industry, or rather businesses within an industry, for making use of diplomatic protection in the case of violation of obligations under the WTO Agreements by other members through the introduction of trade barriers, that is, through any trading rule or practice in violation of the international trade rules. Since only members, that is, states, can initiate and participate in proceedings under the WTO Dispute Settlement Understanding (DSU), private actors need to rely on their home state to make a complaint in case of an alleged violation by another state of its obligations under the WTO Agreements. The TBR attempts to fill this gap by providing for a transparent procedure, allowing EU industries to request Union action in dispute settlement proceedings before the WTO. Initiating proceedings under the DSU constitutes an offensive trade defence mechanism.[183]

4 Protection of the individual before the CJEU

It can be observed that judicial review is traditionally more common, and thus pronounced, as regards anti-dumping and countervailing measures, when compared with safeguard measures relating to complaints made by individuals. Most notably, the reason for this is that anti-dumping and countervailing measures address specific actors exporting their products into the EU. Safeguard measures, on the other hand, are applied to products and, as such, apply *erga omnes* to actors exporting or importing these products into the EU, thus making it difficult for economic actors to demonstrate individual concern.[184] It should be noted, however, that Member States can notify to the Commission contracts concluded on normal terms and conditions before the entry into force of a safeguard measure (Article 15(3)(b) Import Regulation), and thereby enabling economic actors to show their individual concern. According to this so-called 'Plaumann test', introduced by the ECJ in 1963,[185]

---

[181] Opinion 1/09 *Re European Patent Court* ECLI:EU:C:2011:123.
[182] Macdonald MacLean, *EU Trade Barrier Regulation: Tackling Unfair Foreign Trade Practices* (n 72); Herrmann, 'Das Verwaltungsrecht der handelspolitischen Schutzinstrumente' (n 100) § 30 (43).
[183] Herrmann, 'Das Verwaltungsrecht der handelspolitischen Schutzinstrumente' (n 100) 1067 § 30(13) ff.
[184] See Case T-155/02 *VVG International and Others v Commission* ECLI:EU:T:2003:125, para 30; on the problem of legal protection of individuals see Jürgen Schwarze, 'The Legal Protection of the Individual against Regulations in European Union Law' (2004) 10 *European Public Law* 285.
[185] Case C-25/62 *Plaumann v Commission of the EEC* ECLI:EU:C:1963:17.

[p]ersons other than those to whom a decision is addressed may only claim to be individually concerned if that decision affects them by reason of certain attributes which are peculiar to them or by reason of circumstances in which they are differentiated from all other persons and by virtue of these factors distinguishes them individually just as in the case of the person addressed.[186]

With respect to CCP measures, this has the effect that individual concern can be easily established for persons identified explicitly in a given measure, that is, a regulation introducing anti-dumping or countervailing measures, or where they have been directly concerned during any preliminary investigations.[187] Those requirements, as they evolved and were applied, often led to a dismissal of the cases for a lack of locus standi.

With the entry into force of the Lisbon Treaty hopes were high that the situation would change with the introduction of the third alternative of Article 263 fourth paragraph TFEU. This provision now grants individuals the right to institute proceedings against a 'regulatory act which is of direct concern to them and does not entail implementing measures'. The Court has by now clarified 'regulatory act' as including *non-legislative* acts of general application.[188] Direct concern refers to a Union measure that directly affects the legal situation of the individual (exporter or importer), and leaves no discretion to the institution implementing it.[189] This last requirement does not pose any problems with respect to trade defence measures, as they leave no discretion to national authorities regarding their implementation. However, such actions by national customs authorities have now been qualified as implementing measures within the meaning of the provision.[190] It thus appears that everything remains the same regarding the protection of rights of individuals in relation to the effect of trade defence measures.[191]

K Conclusions

The CCP and other rules governing the Union's external trade still embody the backbone of the outer dimensions of the European administrative space.

---

[186] ibid 107.

[187] Case C-239/82 *Allied Corporation and Others v Commission* ECLI:EU:C:1984:68, para 12; for a detailed account of 'individual concern' with respect to anti-dumping regulation see Georg M Berrisch, Hans-Georg Kamann '110. Rechtsschutz im EU-Außenwirtschaftsrecht' in Horst Günter Krenzler, Christoph Herrmann, and Marian Niestedt (eds), *EU-Außenwirtschafts- und Zollrecht* (C H Beck 2016) para 17 ff.

[188] Case C-583/11 *Inuit Tapiriit Kanatami and Others v Parliament and Council* ECLI:EU:C:2013:625, paras 56 ff.

[189] See Joined Cases C-445/07 P and C-455/07 P *Commission v Ente per le Ville Vesuviane and Ente per le Ville Vesuviane/Commission* ECLI:EU:C:2009:529, para 45 and Case T-596/11 *Bricmate v Council* ECLI:EU:T:2014:53, para 74, both with further references.

[190] Case T-551/11 *BSI v Council* ECLI:EU:T:2013:60, para 62.

[191] For a detailed account of the application of Art 263(4) second and third alternative TFEU since the entry into force of the Lisbon Treaty see Herbert Rosenfeldt, 'Das Erfordernis fehlender Durchführungsmaßnahmen: Zu jüngsten Konkretisierungen des Art. 263 IV 3. Var. AEUV durch die Rechtsprechung' (2015) *Europäische Zeitschrift für Wirtschaftsrecht* 174.

Recent developments, such as reform of the CCP and several judgments of the CJEU underline that this area of European law is subject to a 'second wave' of constitutionalization. In the context of EU administrative law, this trend is of major interest: it demonstrates that some of the 'traditional' areas of internal market law are subject to continuing efforts towards increased transparency, democratic legitimacy, and accountability.[192] This tendency is also reflected in the jurisprudence of the Court, regarding so-called 'smart sanctions' based on Article 215 TFEU. These judgments underline the significance of human rights even in external trade, an area which was long seen as untouched by any concerns relating to individual rights. In addition, the new debate on the (potential) role of EU values (Article 21 TEU, and Articles 205 and 206 TFEU) within the CCP marks another facet of this development.

Another important observation is that the administration of the CCP and other fields of external trade is becoming increasingly complex. In particular, the interaction of the EU and Member States within the CCP, and the new role of the European Parliament, lead to more complex procedures, and to demands for even more adjustments between the European institutions and the Member States. The 'CETA-Saga' demonstrates how complex this interaction can potentially be. A 'surplus' of democracy might then harm the effectiveness of the external trade relations of the European Union. The new position of the Parliament within the CCP is, of course, just one further step towards an ultimately comprehensive application of the ordinary law-making procedure (Article 289 TFEU).

Recent developments, such as 'trade wars', or the so-called Brexit, demonstrate that the role of political considerations within international trade is still of pre-eminent importance. Strikingly, the US administration under President Trump has introduced a new approach to national trade policy which may well lead to more trade confrontation than any approaches taken in the past. This approach is accompanied by a distinct scepticism as to whether WTO structures are still capable of solving trade disputes. Such a rapid undermining of international mechanisms demonstrates the ongoing, predominant dependence of international trade on political considerations and the political setting.

From an administrative law perspective, these developments reflect the fact that the CCP and other rules governing external trade are much more amenable to being characterized as (external) politics in action, than other fields of EU policy. Were this field of Union law more strongly shaped by principles of administrative law rather than political twists and turns, one might expect that the core principles of a Union based on clearly articulated goals and values would be more regularly observed and followed.

---

[192] So also in the context of competition law, where transparency, due process and the right to be heard etc are key principles. However, in that context—in contrast to the CCP and external trade policy—the European Parliament as defender of civic interests does not yet really play a role.

APPENDIX

List of Comitology Committees operating the sector

- Trade Defence Instruments Committee[193]
- Generalised Preferences Committee[194]
- Committee on common rules for exports of products[195]
- Committee on the exercise of the Union's rights under international trade rules[196]
- Committee on Safeguards and Common Rules for Exports[197]
- Management Committee on quantitative import or export quotas[198]
- Committee on common rules for imports of textile products from certain third countries (autonomous regime)[199]
- Committee on defence against obstacles to trade which affect the market of the Community or a non-member country (TBR)
- Committee on harmonisation of the provisions concerning export credit insurance for transactions with medium and long-term cover[200]
- Wood Committee[201]
- Committee for Investment Agreements[202]

[193] Established by Art 25(1) of Regulation (EU) 2016/1037 of the European Parliament and of the Council of 8 June 2016 on protection against subsidised imports from countries not members of the European Union [2016] OJ L176/55; the rules of procedure for the trade defence instruments committee are available at http://ec.europa.eu/transparency/regcomitology/OpenSaveDoc.cfm?dc_id=10326&doc_type=application/pdf&com_code=C44100 (last accessed 9 April 2015).

[194] Established by Art 39(1) of Regulation (EU) No 978/2012 of the European Parliament and of the Council of 25 October 2012 applying a scheme of generalised tariff preferences and repealing Council Regulation (EC) No 732/2008 [2012] OJ L303/1.

[195] Established by Art 3(1) Regulation (EU) No 2015/479 (n 69).

[196] Established by Art 8(1) of Regulation (EU) No 654/2014 of the European Parliament and of the Council of 15 May 2014 concerning the exercise of the Union's rights for the application and enforcement of international trade rules and amending Council Regulation (EC) No 3286/94 laying down Community procedures in the field of the common commercial policy in order to ensure the exercise of the Community's rights under international trade rules, in particular those established under the auspices of the World Trade Organization [2014] OJ L189/50; the committee's rules of procedure are available at http://ec.europa.eu/transparency/regcomitology/index.cfm?do=List.list&page=1 (last accessed 11 April 2018).

[197] Established by Art 3(1) of Regulation (EU) 2015/478 of the European Parliament and of the Council of 11 March 2015 on common rules for imports OJ [2015] L83/16.

[198] Established by Art 22(1) of Council Regulation (EC) No 717/2008 of 17 July 2008 establishing a Community procedure for administering quantitative quotas [2008] OJ L198/1.

[199] Established by Art 30(1) Regulation (EU) 2015/936 (n 67).

[200] Established by Art 4 of Council Directive 98/29/EC of 7 May 1998 on harmonisation of the main provisions concerning export credit insurance for transactions with medium and long-term cover [1998] OJ L148/22.

[201] Established by Art 2(1) of Regulation (EU) No 1217/2012 of the European Parliament and of the Council of 12 December 2012 on the allocation of tariff-rate quotas applying to exports of wood from the Russian Federation to the European Union [2012] OJ L351/34.

[202] Established by Art 16(1) of Regulation (EU) No 1219/2012 of the European Parliament and of the Council of 12 December 2012 establishing transitional arrangements for bilateral investment agreements between Member States and third countries [2012] OJ L351/40.

- Advisory Committee on the implementation of activities relating to the Community market access strategy[203]
- Committee on responsible sourcing of tin, tantalum, tungsten, and gold[204]
- Western Balkans Implementation Committee[205]
- Committee for Investment Agreements.[206]

[203] Established by Art 3 of Council Decision 98/552/EC of 24 September 1998 on the implementation by the Commission of activities relating to the Community market access strategy [1998] OJ L265/31; the committee's rules of procedure are available at http://ec.europa.eu/transparency/regcomitology/index.cfm?do=List.list&page=2 (last accessed 11 April 2018).

[204] Established by Art 15(1) of Regulation (EU) 2017/821 of the European Parliament and of the Council of 17 May 2017 laying down supply chain due diligence obligations for Union importers of tin, tantalum and tungsten, their ores, and gold originating from conflict-affected and high-risk areas, [2017] OJ L130/1.

[205] Established by Art 1(7) of Regulation (EU) No 1336/2011 of the European Parliament and of the Council of 13 December 2011 amending Council Regulation (EC) No 1215/2009 introducing exceptional trade measures for countries and territories participating in or linked to the European Union's Stabilisation and Association process [2011] OJ L347/1.

[206] Established by Art 16(1) of Regulation (EU) No 1219/2012 of the European Parliament and of the Council of 12 December 2012 establishing transitional arrangements for bilateral investment agreements between Member States and third countries [2012] OJ L351/40; the committee's rules of procedure are available at http://ec.europa.eu/transparency/regcomitology/index.cfm?do=List.list&page=2 (last accessed 11 April 2018).

5

The Customs Union

Laurence W Gormley

A Introduction

EU customs law has developed enormously since the entry into force of the Common Customs Tariff on 1 July 1968. The move away from issue-by-issue directives[1] towards more generally applicable regulations heralded greater control at EU level over matters such as inward processing, ensuring more uniformity in the customs territory of the then Community which had started to resemble a Swiss Cheese because of national policies concerned to attract business. The logical next step was the development of a single Community Customs Code,[2] subsequently replaced by the somewhat ill-fated Modernised Customs Code.[3] Both have now been succeeded by the Union Customs Code (UCC).[4] The procedural provisions of the latter have been in force since 30 October 2013, and most of the substantive provisions have applied since 1 May 2016. Three major regulations put flesh on the extensive bones of the UCC: the UCC Delegated Act (UCC-DA);[5] the UCC Implementing Act (UCC-IA),[6] and the UCC Transitional Delegated Act (UCC-TDA).[7] The UCC-DA covers all the matters in respect of which the Commission has been granted delegated powers under the UCC, and the UCC-IA covers all the matters in respect of which the Commission has been granted implementing powers under the UCC.

---

[1] See L W Gormley, 'Consolidation, Codification and Improving the Quality Of Community Legislation: the Community Customs Code' in N Emiliou and D O'Keeffe (eds), *The European Union and World Trade Law after the GATT Uruguay Round* (Wiley 1996) 124. As to the earlier legislation see L W Gormley in 52 *Halsbury's Laws of England* (4th edn, Butterworths 1986) Pt 12; D Lasok and W Cairns, *The Customs Law of the European Economic Community* (Kluwer 1983).

[2] Regulation 2913/92 [1992] OJ L302/1, subsequently amended on numerous occasions. As to the implementing provisions see Commission Regulation 2454/93 [1993] OJ 253/1 (known as the CCIP), which was also heavily amended on numerous occasions. See generally L W Gormley, *EU Law of Free Movement of Goods and Customs Union* (Oxford University Press 2009); T Lyons, *EU Customs Law* (3rd edn, Oxford University Press 2018).

[3] Regulation 450/2008 [2008] OJ L145/1. In fact, only the provisions relating to the various procedures for adopting implementing measures, and provisions dealing with charges and costs entered into force; see Art 188.

[4] Art 288(2) Regulation 952/2013 [2013] OJ L269/1, as corrected by [2013] OJ L287/90 and [2016] OJ L267/2.

[5] Commission Delegated Regulation 2015/2446 [2015] OJ L343/1, as corrected by [2016] OJ L87/35 and as amended by Commission Delegated Regulations 2016/341 [2016] OJ L69/1, 2016/651 [2016] OJ L111/1, and 2018/1063 [2018] OJ L192/1.

[6] Commission Implementing Regulation 2015/2447 [2015] OJ L343/558, as corrected by [2016] OJ L87/35 and as amended by Commission Implementing Regulations 2017/989 [2017] OJ L149/19 and 2018/604 [2018] OJ L101/22.

[7] Commission Delegated Regulation 2016/341 [2016] OJ L69/1, as amended by Commission Delegated Regulation 2016/698 [2016] OJ L121/1 and as corrected by [2016] OJ L101/33 and [2017] L281/34.

The dash for all-electronic customs declarations and systems in the context of the Modernised Customs Code proved to be too ambitious for the Member States, which is why much of that instrument never entered into force.[8] While the European Commission's aspirations for electronic customs processing are clearly set out in its Work Programme relating to the development and deployment of the electronic systems provided for in the UCC,[9] it is very hard to predict whether the Member States will meet the current latest deadline for the implementation of all-electronic systems (31 December 2020),[10] hence the adoption of the UCC-TDA, which ensures that paper-based systems can still be used in the meantime.

EU competence in the field of customs law is exclusive.[11] Common Customs tariff duties are fixed by the Council on a proposal from the Commission[12] which, in formulating that, is to be guided by the provisions of Article 32 TFEU.[13] Articles 33,[14] 114,[15] and 207[16] TFEU form the legal basis for the UCC. While the various customs procedures are established and regulated by the UCC, the UCC-DA, and the UCC-IA, the practical application of EU customs law is largely in the hands of the Member States. Union customs law is applied in a decentralized manner, and matters not regulated at EU level are left to the Member States.[17] The latter are bound to respect the duty of Union loyalty imposed by Article 4(3) TEU, as well as the principles of equivalence and effectiveness, and of proportionality.[18] This executive federalism[19] is actually in the nature of a partnership: the national customs authorities are called upon to work with each other and with the Commission,[20] as well as with customs authorities

---

[8] See K Limbach, *Uniformity of Customs Administration in the European Union* (Hart Publishing 2015) 83–92.

[9] See now Commission Implementing Decision 2016/578 [2016] OJ L99/6. Electronic systems are being developed or upgraded in accordance with the Work Programme.

[10] The Commission has proposed that in respect of certain procedures, the deadline for the use of electronic systems be moved to 31 December 2025, COM(2018) 25 final.

[11] Art 3(1)(a) TFEU.   [12] Art 31 TFEU.

[13] See section D of this chapter, below. The provisions of what is now Art 31 TFEU have remained the same (save for renumbering and the substitution of 'Union' for 'Community') since the entry into force of the EEC Treaty.

[14] Which requires the European Parliament and the Council to take measures by the ordinary legislative procedure to strengthen customs cooperation between the Member States and between the latter and the Commission. See Limbach (n 8) 176 ff.

[15] Which deals with harmonization for the establishment and functioning of the internal market.

[16] On the common commercial policy of the EU.

[17] Thus, eg in relation to appeals, Art 44(2) UCC provides that the right of appeal may be exercised in at least two steps. The central, but unstated, requirement is that recourse must be available to a body which is a court or tribunal of the Member State concerned that is capable of making a reference under Art 267 TFEU.

[18] See eg in relation to penalties UCC Art 42 UCC and inter alia Case C-91/02 *Hannl + Hofstetter v Finanzlandesdirektion für Wien, Niederösterreich und Burgenland* [2003] ECR I-12077, ECLI:EU:C:2003:556, paras 18–20; Case C-414/02 *Spedition Ulustrans v Finanzlandesdirektion für Österreich* [2004] ECR I-8633, ECLI:EU:C:2004:551, para 38, and Case C-76/10 *Berel and Others v Administration des Douanes de Rouen and Others* [2011] ECR I-717, ECLI:EU:C:2011:93, para 47.

[19] See H C H Hofmann, G C Rowe, and A H Türk, *Administrative Law and Policy of the European Union* (Oxford University Press 2011) 13 and literature cited there.

[20] See Council Regulation 515/97 [1997] OJ L82/1 on mutual assistance to ensure the correct application of the law on customs and agricultural matters, as corrected by [1998] OJ L288/55, and most recently amended by European Parliament and Council Regulation 2015/1525 [2015] OJ L143/1. Outside the sphere of customs law in terms of traditional customs activities see, essentially dealing with police cooperation, the 'Naples II Convention' [1998] OJ C 24/1–21, most recently amended by Council Decision

of countries with which relevant agreements have been concluded.[21] The consequent cooperation may be central (through the Customs Code Committee), bilateral, or multilateral. The networks, which these forms of cooperation imply, are important in confidence-building, information exchange, the combating of fraud, smuggling and other nefarious activities, and in ensuring the proper functioning of the customs union as a whole.

B Administrative Tasks in the Customs Sector

The Commission's administrative tasks are now set out item-by-item in the UCC. Sometimes the performance of the tasks involves measures directed only to selected Member States,[22] or sometimes measures of a more general interventionist nature.[23] The Commission was obliged by virtue of Article 280 UCC to draw up a Work Programme for the UCC by 1 May 2014;[24] this resulted in the UCC-DA.[25] Most of the Commission's tasks under the UCC concern, or lead to, regulatory acts.[26] All such provisions which have been adopted are now in force. Their making relied on the conferral of powers to adopt delegated acts as well as implementing acts, the following sub-sections providing an overview of the Commission's powers in this regard.

1 Delegated acts

Article 2 UCC empowers the Commission 'to adopt delegated acts ... specifying the provisions of customs legislation and simplifications thereof with respect to the customs declaration, the proof of customs status, and the use of the internal

---

2008/39 [2008] OJ L9/21 as a result of Bulgarian and Romanian accession to the European Union. This Convention requires the Member States, through their customs administrations to cooperate with each other in preventing and detecting infringements of national customs provisions, and in prosecuting and punishing infringements of [Union] and national customs provisions; the convention covers a wide range of actions, including hot pursuit. The Common Information System (CIS) has two separate databases, because they are based on Regulation 515/97 (CIS II) and on the Naples II Convention (CIS I) respectively; see Limbach (n 8) 185–86 and the literature cited there.

[21] See eg Arts 12(2), 13, 47, 116, and 119 UCC; Arts 55(5)(b)(ii) and 64(2)(c) UCC-DA; Arts 54, 65, 70, 71, 72, 75, 84, 108, 116(3), 119(3), 124, and 155 UCC-IA, and Council Regulation 515/97 on mutual assistance, see n 20 above.

[22] For example, Art 6(4) UCC empowers the Commission to adopt in exceptional cases decisions permitting one or several Member States to use means other than electronic data-processing techniques for the exchange and storage of information. The general derogation in UCC-TDA was adopted using a regulation; see n 7 above.

[23] See eg under Art 34(10) UCC, the Commission must notify the customs authorities where the taking of Binding Tariff Information (BTI) or Binding Origin Information decisions, for goods whose correct and uniform tariff classification or determination of origin is not ensured, is suspended, or where such suspension is withdrawn. Art 34(11) UCC empowers the Commission to adopt decisions requesting the Member States to revoke BTI or BOI decisions, to ensure a correct and uniform tariff classification or determination of the origin of goods.

[24] This was initially done by Commission Implementing Decision 2014/255 [2014] O J L134/46, which was repealed and replaced by Commission Implementing Decision 2016/578; see n 9 above.

[25] See n 7 above.

[26] In the post-Lisbon scenario, Delegated Acts and Implementing Acts, not being adopted by the Ordinary or a Special Legislative Procedure, can best be described using this term, which also features in Art 263 4th para TFEU.

Union transit procedure', which apply to the trade in Union goods between those parts of the EU customs territory to which VAT and excise duty directives apply and those where they do not apply, or between those parts of the territory where such provisions do not apply. Such 'acts may address particular circumstances pertaining to the trade in Union goods involving only one Member State'. Further, the Commission is empowered under Article 7 UCC to adopt delegated acts in order to determine:

(a) the common data requirements [for the exchange and storage of information], taking into account the need to accomplish the required customs formalities and the nature and purpose of the exchange and storage of information …;

(b) the specific cases where means for the exchange and storage of information, other than electronic data-processing techniques, may be used … [and]

(c) the type of information and the particulars that are to be contained in the records [for temporary storage facilities and the storage, working or processing of goods, or the sale or purchase of goods in free zones].

Very numerous further powers for the Commission to adopt delegated acts are to be found throughout the UCC. For convenience, these are most simply presented in list-form as follows, in order to make readily apparent the very extensive place of subordinate regulatory measures—that is, legislative rule-making by the Commission—in the context of the Union's customs administration. Such delegated acts, enabled by the UCC, can:

- determine certain matters concerning registration with the customs authorities of authorized economic operators and of others, and the invalidation of such registration (Article 10);

- lay down when the waiver (under Article 18(2) sub-paragraph 2) of the requirement that a customs representative be established within the Union customs territory shall not apply, and when customs authorities are not to require evidence of empowerment to act as a customs representative (Article 20);

- relate to various matters concerning decisions on the application of customs legislation, and the reassessment or suspension of such measures (Article 24);

- determine the cases when 'a favourable decision addressed to several persons may be revoked, also in respect of persons other than the person who fails to fulfil an obligation imposed under that decision', and 'the exceptional cases, in which the customs authorities may defer the date on which revocation or amendment takes effect' (Article 31);

- can concern specific cases in which decisions on Binding Tariff Information (BTI) and Binding Origin Information (BOI) are to be revoked, as well as cases 'where decisions relating to binding information are taken with regard to other factors on the basis of which import or export duty and other measures in respect of trade in goods are applied' (Article 36);

- determine simplifications, facilitations and more favourable treatment for authorized economic operators (Article 40);

- lay down certain rules concerning when goods of non-preferential origin are to be 'considered as wholly obtained in a single country or territory or to have undergone their last, substantial, economically-justified processing or working, in an undertaking equipped for that purpose, resulting in the manufacture of a new product or representing an important stage of manufacture in a country or territory' (Article 62);
- lay down rules on preferential origin (Article 65);
- relate to simplification authorizations concerning certain amounts to be included in the customs value of goods (Article 75);
- address certain aspects of the calculation of import duty and the time limit for determining the duty incurred where certain procedures have not been discharged or ended properly (Article 88);
- relate to certain aspects of the guarantee system (Article 99);
- lay down the conditions under which customs authorities are exempted from the requirement to notify a customs debt (Article 106);
- 'determine the rules for the suspension of the time-limit for payment of the amount of import or export duty corresponding to a customs debt [in certain circumstances,] and the period of suspension' (Article 115);
- lay down the rules with which the Commission itself must comply when considering requests for remission or repayment of duties, and in particular: '(i) the conditions for the acceptance of the file; (ii) the time-limit to take a decision and the suspension of that time-limit; (iii) the communication of the grounds on which the Commission intends to base its decision, before taking a decision which would adversely affect the person concerned; (iv) the notification of the decision, and (v) the consequences of a failure to take a decision or to notify such decision' (Article 122);
- determine, as regards extinguishment of the customs debt, 'the list of failures with no significant effect on the correct operation of the customs procedure concerned' and supplement the rule relating to extinguishment where such failure did not constitute an attempt at deception (Article 126);
- relate to various matters concerning entry summary declarations (Article 131);
- set the conditions for approving the places where goods must be presented to customs, and (Article 142);
- relate to the approval of places for temporary storage, authorization of the operation of such facilities, and the movement of goods in temporary storage (Article 151);
- deal with certain aspects of the customs status of Union goods (Article 156);
- determine the cases where a customs declaration may be lodged using means other than electronic data-processing techniques (Article 160);
- lay down the rules for authorizing economic operators to draw up supporting documents for customs declarations (Article 164);

- relate to various matters concerning simplified declarations, cases where the customs declaration is invalidated after release of the goods, and authorization of central clearance and of entry in the declarant's records as a means of lodging a customs declaration (Articles 168, 175, 180, and 183 respectively);
- relate to self-assessment by authorized economic operators for simplified procedures (Article 186);
- determine where release of goods is not to be conditional upon the provision of a guarantee in respect of goods subject of a drawing request on a tariff quota (Article 196);
- determine when goods are considered to be returned to the state in which they were exported and when relief from import duty shall be granted to goods which have benefited from measures laid down under the common agricultural policy involving their export out of the customs territory of the Union (Article 206);
- set out the conditions: for the authorization of the use of the inward or outward processing procedure, the temporary admission procedure or the end-use procedure; for the operation of storage facilities for the customs warehousing of goods, where the storage facility operator is not the customs authority itself; for exceptions to the requirement to fulfil all the prescribed conditions; and for cases where the economic conditions are deemed to be fulfilled (Article 212);
- lay down the time limit for the discharge of certain special procedures, and the cases and conditions for the movement of goods placed under a special procedure other than transit or in a free zone and to determine the usual forms of handling for goods placed under customs warehousing or a processing procedure or in a free zone (Articles 216 and 221 respectively);
- determine certain matters relating to equivalent goods, and to determine the specific cases where Union goods are to be placed under the external transit procedure, and the conditions for the granting of the status of authorized consignee to receive at an authorized place goods moved in accordance with the TIR Convention so that that procedure is terminated (Articles 224 and 231 respectively);
- set the conditions of authorizing simplifications regarding the placing of goods under the Union transit procedure or the end of that procedure (Article 235);
- determine the specific use of goods under the temporary admission procedure and the conditions for total or partial duty relief (Article 253);
- determine the specific time-limit within which the pre-departure declaration is to be lodged before the goods are taken out of the customs territory of the Union, taking into account the type of traffic, and to determine the specific cases where the obligation to lodge a pre-departure declaration is waived (Article 265); and
- specify the rules on the exchange and storage of data where the electronic systems which are necessary for the application of the provisions of the are not yet operational (Article 279).

This list makes very clear the central role played by the Commission's subordinate legislative competences, all the specific instances of delegation of powers authorized by the UCC. The delegation is regulated by Article 284 UCC, which makes use of the powers conferred by Article 290 TFEU. The Commission is obliged to notify the European Parliament and the Council as soon as it adopts a delegated act. Delegated acts enter into force only if no objection has been expressed either by the European Parliament or the Council within two months of notification of that act to those institutions, or if, before the expiry of that period, they have both informed the Commission that they will not object. The two-month period for objection may be extended by a further two months if either the Parliament or the Council demand such an extension.

As usual, the exercise of delegated powers is permitted for a period of five years, in the first instance until 30 October 2018; the Commission has to present a report in respect of the delegation of power not later than nine months before the end of the five-year period; the first was presented on 22 January 2018.[27] The delegation of power is tacitly extended for five years at a time, unless the European Parliament or the Council opposes such an extension no later than three months before the end of the pertinent period. The delegation may be revoked at any time by a decision of the European Parliament or by the Council, putting an end to the delegation specified. Such a decision may revoke either all the powers delegated under the UCC or one or more specific powers, and takes effect the day following its publication in the *Official Journal* or at a later date specified. Such a revocation does not affect the validity of any delegated acts already in force.

2 Implementing powers

The implementing powers conferred on the Commission are also specified in individual provisions throughout the UCC. The *procedures* for their exercise are those set out in Article 285 UCC, although the precise procedure varies according to the subject-matter of the power concerned. Thus, under Article 8(1) the Commission may, in implementing acts specify 'where necessary, the format and code of common data requirements', and 'the procedural rules on the exchange and storage of information' where this takes place by non-electronic means. Such acts are adopted using the *examination* procedure referred to in Article 285(4) UCC, whereas, for example, derogations under Article 8(2) UCC (authorizing the use of non-electronic means for exchange and storage of data) are adopted under the *advisory* procedure referred to in Article 285(2) UCC.

As with delegated acts, the Commission competence to adopt implementing acts under the UCC is extremely extensive; it too is best captured in overview in list-form. Commission implementing acts, adopted following the *examination* procedure under the UCC, can, in particular, lay down *procedural rules* for vast variety of acts and measures relating to:

---

[27] COM(2018) 39 final.

- the conferral and proving of the entitlement of empowerment under Article 18(3) (Article 21);
- the submission and acceptance of applications for a decision on the application of the customs legislation, and on the taking such a decision, including consultation of the Member States concerned, and monitoring a decision under Article 22 (Article 25);
- the annulment, revocation or amendment of favourable decisions (Article 32);
- the provision and verification of proof of origin (Article 63);
- facilitating the establishment in the Union of preferential origin of goods, and measures granting a beneficiary country or territory a temporary derogation from rules on preferential origin (Article 66);
- the amount, provision and monitoring of guarantees for customs debt, and temporary prohibitions relating to the use of comprehensive guarantees (Article 100(1));
- repayment and remission of import or export duty (and for a customs authority to inform the Commission when it grants such repayment or remission) (Article 123);
- the notification of arrival and the conveyance of goods (Article 138);
- temporary storage (Article 152);
- the provision and verification of the customs status of Union goods (Article 157);
- determining certain competent customs offices and lodging in specific cases customs declarations otherwise than electronically (Article 161);
- lodging the standard customs declaration and making supporting documents available (Article 165), and lodging simplified and supplementary declarations (Article 169);
- customs formalities and controls to be carried out by an authorized economic operator permitted to use self-assessment for certain customs formalities and certain controls (Article 187);
- the destruction, sale and abandonment of goods to the State; (Article 200);
- the provision of information concerning relief from import duty, establishing that the conditions for relief are fulfilled (Article 207);
- the provision of evidence (Article 209);
- examining economic conditions where evidence exists that the essential interests of Union producers are likely to be adversely affected by the use of the inward or outward processing procedure, the temporary admission procedure, or the end-use procedure, and the operation of storage facilities other than by the customs authority itself (Article 213);
- the discharge of a special procedure (Article 217);
- transferring certain rights and obligations, and the movement of goods under special procedures other than transit or in a free zone (Article 222);

- the use of equivalent goods (Article 225);
- external transit, and (Article 232);
- placing of Union goods under the customs warehousing or free zones procedure (Article 239);
- exit of goods from the customs territory of the Union subject to risk-analysis (Article 268); and
- lodging, amending, and invalidating exit-summary declarations (Article 271) and re-export notifications (Article 276).

The *examination* procedure (Article 285(4) UCC) is also used under Article 37(1) in relation to the adoption by the Commission of procedural rules for:

- using a BTI or BOI decision after it ceases to be valid or has been revoked;
- notification by the Commission of the suspension of the taking of such decisions for goods whose correct and uniform tariff classification or determination of origin is not ensured, or the withdrawal of such suspension;
- using decisions relating to binding information with regard to other factors, determined under delegated powers in accordance with Article 36, after such decisions cease to be valid; and
- suspending such decisions, and notifying suspension or withdrawal of suspension, to the customs authorities.

One might validly query in passing whether, under the guise of empowering the Commission to adopting implementing acts in order to make procedural rules in regard to matters such as those listed here, it is not in fact being given rather far-reaching substantive regulatory competence.

Various other implementing acts of the Commission, also adopted under the *examination* procedure, deal not just with procedural rules but can concern:

- the specification of the customs authorities responsible for registering economic operators (Article 11);
- technical requirements for developing, maintaining, and employing electronic systems for exchanging and storing information (Article 17);
- application of the criteria in Article 39 for the grant of the status of authorized economic operator (Article 41);
- uniform application of customs controls, including the exchange of risk information and risk analysis results, common risk criteria and standards, control measures and priority control areas (Article 50);[28]

---

[28] Where it is necessary to rapidly update the common risk management framework and adapt these measures to the evolution of risks, the Commission may on imperative grounds of urgency adopt immediately applicable implementing acts; these may apply for up to six months, subject to their having to be repealed if the Customs Code Committee gives a negative opinion on them under the examination procedure; the Committee's opinion must be requested within 14 days of the act's adoption: see Art 50(1) UCC in conjunction with Art 285(5) UCC. If the Committee's opinion is to be obtained by written

- ports and airports where customs controls and formalities are applied to the cabin and hold baggage of persons taking certain flights, or using certain maritime services or on board pleasure craft and tourist or business aircraft, and cabin and hold baggage (Article 50(2);

- rules on currency conversions for determining the customs value in relation to import and export duty, including value thresholds in the Common Customs Tariff (Article 54);

- uniform management of tariff quotas and tariff ceilings, and the management and surveillance of the release of goods for free circulation or export (Article 58);[29]

- the origin of specific goods (Article 68);[30]

- matters relating to the determination of customs value (Article 76);

- measures temporarily prohibiting recourse to comprehensive guarantees in the context of special procedures or temporary storage (Article 100(2));[31] and

- mutual assistance between the customs authorities in case of incurrence of a customs debt (Article 107);

- specification of rules relating to entry summary declaration (Article 132);

- conditions for approving designated or approved places for the presentation of goods to customs (Article 143);

- verification of the customs declaration, examination and sampling of goods, and the results of the verification (Article 193);

- Union transit (Article 236);

- the time-limit within which risk analysis is carried out primarily for security and safety purposes prior to the exit of goods from the customs territory of the Union (Article 266);

- adoption of the work programme on the development and deployment of electronic systems (Article 281);[32] and

procedure the procedure can be terminated without result only when, within the time limit for the delivery of the opinion, the chair of the committee so decides: see Art 285(6) UCC.

[29] Measures to determine the tariff classification of goods may also be adopted on imperative grounds of urgency to rapidly ensure the correct and uniform application of the Combined Nomenclature; the procedures outlined in fn 28 above apply: see Art 58(2).

[30] Measures to determine the correct and uniform application of rules of origin may also be adopted on imperative grounds of urgency; the procedures outlined in n 28 above apply: Art 68 2nd and 3rd paras.

[31] Measures justified the need to rapidly enhance the protection of the financial interests of the Union and of its Member States may be adopted immediately in accordance with the procedures outlined in fn 28 above: Art 100(2) UCC.

[32] European Parliament and Council Regulation 182/2011 [2011] OJ 55/13 on control of the exercise by the Commission of implementing powers. See generally C F Bergström and D Ritleng (eds), *Rulemaking by the European Commission: The New System for Delegation of Powers* (OUP 2016). If the Customs Code Committee delivers no opinion, then the proposed work programme is not to be adopted, although the Commission may within two months submit an amended proposal or within one month submit the original draft to the appeal committee (Art 281 UCC).

- authorization to one or more Member States to test for a limited period of time simplifications in the application of customs legislation, especially when IT-related (Articles 282 and 283).

By way of contrast, the *advisory* procedure (Article 285(2)) is used (rarely), specifically for Commission decisions

- requesting Member States to revoke BTI or BOI decisions (relating to tariff classification and origin of goods respectively) and decisions relating to binding information with regard to other factors, on the basis of which import/export duty and other measures in respect of trade in goods are applied (Article 37(2));[33] and

- involving questions of such repayment or remission as a result of error by the competent authorities, or in the interests of equity, under Article 116(3) (Article 123).[34]

The examination procedure is thus typically made applicable for implementing measures of a general kind, whereas the advisory procedure (rare as it is) applies essentially to implementing (single) decisions of the Commission.

C Sources of Administrative Law in the Customs Field

While the UCC is presently the fundamental source of the Commission's administrative tasks, the regulatory substance is dealt with either in the UCC-DA or in the UCC-IA (according to whether the matters are delegated powers or implementing powers, as set out above). Relatively few of those provisions actually involve the Commission itself taking measures which are likely to be challenged by traders, although there have been some interesting attempts, but with a very low success rate. These are discussed below, particularly in section H.

The instruments governing administrative cooperation concerning the Member States are Regulation 515/97,[35] which deals with mutual assistance between the administrative authorities of the Member States in customs and agricultural matters, and Council Directive 2010/24,[36] on mutual assistance for the recovery of claims relating to taxes, duties, and other measures.

---

[33] When the opinion of the Customs Code Committee is obtained by written procedure in respect of these latter decisions, the procedure can be terminated without result only when, within the time limit for the delivery of the opinion, the chair of the committee so decides in accordance with Art 285(6) UCC (Art 37(2)).

[34] If the Committee's opinion is to be obtained by written procedure the procedure can be terminated without result only when, within the time limit for the delivery of the opinion, the chair of the committee so decides: Arts 123(2) and 285(6) UCC.

[35] Council Regulation 515/97 [1997] OJ 82/1, as corrected by [1998] OJ L288/55 and most recently amended by European Parliament and Council Regulation 2015/1525 [2015] OJ L243/1. See Limbach (n 8) 181–85.

[36] [2010] OJ L84/1; see also Commission Implementing Regulation 1189/2011 [2011] OJ L302/16.

D Underlying Sector-specific Legal Principles for Customs Administration

The legal principles underlying the customs union within the European Union are essentially expressed rather as principles related to economic policy or goals. Under Article 31 TFEU the Commission, in carrying out its tasks under Articles 30–32 TFEU (essentially when presenting a proposal to the Council relating to the Common Customs Tariff), is to be guided in particular by the specifications in Article 32:

   (a) the need to promote trade between Member States and third countries;

   (b) developments in conditions of competition within the Union insofar as they lead to an improvement in the competitive capacity of undertakings;

   (c) the requirements of the Union as regards the supply of raw materials and semi-finished goods; in this connection the Commission must take care to avoid distortions of competition between Member States in respect of finished goods;

   (d) the need to avoid serious disturbances the economies of Member States and to ensure rational development of production and an expansion of consumption within the Union.[37]

The Court has observed that the Commission does not always have to take account of all the above criteria, as some may not be relevant for the particular act concerned. The criteria act as a guide for the Commission, which must have regard to the system and fundamental rules of the (now) internal market. The criteria specified 'relate to different objectives which may conflict with one another or not be applicable at the same time, so that the complaint that the Commission has not considered all of them is only valid if they were all relevant to the case'.[38] As essentially economic-policy criteria, these principles confer wide discretion on the Commission and the Council. Any review of their assessment is confined to examining whether the appropriate procedural rules and reasoning requirements have been complied with, whether the facts have been accurately stated in the act concerned, and whether there has been a manifest error of appraisal, or a misuse of powers.[39]

---

[37] Art 32 TFEU is identical to the old Art 29 EEC. The principles and legal provisions on the basis of which national tariffs were replaced by the Common Customs Tariff were set out in Arts 18–29 EEC; the rules on the elimination of customs duties and charges having equivalent effect were set out in Arts 12–17 EEC.

[38] Case 34/62 *Germany v Commission* [1963] ECR 131, 144, ECLI:EU:C:1963:18. See also Case 24/62 *Germany v Commission* [1963] ECR 63, ECLI:EU:C:1963:14. Art 32 TFEU is addressed only to the Commission, although it must clearly influence the conduct of the Council insofar as the Council acts on proposals from the Commission. The Commission has a broad discretion to define the subject-matter of tariff headings, but it is not authorized to alter the subject matter of the tariff headings which have been defined on the basis of the Harmonised System; Case C-267/94 *France v Commission* [1995] ECR I-4845, paras 19–20; Case C-309/98 *Holz Geenen GmbH v Oberfinanzdirektion München* [2000] ECR I-1975, para 13, ECLI:EU:C:2000:165.

[39] See eg Case 255/84 *Nachi Fujikoshi v Council* [1987] ECR 1861, para 21, ECLI:EU:C:1987:203; Case C-156/87 *Gestetner Holdings v Council and Commission* [1990] ECR I-781, para 63, ECLI:EU:C:1990:116; Case T-170/94 *Shanghai Bicycle Corporation (Group) v Council* [1997] ECR II-1383, paras 63–64, ECLI:EU:T:1997:134; Case T-164/94 *Ferchimex v Council* [1995] ECR II-2681, paras 66–67,

Article 33 TFEU authorizes the European Parliament and the Council, using the ordinary legislative procedure, to take measures to strengthen customs cooperation between Member States themselves, and between them and the Commission. The placing of this provision in Title II (Free Movement of Goods) of Part Three of the TFEU (Union Policies and Internal Actions) emphasizes that measures taken under this provision relate to customs measures per se. This was even more apparent in the wording of the second sentence of its predecessor provision, Article 135 EC (added by the Treaty of Amsterdam). That measure provided that the 'measures shall not concern the application of national criminal law or the national administration of justice'.[40] Trstenjak A-G opined in *Fazenda Pública*[41] that the separation, in principle, between customs and the criminal justice system, as provided for in Community law, constituted an indication that—essentially administrative—considerations of customs authorities concerning the criminal nature of an act could not substitute for judicial determination.

To a large extent, the legal principles affecting EU customs legislation are essentially general principles of Union law. Given that many of the Commission's tasks involve cooperation by, and with, the Member States, the principle of sincere cooperation (now Article 4(3) TEU), is one that is central to the functioning of the system of EU customs law, although it is certainly not sector-specific.[42] A particular aspect of sincere cooperation concerns administrative cooperation. While this too is hardly sector-specific, it is a particular example of how the effectiveness of EU customs law and implementation is reliant on various actors, mainly national customs administrations, but also their equivalents in third countries. The possibilities of controlling and coordinating these administrations vary considerably. Administrative cooperation is specifically required under Articles 55(2)(c)(ii) and 55(5)(b)(ii) UCC-DA as a condition for regional cumulation of stocks and materials within the same group of countries under the Generalised System of Preferences (GSP). This can also be observed in provisions of the UCC-IA on:

- special non-preferential import arrangements (Article 58);
- checking the accuracy of information contained in suppliers' declarations (Article 65);
- obligations on GSP beneficiary countries within the framework of the REX system (Articles 70, 72, and 84);
- exports from those countries using certificate of origin Form A and invoice declarations (Article 71);
- on invoice declarations (Article 75);

ECLI:EU:T:1995:173. See further H G Schermers and D Waelbroeck, *Judicial Protection in the European Union* (6th edn, Kluwer 2001) 399–400.

[40] Limbach (n 8) 175–76 observes that there are considerable difficulties, not only in 'vertical cooperation' between the Member States and the Commission, but also in 'horizontal cooperation' between the Member States.

[41] Case C-62/06 *Fazenda Pública—Director Geral das Alfândegas v ZF Zefeser—Importação e Exportação de Produtos Alimentares Lda* [2007] ECR I-11995 at para 46 of her Opinion, ECLI:EU:C:2007:264.

[42] See the sector-specific measures mentioned under section C above.

- control of origin in the context of a registered exporter system (Article 108(1));
- and origin verification in relation to preferential tariff arrangements (Article 124).

Principles also find their expression or basis in other specific legislative provisions, especially in the UCC, dealing, for example, with the communication of information, confidentiality and data protection.[43] All information acquired by the customs authorities in the course of performing their duty, which by its nature is confidential, or which is provided on a confidential basis, is covered by the obligation of professional secrecy.[44] Confidential information must normally[45] not be disclosed by the competent authorities without the express permission of the person or authority providing it.[46] It may, though, be disclosed without permission where the customs authorities are obliged or authorized to do so pursuant to the provisions in force, particularly in respect of data protection, or in connection with legal proceedings.[47] Confidential information may be communicated to the customs authorities, and to competent authorities of countries or territories outside the customs territory of the Union for the purpose of customs cooperation with the latter countries or territories, within the framework of an international agreement or of Union legislation in the area of the common commercial policy.[48] Any disclosure of such information must ensure an adequate level of data protection in full compliance with the data protection provisions in force.[49] Where, in respect of the same goods, controls in addition to customs controls are to be performed by competent authorities other than the customs authorities, the latter must, in close cooperation with the former, endeavour to ensure that such controls are, wherever possible, carried out at the same time and place as customs controls (one-stop-shop). In achieving this, customs authorities have the coordinating role.[50]

The principles of legal certainty and the protection of legitimate expectations, again general principles, rather than sector-specific principles, have also been applied by the Court in the customs field. For example, implementing measures could not be applied to transactions which took place before they entered into force, in the absence of evidence from the minutes of the Customs Code Committee that a different policy had been envisaged.[51] However,

---

[43] Art 12 UCC. See also Art 339 TFEU on the general obligation of professional secrecy imposed on members of the institutions of the Union, members of committees, and the officials and other servants of the Union.

[44] Art 12(1) 1st sub-para UCC.

[45] Except as provided by Art 47(2) UCC, which permits customs and other competent authorities in the framework of certain controls of goods, where necessary for the purpose of minimizing risk and combating fraud, to exchange with each other and with the Commission data received in the context of the entry, exit, transit, movement, storage and end-use of goods, including postal traffic, with between the customs territory of the Union and countries or territories outside the customs territory of the Union, the presence and movement within the customs territory of the Union of non-Union goods and goods placed under the end-use procedure, and the results of any control; customs authorities and the Commission may also exchange data with each other for the purpose of ensuring uniform application of the customs legislation.

[46] Art 12(1) 1st sub-para UCC.   [47] Art 12(1) 2nd sub-para UCC.   [48] Art 12(2) UCC.

[49] Art 12(3) UCC.   [50] Art 47(1) UCC. As to Art 47(2) UCC, see n 39 above.

[51] Case C-256/07 *Mitsui & Co Deutschland v Hauptzollamt Düsseldorf* [2009] ECR I-1951, paras 31–37, ECLI:EU:C:2009:167, and case law cited there.

the principle of legitimate expectations cannot be relied upon against an unambiguous provision of European Union law, nor can the conduct of a national authority responsible for applying European Union law, which acts in breach of that law, give rise to a legitimate expectation on the part of a trader of beneficial treatment contrary to European Union law.[52]

The rights of the defence—in particular the right to be heard—are well established in EU law,[53] but they are now given particular prominence in EU customs legislation.[54] However, the obligation to inform and communicate objections to an applicant in writing arises only when the Commission has reached a preliminary view unfavourable to the applicant. This does not amount to an obligation to keep the latter continuously informed of the progress of the procedure.[55]

The principle of fairness is also referred to by the Court of Justice in relation to the customs union,[56] separately from matters such as a right to a fair hearing and other general elements of rights of the defence. In *Riscomos BV v Commission* the then Court of First Instance observed that this principle 'is intended fully to guarantee the adversarial nature of the procedure for the remission or repayment of import and export duties by further securing observance of the rights of the defence'.[57] Moreover, it stated that 'the applicant for remission or repayment must be able to have access to all the non-confidential documents on file including those which have not been used as the basis for the Commission's objections.'[58] Thus,

---

[52] Case C-153/10 *Staatssecretaris van Financiën v Sony Supply Chain Solutions (Europe) BV* [2011] ECR I-2775, para 47, ECLI:EU:C:2011:224, and case law cited there; Case C-568/11 *Agroferm A/S v Ministeriet for Fødevarer, Landbrug og Fiskeri* ECLI:EU:C:2013:407, para 52.

[53] 'The principle of respect for the rights of the defence requires that any person who may be adversely affected by a decision be placed in a position in which he may effectively make his views known, at least as regards the evidence on which the Commission has based its decision (see, to that effect, Case C-135/92 *Fiskano v Commission* [1994] ECR I-2885, paragraph 40, [ECLI:EU:C:1994:267] and Case C-32/95 P *Commission v Lisrestal and Others* [1996] ECR I-5373, paragraph 21) [ECLI:EU:C:1996:402]', Case T-205/99 *Hyper Srl v Commission* [2002] ECR I-3141, para 50, ECLI:EU:T:2002:189. See also eg Case C-349/07 *Sopropé — Organizações de Calçado Lda v Fazenda Pública* [2008] ECR I-10369, para 36, ECLI:EU:C:2008:746.

[54] See Art 22(6) UCC, Arts 8, 9 UCC-IA. See also, under predecessor legislation, eg Case T-53/02 *Riscomos BV v Commission* [2005] ECR II-3173, paras 62–63, ECLI:EU:T:2005:311, affirmed on appeal, Case C-420/05 *Riscomos BV v Commission* [2007] ECR I-67*, ECLI:EU:C:2007:284; Case C-349/07 *Sopropé:Organizações de Calçado Lda v Fazenda Pública* [2008] ECR I-10369, paras 37–38, ECLI:EU:C:2008:746, and case law cited there, and Joined Cases C-29/13 and C-30/13 *Global Trans Lodzhistik OOD v Nachalnik na Mitnitsa Stolichna* ECLI:EU:C:2014:140.

[55] Case T-53/02 *Riscomos BV v Commission* (n 54) paras 62–63.

[56] See eg Case C-86/97 *Woltmann, trading as 'Trans-Ex-Import' v Hauptzollamt Potsdam* [1999] ECR I-1043, para 21, ECLI:EU:C:1999:95; Case C-61/98 *De Haan Beheer BV v Inspecteur der Invoerrechten en Accijnzen te Rotterdam* [1999] ECR I-5003, paras 52–53, ECLI:EU:C:1999:393; Case T-282/01 *Aslantras v Commission* [2004] ECR II-693, paras 52–56, ECLI:EU:T:2004:42; Case C-253/99 *Bacardi GmbH v Hauptzollamt Bremerhaven* [2001] ECR I-6493, para 56, ECLI:EU:C:2001:490; Case T-53/02 *Riscomos BV v Commission* (n 54) para 73. However, as the theft of high-risk goods is one of the most frequently reported incidents, and traders are normally insured against such losses, a plea of fairness to obtain repayment or remission of duty is likely to fall on deaf ears; see Case T-282/01 *Aslantras v Commission* [2004] ECR II-693, para 65, ECLI:EU:T:2004:42. As to the effect of national procedural rules and the effects of non-observance of the rights of the defence see Joined Cases C-129/13 and C-130/13 *Kamino International Logistics BV and Others v Staatssecretaris van Financiën* ECLI:EU:C:2014:2041 and Joined Cases C-29/13 and C-30/13 *Global Trans Lodzhistik OOD v Nachalnik na Mitnitsa Stolichna* ECLI:EU:C:2014:140.

[57] Case T-53/02 *Riscomos BV v Commission* (n 54) para 73.

[58] ibid para 72, and case law cited there.

the Commission must, at the time when it communicates its objections, give the applicant an opportunity to examine all the documents likely to be relevant in support of the request for remission or repayment; in order to do so the Commission must at the very least provide the applicant with a complete list of the non-confidential documents on file containing sufficiently precise information for the applicant to assess, in full knowledge of the facts, whether the documents described are likely to be useful to it.[59]

Articles 116(1)(d) and 120 UCC specifically recognize equity as a ground for the repayment or remission of duty, thus giving further expression to the principle of fairness in this field.

E Sectoral Organization, Institutions and Structures in the Customs Sector

Given that the operation of EU customs law lies essentially in the hands of the Member States, with the Commission having more of a 'back-office' function (despite the extensive competences of the Commission in regard to delegated and implementing acts discussed above), the role of the Customs Code Committee in the functioning of Union customs law is considerable. Even though the opinions of this body 'do not have legally binding force, they constitute an important means of ensuring the uniform application of the Customs Code by the customs authorities of the Member States and as such may be considered as a valid aid to the interpretation of the Code'.[60] The national customs authorities do not have to follow the Committee's conclusions automatically, and are entitled to disregard them, provided they give reasons for doing so.[61] The

---

[59] ibid para 74.

[60] See eg Case C-11/05 *Friesland Coberco Dairy Foods BV v Inspecteur van der Belastingdienst/Douane Noord/kantoor Groningen* [2006] ECR I-4285, para 51, ECLI:EU:C:2006:312, and case law cited there: 'The Court even added that, where appropriate, it may be necessary to consider whether the content of such opinions is in accordance with the actual provisions of the Common Customs Tariff and whether they alter the meaning of such provisions', Case C-165/07 *Skatteministeriet v Ecco Sko A/S* [2008] I-4037, para 47, ECLI:EU:C:2008:302 and case law cited there. The same approach is taken to Explanatory Notes drawn up by the World Customs Organization (WCO), eg Case 2/13 *Directeur général des douanes et droits indirects v Humeau Beaupréau* ECLI:EU:C:2014:48, paras 32, 39. As to the Nature and Legal Value of Guidelines, see the Customs Code Committee Document TAXUD/1406/2006:

> An administrative arrangement on the management of tariff quotas adopted by the Customs Current Committee cannot derogate from rules established in what is now CC-IP, Art 49(3) on the acceptance of a declaration for release for free circulation in the first days of the New Year, Case C-494/09 *Bolton Alimentari SpA v Ufficio delle Dogane d' Alessandria* [2011] ECR I-1647, para. 33, ECLI:EU:C:2011:87; while the Commission, assisted by Customs Code Committee, may adopt measures with regard to the application of the Combined Nomenclature (which is based on the WCO's Harmonized System), and for that purpose has a broad discretion to define the subject-matter of tariff headings, it is not authorised to alter the subject-matter of tariff headings which have been defined on the basis of that Harmonized System, Case C-273/09 *Premis Medical BV v Inspecteur van de Belastingdienst / Douane Rotterdam, kantoor Laan op Zuid* [2010] ECR I-13783, paras 39–40, ECLI:EU:C:2010:809, and case-law cited there. See also Case C-260/08 *Bundesfinanzdirektion West v HEKO Industrieerzeugnisse GmbH* [2009] ECR I-11571, paras. 20–23, ECLI:EU:C:2009:768, and case-law cited there.

[61] Case C-11/05 *Friesland Coberco Dairy Foods BV v Inspecteur van der Belastingdienst/Douane Noord/kantoor Groningen* [2006] ECR I-4285, paras 26–33, ECLI:EU:C:2006:312.

Court of Justice will not, in the course of a reference for a preliminary ruling under (now) Article 267 TFEU, review the validity of a conclusion of the Committee.[62]

The Customs Code Committee is established by Article 285 UCC; its functions in relation to the adoption of implementing acts by the Commission has been discussed in section B, above. This Committee comprises sections dealing with General Customs Legislation; Tariff and Statistical Nomenclature; Duty Relief; Origin; Customs Value; Customs Debt and Guarantees; Import and Export Formalities; Data Integration and Harmonisation; Customs Status and Transit; Special Procedures; Customs Controls and Risk Management, and the Enforcement of Intellectual Property rights.[63] These sections may have joint meetings with other sections, or with other relevant committees (such as the Excise Duty).

The determinations of the Committee are shrouded in confidentiality. Neither the summary record, the approved minutes of the meetings, or the voting sheets of the Committee record the position adopted by particular Member State representatives. References are merely to 'a Member State' or sometimes 'Member State Six' and 'Member State Seven' and so on.[64] This confidentiality (required under Article 14(2) of the Committee's Rules of Procedure) may be supposed to enable free and frank discussions, but it is hardly a model of transparency.[65] Attempts to obtain access to the Committee's documents has given rise to some hard-fought litigation. Attempts by the Commission to argue that the Committee's documents are not documents of the Commission itself for the purposes of public access have not been successful. The Committee has been held to have no separate identity as 'another Community institution or body' for the purposes of authorship relating to access to documents requests;[66] papers of informal working groups established by the Committee likewise do not escape such requests.[67]

A Customs Expert Group has also been established.[68] This is not a regulatory committee[69] and is in functional terms a distinct entity from the Customs Code Committee.[70] The Expert Group comprises sub-groups dealing with: General Customs Legislation; Data Integration and Harmonisation—EU Customs Data Model; Authorised Economic Operators; Customs Control and Risk Management; Tariff and Statistical Nomenclature; Tariff Measures; Duty Relief; Origin; Customs Valuation; Customs Debt and Guarantees; Import and Export Formalities; Custom Status and

---

[62] ibid paras 36–41.

[63] Rules of Procedure for the Customs Code Committee, TAXUD/A2/2013/034 (Ares (2015) 812628–25 February 2015) Art 1. There may also be sub-sections, as eg the section on Tariff and Statistical Nomenclature has a sub-section on Agriculture/Chemistry.

[64] ibid Art 11(2) last sentence.

[65] Access to documents is provided for under the normal scheme of Regulation 1049/2001 [2001] OJ L145/43 through Art 14 of the Rules of Procedure of the Customs Code Committee (n 50). Arguments about full and frank discussions were advanced and rejected in inter alia Case T-144/05 *Muniz v Commission* [2008] ECR II-335*, paras 86–94, ECLI:EU:T:2008:596.

[66] Case T-188/97 *Rothmans International BV v Commission* [1999] ECR II-2463, ECLI:EU:T:1999:156.

[67] Case T-144/05 *Muniz v Commission* (n 65).

[68] As to its Rules of Procedure, see Ares (2016) 2616740 (6 June 2016).

[69] Joined Cases T-134/03 and C-135/03 *Common Market Fertilisers SA v Commission* [2005] ECR I-3923, para 78, ECLI:EU:T:2005:339, upheld on appeal in Case C-455/05 *Common Market Fertilisers SA v Commission* [2007] ECR I-2709, para 104, ECLI:EU:C:2007:511.

[70] Joined Cases T-134/03 and C-135/03 (n 69) para 59; and Case C-455/05 (n 69) para 100.

Transit; TIR Convention and other UNECE customs Conventions; Special Procedures other than transit; Enforcement of Intellectual Property Rights, and International Customs Matters. The Expert Group has various advisory, assistance, and preparatory functions, as the Customs Code Committee itself can only discuss, finalize, and give an opinion on draft implementing acts. The Expert Group thus ensures continuity of the advisory tasks previously undertaken by the Customs Code Committee.[71]

While not involved in implementing legislation, the Council has two working parties which are of interest. The 'Working Party on Customs Union' deals with customs legislation, in particular with Commission proposals for new legislative acts; it is also the obvious vehicle for advising the Council on whether or not to object to a delegated act or revoke a delegation (discussed in section B1). Moreover, it coordinates relations in customs matters with third countries, represents the EU's common position in the World Customs Organization, and is particularly involved with four further matters: the action plan for customs risk management; the legal framework for customs infringements and sanctions; cooperation between customs authorities in the Member States; and cooperation with customs authorities in key third countries. The Council's 'Customs Cooperation Working Party' is a separate group, dealing with operational cooperation between national customs administrations, aimed at increasing their enforcement capabilities. As well, it defines strategic and tactical objectives for joint customs operations, focusing on seizures, identification of new threats, and the disruption of criminal gangs.

F Administrative Procedures in the Customs Sector

Given that the enforcement of EU customs law is in the hands of the Member State customs authorities, administrative procedures in the application of such measures are those specifically provided for in the UCC, UCC-DA, or the UCC-IA (and also the transitional arrangements set out in the UCC-TDA).

A number of provisions stand out as being of particular importance from the point of view of the rights of the defence. In relation to decisions taken on an individual application, Article 22(6) UCC, in conjunction with Article 8 UCC-DA, requires the customs authorities, before taking a decision adversely to the applicant, to communicate the grounds of the intended decision. The applicant must be given the opportunity to express their point of view within 30 days from the date on which they receive that communication or are deemed to have received it.[72] On the expiry of that period, the applicant must be notified, in the appropriate form, of the decision. Where the decision relates to the outcome of the control of goods, for which no summary-declaration, temporary-storage declaration, re-export declaration, or customs declaration has been lodged, the customs authorities may require the person concerned to comment within 24 hours. There are, however, some exceptions to the right to be

---

[71] See the Terms of Reference of the Expert Group, Ares (2016) 2109.
[72] As to the time limits within the customs authorities must react see Art 22(2) and (3) UCC and Art 13 UCC-DA.

heard.[73] Several of the above provisions apply also to decisions taken by the customs authorities without there having been any prior application by the parties concerned, except where the customs authority acts as a judicial authority.[74] Special procedures apply to BTI and BOI applications.[75]

G Legal Rules Governing the Substance of Decision-making in the Customs Field

Decision-making in the customs field is at the meta level usually in the form of a regulation, as the Union Customs Code and other measures show.[76] The procedure for the adoption of delegated powers is set out in Article 284 UCC and that relating to implementing powers in Article 285 UCC. The areas in which such powers may be exercised by the Commission have been examined under heading B, above.

Individual decision-making is primarily in the hands of the national customs authorities. Some decisions are implicit: if at an airport an arriving traveller passes through the 'Nothing to Declare' channel or through the channel for 'Passengers arriving from EU countries', he or she thereby makes a customs declaration, which is (tacitly) accepted, unless during a spot check a breach of customs law is ascertained. Applications for individual decisions (such as BTI or BOI decisions) must be accepted by the customs authorities where the prescribed conditions are satisfied.[77] To that extent they are not discretionary, but if the customs authorities take the view that further information is necessary, they are entitled to require it. If they take the view that the conditions are not satisfied, they may, of course, take a decision refusing the application. Such a refusal, as a national measure, would be open to challenge in the national courts.

An individual decision which adversely affects an applicant must set out the grounds on which it is based, and must refer to the right of appeal provided for in Article 44.[78] The time limit for taking a decision may be extended under certain circumstances.[79]

---

[73] See Art 22(6) 2nd sub-para UCC and Art 10 UCC-DA. These are: (a) in relation to Binding Tariff Information (BTI) decisions or Binding Origin Information (BTO) decisions under Art 33 UCC; (b) in the event of refusal is a benefit would have quota with specified tag quota volume is reached (Art 56(4) 1st sub-para UCC); (c) where nature or the level of a threat to the security and safety of the Union and its residents, to human, animal or plant health, to the environment or to consumers so requires; (d) where the decision aims at securing the implementation of another decision for which Art 66(1) first sub-para UCC has been applied, without prejudice to the law of the Member State concerned; (e) where it would prejudice investigations initiated for the purpose of combating fraud; (e) in other specific cases, Art 22(6) 2nd sub-para UCC. The other specific cases are: (a) where the application for a decision does not fulfil the conditions laid down in Art 11; (b) where the customs authorities notify the person who lodged the entry summary declaration that the goods are not to be loaded in the case of containerized maritime traffic and of air traffic; (c) where the decision concerns a notification to the applicant of a Commission decision as referred to in Art 116(3) UCC; (d) where an EORI number is to be invalidated, Art 10(a)–(f) UCC-DA. An EORI number means an Economic Operators Registration and Identification number: Art 1(18) UCC-DA. As to important requirements relating to communication of information to an applicant under general and specific procedures, see further Arts 8 and 9 UCC-IA. As to the use of electronic procedures for applications for customs decisions or authorizations see https://ec.europa.eu/taxation_customs/business/customs-procedures/customs-decisions_en (last accessed 8 April 2018).

[74] See eg Arts 22(4)–(7), 23(3), and 26–28 UCC.　　　[75] Art 33 UCC and Arts 19–22 UCC-DA.

[76] But they may take the form of a Commission Implementing Decision (see eg n 9).

[77] Art 22 UCC, Art 13 UCC-DA.　　　[78] Art 22(7) UCC.

[79] Art 22(6) UCC and Art 23 UCC-DA.

Except where the effect of a decision is limited to one or several Member States, decisions relating to the application of the customs legislation are valid throughout the customs territory of the Union.[80] Decisions may be reassessed or suspended, and suspensions lifted under certain conditions.[81] Favourable decisions may be annulled, revoked, or amended.[82]

A Customs Decisions System has been introduced, designed by the Commission and the Member States, and contains central and national components; its use has been compulsory since 2 October 2017.[83] The Central Decisions System is accessed via the EU Trader Portal and must be used for all applications and decisions that may have an impact in more than one Member State, as well as for any later event which might affect the original application or decision (amendment, suspension, revocation, or annulment). Belgium, Bulgaria, Cyprus, Denmark, Estonia, Hungary, Ireland, Italy, Latvia, Lithuania, Luxembourg, Malta, the Netherlands, Portugal, Romania, Slovenia, and Sweden require use of the EU Trader Portal for both multi-Member State decisions and single-Member State decisions.[84] At present, Austria, Croatia, the Czech Republic, Finland, France, Germany, Greece, Poland, Slovakia, and the United Kingdom require the use of the EU Trader Portal for multi-Member State decisions and the national trader portal for single-Member State decisions. Spain has a hybrid approach, whereby for multi-Member State decisions either the EU Trader Portal or the national trader portal may be used, but for single-Member State decisions only the national trader portal can be used.

H Abstract-general Administrative Acts and Measures within the Customs Sector

The main abstract-general administrative acts adopted are the UCC-DA, the UCC-IA, and the UCCTDA. In relation to administrative cooperation, Regulation 517/97 and Directive 2010/24 deal with mutual assistance between the Member States authorities, as observed under section D, above. The Council and the Commission also adopt measures relating to the Common Customs Tariff.[85]

---

[80] Art 26 UCC.

[81] Art 23(4) UCC and Arts 15–18 UCC-DA. In specific cases, the customs authorities shall, upon application, take decisions relating to binding information with regard to other factors referred to in Title II of the UCC (ie Arts 56–76 UCC), on the basis of which import export duty and other measures in respect of trade single are applied, Art 35 UCC. The rules on reassessment and suspension do not apply to binding information decisions: Art 22 UCC-DA.

[82] Arts 27–28 UCC.

[83] See https://ec.europa.eu/taxation_customs/business/customs-procedures/customs-decisions_en (last accessed 7 July 2018), which explains the system and gives useful further links. The date was fixed in the Work Programme under Commission Implementing Decision 2106/578 (n 9).

[84] Multi-Member State decisions will be coded: 1 where the application or authorization is to be valid in all Member States; 2 where the application or authorization is limited to certain Member States, and 3 where the application or authorization is limited to one Member State.

[85] The basis of which is set out in Council Regulation 2658/87 [1987] OJ L256/1 (most recently amended by European Parliament and Council Regulation 952/2013 [2013] OJ L269/1. The actual tariff is set out in the Annex to Regulation 2658/87, replaced annually in October each year, published as a stand-alone regulation, see (for 2018) Commission Implementing Regulation 2017/1925 [2017] OJ L282/1. The Taric, which integrates all measures concerning the Common Customs Tariff (the Combined Nomenclature and the tariffs applicable), commercial and agricultural legislation

Abstract-general acts, which may also have features of single-case administrative measures, not infrequently involve action on the centralized Union level in relation to problems concerning Binding Tariff Information (BTI) or Binding Origin Information (BOI). The Commission's determinations, after discussion in the Customs Code Committee, are, however, regarded as acts of general application.[86] Decisions on such information are in fact normally taken by the national customs authorities.[87] The Commission, however, may adopt decisions suspending BTI or BOI decisions,[88] or requesting Member States to revoke BTI or BOI decisions, in order to ensure a correct and uniform tariff classification or determination of the origin of goods.[89] Intervention is likely when it becomes clear that different national customs authorities are issuing divergent interpretations, or where the Commission simply is of the view that binding information issued is incorrect.

As noted in section B (above), the Commission is empowered under Articles 57(4) and 58(2) UCC to adopt implementing acts to determine the tariff classification of goods, and under Articles 67 and 68 UCC to adopt measures to determine the origin of specific goods. In both cases the examination procedure applies.[90] However, on imperative grounds of urgency relating to such measures, duly justified by the need rapidly to ensure correct and uniform application of the Combined Nomenclature, or of rules of origin, the Commission is to adopt applicable implementing acts immediately.[91] In regard to challenges to such measures, see section K (on supervision) below.

In commercial policy matters, in pursuance of powers granted by the Council,[92] the Commission may adopt implementing regulations (such as individual anti-dumping or anti-subsidy measures) having an effect on the actions of Member State customs authorities. The latter are, in effect, instructed by such the implementing regulation concerned to collect anti-dumping or anti-subsidy duties, as the case may be. Although such rules concern specific goods, they are generally applicable measures which may be of direct and individual concern to the various actors affected by them (such as exporters and allied importers), allowing direct challenge before Union courts under Article 263 TFEU. Other parties affected (such as independent importers) will have to have recourse only to indirect challenge through the national courts, in the hope ultimately of obtaining a reference for a preliminary ruling under Article 267 TFEU (see further in section J, below).

---

nowadays takes the form of a database; it may be consulted at http://ec.europa.eu/taxation_customs/dds2/taric/taric_consultation.jsp (last accessed 7 July 2018). The legal basis for the Taric is established in Regulation 2658/87, above.

[86] See eg Case 40/84 *Casteels PVBA v Commission* [1985] ECR 667, paras 11–12, ECLI:EU:C:1985:77.
[87] See Art 33(1) UCC; see further, Arts 33(2)–35 UCC and Arts 16–23 UCC-IA.
[88] See Art 34(10) UCC and UUC-IA Art 23.
[89] See Arts 34(11) and 37(2) UCC. Other implementing powers are conferred by Art 37(1) UCC, see Arts 16–23 UCC-IA.
[90] ie the procedure referred to in Art 285(4) UCC, see section B, above.
[91] ie the procedure referred to in Art 285(5) UCC, see section B, above.
[92] See European Parliament and Council Regulations 2016/1036 [2016] OJ L176/ (anti-dumping); 2016/1037 [2016] L176/55 (anti-subsidies). Both of these regulations have been amended by European Parliament and Council Regulations 2017/2321 [2017] OJ L338/1 and 2018/825 [2018] OJ L143/1.

There are no 'soft law' measures in this sector; the Commission does provide information (closely referring to the relevant legislative, delegated, and implementing provisions) on its website, and manages various electronic platforms (such as the TARIC, EORI checking, and the EU Trader Portal).

I Single-case Administrative Acts and Measures within the Customs Sector

Real single-case administrative acts in the customs sector are rare on the EU level. The Commission may, under Article 6(4) in conjunction with Article 8(2) UCC, adopt derogation decisions in exceptional cases, allowing one or several Member States to use means for the exchange and storage of information other than electronic data-processing techniques. Such Commission measures are (as noted in section B above), adopted in accordance with the advisory procedure.[93] The same procedure is used when the Commission adopts implementing acts under Article 34(11) in conjunction with Article 37(2)(a) UCC, requesting Member States to revoke BTI or BOI decisions, and when it adopts such acts under Article 35 in conjunction with Article 37(2)(b) UCC, relating to binding information with regard to the basis on which import or export duties and other measures are applied. The final set of single-case measures relates to decisions under Article 116(3) adopted as implementing acts by the Commission, in the advisory procedure, under Article 123(2) UCC relating to repayment and remission of customs duty. Administrative acts addressed to individuals are adopted on a daily basis by the customs authorities of the Member States, applying EU customs legislation,[94] some of which are best classified as measures of administrative enforcement under J below.

J Administrative Enforcement of EU Customs Law

Enforcement of EU customs law takes place day-to-day mainly via the customs authorities of the Member States. Each Member State must provide for penalties against such private parties for failure to comply with the customs legislation. Such penalties must be effective, proportionate and dissuasive.[95]

Where administrative penalties are applied, they may take inter alia either one or both of the following forms: (a) a pecuniary charge by the customs authorities including where appropriate, a settlement applied in place of and in lieu of a criminal penalty; (b) the revocation, suspension or amendment of any authorization held by the person concerned.[96] Further powers of customs authorities, for example, to seize goods, and even the vehicles in which goods are being transported (which has

---

[93] ie in accordance with Art 285(2) UCC, see section B, above.
[94] As to the definition of which, see Art 5(2) UCC.   [95] Art 42(1) UCC.
[96] Art 42(2) UCC. Member States must notify the Commission, within 180 days after 1 May 2016, of the national provisions in force, as envisaged in Art 42(1) UCC, and must notify it without delay of any subsequent amendment affecting those provisions, Art 42(3) UCC.

provoked considerable controversy),[97] or to enter premises, inspect documents and goods, audit economic operators or others, or otherwise investigate and act upon breaches of customs legislation, are regulated by national law. However, by virtue of the duty of loyal co-operation set out in Article 4(3) TEU, any action must not jeopardize the proper working of the EU Customs Code and any Union delegated or implementing measure taken thereunder.

The Commission's role, more in the background, is to monitor compliance and to rein in divergence in approaches, with a view to ensuring the uniform application of EU customs law.[98] The Commission will step into the foreground in particular when action is necessary to safeguard such uniform application. In appropriate cases, the Commission can commence infringement proceedings against a Member State under Article 258 TFEU,[99] but this should, strictly understood, be seen as Commission *supervision* (see section K below) over customs administration on the Member State level, as such proceedings are not ones against individual parties (such as exporters or importers).

K Supervision and Control of, and within, the Customs Sector

Administrative supervision of Member State customs authorities is effectively in the hands of the Commission. Such supervision is enhanced by numerous reporting obligations on the Member States, and by the development of electronic information exchange systems (e.g., for BTI and BOI). In particular, in respect of BTI and BOI decisions, the Commission may intervene, as noted under J above.[100] In respect of repayment or remission of duty, the Commission supervises ex post what the Member States have done, through the imposition of reporting obligations.[101] A further form of supervision is effected by the Court of Auditors through reports from time to time, perhaps most significantly where customs and VAT fraud is discovered.[102] National level supervision (apart from through appeals or judicial review) may be effected by

---

[97] At one time the Commission decided to commence infringement proceedings against the United Kingdom (Commission Press Release IP/04/1255, 20 October 2004) http://europa.eu/rapid/press-release_IP-04-1255_en.htm, but it appears that some form of settlement was reached, as the matter never reached the Court of Justice.

[98] See eg by suspending and calling in BTI or BOI decisions which are incorrect or not uniform, or in respect of which the customs authorities of the Member States concerned have been unable to resolve their differences, Art 34(10) UCC and Art 23 UCC-IA.

[99] See eg Case 60/13 *Commission v United Kingdom* ECLI:EU:C:2014:219; Case C-442/08 *Commission v Germany* [2010] ECR I-6457, ECLI:EU:C:2010:390; Case C-372/05 *Commission v Germany* [2009] ECR I-11801, ECLI:EU:C:2010:390. See generally L Prete, *Infringement Proceedings in EU Law* (Kluwer 2017); L W Gormley, 'Infringement Proceedings' in A Jakab and D Kochenov (eds), *The Enforcement of EU Law and Values* (OUP 2017); L Prete and B Smulders, 'The Coming of Age of Infringement Proceedings' (2010) 47 *Common Market Law Review* 9.

[100] See n 98.   [101] Art 121(4) UCC and Art 181 UCC-IA.

[102] See eg Special Report 13/2011 on customs procedures and prevention of VAT fraud: http://www.europarl.europa.eu/document/activities/cont/201201/20120104ATT34854/20120104ATT34854EN.pdf; Special Report 1/2010 on simplified customs procedures: http://www.eca.europa.eu/Lists/News/NEWS1006_07/NEWS1006_07_EN.PDF, both last accessed 7 July 2018.

national audit office investigations and reports, and even on occasion through reports by parliamentary committees. Supervision also occurs through recourse to the European Ombudsman in respect of maladministration on the EU level (in this case mostly by the Commission, or by any bodies operating under it). Similarly, recourse may be had to the relevant ombudsman at national level.

Any person has the right to appeal against a decision taken by the customs authorities relating to the application of the customs legislation which concerns him or her directly and individually.[103] Any person who has applied to the customs authorities for decision and has not obtained a decision on that application within the relevant time limits is also entitled to exercise a right of appeal.[104] The right of appeal may be exercised in at least two steps: (i) initially, before the customs authorities, or before a judicial or other authority designated for that purpose by the Member States; (ii) subsequently, before a higher independent body, which may be a judicial authority or equivalent body, according to the legal provisions in force in the Member States.[105] The idea is that at some stage an appellant must be able to bring his or her case before a court or tribunal capable of making a reference for a preliminary ruling to the Court of Justice under Article 267 TFEU.

Any appeal must be lodged in the Member State where the decision was taken or applied for,[106] and Member States must ensure that the appeals procedure enables prompt confirmation or correction of decisions taken by the customs authorities.[107] The submission of an appeal does not cause implementation of the disputed decision to be suspended.[108] The customs authorities must, however, suspend implementation of such a decision in whole or in part where they have good reason to believe that the disputed decision is inconsistent with the customs legislation or that irreparable damage is to be feared for the person concerned.[109] In either of these latter cases, where the disputed decision has the effect of causing import or export duty to be payable, suspension of the implementation of that decision must be conditional upon the provision of a guarantee. This requirement, though, will not apply if, on the basis of a documented assessment, it appears that such a guarantee would be likely to cause the debtor serious economic or social difficulty.[110]

Judicial supervision is obviously important in this sector, especially where administrative officials make decisions affecting individuals, including taking enforcement actions against them. Commission actions (including eventually supervisory actions against Member States) which affect individuals may be open to challenge before the Court of Justice by those who satisfy the standing requirements of Article 263 TFEU, or by those without *locus standi* before the Union courts but who challenge a national measure in Member State courts and can obtain a preliminary ruling from the ECJ through the Article 267 TFEU procedure.

---

[103] Art 44(1) 1st sub-para UCC. Arts 44 and 45 UCC do not apply to appeals lodged with a view to the annulment, revocation or amendment of a decision relating to the application of customs legislation taken by a judicial authority, or by the customs authorities acting as judicial authorities: Art 43 UCC.
[104] Art 44(1) 2nd sub-para UCC. As to the time limits, see n 72 above.   [105] Art 44(2) UCC.
[106] Art 44(3) UCC.   [107] Art 44(4) UCC.   [108] Art 45(1) UCC.   [109] Art 45(2) UCC.
[110] Art 45(3) UCC.

It is, however, notoriously difficult to succeed in challenging implementing measures of the Commission, as the judgment in *Casteels*[111] well demonstrates. The main obstacle has traditionally been to demonstrate standing, although there have been some rare cases in which issues of standing were not raised[112] or were resolved in favour of the appellant.[113] These cases confirm that a measure can be of general application yet of direct and individual concern to a particular appellant.[114] The relaxation of standing requirements in relation to regulatory acts not entailing implementing measures has not led to an improvement in the chances of challenging Commission action, as the actual determination of a tariff classification or origin in an individual case is seen as an implementing measure.[115] The notion of a distinction between implementing measures and measures of general application has passed the centralized Union judiciary by. The vast majority of judgments of the Court of Justice in challenges to tariff-classification or origin decisions, and even remission of duty, however, come by way of references for a preliminary ruling under Article 267 TFEU in the course of challenges to the individual decisions of customs authorities before the national courts.[116]

In the different Member States customs authorities' individual decisions can be challenged before the appropriate court or tribunal. In the United Kingdom, for example, appeal lies to the Finance and Tax Tribunal, and then on upwards,[117] or to the appropriate magistrates' court (for example against seizure of goods), with further appeals possible. Sometimes, cases acquire a certain degree of notoriety.[118]

---

[111] Case 40/84 *Casteels PVBA v Commission* [1985] ECR 667. See also eg the orders in Case T-120/98 *Alce Srl v Commission* [1999] ECR II-1395, ECLI:EU:T:1999:88 and Case T-49/00 *Industria pugliese olive in salamoia erbe aromatiche Snc (Iposea) v Commission* [2001] ECR II-163, ECLI:EU:T:2001:22.

[112] See eg Joined Cases T-133/98 and T-134/98 *Hewlett Packard France and Others v Commission* [2001] ECR II-613, ECLI:EU:T:2001:49 (the Commission did not raise the issue, as it felt that Hewlett Packard, which held a number of different BTIs in various Member States for the same product was obviously individually concerned by the revocation decision adopted by the Commission addressed to those Member States.

[113] See eg Case T-243/01 *Sony Computer Entertainment Europe Ltd v Commission* [2002] ECR I-4189, ECLI:EU:T:2003:251.

[114] See eg Case T-120/98 *Alce Srl v Commission* [1999] ECR II-1395, para 19, ECLI:EU:T:1999:88, and case law cited there; Case T-243/01 *Sony Computer Entertainment Europe Ltd v Commission* [2002] ECR I-4189, para 59, ECLI:EU:T:2003:251, and case law cited there. The Court found at para 62 that Sony was directly concerned, and at paras 62–77 that Sony was individually concerned.

[115] See eg Case T-35/11 *Kyocera Mita Europe BV v Commission* ECLI:EU:T:2014:795, affirmed on appeal, Case C-533/14 P *Kyocera Mita Europe BV v Commission* ECLI:EU:C:2015:805.

[116] However, appeals against Commission decisions refusing repayment of customs duty are not unknown, see eg Case T-346/94 *France Aviation v Commission* [1995] ECR II 2843, ECLI:EU:T:1995:187.

[117] A trawl through the relevant categories and sub-categories in the list of cases at http://financeandtax. decisions.tribunals.gov.uk//Aspx/default.aspx (last accessed 7 July 2018) produces a list of appeals brought since April 2003.

[118] Such matters may well end up at the Court of Justice; see eg Case 34/79 *R v Henn and Darby* [1979] ECR 3795, ECLI:EU:C:1979:295 (see also *R v Henn, R v Darby* [1980] 2 All ER 166, [1980] 2 CMLR 229, (HL)) on hard-core pornography; Case 121/85 *Conegate Ltd v HM Customs and Excise* [1986] ECR 1007, ECLI:EU:C:1986:114 on blow-up dolls and sexy vacuum flasks; Case 50/80 *Horvath v Hauptzollamt Hamburg-Jonas* [1981] ECR 385, ECLI:EU:C:1981:34; Case 240/81 *Einberger v Hauptzollamt Freiburg* [1982] ECR 3699, ECLI:EU:C:1982:364 (smuggled goods); and Case C-343/89 *Witzemann v Hauptzollamt München-Mitte* [1990] ECR I-4477, ECLI:EU:C:1990:445 (counterfeit banknotes).

L Conclusion

The administrative arrangements for the enforcement of European Union customs law have been greatly clarified and even simplified with the adoption of the Uniform Customs Code and the delegated and implementing acts flowing from it. Nevertheless, from the administrative law point of view, the possibilities for real challenges by traders to EU customs law are, at least on the centralized level, still somewhat limited and even unsatisfactory. Customs law is a highly technical area, in which a number of pressures are significant: the need to safeguard the unity of the Union customs area and policy; the duty to ensure the correct flow of revenue to the Union's coffers (customs duties are own resources); the need to ensure that customs administrations take account of the Union's international obligations in the customs field and in the allied fields of criminal law and international sanctions; and the need to combat customs and VAT fraud, which is more widespread than many would like to admit. The present discussion has concentrated on a number of aspects of the administrative law relating to the customs union, which give a flavour of the complex and yet considerable achievements which have been made. Law and implementation in this field still needs further development, and slippage in moves towards electronic customs administration may still leave major holes in the achievement of uniformity of customs administration throughout the Union. It is clear, however, that some considerable progress in e-customs procedures has already been made by the Commission and by many Member States.[119]

---

[119] See the Commission's Report, COM(2018) 39 final on the implementation of the UCC and on the exercise of the power to adopt delegated acts pursuant to Art 284 UCC.

6

Development Cooperation and Humanitarian Aid

Philipp Dann and Martin Wortmann

A Introduction

Development cooperation and humanitarian aid constitute central instruments of the European Union's foreign policy. They help shape the Union's relation with neighbouring countries, foster ties with traditional and new allies, and advance European interests in the world. They are also central for the Union's position and visibility in the world, as they inject European ideas into developments around the globe. Ultimately, these policy areas are fundamental for the Union's self-perception as an increasingly active, value-based, international actor.

At the same time, these instruments are intensely regulated by EU law. This seems natural as they involve the transfer of European resources to partner countries and are, therefore, about spending public funds; this should be conducted transparently and hence regulated responsibly. The EU's legal approach stands in contrast, however, to co-operation policies of many nation states where cooperation policy is considered part of the prerogative of the government, and shielded against too much interference by law-makers. The EU's detailed regulation of this area might then be testimony to the EU Member States' distrust and caution. In any event, it means that there is a large area of EU external assistance law. It is surprising, however, how little attention by lawyers these policy areas have attracted. Even though the EU as an international actor has been an in-tensely discussed topic in the past years, its cooperation policies have got little scrutiny.[1]

This chapter provides an overview of these areas of EU policy and specifically their administration, in line with the overall structure of this volume. It defines the scope of these sub-sectors of EU foreign policy according to the EU rules. EU *development cooperation* law is based on Articles 208–211 TFEU and defined mainly by two elem-ents: the transfer of funds must be aimed at the reduction and, in the long term, eradi-cation of poverty; and the recipient must be the government of, or a non-state actor operating in, a developing country. *Humanitarian aid*[2] is defined by the objectives

---

[1] See eg Piet Eeckhout, *EU External Relations Law* (Oxford University Press 2011); Marise Cremona, Bruno de Witte, *EU Foreign Relations Law* (Hart Publishing 2008).

[2] Terms such as emergency aid, emergency support, immediate aid, disaster prevention, disaster con-trol, and *disaster management* are partially used synonymously. For details see Marko Kuhn, *Humanitäre Hilfe der Europäischen Gemeinschaft—Entwicklung, System und primärrechtlicher Rahmen* (Bochumer Schriften zur Friedenssicherung und zum humanitären Völkerrecht 37 2000). As this contribution is, however, solely about the law of the European Union, its understanding of the term is to be applied hereafter.

as laid down in Article 214(1) TFEU:[3] humanitarian operations are intended to 'provide ad hoc assistance and relief and protection for people in third countries who are victims of natural or man-made disasters, in order to meet the humanitarian needs resulting from these different situations'. It follows from secondary law that in certain cases not only the reaction to catastrophes, but also preventive measures are part of humanitarian aid in that sense.[4] In *cooperation policies with (industrialized) third countries* (Articles 212 ff TFEU; in the following: cooperation policies), which are regulated in similar ways and shall also be part of our analysis, recipients are not developing countries:[5] no overall thematically primary objective, such as poverty reduction, exists here. This is also a consequence of the fact that the term 'cooperation policies' has per se a procedural connotation, and can therefore probably not be defined substantively.

B Administrative Tasks in External Assistance

The various cooperation and aid policies are unified by one element: they organize the transfer of public funds from the EU to third countries or to recipients operating there. They can therefore be conceptualized as the European and transnational law of benefits administration. It is *benefits* law because it governs the regulation of the systematic allocation of public funds for development-related and humanitarian objectives; it is *European and transnational*, because most regulation is in EU law, but recipients are states or non-state actors outside the EU with whom agreements are concluded; and it is *administrative* in nature because binding and non-binding procedural and substantive rules and principles determine the competences, instruments, decision-making procedures, discretion, and control, as well as the enforcement and review of the allocation of these funds.[6] The transfer rests on an ultimately cyclical process that involves five phases: the long-term planning and programming of cooperation; the budgeting of funds for the cooperation; the concrete case-by-case negotiation of the allocation of funds; the implementation; and ultimately the control of the transfer.[7] All of these steps necessitate an extensive administration structure that organizes and

---

[3] The Treaty of Lisbon for the first time contains an explicit competence in the area of humanitarian aid. As humanitarian aid is de facto mainly necessary in less developed economies, which are often less well equipped to respond to emergencies and catastrophes, secondary legal acts in this field were hitherto based on the legal basis for development cooperation (now Art 209 TFEU). See especially Council Regulation (EC) No 1257/96 of 20 June 1996 concerning humanitarian aid. Often, association agreements also contained norms on humanitarian aid; cf Kirsten Schmalenbach "Artikel 214 §2 AEUV" in Christian Calliess and Matthias Ruffert (eds), *EUV/AEUV* (CH Beck 2011).

[4] For example, Art 2(f) Council Regulation (EC) No 1257/96 (n 3) names as objectives of humanitarian aid to ensure preparedness for natural disasters and to use early warning systems.

[5] It is controversial whether this is also true for Art 213 TFEU. In favour of the inclusion of developing countries see Schmalenbach "Artikel 213 § 3 AEUV", Calliess, Ruffert, and *EUV/AEUV* (n 3) with further references; in favour of a restriction to non-developing countries see Frank Hoffmeister "Artikel 213 § 3" in Martin Nettesheim (ed), *Das Recht der Europäischen Union* (C H 2011). (Grabitz/Hilf/Nettesheim/Hoffmeister).

[6] For a brief introduction to the concept of cooperation law generally see Philipp Dann, 'Global Administrative Law of Development Cooperation' in Sabino Cassese (ed), *Research Handbook of Global Administrative Law* (Edward Elgar Publishing 2016) 415.

[7] See section F below.

controls them. Consequently, the EU has built up administrative structures in the Commission, as well as the European External Action Service (EEAS).[8]

C Sources of Administrative Law in External Assistance

The administration of EU external assistance is based on a 'constitutional' framework of (mainly) norms of public international law, including sovereignty and international human rights, and EU primary law. The main principles and objectives are listed in Article 21 TEU, while the mandate and competences of the EU are established in Article 4(4) TFEU. As the EU has no exclusive competence for external assistance, its Member States are not prevented from exercising theirs, so that all actors must coordinate their politics.[9] Finally, sector-specific provisions for all three areas of external assistance are laid down in Articles 208 ff TFEU. While these norms establish the constitutional framework—objectives, principles, and legislative procedure—for external assistance, the details of the transfer of funds, including institutional competences, procedures, budgetary rules, or monitoring and review mechanisms, are regulated by a web of international agreements, secondary law and non-binding legal norms. Case law of the Court of Justice of the European Union (CJEU) complements the legislative framework.

With regard to EU development cooperation law, it is central to understand the peculiarities that arise from the division between cooperation with ACP and non-ACP countries, a relic of the colonial ties some EU Member States had with mainly African, Caribbean and Pacific (ACP) countries.[10] Already the Treaty of Rome (Article 131 EEC) stipulated that 'the non-European states and territories, which maintain special relations with Belgium, France, Italy and the Netherlands, ... be associated with the Community' with the objective to 'promote economic and social development'. Therefore, a European Development Fund (EDF) was established in 1957 and regularly renewed, and is still today used to fund *development initiatives with ACP countries*. It is financed and controlled by the Member States, but administered by the European Commission. The history of cooperation with ACP countries never took a linear course, not surprising given the repercussions caused inter alia by the decolonization wave, so that the legal basis for cooperation with ACP countries was replaced or modified several times. The international legal basis today is the Cotonou Agreement, while the details of the cooperation and transfer process are largely regulated by different legal instruments within the EU (cf section F below).

---

[8] See section E below.

[9] Explicitly Art 210 TFEU for development cooperation; see also Art 214(1)(3) and (4) sub-para 2 TFEU.

[10] Philipp Dann, *The Law of Development Cooperation* (Cambridge University Press 2013) 170. On the fundamental concepts based on the TEC see Pitschas in Rudolph Streinz (ed), *EUV/AEUV* (2nd edn, C H Beck 2012) Arts 177–181 with further references; summarizing the amendments by the Treaty of Lisbon see Bernd Martenczuk, 'Die Kooperation der Europäischen Union mit Entwicklungsländern und Drittstaaten und der Vertrag von Lissabon' in Sandra Bartelt and Philipp Dann (eds), *Entwicklungszusammenarbeit im Recht der Europäischen Union [The Law of EU Development Cooperation]* (Europarecht-Beiheft Nr 2, Nomos 2008) 36.

Development cooperation with non-ACP countries was first mentioned in primary law by the Treaty of Maastricht.[11] However, the institutional and procedural framework was rather complicated and triggered new conflicts about vertical and horizontal competences. Several of these disputes ended up before the ECJ which, since then, had jurisdiction to resolve conflicts about competences, the applicable legal basis, and the substantive scope of EU development cooperation. Thus, ECJ case law emerged as an additional source to refine the contours of this field of external assistance law. Under the Treaty of Lisbon, the ordinary legislative procedure applies to 'adopt the measures necessary for the implementation of development cooperation policy' (Article 209(1) TFEU), so that the European Parliament is to that extent a co-legislator.

The Lisbon Treaty also establishes the normative basis for 'economic, financial and technical cooperation with third countries' (in the following: cooperation policies), which generally refers to *non-developing countries* (Articles 212 and 213 TFEU). While the state parties had previously excluded balance of payment assistance to third states from the scope of then Article 181a EC (Nice), Articles 212 and 213 TFEU now allow for these forms of macroeconomic financial aid.[12] Additionally, the Lisbon Treaty stipulates the ordinary legislative procedure and thus turns the European Parliament into a co-legislator for both development cooperation (Article 208 TFEU) and cooperation policies (Article 212 TFEU).

Based on this constitutional framework, the administrative part of the transfer of funds is largely governed by *secondary law*. Especially development cooperation with non-ACP countries and cooperation policies are densely regulated by secondary law. In 2006/2007, the formerly extremely high number of different instruments for development cooperation was fundamentally restructured and reduced, from around thirty legal acts and 90 budget lines to seven instruments for the Multiannual Financial Framework (MFF) 2007–2013,[13] and the general structure has been only slightly modified for the MFF 2014–2020.

These secondary law instruments are generally either geographic or thematic. The latter group channels external assistance to support a specific objective but are independent of the level of development or of the location of the recipient state. These are, inter alia, the Instrument contributing to Stability and Peace,[14] the European Instrument for Democracy and Human Rights (EIDHR),[15] or the EURATOM instrument for nuclear safety.[16] Geographical instruments, in contrast, refer to the cooperation with certain states defined either by region or income standards. For example,

---

[11] Art 130 u–y EC (Maastricht).

[12] Grabitz, Hilf, Nettesheim, and Hoffmeister (n 5) Art 212 § 18 AEUV.

[13] For a good overview of the reform see Sandra Bartelt, 'The Legislative Architecture of EU External Assistance and Development Cooperation' in Bartelt and Dann (eds), *The Law of EU Development Cooperation* (n 10) 9; Manuel Manrique Gil, 'A General Survey of Development Policy, European Parliament' (2014) *Fact Sheets of the European Union*, 2015.

[14] Regulation (EU) No 230/2014 establishing an instrument contributing to stability and peace, which succeeds Regulation (EC) No 1717/2006.

[15] Regulation (EU) No 235/2014 establishing a financing instrument for democracy and human rights worldwide, which replaced Regulation (EC) No 1889/2006.

[16] Regulation (EURATOM) No 237/2014 establishing an Instrument for Nuclear Safety Cooperation, which replaced Regulation (EURATOM) No 300/2007.

the Development Cooperation Instrument (DCI)[17] governs the cooperation with developing non-ACP countries. The main secondary law instrument for cooperation with industrialized and other high-income countries and territories is the Partnership Instrument,[18] which claims to pay more attention to new global challenges and to do more justice to the role of emerging economies such as China, India, or Brazil than did its predecessor. Of special political importance are instruments that regulate the cooperation with countries and regions geographically close to the European Union, such as the Instrument for Pre-Accession Assistance (IPA-II)[19] for potential EU candidates, or the European Neighbourhood Instrument (ENI)[20] for those neighbouring countries which are not (yet) 'enlargement countries'.

Humanitarian aid (Article 214 TFEU) is another important area where the EU is globally involved, but with a different objective: instead of long-term development goals, it aims at the prevention of, and the ad hoc response to, human suffering in exceptional emergency situations. Whereas EU development cooperation law especially leaves room for political and diplomatic purposes, humanitarian law requires strict neutrality. In secondary law, the Instrument for Humanitarian Aid is a central source,[21] which stipulates the general goals and administrative guidelines for humanitarian aid.

Finally, *non-binding norms* refine the framework for EU foreign assistance. The European Consensus on Humanitarian Aid and the European Consensus on Development,[22] for example, are joint declarations of the Member States, the European Commission and the European Parliament, confirming and making more concrete the objectives, principles, and methods. Even though non-binding, they have influenced the legislative acts[23] passed subsequently and are used by the ECJ for interpretational guidance.[24]

---

[17] Regulation (EU) No 233/2014 establishing a financing instrument for development cooperation for the period 2014-2020 (DCI-Regulation). It is also of great practical relevance, given that it contains the largest EU funding source for development.

[18] Regulation (EU) 234/2014 establishing a partnership instrument for cooperation with third countries, which replaced Regulation (EC) 1934/2006 (which in turn established a financial Instrument for cooperation with industrialized and other high-income countries and territories).

[19] Regulation (EU) No 231/2014 establishing an instrument for pre-accession assistance (IPA-II), which replaced Regulation (EC) No 1085/2006.

[20] Regulation (EU) No 232/2014 establishing the European Neighborhood Instrument (ENI).

[21] Regulation (EC) No 1257/96 (n 3) (amended by Regulation (EC) No 1882/2003 and Regulation (EC) No 219/2009).

[22] The European Consensus on Humanitarian Aid, Joint Statement by the Council and the Representatives of the Governments of the Member States meeting within the Council, the European Parliament and the European Commission (2008/C 25/01); and the European Consensus on Development, Joint statement by the Council and the representatives of the governments of the Member States meeting within the Council, the European Parliament and the Commission on European Union Development Policy, (2006/C 46/01). On 22 November 2016, the European Commission presented a 'Proposal for a new European Consensus on Development: Our World, our Dignity, our Future', COM(2016) 740 final.

[23] See eg Art 2(1) DCI-Regulation (EU) No 233/2014 (n 17).

[24] ECJ, Judgment of the Court of 20 May 2008, Case C-91/05 *Commission v Council ECOWAS* ECLI:EU:C:2008:288; ECJ, Judgment of the Court of 23 October 2007, Case C-403/05 *European Parliament v Commission of the European Communities (Border Security in the Philippines)* ECLI:EU:C:2007:624.

D Underlying Legal Principles for External Assistance

While external assistance is part of EU external relations law and thus subject to its general principles, it is also governed by sector-specific principles. The overall objective of EU development cooperation law is poverty alleviation,[25] in line with international declarations and commitments.[26] This commitment is laid down in binding EU law and has frequently been used by the Court to identify the correct legal basis of competence.[27] *Development orientation* is thus not only a political commitment but also a binding legal principle, so that the EU must be able legitimately to assert that development-initiatives can be expected to contribute to poverty alleviation, whereas a reference to potentially positive macroeconomic effects in partner countries is not sufficient.

A second principle is *collective autonomy*, which safeguards the right of states to protect and integrate their political preferences. This is mainly an expression of the principle of equal sovereignty. In development cooperation, it reflects the ideal-type situation of a political process where donors and recipients negotiate targets and strategies on an equal footing. But, as a consequence of oft-existing power imbalances, there is the risk that donors use development aid to enforce their preferences on recipient states, and thus to interfere in their internal affairs. Especially after the cold war, where the risk that developing countries might switch 'to the other side' disappeared, donors started to impose conditions regarding structural adjustments and policy reforms in often politically sensitive areas.[28] Normatively, the recipients' collective autonomy is protected by the principles of sovereignty and non-intervention which, at least in extreme cases, could be violated if a donor not only interferes with the internal affairs of recipient states but also exerts improper economic pressure in order to impose its will.[29] A sector-specific concretization of collective autonomy is the concept of 'ownership',[30] which—even though not a legal principle—expresses a political recognition of the leading role and responsibility of recipients in the development process, implying a recipient's right and responsibility to control development initiatives better. It is a recipient's *right* because of its own collective autonomy; it is also a recipient's *responsibility* in order to protect the donor's collective autonomy, namely to make sure its 'taxpayers' money' is not wasted in third countries.

---

[25] Art 21 (2) lit d) TEU; Art 208 (1) TFEU; Art 2 (1) lit a) DCI-Regulation (EU) No 233/2014 (n 17); Art 1 2nd para Cotonou Agreement; European Consensus on Development clause 5.

[26] See eg Sustainable Development Goals (SDGs) or the preceding Millenium Development Goals, cf Dann, *The Law of Development Cooperation* (n 10) 108 ff.

[27] See eg ECJ Case C-403/05 *European Parliament v Commission of the European Communities* (n 24), (Philippine Border Control), 23 Oct 2007, paras 49 ff, especially para 68.

[28] On the historical context see Dann, *The Law of Development Cooperation* (n 10) 108 ff. On the renaissance and signification of the concept of rule of law in development cooperation see Kenneth Dam, *The Law-Growth-Nexus: The Rule of Law and Economic Development* (Brookings Institution Press 2006); David Trubek and Alvarez Santos (eds), *The New Law and Economic Development: A Critical Appraisal* (Cambridge University Press 2006).

[29] For a more detailed analysis cf Dann, *The Law of Development Cooperation* (n 10) 247 ff.

[30] Art 2 1st bullet point Cotonou-Agreement; European Consensus on Development, para 14; Art 3(7) and (8) lit a) DCI-Regulation (EU) No 233/2014 (n 17); Dann, *The Law of Development Cooperation* (n 10) 239 ff.

A third principle is *individual autonomy*, which is largely based on human rights. While the relief of human suffering has always been a primary goal of humanitarian aid, individuals in fact played a rather minor part in the early conceptualization of development cooperation. Development concepts in the aftermath of the Second World War largely relied on macro-economic growth theories. Only in the last decades, has the development discourse begun to focus on the individual, even though from different perspectives: individual (economic) freedoms are the cornerstone of neoliberalism, while approaches focusing on basic needs and capabilities called for a reorientation of development aid to fight extreme poverty explicitly and to empower individuals.[31] Increasingly, the role of the individual in international development cooperation has come to be conceptualized through human rights lenses.[32] For the EU, individual autonomy is relevant in two ways: first, it concerns the promotion of human rights in partner countries.[33] The EU increasingly includes human rights clauses in development and trade agreements[34] and supports human rights programmes.[35] The other side of the coin refers to the EU's own commitment to respect and protect human rights in its own actions. This is less frequently discussed, even though EU-funded development projects or policies can have tremendous social impacts in partner countries and infringe human rights, such as the right to life, health, food, and an adequate standard of living.[36]

Fourthly, the *principle of coherence and efficiency* (PCE)[37] responds to the oft-mentioned criticism that external assistance is inefficient or even ineffective. PCE is rather a broad principle based on, and defined by, different sub-principles, some of which are common to most, if not all, budgetary regimes, while others are sector-specific. A first sub-principle central to EU budgetary law in general is the principle of sound financial management, comprising the principles of economy, efficiency, and effectiveness.[38] Secondly, development-cooperation especially is to be *result-oriented*, meaning that donors should disburse Official Development

---

[31] A prominent example is *Amartya Sens* capabilities approach, cf Amartya Sen, Development as Freedom (Oxford University Press 1999); Amartya Sen, *Commodities and Capabilities*, Elsevier 1985); Martha Nussbaum, *Women and Human Development: The Capabilities Approach* (Cambridge University Press 2000); Martha Nussbaum and Amartya Sen (eds), *The Quality of Life* (Clarendon Press 1993).

[32] Philip Alston, 'Ships Passing in the Night: The Current State of the Human Rights and Development Debate Seen through the Lens of the Millennium Development Goals' (2005) 27 *Human Rights Quarterly* 755.

[33] cf Art 21(2) lit b) TEU.

[34] Lorand Bartels, *Human Rights Conditionality in the EU's International Agreements* (Oxford University Press 2005), especially 7 ff.

[35] Art 21(2) lit b) TEU declares the promotion of human rights as an objective of external action and therewith of development cooperation. Respect for human rights is further defined as an 'integral part of sustainable development' in Art 9(1) Cotonou- Agreement. The DCI equally regards human rights as essential for the development of partner states (DCI-Regulation, Recital 7) and refers 44 times to the term 'human rights'. Regulation (EU) No 235/2014 (n 15) provides a proper developmental line of support which is solely aimed at the promotion of democracy and human rights.

[36] cf section I(iii) below.   [37] Dann, *The Law of Development Cooperation* (n 10) 284.

[38] Art 317(1) TFEU; Art 30(1) and (2) Financial Regulation (EU, EURATOM) No 966/2012. The same principles apply to the EDF by explicit reference to the Financial Regulation made in Art 11(1) Regulation (EU) No 2015/323.

Assistance (ODA) in accordance with result-based and preferably quantifiable indicators.[39] Thirdly, the sub-principle of *concentration* means that donors should focus on specific key areas and/or recipient states in order to bundle experience and to avoid some recipients' being 'oversupplied' with ODA,[40] while others become 'aid orphans'.[41] A fourth sub-principle is coordination. This is important in all three policy areas and can also be understood as a specific expression of 'the principle of loyalty in EU law'.[42] This includes *intersectoral* coordination, for example between development cooperation and humanitarian aid, and *infrasectoral* coordination, namely between different EU initiatives at the implementation stage. External assistance law contains both technical and institutional, and conceptual and programmatic coordination mechanisms. These can be only briefly outlined in the following sections.

While these principles apply similarly to development and cooperation policies, there is one significant difference with regard to humanitarian assistance. Due to its overall commitment to humanity, 'human suffering must be addressed wherever it is found'.[43] This can be understood in the sense that a priori individual—in contrast with collective autonomy—takes a more prominent position. Therefore, unlike in development cooperation law, the inclusion of conditionalities that serve purposes other than the efficient use of aid to relieve human suffering would be illegal.[44]

E Sectoral Organization, Institutions, and Structures in External Assistance

EU external assistance takes place in a complex political and economic context where different public and private actors both within and outside the EU closely interact. The relationship of key public actors *within* the EU can be depicted in two dimensions: first, on the *vertical* EU-Member State dimension, second, on the *horizontal* inter-institutional and infra-institutional dimension between and within different EU organs.

Regarding the vertical dimension, it is sufficient to mention that competences of external assistance are parallel,[45] meaning that national governments often run their

---

[39] This concept was first introduced in the Paris Declaration and taken up by the European Consensus on Development (eg para 115); the use of indicators to measure achievements is ordered by Art 2(1) DCI Regulation (EU) No 233/2014 (n 17).

[40] On the differentiation and regionalization as well as the concentration on the least developed countries, cf Art 2 4th bullet point Cotonou Agreement; Art 3(2) DCI-Regulation (EU) No 233/2014 (n 17).

[41] Andrew Rogerson and Suzanne Steensen, 'Aid Orphans: Whose Responsibility?' OECD Development Brief 1/2009; Council of the European Union, 'EU Code of Conduct on Complementarity and Division of Labour in Development Policy' (9558/07), Guiding Principle 8.

[42] Coordination (Art 214 para 6 TFEU), coherence (Art 21(3) sub-para 2 TEU), complementarity (Art 214(1) sentence 3 TFEU: 'complement and reinforce'); Art 10 Regulation (EC) No 1257/96 (n 3); European Consensus on Humanitarian Aid (n 22) paras 22, 25–30.

[43] European Consensus on Humanitarian Aid (n 22) para 11.

[44] This follows inter alia from the principles laid down in the European Consensus on Humanitarian Aid (n 22) paras 10–14.

[45] Art 4(4) TFEU; ECJ, Case C-316/91 *Parliament v Council*, 2 March 1994, para 26 (for development cooperation); ECJ, Joined Cases C-181/91 and C-248/91 *Parliament v Council and Commission*, 30 June 1993, para 16 (for humanitarian aid).

own development or humanitarian aid institutions. Consequently, European develop-ment cooperation takes place on different levels and vertical coordination becomes a crucial challenge. However, the focus here is on the horizontal organizational struc-ture. Before the Lisbon Treaty, three DGs within the Commission were mainly in charge of EU foreign assistance: DG Development, DG External Relations, and DG Humanitarian Aid.[46] After Lisbon, a new entity emerged: based on Article 27(3) TEU, the European External Action Service (EEAS) was founded as a 'functionally autono-mous body of the Union',[47] gaining many competences from various DGs. In spite of being an autonomous actor, the EEAS and the Commission are closely connected and cooperate in multiple ways.[48] In the area of development cooperation, EEAS has taken over country units that were formerly situated in DG Development, merging them with country units that used to belong to DG External Relations.[49] The remaining competences within the (renamed) DG Development and Cooperation—EuropeAid mainly relate to programming functions in cooperation with EEAS and implementa-tion of specific projects. Oversight structures have changed too: EuropeAid employees in EU delegations abroad, for example, now work under the supervision of EEAS offi-cials.[50] This reform might in some way have contributed to a fragmentation of EU for-eign assistance law through the introduction of an additional actor. Nevertheless, at least programming for ACP and non-ACP countries is now united under the EEAS, and the functional division between development programming (EEAS) and specific project allocation and implementation (EuropeAID)[51] is now in line with the develop-ment law and policy of many Member States.

F Administrative Procedures and Acts within the External Assistance Sector

External assistance law governs a recurring process of budgeting, planning, and implementing of projects and programmes, a characteristic familiar in domestic benefits administration law: instead of the traditional distinction between law-making and law-execution, benefits law consists of a multi-step process in order to concretize and substantiate the goals and targets pursued by the allocation of public funds. This is one of the reason why benefits law is largely determined by budgetary rules and principles, and less by concise substantive legal rules. In spite of the multi-faceted process, it is useful to distinguish between (1) the setting of a legal and budgetary framework and (2) the implementation stage. Exceptions exist, however, for Articles 213 and 214 TFEU, as these provisions refer to financial or hu-manitarian emergencies. As such, they are not amenable to, and cannot be subject to, equally detailed multiannual planning. These characteristics will be discussed below (cf section F3 and F4).

---

[46] Dann, *The Law of Development Cooperation* (n 10) 171.
[47] Art 1(2) and Recital 1, Council Decision 2010/427/EU (EEAS Decision).
[48] Dann, *The Law of Development Cooperation* (n 10) 172 ff.
[49] EEAS Decision (n 47) Annex 2.   [50] ibid Art 5.
[51] Dann, *The Law of Development Cooperation* (n 10) 173 ff.

1 Setting the legal and financial framework

The setting of the legal and budgetary framework is a mostly EU internal procedure dominated by the Union and its Member States.[52] As the substantive and procedural rules and principles are largely determined by general EU budgetary law, great similarities exist between cooperation policies (Article 212 TFEU) and development cooperation with non-ACP countries (Articles 208 ff TFEU). It is only development cooperation with ACP countries which follows a different model, being funded from the EDF outside the general Union budget.

The legal and budgetary framework for *development cooperation with non-ACP countries* and *cooperation policies with industrialized countries* consists of two main elements: the basic act and the Union's budget. The basic act forms the legislative framework as a precondition of budget appropriations.[53] This basic act is based on Articles 209(2) and 212 TFEU, or both, pursuant to the ordinary legislative procedure. Prominent examples for such a basic act are the DCI Regulation and the Partnership Instrument for Cooperation with non-developing countries. They determine, for a period of seven years, the general substantive and financial frame for the respective cooperation activities. However, that frame does not, at that stage, contain specific appropriations to particular countries, which need still to be authorized by the European Parliament and the Council within the limits of the multiannual financial framework.[54] Relying on the basic act, and this is the second step in setting the legal and financial framework, the use of these financial resources is determined in the regular annual Union budget (Article 314(1) TFEU).

The legal and budgetary framework concerning cooperation with *ACP countries* is three-dimensional: first, the normative basis, determining objectives, principles, and specific areas for cooperation initiatives, is laid down in an international treaty (currently the Cotonou Agreement).[55] Secondly, the corresponding budget is established by an internal agreement between the EU Member State governments represented in the Council, thus without recipient states or the EU itself, as the resources are not part of the regular EU budget. This internal agreement mainly determines the contributions of each Member State, but does not at this stage contain specific allocations or appropriations to recipient countries.[56] Thirdly, the Council enacts an implementing regulation,[57] which determines the applicable budgetary and procedural regime for the implementation of the EDF.

[52] From a political science perspective on the EU's internal distribution of power, see Maurizio Carbone, *The European Union and International Development: The Politics of Foreign Aid* (Routledge 2007).

[53] Art 54(1) Financial Regulation (EU, EURATOM) 966/2012 (n 38), as amended by Regulation (EU, EURATOM) 2015/1929.

[54] Art 20 DCI-Regulation (EU) 233/2014 (n 17).

[55] The Cotonou Agreement is a mixed agreement, ie signed and ratified by the EU and its Member States on the as well as the respective partner countries. The legal competence to conclude these agreements is based on what is now Art 217 TFEU. In order to implement the objectives laid down in these agreements, the EU Member States still rely on the aforementioned regularly renewed European Development Fund (EDF).

[56] Art 1 Internal Agreement on the 11th EDF ([2013] OJ L210 of 6 August 2013).

[57] For the 11th EDF see Regulation (EU) 2015/322 on the implementation of the 11th European Development Fund.

In conclusion, the setting of the legal and budgetary frame is, apart from development cooperation with ACP countries, mainly an EU internal legislative process. The fact that it is *internal*, i.e., without any considerable participation of recipients, does not violate their collective autonomy, as this first stage mainly concerns the general supply of funds for external assistance, a decision almost exclusively at the donor's/creditor's discretion, and the process sets only very broad goals, objectives and principles. It is also a truly *legislative* process, with the EP as co-legislator.[58] This is diametrically opposed to development cooperation with ACP states: here, recipient states negotiate and conclude the partnership agreements, while the Parliament may only approve or reject the final text of the agreement and does not participate in the establishment of the EDF budget at all. This exclusion of EP has been criticized as anachronistic[59] and, indeed, as the division between ACP and non-ACP is a consequence of mainly former colonial ties, this bisection is hard to justify. However, as will be seen now, the legal rules governing the implementation stage are being increasingly brought into line.

2 Implementation stage: programming and execution phase

After setting the legal and financial framework, the implementation stage follows, largely governed by the respective budgetary regime. This means that, in principle, general EU budgetary law applies, mainly the Financial Regulation[60] and the Commission Delegated Regulation, which spells out the rules and procedures,[61] but certain exceptions arise from the particularities of the transnational context. Rules and principles relating specifically to the financing of external action have, since 2014, been compiled in one horizontal regulation laying down common implementing rules and procedures (therefore: 'Common Implementing Regulation' (CIR)) for six instruments of development cooperation and cooperation policies.[62] The EDF's special budgetary regime contains mainly identical norms. Therefore, the implementation stage can be presented so as to encompass both the cooperation with ACP and non-ACP countries.

The implementation stage can be divided into a *programming* and *execution* phase.[63] During the multi-year *programming phase*, strategy papers and/or the multiannual

---

[58] R Passos and D Gauci, 'The European Parliament and Development Cooperation: Shaping Legislation and the New Democratic Scrutiny Dialogue' in Bartelt and Dann (eds), *The Law of EU Development Cooperation* (n 10) 138.

[59] Eeckhout, *EU External Relations Law* (n 1) 129.

[60] Financial Regulation (EU, EURATOM) 966/2012 (n 38) as amended by Regulation (EU, EURATOM) 2015/1929.

[61] Commission Delegated Regulation (EU) No 1268/2012 on the rules of application of Financial Regulation (EU, EURATOM) No 966/2012 (n 38) as amended by Commission delegated regulation (EU) 2015/2462.

[62] Regulation (EU) 236/2014 laying down common rules and procedures for the implementation of the Union's instruments for financing external action. The instruments include: (1) Instrument for Pre-accession Assistance (IPA-II); (2) European Neighbourhood Instrument (ENI); (3) Partnership Instrument; (4) Development Cooperation Instrument (DCI); (5) European Instrument for Democracy and Human Rights (EIDHR); (6) Instrument contributing to Stability and Peace (IcSP).

[63] See extensively Philipp Dann, 'Programm- und Prozesssteuerung im europäischen Entwicklungsverwaltungsrecht' in Bartelt and Dann (eds), *The Law of EU Development Cooperation* (n 10) 118–27; Martin Pellens, *Entwicklungshilfe Deutschlands und der Europäischen*

indicative programmes (MIPs) are drawn up.[64] Unlike the legal and financial framework described above, programming is country/region-specific and contains more detailed thematic and budgetary arrangements. On the budgetary side, the indicative allocation of funds by the Commission establishes preliminarily the amount available for a certain period of time for each recipient country.[65] As regards content, the multiannual indicative programmes are based on country strategy papers drawn up by the EU for each partner country or region. These strategy papers are framework documents analyzing the respective economic, political, and social situation and identifying relevant sectors to be addressed.[66] They are intended to provide a coherent framework for development cooperation consistent with the overall goals, objectives, and principles of EU law in general, and with the requirements of the underlying legal instrument in particular.[67] In procedural terms, the programming process can be divided into four steps: First, strategy papers and multi-annual indicative programmes are created jointly by the recipient state governments and the Commission, working with the EEAS. Secondly, these documents are examined by a committee of Member States chaired by the Commission. Thirdly, both documents are adopted by a decision of the Commission, and the multi-year indicative programme is confirmed through agreements with the partner countries. Finally, both documents are subject to review and, where necessary, updated.[68]

After the programming comes the *execution phase* in which tangible form is given to the multiannual programming and funds are actually transferred to recipient states. This phase consists of two important elements. The first element is the approval of an Annual Action Programme (AAP) specifying the 'objectives pursued, the expected results and main activities, the methods of implementation, the budget and an indicative timetable, any associated support measures and performance monitoring arrangements',[69] adopted by the Commission by way of comitology procedures.[70] In legal terms, this element constitutes the financing decision as such required under EU budgetary law.[71] The second element, based on the AAP, is the specific financing proposal or draft Financing Agreement, mainly containing the details of a specific project, the financial conditions for funds transfer, and rules on the implementation. This

---

Union: Rechtsgrundlagen und Verfahren bei der finanziellen und technischen Zusammenarbeit (Berliner Europa-Studien, Verlag Dr Köstner 1996) 87.

[64] Arts 10, 11, 13, and 14 DCI-Regulation (EU) No 233/2014 (n 17); for cooperation with ACP countries see Arts 4 and 5 Council Regulation (EU) 2015/322 on the implementation of the 11th EDF

[65] Arts 10, 11(5), and 13(2) DCI-Regulation (EU) No 233/2014 (n 17); Art 3 para 1 Regulation (EU) No 2015/322 on the implementation of the 11th EDF.

[66] Art 11 DCI-Regulation (EU) No 233/2014 (n 17); Art 5 Regulation (EU) No 2015/322 on the implementation of the 11th EDF. See also Communication from the Commission to the Council and the European Parliament: Increasing the Impact of EU Aid: a Common Framework for Drafting Country Strategy Papers and Joint Multiannual Programming, COM(2006) 0088 final.

[67] See Art 11(2) and (4) DCI-Regulation (EU) No 233/2014 (n 17).

[68] Dann, *The Law of Development Cooperation* (n 10) 330.

[69] Art 2(1) Regulation (EU) No 236/2014 (n 62).   [70] ibid Art 2(2).

[71] Art 84(2) Financial Regulation (EU, EURATOM) No 966/2012 (n 38) in conjunction with Art 94 Commission Delegated Regulation (EU) No 1268/2012 (n 61); Recital 4 Regulation (EU) No 236/2014 (n 62).

proposal or draft instrument becomes externally binding by concluding the (final) Financing Agreement with the recipient state.[72]

3 Macroeconomic measures: budget support and macro-financial assistance

Budget support in EU external assistance law means that funds are transferred directly to the recipient state's general budget. These measures are usually meant to support mutually agreed policy reforms, over which the recipient country ideally has increased 'ownership'.[73] The transfer process follows the aforementioned two-step approach: budget support must be first provided for in a basic act and the EU's budget, before it can be implemented.[74] However, unlike project aid, budget support is usually conditional upon future policy reforms and a certain level of performance of, or achievement by, the recipient state's government institutions. The associated evaluation is, not surprisingly, often a sensitive task. Unexpectedly, EU law is relatively silent as regards not only specific procedural rules on budget support, but indeed also as regards substantive rules.[75]

Three general remarks can, however, be made. First, certain pre-existing financial and non-financial conditions must be fulfilled: the recipient state's management of public finance must be sufficiently transparent and accountable, and the country must be committed to the principles of democracy, human rights, and the rule of law.[76] The assessment of these requirements obviously leaves a broad discretionary space. Secondly, the recipient government must present a detailed proposal for policy reforms or other initiatives aimed at supporting sustainable and inclusive economic growth and, where applicable, eradicating poverty.[77] If generally approved by the EU, the specific goals and requirements are then laid down in the agreements between the EU and each recipient state. It is through this *procedural* allocation process again that general objectives and principles are put into concrete *substantive* terms. Thirdly, the EU must monitor compliance. For this purpose, performance standards are developed and, in case of non-compliance, the disbursement of the next tranche may be suspended where these are not met (cf below). The fact that the EU thus gains an influential mechanism for reviewing and assessing other states' internal policies is not unproblematic with regard to the recipient's collective autonomy.

The EU can also provide *macro-financial assistance* (MFA), as balance-of-payment support, to 'address exceptional external financing needs of countries that are geographically, economically and politically close to the EU'.[78] MFA is generally made conditional on reforms and on structural adjustment programmes of international

---

[72] Art 189 Financial Regulation (EU, EURATOM) No 966/2012 (n 38); Art 85 Financial Regulation (EU, EURATOM) No 966/2012 (n 38) in conjunction with Art 95 Commission Delegated Regulation (EU) No 1268/2012 (n 61); Art 184(2) lit b) Financial Regulation (EU, EURATOM) No 966/2012 (n 38).

[73] For an in-depth overview cf Dann, *The Law of Development Cooperation* (n 10) 412 ff.

[74] Art 186 Financial Regulation (EU, EURATOM) No 966/2012 (n 38).

[75] Mainly Art 4(1) lit c) and (2) Regulation (EU) No 236/2014 (n 62).   [76] ibid Art 4(2).

[77] ibid; see also Art 61(2) Cotonou Agreement.

[78] Report from the Commission to the European Parliament and the Council on the implementation of macro-financial assistance to third countries in 2014, SWD(2015) 115 final.

financial institutions.[79] It usually consists of loans, not grants. Unlike other forms of assistance, MFA is decided upon directly within the ordinary legislative procedure, and the decision is based directly on Article 212 TFEU. An attempt to enact a Framework Regulation in order to expedite the decision-making process has failed so far.[80] After Lisbon, the question arose as to when, and to what extent, MFA could also be based on Article 213 TFEU. As such a decision to grant urgent financial assistance to third countries requires approval only by the Council, reliance on that provision as the legal basis would considerably speed up the decision-making process. However, the term 'urgent' must be narrowly interpreted, especially as the European Parliament does not even have to be consulted under that Article. It would, therefore, be only under exceptional circumstances that Article 213 TFEU could be applied,[81] so far only once, namely at the beginning of the Ukrainian crisis in 2014.[82] The possible achievement of a better balance between the lengthy ordinary procedure of Article 212 TFEU and the extremely rare, Council-based decision foreseen in Article 213 TFEU could indeed be through the adoption of a MFA regulation, even though a first attempt to do so did not meet with success.[83]

4 Humanitarian aid (Article 214 TFEU)

The EU is a major provider of humanitarian aid, the financing of which takes the form of grants.[84] The EU may fund operations of the Commission and Member States, but also those of non-governmental organizations (NGOs) where they fulfil certain eligibility criteria, as well as those of international organizations.[85] The fundamental norm in secondary law is Regulation (EC) No 1257/96,[86] which not only reflects the aforementioned principles of humanitarian aid law, but also governs the procedures for the implementation of humanitarian aid (Chapter II) and humanitarian operations (Chapter III).

Central features of Union external assistance law apply here too: funds for humanitarian aid are generally granted in accordance with the provisions of general EU budgetary law, in particular the Financial Regulation.[87] However, owing to the characteristics of humanitarian aid, mainly a response to unpredictable catastrophes, certain modifications are necessary. The above-mentioned multi-step planning

---

[79] European Commission, Proposal for a Regulation of the European Parliament and of the Council laying down general provisions for macro-financial assistance to third countries, 4 July 2011, COM(2011) 396 final 1.

[80] The Commission had submitted a proposal for such a Framework Regulation in 2011 (seen 79). After the Council and European Parliament found an agreement different from the Commission's preference, the Commission withdrew its proposal. The annulment action lodged against this withdrawal brought by the Council was dismissed by the Court; cf ECJ, Case C-409/13 *Council of the European Union v European Commission* ECLI:EU:C:2015:217.

[81] Grabitz/Hilf/Nettesheim/Hoffmeister (n 5) Art 213 § 6.

[82] Council Decision 2014/215/EU, cf in particular Recital 4 concerning the urgency of the decision.

[83] See Grabitz/Hilf/Nettesheim/Hoffmeister (n 5) Art 213 § 12.

[84] Art 5 Regulation (EC) No 1257/96 (n 3).   [85] Arts 7–9 Regulation (EC) No 1257/96 (n 3).

[86] Calliess, Ruffert, and Schmalenbach, 'EUV/AEUV Artikel 214 § 1 (n 3); Martenczuk, 'Die Kooperation der Europäischen Union mit Entwicklungsländern und Drittstaaten und der Vertrag von Lissabon (n 10) 48.

[87] cf Art 14 Regulation (EC) 1257/96 (n 3).

and programming approach is especially difficult. Nevertheless, the European Commission must annually draft guidelines for humanitarian operations expected to be undertaken in the coming year, and these are adopted in the comitology procedure.[88] In addition, the Commission has, since 2012, adopted a decision which 'covers all humanitarian aid actions which ECHO anticipates to fund during a given period', and prepares 'humanitarian implementation plans' (HIPs), containing more detail on the operational priorities identified.[89] In the light of the particular challenges of humanitarian assistance, provisions to speed up the transfer of funds in emergency situations are necessary. Unlike the case of MFA, secondary humanitarian aid law provides for both regular and emergency aid. The competences and procedures for the implementation of humanitarian operations are based on the interplay of Articles 13 ff. Reg. (EC) No 1257/96 and Regulation (EU) No 182/2011,[90] (which repealed the old 'comitology regulation').[91]

G Legal Rules Governing Decision-making Substance in the External Assistance Sector

Whether funds are transferred is generally discretionary; there is so far no substantive obligation in the law of the European Union to provide development or cooperation assistance. But *how* funds are transferred is quite densely regulated, for example, concerning competences, procedure, or compliance mechanisms. However, EU external assistance law contains mainly procedural provisions and only very few substantive standards—apart from certain broad and general principles. Of course, the significance of principles should not be underestimated as they not only guide ECJ case law, but also the legislative and administrative decision-making process. During the different steps of the implementation phase (described above), the general principles of Union external assistance law are embodied in specific substantive rules and targets. This is a typical feature of benefits administration law: substantive objectives and principles are only broadly defined by constitutional or administrative law. It is during the multi-step legislative and administrative process that, in part unilaterally and in part bi- or multilaterally, substantive standards crystallize and are laid down in legally binding agreements.

H Administrative Enforcement of Sectoral Law for Development and Aid

Due to the transnational character of the development and aid sector, traditional administrative enforcement mechanisms are usually either unavailable or functionally

---

[88] ibid Art 16(1).   [89] http://ec.europa.eu/echo/node/3187 (last accessed 20 May 2017).
[90] Regulation (EU) No 182/2011 laying down the rules and general principles concerning mechanisms for control by Member States of the Commission's exercise of implementing powers.
[91] Regulation (EC) No 1257/96 (n 3), as amended by Regulation (EC)1882/2009 and Regulation (EC) 219/2009) still refers to former Council Decision (EC) No 1999/468, so that the transitional provisions according to Art 13 Regulation (EC) No 182/2011 still apply.

modified.[92] Unlike domestic settings, the European Commission is not (and cannot) be empowered by constitutional or statutory law to enforce legal obligations vis-à-vis third states, but must explicitly reserve the authority to do so in the respective financing agreements. Therefore, Union law requires that the respective EU organs include clauses reserving rights to investigate fraud and corruption, and to monitor compliance. Thus, rights to investigate financial irregularities, to inspect documents, and to visit project sites are spelled out in the General Conditions of the financing agreement between the EU and a recipient state.[93] In case of non-compliance, different consultation procedures are triggered and, as the ultimate sanction, a treaty may be suspended or terminated.

Legal compliance and enforcement instruments can be classified as either ex ante or ex post mechanisms. Ex ante instruments have the task of making sure that certain conditions are met before the transfer of financial assistance, for example, that certain reforms be implemented before the disbursement of the subsequent tranche. The EU frequently uses such an ex ante approach for budget support or macro-financial assistance. In the case of project aid, however, the focus is on ex post control.[94] Here, Union law usually distinguishes between project-specific requirements and general ones. *Project-specific terms and conditions* are laid down in the agreement and comprise, beside specification of project details, clauses on financial management. Politically and legally more problematic, however, are the *general requirements* laid down in the Annex to the agreement concerned. These are conditionalities, similar to those used by other donors in international development law, or increasingly also employed in the management of the EU financial crisis.[95] We define conditionality here as any regulation that one state or international organization attaches unilaterally to an agreement, or any sanction that it attaches to non-fulfilment. 'Unilaterally' here means that the conditions are de facto non-negotiable.[96] Doctrinal similarities with domestic benefits administration law become evident,[97] as subsidies are often linked with conditions in order to promote broader economic, environmental, or social goals. These general conditionalities are also part of a legally enforceable agreement and may, in case of non-compliance, result in the suspension or termination of the agreement.[98] As they are, by definition, unilaterally imposed and often concern sensitive areas such as human rights, or the design of a state's internal economic system, this instrument is not uncontroversial, as the donor's and recipient's claims for collective autonomy often clash.

---

[92] For references cf Dann, *The Law of Development Cooperation* (n 10) 359 n 20.

[93] See Financing Agreement, General Conditions, Annex I Arts 19, 20 for assistance from the EDF and, similarly, for assistance from the EU budget cf http://ec.europa.eu/europeaid/financial-agreement-model-general-conditions-edf_en and http://ec.europa.eu/europeaid/financial-agreement-budget-model-2012_en (last accessed 20 May 2017); Dann, *The Law of Development Cooperation* (n 10) 358, 392.

[94] Dann, *The Law of Development Cooperation* (n 10) 391.

[95] On conditionalities in development cooperation law cf Dann, *The Law of Development Cooperation* (n 10) 358–61, 377, 391–97, 408–409, 420–21, 451, 509.

[96] ibid 360.   [97] ibid 408 ff.   [98] See eg Art 23 f. General Conditions (n 93).

I Supervision and Control of, and within, the Development and Aid Sectors

Supervision and control of EU external assistance is defined by a high level of complexity.[99] There are many answers to the question who controls whom, and subject to what standards. It is, therefore, possible here to provide only a brief overview of the main administrative, political, and judicial review mechanisms.

1 Administrative supervision

EU internal control mechanisms exist within the Commission, which is obliged to regularly evaluate the funded initiatives (and, feeding into political supervision, to inform the Council, the European Parliament, and the competent committees about the findings).[100] For these evaluations, interested parties, including non-state actors, can be involved.[101] However, self-reporting review mechanisms are not sufficient when evaluated against rule-of-law standards. Thus, it is important to look at more independent forms of control. As Union external assistance relies mainly on the EU budget itself, it is also subject to control by the European Court of Auditors (ECA), which 'shall examine the accounts of all revenue and expenditure of the Union'.[102] For assistance to ACP countries, funded by the EDF which is outside the general EU budget, audits are explicitly prescribed,[103] further flattening differences between ACP and non-ACP development cooperation. The ECA reviews both the lawfulness of revenues and expenditures, and the soundness of financial management,[104] thus promoting the principle of effectiveness and efficiency.[105] The instruments available to the ECA are annual reports published in the Official Journal. Special reports focusing on specific issues of development cooperation are also frequently prepared.[106] In order to fulfil its task properly, the ECA may examine Commission documents and visit EU delegations in partner countries in order to investigate 'on the spot': EU external assistance law requires the reservation of such investigative rights in the financing agreement with recipient countries.[107]

---

[99] Schmalenbach, 'Accountability: Who Is Judging the European Development Cooperation?' in Bartelt and Dann (eds), *The Law of EU Development Cooperation* (n 10) 162–87.

[100] Art 13 Regulation (EU) No 236/2014 (n 63).   [101] ibid Art 12(3).

[102] Art 287(1) TFEU.   [103] Art 11(6) Internal Agreement on the 11th EDF.

[104] Art 287(2) TFEU.

[105] Waldhoff in Calliess/Ruffert (eds), *EUV/AEUV* (n 3) Art 287, § 6 ff.

[106] cf Special Report No 10/2008 concerning EC Development Assistance to Health Services in Sub-Saharan Africa http://www.eca.europa.eu/Lists/ECADocuments/SR08_10/SR08_10_EN.PDF (last accessed 20 May 2017); see also Schmalenbach, 'Accountability' (n 99) 167.

[107] See eg: Art 12 Regulation (EC) No 1257/96 (n 3), whereby the financing agreement has to ensure, that 'the Commission and the Court of Auditors may conduct checks on the spot and at the headquarters of humanitarian partners according to the usual procedures'; cf also above n 93.

2 Political control

Political control is mainly exercised by the European Parliament. To a large extent, the instruments available to the Parliament to control the Commission's external actions are not different from those in other policy areas, just as is the case with the right of individuals to file a petition with the Parliament concerning development, cooperation, or humanitarian aid activities.

One accountability mechanism, the full potential of which has not yet unfolded, is supervision through the European Ombudsman (Article 228 TFEU), which can function as a complaint mechanism also in the area of external relations.[108] Its mandate covers investigations into the 'maladministration in the activities of the Union institutions, bodies, offices or agencies ...',[109] and it can receive complaints from 'any citizen of the Union or any natural or legal person residing or having its registered office in a Member State', thus also from non-EU citizens. The residential requirement might seem problematic at first, given that individuals affected by development projects or policies hardly ever reside in the EU. But complainants do not have to be directly or individually affected; consequently, for example, NGOs can (and do) bring complaints as *actio popularis* on behalf of affected individuals or the environment. As a comparison with the World Bank's Inspection Panels or other quasi-judicial review mechanisms makes clear, this is rather the rule than the exception. Admittedly, the Ombudsman's decisions are not legally enforceable. However, the Union's organs have to reply to these Ombudsman reports and recommendations, which at least makes them a significant instrument between formal judicial and more free-ranging political supervision.

3 Judicial supervision

The traditional mechanism for supervising administrative action and enforcing administrative law would be judicial review. To what extent, however, is this viable in external assistance law? To understand the role the EU courts do or could play, it is important to recall the main constellations where justiciable conflicts might arise. These conflicts can be defined by their internal or external, and individual or institutional dimensions.

As regards the *internal-institutional constellation*, i.e., between different Union organs, most legal disputes before EU courts concern the alleged misuse of competences, at first sight only a technical question which, however, relates in fact to the politically sensitive power balance between the EU institutions. Even though many decisions concerning external assistance require complex political and economic analysis, so that judicial review must necessarily be limited,[110] the ECJ nevertheless has drawn relatively specific contours and has on several occasions invalidated a legal act because the legal basis chosen by the Council or Commission was incorrect. For example, in

---

[108] Schmalenbach, 'Accountability' (n 99) 185.
[109] Art 228 TFEU; for more details cf Dann, *The Law of Development Cooperation* (n 10) 464.
[110] Schmalenbach, 'Accountability' (n 99) 172–73.

the *Philippines Border Control* case, the Court held that the Commission had partially exceeded its implementing power by funding a project relating to the border security of the Philippines: in spite of its potentially positive economic impacts, this was not a development project in the sense of EU development law.[111]

Internal-individual conflicts between European Union residents and the EU mainly arise between the Union and entrepreneurs. If the Union hires private contractors to carry out aspects of a development project and EU procurement law applies to this, bidders often claim that the contract was illegally awarded to competitors. This Commission's decision is subject to judicial review, but thus far with limited success for the complainants.[112]

External-institutional disputes are those that can, at least theoretically, arise between the Union and public authorities outside the EU, such as recipient governments. Even though a third-state government can probably not bring an annulment action against the EU,[113] generally it could seek international arbitration as agreed in the respective international agreements.[114] These arbitration clauses, however, have never been used, most likely for political reasons given the voluntary character of the Union's decision to grant ODA.[115]

The *external-individual* constellation, finally, concerns claims brought by individuals residing in third countries for the (alleged) violation of their rights by, or within the framework of, an EU-funded initiative. Negative side-effects of development, cooperation, or humanitarian aid initiatives can infringe fundamental human rights in third countries, ranging from forced evictions or environmentally-induced health impacts through to the impairment of social rights in consequence of budget cuts as a result of EU conditionalities. As complaints against the Union in recipient states' national courts would usually fail owing to jurisdictional immunities,[116] the only potentially promising path would be a suit before EU courts.

Substantively, an action of annulment could be successful if the applicant proves that an EU institution fails to consider human rights impacts adequately; this could be the case, even where these impacts occur outside EU territory.[117] Nevertheless, there

---

[111] ECJ, Case C-403/05 *European Parliament v Commission of the European Communities* (Philippines Border Control) (n 24) para 68.

[112] ECJ, Case C-257/90 *Italsolar SpA v Commission* [1990] ECR I–3841; CFI, Case T-231/97 *New Europe Consulting v Commission* ECLI:EU:T:1999:146; CFI, Case T-185/94 *Geotronics v Commission* [1995] ECR II-2795; Peter Kalbe, 'The Award of Contracts and the Enforcement of Claims in the Context of EC External Aid and Development Cooperation', (2001) 38 *Common Market Law Review* 1217.

[113] This is doctrinally not clear. However, Schmalenbach argues that at least a teleological reading would curtail such an option: two subjects of international law would hardly want that disputes about 'acta iure imperii' were settled in the court of one of them, cf Schmalenbach, 'Accountability' (n 99) 176; Dann, *The Law of Development Cooperation* (n 10) 462.

[114] Art 25 General Conditions (n 93); Art 98 Cotonou Agreement.

[115] Dann, *The Law of Development Cooperation* (n 10) 462; On the problems of other remedies Schmalenbach, 'Accountability' (n 99) 176–77.

[116] Immunities are not only a basic principle of public international law, they are also explicitly included in many partnership agreements. Dann, *The Law of Development Cooperation* (n 10) 463; Paul Craig, *EU Administrative Law* (Oxford University Press 2011) 307; with regard to international organizations see August Reinisch, *International Organizations before National Courts* (Cambridge University Press 2000).

[117] In this sense see recently General Court, Case T-512/12 *Front Polisario v Council* ECLI:EU:T:2015:953, paras 227 ff. However, the judgment was reversed by the ECJ, which held that the application was, in that particular case, inadmissible: ECJ, Case C-104/16 P *Council v Front Polisario* ECLI:EU:C:2016:973.

are several procedural obstacles. An annulment action would, in most cases, be inadmissible. The Financing Decision or Financing Agreement might be of *individual* but generally not of *direct* concern (Article 263 (4) TFEU) to affected persons in third states. The financing agreement would not immediately, and in a quasi 'purely automatic' way, affect individual rights, but require the 'application of other intermediate rules' to the extent that the recipient state would generally have to take additional discretionary decisions in order to realize the project or policy in question.[118]

A different path might be by way of an action for damages (non-contractual liability).[119] An applicant would need to prove that the legal rule infringed was intended to confer rights on individuals; the breach would have to be sufficiently serious, and there would have to have been a direct causal link between the breach and the resultant harm. The decisive test for finding that a breach of EU law is sufficiently serious is whether the institution concerned manifestly and gravely disregarded the limits on its discretion.[120] However, where the institution in question has only considerably reduced discretion (or none at all), the mere infringement of EU law may be sufficient to establish the existence of a sufficiently serious breach.[121]

As most secondary norms of European external assistance do not in fact confer individual rights, an individual claim could probably best be based on an alleged breach of fundamental and human rights. Doctrinally, however, the extraterritorial scope of human rights is itself not uncontroversial and is generally limited to situations where authorities exert effective control over a territory or individuals,[122] not a conclusion easily reached in regard to development assistance or humanitarian aid. Another approach for holding the Union responsible for human rights infringements through development initiatives is provided by the concept of complicity under international law. Even without the necessary effective control over a funded project or policy, the EU might be responsible as an accomplice by providing funds to a recipient state which, in implementing the agreed project or policy, commits human rights violations.[123] Still,

---

[118] On the requirement of 'direct' concern, cf by way of example ECJ, Case C-404/96 P *Glencore Grain v Commission* [1998] ECR I-2435, para 41; Joined Cases C-445/07 P and C-455/07 P *Commission v Ente per le Ville Vesuviane and Others* ECLI:EU:C:2009:529, para 45; Joined Cases C-463/10 P and C-475/10 P *Deutsche Post and Germany v Commission* ECLI:EU:C:2011:656, para 66; General Court, Case T-262/10 *Microban v Commission* ECLI:EU:T:2011:623, para 27; similarly, with regard to EU development cooperation see Schmalenbach, 'Accountability' (n 99) 12 and n 107.

[119] Schmalenbach, 'Accountability' (n 99); Dann, *The Law of Development Cooperation* (n 10) 463.

[120] ECJ, Joined Cases C-46/93 and C-48/93 *Brasserie du Pêcheur SA and Factortame* ECLI:EU:C:1996:79, para 55; Joined Cases C-178/94, C-179/94, C-188/94, C-189/94, and C-190/94 *Dillenkofer and Others* ECLI:EU:C:1996:375, para 25.

[121] ECJ, Case C-352/98 P *Bergaderm* [2000] ECR I-5291, para 42-44. For a detailed analysis see Alexander Türk, *Judicial Review in EU Law* (Edward Elgar Publishing 2009) 250 ff. The *Bergaderm* formula modified the previous test with its distinction between discretionary and non-discretionary acts. See ECJ, Case 5/71 *Schöppenstedt v Council* ECLI:EU:C:1971:116, para 11; CFI, Joined Cases T-481 and 484/93 *Vereniging van Exporteurs in Levende Varkens* [1995] ECR II-2941, para 81.

[122] For a good overview of the extraterritorial scope of human rights in EU law cf Lorand Bartels, 'The EU's Human Rights Obligations in Relation to Policies with Extraterritorial Effects' (2014) 25 *European Journal of International Law* 1071.

[123] For more on the concept of complicity and its limits cf Dann, *The Law of Development Cooperation* (n 10) 265. For a good overview of the EU's own commitment see Bruno Simma, Jo Aschenbrenner, and Constanze Schulte, 'Human Rights Considerations in the Development Cooperation Activities of the EC' in Philip Alston (ed), *The EU and Human Rights* (Oxford University Press 1999); Daniel Thym,

the major challenge here might not be on the legal but rather the factual side, namely that the complainants prove facts that constitute a manifest and grave disregard of the law. Unlike annulment actions, mere errors of assessment,[124] or mere infringements of EU law, are not sufficient where the responsible institution enjoys more than 'considerably reduced' discretion. This will often be the case: in external assistance law, *procedural* norms can be very specific and non-discretionary; however, EU bodies generally enjoy a broad discretion concerning the *substantive* content of the specific project or policy. Understandably, this is often unavoidable due to the highly technical, economic, political, and social complexities of the external measures referred to here, and which can vary considerably from case to case.

In consequence, victims affected by (development) cooperation or humanitarian assistance can usually not challenge illegal acts successfully: annulment actions are generally inadmissible, and actions for non-contractual damages are often unfounded because it is extremely difficult to prove that a breach of law is sufficiently serious. It would be desirable to reduce such obstacles to judicial review, at least as concerns development and humanitarian aid, two policy areas that are ostensibly committed to reduce poverty and human suffering. Making judicial review at least somewhat more accessible for potential victims of the Union's external measures and projects would reaffirm the seriousness of its commitment towards humanity.

J Conclusion and Outlook

The law of EU external assistance is more than an area of foreign politics wrapped up in nothing but broad and vague legal principles. It is rather an area where decision-making is increasingly guided by a set of administrative norms that have been classified here as transnational benefits administration law. This is an area where decisions are not substantively prescribed by legislatures, but rather are based on general principles and objectives which then, during a densely regulated administrative procedure, are turned into specific targets and embodied in substantive rules. It can, thus, be regarded as a fruitful field of study from (at least) two perspectives, which we would call the international politics perspective and the administrative theory perspective.

For the administrative theory perspective, especially the fact that traditional enforcement measures are largely absent turns external assistance law into an interesting field of study. This includes (but is not limited to) the theory and practice of new approaches to the scholarship of administrative management ('*Steuerungswissenschaft*', New Public Management approach, etc). Transnational benefits administration law is, therefore, of its nature situated beyond classic command-and-control approaches. The use of concepts, information-generation techniques, indicators, or principle-based programming and planning are but a few keywords which illustrate where links to general theoretical debates about (international) administrative law and theory might be established.

'Auswärtige Gewalt' in Armin von Bogdandy and Jürgen Bast (eds), *Principles of European Constitutional Law* (Hart Publishing 2006) 464.

[124] Craig, *EU Administrative Law* (n 116) 688.

From the angle of international politics, the emergence of (international) administrative law implies that external financing decisions are not based purely on political or economic considerations, but increasingly governed by legal rules and, in part, judicially reviewable ones. At the same time, though, access to such judicial review is often limited at best, especially for citizens and residents of third countries whose rights might be infringed by a European Union initiative. The role of law in the external assistance sector can therefore, beyond a doctrinal analysis, be subject to further empirical or theoretical research. Such analysis would be both challenging and promising because of the location of external assistance law right at the interface between value-based and real-power politics.

PART III

SECURITY AND JUSTICE

7

European Union Criminal Law

Valsamis Mitsilegas and Niovi Vavoula

A Introduction

The past three decades have witnessed the gradual evolution of a supranational system of criminal law by the European Union. This is a striking development, since criminal law is an area of great significance for state sovereignty and national identity, whereby EU Member States have developed divergent legal traditions and understandings. Although the Treaty of Rome did not confer any express power on the then European Community (EC) in the field of criminal justice, the European integration process proved that it was difficult to disassociate Community action in the main areas of EC competence, including free movement and the completion of the internal market, from criminal justice policy.[1] Thus, the Maastricht Treaty established a Union competence in the field of Justice and Home Affairs, under the (former) Third Pillar, including judicial and police cooperation in criminal matters. However, decision-making in relation to this took place on the basis of unanimity within the Council, with mere consultation of the European Parliament. With the entry into force of the Amsterdam Treaty, the 'policy core' of EU criminal law became more firmly defined, resulting in the adoption of a wide range of framework decisions (e.g. on terrorism, trafficking in human beings, corruption).[2] Importantly, in order to by-pass national resistance to legal harmonization in relation to criminal matters, the mutual recognition mechanism was transplanted from its traditional internal market context into the field of criminal law.[3]

In the post-Lisbon Treaty era, the objectives and tasks in the field of EU criminal law are set out in Articles 82–89 TFEU. The Treaty abolished the pillar structure

---

[1] On that issue see judgments in Case C-68/88 *Commission of the European Communities v Hellenic Republic* (*Greek Maize* case), 21 September 1989, ECR [1989] 02965; Case C-176/03 *Commission v Council* (the environmental crime case), 13 September 2005, ECR [2005] I-07879; Case C-440/05 *Commission v Council* (the *ship-source pollution* case), 23 October 2007, ECR [2007] 09097. For an analysis see V Mitsilegas, *EU Criminal Law* (Hart Publishing 2009) 70–84.

[2] Framework decisions were adopted in relation to the following offences: sexual exploitation of children and child pornography (2004/68/JHA), drug trafficking (2004/757/JHA), corruption in the private sector (2003/568/JHA), attacks against information systems (2005/222/JHA), counterfeiting of the Euro (2000/383/JHA), non-cash means of payment (2001/413/JHA), racism and xenophobia (2008/913/JHA), and organized crime (2008/841/JHA).

[3] The most emblematic EU instrument is the Council Framework Decision of 13 June 2002 on the European arrest warrant and the surrender procedures between Member States—Statements made by certain Member States on the adoption of the Framework Decision [2002] OJ L190/1.

and codified the principle of mutual recognition (Article 82(1) TFEU), leading to a progressive strengthening and harmonization of rights of defence,[4] and for the first time contained an explicit legal basis for Union legislation in the field of criminal procedure (Article 82(2) TFEU). Furthermore, Article 83(1) TFEU conferred upon the EU the competence to 'establish minimum rules concerning the definition of criminal offences and sanctions in the areas of particularly serious crime with a cross-border dimension resulting from the nature or impact of such offences or from a special need to combat them on a common basis'. Moreover, Article 83(2) took over the Court's functionalist interpretation, providing the EU with the competence to adopt criminal laws and regulations if such harmonization is essential to ensure the effective implementation of other EU policies. A significant development in Union competence in the criminal law field has been the introduction, for the first time in EU primary legislation, of an express legal basis for the establishment of a European Public Prosecutor's Office (EPPO, Article 86 TFEU).

European integration in criminal matters has been a multi-level process, whereby efforts towards harmonization of substantive and procedural law have been accompanied by the establishment of EU bodies and agencies and by the development of composite systems of communication and coordination among the various EU structures, but also importantly, across Union and national networks and structures. To that end, the proliferation of information exchange channels, including the setting up of large-scale information systems, of specialized agencies with coordinating tasks, particularly Europol and Eurojust, and of networking structures, lies at the heart of EU criminal law. This chapter will address the elements of EU criminal law relevant to an inquiry into the administrative system of the EU. For the purposes of the analysis, three main strands will be explored and brought to the fore: (a) establishment and operation of EU agencies and bodies; (b) establishment and operation of national bodies and of transnational networks with a view to supporting the administration of EU criminal law; and (c) information exchange platforms of both centralized and decentralized nature.

---

[4] Directive 2010/64/EU of the European Parliament and of the Council of 20 October 2010 on the right to interpretation and translation in criminal proceedings [2010] OJ L280/1; Directive 2012/13/EU of the European Parliament and of the Council of 22 May 2012 on the right to information in criminal proceedings [2012] OJ L142/1; Directive 2012/29/EU of the European Parliament and of the Council of 25 October 2012 establishing minimum standards on the rights, support and protection of victims of crime, and replacing Council Framework Decision 2001/220/JHA [2012] OJ L315/57; Directive 2013/48/EU of the European Parliament and of the Council of 22 October 2013 on the right to access to a lawyer in criminal proceedings and in European arrest warrant proceedings, and on the right to have a third party informed upon deprivation of liberty and to communicate with third persons and with consular authorities while deprived of liberty [2013] OJ L294/1; Directive 2016/343 of the European Parliament and of the Council of 9 March 2016 on the strengthening of certain aspects of the presumption of innocence and of the right to be present at the trial in criminal proceedings [2016] OJ L65/1.

B Sources of Law, Administrative Bodies, Structures, and Tasks in the Field of EU Criminal Law

1 EU agencies

Integration in judicial and police cooperation in criminal matters is substantially facilitated via the establishment, development, and operation of specialized agencies. In particular, according to Article 88 TFEU, *police* cooperation is promoted through Europol, the EU Agency for Law Enforcement Cooperation, that supports cooperation between domestic law enforcement authorities through the collection, storage, further processing, analysis, and exchange of personal data, whether provided by Member States or produced by the agency itself. Operating since 1999, Europol is governed by Regulation 2016/794,[5] replacing Council Decision 2009/371/JHA[6] and the pre-existing Europol Convention.[7] This development of the legislative platform has enhanced its operational effectiveness and has confirmed a gradual shift from an intergovernmental to an increasingly supranational model of governance and accountability. Closely connected to Europol is CEPOL, the EU Agency for Law Enforcement Training, dedicated to developing, implementing, and coordinating training for law enforcement officials, and facilitating cooperation and knowledge-sharing among law enforcement officials of the Member States.[8]

The counterpart of Europol in relation to the *judicial* cooperation domain is Eurojust.[9] Article 85 TFEU constitutes the legal basis of Eurojust, enabling its further development. Eurojust is regulated by Council Decision 2002/187/JHA,[10] as amended by Council Decisions 2003/659/JHA[11] and 2009/426/JHA.[12] A Commission proposal,

---

[5] Regulation (EU) 2016/794 of the European Parliament and of the Council of 11 May 2016 on the European Union Agency for Law Enforcement Cooperation (Europol) and replacing and repealing Council Decisions 2009/371/JHA, 2009/935/JHA, 2009/936/JHA, and 2009/968/JHA [2016] OJ L135/53.

[6] Council Decision of 6 April 2009 establishing the European Police Office (Europol) [2009] OJ L121/37. This Decision equally replaced the original 1995 Europol Convention based on Art K.3 of the Treaty on European Union, on the Establishment of a European Police Office (Europol Convention) [1995] OJ C316/1. It was repealed by three protocols: a) The Protocol drawn up on the basis of Art 43(1) of the Europol Convention amending Art 2 and the Annex to that Convention—(Money Laundering Protocol) [2000] OJ C 358/2; (b) The Protocol amending the Europol Convention and the Protocol on the privileges and immunities of Europol, the members of its organs, the deputy directors and the employees of Europol—(JIT Protocol) [2002] OJ C 312/2; c) The Protocol drawn up on the basis of Art 43(1) Europol Convention amending that Convention—(Danish Protocol) [2004] OJ C002/3.

[7] Council Act of 26 July 1995 drawing up the Convention based on Art K.3 Treaty on European Union, on the establishment of a European Police Office (Europol Convention) [1995] OJ C316/1.

[8] Regulation (EU) 2015/2219 of the European Parliament and of the Council of 25 November 2015 on the European Union Agency for Law Enforcement Training (CEPOL) and replacing and repealing Council Decision 2005/681/JHA [2015] OJ L319/1.

[9] For details see Mitsilegas, *EU Criminal Law* (n 1) ch 4.

[10] Council Decision of 28 February 2002 setting up Eurojust with a view to reinforcing the fight against serious crime [2002] OJ L63/1 (2002 Eurojust Decision).

[11] Council Decision 2003/659/JHA of 18 June 2003 amending Decision 2002/187/JHA setting up Eurojust with a view to reinforcing the fight against serious crime [2003] OJ L245/44 (Eurojust Decision).

[12] Council Decision 2009/426/JHA of 16 December 2008 on the strengthening of Eurojust and amending Decision 2002/187/JHA setting up Eurojust with a view to reinforcing the fight against serious crime [2009] OJ L138/14.

reforming Eurojust, including its administrative structure, is currently subject to ne-gotiation,[13] inextricably linked with the forthcoming establishment of a European Public Prosecutor's Office (EPPO), to be entrusted with the power to investigate and prosecute fraud and other crimes affecting the Union's financial interests. The creation of the EPPO constitutes a significant constitutional innovation of the Lisbon Treaty, as Article 86 TFEU expressly and concretely allows the Council—with the prior consent of the European Parliament—to set up the EPPO. After years of thorny negotiations, Regulation 2017/1939 was adopted to this end in October 2017.[14]

Another EU body tasked with the conduct of administrative investigation within European institutions, bodies, and agencies of possible fraud affecting Union financial interests is OLAF, the European Anti-fraud Office. Its legal basis is nowhere to be found in primary law, being originally established instead in 1987 as an anti-fraud unit within the Commission (the then UCLAF) and replaced[15] in 1999 by OLAF.[16] Following a series of evaluations[17] of its activities, the office is now governed by Regulation 8883/2013.[18]

Two other agencies are relevant to the administration of EU criminal law, with, however, a scope falling broadly within the remits of the Area of Freedom, Security and Justice (AFSJ) and serving to support the administration of other fields of Union policy, particularly immigration. One, eu-LISA (European Agency for the Operational Management of Large-scale IT Systems in the Area of Freedom, Security and Justice), established under Regulation (EU) No 1077/2011,[19] concerns centralized informa-tion systems operating on the EU level mainly for immigration control, but also more broadly under the auspices of the 'Security Union'.[20] In addition, it is worth mentioning Frontex (the European Border and Coast Guard) which, after consecutive reforms, is

---

[13] Commission, Proposal for a Regulation of the European Parliament and of the Council on the European Agency for Criminal Justice Cooperation (Eurojust), COM(2013) 535 final of 17 July 2013. For the latest documents on the negotiations see Council, Documents 14306/17 (8 December 2017) and 15894/17 (21 December 2017).

[14] Council Regulation (EU) 2017/1939 of 12 October 2017 implementing enhanced cooperation on the establishment of the European Public Prosecutor's Office (EPPO) [2017] OJ L283/1. For an analysis see V Mitsilegas, *EU Criminal Law after Lisbon* (Hart Publishing 2016) ch 4.

[15] P Craig, 'The Fall and Renewal of the Commission: Accountability, Contract and Administrative Organisation' (2000) 6 *European Law Journal* 98; A Tomkins, 'Responsibility and Resignation in the European Commission' (1999) 62 *Modern Law Review* 744; and D Georgakakis, 'La démission de la Commission européenne: Scandale et tournant institutionnel (octobre 1998—mars 1999)' (2000) *Cultures et conflits* 38–39 www.conflits.org.

[16] Regulation (EC) No 1073/1999 of the European Parliament and of the Council of 25 May 1999 con-cerning investigations conducted by the European Anti-fraud Office (OLAF) [1999] OJ L136/1.

[17] Special Report No 1/2005 concerning the management of the European Anti-=d Office (OLAF), to-gether with the Commission's replies [2005] OJ C202/1; [2011] OJ C124/9 of 27 April 2011.

[18] Regulation (EU, EUROTOM) No 883/2013 of the European Parliament and of the Council con-cerning investigations conducted by the European Anti-fraud Office (OLAF) and repealing Regulation (EC) No 1074/1999 of the European Parliament and of the Council and Council Regulation (Euratom) No 1074/1999 [2013] OJ L248/1.

[19] Regulation (EU) No 1077/2011 of the European Parliament and of the Council of 25 October 2011 establishing a European Agency for the operational management of large-scale IT systems in the area of freedom, security and justice [2011] OJ L286/1. See also Commission, 'Proposal for a Regulation of the European Parliament and of the Council on the European Agency for the operational management of large-scale IT systems in the area of freedom, security and justice, and amending Regulation (EC) 1987/2006 and Council Decision 2007/533/JHA and repealing Regulation (EU) 1077/2011' COM(2017) 352 final.

[20] See section F below.

currently governed by Regulation 2016/1624.[21] Whilst the origins of this agency are rooted in the border management domain, the mandate of Frontex now explicitly encompasses broader action for mitigating potential future threats at the Union's external borders, thereby contributing to addressing serious crime with a cross-border dimension, and to ensuring a high level of internal security within the Union while safeguarding free movement of persons.[22]

2 EU bodies

Coordination in the field of Union criminal law has not been exclusively the domain of agencies, as a series of other initiatives has emerged in the past two decades also with a view to aiding cooperation here. One such initiative involves the installation of a Counter-terrorism Coordinator, agreed by the European Council in the aftermath of terrorist attacks of March 2004 in Spain.[23] Since September 2007, Gilles de Kerchove has had this position (appointed by the High Representative for Foreign Affairs and Security Policy), charged with coordinating the work of the Council in combating terrorism, presenting policy recommendations, and suggesting priorities for Council action. Another pioneering body, partly falling within the scope of the former Second Pillar of Common Foreign and Security Policy (CFSP), is the EU Intelligence and Situation Centre (INTCEN), an intelligence entity established in 2010 within the Union's External Action Service under the authority of the High Representative. INTCEN lacks a clear legal basis, but its work in monitoring events both inside and outside the EU, in order to provide intelligence analyses and situational awareness to both the Union and Member States in the fields of security, defence, and counterterrorism, is highly influential. Finally, the Council has come to play an important executive role of its own through the establishment in 2009 of the Standing Committee on Internal Security (COSI) within the Council itself,[24] as mandated by Article 71 TFEU to serve as a forum for promoting and strengthening operational cooperation between Member States in the field of internal security.

3 National bodies and transnational networks

In addition to Union bodies and structures aimed at enhancing and strengthening cooperation among Member States, a series of legal instruments has impacted on

---

[21] Regulation (EU) 2016/1624 of the European Parliament and of the Council of 14 September 2016 on the European Border and Coast Guard and amending Regulation (EU) 2016/399 of the European Parliament and of the Council and repealing Regulation (EC) No 863/2007 of the European Parliament and of the Council, Council Regulation (EC) No 2007/2004 and Council Decision 2005/267/EC [2016[OJ L251/1. For the previous legal framework see Council Regulation (EC) No 2007/2004 of 26 October 2004 establishing a European Agency for the Management of Operational Cooperation at the External Borders of the Member States of the European Union [2004] OJ L349/1 as amended by Regulation (EC) No 863/2007 and Regulation (EC) 1168/2011.

[22] Art 1 Frontex Regulation (n 21).

[23] European Council, 'Declaration on Combating Terrorism' (25 March 2004) 13.

[24] Council Decision 2010/131/EU of 25 February 2010 on setting up the Standing Committee on operational cooperation on internal security [2010] OJ L52/50.

national administrations by requiring the establishment of domestic bodies entrusted with specific tasks. A prime example of this decentralization of EU criminal law has been the requirement of establishing a financial information unit in each Member State (FIU), in order to receive and assess reports on suspicious transactions concerning money laundering and terrorism financing.[25] Furthermore, the PNR Directive 2016/681, which is at the time of writing in the national implementation process, requires Member States to establish passenger information units (PIUs) on the national level for the purpose of assessing PNR data of all passengers travelling on international flights between the EU and third countries, as transferred to them by airline carriers.[26] Another form of decentralization has been the requirement for national asset recovery offices (AROs) aimed at identifying assets illegally acquired in Member State territory, and at facilitating the exchange of relevant information.[27] Furthermore, co-operation among national authorities and bodies in relation to VAT frauds, genocide, and cybercrime is ensured through the development of designated networks, as mandated by secondary legislation. However, more generally, facilitation of judicial co-operation in criminal matters is promoted through the development of a European Judicial Network (EJN), comprising contact points in the Member States, designated on the national level from among central authorities in charge of international judicial cooperation.

4 Proliferation of information exchange mechanisms

The third strand of administrative organization and tasks in the field of EU criminal law relates to the facilitation of information exchange across law enforcement authorities on the national level. Initiatives in this respect have been twofold: on the one hand, the establishment of pan-European centralized information systems; and on the other hand, the elimination of obstacles to the exchange of personal data between national authorities. The competence to embark on these measures relies upon Article 87(2)(a) TFEU, providing for the setting up of information exchange mechanisms, which enable the collection, storage, processing, analysis, and exchange of relevant information. In that respect, a series of secondary legislative instruments setting up centralized databases has been adopted, the most emblematic being the Schengen Information System (SIS)—in its newest configuration, SIS II—a database which enables national authorities to register so-called 'alerts' in relation to specific categories of wanted persons and objects. These are essentially requests by an issuing State to the other Schengen countries to take a certain action.[28] Its *sui generis* status, as an instrument aimed at facilitating both law enforcement and border controls, is

---

[25] These reports derive from a wide range of professions, spanning from the banking sector to lawyers.

[26] Directive (EU) 2016/681 of the European Parliament and of the Council of 27 April 2016 on the use of passenger name record (PNR) data for the prevention, detection, investigation and prosecution of terrorist offences and serious crime [2016] OJ L119/132.

[27] Council Decision 2007/845/JHA of 6 December 2007 concerning cooperation between Asset Recovery Offices of the Member States in the field of tracing and identification of proceeds from, or other property related to, crime [2007] OJ L332/103.

[28] J Dumortier, 'The Protection of Personal Data in the Schengen Convention' (1997) 11 *International Review of Law, Computers & Technology* 93, 93.

exemplified by the existence of a complex legal framework (comprising three separate legal instruments governing its operation).[29] That database is supplemented by an auxiliary system, SIRENE, which provides the infrastructure for exchanging information additional to that held in SIS. Furthermore, Europol stores and allows the further processing of vast amounts of data originating either from Member States or its own analyses; the current legal framework does not, however, pre-determine a particular structure for its databases.[30] In addition to these, the Customs Information System (CIS) supports customs cooperation in regard to preventing, investigating, and prosecuting serious contraventions of national law through information exchange.[31] Finally, certain legal instruments allow for the streamlining and simplification of information concerning criminal records,[32] DNA profiles,[33] or information in criminal files.[34] A key concern in this respect has been the need for national authorities to have a full and up-to-date picture of the criminal record status of those who enter their territory, and specifically of those entering from other Member States.

C Organizational and Sector-specific Legal Principles

Within the field of criminal justice, the CJEU has applied general principles of European Union law on numerous occasions. Key principles, such as the primacy of Union law[35] and the duty of sincere cooperation or loyalty, whereby national authorities have the duty to interpret national law as far as possible in conformity with requirements of the then Community law,[36] have been found to be applicable also in this field. Furthermore, whilst information exchange is primarily underpinned by numerous principles, particularly in relation to data protection,[37] two sector-specific principles emerged in the course of the last ten or more years in the context of criminal

---

[29] Regulation (EC) 1987/2006 of the European Parliament and of the Council on the development, operation and use of the second generation Schengen Information System (SIS II) [2006] OJ L381/4 (SIS II Regulation). Regulation (EC) 1986/2006 of the European Parliament and of the Council of 20 December 2006 regarding access to the second generation Schengen Information System (SIS II) by the services in the Member States responsible for issuing vehicle registration certificates [2006] OJ L381/1. Council Decision 2007/533/JHA of 12 June 2007 on the establishment, operation and use of the second generation Schengen Information System (SIS II) [2007] OJ L205/63 (SIS II Decision).

[30] See below. For an analysis of the Europol databases see the contribution of Dimitrova in this volume (ch 9). Also see Mitsilegas (n 1) ch 5.

[31] Council Decision 2009/917/JHA of 30 November 2009 on the use of information technology for customs purposes (CIS Decision) [2009] OJ L323/20.

[32] Decision 2009/316/JHA on the establishment of the European Criminal Records Information System (ECRIS) in application of Art 11 of Framework Decision 2009/315/JHA [2009] OJ L93/13.

[33] Decision 2008/615/JHA on the stepping up of cross-border cooperation, particularly in combating terrorism and cross-border crime [2008] OJ L210/1; Decision 2008/616/JHA on the implementation of Decision 2008/615/JHA [2008] OJ L210/12.

[34] Council Framework Decision 2006/960/JHA of 18 December 2006 on simplifying the exchange of information and intelligence between law enforcement authorities of the Member States of the European Union [2006] OJ L386/89.

[35] Case C-399/11 *Melloni*, 26 February 2013, ECLI:EU:C:2013:107. Although this principle had not been applied to EU criminal law instruments prior to the Lisbon Treaty, post-communitarization, the CJEU clearly extended the primacy principle to the Framework Decision 2002/584/JHA on the EAW. See in particular para 59 of the judgment.

[36] Case C-105/03 *Pupino*, 16 June 2005, ECR [2005] I-05285.

[37] For an analysis on data protection, see the contribution of Dimitrova (ch 9) in this volume.

justice administration. A first step has been the proclamation of the principle of availability, which was first encompassed in the Hague Programme,[38] and subsequently elaborated in the 2005 Commission proposal for a (former) Third-Pillar Framework Decision.[39] This principle seeks to ensure that information be provided to equivalent competent authorities of other Member States and to Europol on a 'need-to-know' basis,[40] with information exchange taking place on the basis of standard, pro forma documents and with very few grounds for refusal available to the requested authorities.[41] That proposal was not very far-reaching. However, automaticity is introduced into such information exchange through the principle of so-called interoperability. This latter principle first emerged in the post-9/11 era,[42] fleshed-out in a Commission Communication on improved effectiveness, enhanced interoperability, and synergies among EU databases, where the concept was defined as the 'ability of IT systems and of the business processes they support to exchange data and to enable the sharing of information and knowledge'.[43] Since November 2015, the connection of the 'data pots'—irrespective of whether these have been set up for border control or law enforcement purposes—has gained fresh impetus,[44] with the Commission proposing the establishment of a framework for interoperability among EU information systems, but excluding decentralized schemes of information exchange.[45] The subtext

[38] Point 2.1, p. 27. Throughout the Union, a law enforcement officer in one Member State who needs information in order to perform his duties can obtain this from another Member State and that the law enforcement agency in the other Member State which holds this information will make it available for the stated purpose, taking into account the requirement for ongoing investigations in that State'.

[39] Commission Proposal for a Council Framework Decision on the exchange of information under the principle of availability, COM(2005) 490 final. In that respect see Council, Documents 13558/05, (24 October 2005) and 5595/06 (25.01.2006, both of which are partially accessible.

[40] ibid Art 6.

[41] ibid Art 14. For criticism see D Bigo, 'The Principle of Availability of Information', Briefing Note for European Parliament Civil Liberties Committee, reproduced in D Bigo and A Tsoukala (eds), *Controlling Security* (L'Harmattan and Centre d'Etudes sur les Conflits 2008); V Mitsilegas, written evidence for House of Commons Home Affairs Committee, inquiry on EU Justice and Home Affairs: reproduced in Report on *Justice and Home Affairs Issues at European Union Level*, 3rd Report, session 2006–07, HC 76-II, Ev 146.

[42] Council Document 13176/01 (24 October 2001).

[43] For a critique see P De Hert and S Gutwirth, 'Interoperability of Police Databases within the EU: An Accountable Political Choice?' (2006) 20(1–2) *International Review of Law Computers & Technology* 21, 22.

[44] See Commission, 'Stronger and smarter information systems for borders and security' (Communication) COM(2016) 205 final. In the Communication on stronger and smarter borders, the Commission identified four different models of interoperability, which correspond to a gradation of convergence among the systems: (a) A single search interface to query several information systems simultaneously and to produce combined results on one single screen; (b) Interconnectivity of information systems where data registered in one system will automatically be consulted by another system; (c) Establishment of a shared biometric matching service in support of various information systems; and (d) Common repository of data for different information systems (core module).

[45] Commission, 'Proposal for a Regulation of the European Parliament and of the Council on establishing a framework for interoperability between EU information systems (police and judicial cooperation, asylum and migration) COM(2017) 794 final; Proposal for a Regulation on establishing a framework for interoperability between EU information systems (borders and visa) and amending Council Decision 2004/512/EC (VIS Decision), Regulation (EC) No 767/2008 (VIS Regulation), Council Decision 2008/633/JHA (regarding law enforcement access to VIS), Regulation (EU) 2016/399 (Schengen Borders Code) and Regulation (EU) 2017/2226 (EES Regulation) COM(2017) 793 final. For a critique of the proposal see European Parliament, 'Interoperability of Justice and Home Affairs Information Systems' (Report for the LIBE Committee conducted by Optimity Advisors, 12 April 2018).

is that, where necessary and feasible, information systems should generally be inter-connected and interoperable. Simultaneous searches of systems should be facilitated, so as to ensure that all relevant information be available to border guards or police officers, when and where this is necessary for their respective tasks, without modi-fying existing access rights.

D Sectoral Organization, Institutions, and Structures in Union Criminal Law

Criminal law and its administration in the European Union constitutes a field of European integration where cooperation across Member States has been largely facilitated and promoted through the establishment, development, and prolifer-ation of Union agencies, bodies, and transnational networks within which Member State officials may exchange views with one another. Here, the structures that have emerged in recent decades, already largely identified in section B above, will be fur-ther mapped as regards their nature, composition, and main activities.

1 Agencies

As already noted, police and judicial cooperation in criminal matters heavily relies on the operation of three agencies, Europol, Eurojust, and OLAF—soon to be supple-mented by the EPPO—the powers of which are regulatory, operational, and linked to core public security functions.

Europol constitutes a mass-scale 'information hub', in order to provide intelligence support without acting as a law enforcement body as such. Under Article 9 Europol Regulation, its main organs are the executive director and the management board, but the latter may, where appropriate, establish advisory bodies. The dual management structure of this agency has always been a central aspect of its legal regime; however, whereas under the 1995 Convention those organs were complemented by the finan-cial controller and the Financial Committee,[46] following the 2009 Council Decision Europol came to be managed solely by these two elements.[47] The Commission proposal for the Europol Regulation[48] foresaw, though, a different structure for the agency,[49] including the merging between Europol and CEPOL. In addition, the Commission had unsuccessfully put forward the option of setting up an Executive Board, to assist

---

[46] Art 27 Europol Convention (n 7).

[47] Art 36 of Council Decision of 6 April 2009 establishing the European Police Office (Europol) (2009/371/JHA) (Europol Decision).

[48] Commission, 'Proposal for a Regulation of the European Parliament and of the Council on the European Union Agency for Law Enforcement Cooperation and Training (Europol) and repealing Decisions 2009/371/JHA and 2005/681/JHA' COM(2013) 173 final.

[49] See Joint Statement of the European Parliament, the Council of the EU and the European Commission on decentralized agencies http://europa.eu/agencies/documents/joint_statement_and_common_approach_2012_en.pdf.

the main organs so as to reinforce supervision of administrative management and to increase the agency's efficiency.[50]

The executive director is essentially the legal representative and manager of the agency.[51] Obliged to act independently, they are responsible for overseeing the performance of the tasks assigned to Europol, for preparing budgetary and planning documents, and for implementing the multiannual programming and annual work programmes of Europol.[52] The management board is composed of one representative from each Member Sate and a representative of the Commission, all with a voting right.[53] The Board is entrusted with a wide range of functions, such as the adoption of the multiannual programming and the annual work programme,[54] the annual budget and activity report, or various internal rules.[55] A 'communitarised' composition of the management board has been progressively achieved. In particular, under the Europol Convention, the Commission was not represented on the board, but was merely invited at the board's discretion to meetings, but without a voting status.[56] The purely intergovernmental nature of the agency was then amplified—indeed, modified—by the 2009 Council Decision, providing for the Commission's participation on the Board through one representative.[57] A new feature under the Europol Regulation is that the management board has the discretion to invite non-voting observers whose opinion may be relevant for discussions.[58]

Another important development towards the gradual communitarization of Europol relates to the voting rules within the management board. Over time, these rules have been subject to significant reforms. Under the Europol Convention, the management board would mostly adopt its decision unanimously,[59] but a two-thirds majority was foreseen for approving the opening of an analysis file,[60] deciding on the detailed provisions for drawing up reports,[61] and for resolving disputes in relation to liability.[62] The 2009 Council Decision revised this framework by setting the majority of two-thirds of its members as the general rule for decision-making unless otherwise specified.[63] However, despite this possible basis for decisions, the management board apparently continued to strive for consensus.[64] The Europol Regulation innovates by

---

[50] See Arts 21 and 22 of the proposal for a Europol Regulation. The merging of agencies and the usefulness of and executive board were disputed. For the reaction of the Commission see Commission, Communication from the Commission to the European Parliament pursuant to Article 294(6) of the Treaty on the Functioning of the European Union concerning the Position of the Council at first reading with a view to the adoption of a Regulation of the European Parliament and of the Council on the European Union Agency for Law Enforcement Cooperation (Europol) and replacing and repealing Council Decisions 2009/371/JHA, 2009/934/JHA, 2009/936/JHA, and 2009/968/JHA, COM(2016) 209 final (8 April 2016) 5.

[51] Arts 16(1) and (4) Europol Regulation (n 50).

[52] For a detailed list of the executive director's tasks see Art 16(5) Europol Regulation (n 50).

[53] ibid Art 10(1); however, according to Art 15(3) of that Regulation, the executive director does not take part in the vote.

[54] ibid Art 12.   [55] ibid Art 11(1).   [56] Art 28(2) and (4) Europol Convention (n 7).

[57] Art 37(1) Europol Decision (n 47).   [58] Recital 20 Europol Regulation (n 50) (see below).

[59] See in particular Arts 5(1), 5(7), 5(9), 11(3), 28(7), 28(10), 35(4), 37, and 42(1) Europol Convention (n 7).

[60] ibid Arts12(1) and 28(1)(7).   [61] ibid Art 16.   [62] ibid Art 38(3).

[63] Art 37(8) Europol Decision (n 47).

[64] E Disley and others, *Evaluation of the Implementation of the Europol Council Decision and of Europol's Activities* (RAND Europe 2012) xvi–xvii.

stipulating majority voting as a general rule.[65] Although a number of exceptions still remain,[66] unanimity as a threshold seems to have been abandoned.

Closely connected to Europol, CEPOL is an agency dedicated to develop, implement, and coordinate training for law enforcement officials.[67] Retaining its self-standing status as an EU agency, CEPOL facilitates cooperation and knowledge sharing among law enforcement officials of the Member States. The agency's structure combines supranational elements alongside decentralized features. It is headed by an executive director, who is accountable to a management board.[68] The latter is made up of representatives of the Member States and the Commission, meets at least twice a year, and takes decisions by way of majority, but the executive director does not have voting rights.[69] In addition, CEPOL has dedicated national units (CNUs) in every Member State, to provide information and assistance to law enforcement officials who wish to participate in the agency's activities.[70]

Eurojust promotes exchange of information, coordination, and cooperation among the competent authorities, the application of mutual recognition instruments, and the consolidation of best practice. The structure of governance of Eurojust reflects a delicate balance between agencification on the EU level and attempts by Member States to maintain intergovernmental elements in the functioning of the body as far as possible. Eurojust comprises one national member from each Member State who can be a judge, prosecutor or police officer of equivalent competence, seconded and remunerated by their Member State of origin in accordance with national practice.[71] These members together form the College of Eurojust, which is itself responsible for the organization and operation of the agency.[72] The agency is staffed by administrative personnel, headed by an administrative director.[73] The governance of Eurojust is hybrid in nature: the national members of Eurojust both cooperate with the competent national authorities in relation to ongoing investigations and prosecutions against serious cross-border crime, while simultaneously constituting the College of Eurojust, which oversees the organization.[74] In accordance with the rules of procedure of Eurojust, the President calls, and presides over, the meetings of the College, signs all official communication on behalf of the College, and represents the agency. Further, the President monitors the daily management conducted by the administrative director and directs the work of the College. The College undertakes operational, support, and coordination tasks in connection with national investigations. These are its 'core business'.[75]

---

[65] Art 15 Europol Regulation (n 50).
[66] There are a few exceptions to this rule: Art 11(1)(a) and (b) on the adoption of the multiannual programming, annual reports and annual budget, Art 13(2) on the election of a chairperson and deputy chairperson of the management board, Art 50(2) on the resolution of disputes between Europol and Member States as regards the compensation of individuals in cases of improper data processing, Art 54(8) regarding the procedure for selecting the executive director or the renewal of his or her appointment and Art 64 on language arrangements within the meetings of the board.
[67] CEPOL Regulation (n 8).   [68] ibid Arts 8–9 and 14.   [69] ibid Art 13.
[70] ibid Art 6.
[71] Art 2(1) 2002 Eurojust Decision (n 10); for the consolidated version see Decision 2009/426/JHA [2009] OJ L138 of 4 June 2009 at 14.
[72] ibid Art 28(1).   [73] ibid Art 29.   [74] ibid Arts 6 and 7.
[75] M Coninsx, 'Eurojust' in V Mitsilegas, M Bergström, and T Konstadinides (eds), *Research Handbook on EU Criminal Law* (Edward Elgar Publishing 2016) 443.

The Commission proposal for a Eurojust Regulation[76] aims at restructuring the agency so as to alleviate the administrative burden on national members, allowing them to focus on their operational tasks. In this context, it proposes a new governance structure, according to which the College would meet in two distinct formations—one for operational issues, the other for administrative issues[77]—and an executive board would be set up to assist the College and the administrative director.[78] Furthermore, the Commission would be represented in the College by two Commission officials when discussing managerial matters[79] and in the executive board.[80] An innovative feature foresees two Commission representatives joining the College when it is undertaking its administrative tasks, adopting the budget or the annual report, appointing the administrative director, or adopting the Rules of Procedure.[81] The executive board would be installed as a new body and would prepare the College's administrative decisions and assume some administrative tasks directly. It would comprise of a Commission representative, national members, and the administrative director.[82] In its General Approach,[83] the Council favoured an alternative model of governance for Eurojust, designed to allow the College to focus primarily on its operational tasks by designating the preparation of all managerial matters for the new executive board.[84] At the time of writing, the negotiations for the Eurojust Regulation are moving ahead speedily, with trilogues focusing on the revised structure of the agency. The compromise draft lists those managerial duties that are to be conducted by Eurojust as a College, where the latter is to be assisted by an executive board, responsible for taking administrative decisions which ensure the proper functioning of Eurojust. The board would review the necessary preparatory work of the administrative director on other administrative matters for adoption by the College, but it would not be involved in Eurojust's operational activity.[85]

OLAF has a *sui generis* status, being on paper an independent body, yet structurally located within the Commission.[86] OLAF's tasks comprise the conduct of external administrative investigations in Member States wherever the EU's financial interests are at stake, and in third countries and on the premises of international organizations in accordance with international agreements or other legal instruments in force. OLAF also conducts internal administrative investigations within Union institutions, bodies, agencies, and offices, in relation to the protection of EU financial interests and

---

[76] Commission, 'Proposal for a Regulation of the European Parliament and of the Council on the European Agency for Criminal Justice Cooperation (Eurojust)' COM(2013) 535 final of 17 July 2013.

[77] ibid Arts 4, 5, and 14.   [78] ibid Art 16.   [79] ibid Arts 10(1)(b).   [80] ibid Art 16(4).

[81] For voiced concerns on the *raison d'être*, functions, and competences of the two Commission representatives see European Parliament, 'Working Document on the European Union Agency for Criminal Justice Cooperation (Eurojust)' (LIBE Committee, 14 March 2014).

[82] To a large extent, the proposed structural duality of Eurojust is largely in line with the common approach on EU decentralized agencies endorsed by the European Parliament, the Council and the Commission in July 2012, but some discrepancies are still evident (eg accountability of administrative director).

[83] Council of the European Union Document 6643/15 (27 February 2015).

[84] For the discussions on the revised model see Council of the European Union Document 8839/14 (16 April 2014) and Document 9486/14 (19 May 2014).

[85] For the compromise text see Council of the European Union Document 14306/2/17 (8 December 2017).

[86] On this paradox see Mitsilegas, *EU Criminal Law* (n 1) ch 4.

serious issues concerning the discharge of professional duties, and the coordination of investigative activities by Member States' authorities and assistance to them. OLAF's investigations are conducted under the authority of its director-general, who is fully independent and not subject to instruction by other EU institutions, bodies, or agencies.[87] The director-general, appointed by the Commission for a non-renewable term of seven years,[88] may open an investigation where there is sufficient suspicion that there has been fraud, corruption, or other illegal activity affecting the financial interests of the Union, acting on their own initiative or following a request from a Member State or an EU institution.[89] Direction of the conduct of the investigation is entrusted to the director-general, who may provide written instructions where appropriate.[90] Each year they determine the policy priorities of the office's investigations, forwarding them prior to publication to the Supervisory Committee.[91] The director-general informs the Supervisory Committee on the office's activities, the implementation of its investigative function, and the action taken by way of follow-up to investigations. In particular, he or she shall inform the Committee of cases in which their recommendations have not been followed, of cases in which information has been transmitted to national judicial authorities, or about the duration of investigations.[92]

The forthcoming EPPO will be responsible for investigating, prosecuting, and bringing to judgment the perpetrators of, and accomplices in, offences against the EU's financial interests. The EPPO will exercise the functions of prosecutor in the competent courts of the Member States in relation to such offences.[93] Prior to the adoption of the EPPO Regulation, a number of models were put forward as regards its structure and powers, with some scholars conceiving the agency from the perspective of a vertical/hierarchical structure in relation to Member States, juxtaposing this model to strengthening horizontal cooperation under Eurojust. Others focused more on the degree of centralization of prosecutorial power within the EPPO, and on the relationship between a centralized and a decentralized prosecutorial model in this context.[94] In the course of the negotiations on the establishment of an EPPO, various incarnations of these models emerged. These ranged from a centralized, vertical model put forward by the Commission to a more intergovernmental, collegiate model, which was preferred by the Council.[95] The chosen version foresees a complex structure for the EPPO, organized on both a central and a decentralized level, whereby supranational and intergovernmental elements co-exist, thus addressing Member State concerns regarding

---

[87] Art 17 OLAF Regulation (n 16).

[88] ibid Art 17(1); concerning the appointment see Art 17(2). Compare with Art 5(1) of Commission Decision 1999/352/EC (ECSC, Euratom) of 28 April 1999 establishing the European Anti-fraud Office (OLAF Decision).

[89] Art 5 OLAF Regulation (n 16).   [90] ibid Art 7(1).   [91] ibid Art 17(5).

[92] ibid Art 17(5).   [93] Art 86(2) TFEU.

[94] On key academic and policy discussions of various EPPO models see V Mitsilegas (ed), 'The Future of Prosecution After Lisbon' (2013) 4 *New Journal of European Criminal Law*. See in particular K Ligeti and M Simonato, 'The European Public Prosecutor's Office: Towards a Truly European Prosecution Service?' (2013) 4(1–2) *New Journal of European Criminal Law* 7; S White, 'Towards a *Decentralised* European Public Prosecutor's Office?' (2013) 4(1–2) *New Journal of European Criminal Law* 22; L Harman and E Szabova, 'European Public Prosecutor's Office: *Cui Bono?*'(2013) 4(1–2) *New Journal of European Criminal Law* 40.

[95] For an overview of the discussions see Mitsilegas, *EU Criminal Law after Lisbon* (n 14) 104–09.

the establishment of an overtly centralized arrangement deviating from the more collegiate structure of Eurojust.[96]

The central office comprises the College, the Permanent Chambers, the European chief prosecutor and deputies, the European prosecutors, and the administrative director.[97] On the other hand, the European delegated prosecutors (EDPs), acting on behalf of the EPPO, will operate on the decentralized level.[98] The College composed of the European chief prosecutor and one European prosecutor for each Member State is the management body of the agency. It will be responsible for the general oversight of EPPO activities and for taking decisions in strategic matters and on general issues, but will not be involved in taking operational decision in individual cases.[99] It adopts the budget of the agency and sets up the Permanent Chambers, the 'heart' of the EPPO. The Permanent Chambers are to have three members, the chair and two permanent members, with the task of monitoring and directing the casework of the EPPO.[100] Furthermore, as head of the EPPO, the European chief prosecutor, appointed by common accord of the European Parliament and the Council, has the function of organizing the work, directing activities, and taking decisions.[101] As for the EDPs, they play a key role in the EPPO by carrying out investigations under the direction of the Central Office and putting into practice the decisions of the Permanent Chambers in their Member States.[102] Finally, there is an additional layer in the organizational structure, between the Chambers and the EDPs, namely the supervisory European Prosecutor, who oversees the activities of the EDPs, instructing in a specific case if deemed necessary.[103] This official is one of the European Prosecutors of the College, coming from the same Member State as the EDP concerned, acting as a liaison for information sharing between the Chambers and the EDP.[104]

This structure demonstrates a rather complex and bureaucratic system for European prosecution,[105] composed of 'too many chiefs and not enough Indians'.[106] Key concerns involve the similarities of the EPPO structure with that of Eurojust in terms of intergovernmental elements. The centrality of Permanent Chambers, which will operate collegiately and involving in decisions the Member State(s) where investigations are being conducted, indicates that priority has been given to the ownership of the procedure by Member States, above the need for an authority able to take speedy decisions in the context of investigations.[107] The insertion of intergovernmental elements is also evident in the provisions on the appointment of the EPPO: the European prosecutors will be nominated by their respective Member States and be appointed by the Council, acting by a simple majority and taking into account the opinion of a selection panel;[108] the EDPs, nominated by Member States, will be appointed by the College

---

[96] Art 8(1) and (2) EPPO Regulation (n 14).   [97] ibid Art 8(3).   [98] ibid Art 13.
[99] ibid Art 9.   [100] ibid Art 10.   [101] ibid Art 11.   [102] ibid Art 13.
[103] ibid Art 10(5).   [104] ibid Art 12(5).
[105] F Giuffrida, 'The European Public Prosecutor's Office: King without Kingdom?' (CEPS Research Report No 2017/03, February 2017) 16.
[106] A Csúri, 'The Proposed European Public Prosecutor's Office—from a Trojan Horse to a White Elephant?' (2016) *Cambridge Yearbook of European Legal Studies* 24.
[107] V Mitsilegas and F Giuffrida, 'Raising the Bar? Thoughts on the Establishment of the European Public Prosecutor's Office' (CEPS 2017/39, 30 November 2017) 7.
[108] Art 16 EPPO Regulation (n 14).

on a proposal from the European chief prosecutor.[109] Another issue involves the possibility of conflict of opinion between the Chambers and the supervising European prosecutor, and the extent to which the latter should have the final say, since in any given case he or she will definitely be more acquainted with the legal system in which the investigation is carried out.[110]

A key issue in this context involves the relationship between the different EU bodies, and specifically that of the EPPO with Eurojust and OLAF. In addition to providing access to the case management systems of Eurojust and OLAF (as explained below),[111] the EPPO Regulation envisages a close link with OLAF. The latter may be requested to provide information, analysis, expertise, and operational support, facilitate coordination of specific actions of the competent national administrative authorities and EU bodies, and conduct administrative investigations. However, due to their different natures, whilst OLAF is to support the activities of the EPPO, parallel investigations of the same facts are explicitly proscribed.[112] The special relationship of the EPPO with Eurojust, as set out in Article 86(1) TFEU, envisages mutual cooperation within their respective mandates, and the development of 'operational, administrative and management links'.[113] Crucially, Eurojust is to enable coordination, and facilitation of judicial cooperation, in regard to serious crimes falling within the scope of the EPPO, but also encompassing non-participating Member States or third countries.[114] Overall, there is a degree of complementarity between the work of these bodies, and one can imagine that their relationships will be moulded and evolve over time. Without the participation of eight Member States in the enhanced cooperation of the EPPO, a close relationship based on mutual trust, avoidance of duplication of tasks and exchange of information will be important.[115]

In addition, the role of **eu-LISA** is entangled with the operational management of the centralized databases established within the AFSJ, including responsibility for the communication infrastructure.[116] At the time of writing, eu-LISA's mandate encompasses the functioning of the SIS II, the Visa Information System (VIS), which stores personal data of visa applicants, and the Eurodac, which registers the fingerprints of asylum seekers and irregular migrants. Eu-LISA's structure comprises a management board, an executive director, and advisory groups.[117] In addition, a data protection officer, a security officer, and an accounting officer are foreseen.[118] The day-to-day administration, management, and representation of the agency is entrusted to the executive director, appointed by the management board for a five-year term.[119] The management board is composed of one representative from each Member State and two representatives of the Commission.[120] It exercises disciplinary authority, oversees the performance of the executive director, and is responsible for the multi-annual and annual programmes, as well as the drafting of the annual reports.[121] A peculiarity

---

[109] ibid Art 17.   [110] Giuffrida (n 105) 15.   [111] See section E(c) below.
[112] Art 101(2) EPPO Regulation (n 14).   [113] ibid Art 100(1).   [114] ibid Art 100(2)(b).
[115] Mitsilegas and Giuffrida (n 107) 17. A Weyembergh and C Brière, 'The Future Cooperation between OLAF and the European Public Prosecutor's Office' (Study for the CONT Committee of the European Parliament, 2017).
[116] Art 1 eu-LISA Regulation (n 19).   [117] ibid Art 11.   [118] ibid.   [119] ibid Art 18.
[120] ibid Art 13.   [121] ibid Art 12.

of eu-LISA is the existence of three advisory groups, one for each database within the mandate of the agency, striving for consensus in drafting opinions on the annual work programme and the annual activity reports.[122] Each Member State, which is bound under Union law by any legislative instrument governing the development, establishment, operation, and use of a particular large-scale IT system, along with the Commission, appoints a member to the Advisory Group relating to the system concerned, for a (renewable) three-year term. Arguably, eu-LISA is to be characterized as an agency of rather technical nature, where fundamental rights concerns are apparently side-lined in lieu of burgeoning digitalization and the efficient, speedy, and automatic identification and management of persons and their personal data. Consequent upon the principle of interoperability, the role of eu-LISA is to be further expanded, but the proposal does not appear to address the technical underpinning of the agency.

Finally, Frontex has been established with a view to the efficient management of the crossing of the EU external borders, a task which involves addressing the challenges of (illegal and/or large-scale) migration and potential threats at those borders, and thus contributing to addressing serious crime with a cross-border dimension, in order to ensure a high level of internal security for the Union.[123] Consequently, the work of Frontex should be seen as an awkward combination of law enforcement and border control, including activities related to the prevention and detection of cross-border crime (e.g., migrant smuggling, trafficking in human beings, terrorism) and support and coordination of the analysis of risks for internal security across Member States.[124] The main organs of this agency are the management board, the executive director, the consultative forum, and the fundamental rights officer. Arguably, an intergovernmental imprint prevails, as the strategic governance of Frontex is entrusted to the management board, composed of one representative of each Member State and two of the Commission, without participation of the European Parliament or other Union body,[125] with most decisions being adopted by absolute majority.[126] The Executive Director is appointed by a two-thirds majority of the management board from a list of at least three candidates drawn up by the Commission,[127] and is responsible for the daily management, preparing and implementing decisions, programmes, and activities approved by the Board.[128] An attempt to introduce a 'supervisory board' to advise the executive director, which would have given a firmer grip on the agency

---

[122] ibid Art 19.
[123] Emphasis added. See also recital 2 of the preamble to the Regulation, which states that the aim is to manage the crossing of the external borders efficiently and address migratory challenges and potential future threats at those borders, thereby contributing to addressing serious crime with a cross-border dimension and ensuring a high level of internal security within the Union.
[124] Emphasis added. According to recital 19 of the preamble: 'Given its activities at the external borders, the Agency should contribute to preventing and detecting serious crime with a cross-border dimension, such as migrant smuggling, trafficking in human beings and terrorism, where it is appropriate for it to act and where it has obtained relevant information through its activities ... Cross-border crimes necessarily entail a cross-border dimension. Such a cross-border dimension is characterised by crimes directly linked to unauthorised crossings of the external borders, including trafficking in human beings or smuggling of migrants'.
[125] Art 63(1) EBCG Regulation (n 21). See V Moreno-Lax, *Accessing Asylum in Europe: Extraterritorial Border Controls and Refugee Rights under EU Law* (OUP 2017) 160.
[126] Art 67(1) and (3) EBCG Regulation (n 21).   [127] ibid Art 68.   [128] ibid Art 68.

to the Commission, was not included in the latest EBCG Regulation.[129] The addition of the Consultative Forum and a fundamental rights officer results from the reform of the agency's legal framework in 2011, obliging Frontex to adopt a Fundamental Rights Strategy (FRS). The Consultative Forum, composed of representatives from the European Asylum Support Office (EASO), the Fundamental Rights Agency (FRA), UNHCR, and other relevant organizations has been established to advise on fundamental rights matters,[130] while the fundamental rights officer contributes to the effective monitoring of the impact of agency's activity on fundamental rights. In addition, the tasks of Frontex require a certain level of decentralization, in deployment of border guards and other relevant staff as members of Frontex teams in joint operations, rapid border interventions, and within the framework of migration management support teams.[131] The profiles and the number of the members in each team are decided by the management board on a proposal from the executive director.[132] For each joint operation or rapid border intervention the executive director appoints one or more experts as a coordinating officer.[133] In addition, liaison officers of the agency (appointed by the executive director), monitor the management of external borders on the national level in the Member States, and in relations with third states, and are responsible for fostering cooperation and dialogue between the agency and national authorities.[134]

2 EU bodies

Since its introduction, the position of the EU Counter-terrorism Coordinator (CTC) has been answerable to the European Council's General Secretariat. The CTC acts as a guardian of counter-terrorism, coordinates the work of the European Council in combating terrorism, and oversees all existing counter-terrorism measures. It reports to the Council on the functioning and implementation of such measures, and gives detailed policy recommendations for priority areas of action twice a year, as well as otherwise when deemed necessary. Therefore, the CTC operates as a 'political, strategic and operational guide'.[135] Appointments of both coordinators—as noted above, presently de Kerchove, and before that Gijs de Vries—have been decided by the previous High Representative for Foreign Affairs and Security Policy, Javier Solana, whose function and role fall within the scope of the CFSP. Arguably, the legality of these appointments might be called into question in view of the lack of a legal basis for the establishment of this body, and of the lack of transparency as regards appointment decisions. These concerns are exacerbated by the increasingly important role of

---

[129] Commission, 'Proposal for a Regulation of the European Parliament and of the Council on the European Border and Coast Guard and repealing Regulation (EC) No 2007/2004, Regulation (EC) No 863/2007 and Council Decision 2005/267/EC COM(2017) 261 final.

[130] Art 70(1) EBCG Regulation (n 21).   [131] ibid Art 20.

[132] In cases of rapid reaction the management board decides by a three-quarters majority. See Art 20(3) EBCG Regulation (n 21).

[133] ibid Art 22.   [134] ibid Art 12.

[135] H Busch and M Monroy, 'Who Drives EU Counter-terrorism? On the Legislation of the European Union' *Statewatch Analysis* (May 2017) 2.

the Coordinator in proposing new legislation, or amendment of existing legal instruments on terrorism, falling within the scope of the AFSJ, rather than within that of the CFSP.

Similar legality concerns are raised in connection to INTCEN, entrusted with the task of collecting, processing, and analysing intelligence from Member States. The history of the emergence of this rather small agency is somewhat foggy: in 2002, INTCEN's predecessor organization was established as a directorate of the General Secretariat of the Council as the ' Joint Situation Centre' (SITCEN), for which staff from national intelligence services would be seconded, so as to exchange sensitive intelligence.[136] The legal basis of such transfers was unclear, although it is reported that it took place on the initiative of the High Representative.[137] Pursuant to the decision to establish the European External Action Service (EEAS), SITCEN was transferred to it in 2010, without reference to its formal legal basis or any constitutive document, thus accentuating already existing concerns regarding its legality. Since 2012, renamed INTCEN, it is managed by a secretary-general answerable to the head of the EEAS (who is in fact the High Representative).

The tasks of COSI are to set priorities and coordinate operational cooperation between Member States. In this capacity, it acts in a number of different areas, including police and customs cooperation, protection of external borders, and judicial cooperation in criminal matters. It must submit a regular report on its activities to the Council, which then informs the European Parliament and the national parliaments. COSI does not take part in the preparation of new legislation or the conduct of operations, but plays a strategic role in evaluating the operational measures of the agencies of the Member States and to coordinate them if necessary. With a presidency which rotates twice annually, COSI is composed of members of the competent national ministries, assisted by permanent representatives of the Union and by the European Council's secretariat. Members of the Commission and the EEAS also participate and representatives from agencies may be invited as well, particularly from Europol and Frontex.[138] Its membership was initially contemplated as consisting of permanent members, but non-fixed membership has prevailed as the rule.[139] It has been pointed out that, in practice, the representation of Member States in COSI is unbalanced both in terms of rank and as regards the background of participants (ministries/law enforcement authorities/Brussels staff).[140] COSI has attracted criticism for becoming, in effect, a Union interior ministry in the making, or—at another extreme—a toothless standing committee struggling to define its role. Indeed, the rotating presidency and the changing membership may jeopardize the continuity of COSI's work, while other actors, such as the Council's secretariat and agencies, may come to exert a dominating influence on its deliberations.

---

[136] C Jones, 'Secrecy Reigns at the EU's Intelligence Analysis Centre' *Statewatch Analysis* (January 2013).
[137] ibid.   [138] European Council 'Declaration on Combating Terrorism' (n 23) 4.
[139] Council of the European Union Document 5949/10 (5 February 2010).
[140] J Jeandesboz and others, 'Developing an EU Internal Security Strategy, Fighting Terrorism and Organised Crime' (Study for the LIBE Committee PE 462.423011) 41.

3 The proliferation of transnational networks

The wide divergences among national criminal justice systems, coupled with the increasing cross-border dimension of criminality, have necessitated increased cooperation between national authorities and the exchange of expertise by way of platforms facilitating such interaction. A primary example of this is the European Network of National Officials to Detect and Combat New Cases of Cross-Border VAT Fraud (Eurofisc), a decentralized network of national officials responsible for the detection and prosecution of cross-border VAT fraud.[141] Its main task is to ensure that VAT is correctly applied in cross-border transactions taxable in a Member State other than that in which the supplier is established and to act appropriately when VAT fraud in fact takes place. These tasks are pursued through an information system which includes an early identification mechanism that permits rapid and accurate information storage and exchange. Similar platforms have been introduced in relation to cybercrime (National Cybercrime Alert Platforms),[142] genocide (Genocide Network), and corruption (Contact-Point Network against Corruption).[143]

Alongside these structures, dedicated to specific criminal offences, a series of other networks has emerged. The prime example here is the European Judicial Network (EJN), a network of national contact points for the facilitation of judicial cooperation in criminal matters.[144] Its aim is to assist with establishing direct contact between competent authorities, to provide legal and practical information necessary for preparing an effective request for judicial cooperation, and to improve judicial cooperation in general. In this context, EJN contact points, appointed under internal (national) rules and procedures, are meant to function as 'active intermediaries' by facilitating direct contact between competent authorities and by providing legal and practical information. Moreover, the EJN Contact Points are involved in, and promote, the organization of training sessions on judicial cooperation. Eurojust and the EJN maintain 'privileged relations with each other, based on consultation and complementarity', including informing the EJN on cases where it may be the more suitable body to deal with these.[145] An additional structure is the Joint Investigation Team Experts Network, established in July 2005 in accordance with The Hague Programme

---

[141] Eurofisc was established in line with the Conclusions of the Economic and Financial Affairs Council on 7 October 2008 and it was officially created via the Council Regulation (EU) No 904/2010 of 7 October 2010. Council Regulation (EU) No 904/2010 of 7 October 2010 on administrative cooperation and combating fraud in the field of value added tax (recast) [2010] OJ L28/1 of 12 October 2010.

[142] The legal basis for establishing national cybercrime platforms is nowhere to be found in either primary or secondary legislation. Their setting up at the national level has rather been mandated by JHA Council Conclusions adopted in October 2008. Council Conclusions on setting up national alert platforms and a European alert platform for reporting offences on the Internet, JHA Council of 24 October 2008. See also Council Conclusions concerning an action plan to implement the concerted strategy to combat crime (General Affairs Council, 26 April 2010).

[143] Both these networks have been established through Eurojust. See Council Decision 2002/494/JHA [2002] OJ L167/1 of 26 June 2002.

[144] Council Decision 2008/976/JHA of 16 December 2008 on the European Judicial Network [2008] OJ L348/130.

[145] Art 25a Eurojust Decision (n 11).

'with a view to encouraging the use of JITs [Joint Investigation Teams] and exchanging experiences and best practices'.[146]

Finally, the establishment and operation of the High-level Expert Group on Information Systems and Interoperability (HLEG) also deserves mention here.[147] The Group was appointed for a limited duration until mid-2017 and comprised authorities from Schengen states, as well as relevant EU agencies, the Counter-terrorism Centre (CTC), and the EDPS, with the overarching objective of improving the functioning of information systems and exploring various tasks in relation to interoperability.[148] A key concern, however, regarding its operation was the lack of transparency as regards the identity and status of its members, appointed by Member States on the basis of their expertise and position in the national administration, but without further information revealed in public documentation.

E Administrative Procedures in the EU Criminal Policy Field

The previous section highlighted the emergence of transnational structures and bodies aimed at bringing together officials from Member States or coordinating their activities. Beyond this, the administrative law in this field also encompasses the numerous administrative procedures embedded within criminal law instruments. Broadly centred upon the exchange of information among Member States, these procedures relate to three main areas of action: first, in relation to information exchange channels, the Commission is entrusted with the adoption of rules through comitology procedures; secondly, with a view to facilitating information exchange for the fight against terrorism and other serious offences, Member States have been increasingly required by EU criminal law to establish or assign specific roles to national bodies; and, thirdly, information exchange necessarily requires a series of administrative procedures in regard to information management. This section considers the administrative law rules applicable to each of these key areas.

1 The role of the Commission in adopting implementing decisions

The field of EU criminal law is admittedly not one where the Commission has an extensive role in adopting delegated or implementing acts generally. It is only in the domain of information exchange that the Commission has been entrusted with specific powers to establish such rules. A prime example here has been the elaboration of the rules governing the operation of SIRENE (the necessary corollary of SIS II), known as the SIRENE Manual, set up by the Commission under a power delegated to it.[149]

---

[146] The Hague Programme: Strengthening Freedom, Security and Justice in the European Union [2004] OJ C53/1 at 13.

[147] Commission Decision of 17 June 2016 setting up the High-level Expert Group on Information Systems and Interoperability (2016/C 257/03).

[148] High-level expert group on information systems and interoperability, Final report (May 2017).

[149] The current legal framework is Commission Implementing Decision (EU) 2017/1528 of 31 August 2017 replacing the Annex to Implementing Decision 2013/115/EU on the SIRENE Manual and other implementing measures for the second generation Schengen Information System (SIS II) (notified under document C(2017) 5893) [2017] OJ L231/6.

That Manual prescribes detailed technical rules on the functioning of the national SIRENE Bureaux, including the relationship with EU agencies, such as Europol and Eurojust explains best practices, and sets quality standards as a regards information exchange (also taking into account different categories of alert). Another example of the Commission's role in this field has been the adoption of a decision on the setting up of the HLEG.[150] The Decision defined the tasks of the HLEG, the duration of its functioning, and its composition. Finally, whilst that aspect is no longer now being pursued, it is noteworthy that, in the Commission proposal on the principle of availability, a comitology procedure was prescribed for determining the definition of equivalence between national law enforcement authorities, thus evading full parliamentary scrutiny.[151]

2 Composite procedures

Cooperation in criminal matters has been promoted through the establishment of designated bodies within the Member States, entrusted with specific tasks defined on the Union level, with a view to their becoming the focal points for cooperation in a particular segment of this policy area. The first example in this respect has been the establishment and operation of financial information units (FIUs) in each Member State. These units access financial data transmitted or retrieved by the private sector, the purpose being to combat money-laundering and the financing of terrorism. Their setting up was mandated in the first Anti-Money Laundering Directive of 1991 but, for many years, until the adoption of the fourth Anti-money Laundering (AML) Directive in 2015, their operation was regulated in very brief form, with few general provisions in the AML Directives and a Third-Pillar Decision on FIU cooperation[152] concerning arrangements between national FIUs for information exchange. In particular, the third AML Directive stated merely that coordination and cooperation between FIUs, including the establishment of a decentralized network named FIU. net, should be encouraged as much as possible, for which purpose the Commission would provide assistance.[153] Importantly, EU law had not imposed upon Member States any specific model of FIUs. Hence, these developed organically on the national level and have taken many different forms, broadly categorizable into four alternative models: police FIUs; administrative FIUs; judicial FIUs; and independent FIUs.[154]

---

[150] Commission Decision of 17 June 2016 setting up the High Level Expert Group on Information Systems and Interoperability [2016] OJ C257/3 (n 147).

[151] ibid Art 5. Moreover, measures adopted under this procedure will be classified as 'confidential'.

[152] Council Decision of 17 October 2000 concerning arrangements for cooperation between financial intelligence units of the Member States in respect of exchanging information [2000] OJ L271/4.

[153] See Recital 40 and Art 38 of the third AML Directive (Third Money Laundering Directive (2005/60/EC) (MLD3)).

[154] For an early such categorization see V Mitsilegas, 'New Forms of Transnational Policing: The Emergence of Financial Intelligence Units in the European Union and the Challenges for Human Rights: Part 1' (1999) 3 *Journal of Money Laundering Control* 147; V Mitsilegas, 'New Forms of Transnational Policing: The Emergence of Financial Intelligence Units in the European Union and the Challenges for Human Rights: Part 2' (2000) 3 *Journal of Money Laundering Control* 250. A more recent analysis confirms the substance of this categorization: see I. Deleanu, 'FIUs in the European Union: Facts and Figures, Functions and Facilities' in B Unger et al. (eds), *The Economic and Legal Effectiveness of the European Union's Anti-Money Laundering Policy* (Edward Elgar Publishing 2014) 97–124.

These differences in national types of FIUs can be explained by variations in Member States' efforts to accommodate the new, preventive anti-money laundering framework within their legal and financial systems.[155] Against this background, the fourth AML Directive calls for the setting up of 'operationally independent and autonomous FIUs' on the national level, in order to collect and analyse the information received with the aim of establishing links between suspicious transactions and underlying criminal activity, so as to prevent and combat money laundering and terrorism financing.[156] FIUs are also responsible for disseminating the results of their analyses to competent authorities where there are grounds to suspect money laundering, associated predicate offences, or terrorism financing, and may require additional information from obliged entities.[157] They enjoy maximized access to administrative and law enforcement data, and may cooperate through the EU Financial Intelligence Units' Platform (EU FIUs Platform), an informal group composed of representatives from FIUs, active since 2006. Cooperation between FIUs takes place 'to the greatest extent possible' under highly favourable rules,[158] irrespective of the model adopted (as noted above) for their organization in a given Member State.[159] This effectively permissive approach is characterized by limited possibilities for denying disclosure of information in response to a request by another FIU.[160] At the time of writing, the European Union institutions have reached political agreement on a fifth AML Directive, which will further strengthen the powers of FIUs. In particular, this new Directive eliminates the requirement that a suspicious transaction report must have been filed beforehand by an obliged entity, before an FIU can require (additional) information from such an entity.[161] As the Commission has hinted, the nature of FIUs seems to be evolving from suspicion-based systems of disclosure into more intelligence-based disclosure systems.[162]

Similar to the data management of the FIUs, the PNR Directive requires that passenger data transmitted by airline companies will be stored and analysed by Passenger Information Units (PIUs), designated bodies on the national level to become operational by May 2018. Two or more Member States (the participating Member States) may establish or designate a single authority to serve as their (joint) PIU.[163] The operation of these bodies will be largely based on profiling and on extensive risk assessment

---

[155] In particular, the placement of FIUs outside the criminal justice sector (preferred in the majority of EU Member States) reflects the view that suspicious transaction reports—which are transferred by the private sector to be filtered by FIUs—are not necessarily relevant to criminal proceedings.

[156] See Art 32(3) of the fourth AML Directive (Fourth Money Laundering Directive ((EU) 2015/849) (MLD4)).

[157] ibid.

[158] ibid Art 53(1), which prescribes that FIUs are empowered to exchange, spontaneously or upon request, any information that may be relevant for the processing or analysis of information by the FIU related to money laundering or terrorist financing, 'even if the type of predicate offence that may be at stake is not identified at the time of the exchange'.

[159] ibid Art 52. In this regard, the European Parliament had suggested specific reference to the need to ensure compliance with data protection rules. See Council Document 7387/14 (13 March 14) 67.

[160] ibid Art 53(3).

[161] Council of the European Union Document 15849/17 (19 December 2017).

[162] Commission, 'Communication from the Commission to the European Parliament and the Council on an Action Plan for strengthening the fight against terrorism financing' COM(2016) 050 final.

[163] Art 4(4) EU PNR Directive (n 26).

and cross-referencing with national and EU-wide databases and screening criteria, aimed at identifying 'persons who were previously unsuspected of involvement in terrorism or serious crime' requiring further investigation by competent authorities in relation to serious crimes. The PIUs are also to be tasked exclusively with the exchange of data or of data-processing outcomes with competent national authorities, other Member State PIUs, Europol, and third countries. A PIU.net system will ensure secure communication and matching among PIUs themselves and between them and Europol and third countries for PNR information exchange. The rules underpinning the cooperation among PIUs do not, however, fully correspond to those relating to the FIUs as, for example, information exchange between PIUs needs to be based on reasoned requests.

Another example of national administrations coming together is the establishment and operation of Asset Recovery Offices (AROs) as national central contact points which facilitate, through enhanced cooperation, the fastest possible EU-wide tracing of assets derived from crime. Cooperation between AROs is ensured by exchanging information and best practice data, both upon request[164] and spontaneously. Since 2009, an informal Asset Recovery Offices Platform exists in order to enhance cooperation and coordination on the Union level. Cooperation is not obstructed or limited by (differences in) the status of AROs under Member State law, under which they may form part of an administrative, law-enforcement, or judicial authority. Primarily the designated AROs have been established within national law-enforcement services. The rest are divided almost equally between judicial AROs and AROs with a multi-disciplinary structure.[165]

3 Information management

Due to the heavy reliance on national law enforcement authorities and EU agencies for enhancing information exchange in the course of investigations or criminal proceedings, it has been necessary to adopt elaborate sets of rules in relation to each particular channel or database. Reflecting the particularities of each system, the rules on information management are, therefore, quite diverse, depending also upon the degree to which each mechanism is of centralized or decentralized nature.

In particular, the SIS II has been designed by default to perform as a hybrid instrument: on the one hand, as a tool for police and judicial cooperation in criminal matters (through the storage of alerts on persons wanted for arrest or surrender), and on

---

[164] See Art 3 of Council Decision 2007/845/JHA. When filling out the form provided for under Framework Decision 2006/960/JHA, the requesting Asset Recovery Office shall specify the object of and the reasons for the request and the nature of the proceedings. It shall also provide details on property targeted or sought (bank accounts, real estate, cars, yachts and other high value items) and/or the natural or legal persons presumed to be involved (eg names, addresses, dates and places of birth, date of registration, shareholders, headquarters). Such details shall be as precise as possible.

[165] Commission, 'Report from the Commission to the European Parliament and to the Council based on Article 8 of the Council Decision 2007/845/JHA of 6 December 2007 concerning cooperation between Asset Recovery Offices of the Member States in the field of tracing and identification of proceeds from, or other property related to, crime' COM(2011) 176 final.

the other hand, as an instrument for immigration and border control.[166] The SIS II is composed of a central EU system (Central SIS II) and a national system (N.SIS II),[167] in each Member State, each of the latter being the responsibility of a designated national authority.[168] SIRENE, on the other hand, is meant as the depository for supplementary information in relation to all national entries, at the disposal of other participating Member States if so required. In that sense, the SIS II practically serves as an index to the SIRENE system. After lengthy negotiations, the management of the SIS II was not entrusted to the Commission but rather, after a transitional period, to a Management Authority.[169] Under the SIS II legislation the Commission formally had the interim operational management of the system,[170] but in reality this was delegated to France and Austria (where the back-up of the system will be located). The management authority, which became responsible for supervision, security, and coordination of relations between the Member States and the provider, was replaced by eu-LISA.

The key information management tool of criminal law cooperation in relation to customs, the Customs Information System (CIS), consists of a centralized database accessible via terminals in each Member State, the Commission, Europol, and Eurojust.[171] In addition, the CIS Decision prescribes the creation of a special database, the Customs Files Identification Database (FIDE), whereby national authorities responsible for carrying out customs investigations are enabled to identify the competent authorities of other Member States which are carrying out or have carried out investigations of the persons or businesses concerned.[172]

Furthermore, as mentioned above, the management of Europol information has undergone a series of changes since the development of the system. Whilst this topic is examined in another contribution in the present volume,[173] it is worth noting certain key elements here. Before the adoption of the Europol Regulation, information processing in Europol took the form of the establishment and operation of two main data processing schemes: the Europol Information System (EIS) and the analysis work files that could be opened by Europol for specific cases.[174] The EIS interconnected the computerized networks of the national authorities with Europol, and enabled the introduction and retrieval of data from itself. As for the analysis work files, these could contain information about witnesses, victims, contacts, associates, and informants.[175] A key change of the Europol Regulation is that it no longer pre-defines databases, and it makes no explicit reference to the aforementioned systems. Instead, emphasis is placed on the exact purpose for which the data can be processed, rather than on the

---

[166] Mitsilegas, *EU Criminal Law* (n 1) 237. Under its function as a law enforcement reporting tool, alerts are stored in relation to: (a) persons wanted for arrest or surrender purposes (Art 26 Council Decision 2007/533); (b) missing persons (Art 30 Council Decision 2007/533); (c) persons sought to assist with a judicial procedure (Art 34 Council Decision 2007/533); (d) persons and objects for discreet checks or specific checks (Art 36 Council Decision 2007/533); and (e) objects sought for the purpose of seizure or use as evidence in criminal proceedings (Art 38 Council Decision 2007/533).

[167] Art 4(1) SIS II Decision (n 29).   [168] ibid Art 7(1).   [169] ibid Art 15.

[170] ibid Art 15(3).   [171] Art 3(1) CIS Decision (n 31).   [172] ibid Arts 15–19.

[173] See the contribution of Dimitrova (ch 9) in this volume.

[174] For an analysis of these systems see F Boehm, *Information Sharing and Data Protection in the Area of Freedom, Security and Justice: Towards Harmonised Data Protection Principles for Information Exchange at EU-level* (Springer 2013) 192–93.

[175] Art 14 Europol Decision (n 47).

forum of processing as such.[176] Data is indirectly accessed by Eurojust and OLAF,[177] and will be accessed by the EPPO.[178] In order to ensure the application of data protection rules, a Data Protection Officer is appointed for four years by the management board.[179]

Each agency maintains its personal and non-personal data within information systems. The Case Management System of Eurojust (CMS), supported by the Eurojust National Coordination Systems (ECNSs),[180] comprises temporary work files and an index, and is primarily aimed at supporting and facilitating the management and coordination of investigations and prosecutions.[181] The OLAF Content Management (OCM) is a case and document management tool used to conduct OLAF investigations and other activities to protect the financial interests of the EU. The forthcoming EPPO will also set up its own case management system (EPPO CMS), aimed at supporting the management of investigations and prosecutions conducted by the EPPO, in particular by managing internal information workflows and by supporting investigative work in cross-border cases. That system will comprise a register of information obtained by the EPPO, including any decisions in relation to that information, information on the case files opened when an investigation commences, and an index of the case files.[182] Exchange of information held by the relevant agencies is foreseen and regulated in a rather general manner, leaving to the agencies the discretion to conclude working agreements with more elaborated rules. Overall, Article 21 of the Europol Regulation prescribes that Eurojust and OLAF should be enabled to have indirect access to its database on the basis of a hit/no hit system. The EPPO will be able to obtain, upon request, any relevant information held by the agency, and may in addition request Europol to provide analytical support for a specific investigation.[183] Where necessary for coordination or cooperation between national investigating and prosecuting authorities, or in cases where Member States have forwarded information on cases of suspected fraud against EU financial interests, OLAF is required to transmit pertinent information to Eurojust. EPPO will have indirect access to the information in OLAF's case management system on the basis of a hit/no hit basis.[184] It will be granted the same access to Eurojust's case management system.[185]

Frontex has developed and operates an information system, capable of exchanging classified information with the Commission and the Member States.[186] The agency is empowered to send personal data of suspected criminals to Europol. The transfer of personal data is limited to information gathered by Member States during operations coordinated by Frontex about people suspected of being involved in cross-border criminal activities. Furthermore, in order to prevent and combat criminal activities,

---

[176] Art 18 Europol Regulation (n 50).   [177] ibid Art 21.
[178] Art 102 EPPO Regulation (n 14).   [179] Art 41 Europol Regulation (n 50).
[180] A Eurojust National Coordination System is located in each of the Member State and connects: the national correspondents for Eurojust (including those for terrorism matters), the European Judicial Network (EJN) and certain other contact points of national correspondents for Eurojust, and the National Members (or contact points) of the networks relating to Joint Investigation Teams, genocide, crimes against humanity and war crimes, and asset recovery and corruption.
[181] Art 16 Eurojust Decision (n 11).   [182] Art 46 EPPO Regulation (n 14).
[183] ibid Art 102(2).   [184] ibid Art 101(5).   [185] ibid Art 100(3).
[186] Art 44 EBCG Regulation (n 21).

those agencies share strategic and operational information.[187] In addition, Frontex and Eurojust have agreed to further their cooperation concerning terrorism, human trafficking, and illegal immigrant smuggling.[188]

In relation to the decentralized forms of information exchange, the European Criminal Records Information System (ECRIS),[189] is an information-technology system based on the criminal records databases in each Member State, composed of an interconnection software enabling the exchange of information between Member State criminal records databases and a common communication infrastructure that provides an encrypted network.[190] Each Member State is the central data repository regarding all criminal convictions of its own nationals (or residents), regardless of where in the EU the conviction was handed down. Each Member State must notify convictions of a national of another Member State to the latter's authorities. Such authorities must store and update all information received, and retransmit it, if and when requested. As a result, each Member State is in the position of providing exhaustive, up-to-date information from its criminal records in regard to its own nationals, irrespective of the location of the original conviction(s). Information on criminal convictions is transmitted electronically, through a standardized European format, using two reference tables listing categories of offences and penalties. The relevant legislation has provided a solid Union-wide mechanism for the exchange of criminal record data, which, according to the Commission, has led to significant progress in the sharing of criminal record information across the EU.[191] On the basis of a proposal, currently subject to negotiation, this mechanism will be supplemented by an additional centralized database specifically directed towards storing information on criminal convictions occurring in third countries.[192] Furthermore, law enforcement authorities may exchange existing information and intelligence effectively and expeditiously for the purposes of conducting criminal investigations or criminal intelligence operations under the so-called Swedish Initiative.[193] This measure does not in itself provide for special rules as regards the transmission of information, but rather gives leeway to

---

[187] Strategic Cooperation Agreement between the European Agency for the Management of Operational Cooperation at the External Borders of the Member States of the European Union and the European Police Office (2010).

[188] http://www.eurojust.europa.eu/press/News/News/Pages/2017/2017-02-24-Eurojust-and-Frontex-agree-to-develop-operational-cooperation.aspx (Eurojust, 24 February 2017) (last accessed 4 February 2018).

[189] Decision 2009/316/JHA on the establishment of the European Criminal Records Information System (ECRIS) in application of Article 11 of Framework Decision 2009/315/JHA [2009] OJ L93/13.

[190] ibid Art 3(2).

[191] Commission, 'Report from the Commission to the European Parliament and the Council on the implementation of Council Framework Decision 2009/315/JHA of 26 February 2009 on the organisation and content of the exchange of information extracted from criminal record between Member States' COM(2016) 6 final.

[192] Commission, Proposal for a Regulation of the European Parliament and of the Council establishing a centralised system for the identification of Member States holding conviction information on third country nationals and stateless persons (TCN) to supplement and support the European Criminal Records Information System (ECRIS– TCN system) and amending Regulation (EU) No 1077/2011 COM(2017) 344 final.

[193] Council Framework Decision 2006/960/JHA of 18 December 2006 on simplifying the exchange of information and intelligence between law enforcement authorities of the Member States of the European Union [2006] OJ L386/89 (Swedish Initiative).

Member States to exploit any existing channels for international law enforcement co-operation.[194] The final mechanism of note concerning decentralized information exchange is enshrined in the Prüm Decision, which effectively obliges Member States to establish national DNA analysis files for the investigation of criminal offences.[195] Member States must ensure the availability of DNA data from their national DNA files,[196] and allow automated searches for comparing DNA profiles in these databases conducted by other Member States' national contact points.[197] The same applies to automated fingerprint identification systems and vehicle registration data. DNA and fingerprint exchanges take place based on a 'hit/no-hit' approach, which means that DNA profiles or fingerprints found at a crime scene in one EU Member State can be compared automatically with profiles held in the databases of the others.

F Abstract-general Administrative Acts—Agenda-setting in EU Criminal Law

Due to the intergovernmental origins of the AFSJ, agenda-setting in the sphere of EU criminal law remains a battlefield of inter-institutional competition as to who has the final say. The activity itself could be divided in three broad tasks, (a) the preparation and issuance of general agenda-setting documents underpinning the field more broadly; (b) cross-cutting agenda-setting involving wider areas within the overall field of EU criminal law; and (c) specific agenda-setting dedicated to particular areas of criminality. In all this, the necessary impetus for the development of EU criminal law, and the establishment of its general political direction and priorities, are circumscribed by the European Council in its multi-annual programmes: the Tampere Conclusions,[198] the Hague Programme,[199] the Stockholm Programme,[200] and the Strategic Guidelines[201] have each underlined the five-year programmes, setting out priorities on the basis of which the Commission has adopted its proposals for legislation. On the basis of such guidelines, the Commission draws up action plans for concrete implementation. The emphasis on the role of the European Council, as evidenced by the wording of Article 68 TFEU, sits at odds with the supranationalization of EU criminal law post-Lisbon, and with the central role of the Commission as the initiator of legislation. These tensions between Member States and the Commission culminated, for example, in a critical reaction to the publication of the Commission's Action Plan for implementing the Stockholm Programme: in the Justice and Home Affairs Council (JHA) of June 2010 it was highlighted that 'the Stockholm Programme is the exclusive frame of reference for the political and operational agenda of the European Union in the Area of Freedom,

---

[194] ibid Art 6.
[195] Decision 2008/615/JHA on the stepping up of cross-border cooperation, particularly in combating terrorism and cross-border crime [2008] OJ L210/1; Decision 2008/616/JHA on the implementation of Decision 2008/615/JHA [2008] OJ L210/12 (Prüm Decision).
[196] ibid Art 8.   [197] ibid Art 3(1).
[198] European Council, Tampere Conclusions of 15 and 16 October 1999.
[199] The Hague Programme (n 146).
[200] The Stockholm Programme: An open and secure Europe serving and protecting citizens [2010] OJ C115/1.
[201] Council of the European Union Document EUCO 79/14 (27 June 2014).

Security and Justice', noting that 'some of the actions proposed by the Commission are not in line with the Stockholm Programme'.[202] These pronouncements were aimed at (re)asserting the exclusivity of the Member States' strategic initiative in the AFSJ, and pushing the exclusivity of Member State priorities under Stockholm, disregarding Commission views. In its post-Stockholm follow-up, the European Council has again departed from the positions of the other institutions[203] and demonstrated a marked lack of ambition with regard to the adoption of new EU legislation in the field of criminal law, strongly emphasizing consolidation and implementation.[204]

The competition between Union institutions has persisted until now. The Commission has acquired an important role in the configuration of the EU criminal justice sphere by releasing pioneering documents, for example the European Agenda on Security of 2015 that called for better information exchange, increased operational cooperation, and mutual trust.[205] In essence, the Agenda has replaced the previous Internal Security Strategy (ISS), as drawn up by the Council,[206] thus—so it seems— lifting the Third Pillar shadow off operational cooperation. However, the Commission has cautiously stated that the ISS objectives 'remain valid and should continue to be pursued'.[207] One way through which the ISS has been implemented is the EU Policy Cycle for serious and organized crime, whereby national authorities coordinate common priorities and operational actions, with COSI playing a key role in overseeing development and implementation. That Policy Cycle is a model for an intelligence-led approach to internal security, based on joint-threat assessments coordinated within Europol. It provides the methodology for setting out priorities in this area, and for their translation of into concrete action.[208] With regard to information exchange, the blueprint for further integration is also determined by the Council through the elaboration of non-binding action lists, having a life-span of eighteen months, so as to develop an Information Management Strategy (IMS), renewed from time to time.[209]

---

[202] Council Conclusions on the Commission Communication 'Delivering an area of freedom, security and justice for Europe's citizens: Action Plan Implementing the Stockholm Programme'—3018th Justice and Home Affairs Council meeting, Luxembourg, 3 June 2010.

[203] On the Commission's views see Communication from the Commission to the European Parliament, the Council, the European Economic and Social Committee and the Committee of the Regions: An open and secure Europe: making it happen, Brussels, 11 March 2014 COM(2014) 154 final; European Parliament, Motion for a Resolution on the mid-term review of the Stockholm Programme, 2013/2024 (INI), 4 March 2014.

[204] European Council Conclusions, 26–27 June 2014, Brussels, EUCO 79/14, para 3.

[205] Commission, 'Communication from the Commission to the European Parliament, the Council, the European Economic and Social Committee and the Committee of the Regions: The European Agenda on Security' COM(2015) 185 final.

[206] Council Conclusions of 25 February 2010 on the Internal Security Strategy for the European Union: Towards a European security model; COM(2014) 154 final of 11 March 2014.

[207] Commission, 'The European Agenda on Security' (n 205) 2.

[208] JHA Council Conclusions on the Creation and Implementation of an EU Policy Cycle for Organised and Serious International Crime, 8 and 9 November 2010.

[209] The IMS arose as an idea in June 2009 (see Council, Document 16637/09, 25 November 2009), with a view to providing a methodology to ensure that decisions about the need for managing and exchanging data, and decisions about the ways to do so are taken in a coherent, professional, efficient, cost-effective way, accountable and comprehensible to the citizens and the professional users. The Strategy has a long-term focus and can be further developed and updated as the overarching vision develops. Currently, there have been five action lists completed, which entail different actions such as the streamlining of national procedures after a 'hit' or the enhancement of data quality. A renewed IMS was approved in

Building on the initial IMS, the Commission released a Communication on the development of a European Information Exchange Model (EIEM) that would take stock of the existing information exchange mechanisms and assess their operation.[210] More recently, the Council has endorsed a roadmap encompassing the key elements needing modification in order to enhance information exchange and information management.[211] In relation to particular offences, a series of action plans has been released over time by the Commission in the form of Communications. These have identified gaps in the fight against certain offences and the reforms needed in legal instruments or their implementation. Recent key examples in this context are the Action Plan for strengthening the fight against terrorist financing,[212] and the Action Plan against migrant smuggling.[213]

Apart from the central role of Europol in carrying out the Policy Cycle, overall agenda-setting is increasingly influenced by the analyses and reports provided by specific agencies and bodies, with the EU Terrorism Situation and Trend Report (TE-SAT), itself drafted by Europol, being a prime example in this respect. TE-SAT reports provide an overview of terrorism phenomena in the EU in any given year, and offer facts and figures based on information provided by Member States to Europol. Eurojust also produces numerous reports each year, particularly an annual report that lists challenges in judicial cooperation arising from divergences in national laws. The function of the CTC in pointing out perceived loopholes in Union legislation or their practical implementation should also not be omitted here. The role of these actors in agenda-setting cannot be underestimated; the influence of Europol, Eurojust, and Frontex in drafting the Internal Security Strategy and in the EU Policy Cycle is exemplary in this respect.[214] Furthermore, in the European Agenda on Security the Commission has expressly conceded the assistance provided by the various agencies in defining priorities for operational action.[215] On the one hand, the challenges and risks identified by these actors may bring to the attention of EU institutions issues that have arisen in practice, leading to targeted solutions and speedy action on the Union level, particularly in cases of urgency, such as following terrorist offences. On the other hand, the law-enforcement vector of all these actors risks over-focusing on effective police and judicial cooperation, and thereby trumping considerations relating to the protection of fundamental rights.

December 2014 (Council Document 15701/1/14 18 December 2014). For the current state of play and the drafting of the sixth action list see Council Document 13546/17 (28 November 2017).

[210] Commission, 'Communication from the Commission to the European Parliament and the Council—Strengthening law enforcement cooperation in the EU: the European Information Exchange Model (EIXM)' COM(2012) 735 final.

[211] Council Document 9368/1/16 REV 1 (9–10 June 2016).

[212] Commission, 'Communication from the Commission to the European Parliament and the Council on an Action Plan for strengthening the fight against terrorist financing' COM(2016) 50 final.

[213] Commission, 'Communication from the Commission to the European Parliament, the Council, the European Economic and Social Committee and the Committee of the Regions on an EU Action Plan against migrant smuggling (2015–2020)' COM(2015) 285 final.

[214] See Council Document 9359/1 (7 May 2010); J Parkin, 'EU Home Affairs Agencies and the Construction of EU Internal Security' CEPS Papers No 53 (2012).

[215] Commission, 'The European Agenda on Security' (n 205) 8–9.

G Supervision

1 Supervision in criminal law information exchange mechanisms

Supervision of the lawfulness of the SIS II activities is entrusted to national data protection authorities in regard to data-processing on the national level. On the other
hand, supervision of eu-LISA (formerly the management authority) is now conducted
by the European Data Protection Supervisor (EDPS).[216] Similar rules and distribution
of responsibilities apply as regards the supervision of the CIS.[217]

2 Supervision of EU agencies

(a) Administrative supervision within agencies and other bodies

In the case of Europol, the task of ensuring that individual rights are not violated and
of monitoring the transmission of data originating from Europol was originally entrusted to a Joint Supervisory Body (JSB).[218] However, under the Europol Regulation,
supervision is now conducted by the EDPS.[219] Furthermore, Article 45 of the Europol
Regulation provides for the establishment of a cooperation board having an advisory
role. The board comprises a representative of a national supervisory authority of
each Member State and of the EDPS. In view of the establishment of the European
Data Protection Board (EDPB) (under the Data Protection Directive),[220] the role of
the Cooperation Board will be taken up by that new body. Furthermore, as in the
case of Europol, the 2002 Eurojust Decision stipulated the establishment of a Joint
Supervisory Body (JSB), comprising national judges, the task of which was collectively to monitor Eurojust's activities with regard to the processing of personal data.[221]
According to the Commission proposal on revising the structure of Eurojust, the
monitoring of the agency's activities with regard to such data-processing should be
entrusted to the EDPS, thus taking over the tasks of the JSB.[222] At the time of writing,
the role of the EDPS is still subject to negotiation, but with its duties and functions
mirroring those found in the Europol Regulation.[223] That instrument has been the
model for the supervision provisions of the EPPO Regulation.[224]

The structural independence of OLAF has been reinforced by according the monitoring of its investigative functions to the Supervisory Committee,[225] appointed for

---

[216] Art 45 SIS II Regulation (n 29), Art 61 SIS II Decision (n 29).
[217] Arts 24–26 CIS Decision (n 31).   [218] Art 24(1) Europol Convention (n 7).
[219] Art 43 Europol Regulation (n 50).
[220] Directive (EU) 2016/680 of the European Parliament and of the Council of 27 April 2016 on the
protection of natural persons with regard to the processing of personal data by competent authorities for
the purposes of the prevention, investigation, detection or prosecution of criminal offences or the execution of criminal penalties, and on the free movement of such data, and repealing Council Framework
Decision 2008/977/JHA [2016] OJ L199/89 Art 51.
[221] Art 23 2002 Eurojust Decision (n 10).
[222] Explanatory Memorandum to the Eurojust proposal (n 76) p 5.   [223] See n 88.
[224] Art 85 EPPO Regulation (n 14).
[225] The 1999 Decision called for the establishment of a 'surveillance committee' responsible for monitoring the investigative functions of OLAF. See Art 4 OLAF Decision (n 88).

a non-renewable five-year period.[226] According to the OLAF Regulation, this monitoring explicitly involves the application of procedural guarantees and oversight of
the duration of investigations.[227] The Committee's main task is to issue opinions
including, where appropriate, recommendations to the Director-General concerning
OLAF's activities 'without however interfering with the conduct of investigations in
progress'.[228] The OLAF Supervisory Committee is composed of five independent members, having experience in senior judicial or investigative functions or comparable
functions relating to the areas of activity of the Office, appointed by common accord
of the European Parliament, the Council, and the Commission.[229] By way of contrast
to the bodies already mentioned, no rules on supervision are envisaged in the eu-LISA
Regulation. In addition, the Frontex legal framework (the EBCG Regulation) does not
contain a provision on supervision. However, it could be argued that its Fundamental
Rights Officer acts as a quasi-supervisor, at least as regards the protection of fundamental rights if not other matters. Otherwise, that Regulation cautiously refrains from
explicitly referring to supervision functions as such.

(b) Political supervision

Political supervision is increasingly relevant so as to improve democratic accountability. In the case of Europol, this has been a particularly problematic issue. The
Europol Convention included an extremely weak provision calling for the submission of an annual 'special' report by the Council Presidency to the Parliament.[230] This
was then substituted by a still weaker provision according to which the Presidency or
its representative could appear before the European Parliament 'with a view to discuss general questions relating to Europol'.[231] A modest shift from the intergovernmental focus of the agency was made with the 2009 Council Decision, which granted
the European Parliament more binding and broader information rights in requiring
the presidency, the Europol director, and the chairperson of the management board
to appear before the Parliament at the latter's request, with a view to discussing matters touching the agency.[232] The now applicable Europol Regulation prescribes the
establishment of a specialized Joint Parliamentary Group (JPSG), composed of representatives of national parliaments and the competent committee of the European
Parliament. The Group monitors Europol's activities as an instance of political accountability.[233] To this end, the chairperson of the management board, the executive
director, or the deputies of either, shall appear before the JPSG, at its request, to discuss matters relating to the agency's activities, including its budget and structural organization. In addition, the Group must be consulted in relation to the multi-annual

---

[226] ibid Art 15(3). Compare with Art 11(3) OLAF 1999 Regulation (n 16).
[227] Art 15(1) second indent OLAF Decision (n 88). This is an addition in comparison to the OLAF 1999
Regulation (n 16), however, as the Commission admits, the 2013 Regulation did not change so much in
this respect.
[228] Art 15(1) third indent OLAF Decision (n 88).   [229] Art 15(2) OLAF Regulation (n 16).
[230] Art 34(1) Europol Convention (n 7); according to Art 34(2), however, the presidency should take
into account the obligations of discretion and confidentiality.
[231] Danish Protocol (n 6) amended Art 34(2).   [232] Art 47 Europol Decision (n 47).
[233] Art 51(2) Europol Regulation (n 50).

programming of Europol. In order to exercise effective scrutiny, the JPSG must have access to certain documents produced by the agency, and to information processed by, or passing, through Europol.[234]

The democratic oversight of Eurojust is somewhat limited at the time of writing. In accordance with Article 32(2) of the Eurojust Decision, the European Parliament receives an annual report from the Presidency of the Council 'on the work carried out by Eurojust and on the activities of the Joint Supervisory Body'.[235] However, the President of the Eurojust College reports annually to the Council in writing every year on the activities and management, including budgetary management, of Eurojust.[236] This weak standard of accountability will be rectified to some extent by the forthcoming Eurojust Regulation, by requiring the Eurojust President to appear before the European Parliament to discuss matters relating to Eurojust, and both the European Parliament and the national parliaments will receive the agency's annual reports and other relevant documentation.[237] However, the proposal has been watered down by the Council, which called for its direct involvement in evaluating the activities of Eurojust, thus underscoring the intergovernmental dimension. As a consequence, the Annual Report of Eurojust will be transmitted to the Council as well, whereas the President of the College may appear either before the European Parliament or the Council.[238]

Article 16 OLAF Regulation provides that the Parliament, the Council, and the Commission shall meet the Director-General annually to exchange views on OLAF's policy. The Supervisory Committee is to participate in such meetings, and representatives of the Court of Auditors, Eurojust, and/or Europol may be invited. Such an exchange of views should cover, inter alia, the strategic priorities for OLAF investigation policy and the effectiveness of the office in regard to the performance of its mandate, without, however, interfering with OLAF's independence.[239] These rules supplement the pre-existing regime, maintained in the current Regulation, according to which the director-general shall report regularly to the European Parliament, the Council, the Commission, and the Court of Auditors, on the findings of investigations carried out by the office, actions taken, and problems encountered, whilst respecting the confidentiality of the investigations, and the legitimate rights of persons concerned and of informants.[240]

In addition, according to the EPPO Regulation, the EPPO is to be an independent body, accountable to the European Parliament, the Council, and the Commission for its general activities by sending its annual report to these institutions.[241] In this respect, the European chief prosecutor appears annually before the European Parliament and the Council to give an account of the general activities of the EPPO.[242]

Channels for the political—democratic—oversight over eu-LISA and Frontex are weak. In the case of the former, the European Parliament or the Council may invite the executive director to report on the implementation of its tasks, but there appears

---

[234] ibid Arts 51(3) and 52.   [235] Art 32(2) Eurojust Decision (n 11) 2002/187/JHA.
[236] ibid Art 32(1). See Art 85(1) TFEU.   [237] Art 55 Commission Proposal (n 13).
[238] Council of the European Union Document 14306/2/17 (9 December 2017) 254–57.
[239] Recital 41 and Art 16(2) OLAF Regulation (n 16).
[240] ibid Art 17(4). Compare with Art 12(3) 1999 OLAF Decision (n 88).
[241] Art EPPO Regulation (n 14).   [242] ibid Art 7.

to be no obligation either to issue such an invitation, nor indeed to respond to it.[243] Furthermore, the agency is to keep the European Parliament, the Council, and the Commission informed on any research developments relevant for the operational management of the centralized databases.[244] As for Frontex, the European Parliament has exerted limited control through budgetary procedures, but it has not been possible to hold the agency accountable.[245] Article 7 EBCG Regulation stipulates that the agency 'shall' be accountable to the European Parliament, whereas Article 68 provides that the Executive Director must make a statement before the European Parliament, if requested, and report to it regularly. These provisions are certainly a step forward, but it remains to be seen how these will play out in the future.

3 Judicial control

Judicial control of EU agencies and bodies is another complex issue in the field of criminal justice, where developments in rules have progressively expanded the jurisdiction of the CJEU. In particular, in the case of Europol, where the Convention provided that disputes would be discussed at the Council, the Europol Decision inserted provisions for judicial review, subject to certain limitations.[246] Post-Lisbon, judicial control increased through the introduction of Article 263 TFEU and, since 1 December 2014, a Council Decision is subject to the full supervisory jurisdiction of the CJEU.[247] However, this is limited by Article 263(5), which stipulates that acts setting up bodies, offices, and agencies of the EU may lay down specific conditions and arrangements in regard to legal actions brought by natural or legal third parties against acts of such bodies intended to produce legal effects in relation to them. In that respect, individuals seeking a remedy against Europol, in regard for example to the processing of data, would first have to refer the matter to the EDPS by lodging a complaint. An action against a decision of the EDPS might then be brought before the CJEU.[248]

Furthermore, the 2002 Eurojust Decision contains no express provision with regard to the judicial control or the interpretation of Eurojust acts. In effect, the CJEU was called to rule in the case of *Spain v Eurojust*[249] concerning the annulment of calls for applications in the recruitment of temporary staff issued by Eurojust, but the Court dismissed the action as inadmissible. As with Europol, however, after the entry into force of the Lisbon Treaty, Eurojust became subject to the full jurisdiction of the CJEU.[250]

---

[243] Art 17(4) See eu-LISA Regulation.   [244] ibid Arts 8 and 9.

[245] Moreno-Lax (n 125) 163.

[246] According to Art 35(5) TFEU, the Luxembourg Court could not 'review the validity or proportionality of operations carried out by the police or other law enforcement services of a Member State or the exercise of the responsibilities incumbent upon Member States with regard to the maintenance of law and order and the safeguarding of internal security'.

[247] See also Protocol No 36, Lisbon Treaty.

[248] Arts 47–48 Europol Regulation (n 50). See S Gless, 'Europol' in V Mitsilegas, M Bergström, and T Konstadinides (eds), *Research Handbook on EU Criminal Law* (Edward Elgar Publishing 2016).

[249] Case C-150/03 *Spain v Eurojust* [2005] ECR I-02077.

[250] For an analysis on the need for judicial review M Wade, 'Judicial Control: The CJEU and the Future of Eurojust' (2013) 14(2) *ERA Forum* 201.

Judicial review of OLAF's acts by the Court is still very restricted, an approach that has resulted in the failure of legal actions brought for the annulment of OLAF acts but which have routinely been declared to be inadmissible.[251] In *Tillack*, the Court of First Instance (CFI) held that, while national authorities are under a duty to examine the information forwarded by OLAF carefully, this does not mean that such forwarded information has binding effect, 'in the sense that the national authorities are obliged to take specific measures, since such an interpretation would alter the division of tasks and responsibilities as prescribed for the implementation of Regulation No 1073/99'.[252] The CFI thus shielded OLAF from judicial scrutiny by refusing to examine the substance of the OLAF report that had triggered the national investigations concerned, and notwithstanding the fact that, earlier in the procedure, the European Ombudsman had found that the publication of allegations was disproportionate and constituted an act of maladministration.[253]

In relation to the EPPO, the Court of Justice is to have jurisdiction to give preliminary rulings concerning: (a) the validity of procedural acts of the EPPO 'insofar as such question of validity is raised before any court or tribunal of a Member State directly on the basis of Union law';[254] (b) the interpretation or the validity of provisions of EU law;[255] and (c) the interpretation of the provisions of the Regulation concerning the material competence of the EPPO.[256] Furthermore, the Court is empowered to review decisions of the EPPO to dismiss a case, insofar as they are contested directly on the basis of EU law.[257] In effect, judicial review of the acts of the EPPO will be mostly carried out on the national level, which, however, overlooks the nature of the EPPO as in reality a Union body.[258] However, the special nature of the agency—whose action may significantly affect fundamental rights for persons across the whole of the EU— renders the need for judicial review even more imperative.[259] Consequently, the fragmentary approach to judicial review constitutes a direct attack on the rule of law, and challenges the obligation on the Union to uphold fundamental rights, particularly the right to effective judicial protection. On the contrary, judicial review should apply as extensively as possible. It is difficult to distinguish between acts of the EPPO in its centralized functions on the one hand from those under its decentralized formations on the other. Nor is it possible to draw a line between the different types of acts, with pre-prosecutional (investigatory) acts being left to national courts to deal with,

---

[251] J F H Inghelram, 'Fundamental Rights, the European Anti-Fraud Office (OLAF) and a European Public Prosecutor's Office (EPPO): Some Selected Issues' (2012) 95 *Kritische Vierteljahresschrift für Gesetzgebung und Rechtswissenschaft* 67; V Covolo, 'The Legal Framework of OLAF Investigations. What Lessons for the European Penal Area?' (2011) 2 *New Journal of European Criminal Law* 201.

[252] See para 72.

[253] European Ombudsman, Special Report to the European Parliament following the draft recommendation to the European Anti-fraud Office in complaint 2485/2004/GG, Strasbourg, 12 May 2005, at: ombudsman.europa.eu/special/pdf/en/042485.pdf. The judgment is in striking contrast with the subsequent ruling of the European Court of Human Rights. See *Affaire Tillack c Belgique*, Requête no 20477/05, 27 November 2007 (final version 27 February 2008), para 68.

[254] Art 42(2)(a)EPPO Regulation (n 14).   [255] ibid Art 42(2)(b).   [256] ibid Art 42(2)(c).

[257] ibid Art 42(3).

[258] V Mitsilegas, 'The European Public Prosecutor before the Court of Justice: The Challenge of Effective Judicial Protection' in G Giudicelli and others (eds), *Le Contrôle Judiciaire du Parquet Européen—Nécessité, Modèles, Enjeux* (Société de Legislation Comparée 2015) 78–84.

[259] Mitsilegas and Giuffrida (n 107) 13.

whereas decisions on prosecution itself might be subject to judicial review on the EU court level.[260]

H Conclusion

The administrative dimension of EU criminal law, as exemplified by the establishment and proliferation of EU agencies, other Union bodies, and national bodies, as well as networks in the field of criminal justice, is a significant component in the development of European integration in this field. The evolution of European criminal law, in parallel with the ongoing development of Union constitutional law (resulting in a number of Treaty reforms and the move from the Third Pillar structure to an integrated and largely supranational Treaty structure post-Lisbon) has led to the internal development of numerous bodies and entities in this field.

A common characteristic underpinning the administration of EU criminal law is the relative flexibility of the rules governing the setting up and operation of EU agencies and information exchange mechanisms. This flexibility appears to exist mainly to address the perceived impact of Europeanization on state sovereignty. The case of the two main EU agencies which are operational at the time of writing, Europol and Eurojust, demonstrates an incremental evolution in their mandates and powers, although without their replacing key national law enforcement functions. Furthermore, the safeguarding of national administrative structures and respect for national organizational arrangements is evident in the leeway allowed to Member States when designating or creating national bodies for conducting law enforcement tasks prescribed by EU legislation. At the same time, the reinforcement of law enforcement cooperation as a response to perceived threats of terrorism and organized crime has led to the adoption of a series of information exchange mechanisms under rules that prioritize fast and simplified information exchange and which allow for constant adaptation and reform at any time depending on operational needs or perceived gaps. Such gaps have been identified by a multiplicity of actors; amidst inter-institutional battles, Member States retain the leading role as regards the shaping of EU strategy and priorities.

However, EU agencies as well as certain other bodies, such as the CTC or COSI, have increasingly emerged as key players through their monitoring of both EU and Member State laws and policies. Importantly, such bodies have been created and legitimized through dubious procedures involving minimal accountability. In addition, in certain cases their mandates may not necessarily fall only within the scope of the AFSJ, but also be referable to the former Second Pillar of CFSP, thus inherently invoking secrecy and lack of transparency. Moreover, the relationship between the CTC, INTCEN, and COSI has remained thus far ill-defined. As well, the blurring of boundaries between separate fields of European Union law is also evident in the case of eu-LISA and Frontex, the tasks of which are principally attached to the area of immigration law. It is true that, with the entry into force of the Lisbon Treaty, the promotion of further cooperation among Member States through the EPPO or the

---

[260] ibid.

simplification of rules for the cooperation of FIUs and PIUs has been coupled with calls for enhanced accountability and for democratic and judicial scrutiny of the EU agencies. In this context, stronger supranational elements (in particular in the design of governance structures and in judicial review) have been inserted into revised EU rules. However, the delicate balance between Europeanization and the maintenance of state sovereignty in criminal justice is still evident. What is essential, as this complex field evolves further, is heightened vigilance so that the development of the administrative dimension of EU criminal law is accompanied by robust safeguards of fundamental rights and the rule of law.

8

The Common European Asylum System

Elspeth Guild

A Introduction

Administrative law relating to the Common European Asylum System (CEAS) developed rapidly following the introduction of a European Union competence for asylum. The Amsterdam Treaty 1999 brought an end to the rather chaotic European field of law and policy on borders, immigration, and asylum. This area had not been included in EU competences at all until the Maastricht Treaty (in force from 1993) which fragmented the legal framework of the then EC by creating three so-called pillars, the first pillar of EU law proper (as had been contained in the then EC Treaty), the second on the Common Foreign and Security Policy (which was entirely intergovernmental), and the third pillar on justice and home affairs which included then (most of) border policy, migration, and asylum.[1]

In the infamous third pillar a range of measures, the Resolutions and Recommendations, were adopted in the field of asylum (among others).[2] While the Single European Act 1987 had established, as part of the 1992 project to complete the internal market,[3] the abolition of intra-EU border controls on the movement of goods, persons, services, and capital, it became clear that this objective would not be achieved by the specified deadline of 31 December 1992. Instead, abolition of border controls took place in the context of the Schengen Implementing Agreement 1990[4] and became a reality for (most) people moving among the participating states only on 25 March 1995.[5] In the 1990 Agreement (following on from the first Schengen Agreement 1985), the initial five participant states[6] agreed on the abolition of border controls on persons moving among them, as well as on a range of flanking measures regarding visas,

---

[1] Pieter-Jan Kuijper, 'Some Legal Problems Associated with the Communitarization of Policy on Visas, Asylum and Immigration under the Amsterdam Treaty and Incorporation of the Schengen *Acquis*' (2000) 37 *Common Market Law Review*) 345.

[2] E Guild and J Niessen, *The developing immigration and asylum policies of the European Union: adopted conventions, resolutions, recommendations, decisions and conclusions.* (1996). (Kluwer Law International).

[3] Claus-Dieter Ehlermann, 'The 1992 Project: Stages, Structures, Results and Prospects' (1989) 11 *Michigan Journal of International Law* 1097.

[4] European Union, Convention Implementing the Schengen Agreement of 14 June 1985 between the Governments of the States of the Benelux Economic Union, the Federal Republic of Germany and the French Republic, on the Gradual Abolition of Checks at their Common Borders (Schengen Implementation Agreement), 19 June 1990 http://www.refworld.org/docid/3ae6b38a20.html (last accessed 24 January 2017).

[5] Eckart Wagner, 'The Integration of Schengen into the Framework of the European Union' (1998) 25 *Legal Issues of European Integration* 1.

[6] Belgium, France, Germany, Luxembourg, and the Netherlands.

external border controls, and policing.[7] All EU Member States, with the exception of Ireland and the UK, became parties to the Schengen Agreements, including those acceding to the Union in every enlargement after 1990.

One of a variety of reasons for the delay in achieving the abolition of intra-EU border controls on movement of persons (let alone this aspect of the then EC Treaty) was the question of asylum-seekers and refugees. The fall of the Berlin Wall in 1989 coincided with a substantial increase in the number of people seeking asylum in the European Union. This situation was then aggravated by the Yugoslav wars from 1992.[8] As asylum-seekers arrived in an EU without common policies in the field of asylum each Member State had to cope on its own. The fact that the majority of the Balkan refugees went to Germany was a matter for some hand-wringing in Germany and led to a call for the coordination of asylum policy among the Member States.[9]

The first measure which the Member States adopted in order to determine which state should carry responsibility for an asylum-seeker was the Dublin Convention 1990[10] (in force in 1997, year in which negotiations for the Amsterdam Treaty were completed). Mirror provisions of the Dublin Convention were then included in the Schengen Implementing Agreement 1990. Basically, the Member States agreed among themselves, and outside the competence of the then EEC, that in the absence of a first degree family relation with a residence permit in a Member State, or of a visa or a residence permit, an asylum-seeker should be the responsibility of the first Member State through which he or she had entered the EEC (and from 1993 the EU). This so-called Dublin principle is still applicable in the EU and is the source of much friction among the Member States of (predominant present) arrival (Greece and Italy) and the others, some of which have for various reasons in fact received large numbers of asylum-seekers (Germany and Sweden being, in January 2017, the front runners). The idea behind the Dublin arrangements was that an asylum-seeker would have only one chance to make an asylum application in the EU and that the country in which such application had to be made would be determined by the Member States (and not by the asylum-seeker). Thereafter, if the asylum-seeker were recognized as a refugee, he or she would have to stay in that original Member State. If that state rejected the application, then it was its responsibility to expel the person from the EU.[11] All this was presented at the time as a measure in support of asylum-seekers by providing them with more certainty and a quicker determination of their claims. The experience in applying the Dublin principle in practice does not

---

[7] Evelien Brouwer, *Digital Borders and Real Rights: Effective Remedies for Third-Country Nationals in the Schengen Information System* (Brill 2008).

[8] Elspeth Guild, Cathryn Costello, and Madeline Garlick in V Moreno-Lax, *Enhancing the Common European Asylum System and Alternatives to Dublin* (Study for the Libe Committee, European Union's Publications Office 2015) 1–89.

[9] Dietrich Thränhardt, 'Germany: An Undeclared Immigration Country' (1995) 21 *Journal of Ethnic and Migration Studies* 19.

[10] European Union, Convention Determining the State Responsible for Examining Applications for Asylum lodged in one of the Member States of the European Communities (Dublin Convention), 15 June 1990, OJ C254/1 of 19 August 1997 http://www.refworld.org/docid/3ae6b38714.html (last accessed 24 January 2017).

[11] Elspeth Guild, 'The Europeanisation of Europe's Asylum Policy' (2006) 18(3–4) *International Journal of Refugee Law* 630.

provide unqualified support for these (essentially political) claims about the bene-fits for asylum-seekers.[12]

B Administrative Law and the Development of an EU Competence in Asylum

Despite the apparent settling of the underlying principles, as just outlined, the Member States fell to quarrelling with one another about their duties in respect of asylum-seekers from 1990 onwards. The intersection with the abolition of intra-EU border controls only exacerbated these disagreements as the absence of border officials at internal EU borders (excepting, as noted, Ireland and the UK) meant that there was no one to ensure that stray asylum-seekers were penned into the states which the EU had determined were responsible and did not enter a Member State, which was under that principle not responsible. This issue has continued to be a source of difficult and, during the movement of asylum-seekers across Europe in 2015–2016 in much larger numbers than had ever been anticipated, some Member States reintroduced intra-EU border controls in an attempt to slow down the movement.[13]

As the legal framework established under the Schengen Agreements, the Dublin Convention, and the Maastricht Third Pillar were failing to provide any certainty on the issue of border controls, migration, and asylum—indeed rather creating more tensions and disagreements among the Member States—towards the end of the negotiations leading to the Amsterdam Treaty, the Dutch Presidency recommended that the whole regulatory package be contained in the EU Treaty. This led to the end of an independent life for the Schengen Agreements and Dublin Convention, and to the so-called 'communitarisation' of all three areas—borders, migration, and asylum.[14]

It is undoubtedly the case that the less than satisfactory experiences of the Member States in dealing with asylum through the prior intergovernmental mechanisms had a strong effect on the competences which were then established for the Union in regard to the creation of the CEAS. The core elements which went into the Amsterdam Treaty (now Article 78 TFEU) for the creation of the CEAS were

> measures on asylum, in accordance with the Geneva Convention of 28 July 1951 and the Protocol of 31 January 1967 relating to the status of refugees and other relevant treaties, within the following areas:
>
> (a) criteria and mechanisms for determining which Member State is responsible for considering an application for asylum submitted by a national of a third country in one of the Member States;
> (b) minimum standards on the reception of asylum seekers in Member States;
> (c) minimum standards with respect to the qualification of nationals of third countries as refugees,
> (d) minimum standards on procedures in Member States for granting or withdrawing refugee status.

---

[12] Guild, Costello, and Garlick (n 8).
[13] E Guild and S Carrera, EU Borders and Their Controls: Preventing Unwanted Movement of People in Europe? (14 November 2013). CEPS Essays No 6 at SSRN: https://ssrn.com/abstract=2360491.
[14] Guild 'The Europeanisation of Europe's Asylum Policy' (n 11).

This prescriptive list of measures to be adopted as EU law was accompanied by a require-ment that they be achieved within five years of the entry into force of the Amsterdam Treaty.[15] (Annex I to this chapter sets out the legislation which has been adopted under this competence together with references to relevant case law).

C The Development of Administrative Law Procedures in the Asylum Sector

From the perspective of European procedural administrative law, the most interesting as-pect flowing from the development of the CEAS is the Procedures Directive.[16] Here, the Union lays down obligatory administrative procedures which the Member States must follow in a specific field, namely in the determination of claims for international protection. Unlike the usual approach of the EU legislator to rely on national administrative procedures regarding the determination of rights and obligations in the implementation of European law, the Union and its own procedural standards have, in effect, moved to centre stage.

There are a number of reasons for this, the most important being the inability of the CEAS to become a common system without the confidence among all participating Member States that each is taking its fair share of responsibility for asylum applica-tions, including the determination of applications fairly and consistently. The con-cern, in particular of those Member States which have been traditional destination countries for asylum-seekers, was that, by failing to establish efficient and effective asylum determination systems, some Member States would shirk their duties. This would then have the consequence that asylum-seekers would leave those states and seek asylum in states with more efficient and fairer procedural systems. This is indeed exactly what has occurred as a consequence of the rather sclerotic Greek and Italian asylum systems in particular, which both the European Court of Human Rights (ECtHR)[17] and the Court of Justice[18] regarded as so substandard that Dublin returns to either of those countries were barred in 2011. Notwithstanding valiant efforts by the European Commission and the authorities of the two states, Dublin returns to Greece were, at the time of writing, still not possible on account of substantive failures in re-ception and procedures.[19]

---

[15] Steve Peers, 'Legislative Update: EU Immigration and Asylum Competence and Decision-making in the Treaty of Lisbon' (2008) 10 *European Journal of Migration & Law* 219.

[16] Steve Peers, *EU Justice and Home Affairs Law: EU Immigration and Asylum Law, Vol 1* (Oxford University Press 2016).

[17] ECtHR, *MSS v Belgium and Greece*, Application no 30696/09 21 January 2011 http://www.refworld.org/docid/4d39bc7f2.html (last accessed 21 January 2017); ECtHR, *Tarakhel v Switzerland*, Application no 29217/12, 4 November 2014 http://www.refworld.org/docid/5458abfd4.html (last accessed 21 January 2017).

[18] CJEU, Joined Case *N S (Case C-411/10) v Secretary of State for the Home Department and M. E. and Others (Case C-493/10) v Refugee Applications Commissioner and Minister for Justice, Equality and Law Reform* ECLI:EU:C:2011:865, 21 December 2011 http://www.refworld.org/docid/4ef1ed702.html (last ac-cessed 21 January 2017).

[19] Commission Recommendation of 8 December 2016 addressed to the Member States on the resump-tion of transfers to Greece under Regulation (EU) No 604/2013 C(2016) 8525.

Thus, the pressure for common asylum procedures to prevent Member States from shirking their duties towards asylum-seekers was a key component in the construction of the CEAS. The fact that this amounted to an incursion into national sovereignty regarding administrative law was seen as less important than achieving the objective of a common system working as the Member States had intended.[20] The possibility that making a system of asylum reception and determination work effectively might only be achievable if it also actually took account of the needs and legitimate expectations of asylum-seekers themselves was, however, not entertained by the Member States either then or ever afterwards.

D Administrative Law and Minimum Standards in the CEAS: Round I

In 2000, the Commission produced a proposal for a directive on minimum procedural standards in Member State decision-making in granting, denying, and withdrawing refugee status.[21] This proposal followed on from a Commission working paper in 1999 on the same subject, to which thirteen Member States had responded with suggestions. The European Parliament had also considered the paper and a number of non-governmental organizations had commented on it. According to the Commission, the key issue was that of producing a simple and quick system for dealing with applications. Common standards and time limits were essential to its effective operation but, from the start, as the Commission stated in its explanatory memorandum, the objective was 'to dismiss quickly inadmissible and manifestly unfounded cases so that each national system can operate smoothly for the benefit of Geneva Convention refugees [be widened in the negotiations to cover all beneficiaries of international protection]'.[22] This emphasis on separating 'real' from 'false' protection seekers would haunt the system ever since. The controversy which has dogged procedural arrangements since then has been whether there are sufficient systemic guarantees for asylum applicants in order to ensure that their applications are in fact fairly considered on the facts, and that they have effective rights of appeal.[23]

A corrective mechanism against unfair procedures would eventually be found in decisions of the ECtHR, which has taken ever more seriously procedural failures of Member States resulting in the risk of refoulement (return to torture, prohibited by Article 3 of the European Convention on Human Rights (ECHR)). The 2016 judgment

---

[20] Vincent Chetail, Philippe De Bruycker, and Francesco Maiani (eds), *Reforming the Common European Asylum System: The New European Refugee Law* (Brill 2016).

[21] COM(2000) 578 final.

[22] Explanatory Memorandum: Proposal for a Council Directive on minimum standards on procedures in Member States for granting and withdrawing refugee status/*COM/2000/0578 final; CNS 2000/0238*/ Official Journal 062 E, 27/02/2001 P 0231–0242.

[23] Volker Türk and Madeline Garlick, 'From Burdens and Responsibilities to Opportunities: The Comprehensive Refugee Response Framework and a Global Compact on Refugees' 2016) 28(4) *International Journal of Refugee Law* 656.

in *MD & MA v Belgium* provides a classic example of the problem.[24] In that case, two Russian nationals of Chechen origin had applied for asylum four times in Belgium, the applications being rejected on grounds which were superficial, which failed to take into account relevant facts, or which were based simply on a finding of lack of credibility of the applicants. The Court held that, by refusing to consider the fourth asylum claim (in a full procedure untainted by the errors of the prior procedures), the Belgian authorities' approach to considering whether there were new elements was too restrictive, failing to meet the standard of careful and rigorous examination. There had been no assessment of the relevance, authenticity, or probative value of the new evidence put forward, rejected on the basis of the assumption that, according to the dates, it could have been produced in an earlier claim. The applicants' explanations for not submitting these documents earlier had, however, not been considered, and were held to have put an unreasonable burden of proof on the applicants. Due to the absence of review of the risks faced by the applicants, in view of the documents submitted in support of their fourth asylum claim, the ECtHR held that there had been insufficient evidence for the Belgian authorities to be assured that the applicants would not be at risk of harm if deported to Russia (and thus a breach of Article 3 ECHR).

The Commission's 2000 proposal for a directive reassured Member States that it would not require them to apply uniform procedures, although this would come in 2016 when the Commission proposed to transform the directive into a regulation (see below).[25] One of the key issues of concern to Member States was whether the right of appeal against a negative decision on an application would give rise to a suspensive effect, that is, that the asylum-seeker could not be expelled (possibly refouled) until such time as the appeal had been finally determined. This principle of law, the suspensive effect of asylum appeals, is the outcome, once again, of the jurisprudence of the ECtHR. The Court had, in 1991, found that the risk of torture included return to a country where there is a real risk of torture and the consequences of such a return are contrary to ECHR member state's obligations. In order to determine the question of risk sufficiently, an appeal with suspensive effect is necessary.[26] The Commission's solution to Member States' opposition to a suspensive appeal right was to allow for derogations.

According to the Commission, the directive had eight central aims which were: (1) to implement the Treaty obligation to adopt such a measure; (2) to introduce measures essential to the effectiveness of Member States' procedures; (3) to provide common definitions of, and requirements, for inadmissibility and for manifestly unfounded cases, including the safe country concept, in order to achieve a common approach among the Member States; (4) to set out time limits for deciding first instance appeals; (5) to enhance the ability of Member States to examine applications; (6) to set out minimum procedural safeguards for asylum applicants and ensure a

---

[24] *MD and MA v Belgium*, Application no 59689/12 [Articles 3 & 13 ECHR], 19 January 2016 http://www.refworld.org/cases,ECHR,569e61664.html (last accessed 31 January 2017).

[25] COM(2016) 467.

[26] *Vilvarajah v UK* (45/1009/236/302-306) Series A No 215; *Chahal v UK* (22414/93) 15 November 1996, COM(2016) 467.

common level of procedural fairness; (7) to lay down specific safeguards for fair procedures for persons with special needs; and (8) to set out minimum requirements for decisions and decision-making authorities in order to reduce disparities in examination processes and to ensure high standards across the Union as a whole.[27]

In order to achieve these objectives, the directive contained three quite distinct sets of provisions. First, there were procedural guarantees for determining asylum applications including rights of appeal and entitlements to information. The second set of provisions related to minimum standards of decision-making. While Member States could continue to use their national rules, those rules were to be adjusted to include all the minimum standards of the directive. In particular, there needed to be a three-tiered system, including an authority to determine applications, an authority to hear appeals against decisions, and an appellate court to consider further appeals.

The third set of provisions of the directive set out all the 'dirty laundry'—derogations and exceptions which Member States wanted to apply so as to circumvent the full effect of the guarantees for various categories of asylum-seekers. Accelerated processing and border procedures (where a presumption of inadmissibility or unfoundedness is allowed) permit the Member State to dispense with a variety of guarantees for the individual, including both in-depth examination of the claim and suspensive appeal rights. These procedures also applied where a claim was determined to be inadmissible on the basis that the Member State was not 'Dublin' responsible. In such a case, another country should be responsible in any event for the individual or the applicant in fact came from a country considered a safe third country en route to the Member State.

A Policy Plan on Asylum in 2008[28] called for a revision of the directive (itself introduced in 2009). Although the new proposal was stated to have been based on the information gained by the Commission in an assessment of the directive, that assessment was, however, not actually published until the following year.

E Common Administrative Standards in the Recast Asylum Procedures Directive

The Commission's first assessment of the implementation of the Directive was duly published in 2010.[29] Examining each contentious provision of the Directive, the Commission concluded:

> This evaluation confirms that some of the Directive's optional provisions and derogation clauses have contributed to the proliferation of divergent arrangements across the EU, and that procedural guarantees vary considerably between Member States. This is notably the case with respect to the provisions on accelerated procedures, 'safe country of origin', 'safe third country', personal interviews, legal assistance, and access to an effective remedy. Thus, important disparities subsist.

---

[27] Chetail, De Bruycker, and Maiani (n 20).   [28] COM(2008) 360.
[29] COM(2010) 465 final.

However, the Commission had already introduced its proposal for amendments to the Directive which was already facing opposition. There was no agreement in the Council on the draft and, after fruitless discussions, the Commission withdrew it.[30] Instead, it presented a revised proposal for a new, improved Procedures Directive in 2012 which would finally be adopted the following year.[31] In the proposal, which eventually led to the recast directive, the Commission stressed that it was seeking a system which would be efficient and protective. It promised that the changes would make the system more cost-effective and assist in tackling abusive claims to asylum. Thus, the move towards increasing convergence in a field not only of administrative law but also as regards on administrative procedures were justified vis-à-vis the Member States on cost grounds and—once again—with the promise that the rules would allow Member States to act more effectively and rapidly to exclude people from protection.

1 Objective of the recast directive

The objective of the recast directive was to develop further the standards and procedures obtaining in Member States for granting, denying, and withdrawing international protection, with a view to establishing a common asylum procedure in the EU. Thus, the system had moved from aiming to establish minimum guarantees to merely the objective of achieving common procedures. The mechanism for reaching this objective was the approximation of rules on procedure, with the specific aim of limiting what was now called 'secondary movement', i.e., movement of asylum-seekers from one Member State to another to seek asylum, where such movement would be encouraged by differences in the legal frameworks of the Member States. In this way the proposal responded to Member States' concerns asylum-seekers moving across the border-control free area, in order to seek asylum where they themselves preferred rather than in the Member State in which, under the Dublin rules, they were obliged to do so.[32] This first principle of EU asylum law continued then to be one related to organization, even in aspects of asylum determination procedure.[33]

Although one of the claims regarding the new measure was that it would provide a common procedure, under the new proposal Member States were in fact permitted to maintain—or introduce procedures –which are more or less beneficial to asylum-seekers, thus arguably undermining the principle of common procedure, and ending up with something more closely resembling minimum procedures, or procedures with minimum safeguards.[34]

Specifically, the recast Directive extended the provisions on the relationship of entry on to territory and the procedure applicable in respect of an asylum application.

---

[30] COM(2011) 319 final.

[31] Revised Asylum Procedures Directive 2013/32 [2013] OJ L180/60.

[32] Bruno Nascimbene, 'Refugees, the European Union and the "Dublin System": The Reasons for a Crisis' (2016) 1 *European Papers* 101.

[33] Maarten den Heijer, Jorrit J Rijpma, and Thomas Spijkerboer, 'Coercion, Prohibition, and Great Expectations: The Continuing Failure of the Common European Asylum System' (2016) 53 *Common Market Law Review* 607.

[34] Cathryn Costello, Minos Mouzourakis; 'EU Law and the Detainability of Asylum-Seekers' (2016) 35(1) *Refugee Survey Quarterly* 47 https://doi.org/10.1093/rsq/hdv020.

The scope was widened to include the territorial waters of Member States as well as transit zones, in recognition that these areas were the subject of dubious practices designed at shifting responsibility for asylum-seekers on to other countries. The revision presaged the outcome of a legal action pending at the time before the ECtHR regarding the pushing back to Libya of asylum-seekers by the Italian navy in order to prevent their arrival in Italy.[35] The ECtHR's judgment, delivered in 2012, found that such steps were illegal as Italy had exercised extraterritorial sovereignty over the asylum-seekers by rescuing them at sea outside Italian territorial waters and was thus responsible under the ECHR to ensure that they had an opportunity to present their asylum claims. Even more controversially, the ECtHR found that the push backs to Libya constituted collective expulsion.[36] The revision of the directive did not go so far as the ECtHR did then in the year following, but already the issue was firmly in the sights of EU institutions.

2 Reframing procedural fairness

The recast directive provided that Member States were not under a duty to consider applications in the order of their arrival or presentation. Instead, Member States were permitted to postpone taking decisions, in particular, where the situation in the country of origin was temporarily uncertain. This new power was for the individual countries to exercise as they wished, and thus a move away from, rather than toward, an approximation of procedures. It also ran contrary to the Commission's claim that speed in the determination of application was of the essence so as to ensure both that asylum-seekers did not remain in limbo and that so-called abusive applications were dealt with rapidly. The standard time limits which were introduced, not only for appeal procedures but now also for first determinations of asylum applications, were thereby relaxed in these circumstances.[37] Further, in response it would seem, to some Member States' pressure, an exception permitting more flexibility regarding access to procedures, conduct of personal interviews and time limits was introduced where Member States had to deal with a large number of simultaneous asylum claims. This was rather curious, not least because the EU had in 2001 already adopted a Temporary Protection Directive[38] containing a comprehensive range of procedures to assist Member States in the event of a mass influx. However, it was clear from the arrivals of substantial numbers of Eritreans, Afghans, Iraqis, and, in due course, Syrians, that Member States were averse to opening temporary protection schemes. Instead, the Commission provided an alternative in the event of a 'large number of simultaneous asylum claims' by changing the Procedures Directive so as to allow flexibility in respect of guarantees otherwise central to applicable procedures.

---

[35] *Hirsi Jamaa and Others v Italy*, Application no 27765/09, judgment of 23 February 2012.
[36] Prohibited by Art 4 Protocol 4 ECHR.
[37] Jens Vedsted-Hansen, *Asylum Procedures Directive 2013/32/EU: EU Immigration and Asylum Law* (Nomos 2016).
[38] Directive 2001/55 on temporary protection.

3 Administrative abuse

As had by now become the norm, presumably to encourage some Member States to engage with the legislation proposed, the Commission offered new powers and possibilities to better address potential abuse. New rules were introduced to permit Member States to accelerate procedures at a border (dispensing with guarantees to asylum-seekers) where the applicant had made clearly false or obviously improbable representations contradicting sufficiently verified country of origin information such that the applicant's claim was unconvincing. The test here is problematic: it appears to assume that in border procedures there is full access to reliable country of origin information, that countries act in coherent and consistent ways if persecuting and torturing their citizens, and that it should thus be evident from country of origin information whether one of its citizens is likely to suffer such treatment.[39] This is additionally problematic as many states in respect of which there is substantiated evidence of severe human rights abuses also lack functional rule of law mechanisms preventing officials from exercising coercive powers in arbitrary or self-interested ways, whether or not consistent with country of origin evidence.

Also in regard to abuse of the administrative asylum system, the directive was amended to permit states to deem applications abandoned and to make assumptions as to whether the asylum-seeker has absconded or failed to comply with conditions.[40] Here too this is problematic, not least since in Member States where asylum systems have been most criticized, such as Greece, reception conditions and procedures have been either non-existent or extremely difficult to access. Thus, asylum-seekers such as those whose situation was considered by the ECtHR in *MSS*, were living in parks or under bridges in the host state, with no protection from assault or access to fresh water. Thus, when due to be called by the authorities to an asylum interview, they had no address to which the summons could be sent. The failure to appear at the scheduled interview was taken as evidence that they had absconded, and had failed to comply with their obligations, with the consequence that their asylum application was deemed to have lapsed and they became in effect standard irregular migrants. While the introduction of a provision in the directive effectively legalizing such practices was popular with some Member States, it was not something which provided increased confidence in the correct application of the EU's asylum procedures (as is apparent in the decision of the ECtHR in *MSS*).

The directive revision did introduce an obligation that Member States provide legal assistance to asylum-seekers, including for first instance procedures, thus strengthening the initiation of the process by ensuring better prepared and presented applications, a contribution to rapid decision-making. This requirement was among those which convinced the United Kingdom to participate no longer in this part of the CEAS, choosing to opt out. This had the rather odd consequence that the first Asylum Procedures Directive has remained operable only for the UK, while all the

---

[39] Galina Cornelisse, 'Territory, Procedures and Rights: Border Procedures in European Asylum Law' (2016) 35 *Refugee Survey Quarterly* 74.

[40] Costello and Mouzourakis, 'EU Law and the Detainability of Asylum-Seekers' (n 34); Helen O'Nions, *Asylum—A Right Denied: A Critical Analysis of European Asylum Policy* (Routledge 2016).

other Member States (except Denmark and Ireland, which had never participated, having opted out from the CEAS entirely) had moved across to the revised requirements. It was also provided in the directive that an asylum procedure should take no longer than six months, but a substantial number of exceptions allow more time where a Member State may need it.

Notwithstanding the criticisms expressed here, the recast directive moved substantially in the direction of a more coherent system of, and the procedures for, the determination of asylum applications. The original aim of closer approximation of asylum procedures across Member States was, however, much less couched in the terms of general objectives without interfering with national procedures than in setting out in effect a comprehensive administrative procedural code.

F Administrative Standards without Transposition: Moving to an Asylum Procedures Regulation

Between the recast Directive of 2011 and the proposal for a regulation in 2016, the European Asylum Support Office (EASO) was established.[41] This body was given a wide range of tasks: acting as a centre of expertise on asylum; contributing to the development of the CEAS by facilitating, coordinating, and strengthening practical cooperation among Member States on the many aspects of asylum; helping Member States fulfil their European and international obligations to protect people in need; providing practical and technical support to Member States and the Commission; providing operational support to Member States with specific needs and where asylum and reception systems are under particular pressure; and providing evidence-based input for EU policy-making and legislation in all areas having direct or indirect impact on asylum. This agency became operational in February 2011, just at the time when the Union and the Member States were confronted with the policy and practical implications of ECtHR judgment in *MSS* (above).

Equipped now with an agency to support Member States in dealing with asylum issues, including providing them with at least a some country of origin information,[42] the EU was ready to go a step further and to propose the making of regulation on asylum procedures.[43] The arrival of about 1 million asylum-seekers in dramatic circumstances from across the Mediterranean toward either the Greek islands or southern Italy in 2015 concentrated the minds of many EU and Member State officials as to need for a CEAS capable of responding commensurately.[44]

1 From transposition to directly applicable procedural standards

In July 2016, a package of proposed measures was published with the intent of reforming the then applicable system and providing 'a more coherent European approach, reflecting the extent to which the strain of refugee arrivals in the year before

---

[41] Regulation 439/2010 on European Asylum Support Office [2010] OJ L132/11.
[42] Cathryn Costello, 'Safe Country? Says Who?' (2016) 28(4) *International Journal of Refugee Law* 601.
[43] COM(2016) 467 final.   [44] Guild, Costello, and Garlick (n 8).

had led to much friction among Member States. The intent was the amendment of all CEAS measures, in particular transforming some directives (e.g., Asylum Procedures Directive) into (directly applicable) regulations and enhancing Union administrative capacity through a new Agency for Asylum providing operational and technical support to Member States and ensuring efficient management of asylum applications. The proposed agency is seen as having an important capacity building mandate. This might—perhaps validly—be considered as an attempt to police Member States' fulfilment of their CEAS obligations. Undoubtedly for a UK claiming concerns about regaining its state sovereignty, such an agency represents just what it does not like about the EU.

The Commission had three priorities as regards the reforms proposed. First, it sought to change the Dublin system (theoretically in place since 1997, but never actually effective in ensuring that asylum-seekers stay and be processed in the country which the Dublin rules determine) so that it provide a sustainable and fair system of shared responsibility among Member States.[45] While this ambition can be welcomed, thus far other, even concerted, efforts have not achieved this aim, and this proposal appears unlikely to do so. Secondly, the measures are aimed at reinforcing the EURODAC fingerprint database of all asylum-seekers and all those apprehended crossing an EU external border irregularly, made available to Member States to determine which of them is responsible for processing the asylum application. Thirdly, the Commission seeks to establish a 'genuine European Agency for Asylum'—one wonders whether this is an oblique criticism of EASO—to ensure the proper functioning of the CEAS.

The proposal for an Asylum Procedures Regulation is a flanking measure to these three aims. The stated objective of that Regulation is to establish a 'truly common procedure for international protection which is efficient, fair and balanced'. Its instrumental form makes it directly applicable in the Member States, and is thus intended to remove elements of national discretion, as well as to streamline and consolidate procedural arrangements.

2 Relating procedure and outcome

The Commission's proposed regulation seeks a higher degree of harmonization and uniformity in outcomes across the Member States. This is the first time in the development of asylum procedures that the thorny issue of the outcomes of asylum application has been addressed: the Achilles heel of the CEAS is that, after more than ten years, outcomes for asylum-seekers in very similar situations have regularly been very different in different Member States.

Quarterly statistics on asylum in the EU are provided by EUROSTAT, the EU statistical agency. According to two reports (June[46] and December

---

[45] Vincent Chetail, 'Looking beyond the Rhetoric of the Refugee Crisis: The Failed Reform of the Common European Asylum System' (2016) 5 *European Journal of Human Rights* 584 https://ssrn.com/abstract=2898063.

[46] http://ec.europa.eu/eurostat/documents/2995521/7662180/3-22092016-AP-EN.pdf/22f5de3b-b5a8-4195-82fe-3072a4a08146 (last accessed 23 January 2016).

2016[47]), Syrian asylum-seekers have a 98 per cent average success rate (for both quarters), Eritrean asylum-seekers 93 per cent (2nd quarter) and 90 per cent (3rd quarter), and stateless persons 91 per cent (2nd quarter) and 89 per cent (3rd quarter). However, such overall statistics do not reveal the differences in recognition rates among Member States. For instance, according to UNHCR in 2014, only 15 per cent of new asylum applications by Eritreans in France resulted in recognition. In Hungary, the percentage for Eritreans was 49 per cent but in Austria it was 100 per cent.[48] The UNHCR statistics reveal a similar range for Syrian refugee recognition rates in 2014: positive decisions in 64 per cent of first instance applications in Italy, 74 per cent in Greece, 65 per cent in Hungary but 100 per cent in Poland. These differences in recognition rates across the EU are not as pronounced as those for some other nationalities, but their comparisons here are significant because the mentioned nationalities are the only ones which qualify for relocation from Italy and Greece.

Not only does the Commission's proposal for a regulation for the first time allude to the impact of procedures on outcomes. In addition, there is confirmation that these differences in outcomes for individuals may constitute an incentive for people to move from one Member State to another to pursue their claims (the secondary movement issue referred to above).[49] It comes as no surprise that the proposal seeks to offer 'fast but high quality decision-making', now stressing that the decisions will be solid, presumably an acknowledgement that rapid decision-making has resulted in poor decision-making in many Member States, associated with multiple, repeated asylum claims until eventually fair consideration is given (see again, above, the ECtHR in *MSS*). There is still a six-month benchmark for the determination of applications, but with shorter periods for those classified as manifestly unfounded or inadmissible. New time limits are proposed for registering, lodging, and examining applications, with exceptions available on specific grounds. Member States will be obliged to make available sufficient resources to fulfil these obligations and the implementation will be policed by the new agency.

The procedural guarantees for asylum-seekers are maintained in the regulatory proposal, and the need for applicants to be given an effective opportunity to cooperate and properly communicate the elements of their claims is stressed. These issues have been sources of friction as asylum authorities have been accused of cutting corners regarding the provision of a genuine opportunity to make a claim, in order to meet their deadlines.[50] The principle of a procedure with suspensive effect is maintained, but this is to be weakened in respect of appeals. Once again, stricter rules on perceived abuse of the system are introduced. Sanctions are to be mandatory for asylum-seekers who move on (secondary movement) and where claims are classified as manifestly

---

[47] http://ec.europa.eu/eurostat/statistics-explained/index.php/Asylum_quarterly_report (last accessed 23 January 2017).

[48] UNHCR Statistical Yearbook 2014, table 13 http://www.unhcr.org/56655f4b3.html (last accessed 23 January 2017).

[49] Maryellen Fullerton, 'Asylum Crisis Italian Style: The Dublin Regulation Collides with European Human Rights Law' (2016) 29 *Harvard Human Rights Journal* 57.

[50] G Garelli and M Tazzioli http://societyandspace.org/2016/11/08/hotspot-beyond-detention-spatial-strategy-of-dispersal-and-channels-of-forced-transfer/ (last accessed 30 January 2017).

unfounded. Accelerated procedures become obligatory for claims designated as manifestly unfounded and there are new provisions on repeat applications.[51]

A big innovation of the proposal is that the EU should have a common list of countries which are designated as safe countries of origin (and thus not countries giving rise to asylum claims). The consequence for a national of a state so designated would be a strong presumption that an asylum application in the EU is inadmissible, coupled with accelerated procedures and non-suspensive appeal rights, making it extremely difficult for the presumption to be rebutted. The Commission proposes here to harmonize these rules for the first time. Similarly, new rules would govern the return of asylum-seekers where the applicable rules identify the first country of asylum as outside the EU.[52] All of this is contentious, but points in one direction: a move away from approximation (the approach in the recast directive) to harmonization, coupled with a policing mechanism.[53]

G Conclusions

The purpose of this chapter has been to set out the development of EU administrative law in the field of asylum. The overall picture of this field of law is one of (by EU standards) fairly rapid legislative development from minimum standards, through common standards, to full harmonization. This approach is consistent across the field of EU asylum law, made more complex by various judgments, in particular by the ECtHR, but also the CJEU, limiting some of the more restrictive approaches preferred by some of the administrative actors of the Member States.

Even fifteen years ago asylum procedures in the Member States were determined primarily by national administrative procedural law, often with some modifications to adjust to the subject matter. However, since 2005 when the first directive was adopted, this area of administrative law has moved away from its normal place in national procedural, adopting as a result of EU law characteristics which might be quite foreign to the national system. One might suggest that asylum procedures became divorced from their national administrative law setting, becoming part of a European system of administrative rules. Even issues as banal as time limits on administrative decision-making is no longer a matter for national law but rather for Union law, which also imposes an obligation of Member States to provide sufficient administrative resources to meet the various obligations of the directive(s), with substantial consequences for national budgets.

There has been a clear path in the way in which this process has taken place, beginning with minimum procedural standards demanded of Member States but overtly tacked on to national procedural rules. Within eight years (2005–2013), this approach fell out of favour as insufficient and instead the EU moved to approximation of asylum

---

[51] Chetail, De Bruycker, and Maiani (n 20).

[52] Madeline Garlick, 'The Road More Travelled? Onward Movement of Asylum Seekers and Refugees' (2016) 51 *Forced Migration Review* 42.

[53] Leonie Ansems De Vries, Elspeth Guild, and Sergio Carrera, 'Documenting the Migration Crisis in the Mediterranean: Spaces of Transit, Migration Management and Migrant Agency' CEPS Liberty and Security in Europe No 94 (13 September 2016).

procedures, rather than imposing minimum standards. All manner of variations were still permitted under the Union directive, but these were now the exception and not merely left unregulated. Finally, in the most recent 2016 proposals, full harmonization is planned, involving common rules in even very specific aspects of procedure. In addition, an EU agency has been proposed to police implementation and the application of those procedural rules by Member States and to provide them with technical and operational support to achieve the intended results.

9

Data Protection within Police and Judicial Cooperation

Diana Dimitrova

A Introduction

The main focus of this chapter is on administrative procedures for data protection in the area of Police and Judicial Cooperation (PJC), an integral part of the Area of Freedom, Security and Justice (AFSJ) in the European Union. This includes *public security*, as far as it falls within the scope of Union law, and the AFSJ. This is to be distinguished from *national security* which falls outside the scope of EU law. The administrative procedures discussed here concern the *compliance* with, and *supervision* and *enforcement* of data protection provisions applicable to EU and national authorities competent in the police and justice sector. As well, the mechanisms for EU–Member State cooperation in protecting personal data in the course of police and justice operations fall within this scope.

The analysis is based on administrative law provisions on data protection within the PJC sector. These are scattered throughout several different legal instruments. The focus here is mainly on EU instruments: relevant articles in the Treaties, the Charter of Fundamental Rights (CFR) and several secondary law instruments, including those containing specific rules on data protection applicable to Eurojust and Europol.

When examining different administrative procedures, certain key characteristics should be noted:

- Data protection provisions in the PJC sector represent a *patchwork of rules*, with different administrative provisions applying depending on which EU and/or national actors are involved in a given data processing operation. In principle EU and national authorities competent in the PJC sector are subject to different legal frameworks, which, however, contain similar provisions on data protection. However, they are subject to different supervision and enforcement mechanisms and procedures.

- The changes brought about by the Lisbon Treaty, pursuant to which PJC has become a 'normal' Union policy, import many principles and procedures from existing data protection laws into the PJC sector. These would now cover the *whole life-cycle of data processing* by competent Member State authorities. At the same time, they would *strengthen* the *data protection standards* applicable to EU entities such as Europol.

- The 'Lisbonisation' of the PJC sector is manifested also in the *stronger control, supervision, and enforcement mechanisms*. In addition, it results in *more cooperation* between the EU and national independent supervisory authorities (ISAs) in ensuring the protection of personal data in the PJC framework.

To elaborate on the points above, the chapter will examine the different applicable legal instruments on data protection, analysing both the administrative procedures they have created and how these mechanisms interact with one another in order to ensure adequate data protection in the PJC sector. The chapter will present first the various sources of data protection law in this sector (section B). Then it will elaborate on the substantive legal principles of that law (section C). Section D will deal with the sectoral organization, institutions, and structures which have responsibilities for compliance with the legal framework. The administrative procedures to which institutional actors here are subject is treated in section E, while legal rules on decision-making substance are examined in section F. The legal acts and measures which the different actors may adopt will be analysed in sections G and H. Section I focuses on the supervision and control, including the judicial remedies. Before the concluding remarks (section K), section J will delve into matters of enforcement within the sector.

B Sources of Law and the Definition of Data Protection in Police and Justice

The relevant administrative tasks and secondary law measures can be traced back to several sources in the Lisbon Treaty, namely provisions on data protection and those on the AFSJ provisions which apply to PJC. As to AFSJ matters generally, the EU has a *shared competence* to legislate in this field (since the Lisbon Treaty),[1] as a result of the abolition of the pillar structure and bringing the AFSJ under the former Union Pillar.[2] This means that both the EU and its Member States may pass legally binding acts in this field. Member States may exercise their competence, though, only insofar as the Union has either not exercised its competence, or has ceased to do so.[3]

As to data protection as such, this is not assigned to a specific policy field. Instead, the Lisbon Treaty enshrined it separately, as an independent right with horizontal application, in Article 16 TFEU. Its fundamental right status is acknowledged also by Article 8 CFR. Article 16 TFEU provides the Union with the legal basis for adopting legislative measures on data protection in all its policy fields, including within the AFSJ. However, there are several caveats to be made. First, data protection rules in the Common Foreign and Security Policy (CFSP) are subject to a separate

---

[1] Art 4(2)(j) of the Consolidated Version of the Treaty on the Functioning of the European Union [2012] OJ C326/47 of 26 October 2012 (TFEU).

[2] D Bigo and others, 'Towards a New EU Legal Framework for Data Protection and Privacy: Challenges, Principles and the Role of the European Parliament' *Study for the European Parliament* (September 2011) 16; F Boehm, *Information Sharing and Data Protection in the Area of Freedom, Security and Justice: Towards Harmonized Data Protection Principles for Information Exchange at EU-level* (Springer 2012) 116.

[3] Art 2(2) TFEU.

decision-making procedure[4] (outside the scope of this chapter). Secondly, pursuant to Declaration 21 TFEU, in the field of *police and judicial cooperation in criminal matters* specific rules on data processing and data protection may be necessary due to the peculiar nature of that field.[5] This means that PJC is still treated differently, although now the same level of data protection is to be ensured. So far, this has resulted in a directive on the processing of data in the law-enforcement sector (DPLEA Directive).[6] This 'sectoralization' of the EU rules on data protection, in addition to which various exemptions and derogations also exist (see below), makes it difficult to give an exhaustive overview and analysis of all applicable data protection procedures. Thus, the chapter concentrates on the *main* actors, instruments, mechanisms, and procedures, without striving for exhaustiveness.

1 Sources: primary law

Administrative procedures in the PJC are enshrined in *secondary law* instruments, which have their legal basis in the following EU primary law sources.

(a) On privacy and data protection

(i) Article 6(1) TEU, pursuant to which *fundamental rights*, as enshrined in the CFR, e.g. privacy and data protection, are to be respected and are accorded the status of primary law. These are enshrined in Articles 7 and 8 CFR on privacy and data protection respectively. Article 8 CFR establishes data protection as a fundamental right and specifies that: (a) data shall be processed fairly for specified purposes, with some legitimate basis, e.g., consent; (b) data subjects should have the right to access their data and have data rectified; and (c) an independent authority should ensure compliance with these rules.

(ii) Article 16(1) TFEU enshrines the *right to data protection*. Article 16(2) of the Treaty provides the *legal basis for secondary legislation* in the field of data protection, pursuant to which the Council and the Parliament are to act in accordance with the *ordinary* legislative procedure to pass legislation. Thus, the Lisbon Treaty has empowered the Union to legislate in the field of data protection, including within the AFSJ. However, sometimes Member States must transpose EU measures into their national laws, e.g., they currently have to implement Directive 2016/680 (DPLEA Directive), and thus spell out the

---

[4] Pursuant to Art 16(2) TFEU and Art 39 of the Treaty on the European Union (TEU), the Council may adopt decisions on the processing of personal data in the CFSP.

[5] Declaration (No 21) to the TFEU on the protection of personal data in the fields of judicial cooperation in criminal matters and police cooperation.

[6] Directive (EU) 2016/680 of the European Parliament and of the Council of 27 April 2016 on the protection of natural persons with regard to the processing of personal data by competent authorities for the purposes of the prevention, investigation, detection or prosecution of criminal offences or the execution of criminal penalties, and on the free movement of such data, and repealing Council Framework Decision 2008/977/JHA [2016] OJ L119/89 of 4 May 2016 (DPLEA Directive).

directive's provisions. The Member States thus retain certain legislative powers and degrees of freedom.

Although this chapter focuses primarily on the Union's administrative law provisions in the sphere of data protection and privacy, it is worth mentioning that Article 8 of the European Convention on Human Rights (ECHR), to which all EU Member States are parties, is also a source of law on data protection. It regulates the conditions under which Member State authorities may interfere with the *right to privacy*, into which the European Court on Human Rights (ECtHR) has also read—and strengthened—the right to data protection.[7] The ECHR and its interpretation by the ECtHR have inspired both the EU legislator and the Court of Justice, and will therefore, where relevant here, be examined. Other Council of Europe sources of data protection standards for PJC are Convention No. 108 (1981) and Recommendation R (87) 15. In the absence of a comprehensive PJC data protection package in the EU until recently, these two international instruments have also been an inspiration in this sector.

(b) On police and justice cooperation

(i) According to Article 3(2) TEU, one of the aims of the Union is to create an Area of Freedom, Security and Justice (AFSJ).

(ii) Part III, Title V TFEU sets out *further provisions* on the AFSJ. Chapter 1 (General Provisions) regulates the decision-making procedures and provides the legal basis for measurers in the several policies fields: border checks, asylum, and immigration (Chapter 2), judicial cooperation in civil matters (Chapter 3), judicial cooperation in criminal matters (Chapter 4), and police cooperation (Chapter 5). Since the focus of the present chapter is on Police and Justice in criminal matters, it will not consider the areas of border checks, asylum and immigration or judicial cooperation in civil matters.

Certain articles in the TFEU relating to PJC deserve special attention. Pursuant to Article 67(3) TFEU:

> The Union shall endeavour to ensure a high level of security ... through measures for *coordination and cooperation* between police and judicial authorities and other competent authorities, as well as through the *mutual recognition* of judgments in criminal matters and, if necessary, through the *approximation of criminal laws*.[8]

Reflecting the intergovernmental spirit which governed the area prior to the Lisbon Treaty, Article 68 TFEU provides that the European Council shall set the strategic guidelines for *legislative and operational planning* in the AFSJ. Article 76 TFEU provides that the acts adopted to advance *administrative cooperation* in the PJC sector should be passed either on a proposal by the Commission or on the initiative of a quarter of the Member States. Articles 85 and 88 TFEU provide for the legal basis for

---

[7] Bigo and others (n 2) 102.   [8] Emphasis added.

Eurojust and *Europol* respectively, the tasks, activities, and structure of which are to be adopted by the European Parliament and the Council pursuant to the ordinary legislative procedure. As to judicial cooperation, Article 82 TFEU establishes that it should be based on the principle of *mutual recognition* of judgments and judicial decisions. Although it does not explicitly mention the processing of personal data, it is self-explanatory that mutual recognition can work only on the basis of exchange of personal data of the concerned individuals. Finally, Article 87 TFEU establishes *police cooperation* between the Member States. Article 87(2)(a) TFEU provides that for the purposes of such cooperation the European Parliament and the Council, acting in accordance with the ordinary legislative procedure, may law down rules on the processing of 'relevant information', which includes also personal data. Therefore, one of the instruments for realizing the cooperation between the competent national law enforcement authorities is *personal data processing*.

In order to ensure the fair and lawful processing of personal data, however, specific data protection rules are needed. The purpose of such rules is to prevent the arbitrary exercise of state powers against citizens, as well as allow for the correction of mistakes and inaccuracies. Such rules are necessary so as to mitigate and remedy the possible negative impact on the data subjects concerned, e.g., wrongful identification of an innocent person as a criminal, purposeful but wrongful listing of an innocent individual as a suspect, the leaking of data about someone's criminal past which might prejudice their re-integration in society, and so on.[9]

Data protection rules thus play an important role in the PJC sector in the EU, ensuring the fairness of personal data processing, essential for the integrity of the outcomes of police and judicial operations in the EU and of cooperation between authorities in that field. Such data protection rules include: (1) data protection and criminal justice principles, (2) the rights of data subjects, e.g., suspects or victims of crime; (3) transparency of procedures; and (4) framework of supervision, enforcement, sanctions, and remedies. Rules of this kind (belonging to the core of the administrative procedural law) are found mainly in secondary law instruments, clarified by case law (and are discussed further below).

2 Sources: secondary law

The specific administrative procedures have been detailed in the following secondary law instruments (without making a strict distinction adoption under Article 16 TFEU and that under Title V TFEU, as in any case some instruments pre-date the Lisbon Treaty framework):

(i) Directive 95/46/EC on *personal data protection in the framework of the internal market*. It excludes from its scope the PJC sector, e.g., public security. It applies to all private controllers and processors, but sometimes data which are processed by these are needed for purposes of criminal investigations, detections, or prosecutions. In such cases, certain rights of data subjects may be restricted

---

[9] Boehm (n 2) 8–11.

under specific conditions, as regulated in Article 13. Therefore, Directive 95/46/EC is not totally irrelevant for the present discussion.

(ii) Framework Decision (FD) 2008/977/JHA, although focused specifically on the *processing* of personal data in the framework of PJC in criminal matters, had a significantly restricted scope as it applies only to exchanges of personal data between the respective competent Member State authorities, between them and Europol and Eurojust, and their transfer to third countries.[10] This means that it did not apply to data processing activities within a purely national context. The Framework Decision was repealed and replaced by Directive 2016/680 (DPLEA Directive).[11]

(iii) The Directive 2016/680 (DPLEA Directive), in force since 6 May 2016 and applicable by the Member States two years after that,[12] remedies the hitherto existing lack of EU-regulation of the entire personal data processing cycle *by Member State law-enforcement authorities* for the purposes of prevention, investigation, detection, or prosecution of criminal offences or the execution of criminal penalties. This directive will constitute the *lex generalis* for data protection in the PJC sector.

(iv) Regulation 45/2001 applies to personal data processing operations *by EU institutions, bodies and agencies*, e.g. Europol and Eurojust. It is the *lex generalis* on data protection for all EU entities. It is set to be replaced by a new Regulation, which is still being negotiated.[13]

(v) Several Europol and Eurojust instruments contain relevant provisions on *data protection procedures* to be followed by Europol and Eurojust, to be seen as *lex specialis* to Regulation 45/2001.[14]

---

[10] See Art 1 of Council Framework Decision 2008/977/JHA of 27 November 2008 on the protection of personal data processed in the framework of police and judicial cooperation in criminal matters [2008] OJ L350/60 of 30 December 2008.

[11] Art 59 DPLEA Directive (n 6).   [12] ibid Art 63(1).

[13] Proposal for a Regulation of the European Parliament and of the Council on the protection of individuals with regards to the processing of personal data by the Union institutions, bodies, offices and agencies and on the free movement of such data, and repealing Regulation (EC) No 45/2001 and Decision No 1247/2002/EC, COM(2017) 8 final, Brussels, 10 January 2017.

[14] Council Decision of 6 April 2009 establishing the European Police Office (Europol) (2009/371/JHA) [2009] OJ L 121/37 of 15 May 2009 (Europol Decision); Regulation 2016/794 of the European Parliament and of the Council of 11 May 2016 on the European Union Agency for Law Enforcement Cooperation (Europol) and replacing and repealing Council Decisions 2009/371/JHA, 2009/934/JHA, 2009/935/JHA, 2009/936/JHA, and 2009/968/JHA [2016] OJ L135/ of 25 May 2016 (Europol Regulation, which entered into force on 1 May2017); Rules of procedure on the processing and protection of personal data at Eurojust (Text adopted unanimously by the college of Eurojust during the meeting of 21 October 2004 and approved by the Council on 24 February 2005) (2005/C 68/01) http://www.eurojust.europa.eu/doclibrary/Eurojust-framework/dataprotection/Eurojust%20Data%20Protection%20Rules/Eurojust-Data-Protection-Rules-2005-02-24-EN.pdf; Additional rules defining some specific aspects of the application of the rules on the processing and protection of personal data at Eurojust to non-case-related operations (adopted by the College of Eurojust on 27 June 2006) http://www.eurojust.europa.eu/doclibrary/Eurojust-framework/dataprotection/Additional%20rules%20defining%20specific%20aspects%20of%20the%20application%20of%20Rules%20on%20Processing%20and%20Protection%20of%20Personal%20Data/additional_dp_rules.pdf; Council of the European Union, Council Decision on the strengthening of Eurojust and amending Decision 2002/187/JHA, Brussels (15 July 2009) http://www.eurojust.europa.eu/doclibrary/Eurojust-framework/ejdecision/Consolidated%20version%20of%20the%20Eurojust%20Council%20Decision/Eurojust-Council-Decision-2009Consolidated-EN.pdf.

(vi)   Council Decision 2007/533//JHA on the Second Generation *Schengen Information System* (SIS II), a single database, which contains two types of alerts, entered by, and shared between, the Member States. The first type of alerts concerns individuals who are of interest to law enforcement authorities, e.g., criminals and victims, and stolen objects, e.g., identity papers. The other type of alerts concerns third country nationals (TCNs) who should be denied entry into the Schengen Area (outside the scope of this chapter).[15] The Council Decision contains several data protection provisions as they apply to the Member States, Europol and Eurojust.

(vii)   Council Decision 2008/633/JHA on Member State police and Europol *access to VIS data*. The Visa Information System (VIS) is a database on TCN Schengen visa applicants and holders, i.e., it is an administrative database, unlike SIS II. However, competent Member State authorities, as well as Europol, may access the personal data stored on it (e.g., names, passport and visa details, ten fingerprints and a facial image) for law-enforcement purposes, under certain conditions. This Council Decision contains special provisions on data protection safeguards and supervision mechanisms.

(viii) Regulation (EU) No 603/2013 on Member State police authorities and Europol *access to Eurodac data*.[16] Eurodac is a database of TCNs who claim refugee or asylum status in the EU, of those who have been apprehended as residing illegally on EU territory or crossing the EU borders illegally, and of stateless people. It is also an administrative database which may be accessed under certain conditions by the competent national law enforcement authorities, as well as Europol, for law-enforcement purposes. Similarly to the VIS and SIS II case, it too contains a series of data protection provisions.

ix)   The Prüm Convention on exchange of DNA, fingerprint and vehicle registration data to combat serious crime such as terrorist offences.[17] It has several data protection provisions.

In addition, *national (implementing) provisions*, e.g., national criminal procedural law such as Article 136a of the *Strafprozeßordnung* (StPO) [Criminal Procedure Act]

---

[15] This second type of alerts form a separate section in the SIS II and has a separate legal basis, namely Regulation (EC) No 1987/2006, which is not analysed in this chapter.

[16] Regulation (EU) No 603/2013 of the European Parliament and of the Council of 26 June 2013 on the establishment of 'Eurodac' for the comparison of fingerprints for the effective application of Regulation (EU) No 604/2013 establishing the criteria and mechanisms for determining the Member State responsible for examining an application for international protection lodged in one of the Member States by a third country national or a stateless person and on requests for the comparison with Eurodac data by Member States' law enforcement authorities and Europol for law enforcement purposes, and amending Regulation (EU) No 1077/2011 establishing a European Agency for the operational management of large-scale IT systems in the area of freedom, security and justice (recast) [2013] OJ L180/1 of 29 June 2013 (Eurodac Regulation).

[17] Council of the European Union, Convention the Kingdom of Belgium, the Federal Republic of Germany, the Kingdom of Spain, the French Republic, the Grand Duchy of Luxembourg, the Kingdom of the Netherlands and the Republic of Austria on the stepping up of cross-border cooperation, particularly in combating terrorism, cross-border crime and illegal migration (Prüm Convention), Council Document No 10900/05, Brussels (7 July 2005) https://ec.europa.eu/anti-fraud/sites/antifraud/files/docs/body/prumtr.pdf.

in Germany (on the so-called *Beweisverwertungsverbot*, i.e., exclusion of improperly obtained evidence), apply to national authorities. This represents an additional layer of regulation of the activities of criminal authorities as regards the information/personal data they process.

3 Sources: soft law

There are also soft law measures (recommendations, best practices, guidelines on the interpretation and application of data protection rules), which frame the processing of personal data in the AFSJ. Of particular importance are the thematic guidelines and opinions of the European Data Protection Supervisor (EDPS), the Article 29 Working Party (to be soon replaced by the European Data Protection Board (EDPB)), the earlier Working Party on Police and Justice,[18] and the national independent supervisory authorities (ISAs).

From the above mapping out of the sources of administrative data protection law in the PJC sphere one can conclude that these sources represent a *patchwork of regimes and rules*. However, as shown below, there is a move towards increased *harmonization* of the substantive sectoral data protection rules and increased mechanisms for *cooperation* between national and EU supervisory authorities.

C Substantive Legal Principles of Data Protection in Police and Justice

A number of substantive principles have their origin in Article 4 DPLEA Directive (1-6 below). These, or at least some of them, are also to be found in Recommendation (87) 15, Convention 108, and in the instruments on SISII, VIS, Eurodac, Europol, and Eurojust. The other five (7–12 below), have been derived from various DPLEA Directive provisions and/or the TFEU, the CFREU, and international law instruments (as noted accordingly). The key principles are:

1 *Fair and lawful processing.* This means that the applicable data protection rules, as well as other applicable provisions, e.g., on criminal law procedure, should be respected. This in itself entails compliance with other principles, e.g. non-discrimination.[19] Lawfulness requires compliance with legitimizing principles. For example, that investigative measures should have a basis in law which is accessible, foreseeable, and prevents arbitrariness, is a requirement under Article 8(2) ECHR and ECtHR case law.[20] Advocate General Øe argued for the endorsement of this principle by the Court of Justice in his opinion in *Tele2*.[21] Article 8

---

[18] Commission for the protection of privacy, Working Party on Police and Justice, https://www.privacycommission.be/en/wppj.

[19] Boehm (n 2) 130–32.

[20] See eg European Court of Human Rights (ECtHR), *Kruslin v France*, Application no 11801/85, 24 April 1990; Art 8 DPLEA Directive (n 6), Art 8(2) European Convention of Human Rights (ECHR).

[21] CJEU, Opinion of Advocate General Saugmandsgaard ØE, Joined Cases C-203/15 and C-698/15 *Tele2 Sverige AB v Postoch telestyrelsen* and *Secretary of State for the Home Department v Tom Watson, Peter Brice, Geoffrey Lewis* ECLI:EU:C:2016:970, para 143.

DPLEA Directive spells out some criteria for lawfulness, namely *necessity* for ful-filling the task of preventing, detecting, and prosecuting crimes, as well as having an existing *legal basis* in Union or national law. The latter should specify at least the *objectives* and the *purposes* of the processing, as well as the type of *personal data* to be processed.

2   *Purpose limitation* (i.e., purpose specification and compatible use). The respon-sible data controller should specify the exact purposes of the data processing activity, e.g., for investigating a *specific* crime. However, the DPLEA Directive contains several *exceptions* to this principle. There, Article 9 allows personal data processing only for law enforcement purposes, *unless* further processing is authorized by Union or national law for other, non-criminal law related pur-poses (including scientific, historical, and statistical purposes, and archiving in the public interest).[22] Article 4(2) DPLEA Directive provides also that the processing of personal data for law enforcement purposes (including scientific, historical, statistical and archiving purpose) other than those for which they were collected is permitted. Such further processing by the same *or another con-troller* is allowed where: (1) the controller is authorized by EU or Member State law to process such personal data for the new purpose and (2) the processing is necessary and proportionate to the new purpose under Member State or Union law. Thus, the 'purpose limitation' principle, 'a cornerstone of data protection law',[23] can be easily circumvented, thus opening the door for future function creep and making it difficult to stick by other principles (1, 3–6) as their ap-plication relates to the purpose. Framework Decision 2008/977/JHA contained similar exceptions.[24]

3   *Data minimization, adequacy and relevance.* The controller should use only the minimum data necessary, i.e., the minimum in relation to the purpose. For ex-ample, in the context of a specific investigation or prosecution, this requires a determination as to which data might be necessary for solving a certain crime, or set of crimes, and deleting, or not collecting, data not deemed irrelevant.

4   *Accuracy.* This principle implies verifying that the data are actually correct and up-to-date. Related to this, Article 7 DPLEA Directive provides that fact-based personal data should be distinguished from data based on personal assessments. The controller is thus required to verify the data-quality before they are trans-mitted or made available. This should avoid negative consequences for an investi-gation based on inaccurate data, and negative consequences for those whose data are processed.

---

[22] For such other processing Regulation 2016/679 of the European Parliament and of the Council of 27 April 2016 on the protection of natural persons with regard to the processing of personal data and on the free movement of such data, and repealing Directive 95/46/EC (General Data Protection Regulation) [2016] OJ L119/1, of 4 May2016 (GDPR) applies only if the new processing is within the scope of Union law. The GDPR (n 22), which applies as of 25 May 2018, regulates the majority of data processing oper-ations, ie those which do not fall within the area of law-enforcement, security and the CFSP or processing by Union entities.

[23] European Data Protection Supervisor, 'Opinion of the European Data Protection Supervisor on the Communication from the Commission to the European Parliament and the Council on an area of freedom, security and justice serving the citizen' [2009] OJ C276/8 of 17 November 2009, at 19.

[24] Boehm (n 2) 133; and Art 3 Council Framework Decision 2008/977/JHA (n 10).

5 *Limitation of storage period.* Personal data should be retained only as long as necessary for the specific purpose. This implies a need for periodic review of stored
data, deleting those not relevant and or any longer necessary. For example, *S and
Marper*, acquitted individuals' (sensitive) data were kept on a UK police database after the acquittal, considered an infringement to the right to privacy under
Article 8 ECHR.[25] Periodic review of the necessity for storing data is enshrined
also in Article 5 DPLEA Directive, which requires the establishment of *procedural
measures* to ensure that the storage time-limits are respected.

6 *Data security.* Measures are needed to prevent unauthorized or unlawful processing and accidental loss, destruction or damage (e.g., through leaking or
hacking), whereby data falls in the hands of those who are not charged with
the detection/investigation/prosecution of a crime (e.g., hackers who may compromise investigations or those subject to them). Steps must exist to prevent internal abuse (e.g. by police officer who might copy and distribute data). The loss,
destruction, or damage of data may be detrimental to investigations themselves
(e.g., loss of evidence or investigatory leads) as well as harming individuals subject
to investigations or otherwise affected by them.

7 *Necessity and proportionality. Necessity* is one of the main criteria of EU law, with
multi-faceted application. The EDPS distinguishes between two applications of
this principle in data protection law. On the one hand, it is an essential criterion
when assessing: (1) the lawfulness of data processing operations, i.e., whether a
processing operation is necessary for carrying out a task with which the controller is entrusted or one in the public interest; and (2) the legality of restrictions
on fundamental rights, e.g., whether interception of everybody's' telecommunications is necessary in order to fight serious crime.[26] With regard to the latter, the
ECtHR requires a limitation on a right to be 'necessary in a democratic society'
and, in cases of secret surveillance, to be 'strictly necessary'.[27] 'Strict necessity' is
also demanded by the CJEU.[28]

Proportionality refers to the balance to be struck between the means, i.e., the intended data-processing operations (such as interception of a suspect's communications) and the intended aim or the results achieved, e.g., finding evidence of a
crime. In addition, the chosen means should as such be appropriate for achieving
the intended purpose.[29]

8 *Confidentiality of processing*[30] requires data to be processed only those members
of staff working under the instruction of the competent authority. These staff
members are themselves bound by the data protection rules applicable to that
authority.

---

[25] ECtHR, *S and Marper v United Kingdom,* Application nos 30562/04 and 30566/04, 4 December 2008,
para 125.
[26] European Data Protection Supervisor (EDPS), 'Developing a "toolkit" for assessing the necessity of
measures that interfere with fundamental rights. Background paper for consultation' 16.62016, 4.
[27] ECtHR, *Szabo and Vissy v Hungary,* Application no 37138/14, 12 January 2016, para 73.
[28] CJEU, Joined Cases C-293/12 and C-594/12 *Digital Rights Ireland* ECLI:EU:C:2014:238, para 52 and
CJEU, Case C-362/14 *Schrems* ECLI:EU:C:2015:650, paras 92–93.
[29] EDPS (n 26) 6.
[30] Art 23 DPLEA Directive (n 6) and Art 12 Framework Decision 2008/977/JHA (n 10).

9   *Functional categorization of the personal data of different types of data subjects,* i.e., distinguishing between the personal data of suspects, those charged with crimes, those convicted, victims, witnesses, and informants.[31] This is necessary because the implications for affected individuals may be very different depending on how they and their personal data are categorized.

10 *Independent supervision.*[32] This principle requires control exercised by a supervisory authority, e.g., by ISAs when it comes to national law-enforcement authorities, or by the EDPS when it comes to Europol and Eurojust. Other supervisory bodies, set up to supervise e.g. Europol and Eurojust, may also participate in the supervision of their data processing practices.[33]

11 *Transparency.* This is a multi-faceted principle, which the ECtHR interprets to mean transparency of the limitations on the rights to privacy and data protection. In other words, such limitations have to be based on law which is clear, accessible, and foreseeable by the potential data subjects. For example, individuals need to be able know which offences might give rise to measures such as telephone tapping, and what the categories of individuals likely to be subject to such measures.[34] On the other hand, the controller, very often a competent law-enforcement authority, has to be make clear to data subjects what data it is collecting and processing further in regard to them, for what purposes, for how long, etc, as well as what subjective rights under the DPLEA Directive such data subjects enjoy.[35]

12 *Consistency, mutual assistance, and cooperation between supervisory authorities.* The purpose of the cooperation is to ensure the *'consistent application'* of the Directive throughout the Union.[36] Such cooperation should consist in the *exchange of information* and *mutual assistance* between ISAs. Mutual assistance in this setting should cover responding to information requests and the undertaking of supervisory measures, e.g., requests to carry out consultations, inspections, and investigations. The requested supervisory authority should be subject to a time-limit of one month for responding to a request, and should inform the requesting authority of the result, or the state of progress. Reasons should be provided if the requested authority refuses to cooperate.[37] In the future, cooperation among ISAs will occur within the framework of the European Data Protection Board (EDPB)[38] (see further below D(viii)).

The above principles are not new in the data protection scene. However, their full application to the PJC sector is a significant step forward in ensuring fair data processing practices. The ultimate achievement of this will, however, largely depend on a strict interpretation of the purpose limitation principle (number 2 above).

---

[31] Art 6 DPLEA Directive (n 6).
[32] Art 16(2) TFEU, Art 42 DPLEA Directive; Principle 1 Council of Europe Recommendation (87) 15; Art 8(2) CFREU and in all the other instruments mentioned in section B of this chapter.
[33] Bigo and others (n 2) 22.   [34] ibid 21–22. See also *Kruslin v France* (n 20) para 35.
[35] Arts 12 and 13DPLEA Directive (n 6).   [36] ibid Art 41(2) (emphasis added).
[37] ibid Art 50.   [38] ibid Art 51 in conjunction with Art 68 GDPR (n 22) GDPR.

D Organization, Institutions, and Structures for Data Protection in the PJC Sector

Organizational structures within the sector are, as in other EU policy fields, established on national and European levels, and do not work in isolation. On the contrary, they operate cooperatively through the mechanisms and fora established by EU secondary law. The discussion here mainly focuses on how the framework contributes to ensuring compliance with the EU data protection law and its harmonized application across the PJC sector. This sector concerns tasks in the public sphere, and therefore the actors here are public sector ones. Private actors are not dealt with given the dearth of legal provisions concerning them, even though they may play a role with data protection relevance, e.g., in regard to the Passenger Name Record (PNR).[39] In general, any private actor could be invited to cooperate with the police and judicial authorities in the framework of investigations when these authorities request information from them (e.g., private banks could be asked to provide transaction details related to money-laundering investigations). Such a cooperation should follow the procedures as established in national law, e.g., requiring the presentation of a judicial warrant.

1 Organization on Member State level

(i) In data protection law, the concept of the (data) controller plays a central role. The *controller* is defined as:

the competent authority which, alone or jointly with others, determines the purposes and means of the processing of personal data; where the purposes and means of such processing are determined by Union or Member State law, the controller or the specific criteria for its nomination may be provided for by Union or Member State law.[40]

This means that the controllers would be normally staff of the police, investigative, prosecutorial, and similar departments, with sufficient decision-making powers in terms of the personal data processing operations. According to the DPLEA Directive, the controller would have several responsibilities to ensure compliance with the Directive through implementing appropriate technical and organizational

---

[39] Pursuant to Directive (EU) 2016/681 of the European Parliament and of the Council of 27 April 2016 on the use of passenger name record (PNR) data for the prevention, detection, investigation and prosecution of terrorist offences and serious crime OJ L. 119/132 of 4 May 2016, air carriers are obliged to transfer all booking details information to specially established passenger information units (PIU) in each Member State, where the personal data of the passengers is analysed to detect profiles which could correspond to serious criminals (Art 8). However, beyond the collection and transfer of the passengers' details, air carriers do not seem to play a role in the processing of the personal data for *criminal law purposes*.

[40] Art 3(8) DPLEA Directive (n 6).

measures, *inter alia* data protection policies.[41] Controllers thus represent a first level of control over the data processing operations within their department(s), similar to self-monitoring.

(ii) *Data protection officers* (DPOs) of Member State authorities: These should be experts in data protection involved properly and punctually in all matters related to data protection and with whom the controller should cooperate. Their role is to collaborate with, i.e., inform and advise, the controller and other employees on data-protection matters, monitor compliance, advise on the Data Protection Impact Assessment process and monitor its performance, and cooperate with the national ISAs (see following section) and be the contact point for them.[42] Thus, while the responsibility for data protection compliance strictly lies with the controller, the expert knowledge of data protection and its daily application would normally come from the DPO, who acts as a reference point both within his organization and towards the ISAs.

(iii) *Independent supervisory authorities* (ISAs) in the Member States (sometimes known as National Data Protection Authorities, or as National Supervisory Authorities):[43] Each Member State should designate at least one such authority, which shall be *public* and *independent*.[44] The main task of such authority would be to *monitor and enforce* the application of the provisions adopted in implementation of the directive.[45] The directive enumerates the specific tasks of this authority in detail. These can be broadly summarized as advising national authorities (e.g., the legislature, the public, and controllers) on data protection topics, handling and investigating complaints by data subjects or initiating investigations *ex officio*, giving advice in cases of data transfers to third countries, and cooperating with other ISAs pursuant to mutual assistance and cooperation requirements (as in Articles 50 and 51 DPLEA Directive).[46] To fulfil these tasks, such authorities need to be equipped with *effective investigative, corrective and advisory powers*.[47]

ISAs already exist in each Member State pursuant to a number of other legal measures, the supervisory and enforcement tasks reflecting the particular law establishing them. These laws are specifically: (1) **Directive 95/46/EC** and its successor the General Data Protection Regulation (**GDPR**) (in force since 25 May 2018).[48] The same supervisory authorities under the GDPR may now be designated as competent supervisory authorities under the DPLEA Directive.[49] As to the law-enforcement sector, there have existed other supervisory authorities, namely pursuant to the now repealed (2) **Framework Decision 2008/977/JHA**, which required data-processing to be supervised by an independent authority with investigative and advisory powers, powers to hear complaints by data subjects, and powers to engage in legal proceedings and to bring

---

[41] ibid Art 19.   [42] ibid Arts 32–34.   [43] ibid Chapter VI.   [44] ibid Art 42.
[45] ibid Arts 41(1) and 46(1)(a).   [46] ibid Art 46.   [47] ibid Art 47.   [48] GDPR (n 22).
[49] Art 41(3) DPLEA Directive (n 6).

infringements to the attention of judicial authorities.[50] Additionally, pursuant to (3) the **SIS II Council Decision**, the **Prüm Convention**, **Eurodac**, and **VIS**, the processing of personal data by the competent law-enforcement authorities should be supervised by ISAs.[51]

A possible future scenario, in application of the DPLEA Directive, is that one ISA per Member State might become competent under all the above-mentioned instruments. This could lead to an increased harmonization of data protection rules and practice across the PJC sector, and between it and other sectors (specifically where private actors are involved).

2 Organization on the EU level

Within the Union administration in the narrower sense there is a similar architecture to ensure compliance of EU entities with the applicable data protection provisions:

(iv) The *controller* within the different EU authorities is defined as the organizational entity which defines the means and purposes of the processing, alone or jointly with the others. He or she may be appointed by Union law, if the means and purposes of the data processing are laid down by such law.[52]

In the specific case of Eurojust, the definition of a controller is identical to the definition above.[53] As for Europol, the responsibility for data processing is shared between the Member States and Europol itself (and this will not change under the new Europol Regulation).[54] Europol can be seen as an information hub to which Member States and third countries or organizations provide data. The data provider is the entity which *defines the purposes of, and limitations on,* the data processing, sometimes together with Europol.[55] Thus, it should not come as a surprise that no one in Europol is designated as a controller. However, pursuant to the Council Decision on implementing rules for

---

[50] Art 25 Framework Decision 2008/977/JHA (n 10).

[51] See Art 60 SIS II Council Decision 2007/533/JHA, Art 8(5) and (6) Council Decision 2008/633/JHA on Member State police and EUROPOL access to VIS data, Art 33(2) Eurodac Regulation (n 16), Art 39(5) Prüm Convention (n 17).

[52] See Art 2(d) of Regulation (EC) No 45/2001 of the European Parliament and of the Council of 18 December 2000 on the protection of individuals with regard to the processing of personal data by the Community institutions and bodies and on the free movement of such data [2001] OJ L8/1 of 12 January 2001.

[53] See Art 1(k) of the Rules of procedure on the processing and protection of personal data at Eurojust (Text adopted unanimously by the college of Eurojust during the meeting of 21 October 2004 and approved by the Council on 24 February 2005) (2005/C 68/01) (19 March 2005) http://eurojust.europa. eu/doclibrary/Eurojust-framework/dataprotection/Eurojust%20Data%20Protection%20Rules/Eurojust-Data-Protection-Rules-2005-02-24-EN.pdf. See also Art 4 of the 'Additional rules defining some specific aspects of the application of the rules on the processing and protection of personal data at Eurojust to non-case-related operations on the responsibilities of the controller in non-case-related data (adopted by the College of Eurojust on 27 June 2006)' http://www.eurojust.europa.eu/doclibrary/Eurojust-framework/dataprotection/Additional%20rules%20defining%20specific%20aspects%20of%20the%20 application%20of%20Rules%20on%20Processing%20and%20Protection%20of%20Personal%20Data/ additional_dp_rules.pdf.

[54] Art 38 Europol Regulation (n 14).   [55] Art 19 Europol Regulation.

Europol analysis work files, it is the *Director of Europol*, who should ensure data protection compliance, on advice from the designated DPO,[56] a responsibility borne by controllers. It is assumed that the executive director will have the same responsibility under the new Regulation.

(v) The *internal DPO* of each EU body: These DPOs are a member of the staff of the respective entity but acting independently to: ensure compliance with the data protection rules applicable to that entity; advise the controller on data protection topics; inform data subjects of their rights; serve as a contact point for the EDPS; and keep a register of the data processing operations carried out by the controller.[57] The DPOs of Eurojust[58] and Europol[59] are vested with similar powers.

(vi) The European Data Protection Supervisor (EDPS) supervises and enforces the application of Regulation 45/2001 on the EU level, i.e., as regards data processing operations of EU bodies such as Europol and Eurojust, as well as being consulted on various data protection topics and handling complaints.[60]

vii) Additional supervisory structures have, amongst others, certain data protection responsibilities, varying dependent on the structure but, in principle, encompassing supervisory functions, including reacting to infringements. These additional structures are (1) the Joint Supervisory Body (JSB) for Europol, which supervises the activities of Europol in view of ensuring that the rights and freedoms of data subjects are not prejudiced by its personal data processing. The JSB used to be composed of up to two representatives from each ISA,[61] but, as of 1 May 2017, has been replaced by the *Cooperation Board*, composed both of ISAs *and* the EDPS;[62] and (2) the *Joint Supervisory Body (JSB) for Eurojust*, which also supervises the compliance of that body's data processing operations with the provisions of the Eurojust Decision. It is composed of three permanent members, as well as ad-hoc members, being one judge (not him- or herself a member of Eurojust) from each EU Member State.[63]

There are other cases in which the responsibility for ensuring compliance with the respective data protection law is shared between the EU and the Member State supervisory authorities, e.g. in the case of SIS II, VIS, and Eurodac. Since the data stored on these databases is accessible both by Member State competent authorities and certain EU entities, e.g. Europol, supervision lies both with the ISAs (for the processing by competent national law-enforcement authorities) and with the European Data

---

[56] See Art 10 of Council Decision 2009/936/JHA of 30 November 2009 adopting the implementing rules for Europol analysis work files [2009] OJ L325/14 of 11 December 2009.

[57] Art 24 Regulation 45/2001 (n 52).

[58] See Art 17 of Council Decision on the strengthening of Eurojust and amending Decision 2002/187/JHA of 15 July 2009 (Eurojust Decision).

[59] Art 28 Europol Decision (n 14) and Art 41 Europol Regulation (n 14).

[60] Chapter V Regulation 45/2001 (n 52), Art 43 Europol Regulation (n 14).

[61] Art 34 Europol Decision (n 14).   [62] Art 45 Europol Regulation (n 14).

[63] Art 23 Eurojust Decision (n 58); Act of the joint supervisory body of Eurojust of 23 June 2009 laying down its rules of procedure (adopted unanimously at the plenary meeting of the Joint Supervisory Body of Eurojust on 23 June 2009) (2010/C 182/03) of 7 July 2010.

Protection Supervisor (EDPS) for the processing by, for instance, Europol. As to the overall supervision of data processing by Europol, this will in future be split between the ISAs and the EDPS, which have an obligation of mutual cooperation.[64] To encourage further cooperation between ISAs, and between them and the EU, several *hybrid Member State and European structures* have been set up:

viii) The European Data Protection Board (EDPB), established under the GDPR,[65] is a forum for exchange of ideas and expertise between the national ISAs and between them and the EDPS. This demonstrates the narrowing distance between the data protection provisions for the law-enforcement sector on the one hand and, on the other hand, the sectors to which the GDPR is applicable, i.e., the private sector, and the public sector when it processes personal data for administrative purposes, or entities that combine private and public sectors. This Board will replace the present Article 29 Working Party (from 6 May 2018). Pursuant to the DPLEA Directive, its tasks will be to: advise the Commission on any data protection related issue, including any proposed Directive amendments; examine and issue guidelines on the application of the Directive (with a view to consistency); issue guidelines, best practices and recommendations on the investigative and advisory functions of the national supervisory authorities and on data breaches; review the practical application of the guidelines issued; contribute to Commission assessments carried out on adequacy of protections adopted by third countries; promote cooperation between supervisory authorities; organize mutual trainings; and cooperate with third countries on data protection topics.[66]

ix) ISAs and EDPS will be required to meet and collaborate more frequently in the framework of supervising and auditing the compliance of operations in the SIS II,[67] Eurodac,[68] and Europol frameworks (see again above).

E Administrative Procedures within the PJC Sector

Several *enforcement* procedures, e.g., investigations by ISAs in reaction to a complaint, form part of the administrative procedures within the sector. These procedures, however, will be examined in Section I, which looks at *enforcement* mechanisms within the sector. Here the focus is on other administrative procedures ensuring the correct application of the law (touching, however, where needed upon elements of enforcement).

1 Prior consultation of the supervisory authority

Pursuant to Article 28 DPLEA Directive, the controller or processor should consult the respective ISA before setting up new filing systems where either a Data Protection Impact Assessment has indicated that the intended data processing operation would

---

[64] Arts 42 and 43 Europol Regulation (n 14).   [65] Art 68 GDPR Regulation (n 22).
[66] Art 51 DPLEA Directive (n 6).   [67] Art 62(3) SIS II Council Decision 2007/533/JHA (n 60).
[68] Art 32 Eurodac Regulation (n 16).

pose high risks to the data subjects in the absence of adequate safeguards *or* the data processing poses high risks for the rights and freedoms of data subjects (e.g., because of the capacities of new technologies or the chosen mechanisms and procedures). This requirement mirrors the one established by Article 23 Framework Decision 2008/977/JHA.

As to EU entities, the respective controller should first submit a notification to the DPO before commencing any processing operation.[69] If the DPO finds that the intended data processing poses high risks (e.g., because of the nature, scope, and purposes of the processing), it should submit a notification for prior checking to the EDPS (which must deliver an opinion within two months of the notification, a deadline which may be suspended where the EDPS needs further details of the operation or because of its complexity).[70]

2 Transfers of personal data to third countries or international organizations

If the competent authorities of one Member State wish to transfer personal data to law-enforcement authorities in third countries, then several conditions would need to be fulfilled, namely:

- The transfer should be only for purposes of criminal detection, investigation, prosecution, etc, as listed in Article 1(1) of the DPLEA Directive.
- The receiving authority should have the competence and responsibility for such tasks.
- If the transferring Member State has obtained the data from a controller in another Member State, then the consent of this -controller is necessary. Under certain conditions derogations to this requirement can apply.[71]
- The transfer should be based either on an adequacy decision or in the absence thereof—on adequate safeguards or a derogation for that specific transfer.
- In cases of onward transfer to another third country, the Member State which carried out the first transfer should authorize the new transfer.[72]

Adequacy decisions (one of the possible conditions for data transfer) are implementing acts adopted by the Commission in respect of a specific third country where the latter ensures an 'adequate level of protection'. In that case no specific authorization for the transfer would be necessary.[73] As the Court ruled in the *Schrems* case, 'adequate' shall mean 'essentially equivalent' to the level of protection in the Union.[74] Article 36(2) DPLEA Directive provides a number of criteria for assessing the level of data protection in third countries, e.g., respect for the rule of law, independent supervision of data processing operations, etc.

---

[69] Art 25 Regulation 45/2001 (n 52).   [70] Art 27 Regulation 45/2001 (n 52).
[71] Art 35(2) DPLEA Directive (n 6).   [72] ibid Art 35(1).   [73] ibid Art 36(1) and (3).
[74] Case C-362/14 *Schrems* (n 28), para 73.

Transfers may also be effected if the controller adduces *appropriate safeguards* in the absence of an adequacy decision. These safeguards should fulfil one of the following conditions: (1) they are adduced in a *legally binding document* or (2) the controller concludes that appropriate safeguards exist concerning the protection of personal data, after having assessed all the circumstances surrounding the transfer. In that latter case he or she should inform the ISA of the categories of transfer, document the transfer, and make it available to the ISA upon request.[75]

The third option for a transfer is based on *a derogation in specific situations* only if the transfer is *necessary* for one of the following purposes:

- to protect the vital interests of the data subject or another natural person
- to safeguard legitimate interests of the data subject, where the law of the Member State transferring the data so provide
- to prevent an immediate and serious threat to public security of a Member State or third country
- to fulfil one of the purposes in Article 1(1) in an individual case or
- to establish, exercise or defend legal claims for the purposes in Article 1(1) in an individual case.[76]

In the latter two cases, the competent transferring authority should carry out a balancing test on whether the rights and freedoms of the data subjects outweigh the public interest and, if so, then desist from the transfer.[77] As in the case of transfers based on appropriate safeguards, transfers which are qualified as a derogation should be thoroughly documented, and the documentation available to the ISA upon request.[78]

3 Transfers under the Framework Decision

Article 13 of Framework Decision 2008/977/JHA provided for transfers of personal data under similar conditions to those enumerated above. Pursuant to it, the prior consent of the Member State providing the data to the Member State wishing to transfer it outside the EU is always necessary, unless one of the derogations in Article 13(2) apply.

4 Mutual assistance mechanism

Mutual assistance under the DPLEA Directive refers to that rendered between the ISAs. If requested (e.g. to transmit relevant information on the conduct of a data protection investigation by another supervisory authority), an ISA should reply with no undue delay to the request, and certainly no later than one month after receiving the request.[79] Such assistance is to be rendered by electronic means, using a standardized format.[80]

---

[75] Art 37(1)(j), (2) and (3) DPLEA Directive (n 6).   [76] ibid Art 38(1).   [77] ibid Art 38(2).
[78] ibid Art 38(3).   [79] ibid Art 50(2).   [80] ibid Art 50(6).

Such requests should contain all information that is necessary, such as the purpose of, and reasons for, the request, and the information provided is to be used only for the purposes for which it was requested.[81] The requested supervisory authority[82] may refuse to cooperate only if it is not competent to respond to the request or if compliance with the request would infringe the Directive, or Union or Member State law to which the requested ISA is subject.[83] Requested supervisory authorities shall inform the requesting authority of the results or the progress of the requested measure, or the reasons for the refusal to accede to the request.[84] In principle assistance should be provided without charge but supervisory authorities may agree on rules governing mutual indemnification for expenditures in exceptional circumstances.[85]

5 Consulting the European Data Protection Board (EDPB)

Should the European Commission request advice from the Board on a certain topic, it may indicate a time limit for the delivery of the Board's opinion in accordance with the urgency of the matter.[86] The EDPB should forward its opinions or guidelines to the Committee which assists the Commission, composed of representatives of the Member States and chaired by a Commission representative,[87] and publish them.[88] The Commission informs the EDPB of the actions taken in response to its advice. When the Board assists the Commission in assessing the adequacy of a third country, the Commission should provide it with full access to the documentation on the case.[89]

6 Data breach notification

Data breaches could occur under different forms, e.g., personal data could be accidentally lost or leaked. In certain cases, the controller has the responsibility to notify the ISA and the data subjects of such breaches.

(a) Notification to the supervisory authority

The controller shall communicate to the ISA without undue delay and where feasible within 72 hours of becoming aware of it the data breach where a risk to the rights and freedoms of natural persons is likely to result. Delays in the notification should be accompanied by a justification.[90] In cases where the breach is detected by the processor, he should notify the controller without undue delay.[91] All data breaches are to be documented by the controller.[92]

The content of the notification should include a description of nature of the breach, e.g., categories and approximate number of data subjects possibly affected, the consequences of the breach, the measures (to be) taken to mitigate the consequences, and

---

[81] ibid Art 50(3).
[82] The supervisory authority requested to assist another supervisory authority.
[83] Art 50(4) DPLEA Directive (n 6).   [84] ibid Art 50(5).   [85] ibid Art 50(7).
[86] ibid Art 51(2).   [87] Art 3(1) and (2) Regulation 182/2011.
[88] Art 51(3) DPLEA Directive (n 6).   [89] ibid Art 51(1)(g).   [90] ibid Art 30(1).
[91] ibid Art 30(2).   [92] ibid Art 30(5).

the contact details of the DPO.[93] All information is to be provided at once, or as soon as available.[94] Where the matter concerns personal data transmitted by or to a controller of another Member State, information should be provided to this controller as required by Article 30(3) DPLEA Directive.

(b) Notification to the data subject

The controller must also inform data subjects of personal data breaches where the breach might put their rights and freedoms at risk.[95] The information should be in clear and plain language, explaining the nature of the breach and the information as required by Article 30(3) DPLEA Directive.

An exemption from the notification to individual natural persons applies only if: (1) the controller has applied proper technological and organizational measures to minimize the consequences, e.g., through encryption; or (2) the controller has taken measures following the breach to ensure that risks of substantial injury to the rights and freedoms of data subjects would not materialize; or (3) if it would require disproportionate effort, in which case a public communication can substitute for individual notifications.[96] If the controller has not yet communicated the breach to the data subject(s), the *supervisory authority* (1) may require it to do so if the risks are deemed to be high, or (2) may decide that any of the above conditions are met, and thus exempting the controller from obligation to notify.[97] Another exemption could arise under Article 13(3) DPLEA Directive, e.g., where providing the information might prejudice ongoing investigations, harm the rights and freedoms of the others, and so on.[98] Finally, the competent law-enforcement authorities should themselves encourage the confidential reporting of infringements of the provisions of the Directive (in effect, whistle-blowing).[99]

F Legal Rules Governing the Substance of Sector-specific Decision-making

Since the Lisbon Treaty, legislative acts in the AFSJ are made through co-decision, i.e., the ordinary legislative procedure.[100] Thus, the European Parliament is on a footing equal to that of the Council and has a decisive influence on the content of the new law.[101] The same is true in regard to secondary data protection law. The DPLEA Directive, which takes on a central position *inter alia* in the PJC sector, was adopted following this ordinary procedure. There are also other decision-making procedures in relation to data protection in this sector. This present section examines such law in relation to *predefined administrative decision-making procedures* relating to the processing personal data in the PJC sector, and the *discretionary powers* that apply to the decision-makers.

---

[93] ibid Art 30(3).   [94] ibid Art 30(4).   [95] ibid Art 31(1).   [96] ibid Art 31(3).
[97] ibid Art 31(4).   [98] ibid Art 31(5).   [99] ibid Art 48.   [100] Boehm (n 2) 120.
[101] Bigo and others (n 2) 18.

1 The controller and the DPO

In general, the controller, assisted by the DPO, is the actor who has to ensure that, when personal data are processed in the framework of the DPLEA Directive, this complies with the Directive. This official also has to be able to demonstrate this compliance.[102] While their duties may be strictly prescribed by national implementing law, there are still certain discretionary powers. e.g., to decide whether to allow *data transfers to third countries* on the basis of safeguards or derogations where no adequacy decision as such exists. In those two cases, however, the controller should inform on request or on its own initiative, as the case may be, the respective supervisory authority, either the national body or the EDPS (in case of EU entities).[103] On the other hand, if the Commission has taken a decision that a certain third country offers an adequate level of protection, Member State and Union authorities *should comply* with such a determination.[104]

The controller must also take a decision based on his assessment of the risks of the intended data processing, e.g., whether to carry out a Data Protection Impact Assessment (DPIA) and whether to consult the ISA before carrying out certain operations. In the case of Europol and Eurojust, for example, both agencies must consult the EDPS when drawing up administrative measures relating the processing of personal data.[105] As to Europol, if it intends to conclude cooperative or working agreements with EU bodies or third parties which would involve the processing of personal data, then the Management Board should first seek the opinion of the JSB before granting approval.[106]

2 ISAs and the EDPS

The supervisory authorities enjoy a certain margin of discretion as to when and how to exercise their investigative, corrective, and advisory powers, as well as their powers to bring infringements before the courts. In cases of a complaint, the supervisory authorities are under a duty to inform the data subject of the progress and outcome of the complaint,[107] and the EDPS, when hearing complaints, to notify the data subject of the outcome 'within a reasonable period'.[108]

As to transfers to third countries, in the recent *Schrems* judgment the Court of Justice established that if an ISA deems that a certain third country, in respect of which a Commission adequacy decision exists, is not (or no longer) adequate, then this ISA may suspend the flow of data. However, for such a Commission decision to be invalidated, ISAs are required to refer the matter to the national courts, e.g., in response to a complaint. These courts may in turn refer the question for a preliminary

---

[102] Art 19 DPLEA Directive (n 6).
[103] ibid Arts 37 (2) and (3), 38 (3) and 39 (3) DPLEA Directive, Art 9(8) Regulation 45/2001 (n 52).
[104] Art 9(5) Regulation 45/2001 (n 52), Art 36(1) DPLEA Directive (n 6).
[105] Art 28(1) Regulation 45/2001 (n 52).
[106] See Arts 4(4), 5(4), and 6(4) of Council Decision 2009/934/JHA of 30 November 2009 adopting the implementing rules governing Europol's relations with partners, including the exchange of personal data and classified information [2009] OJ L325/12 of 11 December 2009.
[107] Art 52(4) DPLEA Directive (n 6).   [108] Art 46(1) Regulation 45/2001 (n 52).

ruling by the ECJ, the only instance competent to declare such a Commission decision invalid.[109]

3 The European Commission

The Commission has been granted specific powers for the implementation of two major topics of data protection: adequacy determinations on the level of protection obtaining in third countries, and determining the format and procedures for mutual assistance applicable between the ISAs, and between those bodies and the EDPB. These decisions are subject to the comitology procedures of Regulation (EU) No 182/2011.[110] Before an adequacy decision is adopted, the Board shall provide the Commission with an opinion about the data protection adequacy assessment of the third country concerned, while the Commission shall provide it with the necessary documentation, e.g., correspondence with the third country government in question.[111] The Commission should regularly monitor the situation in an 'adequate' third country and make periodic reviews of any adequacy decision. Where the Commission discovers that the third country no longer fulfils the adequacy criteria, it may decide to repeal, amend, or suspend its decision by means of implementing acts, which do not have retroactive effect.[112] The Commission may also enter into negotiations with the third country concerned in order to attempt to remedy the situation.[113]

4 National and EU (legislative) authorities

Member State law shall provide for each ISA to have effective power to issue advisory opinions to its national parliament or other governmental institutions on personal data protection issues. ISAs may themselves initiate such advisory steps or may be requested to do so by such bodies. In addition, national legislative authorities are to consult ISAs when preparing a legislative or subordinate legislative measure concerning personal data processing.[114]

The Union legislature is obliged always to consult the EDPS when preparing laws touching personal data processing. EU bodies generally must consult the EDPS when adopting administrative measures on data processing.[115] When it comes to international agreements, pursuant to Articles 300(6) and 218(11) TFEU, the European Parliament may request the Court's opinion on the compatibility of international agreements with EU law. Following that procedure, the European Parliament referred the draft EU-Canada PNR agreement to the ECJ for a determination on its compatibility with the provisions of the TFEU and the CFREU.[116] In addition, where

---

[109] Case C-362/14 *Schrems* (n 28), paras 99–104 and 61–66. Alternatively, if the ISA rejects a complaint, the data subject should still be allowed to take the decision of an ISA to national courts, which can again make a reference for a preliminary ruling to the CJEU.

[110] Recital 90 DPLEA DirectiveDPLEA Directive (n 6).

[111] ibid Art 51(1)(g) and last line of Art 51(1).   [112] ibid Art 36(5).   [113] ibid Art 36(7).

[114] ibid Art 28(2) and 47(3).   [115] Art 28 Regulation 45/2001 (n 52).

[116] Court of Justice of the European Union, 'Request for an opinion submitted by the European Parliament pursuant to Art 218(11) TFEU (Opinion 1/15)' http://curia.europa.eu/juris/document/

an international agreement in the AFSJ is adopted under the ordinary legislative procedure, the Parliament's consent is necessary,[117] as with the Umbrella Agreement between the EU and the USA on the transfer of personal data from the EU to the USA
authorities in the framework of law-enforcement cooperation.[118]

G Abstract-general Administrative Measures for Data Protection in the PJC Sector

This section provides a broad overview of the political guidelines on data protection
in AFSJ provided for in communications and framework programmes. On a very general level the European Commission, in a 2009 Communication on the future of the
AFSJ, advocated the 'utmost respect for the protection of privacy'. In addition, it called
for a comprehensive scheme and strategy for data protection within the EU and in
its relations with third countries. In view of recent and rapid technological developments, new (non)-legislative instruments would be needed to maintain a high level of
protection.[119]

1 Multi-annual programmes in the AFSJ

There have been several five-year programmes which have set the tone for measures
in the AFSJ. These programmes were namely the Tampere Programme (1999–2004),
the Hague Programme (2004–2009), and the Stockholm Programme (2009–2014).
Although absent in the previous programmes, data protection in the AFSJ had been
on the agenda in the Stockholm Programme.[120] On its expiry, the Union relied on
the application of Article 68 TFEU, pursuant to which the Council is to establish the
strategic guidelines for legislative and operational measures in the AFSJ.[121] The guidelines for the five-year period of 2014–2019 were published in June 2014, and emphasize
policy *coherence* and *synergies*, including those between the EU's internal and external
policies. As to personal data processing, these Council guidelines refer to police cooperation measures such as PNR and transborder exchange of information (such as
criminal records). Exchange of information is explicitly seen as a means of achieving
judicial cooperation.[122] Special attention is paid also to the role of information and

---

document.jsf?text=&docid=163590&pageIndex=0&doclang=EN&mode=lst&dir=&occ=first&part=1&
cid=1038481.

[117] Art 218 TFEU and Bigo and others (n 2) 18.

[118] European Council and Council of the European Union, 'Enhanced data protection rights for EU
citizens in law enforcement cooperation: EU and US sign "Umbrella agreement"' (2 June 2016) http://
www.consilium.europa.eu/en/press/press-releases/2016/06/02-umbrella-agreement/.

[119] European Commission, Communication from the Commission to the European Parliament and
the Council: An area of freedom, security and justice serving the citizen, COM(2009) 262 final, Brussels,
10 June 2009, at 8–9.

[120] Bigo and others (n 2) 16.

[121] European Parliamentary Research Service Blog, 'Justice and Home Affairs after the Stockholm
Programme' (25 June 2014) https://epthinktank.eu/2014/06/25/justice-and-home-affairs-after-the-
stockholm-programme/.

[122] European Council, 'Conclusions: 26/27 June 2014' Brussels, 27 June 2014, paras 10–11.

communication technologies (ICTs) in intensifying operational cooperation. The guidelines explicitly mention the importance of respecting fundamental rights (such as the right to data protection) in the context of addressing security concerns, also vis-à-vis third countries.[123]

2 Internal security strategy (ISS)

The Internal Security Strategy (2015) emphasizes that, in its implementation, full compliance with fundamental rights, including the protection of personal data, privacy, and the principles of confidentiality of communication, necessity, proportionality, and legality, should be ensured.[124] Information exchange and accessibility of information on Union and Member State level, e.g., through interoperability of information systems, is given special attention.[125] The ISS calls for respect of the principle of mutual recognition in the sphere of judicial cooperation. In the adoption of European PNR and of PNR with third countries, it also calls for 'solid' data protection safeguards.[126]

3 Negotiated administrative rules

Union institutions inter se, and the EU and Member States among themselves, sometimes choose to adopt negotiated administrative rules by way of agreement. This may occur also in, or be relevant to, the data protection context subject of this chapter. For example, in 2010 Eurojust and Europol concluded a cooperation agreement to combat international crime more effectively through exchange of operational, strategic, and technical information, including personal data.[127] Pursuant to that agreement, Europol's Director and Eurojust's President were required to conclude a memorandum of understanding containing a table of equivalence of the level of confidentiality of the data exchanged between them.[128] Such a table is an example of negotiated or consensual administrative rulemaking.

H Single-case Administrative Acts and Measures in Police and Justice

In the AFSJ there are several types of single-case administrative acts and measures aimed at implementing EU data protection law in this field.

Some of these measures are directed to or concern public bodies or actors. The most notable example of such an act is the above mentioned *adequacy decision* taken by the Commission is respect of third countries,[129] currently taken under Article 25(6)

---

[123] ibid para 4.
[124] Council of the European Union, 'Draft Council Conclusions on the Renewed European Union Internal Security Strategy 2015-2020' Brussels, 10 June 2015. These draft Conclusions were adopted by the 3396th Council Meeting on Justice and Home Affairs in Luxembourg, 15–16 June 2015, Doc No 9951/15.
[125] ibid 9.   [126] ibid 10.
[127] Art 2 Cooperation Agreement between Eurojust and Europol (2010).   [128] ibid Art 19.
[129] Art 36 DPLEA Directive (n 6).

Directive 95/46/EC (and published on the Commission's website).[130] It is assumed that adequacy decisions taken on that basis will continue to apply in the framework of the new DPLEA Directive.

A further example of such single-case measures is the *written agreement between controller and a processor* where the latter processes personal data on behalf of the controller, the purpose being to bind the processor to meet the same data protection standards as are applicable to the controller.[131]

As to measures directed at individuals, one example is the decision taken by *controllers* acceding to, or refusing, a *data subject's request* to have access to his or her data or to have it rectified, erased, or blocked.[132] Another type of decision, addressed directly to individuals, are decisions taken by ISAs in response to *complaints* by data subjects. Such decisions can be whether the complaint will be investigated or rejected and to provide some other outcome of the investigation.[133]

I Administrative Enforcement of Data Protection Rights and Obligations in Relation to PJC

The obligations and duties provided for in the legislation on data protection in the AFSJ field are largely addressed to *public bodies*: the law enforcement authorities of the Member State; Union authorities with responsibilities in the AFSJ field (notably Europol and Eurojust); and to public authorities with supervisory responsibilities for all of these. Thus, one needs to keep separate the case of EU or Member State laws and implementing measures relating, more or less, just to *private parties* (e.g. in the case of competition law). Therefore, the following section will discuss the enforcement of data protection in the PJC sector against the EU and Member State authorities.

Data protection law establishes (or protects) the rights of individuals, and comes, therefore, with commensurate obligations on (administrative) supervisory authorities to enforce these, or to assist in their enforcement. Data subjects enjoy rights of information, and rights to access their data, and to its rectification, erasure, and blocking. There is an *obligation* on a controller to assist them to exercise their rights,[134] in particular by establishing mechanisms and procedures to allow this to occur. The controller must also inform the data subject of any follow-up to a request for assistance without undue delay.[135] If data subjects believe their data protection rights pursuant to the DPLEA Directive have been breached by national law enforcement authorities, e.g., data has been illegally processed by the controller (or the latter does not react to requests as noted), they may submit a *complaint* to any ISA. Where the supervisory authority receiving the complaint is

---

[130] European Commission, 'Commission decisions on the adequacy of the protection of personal data in third countries' http://ec.europa.eu/justice/data-protection/international-transfers/adequacy/index_en.htm.

[131] Art 22(3) DPLEA Directive (n 6).   [132] ibid Chapter III.   [133] ibid Art 52.
[134] ibid Art 12(2).   [135] ibid Art 12(3).

not competent in the particular context, its officials must transmit the complaint to the correct authority and notify the data subject of this transmission. The complainant should be kept informed of the progress and outcome of the treatment the complaint, as well as of any possibilities of judicial remedies in accordance with the Directive.[136]

In the case of infringements of the DPLEA Directive, the Member States must provide for 'effective, proportionate and dissuasive' *penalties*[137] and ensure that these can be imposed. Anyone who has suffered from material or non-material damage as a result of infringement of the DPLEA Directive or its implementing provisions is to have the right to appropriate *compensation*, pursuant to applicable national law.[138]

An individual who believes that his right to data protection pursuant to Article 16 TFEU has been breached by a Union body may submit a *complaint to the EDPS*. The EDPS has 6 months to react, otherwise the complaint is considered rejected.[139] A civil servant of the Union who breaches Regulation 45/2001 may be subject to sanctions and to disciplinary actions in accordance with the staff regulations of officials of the EU.[140] This includes the EDPS staff, as well as any other EU official. The European Ombudsperson also has the power to take action in cases of maladministration within the Union, e.g., in case of breaches of personal data provisions by EU institutions and authorities.[141]

In addition to the above measures, where the DPO of *Eurojust* establishes non-compliance with the data protection rules to which Eurojust is subject, it shall inform the College. If the situation is not remedied by the College, the issue shall be removed to the JSB.[142] In the case of *Europol*, if the DPO registers a case of non-compliance, it is referred first to the Director who is obliged to resolve it within a specified time. If he does not do so, the case is brought to the attention of the JSB.[143] The new Europol Regulation does not radically change this workflow, except that, if the Management Board does not resolve the issue, the DPO is to refer the matter to the EDPS.[144] It is assumed that the latter will collaborate with the ISAs in resolving a non-compliance by a national authority.[145] Currently, the JSB may, on its own initiative, refer cases of non-compliance to the Management Board.[146] Also, if data subjects wish to appeal against Europol decisions, e.g., if denied access to their data or their rectification, they too can appeal to the JSB.[147]

---

[136] ibid Art 52.   [137] ibid Art 57.   [138] ibid Art 56.

[139] Art 32(2) Regulation 45/2001 (n 52); Art 47 Europol Regulation (n 14).

[140] Art 49 Regulation 45/2001 (n 52).

[141] European Ombudsman, 'The European Ombudsman's Guide to complaints. A publication for staff of the EU institutions, bodies, offices, and agencies' *European Union 2011* http://www.ombudsman. europa.eu/en/resources/staffguide.faces#/page/7, Decision of the European Ombudsman adopting implementing provisions (adopted on 8 July 2002 and amended by decisions of the Ombudsman of 5 April 2004 and 3 December 2008) http://www.ombudsman.europa.eu/en/resources/provisions.faces.

[142] Art 17 Eurojust Decision (n 58).   [143] Art 24(5) Europol Decision (n 14).

[144] Art 41(9) Europol Regulation (n 14).   [145] ibid Art 44.

[146] Art 34 Europol Decision (n 14).   [147] ibid Art 32.

J Supervision and Control of Data Protection Administrators in the PJC Sector

As far as 'enforcement' of data protection law is concerned, that has been the subject matter of the preceding section. This section now discusses the supervisory mechanisms relating to the administration of data protection in the PJC sector.

1 Administrative supervision and control

With regard to supervision of the various *controllers*, including within Europol and Eurojust, this is mainly entrusted to the ISAs and to the EDPS. One of the mechanisms there is the *prior-consultation* procedure (see section E above). Abstract-general measures, e.g., guidelines, also have the function of ex ante supervision of 'subordinate' administrative authorities with date protection responsibilities (see section G above). The EDPB, providing as it does for exchange of ideas and expertise between the EDPS and the ISAs, and the requirement of regular collaboration between theses bodies, as well as the cooperation between DPOs and ISAs in each national jurisdiction, and between the DPOs and the EDPS on the EU level are, arguably, not supervision in the strict sense. Nevertheless, the implicit networking of these bodies with one another, and their associated communications, do perhaps take on at least some of the character of both ex ante and possibly ex post guidance, even if not actually binding (see D above).

2 Political supervision

As of 1 May 2017 (in addition to the administrative supervision exercised by the EDPS and the ISAs), *Europol* shall be subject to a special parliamentary scrutiny, i.e., political monitoring, by the European Parliament and the national parliaments. This supervision is conducted by Joint Parliamentary Scrutiny Group (JPSG) with the purpose of monitoring Europol's activities generally, including their effect on fundamental rights including privacy and data protection. In the framework of such a scrutiny the EDPS might also be called to appear before the JPSG to discuss matters related to personal data protection in respect of Europol (and thus an interaction of internal, i.e. administrative, supervision with political supervision).[148] Similarly, under the current Europol Decision, the Joint Supervisory Body (JSB) should submit reports, the scope of which includes data protection compliance, to the Parliament and to the Council.[149] In addition, the Council, the Chairman of the Management Board and Europol's Director can be requested to appear before the European Parliament to report on its activities.[150]

As to the political control over the ISAs themselves, this is partially exercised through the appointment procedures. The EDPS and the Assistant EDPS are appointed after the joint approval by the European Parliament and of the Council.[151]

---

[148] Art 88 TFEU and Art 51 Europol Regulation (n 14).
[149] Art 34(6) Europol Decision (n 14).   [150] ibid Art 48.
[151] Art 42(1) and (2) Regulation 45/2001 (n 52).

With regard to ISA staff, each staff member is to be appointed by parliament, or the government, or the Head of State or an independent body entrusted by national law to make such appointments, following a transparent procedure.[152]

In addition, the EDPS and the ISAs have to submit activity reports. The EDPS must submit activity reports annually to the European Parliament, the Commission and Council and make them public. Such reports are also to be forwarded to the other Union entities. They are then able to comment on the action taken by an EU authority in response any EDPS intervention relating to an alleged breach of Regulation by that authority. Any such comments may be possibly subject to examination by the European Parliament.[153] ISAs should also submit annual activity reports to their respective national parliaments, governments and other authorities designated by national law, and they should be published and made available to the Commission and the EDPB. Such submission should report on actions undertaken by that supervisory authority, e.g., on the types of infringements notified and penalties imposed.[154]

3 Judicial supervision and remedies

The PJC field has, since Lisbon, been part of the Union 'pillar' and is therefore subject judicial control by the Court of Justice. Infringement proceedings against the Member States can thus be initiated before the Court just as in any other EU policy field.[155] This also means that any national court may refer an AFSJ matter for a preliminary ruling to the Court.[156] In addition, anyone can invoke the right to data protection before the courts, both national and European, when the processing of data concerns EU actors, including administrative ones.[157]

The novelties introduced by the Lisbon Treaty are already evident in the case of Europol. The new Europol Regulation explicitly refers to the right of individuals to take Europol to the CJEU (and/or to national courts) when they have suffered damage as a result of the unlawful processing of their data. In such a case they would be entitled to compensation. Where there is dispute over the responsibility for the compensation, i.e., whether it lies with Europol or with a Member State, this is to be resolved by the (Europol) Management Board. Its decision can be challenged before the ECJ in accordance with Article 263 TFEU.[158] The Court has always been competent to rule on actions brought against the EDPS and award damages to individual if they have suffered as a result of a breach of Regulation 45/2001.[159] In addition, now the EDPS can be taken to the Court over its action—or inaction—in respect to Europol.[160] The EDPS itself may refer a matter to the Court of Justice and intervene in actions brought before it.[161] The EDPS may intervene in any case related to personal data processing, i.e. not only in cases which concern data processing by Union institutions, agencies and bodies. In addition, the EDPS's right to intervene extends to cases before the General

---

[152] Art 43(1) DPLEA Directive (n 6).   [153] Art 48 Regulation 45/2001 (n 52).
[154] Art 49 DPLEA Directive (n 6).   [155] Arts 258–59 TFEU and Boehm (n 2) 121–22.
[156] Bigo and others (n 2) 17–18; exceptions may apply to the UK.   [157] ibid 23.
[158] Art 50 Europol Regulation (n 14).   [159] Art 32 Regulation 45/2001 (n 52).
[160] Art 48 Europol Regulation (n 14).   [161] Art 47(1)(h) and (i) Regulation 45/2001 (n 52).

Court, but not to preliminary ruling questions.[162] The Commission may also initiate infringement proceedings against Member States for incorrect implementation of secondary EU law. For example, it took Germany, Austria and Hungary to the CJEU over the lack of independence of their ISAs.[163] In addition, Commission Decisions (e.g., adequacy determinations), can also be challenged before the Court. Furthermore, an ISA, in reaction to a data subject's complaint, may take a certain matter before national courts, which may then trigger the preliminary ruling procedure before the European Court for its decision on the matter.[164]

As far as the national context is concerned, Article 53 DPLEA Directive confers on each individual the right to an *effective* judicial remedy against a legally binding decision of a *supervisory authority* which concerns that person.[165] This right applies, too, when the competent supervisory authority fails either to handle the complaint or to inform the data subject on the progress or the outcome within three months.[166] In its implementation of the directive, Member States must ensure that proceedings can be brought against a supervisory authority before its own courts.[167] Article 54 DPLEA Directive confers on individuals the right to an *effective* judicial remedy against a controller or processor, where these have infringed the data subject's rights by acting in contravention of the relevant legal provisions. This is without prejudice to other available remedies. When exercising their right to judicial remedies, data subjects also have the right to be represented by non-for-profit organizations properly constituted under national law and having the necessary expertise.[168] ISAs are to be granted the power under national law to bring infringement action in the courts and to commence or engage in other legal proceedings in order to enforce the DPLEA Directive.[169]

K Conclusion

The discussion here has sought to elaborate on the principles and procedures which the EU legislator has established in order to ensure the adequate administration of data protection in the field of Police and Justice Cooperation as part of the AFSJ. The analysis shows that the entry into force of the Lisbon Treaty has led to significant improvements in this area. New legislative measures, in particular the DPLEA Directive and the new Europol Regulation import into the PJC sector additional data protection principles and provide for significantly more sophisticated procedures for both administrative and judicial enforcement of data protection provisions. These developments also call for more cooperation and collaboration between the European Data Protection Supervisor and national Independent Supervisory Authorities, ensuring greater consistency in the interpretation and application of data protection rules and principles.

---

[162] EDPS, 'Court Cases' https://secure.edps.europa.eu/EDPSWEB/edps/cache/offonce/Consultation/Court.

[163] CJEU, Case C-518/07 *Commission v Germany* ECLI:EU:C:2010:125; Case C-614/10 *Commission v Austria* ECLI:EU:C:2012:631; Case C-288/12 *Commission v Hungary* ECLI:EU:C:2014:237.

[164] Case C-362/14 *Schrems* (n 28) para 65.   [165] Art 53(1) DPLEA Directive (n 6).

[166] ibid Art 53(2).   [167] ibid Art 53(3).   [168] ibid Art 55.

[169] ibid Art 47(5).

These innovations do not, however, necessarily depart from the rather patchwork nature of data protection law and procedure in the PJC sector. Nevertheless, the increased harmonization and the numerous enforcement mechanisms hold the potential to bridge gaps among numerous legal acts, a potential which can be measured only once all the new instruments have become applicable.

PART IV

ECONOMIC GOVERNANCE

10

Monetary Policy and Euro Area Governance in the EMU

Herwig C H Hofmann

A Introduction

One of the European Union's most ambitious policy projects to date is the 'economic and monetary union whose currency is the euro' (EMU, Article 3(4) TEU). The EMU's two polices—the economic union and the monetary union—are an unequal set of twins. On one hand, the *monetary union*'s central elements are well developed: as an element of substance, the introduction of the euro as a single currency; as an institutional achievement, the creation of the European System of Central Banks (ESCB) together with the European Central Bank (ECB) on the EU level as a highly independent body having the power to adopt a diverse range of measures. Additionally, the Treaties contain specific provisions on the goals and principles of monetary policy.

Economic union within the European Union is, on the other hand, much less developed. The Maastricht Treaty's approach was to leave economic—and fiscal—policies largely within the competence of the Member States establishing only loose mechanisms of intergovernmental cooperation. Market pressures, so the original thinking behind the loose structure, would in the long run ensure that national policy choices by the democratic parliaments and governments on Member State level align to form a coherent whole. Since 2009, though, a host of more or less directly binding measures for enhancing economic policy cooperation have emerged in Union law, adding to the initial 'light-touch' approach.

Irrespective of the very different treatment of the monetary and economic policies in the EMU, the two are highly inter-related, not least due to the fact that monetary policy often indirectly affects the conditions under which economic policy can be exercised.[1] Monetary policy takes place alongside, and in coordination with, fiscal policy measures (including taxation, debt-financing of public budgets, and allocation of available funds through national budgets, including social security systems). The broader economic policy orientation of Member States also includes issues of regulation, for example, through labour, competition, environmental, or energy law. Monetary policy is created by reacting to, and in effect commenting upon, the economic policy decisions of Member States. In carrying out its task of constructing an efficacious monetary policy for the eurozone (officially, the 'euro area'), the ECB cannot ignore either

---

[1] This is explicitly acknowledged by the Court of Justice of the European Union (CJEU) in Case C-62/14 *Peter Gauweiler and Others v Deutscher Bundestag*, 16 June 2015, ECLI:EU:C:2015:400, paras 52 and 58.

the structure nor the state of the economy. In fact, it may well have available to it more information about the reality of the economic situation than some Member State governments themselves. Therefore, drawing the boundary between the two policy fields is not easy. The ECB, as a highly specialized European body with key monetary policy functions may risk, directly or indirectly, affecting the conditions for the creation of an economic policy.

Against this background, this chapter addresses the elements of the EMU relevant to an enquiry into the administrative system, workings, and law of the Union specifically in this sector. These elements include the role of the ECB—a highly independent body, functioning on a non-majoritarian and expertise-driven basis—in the field of monetary policy. The chapter also enquires into economic governance, which relies on *intergovernmental cooperation* leading to a wide range of forms of executive action (under EU, public international, and private law). Yet a further element for the consideration of sectoral administration and administrative law, is the emergence of new types of reporting, surveillance, and compliance mechanisms. This chapter, therefore, enquires, first, into the concepts of (EU) administrative law which can be successfully applied to the fields of monetary and perhaps even economic policy, and, secondly, into what can be learnt for the wider field of (EU) administrative law from the EMU as a sectoral focus. Where appropriate, the chapter compares the approaches taken with regard to the monetary as opposed to economic policy.

B Sources of Law and the Definition of Administrative Tasks in the Economic and Monetary Union

The objectives and administrative tasks of the EMU are outlined in Article 119 TFEU, according to which the activities of the Member States and the Union within the field of monetary policy include:

- 'the adoption of an economic policy which is based on the close coordination of Member States' economic policies, on the internal market and on the definition of common objectives, and conducted in accordance with the principle of an open market economy with free competition';[2] and

- creating and administering 'a single currency, the euro, and the definition and conduct of a single monetary policy and exchange-rate policy ...'.[3]

The distinction between economic and monetary policy reflects the mixed approach to the legal competences of the Union. Under Article 3(1)(c) TFEU, the monetary policy of Members States who have adopted the euro is an exclusive competence of the Union. Economic policy, on the other hand, as identified in Article 5(1) TFEU, is a policy field of coordination, with the possibility of a (not further defined) third category of 'specific provisions', applicable to euro member states. A possible explanation for the distinction between the monetary and the economic policy in the Treaties is the earlier assumption that the key to stable economic growth was a 'sound' monetary

---

[2] Art 119(1) TFEU.   [3] Art 119(2) TFEU.

policy, conducted by technical experts in independent central banks.[4] Active fiscal policy was deemed counterproductive for this purpose, and it thus appeared inopportune to give to the monetary union governance or regulatory capacities for coordinating its member states' fiscal policies.[5] The fact that the distinction identified here allowed for the creation of a monetary union without the necessary transfer to the EU of a wide range of powers over fiscal and general economic policy might help explain the striking structural differences in the monetary and the economic union within the EMU.

1 Sources of law and definition of tasks in the Monetary Union

Articles 127 ff TFEU constitute the legal basis for the policies pursued in the EU's monetary union. These provisions provide for the specific institutional design necessary in the field of monetary policy of the eurozone, as well as the administrative powers in regard to monetary law and policy in the Union.

According to Article 127 TFEU itself, 'the primary objective of the European System of Central Banks (ESCB) is to maintain price stability'. Without prejudice to this objective, monetary policy is to support the 'general economic policies in the Union with a view to contributing to the achievement of the objectives of the Union as laid down in Article 3 of the TEU'. To that end, the ESCB shall (under Article 127(2) TFEU):

- 'define and implement the monetary policy of the Union'
- conduct foreign-exchange operations (consistent with the provisions of Article 219 TFEU)
- hold and manage the foreign reserves of the Member States and
- 'promote the smooth operation of payment systems'.

The ECB has, under Article 282(3) TFEU, the central function to 'authorize the issue of the euro'. In that respect, Article 128(1) TFEU and Article 16 ESCB/ECB Statute accordingly empower the ECB's Governing Council with the 'exclusive right to authorize the issue of euro banknotes within the Union'. The latter are issued by the ECB and the National Central Banks (NCBs). Coinage, by way of contrast, is a prerogative of the NCBs but this power also is exercise within the strict coordination of the ESCB.

Irrespective of this essentially technical function, one of the distinctive specificities of the policy area of monetary policy is the fundamentally political nature of the powers conferred on a very independent administrative body designed with a maximum concentration of expertise. Under the system established by the Treaties, the ECSB and the ECB are in charge of defining monetary policy, and subsequently implementing it by means of rule-making and single-case implementation by means of decisions, information management, and engaging in contractual activities. These

---

[4] Peter A Hall, 'The Mythology of European Monetary Union' (2012) 18 *Swiss Political Science Review*, 508, 508.

[5] Tal Sadeh, Amy Verdun, 'Explaining Europe's Monetary Union: A Survey of the Literature' (2009) 11 *International Studies Review* 277, at 285, with further references.

tasks and modes of operation are further underpinned by Article 282(4) TFEU, which established that the ECB 'shall adopt such measures as are necessary to carry out its tasks'. Its 'monetary functions', specified in Articles 18–20 ESCB/ECB Statute, are to be exercised either by the ECB or by the NCBs:

- First, under Article 18 ESCB/ECB Statute, the 'ECB shall establish general principles for open market and credit operations carried out by itself or the national central banks', 'open market' activities being contractual activities including:
  - 'buying and selling outright (spot and forward) or under repurchase agreement'
  - 'lending or borrowing claims and marketable instruments, whether in euro or other currencies, as well as precious metals'
  - conducting 'credit operations with credit institutions and other market participants, with lending being based on adequate collateral'.
- Secondly, again under Article 18 ESCB/ECB Statute, the ECB is obliged to conduct an information policy 'for the announcement of conditions under which they stand ready to enter into such transactions'.
- Thirdly, Article 19 ESCB/ECB Statute specifies that the ECB holds minimum reserves. This activity is typically regulatory in nature, in that the 'ECB may require credit institutions established in Member States to hold minimum reserve on accounts with the ECB and national central banks in pursuance of monetary policy objectives'. The ECB's Governing Council has the power to establish 'Regulations concerning the calculation and determination of the required minimum reserves'. These regulations may also identify sanctions since in 'cases of noncompliance the ECB shall be entitled to levy penalty interest and to impose other sanctions with comparable effect'. The regulatory activity, therefore, takes place vis-à-vis private actors.
- Fourthly, under Article 20, the 'ECB and national central banks may provide facilities, and the ECB may make regulations, to ensure efficient and sound clearing and payment systems within the Union and with other countries'. That authorization is, according to the General Court, to be interpreted narrowly, as are all specific allocations of powers. In *UK v ECB* the court held, for example, that the power to ensure clearing and payment systems confers powers explicitly only for clearing of payment systems, but not for clearing of securities, even though one might argue that the latter may, in some transactions, be linked to the former.[6]
- Additionally, the ESCB/ECB Statute contains further, in Article 20, an open empowerment, allowing the ECB Governing Council (by a majority of two-thirds of the votes cast), to 'decide upon the use of such other operational methods

---

[6] Case T-496/11 *United Kingdom v European Central Bank* ECLI:EU:T:2015:133, 4 March 2015, paras 99–105: 'the existence of an implicit regulatory power, which constitutes a derogation from the principle of conferral laid down by Art 13(2) TEU, must be appraised strictly. It is only exceptionally that such implicit powers are recognised by case-law and, in order to be so recognised, they must be necessary to ensure the practical effect of the provisions of the Treaty or the basic regulation at issue' (citation omitted).

of monetary control as it sees fit' as long as the general provisions of Article 2 ESCB/ECB Statute are complied with. Measures under Article 20 can, therefore, be adopted to ensure any of the objectives listed in Article 127(1) and Article 282(2) TFEU.

Primary law is fleshed out by secondary legislation, for example, concerning the 'use of the euro as single currency', which can be adopted under the ordinary legislative procedure (Article 133 TFEU). The Council may also adopt, under the special legislative procedure of Article 127(6) TFEU, regulations for the conferral on the ECB of special tasks concerning policies relating to supervision of banks and other financial institutions.[7] Another special legislative procedure applies under Article 129(4) TFEU regarding subordinate regulatory powers on matters such as minimum reserves (Article 19(2) ESCB/ECB Statute), methods of monetary control (Article 20), the conditions of capital increases of the ECB (Article 28(1)), and the imposition of fines or periodic penalty payments on undertakings for failure to comply with obligations under the ECB's regulations and decisions.

The ECB has its own regulatory powers conferred on it pursuant to Article 132(1) TFEU and Article 34 ESCB/ECB Statute. There is a delicate balance between acts of the Council and those of the ECB. This can be illustrated by the fact that fundamental decisions regarding, for example, minimum reserves of banks are reserved to Council regulations adopted in the special legislative procedure. Within this framework, Council provisions may require credit institutions established in Member States to hold minimum reserves on accounts with the ECB and with national central banks in pursuance of monetary policy objectives. Regulations concerning the calculation and determination of the required minimum reserves may be established, however, by the ECB.[8]

Monetary policy of the Union is further implemented by NCBs for which national administrative law and private law is applicable. Some aspects of Union monetary policy also need to be implemented in national law by Member States which have not adopted the euro.

2 Sources of law and definition of tasks in the Economic Union

A very different picture emerges regarding economic policy of the Union. Very few legal provisions had been adopted in relation to this policy prior to the onset of the economic crises in 2008. The Treaty of Maastricht had left a potential 'economic policy union' incomplete despite fact that the 'the monetary and economic union' (Article 3 TEU) contained 'two integral parts of a single whole' which would have to be implemented in parallel.[9]

---

[7] One example for this is Council Regulation (EU) No 1024/2013 of 15 October 2013 conferring specific tasks on the European Central Bank concerning policies relating to the prudential supervision of credit institutions [2013] OJ L287/63.

[8] One ECB regulation with a considerable impact on the relation between these bodies is Regulation 1745/2003 ([2003] OJ L251/10), which delegates powers especially in the field of administration of minimum reserves of banks to the national central banks (see eg Articles 9, 10 Regulation 1745/2003).

[9] Committee for the Study of Economic and Monetary Union, Report on economic and monetary union in the European Community (Brussels 1989).

In this respect, the measures concerning economic policy coordination developed in the wake of the economic and financial crises have, inter alia, aimed at developing the conditions of a more integrated monetary—as well as economic—policy in the EU. Not only has economic policy been increasingly coordinated through the use of a great diversity of tools (often developed in an ad-hoc manner), which arguably have taken the design of economic policy away from a more political to a more expert-driven administrative setting. Moreover, *Gauweiler* highlights how the exercise of tools belonging primarily to monetary policy can, and will, have effects on the conditions of the exercise of economic policy.[10]

Initially, the economic union was shaped primarily through mutual information and evaluation procedures which were introduced as means of coordinating Member States' economic policies.[11] Under the Lisbon Strategy for the coordination of the economic and employment developments of the Member States, one of the key measures employed was the so-called open method of cooperation (OMC) of the time,[12] within which Member States produced National Reform Programmes co-evaluated on the EU level. The establishment and reporting of such national programmes entailed the reporting of key data on economic development and employment.

The first step in giving this executive cooperation more solid form by means of 'multilateral surveillance' (Article 126(3) TFEU) came with the Stability and Growth Pact (SGP) concluded in 1997. This involved the production of so-called stability and convergence reports by Member States, to be substantiated by relevant data, and their subsequent review of by the Commission and the Council. The SGP, based on Article 126 TFEU (ex Article 104c TEC) in conjunction with the Protocol on the Excessive Deficit Procedure annexed to the Treaty, was the means by which the European Council concluded measures designed to address the disparity between a common monetary policy and the divergent economic and fiscal policies of the Member States. The SGP in force today has seen several amendments and enhancements, mostly ad hoc in reaction to economic problems, without having a pre-existing constitutional template and list of administrative tasks.[13] These amendments have been marked by an intensification of the coordination between the Member States, and an increase in prescriptive rules for compliance.[14]

---

[10] Case C-62/14 *Peter Gauweiler and Others v Deutscher Bundestag* (n 1) paras 52 and 58 and Opinion of Advocate General Cruz Villalón of 14 January 2015 ECLI:EU:C:2015:7. At the heart of the dispute in *Gauweiler* was whether the European Central Bank's (ECB) announcement in the summer of 2012 that it would be purchasing on a large scale government bonds issued by states of the euro area, known as the 'OMT programme', was in fact an economic policy measure, which would fall outside of the ECB's mandate in the field of monetary policy.

[11] See Arts 102a and 103 EC. Multilateral surveillance formally began in 1990 and was subsequently governed by Council Decision 90/141/EEC of 12 March 1990 on the attainment of progressive convergence of economic policies and performance during stage one of economic and monetary union [1990] OJ L78/3. See also Art 104c EC and the Protocol on the Excessive Deficit Procedure.

[12] D Curtin, 'Democratic Accountability of Executive Power' in Federico Fabbrini, Ernst Ballin, and Han Somsen (eds), *What Form of Government for the European Union and the Eurozone* (Hart Publishing Oxford 2015) 171–96, at 179; Kenneth Armstrong, 'The New Governance of EU Fiscal Discipline' (2013) 38 *European Law Review* 601, 609.

[13] For an overview see https://ec.europa.eu/info/business-economy-euro/economic-and-fiscal-policy-coordination/eu-economic-governance-monitoring-prevention-correction/stability-and-growth-pact_en (last accessed 1 March 2017).

[14] Curtin (n 12) 179.

In reaction to further economic crises since 2008, the EU has had to find ways to deal with various emergency situations, including threats of collapse of individual Member State economic systems. Thus, between late 2010 and 2012, a comprehensive reinforcement of economic governance in the EU and the euro area saw the establishment of institutional structures such as the European Stability Mechanism (ESM),[15] the European Financial Stabilisation Mechanism (EFSM),[16] and the European Financial Stability Facility (EFSF),[17] as agreements under public international law outside the Treaty framework. Reliance on public international law was not uncontroversial, but had become necessary because of the lack of unanimity in Council. In *Pringle,* the CJEU declared this approach legal.[18] However, the negative consequence of the intergovernmental approach is that it excludes recourse to existing mechanisms of democratic accountability within the Union, while considerably strengthening powers of the executive branch of Member States. (The latter may be sometimes subject to parliamentary—national democratic—scrutiny, but not necessarily thereby contributing to or strengthening a pan-European policy perception.) One example of this was the creation and empowerment, in matters of fiscal and economic policy, of the 'Eurogroup', an informal gathering of national finance ministers (recognized, however, in Article 137 TFEU and Protocol No 14) for, inter alia, the adoption of semi-annual work programmes. The Eurogroup, supported by the Eurogroup Working Group, has a president with agenda-setting powers, supported by a secretariat. Its president is also the chair of the board of governors of the ESM. Despite being able to exercise significant influence in the context of economic cooperation, Working Group decisions are not binding, as confirmed by the General Court in *Mallis.*[19]

On the basis of Union law, the first step towards the coordination of the budgetary, structural, and macroeconomic policies of the eurozone states was the adoption,[20]

---

[15] The European Stability Mechanism (ESM) is the permanent crisis resolution mechanism for the countries of the euro area. The intergovernmental treaty establishing the ESM was adopted on 2 February 2012.

[16] The European Financial Stabilisation Mechanism, legally based on Art 122(2) TFEU, is a programme whose purpose is to provide loans to EU Member States in financial difficulty.

[17] The European Financial Stability Facility is a special purpose vehicle, outside the EU Law framework, established as a private company under Luxembourg law with the Member States as shareholders.

[18] Case C-370/12 *Pringle* ECLI:EU:C:2012:756, with much literature having discussed the legality of the structure. See eg Mathias Ruffert, 'The European Debt Crisis and European Union Law' (2011) 48 *Common Market Law Review* 1777, 1785; Richard Palmstorfer, 'To bail out or not to bail out? The Current Framework of Financial Assistance for Euro Area Member States Measured against the Requirements of EU Primary Law' (2012) 37 *European Law Review* 771; Jean-Victor Louis, 'The No-bailout Clause and Rescue Packages' (2010) 47 *Common Market Law Review* 971, 977; Jörn Pipkorn, 'Legal Arrangements in the Treaty of Maastricht for the Effectiveness of the Economic and Monetary Union' (1994) 31 *Common Market Law Review* 275; Harald Hofmeister, 'To bail out or not to bail out?—Legal Aspects of the Greek Crisis' (2010–2011) 13 *Cambridge Yearbook of European Legal Studies* 113.

[19] Case T-327/13 *Mallis* EU:T:2014:909, paras 41–44, 53.

[20] The European Semester was approved by the Member States on 7 September 2010 and the first European Semester cycle was launched in January 2011. See Regulation (EU) No 1173/2011 of the European Parliament and of the Council of 16 November 2011 on the effective enforcement of budgetary surveillance in the euro area [2011] OJ L306/1; Regulation (EU) No 1174/2011 of the European Parliament and of the Council of 16 November 2011 on enforcement measures to correct excessive macroeconomic imbalances in the euro area [2011] OJ L306/8; Regulation (EU) No 1175/2011 of the European Parliament and of the Council of 16 November 2011 amending Council Regulation (EC) No 1466/97 on the strengthening of the surveillance of budgetary positions and the surveillance and coordination of economic policies [2011] OJ L306/12; Regulation (EU) No 1176/2011 of the European Parliament and of the Council

upon the Commission's proposal,[21] of the so-called 'European Semester',[22] legally en-shrined in Articles 121 and 148 TFEU. This consists of a six-month cycle based on surveillance and ex ante monitoring of the Member States' economic, structural, and budgetary policies. This process grants to the Commission far reaching administra-tive powers, allowing it to review the Member States' budgets, and to assess whether the national draft budgetary plans comply with the SGP criteria as further established by the Commission in guidance documents.[23] The analysis by the Commission re-sults, at the end of the calendar year marking the beginning of the 'semester cycle', in two reports: an 'annual growth survey' and an 'alert mechanism report'. These reports are adopted by the Council, and the conclusions adopted by the European Council, in an effort directed at taking the old OMC approach to both of these institutions. The Commission, then, on this basis, drafts Country Specific Recommendations, again to be adopted by the Council. Based on the findings of these reviews, the Commission may trigger procedures to pressure Member States into changing their economic policies through the so-called 'European semester macroeconomic imbalances pro-cedure' (MIP). The Commission's recommended policy responses to the imbalances are integrated into its 'country specific recommendations' (CSR), published annually in respect of all Member States.[24] These recommendations are, then, documents emer-ging from the Union administration with the objective of guiding Member State eco-nomic policy, and of intensifying economic policy coordination.

A further set of measures, the 'Six-Pack Agreement' (based on Articles 121, 126, and 136 TFEU) comprises five regulations and one directive on macroeconomic im-balances and fiscal policies.[25] These measures are complementary to the European Semester, in that they provides for strengthened and broadened economic and budgetary surveillance of the Member States (Regulation 1175/2011 and Regulation

---

of 16 November 2011 on the prevention and correction of macroeconomic imbalances [2011] OJ L306/25; Council Regulation (EU) No 1177/2011 of 8 November 2011 amending Regulation (EC) No 1467/97 on speeding up and clarifying the implementation of the excessive deficit procedure [2011] OJ L306/33; Council Directive 2011/85/EU of 8 November 2011 on requirements for budgetary frameworks of the Member States [2011] OJ L306/41.

[21] European Commission, 'Mastering economic interdependence: Commission proposed reinforced economic governance in the EU', IP/10/561, 12 May 2010 and European Commission, 'EU economic governance: the Commission proposes a reinforced macro-economic, budgetary and structural surveil-lance, IP/10/859, 30 June 2010.

[22] http://europa.eu/rapid/press-release_MEMO-11-14_en.htm.

[23] See eg the 2015 Communication from the Commission to the European Parliament, the Council, the ECB, the Economic and Social Committee, the Committee of the Regions and the EIB making the best use of the flexibility within the existing rules of the Stability and Growth Pact, COM(2015) 012 final.

[24] See eg the 'Alert Mechanism Report 2015', Report from the Commission to the European Parliament, the Council, the European Central Bank and the European Economic and Social Committee, 28 November 2014, COM(2014) 904 final.

[25] Regulation 1175/2011 amending Regulation 1466/97 on the strengthening of the surveillance of budgetary positions and the surveillance and coordination of economic policies [2011] OJ L306/12; Regulation 1177/2011 amending Regulation 1467/97 on speeding up and clarifying the implementation of the excessive deficit procedure [2011] OJ L306/33; Regulation 1173/2011 on the effective enforcement of budgetary surveillance in the euro area [2011] OJ L306/1; Directive 2011/85/EU on requirements for budgetary frameworks of the Member States [2011] OJ L306/41; Regulation 1176/2011 on the prevention and correction of macroeconomic imbalances [2011] OJ L306/25; Regulation 1174/2011 on enforcement measures to correct macroeconomic imbalances in the euro area [2011] OJ L306/8.

1173/2011), for the implementation of the excessive deficit procedure (EDP, Regulation 1177/2011). Furthermore, Regulation 1176/2011 lays out the details of the macroeconomic imbalance surveillance procedure,[26] while Regulation 1174/2011 applies to all eurozone states and lays out the procedural requirements for sanctions and the 'corrective action plan'. As just noted, the Six-Pack legislation introduces a so-called 'excessive deficit procedure' (EDP) which applies to Member States that have breached either the deficit or the debt criterion, imposing through the Council financial sanctions in a gradual way as enforcement mechanisms vis-à-vis non-compliant Member States.[27] Most sanctions will be determined in the Council under a reverse qualified-majority voting procedure,[28] increasing the likelihood for the eurozone member states to be sanctioned and strengthening the position of the Commission.

As a result, the Union's economic policy has led to a significant strengthening and widening of EU administrative powers. These are exercised through cooperation and coordination but they can be toughened specifically, when applied in concert with the powers of monetary policy. The result is a considerable de facto transfer of power in the field of economic, fiscal, and social policies to the Union, especially from those Member States within some financial assistance programme or who benefit from ECB measures. This transfer is one from parliamentary law-making and democratically elected governments to a highly complex system of executive cooperation and administrative procedures. As a consequence, although a nascent intergovernmental, European economic executive governance is evolving, it is based largely on administrative action.[29] Whether such expansion of the 'administrative state' is endowed with adequate tools of accountability will be taken up below.

C Organizational and Substantive Principles in the Monetary and Economic Policy Sector

1 Principles regarding the Monetary Union

When compared with other areas of European administrative law, European monetary union law contains many familiar features, but also ones characterized by certain specificities. Monetary policy for the EU is conducted by the European Central Bank (ECB) in conjunction with the NCBs of those EU Member States belonging to

---

[26] Regulation 1176/2011 on the prevention and correction of macroeconomic imbalances [2011] OJ L306/25; Regulation 1174/2011 on enforcement measures to correct macroeconomic imbalances in the euro area [2011] OJ L306/8.

[27] According to Art 4 of Regulation 1173/2011 countries will now face lodging an interest-bearing deposit of 0.2% of gross domestic product (GDP), upon the Commission's recommendation, if they fail to comply with the recommendations by the Council regarding the preventative arm of the SGP (Medium Term Objective).

[28] That is, a recommendation is deemed to be adopted unless the Council decides by qualified majority to reject it within a given deadline.

[29] Christoph Herrmann, 'Die Bewältigung der Euro-Staatschulden-Krise an den Grenzen des deutschen und europäischen Währungsverfassungsrechts' (2012) *EuZW* 805; Herrmann Joseph Blanke, Stefan Pilz, 'Solidarische Finanzhilfen als Lackmustest föderaler Balance in der EU' (2014) *Europarecht* 541, 555.

the euro area.[30] The ECB and the NCBs are the components of the European System of Central Banks (ESCB). The ECB, in some ways structured similarly to an EU agency having its legal basis in the Treaties,[31] is, again like many agencies, a centre of Union expertise.

However, there are some important differences between the ECB and the organization of other Union agencies. The management of monetary policy is an area requiring great technical expertise, and entailing large and substantive risks for the economic wellbeing of all citizens and for the financial positions of Member States. For that reason, it is an eminently political area of law. The relevant Treaty provisions regulate in great detail the internal structure and the independence of the ECB. The ESCB, under Article 130 TFEU, and the ECB according to its statutes are strictly independent. Under Article 130 TFEU 'neither the ECB, nor a national central bank, nor any member of their decision-making bodies shall seek or take instructions from Union institutions, bodies, offices or agencies, from any government of a Member State'.

EU law also requires each Member State to ensure the independence of its own NCB. Article 131 TFEU as well as Article 14(3) ESCB/ECB Statute (Protocol No 4) require that 'each Member State shall ensure that its national legislation including the statues of its national central bank is compatible with the Treaties and the Statute of the ESCB and of the ECB'. It appears from the legal context of EU monetary policy that independence of the NCBs includes de jure and de facto independence and the possibility for these NCBs to adopt legal acts necessary for implementing ECB policies and guidelines within the ESCB.

Regarding EU monetary policy the ESCB is the central *structural innovation* established by the Treaties. It is based on a rather unique concept, namely that within the ESCB, the ECB and the NCBs are linked in a very particular way. One factor of this relation touches the role of the NCBs as components of the ESCB. Although the NCBs of those EU Member States whose currency is the euro subscribe to the capital of the ECB,[32] and the shareholders have the right to receive dividend payments, shareholder voting rights are not linked to the share volume held (except as regards decisions on matters such as the distribution of dividends) (Article 10 ESCB/ECB Statute). Another specific factor in the idiosyncratic linkage concerns the distribution of powers within

---

[30] As of 2015, the following 18 Member States who had adopted the euro as their currency: Austria, Belgium, Cyprus, Estonia, Finland, France, Germany, Greece, Luxembourg, Ireland, Italy, Latvia, Lithuania, Netherlands, Portugal, Slovenia, and Spain.

[31] The ECB evolved out of the European Monetary Cooperation Fund (EMCF), which had been set up by Council Regulation (EEC) No 907/73 of 3 April 1973 ([1972] OJ L89/2). The EMCF was superseded and its functions assumed by the European Monetary Institute (EMI). This was a temporary body created at the beginning of stage two of the EMU (Art 109f TEC and the EMI statutes attached as a protocol to the TEC). The legal basis of the ECB, together with the ESCB, is Protocol (No 4) on The Statute of the European System of Central Banks and of the European Central Bank, to the Consolidated Versions of the Treaty on European Union and the Treaty on the Functioning of the European Union (2016/C 202/01), [2016] OJ C202/1 at 230 (ESCB/ECB Statute).

[32] Their participation is calculated under Articles 10(1) and 29 ESCB/ECB Statute, taking into account two factors: 50% on the basis of population size of the Member State and 50% on the basis of its GDP—for the current calculation see https://www.ecb.europa.eu/ecb/orga/capital/html/index.en.html.

the ESCB, where much power is concentrated in the ECB, coupled with an important structural element of this administration of monetary policy, namely the decentralization of duties within the ESCB.[33] The NCBs are obliged generally to report to the ECB. Also, they are required to implement very detailed policies established by the ECB in Frankfurt.[34] So, the ECB may give 'the necessary instructions to national central banks' but, as well, may 'have recourse to the national central banks to carry out operations which form part of the tasks of the ESCB'.[35] The relation might, then, be regarded as of both a hierarchical and a decentralized nature.[36] This shows that while, normally, Member State bodies, despite their obligation to comply with EU law and to implement it, do not receive direct administrative instructions from Union bodies, in the field of monetary policy the members of the ECSB are more tightly interlinked, with the NCBs' acting, at least de facto, much as decentralized EU agencies, being obliged to conforms to ECB guidelines.

The ECB's organs are the Governing Council and the executive board (Article 129(1) TFEU). The Governing Council comprises the members of the ECB executive board, together with the governors of each of the NCBs of the eurozone states (Article 283 TFEU). The NCBs are thus not represented as institutions, but rather by individuals as members of an ECB organ. Each member of the Governing Council has one vote, exercised in confidential proceedings. However, voting rights are not allocated on a one-Member-State-one-vote basis, as the number of governors with voting rights is limited to fifteen.

The executive board of the ECB comprises the president, the vice-president, and four other members who are appointed by the Council (Article 283(2) first sub-paragraph TFEU). Its function is the implementation of monetary policy in accordance with the guidelines and decisions laid down by the Governing Council. Under Article 12 ESCB/ECB Statute

> the Governing Council shall adopt the guidelines and take the decisions necessary to ensure the performance of the tasks entrusted to the ESCB under these Treaties and this Statute. The Governing Council shall formulate the monetary policy of the Union including, as appropriate, decisions relating to intermediate monetary objectives, key interest rates and the supply of reserves in the ESCB, and shall establish the necessary guidelines for their implementation.

The Governing Council has committees (themselves supported by working groups comprising NCB staff) which prepare decisions, exchange information, and support uniform implementation of decisions taken. Probably the best known of these was the Banking Supervisory Committee, now transformed into the so-called Single Supervisory Mechanism (SSM), ensuring that banking supervision by the ECB occurs in an organizationally separate unit.

---

[33] Jochen Hoffmann, 'Europäisches Währungsverwaltungsrecht' in Jörg Phillip Terhechte (ed), *Verwaltungsrecht der Europäischen Union* (Nomos 2011) 984, § 27, para 8.

[34] For the reporting obligations see Regulation EC 2533/98 of the Council of 23 November 1998 [1998] OJ L318/8.

[35] See Art 12(1) ESCB/ECB Statute.   [36] Hoffmann (n 33) 984–86 (§ 27, paras 8–11).

Additionally, 'without prejudice to Article 129(1) TFEU, the *General Council* shall be constituted as a *third decision-making body* of the ECB', under Article 44 ESCB/ECB Statute (emphasis added). This body is composed of the 'President and Vice-President of the ECB and the Governors of the national central banks. The other members of the Executive Board may participate, without having the right to vote'. Its duties are stated in Article 46 ESCB/ECB Statute.

When reflecting upon the structure of the ESCB in the context of its legal provisions, it appears that it is a highly organized and institutionalized form of interaction, a network of NCBs both within the single structure of, and together with, the ECB. The ECB and NCBs ensure the implementation of the EU monetary policy, the NCBs undertaking much of the supervisory work and the management of minimum reserves, the ECB playing a more policy-setting role. With the introduction of the SSM, the ECB is now also increasingly involved in the supervision of banking and finance, noting (as above), however, that in doing so a special—rather distinct—substructure has been created within the ECB. The structure of the ESCB, largely subject as it is to the authority of the ECB (to which the NCBs stand in a subordinate position, under an obligation to comply with ECB decisions), is a unique construct in the institutional design of the European Union. It is possibly the most centralized approach to agency design so far established in the Union.

2 Principles regarding the Economic Union

Economic policy of the Union, however, might be regarded—even more than monetary policy—as a field of experimental approaches, not least owing to the much less developed set of primary and secondary law provisions. Much of the field of cooperation in economic policy was developed ad hoc in response to the economic crises since 2008. The central legal norm has been Article 126 TFEU, on the prohibition of excessive government deficits and the key means for achieving adherence with this. However, those basic provisions have been expanded by establishing structures, some of which have seemed to be testing notions of constitutionality through the use of existing forms of act in rather creative ways. The pre-ESM 'emergency' response to the 2008 crisis was, for example, heavily premised on *private law*, notably Memoranda of Understanding (MoU). These often contained strict conditions to be fulfilled by Member States recipient of credit-based funding. This conditionality was spelled out in adjustment programmes to which the recipient countries needed to commit themselves as a prerequisite for loan disbursement. With this, the tool of 'conditionality' entered into the mainstream of EU governance techniques.[37] Greece, as the first potential defaulter, was also the first Member State to seek assistance within the MoU framework. The Greek MoU provisions were then incorporated into the Council Decision

---

[37] Carol Harlow, Richard Rawlings, *Process and Procedure in EU Administration* (Hart Publishing 2014) 47, referring to this as the 'tough love' approach.

2010/320/EU[38] which, based on Article 126(9) and 136 TFEU, thereby brought the MoU within the realm of EU law—and thus generating a potential for ensuring its supremacy vis-à-vis national law.[39] While the idea behind the MoU, and the Council Decision that implemented it, was broadly to reinforce fiscal supervision and reduce the Greek deficit, both the MoU and the subsequent adjustment programmes[40] in fact contained a list of very specific, even precise, measures to be undertaken by the country, including measures pertaining to direct taxation, pension maxima, and the abolition of the solidarity allowance.

Another example of the use of forms of private law for achieving macroeconomic goals can be found in the European Financial Stability Facility (EFSF), established as a *private* company under Luxembourg law, with Member States as shareholders. This structure, a temporary crisis-resolution mechanism, functioned by issuing bonds and other debt instruments on capital markets, in order to provide financial assistance to Greece, Ireland and Spain.[41] Finding a linguistically telling characterization of this construction is not easy. We might borrow the very specific German specific term which emerged for this kind of private law arrangement between states for achieving public goals, *Völkerprivatrecht*, which might best be translated as 'intergovernmental private law'.[42]

From the perspective of the history of European integration it might not come as a surprise that, in its initial response to these questions, the EU relied to a large extent on the intergovernmental method and the associated need for unanimity. Whether by necessity and/or by design, Union law led to the integration of executive powers through cooperative structures linking governments and executives of Member States and the EU on the basis of public international law, private law, and some European law. The subsequent 'constitutionalisation' of such arrangements, that is, their integration into the Union's general constitutional framework is an ongoing process. This process includes, however, finding answers to questions of the compatibility of the macroeconomic policy elements addressed here with the principles of democracy and of institutional and administrative transparency, as well as with other underlying constitutional values including fundamental rights.

---

[38] See Council Decision 2010/320/EU of 20 December 2010 addressed to Greece, with a view to reinforcing and deepening fiscal surveillance and giving notice to Greece to take measures for the deficit reduction judged necessary to remedy the situation of excessive deficit, as amended by Council Decisions 2011/57/EU of 7 March 2011.

[39] A series of additional or amending Decisions followed, founded directly on Art 121(4) Council Decision 2010/190/EU, Art 126(8) Council Decision 2010/29/EU, and Art 136 TFEU Council Decision 2010/182/EU.

[40] Similarly, the Commission's 'Economic Adjustment Programme for Greece', May 2010 which aims at imposing fiscal stability and a quick reduction in the fiscal deficit, includes immediate increases of VAT and excise taxes, cuts to public sector wages, pensions, social expenditures and public investments.

[41] The EFSF no longer provides financial assistance, since this task is now exclusively performed by the ESM. The EFSF, however, continues to operate to service existing obligations.

[42] An alternative, but arguably less telling, translation might be 'public international *private* law', where the emphasis is crucial for capturing the essence of the idea.

D Administrative Procedures within the Fields of Monetary and Economic Policy

1 Administrative procedures within the Monetary Union

In the area of the monetary policy, procedural rules are largely established within the legal framework of the ESCB, and it is the decision-making authorities of the ECB which govern the ESCB (Articles 8 ESCB/ECB Statute). The ECB's sometimes far reaching decision-making powers emerge from the TFEU, as well as from the Statutes of the ESCB/ECB (in Protocol No 4). In order to underpin its decision-making authority, Article 132(1) TFEU confers on the ECB powers to adopt binding acts in the form of both regulations and decisions (under Article 288 TFEU), following special procedures laid down in the Statute. Additionally, Article 132(3) TFEU grants the ECB power to impose pecuniary sanctions on private parties for non-compliance with its acts.

The central task of formulating the monetary policy of the Union is given to the Governing Council of the ECB. Under Article 12(1) ESCB/ECB Statute, it adopts guidelines and takes the decisions 'necessary to ensure the performance of the tasks entrusted to the ESCB under these Treaties and this Statute', including decisions relating to 'intermediate monetary objectives, key interest rates and the supply of reserves in the ESCB'. The ECB president chairs the Governing Board as well as its Executive Board. The latter is responsible for the ECB's current business, defined in Article 12(2) ESCB/ECB Statute as the responsibility to 'implement monetary policy in according with the guidelines and decisions laid down by the Governing Council. In doing so the Executive Board shall give the necessary instructions to national central banks'. Generally, the Governing Board decides by a majority vote. Exceptionally, Article 20 ESCB/ECB Statute, in an open empowerment, allow the Governing Council, by a majority of two-thirds of the votes cast, to 'decide upon the use of such other operational methods of monetary control as it sees fit'.

The position of the participant NCBs is clarified in Article 14(3) ESCB/ECB Statute. According to this, 'national central banks are an integral part of the ESCB and act in accordance with the guidelines and instructions of the ECB. The Governing Council shall take the necessary steps to ensure compliance with the guidelines and instructions of the ECB'.

Monetary policy decisions rely on large quantities of detailed statistical information. In the ESCB, such information is collected predominantly by NCBs from the competent national authorities or economic actors in collaboration with the EU institutions, bodies, offices, and agencies (Article 5(1), (2) ESCB/ECB Statute). For this purpose, specific rule-making powers on collection and classification of statistical information has been conferred on the ECB (Article 5(3)) and on the Council in the special legislative procedure of Article 129(4) TFEU and Article 41 ESCB/ECB Statute, to define the natural and legal persons subject to reporting requirements, and to cover issues of confidentiality and powers of enforcement.

2 Administrative procedures within the Economic Union

As mentioned, the area of economic policy could be regarded as even more experimental than the field of monetary policy, seen from the point of view of EU structure, design, and competence. One reason for this may be that, for monetary policy, frameworks for establishing innovative and highly integrative institutional structures already existed. For economic policy, the initial hope that market forces would ensure policy alignment and thus convergent monetary policies went unfulfilled. Instead, institutional structures had to be created ad-hoc, often in situations of acute crisis. In so proceeding, the linking of instruments under public international law with those of Union law has been used to creatively develop the new elements of the EU 'economic constitution'. The 2011 intergovernmental Euro Plus Pact (EPP)[43] between EU Member States was aimed at strengthening economic policy coordination.[44] This was later implemented in Union legislation through the above discussed 'Two-Pack' regulations. These were designed to enhance economic integration amongst the euro area Member States, allowing in-depth budgetary-policy monitoring, involving a process which foresees the submission of national budget plans for initial surveillance by the Commission's administration.[45] Next to the procedural dimension, the Two-Pack contains substantive criteria, obliging Member States to base their draft budgets on macroeconomic forecasting.[46] As an overall procedural framework for coordinating EU economic policy, Article 121 TFEU establishes so-called 'multilateral surveillance', involving the Commission, the European Council, the Council, the European Parliament, and the Member States all performing certain functions, taking on certain tasks, and having certain responsibilities.[47]

With regard to certain key areas of economic policy, agreements under public international law have played a major role in the European context. For the granting of financial assistance to Member States of the euro area, the ESM Treaty, a 2012 agreement under public international law, established a mechanism and procedure for the making of loans on the basis of conditionality, in a way similar to that of the earlier forms of assistance.[48] In the same year, twenty-five Member States of the

---

[43] Initially called the Competitiveness Pact or later the Pact for the Euro. See http://www.consilium. europa.eu/uedocs/cms_data/docs/pressdata/en/ec/120296.pdf.

[44] Conclusions of the EU Summit of 24–25 March 2011 http://register.consilium.europa.eu/pdf/en/11/st00/st00010.en11.pdf.

[45] The milestones of this timeline can be summarized, in the framework of the budgetary cycle as follows: By 30 April, euro area member states must publish their medium-term fiscal plans (Stability Programmes), together with their policy priorities for growth and employment for the forthcoming 12 months (National Reform Programmes) in the context of the European Semester on economic policy coordination; by 15 October, euro area Member States must publish their draft budgets for the following year; by 31 December, euro area member states must adopt their budgets for the following year.

[46] According to Art 4(4) of Regulation 473/201: 3 'National medium-term fiscal plans and draft budgets referred to in paragraphs 1 and 2 shall be based on independent macroeconomic forecasts, and shall indicate whether the budgetary forecasts have been produced or endorsed by an independent body. Those forecasts shall be made public together with the national medium-term fiscal plans and the draft budgets that they underpin'.

[47] Under Art 121(6) the Council and the European Parliament are empowered to adopt detailed rules governing the procedures to apply in this multilateral surveillance, the legal basis for inter alia the Six-Pack measures.

[48] According to Bruno de Witte, the addition of para 3 in Art 136 TFEU would serve, first of all, to discard any doubts as to the legality of the establishment of a financial support mechanism for countries in

EU concluded the public international law Treaty on Stability, Coordination and Governance in the Economic and Monetary Union (TSCG, also known as the Fiscal Compact). The TSCG could arguably have been adopted under EU law as such, either under the enhanced cooperation procedure,[49] or through an amendment of TEU Protocol No 12 on the excessive deficit procedure.[50] However, public international law was chosen in order to overcome the opposition—and veto—of two Member States.[51] The TSCG was implemented in tandem with above mentioned Six-Pack legislation (and there, is in any case, arguably a considerable overlap between it and the existing EU *acquis*)[52] and its full integration into Union law has been proposed.[53] The Six-Pack measures involved highly complex technical provisions, introducing a managerial type of review of national policy preferences in a host of economic policy areas. The results are computed in seemingly objective approaches based on well-defined calculations, the input into which is, however, subject to much arbitration.[54] The ESM and the TSCG were both designed to foster budgetary discipline, to enhance coordination of economic policies, to improve the economic governance of the euro area, and to reinforce the provisions of the initial post-Maastricht Stability and Growth Pact (SGP).[55]

E Legal Rules Governing the Substance of Sector-specific Decision-making

1 Decision-making within the Monetary Union

According to its legal basis in the Treaties, the ECSB defines and implements the monetary policy of the Union, conducts foreign-exchange operations, manages the official foreign reserves of the Members States, and promotes the 'smooth operation of payment systems' (as noted at the outset of this chapter). In all of this, its prime objective is to maintain 'price stability' (Article 127 TFEU). Additional objectives are adjuvant to the general economic policies in the Union. The competences of the ECB are circumscribed by the prohibition in Article 123(1) TFEU of monetary financing

---

budgetary difficulties and secondly, to neutralize the no bail out prohibition of Art 125 TFEU, by a complementary norm with the same Treaty rank. See Bruno de Witte, 'International Treaties on the Euro and the EU Legal Order' (2012) paper presented in the framework of the EUDO Dissemination Conference 'The Euro Crisis and the State of European Democracy', Florence 22–23 November 2012.

[49] Art 20 TEU and Arts 326–334 TFEU.

[50] Protocol (No 12) on the Excessive Deficit Procedure annexed to the TEU.

[51] The only two Member States that did not sign the TSCG were the United Kingdom and the Czech Republic.

[52] See eg Michael Dougan and Michael Gordon, Written Evidence, UK House of Commons, Select Committee on Foreign Affairs 22 May 2012, paras 7–8 https://publications.parliament.uk/pa/cm201314/cmselect/cmfaff/87/87we18.htm.

[53] Jean-Claude Juncker, State of the Union Address 2017, European Parliament, Brussels, 13 September 2017 http://europa.eu/rapid/press-release_SPEECH-17-3165_en.htm.

[54] See for detail especially Annexes 5 and 6 of the European Commission, Vademecum on the Stability and Growth Pact, May 2013, European Economy Occasional Papers 151, ISSN 1725-3209, at 90–99 http://ec.europa.eu/economy_finance/publications/occasional_paper/2013/pdf/ocp151_en.pdf.

[55] Art 1 of the Treaty on Stability, Coordination and Governance in the Economic and Monetary Union (Fiscal Compact Treaty).

of Member State debt by means of direct purchases (as opposed to open market operations of the ECB, involving Member State bonds).

This broad definition of the tasks, combined with the constitutionally guaranteed independence of the ECB, and the formal obligation of independence of the NCBs as members of the ESCB, results in according a very broad discretion to the ECB in monetary policy decisions. The framing and implementation of monetary policy is undertaken by the ESCB predominantly through the ECB. To exercise this task it has at its disposal, as Cruz Villalón AG observed in *Gauweiler*, technical expertise and access to crucial information enabling it to devise monetary policies which actually influence economic realities.[56]

Such highly technical, very complex, and information-intensive activity is, consequently, very difficult to monitor through the 'traditional' legal means of a framework of power coupled with judicial review. Another, albeit more practical, reason for the difficulty of employing judicial review as a means of enforcing accountability is that most of the decisions of the ECB are directed to the NCBs by way of guidelines. For example, interest rate decisions are directed to the NCBs, without any per se external effect. In principle, this approach makes it exceedingly difficult to ensure judicial review of ECB decisions through direct legal action. More likely to succeed is an approach involving indirect review, by means of preliminary references to the Court, within legal actions relating to national measures and procedures before national courts which grant more liberal standing than a direct approach to the CJEU would encompass.[57]

Criteria of accountability can be decisive in cases involving broad discretion. The fewer the possibilities of judicial review as to the substance of an administrative decision, the more important are procedural considerations as to, for example, satisfaction of a duty of care (specifically, the full and independent assessment of all relevant facts prior to decision-making), compliance with the requirement of having and providing reasons for a measure and, finally, compliance with the principle of proportionality.[58] With respect to developments in the EMU, it is important to note that 'the principle that powers be exercised proportionally' should not, in the words of Somek, be 'replaced with the principle that powers be proportionate to unpredictable challenges' in times of economic crises or otherwise.[59]

The system for the implementation of EU monetary policy is a highly integrated administrative system in which a special (constitutional) agency—the ECB—is institutionally linked in with the NCBs within the structural and procedural framework of the ESCB. The NCBs themselves must comply with the independence requirements established by primary EU law. They are part of a hierarchical agency structure in which ECB guidelines and decisions are binding. NCBs are, therefore, more like decentralized implementation bodies for centralized decision-making than the more

---

[56] See Opinion of AG Cruz Villalón in Case C-62/14 *Peter Gauweiler and Others v Deutscher Bundestag* (n 10).

[57] An example is the already mentioned Case C-62/14 *Peter Gauweiler and Others v Deutscher Bundestag* (n 1).

[58] ibid paras 66–92.

[59] Alexander Somek, 'Authoritarian Liberalism' (2015) 21 *European Law Journal* 340, 359.

networked structures found in many other areas, where decision-making authority can be seen as more dispersed, distributed and, particularly, shared. That said, the NCBs are bodies established under national law, financed by the Member States, and of which the employees are subject to Member State law.

2 Decision-making within the Economic Union

On the other hand, as far as economic policy is concerned, much less clear-cut institutional approaches have been laid down by primary law, or by the case law of the courts. Article 119(3) TFEU contains a set of guiding principles for Member State economic policy based on the internal market and an 'open market economy with free competition'. This is applicable 'concurrently', that is, in parallel, with the implementation of Union monetary policy. Therefore, the just cited provision obliges the Member States to maintain sound public finances and a sustainable balance of payments, the reference to the single market being directed at ensuring free movement of capital (Article 63 TFEU). One of the structural duties of EU monetary policy is the combination of macro-prudential activities (such as those listed in Article 18 and 19 ESCB/ECB Statute) and banking supervision, now undertaken by the Single Supervisory Mechanism (SSM) located at the ECB and the NCBs.

Further principles are evolving—and are regularly challenged. One example is the so-called 'no bail-out clause' (Article 125 TFEU), which was introduced (pre-crisis) in the Treaty of Maastricht, in the absence of a fiscal union, apparently in order to avoid (economic) moral hazard within the EU.[60] This clause, and the subsequent possibility of default for undisciplined participant countries, was the expression of a 'market-based model' assumed to ensure fiscal discipline by states through the pressure emanating from financial markets. This was supposed to imply a 'competitive' and 'decentralized' model for the European macroeconomic constitution.[61] Such a market-based system is premised on the fact that states should, in principle, have direct access to financial markets in order to fund their expenditures. Lack of fiscal discipline and unsound public finances would be punished, so the market-based model goes, directly through the markets which would stop the lending to the refractory state. The original EMU approach, as enshrined in the Maastricht Treaty, combined elements of both 'competing' approaches.[62] On the 'market-based side', Article 103 TEC (now 125 TFEU)[63] established the 'no bail-out clause' in combination with a strict prohibition

---

[60] The 'moral hazard' in this case would consist in the reduced budgetary discipline of the Member States if the possibility of endless financing by the EU or the ECB was institutionalized. Note, however, a strand of economic theory, which argues that 'compulsory' fiscal discipline is not necessary in a Monetary Union as it would not leave any instruments in the Member States' hands to respond to shocks; see W Buiter, G Corsetti, and N Roubini, '"Excessive Deficits": Sense and Nonsense in the Treaty of Maastricht' (1993) *Economic Policy*, reprinted in P de Grauwe, *The Political Economy of Monetary Union* (Edward Elgar Publishing 2001) 297–331.

[61] Miguel Poiares Maduro, *We the Court* (Hart Publishing 1998) 103 ff.

[62] By 'original EMU approach' we refer to the broad understanding of the 'no bail-out clause' as was perceived by the biggest part of the literature before the *Pringle* judgment; see Case C-370/12 *Pringle* (n 18).

[63] Art 125 (1) TFEU reads: 'The Union shall not be liable for or assume the commitments of central governments, regional, local or other public authorities, other bodies governed by public law, or public

on 'monetising' debt through the ECB (Article 101 TEC, now 123 TFEU),[64] while, in respect of the 'central rules system', the Excessive Deficit Procedure (EDP)[65] and the Stability and Growth Pact (SGP) were directed towards guaranteeing fiscal discipline.

F Sector-specific Forms of Acts and Measures

1 Forms of acts and measures within the Monetary Union

The forms of act which have been developed for EU monetary policy are adapted to the particularities of the ESCB. Along with binding regulations and decisions (Article 288 TFEU and Article 34(1) ESCB/ECB Statute) a specific instrument available to the ECB is that of *guidelines* (Article 12(1), 14(3) ESCB/ECB Statute) which are binding upon the NCBs. Additionally, *contractual forms* of act play an important role.

In practice, *regulations* are used to outline basic tasks and provide for possible limits on individual rights.[66] Regulations can be used to establish methods of calculation and determine minimum reserves (Article 19(1) ESCB/ECB Statute) or to ensure the proper design of payment clearing systems (Article 22). *Decisions* can be adopted as 'externally' binding acts, addressing both public and private actors not within the ESCB. Practically, this is predominantly the case in the field of supervision or in requiring minimum reserves. ECB decisions may also be addressed to actors within the ESCB, specifically orders or directions by the ECB to the NCBs, but may also be adopted in the context of self-organization.[67]

A specifically designed tool of the ECB is the *guideline*, setting out the general rules within the ESCB and binding the NCBs in their implementation actions. Most of such regulatory activity has occurred through abstract-general guidelines.[68] Under Article 14(3) ESCB/ECB Statute, NCBs 'are an integral part of the ESCB and shall act in accordance with the guidelines and instructions of the ECB. The Governing Council [of

---

undertakings of any Member State, without prejudice to mutual financial guarantees for the joint execution of a specific project. A Member State shall not be liable for or assume the commitments of central governments, regional, local or other public authorities, other bodies governed by public law, or public undertakings of another Member State, without prejudice to mutual financial guarantees for the joint execution of a specific project'.

[64] The Outright Monetary Transactions (OMT) Programme launched by the ECB has been also called into question. The German Constitutional Court recently referred a preliminary ruling to the CJEU (BVerfG, 2 BvR 1390/12 vom 17 December 2013, http://www.bverfg.de/entscheidungen/rs20131217_2bvr139012.html), asking, among other questions, whether the governments' bond buying in secondary markets by the ECB infringes Art 123 TFEU and the prohibition of debt monetizing by the ECB. AG Cruz Villalon delivered his Opinion in Case C-62/14 *Gauweiler* (n 10) on the legality of the OMT scheme of the European Central Bank (ECB) on 14 January 2015, according to which the ECB's OMT programme is compatible, in principle, with the TFEU.

[65] Art 126 TFEU (ex Art 104 TEC).

[66] See eg Regulation (EC) No 2532/98 and Regulation (EC) No 2157/1999 of the European Central Bank of 23 September 1999 on the powers of the European Central Bank to impose sanctions (ECB/1999/4) [1999] OJ L264/21, as last amended by Regulation of the ECB of 16 April 2014 amending Regulation (EC) No 2157/1999 on the powers of the ECB to impose sanctions (ECB/2014/18) [2014] OJ L141/51.

[67] See eg Decision of the ECB of 12 October 1999 concerning the Rules of Procedure of the Executive Board of the ECB (ECB/1999/7) [1999] OJ L314/34 and the Decision concerning the establishment of the Administrative Board of Review and its Operating Rules (ECB/2014/16) [2014] OJ L175/47.

[68] Hoffmann (n 33) 989, § 27, para 19.

the ECB] shall take the necessary steps to ensure compliance with the guidelines and instructions of the ECB, and shall require that any necessary information be given to it [by the NCBs]'. One of the difficulties regarding the accountability of the ESCB system (already referred to above) lies in the very instrument of the ECB guideline, binding directly as it does only on the NCBs as participants of the ESCB itself.[69]

Especially in the context of any open market activity, the ECB can act on a contractual basis with creditors, debtors, or any other entity. Article 35(2) ESCB/ECB Statute explicitly acknowledges such activity by stating that disputes arising from such activities 'shall be decided by the competent national courts, save where jurisdiction has been conferred upon the Court of Justice of the European Union'. However, in practice, the ECB, despite explicit empowerment in Article 18(1), does not itself give effect to monetary transactions with financial institutions. Instead, decentralized implementation of so called 'open market' operations is the norm, in turn explaining the absence of an explicit legal framework for ECB-triggered monetary transactions. Instead, open market operations conducted by the NCBs are carried out under national law and it is, therefore, for that law to determine the forms of act for such operations within its jurisdiction. It is specifically for national administrative law to determine whether an NCB has a choice between forms of act and what the consequences of such a choice might be as regards, for example, judicial review and enforceability. However, the choice of contract law under national provisions—public or private law—may lead to varied consequences regarding ECB guidelines, both with respect to enforcement and for the sanctioning of non-compliance.

2 Forms of acts and measures within the Economic Union

Given the very different configuration of actors in the field of EU economic policy, an entirely different, but specific, typology of acts has developed. Forms of act with abstract-general content can, in some instances, be adopted as Union acts under Article 288 TFEU (e.g., Two-Pack and Six-Pack legislation). Additionally, forms of what have been called 'intergovernmental private law' and international agreements have been developed. A powerful instrument under the former is the Memorandum of Understanding (MoU), attached to intergovernmental financial support agreements establishing the conditions of loans and the terms of repayment. As such, they have the power indirectly to shape the creation and enforcement of national law. MoUs applicable in a specific loan agreement have in the past been attached to a Council measure and have thereby changed their nature from *inter partes* agreements to that of a generally applicable Union act, endowed with the principles of supremacy and direct effect (see above C.2 of this chapter). That practice is, however, rather problematic, since the transfer of contractual terms into binding Union legal acts changes the enforcement possibilities, and may need to be reviewed regarding the procedural conditions for its occurrence. On the other hand, economic policy of the Union is per se not a field of single-case

---

[69] The implementation of ECB monetary policy takes place within the rules established by ECB/2011/14, Guideline of the ECB of 20 September 2011 on monetary policy instruments and procedures of the Eurosystem [2011] OJ L331/1.

decision-making, but realized rather through broad, macroeconomic policy choices and associated measures.

G Administrative Enforcement in Monetary and Economic Policy

1 Enforcement within the Monetary Union

With regard to individuals, the ECB has the power to sanction non-compliance with monetary policy established by the ESCB. Under Article 34(3) ESCB/ECB Statute, the Council can empower both the ECB and NCBs to impose financial penalties on banks and other financial institutions directly: 'Within the limits and under the conditions adopted by the Council under the procedure laid down in Article 41, the ECB shall be entitled to impose fines or periodic penalty payments on undertakings for failure to comply with obligations under its regulations and decisions'. Further details on the powers of the ECB to impose sanctions are established in ECB Regulations 2532/98 and 2157/1999.[70]

With respect to Member States, the ECB has considerable de facto powers to influence even economic policies, as a result of its powers in the context of monetary policy. The main tool for this is, alongside the formal conditionality of financial instruments, also the informal conditionality of ECB actions upon Member States' action in carrying out specific measures of economic reform. Beukers reports that this has been part of the ECB's unconventional monetary policy, examples being sovereign bond buying under the Securities Markets Programme,[71] the Outright Monetary Transactions,[72] and measures related to the solvency of financial institutions in granting—or withholding—Emergency Liquidity Assistance in cases where the solvency of financial institutions is not secured through EU/IMF programmes.[73] The ECB has in practice been involved in formulating the conditionality of the EU/IMF programmes, not least by supplying expertise and information, but sometimes through more direct intervention, e.g., as part of the 'Troika' (now known—perhaps less pejoratively—as the 'institutions'). In these instances, the ECB acts in assisting the formulation of economic policy measures for a Member State, non-compliance with which can be sanctioned by the Bank with serious threats to the liquidity of the banking system (and with it the functioning of the entire economy) of the Member State concerned. The expertise-driven independent EU agency that is the ECB thus has at its disposal extremely

---

[70] Regulation (EC) No 2532/98 and Regulation (EC) No 2157/1999 of the European Central Bank of 23 September 1999 on the powers of the European Central Bank to impose sanctions (ECB/1999/4) [1999] OJ L264/21 as last amended by Regulation of the ECB of 16 April 2014 amending Regulation (EC) No 2157/1999 on the powers of the ECB to impose sanctions (ECB/2014/18) [2014] OJ L141/51.

[71] Thomas, Beuckers, 'The New ECB' 50 CMLRev (2013) 1579–1620 referring to a Press Release of 21 February 2013 on the Eurosystem's holdings of securities acquired under the Securities Markets Programme (SMP).

[72] ECB Press Release of 11 March 2016 on OMTs and their conditions which led to Case C-62/14 *Peter Gauweiler and Others v Deutscher Bundestag* (n 1).

[73] ECB Press Release of 21 March 2012 stating that, as of 25 March 2013, 'Emergency Liquidity Assistance (ELA) could only be considered if an EU/IMF programme is in place' that would ensure the solvency of the banks concerned, as was the case of Cyprus, Ireland, and Greece.

powerful tools for demanding compliance with centrally—or at least collectively—determined economic policy approaches.

Beukers cites three cases in which the ECB also tried to link its support for Member States' financial institutions through secretly issuing warnings regarding compliance with economic policy goals. Letters of this kind have demonstrably been sent by the president of the ECB to Italy, Spain, and Ireland at various times during the crises. The letter to Ireland warned, for example, that 'future decisions of the Governing Council of the ECB regarding the terms of liquidity provision to Irish banks will thus need to take into account appropriate progress in the areas of fiscal consolidation' by the Republic of Ireland.[74]

2 Enforcement within the Economic Union

In economic policy, the options for enforcement are spelled out essentially in Article 126(11) TFEU and Regulations 1173/2001[75] and 1174/2011[76] (part of the Six-Pack legislation), requiring budgetary surveillance and the prohibition of excessive debt and economic imbalances. The budgetary surveillance mechanism (Regulation 1173/2011) lists various infractions, such as not taking action to tackle excessive deficits or misrepresentation of deficits, and establishes enforcement mechanisms. Sanctions include ordering Member States to make interest bearing deposits (Article 4) or non-interest bearing deposits (Article 5), or to pay fines 'amounting to 0.2% of the Member State's GDP' imposed by the Council acting under Article 126(8) TFEU (Article 6). Enforcement powers regarding the policing of the prohibition of excessive debt and economic imbalances are thereby conferred on the Council. Also, under Article 3(1) Regulation 1174/2011, Council decisions establishing non-compliance in accordance with Article 10(4) Regulation 1176/2011 may lead to interest-bearing and non-interest bearing deposits, as well as, under Article 3(2), to fines. In these cases, the Council acts on a Commission recommendation. In certain cases, the Council may further transpose the interest-bearing deposit into an annual fine. However, in view of the difficulties in finding majorities in the Council for such actions—especially since Member States are called upon to sanction each other, and to impose fines on countries already in financial difficulty—the decision-making procedure for the imposing fines is simplified in that the 'decisions referred to in paragraphs 1 and 2 [of Article 3 Regulation 1174/2011] shall be deemed adopted by the Council unless it decides, by qualified majority, to reject the recommendation within 10 days of its adoption by the Commission'. However, the Council has also some leeway with regard to the decision as there is no need for unanimity because, under the Regulation, 'the Council may decide, by qualified majority, to amend the [Commission's] recommendation'. This is not atypical for

---

[74] Letter of Jean Claude Trichet, President of the ECB to Brian Lenihan, Minister for Finance of Ireland, of 15 October 2010.

[75] Regulation (EU) No 1173/2011 of the European Parliament and of the Council of 16 November 2011 on the effective enforcement of budgetary surveillance in the euro area [2011] OJ L306/1.

[76] Regulation (EU) No 1174/2011 of the European Parliament and of the Council of 16 November 2011 on enforcement measures to correct excessive macroeconomic imbalances in the euro area [2011] OJ L306/8.

Council *administrative* action, in contrast with its procedures when acting in a legislative capacity. The Regulations provide the Member States with certain rights of defence. These may be further developed in case law should challenges come before the Court, but this has so far not occurred given the rarity of the Council's use of these enforcement measures. Nonetheless, this is an impressive example of the reach of administrative powers (and the significance of the associated legal framework, procedures and structures) in European Union law. A 'recommendation' by the Commission, followed by a Council decision, can be enforced by the imposition of deposit requirements and fines, large enough so as to be able to influence a Member State's economic development and force it to take certain economic policy decisions.

Additionally, Regulation 1303/2013 allows for suspension of payments under the European Structural Funds (ESF) mechanism in cases of established violations of the conditionality of funding (such as complying with rules on budgetary surveillance, on excessive debt as well as on economic imbalances).[77]

H Supervision and Control of European Economic and Monetary Policy

1 Supervision within the Monetary Union

In the realm of monetary policy, the strict independence of the ECB does not exclude its being subject to certain forms of supervision. Nevertheless, there is very little anticipatory control, other than through the policy and structural frameworks deriving from the specific legislative acts applying to the ESCB. One such ex ante (political) control emerges from the nomination process for the chief personnel of the ECB. For example, the president of the ECB, who chairs the Executive Board, the Governing Council and the General Council, is appointed (by majority vote) in the European Council for an eight-year non-renewable term. However, this long-term appointment and the non-renewability, while underlining the legislative objective of genuine independence, clearly weakens such control in comparison with other policy fields.

Ongoing supervision—broadly ex post, because in the form of reporting—relies very much on the accuracy of the ECB's own reporting. In that regard, an important supervisory instrument under Article 15(2) ESCB/ECB Statute (Protocol No 4) consists of the 'consolidated financial statement of the ESCB', published weekly and 'available to interested parties free of charge' (Article 15(4)). These statements are important especially with regard to the ECB's financial arrangements, which are separate from those of the EU, the ECB having its own budget and its capital being subscribed and paid up by the euro area NCBs. Whether such 'supervision' is to be regarded

---

[77] Regulation (EU) No 1303/2013 of the European Parliament and of the Council of 17 December 2013 laying down common provisions on the European Regional Development Fund, the European Social Fund, the Cohesion Fund, the European Agricultural Fund for Rural Development and the European Maritime and Fisheries Fund and laying down general provisions on the European Regional Development Fund, the European Social Fund, the Cohesion Fund and the European Maritime and Fisheries Fund and repealing Council Regulation (EC) No 1083/2006 [2013] OJ L347/320. See eg Art 23: 'Measures linking effectiveness of ESI Funds to sound economic governance'.

as administrative or political in nature is perhaps a moot point, not needing further clarification here.

Subsequent, ex post (administrative) supervision also takes place, according to the Statute of the ESCB, through two interacting layers of auditing, one by external private auditors, the other by the EU's own auditing body, the European Court of Auditors (ECA). External auditors' assessments of the ECB's annual accounts (Article 27(1) ESCB/ECB Statute) are published as part of the ECB Annual Report. The European Court of Auditors, on the other hand, examines the operational efficiency of the management of the Bank (Article 27(2)). The reason for such distinction, and for a layer of external audit in addition to the scrutiny by the ECA, is not entirely clear.

The ECB Governing Council had initially attempted to prevent anti-fraud review of the Bank by the Commission's anti-fraud office (OLAF),[78] with the argument that the ECB's independent position and its statutory tasks precluded application of the OLAF Regulation to it. The Court of Justice held this to be in violation of EU law.[79] According to the Court, the guarantee of independence for the ECB does not have the consequence of separating it entirely from the whole framework of the Union and exempting it from every rule of EU law. In adapting to this judgment, the Governing Council has accepted OLAF investigations.[80] Tensions, however, linger, with the ECB's assertion that application of the OLAF Regulation could be a threat to the independent performance of its tasks. For this reason, special working arrangements were agreed between OLAF and the ECB in 2016.[81] As well as being subject to OLAF review, the ECB is also subject to scrutiny by the European Ombudsman (and its powers of reporting to the European Parliament). Data processing by the ECB is subject to control by the European Data Protection Supervisor (EDPS).[82]

Judicial review in respect of the administration of EU monetary policy is limited, as a consequence of the highly technical and discretionary procedures of the ESCB, as well as of the general lack of individual standing in annulment actions against ECB measures.[83] Nonetheless, judicial review plays an important role in the overall control

---

[78] In 1999, the European Parliament and the EU Council adopted Regulation (EC) No 1073/1999 concerning investigations carried out by the European Anti-Fraud Office (OLAF Regulation) in order to step up the fight against fraud, corruption and other illegal activities detrimental to the Communities' financial interests. It mainly provides for the internal investigation by OLAF of suspected fraud within EU institutions, bodies, offices, and agencies.

[79] See Case C-11/00 *Commission v ECB* [2003] ECR I-7147, ECLI:EU:C:2003:395.

[80] ECB Decision on the rules applying to OLAF investigations—The Governing Council of the European Central Bank adopted on 3 June 2004 a Decision (ECB/2004/11) concerning the terms and conditions for European Anti-Fraud Office investigations of the European Central Bank, in relation to the prevention of fraud, corruption and any other illegal activities detrimental to the European Communities' financial interests and amending the Conditions of Employment for Staff of the European Central Bank. This Decision entered into force on 1 July 2004.

[81] Administrative Arrangements between the European Central Bank and the European Anti-Fraud Office of 16 June 2016 https://www.ecb.europa.eu/ecb/pdf/orga/Administrative-Arrangements-between-ECB-and-European-Anti-Fraud-Office.pdf (last accessed 1 March 2017).

[82] See Art 46 of Regulation (EC) No 45/2001 of 18 December 2000 on the protection of individuals with regard to the processing of personal data by the Community institutions and bodies and on the free movement of such data [2001] OJ L8/1.

[83] For difficulties to bring cases against decisions or guidelines of the ECB by individuals see eg Case C-64/14P *Sven A von Storch and Others v European Central Bank* ECLI:EU:C:2015:300 (on appeal against the order of the General Court of 10 December 2013 in Case T-492/12).

of ECB activity. The *Gauweiler* OMT case is an example of highly publicized disputes in regard to the legality of ECB monetary policy decisions.[84] Judicial review also takes place with regard to personnel matters, access to documents, and transparency issues.[85] Article 35 ESCB/ECB Statute enables the Court to review and interpret 'the acts or omissions of the ECB'. Problematic for this, though, are the 'open market operations' in which the ECB may act merely on a contractual basis, where disputes may arise between the ECB and its creditors. These disputes 'shall be decided by the competent national courts [under the national law applicable], save where jurisdiction has been conferred upon the Court of Justice of the European Union' (Article 35(2) ESCB/ECB Statute). Irrespective of such national court review over the legal position of the ECB, the Bank is subject to the liability regime provided for in Article 340 TFEU. Since the NCBs are themselves liable in accordance with their respective national laws, cases of the possible joint liability with the ECB will result in complex legal questions.

Beyond such judicial review possibilities, the ECB itself has standing to bring legal action (Article 35 ESCB/ECB Statute). Further, it may be able to avail itself of the jurisdiction of the CJEU within an arbitration clause contained in a contract concluded by, or on behalf of the ECB, whether that contract be governed by public or private law (Article 35(5) ESCB/ECB Statute). Under that provision, the CJEU has jurisdiction 'in disputes concerning the fulfilment by a national central bank of obligations under the Treaties and this Statute'.

In order to address disputes between the ECB and the NCBs, a simplified action under the infringement procedure is available. Article 35(6) ESCB/ECB Statute provides that if

> the ECB considers that a national central bank has failed to fulfil an obligation under the Treaties and this Statute, it shall deliver a reasoned opinion on the matter after giving the national central bank concerned the opportunity to submit its observations. If the national central bank concerned does not comply with the opinion within the period laid down by the ECB, the latter may bring the matter before the Court of Justice of the European Union.

Article 271(d) TFEU explicitly states that the powers given to the ECB Governing Council in respect of alleged violations of NCB obligations shall be 'the same as those conferred upon the Commission in respect of Member States by Article 258 TFEU'. The ECB can then ensure that the national banks comply with their obligations established by ECB guidelines. So far, however, no case law, equivalent to that where fines under Articles 258–260 TFEU have been imposed, especially for repeat violations of EU law, has emerged under these provisions.

2 Supervision within the Economic Union

In the context of the economic union, possibilities of judicial review reflect a particular intergovernmental (public international law) approach. Any Commission finding of

---

[84] Case C-62/14 *Peter Gauweiler and Others v Deutscher Bundestag* (n 1).
[85] See eg Order of the Court in Case C-28/13 P *Thesing and Bloomberg Finance v ECB* ECLI:EU:C: 2014:230.

inadequate implementation of the balanced budget rule requires the country concerned to be brought before the Court of Justice by another state.[86] Article 8(1) TSCG
provides for recourse to the CJEU via Article 273 TFEU (which accords jurisdiction to
the Court in any dispute between Member States which relates to the subject matter
of the EU Treaties) if the dispute is submitted to it under a special agreement between
the parties.[87] However, experience shows that Member States will only very rarely take
each other to court. If the Commission is not empowered to start infringement proceedings against a Member State—and judging by the letter of the Fiscal Compact
(FCT), as well as the TEU and TFEU, it is not able to do so—and one country within
the TSCG does not bring another member before the Court, it seems likely that a violation of Article 3 TSCG (on the FCT) will not trigger a sanction for the non-compliant state. Many elements of this approach have been criticized in the literature.[88]
Perhaps, most centrally, the nature of this economic framework as an international
treaty means that it does not prevail over national constitutions, thus arguably weak-
ening its supervision and enforcement mechanisms. The indirect possibility of the
conferral of new powers to the EU institutions, notably the Commission, by the TSCG
has further raised concerns about legality.[89] Arguably, however, the agreement should
be seen as carefully drafted in such a way so as not to give EU institutions new competences—which might have triggered the necessity for referenda in certain states prior
to ratification—but rather new tasks falling within their existing competences, which
the Commission and the Council are under no obligation to perform.

I Conclusion

Although monetary and economic policies are highly inter-related, as in most national systems, there are in the Union context also great differences in the legal and
administrative framework governing the two fields. The implementation of European
monetary policy is set within a system of independent but tightly linked 'agencies'
consisting of the European Central Bank and the national central banks, within the
European System of Central Banks. These bodies have powers guaranteed in the

---

[86] Treaty on Stability, Coordination and Governance in the Economic and Monetary Union (Fiscal
Compact Treaty), Art 8(1): 'Where a Contracting Party considers, independently of the Commission's
report, that another Contracting Party has failed to comply with Art 3(2), it may also bring the matter to
the Court of Justice. In both cases, the judgment of the Court of Justice shall be binding on the parties to
the proceedings, which shall take the necessary measures to comply with the judgment within a period
to be decided by the Court of Justice. According to Art 8(2), failure to comply with a judgment may result
in further proceedings in which the Court of Justice may impose a lump-sum or penalty payment of 0.1%
of GDP. For eurozone members, this money will be paid into the European Stability Mechanism, while
for non-eurozone states it will be paid into the general EU budget.

[87] See Council of the European Union 5788/12 (Brussels, 26 January 2012) and Paul Craig, 'The
Stability Coordination and Governance Treaty: Principle, Politics and Pragmatism' (2012) 37 *European
Law Review* 245.

[88] Bruno de Witte, 'Another Legal Monster? An EUI Debate on the Fiscal Compact Treaty' EUI
Working Paper Law 2012/09, 5–7.

[89] According to Art 13(2) TEU, the EU institutions shall act within the limits of the powers given to
them under 'the Treaties' (ie the TEU and the TFEU). For the doubts as to the legality of the attribution
of new powers see House of Lords—European Union Committee, 'The Euro Area Crisis: 25th report of
session 2010-2012' (14 February 2012). However, see also Dougan and Gordon (n 52) paras 11–13.

primary law of the European Union. Much of the specification of the instruments and procedures for ECB decision-making is concentrated in the Treaties, together with the Statute of the ESCB/ECB (in Protocol No 4 to the TEU and the TFEU).

Monetary policy conducted within the ESCB's specific structure of decentralized Union administration is a case study of a highly integrated agency regime in which a Union authority—the ECB—takes the decisions, and the national agencies implement the (binding) 'guidelines' issued by it. No other EU policy area has reached this level of quasi-federal agency-structure. At the same time, EU monetary policy has become a revealing field for the study of agency independence, and of the powerful role which specialist expertise can play in articulating a highly important and precisely focused objective: that of guaranteeing price stability. This closely defined policy goal is one to be exercised, where possible, so that the maintenance of price stability contributes to the 'general economic policies in the Union'. It is thus a technical objective, but one ssto be exercised in the context of politically defined goals. Therefore, one must conclude that the 'administration' of the Union's monetary policy is a highly *political* one.

The legal framework of the other major branch of the sector addressed in this chapter, European Union economic policy, has been, and is, in the process of continuous transformation or evolution. The economic and financial crises after 2008 has been catalytic for accelerating integration. Some of the measures adopted in that context have gone more deeply than simply strengthening the previous policy framework.

Under this umbrella the EU was, in the bid to find new 'governance techniques', compelled to supplement its economic policy toolbox with novel instruments of governance and administration. It has resorted to public international law instruments (such as the Fiscal Compact) and intergovernmental private law instruments (ESM, MoUs). Arguably, it was possible by these means to circumvent both EU procedural rules, which allowed for national vetoes, and—in part—even Union constitutional principles. For example, the adjustment programmes premised on the MoUs laid out very specific lists of measures to be undertaken by the recipient Member States, including measures pertaining to direct taxation and social policy.[90] Limits on further integration in this field result both from the Treaties (e.g., the prohibition of monetary financing of national budgets) and from national constitutional law limiting steps towards further financial integration. That said, it should be noted—and can be persuasively argued—that the 'TSCG is an international agreement entirely separate from and constituting no [at least formal] part of the EU legal order … [and] must be interpreted and applied in conformity with EU law, the latter taking precedence in the event of any conflict between the two regimes'.[91]

Whilst these ad hoc 'crisis measures' are, on the one hand, highly technical, requiring sophisticated mastery of detail by expert regulators, they are also deeply political. The conditionalities attached to any (pre- or post-ESM) financial assistance, as well as the Country Specific Recommendations made by the Commission to the

---

[90] See section 3.2.1.   [91] Dougan and Gordon (n 52) para 7.

Member States, have direct and immediate implications for the economic and social policy choices for the future of Europe and its Member States, pertaining, for instance, to employment, social security, and taxation. By being brought within the realm of the Union, they are, however, transformed. No longer exclusively subject to national legislative and political choices, they are, instead, brought within the realm of the supranational governance of the European Union, and thereby that of its public administration and administrative law. This is not, per se, objectionable, but needs to be acknowledged squarely. The reasoning behind such a shift from purely national policy-making and implementation to the setting of supranational policy and European administrative law lies in the objective of a strengthened and more efficient achievement of the objectives of Union economic policy and law, based in particular on the perceived need for stronger technocratic oversight of national economic management.[92] Economic policy cooperation has, therefore, led to profoundly technocratic attempts at ensuring compliance with certain framework parameters, in particular those of indebtedness and growth. The *means* of achieving these objectives are now prescribed by the Commission as an executive body, issuing policy suggestions regarding tax reform, as well as transport, environmental, educational, health and much other policy, suggestions which can be made quasi-binding for, in particular, so-called 'programme countries'.

For the legitimate exercise of this economic policy role, the Commission and indeed the Union as a whole—seen at least from the classic perspective of the principles of democracy and the rule of law—arguably need a very different democratic mandate from the one that exists today. European economic governance as it has been evolving, requires a 'higher' level of democratic legitimacy than that provided for the various recent intergovernmental policies and their formal EU equivalents. Strongly intergovernmental or purely administrative-technocratic approaches cannot claim this legitimacy, since they cannot ensure that the views and interests of those affected by such decisions and measures have influenced, or can potentially influence, the policy choices made. Here inevitably follow two profound, interlinked future research questions: Does the European Union in its existing political-institutional conception and architecture have the capacity of providing such a framework of legitimacy. Secondly, if so, what means and specific steps are needed in order to usher in the actions necessary for realising and extending this potential, and within what timeframe?

Overall, one can observe that the policy field of economic and monetary union has many specificities. The highly integrated monetary union relying on an administrative-intergovernmental economic policy review creates a very particular and interrelated set of policies and implementation tools. However, despite the many individual—perhaps unique—features, this area actually also offers itself as one with a wealth of examples for many of the general characteristics—and the problems—of the fast-evolving administrative law of Union seen as a whole.[93] In this respect, we see

---

[92] Huw Macartney, 'The Paradox of Integration? European Democracy and the Debt Crisis' (2014) *Cambridge Review of International Affairs* 12.

[93] Herwig C H Hofmann, Gerard C Rowe, and Alexander H Türk, *Administrative Law and Policy of the European Union* (Oxford University Press 2011) 18.

that the policy objectives of the economic and monetary union are clearly defined in Treaty provisions, and that therefore the functional objectives of this policy clearly have a (pan-)European focus and orientation. Nonetheless, the (administrative) actors involved are themselves located either on the European level (ECB, Commission, Council, European Council, European Parliament) or on the national level under national law (NCBs, national governments and parliaments). No actors can be described as truly joint EU and Member State bodies, that is, from an organizational point of view, there is no strictly joint and/or fused national and European organizational entity. However, the two levels are indeed integrated, through intricate procedural—and to some extent structural—*cooperation*.

In monetary policy this cooperation occurs through the ESCB in which, quite atypically, a hierarchic command relation exists between the ECB and the NCBs. And although the ESCB is, in effect, a classic example of an EU network, such networks typically have no hierarchical decision-making element. More particularly, such networked structures—which run throughout EU administrative law—are mostly so constructed that, where a central Union body is involved, it has only a steering function, but no vote in final decision-making (e.g., the Commission in comitology committees). Here in the field of monetary policy, however, the ECB is considerably more than a *primus inter pares* in the ESCB; rather it has a virtually dominant role.

In the area of economic policy, intergovernmental cooperation is supplemented by the administrative review of national policies of the Member States, and by what I have referred to above as intergovernmental private law. The unusual nature of this as a European administrative phenomenon and its complicating implications for EU administrative law arise here from the elaborate procedures which link the various actors together in diverse arrangements which make use of creatively devised forms of act. Problems arise in a context of such variable character, then, in regard to the allocation of responsibilities, issues of transparency, and accountability mechanisms. The stronger the moves toward more multi-level but integrated, administrative procedures of these kinds, the more pronounced and urgent becomes the need for clear democratic legitimation of European executive action.

PART V

INTERNAL MARKET

11

The Single European Market in Goods

Isidora Maletić and Catherine Barnard

A Introduction

The focus of this chapter is on the European Union administrative law[1] that has arisen in the specific policy setting of the internal market. The creation of the internal market, which 'shall comprise an area without internal frontiers in which the free movement of goods, persons, services and capital is ensured',[2] is at the heart of the European Union integration project and consequently also of the EU's administrative network structure. A number of the other chapters that follow in this collection are closely related to the present discussion, either through the specific type of product concerned, or by virtue of exploring a particular policy objective intertwined with the broader framework of the internal market. This chapter concentrates on the internal market and its administration more narrowly understood. Its focus is mainly on the administrative tasks, structures, procedures, and enforcement in the field of product regulation. However, this should not overlook the extent to which the underlying provisions, principles, and practices in this field relate, more widely, to the whole body of EU administrative law.

The chapter will be structured as follows. First, it looks at what constitutes the administrative law of the internal market, focusing on sources of the administrative law of the internal market, outputs of the rule-making process in this setting, and the associated actors. Secondly, it looks at the scope of the power conferred on the EU in the key legal basis of the internal market, Article 114 Treaty on the Functioning of the European Union (TFEU), before considering the scope of the powers to enable agencies to fulfil the Union's functions under Article 114 TFEU. Thirdly, it examines other types of rule-making which govern the single market, notably the new approach to harmonization. Finally, it considers the question of enforcement.

---

[1] 'Administrative law' has been described as 'part of public law enabling and constraining administrative conduct, that is, activity designed to implement EU law'. See H C H Hofmann, 'General Principles of EU Law and EU Administrative Law' in C Barnard and S Peers (eds), *European Union Law* (Oxford University Press 2014) 196–225, at 197.

[2] Art 26 TFEU.

B Sources, Acts, and Actors

1 Sources of (administrative) law in the internal market

In the internal market context, the (administrative) law sources (of which only an indicative overview can be provided here) are wide-ranging and, in the light of the progressive experimentation with varying regulatory techniques, have evolved over time. First of all comes the Treaty framework and its provisions on negative integration, notably in this context Articles 34–36 TFEU on the free movement of goods. This is supplemented by the case law of the Court of Justice of the European Union (CJEU) which provides a significant source of internal market law. The evolution of principles, such as mutual recognition and market access,[3] through the Court's jurisprudence has prominently affected both the substantive and administrative scope of product regulation within the internal market.

Next comes the legislative power for the EU to adopt positive integration measures. Article 26 TFEU provides that the 'Union shall adopt measures with the aim of establishing or ensuring the functioning of the internal market'.[4] The principal legal basis for the attainment of this objective is Article 114 TFEU, introduced by the Single European Act (as ex Article 100a EEC). Unlike its predecessor, Article 100 EEC (now Article 115 TFEU),[5] the present provision did not require unanimity, but only qualified majority voting (QMV).[6] Article 114 TFEU provides:

Save where otherwise provided in the Treaties, the following provisions shall apply for the achievement of the objectives set out in Article 26. The European Parliament and the Council shall, acting in accordance with the ordinary legislative procedure and after consulting the Economic and Social Committee, adopt the measures for the approximation of the provisions laid down by law, regulation or administrative action in Member States which have as their object the establishment and functioning of the internal market.

The relevant European Union institutions are bound, in the exercise of their legislative (including related administrative) powers in the internal market, not only by the principle of conferral, but also by further general principles of law, such as the principles of proportionality and subsidiarity, as well as fundamental rights compliance.[7] We shall

---

[3] On the principle of mutual recognition see Case 120/78 *Cassis de Dijon* [1979] ECR 649. On the evolution of the jurisprudence relating to the internal market Treaty provisions more generally see C Barnard, *The Substantive Law of the EU* (5th edn, Oxford University Press 2016).

[4] Under Art 26(3) TFEU 'The Council, on a proposal from the Commission, shall determine the guidelines and conditions necessary to ensure balanced progress in all the sectors concerned'.

[5] Art 115 TFEU provides that: 'Without prejudice to Article 114, the Council shall, acting unanimously in accordance with a special legislative procedure and after consulting the European Parliament and the Economic and Social Committee, issue directives for the approximation of such laws, regulations or administrative provisions of the Member States as directly affect the establishment or functioning of the internal market'.

[6] Art 114(2) TFEU identifies certain fields where the use of QMV is deemed too contentious, providing that: 'Paragraph 1 shall not apply to fiscal provisions, to those relating to the free movement of persons nor to those relating to the rights and interests of employed persons'.

[7] Pursuant to Art 5(1) TEU 'The limits of Union competences are governed by the principle of conferral. The use of Union competences is governed by the principles of subsidiarity and proportionality'.

return to this issue below. The conduct of administrative tasks and the behaviour of administrative actors in the internal market sector are shaped by broad-ranging legislative measures dictating, for example, notification requirements with respect to the prevention of technical barriers, the provision of information, or attention to product safety requirements (see further below).

However, legislation is no longer the sole means for effectuating Union policy. As Hofmann has pointed out, the Union moved from being an organization primarily engaged in setting the legal framework through legislative action into an organization increasingly active in the field of the administrative implementation of such Union law.[8] For example, agencies are

> not only coordinators of composite procedures in which EU and Member States cooperate by means of joint implementation and enforcement of EU law, but they are also increasingly authors of standards to be used in implementation of EU law by Member States [with such agencies' roles developing] next to and alongside the more 'traditional' approach of regulatory law which consists of references to 'outside' standards set by private and semi-private standardisation bodies and scientific expertise.[9]

Finally, substantive and administrative product regulation within the internal market occurs against the backcloth of international trade law, including, for example, the rules of the World Trade Organization (WTO) and other international instruments, such as inter-governmental mutual recognition agreements between the EU and third countries.

2 The variety of forms of rule-making within the internal market

Legislation is the most obvious output of the Article 114 TFEU process (considered in more detail below). There is now much sector-specific regulation within the broader internal market context, e.g. in respect of financial services, transport, chemicals, foodstuffs, environment, energy, and public health, some of which are the focus of later chapters. However, experimentation with different regulatory techniques within the internal market has resulted in the creation of a number of actors and structures which contribute to the administrative law of the Union. Administrative tasks related to product regulation include:

- the '*planning* of joint actions and framework plans'
- the '*regulatory activities* such as administrative rule-making'
- 'the interpretation and further specification of conditions for implementation of legislative provisions'

On fundamental rights compliance see eg Joined Cases C-293/12 and C-594/12 *Digital Rights Ireland* EU:C:2014:238.

[8] H C H Hofmann, 'European Regulatory Union? The Role of Agencies and Standards' in P Koutrakos and J Snell (eds), *Research Handbook on the Law of the EU's Internal Market* (Edward Elgar Publishing 2017) 460–76, at 476.

[9] ibid 460–76, at 470–71.

- the adoption of '*single case decisions*'
- the '*making of recommendations, opinions and reports*'
- the '*coordination and supervision* of private actors involved in administrative activities such as standard setting and normatisation'
- the '*coordination of networks* of administration for implementation of EU policies' and
- 'information management' arrangements.[10]

3 Institutions and structures

Administrative functions within the internal market are performed by a variety of actors, both on the EU and national levels. Pursuant to Article 4(2) TFEU, the internal market is an area of shared competence. In those instances where 'the Treaties confer on the Union a competence shared with the Member States in a specific area, the Union and the Member States may legislate and adopt legally binding acts in that area'.[11] The principal actors under Article 114 TFEU in the ordinary legislative procedure are the Commission, which makes a proposal, with adoption by the Council and by the Parliament. More recently, national parliaments have gained, through a preventive subsidiarity scrutiny mechanism, a more prominent role in the evolution of the internal market.

Legislation is, however, merely the tip of the administrative law iceberg. It is supplemented by extensive administrative procedures which can take the form of:[12]

- direct administration[13]
- agency/comitology procedures[14]
- composite procedures.[15]

---

[10] For a general overview of the possible classification of such administrative tasks see H C H Hofmann, 'Seven Challenges for EU Administrative Law' (2009) 2(2) *Review of European Administrative Law* 37-59, at 39, n 7.

[11] See Art 2(2) TFEU, which stipulates further that: 'The Member States shall exercise their competence to the extent that the Union has not exercised its competence. The Member States shall again exercise their competence to the extent that the Union has decided to cease exercising its competence'.

[12] See generally on the possible classification of administrative procedures, H C H Hofmann, G C Rowe, and A H Türk, *EU Administrative Law and Policy* (Oxford University Press 2011).

[13] Instances of direct administration can, for example, be found in the context of the Treaty provisions on competition and State aid rules (eg Arts 105 and 108 TFEU).

[14] See Hofmann, 'Seven Challenges for EU Administrative Law' (n 10) 41, n 10, observing that: 'Structures to coordinate actors include comitology committees for development and coordination of implementation of EU law between Member States and the Commission, as well as agencies fulfilling special tasks of network administration'.

[15] 'Composite procedures' have been described as 'multiple-step procedures with input from administrative actors from different jurisdictions. These cooperate either vertically (between EU institutions and bodies, on the one hand, and Member States' institutions and bodies, on the other), horizontally (between various Member State institutions and bodies) or in triangular procedures (in which institutions from various Member States' as well as EU institutions and bodies are involved). The final acts or decisions emanating from such procedures are issued by a Member State body or an EU institution or body'. See Hofmann, 'Seven Challenges for EU Administrative Law' (n 10) 52.

Of particular importance are the extensive procedures for, and in relation to, information management,[16] such as the obligation on Member States to furnish information and notify the Commission of any new relevant technical regulations prior to their adoption.[17] The obligation enables preventive scrutiny of national rules for products and Information Society services (online services, including e-commerce) that may pose a restriction on free movement, thereby preventing the creation of new trade barriers and diminishing the need for enforcement action by the Commission. The obligation has been enhanced by the Court's jurisprudence, which has confirmed that a national measure that has not been notified may not be relied on.[18] Pursuant to Regulation 2679/98,[19] Member States are also under an obligation to provide information to the Commission relating to obstacles to the free movement of goods that may lead to serious trade disruption and loss to the individuals affected. Member States are further required to take all necessary and proportionate action to ensure the free movement of goods, and to inform the Commission of such action.

Such a multi-actor approach can also be seen on the EU level itself, with Union agencies being responsible, together with the Commission, for the administration of the internal market. However, this raises the issue that where 'administrative functions are undertaken on the EU level ... their exercise is organisationally fragmented'.[20] Closer scrutiny of the regulatory and administrative functions performed within the context of the internal market reveals increasingly onerous obligations being placed on national, EU, and international standardization entities, as well as the need for administrative networks and cooperative arrangements. In addition, because the internal market and the rules and practices applying to it, have been consistently subjected to revision, this has entailed the preparation of action plans, the updating of agenda-setting, and the evolution in organizational arrangements and programme management processes.

Beyond this, product regulation procedures are subject to compliance with international trade rules, including those of the World Trade Organization (WTO), e.g., product regulation under the Technical Barriers to Trade Agreement (TBT) (which includes notification procedures designed to prevent the emergence of international

---

[16] It has been suggested that '[i]ncreasingly, information is the key input and commodity for decision-making through administrative cooperation in the EU. Composite procedures, referred to above, can themselves generally be reduced to steps, measures and decisions concerning the joint creation, use and sharing of information'. See Hofmann, 'Seven Challenges for EU Administrative Law' (n 10) 53.

[17] The procedure was initially set up in Directive 83/189 laying down a procedure for the provision of information in the field of technical standards and regulations [1983] OJ L109/8; replaced by Directive 98/34, laying down a procedure for the provision of information in the field of technical standards and regulations [1998] OJ L204/37; modified by Directive 98/48, amending Directive 98/34/EC laying down a procedure for the provision of information in the field of technical standards and regulations [1998] OJ L217/18, to extend to Information Society services; and superseded by Directive 2015/1535 laying down a procedure for the provision of information in the field of technical regulations and of rules on Information Society services [2015] OJ L241/1.

[18] Case C-194/94 *CIA Security* [1996] ECR I-2201; Case C-443/98 *Unilever* [2000] ECR I-7535; Case 26/11 *Belgische Petroleum* EU:C:2013:44.

[19] Regulation 2679/98 on the functioning of the internal market in relation to the free movement of goods among Member States [1998] OJ L337/8. For an overview of some of the perceived challenges in this field see the Commission's Report on the application of Regulation 2679/98, COM(2001) 160.

[20] Hofmann, 'General Principles of EU Law and EU Administrative Law' (n 1) 198.

technical barriers to trade). Further, international instruments, such as inter-governmental mutual recognition agreements between the EU and third countries regarding, e.g., conformity assessment, certification, and marking to facilitate the mutual recognition of technical standards, also play a role here.

C Legal Rules Governing the Substance of Internal Market Decision-making

1 The powers under Article 114 TFEU

This chapter does not aim to provide a detailed account of the legal substance of the internal market policy area and of substantive, i.e., non-administrative, sectoral law which is necessarily left to detailed works on such topics. Rather, as already noted, the present analysis focuses on the law of the *administration* of this field. Nevertheless, the basic tenets of internal market substantive law need some exploration here, insofar as this is closely linked to an understanding of the legal operation of the sectoral administration. Indeed, the scope of the EU internal market sectoral administrative law stems in part from the broad interpretation of the underlying substantive legal provisions.

As mentioned above, the principal legal basis for attaining legal harmonization in the internal market is Article 114 TFEU,[21] which applies '[s]ave where otherwise provided in the Treaties'.[22] The 'residual' nature of the provision means that Article 114 cannot be used where a more specific legal basis exists for a relevant measure.[23] Thus, for example, the Court has held that where certain measures are intended to strengthen administrative cooperation in the field of value added tax (VAT), the more specific taxation law basis, rather than what is now Article 114, should be relied upon for their adoption.[24] Similarly, the powers under Article 114 cannot be deployed where the measures adopted do not seek to harmonize a particular aspect of the internal market, but rather leave existing national laws unchanged.[25]

However, while the enabling competence pursuant to Article 114 TFEU is not intended to confer 'a general power to regulate the internal market',[26] the scope of the legal basis has been interpreted rather permissively.[27] The Court has said that a mere

---

[21] Despite the strong integrationist function of Art 114 TFEU, the provision allows deviations from attained harmonization—see Art 114 TFEU, paras 4–10. For a detailed exploration of the ability of Member States to derogate from Art 114 TFEU harmonization norms see I Maletić, *The Law and Policy of Harmonisation in Europe's Internal Market* (Edward Elgar Publishing 2013); I Maletić, 'Derogations from the Regulation of Free Movement: Article 114 TFEU' in P Koutrakos and J Snell (eds), *Research Handbook on the Law of the EU's Internal Market* (Edward Elgar Publishing 2017) 384–400.

[22] Art 114(1) TFEU.

[23] For a legal basis dispute example involving Art 114 TFEU, see Case C-137/12 *Commission v Council (Conditional Access)* EU:C:2013:675.

[24] C-533/03 *Commission v Council* [2006] ECR I-1025.

[25] See Case C-436/03 *Parliament v Council* [2006] ECR I-3733, where the Court thought that the contested legislation, insofar as it left unchanged the various national laws already in existence, did not purport to approximate the laws of the Member States relating to cooperative societies, but aimed rather at the creation of a new form of cooperative society in addition to the national forms.

[26] Case C-376/98 *Germany v Parliament and Council* [2000] ECR I-8419, para 83.

[27] Case C-380/03 *Germany v Parliament and Council* [2006] ECR I-11573; Case C-58/08 *Vodafone* [2010] ECR I-4999; C-398/13 *Inuit* EU:C:2015:535; Case C-358/14 *Poland v Parliament and Council*

finding of disparities between national rules is not sufficient to justify recourse to Article 114. It is, however, otherwise where 'there are differences between the laws, regulations or administrative provisions of the Member States which are such as to obstruct the fundamental freedoms and thus have a direct effect on the functioning of the internal market'.[28] So, in the *Product Safety* ruling, the Court reasoned that Article 114 TFEU 'must be interpreted as encompassing the Council's power to lay down measures relating to a specific product or class of products and, if necessary, individual measures concerning those products'.[29] Subsequently, in *Swedish Match* the Court said that the notion of 'measures for the approximation' in Article 114 could require all the Member States to 'authorise the marketing of the product or products concerned, subjecting such an obligation of authorisation to certain conditions, or even provisionally or definitively prohibiting the marketing of a product or products'.[30] In the *Food Supplements* case, for example, it was held that the current Article 114 TFEU authorizes even *preventive* intervention, such as

> when there are obstacles to trade, or it is likely that such obstacles will emerge in the future, because the Member States have taken, or are about to take, divergent measures with respect to a product or a class of products, which bring about different levels of protection and thereby prevent the product or products concerned from moving freely within the Community.[31]

As mentioned above, the relevant Union institutions are bound, in the exercise of their legislative (and administrative) powers in the internal market, not only by the principle of conferral, but also by further general principles of law, such as the principles of proportionality and subsidiarity.[32] Subsidiarity has, however, not, in fact, played a significant role in this area. With respect to the principle of proportionality,[33] the Union legislature has also been accorded a 'broad discretion' in the context of the adoption of measures based on Article 114 TFEU,[34] with the possibility of such measures being called into question only where 'manifestly inappropriate having regard to the objective which the competent institution is seeking to pursue'.[35]

EU:C:2016:323. For further exploration of the Court's jurisprudence under Art 114 TFEU, see C Barnard, *The Substantive Law of the EU* (n 3) 557–610; Maletić, *The Law and Policy of Harmonisation in Europe's Internal Market* (n 21).

[28] Joined Cases C-154/04 and C-155/04 *Alliance for Natural Health* [2005] ECR I-6451, para 28.

[29] Case C-359/92 *Germany v Council* [1994] ECR I-3681, para 37, concerning Directive 92/59 on general product safety [1992] OJ L228/24, which has subsequently been replaced by Directive 2001/95 on general product safety [2002] OJ L11/4.

[30] Case C-210/03 *Swedish Match* [2004] ECR I-11893, para 34 (emphasis added).

[31] Joined Cases C-154/04 and C-155/04 *Alliance for Natural Health* (n 28), para 32.

[32] Art 5(1) TEU. Further to Art 5(2) TEU 'Under the principle of conferral, the Union shall act only within the limits of the competences conferred upon it by the Member States in the Treaties to attain the objectives set out therein. Competences not conferred upon the Union in the Treaties remain with the Member States'.

[33] Pursuant to Art 5(4) TEU 'Under the principle of proportionality, the content and form of Union action shall not exceed what is necessary to achieve the objectives of the Treaties. The institutions of the Union shall apply the principle of proportionality as laid down in the Protocol on the application of the principles of subsidiarity and proportionality'.

[34] Case C-491/01 *BAT* [2002] ECR I-11453, para 123.   [35] ibid para 123.

2 Internal market administrative structure development through Article 114 TFEU

The broad interpretation of the enabling competence conferred by Article 114 TFEU also has extensive implications for the administrative law of the internal market, the development of which has been greatly influenced by the substantive reading of that Treaty provision. Indeed, the jurisprudence concerning Article 114 reveals the deployment of this legal basis for 'the creation of the Union's own administrative infrastructure'.[36] This can be seen most clearly in the context of the *Smoke Flavourings* case,[37] where the Court recognized that harmonization can be done in a variety of ways, including in stages such as 'the fixing of a number of essential criteria set out in a basic regulation followed by scientific evaluation of the substances concerned and the adoption of a positive list of substances authorised throughout the Community'.[38] Such successive, delegated harmonization is subject to satisfying two conditions: first, the 'legislature must determine in the basic act the essential elements of the harmonising measure in question'; and, secondly, 'the mechanism for implementing those elements must be designed in such a way that it leads to a harmonisation' within the meaning of what is now Article 114 TFEU.[39] The Court reasoned that this 'is the case where the Community legislature establishes the detailed rules for making decisions at each stage of such an authorization procedure, and determines and circumscribes precisely the powers of the Commission as the body which has to take the final decision'.[40]

This flexible approach to what can be delivered using the powers in Article 114 TFEU can be seen in *ENISA*,[41] which represented a further step in the construction of an administrative framework for the internal market. There the United Kingdom sought the annulment of a regulation, adopted on the basis of what is now Article 114 TFEU, establishing the European Network and Information Security Agency (ENISA). The UK contested the choice of legal basis, arguing that Article 114 TFEU entailed only the power to harmonize national laws, and not to set up Union bodies and confer tasks upon them. The Court adopted the position that the

> legislature may deem it necessary to provide for the establishment of a Community body responsible for contributing to the implementation of a process of harmonisation in situations where, in order to facilitate the uniform implementation and application of acts based on that provision, the adoption of non-binding supporting and framework measures seems appropriate.[42]

The Court emphasized, however, that 'the tasks conferred on such a body must be closely linked to the subject matter of the acts approximating the laws, regulations

---

[36] R Schütze, *European Union Law* (Cambridge University Press, 2015) 328.
[37] Case C-66/04 *United Kingdom v Parliament and Council* [2005] ECR I-10553, para 45.
[38] ibid para 47.   [39] ibid para 48–49.
[40] ibid para 49, with the Court proceeding to clarify that this 'applies in particular where the harmonisation in question consists in drawing up a list of products authorised throughout the Community to the exclusion of all other products'.
[41] Case C-217/04 *United Kingdom v Parliament and Council (ENISA)* [2006] ECR I-3771.
[42] ibid para 44.

and administrative provisions of the Member States': in the Court's view '[s]uch is the case in particular where the Community body thus established provides services to national authorities and/or operators which affect the homogenous implementation of harmonising instruments and which are likely to facilitate their application'.[43]

The significance of ENISA, in particular, lies in the fact that, as Hofmann points out, the new(ish) Treaty provisions on delegation of powers, set out in Articles 290 and 291 TFEU, favour delegation to the Commission. The provisions make no reference to agencies as possible recipients of delegation.[44] This issue was addressed directly in the *Short-selling ban* case,[45] which arose in the aftermath of the financial crisis, where the UK sought annulment of a provision in a regulation on short selling and certain aspects of credit-default swaps. The challenge focused on certain intervention powers conferred on the European Securities and Markets Authority (ESMA), established as part of the European System of Financial Supervision, entrusted with the oversight of the Union's financial system. The UK objected, in particular, to the degree of discretion conferred on ESMA, arguing that this contravened the principles on delegation of powers as established in *Meroni*;[46] that the delegation enabled ESMA to adopt quasi-legislative measures of general application, contrary to the principles established in *Romano*;[47] that the delegation of powers was incompatible with Articles 290 and 291 TFEU; and that Article 114 TFEU was not an acceptable choice of legal basis for the contested provisions.

Consistent with the earlier case law, the Court was unmoved and dismissed the claim. It found that the EU legislature, in its choice of method of harmonization, could delegate to a Union body, office, or agency powers for the implementation of the harmonization sought, particularly 'where the measures to be adopted are dependent on specific professional and technical expertise and the ability of such a body to respond swiftly and appropriately'.[48] The Court, recalling its *ENISA* ruling, to the effect that 'nothing in the wording of Article 114 TFEU implies that the addressees of the measures adopted by the EU legislature on the basis of that provision can only be Member States',[49] was satisfied that 'faced with serious threats to the orderly functioning and integrity of the financial markets or the stability of the financial system in the EU', the EU legislature had sought 'to provide an appropriate mechanism which would enable, as a last resort and in very specific circumstances, measures to be adopted throughout the EU which may take the form, where necessary, of decisions directed at certain participants in those markets'.[50]

---

[43] ibid para 45.
[44] Hofmann, 'General Principles of EU Law and EU Administrative Law' (n 1) 201.
[45] C-270/12 *United Kingdom v Parliament and Council (Short-selling ban)* EU:C:2014:18.
[46] Case 9/56 *Meroni v High Authority* [1957–1958] ECR 133.
[47] Case 98/90 *Romano* [1981] ECR 1241.
[48] Case C-270/12 *United Kingdom v Parliament and Council (Short-selling ban)* (n 45) para 105.
[49] C-270/12 *United Kingdom v Parliament and Council (Short-selling ban)* (n 45) para 107; Case C-217/04 *United Kingdom v Parliament and Council (ENISA)* (n 41) para 44.
[50] C-270/12 *United Kingdom v Parliament and Council (Short-selling ban)* (n 45) para 108.

D Other Types of Rule-making

Alongside the immediate significance of Article 114 TFEU for the development of the internal market administrative structure, 'rule-making' governing this area can take several forms, including decentralized administrative enforcement, as well as a range of further techniques that have evolved through regulatory experimentation over time.

1 Decentralized administrative enforcement

Even in the absence of harmonization in the application of the free movement rules,[51] there may be an indirect approximation of standards in the internal market through reliance on decentralized administrative enforcement. By virtue of the principle of mutual recognition, subject to possible, objective justifications, host state administrators must be open, where products have been lawfully placed on the market, to home state regulation. The Mutual Recognition Regulation, Regulation 764/2008,[52] sets out the rights and obligations for public authorities and enterprises purporting to market their products in another Member State. The 'philosophy of the Regulation' has been described as:

> 'the twofold approach of combining transparency and efficiency: transparency of information to be exchanged between enterprises and national authorities, efficiency by avoiding any duplication of checks and testing' with the 'preventive dialogue established between enterprises and administrations' taking 'full advantage of the instruments for preventing and for amicably and effectively settling problems of free movement'.[53]

The Commission has argued that the Mutual Recognition Regulation 'has been crucial in transferring the burden of proof that products are lawfully marketed elsewhere from economic operators to national authorities'.[54] It has also suggested, however, that

> national regulations and practices continue to create barriers [since] [n]ational authorities often require specific proof of lawful marketing or simply refuse access to their national market [and] [e]conomic operators are often required to produce specific documentation or carry out additional tests for their products [so that] [t]his increases the costs for economic operators or discourages them from expanding to new markets.[55]

---

[51] Case 120/78 *Cassis de Dijon* (n 3).

[52] Regulation 764/2008 laying down procedures relating to the application of certain national technical rules to products lawfully marketed in another Member State (Mutual Recognition Regulation) [2008] OJ L218/21, repealing Decision 3052/95 establishing a procedure for the exchange of information on national measures derogating from the principle of the free movement of goods within the Community [1995] OJ L321/1.

[53] Commission Communication, First Report on the application of Regulation 764/2008, COM(2012) 292, para 2.2.

[54] Commission Communication, Upgrading the Single Market: more opportunities for people and business, COM(2015) 550, para 4.3.

[55] ibid.

The Commission has suggested the need to 'revise the Mutual Recognition Regulation to address administrative fragmentation and streamline the documentation required to prove that a product is being marketed lawfully in a Member State'.[56] In addition, while the mutual recognition principle is capable of obviating the need for detailed rules, due to the inherent limitations of the principle, it has long been recognized that harmonization may still be required.[57] Indeed, the Commission has acknowledged that

> mutual recognition in general and the application of the Regulation in particular, cannot always offer a solution for ensuring the free movement of goods in the single market [and that therefore] [h]armonisation remains one of the most effective instruments, both for economic operators and for the national administrations.[58]

2 The 'New Approach' to product regulation

The perceived shortcomings of available harmonization techniques for the internal market have, over time, prompted the search for additional variations in regulatory possibilities. The 'New Approach'[59] to harmonization of product requirements, seeking swifter harmonization, sets out general principles rather than more elaborate rules, relying on private standard-setting bodies to define voluntary standards. Harmonization under the relevant legislation is confined to the essential safety requirements with which products must conform in order to be placed on the market. Specialized European Standardisation Organisations (ESOs)—the European Committee for Standardisation (CEN), the European Committee for Electrotechnical Standardisation (CENELEC), and the European Telecommunications Standards Institute (ETSI)—are all entrusted with drawing up the technical specifications for products through standards that meet the relevant essential requirements.[60] Compliance with the standards is of a voluntary nature, in the sense that market players may either conform with those standards, or follow different standards but proving that the latter meet the essential requirements (although cost efficiencies may present strong incentives for compliance with those set by the organizations mentioned).

Compliance with prescribed requirements results in the presumption that the product concerned may circulate in the market. Member States are given the task of enforcement, including through market surveillance mechanisms, so as to ensure the suppression or withdrawal of non-conforming products from the market. The General Product Liability Directive[61] 'is intended to ensure a high level of product safety throughout the EU for consumer products that are not covered by sector-specific EU harmonisation legislation' and 'also complements the provisions of sector legislation in

---

[56] ibid.

[57] Report from the Commission to the Council, the European Parliament and the Economic and Social Committee—Second biennial Report on the Application of the Principle of Mutual Recognition in the Single Market, COM(2002) 419.

[58] Commission Communication, First Report on the application of Regulation 764/2008 (n 53) para 6.

[59] The New Approach legislative technique was approved on 7 May 1985 by the Council of Ministers in its Resolution on a new approach to technical harmonisation and standards [1985] OJ C136/1.

[60] See further Regulation 1025/2012 on European standardisation [2012] OJ L316/12.

[61] Directive 2001/95 on general product safety [2002] OJ L11/4.

some aspects'.[62] This directive also contains market surveillance provisions, including through the Rapid Alert System RAPEX on notifications, and through the rapid exchange of information for dangerous non-food products[63] between the Member States and the Commission.[64]

A 'New Legislative Framework' was adopted in July 2008, building on the New Approach, with elements relating to effective conformity assessment, accreditation, and market surveillance. Alongside the Mutual Recognition Regulation 764/2008, examined above, key components of the New Legislative Framework include Regulation 765/2008,[65] setting out the requirements for accreditation and market surveillance relating to the marketing of products, and Decision 768/2008,[66] on a common framework for the marketing of products to allow greater coherence across sectoral legislation, including future harmonizing legislation.

While the new approach has obviated the need for much detailed legislation on the Union level, the 'New Approach' also entails certain implementational difficulties. Thus, the 'Blue Guide' on the implementation of EU products rules, notes, for example, that:

> [s]ince the New Approach calls for common essential requirements to be made mandatory by legislation, this approach is appropriate only where it is possible to distinguish between essential requirements and technical specifications. Further, as the scope of such legislation is risk-related, the wide range of products covered has to be sufficiently homogeneous for common essential requirements to be applicable. The product area or hazards also have to be suitable for standardisation.[67]

Standard-setting techniques have furthermore been questioned in terms of stakeholder participation and consensus, as well as the ability to adapt sufficiently rapidly to evolving market priorities.[68]

As will be seen further below, the approach also poses enforcement challenges: whilst arguably

> technical harmonisation has created a single market, where products move over national borders, market surveillance is carried out on a national basis, [demanding] [a]dministrative cooperation mechanisms between national surveillance authorities [in order to] increase the efficiency of surveillance, to minimise the effect of different surveillance practices and to reduce the overlapping of national surveillance operations.[69]

---

[62] Commission Notice, The 'Blue Guide' on the implementation of EU products rules 2016/C 272/1 at 12.

[63] In the case of medical devices, a specific vigilance system applies. See Commission Notice, The 'Blue Guide' on the implementation of EU products rules (n 62) 117.

[64] The Rapid Alert System has been extended by Regulation 765/2008 (see below).

[65] Regulation 765/2008 setting out the requirements for accreditation and market surveillance relating to the marketing of products and repealing Regulation 339/93 [2008] OJ L218/30.

[66] Decision No 768/2008/EC of the European Parliament and of the Council on a common framework for the marketing of products, and repealing Council Decision 93/465/EEC [2008] OJ L218/82.

[67] Commission Notice, The 'Blue Guide' on the implementation of EU products rules (n 62) 8.

[68] Commission Communication, A strategic vision for European standards: Moving forward to enhance and accelerate the sustainable growth of the European economy by 2020, COM(2011) 311.

[69] Commission Notice, The 'Blue Guide' on the implementation of EU products rules (n 62) 112.

3 Experimentation with other techniques

The search for more flexible harmonisation, technical expertise, swiftness, and adaptability has led, alongside the new-approach directives, to experimentation with a range of regulatory techniques within the internal market, such as 'reflexive harmonisation', the open method of coordination (OMC), and the Lamfalussy process,[70] involving a blend of (public and private) actors at the national and EU level. Whilst each of the techniques has, at least to some extent, been exposed to critique, with perceived shortcomings often seen as including issues of public engagement, democratic input, representation, transparency, accountability, access, and success of outcome, they reveal close interdependence of the multiplicity of actors and administrative coordination necessary in the context of internal market integration. Such integration may not always take place at a comparable speed across all Member States. Thus, the Treaty recognizes the possibility, under specified circumstances, for a group of Member States to engage in enhanced cooperation where this is not attainable by all members of the Union as a whole.[71]

E Enforcement and Supervision

1 Administrative enforcement of the EU internal market

Having rules is one thing, getting them observed is another. Here again we see the interplay between national and Union authorities. This means, however, that—just as with other administrative functions—administrative enforcement of EU law is similarly fragmented, requiring wide-ranging action, including on the level of the Union, Member State and private level.

Enforcement may be carried out by the Commission through its use of the Article 258 TFEU infringement procedure. Infringement proceedings may not only be commenced for incorrect implementation, but also for failure by national administrations to apply the relevant national transposition measures correctly. The possibility to bring infringement proceedings also extends to unjustifiable breaches of Articles 34 and 35 TFEU. However, the Commission has emphasized its reliance, in the first instance, on informal problem-solving devices. Where 'these problem-solving efforts are not successful, the Commission may start a formal infringement procedure', with the possibility of a continued Member State failure to comply being pursued before the Court of Justice and, as a 'final step', financial penalties being 'proposed when a Member State fails to implement a Court

---

[70] For further discussion of such regulatory techniques see C Barnard, *The Substantive Law of the EU* (n 3) 557–610.

[71] Art 20 TEU and Articles 326–334 TFEU. The decision authorizing enhanced cooperation must be adopted by the Council as a last resort and enhanced cooperation must involve at least nine Member States. In addition, enhanced cooperation must aim to further the objectives of the Union, comply with the Treaties and Union law and must not undermine the internal market. For an example of its use see the proceedings relating to the Unitary Patent in Joined Cases C-274/11 and C-295/11 *Spain and Italy v Council of the European Union* ECLI:EU:C:2013:240.

judgement or to communicate the transposition measures of a legislative directive to the Commission'.[72]

Private enforcement before the national courts (possibly backed by state liability in damages) constitutes another key aspect of internal market compliance. The Commission has recognized that preliminary rulings under Article 267 TFEU may present the Court with the possibility to

> address conformity issues of national laws in regard of EU legislation [and that even though] preliminary rulings are distinct from infringement judgments, this gives the Commission an additional opportunity to ensure that violations of Union law deriving from national legislation or its application are remedied [with the Commission] systematically following-up on Court's preliminary rulings where the Court identified non-conformities of national legislations.[73]

As can be seen from the discussion above regarding deployment of Article 114 TFEU for decision-making in the context of the internal market, the Courts (along with, to a certain degree, the national parliaments through the ex ante subsidiarity mechanism) will also have an important role, not only in the monitoring of the boundaries of the administrative scope of product regulation, but also the administrative structure available for this purpose.[74]

Nevertheless, it has been recognized that the 'high number of infringement procedures in 2015 shows that ensuring timely and correct application of EU legislation in the Member States remains a serious challenge'.[75] The Commission has noted that '[i]n mid-2015, around 1090 infringement proceedings were pending in the area of the Single Market' and that '[o]n average, national administrations, with the help of the Commission, need almost 30 months to resolve an infringement proceeding'.[76] On 28 October 2015, the European Commission presented a new Single Market Strategy, as part of which, highlighting the importance of '[e]ffective compliance' and the difficulty of attaining this objective in the internal market, it has sought to promote 'a smart enforcement strategy'.[77] As the Commission has stated,

> [m]onitoring and enhancing the application of EU law [therefore remains] a priority [, with monitoring outcomes feeding into] evaluations of the law, into impact assessments of new initiatives and, more generally, into the legislative life cycle [, in order] to improve the implementation and enforcement of existing legislation as well as the quality of new legislation.[78]

---

[72] Commission Report, Monitoring the application of European Union law, 2015 Annual Report, COM(2016) 463, pt I.

[73] ibid pt III.

[74] For consideration of potential challenges in the review of administrative activities and procedures see H C H Hofmann, 'The Court of Justice of the European Union and the European Administrative Space' in M W Bauer and J Trondal (eds), *The European Administrative System* (Palgrave 2014); A H Türk, 'Oversight of Administrative Rule-making: Judicial Review' (2013) 19(1) *European Law Journal* 126.

[75] Commission Report, Monitoring the application of European Union law, 2015 Annual Report (n 72) pt III.

[76] Commission Communication, Upgrading the Single Market (n 54) para 4.1.   [77] ibid.

[78] Commission Report, Monitoring the application of European Union law, 2015 Annual Report (n 72) pt I.

2 Supervision and control of, and within, the internal market

However, enforcement is not just conducted by the standard actors (the Commission under Article 258 TFEU, or private parties through the national courts via actions involving rulings under Article 267 TFEU). Supervision and control of, and within, the internal market occurs through enforcement and supervisory arrangements involving a multitude of actors. Nevertheless, such supervision has not been without difficulties.

Administrative supervision constitutes a key type of supervision and control within product regulation. Alongside the possibility for infringement proceedings examined above, the SOLVIT initiative purports to facilitate through administrative co-operation redress for, broadly, improper application of the internal market rules.[79] Moreover, there may be additional control functions and rules for supervision conducted within specialist structures and organizations of the internal market sector itself, e.g., within agencies.

More generally, the 'proper application of Union law depends on a smooth administrative cooperation to ensure uniform and efficient enforcement of Union legislation in all Member States'.[80] As we saw above, the New Legislative Framework has sought to deal with challenges presented by the decentralized administration of certification, with the possible 'irony that minimising the harmonisation of products is only possible by increasing the harmonisation of the procedure'.[81]

In a similar vein, as seen above, it has been noted that, whilst 'technical harmonisation has created a single market, where products move over national borders, market surveillance is carried out on a national basis'.[82] Thus, '[a]dministrative co-operation calls for mutual trust and transparency between national surveillance authorities'.[83] The Commission has highlighted the perceived underlying challenges to market surveillance, suggesting that '[m]any economic operators disregard the rules either through lack of knowledge or intentionally to gain a competitive advantage' and that 'the responsible market surveillance authorities are often underfunded and constrained by national boundaries, while economic operators are active at European or even global level'.[84] Accordingly, the Commission has suggested the need 'to strengthen product compliance by providing the right incentives to economic operators, intensifying compliance checks and promoting closer cross-border cooperation among enforcement authorities, including through cooperation with customs authorities' and to 'consolidate the existing framework for market surveillance activities'.[85]

Administrative supervision within the internal market will often (but not always) be of an anticipatory nature, particularly with the intent of minimizing disruption

---

[79] Commission Communication, Effective Problem Solving in the Internal Market (SOLVIT), COM(2001) 702; Commission Recommendation on principles for using SOLVIT—the Internal Market Problem Solving Network [2001] OJ L331/79.

[80] Commission Notice, The 'Blue Guide' on the implementation of EU products rules (n 62) 112.

[81] D Chalmers, G Davies, and G Monti, *European Union Law* (3rd edn, Cambridge University Press 2014) 692.

[82] Commission Notice, The 'Blue Guide' on the implementation of EU products rules (n 62) 112.

[83] ibid.   [84] Commission Communication, Upgrading the Single Market (n 54) para 4.3.

[85] ibid.

of trade. This, though, does not obviate the need for subsequent judicial control. The Commission, commenting on the Mutual Recognition Regulation, has suggested that, in view of its 'directly enforceable' nature,

> any decision to which it applies should specify the remedies available so that an economic operator can bring proceedings before the competent national court or tribunal [, with the result that] the matters regarding the correct application of the Regulation in concrete situations, while not precluding any possible Commission's action, should be dealt with by the competent national bodies.[86]

Again, it has been lamented that

> inadequate application of mutual recognition makes it harder for companies seeking access to markets in other Member States [and] the increasing presence on the market of products that are not compliant with EU rules puts law-abiding operators at a disadvantage and endangers consumers [so that] [d]espite the high degree of market integration in the area of goods, this leads to lost opportunities for the economy at large.[87]

In this sense, the CJEU retains an important function in supervising mutual recognition and the policing of decentralized enforcement in the context of the rules on the free movement of goods, including in particular the interpretation of Articles 34–36 TFEU and the determination of the acceptability of national justifications for restrictions on trade.

F Concluding Remarks

As has been seen throughout, the specific role and interaction of Union and Member State institutions and bodies, as well as that of private parties, international organizations, and third countries, has not been without challenges, either in the administrative responsibilities for product regulation or the administrative enforcement thereof. The administrative law and practice in the internal market sector reveals a multiplicity of techniques and a plethora of often decentralized structures, resulting in a somewhat fragmented character of administrative integration across the internal market.

Yet the specific legal problems affecting the administration of product regulation as an individual policy area, may be of wider significance. Thus, it has, for example, been suggested with regard to the development of administrative cooperation mechanisms between national surveillance authorities, that

> [c]ooperation between market surveillance authorities can also spread good surveillance practice and techniques across the Union, as it allows national authorities to compare their methods with those of other authorities, for example in the framework of comparisons and joint surveys or study visits [and that] cooperation can be useful for exchanging views and solving practical problems.[88]

---

[86] Commission Communication, First Report on the application of Regulation 764/2008 (n 53) para 5.
[87] Commission Communication, Upgrading the Single Market (n 54) para 4.3.
[88] Commission Notice, The 'Blue Guide' on the implementation of EU products rules (n 62) 112.

Furthermore, the sector-specific administrative structures, bodies, competences, procedures, forms of action, and controls in the internal market are influenced by, and themselves influence, generally applicable EU administrative law. This can be readily seen when analysing the impetus of Article 114 TFEU, whose far-reaching substantive interpretation is not only of import for the internal market, but also for European Union administrative law more widely.

At the same time, the

> trend to new governance has undoubtedly been influenced by developments in the fields of public administration and law, [with elements of new governance practices] in domestic administrative law and public administrative practice [where it has been observed that] there has been a growing recognition of the limits of traditional top-down regulatory approaches, and repeated calls for things like power sharing, participation, management by objectives, and experimentation.[89]

Thus, examination of the administration of product regulation reveals a level of mutual influence upon, and relevance to, general European Union administrative law, and indeed Union public law in a broader sense.

---

[89] J Scott and D Trubek, 'Mind the Gap: Law and New Governance in the EU' (2002) 8 *European Law Journal* 1, describing 'new governance' as covering 'a number of very disparate mechanisms each of which has its own particular history' where '[m]ost, if not all, have emerged as pragmatic forms of accommodation between emerging needs of the Union and available mechanisms for policy-making'.

12

Transport Policy and Trans-European Networks

Roland Bieber

A Introduction

Transport is one of the foundations of modern society; it is a precondition of a functioning economy and an important economic factor in itself. Transport, by definition, vanquishes space, and hence borders. On the other hand, transport has social implications, and gives rise to secondary effects and to risks in respect of the environment and people's health. For these and additional strategic reasons, public intervention at national level, on the basis of national criteria and preferences, has a long tradition in the field. Moreover, the notion of transport covers in practice the very wide range of modes: road, inland waterway, rail, sea, and air, with many variations and combinations.

Those factors explain the initial difficulties of bringing into effect a truly 'common' transport policy as provided for by Title VI ('Transport', Article 90 TFEU). In order to implement that policy, the Treaty entrusts extensive legislative powers to the European Parliament and the Council and grants certain administrative functions to the European Commission. The task of contributing to the 'establishment and development' of transnational networks is entrusted to the Union by Article 170 TFEU, providing to that end mainly administrative instruments.

Only after a landmark 1985 decision of the ECJ,[1] and under pressure at the same time to complete the internal market, did the Union legislature feel compelled to enact the necessary measures, initially to ensure the freedom to provide transport services, but increasingly to deal with questions of safety, security, technical harmonization, and the setting up and improvement of infrastructures of transnational interest. At present, over a hundred pieces of European legislation are applicable in the field.[2] This legislation has become increasingly diverse and detailed in recent years. It has generated complex implementation mechanisms, providing to that end new means of action (e.g., binding and non-binding 'guidelines'), provided for the intervention of numerous committees and agencies at European level, required Member States to set up new bodies at national level, and established cooperation among them in the form of 'networks'.

Implementation of the Treaties, and of the legislation based upon them, is a task conferred upon the Member States and the Union either explicitly, in the corresponding

---

[1] Case 13/83 *European Parliament v Council* ECLI:EU:C:1985:220.
[2] See list in Appendix I. For a detailed presentation of European transport law see Roland Bieber and Francesco Maiani, *Europäisches Verkehrsrecht* (Nomos 2015).

Treaty provisions, or in accordance with general rules, namely Articles 290 and 291 TFEU. Moreover, in the areas of transport and trans-European networks, the Union has to share legislative competence with the Member States.[3] Hence, in this field national authorities have simultaneously to implement European law and national provisions, which continue to apply so long as no European law has been passed on a specific matter.

A full presentation of the multiple facets of the administrative implementation of current European transport law is not possible within the confines of this chapter. Each sub-topic has therefore been addressed by reference to indicative examples only.

B Administrative Tasks within the Transport Sector of the EU

Administrative tasks in the field of transport arise either from the general monitoring powers entrusted to the Commission (Article 17(1) TEU) or from specific transport-related provisions on the monitoring of Member States' action, in particular as concerns the prohibitions spelled out in Title VI TFEU. Further administrative tasks arise directly from Article 171(2) TFEU, providing for coordination measures to be undertaken by the Commission in respect of trans-European networks. Monitoring and coordination and are discussed here together (1 below). Considerably more diverse tasks result from legislation based on the relevant provisions of the TFEU (section 2 below).

1 Monitoring and coordination

Administrative tasks explicitly mentioned by the Treaties in the area of transport are entrusted to the Union in Articles 93, 95, 96, and 97 TFEU. They concern supervisory functions to be exercised by the Commission in respect of state aid, and of the prohibitions of discrimination and protective measures. Further tasks result from Article 92 TFEU, prohibiting new national discrimination against carriers of other Member States.[4] Administrative tasks are also foreseen in Article 171(2) TFEU, relating to coordination among Member States concerning the establishment and development of trans-European networks, and empowering the Commission to 'take any useful initiative to promote such coordination'.

2 Administrative tasks resulting from legislation

The transport policy of the EU is subject to the aims listed in Article 3(3) TEU, namely the establishment of the internal market. Its main elements represent a special case of the more general rules on the freedom to provide services (Articles 56–62 TFEU), free

---

[3] Art 4 TFEU: 'The Union and the Member States may legislate and adopt legally binding acts in that area. The Member States shall exercise their competence to the extent that the Union has not exercised its competence'.

[4] See eg ECJ Case C-195/90 *Commission v Germany*, ECLI:EU:C:1992:219 (Road tax for heavy goods vehicles).

movement of goods (Articles 34–37 TFEU) and approximation of laws (Articles 114–117 TFEU). Union transport policy increasingly extends, however, to areas outside the internal market (e.g. transport safety, protection of the environment, competition policy, statistics, external relations).

The freedom to provide services specifically in the field of transport does not, as such, follow from the wording of the Treaty. Those Treaty provisions do not have 'direct effect'. They require first and foremost the adoption of legislation and its implementation, before an individual can rely on them.[5] The legislature is required to ('shall') extend freedom to provide services to the transport sector pursuant to Article 91(1)(a) and (2), in so far as such an extension relates to

- common rules applicable to international transport to or from the territory of a Member State or passing across the territory of one or more Member States (a)
- the conditions under which non-resident carriers may operate transport services within a Member State ('cabotage') (b).

The legislature is furthermore empowered to adopt:

- 'measures to improve transport safety' (c) and
- 'any other appropriate provisions' (d).

An extraordinarily large margin of discretion for the EU legislature, as far as the definition of the substance of the transport policy is concerned, results from the last-mentioned category in Article 91(1)(d) TFEU. Such discretion is, however, limited by the result to be achieved ('common transport policy', Article 90 TFEU).

The provisions on trans-European networks (Articles 170 to 172 TFEU) were introduced only in 1993, aimed at the coordination and promotion of the interconnection and interoperability of national networks.[6] The main task of the Union here consists in the establishment of (binding) 'guidelines' covering the objectives, priorities, the broad contours of measures, and identifying projects of common interest. The Union can also take steps in the field of technical standardization, finance specific projects, and provide feasibility studies, loan guarantees, and interest rate subsidies (Article 171(1) TFEU).

In 2017, approximately 120 acts were in force relating to transport and infrastructure, based directly on Treaty provisions. Fifty of these concerned the approximation of technical requirements, safety, and security. Their implementation requires particularly intensive administrative action. This factor alone explains why secondary legislation in the transport sector under Article 291(2) TFEU systematically confers administrative tasks on the Commission, acting alongside or jointly with the Member States. Those tasks concern, inter alia, the uniform implementation of technical provisions, monitoring of national legislation, and the adoption of individual acts. Moreover, administrative tasks result from delegation of powers to the Commission in accordance with Article 290 TFEU and consist of the adoption of delegated acts

---

[5] ECJ Case 13/83 *European Parliament v Council* ECLI:EU:C:1985:220, paras 62, 63.
[6] This Title in the TFEU is not exclusively devoted to transport but concerns telecommunications and energy as well (Art 170(1) TFEU).

aimed at supplementing or amending non-essential elements of legislation. Most of those acts concern amendments to technical provisions which are set out in the annex to the act in question.

A characteristic pattern in respect of administrative functions in this area emerges from Regulation 165/2014 on tachographs in road transport.[7] This sets out requirements in relation to the construction, installation, use, testing, and control of tachographs used in road transport. Whereas Member States are responsible for the general implementation of the various technical requirements, the Commission

- is mandated to adopt certain acts of *direct administration* in so far as it is given the 'the authority and responsibility' to supervise a single laboratory which issues 'interoperability certificates' to the manufacturers (Article 12(3))
- has to adopt detailed provisions assuring uniform application by way of '*implementing acts*'[8]
- is given the task of *publishing certain information* concerning the competent national authorities and approved fitters and workshops (Articles 12(2) and 24(5))
- is also obliged to *monitor* the issuing of 'driver cards' by the competent authorities of the Member States (Article 26(4)) and
- is to *report* its findings every two years to the European Parliament and to the Council.

According to Article 42 of this Regulation, the Commission, when adopting implementing acts, is to be assisted by a committee within the meaning of Regulation (EU) 182/2011.

Following the same pattern, many acts in the field of transport have been based on Article 114 TFEU (approximation of laws).[9]

C Sources of Administrative Law in the Sector Concerned

1 Primary sources

The primary sources of administrative law in the field of transport and infrastructure are Articles 92, 93, 95, 97, 99, and 171(2) TFEU. Those provisions either impose obligations on carriers not to discriminate on grounds of the country of origin or of destination (Article 95) or impose limits on Member States' autonomy in respect of state aid (Article 93), discrimination against carriers of other Member States (Article 92), discriminatory rates and conditions imposed on transport operations (Article 96) and charges or dues in respect of the crossing of frontiers (Article 97).

In all cases the Commission has the task of securing compliance with the obligations in question. Whilst Article 92 and 93 do not provide for a specific procedure for their implementation, thus implying the applicability of the general supervisory

---

[7] [2014] OJ L60/1.
[8] See eg Arts 11(1), 12(7), 14, 21(3), 31(5), and 39(3) of Regulation 165/2014.
[9] See eg Regulation 167/2013 on the approval and market surveillance of agricultural and forestry vehicles [2013] OJ L60/1.

functions to be exercised by the Commission, Articles 95(3) and (4) and 97[10] lay down details of the administrative procedure to be followed for ensuring compliance. Articles 95(4) and 96(2) establish a special procedure for the adoption of the implementing legislation.[11] Moreover, Article 99 provides for the establishment of an 'Advisory Committee' to be attached to the Commission. Although formally constituted, this committee has not met for more than 30 years. A large number of active specialized committees has, however, been created on the basis of secondary legislation.[12] Administrative activities concerning the coordination of Member States' policies concerning trans-European networks can be undertaken by the Commission (Article 171(2) TFEU).

2 Secondary law

By far the largest part of administrative law in the area of transport and infrastructure results from legislation adopted pursuant to Articles 91, 114, and 171 TFEU. A separate category of administrative law arises in the context of international agreements and from the activities of international organizations in which the Union participates either directly or indirectly through its Member States.

According to its subject matter, the most important legislation can be grouped in eleven specific categories (numbered here in accordance with the more complete list of legislation provided in Appendix I), comprising rules on:

- access to the occupation of transport operator (freedom of establishment, recognition of diplomas) (i)
- access to the market (freedom to provide services) (ii)
- transport rates and fares (iii)
- access to infrastructure, infrastructure costs (iv)
- passenger rights (v)
- approximation of technical requirements, safety and security, insurance (vi)
- social provisions (vii)
- competition and fiscal matters (viii)
- measures concerning infrastructure and conditions and procedures for establishing and promoting projects of common interest (trans-European networks) (ix)
- establishment of specialized agencies and other bodies (x)
- external relations (xi).

---

[10] Art 97 TFEU has also lost its significance, since border controls of transport by road and internal waterways were abolished by Regulations Nos 1100/2008 [2008] OJ L304/63 and 3912/92 [1992] OJ L395/6.

[11] See Regulation 11 [1960] OJ 52/1121, as amended by Regulation 569/2008 [2008] OJ 161/1.

[12] See section E.

A twelfth group (miscellaneous) contains acts which do not fall within any of those specific categories.

D Sectoral Organization, Institutions, and Structures

In the area of transport and infrastructure, the implementation of the above-mentioned legislation has first and foremost to be carried out by the Member States (1). Most acts provide, however, for additional intervention on the part of the institutions of the European Union (2). Certain specific administrative tasks are carried out on the Union level by specialized agencies under the control of the Commission (3). Moreover, the Commission frequently has to act in accordance with a specific procedure involving the participation of specialized committees (4) and/or is assisted by advisory bodies (5).

1 National bodies

Under normal circumstances Member States implement EU legislation autonomously. However, the European Commission and the European Court of Justice supervise the conformity of implementation with primary and secondary Union law, in particular with the particular act in question. In most cases, Member States rely in their implementation on their own existing institutions. Depending on the nature of the specific implementing measure, and according to the rules and structures internal to the jurisdiction concerned, the competent national authority may be the national (or possibly regional) Parliament, the competent ministry (in most cases ministry of transport and/or of infrastructure), governmental bodies at regional level and/or independent agencies. For purposes of implementation, European legislation may require in certain cases the creation of new institutions on national level (e.g., '[e]ach Member State shall establish a single national regulatory body for the railway sector'[13] or '[e]ach Member State shall designate a body responsible for the enforcement of this Regulation'[14]).

Cooperation between the various bodies is also expressly provided for in certain cases. According to the Directive establishing a single European railway area, the regulatory bodies of the different Member States 'shall participate and work together in a *network* that convenes at regular intervals. The Commission shall be a member, shall coordinate and support the work of the network, and make recommendations to the network, as appropriate. It shall ensure active cooperation of the appropriate regulatory bodies'.[15]

---

[13] See Art 55(1) of Directive 2012/34 establishing a single European railway area [2012] OJ L343/32.

[14] See Art 16(1) of Regulation 261/2004 establishing common rules on compensation and assistance to passengers in the event of denied boarding and of cancellation or long delay of flights [2004] OJ L46/1. A list of national enforcement bodies has been published by the Commission http://ec.europa.eu/transport/themes/passengers/air/doc/2004_261_national_enforcement_bodies.pdf. On the limits of their tasks see ECJ Joined Cases C-145/15 and C-146/15 *Ruijssenaars* [2015] OJ C198/22; ECLI:EU:C:2016:12.

[15] See Art 57(1) Directive 2012/34 (n 13).

2 EU institutions

The central role in the implementation of transport policy on the level of the Union is performed by the European Commission and by EU agencies. The European Parliament and the Council are, however, also closely involved in the process of implementation when the Commission is entrusted with the task of adopting 'delegated acts' in accordance with Article 290 TFEU. Other measures require regular reporting by the Commission to those two institutions.

The scope and intensity of the Commission's intervention vary considerably. Only very few acts do not mention the Commission at all or only as the recipient of information provided by Member States. In such cases, the Commission is limited to exercising its general supervisory functions (Article 17(1) TEU).[16] Other acts provide merely for consultation.[17] Those two categories represent, however, only a small fraction of the totality of measures in the transport field. In the vast majority of cases, the Commission is given the additional tasks of adopting specific implementing measures and delegated acts, of scrutinizing Member States' implementation, of collecting and distributing information in the field in question, of promoting the exchange of information among Member States, and of evaluating the outcomes of any particular measure. Examples of acts which provide for particularly intensive administrative activity on the Commission's part are Regulation 549/2004 laying down the framework for the creation of the single European sky,[18] the connected air navigation services under Regulation 550/2004,[19] and Directive 2012/34 establishing a single European railway area.[20] Within the Commission, the DG 'Mobility and Transport' (MOVE) is in charge of preparing and managing the institutions' activities in the transport and infrastructure sector.

The Union's legislative arm is also involved. The European Parliament has set up a 'Transport and Tourism' committee.[21] Moreover, it can make use of its right of inquiry and has, to that end, set up a special Committee of Inquiry (Article 226 TFEU).[22] The Council meets in the configuration 'Transport, Telecommunications and Energy'.[23] Assistance to this configuration is provided by Directorate-General E 'Environment, Education, Transport and Energy', part of the Council's General Secretariat. The Council has in addition set up a certain number of specialized preparatory bodies, for example, 'Working Party on Land Transport', 'Shipping Working Party', 'Working Party on Transport Intermodal Questions and Networks', and 'Aviation Working Party'.[24]

---

[16] See eg Arts 6(1) and 7(2) of Directive 89/629 on the limitation of noise emission from civil subsonic jet aeroplanes [1989] OJ L363/27.

[17] See eg 'The Member States and the Commission shall consult each other …'; see Art 1 of Decision 77/587 setting up a consultation procedure on relations between Member States and third countries in shipping matters and on action relating to such matters in international organizations [1977] OJ L239/23.

[18] [2004] OJ L96/1, as amended by Regulation 1070/2009 [2009] OJ L300/34.

[19] [2004] OJ L96/10, as amended by Regulation 1070/2009 [2009] OJ L300/34.

[20] [2012] OJ L343/32.   [21] EP Rules of Procedure, Annex VII, as amended on 15 January 2014.

[22] See eg Decision 2016/34 on setting up a Committee of Inquiry into emission measurements in the automotive sector [2016] OJ L10/13.

[23] Council Rules of Procedure, Annex I [2009] OJ L325/36.

[24] For a list of Council preparatory bodies see http://data.consilium.europa.eu/doc/document/ST-10356-2015-INIT/en/pdf.

The work of the consultative body, the European Economic and Social Committee (Article 13(4) TEU), is supported in the transport field by its Commission 'Transport, Energy, Infrastructure and Information Society (TEN)'. In addition, the consultative Committee of the Regions (Article 13(4) TEU), has established a Commission for Territorial Cohesion Policy and EU Budget (COTER) for the preparation of discussions in the plenary on transport.

3 Agencies

Three specialized agencies have been established by legislative acts:

- European Aviation Safety Agency (EASA)
- European Maritime Safety Agency (EMSA)
- European Railway Agency (ERA).

These have, in their respective fields, been entrusted with administrative tasks which require a high degree of expert knowledge. They perform important functions at the interface between national administrations and the European Commission, thus blurring any imagined dichotomy between national and common implementation. A fourth agency, the Innovation and Networks Executive Agency (INEA), was established in 2013 by the Commission pursuant to Regulation 58/2003,[25] laying down the statute for executive agencies.

(a) *The European Aviation Safety Agency (EASA)*

The EASA is a Union body with separate legal personality, independent as regards technical matters and with legal, administrative, and financial autonomy.[26] It is represented by its executive director, appointed by the management board. The board, composed of one representative of each Member State and one from the Commission, takes its decisions by a two-thirds majority of its members, each having one vote.[27] Its main task consists of developing expertise in all aspects of civil aviation safety and environmental protection. It assists the Commission in the preparation of pertinent legislation, and the Member States and industry in its implementation. It is empowered to issue certification specifications and guidance material, to make technical findings, and to issue certificates. It assists the Commission in monitoring the application of Regulation 2018/1139 and its implementing rules. In addition, the Agency may adopt single-case acts relating to the operation of aircraft, the qualification of crew, or the safety of third-country aircraft.

---

[25] [2003] OJ L11/1.
[26] Regulation 2018/1139 [2018] OJ L 212/1.
[27] Arts 28, 34, and 37 Regulation 216/2008.

(b) *The European Maritime Safety Agency (EMSA)*

The EMSA[28] is constructed identically to the EASA, having the comparable autonomy and structure. However, there are, together with the representatives of the Member States, four representatives of the Commission, together with four professionals from the sectors most concerned, nominated by the Commission but not having the right to vote. It takes its decisions by a two-thirds majority of its voting members.[29] Its activities concern maritime safety, maritime security, and prevention of, and response to, pollution caused by ships, as well as response to marine pollution caused by oil and gas installations. To that end, the Agency assists the Commission, works with Member States, facilitates cooperation between the Member States and the Commission and, at the request of the Commission, provides technical assistance to third countries. The Agency carries out visits to Member States in order to assess the effective implementation of relevant Union law, and to recognized organizations for ship inspection and survey purposes. Moreover, the Agency provides, upon request, relevant positioning data and Earth observation data on vessels flying the flag of Member States, both to competent national authorities and to Union bodies, such as Frontex and Europol, to facilitate prevention of intentional unlawful acts.

(c) *European Union Agency for Railways (ERA)*

Again, status, structure, and decision-making resemble closely the two preceding bodies, but here there are two representatives of the Commission, together with six other non-voting members representing, on the European level, railway undertakings, infrastructure providers, railway industry worker unions, passengers, and freight customers. Decisions are reached by simple majority vote.[30]

The Agency's main tasks are to contribute to the further development and effective functioning of a single European railway area by guaranteeing a high level of railway safety and interoperability, while improving the competitive position of the railway sector.[31] In particular, the Agency is to contribute to the implementation of Union legislation in technical matters by developing a common approach to safety on the Union rail system and by enhancing its level of interoperability (Article 2 Regulation 2016/796). It addresses recommendations and opinions to the Commission and to Member State authorities, issues guidelines and technical documents, and adopts specific administrative measures. The Agency issues authorizations for the placing of railway vehicles on the market (Article 20) and keeps inter alia a European Vehicle Register in accordance with Article 47 of Directive 2016/797 (Article 37 of Regulation 2016/796). The Agency also carries out a technical examination of new national rules submitted to the Commission in accordance with Article 8 of the Railway Safety Directive 2016/798.

---

[28] Regulation 1406/2002 [2002] OJ L208/1, as amended by Regulation 2016/1625 [2016] OJ L251/77.
[29] Arts 5, 10, 11, and 14 Regulation 1406/2002.   [30] Arts 46, 47, and 50 Regulation 2016/796.
[31] Regulation 2016/796 [2016] OJ L138/1.

The Agency is also required to establish a *network with the national authorities* responsible for safety, and for the investigations provided for by the Railway Safety Directive in order to define the content of 'common safety indicators' (i.e., technical standards) and to collect relevant data on railway safety. More generally, the Agency is to 'form an essential tool of dialogue, consultation and exchange between all the actors in the railway sector'.[32] On the basis of the common safety indicators, national reports on safety and accidents, and its own information, the Agency submits a publicized report on safety performance at regular intervals. The detailed tasks of the Agency are set out in mandates given by the Commission.[33]

(d) Innovation and Networks Executive Agency (INEA)

The INEA carries out implementing tasks which have been entrusted to the Commission but which, for reasons of efficiency, have been 'outsourced'. In contrast to the previously listed Agencies, the INEA's activities remain entirely under the aegis of the European Commission.[34] As an executive agency pursuant to Regulation 58/2003,[35] it is a body of the European Union, under the control and responsibility of the Commission, albeit with separate legal personality. It is managed by a Steering Committee and a Director. The Steering Committee consists of five members, all appointed by the Commission (Articles 4, 7, and 8).

The most important task of this executive agency consists of the management of the 'Connecting Europe Facility'.[36] In accordance with specific delegations conferred by the Commission, this task involves programme implementation, implementation of technical projects, the adoption of the instruments of budget execution for revenue and expenditure, and the carrying out of all the operations necessary for the management of the programme (Article 3).

4 Specialized Committees

Most implementing acts provide for the intervention, alongside the European Commission, of specialized committees, composed of one representative of each Member State and presided over by a Commission representative. Most of their members are experts in their respective fields. Pursuant to Article 291(3) TFEU, those committees perform the task of controlling, on behalf of the Member States, the Commission's exercise of implementing powers. In accordance with Regulation

---

[32] Recital 7 Regulation 881/2004.

[33] See Commission Decisions of 13 July 2007 and 29 April 2010, Documents C(2007) 3371 and C(2010) 2576 concerning a mandate to the European Railway Agency to develop and review Technical Specifications for Interoperability (TSIs). This mandate was given pursuant to Art 6(1) of Directive 2008/57 [2008] OJ L191/1: ('Draft TSIs and subsequent draft amendments to TSIs shall be drafted by the Agency under a mandate from the Commission'). Subsequently, the Agency submitted Recommendations concerning interoperability to the Commission, which transposed them into Regulations 1299/2014–1305/2014 [2014] OJ L356/1, 179, 228, 394, 421, and 438.

[34] Commission Decision 2013/801 [2013] OJ L352/65, implemented by Commission Decision C(2013) 9235, as amended by Decision C(2015) 2256 (not published in the OJ).

[35] [2003] OJ L11/1.   [36] Regulation 1316/2013 [2013] OJ L348/129.

182/2011[37] laying down the rules and general principles concerning the mechanisms for control of the exercise of those powers, the committees perform either an advisory function or a function of examination, the choice between the two being made within the legislative act in question. A third category of control, the 'regulatory procedure with scrutiny', applies temporarily to certain committees pursuant to Article 5a of the 1999 Comitology Decision (as amended in 2006)[38] (for details see section F below).

The Commission's 2015 Report on the Working of the Committees mentions 30 committees for this sector.[39] The total number in transport matters is, however, greater, because other committees deal with matters of transport as well, despite having been set up on a non-transport-related legal basis (e.g., the Climate Change Committee,[40] which acts in the field of transport as well; similarly, the European Statistical System Committee deals inter alia with transport statistics[41]). Some such committees exercise control functions only with regard to the implementation of a single legal act, others are referred to in several acts, the most frequently mentioned being the Committee on Safe Seas and Prevention of Pollution from Ships (COSS), which acts pursuant to 25 Regulations or Directives.[42]

A specific form of committee is provided for in several international agreements between the Union (and the Member States) and third states. Those 'mixed committees' consist of an equal number of representatives of the contracting parties. They perform administrative tasks as well. In contrast to the committees which act entirely within the framework of the European Union, they act autonomously, in accordance with the provisions of agreement in question. For example, the Community/Switzerland Inland Transport Committee monitors and applies the provisions of the corresponding agreement, and adopts, among other things, measures aimed at safeguarding its proper functioning.[43] Situated at the outer limits of EU law is the European Committee for Drawing up Standards in the field of Inland Navigation (CESNI), established by the Central Commission for Navigation on the Rhine (CCNR),[44] an organization separate from the European Union.[45] CESNI is composed of experts representing Member States of the CCNR and of the EU, and has adopted a standard concerning technical requirements for inland waterway vessels. That standard is mandatory within the framework of the application of the Revised Convention for Rhine

---

[37] [2011] OJ L55/13.

[38] [1999] OJ L184/23, as amended by Council Decision of 17 July 2006 [2006] OJ L200/11.

[39] Commission Report COM(2016) 772 of 5 December 2016.

[40] Established by Decision 280/2004, referred to in in Regulation 443/2009 setting emission performance standards for new passenger cars [2009] OJ L140/1 and in Regulation 510/2011 setting emission performance standards for new light commercial vehicles [2011] OJ L145/1.

[41] Established by Regulation 223/2009 [2009] OJ L87/164, in respect of transport referred to in Regulations 70/2012; 91/2003; 437/2003; 1365/2006; 1172/98; Directive 2009/42.

[42] Regulation 2099/2002 [2002] OJ L324/1 as amended by Regulation 2016/103 (2016) OJ L21/67.

[43] See Art 51 of the Agreement between the European Community and the Swiss Confederation on the Carriage of Goods and Passengers by Rail and Road of 1999 [2002] OJ L114/91.

[44] Resolution CCNR 2015-I-3 of 3 June 2015 http://www.ccr-zkr.org/files/documents/resolutions/ccr2015_If.pdf (last accessed 11 July 2018).

[45] On the relationship between the European Union and the CCNR see Bieber and Maiani (n 2) 137–56.

Navigation, and is applicable within the European Union albeit indirectly.[46] A complete list of the various committees is provided in Appendix II.

5 Advisory bodies

Many *specialized advisory bodies* have been either set up in legislative acts or established by the Commission on its own initiative. Those bodies act under the auspices of the Commission. One example is the *Bodies Coordination Group*, composed of representatives of national bodies responsible for carrying out assessments of conformity or suitability in regard to interoperability in railway transport.[47] Another example is the *Tachograph Forum* whose task it is to support dialogue on technical matters concerning tachographs. It is composed of delegates of the Member States and is open to participation by experts from interested third countries. Stakeholders, representatives of vehicle manufacturers, tachograph manufacturers, social partners, and the European Data Protection Supervisor are invited to attend its meetings.[48] A specific advisory body has been established by the Agreement between the European Community and the Swiss Confederation on the Carriage of Goods and Passengers by Rail and Road of 21 June 1999, the *Observatory for the monitoring of road, rail and combined traffic in the Alpine region*.[49] Presently, 52 advisory groups are active in the transport and infrastructure sector[50] (listed in *Appendix III*).

E Administrative Procedures within the Sector

The procedures for adopting implementing measures in the field of transport do not differ fundamentally from procedures in other areas of EU law. Primary law (1) refers in most cases to the ordinary legislative procedure (i.e., Article 294 TFEU), albeit with additional requirements concerning consultation, whilst secondary legislation (2) provides in general for implementation by Member States without imposing procedural requirements (Article 291(1) TFEU). In addition, most acts of secondary legislation envisage intervention on the part of the Commission (Article 291(2) TFEU), in some cases acting autonomously, or on a proposal from an agency,[51] in most cases in conjunction with committees[52] (in accordance with the general procedure laid down in Regulation 182/2011[53] and Decision 2006/512).[54] Some acts of implementation have to be adopted by agencies acting autonomously. According to the specific act of legislation, delegated acts supplementing or amending it have to be adopted by the Commission pursuant to one of the procedures listed in Article 290(2) TFEU.

---

[46] See Council Decision 2015/2176 [2015] OJ L307/25 and the corresponding explanatory memorandum from the Commission, COM(2015) 549 of 27 October 2015.

[47] Art 28, Directive 2008/57 on the interoperability of the rail system within the Community [2008] OJ L191/1.

[48] Art 43, Regulation 165/2014 on tachographs in road transport [2014] OJ L60/1.

[49] [2002] OJ L114/91.

[50] European Commission, Register of Expert Groups and Other Similar Entities' http://ec.europa.eu/transparency/regexpert/index.cfm?do=search.result (last consulted on 30 March 2017).

[51] *supra E, iv).*   [52] *supra E, v).*   [53] [2011] OJ L55/13.   [54] [2006] OJ L200/11.

1 Primary law

Legislation in the field of transport provided for by Articles 91(1) and 100(2) TFEU has to be adopted in accordance with the ordinary legislative procedure, but with the specific feature of prior mandatory consultation of the Economic and Social Committee and the Committee of the Regions. The same procedure applies to the adoption of acts concerning trans-European networks (Article 172 TFEU). This latter provision requires, however, the approval of the Member State concerned, if guidelines or projects of common interest relate to its territory.

Equally, approximation of laws concerning the *functioning* of the internal market in the field of transport is effected in accordance with the ordinary legislative procedure (Article 114 TFEU). In this case, only consultation of the Economic and Social Committee is required. In the exceptional case of Article 115 TFEU (approximation of national laws that *directly affect* the establishment or functioning of the internal market), a special legislative procedure applies. It provides for a unanimous decision of the Council, together with consultation of the European Parliament and the Economic and Social Committee.

Special procedures have to be followed for implementation of the prohibition of discrimination as regards transport rates and conditions (Article 95(1) TFEU). Those procedures have to be laid down by the Council, on a proposal from the Commission and after consulting the European Parliament and the Economic and Social Committee (Article 95(3) TFEU). Regulation 11, which was adopted on this basis, provides for scrutiny by the Member States of compliance of carriers with the prohibition, and simultaneously empowers the Commission to carry out verification on the spot and to impose fines in case of breach.[55]

Individual implementing acts may be adopted by the Commission in respect of the prohibition of rates and conditions involving any element of support or protection in the interest of undertakings or industries (Article 96(2) TFEU). Such acts can be adopted either on the Commission's own initiative or on application by a Member State. Moreover, the Commission may make 'recommendations' relating to 'charges or dues in respect of the crossing of frontiers which are charged by a carrier in addition to the transport rates' (Article 97 TFEU).[56]

2 Secondary legislation

Procedures for the implementation of secondary legislation in the field of transport and infrastructure within the framework of Article 291(2) TFEU vary over the many legislative acts. Some complex acts provide simultaneously for implementation according to several procedures and/or imply the participation of different actors. Six categories of procedure (one of which has four sub-categories) can be distinguished. Moreover, the procedure for the adoption of delegated acts pursuant to Article 290(2) TFEU is frequently referred to:

---

[55] (1960) OJ 52, 1121, as amended by Regulation 569/2008 [2008] OJ L161/1.
[56] This Article has lost practical significance.

(i) Implementation *solely by the Commission* (with or without the voluntary con-sultation of Member States and/or experts), for example, Regulation 3577/92 applying the principle of freedom to provide services to maritime transport within Member States (maritime cabotage),[57] Article 5.

(ii) Implementation with committee participation:

- *advisory committee procedure* (Article 4, Regulation 182/2011), for example Regulation 391/2009 on common rules and standards for ship inspections and survey organizations,[58] Articles 6 and 12(2);

- *examination procedure* (Article 5, Regulation 182/2011), for example, Regulation 376/2014 on the reporting, analysis and follow-up of occurrences in civil aviation,[59] Articles 4(5), 7(7), 8(4) and 19(2);

- cumulative application of *advisory committee and examination procedure* (Articles 4 and 5 of Regulation 182/2011), for example, Regulation 551/2004 on the organization and use of the airspace in the single European sky (the Airspace Regulation),[60] Article 6(7); and

- *regulatory procedure with scrutiny* (Article 5a, Decision 2006/512[61]), for example, Regulation 725/2004 on enhancing ship and port facility security,[62] Articles 10 (2), (3) and 11(4), (5).

iii) Implementation by the Commission on a proposal by, or in other forms of *cooperation with, an agency*, for example, Regulation 1371/2007 on rail passen-gers' rights and obligations (intervention by the European Railway Agency),[63] Article 10(3).

iv) Implementation by an *agency* without any intervention on the part of the Commission, for example, Regulation 2018/1139 on common rules in the field of civil aviation and establishing a European Aviation Safety Agency,[64] Articles 79–90.

v) Implementation by an *executive agency*, for example, entrusting the *Innovation and Networks Executive Agency* with implementation of parts of the Union programme, 'Connecting Europe Facility'. To that end an 'instrument of dele-gation' was issued by the Commission, establishing the detailed tasks of the agency and the procedures to be followed for their accomplishment.[65]

vi) Adoption of *delegated acts* in accordance with Article 290(2) TFEU empowering the Commission (following the procedure specified there, involving the EP

---

[57] [1992] OJ L364/7, as amended by the 2012 Accession Treaty [2012] OJ L112/21, 74.

[58] [2009] OJ L131/11, as amended by Regulation 1355/2014 [2014] OJ L365/82.

[59] [2014] OJ L122/18.

[60] [2004] OJ L96/20, as amended by Regulation 1070/2009 [2009] OJ L300/34.

[61] Council Decision amending Decision 1999/468 laying down the procedures for the exercise of implementing powers conferred on the Commission, OJ 2006, L200/11 (Article 5a is still applicable in 2018).

[62] [2004] OJ L129/6, as amended by Regulation 219/2009 [2009] OJ L87/109, 148.

[63] [2007] OJ L315/14.   [64] [2008] OJ L79/1, as amended by Regulation 2016/4 [2016] OJ L3/1.

[65] See Annex I to Commission Document C(2013) 9235 (not published but referred to in Art 7 (3) of Decision 2013/801 [2013] OJ L352/65).

and the Council, under which one of the two may revoke the delegation and/or object to the entry into force of the act envisaged), for example, Directive 2012/34 establishing a single European railway area,[66] Article 60 (containing both possible limits, applicable under certain conditions). Under the terms of Article 290 TFEU, the participation of national experts is not required within this procedure. Recent legislation stresses, however, that '[i]t is of particular importance that the Commission carry out consultations with experts, including Member States' experts, during the preparation of such delegated acts'.[67]

F Legal Rules Governing the Substance of Sector-specific Decision-making

Implementation of the TFEU provisions on transport and trans-European networks is governed by a particular combination of non-discretionary and discretionary action on the part of the Union institutions and Member States. In so far as the freedom to provide the service of transport is concerned, implementation of the Treaty imposes an unconditional obligation on the EU legislature to adopt the measures mentioned in Article 91(1)(a) and (b) TFEU (conditions under which non-resident carriers may operate transport services within a Member State, and under which international transport to or from the territory of a Member State, or across the territory of one or more Member State, takes place).[68] In this connection no discretion exists. As far as general transport policy is concerned, and in particular with regard to the aims mentioned in Article 91(1)(c) and (d), a large margin of discretion is, however, available for its implementation (see, in particular, the terms of (d): adoption of 'any other appropriate provisions').[69]

The discretion both of the EU institutions and the Member States in matters of transport is, however, restricted by several specific or general qualifications. The adoption of implementing measures at Union level is made subject to two conditions, mentioned in Article 91(1) and (2) respectively: the taking into account of 'the distinctive features of transport'; and taking into account 'cases where their application might seriously affect the standard of living and level of employment in certain regions, and the operation of transport facilities'. Those conditions can be seen as an expression of the intention, on the one hand, to consider transport policy as part

---

[66] [2012] OJ L343/32.

[67] See Art 8(2), (3) of Directive 2014/90 on marine equipment [2014] OJ L257/146. See also Art 6(11), (12) of Directive 2014/94 on the deployment of alternative fuels infrastructure [2014] OJ L307/1:

> In the 'Common Understanding on Delegated Acts', attached to the *Interinstitutional Agreement on Better Regulation* of 2016, the Commission 'commits to gathering, prior to the adoption of delegated acts, all necessary expertise including through the consultation of experts from the Member States and through public consultations'. COM(2015) 216.

[68] ECJ, Case 13/83 *European Parliament v Council* ECLI:EU:C:1985:220, paras 62, 65.

[69] ibid para 78: '[t]hey belong to the class of accompanying measures which may be adopted in addition to the requisite measures for liberalization and their adoption lies *within the discretion* of the Council' (emphasis added).

of the internal market (which, according to Article 119(1) TFEU, is to be conducted 'in accordance with the principle of an open market economy with free competition') and, on the other hand, to protect certain prevailing values (e.g., protection of 'services of general economic interest' (Article 14 TFEU)). Accordingly, Articles 93 and 94 TFEU establish specific qualifications as regards implementation in the field of transport. Furthermore, the exercise of discretionary powers in this area has to take into account the horizontal clauses of Articles 7–17 TFEU. Of particular importance in this respect is the obligation to integrate environmental protection requirements in the definition and implementation of a policy. The TFEU also imposes restrictions on Member States concerning their implementation of transport policy (Article 92, 95: prohibition of discrimination; Article 96 prohibition of protective measures).

As regards trans-European networks and the contribution of the Union to their establishment and development, Article 171(1) TFEU obliges the Union 'to establish … guidelines' and to 'implement any measures', which 'shall take into account the potential economic viability of the projects'. The EU institutions enjoy, however, wide discretion in regard to choices in policy substance. Moreover, the power 'to support projects of common interest' can be exercised fully within their discretion, subject to the limits resulting from general principles of EU law.

A similar combination of *discretionary* and *non-discretionary* powers exists at the level of *secondary legislation*. This observation applies to implementation both by the *Member States* and by the *Union*. Frequently all four variations for implementation can be found within one act, for example, Regulation 551/2004 on the organization and use of the airspace in the single European sky (Airspace Regulation):[70] in certain cases of implementation by Member States the Regulation provides for *no discretion* (Articles 6(6), 7(1)), in others it provides for *discretion* (Articles 1(3), 8). Similarly, when implementation by European Commission is foreseen, Articles 3a, 4, 6(2), (4) establish *no discretion*, whilst Article 6(3) establishes *discretion*.

G Abstract General Administrative Acts and Measures within the Sector Concerned

1 Agenda setting and framework measures

According to the terms of the TFEU, the common transport policy pursuant to Article 91 is to be implemented by *common rules* (Article 91(1)(a); *conditions* (Article 91(1) b), *measures* (Article 91(1)(c), *appropriate provisions* (Article 91(1)(d)). Moreover, the Treaty empowers the Commission to take *decisions* (Article 95(4), 96(2)) and *recommendations* (Article 97 TFEU). In the field of trans-European networks, the Union is given the power to establish *guidelines* and *measures* (Article 171(1)). The prevailing legal forms for rendering those abstract notions operational in the field of transport are the acts mentioned in Article 288 TFEU (*regulations, directives,* and, less

---

[70] [2004] OJ L96/20, as amended by Regulation 1070/2009 [2009] OJ L300/34.

frequently, *decisions* and *recommendations*). Binding programmes are adopted in one of the above-mentioned forms (regulations or decisions).[71]

Agenda setting is effected either in the form of binding mandates given to the Commission in legislative acts, or in the form of non-binding statements made by one of the institutions. An example of the former is Regulation 168/2013 on the approval and market surveillance of two- or three-wheel vehicles and quadricycles. Article 23 of that Regulation mandates the Commission 'to carry out a comprehensive environmental effect study'. On the basis of the findings of that study, the Commission has to present to the European Parliament and the Council a report and 'make any appropriate legislative proposals'.[72] Among the non-binding measures for agenda setting, the most important are issued by the Commission in the form of 'Communications'[73] and 'White Papers'.[74] They are systematically commented upon by the European Parliament in the form of 'resolutions'.[75] For the programming of future implementing measures, the Council occasionally adopts 'resolutions'[76] and 'conclusions'.[77]

2 Subordinate legislation

In the various sectors of transport, large competences have been bestowed on the Commission for the making of delegated and implementing acts of non-typical, albeit binding, form, an example of which is Regulation 300/2008 (aviation security)[78]: Article 4 of that Regulation governs the adoption, amendment and implementation of mandatory *basic standards* for safeguarding civil aviation against acts of unlawful interference that jeopardize the security of civil aviation. To that end, *Common Basic Standards* are laid down in the Annex to the Regulation. Moreover, where necessary, *Additional Common Basic Standards,* not provided for when the regulation entered into force, need to be added to the Annex in accordance with the ordinary legislative procedure. Both are supplemented by general measures, designed to amend non-essential elements thereof, to be adopted in accordance with the regulatory procedure with scrutiny (Article 5a, Decision 2006/512) (Article 19(3)). Detailed measures for the implementation of the Common Basic Standards and general measures have to be laid down in accordance with the *examination procedure* (Article 5, Regulation 182/2011) (Article 19(2)).[79]

---

[71] See eg Regulation 1316/2013 establishing the Connecting Europe Facility [2013] OJ L348/129, as amended by Regulation 2017/2396 [2017] OJ L345/34.

[72] [2013] OJ L60/52.

[73] See eg Commission communication 'A sustainable future for transport: Towards an integrated, technology-led and user-friendly system', COM(2009) 0279.

[74] See eg White Paper 'Roadmap to a Single European Transport Area: Towards a competitive and re-source efficient transport system', COM[2011] 0144.

[75] See eg European Parliament Resolution of 6 July 2010 on a sustainable future for transport [2011] OJ CE315/13.

[76] See eg Council Resolutions of 14 February 2000 on the promotion of intermodality and intermodal freight transport and on the promotion of short sea shipping [2000] OJ C56/1, 3.

[77] See eg Council conclusions on developing the agenda for the Community's external aviation policy [2005] OJ C173/1.

[78] [2008] OJ L97/72, as amended by Regulation 18/2010 [2010] OJ L7/3.

[79] E.g Implementing Regulation 2015/1998 laying down detailed measures for the implementation of the common basic standards on aviation security [2015] OJ L299/1.

3 Administrative rule-making within the sector

Because of the detailed, and often very technical nature of many topics related to transport, implementation of abstract EU legislation frequently meets micro-obstacles at national level. An extension of the range of available instruments to include non-binding instruments is likely to enhance the flexibility of the implementation process. It is, therefore, not surprising that law-making in the field of transport has brought about, alongside the aforementioned legally binding instruments, several forms of non-binding measures to be issued by the Commission. They are aimed at 'promoting a harmonised application'[80] of the relevant provisions of a binding act. Most frequently (non-binding) *guidelines* are published in the legal form of *recommendations*.[81] Certain guidelines are very detailed and are, therefore, de facto binding. Occasionally, the form of the Commission's action is not specified in the relevant act ('The Commission may adopt guidelines and *other non-binding measures* to facilitate Member States' cooperation').[82]

Another form of non-binding act ('*common principles and practices*') is envisaged in recent directives which provide for the setting up of national 'regulatory bodies'. Such bodies are entrusted with the issuing of authorizations required by the directive for certain transport activities. The common principles and practices referred to are intended to facilitate the implementation of the directive.[83]

In the aviation sector the setting up of *performance targets* for the air traffic management network is provided for by Regulation 549/2004 (as amended by Regulation 1070/2009).[84] Those targets are not, as such, legally binding for the Member States. If, however, they are not met, the Commission 'may decide ... that the Member States concerned *shall take* corrective measures', thus rendering the targets de facto mandatory.

4 Rule-making by private parties

Three examples of rule-making by private parties can be mentioned here. They concern agreements between unions and employers in the field of air,[85] ship,[86] and

---

[80] See Art 21 (1), Regulation 561/2006 on the harmonisation of certain social legislation relating to road transport [2006] OJ L102/1, as amended by Regulation 165/2014 [2014] OJ L60/1 ('guidelines').

[81] See eg the respective 'guidelines' annexed to Recommendation 2010/378 on the assessment of defects during roadworthiness testing [2010] OJ L173/74 and to Recommendation 2010/379 on the risk assessment of deficiencies detected during technical roadside inspections (of commercial vehicles) [2010] OJ L173/97.

[82] Art 9, Directive 2010/40 on the framework for the deployment of Intelligent Transport Systems in the field of road transport and for interfaces with other modes of transport [2010] OJ L207/1.

[83] See eg Directive 2012/34 establishing a single European railway area [2012] OJ L343/32.

[84] Art 11(3), Regulation 549/2004 (as amended by Regulation 1070/2009) [2004] OJ L96/1; [2009] OJ L300/34.

[85] Directive 2000/79 concerning the European Agreement on the Organisation of Working Time of Mobile Workers in Civil Aviation [2000] OJ L302/57.

[86] Directive 1999/63 concerning the Agreement on the organisation of working time of seafarers concluded by the European Community Shipowners' Association (ECSA) and the Federation of Transport Workers' Unions in the European Union (FST), [1999] OJ L167/33.

railway[87] transport. They have been transposed into formal EU law pursuant to Article 155 TFEU.

H Single-case Administrative Acts and Measures within the Sector Concerned

1 Individual administrative decisions

The main elements of the common transport policy and of activities concerning trans-European networks, resulting from the corresponding provisions of the TFEU, require, first of all, activity on the part of the EU legislature. On the levels of both that Treaty and secondary legislation the adoption of single-case administrative acts is almost entirely a matter for the Member States. The few single-case acts provided for by the TFEU concern the exercise of supervisory functions by the Commission in the area of transport (Articles 92, 95(3), and 96(2)). If any of the prohibitions spelled out in those articles is breached by Member States, or by carriers (the latter in the case of Article 95(1) TFEU), the Commission 'shall take the necessary decisions'. As far as trans-European networks are concerned, the measures provided for in Article 171(1) comprise single cases (e.g. support of specific projects) or specific measures concerning the interoperability of networks.

Implementation of legislative acts adopted pursuant to Articles 91, 100, and 114 TFEU requires that individual administrative decisions be taken by the institutions of the Union (i.e., the Commission and/or an agency) only in exceptional cases. Examples are:

- Directive 2004/54 on minimum safety requirements for tunnels in the Trans-European Road Network:[88] the Commission may adopt a binding negative decision with regard to possible requests from national authorities for derogations in specific cases from the prescriptions of the Directive, Article 14(4), (5));

- Regulation 561/2006 on the harmonization of certain social legislation relating to road transport:[89] the Commission may, in specific cases, 'approve' or 'authorize' exemptions from the rules on driving times, breaks, and rest periods for drivers, Articles 13(3) and 14(1));

- Directive 2007/46 establishing a framework for the approval of motor vehicles and their trailers, and of systems, components and separate technical units intended for such vehicles:[90] the Commission may in specific cases authorize Member States to grant exemptions from the technical prescriptions of the Directive, Article 20(1), (4)).

---

[87] Directive 2005/47 on the Agreement between the Community of European Railways (CER) and the European Transport Workers' Federation (ETF) on certain aspects of the working conditions of mobile workers engaged in interoperable cross-border services in the railway sector [2005] OJ L195/15.

[88] [2004] OJ L167/39, as amended by Regulation 596/2009 [2009] OJ L188/14, 87.

[89] [2006] OJ L102/1, as amended by Regulation 165/2014 [2014] OJ L60/1.

[90] [2007] OJ L263/1, as amended by Regulation 2015/758 [2015] OJ L123/77.

In the above-mentioned cases, single-case decisions are addressed to a particular Member State.

In matters of aviation safety and of railway safety, single-case decisions may be addressed to individual persons. To this end Regulation 2018/1139[91] authorizes the European Aviation Safety Agency to issue and renew, for example, the certificates of pilot training organizations and of flight simulation training devices (Articles 76–78). Similarly, Directive 2016/798 on railway safety provides for issuing 'safety certificates' to railway undertakings by the European Union Agency for Railways (Article 10).

2 Administrative agreements

Cooperation between national regulatory bodies is provided for in several acts in the field of transport. For example, Regulation 2016/796 requests the Railway Agency to establish a network of the national safety authorities referred to in Article 16 of Directive (EU) 2016/798. The Agency shall provide the network with a secretariat (Article 38). Although such cooperation does not necessarily imply the conclusion of formal agreements, especially when the setting up of 'networks' is envisaged, it certainly has the potential for their adoption. For example, Article 57 of Directive 2012/34 (European railway area) provides for cooperation between national regulatory bodies 'for the purpose of coordinating their decision-making across the Union. For this purpose, they shall participate and work together in a network …'. Moreover '[r]egulatory bodies shall develop *common principles and practices* for making the decisions for which they are empowered under this Directive'.[92] Similarly, Article 15 of Directive 2006/126 on driving licences states: 'Member States shall assist one another in the implementation of this Directive and shall exchange information on the licences they have issued, exchanged, replaced, renewed or revoked. They shall use the *EU driving licence network* set up for these purposes, once this network is operational'.[93]

The potential for administrative agreements is inherent in Directive 2006/22 on minimum conditions for the implementation of Council Regulations 3820/85 and 3821/85, concerning social legislation relating to road transport activities.[94] The Directive expressly provides for the adoption of implementing measures which are aimed at promoting a *common approach* to the implementation of the Directive, at encouraging a coherence of approach between enforcement authorities and a harmonized interpretation of Regulation (EEC) 3820/85 between enforcement authorities and at facilitating dialogue between the transport sector and enforcement authorities.[95]

[91] Regulation 2018/1139 on common rules in the field of civil aviation and establishing a European Aviation Safety Agency [2018] OJ L 212/1.

[92] See Art 57(1), (8) of Directive 2012/34 establishing a single European railway area (n 85).

[93] [2006] OJ L403/18, as amended by Directive 2015/653 [2015] OJ L107/68. See also Regulation 1073/2009 [2009] OJ L300/88, Art 20: 'Member States shall assist one another in ensuring the application and monitoring of this Regulation. They shall exchange information via the national contact points established pursuant to Art 18 of Regulation (EC) 1071/2009'. On a failure to cooperate with the 'European driving licence network' cf ECJ case C– 665/15 (Commission/Portugal), ECLI:EU:C:2017:231.

[94] [2006] OJ L102/35, as amended by Directive 2009/5 [2009] OJ L29/45.

[95] See also Art 18, Regulation 1071/2009 establishing common rules concerning the conditions to be complied with to pursue the occupation of road transport operator [2009] OJ L300/72: 'Member States

I Administrative Enforcement of EU Sectoral Law

In the field of EU transport and infrastructure law there exists only one specific mechanism which provides for the administrative enforcement of a Treaty provision. It concerns the enforcement of the prohibition laid down in Article 95 TFEU (discrimination). Regulation 11 concerning the abolition of discrimination in transport rates and conditions[96] provides for enforcement by the Member States and empowers the Commission to send its officials or any experts on visits of inspection to check and supervise compliance with the obligations imposed on undertakings (Article 14). Moreover, the Commission may, in cases of discrimination within the meaning of Article 95(1) TFEU, impose on the carrier responsible a penalty not exceeding twenty times the carriage charge obtained or demanded (Article 18).

Secondary legislation only exceptionally provides for sanctions to be imposed by the Commission in case of non-compliance. One example is Article 84 of Regulation 2018/1139 on common rules in the field of civil aviation,[97] which empowers the Commission to impose fines on persons and undertakings where there is a breach of the provisions of the Regulation.

Hence, enforcement of EU legislation in this field is, as a general rule, framed by the national administrative law concerned. In order to promote compliance, however, several legislative acts in this area explicitly require Member States to adopt *sanctions* in case of breach. Examples are:

- Regulation 785/2004 on insurance requirements for air carriers and aircraft operators[98] (Article 8(1) and (4)): 'Member States shall ensure that air carriers and aircraft operators referred to in Article 2 comply with this Regulation'; 'Sanctions for infringement of this Regulation shall be effective, proportional and dissuasive'.

- Regulation 725/2004 on enhancing ship and port facility security (Article 9(3): 'Each Member State shall adopt a national programme for the implementation of this Regulation'; and 'Member States shall ensure that effective, proportionate and dissuasive sanctions for breaching the provisions of this Regulation are introduced' (Article 14). [99]

J Supervision and Control of, and within, the Sector Concerned

Supervisory functions in respect of the correct implementation and observance of the TFEU provisions on transport and of the corresponding EU legislation, and the underlying political choices, are exercised at the level both of the EU institutions and

---

shall designate a national contact point responsible for the exchange of information with the other Member States with regard to the application of this Regulation'.

[96] (1960) 1121, as amended by Regulation 569/2008 [2008] OJ L161/1.
[97] [2018] OJ L 212/1.
[98] [2004] OJ L138/1, as amended by Regulation 285/2010 [2010] OJ L87/19.
[99] [2004] OJ L129/6 (as amended by Regulation 219/2009 [2009] OJ L87/109.

of the Member States. In accordance with its general function 'to oversee the application of Union law' attributed by Article 17 TEU, the European Commission is the principal actor, undertaking, in effect, *administrative* supervision. Legislation has introduced mechanisms which increasingly provide for interaction between the national implementing authorities and the Commission, assisted in the field of sea, air and rail transport by one of the three agencies. In certain cases, the Commission or its agencies may check and supervise compliance with EU law by means of *investigations*[100] or *inspections*.[101] Administrative supervision of agencies themselves is bestowed on special bodies, composed of representatives of Member States and of the Commission. For example, pursuant to Article 51 of Regulation 2016/796 the activities of the Railway Agency are subject to an administrative supervision by the management board, established in accordance with Article 47 of that Regulation. The board is composed of representatives from the Member States and the Commission. Moreover, an appeal against decisions taken by the Agency may be brought before a board of appeal (Article 58 of Regulation 2016/796), probably still to be regarded as a component of administrative supervision, although one can observe a quasi-judicial character beginning to emerge.

The Commission is in turn subject to *political* supervision by the European Parliament and the Council, specifically in the framework of the procedure for delegated legislation pursuant to Article 290(2) TFEU. Legislation frequently provides for *ex ante* monitoring of acts of implementation by one of the specialized committees of the EP. It normally consists of a right to be *consulted*, but may also consist of a *power to approve or reject* a draft implementing act.[102] Ex post monitoring exists in various forms. The most frequently used instrument is mandatory *transparency* of implementation. To this end, many regulations and directives provide for duties of *reporting*[103] and for duties of *publication* of certain information relevant to the specific transport issue.[104] Those duties may have to be fulfilled by national authorities or by the Commission.

The 'Volkswagen case' furnishes a recent example of political control exercised by the European Parliament over the Commission and over national public and private actors. On 17 December 2015 the European Parliament decided to set up a Committee of Inquiry into emission measurements in the automotive sector pursuant to Article 226 TFEU.[105] The committee is mandated 'to investigate alleged contraventions and

---

[100] See eg Art 69(1) of Regulation 168/2013 [2013] OJ L60/52: Investigation by the Commission concerning the competence of technical services designated by national authorities for the purpose of implementation of the Regulation.

[101] See eg Art 3 of Regulation 1406/2002 establishing a European Maritime Safety Agency [2002] OJ L208/1, as amended by Regulation 100/2013 [2013] OJ L39/30.

[102] See section C2(v), (vi), and F(ii).

[103] See eg Reports by the Commission to be submitted to the European Parliament and the Council; Arts 10(2), 17, of Regulation 391/2009 [2009] OJ L131/11, as amended by Regulation 1355/2014 [2014] OJ L365/82.

[104] See eg (Special procedures for notification by Member States and of subsequent publication by the Commission): Art 43(1), (5) of Directive 2007/46 (OJ L263/1 (as amended by Regulation 2015/758) and Art 63 of Regulation 167/2013 [2013] OJ L60/1.

[105] Decision 2016/34 (2016) OJ L10/13. The report of the Committee is published as European Parliament document A8-0049/2017 of 2 March 2017.

maladministration in the application of Union law in relation to emission measurements in the automotive sector, without prejudice to the jurisdiction of national
or Union courts'. To that end, it will in particular investigate alleged failures of the
Commission and of the Member States' authorities to comply with obligations imposed by Regulation 715/2007 on type approval of motor vehicles with respect to
emissions from light passenger and commercial vehicles (Euro 5 and Euro 6), and on
access to vehicle repair and maintenance information.[106]

Supervisions via *judicial review* is of particular importance in the area of transport. It has given rise to some of the leading cases of Union law, for instance, *AETR*,[107]
'transport policy',[108] 'open skies agreements',[109] and *Intertanko*.[110] Up to 2017, more
than 150 decisions (including cases decided by the General Court) have been delivered by the Court in the field of transport law.[111] In the preliminary ruling procedure pursuant to Article 267 TFEU, the Court contributes to the interpretation of
the Treaty and of secondary law, and transport law provides no exception to this.
Examples of cases relating specifically to implementation issues are Cases C-627/10;
C-473/10, and C-483/10 concerning the implementation of Directive 2001/14 (railway
infrastructure);[112] Case C-150/11 concerning the implementation of Directive 1999/
37 (registration documents for road vehicles);[113] Case C-299/02 (freedom of establishment of shipowners);[114] and Case C-195/90 (road tax for heavy goods vehicles).[115] On
passenger rights, a rich stream of case-law is developing on the interpretation of secondary legislation, a recent example of the latter being Joined Cases C-145/15 and 146/
15 concerning the interpretation of the rules on national bodies responsible for the enforcement of Regulation 261/2004[116] on compensation and assistance to passengers in
the event of denied boarding, and of cancellation or long flight delay.[117]

K Conclusion

To date, the 'common transport policy', which, in accordance with Title VI TFEU, is
one of the many policy fields to be pursued by the European Union, has been one of
the most complex areas of EU legislation. On the one hand, this complexity results
from the fact that it does not consist of one harmonious set of rules but comprises rather provisions applicable to five different means of transport, each of which has specific economic and technical requirements. Moreover, any governance of transport
has to take into account a particularly large number of variables which include, apart

---

[106] [2007] OJ L171/1, as amended by Regulation 459/2012 [2012] OJ L142/16.
[107] Case 22/70 *Council v Commission* ECLI:EU:C:1971:32.
[108] Case 13/83 *European Parliament v Council* ECLI:EU:C:1985:220.
[109] Joined Cases C-466/98 *Commission v UK*, C-467/98 *Commission v Denmark* ECLI:EU:C:2002:624.
[110] Case C-308/06 *Intertanko* ECLI:EU:C:2008:312.
[111] A list of cases decided up to 2015 is published by Bieber and Maiani (n 2) 315.
[112] Cases C-627/10 *Commission v Slovenia* ECLI:EU:C:2012:793; C-473/10 *Commission v Hungary* ECLI:EU:C:2013:113; Case C-483/10 *Commission v Spain* ECLI:EU:C:2013:114.
[113] Case C-150/11 *Commission v Belgium* ECLI:EU:C:2012:539.
[114] Case C-299/02 *Commission v Netherlands* ECLI:EU:C:2004:620.
[115] Case C-195/90 *Commission v Germany* ECLI:EU:C:1992:219.   [116] [2004] OJ L46/1.
[117] Joined Cases C-145 and C-146/15 *Ruijssenaars* and *Jansen* ECLI:EU:C:2016:12.

from the establishment of the conditions for free movement of services and aspects of economic and regional policy, inter alia aspects of safety, security, social protection, environmental protection, and the harmonization of many detailed technical provisions.

This complex background has led to correspondingly complex legislation which, in turn, has generated complex forms of implementation, stimulating vertical and horizontal osmosis both between national bodies and between national and European bodies that goes beyond the binary model of isolated implementation by the Member States *or* the Union (which seems to have inspired the wording of Article 291 TFEU). We observe in fact an increasing role for *agencies*, the continuing activity of more than thirty committees which participate in the shaping of secondary law, and of an even higher number of advisory bodies, all of which are composed of national experts. Moreover, specially created national implementing bodies and their transnational co-operation through 'networks' of national bodies illustrate the trend of diversified implementation in this field. This evolution has not come to an end; rather is likely to intensify in the future.

APPENDIX I

List of secondary legislation in the field of transport and infrastructure

(Selected according to importance and to relevance for administrative law. Several acts of the following inventory cover more than one of the sub-headings. For the purpose of this overview, they are mentioned only once. Within each sub-heading the different means of transport are grouped together in the following order: road, rail, inland waterway, sea, air. Sources in footnotes are given without reference to sources for subsequent amendments)

(i) Access to the occupation of transport operator (freedom of establishment, recognition of diploma)

Regulation 1071/2009 establishing common rules concerning the conditions to be complied with to pursue the occupation of road transport operator[118]

Directive 87/540 on access to the occupation of carrier of goods by waterway in national and international transport and on the mutual recognition of diplomas, certificates and other evidence of formal qualifications for this occupation[119]

Directive 2012/34 establishing a single European railway area[120]

Regulation 1008/2008 on common rules for the operation of air services in the Community.[121]

(ii) Access to the market/freedom to provide services

Regulation 1072/2009 on common rules for access to the international road haulage market[122]

Regulation 1073/2009 on common rules for access to the international market for coach and bus services[123]

Regulation 3577/92 applying the principle of freedom to provide services to maritime transport within Member States (maritime cabotage)[124]

Regulation 4055/86 applying the principle of freedom to provide services to maritime transport between Member States and between Member States and third countries[125]

Directive 96/67 on access to the ground handling market at Community airports.[126]

(iii) Transport rates and fares

Regulation 4058/89 on the fixing of rates for the carriage of goods by road between Member States[127]

Directive 96/75 on the systems of chartering and pricing in national and international inland waterway transport in the Community[128]

Regulation 1370/2007 on public passenger transport services by rail and by road[129]

Regulation 11 concerning the abolition of discrimination in transport rates and conditions[130]

Regulation 4057/86 on unfair pricing practices in maritime transport.[131]

(iv) Access to infrastructure, infrastructure costs

Directive 1999/62 on the charging of heavy goods vehicles for the use of certain infrastructures[132]

Regulation 95/93 on common rules for the allocation of slots at Community airports[133]

Directive 2009/12 on airport charges.[134]

---

[118] [2009] OJ L300/51. [119] [1987] OJ L322/20. [120] [2012] OJ L343/32.
[121] [2008] OJ L293/3. [122] [2009] OJ L300/72. [123] [2009] OJ L300/88.
[124] [1992] OJ L364/7. [125] [1986] OJ L378/1. [126] [1996] OJ L272/36.
[127] [1989] OJ L390/1. [128] [1996] OJ L304/12. [129] [2007] OJ L315/1.
[130] [1960] OJ 52/1121. [131] [1986] OJ L378/14. [132] [1999] OJ L187/42.
[133] [1993] OJ L14/1. [134] [2009] OJ L70/11.

(v) Passenger rights

Regulation 181/2011 concerning the rights of passengers in bus and coach transport[135]

Regulation 1177/2010 concerning the rights of passengers when travelling by sea and inland waterway[136]

Regulation 1371/2007 on rail passengers' rights and obligations[137]

Regulation 392/2009 on the liability of carriers of passengers by sea in the event of accidents[138]

Regulation 2027/97 on air carrier liability in the event of accidents[139]

Regulation 261/2004 establishing common rules on compensation and assistance to passengers in the event of denied boarding and of cancellation or long delay of flights.[140]

(vi) Technical requirements, safety and security, insurance

Directive 2006/126 on driving licences[141]

Directive 2003/59 on the initial qualification and periodic training of drivers of certain road vehicles for the carriage of goods or passengers[142]

Directive 2007/46 establishing a framework for the approval of motor vehicles and their trailers, and of systems, components and separate technical units intended for such vehicles (Framework Directive)[143]

Regulation 715/2007 on type approval of motor vehicles with respect to emissions from light passenger and commercial vehicles (Euro 5 and Euro 6) and on access to vehicle repair and maintenance information,[144]

Regulation 168/2013 on the approval and market surveillance of two- or three-wheel vehicles and quadricycles[145]

Directive 2014/45 on periodic roadworthiness tests for motor vehicles and their trailers[146]

Regulation 443/2009 setting emission performance standards for new passenger cars as part of the Community's integrated approach to reduce CO_2 emissions from light-duty vehicles[147]

Regulation 510/2011 setting emission performance standards for new light commercial vehicles as part of the Union's integrated approach to reduce CO_2 emissions from light-duty vehicles[148]

Regulation 595/2009 on type-approval of motor vehicles and engines with respect to emissions from heavy duty vehicles (Euro VI) and on access to vehicle repair and maintenance information[149]

Directive 2014/47 on the technical roadside inspection of the roadworthiness of commercial vehicles circulating in the Union[150]

Directive 91/671 on the approximation of the laws of the Member States relating to compulsory use of safety belts in vehicles of less than 3,5 tonnes[151]

Regulation 661/2009 concerning type-approval requirements for the general safety of motor vehicles, their trailers and systems, components and separate technical units intended therefor[152]

Directive 92/6 on the installation and use of speed limitation devices for certain categories of motor vehicles in the Community[153]

Directive 96/53 laying down for certain road vehicles circulating within the Community the maximum authorized dimensions in national and international traffic and the maximum authorized weights in international traffic[154]

Directive 2008/68 on the inland transport of dangerous goods[155]

---

[135] [2011] OJ L55/1.   [136] [2010] OJ L334/1.   [137] [2007] OJ L315/14.
[138] [2009] OJ L131/24.   [139] [1997] OJ L285/1.   [140] [2004] OJ L46/1.
[141] [2006] OJ L403/18.   [142] [2003] OJ L226/4.   [143] [2007] OJ L263/1.
[144] [2007] OJ L171/1.   [145] [2013] OJ L60/52.   [146] [2014] OJ L127/51.
[147] [2009] OJ L140/1.   [148] [2011] OJ L145/1.   [149] [2009] OJ L188/1.
[150] [2014] OJ L127/134.   [151] [1991] OJ L373/26.   [152] [2009] OJ L200/1.
[153] [1992] OJ L57/27.   [154] [1996] OJ L235/59.   [155] [2008] OJ L260/13.

Directive 95/50 on uniform procedures for checks on the transport of dangerous goods by road[156]

Directive 2015/413 facilitating cross-border exchange of information on road safety-related traffic offences[157]

Directive 2016/1629 laying down technical requirements for inland waterway vessels[158]

Directive 2016/798 on railway safety[159]

Directive 2007/59 on the certification of train drivers operating locomotives and trains on the railway system in the Community,[160]

Directive 2008/68 on the inland transport of dangerous goods[161]

Regulation 725/2004 on enhancing ship and port facility security[162]

Directive 2002/59 establishing a Community vessel traffic monitoring and information system[163]

Directive 2010/65 on reporting formalities for ships arriving in and/or departing from ports of the Member States[164]

Directive 98/41 on the registration of persons sailing on board passenger ships operating to or from ports of the Member States of the Community[165]

Directive 2014/90 on marine equipment[166]

Directive 2001/96 establishing harmonised requirements and procedures for the safe loading and unloading of bulk carriers[167]

Directive 97/70 setting up a harmonised safety regime for fishing vessels of 24 metres in length and over[168]

Regulation 336/2006 on the implementation of the International Safety Management Code within the Community[169]

Directive 2009/45 on safety rules and standards for passenger ships[170]

Directive 2003/25 on specific stability requirements for ro-ro passenger ships[171]

Regulation 2015/757 on the monitoring, reporting and verification of carbon dioxide emissions from maritime transport[172]

Directive 2009/16 on port State control[173]

Regulation 391/2009 on common rules and standards for ship inspection and survey organisations[174]

Directive 2009/15 on common rules and standards for ship inspection and survey organisations and for the relevant activities of maritime administrations[175]

Regulation 530/2012 on the accelerated phasing-in of double-hull or equivalent design requirements for single-hull oil tankers[176]

Directive 2000/59 on port reception facilities for ship-generated waste and cargo residues[177]

Regulation 782/2003 on the prohibition of organotin compounds on ships[178]

Directive 2009/18 establishing the fundamental principles governing the investigation of accidents in the maritime transport sector[179]

Regulation 549/2004 laying down the framework for the creation of the single European sky (the Framework Regulation)[180]

Regulation 550/2004 on the provision of air navigation services in the single European sky (the Service Provision Regulation)[181]

Regulation 551/2004 on the organisation and use of the airspace in the single European sky (the Airspace Regulation)[182]

---

[156] [1995] OJ L249/35.　　　[157] [2015] OJ L68/9.　　　[158] [2016] OJ L252/118.
[159] [2016] OJ L138/102.　　[160] [2007] OJ L315/51.　　[161] [2008] OJ L260/13.
[162] [2004] OJ L129/6.　　　[163] [2002] OJ L208/10.　　[164] [2010] OJ L283/1.
[165] [1988] OJ L188/35.　　[166] [2014] OJ L257/146.　　[167] [2002] OJ L13/9.
[168] [1988] OJ L34/1.　　　[169] [2006] OJ L64/1.　　　[170] [2009] OJ L163/1.
[171] [2003] OJ L123/22.　　[172] [2015] OJ L123/55.　　[173] [2009] OJ L131/57.
[174] [2009] OJ L131/11.　　[175] [2009] OJ L131/47.　　[176] [2012] OJ L172/3.
[177] [2000] OJ L332/81.　　[178] [2003] OJ L115/1.　　[179] [2009] OJ L131/114.
[180] [2004] OJ L96/1.　　　[181] [2004] OJ L96/10.　　　[182] [2004] OJ L96/20.

Regulation 552/2004 on the interoperability of the European Air Traffic Management network (the interoperability Regulation)[183]

Regulation 3922/91 on the harmonization of technical requirements and administrative procedures in the field of civil aviation[184]

Regulation 785/2004 on insurance requirements for air carriers and aircraft operators[185]

Regulation 996/2010 on the investigation and prevention of accidents and incidents in civil aviation[186]

Regulation 376/2014 on the reporting, analysis and follow-up of occurrences in civil aviation[187]

Regulation 300/2008 on common rules in the field of civil aviation security[188]

Regulation 2015/340 laying down detailed rules for air traffic controllers' licences and certain certificates[189]

Regulation 1178/2011 laying down technical requirements and administrative procedures related to civil aviation aircrew[190]

Regulation 748/2012 laying down implementing rules for the airworthiness and environmental certification of aircraft and related products, parts and appliances, as well as for the certification of design and production organisations[191]

Directive 89/629 on the limitation of noise emission from civil subsonic jet aeroplanes[192]

Regulation 598/2014 on the establishment of rules and procedures with regard to the introduction of noise-related operating restrictions at Union airports within a Balanced Approach[193]

Directive 2003/87 establishing a scheme for greenhouse gas emission allowance trading within the Community.[194]

(vii) Social provisions

Regulation 561/2006 on the harmonisation of certain social legislation relating to road transport[195]

Regulation 165/2014 on tachographs in road transport[196]

Directive 2006/22 on minimum conditions for the implementation of Council *Regulations 3820/85* and *3821/85* concerning social legislation relating to road transport activities[197]

Directive 2003/88 concerning certain aspects of the organisation of working time[198]

Directive 2002/15 on the organisation of the working time of persons performing mobile road transport activities[199]

Directive 2005/47 on the Agreement between the Community of European Railways (CER) and the European Transport Workers' Federation (ETF) on certain aspects of the working conditions of mobile workers engaged in interoperable cross-border services in the railway sector[200]

Directive 1999/63 concerning the Agreement on the organisation of working time of seafarers concluded by the European Community Shipowners' Association (ECSA) and the Federation of Transport Workers' Unions in the European Union (FST)[201]

Directive 1999/95 concerning the enforcement of provisions in respect of seafarers' hours of work on board ships calling at Community ports[202]

Directive 2008/106 on the minimum level of training of seafarers[203]

Directive 2000/79 concerning the European Agreement on the Organisation of Working Time of Mobile Workers in Civil Aviation.[204]

---

[183] [2004] OJ L96/26. [184] [1991] OJ L373/4. [185] [2004] OJ L138/1.
[186] [2010] OJ L295/35. [187] [2014] OJ L122/18. [188] [2008] OJ L97/72.
[189] [2015] OJ L63/1. [190] [2011] OJ L311/1. [191] [2012] OJ L224/1.
[192] [1989] OJ L363/27. [193] [2014] OJ L173/65. [194] [2003] OJ L275/32.
[195] [2006] OJ L102/1. [196] [2014] OJ L60/1. [197] [2006] OJ L102/35.
[198] [2003] OJ L299/9. [199] [2002] OJ L80/35. [200] [2005] OJ L195/15.
[201] [1999] OJ L167/33. [202] [2000] OJ L14/29. [203] [2008] OJ L323/33.
[204] [2000] OJ L302/57.

(viii) Competition and fiscal matters

Regulation 169/2009 applying rules of competition to transport by rail, road and inland waterway[205]

Regulation 1370/2007 on public passenger transport services by rail and by road[206]

Regulation 246/2009 on the application of Article 81(3) of the Treaty to certain categories of agreements, decisions and concerted practices between liner shipping companies (consortia)[207]

Regulation 4057/86 on unfair pricing practices in maritime transport[208]

Regulation 4058/86 concerning coordinated action to safeguard free access to cargoes in ocean trades[209]

Directive 2003/96 restructuring the Community framework for the taxation of energy products and electricity[210]

Regulation 487/2009 on the application of Article 81(3) of the Treaty to certain categories of agreements and concerted practices in the air transport sector[211]

Regulation 868/2004 concerning protection against subsidisation and unfair pricing practices causing injury to Community air carriers in the supply of air services from countries not members of the European Community.[212]

(ix) Measures concerning infrastructure and conditions and procedures for establishing and promoting projects of common interest (trans-European networks)

Directive 2004/54 on minimum safety requirements for tunnels in the Trans-European Road Network[213]

Directive 2016/797 on the interoperability of the rail system within the European Union[214]

Directive 2014/94 on the deployment of alternative fuels infrastructure[215]

Regulation 1315/2013 on Union guidelines for the development of the trans-European transport network[216]

Regulation 1316/2013 establishing the Connecting Europe Facility[217]

Regulation 913/2010 concerning a European rail network for competitive freight.[218]

(x) Establishment of specialized agencies and bodies

Regulation 216/2008 on common rules in the field of civil aviation and establishing a European Aviation Safety Agency[219]

Regulation 1406/2002 establishing a European Maritime Safety Agency[220]

Regulation 2016/796 establishing a European Union Agency for Railways[221]

Implementing Decision 2013/801 establishing the Innovation and Networks Executive Agency[222]

Regulation 2099/2002 establishing a Committee on Safe Seas and the Prevention of Pollution from Ships (COSS)[223]

Decision 2010/302 on the conclusion of a Memorandum of Cooperation between the International Civil Aviation Organisation and the European Community regarding security audits/inspections and related matters.[224]

(xi) External relations

Regulation 847/2004 on the negotiation and implementation of air service agreements between Member States and third countries[225]

Agreement between the European Community and the Swiss Confederation on Air Transport[226]

---

[205] [2009] OJ L61/1.   [206] [2007] OJ L315/1.   [207] [2009] OJ L79/1.
[208] [1986] OJ L378/14.   [209] [1986] OJ L378/21.   [210] [2003] OJ L283/51.
[211] [2009] OJ L148/1.   [212] [2004] OJ L162/1.   [213] [2004] OJ L167/39.
[214] [2016] OJ L138/44.   [215] [2014] OJ L307/1.   [216] [2013] OJ L348/1.
[217] [2013] OJ L348/129.   [218] [2010] OJ L276/22.   [219] [2008] OJ L79/1.
[220] [2002] OJ L208/1.   [221] [2016] OJ L138/1.   [222] [2013] OJ L352/65.
[223] [2002] OJ L324/1.   [224] [2010] OJ L129/68.   [225] [2004] OJ L157/7.
[226] [2002] OJ L114/73.

Agreement between the European Community and the Swiss Confederation on the Carriage of Goods and Passengers by Rail and Road[227]

Decision 2006/682 on the signature and provisional application of the Multilateral Agreement on the establishment of a European Common Aviation Area[228]

Decision 2007/339 on the signature and provisional application of the Air Transport *Agreement* between the European Community and its Member States, on the one hand, and the United States of America, on the other hand[229]

Agreement on maritime transport between the European Community and its Member States, of the one part, and the government of the People's Republic of China[230]

Agreement on the international occasional carriage of passengers by coach and bus (Interbus Agreement)[231]

Decision 2010/302 on the conclusion of a Memorandum of Cooperation between the International Civil Aviation Organisation and the European Community regarding security audits/inspections and related matters.[232]

(xii) Miscellaneous

Regulation 718/1999 on a Community-fleet capacity policy to promote inland waterway transport[233]

Directive 92/106 on the establishment of common rules for certain types of combined transport of goods between Member States[234]

Decision 93/704 on the creation of a Community database on road accidents[235]

Regulation 91/2003 on rail transport statistics[236]

Regulation 437/2003 on statistical returns in respect of the carriage of passengers, freight and mail by air[237]

Regulation 1365/2006 on statistics of goods transport by inland waterways[238]

Directive 2009/42 on statistical returns in respect of carriage of goods and passengers by sea[239]

Regulation 70/2012 on statistical returns in respect of the carriage of goods by road.[240]

---

[227] [2002] OJ L114/91.　　[228] [2006] OJ L285/1.　　[229] [2007] OJ L134/1.
[230] [2008] OJ L46/23.　　[231] [2002] OJ L321/13.　　[232] [2010] OJ L129/68.
[233] [1999] OJ L90/1.　　[234] [1992] OJ L368/38.　　[235] [1993] OJ L329/63.
[236] [2003] OJ L14/1.　　[237] [2003] OJ L66/1.　　[238] [2006] OJ L264/1.
[239] [2009] OJ L141/29.　　[240] [2012] OJ L32/1.

APPENDIX II

Comitology Committees assisting the European Commission in the transport sector

(This list is based on the Comitology Register published by the European Commission.)[241]

Advisory Committees

1. Advisory Committee on application of the legislation on access for Community air carriers to intra-Community air routes[242]

2. Advisory Committee on measures taken in the event of a crisis in the market in the carriage of goods by road and for laying down the conditions under which non-resident carriers may operate national road haulage services within a Member State (cabotage)[243]

3. Advisory Committee on unfair pricing practices in maritime transport[244]

4. Advisory Committee on Restrictive Practices and Dominant Positions[245]

Road transport

5. Committee on Road Transport[246]

6. Committee on driving licences[247]

7. Committee on initial qualification and periodic training of drivers of certain road vehicles for the carriage of goods or passengers[248]

8. Technical Adaptation Committee on Roadworthiness Testing[249]

9. Technical Committee — Motor Vehicles' (TCMV)[250]

10. Committee for the compulsory use of safety belts and child-restraint systems in vehicles[251]
11. Committee on the promotion of clean and energy-efficient road transport vehicles[252]
12. Committee on the transport of dangerous goods[253]

---

[241] See http://ec.europa.eu/transparency/regcomitology/index.cfm?do=search.search.For each committee the basic legal act(s) is given in the associated footnote.

[242] Regulations 868/2004; 847/2004; 785/2004; 1008/2008; Directive 2002/30.

[243] Regulation 3916/90.   [244] Regulation 4057/86.

[245] Regulation 1/2003, referred to in Regulation 246/2009 (liner shipping companies).

[246] Regulations 165/2014; 561/2006; 1073/2009; 1072/2009; 1071/2009; 3821/85; Directives 2006/22; 96/53.

[247] Directive 2006/126; Directive 91/439.   [248] Directive 2003/59.

[249] Directives 2009/40; 2000/30; 96/96.

[250] Directive 2007/46, referred to in Regulations 595/2009; 168/2013.

[251] Directive 2003/20.   [252] Directive 2009/33.   [253] Directives 2008/68; 95/50; 1999/36.

13. European ITS Committee (EIC)[254]
14. Climate Change Committee;[255]

Inland waterways

15. Committee on adaptation of the legislation concerning reciprocal recognition of national boat masters' certificates for the *carriage of goods and passengers by inland waterway*;[256]

Rail

16. Single European Rail Area Committee[257]
17. Committee for the establishment of conditions for the interoperability of the trans-European high-speed rail system[258]

Aviation

18. Single Sky Committee[259]
19. Committee for the application of common safety rules in the field of civil aviation[260]
20. Committee on application of the common rules for the allocation of slots at Community airports[261]
21. Committee on common rules for the operation of air services in the Community[262]
22. Committee on application of the legislation on access to the ground handling market at Community airports[263]
23. Committee on application of the legislation on harmonisation of technical requirements and administrative procedures in the field of civil aviation[264]
24. Committee on the application of legislation and common rules on the security of civil aviation[265]
25. Climate Change Committee;[266] (see supra 14)

Maritime transport

26. Committee on Safe Seas and prevention of pollution from ships (COSS)[267]
27. Committee on the implementation of legislation on improving ship and port installation security[268]

---

[254] Directive 2010/40.
[255] Decision 280/2004, referred to in Regulations 443/2009 and 510/2011.
[256] Directives 2005/44; 96/75; 96/50; 91/672; 2006/87; 2006/137.
[257] Regulations 913/2010; 1371/2007; Directive 2012/34.
[258] Directives 2008/57; 2007/59; 2001/16; 96/48; 2016/797.
[259] Regulations 552/2004; 551/2004; 550/2004; 549/2004; 219/2007.
[260] Regulations 376/2014; 216/2008; 1592/2002; 3922/91. [261] Regulation 95/93.
[262] Regulation 1008/2008, referred to in Regulations 868/2004; 847/2004.
[263] Directive 96/67.
[264] Regulation 2111/2005; Directive 2004/36; Directive 2003/42; Regulation 3922/91.
[265] Regulation 300/2008. [266] Decision 280/2004, referred to in Directive 2003/87.
[267] Regulations 789/2004; 782/2003; 417/2002; 392/2009; 391/2009; 336/2006; 2099/2002; Directives 2014/90; 2009/45; 2009/21; 2009/18; 2009/17; 2009/16; 2009/15; 2008/106; 2005/35; 2003/25; 2002/6; 2002/59; 2001/96; 2000/59; 98/41; 97/70; 96/98; 95/21; 94/57; 93/75; 1999/35; 1999/32.
[268] Regulation 725/2004; Directive 2005/65.

Infrastructure

28. Committee for road infrastructure safety management[269]
29. Committee for the interoperability of electronic road toll systems[270]
30. Transport infrastructure charging[271]
31. Committee on adaptation to technical progress and the possible adoption of a harmonised risk analysis method concerning the minimum safety requirements for tunnels in the European road network[272]
32. Connecting Europe Facility Coordination Committee[273]
33. Trans-European Transport Network Committee[274]
34. Marco Polo Committee[275]

Transport Statistics

35. European Statistical System Committee (ESS Committee)[276]
36. Committee on the Statistical Programmes[277]

'Mixed' Committees in International Agreements

37. Community/Switzerland Air Transport Committee[278]
38. Community/Switzerland Inland Transport Committee[279]
39. Joint Committee of the Multilateral Agreement on the establishment of a European Common Aviation Area[280]
40. Joint Committee of the Air Transport Agreement between the European Community and its Member States, on the one hand, and the United States of America, on the other hand[281]
41. Joint Committee of the Agreement on the international occasional carriage of passengers by coach and bus (Interbus Agreement)[282]
42. European Economic Area Joint Committee.[283]

---

[269] Directive 2008/96.   [270] Directive 2004/52.
[271] Regulation 1108/70; Directive 1999/62; Decision No. 64/389.   [272] Directive 2004/54.
[273] Regulation 1316/2013.   [274] Regulation 1315/2013.   [275] Regulation 1692/2006.
[276] Regulations 70/2012; 91/2003; 437/2003; 1365/2006; 1172/98; Directive 2009/42.
[277] Decision 89/382, referred to in Decision 93/704.
[278] Agreement between the European Community and the Swiss Confederation on Air Transport of 21 June 1999 [2002] OJ L114/73.
[279] Agreement between the European Community and the Swiss Confederation on the Carriage of Goods and Passengers by Rail and Road of 21 June 1999 [2002] OJ L114/91.
[280] Multilateral Agreement between the European Community and its Member States, the Republic of Albania, Bosnia and Herzegovina, the Republic of Bulgaria, the Republic of Croatia, the former Yugoslav Republic of Macedonia, the Republic of Iceland, the Republic of Montenegro, the Kingdom of Norway, Romania, the Republic of Serbia and the United Nations Interim Administration Mission in Kosovo on the establishment of a European Common Aviation Area [2006] OJ L285/1.
[281] Air Transport Agreement of 25 April 2007 [2007] OJ L134/1.
[282] Interbus Agreement of 14 April 2000 [2002] OJ L321/13.
[283] Agreement on the European Economic Area of 2 May 1992 [1994] OJ L1/3.

APPENDIX III

Advisory groups in the sector of transport and infrastructure[284]

- Advisory body on accessibility of the EU rail system for PRM
- Best practices in Road Safety
- Commission group of experts on SESAR Interim Deployment Steering
- Commission expert group on rail market access
- Commission expert group on the technical pillar of the 4th Railway Package
- Consultative Forum on EU External Aviation Policy
- Digital Transport and Logistics Forum
- European eCall Implementation Platform
- European ITS Advisory Group
- European Network of Rail Regulatory Bodies
- European Observatory on Airport Capacity & Quality
- European Sustainable Shipping Forum (ESSF)
- Expert Group established to Support the Enforcement of Road Safety-related Traffic Offences
- Expert Group for the Priorities of the Connecting Europe Facility
- Expert Group on alternative transport fuels ('the Sustainable Transport Forum')
- Expert Group on Aviation Internal Market
- Expert Group on laboratory alignment for the measurement of tyre rolling resistance
- Expert Group on Land Transport Security
- Expert Group on Maritime Administrative Simplification and Electronic Information Services
- Expert Group on Passenger Rights
- Expert group on technical requirements for inland waterway vessels
- Expert Group on Tyres Labelling
- Market Surveillance Administrative Cooperation
- Expert Group on Urban Mobility
- Focal Points and Short Sea Promotion Centres for Shortsea Shipping and Motorways of the Sea
- GEAR 2030 High Level Group
- GNSS Security Board
- Group of Experts on Aviation Security Inspections
- High Level Platform of Rail Infrastructure Managers in Europe
- High Level Steering Group for Governance of the Digital Maritime System and Services
- Horizon 2020 Advisory Group for the Societal Challenge 4 on Smart, green and integrated transport 2014–2020
- Horizon 2020 Commission expert group to assist the Strategic Research and Innovation Agenda (STRIA) initiative
- Inland Waterway Transport (IWT)
- Naiades II implementation expert group
- Intelligent Transport Systems
- Marine Equipment Expert Group
- Maritime and Port Security
- Maritime Safety Group
- Observatory for the Monitoring of Road, Rail and Combined Traffic in the Alpine Region[285]

---

[284] European Commission, Register of Expert Groups and Other Similar Entities, http://ec.europa.eu/transparency/regexpert/index.cfm?do=search.result (last accessed 30 March 2017).

[285] Established by the Agreement between the European Community and the Swiss Confederation on the Carriage of Goods and Passengers by Rail and Road of 21 June 1999 (Art 45).

- Platform for the Deployment of Cooperative Intelligent Transport Systems in the EU
  - Rail Transport
  - Reference scenario experts group
  - Road Accidents (CARE)
  - Search and Rescue Galileo Operations Advisory Board
  - Social issues in inland navigation
  - Stakeholders' Advisory Group on Aviation Security
  - Tachograph Forum
- Telematic Applications for Passengers (TAP) Steering Committee
- The Expert Group on the Single European Sky
- Thessaloniki Forum of Airport Charges Regulators
- Trans-European Transport Network (TEN-T) Article 49

13

Environmental Protection

André M Latour and Gerard C Rowe

A Introduction

The effective implementation of European Union environmental policy depends upon the efficient cooperation and coordination of various administrative levels and actors. Key to this are the sharing of environmentally relevant information, mutual support, and common agreement aimed at the 'high level of protection'[1] of the environment sought by the Union. The transboundary nature of environmental issues, whether through emissions, transterritorial waste transport, or management of shared water resources, or of climate and nature resources, and administrative action related to such matters, pose particular challenges. Were there insufficient collaborative interaction of all the relevant actors in the field of EU environmental protection, and were this field to be characterized primarily by Member States' acting on their own, the fate of environmental protection in Europe would be bleak. The generation, management, and sharing of information play here a vital, perhaps even dominant, role. The concept of a highly (inter-)networked, indeed integrated, European administration can thus be illustrated very strikingly through a consideration of this policy sector. Indeed, a great deal of EU environmental administration, while not alone within the general setting of Union administration, appears characterizable only through the epithet 'integrated'.

The scope of Union environmental policy is extremely wide, both because environmental protection is a cross-sectional task of the EU, and because there are numerous, specific sub-sectors subject to Union regulation for a variety of reasons. These sub-sectors include: climate change and related issues such as emissions trading; nature conservation; bio-diversity and soil protection; ecological sustainability; water resource protection and management; air pollution control; waste and resource efficiency; civil protection; measures against noise pollution; and chemicals regulation. Other Union policy sectors also have important tangential interactions with environment fields as such, in particular, transport, energy, and regional funds, to name but a few. Taken together, the matters listed here show that the environmental protection sector of Union policy has, quite simply, an enormous scope. This overview of the various heads of Union environmental action also makes clear that it is possible in this essay to provide only an indicative and highly selective treatment of the public administration and administrative law of the sector.

---

[1] Art 191(2) TFEU.

The European nature conservation network, Natura 2000,[2] provides an opportunity to observe a number of key elements typical of EU (environmental) administration, specifically in respect of:

- the *preparation* of programmes and measures
- the *structure* and organization applicable (e.g., comitology committees, Scientific Working Groups, expert groups, European Topic Centres (ETCs), DG-Environment)
- implementation via *administrative rule-making*
- development of support *documentation* (e.g., guidelines or interpretive rules of the Commission or documents of participant groups and committees)[3]
- *procedures* which embody the active, cooperative participation of Member State representatives in round-table meetings, etc
- both administrative and curial *supervision*
- participation of *other supranational actors* (e.g. the Council of Europe) and
- cooperative participation of *private actors* including, e.g., non-governmental organizations (NGOs) and landowners in administrative steps within the Union in relation to nature and environmental protection.

This conservation network will serve as a thread for illustrating aspects of the Union's environmental administration as a whole, although many examples from other sub-sectors of the environmental field will also be treated.

B Administrative Tasks in the Environment Sector

Only in the light of an understanding of the complete setting of Union environmental policy can the environmental administrative tasks of the EU can be appreciated. That setting can be perceived indicatively, through the list of sub-sectors in this field given above. In relation to those sub-sectors, and to the obligation to take environmental

---

[2] As to this see further below. Natura 2000 is a coherent network of conservation areas based upon two key directives. Once the Member States, proceeding according to the criteria in Appendix III of Council Directive 92/43/EEC of 21 May 1992 on the conservation of natural habitats and of wild fauna and flora [1992] OJ L206/7–50 (Habitats Directive), have selected potential areas, these are put forward to the Commission (Art 4(1)). The latter then declares the areas of European significance after a process of evaluation (Art 4(2)). The Member States are then obliged to establish full protection for these areas swiftly, at the latest within six years (Art 6). Areas in accordance with Directive 2009/147/EC of the European Parliament and of the Council of 30 November 2009 on the conservation of wild birds [2010] OJ L20/7–25 (Birds Directive), gain special protected status immediately upon their nomination to the Commission, without any evaluation process.

[3] See eg European Topic Centre on Nature Protection & Biodiversity, *Some general principles for biogeographical seminars—a discussion paper for the Scientific Working Group meeting* (Paris, 16 September 2002): 'The first round of biogeographical seminars has been completed and the second and final round has now started. It has become apparent to the ETC-NPB and others that there is a need to learn from our collective experience and to try to have a greater degree of conformity between the various regions and Member States. This document is intended to suggest a common understanding of a number of points based on discussions at previous seminars' (Habitats SWG 2002-02 rev1 (ETC/NPB)) 1.

protection into account cross-sectionally in all sectors of the EU, environmental administrative tasks and activities include at least the following elements:

- coordination of administrative networks
- conduct of activities internal to specific administrative bodies
- planning and coordination of joint measures and the preparation of framework plans
- delegated and administrative rule-making
- preparation of legislative measures
- individual decision-making
- preparation of recommendations, assessments, and reports
- information management
- outsourcing of particular tasks to private actors and the consequent coordination and supervision of these
- actions for the enforcement of EU law and decisions; and
- supervisory measures, especially of the Commission, in particular vis-à-vis the Member States, and sometimes centralized (Union) decision-making, in order to ensure coordinated and consistent implementation of Union environmental policy.

The role and place of each of these kinds of administrative tasks in the implementation of EU environmental policy will be illustrated in the subsequent discussion.

C Sources of Administrative Environmental Law

The environmental administration of the EU is based, not surprisingly, on elements of primary Union law. Many of these are of general import (e.g., Article 197 TFEU on administrative cooperation), and these will not be rehearsed here. Elements with a specifically environmental focus include Article 3(3) TEU which requires efforts towards the 'sustainable development of Europe based on … a high level of protection and improvement of the quality of the environment'.[4] This can been seen as feeding into Article 11 TFEU, which contains the cross-sectional requirement that 'environmental protection requirements must be integrated into the definition and implementation of the Union's policies and activities, in particular with a view to promoting sustainable development'. These provisions in themselves establish a basis for, inter alia, administrative action directed to environmental protection (even if such action must itself rely on concrete policy expression in EU secondary legislation), demanding at the same time that activities be avoided which may compromise the achievement of these environmental goals.[5] The Commission has, from time to time, sought to draw

---

[4] See, for discussion of the effect of this provision, M Wasmeier, 'The Integration of Environmental Protection as a General Rule for Interpreting Community Law' (2001) 38 *Common Market Law Review* 164.

[5] A Wasilewski, 'Der Europäische Verwaltungsraum–Bemerkungen über die Europafähigkeit der mitgliedstaatlichen Verwaltungen anhand von Beispielen aus dem Umweltschutzbereich' in S Magiera,

out the consequences of the provisions for the development of Union policy generally.[6] Articles 191–193 TFEU provide more explicit primary legislative articulation of
Union environmental policy (see further below, concerning principles). In particular,
Article 192(1) determines that the Parliament and the Council decide 'what action is
to be taken', subject to the principle of procedural autonomy, which finds expression
in this context in Article 192(4) (touched on again below). Whether, and to what extent, Article 192(1) itself provides a legal foundation for environmental administrative
action as such, and in particular for legal harmonization, is still subject to debate.[7] For
example, Regulation 880/92 on the eco-label[8] displays a specific application of such legislative competence: a national authority is given the task of awarding an eco-label
for a product or firm, but where the Member States are unable to agree cooperatively
and uniform criteria are not applied throughout the Union, the Commission can exceptionally intervene.[9]

One should also note in passing certain other primary sources which at least have
implications for administrative implementation. Article 192(2) TFEU provides for legislation of a fiscal nature by the Council, and for measures dealing with land-use
planning, quantitative water resource management, and national choices regarding
energy sources and energy supply. In addition, under Article 192(3), the Council and
the Parliament are to adopt action programmes and 'measures necessary for the implementation of these programmes'.

All of such primary law provisions can, then, be regarded, if only indirectly, as
sources of sectoral environmental administrative law. Yet, even within that category, it
is possible to make a (subtle) distinction, involving further sub-categorization within
environmental administrative law itself, namely between general and specialized
environmental administrative law (referred to again below). General EU environmental administrative law includes all of the primary law provisions (although
very far from a complete codification) just referred to, as well as certain secondary
laws dealing mainly, and very importantly, with the management of environmental

---

K-P Sommermann, and J Ziller (eds), Verwaltungswissenschaft und Verwaltungspraxis in nationaler
und transnationaler Perspektive – Festschrift für Heinrich Siedentopf zum 70. Geburtstag, (Duncker &
Humblot 2008) 132 ff.

[6] See Communication from the Commission to the European Council—Partnership for integration: a strategy for Integrating Environment into EU Policies, Cardiff, June 1998, COM/98/0333 final;
Communication from the Commission to the European Parliament and the Council—Single Market
and Environment, COM/99/0263 final; Communication from the Commission to the Council and the
European Parliament—Integrating environment and sustainable development into economic and development co-operation policy: elements of a comprehensive strategy, COM/2000/0264 final.

[7] In support of this see, W Kahl, 'Hat die EG die Kompetenz zur Regelung des Allgemeinen
Verwaltungsrechts?' (1996) 15 *Neue Zeitschrift für Verwaltungsrecht* 865, 866, and R Streinz (ed), *EUV/
AEUV–Vertrag über die Europäische Union und Vertrag über die Arbeitsweise der Europäischen Union*
(2nd edn, Beck 2012) 99. To the contrary see M Hilf, 'Möglichkeiten und Grenzen des Rückgriffes auf
nationale verwaltungsrechtliche Regeln bei der Durchführung von Gemeinschaftsrecht' in J Schwarze
(ed), *Europäisches Verwaltungsrecht im Werden* (Nomos 1982) 76. See also D Nitschke, *Harmonisierung
des nationalen Verwaltungsvollzugs von EG-Umweltrecht* (Mohr Siebeck 2000) 99.

[8] Council Regulation (EEC) No 880/92 of 23 March 1992 on a Community eco-label award scheme
[1992] OJ L99/1–7.

[9] See eg D Nitschke (n 7) 132 ff.

information: provisions on environmental impact assessment,[10] freedom of environmental information,[11] and environmental audit.[12] One could also include here the law on integrated environmental protection[13] (as being of *general* environmental import, in the sense that its regulatory scope goes beyond individual environmental media (water, air, soil, etc), in order to lay down rules governing the interaction between a number of media with one another).

On the other hand, most Union environmental law is in fact (sub-sectorally) specialized—and legion—and coming with substantial amount of (specialized) specialized administrative law. The sources of this include numerous secondary legal measures (directives and regulations) dealing with air and water quality, chemicals, nature conservation, river systems, and many more. For the purposes of illustration—but pointing only to a tiny fraction of such measures—we can refer here to the secondary legislative basis of the nature conservation programme, Natura 2000. That conservation network relies in particular on the Habitats Directive[14] and the Birds Directive,[15] as the legislative basis for the establishment of the world's largest network of nature conservation areas. Additionally illustrative of the sources of law, but again *pars pro toto*, we can refer to the decision of the European Court of Justice (ECJ) in *Commission v United Kingdom*,[16] which had the effect of establishing that the physical network of conservation areas could take in maritime zones (an issue which was, hitherto, in dispute, so that the physical-geographical compass subject to the networked EU environmental administration was thus significantly enlarged).

D Underlying Legal Principles in the Environmental Sector

The general principles of the Union's environmental policy are found expressed, first, in the primary sources already referred above. The foremost of these principles is a (high level of) 'protection' and 'improvement', but is followed closely by: sustainability;

---

[10] Directive 2011/92/EU of the European Parliament and of the Council of 13 December 2011 on the assessment of the effects of certain public and private projects on the environment [2012] OJ L26/1–21.

[11] Directive 2003/4/EC of the European Parliament and of the Council of 28 January 2003 on public access to environmental information and repealing Council Directive 90/313/EEC [2003] OJ L41/26–32.

[12] Regulation (EC) No 1221/2009 of the European Parliament and of the Council of 25 November 2009 on the voluntary participation by organisations in a Community eco-management and audit scheme (EMAS) [2009] OJ L342/1–45.

[13] Directive 2010/75/EU of the European Parliament and of the Council of 24 November 2010 on industrial emissions (integrated pollution prevention and control) [2010] OJ L334/17–119. See also, indicatively, European Commission, Integrated Environmental Management—Guidance in relation to the Thematic Strategy on the Urban Environment (Brussels, 2007). For discussion of the concept see G C Rowe, 'Wieviel Integration braucht der "integrierte Umweltschutz"? Der Weg zum integralen und integeren Umweltschutz' in E Gawel, G Lübbe-Wolff (eds), *Effizientes Umweltordnungsrecht—Kriterien und Grenzen* (Nomos 2000) 205–49.

[14] Council Directive 92/43/EEC of 21 May 1992 on the conservation of natural habitats and of wild fauna and flora (n 2).

[15] Directive 2009/147/EC of the European Parliament and of the Council of 30 November 2009 on the conservation of wild birds (n 2).

[16] Case C-6/04 *Commission v United Kingdom* [2005] ECR I-09017.

precaution; prevention; rectification at source;[17] polluter pays;[18] rational use of resources; and promotion of measures on the international level, in particular regarding climate change. These are all, broadly speaking, not underlying principles of environmental *administration* as such. Nevertheless, they certainly can be regarded as necessarily informing, shaping and constraining the Union's administrative action in this sector.[19] Other principles, however, emerging from primary law come closer to having a direct relation to administration: taking into account available scientific and technical data, local environmental conditions, cost and benefits, and economic and social development. Such standards are, without doubt, ones which must guide legislative action, but equally also provide a framework for administrative action. The Union and the Member States are also charged with environmental cooperation with third countries and with international organizations in this sphere, a demand which can be said to have specifically administrative implications (and the achievement of which can certainly be observed, as will be noted further below). Finally, in respect of principles emerging from primary law, one should note Article 192(4) which expressly places the obligation for implementation of environmental policy on the Member States (a characteristic not unique to environmental protection, considering in particular the general principle of 'procedural autonomy'),[20] and Article 192(5) which, in giving acknowledgement of the principle of proportionality (here relating to costs imposed on national authorities), allows for temporary derogations and for support from the Cohesion Fund.

All of the principles noted here,[21] together with other 'meta'-principles of the EU (e.g., proportionality, subsidiarity, sincere cooperation, administrative cooperation),[22] inform the generation and the interpretation of primary and secondary EU environmental law, and of its application in practice. The specifically environmental principles just listed find their concrete expression again and again in EU secondary environmental law. No attempt to catalogue such instances will be undertaken here; just one example can be offered, standing for the many others, namely the specific expression

---

[17] M Kloepfer, *Umweltrecht* (2004) § 9, para 102 ff; C Vedder, W Heintschel von Heinegg, *Europäisches Unionsrecht–EUV, AEUV, Grundrechte-Charta—Handkommentar mit vollständigen Texten der Protokolle und Erklärungen und des EAGV* (Nomos 2012) 748.

[18] Case C-378/08 *Raffinerie Mediterranee (ERG) SpA, Polimeri Europa SpA and Syndial SpA v Ministero dello Sviluppo economico and Others* [2010] ECR I-1919; Joined Cases C-379/08 and C-380/08 *Raffinerie Mediterranee (ERG) SpA, Polimeri Europa SpA and Syndial SpA v Ministero dello Sviluppo economico and Others and ENI SpA v Ministero Ambiente e Tutela del Territorio e del Mare and Others* [2010] ECR I-2007. See also G C Rowe, 'Das Verursacherprinzip als Aufteilungsprinzip im Umweltrecht: Juristische und ökonomische Überlegunegn auf der Basis des Coase-Theorems' in E Gawel, *Effizienz im Umweltrecht* (Nomos 2001) 397–426; B Wegener, 'Europäisches Umweltverwaltungsrecht' in J P Terhechte (ed), *Verwaltungsrecht der Europäischen Union* (Nomos 2011) 1308.

[19] See, for a general coverage of the interpretation of environmental protection in the EU, Wasmeier (n 4) 159).

[20] B Grzeszick, 'Das Grundrecht auf eine gute Verwaltung–Strukturen und Perspektiven des Charta-Grundrechts auf eine gute Verwaltung', (2006) 41 *Europarecht* 161–81, 161; W Weiß, *Der Europäische Verwaltungsverbund—Grundfragen, Kennzeichen, Herausforderungen* (Duncker & Umblot 2010) 45.

[21] Certain subsidiary principles could be added, eg 'cradle-to-grave' and, arguably, the principle of environmental restoration.

[22] G Sydow, *Verwaltungskooperation in der Europäischen Union–Zur horizontalen und vertikalen Zusammenarbeit der europäischen Verwaltungen am Beispiel des Produktzulassungsrechts* (Mohr Siebeck 2004) 22.

and application of the precautionary principle in relation to the regulation of pesticides.[23] Also, the more general principles of Union law are reflected repeatedly in secondary environmental legislation. Cooperation, for example, as a principle pointing to various means of collaborative action,[24] including especially information exchange and mutual assistance, particularly within networks, underlies numerous rules in sectoral environmental law laying down methods, standards, and procedures for environmental information management (see below). We can indeed see such rules as demonstrating that the idea of a real separation of levels, actors and procedures loses ground to the concept of integrated administration, even despite the above-mentioned emphasis on national implementation.

E Organization, Institutions, and Structures for Environmental Protection

Just as in most other sectors, structural aspects play a central role in the integrated—inter-administrative and transnational—environmental administration of the Union, seeking to reflect, or indeed provide, optimal 'European fitness',[25] and thereby to satisfy aspects of the principle of good administration.[26] The latter demands an identifiable structure of communication as the basis of an efficient and enduring willingness to cooperate.[27] Key actors and bodies at the core of EU environmental management are DG Environment (DG ENV), the European Environment Agency (EEA) and the European Chemical Agency (ECHA). One should note that other elements of the EU bureaucracy also have at least some explicit focus on the implementation of environmental policy, for example, DG Health and Food Safety (DG SANTE) and DG Energy (DG ENER), so that responsibilities in their fields are, to a certain degree, somewhat dispersed (but that reflects arguably the underlying, cross-sectoral impact of Article 11 TFEU).

Emerging from Commission initiatives,[28] the establishment by the Member States of national bodies as coordinating nodes between the national and supranational levels has specifically resulted in so-called National Reference Centres (NRCs) and Primary Contact Points (PCPs).[29] These specialist centres are responsible for links between the EEA (see below) and the European Topic Centres (ETCs). The latter, consortia of national bodies specialized in particular environmental fields, are contractually

---

[23] See eg Art 1(4) of Regulation (EC) No 1107/2009 of the European Parliament and of the Council of 21 October 2009 concerning the placing of plant protection products on the market [2009] OJ L309/1–50. See also, in relation to nitrates in rivers, Case C-543/16 *Commission v Germany*, 21 June 2018 ECLI:EU:C:2018:481.

[24] J. Sommer, *Verwaltungskooperation am Beispiel administrativer Informationsverfahren im europäischen Umweltrecht* (Duncker & Humblot 2003) 74.

[25] H Siedentopf, B Speer, 'Europäischer Verwaltungsraum oder Europäische Verwaltungsgemeinschaft? Gemeinschaftsrechtliche und funktionelle Anforderungen an die öffentliche Verwaltung in den EU-Mitgliedstaaten' (2002) 55 *Die Öffentliche Verwaltung* 753, 754.

[26] Art 41 CFR.

[27] C Koch, *Arbeitsebenen der Europäischen Union—Das Verfahrensrecht der Integrationsverwaltung* (Nomos 2003) 28 ff; Sydow (n 22) 112.

[28] Report from the Commission to the Council and the European Parliament—Cooperation between administrations for enforcement of internal market law: a progress report, COM/96/0020 final.

[29] Sommer (n 24) 22. Such centres are financed by the Member States.

entrusted with particular tasks by the EEA in support of its programmes.[30] Among other things, they conduct so-called EIONET-Workshops with the goal of strengthening contact with the NRCs. There are currently seven ETCs, for discussion and agreement on the evolution of EU environmental policy, specifically in the fields of:

- air pollution and climate change mitigation
- biological diversity
- climate change impacts, vulnerability and adaptation
- inland, coastal and marine waters
- spatial information and analysis
- sustainable consumption and production and
- waste and materials in a green economy.[31]

The structure of the NRCs varies, depending on the demands and priorities emerging from the strategies of the EEA. The relevant areas are very diverse (environment and agriculture; air quality; biodiversity data and information; biodiversity and ecosystem indicators and assessment; climate change impacts, vulnerability, and adaptation; communication; environment and energy; environmental information systems; forward-looking information and services; environment and health). EIONET PCPs and NRCs exist for industrial pollution; land cover; land use and spatial planning; marine, coastal, and maritime areas; mitigation of air pollution and climate change; noise; resource-efficient economy and the environment; soil; environment and transport; waste; water emissions; water quality and ecological status; water quantity, and state of environment (SOE) review.[32] The activity of national reporting coordinators for the Water Information System for Europe (WISE) also falls within the EIONET framework. In addition to the reference centres, there are the so-called National Focal Points (NFPs) which, in conjunction with the EEA, address transterritorial resources in particular areas (e.g., nature conservation). There are currently 38 of these, typically Member State ministries or environment departments. Regular meetings (several per year) take place between representatives of the NFPs, the Commission, and managers of the ETCs. The outcomes of these discussions are taken up in the meetings of the administrative committee of the EEA, and thus enter into decision-making processes on the Union political level.

No real structure of hierarchy can be identified within this rather complex framework of multi-nodal environmental administration. That said, the Commission has certain coordinative competences[33] vis-à-vis the Member

---

[30] See N Khuchua, 'Die Europäische Umweltagentur (EUA): Überblick und Bewertung der Effizienz' (2009) 5 *Hanse Law Review* 79, 88.

[31] COM(2003) final.

[32] For further information on EIONET NRCs and PCPs see https://www.eionet.europa.eu/ldap-roles/?role_id=eionet-nrc.

[33] This does not amount to supervision, however; rather, there may be a contingent shift in decision-making competence; see G C Rowe, 'Controlling Administrative Action: Internal Administrative Supervision in the European Union' (2009) 61 (Special Edition) *Administrative Law Review* 223, 228.

States.[34] Such competences come into play where deficits in collaborative implementation emerge, for example, concerning nature conservation (especially, e.g., the Natura 2000 network).[35] In relation to information management the Commission can take on a coordinating role by prescribing technical processes for data transfer by the Member States as a consequence of Article 5(5) of Council Decision 97/101/EG.[36] To facilitate emissions-trading the Commission has the competence to reduce the volume of tradable permits when this appears necessary.[37] Despite such opportunities for intervention, there is no doubt that it is the cooperative model which dominates, and not a hierarchical one. A decision on the supranational ('central') level occurs only under strictly predetermined conditions set out in the relevant legislative measure, as in the examples just given. The transition from horizontal cooperation through Commission-based coordination to ultimate determination by the Commission is gradual and fluid, but may display a certain vagueness. This lack of a sharp differentiation, may, in certain circumstances, be disadvantageous, and has generated demands for change. Where legal acts do not explicitly afford the Commission a coordinative competence, a more precisely defined coordinational or determinative capacity may be necessary for a higher standard of environmental protection.[38]

[34] Such can already be taken out of Art 17(1) TFEU (the Commission's power to control the observance of the treaty by the Member States) and, more concretely, the role of the Commission in setting the agenda of and chairing comitology committees (but, notably, without having voting rights).

[35] Based on Directive 2001/18/EC of the European Parliament and of the Council of 12 March 2001 on the deliberate release into the environment of genetically modified organisms and repealing Council Directive 90/220/EEC[2001] OJ L106/1–39, the Commission has a dispute-resolution function where national authorities' divergent points of reference and recognitions determinations which cannot be resolved in follow-up clarification discussions. The Commission then issues a decision directed to a state in the sense of Art 288 fourth paragraph TFEU, from which the decision-making authority can depart only in special circumstances. See also Sydow (n 22) 152. EU energy law also provides that the Commission can require the amendment of a national regulatory decision and can eventually call in the decision-making competence to itself; see eg Art 42 of Directive 2009/72/EC of the European Parliament and of the Council of 13 July 2009 concerning common rules for the internal market in electricity and repealing Directive 2003/54/EC, OJ L 211, 14.8.2009, pp. 55–93, and Art 46 of Directive 2009/73/EC of the European Parliament and of the Council of 13 July 2009 concerning common rules for the internal market in natural gas and repealing Directive 2003/55/EC, OJ L 211, 14.8.2009, pp. 94–136.

[36] Council Decision 97/101/EC of 27 January 1997 establishing a reciprocal exchange of information and data from networks and individual stations measuring ambient air pollution within the Member States [1997] OJ L35/14–22.

[37] Under Art 9 Directive 2009/29/EC of the European Parliament and of the Council of 23 April 2009 amending Directive 2003/87/EC so as to improve and extend the greenhouse gas emission allowance trading scheme of the Community [2009] OJ L140/63–87. See Case C-267/11 *P European Commission v Republic of Latvia* ECLI:EU:C:2013:624; Case T-374/04 *Federal Republic of Germany v Commission of the European Communities* ECLI:EU:T:2007:332; Case T-183/07 *Republic of Poland v Commission of the European Communities* ECLI:EU:T:2009:350; Case T-370/11 *Republic of Poland v European Commission* ECLI:EU:T:2013:113; Case C-504/09 *P European Commission v Republic of Poland* ECLI:EU:C:2012:178).

[38] A typical example of competences expressed only generally or vaguely, is given by the following:

Without prejudice to the division of responsibilities between Member States and the Commission, the Commission shall implement the actions under the framework for cooperation, as set out in Annexes I and II ... The Commission may, where necessary, arrange additional actions to those set out in Annex II. Such additional actions shall be assessed in the light of the priorities set and the financial resources available and shall be adopted in accordance with the [committee] procedure laid down in Article 4(2);

from Art 2 of Decision No 2850/2000/EC of the European Parliament and of the Council of 20 December 2000 setting up a Community framework for cooperation in the field of accidental or deliberate marine pollution [2000] OJ L332/1–6 (no longer in force, but still relevant for certain purposes under Arts 10 and 14, Directive

Such structural features can be observed very readily in the context of Natura 2000, the Union's pan-European network of nature conservations areas, established in order to increase biodiversity protection through protection of habitat. This measure finds its justification, among others, particularly in the realization that habitat protection can scarcely be effective unless it transcends national borders.[39] The tracts affected are bird-protection areas[40] and flora and fauna habitats, including the maritime sphere.[41] Natura 2000 in fact provides an outstanding example of the integrated system of European environmental administration, characterized by the most intensive administrative cooperation among, and between, repeated and assorted constellations of actors for manifold purposes, on the basis of cooperative procedures coordinated by Union bodies. Thus, the actors and organizational elements which contribute to the realization of Natura 2000 include:

- the Commission, especially DG-Environment

- the European Topic Centres (ETCs), especially the European Topic Centre on Nature Protection and Biodiversity (ETC-NPB)

- Member State representatives on comitology committees

- Member State representatives in the Scientific Working Groups of comitology committees

- Member State representatives and observers for certain procedures specifically related to Natura 2000

- experts groups led and installed by the Commission, including independent experts

- elected and appointed representatives of numerous national and supranational NGOs, including experts from the European Habitats Forum, and landowners' representatives through the European Landowners Organization[42]

2005/35/EC of the European Parliament and of the Council of 7 September 2005 on ship-source pollution and on the introduction of penalties for infringements [2005] OJ L255/11–21).

[39] As expressed also in eg Berne Convention on the Conservation of European Wildlife and Natural Habitats of 19 September 1979, ratified by the EC in 1982.

[40] Special Protection Areas (SPAs) in respect of species falling under Directive 2009/147/EC of the European Parliament and of the Council of 30 November 2009 on the conservation of wild birds (n 2) (esp under Appendix 1).

[41] Sites of Community Importance (SCIs) preparatory to designation, or Special Areas of Conservation (SACs) after designation under Council Directive 92/43/EEC of 21 May 1992 on the conservation of natural habitats and of wild fauna and flora (n 2) (which emerged from the extension of EC competences under the Single European Act). Proposed SCIs are given the name of a proposed sites of Community importance' (pSCI).

[42] European Habitats Forum (EHF) (since1991), a grouping of NGO-Netzwerks which advises and inform DG Environment and the nature conservation authorities of the Member States, especially as regards the introduction of the Habitats and Birds Directives and of Natura 2000. The EHF meet twice yearly with representatives of DG Environment. It has a seat in the Coordination Group for Biodiversity and Nature (comprising representative of the Commission, the Member States, the EEA and other interest groups. The EHF provides a bridge from communication between the DG and European nature conservation organizations. Its members are: A Rocha, BirdLife International, Buglife, Butterfly Conservation Europe, Central & East European Working Group for the Enhancement of Biodiversity (CEEWEB), EUROPARC Federation, European Environmental Bureau (EEB), European Nature Heritage Fund (Euronatur), Eurosite, Fedenature, International Mire Conservation Group (IMCG), International Union

- representatives of the Emerald Network of the Council of Europe
- representatives of applicant states (CEECs) (where necessary or appropriate)
- voluntary representation of non-affected Member States and
- private participants, such as the observational network, the European Bird Census Council.

Beyond the example of the Natura 2000 (physical and organizational) network, other organizational structures in the environmental sector can be drawn upon to typify EU environmental administration. Transborder collaboration in respect of transnational river basin districts[43] offers a classical example of both horizontal and vertical co-ordination, involving agreement among affected Member States, administrative units within Member States (especially in (quasi-)federally organized ones), and third countries, in relation to the management of river systems and catchment areas.[44]

Further, we can also mention the Global Climate Change Alliance (GCCA/ GCCA+).[45] This framework, established in 2007 in order to provide for climate-related dialogue and cooperation with developing countries, in particular with least developed countries (LDCs) and small island developing states (SIDS), involves the interaction of, and partnerships with, a very diverse range of participants, including many which go beyond the confines of the EU itself.[46] Other undertakings, such as the Commission-managed Community Research and Development Information Service (CORDIS), even though encompassing matters going well beyond those within the environmental sphere, also provide platforms for information dissemination and exchange of significance to environmental protection in the Union.

The examples mentioned here merely scratch the surface of the organizational arrangements at work within, and under umbrella of, the EU for the purposes of environmental administration, but should be seen as indicative—and characteristic—of arrangements which can be experienced in virtually every environmental sub-sector.

F Administrative Procedures in the Environmental Sector

In section B above, the Union's administrative tasks (including Member State implementation and single-case enforcement of Union law) in the environment sector were

---

for Conservation of Nature (IUCN), Planta Europa, Societas Europea Herpetologica, The Coastal Union (EUCC), Wetlands International, and the Worldwide Fund for Nature (WWF) European Policy Office.

[43] On the basis of the Water Framework Directive (Directive 2000/60/EC of the European Parliament and of the Council of 23 October 2000 [2000] OJ L327/1–73.

[44] See eg W Köck, J Bovet, 'Koordinierung der Flussgebietsbewirtschaftung: unter besonderer Berücksichtigung der Abstimmung mit der Raumordnung' in H Karl (ed), *Koordination raumwirksamer Politik, Mehr Effizienz und Wirksamkeit von Politik* (EconStor 2015; http://hdl.handle.net/10419/109651); J Albrecht, 'Rechtliche und organisatorische Aspekte grenzübergreifender Flussgebietsverwaltung dargestellt am Beispiel des Elbeeinzugsgebietes' (2008) 123 *Deutsches Verwaltungsblatt* 1027.

[45] See Communication from the Commission to the Council and the European Parliament—Building a Global Climate Change Alliance between the European Union and poor developing countries most vulnerable to climate change, COM(2007) 0540 final.

[46] The categories of partners in the GCCA+ are EU Member States, the Commission, partner countries, implementing partners, development partners, NGOs, EU delegations, the Global Support Facility, local authorities, the ACP Secretariat and Assistance Facility, and regional organizations.

set out in rather schematic and summary form. Associated with the execution of all such tasks are invariably administrative procedures, some more formal and/or systematic than others, some regular and others sporadic, some involving the interaction of many actors and some of fewer, and some within complex organizational frameworks while others take place within simpler structures. Among the most significant tasks of EU administration is the preparation of legislation, and of other measures which then implement environmental legislative schemes. We turn now to procedures typically applicable to those actions.

1 Consultations and hearings

The work of the Council is supported by the Committee of Permanent Representatives of the Governments of the Member States to the European Union (*Coreper—Comité de représentants permanents*) (strictly Coreper I and Coreper II, each with different policy bundles). The Council, as a legislative institution, would itself not properly be characterized as 'administrative'. Even so, it would be more than plausible to describe the preparatory role and associated procedures of Coreper, which meets every week, in this way. The involvement of this committee, composed of permanent national representatives—from the national administrations —, is provided for in Article 240(1) TFEU.[47] The work of Coreper is amplified by in excess of 150 specialized working parties and committees, known together as 'Council preparatory bodies'. They can be viewed as an additional political-administrative element lying between the Commission (in its role as proponent of legislation) and the Council (as co-legislator), with the specific aim of reflecting Member State policy positions.[48] Among these bodies, the Working Party on the Environment and the Working Party on International Environment Issues deserve special mention in the present context. Other standing and ad hoc committees and working parties, usually set up by Coreper (such as the Working Party on Plant Health, the Working Party on Agricultural Questions, the Working Party on Forestry, and the two working parties on external and internal fisheries policy) may also be expected to intersect with environmental policy. In passing, one should note the regular conferences which take place between the representatives of Commission and the European Parliament in the legislative preparatory phase; again, these might justifiably be characterized as political-administrative procedures.[49]

---

[47] In addition to Coreper, special mention should be made of the Special Committee on Agriculture (SCA) (established by a decision of COREPER on 12 May 1960) which prepares the work of the Agriculture and Fisheries Council, i.e., matters relating to the Common Agriculture Policy, which may also have environmental implications.

[48] See generally C Neuhold, E Radulova, 'The Involvement of Administrative Players in the EU Decision-making Process' in H C H Hofmann, A H Türk, *EU Administrative Governance* (Edward Elgar Publishing 2006) 47; T Christiansen, T Larsson, 'Introduction: The Role of Committees in the Policy-process of the European Union' in T Christiansen, T Larsson, *The Role of Committees in the Policy-Process of the European Union–Legislation, Implementation and Deliberation* (Edward Elgar Publishing 2007) 4.

[49] As just one example, the Directive 2002/96/EC of the European Parliament and of the Council of 27 January 2003 on waste electrical and electronic equipment (WEEE)—Joint declaration of the European Parliament, the Council and the Commission relating to Article 9 [2003] OJ L37/24–39, emerged only after long negotiations between the Commission and the European Parliament, involving such preparatory procedures; see E Vogelezang-Stoute, 'Regulating uncertain risks of new technologies: Nanomaterials

In the preparation of legislative proposals, discussion papers, and administrative rules, the Commission regularly conducts both formal and non-formal consultations. Agenda-setting through green and white papers (see below) is always associated with arrangements for discussion in some form, sometimes with proposals for the establishment of specific mechanisms and procedures for the exchange of views, such as the European Forum on Renewable Energy.[50] The conduct of such consultation procedures and public hearings can be traced in part to the 1997 resolution of the Council calling on the Commission to undertake such steps preparatory to legislative proposals,[51] including opening up possibilities for interventions by administrators, external organizations, and citizens.[52] We have in passing already noted above the role of environmental NGOs in consultations, even if not in a formalized way; they are a source of (often indispensable) information for the Commission,[53] themselves linked with one another within the framework of the European Environmental Bureau (EEB). Their involvement can be seen as an example of the place of private actors within implementation in this policy field. In a comparable, but somewhat differently oriented, way, representatives of industry and commerce, also in various groupings and federations—and invariably better resourced than environmental groups—reflect private business influence on Union environmental policy and its administration.

While such processes are of key importance, it has to be noted that they can also allow arguably excessive influence of special interests and professional lobbyists, often supported by substantial financial resources, which may lead to a lack of balance among participants in the political process. A classic illustration of such a constellation is provided by the (now, somewhat older) internet consultations prior to the emergence of the REACH regulation:[54] 250 economic umbrella-groups, 700 individual firms, and 50 environmental and consumer organizations were involved.[55] The key antidote to such imbalance is transparency, supervision, and the observance of basic principles of procedure,[56] but there are deficits, in particular due to the voluntary nature of control structures and the lack of effective application of

---

as a challenge for the regulator' in M Peeters, R Uylenburg (eds), EU Environmental Legislation—Legal Perspectives on Regulatory Strategies (Edward Elgar Publishing 2014) 226.

[50] Green Paper on Energy Efficiency or Doing More with Less, COM(2005/) 0265 final.

[51] Council Resolution of 7 October 1997 on the drafting, implementation and enforcement of Community environmental law [1997] OJ C321/1–5. See also the Commission Communication 'Towards a reinforced culture of consultation and dialogue—General principles and minimum standards for consultation of interested parties by the Commission', COM(2002) 0704 final.

[52] The Commission publishes information about current and concluded consultations at: https://ec.europa.eu/info/consultations_en.

[53] A Epiney, *Umweltrecht der Europäischen Union* (3rd ed, Nomos 2013).

[54] Regulation (EC) No 1907/2006 of the European Parliament and of the Council of 18 December 2006 concerning the Registration, Evaluation, Authorisation and Restriction of Chemicals (REACH), establishing a European Chemicals Agency [2006] OJ L396/1–849. (REACH = Registration, Evaluation, Authorisation and Restriction of Chemicals).

[55] K Meßerschmidt, *Europäisches Umweltrecht* (Beck 2011) 477.

[56] The Commission's 'transparency register' and code of conduct are intended to serve these goals. See Annex III of the Agreement between the European Parliament and the European Commission on the transparency register for organisations and self-employed individuals engaged in EU policy-making and policy implementation [2014] OJ L277/11–24.

sanctions.[57] As a matter of achieving a balanced environmental policy, one could argue that the Union should provide financial support for environmental NGOs in such processes.[58]

In the specific context of Natura 2000 the European Bird Census Council (EBCC), a Europe-wide union of ornithologists based in the Netherlands, offers a key example of the place of private actors in the procedures of Union nature conservation administration. This organization is responsible for a major monitoring project in this field, the Pan-European Common Bird Monitoring Scheme (PECBMS), contributing data necessary for the conduct of various political and administrative tasks, for example, feeding into Eurostat statistics on biological diversity and thus providing measures of the appropriateness of area conservation under the habitat and bird protection regimes or in relation to the European index of common farmland birds. Such monitoring also serves Eurostat's construction of indicators for sustainable development in connection with national data under Regulation 1305/ 2013 on support for rural areas through the European Agricultural Fund for Rural Development (EAFRD),[59] and the EEA, as the basis of its 'Impact of climate change on bird populations—SEBI 011' (EEA Assessment, May 2010). Other international/ global organizations too play a role in these processes, for example, the International Union for the Conservation of Nature (IUCN) and BirdLife International (a global partnership of conservation NGOs focused on conservation of bird and their habitats and biodiversity generally).

One should note here that an actor like EBCC, and a project like PECBMS, are not just examples of cooperation and interaction between private actors and the EU environmental administration, in the ways just outlined. They also exemplify, in themselves, in their own multi-level and networked operation, the cooperative and indeed integrated administrative elements profoundly characteristic of the European Union itself. Specifically, the example of the employment of the PECBMS by the EEA is highly instructive: an EU-body, itself comprising Member State representation (in other words, in effect itself a network) carries out its responsibilities through the use of data gathered via an international network of private persons and organizations in various Member States, in order to serve the needs of a (vast) physical network of conservation areas spread across all (presently) twenty-eight Member States of the Union. There could scarcely be a more telling example of the essential character of European administration of environmental protection, one which is arguably indicative of much of EU administrative implementation, irrespective of the sector concerned.

---

[57] Meßerschmidt, *Europäisches Umweltraecht* (n 55) 473.

[58] See eg Decision No 466/2002/EC of the European Parliament and of the Council of 1 March 2002 laying down a Community action programme promoting non-governmental organisations primarily active in the field of environmental protection [2002] OJ L75/1–6 (now repealed by Council Decision 2007/ 614/Euratom); see also H C H Hofmann, G C Rowe, and A H Türk, *Administrative Law and Policy of the European Union* (Oxford University Press 2011) 31 ff.

[59] Regulation (EU) 1305/2013 of the European Parliament and of the Council of 17 December 2013 on support for rural development by the European Agricultural Fund for Rural Development (EAFRD) [2013] OJ L347/487–548.

2 Consultation with the Committee of the Regions

Environmental measures often have a direct relationship with the activities of municipal and regional authorities, and in particular often impose additional administrative burdens on them. For this reason, hearings involving the European Committee of the Regions (CoR) will normally be held before Union measures in this field (and others) are adopted. This consultative body consists of elected representatives of local and regional governmental bodies throughout Europe (members of local councils, city mayors, chairs or presidents of larger regions, etc).[60] It has six specialized sub-committees which can respond to, or develop their own, proposals. Apart from areas of specifically environmental focus (such and energy and climate), issues addressed include those arising in many other policy fields and the observance of certain basic principles, including proportionality and subsidiarity, for example specifically through the CoR's Subsidiarity Monitoring Network (the CoR being seen as the 'guardian' of the principle). The activity of the CoR preparatory to the adoption of EU legislation and in the supervision of political-legislative actors and, at least incidentally, of administrative actors too, echoes that of the European Parliament and its committees. Measures proposed or adopted by the Commission with the support of any of those bodies are likely to attain a greater level of legitimacy, even though the Commission is not bound by the outcomes of such consultative steps.

3 Expert working groups

Over and above formal or semi-formalized hearings and consultations, various, more formal, procedures are at the Commission's disposal, especially those involving scientific committees and expert working groups.[61] For the purposes of environmental policy, such advisory bodies are almost invariably concerned with complicated technical and scientific subject matter; some may be virtually indispensable in the emergence of solutions to environmental problems.[62] They may be ad hoc or standing bodies. Some have a direct influence on agenda setting, others will merely aid in co-ordinating the interaction of environmental actors. Among other things, they have the task of informing the Commission of the existing regulatory and implementational framework in the several Member States, and alerting it to possible difficulties in the application of proposed legislation.[63] The composition of such groups varies considerably depending on the subject matter and on the Commission's informational needs. The participants will typically represent certain (environmental) political perspectives

---

[60] Meßerschmidt, *Europäisches Umweltrecht* (n 55) 461; L van den Brande in Committee of the Regions, *Political Priorities 2008-2010* (European Union Committee of the Regions 2008) 2.

[61] G F Schaefer, 'Committees in the EC Policy Process: A First Step Towards Developing a Conceptual Framework' in R H Pedler, G F Schäfer (eds), *Shaping European Law and Policy: The Role of Committees and Comitology in the Political Process* (European Institute of Public Administration 1996) 8; C. Demmke, *Europäische Umweltpolitik und nationale Verwaltungen–Rolle und Aufgaben nationaler Verwaltungen im Entscheidungsprozeß* (1998) 9.

[62] T Larsson, T Trondal, 'Agenda-setting in the European Commission: How the European Commission Structure and Influence the EU Agenda' in H C H Hofmann, A H Türk (eds), *EU Administrative Governance* (Edward Elgar Publishing 2006) 33.

[63] Sommer (n 24) 237.

which may well then receive more emphasis than either supranational or national interests and priorities as such,[64] so that finding a suitable balance constitutes much of the policy development process. A general framework for scientific committees has been established by the Commission.[65] Key examples are the (advisory) Scientific Committee of the EEA, the Scientific Committee on Health, Environmental and Emerging Risks (SCHEER),[66] the Advisory Committee on the Control and Reduction of Pollution Caused by Hydrocarbons Discharged at Sea,[67] the Advisory Committee on the Protection of the Environment in Areas under Serious Threat (Mediterranean basin),[68] and the European Consultative Forum on the Environment and Sustainable Development.[69] The last of these consists of representatives of industry, union, national authorities and consumer and environmental organizations and seeks to gather ideas and concepts, and to sense the political and social achievability of measures for environmental protection.[70]

The Commission also relies on a (general) Scientific Advice Mechanism (SAM), the key component of which is the Group of Chief Scientific Advisors (until 2018 known as the High-level Group of Scientific Advisors (HLG).[71] Although its advisory functions are very broad, the expressly scientific nature of its brief creates inevitable links with the development of environmental policy within the European executive.

4 Comitology and the environment

In the environmental sector, as in others, administrative action and the associated evolution of environmental policy is characterized by complex committee activity, particularly within the framework of comitology.[72] As distinct from the extensive place of experts groups in the context of the exercise of the Commission's virtual monopoly in initiating legislative proposals (Article 294(2) TFEU),[73] the application of

---

[64] Demmke (n 61)) 15.

[65] Commission Decision of 7 August 2015 on establishing Scientific Committees in the field of public health, consumer safety and the environment, C(2015) 5383 final.

[66] This is a standing body primary set in the context of relation health, food and safety but, because of its part focus on environmental matters, provides an example of the cross-sectoral application of environmental factors, reflecting Art 11 TFEU. This committee reaches back to a predecessor based on Commission Decision 78/618/EEC of 28 June 1978 setting up a Scientific Advisory Committee to examine the toxicity and ecotoxicity of chemical compounds [1978] OJ L198/17–18.

[67] Commission Decision 80/686/EEC on establishing an Advisory committee on the control and reduction of pollution caused by hydrocarbons discharged at sea [1980] OJ L188/11–12.

[68] Commission Decision 86/479/EEC of 18 September 1986 establishing an Advisory Committee on the protection of the environment in areas under serious threat (Mediterranean basin) [1986] OJ L282/23–24.

[69] Commission Decision 2001/704/EC of 26 September 2001 repealing Decision 97/150/EC on the setting-up of a European consultative forum on the environment and sustainable development (notified under document number C(2001) 2863) [2001] OJ L258/20–20. See Sommer (n 24) 239 ff.

[70] Sommer (n 24) 243.

[71] Based on Commission Decision C(2015) 6946 of 16 October 2015 on the setting up of the High Level Group of Scientific Advisors, as amended by Commission Decision C(2018) 1919 of 5 April 2018.

[72] T Christiansen and Larsson (n 48) 2 ff, 6; Larsson and Trondal (n 62) 16; G Roller, 'Comitology in Environmental Policy: Practical Experiences between Efficiency and Legitimacy' in H C H Hofmann, A H Türk, *EU Administrative Governance* (2006) 115.

[73] See generally T Larsson, *Precooking in the European Union–: The World of Expert Groups* (Stockholm: ESO Report 2003/16).

comitology procedures is more formalized. Comitology committees in effect control the Commission in its preparation of Union subordinate legislation (delegated and implementing acts),[74] thus profoundly shaped by the participation of Member State representatives. In the context under discussion are numerous committees, presently 30, covering virtually the whole spectrum of the environmental sector (see Appendix I for a complete list), of great significance in particular because of the numerous administrative rules emerging from the Commission for purposes of environmental implementation.[75] Although the Commission has the role of convening the committees and setting their agendas, it has no vote in the decision-making. The committees are usually supported by scientific working groups (SWGs).

Among the more important committees are those relating to waste,[76] and dangerous substances.[77] So, for example, in 1976 the Committee on Waste Management[78] was established, with the task of supporting the Commission in its development of waste management policy in relation to the technical, economic and legal means of reducing waste quantities, to recycling, and to waste disposal as well as in the preparation of new proposals for directives. The activity of the committees is aimed, on the one hand, at integrating scientific and economic expertise (e.g., in updating legal measures in accordance with technical advances), and on the other hand at allowing the interests of the Member States and others to be heard at an early stage in decision-making processes. Among other things, such committees deal with establishing financing programmes for purposes of environmental implementation or, for example, preparing lists of dangerous substances,[79] for example, the European Waste Catalogue (EWC)[80]

---

[74] B G Peters, 'Forms of Informal Governance: Searching for Efficiency and Democracy' in T Christiansen and T Larsson (eds), *The Role of Committees in the Policy-Process of the European Union—Legislation, Implementation and Deliberation* (Edward Elgar Publishing 2007) 39, 46); see generally Hofmann, Rowe, and Türk (n 58)) 264 ff.

[75] Epiney (n 53) 36 ff; Roller (n 72) 115 ff; on comitology under the REACH-Regulation (EC) No 1907/2006 see especially D Martel, 'REACH: Komitologie und Rechtsschutz' (2008) 12 *Zeitschrift für Europarechtliche Studien*) 601, 622 ff. See also Directive 2008/98/EC of the European Parliament and of the Council of 19 November 2008 on waste and repealing certain Directives [2008] OJ L312/3–30; Commission Directive 94/3/EC of 21 January 1994 establishing a procedure for the notification of interception of a consignment or a harmful organism from third countries and presenting an imminent phytosanitary danger [1994] OJ L32/37–39; Regulation (EC) No 1013/2006 of the European Parliament and of the Council of 14 June 2006 on shipments of waste [2006] OJ L190/1–98.

[76] See especially Art 18 of Council Directive 75/442/EEC of 15 July 1975 on waste [1975] OJ L194/47–49, in the form of Council Directive 91/156/EEC of 18 March 1991, amending Directive 75/442/EEC on waste [1991] OJ L78/32–37; see now Directive 2008/98/EC of the European Parliament and of the Council of 19 November 2008 on waste and repealing certain Directives (n 75); NB: Council Directive 91/156/EEC of 18 March 1991 amending Directive 75/442/EEC on waste [1991] OJ L78/32–37.

[77] Council Directive 67/548/EEC of 27 June 1967 on the approximation of laws, regulations and administrative provisions relating to the classification, packaging and labelling of dangerous substances [1967] OJ 196/1–98, most recently amended through Regulation (EC) No 1272/2008 of the European Parliament and of the Council of 16 December 2008 on classification, labelling and packaging of substances and mixtures, amending and repealing Directives 67/548/EEC and 1999/45/EC, and amending Regulation (EC) No 1907/2006 [2008] OJ L353/1–1355. See also Roller (n 72) 115, 119.

[78] Commission Decision 76/431/EEC of 21 April 1976 setting up a Committee on Waste Management [1976] OJ L115/73–74.

[79] Epiney (n 53) 36 ff; G C Azzi, 'Comitology and the European Commission' in C Joerges, E Vos (eds), *EU Committees: Social Regulation, Law and Politics* (Oxford University Press 1999) 51 (51); Roller (n 72) 115, 118 ff.

[80] Commission Decision 94/3/EC of 20 December 1993 establishing a list of wastes pursuant to Art 1a of Council Directive 75/442/EEC on waste [1994] OJ L5/15–33.

and the Hazardous Waste Catalogue (HWC),[81] leading ultimately then to a unified European waste catalogue.[82] A further example of significant comitology activity is provided by the work of the committee under the Water Framework Directive,[83] the Committee for implementing the directive establishing a Community policy regarding water, initially resisted by the Member States,[84] where Commission proposals for the further development of the Directive itself have been subject of discussion, and binding technical and analytical guidelines on its implementation have been adopted. The list of such activities can be extended by reference to the fields of the release of genetically modified organisms,[85] crop protection,[86] radioactive substances,[87] or foodstuffs.[88]

Specifically in the field of nature conservation, the Habitats Committee[89] and the Ornis-Committee[90] (composed of specialists from the ministries of the Member States) are of central importance, inter alia for ensuring that the management of the conservation areas of Natura 2000 satisfies evolving technical and scientific standards.[91] So, for example, the 2011 'Explanatory Notes & Guidelines' emerging from the Habitats Committee, setting out monitoring and reporting requirements which go

---

[81] Council Decision 94/904/EC of 22 December 1994 establishing a list of hazardous waste pursuant to Art 1(4) of Council Directive 91/689/EEC on hazardous waste [1994] OJ L356/14–22; now replaced (see following footnote).

[82] Commission Decision 2000/532/EC of 3 May 2000 replacing Decision 94/3/EC establishing a list of wastes pursuant to Art 1(a) of Council Directive 75/442/EEC on waste and Council Decision 94/904/EC establishing a list of hazardous waste pursuant to Art 1(4) of Council Directive 91/689/EEC on hazardous waste (notified under document number C(2000) 1147) [2000] OJ L226/3–24.

[83] Directive 2000/60/EC of the European Parliament and of the Council of 23 October 2000 establishing a framework for Community action in the field of water policy [2000] OJ L327/1–73.

[84] The Member States opposed this committee which, in their view would change decision-making practice and in particular impose extra costs; see T Gehring, 'Bargaining, Arguing and Functional Differentiation of Decision-making: The Role of Committees in European Environmental Process Regulation' in C Joerges, E Vos, *EU Committees: Social Regulation, Law and Politics* (Oxford University Press 1999) 205 ff.

[85] Directive 2001/18/EC of the European Parliament and of the Council of 12 March 2001 on the deliberate release into the environment of genetically modified organisms(n 35), as amended by Directive 2008/27/EC of the European Parliament and of the Council of 11 March 2008 amending Directive 2001/18/EC on the deliberate release into the environment of genetically modified organisms, as regards the implementing powers conferred on the Commission [2008] OJ L81/45–47. See also Roller (n 72) 123.

[86] Council Decision 76/894/EEC of 23 November 1976 establishing a Standing Committee on Plant Health [1976] OJ L340/25, now repealed by Regulation (EU) No 652/2014 of the European Parliament and of the Council of 15 May 2014 laying down provisions for the management of expenditure relating to the food chain, animal health and animal welfare, and relating to plant health and plant reproductive material [2014] OJ L189/1–32.

[87] Council Decision 80/237/Euratom of 18 February 1980 on the setting up of an 'ad hoc' Advisory Committee on the Reprocessing of Irradiated Nuclear Fuels [1980] OJ L52/9–10.

[88] In this regard see Sommer (n 24) 240 ff.

[89] Committee (C13400) on the conservation of natural habitats and of wild fauna and flora, under Council Directive 92/43/EEC of 21 May 1992 on the conservation of natural habitats and of wild fauna and flora (n 2).

[90] Committee (C11800) for the adaptation to scientific and technical progress of the directive on conservation of wild bird, under Directive 2009/147/EC of the European Parliament and of the Council of 30 November 2009 on the conservation of wild birds (n 2).

[91] Report from the Commission on the application of Directive 79/409/EEC on the conservation of wild birds—Update for 1993–1995 based on information supplied by the Member States on the application of national measures adopted pursuant to the Directive, COM(2000) 0180 final.

back to Article 11 Habitats Directive,[92] themselves exemplify the documentary expression of administrative integration reflected in Natura 2000. Also contributing to nature conservation activity is the LIFE+ Committee, dealing with the financing of environmental protection measures.[93] One could add here a longer list of committees relevant to this sub-sector, addressing the issues of spatial data, maritime zone strategy, and trade in endangered species.[94]

5 Information sharing procedures in environmental administration

We stressed above that the administrative implementation of environmental policy in the European Union relies significantly—perhaps predominantly—on the sharing of relevant information. It is, therefore, not surprising that key procedures relate exactly to this factor.

(a) Exchange of information and coordination

Information sharing can occur only through cooperative processes and relations in the service of a common goal, and in some way can be seen to suppress any distinction between the national and the supranational administrative levels. Key players in such processes are the Commission and the EEA. To a certain extent, the Commission possesses certain powers in relation to information which go beyond those of the individual Member States,[95] although the latter have informational competences and responsibilities flowing from the tasks they must themselves undertake, as well as sometimes from national practice.[96]

---

[92] Cf European Topic Centre on Biological Diversity, 'Assessment and reporting under Article 17 of the Habitats Directive – Reporting Formats for the period 2007-2012' (July 2011) https://circabc.europa.eu/sd/a/2c12cea2-f827-4bdb-bb56-3731c9fd8b40/Art17%20-%20Guidelines-final.pdf.

[93] See Arts 19(6), 20(1)c)(ii), 30 of Regulation (EU) No 1293/2013 of the European Parliament and of the Council of 11 December 2013 on the establishment of a Programme for the Environment and Climate Action (LIFE) [2013] OJ L347/185–208.

[94] Committee (C33600) on Infrastructure for Spatial Information in the European Community (INSPIRE) (Directive 2007/2/EC); Committee (C36400) for implementing the marine strategy framework directive (Directive 2008/56/EC); Committee (C13100) for the protection of species of wild fauna and flora by regulating trade therein (Regulation 1007/2009/EC and Regulation 338/97/EC).

[95] See A von Bogdandy, 'Die Informationsbeziehungen im europäischen Verwaltungsverbund' in M Albers, W Hoffmann-Riem, E Schmidt-Aßmann and others, *Grundlagen des Verwaltungsrechts–Informationsordnung, Verwaltungsverfahren, Handlungsformen* (Beck Verlag 2008) 347, 353.

[96] In federal systems, such Germany, there are typically coordinating responsibilities imposed on the central (federal) level, vis-à-vis the individual states, e.g. in nature conservation, where the latter have legislative competences. In relation to EU committee activity see Neuhold and Radulova (n 48)H C H Hofmann, A H Türk 44, at61 ff; A Bücker, S Schlacke, 'Die Entstehung einer "politischen Verwaltung" durch EG-Ausschüsse: Rechtstatsachen und Rechtsentwicklungen' in C Joerges, J Falke, *Das Ausschußwesen der Europäischen Union–Praxis der Risikoregulierung im Binnenmarkt und ihre rechtliche Verfassung* (Nomos 2000) 161, 234; C Demmke, M Haritz, 'Die Europäisierung des öffentlichen Dienstes in den Mitgliedstaaten und die Rolle der einzelstaatlichen Bediensteten im Entscheidungsprozess' in C Demmke (ed), *Europäische Umweltpolitik und nationale Verwaltungen—Rolle und Aufgaben nationaler Verwaltungen im Entscheidungsprozeß* (European Institute of Public Administration 1998) 9, 16.

(b) Informational obligations

One of the key elements of all administrative interaction in the Union is the obligation of generating and passing on certain kinds of information. The environmental sector is no exception.

(i) Generation of environmental information

The obligation to generate environmental information arises in diverse sub-sectoral areas. The Member States are required in numerous environment-protection settings to generate or obtain information, by way of monitoring measures, by requiring private parties to provide information to regulatory authorities, by conducting certain procedures in order to generate and process information (foremost among these, environmental impact assessment), through consultations with member of the public, or sometimes in conjunction with experts or industry representatives, and more besides.[97] Often, though, the need to generate information is not the result of an explicit obligation to this effect, but rather the indirect consequence of being obliged to provide information to another authority, typically on the supranational level of the Union, or via a common platform for information sharing across the EU.[98] Very obviously in the field of transboundary air pollution, there is a need to have recourse to information from authorities in the source-jurisdiction(s). This is most telling when the nature of the transboundary pollution is such that its effects are felt not just by adjacent or neighbouring countries, but by many countries in common (as, for example, ozone), where plans and programmes must perforce be developed in common.[99] In the case of ozone, national monitoring information is transmitted via the Commission to the EEA, so that in this case even an indirect obligation to generate information could be seen as being imposed upon the Commission due to its obligation to enforce the requirements of the Directive 2002/3/EC. Comparable (indirect) obligations have arisen under Council Decision 97/101/EC[100] for the monitoring of air pollution in the Member States. Perhaps a rare example of a direct obligation to produce environmental information is given by the case of measurements of water quality serving to designate waters endangered by nitrates,[101] or for waters under the Bathing Water Directive.[102]

---

[97] See, inter alia, Council Decision 93/389/EEC of 24 June 1993 for a monitoring mechanism of Community CO_2 and other greenhouse gas emissions [1993] OJ L167/31–33; concerning air pollution see Art 6 Directive 2008/50/EC of the European Parliament and of the Council of 21 May 2008 on ambient air quality and cleaner air for Europe [2008] OJ L152/1–44, under which the Member State must carry out an initial evaluation of air quality through representative measurement and so generate the information relevant to fulfilling the policy; Sommer (n 24) 166 ff, with further references.

[98] Sommer (n 24) 166 ff.

[99] See eg Directive 2008/50/EC of the European Parliament and of the Council of 21 May 2008 on ambient air quality and cleaner air for Europe (n 97). See also H C H Hofmann, 'Composite Decision-making Procedures in EU Administrative Law' in H C H Hofmann, A H Türk, *Legal Challenges in EU Administrative Law: Towards an Integrated Administration* (Edward Elgar Publishing 2009) 145.

[100] Council Decision 97/101/EC of 27 January 1997 establishing a reciprocal exchange of information and data from networks and individual stations measuring ambient air pollution within the Member States (n 36).

[101] Council Directive 91/676/EEC of 12 December 1991 concerning the protection of waters against pollution caused by nitrates from agricultural sources [1991] OJ L375/1–8.

[102] Directive 2006/7/EC of the European Parliament and of the Council of 15 February 2006 concerning the management of bathing water quality and repealing Directive 76/160/EEC [2006] OJ L64/37–51.

(ii) Disclosure and transfer of information

As just noted, it is more the obligation to provide, disclose or transfer information, typically to an authority in another Member State or on the Union level, which characterizes EU informational obligations, rather than an express duty to produce the information in the first place. The obligation is usually in fact a correlative of a demand, or request, for information in a particular instance.[103] Numerous provisions in secondary law impose a duty on national authorities to make information available, or to transfer it, upon request.[104] The Urban Waste Water Directive[105] requires that information held by national bodies should be provided to the Commission as requested; a similar obligation arose under the (now repealed) Plant Protection Products Directive.[106] The replacement legislation for the latter Directive, Article 9(3) of Regulation 1107/2009,[107] now provides a key illustration of the nature of information sharing in EU composite (product approval) procedures within the environmental sector:

> Where the dossiers submitted with the application contain all the elements provided for in Article 8, the rapporteur Member State shall notify the applicant, the other Member States, the Commission and the Authority of the admissibility of the application and start assessing the active substance.
>
> After receiving that notification, the applicant shall immediately forward the dossiers ... to the other Member States, the Commission and the Authority, including the information about those parts of the dossiers in respect of which confidentiality has been requested as referred to in Article 7(3).

The Commission itself can be subject to duties to provide information to a Member State as regards information of transborder relevance obtained from (another) Member State, usually arising from documentation on national environmental protection measures or concerning product-related installations submitted to the Commission.

Such duties to 'provide' information should be clearly distinguished from obligations to *distribute* information, or, more simply, to inform (despite rather varied formulations). The differentiation here lies in the body which has to take the initiative. In the preceding paragraph, information was made available after the initiative

---

[103] Sommer (n 24) 102 ff.

[104] See eg Art 19(2) of Directive 2008/50/EC of the European Parliament and of the Council of 21 May 2008 on ambient air quality and cleaner air for Europe (n 97); Arts 4, 5, 7, and 17 of Commission Regulation (EC) No 1737/2006 of 7 November 2006 laying down detailed rules for the implementation of Regulation (EC) No 2152/2003 of the European Parliament and of the Council concerning monitoring of forests and environmental interactions in the Community [2006] OJ L334/1–73, as the basis of the European Forest Fire Information System (EFFIS).

[105] Council Directive 91/271/EEC of 21 May 1991 concerning urban waste-water treatment [1991] OJ L135/40–52.

[106] Council Directive 91/414/EEC of 15 July 1991 concerning the placing of plant protection products on the market [1991] OJ L230/1–32.

[107] Regulation (EC) No 1107/2009 of the European Parliament and of the Council of 21 October 2009 concerning the placing of plant protection products on the market and repealing Council Directives 79/117/EEC and 91/414/EEC (n 23). See also Art 65 of that Regulation.

was taken to request it. Here, the initiative is with a body to provide it, whether in a single case or generally, without being asked.[108] We are, then, often concerned with a duty to warn of environmental danger, or with the making of an application for approval of an installation or a product and the concomitant requirement to provide information relevant to this.[109] An example is offered by the Euratom Decision in relation to a radioactive emergency, where the Commission is to be informed without delay, and it, in turn, is to inform the Member States.[110] What should be generally noted here is that the chain of information transmission imposed can take different forms:

- Member State(s) to the Commission
- Member State(s) to the Commission, and then on to (other) Member State(s) and
- Member State(s) to Member State(s).

(iii) Reporting obligations

Reporting obligations can take a range of forms. Some require not only a transmission of bare data, but rather systematic, regular, and comprehensive compilation of relevant information.[111] These are sometimes monitoring prerequisites set down in provisions of secondary law, such as the REACH Directive,[112] or in the context of integrated avoidance and reduction of environmental harms,[113] (in the latter case a requirement of a national report on the operational implementation of the legislation (Article 17)). Many such obligations require the publications of reports addressing the conditions of environmental protection in the Member State concerned, and the transmission of these to the Commission (e.g., on urban waste water,[114] or on Union joint action in the

---

[108] Sommer (n 24) 107.

[109] J Sommer, 'Informationskooperation am Beispiel des Europäischen Umweltrechtes' in E Schmidt-Aßmann, B Schöndorf-Haubold, *Der europäische Verwaltungsverbund–Formen und Verfahren der Verwaltungszusammenarbeit in der EU* (Mohr Siebeck 2005) 61.

[110] See Arts 4, 5 of Council Decision 87/600/Euratom of 14 December 1987 on Community arrangements for the early exchange of information in the event of a radiological emergency [1987] OJ L371/76–78. The Commission is also obliged to transmit all information at its disposal regarding raised radioactivity levels in third countries to the Member States, art 5(1) of Council Decision 87/600/Euratom. Similarly, Art 25(2) of Directive 2008/50/EC of the European Parliament and of the Council of 21 May 2008 on ambient air quality and cleaner air for Europe (n 97), under which the Commission shall be invited to be present and to assist in any cooperation of the member states, or Art 25(2) of Directive 2008/50/EC of the European Parliament and of the Council of 21 May 2008 on ambient air quality and cleaner air for Europe (n 97).

[111] See von Bogdandy, 'Die Informationsbeziehungen im europäischen Verwaltungsverbund' (n 95) 354.

[112] Consider Recital 121 Regulation (EC) No 1907/2006 of the European Parliament and of the Council of 18 December 2006 concerning the Registration, Evaluation, Authorisation and Restriction of Chemicals (REACH), establishing a European Chemicals Agency (n 54); see also the reporting obligations within the framework of Council Directive 96/82/EC (Seveso II) of 9 December 1996 on the control of major-accident hazards involving dangerous substances [1997] OJ L10/13–33 (repealed by Directive 2012/18/EU [2012] OJ L197/1–37).

[113] Directive 2010/75/EU of the European Parliament and of the Council of 24 November 2010 on industrial emissions (integrated pollution prevention and control) [2010] OJ L334/17–119.

[114] Council Directive 91/271/EEC of 21 May 1991 concerning urban waste-water treatment (n 105).

field of water policy).[115] With respect to the Habitats Directive, one of the central legislative pillars of Natura 2000, the Member States must report every six years on measures of implementation.[116] Obligations to report periodically to the Commission have at times led to considerable variation across the Member State concerning form, content, and frequency. Attempts were, therefore, made to establish greater uniformity, particularly in Directive 91/692/EC,[117] which aimed at in effect a standardized model for reports, and standardized periodicity and format, including a consolidated implementation report. (Article 2(1)).

The Commission also has reporting obligations vis-à-vis the Member States, for example under Article 72(3) fifth paragraph Directive 2010/75/EU,[118] and these are basically associated with the obligation to *publish* information and to focus on the distribution or transfer of scientific and technical material. The Commission will usually receive such information from Member States and evaluate and summarize it itself. Before placing its report in a database accessible to all Member State, it may request a national authority to check certain aspects. A typical example of such a way of proceeding is provided under the Birds Directive, in respect of three-yearly reports,[119] or reporting in regard to freshwater quality.[120] Progress reports which must be made by the Commission may follow a similar pattern, often with recommendations for improvement in implementation or legislative change, but such documents are characterized by greater freedom of form.[121] The EEA is also subject to reporting duties.[122] As the Agency does not have a measuring, observational, and monitoring competence of its own in national territory,[123] it relies on the environmental reports of the Member State authorities, on the basis of informational cooperative arrangements with them.

[115] Directive 2000/60/EC of the European Parliament and of the Council of 23 October 2000 establishing a framework for Community action in the field of water policy (n 83).

[116] Council Directive 92/43/EEC of 21 May 1992 on the conservation of natural habitats and of wild fauna and flora (n 2).

[117] Council Directive 91/692/EEC of 23 December 1991 standardizing and rationalizing reports on the implementation of certain Directives relating to the environment [1991] OJ L377/48–54, together with Directive 2010/75/EU of the European Parliament and of the Council of 24 November 2010 on industrial emissions (integrated pollution prevention and control) (n 113).

[118] Sommer (n 24) 200 ff. In exceptional cases, the Commission's obligation to inform Member States with information may be limited merely to providing an overview in tabular form; see Art 5 Council Decision 82/459/EEC of 24 June 1982 establishing a reciprocal exchange of information and data from networks and individual stations measuring air pollution within the Member States [1982] OJ L210/1–7.

[119] See Art 12(2) of Directive 2009/147/EC of the European Parliament and of the Council of 30 November 2009 on the conservation of wild birds (n 2) (ORNIS). That part of the draft report covering the information supplied by a Member State shall be forwarded to the authorities of the Member State in question for verification. The final version of the report is to be forwarded to the Member States.

[120] See also Art 3(8) and Annex I of Directive 2000/60/EC of the European Parliament and of the Council of 23 October 2000 establishing a framework for Community action in the field of water policy (n 83).

[121] See especially Art 37 Directive 2008/98/EC of the European Parliament and of the Council of 19 November 2008 on waste (n 75); Sommer (n 24) 204.

[122] Regulation (EC) No 401/2009 of the European Parliament and of the Council of 23 April 2009 on the European Environment Agency and the European Environment Information and Observation Network (Codified version) [2009] OJ L126/13–22.

[123] Sommer (n 24) 203, with further references.

The satisfaction of reporting obligations on the Union level has repeatedly been jeopardized by the insufficiency of national reports to Union authorities.[124] A telling example from the past is provided by the requirement under the Waste Shipment Directive[125] to provide biannual reports on hazardous wastes to the Commission; none was ever provided. Although the Commission would have been entitled to have brought infringement procedures under the Treaties for such breaches, it scarcely did so, rare exceptions being actions against Germany and Belgium.[126] Along the same line, the Drinking Water Directive provided that the Member States could deviate from certain legislative requirements, provided this was notified to the Commission. In its turn, Germany permitted its *Länder* to deviate, but without a notification requirement; this was invalidated by the Court at the behest of the Commission.[127] Since the standardizing of reporting, mentioned above, the Member States now, as a rule, satisfy such reporting obligations, so that the Commission is in turn able to fulfil its own reporting and publication duties.[128]

As we noted above concerning duties to 'provide' information, one can in summary also identify certain typical chains for the distribution of information by the making of (regular) reports. These are:

- Member State(s) to the Commission
- Commission to the Member States
- Member State(s) to Commission to Member States
- Member State(s) to EEA to Commission/Member States.

---

[124] L Krämer, 'Defizite im Vollzug des EG-Umweltrechts und ihre Ursachen' in G Lübbe-Wolff (ed), *Der Vollzug des europäischen Umweltrechts* (Nomos 1996) 24.

[125] See Art 13(1) of Council Directive 84/631/EEC of 6 December 1984 on the supervision and control within the European Community of the transfrontier shipment of hazardous waste [1984] OJ L326/31–41 (that particular requirement has now changed, the Directive having been replaced by Regulation (EC) No 1013/2006 of the European Parliament and of the Council of 14 June 2006 on shipments of waste (n 75).

[126] Case C-237/90 *Commission v Germany* [1992] ECR I-05973; Case C-162/89 *Commission v Belgium* [1990] ECR I-02391.

[127] Case C-237/90 *Commission v Germany* (n 126).

[128] Such Commission reports in the environmental field are illustrated by the following few examples: Report from the Commission to the European Parliament and the Council on the exercise of the power to adopt delegated acts conferred on the Commission pursuant to Regulation (EU) No 525/2013 of the European Parliament and of the Council of 21 May 2013 on a mechanism for monitoring and reporting greenhouse gas emissions and for reporting other information at national and Union level relevant to climate change and repealing Decision No 280/2004/EC, COM(2018) 052 final; Report from the Commission to the European Parliament and the Council on progress in implementing Regulation (EC) 166/2006 concerning the establishment of a European Pollutant Release and Transfer Register (E-PRTR), COM(2017) 0810 final; Report from the Commission to the European Parliament and the Council on the review of implementation of Regulation (EC)No 122/2009 of the European Parliament and of the Council on 25 November 2009 on the voluntary participation by organisations in a Community eco-management and audit scheme (EMAS) and the Regulation (EC) No 66/2010 of the parliament and of the Council of 25 November 2009 on the EU Ecolabel, COM(2017) 0355 final; Report from the Commission to the European Parliament and the Council on the exercise of the power to adopt delegated acts conferred on the Commission pursuant to Directive 2016/802/EU of the European Parliament and of the Council of 11 May 2016 relating to a reduction in the sulphur content of certain liquid fuels, COM(2017) 0342 final; Report from the Commission to the European Parliament, the Council, the European Economic and Social Committee and the Committee of the Regions, Actions to Streamline Environmental Reporting, COM(2017) 0312 final.

Such a list is a simplification: the activities of other actors—working groups, committees, NGOs, foreign authorities—actually mean that there are further, more complicated information streams and sequences, but typically less formal and usually without a strict legislative framework regarding obligation, content, or form.

(iv) Notification

Beyond provision with or without request, and obligation to report and/or distribute, there are requirements to *notify*. Such obligations are in legal terms typically more formalized, and generally associated with legal consequences.[129] For example, the Waste Shipments Regulation[130] explicitly requires the notification of transborder movement of waste (Articles 4 ff), using prescribed forms which call for specific information. The requirement under the Euratom Directive concerning radioactive waste is similar.[131] The Court has regularly issued declaratory relief relating to breaches of notification obligations.[132]

(v) Notice and communication within consultation procedures

A further, special context for the provision or communication of information is that which arises where consultation processes occur. Such obligations are familiar under public international law, but emerge also from EU secondary law.[133] This occurs especially in legal relations between neighbouring jurisdictions, and correspondingly usually involves a mutuality of exchange.[134] This can occur voluntarily as well as being the result of a legal requirement. So, for example, under the Water Framework Directive,[135] a Member State experiencing difficulty in water resource management can consult other states and/or the Commission in order to generate an exchange of views (Article 12).[136] If the Commission is drawn into this, it has indeed the obligation to express its position, just as in the case where a Member State has difficulties in implementing Union secondary law.[137] Such exchange takes places on the basis of reciprocity and

---

[129] See von Bogdandy, 'Die Informationsbeziehungen im europäischen Verwaltungsverbund' (n 95) 354.

[130] Regulation (EC) No 1013/2006 of the European Parliament and of the Council of 14 June 2006 on shipments of waste (n 75).

[131] See Art 7 of Council Directive 2006/117/Euratom of 20 November 2006 on the supervision and control of shipments of radioactive waste and spent fuel [2006] OJ L337/21–32.

[132] See eg under Directive 98/34/EC, Case C-139/92 *Commission v Italy* [1993] ECR I-04707; Case C-317/92 *Commission v Germany* [1994] ECR I-02039; Case C-52/93 *Commission v Netherlands* [1994] ECR I-03591; Case C-61/93 *Commission v Netherlands* [1994] ECR I-03607.

[133] See generally Sommer (n 24) 136 ff.

[134] See von Bogdandy, 'Die Informationsbeziehungen im europäischen Verwaltungsverbund' (n 95) 355. Based on its responsibilities as 'guardian of the Treaties' (Art 17(1) TEU), the Commission has a certain right to be part of horizontal procedures: see eg Art 25(2) of Directive 2008/50/EC of the European Parliament and of the Council of 21 May 2008 on ambient air quality and cleaner air for Europe (n 97), under which the Commission is to be invited to be present and to aid cooperation among the Member States.

[135] Directive 2000/60/EC of the European Parliament and of the Council of 23 October 2000 establishing a framework for Community action in the field of water policy (n 83).

[136] Regarding reporting obligations in the context of consultation procedures see Art 3 of Directive 2000/60/EC of the European Parliament and of the Council of 23 October 2000 establishing a framework for Community action in the field of water policy (n 83).

[137] Case 254/83 *Commission v Italy* [1984] ECR 3395; see von Bogdandy, 'Die Informationsbeziehungen im europäischen Verwaltungsverbund' (n 95) 355.

equivalence. This is of particular significance where a Member State establishes that a facility on its territory may cause serious environmental damage on the territory of another Member State. The former is obliged to consult with the latter and to take the results of such consultation into account in any decision-making relating to approval of that facility.[138] The Habitats Directive also contains provisions relating to information exchange in such settings, here vis-à-vis the Commission.[139]

(c) Information systems linked with specific environmental media

Environmental information systems taking in the EU as a whole go beyond mere co-operation between administrative actors. Such systems ensure a coordinated basis for addressing environmental risks and harms,[140] regularly having the goal of central collection and processing of environmentally relevant information in order then to make it available to environmental decision-makers in the EU both vertically and horizontally, in order in particular to point to reactive possibilities and cooperative analysis of problems. This is an essential component of efficient and effective environmental policy.[141] One of the most significant of such systems, particularly—but not only—for nature conservation, is the European Environment Information and Observation Network (EIONET).[142] Based on it, the EEA can unify environmental data on the supranational (Union) level, making possible a Union-wide informational structure upon which the pertinent political and administrative actors can rely for the achievement of their tasks.[143] This is not to be seen merely as a database in the narrow sense, but rather as a form of networked coordination of the totality of expertise in the field across the Union, for which the EEA plays the central role.[144] The Agency achieves this through the conduct of annual work programmes,[145] but lacking investigative and sanctioning authority itself, it is dependent upon national cooperation to see these

---

[138] See Art 26 of Directive 2010/75/EU of the European Parliament and of the Council of 24 November 2010 on industrial emissions (integrated pollution prevention and control) (n 113). Horizontal obligations to consult exist also under Art 7 of Directive 2011/92/EU of the European Parliament and of the Council of 13 December 2011 on the assessment of the effects of certain public and private projects on the environment (n 10); and Art 7(2) of Directive 2001/42/EC of the European Parliament and of the Council of 27 June 2001 on the assessment of the effects of certain plans and programmes on the environment [2001] OJ L197/30–37; see also n 134 above.

[139] Council Directive 92/43/EEC of 21 May 1992 on the conservation of natural habitats and of wild fauna and flora (n 2); see in particular Art 6(4).

[140] See T von Danwitz, *Europäisches Verwaltungsrecht* (Duncker & Humblot 2008) 620.

[141] See Sixth Environmental Action Programme; No 3 of the Communication from the Commission to the Council, the European Parliament, the European Economic and Social Committee and the Committee of the Regions—Towards a Shared Environmental Information System (SEIS) SEC(2008) 111, SEC(2008) 112, COM(2008) 0046 final.

[142] Now based on Regulation (EC) No 401/2009 of the European Parliament and of the Council of 23 April 2009 on the European Environment Agency and the European Environment Information and Observation Network (Codified version) (n 122).

[143] E Chiti, 'The Emergence of a Community Administration: The Case of European Agencies' (2000) 37 *Common Market Law Review* 309, 324; Hofmann, Rowe, and Türk (n 58) 308.

[144] H C H Hofmann, A H Türk, 'Policy implementation' in H C H Hofmann, A H Türk (eds), *EU Administrative Governance* (Edward Elgar Publishing 2006) 74, 91; Chiti (n 143) 309, 324 ff; K Heußner, *Informationssysteme im Europäischen Verwaltungsverbund* (Mohr Siebeck 2007) 63.

[145] T Runge, 'Zehn Jahre Umweltinformationsmanagement für Europa: die Tätigkeit der Europäischen Umweltagentur' (2005) 120 *Deutsches Verwaltungsblatt* 542, 544; Chiti (n 143) 309, 325.

through (eventually relying upon the Commission to exercise supervisory power vis-à-vis the Member State where necessary).[146] As part of the EIONET structure, the Member States are required to nominate the most important parts of their national information networks (Article 4, Regulation 401/2009), usually the NRCs.[147] Member States are also entitled to act jointly to generate and analyse such data.[148]

Specialized information systems in the environmental field include those covering:

- accidental or deliberate maritime pollution[149]
- the monitoring of forests and forest fire (EFFIS)[150]
- measurement of air pollution in the Member States[151] and
- information generation and management for Natura 2000.

Concerning all of these, the Commission plays the key coordinating role. The information system for Natura 2000 will serve to illustrate the central place of information management in environmental administrative procedures. As already noted, Natura 2000 is a physical network of nature conservation areas, supported in essence by an administrative network. The physical network of protected areas has been established in four phases, in each of which certain—relatively similar—procedures have been followed. These procedures have included so-called *biogeographical seminars*, cooperative working meetings designed to establish the protection value, or need, of particular areas (a methodology adopted by the Commission, the Member States and the ETC, emerging from Article 4 of the Birds Directive). The first meeting (1994) produced the concept of reference lists, cataloguing the bird species set out in the appendices to the Directive in relation to different regions. Regional seminars generated such lists in preparation for the making of Member State proposals for areas to be made subject to protection. The diverse participation in such seminars is indicative of the cooperative-integrated character of the administration of the physical network (see the list in section E above). The meetings can also be merely bi-lateral, typically then with representation of the Commission and the ETC, and of one affected Member State. One should also stress the role of NGOs in these fora.

---

[146] Thus, reflecting Recital (9) of Regulation (EC) No 401/2009 of the European Parliament and of the Council of 23 April 2009 on the European Environment Agency and the European Environment Information and Observation Network (Codified version) (n 122), the EEA is required to work together with the Commission and specifically to report breaches of the law to it. It is only by this means that the Commission can ensure the unrestricted application of the provisions of EU environmental law.

[147] Heußner (n 144) 66.

[148] See Art 4(2) of Regulation (EC) No 401/2009 of the European Parliament and of the Council of 23 April 2009 on the European Environment Agency and the European Environment Information and Observation Network (Codified version) (n 122).

[149] Decision No 2850/2000/EC of the European Parliament and of the Council of 20 December 2000 setting up a Community framework for cooperation in the field of accidental or deliberate marine pollution (n 38); cf in relation to water resources, also the medium-specific information system under Directive 2000/60/EC of the European Parliament and of the Council of 23 October 2000 establishing a framework for Community action in the field of water policy (n 83).

[150] Regulation (EC) No 2152/2003 of the European Parliament and of the Council concerning monitoring of forests and environmental interactions in the Community (n 104).

[151] Council Decision 97/101/EC of 27 January 1997 establishing a reciprocal exchange of information and data from networks and individual stations measuring ambient air pollution within the Member States (n 36).

A further element of information generation with a direct relation to Natura 2000 is that the details of the (proposed) areas of protection, short-listed for final selection, are encapsulated in the Standard Data Form (SDF) for nomination to the Commission. This raises the level of transparency of the process, ensures the equal treatment of the Member States in the evaluation of proposal by the Commission, supports the national bodies in their adherence to standards of protection, and makes possible a regular supervision of that adherence. This standardized method of submission enables the incorporation of the relevant information in a database.

(d) Challenges for information management

The standards applicable to information systems of the kind just referred to can make reference to some of the key underlying principles of Union administration. So, the principle of transparency (Article 15 TFEU), directed to both Union bodies and Member State ones, should be noted here;[152] it obtains specific expression in freedom of information legislation, both general[153] and specifically related to environment.[154] There may well also be issues of data protection. While this may, in the environmental field, sometimes be of importance to individual citizens, it is rather of particular significance where environmentally relevant information may relate to business secrets.[155]

6 Consultations in preparation of unilateral administrative measures

Unilateral administrative acts (addressed as such below), such as decisions (under Article 288 fourth paragraph TFEU) or implementing measures of the Commission (under Article 291(2)), as well as non-binding recommendations and opinions (Article 288 fifth paragraph) make an important but perhaps indirect contribution to shaping multilevel and national administrative action, providing inter alia for developing cooperation.[156] Such measures, especially on the national level, typically involve preparatory consultation (much of which falls under the previously discussed topic of information

---

[152] It is above all the publication of information which supports transparency; cf Hofmann, Rowe, and Türk (n 58) 460 ff.

[153] Regulation (EC) No 1049/2001 of the European Parliament and of the Council of 30 May 2001 regarding public access to European Parliament, Council and Commission documents [2001] OJ L145/43–48; see also Art 38(1) of Regulation (EC) No 178/2002 of the European Parliament and of the Council of 28 January 2002 laying down the general principles and requirements of food law, establishing the European Food Safety Authority and laying down procedures in matters of food safety [2002] OJ L31/1–24.

[154] Regulation (EC) No 1367/2006 of the European Parliament and of the Council of 6 September 2006 on the application of the provisions of the Aarhus Convention on Access to Information, Public Participation in Decision-making and Access to Justice in Environmental Matters to Community institutions and bodies [2006] OJ L264/13–19; Art 4 Directive 2003/35/EC of the European Parliament and of the Council of 26 May 2003 providing for public participation in respect of the drawing up of certain plans and programmes relating to the environment and amending with regard to public participation and access to justice Council Directives 85/337/EEC and 96/61/EC—Statement by the Commission [2003] OJ L156/17–25.

[155] See generally Hofmann, Rowe, and Türk (n 58) 480 ff.   [156] Koch (n 27) 387 ff.

management). Such consultations may be obligatory or voluntary. So, before granting approval for an industrial facility, Member State authorities must carry out consultations (Article 5(2), Directive 2010/75),[157] in particular those which involve the participation and coordination of a range of authorities in accord with the principle of integrated environmental protection. Such a demand for consultation becomes extended when there are potential cross-border effects (Article 18(1)). No approval decision can be made before this procedure. Comparable procedures are envisaged by environmental impact assessment law.[158]

Consultations are also part of the nature conservation decisions within Natura 2000. The Habitats Directive provides that the Member States are to select and then to propose the Commission a list of areas of Union-wide significance. Within the framework of an evaluation procedure, the Commission, with the concurrence of the Member States, then establishes a conclusive list of areas in which one or more priority habitats or species have been identified (Article 4(2) Directive 92/43). Only after that does the Commission conclusively determine the areas to fall within the Natura 2000 network, with the consequence that the Member State must then (within six years) declare them protected areas (Article 4(4) Directive 92/43). In coming to its decision, the Commission is supported by the Habitats Committee (Article 20 Directive 92/43). A similar process is followed for areas of special protection (Article 8(1) Directive 92/43).

A final example of obligatory consultation procedures is provided by the Water Framework Directive.[159] Member States are obliged to act in a coordinated way in regard to international river basin districts. Article 3 can be offered as, in effect, a paradigm example of the processes and steps (including the coordinative role of the Commission), laid down in order to achieve this:

3. Member States shall ensure that a river basin covering the territory of more than one Member State is assigned to an international river basin district. At the request of the Member States involved, the Commission shall act to facilitate the assigning to such international river basin districts.

   Each Member State shall ensure the appropriate administrative arrangements, including the identification of the appropriate competent authority, for the application [the] Directive within the portion of any international river basin district lying within its territory.

4. Member States shall ensure that the requirements of this Directive for the achievement of [its] environmental objectives ... and in particular all programmes of measures are coordinated for the whole of the river basin district. For international river basin districts the Member States concerned shall together ensure

---

[157] Directive 2010/75/EU of the European Parliament and of the Council of 24 November 2010 on industrial emissions (integrated pollution prevention and control) (n 113).

[158] Directive 2011/92/EU of the European Parliament and of the Council of 13 December 2011 on the assessment of the effects of certain public and private projects on the environment (n 10). See also Arts 6 ff of Directive 2001/42/EC of the European Parliament and of the Council of 27 June 2001 on the assessment of the effects of certain plans and programmes on the environment (n 138).

[159] Directive 2000/60/EC of the European Parliament and of the Council of 23 October 2000 establishing a framework for Community action in the field of water policy (n 83).

this coordination and may, for this purpose, use existing structures stemming from international agreements. At the request of the Member States involved, the Commission shall act to facilitate the establishment of the programmes of measures.

5. Where a river basin district extends beyond the territory of the [Union], the ... Member States concerned shall endeavour to establish appropriate coordination with the relevant non-Member States, with the aim of achieving the objectives of this Directive throughout the river basin district. Member States shall ensure the application of the rules of this Directive within their territory.

7 Composite coordination strategies

The elements discussed above in this section reflect a considerable range of procedural steps available for environmental implementation. Sometimes all or some such steps are combined into a greater whole, in order to construct an even more multi-facetted strategy. As an example, we can refer briefly to the Common Implementation Strategy (CIS) for the Water Framework Directive (WFD),[160] based on an agreement between the Member States, Norway and the Commission. The aim of this is to address, in a series of practical steps and processes, the shared technical challenges associated with the implementation of the WFD (together with certain other directives, in particular the Floods Directive). Those challenges relate in part to the great breadth of the potential participants in the implementation process: Member States, the Commission, candidate countries, EEA countries, regional and municipal authorities, NGOs, and affected individuals, businesses, and industries. Also, many European river basins, key foci of the WFD, are international, crossing territorial and administrative boundaries, adding considerable complexity to the implementational tasks. A common framework is, therefore, crucial to the successful and effective operation of the Directive, and the CIS-WFD is intended to provide this.

The Strategy relies on working groups,[161] and its actions are organized within work programmes,[162] informally established by the EU Water Directors (the responsible representatives of the Member States for the policy sub-area). Guidance and resource documents[163] emerge from the CIS-WFD, and meetings and events are aimed at enhancing communication and information exchange. The Strategy provides a basis for Commission action in the continued development of Union water resource policy, and this has been embodied in further legal acts, in particular in the

---

[160] Directive 2000/60/EC of the European Parliament and of the Council of 23 October 2000 establishing a framework for Community action in the field of water policy (n 83).

[161] The Commission has an open application process for organizations wishing to join the CIS Strategic Co-ordination Group, or any of the CIS Working Groups, so that the composition of the participants is not static.

[162] See https://circabc.europa.eu/faces/jsp/extension/wai/navigation/container.jsp.

[163] See https://circabc.europa.eu/faces/jsp/extension/wai/navigation/container.jsp. Further documents prepared in the context of the CIS and others are accessible on a specific information exchange platform established for this purpose, the WFD CIRCA Interest Group 'Implementing the Water Framework Directive and the Floods Directive' https://circabc.europa.eu/faces/jsp/extension/wai/navigation/container.jsp.

daughter directives to the WFD, namely the Groundwater Directive[164]and the Priority Substances Directive,[165] as well as in the Flood Risks Directive[166] (which has its own Working Group on Floods). Part of the work of the CIS-WFD has concerned the establishment of the so-called Pilot River Basins, a key aim being to try out, on selected river systems across the Union,[167] certain guidance documents as a lead into long-term development of River Basin Management Plans and related management programmes. Linked to the CIS-WFD, the international river basin commissions for the geographical area of the EU,[168] as well as other frameworks governing, for example, Lake Constance and Lake Geneva, also play an important role in coordinating WFD implementation, adding yet further layers of networking, coordination, and cooperation to those already noted in relation to the Union itself.

Very similar to the CIS-WFD is the Common Implementation Strategy (CIS-MSFD) of the Marine Strategy Framework Directive (MSFD).[169] Indeed, taken together, the WFD and the MSFD provide an overarching framework for the management of water resources in the European Union. In certain respects, both the CIS-WFD and the CIS-MSFD appear rather similar to, but are rather more formalized than, the sum of the measures and procedures which apply under Natura 2000 (discussed above).

G Legal Rules Governing Sector-specific Decision-making on Environmental Protection

Decision-making in the environmental sector covers a vast range of—mostly technical—matters, whether it be in relation to the approval of facilities with a potentially damaging effect on the environment, or the introduction of, for example, new herbicides or pesticides on to the common market, the release of genetically modified organisms, the carrying out of water resources projects with effects on shared waterways, or the cross-border movement of hazardous waste, the establishment of national allocation plans (NAPs) within the EU Emissions Trading Scheme (EU ETS), or the management of nature conservation areas of European significance under Natura 2000. Such decisions are mainly ones for national authorities, often with transterritorial (cross-EU) effect, or possibly for the Commission, where the

---

[164] Directive 2006/118/EC of the European Parliament and of the Council of 12 December 2006 on the protection of groundwater against pollution and deterioration [2006] OJ L372/19.

[165] Directive 2008/105/EC of the European Parliament and of the Council of 16 December 2008 on environmental quality standards in the field of water policy [2008] OJ L348/84–97; there is a Commission Proposal for the amendment of this Directive: Proposal for a Directive of the European Parliament and of the Council amending Directives 2000/60/EC and 2008/105/EC as regards priority substances in the field of water policy, COM(2011) 876.

[166] Directive 2007/60/EC of the European Parliament and of the Council of 23 October 2007 on the assessment and management of flood risks [2007] OJ L288/27–34.

[167] See eg L Galbiati, F Somma, J M Zaldivar-Comenges (eds), *Pilot River Basin Activity Report Phase II: 2005-2006—-Water Framework Directive implementation pilot activities—Key challenges and recommendations from the Pilot River Basins* http://publications.jrc.ec.europa.eu/repository/bitstream/JRC43751/prb_report_150508.pdf.

[168] Most notably in relation to the Odra, Elbe, Meuse, Danube, Rhine, Sava, and Scheldt.

[169] Directive 2008/56/EC of the European Parliament and of the Council of 17 June 2008 establishing a framework for community action in the field of marine environmental policy [2008] OJ L16419–40.

decision-making power is transferred to it under specified conditions. Other kinds of decisions include, for example, determinations by the Commission to include areas proposed by Member States into the nature conservation network of Natura 2000, or Commission approval of NAPs in the EU ETS.[170] This list of examples could, however, be augmented very substantially indeed.

A detailed treatment of such rules, however, would shed little additional light on the specifically administrative side of Union environmental policy. Rather, it would take us into the legal-policy substance of the field, which is not the intention here. Nevertheless, one can, as merely one indicative example of the myriad possibilities, make brief reference to the recent decision of the Court regarding the management of a conservation area under Natura 2000 in *Commission v Poland*,[171] noting here the salient elements for the present discussion. Having had certain areas of ancient Polish forest placed within the Natura 2000 network, national administrative authorities subsequently gave approval for expanded forestry activity in these areas. The Court held that, in doing so, national administrators had failed to respect the substantive protection requirements of both the Habitats Directive and the Birds Directive, upon which Natura 2000 rests. Notably, the national administration had failed to establish conservation measures which corresponded to the ecological needs of the areas concerned. The Member State administration had failed to meet its EU legal obligation both in not ensuring a sufficiently protective framework and in adopting a forestry plan which did not guarantee the integrity of the areas concerned. In addition to reflecting the demands imposed by Union law on national administrative decision-making, the facts of that case also remind us of the supervisory roles of the Commission and of the Court, to which we return below.

Although it is not possible, nor useful, to offer here a comprehensive coverage of such environmental decision-making rules, one set of rules from *general environmental* administrative law (in the sense that this expression has been used above, section C) deserves explicit mention, namely the law on *environmental impact assessment* (EIA), touching the administration of a very wide range of environmental sub-sectors and decision-making in them. That law relates in fact to a number of the different topics covered throughout this chapter: procedures (demanding, for example, certain forms of consultations), administrative information (being indeed a rule specifically about the generation of information), and even structures and actors (for example, requiring public participation, and under some circumstances the involvement of transboundary national authorities). EIA finds its basis in Directive 2001/92.[172]

---

[170] See eg Case C-267/11 P *Commission v Latvia* ECLI:EU:C:2013:624; Case T-374/04 *Germany v Commission* ECLI:EU:T:2007:332; Case T-183/07 *Poland v Commission* ECLI:EU:T:2009:350; Case T-370/11 *Poland v Commission* ECLI:EU:T:2013:113; Case C-504/09 P *Commission v Poland* ECLI:EU:C:2012:178; Case T-263/07 *Estonia v Commission* ECLI:EU:T:2009:351.

[171] Case C-441/17 *Commission v Poland (Forêt de Białowieża)* ECLI:EU:C:2018:255.

[172] Directive 2011/92/EU of the European Parliament and of the Council of 13 December 2011 on the assessment of the effects of certain public and private projects on the environment (n 10). The EIA procedure ensures that environmental consequences of projects and plans are identified and assessed before a final authorization can be given in an administrative procedures under national law. The European provisions implemented into national law provide inter alia for the public to give its opinion and provides that the results arising from the impact assessment exercise will be taken into account in the authorization procedure of the project. For a comparative study see G C Rowe, 'Rechtsangleichung und

It is, in essence, a special *procedure* for the generation of (particular, perhaps hard-to-come-by) *information,* in order to ensure that the ultimate decision-maker is as *fully informed* as possible (thus satisfying some of the demands of the principle of *good administration* and administrative rationality). A key element of all EIA regimes is that the outcomes of the assessment be *taken into account* by the responsible decision-maker in the final decision, without, however, meaning that those outcomes determine the decision in a binding way. The significance of EIA as a legal rule governing sector-specific decision-making lies in the fact that the normal (but typically informal) obligation of decision-makers to take into account all relevant matter and to ignore, indeed exclude, irrelevant matters has become a procedurally formalized one. Broadly, this rule affects primarily the decision-making of national administrators, as it is they who make plans, carry out projects, and give approvals.

Beyond the EIA rule—which, as procedurally formalized information-gathering, appears almost unique in administrative decision-making, irrespective of the sectoral focus—we should, for completeness, refer again to the cross-sectional requirement of Article 11 TFEU, requiring that 'environmental protection requirements ... be integrated into the definition and *implementation* of the Union policies and activities, in particular with a view to promoting sustainable development' (emphasis added). On one perspective this requirement might actually be regarded as not a sector-specific decision-making rule at all, because, strictly understood, it applies to *all sectors* of Union decision-making. That, however, would be an almost perverse view of the provision. A better—but admittedly challenging—view is to see this treaty provision as having the effect of making environmental protection a policy focus which actually *transcends* individual policy sectors as such (arguably comparable with data protection). That perception needs, nevertheless, to be relativized by reminding ourselves of the many sub-sectors of environmental policy as such, as we have noted at the outset. In the result, then, we can see Article 11 TFEU as being a Union environmental regulation which is double-edged, but continuous:

- *all* policy areas of the Union are (at least potentially) areas of *environmental* decision-making, in the sense that environmental protection must inform *all* Union decision-making, and Article 11 is therefore a relevant—and significant—legal rule governing this activity; and

- environmental decision-making includes at the same time a substantial number of specifically identified sub-fields, each of which has its own sub-sectoral, specialist (substantive) decision-making rules, of the kind noted at the opening of this section.

In fact, no matter how we view Article 11 in a theoretical or categorical sense, its effect is undoubtedly to require administrative decision-makers, whether generally or specifically, to have environmental protection at the forefront of their decision-making criteria. One can, therefore, bring the demands both of Article 11 TFEU and

---

Rechtsdivergenz: Das Beispiel der Umweltverträglichkeitsprüfung' in J Basedow, K J Hopt, and H Kötz, *Festschrift für Ulrich Drobnig zum siebzigsten Geburtstag* (Mohr Siebeck 1998) 629–60; and the summary in Hofmann, Rowe, and Türk (n 58) 505–06.

of EIA together: in order to integrate environmental protection into the shaping and implementation of all EU policy fields, as the Treaty clearly requires, it is—at least in substance, if not in the strictest procedural form—necessary that some assessment of environmental impact *always* take place, whether in reaching conclusions in the European Council, in legislation by the Council and the Parliament, in the legislative implementation of European directives in the Member States, and (especially from the administrative law standpoint of this chapter) in all administrative implementation activity of both Union and national authorities. It is, therefore, incumbent on all actors within the Union's integrated administration to carry out *substantive* environmental impact assessment, even where formal EU or national law does not require the conduct of formal-procedural EIA. This is then both a sector-specific decision-making legal rule, and a cross-sectoral one.

H Abstract-general Administrative Acts in the Environmental Sector

1 Preparatory measures

As in virtually all areas of Union competence the Commission has the task of agenda setting and making proposals for legislation in the environmental field. In this process both green papers[173] and white papers[174] (issued as Commission communications) play a role in stimulating public discussion, often anticipatory of hearings and consultations (noted above) and allowing the Commission to test the water, calling in particular on the Member States to express their view on policy development.[175] Following on from white papers and associated consultations, the Commission typically prepares 'action plans' or 'action programmes' (adopted then as decisions of the Council and European Parliament), of which there have been seven for environmental matters, the most recent intended to guide EU policy until 2020[176] (focusing on natural capital, resources efficiency, low-carbon economy, and environment-related pressures and risks). Such plans have no binding legal status. They take their place with certain other documents, such as working papers, which also play an important role in guiding environmental action.[177] National

---

[173] See eg Green Paper—A European Strategy for Sustainable, Competitive and Secure Energy SEC(2006) 317, COM(2006) 0105 final; Hofmann, Rowe, and Türk (n 58) 515.

[174] See eg White Paper—Adapting to climate change: towards a European framework for action SEC(2009) 386, SEC(2009) 387, SEC(2009) 388, COM(2009) 0147 final; White Paper on environmental liability, COM(2000) 0066 final.

[175] See eg Green Paper—A European Strategy for Sustainable, Competitive and Secure Energy SEC(2006) 317, COM(2006) 0105 final; Hofmann, Rowe, and Türk (n 58) 515.

[176] Decision No 1386/2013/EU of the European Parliament and of the Council of 20 November 2013 on a General Union Environment Action Programme to 2020 'Living well, within the limits of our planet' [2013] OJ L354/171–200.

[177] See Commission staff working document accompanying the White paper—Adapting to climate change: towards a European framework for action—Summary of the impact assessment. COM(2009) 147 final, SEC(2009) 386, SEC(2009) 387, SEC(2009) 0388 final; Commission staff working document accompanying the White paper—Adapting to climate change: Towards a European framework for action—Adapting to climate change: the challenge for European agriculture and rural areas, COM(2009) 147 final, SEC(2009) 0417 final; Hofmann, Rowe, and Türk (n 58) 517.

allocation plans, within the Emissions Trading Scheme, formally have a similar character, but can fall under Commission supervision in relation to their objectivity and transparency.[178]

2 Subordinate legislation and legislative rule-making

In the environmental field, decisions under Article 288 fourth paragraph (whatever their function and application in other fields), can be seen as instruments of administrative-procedural coordination. They are, then, not so much measures restricted to individual cases but take on an abstract-general character, alongside secondary legislation and Commission rule-making.[179] Examples are offered by Commission Decisions 2009/770[180] and 2003/701[181] on standardized reporting regarding GMOs, or the guidance issued concerning entities capable of coming within the EU eco-audit scheme.[182] Some decisions, though, take on the appearance of Union *secondary* law, for example, the Decision of the *Council* and the *Parliament* on the EU's 7th Environmental Action Plan.[183]

Implementing measures of the Commission on the basis of Article 291(2) are of considerable importance, for example, the Commission Decision on standardized provision of site information for areas to be protected within the Natura 2000 network.[184] One should note here that the standardized elements which the Member State authorities must provide under that decision were settled by national representatives in the framework of the Habitats Committee (referred to in the discussion of comitology, above). Further cases are provided by the Commission's regulation in relation to

[178] See Hofmann, Rowe, and Türk (n 58) 520, with further references. See also the cases noted above, n 170, and generally M Hartmann, *Europäisierung und Verbundvertrauen: Die Verwaltungspraxis des Emissionshandelssystems der Europäischen Union* (Mohr Siebeck 2015).

[179] Further as to this see B Schöndorf-Haubold, 'Gemeinsame Europäische Verwaltung: die Strukturfonds der Europäischen Gemeinschaft' in E Schmidt-Aßmann, B Schöndorf-Haubold, *Der europäische Verwaltungsverbund–Formen und Verfahren der Verwaltungszusammenarbeit in der EU* (Nomos 2005) 219 ff; T von Danwitz, *Verwaltungsrechtliches System und europäische Integration* (Duncker & Humblot 1996) 239 ff.

[180] Commission Decision 2009/770/EC of 13 October 2009 establishing standard reporting formats for presenting the monitoring results of the deliberate release into the environment of genetically modified organisms, as or in products, for the purpose of placing on the market, pursuant to Directive 2001/18/EC of the European Parliament and of the Council [2009] OJ L2759.

[181] Commission Decision 2003/701/EC of 29 September 2003 establishing pursuant to Directive 2001/18/EC of the European Parliament and of the Council a format for presenting the results of the deliberate release into the environment of genetically modified higher plants for purposes other than placing on the market [2003] OJ L254/21.

[182] Commission Decision 2001/681/EC of 7 September 2001 on guidance for the implementation of Regulation (EC) No 761/2001 of the European Parliament and of the Council allowing voluntary participation by organisations in a Community eco-management and audit scheme (EMAS) (notified under document number C(2001) 2504) [2001] OJ L247/27–47.

[183] Decision 1386/2013/EU of the European Parliament and of the Council of 20 November 2013 on a General Union Environment Action Programme to 2020 'Living well, within the limits of our planet' (n 176), or previously, Decision 1230/2003/EC of the European Parliament and of the Council of 26 June 2003 adopting a multiannual programme for action in the field of energy: 'Intelligent Energy—Europe' (2003–2006) [2003] OJ L176/29–36 (no longer in force).

[184] Commission Implementing Decision of 11 July 2011 concerning a site information format for Natura 2000 sites (notified under document C(2011) 4892) [2011] OJ L198/39–70.

foodstuffs possibly affected by the Fukushima nuclear incident,[185] or in relation to timber products and their monitoring.[186]

Delegated legislation under Article 290 TFEU (in the form of both regulations and directives of the Commission), plays a major role in implementation through administrative rule-making in this sector. For example, the Commission has issued a rule on the notification to it of information on agriculture, potentially significant for environmentally relevant material.[187] The field is indeed very wide, including—as an illustrative selection—measures on environmental standards for agricultural vehicles,[188] budgetary allocations to projects for nature conservation and biodiversity,[189] fisheries conservation and the marine environment of the Baltic,[190] the recognition of monitoring organizations in relation to timber products,[191] restricted substances,[192] risk assessments of invasive alien species,[193] import and export of hazardous substances,[194] and wastewater engineering products.[195] Concerning all measures of

---

[185] Commission Implementing Regulation (EU) 996/2012 of 26 October 2012 imposing special conditions governing the import of feed and food originating in or consigned from Japan following the accident at the Fukushima nuclear power station (no longer in force) [2012] OJ L299/31–41 (and its predecessors).

[186] Commission Implementing Regulation (EU) No 607/2012 of 6 July 2012 on the detailed rules concerning the due diligence system and the frequency and nature of the checks on monitoring organisations as provided for in Regulation (EU) No 995/2010 of the European Parliament and of the Council laying down the obligations of operators who place timber and timber products on the market [2012] OJ L177/16–18.

[187] Commission Delegated Regulation (EU) 2017/1183 of 20 April 2017 on supplementing Regulations (EU) No 1307/2013 and (EU) No 1308/2013 of the European Parliament and of the Council with regard to the notifications to the Commission of information and documents [2017] OJ L171/100–102.

[188] Commission Delegated Regulation (EU) 2015/96 of 1 October 2014 supplementing Regulation (EU) No 167/2013 of the European Parliament and of the Council as regards environmental and propulsion unit performance requirements of agricultural and forestry vehicles [2015] OJ L16/1–21.

[189] Commission Delegated Regulation (EU) 2018/93 of 16 November 2017 on the increase of the percentage of the budgetary resources allocated to projects supported by way of action grants under the sub-programme for Environment dedicated to projects supporting the conservation of nature and biodiversity according to Article 9(4) of Regulation (EU) No 1293/2013 of the European Parliament and of the Council on the establishment of a Programme for the Environment and Climate Action (LIFE) and repealing Regulation (EC) No 614/2007, C(2017) 7538 [2018] OJ L17/5–6.

[190] Commission Delegated Regulation (EU) 2017/117 of 5 September 2016 establishing fisheries conservation measures for the protection of the marine environment in the Baltic Sea and repealing Delegated Regulation (EU) 2015/1778, C(2016) 5562 [2017] OJ L19/1–9.

[191] Commission Delegated Regulation (EU) No 363/2012 of 23 February 2012 on the procedural rules for the recognition and withdrawal of recognition of monitoring organisations as provided for in Regulation (EU) No 995/2010 of the European Parliament and of the Council laying down the obligations of operators who place timber and timber products on the market [2012] OJ L115/12–16.

[192] Commission Delegated Directive (EU) 2015/863 of 31 March 2015 amending Annex II to Directive 2011/65/EU of the European Parliament and of the Council as regards the list of restricted substances, C(2015) 2067 [2015] OJ L137/10–12.

[193] Commission Delegated Regulation (EU) 2018/968 of 30 April 2018 supplementing Regulation (EU) No 1143/2014 of the European Parliament and of the Council with regard to risk assessments in relation to invasive alien species [2018] OJ L 174, 5–11, C(2018) 2526 final.

[194] Commission Delegated Regulation (EU) 2018/172 of 28 November 2017 amending Annexes I and V to Regulation (EU) No 649/2012 of the European Parliament and of the Council concerning the export and import of hazardous chemicals, C(2017) 7828 [2018] OJ L32/6–11.

[195] Commission Delegated Decision (EU) 2015/1959 of 1 July 2015 on the applicable systems to assess and verify constancy of performance of wastewater engineering products pursuant to Regulation (EU) No 305/2011 of the European Parliament and of the Council [2015] OJ L284/184–86.

this kind the Union now provides a useful research tool, the Interinstitutional Register of Delegated Acts.[196]

3 Unilateral non-binding measures

Non-binding measures are widespread in the environmental context, especially for purpose of information exchange, particularly in the form of recommendations and opinions (under Article 288(5) TFEU). Depending on their origin, such measures may be directed to Commission (services) and (perhaps most often) to Member State authorities.[197] As an example, one can refer to the opinion of the Committee of the Regions on the Commission's proposal for LIFE+,[198] in particular giving attention to the implementation role accorded to municipal authorities and, vis-à-vis the Commission, demanding a higher level of financial support. Many other examples of a similar kind from that Committee should also be noted.[199] Similarly, recommendations also take their place in the administrative arrangements in this sector, for example, from the Commission to the Netherlands in relation to environmental protection measures which should be adopted in relation to unintended release of genetically modified plant species,[200] or to Member States concerning standardized information regarding radioactive substances derived from the ventilation and waste water of nuclear facilities under normal operating conditions.[201] To these measures we can also add resolutions and guidelines. Although the former are usually measures specific to the Council, they have more the character of executive (i.e., not legislative) acts, especially in the light of their flexible and non-binding nature.[202] Resolutions can also emerge from other bodies, for example, from the Committee of the Regions in relation to legislative and work programmes of the Commission, where the Committee has, for example, called for a maintenance of certain priorities in energy and climate policy.[203]

---

[196] See https://webgate.ec.europa.eu/regdel/#/delegatedActs. The Register, begun in 2017, enables searches which follow the development of delegated acts from their planning through Commission until their publication in the Official Journal, and provides access to the various steps taken by the Parliament and the Council, and of Commission expert groups in the preparation of such acts.

[197] See von Danwitz (n 140) 246.

[198] Opinion of the Committee of the Regions on the Proposal for a Regulation of the European Parliament and of the Council concerning the Financial Instrument for the Environment (LIFE+) [2005] OJ C231/72–74.

[199] Opinion of the Committee of the Regions on the maritime and coastal package [2009] OJ C211/65–72; Opinion of the Committee of the Regions on the Green Paper on territorial cohesion [2009] OJ C120/23–28.

[200] Commission Recommendation of 16 August 2005 concerning the measures to be taken by the consent holder to prevent any damage to health and the environment in the event of the accidental spillage of an oilseed rape (Brassica napus L., GT73 line—MON-00073-7) genetically modified for tolerance to the herbicide glyphosate (notified under document number C(2005) 3073) [2005] OJ L228/19–20.

[201] Commission Recommendation of 18 December 2003 on standardised information on radioactive airborne and liquid discharges into the environment from nuclear power reactors and reprocessing plants in normal operation (notified under document number C(2003) 4832) [2004] OJ L2/36–46.

[202] See von Bogdandy, 'Die Informationsbeziehungen im europäischen Verwaltungsverbund' (n 95) 360; T von Danwitz, *Europäisches Verwaltungsrecht* (n 140) 193 ff, 376.

[203] Resolution of the Committee of the Regions on the Priorities of the Committee of the Regions for 2009 based on the Legislative and Work Programme of the European Commission [2009] OJ C76/66–69.

Perhaps the most important, formally non-binding, instruments to be noted here are Commission guidelines in relation to the implementation and application of substantive and procedural rules. It suffices to mention just one example: guidelines for the definition of environmental risks within the framework of the Directive on veterinary medications[204] (and, as such, again a reflection of the cross-sectoral nature of environmental protection, in the light of Article 11 TFEU). One should recall here that such guidelines, even though not formally binding, can in certain circumstances nevertheless take on a substantially binding effect.[205]

In addition, one should also note here the example, in the nature conservation setting, of the 'Working Documents' of the European Topic Centre (ETC) on Biological Diversity. Some of these relate to procedures in the selection and management of Natura 2000 conservation areas, sometimes they are of more technical character (e.g., maps, summary description of areas, preliminary analyses of species or habitats). They find their basis in various data sources, including national handbooks relating to the protection species or habitats, or contributions from conservation NGOs (e.g., WWF). So, for example, the 'Working Document: Implementation of the Habitats Directive' on the organization of the biogeographical seminars (referred to above) illustrates procedural documentation (but lacking external binding force). For the practical implementation of the Natura 2000 network and the effectuation of administrative cooperation in this fundamental project of European nature conservation, such measures are of great importance. Through them, guidance is provided for the evaluation of areas proposed for protection, and in regard to the procedures to be conducted for that purpose, including the integration of the very diverse participants (e.g., in round-table meetings). Further documents exemplifying these elements are provided by the 'Interpretation Manual of European Union Habitats – EUR 28' (April 2013), the Commission Decision on standardized formats for data about proposed conservation areas (1997),[206] the 'Criteria for assessing National Lists of potential SCIs at Biogeographical Level Hab' (1997)[207] (an example of the interactive work of the Habitats Committee and its Scientific Working Group), and the 'Guidelines for the establishment of the Natura 2000 network in the marine environment' (May 2007).[208]

4　Rule-making and other activity of private parties

As in other administrative fields, the environmental sector relies not just on public officials. We have already noted that scientific and technical experts are often involved in consultations and other procedures, whether in an oral setting or by submitting expert reports. Beyond that, however, the role of private actors cannot be overlooked as an

---

[204] Directive 2001/82/EC of the European Parliament and of the Council of 6 November 2001 on the Community code relating to veterinary medicinal products [2001] OJ L3111–66.

[205] See Hofmann, Rowe, and Türk (n 58) 548 ff.

[206] Commission Implementing Decision of 11 July 2011 concerning a site information format for Natura 2000 sites (notified under document C(2011) 4892) (n 184) (originally 97/266/EC: Commission Decision of 18 December 1996 concerning a site information format for proposed Natura 2000 sites (no longer in force) [1997] OJ L107/1–156.

[207] HAB 97/2 rev 4 of 18 November 1997 http://bd.eionet.europa.eu/activities/Natura_2000/crit.

[208] See http://ec.europa.eu/environment/nature/natura2000 /marine/docs/marine_guidelines.pdf.

expression of the so-called 'new modes of governance',[209] specifically in co-regulation and self-regulation.[210] In respect of the former, EU legal acts may entrust the realization of policy goals to private bodies and environmental organizations (NGOs, etc).[211] The Union's Eco-Management and Audit Scheme, under the EMAS Regulation,[212] can be seen as a case in point, where private firms and businesses voluntarily participate in an environmental compliance framework, the forms and procedures of which are governed by inter-connected EU and national law, involving inter alia the regular provision of environmentally relevant data to both the authorities and the public. On the other hand, the broad concept of self-regulation includes, for example, the possibility for private parties individually and collectively to adopt common frameworks (e.g., codes of practice or environmental agreements), operating on the European level, as the basis of their satisfaction of environmental requirements,[213] in sectoral sub-areas where binding EU measures are seen as unnecessary or undesirable. In particular, one can refer here to administrative agreements involving voluntary commitments of industry, for example in relation to waste management, emissions reduction, or the lowering of pollution in various areas of production.[214] How appropriate such arrangements are, especially relating to ensuring the 'high level of protection' demanded by the Treaty, needs to be answered in each individual application, and always depends on the commitment of the participants and, perhaps more particularly, on the possibilities of monitoring, control and ultimately the plausibility and traceability of the outcomes. In any case, from the standpoint of environmental protection, it is essential that there be clear and unambiguous environmental goals, transparency in the agreement(s), and the carrying through of sanctions where decisive elements of agreements are not observed.

In addition to such interactive regulatory arrangements involving private actors, the EU environmental sector makes use of out-sourcing for regulatory purposes, specifically for the development of administrative rules which can then be adopted by the Commission and/or the Member States. The European Committee for Standardisation (CEN—Comité Européen de Normalisation), a non-profit body comprising 31 national members, has the aim of establishing supranational technical standards for the purpose of furthering and harmonizing technical specifications, inter alia in order to strengthen the level of environmental protection. So, the CEN has contributed to the criteria of sustainability in relation to bio-mass and greenhouse gas emissions.[215]

---

[209] H Hill, 'Exekutivische Normsetzung' in M Albers, W Hoffmann-Riem, E Schmidt-Aßmann and others, *Grundlagen des Verwaltungsrechts–Informationsordnung, Verwaltungsverfahren, Handlungsformen* (Beck 2008) 1017.

[210] See European governance—A White paper [2001] OJ C287/1–29.

[211] Interinstitutional Agreement between the European Parliament, the Council of the European Union and the European Commission on Better Law-making, OJ L123, 12.5.2016, pp. 1–14; Hofmann, Rowe, and Türk (n 58) 587.

[212] Regulation (EC) No 1221/2009 of the European Parliament and of the Council of 25 November 2009 on the voluntary participation by organisations in a Community eco-management and audit scheme (EMAS) L (n 12).

[213] Interinstitutional Agreement between the European Parliament, the Council of the European Union and the European Commission on Better Law-making (n 211).

[214] See Communication from the Commission to the Council and the European Parliament on environmental agreements, COM(96) 0561 final.

[215] European Committee for Standardization, *Annual Report 2010* (2010) 121.

In this process of standards-setting, reliance is placed on transterritorial networks, within which working groups are able to exchange views and develop new partnerships both among one another and with EU bodies.

I Single-case Administrative Acts in Environmental Protection

Two key forms of administrative measure in relation to single cases deserve attention in this sectoral setting: the transnational administrative act, and the administrative contract. Before addressing these as such, it needs to be observed that multitudes of single case decisions of environmental relevance are taken on the national level regularly. The approval of industrial facilities, for example, occurs repeatedly, and indeed substantially within the framework of (integrated) environmental protection derived from Union law, just as the approval of land use with regard to an area protected within Natura 2000 occurs under the substantive standards of EU nature conservation law. The decision of the national authority must, then, be in accord with EU legislation (implemented in national law), but in many respects—organizationally, procedurally—such decision-making is not necessarily characterizable in some specific way as 'EU administration'. For our purposes, such single-case decision-making comes to be of significance when, for example, the procedural demands are traceable to Union law (as, for example, where EIA is required), or where a national administrative authority fails to decide in accordance with that law (but then, on the assumption that Union legislation has properly been transposed into national law, such behaviour will essentially be a breach of the latter) and Union supervision may be needed. Most importantly, it will a cross-border element in single cases—transboundary pollution, substances destined for the EU market, etc—which will typically invoke the issue of its character as part specifically of the administration of EU environmental policy.

1 Transnational administrative acts

Certain single case measures (typically: decisions) of national origin to some extent breach the principle of territoriality, in order to attain a Union-wide effect.[216] Such measures are complementary to supranational measures of Union bodies and to individual measures of national authorities with effect solely within national territory (of the kind just noted above).[217] In the environmental context we find examples of approvals given within a particular Member State, for example, for the release of genetically modified organisms,[218] which then are valid throughout the whole of the Union.[219]

---

[216] M Gautier, 'Acte Administratif Transnational et Droit Communautaire' in J-B Auby (ed), *Droit Administratif Européen* (Bruylant 2007) 1069; Hofmann, Rowe, and Türk (n 58) 310.

[217] See Hofmann (n 99) 136, 149.

[218] Directive 2001/18/EC of the European Parliament and of the Council of 12 March 2001 on the deliberate release into the environment of genetically modified organisms (n 35).

[219] V Neßler, 'Der transnationale Verwaltungsakt: Zur Dogmatik eines neuen Rechtsinstituts' (1995) 14 Neue *Zeitschrift für Verwaltungsrecht* 863, 865.

Such administrative measures are preceded by multi-stage participatory procedures.[220] Again, Directive 2001/18[221] on the release of GMOs into the environment,
or their introduction in products on the market, provides a setting for illustrating
this.[222] Where the responsible national authority favours granting approval for a
product, it must pass on its evaluation report to the Commission which in turn for-
wards this to the relevant authorities of the remaining Member States (Article 14(2)
and (3) letter a of Directive 2001/18). Those authorities then have the possibility
of requesting further information and expressing environmental objections to the
granting of approval. Where there are no objections, the product can be approved
for the market (Article 15(3)) but, if there are objections by other Member States
or the Commission, and no agreement is reached, a decision is made through a
comitology procedure under Article 30 (Article 18). The Commission, subject to the
binding majority opinion of the relevant committee, makes a decision on the basis
of Article 288 fourth paragraph TFEU.[223] The participation rights of the Member
States arising from secondary law in these kinds of cases can range from a mere expression of views through to a right of veto. A Member State can depart from the
final determination of the Commission under unforeseen circumstances where this
would be justified by a risk to health or the environment.[224] Such multi-stage procedures strengthen the Union-wide acceptance of the outcome through the direct
cooperation of national authorities. A further case where such a process is employed
is that of waste transport (under Regulation 1013/2006),[225] where the responsible national authority in the destination state issues a transport permit subject to the participation of the authorities of the state of origin (and of the states through which
the waste might pass).

A further legal facet of such a Union-wide decision-making effect is provided
by transnational administrative acts subject to scrutiny in a recognition procedure.
So, a determination made in one Member State (sometimes in cooperation with,
or in work-sharing arrangements with, other Member States)[226] is then treated as
its own administrative decision by each other Member State, subject only to an-
swering limited additional questions.[227] The original determination emerges typically through recourse to a so-called 'reference method' in the initial Member
State (a method used in a number of EU regulatory fields, including, for example,

---

[220] K Reinacher, *Die Vergemeinschaftung von Verwaltungsverfahren am Beispiel der Freisetzungsrichtlinie*
(Duncker & Humblot 2005) 72; Sydow (n 22) 151.

[221] Directive 2001/18/EC (n 35).

[222] See von Danwitz (n 140) 630 ff; U Lienhard, 'Der mehrstufige gemeinschaftliche Verwaltungsakt
am Beispiel der Freisetzungsrichtlinie', *Natur und Recht* (2002) 13, 15 ff.

[223] Sydow (n 22) 152.

[224] See eg Case C-6/99 *Greenpeace France v Ministère de l'Agriculture et de la Pêche* [2000] ECR I-1652,
para 47.

[225] Regulation (EC) No 1013/2006 of the European Parliament and of the Council of 14 June 2006 on
shipments of waste (n 75).

[226] See Art 35 of Regulation (EC) No 1107/2009 of the European Parliament and of the Council of 21
October 2009 concerning the placing of plant protection products on the market (n 23).

[227] See E Schmidt-Aßmann, 'Verwaltungskooperation und Verwaltungskooperationsrecht in der
Europäischen Gemeinschaft', (1996) 30 *Europarecht* 301.

foodstuffs, as well as in the environmental sector). That method is a mode of assessment which relies on applying an established and adopted standard and/or following a strictly set procedure.[228] It may sometimes be applied in regard to the type and quality of measurement which a Member State authority must use in order to generate information to be provided to the Commission (or to other Member States), in the satisfaction of monitoring or similar obligations, for example in relation to air quality.[229] In the context of a discussion of transnational acts as such, though, its application is to authorization applications, typically in relations to good or products with (potentially) harmful environmental effects.[230] Similarly, the admission of certain detergents to the internal market, and the standards of bio-degradability demanded of them, relies on such methods,[231] in that case on the application of a harmonized product standard, coupled with possible scrutiny and objection by any Member State.[232]

Where an authorization decision has been made under the reference method, the decision (if need be) then undergoes a recognition procedure in other national systems. Reciprocal or mutual recognition[233] follows upon the prior employment of the standardized processes in the original decision. So, in relation to bringing plant protection products on to the market, there is a two-stage procedure: the authorization by the Member State where the application has been made, followed (where sought by the producer or user) by the (mutual) recognition in the other Member State(s) where

---

[228] See Art 36 of Regulation (EC) No 1107/2009 of the European Parliament and of the Council of 21 October 2009 concerning the placing of plant protection products on the market (n 23).

[229] See eg European Commission, EC Working Group on Guidance for the Demonstration of Equivalence, Report—Guide to the Demonstration of Equivalence of Ambient Air Monitoring Methods (January 2010). That guidance indicates that a Member State should use the reference method when implementing the directives, but that the directives allow a Member State to 'use any other method which it can demonstrate gives results equivalent to the above (reference) method' (p 5). See also European Commission, EC Working Group on Particulate Matter, *A Report on Guidance to Member States on Pm10 Monitoring and Intercomparisons with the Reference Method* (January 2002). See also eg Art 9 of Commission Implementing Decision 2011/850/EU of 12 December 2011 laying down rules for Directives 2004/107/EC and 2008/50/EC of the European Parliament and of the Council as regards the reciprocal exchange of information and reporting on ambient air quality (notified under document C(2011) 9068) [2011] OJ L335/86–106.

[230] There is thus an interaction between regulation of the internal market for goods as such (and mutual recognition procedures for goods) with the policy of environmental protection.

[231] See eg Annexes II, III, and VIII of Regulation (EC) No 648/2004 of the European Parliament and of the Council of 31 March 2004 on detergents [2004] OJ L104/1–35.

[232] See Art 15 of Regulation (EC) No 648/2004 of the European Parliament and of the Council of 31 March 2004 on detergents (n 231), provides, as a 'safeguard clause':

1. Where a Member State has justifiable grounds for believing that a specific detergent, although complying with the requirements of this Regulation, constitutes … a risk to the environment, it may temporarily prohibit the placing on the market of that detergent in its territory …
   It shall immediately inform the other Member States and the Commission thereof, giving the reasons for its decision.
2. After consultation of the Member States, or, if appropriate, of the relevant technical or scientific committee of the Commission, a decision shall be taken on the matter within ninety days in accordance with [a specified] procedure.

[233] This process is variously described as 'mutual recognition'/ 'reconnaissance mutuelle'/'gegenseitige Anerkennung': see Sydow, *Verwaltungskooperation in der Europäischen Union–Zur horizontalen und vertikalen Zusammenarbeit der europäischen Verwaltungen am Beispiel des Produktzulassungsrechts* (n 22) 181; Reinacher (n 220) 162.

the product is to be marketed.[234] In the latter, matters such as the comparability of the environmental circumstances with those of the authorizing state can be taken into account.[235] In such a framework, a *transnational* element is, perhaps, on the face of it, not immediately apparent, as individual applications are in fact necessary in relation to each relevant national market. That element nevertheless emerges from the fact that reciprocal recognition is, as a rule, to be accorded on the basis that the (original) authorization satisfied the standards and demands laid down by EU law. The fact that other Member States are not entitled to pursue their own independent policy and procedure, without acknowledgement of the prior authorization, reflects this. Where, in the recognition procedure, divergences emerge between or among the Member States, a resolution procedure must be conducted. This initially entails the attempt to achieve unity among the Member States, but, should this fail, centralized decision-making takes place through the Commission (under Article 288 fourth paragraph TFEU), involving comitology procedures and the participation of scientific committees.[236] In this way, the (original) authorization procedure does not then need to be rehearsed in each Member State.

2 European administrative agreements

As in national administrations, contractual arrangements complement methods of command-and-control for administrative implementation in EU environmental policy, although not (yet) in great numbers. Nevertheless, of special significance here are multi-level accords, for example between the Commission (or the EEA)[237] and national, municipal, and other public authorities in the Member States,[238] or among the latter inter se. These measures aid the coordination of administrative implementation and reflect various forms of multilateral cooperation for Union measures with distinctly regional or geographical focus or effect,[239] often with a particular relevance for nature conservation. They may form the basis of planning measures with a

[234] See Arts 29 and 40 of Regulation (EC) No 1107/2009 of the European Parliament and of the Council of 21 October 2009 concerning the placing of plant protection products on the market (n 23).

[235] See Art 41(1) of Regulation (EC) No 1107/2009 of the European Parliament and of the Council of 21 October 2009 concerning the placing of plant protection products on the market (n 23).

[236] See eg Arts 38 and 79 of Regulation (EC) No 1107/2009 of the European Parliament and of the Council of 21 October 2009 concerning the placing of plant protection products on the market [2009] OJ L309/1–50. The description offered in the text is a somewhat simplified account of the framework for pesticides: in fact under Arts 7–13 Regulation 1107/2009 active substances are authorized under a strict procedure (by a rapporteur Member State, lodgement of a draft assessment with the Commission, conduct of expert consultations by the European Food Safety Authority, and a determination including comitology procedures, leading to a Commission regulation). The introduction of a product, containing such an active substance, on to the market takes place against this extended regulatory framework. Where there is a divergent view among the Member States concerning the equivalence of the substance (under Art 29(1) (b)) with that covered by a regulation, comitology procedures are then triggered (Art 38(4)).

[237] Sommer sees agreements as the principal tool of the EEA in its relations with Member States: Sommer (n 24) 544 ff.

[238] I Härtel, *Handbuch Europäische Rechtsetzung* (2006) 455; C Koch, *Arbeitsebenen der Europäischen Union—Das Verfahrensrecht der Integrationsverwaltung* (Nomos 2003) 395; von Danwitz (n 140) 375; see eg Agreement on the Protection and Sustainable Development of the Prespa Park Area [2011] OJ L258/2–8.

[239] Initiated in the White Paper 'European Governance' COM(2001) 428 final [2001] OJ C 287/1; see also Härtel, *Handbuch Europäische Rechtsetzung* (n 238) 455.

specifically environmental focus.[240] In the setting of Union water management policy, Member States are required to embark on suitable agreements in order to apply the Water Framework Directive in each river basin area on its territory, in order to achieve waterway management properly suited to it.[241] For that, programmes and plans are to be instituted and, where such a basin (not rarely) crosses national borders, the affected Member States can enter into administrative agreements to give effect to these steps, eventually with the collateral assistance of the Commission.[242]

The Commission also enters into contractual arrangements with private parties or consortia, specifically 'framework contracts', in pursuit of advice, enquiry, proposals, and above all technical assistance in various fields, including the environmental sector. For example, a Framework Contract on the Evaluation, Review and Development of EU Water Policy,[243] has been made for a comprehensive examination of the implementation of the Water Framework Directive[244] and of compliance with it by the Member States, and on the operation of the Common Implementation Strategy (CIS-WFD, see above). Such contracts involve, in effect, the provision of technical support for the (networked) administration of the Union through research and scientific advice, received from a transnational network of external (private or public) bodies.

J Administrative Enforcement in the Environmental Sector

Enforcement in the environmental sector relies, as elsewhere, on enforcement networks (or networking). A 'vertical' form of enforcement is seen in the form of inspections, at least insofar as these are not actually passed over to third parties outside the administration as such (especially in the context of co-regulation, such as that under EMAS). Cooperative enforcement measures are exemplified, under the Article 28(1) of Regulation 1005/2009 on substances damaging to the ozone layer,[245] by the reliance on national authorities acting on behalf of the Commission (and obliged after the event to report to it on the outcome).[246] The adoption of such an enforcement procedure demonstrates a

---

[240] A conservation area under Habitat Directive (and thus within Natura 2000) can be established by a contractual accord: Art 1 letter l of Council Directive 92/43/EEC of 21 May 1992 on the conservation of natural habitats and of wild fauna and flora (n 2), following establishment of a special area of protection durch a contractual agreement.

[241] 'International agreements' and 'negotiated environmental agreements': see Arts 3(4) and 11(4) of Directive 2000/60/EC of the European Parliament and of the Council of 23 October 2000 establishing a framework for Community action in the field of water policy (n 83).

[242] This does not necessarily an easy task or in the result effective: see Meßerschmidt, *Europäisches Umweltrecht* (n 55) 365.

[243] Led by the Water Research Centre (WRc), United Kingdom, with participation of Ecologic Institute, (Germany), Aarhus University, Danish Centre for Environment and Energy (DCE) (Denmark), ARCADIS Belgium (Belgium), Ecosphere Consultants (Portugal), Environmental Institute (EI), (Slovakia), Fresh Thoughts (Austria), INTECSA-INARSA (Spain), InterSus Sustainability Services (InterSus) (Germany), Milieu (Belgium), Norwegian Institute for Water Research (NIVA) (Norway), Federal Environment Agency (UBA), Germany.

[244] See Arts 3(4) and 11(4) of Directive 2000/60/EC of the European Parliament and of the Council of 23 October 2000 establishing a framework for Community action in the field of water policy (n 83).

[245] Regulation (EC) No 1005/2009 of the European Parliament and of the Council of 16 September 2009 on substances that deplete the ozone layer [2009] OJ L286/1–30.

[246] E Schmidt-Aßmann, 'Einleitung: Der Europäische Verwaltungsverbund und die Rolle des Europäischen Verwaltungsrechts' in E Schmidt-Aßmann, B Schöndorf-Haubold, *Der europäische*

recognition that local authorities are likely to be more familiar with local circumstances, and capable of reacting more quickly (quite apart from difficulties which might arise attempting to conduct enforcement operations with external actors within the local legal framework). It also emerges from the fact that the supranational authorities rarely will have resources sufficient to these purposes.[247] Even in such cases, notwithstanding that, the Commission will be at liberty to accompany local officials, so that the enforcement actually then becomes joint.[248] In a horizontal sense there can also be cooperative measures of enforcement. The basis for these lies in the duty of the Member States 'in the light of the duty of faithful cooperation with the Commission … to set up comprehensive administrative checks and on-the-spot inspections thus guaranteeing the proper observance of the substantive and formal conditions',[249] corresponding to obligations arising Article 4(3) TEU.[250] Specific obligations relating to inspection and the sharing of relevant information between Member States can be illustrated by reference to waste electrical equipment,[251] major-accident hazards involving dangerous substances,[252] geological storage of carbon dioxide,[253] and landfill of waste.[254]

K Supervision in the Administration of Environmental Policy

Ensuring the accountability of administrative actors is essential, above all to reflect inter alia the principles of the rule of law and of good administration, and effective mechanisms are needed for this.[255] There must be means for holding administrative actors to their various legal obligations, including the meeting of deadlines, the generation and provision of required information, the undertaking of actions of

---

Verwaltungsverbund–Formen und Verfahren der Verwaltungszusammenarbeit in der EU (Mohr Siebeck 2005) 22; although the word 'inspection' is not used explicitly in Art 20(3) of Regulation 2037/2000/EG, it is used in the title to Chapter V.

[247] Epiney, *Umweltrecht in der Europäischen Union–Primärrechtliche Grundlagen, Gemeinschaftliches Sekundärrecht* (n 53) 160; Demmke (n 61)) 112.

[248] As under Art 98(1) 2nd sentence of Council Regulation (EC) No 1224/2009 of 20 November 2009 establishing a Community control system for ensuring compliance with the rules of the common fisheries policy [2009] OJ L343/1–50.

[249] Case C-247/98 *Greece v Commission* [2001] ECR I-1, para 81.

[250] Cooperative enforcement measures can be illustrated by the requirements of Articles 71(3), 79, and 83 of Council Regulation (EC) No 1224/2009 of 20 November 2009 establishing a Community control system for ensuring compliance with the rules of the common fisheries policy (n 248).

[251] See Arts 18 and 23 of Directive 2012/19/EU of the European Parliament and of the Council of 4 July 2012 on waste electrical and electronic equipment (WEEE) [2012] OJ L197/38–71.

[252] See Arts 17, 19, and 20 Directive 2012/18/EU of the European Parliament and of the Council of 4 July 2012 on the control of major-accident hazards involving dangerous substances, amending and subsequently repealing Council Directive 96/82/EC [2012] OJ L197/1–37.

[253] See Arts 11 and 15 of Directive 2009/31/EC of the European Parliament and of the Council of 23 April 2009 on the geological storage of carbon dioxide [2009] OJ L140/114–35.

[254] See Arts 11 and 13 of Council Directive 1999/31/EC of 26 April 1999 on the landfill of waste [1999] OJ L182/1–19.

[255] See G C Rowe, 'Administrative Supervision of Administrative Action in the European Union' in H C H Hofmann, A H Türk (eds), *Legal Challenges in EU Administrative Law: Towards an Integrated Administration* (Edward Elgar Publishing 2009) 179; A M Latour, *Die integrierte Umweltverwaltung in der Europäischen Union* (Nomos 2013) 220 ff, with further references.

enforcement,[256] and so on. As the preceding material demonstrates, environmental administration relies little upon hierarchical relationships. Supervisory mechanisms must reflect the heterarchy which in fact obtains, for example, responding to composite procedures and transnational administrative acts. In doing so, one can rely in part on the conceptual figure of the 'counter-flow' (or alternate-current) principle,[257] as at least one applicable model. Administrative implementation in the EU environmental sector employs all of the usual categories of supervision and control over public official and authorities: administrative, political and judicial. In the following discussion, we also rely on the accepted distinction between ex ante and ex post control,[258] where judicial control and political supervision (apart from legislation as such) almost invariably operate subsequent to the action concerned, and administrative (internal) control is more likely (but not invariably) to be exercised in advance.

1 Administrative supervision

Administrative supervision ex ante classically takes the form of instruction or guidance of a 'lower' administrative level by a 'higher' one, but that is not the general relationship of the different levels in Union administration. Nevertheless, the Commission does have competences to impose rules for national administrations, especially through delegated and implementing measures. Examples of these, and of non-binding guidelines have been offered above, as have instruments of (formally non-binding) guidance (section H), and these will not be rehearsed here. The role of comitology when the Commission is preparing administrative rules, could itself be conceived of as one further form of (administrative) supervision. However, it would be better to see it as an integrated part of a composite procedures for the *making* of EU subordinate legislation (see above).[259] Also, the procedure associated with the issue of a transnational administrative act, involving reciprocal consultation, offers in effect considerable opportunity for incidental control, and this is intensified in the multi-level procedures aimed at the resolution of divergent national positions, where the Commission makes the final decision in conjunction with comitology under Article 288 fourth paragraph TFEU.[260]

---

[256] The accountability of administrative officials specifically for their enforcement action, and the implications of that for political and judicial supervision, has been extensively examined in M Scholten, M Luchtman (eds), *Law Enforcement by EU Authorities--Implications for Political and Judicial Accountability* (Edward Elgar Publishing 2017).

[257] Well known in fluid science, but also used in German constitutional law, under the term *Gegenstromprinzip*, the idea being that control and influence does not always flow in the same direction but can alternate in a reflexive way, depending on the context and subject-matter; cf E Schmidt-Aßmann in E Schmidt-Aßmann, B Schöndorf-Haubold, *Der europäische Verwaltungsverbund—Formen und Verfahren der Verwaltungszusammenarbeit in der EU* (Mohr Siebeck 2005) 1, 20 ff; Rowe, 'Administrative Supervision of Administrative Action in the European Union' (n 255) 179, 194.

[258] The central purpose of ex ante mechanisms and procedures is to avoid the situation that illegality in decision-making or other administrative action is discovered, but only after the event, that is, to avoid it in the first place; see Rowe, 'Controlling Administrative Action' (n 33) 223, 227.

[259] Specifically when the competence to make a decision shifts from one decision-maker to another; see Rowe, 'Administrative Supervision of Administrative Action in the European Union' (n 255) 179, 206.

[260] Sydow (n 22) 152.

In exercising its responsibilities of supervision vis-à-vis the Member States, the Commission can have recourse to actions before the Union courts, a form of *ex post* control, but in essence transmuting the supervision from 'administrative' into 'judicial' control (see below) (usually finally concluded only after rather long periods of time). The conduct of the Commission's (administrative) *infringement procedure* (typically in anticipation of legal action) is itself an often effective means of exercising supervisory control. Other *ex post* supervisory procedures include the Commission's so-called 'package meetings', within which practical solutions to implementation deficits can be sought.[261] An example is provided by the public discussions in Spain, organized by the Commission, concerning compensatory measures for disturbances of nature and environment. There, environmentalists, administrators, advisors, and local experts were able to participate,[262] offering procedural means for ensuring—or at least encouraging—conformity with administrative obligations.

The Commission appears to be showing new resolve in pursuing its supervisory role, and, where appropriate, to trigger supervision through the Union courts in initiating infringement proceedings. Nevertheless, there has in fact been significant criticism of the Commission's failure to conduct infringement procedures, and then to go on to the Court, in relation to the failure of many Member States to fulfil the requirements of Union air pollution law, especially concerning urban air pollution due to motor vehicles.[263] This is despite the fact that the Commission has said it

> will therefore give high priority to infringements that reveal systemic weaknesses which undermine the functioning of the EU's institutional framework. This applies in particular to infringements which affect the capacity of national judicial systems to contribute to the effective enforcement of EU law.[264]

Coupled with this apparent—but as yet unfulfilled—resolve, the Commission has established a standardized way of proceeding in dealing with *individual complaints* made to it in relation to the inadequate application of European law on the Member State level.[265]

2 Political supervision

The Committee on the Environment, Public Health and Food Safety (ENVI) of the European Parliament is, as one of the leading legislative committees of the EP, a key organizational element of political supervision in this sector. The Committee (of sixty-nine Members of the European Parliament (MEPs)), addresses a comprehensive range

---

[261] Together with national authorities, all current processes are examined, in order to avoid, in any applicable case, the commencement of infringement procedures; see No III of the Communication from the Commission—A Europe of Results—Applying Community Law, COM(2007) 0502 final.

[262] Krämer (n 124) 7, 13 ff.

[263] See eg the complaints of the EEB http://eeb.org/delays-and-secrecy-surround-governments-plans-to-tackle-air-pollution.

[264] Commission Communication—EU law: Better results through better application C(2016) 8600) [2017] OJ C18/10–20, at 14.

[265] ibid Annex: 'Administrative procedures for the handling of relations with the complainant regarding the application of European Union law' (at 18–20).

of environmental topics: climate change; air, soil and water pollution; waste management and recycling; dangerous substances and preparations; noise; biodiversity;
sustainable development; and civil protection. Part of its focus is of an institutional
kind, on the one hand in supervising the activities of the European Environment
Agency (EEA) and the European Chemicals Agency (ECHA), and on the other hand
attending to international and regional dimensions of environmental protection.
The Committee, for example, scrutinizes legislative proposals from the Commission
(for both secondary legislation, and delegated regulations and directives by the
Commission itself).[266] A striking element of its assumed responsibilities is the issue of
the *restoration* of environmental damage, an environmental principle thus far insufficiently recognized. Within the general annual process of the Parliament's scrutiny of
the implementation of Union law, the ENVI Committee gives its opinion in relation to
the environmental sector. While its comments here are typically somewhat anodyne,
it has drawn attention to enforcement deficits and underscored the broader socio-economic costs of inadequately implemented environmental protection.[267]

The work of the Committee is supported by external bodies, such as think-tanks
like the Institute for European Environmental Policy (which provide reports and advice to various Union institutions and bodies), sometimes through framework contracts (e.g., Framework Contract on European Environmental Policies and Sustainable
Development) with the European Parliament for the conduct of research, the preparation of reports, and provision of advice.[268] Like such contracts with the Commission,
we see the networked administration of the Union itself being supported by a transnational network of external (private or public) research and technical organizations.

The European Parliament's Office for Scientific and Technological Option
Assessment (STOA), while not having an exclusively environmental focus, also addresses significant topics in this field, in particular eco-efficiency in transport and energy, and the sustainable management of natural resources. The STOA Panel consists
of members nominated by the Parliament's standing committees. Its role is to provide
EP committees with independent studies, information, and advice for assessing new
technologies. Moreover, it conducts fora for politicians, scientific representatives, and
civil society representatives for consideration of scientific and technological developments. One particular aim is the support of parliamentary assessment activity in the
Member States, thus strengthening political supervision on that level.

One can notice that the key bodies of parliamentary scrutiny in this field emulate,
in a certain way at least, the organizational, structural, and procedural character of EU

---

[266] A full list of its legislative scrutiny activity is available at http://www.europarl.europa.eu/commit-
tees/en/envi/work-in-progress.html.

[267] See eg Opinion of the Committee on the Environment, Public Health and Food Safety for the
Committee on Legal Affairs on monitoring the application of EU law 2016 (2017/2273(INI) (accessible
at: www.europarl.europa.eu/sides/getDoc.do?pubRef=-%2f%2fEP%2f%2fNONSGML%2bCOMPARL%
2bPE-616.822%2b03%2b%2bDOC%2bPDF%2bV0%2f%2fEN).

[268] Led by the Institute for European Environmental Policy (IEEP) (UK) with participation of Ecologic
Institute (Germany), denkstatt Bulgaria (Bulgaria), Cambridge Econometrics (UK), VU University
Amsterdam, Institute for Environmental Studies (Netherlands), Finish Environment Institute (Finland),
and BIO by Deloitte (France).

environmental administration: they are all characterizable as multi-level, representative, participatory, and technocratic.

3 Judicial supervision

Judicial supervision is often concerned with the breach of obligations by Member States to provide information required under Union law. One can point to numerous actions by the Commission against Member States for failing to satisfy reporting obligations contained in secondary law, where the Court has granted declaratory relief (including cases where the Member State has acknowledged, in the course of the proceedings, its own failure to meet such obligations).[269] There have been actions against virtually every Member State for the unpunctual implementation of the Birds Directive, and thereby in failing to meet administrative deadlines for the proposal of areas to be brought within the framework which ultimately became Natura 2000.

The Court's supervisory role also includes enforcing the obligation on Member States to conduct (adequate) environmental impact assessment of a project or plan. This can also occur, for example, in relation to projects which can have a significant effect on a nature conservation site within Natura 2000, according to measures understood in the light of Commission guidelines (e.g., a Special Protection Area (SPA) on the Waddenzee, in the Netherlands),[270] or in deciding what factors a Member State may (or may not) take into account (e.g., when selecting a site in the Severn Estuary for inclusion in Natura 2000 as a site of 'Community importance'),[271] or the failure of a Member State to classify a site as a SPA and not adopting sufficient conservation measures (e.g., the Basses Corbières site, France),[272] or determining the scope of the discretion available to a Member State in selecting sites for nomination to the Natura 2000 network (e.g., contradicting Germany's claim that the relevant directive accorded national authorities a wide margin of discretion).[273]

In all areas of environmental protection there are numerous comparable determinations by the Court in the context of infringement proceedings, for example, as regards the unlawful disposal of hazardous waste in landfill (with a substantial financial penalty imposed on Italy).[274] No attempt can be made here at a comprehensive presentation of such actions and judicial determinations.[275]

---

[269] Generally in relation to technical standards and regulations eg Case C-139/92 *Commission v Italy* (n 132); specifically in relation to environmentally relevant notifications see eg Case C-162/89 *Commission v Belgium* (n 126); Case C-237/90 *Commission v Germany* (n 126).

[270] Commission Guidelines, 'Managing Natura 2000 Sites: The provisions of Article 6 of the Habitats Directive (92/43/EEC)'. See Case C-127/02 *Waddenvereniging and Vogelbeschermingsvereniging* [2004] ECR I-7405.

[271] Case C-371/98 *'First Corporate Shipping': Queen v Secretary of State for the Environment, Transport and the Regions, ex parte First Corporate Shipping* [2000] ECR I-9235.

[272] Case C-374/98 *Commission v France* [2000] ECR I-10799, ECLI:EU:C:2000:670. As a further example, of many, see Case C-6/04 *Commission v UK* (n 16); Case C-117/00 *Commission v Ireland* [2002] ECR I-5335; Case C-221/04 *Commission v Spain* [2006] ECR I-4515 ff; Case C-535/07 *Commission v Austria* [2010] ECR I-9483; Case C-383/09 *Commission v France* [2011] ECR I-4869.

[273] Case C-71/99 *Commission v Germany* [2001] ECR I-5811.

[274] Case C-196/13 *Commission v Italy Republic* ECLI:EU:C:2014:2407.

[275] Statistics on infringement actions taken by the Commission against Member State in the environmental field can be found at http://ec.europa.eu/environment/legal/law/statistics.htm.

4 Supervision considered overall

The system of control, relying on the components just discussed, is—not just in the environmental sector—arguably rather complex and lacking in clear contours.[276] On the one hand, this may reflect nothing more than the true, multi-facetted nature of the administrative system which is the subject of such supervision, and thus perhaps no cause for concern On the other hand, the possibly convoluted nature of supervisory arrangements may jeopardize the purposeful achievement of Union environmental policy, and under certain circumstances weaken the protection of individual rights. If, as a result of a somewhat confused system of control—in which the need for correction may be overlooked, or difficult to pursue—the administrative implementation of environmental policy is less efficient and effective than it should be, this must be seen as undesirable. In particular, it has been argued that EU secondary law lacks sufficient express means of achieving judicial enforcement of the duties of cooperation which are, as we have been at pains to underscore, a distinctive characteristic of Union (environmental) administration.[277]

Just what form such means should or could take, however, is hard to imagine, again because the complex and intertwined nature of the administrative system also makes it difficult to put one's finger on the critical nodes with a view to improving supervision. Nevertheless, a certain standardization of steps, procedures, and mechanisms of supervisory control may well contribute to improvement here. In particular, any attempt to improve supervision should be based on an open acknowledgement and understanding of the particular networked-cooperative administrative system of the Union, and supervisory methods should indeed themselves almost certainly emulate the methodology of the underlying system.[278]

Supervision aimed at improving cooperative interaction, and in connection with the allocation of competences, should not ignore the possibility of a heightened form of supranational control, through perhaps the establishment of special authorities on the European level, with corresponding powers of implementation. Especially in a setting where executive coordination in response to transborder environmental phenomena is insufficient,[279] such a step may well improve the harmonized implementation of Union environmental law. The decisions of the Court noted above concerning the insufficiency of implementation of the legislation for Natura 2000 might offer further argument in favour of some such supranational supervisory

---

[276] Rowe, 'Controlling Administrative Action' (n 33) 223, 256 ff; E Schmidt-Aßmann in E Schmidt-Aßmann, B Schöndorf-Haubold, *Der europäische Verwaltungsverbund—Formen und Verfahren der Verwaltungszusammenarbeit in der EU* (Mohr Siebeck 2005) 1, 20.

[277] See von Danwitz (n 140) 635.

[278] See, in this regard, Rowe, 'Administrative supervision of administrative action in the European Union' (n 255) 179, 216 ff, who argues in favour of some form of cost-benefit assessment of control mechanisms. Gil Ibanez makes the case for the detailed elaboration of rules in respect of procedural breaches within a clear delimitation of national and supranational competences; A J Gil Ibanez, 'The "Standard" Administrative Procedure for Supervising and Enforcing EC Law: EC Treaty Articles 226 and 228' (2004) 68 *Law and Contemporary Problems* 135, 158.

[279] In relation to the restricted capacity of the Commission concerning such coordination see Latour, *Die integrierte Umweltverwaltung in der Europäischen Union* (n 255) 88 ff, with further references.

agency,[280] and comparison might be made here with the EU energy sector.[281] One can note that the Member States are, as already noted, obliged to establish NRCs and comparable topic centres, but these are subject just to national supervisory control, so that transfer of comprehensive environmental information might well be jeopardized particularly where a Member State might have something to hide. Nevertheless, any such move toward stronger supranational supervision would be subject to strict caveats in the light of national procedural autonomy. It might, despite that, be justified if it were clear that uniform and efficient implementation could not otherwise be attained. On the other hand, it may be precisely the cooperative nature of environmental administration which may enhance the effectiveness of Member States: it may well be only through cooperation that (at least some) Member States are actually capable of meeting their obligations.

5 Individual rights and supervision

Within the context of supervision, one must also note the important issue of the protection of individual rights.[282] Threats to individual rights in the environmental sector are, arguably, less obvious than perhaps in certain other fields. Nevertheless, in particular as regards business and commercial interests (rights to sell certain products, for example, or to operate certain facilities), such concerns should not be overlooked. Enforcement methods, such as inspections may, for example, potentially interfere with the integrity of private property. Informational demands in environmental administration may raise issues of data protection and privacy, especially business secrets.[283]

The heavily networked involvement of administrative actors from different legal orders may make such protection more difficult, especially where it may not be clear which judicial system might provide a remedy.[284] A typical situation is that of a Commission decision (or other measure), directed to national authorities, that the latter then take

---

[280] Demmke sees the possibility of installing such an authority within *IMPEL*-Network or the EEA; C Demmke, 'Nationale Verwaltung und europäische Umweltpolitik–die Umsetzung und der Vollzug von EG-Umweltrecht' in Demmke (n 61)) 85, 117.

[281] See Art 35 of Directive 2009/72/EC of the European Parliament and of the Council of 13 July 2009 concerning common rules for the internal market in electricity and repealing Directive 2003/54/EC (n 35), and Art 39 of Directive 2009/73/EC of the European Parliament and of the Council of 13 July 2009 concerning common rules for the internal market in natural gas and repealing Directive 2003/55/EC (n 35).

[282] See in detail W Kahl, K F Gärditz, 'Rechtsschutz im europäischen Kontrollverbund am Beispiel der FFH-Gebietsfestsetzungen' (2005) 27 *Natur und Recht* 555 ff., and M Lottini, 'From "Administrative Cooperation" in the Application of European Union Law to "Administrative Cooperation" in the Protection of European Rights and Liberties' (2012) *European Public Law* 127, 134 ff. Regarding individual rights in the context of REACH see M Tiedemann, 'Unionsrechtlicher Rechtsschutz gegen Eingriffe im Rahmen der Chemikalienregulierung nach der REACH-VO (EG), (2011) 126 *Deutsches Verwaltungsblatt* 993 ff; Martel (n 75) 601, 637 ff.

[283] Some rules covering data systems provide certain rights for individuals whose personal data may be stored in them (see eg Heußner (n 144) 380), but usually in regard to access, deletion, and correction regarding the data held. This is rarely of relevance for environmental databases eg European Forest Information and Communication System (EFICS), cf Art 2 of Regulation 1615/89, and Eurostat (in regard to the latter see Art 10(8) of Regulation 322/97).

[284] See eg W Kahl, 'Lücken und Ineffektivitäten im Europäischen Verfahrensverbund am Beispiel des Rechts auf Anhörung' (2012) 127 *Deutsches Verwaltungsblatt* 602 ff.

certain measures against third parties,[285] for example, in the resolution of divergent national positions relating to the release or use of genetically modified organisms (GMOs),[286] usually involving the participation of a comitology committee where the Commission (formally) makes the final determination.[287] Were the Commission's measure to be unlawful for whatever reason, an individual—directly and negatively affected only by the 'national' determination—could complain to the national court referring to the invalidity of the supranational legal basis (the Commission's decision) of the national measure, and call on that court to seek a preliminary ruling from the CJEU under Article 267 TFEU. However, in such cases it is not entirely clear whether it would be possible—perhaps even necessary—to proceed directly by way of an action for annulment under Article 263 fourth paragraph TFEU,[288] in order to avoid the Commission's measure from becoming enforceable, which might then prevent the national court from putting the question to the Court.[289] The need, in the course of announcing the (national) decision, to inform potentially affected parties of the remedies available in such a case cannot be underestimated.

Parallel to clarifying the contestability of such measures, the need for clarity and certainty concerning liability for erroneous determinations is also obvious, but this becomes more complicated because of the web of administrative actors involved in the emergence of the decision itself.[290] Should, for example, a comitology committee be legally liable for a determination which follows from its conclusions? Some form of joint liability might be plausible. The exclusive liability of any one responsible authority would be particularly problematic. Some system of surrogate liability (established under secondary law) might be considered. Member State responsibility, for example, for incorrect information in a data base relied upon in the decision-making process, ought to be a minimum requirement.[291]

L Conclusion

The administration of environmental protection in the European Union demands and displays a considerable array of structures, measures, procedures, and techniques. These reflect the fact the environmental policy requiring implementation is itself made up of diverse elements (as well as emerging within a uniquely constructed

---

[285] See eg Art 13 of Directive 2001/95/EC of the European Parliament and of the Council of 3 December 2001 on general product safety [2002] OJ L11/ 4–17.

[286] Directive 2001/18/EC (n 35).

[287] See Latour, *Die integrierte Umweltverwaltung in der Europäischen Union* (n 255) 189.

[288] See C Nowak, 'Rechtsschutz im europäischen Verwaltungsrecht' in J Terhechte, *Verwaltungsrecht der Europäischen Union* (Nomos 2011) 459, 478 ff.

[289] Heußner (n 144) 390.

[290] On state liability for transboundary administrative action see K. Reinacher, *Die Vergemeinschaftung von Verwaltungsverfahren am Beispiel der Freisetzungsrichtlinie* (2005) 175 ff; see also Sydow (n 22) 277; A H Türk, 'Judicial Review of Integrated Administration in the EU' in H C H Hofmann, A H Türk, *Legal challenges in EU Administrative Law: Towards an Integrated Administration* (Edward Elgar Publishing 2009) 218 ff.

[291] Weiß (n 20) 160.

supranational compact). There are, after all, considerable differences between the establishment of environment protection mechanisms of a largely geographic-spatial kind (such as we find in the Natura 2000 conservation network, or the European river basin management system) and those which relate to the testing and approval of (possibly environmentally hazardous) products, including vehicles, destined for European markets. Again, there are many features which distinguish the regime for the approval of industrial facilities with potentially environmentally damaging character, from that for the operation of an emissions trading system aimed at stemming greenhouse gases, or from that for the regulation of the transborder transport of hazardous wastes. This list could be extended significantly further.

To this diversity of subject matter, one needs to note the spread of administrative actors, each of which has its own degree of autonomy and its own specific functions, but with the need to achieve effective interaction in the service of (usually) common goals. We have identified repeated patterns of interaction and coordination in (but by no means unique to) this sector. The key element characterising these patterns is that there is scarcely any structural element which does not involve Member State representation. While there is a coordinating and sometimes supervising role for the Commission (itself hardly lacking Member State input), its role is predominantly that of bringing together national actors and of providing a framework for their effective interaction. Even where (quasi-binding) instruments emerge from the Commission, these virtually never emerge without Member State participation and, almost invariably, their determinative input. Truly 'centralized' elements can almost be reduced to formal steps (e.g., the publication in the *Official Journal* of the official designations of protected areas with Natura 2000), or perhaps to Union financing of cooperative measures (e.g., under LIFE+).

Such variation in subject matter and method means that the nature of (environmental) administrative implementation in the Union can scarcely be summarized as a single phenomenon. Nevertheless, the present chapter does allow us to identify certain recurring elements, even in rather different regulatory settings with rather different regulatory challenges. The features which emerge underscore the distinctively cooperative and interactive nature of EU administration. The various administrative actors of the Union are so interwoven with one another in this field that one can—almost—claim the existence of a homogeneous fulfilment of European environmental policy emerging from cooperative arrangements. The informational interdependence of the Member States in the environmental area can hardly go unnoticed in the regard. Among such cooperative aspects of environmental implementation, one should—perhaps rather surprisingly—draw attention in particular to the willingness to trust the administrative authorities of other Member States in making decisions which might affect the environment of one's own territory or people. Such a willingness is—not unreasonably—not unconditional, so that 'correction' (through recourse to a 'higher' authority, specifically the Commission plus comitology) is available for critical cases of divergence. The regular reliance on comitology, whether for subordinate legislative measures, or for resolving divergences between Member States in relation to transnational administrative acts, is, though, in itself a further element which reminds us of the shared and integrated nature of implementation in this sector. These features are particularly prominent in the administration of nature conservation under Natura 2000, but not only there.

The reliance on standardized elements, be it in information sharing or in the reference method for environmental approvals and for monitoring methodology, can be regarded as good examples of administrative efficiency. There appear to be further possibilities of this. Why, for example, would it not be possible to have standardized regulatory provisions laying down the procedures for resolving divergences between Member States, rather than repeating (very similar) provisions in each legislative act. This would not only reduce the bulk of the legislative instruments but also avoid the impression that, with each new measure, the wheel has to be re-invented.

We noted at the outset that the nature conservation scheme of Natura 2000 for a 'coherent European ecological network'[292] would constitute a thread through this chapter. Here we draw on it again to offer a thumbnail image of EU environmental administration, even if not absolutely applicable to every sub-field: Natura 2000 is a highly successful physical-geographical network of conservation areas (over 27,000 in all, covering almost 20 per cent of Union territory, and including approximately one million km² of terrestrial and maritime areas—the largest such network in the world). This is emblematic of the regime which has given rise to it: an impressive spatial network which has emerged from, and is managed by, an equally impressive structural, procedural and legal network of actors and organizations, both within the Union itself and outside its formal and geographical framework.

An inevitable question hangs in the shadows of this study, the question of policy substance and policy achievement. Has a *high* level of protection of the environment—or even a *high* level of protection of human beings from environmental harm—in fact been attained? The answer can only be negative: while it is undeniable that a *certain* level has been reached, indications contradicting the attainment of that aspirationally high level simply cannot be overlooked. Undoubtedly, via the European Union a level of environmental protection has been achieved which would not have been attained without it (if only because of the transterritorial nature of many of the problems addressed, but also for other reasons). Nevertheless, whether they be unsolved 'old' problems, or insufficiently addressed 'new' ones, there are many serious, pressing environmental and ecological concerns being dealt with disturbingly *inadequately*:

- climate change
- threats to bio-diversity generally (including that of waterways) and significant, possibly existential declines in insects (most notably, bees) and in bird populations
- increasing threats from (micro-)plastics and their waste disposal
- urban air pollution (notably in relation to the illegal practices of motor vehicle manufacturers)
- serious declines of fisheries stocks and
- unresolved issues of the (very long-term) safe management of atomic wastes.

---

[292] See Art 3(1) of Council Directive 92/43/EEC of 21 May 1992 on the conservation of natural habitats and of wild fauna and flora (n 2).

All of these issues (together with others) make ineluctably clear that environmental protection, whether on the local, regional, national or supranational level confronts—and will continue, repeatedly, to confront—enormous challenges, and be burdened by very significant policy and implementational deficits. Is the EU administrative system in the environmental sector to be blamed for such deficits? Does its essentially shared-decentralized-networked administrative implementation contribute significantly to such problems? Is this system indeed inadequate to such challenges? These may, in fact, all be the wrong questions, simply because a fundamentally different system of implementation for the Union is scarcely imaginable. Nevertheless, the dispersed, heavily technocratic character of this system, lacking in particular a *political* concentration, raises important concerns. Our environmental protection relies heavily, both in its policy formation and its practical implementation, on the virtually *decisive* (or exceedingly influential) role of dispersed, de-centrally nominated (expert) representatives, agreeing almost invariably on (commonly, environmentally inadequate) compromises. In that light, we need to ask: who are these representatives; who selects them and how; what (particular) interests do they reflect and represent; and what corrective influences might be channelled to positive effect? Critical elements of the administrative system of European environmental protection need reflection and adjustment. We noted above that measures promoting the intensity and realization of political-administrative cooperation were needed, but that cooperation must provide the substantive policy results which environmental challenges demand. Above all, the strengthening of the influence of civil society—specifically through environmental NGOs—appears increasingly vital in order to realize the level of protection necessary.

APPENDIX

Table of comitology committees in the sector of environmental protection

C49700 The Mercury Regulation Art. 22 Committee

C37000 The Committee for the adaptation to scientific and technical progress and implementation of Directive 2008/98/EC on waste

C35500 The Ambient Air Quality Committee

C48100 Ship Recycling Regulation Committee

C30200 Regulatory Committee on the implementation of the European PRTR

C13700 Management Committee for application of the directive on the standardisation and rationalisation of reports on the implementation of certain directives relating to the environment

C43600 LIFE Committee for Environment and Climate Action

C40000 Industrial Emissions Directive (IED) Article 75 Committee

C33800 Forest Law Enforcement Governance and Trade (FLEGT) Committee

C13400 Committee on the conservation of natural habitats and of wild fauna and flora (HABITAT)

C38800 Committee on the Community eco-management and audit scheme (EMAS)

C47600 Committee on invasive alien species

C33600 Committee on Infrastructure for Spatial Information in the European Community (INSPIRE)

C14000 Committee of Competent Authorities established under the directive on the control of major-accident hazards involving dangerous substances (Seveso Directive 2012/18/EU)

C13100 Committee for the protection of species of wild fauna and flora by regulating trade therein

C33500 Committee for the implementation of the Directive on Sulphur content in Marine Fuels

C42200 Committee for the adaptation to technical progress of the directive on the Stage II control of volatile organic compound emissions resulting from the refuelling of motor vehicles at service stations (VOC)

C12500 Committee for the adaptation to technical progress of the directive on the control of volatile organic compound emissions resulting from the storage of petrol and its distribution from terminals to service stations (VOC)

C12400 Committee for the adaptation to technical progress of legislation to remove technical barriers to trade in dangerous substances and preparations

C34300 Committee for the adaptation to technical progress of Directive 2006/7/EC concerning the management of bathing water quality

C38700 Committee for the adaptation to technical progress and application of the Community award scheme for an eco-label (ECO-LABEL)

C11900 Committee for the adaptation to technical and scientific progress of the directive on the quality of water intended for human consumption

C11800 Committee for the adaptation to scientific and technical progress of the directive on conservation of wild birds (ORNIS)

C11600 Committee for the adaptation to scientific and technical progress and implementation of the directive on urban waste water treatment

C11400 Committee for the adaptation to scientific and technical progress and implementation of the directive on protection of waters against pollution caused by nitrates from agricultural sources

C36400 Committee for implementing the marine strategy framework directive

C11300 Committee for implementing the directive establishing a Community policy regarding water

C11100 Committee for implementation of the directive on packaging and packaging waste

C40800 Animals in Science Committee

C46900 'Access and benefit sharing' Committee

14

Energy and Trans-European Networks

Jens-Peter Schneider

A Introduction

The European Union has established a growing and increasingly complex legal framework for production, trade and consumption of energy during the last decades. In the beginning, the former European Communities played only a very limited role, as energy policy fell mainly into the competences of the Member States.[1] Neither the Treaty on the European Community for Coal and Steel (1951) nor the EURATOM-Treaty (1957) limited the national competences to regulate the national energy mix or the structure of energy industries.[2] A remnant of this former primacy of national competencies can be found in Article 192(2) TFEU.

Today the picture has, however, changed dramatically.[3] First, general treaty provisions such as those on the freedom of goods and services or on competition law and state aids have been applied to an increasing extent to energy industries.[4] Secondly, the EU legislator has become more and more active, especially in the field of the internal energy market with three market liberalization packages of 1996/1998, 2003/2005 and 2009,[5] and a so-called 'winter package' of November 2016 which consists of various reform proposals of the Commission concerning electricity regulation (at present the subject of intensively discussion in the EU legislative bodies: see section C1 below and passim). Thirdly, the negative external effects of energy production and energy consumption have been realized, and been made increasingly the subject of regulation on the EU level.[6] Fourthly, the Treaty of Lisbon integrated an energy-specific provision into the Union's primary law with Article 194 TFEU.[7] Finally, in the last few years, the

---

[1] See Kim Talus, *EU Energy Law and Policy* (OUP 2013) 15 ff; Jörg Gundel, 'Europäisches Energierecht' in Wolfgang Danner and Christian Theobald (eds), *Energierecht* (C.H. Beck 2016) paras 1 ff; Jens-Peter Schneider, 'Vorgaben des europäischen Energierechts' in Jens-Peter Schneider and Christian Theobald (eds), *Recht der Energiewirtschaft* (4th edn, C.H. Beck 2013) § 2 paras 2 ff.

[2] Schneider, 'Europäisches Energierecht' (n 1) § 2 paras 2 ff; see also Angus Johnston and Guy Block, *EU Energy Law* (OUP 2012) paras 13.01 ff, 14.01 ff.

[3] For an overview see Johnston and Block (n 2) paras 2.01 ff; Schneider, 'Europäisches Energierecht' (n 1) § 2 paras 33 ff; Talus (n 1) 15 ff; Hans Vedder and others, 'EU Energy Law' in Martha M. Roggenkamp and others (eds), *Energy Law in Europe* (3rd edn, OUP 2016) paras 4.01 ff.

[4] See Talus (n 1) 110 ff; Vedder and others (n 3) paras 4.55 ff; Schneider, 'Europäisches Energierecht' (n 1) § 2 paras 12 ff.

[5] See Johnston and Block (n 2) 2.19 ff; Talus (n 1) 66 ff; Schneider, 'Europäisches Energierecht' (n 1) § 2 paras 33 ff; Gundel (n 1) paras 37 ff.

[6] See Johnston and Block (n 2) paras 12.01 ff; Talus (n 1) 175 ff; Vedder and others (n 3) paras 4.375 ff; Gundel (n 1) paras 74 ff; Jens-Peter Schneider, 'Energieumweltrecht' in Jens-Peter Schneider/Christian Theobald (ed), Recht der Energiewirtschaft (4th edn, C.H. Beck, 2013) § 21 paras 27 ff, 33 ff, 189 ff.

[7] Vedder and others (n 3) paras 4.26 ff; Schneider, 'Europäisches Energierecht' (n 1) § 2 paras 10 ff; see also paras 7 ff.

EU has extended the use of its external trade competences to energy markets, thereby adding an international dimension to EU energy policy.[8]

The wide-ranging scope of EU energy policies is captured in Article 194(1) TFEU, which provides that

> Union policy on energy shall aim, in a spirit of solidarity between Member States, to:
> (a) ensure the functioning of the energy market;
> (b) ensure security of energy supply in the Union;
> (c) promote energy efficiency and energy saving and the development of new and renewable forms of energy; and
> (d) promote the interconnection of energy networks.

Thus, the Commission could publish, with some justification, a comprehensive communication introducing an 'Energy Union Package', with a framework strategy for a resilient Energy Union and a forward-looking climate change policy in 2015.[9]

The following analysis cannot cover all legal aspects of the Energy Union, which range from issues of international agreements with third countries to problems of EU constitutional law. Instead, the chapter will focus on those aspects of the Energy Union which are especially instructive and important for EU administrative law. The two centre-pieces of Union energy policies, and accordingly of this analysis are (1) the establishment of an internal energy market providing a secure supply of energy, and (2) the implications of EU environmental law for energy industries with a specific focus on their decarbonization in order to combat climate change. These two objectives will structure the following analysis.

B Administrative Tasks within the Energy Sector

1 Internal energy market law

As mentioned above the establishment of the internal energy market began with the application of general internal market provisions to energy industries. The electricity and gas markets especially are characterized by their dependency on transport networks qualifying as natural monopolies. In addition, electricity generation and its consumption must be balanced at all times in order to ensure the stability of the overall electrical system. Consequently, the liberalization of electricity markets and of natural gas markets needed a proactive legal framework of positive coordination, and could not rely simply on negative coordination through the application of the EU fundamental freedoms as with any other product market. For the sake of clarity, the following analysis will focus generally on the legal framework for electricity markets and networks in the text, natural gas markets being treated principally in the footnotes only.

---

[8] See Talus (n 1) 212 ff; Gundel (n 1) paras 86 ff.
[9] COM(2015) 80 final; see also the communication 'Clean Energy For All Europeans', COM(2016) 860 final, accompanying the so-called 'winter package' of 2016.

The regulatory framework considered here was set up successively through the three market liberalization packages of the 1990s and 2000s already mentioned. The administrative tasks emerging from these concern (1) the elimination of market entry barriers (such as those of formally protected monopolies),[10] (2) the unbundling of (liberalized) market components like production, trading, and supply, from enduring natural monopoly components, specifically grid operations,[11] (3) regulatory safeguards for the non-discriminatory third-party access to transport networks,[12] (4) regulation of sufficient and efficient network investments, especially with regard to cross-border interconnectors,[13] and (5) regulatory safeguards for energy security,[14] and against misuse of market power,[15] in the energy production and supply markets.

2 Energy Environmental Law

Energy generation and energy consumption have obvious impacts on the environment. These entail especially the problems of climate change, nuclear security, and consumption of scarce resources. With regard to climate change, decarbonization policies are a focus of EU environmental law, the key instrument being the Emissions Trading System (ETS). The ETS is itself complemented by a broad mix of additional instruments: national climate policy plans; mere EU targets for national policies concerning the promotion of renewables in energy markets; and command-and-control instruments in the field of energy efficiency.[16] In 2007, the European Council announced the 2020 strategy aimed at the reduction of greenhouse gas emission by 20%, achieving a share of 20% for renewables in energy consumption, and an increase in energy efficiency of 20% until 2020.[17] In 2014, the European Union published the

---

[10] Talus (n 1) 269 ff; Schneider, 'Europäisches Energierecht' (n 1) § 2 para 47.
[11] Johnston and Block (n 2) paras 3.01 ff; Talus (n 1) 77 ff; Vedder and others (n 3) paras 4.229 ff; Schneider, 'Europäisches Energierecht' (n 1) § 2 paras 48 ff.
[12] Johnston and Block (n 2) paras 4.01 ff; Talus (n 1) 70 ff; Vedder and others (n 3) paras 4.256 ff; Schneider, 'Europäisches Energierecht' (n 1) § 2 paras 58 ff.
[13] Johnston and Block (n 2) paras 6.01 ff; Talus (n 1) 96 f.; Vedder and others (n 3) paras 4.290 ff; Schneider, 'Europäisches Energierecht' (n 1) § 2 paras 63 ff; see also Regulation (EU) No 347/2013 of the European Parliament and of the Council on guidelines for trans-European energy infrastructure and repealing Decision No 1364/2006/EC and amending Regulations (EC) No 713/2009, (EC) No 714/2009 and (EC) No 715/2009, [2013] OJ L115/39a.
[14] Johnston and Block (n 2) paras 9.01 ff; Talus (n 1) 98 ff; Vedder and others (n 3) paras 4.481 ff; Schneider, 'Europäisches Energierecht' (n 1) § 2 para 68; see also Directive 2005/89/EC of the European Parliament and of the Council concerning measures to safeguard security of electricity supply and infrastructure investment [2005] OJ L33/22 (hereafter Directive 2005/89 (Energy Security)); see also the recent proposal for a Regulation on risk-preparedness in the electricity sector, COM(2016) 862 final.
[15] Johnston and Block (n 2) paras 7.01 ff; Vedder and others (n 3) paras 4.513 ff; Schneider, 'Europäisches Energierecht' (n 1) § 2 para 67; see also Regulation (EU) 1227/2011 of the European Parliament and of the Council on wholesale energy market integrity and transparency [2011] OJ L326/1; Directive 2008/92/EC of the European Parliament and of the Council concerning a Community procedure to improve the transparency of gas and electricity prices charged to industrial end-users (recast) [2008] OJ L298/9; one major objective of the recent 'winter package' reform proposals is to put consumers at the heart of the energy markets by reinforcing pre-existing rights and introducing of new rights: COM(2016) 864, p. 19.
[16] Talus (n 1) 175 ff; Vedder and others (n 3) paras 4.375 ff; Schneider 'Energieumweltrecht' (n 6) § 21 paras 27 ff, 33 ff, 176 ff; Gundel (n 1) paras Rn. 13.
[17] See Vedder and others (n 3) para 4.10 with fn 11.

following updated key targets of its future climate and energy policy for the period 2021–2030:[18]

 (i) reduce the EU's domestic greenhouse gas emissions internally by at least 40% by 2030 relative to 1990 levels ('GHG reduction target'; binding), to be achieved by GHG emissions reductions in

   (a) ETS sectors of at least 43% (base year 2005), and
   (b) non-ETS sectors of at least 30% (base year 2005);

 (ii) increase the proportion of renewable energy to at least 27% of overall EU energy consumption ('renewables target'; binding at EU level with flexibility on national level);

 (iii) reduce projected energy consumption for 2030 by at least 27% (indicative 'energy efficiency target');

 (iv) increase the level in each Member State of electricity interconnections to other Member States to at least 15% of their installed production capacity by 2030 ('electricity inter-connections target').

A matter of close attention are the interdependencies, on the one, hand between different environmental instruments like the ETS and other schemes supporting renewables and, on the other hand, between environmental instruments and the liberalization policies. For example, the integration into supply chains of a growing share of electricity produced with fluctuating renewable energy sources has implications for safeguarding short-term energy security, as well as for the demand for transmission investments. Support schemes for renewables (e.g., feed-in tariffs with a guaranteed access to networks with a primacy given to conventional electric power) may place limits on sharing a market coordinated by competition, and may even restrict transmission capacities for cross-border exchange of electricity.

C Sources of EU Energy Law

1 Internal energy market law

The EU has wide-ranging legislative competences with regard to the establishment of an internal energy market. These are conventionally located in Article 114 TFEU, which was the legal basis for the three liberalization packages. Since the Treaty of Lisbon, this horizontal competence has been complemented, or even derogated from, by the energy-specific competence clause enshrined in Article 194 TFEU.[19]

---

[18] European Council, Conclusions of the meeting of 23 and 24 October 2014, EUCO 169/14, pp. 1, 5, 6; see also the respective Commission's proposal COM(2014) 15 final; in order to implement these targets the Commission proposed obligations for national integrated energy and climate plans as well as rules on respective monitoring and implementation mechanisms: COM(2016) 759 final; this proposal for a Governance-Regulation shall replace and significantly extend Regulation (EU) No 525/2013 of the European Parliament and of the Council of 21 May 2013 on a mechanism for monitoring and reporting greenhouse gas emissions and for reporting other information at national and Union level relevant to climate change.

[19] See n 7.

Energy secondary law consists of several directives and regulations concerning electricity and natural gas markets. The regulations establish the EU Agency for the Cooperation of Energy Regulators (ACER)[20] and govern the conditions for access to the network for cross-border exchanges in electricity,[21] as well as laying down the conditions for access to the natural gas transmission networks,[22] and providing for transparency in wholesale energy markets.[23] These rules are substantially complemented by (regulated) industry self-regulation through ENTSO network codes (which requires ACER and Commission approval).[24] In contrast, other core issues of the liberalization of national energy markets are covered by directives[25] (and thus needing transposition into national law). Although the directives of the third liberalization package (2009) have tightened the Union framework in order to accelerate the liberalization process,[26] they still leave some leeway for the national legislators or administrations (for instance, by providing different options for the unbundling of transmission system operators, or by constituting only rather abstract and vague principles concerning network-access tariffs and similar regulatory issues). In addition, the directives provide for Commission competences to adopt guidelines on a wide range of matters. Thus, regulatory power has clearly shifted extensively to the Commission—or to ACER—although national regulatory authorities are still basically competent for the administrative implementation of Europeanized energy law through single-case decision-making (see sections E1(b); G below).

[20] Regulation (EC) No 713/2009 of the European Parliament and of the Council establishing an Agency for the Cooperation of Energy Regulators [2009] OJ 211/1; see also the Commission's reform proposal COM(2016) 863 final.

[21] Regulation (EC) No 714/2009 of the European Parliament and of the Council on conditions for access to the network for cross-border exchanges in electricity and repealing Regulation (EC) No 1228/2003 [2009] OJ L211/15; see also the Commission's reform proposal COM(2016) 861 final.

[22] Regulation (EC) No 715/2009 of the European Parliament and of the Council on conditions for access to the natural gas transmission networks and repealing Regulation (EC) No 1775/2005 [2009] OJ L211/36.

[23] Regulation 1227/2011 (REMIT) (n 15); Commission Implementing Regulation (EU) No 1348/2014 of 17 December 2014 on data reporting [2014] OJ L363/121.

[24] See section G2 below.

[25] Directive 2009/72/EC of the European Parliament and of the Council concerning common rules for the internal market in electricity and repealing Directive 2003/54/EC [2009] OJ L211/55; see also the Commission's reform proposal COM(2016) 864 final; Directive 2009/73/EC of the European Parliament and of the Council concerning common rules for the internal market in natural gas and repealing Directive 2003/55/EC [2009] OJ L211/94. See also Directive 2005/89 (Energy Security) (n 14); Directive 2008/92 (RECAST) (n 15); Directive 2004/17/EC of the European Parliament and of the Council co-ordinating the procurement procedures of entities operating in the water, energy, transport and postal services sectors [2004] OJ L134/1.

[26] Most noteworthy, Directive 2009/72 (Elec) (n 25) obliges the Member States to implement the model of a regulated third-party access to electricity grids. Consequently, Germany had to abandon its model of a negotiated network access; on this former German model: Schneider, 'Solving Conflicts and Securing Democratic Legitimation in the Energy Sector: A Legal Perspective on Associations' Agreements as a Conflict Solving Mechanism, in Christoph Engel and Adrienne Héritier (eds), *Linking Politics and Law* (Nomos 2003) 169 ff.

2 Energy Environmental Law

The European Union also has, under Article 192 TFEU, broad competences for legislative acts relating to the environmental impacts of energy production and consumption. However, Article 192(2) establishes an unanimity requirement for legislative acts significantly affecting the Member States' choices between competing energy sources and concerning general structure of their energy supply. All the same, as mentioned above, EU energy environmental law is characterized by a diverse instrumental mix and a complex set of legislative acts. Following an amendment of Directive 2003/87/EC in 2009, the emission rights (certificates) within the Emissions Trading System (ETS) are no longer allocated only by the Member States. Instead, the Commission regulates this allocation in the current third trading period (2013–2020) rather intensively through an implementing regulation. Thus, the national allocation plans of the Member States are pre-structured by a central framework.[27]

Apart from the reduction of adverse effects on the environment as such, the second main objective of EU energy environmental law is energy efficiency, a field regulated by a set of quite diverse directives,[28] sometimes with rather strict and detailed efficiency requirements. Nevertheless, the Member States still possess broad margins for own efficiency policies. At the moment, this is particularly the case with regard to support for renewable sources, being the third column of EU energy environmental law. Neither the Renewables Directive 2001,[29] nor its update (2009),[30] obliges Member States to establish a specific support scheme, or to abandon existing national support schemes. Rather, the directives provide only for national targets for increased energy supply from renewable sources.[31] As a result, such support schemes within Europe vary extensively, having a distinctly national focus. These schemes can conflict with the fundamental freedoms of the Union, especially free movement of goods, and with the prohibition of state aid in certain instances.[32] Recent judgements of the Union's courts demonstrate that the classification of scheme elements as state aid will be considered with due regard to the specifics of the scheme in question.[33] Nevertheless, even if a scheme is qualified as a restriction of free movement of goods or as state aid, the

---

[27] See section E2; see also the Commission's reform proposal for the 4th trading period (2021–2030): COM(2015) 337 final.

[28] Johnston and Block (n 2) paras 17.01 ff; Talus (n 1) 189 f.; Vedder and others (n 3) paras 4.418 ff; Gundel (n 1) paras 83 f.; see also the Commission's reform proposals COM(2016) 761 final; COM(2016) 765 final; COM(2016) 773 final.

[29] Directive 2001/77/EC of the European Parliament and of the Council on the promotion of electricity produced from renewable energy sources in the internal electricity market [2001] OJ L283/33.

[30] Directive 2009/28/EC of the European Parliament and of the Council on the promotion of the use of energy from renewable sources and amending and subsequently repealing Directives 2001/77/EC and 2003/30/EC [2009] OJ L140/16; this approach would be relinquished by the Commission's reform proposal COM(2016) 767 final.

[31] See art 3 Directive 2009/28/EC (Renewables) (n 30). See generally on this topic: Johnston and Block (n 2) paras 12.01 ff; Talus (n 1) 190 ff; Vedder and others (n 3) paras 4.375 ff.

[32] For details: Talus (n 1) 137 ff; Vedder and others (n 3) paras 4.55 ff, 4.169 ff; Schneider 'Energieumweltrecht' (n 6) § 21 paras 138 ff.

[33] Case C-262/12 *Vent de Colère and Others* [2013] ECLI:EU:C:2013:851; Case T-251/11 *Österreich v Kommission* [2014] ECLI:EU:T:2014:1060.

courts may still accept it as being a justified environmental instrument, at least in the current state of the internal energy market.[34] It is also noteworthy, that in 2014 the Commission adopted informal guidelines on state aid for environmental protection and energy (for the period 2014–2020),[35] obliging Member States inter alia to establish procurement procedures for new energy generation capacity from renewable sources. It is obvious that the complex interdependencies between market liberalization and the increasing market shares of renewables need a more structured legislative approach than the recent, mainly negative coordination involving the application of horizontal provisions. The Commission recently adopted proposals for such an integrated approach with the 4th legislative energy package.

D Underlying Legal Principles of EU Energy Law

Union law on the internal energy market relies on certain traditional principles of the internal market generally, e.g., non-discrimination with regard to network access. This principle informs energy-specific instruments and measures, such as unbundling of network operators or regulated third-party access to networks. There are, too, more specific principles, such as that of independent regulatory supervision or of energy security, to be analysed in more detail in other parts of this chapter (see section E1 below). Similarly, energy environmental law relies on the general principles of Union environmental law, above all the requirement of integrating environmental protection into all Union policy making, including the concept of environmental sustainability (Article 11 TFEU), as well as other elements such as the polluter-pays principle, or the cautionary principle.

E Organizational and Institutional Structures of EU Energy Law

1 Internal energy market law

As typical for other fields, 'indirect' implementation through national regulatory authorities is dominant in the energy sector. Nevertheless, the growing role of the Commission, of informal and formal administrative networks, and of 'regulated' industry self-regulation must be highlighted. This increasing Europeanization of energy governance structures has been complemented by the establishment of a sector-specific EU agency (ACER).

(a) Implementation of EU energy law by national regulatory authorities

Union energy law is mainly implemented by national regulatory authorities. The second and third liberalization packages retained this general structure, but significantly

---

[34] Case C-379/98 *PreussenElektra* [2001] ECLI:EU:C:2001:160; see also Case C-573/12 *Ålands Vindkraft* [2014] ECLI:EU:C:2014:2037.
[35] [2014] OJ C200/1.

intensified European intervention into national organizational autonomy.[36] Thus, all Member States are to designate a *single* national regulatory authority at national level, although federal Member States may derogate from such a centralization of administrative competence to some extent, passing responsibility to constituent federal units (states, regions).[37] Member States are also free to bundle regulatory competences concerning different industries like energy, telecommunications, railroads, and postal services within one agency, in order to reduce the potential for regulatory capture, and to enhance the possibility of institutional learning.

The directives require that the national regulatory authorities be assigned, inter alia a set of market surveillance or monitoring duties and powers, and that they be set certain objectives.[38] Most notably, the 2009 package obliges the Member States to guarantee the independence of their regulatory authorities from any market interest. In addition to this standard feature, they shall also be legally distinct and functionally independent of any other public entity and not seek—or take—direct instructions from any government in carrying out regulatory tasks.[39] However, this requirement is to be imposed without prejudice to possible close cooperation with other relevant national authorities, or to adherence to general policy guidelines not related to the regulatory powers and duties.[40] Recent discussion has raised the questions of whether this 'political' independence is unlawfully compromised by the German model under which certain third-party access, required and pre-structured by detailed statutory instruments, may significantly reduce the discretion of the regulatory authority.[41] Another (contentious) matter of discussion, with regard to political independence, concerns accountability safeguards of independent agencies required to ensure a sufficient level of democratic legitimation.[42]

(b) Europeanized governance structures within the energy sector

A central feature of the Third Energy Market Package, as well as of later legislative acts, such as the TEN-E Regulation, is the more detailed framework for an enhanced European regulatory network.[43] A first element of this is the requirement that national regulatory authorities closely consult, cooperate with, and provide each other (and

---

[36] Johnston and Block (n 2) paras 5.01 ff; Vedder and others (n 3) paras 4.293 ff; Gundel (n 1) paras 35, 39 ff, 52; Schneider, 'Europäisches Energierecht' (n 1) § 2 para 70.

[37] See Art 35(1), (2) Directive 2009/72 (Elec) (n 25); Art 39(1), (2) Directive 2009/73 (Gas) (n 25).

[38] See Art 37(1) Directive 2009/72 (Elec) (n 25); Art 41(1) Directive 2009/73 (Gas) (n 25).

[39] See Art 35(4), (5) Directive 2009/72 (Elec) (n 25); Art 39(4), (5) Directive 2009/73 (Gas) (n 25).

[40] See Art 35(4) Directive 2009/72 (Elec) (n 25); Art 39(4) Directive 2009/73 (Gas) (n 25).

[41] European Commission, 'The April Infringements' Package: Key Decisions' (28 April 2016) 2 Energy http://europa.eu/rapid/press-release_MEMO-16-1452_en.htm (last accessed 14 July 2016); Case C-424/07 *Kommission v Deutschland* [2009] ECLI:EU:C:2009:749.

[42] See Jörg Gundel and Claas Friedrich Germelmann, 'Kein Schlussstein für die Liberalisierung der Energiemärkte: Das Dritte Binnenmarktpaket' (2009) *Europäische Zeitschrift für Wirtschaftsrecht* 763, 768; Schneider, 'A Common Framework for Decentralised EU Agencies and the Meroni Doctrine' (2009) 61 *Administrative Law Review* 29.

[43] Vedder and others (n 3) paras 4.317 ff; Gundel (n 1) paras 41–43, 55 ff; Janine Haller, *Der Verwaltungsverbund in der Energieregulierung* (Nomos 2013204 ff.

ACER) with any information necessary for the fulfilment of their regulatory tasks,[44] especially with regard to cross-border exchange of energy.[45] This cooperation is institutionalized and supported by the establishment of the Council of European Energy Regulators (CEER), a private non-profit association.[46] An even more advanced form of administrative network is established with ACER (see below), the successor of the European Regulators' Group for Electricity and Gas (ERGEG), established in 2003 in order to advise the European Commission on internal energy-market issues in Europe.[47]

(i) Increased importance of Commission guidelines

The most important new element in the administration of this sector comprises the significantly expanded regulatory powers of the Commission, additional to its already existing powers under general competition law.[48] It is now able to influence the regulatory performance and practices of national authorities through guidelines. These, adopted in a comitology process, can concern a wide range of regulatory issues. They are attributed legally binding force by the relevant regulations and directives, as the Commission may set aside national regulatory decisions not complying with them.[49] For example, such guidelines may relate to the inter-transmission system-operator compensation mechanism, (concerning the operational coordination between Union-wide transmission system operators (TSOs), with rules on the progressive harmonization of the principles for setting charges applying to producers and consumers (load) under national tariff systems, as well as on investment incentives for interconnector capacity). Moreover, the Commission has to approve national TSO certifications,[50] as well as national decisions on third-party access obligation exemptions for new cross-border infrastructures.

(ii) The Agency for the Cooperation of Energy Regulators (ACER)

As already mentioned, the Third Energy Market Package established ACER. Its tasks are defined especially by Regulation 713/2009 (ACER).[51] Its overall mission is to complement and coordinate the work of national energy regulators on Union

---

[44] See Art 37(1)(c), (e), 38 Directive 2009/72 (Elec) (n 25); Art 41(1)(c), (e), 42 Directive 2009/73 (Gas) (n 25); Art 19 Sentence 2 Regulation 714/2009 (Elec) (n 21); Art 24(2) Regulation 715/2009 (Gas) (n 22); Haller (n 43) 51 ff.

[45] See Art 38 Directive 2009/72 (Elec) (n 25); Art 42 Directive 2009/73 (Gas) (n 25); Art 17(4) Regulation 714/2009 (Elec) (n 21); Art 36(3) Regulation 715/2009 (Gas) (n 22); Haller (n 43) 216 ff. These obligations are emphasized in the recent 'winter package' and are complemented with new supervisory tasks with respect to the newly created Regional Operational Centres: see Chap VII of the Electricity Directive, COM(2016) 864.

[46] Johnston and Block (n 2) para 5.30; Haller (n 43) 157 ff.

[47] Commission Decision 2003/796/EC on establishing the European Regulators Group for Electricity and Gas [2003] OJ L296/34.

[48] Talus (n 1) 110 ff; Vedder and others (n 3) paras 4.90 ff; Gundel (n 1) para 33.

[49] See section G1 below.   [50] See section F1(a).

[51] See n 20; see also Arts 6, 9, and 17(5) Regulation 714/2009 (Elec) (n 21); Arts 6, 9 Regulation 715/2009 (Gas)) (n 22) with Art 36(4) Directive 2009/73 (Gas) (n 25); Art 6(2), (4), 22(5), 39(1)–(3) Directive 2009/72 (Elec) (n 25); Art 6(2), (4), 22(5), 43(1)–(3) Directive 2009/73 (Gas) (n 25); Johnston and Block (n 2) paras 5.57 ff; Vedder and others (n 3) paras 4.41 ff; Gundel (n 1) paras 55, 60; Haller (n 43) 95 ff; Schneider, 'Europäisches Energierecht' (n 1) § 2 para 74.

level, and to work towards the completion of the single EU energy market for electricity and natural gas. ACER coordinates regional and cross-regional initiatives
which favour market integration. It monitors the work of European networks of
transmission system operators (ENTSOs) and notably their EU-wide network development plans. In 2011, ACER received additional tasks under Regulation (EU)
No 1227/2011 on wholesale energy market integrity and transparency (REMIT)[52]
and in 2013 under Regulation 347/2013 (TEN-E) on guidelines for trans-European
energy infrastructures.[53]

ACER is composed of a permanent staff together with experts seconded by national
regulatory authorities for energy. Most of its regulatory activities are overseen by a board
of regulators, composed of senior representatives of the national regulatory authorities
for energy from the 28 Member States. The Board generally decides by a qualified majority of two-thirds, each national regulator having one vote irrespective of country size.
This important role of national representatives on the Board is a distinctive feature of
ACER—as of the more recently established European supervisory authorities in the finance sector—diverging from traditional EU agency structures.[54] Thus, ACER can be
characterized as a highly advanced example of the European composite administration. A more traditional component of ACER's organization is its Administrative Board,
whose members are appointed by European institutions and which supervises ACER's
administrative and budgetary activities.[55]

ACER can issue non-binding opinions and recommendations to national energy
regulators, transmission system operators, and the EU institutions.[56] Upon request
from the European Commission, ACER submits draft framework guidelines which
serve as the basis for the drafting of network codes.[57] It is especially noteworthy that
ACER is one of few Union agencies which can take binding individual decisions in
specific cases,[58] inter alia on cross-border infrastructure issues.[59] Complaints lodged
against such binding ACER decisions are not dealt with by the Commission (contrary to the case of certain other EU agencies), but by the ACER Board of Appeal,

---

[52] See especially Arts 7 ff and 16.   [53] See section F1(d)(iv) below.

[54] The board of regulators represents a major deviation from the 'Joint Statement of the European
Parliament, the Council of the EU and the European Commission on decentralised agencies of
19.7.2012' and this deviation shall be preserved during the recent reform Regulation 713/2009 (ACER)
(n 20): COM(2016) 863, at 22–23. An innovative feature of the 'winter package' is a regional decision-
making procedure by regional sub-committee of the board of regulators.

[55] Nevertheless, the composition of ACER's Administrative Board deviates from the model
Management Board as established in the 'Joint Statement of the European Parliament, the Council of the
EU and the European Commission on decentralised agencies of 19.7.2012'. This deviation shall be pre-
served during the recent reform of Regulation 713/2009 (ACER) (n 20): COM(2016) 863, at 23.

[56] See Art 6(7), (9), 7(2), 8(2), (11), 9, 17(4) Regulation 714/2009 (Elec) (n 21); Arts 6(7), (9), 7(2), 8(2),
and 9 Regulation 715/2009 (Gas) (n 22); Art 36(4) Directive 2009/73 (Gas) (n 25); see also Art 6(2), 22(5),
39(1)–(3) Directive 2009/72 (Elec) (n 25); Art 6(2), 22(5), 43(1)–(3) Directive 2009/73 (Gas) (n 25).

[57] See Art 6(2)–(4) Regulation 714/2009 (Elec) (n 21); Art 6(2)–(4) Regulation 715/2009 (Gas) (n 22).

[58] From a general perspective: Herwig CH Hofmann/Gerard C Rowe and Alexander H Türk,
Administrative Law and Policy of the EU (OUP 2011) 285 ff; Schneider 'EU Agencies and the Meroni
Doctrine' (n 42) 29.

[59] See Art 8(1) Regulation 713/2009 (ACER) (n 20); Art 17 Regulation 714/2009 (Elec) (n 21); Art 36
Directive 2009/73 (Gas) (n 25); these powers shall be extended by the reform of Regulation 713/2009
(ACER) (n 20): COM(2016) 864 final, at 22.

strictly a part of the Agency but independent from its administrative and regulatory structures.[60]

(iii) Industry self-regulation and the European Network of Transmission System Operators (ENTSO)

Another feature of the recent energy regulatory framework and governance structure under the Third Energy Market Package is the co-regulation framework of regulated industry self-regulation. Co-regulation is a general Commission strategy for better regulation in the EU.[61] Under the 2nd Energy Market Package the Commission initiated fora with representatives from either the electricity industry (Florence Forum) or the natural gas industry (Madrid Forum).[62] With the Third Energy Market Package these institutions have been further developed and integrated into a quite formal co-regulation framework.

The relevant regulations provide for the establishment of two European Networks of Transmission System Operators (ENTSOs) responsible for either the natural gas and the electricity transmission infrastructures (ENTSO-G, ENTSO-E) respectively. ENTSO-E represents 42 electricity TSOs from 35 countries—obviously, then, including a non-EU members—across Europe. It is governed by an Assembly representing the TSOs and by a Board consisting of 12 elected members.[63] ENTSO is concerned with the preparation and formulation of network codes, infrastructure planning, and adequacy forecasts as well as ten-year network development plans. Network codes regulate not merely technical issues but also sensitive matters such as requirements for network stability, and harmonized structures for transmission fees.[64] Thus, it is appropriate that regulators do not simply trust in self-regulation. Instead, the legislator introduced a framework of co-regulation or 'regulated self-regulation'.[65] This applies also to ENTSO's transmission expansion plans cited above.[66] Provisions on regional cooperation between TSOs and their respective national regulatory authorities, in order to establish the internal energy market in a kind of bottom-up process, are also worth noting here.[67]

2 Energy Environmental Law

The most important organizational arrangement in the Union's energy environmental law is the EU Emissions Trading System (ETS).[68] The ETS works on the 'cap

---

[60] See Arts 18–20 Regulation 713/2009 (ACER) (n 20); see also Case T-411/06 *Sogelma v EAR* [2008] ECLI:EU:T:2008:419, paras 36 ff.

[61] European Commission, *'European Governance: A White Paper'*, COM(2001) 428 final.

[62] Johnston and Block (n 2) paras 5.50 ff; Vedder and others (n 3) paras 4.37 ff; Haller (n 43) 152 ff; Gundel (n 1) paras 59 ff.

[63] Vedder and others (n 3) para 4.44; for more details on ENTSO-E's governance structure see the chart at https://www.entsoe.eu/about-entso-e/inside-entso-e/entso-e-structure/structure/Pages/default.aspx; the recent 'winter package' shall introduce a new European entity for distribution system operators: COM(2016) 861, at 20.

[64] See Art 8(6)(k) Regulation 714/2009 (Elec) (n 21); Art 8(6)(k) Regulation 715/2009 (Gas) (n 22).

[65] For details see section G2 below.   [66] For details see section F1(d)(iii) below.

[67] See Art 12 Regulation 714/2009 (Elec) (n 21); Art 12 Regulation 715/2009 (Gas) (n 22); Art 38(2)–(4) Directive 2009/72 (Elec) (n 25); Art 42(2)–(4) Directive 2009/73 (Gas) (n 25).

[68] For details Talus (n 1) 196 ff; Vedder and others (n 3) paras 4.434 ff; the ETS is complemented by an effort sharing decision establishing binding annual greenhouse gas emission targets for

and trade' principle, the overall volume of greenhouse gases to be emitted each year by the power plants, factories and certain other industries, being subject to a cap. During the first and second trading periods (2005–2007, 2008–2012) the Member States had set national emission caps, requiring approval by the Commission. Under the amended rules for the third trading period (2013–2020) a decreasing cap is set on EU level.[69] On the second stage of the system, the Member States allocate allowances to businesses in the sectors within the ETS, and track and validate the actual emissions. During the first two trading periods allowances were allocated free-of-charge, based on historical emissions ('grandfathering'). Since 2013, auctioning has become the main method of allocation.[70]

The operators within the ETS may reassign or trade their allowances by several means:[71]

- privately, transferring allowances between operators within a company and across national borders
- over the counter, using a broker to match buyers and sellers privately
- trading on the spot market of one of Europe's climate exchanges.

Each transfer of an allowance has to be registered. During the first and second trading periods national registries were used, the European Commission being notified in order to validate the transaction. Since 2013 a single registry on EU level has been installed for the third trading period (2013–2020),[72] representing a significant centralization of the ETS.[73]

Member States for the period 2013–2020 concerning emissions from most sectors not included in the ETS: Decision 406/2009/EC; see also the Commission's proposal for the period of 2021–2030: COM(2016) 482 final; other institutional arrangements concern the European Environmental Agency (see Regulation (EC) No 401/2009 of the European Parliament and of the Council on the European Environment Agency and the European Environment Information and Observation Network [2009] OJ L126/13).

[69] See Art 9 Directive 2003/87/EC of the European Parliament and the Council establishing a scheme for greenhouse gas emission allowance trading within the Community and amending Council Directive 96/61/EC [2003] OJ L275/32; see also Gundel (n 1) para 77.

[70] See Arts 10 ff Directive 2003/87 (ETS) (n 69); see also Decision 2015/1814 concerning the establishment and operation of a market stability reserve for the Union greenhouse gas emission trading scheme.

[71] See Art 12 Directive 2003/87 (ETS) (n 69).

[72] See Arts 19 and 20 20 Directive 2003/87 (ETS) (n 69).

[73] Gundel (n 1) para 76. For the 4th trading period (2021–2030), the Commission proposes an even stricter centralization by extended competencies for delegated rulemaking: Moritz Hartmann, 'Emissionshandel in der vierten Zuteilungsperiode (2021–2030)' *NVwZ* (2016) 189; for details see COM(2015) 337 final, the European Parliament adopted on 15 February 2017 a number of amendments to this proposal, P8_TA-PROV(2017)0035; in addition, the Commission proposed a Regulation on the Governance of the Energy Union with a mix of pre-structured national integrated energy and climate plans and of decentral as well as central monitoring and implementation mechanisms: COM(2016) 759 final.

F Administrative Procedures and their Substantive Framework within the Energy Sector

European energy law provides a wide range of interesting examples of complex, often composite procedural arrangements. These procedures follow a common structure only in some cases. They are in fact quite diverse, offering very different allocations of competences to both public and private bodies, whether on national or European level. Hence, the legislator has established rather task-specific procedural frameworks to implement the various substantive objectives of Union energy law. This close interdependency of substantive and procedural law justifies the combination of these two dimensions of administrative law in the present discussion.

1 Internal energy-market law

Internal energy-market law provides a large range of varied procedures, of which some particularly relevant examples are offered here.

(a) Certification of Transmission System Operators

The Transmission System Operators (TSOs) serve a very important function in liberalized energy markets, controlling the central monopolized infrastructure needed by other competing market actors. As mentioned above, the Third Energy Package introduced a tougher unbundling regime, in order to neutralize the market position of the formerly vertically integrated TSOs. In order to ensure that such unbundling requirements are complied with, each TSO needs to be certified by the respective national regulatory authority, which also monitors continuing compliance. The Commission is empowered to interfere in national procedures to a limited extent.[74] It can request national authorities to open a certification procedure to ensure continuing compliance and require information from TSOs, as can the competent national regulatory authority. Additionally, the national authorities have to notify certification decisions to the Commission, upon which it delivers an opinion. Within two months of that, the national authority is to adopt its final decision, taking utmost account of the Commission's view, which is not considered legally binding and thus not an act reviewable in the Union's courts.[75]

---

[74] See Art 3 Regulation 714/2009 (Elec) (n 21); Art 10 Directive 2009/72 (Elec) (n 25); Art 10 Directive 2009/73 (Gas) (n 25); Johnston and Block (n 2) paras 3.99 ff; Vedder and others (n 3) paras 4.241 ff; Gundel (n 1) paras 49, 53, and 57.

[75] Gundel (n 1) para 57 f. referring to the jurisprudence concerning a similar provision in telecommunication law: Case T-109/06 *Vodafone España und Vodafone Group v Kommission* [2007] ECLI:EU:T:2007:384, paras 69 ff.

(b) Regulation of charges for access to energy networks

Generally, the national regulatory authorities are responsible for regulating transmission charges and the methods for their calculation.[76] However, the regulations on cross-border access to electricity or natural gas networks provide powers to the Commission to adopt binding guidelines via the examination procedure of the Comitology Regulation 182/2011.[77] Such guidelines relate to inter-transmission system operator compensation mechanisms for (unintended) cross-border energy flows, as well as to charges for access to networks.[78] The Commission must consult ACER and ENTSO before presenting a draft of such guidelines to the relevant comitology committee.[79] The regulations and Commission's guidelines do not govern network access charges comprehensively, but rather set a framework of rules and principles of strategic importance for access policies.[80] Prices charged by network operators are to be transparent, must take into account the need for network security, and have to reflect actual costs incurred insofar as they correspond to those of an efficient and structurally comparable network operator, applied in a non-discriminatory manner. Such charges may not be distance-related, but may provide locational signals on the Union level. Additionally, they should take into account network losses and congestion, as well as infrastructural investment costs. Some special rules apply to the economic regulation of cross-border infrastructures according to Regulation 347/2013 (TEN-E).[81] The guidelines are implemented by the national authorities but, under to the Internal Energy Market Directives, ACER and the Commission have supervisory powers.[82]

(c) Congestion management and cross-border market coupling

The framework for cross-border congestion management and cross-border market coupling follows a similar pattern, with basic principles laid down in secondary law,[83] more detailed rules in binding Commission guidelines,[84] and cooperative

---

[76] See Art 37(1)(a), (6)(a), (7), (8) Directive 2009/72 (Elec) (n 25); see also Johnston and Block (n 2) paras 4.01 ff; Vedder and others (n 3) paras 4.256 ff.

[77] For details about this special instrument of administrative rulemaking see section G1 below.

[78] See Arts 13, 14, and 18 Regulation 714/2009 (Elec) (n 21); Arts 13, 23 Regulation 715/2009 (Gas) (n 22).

[79] See Art 18(3) Sentence 2 Regulation 714/2009 (Elec) (n 21); Art 23(3) Sentence 2 Regulation 715/2009 (Gas) (n 22).

[80] Vedder and others (n 3) paras 4.260 ff; Schneider, 'Europäisches Energierecht' (n 1) § 2 paras 61 ff; Kai Uwe Pritzsche and Anke Reimers, 'Die Stromhandelsverordnung (EG) Nr 714/2009' ch 17 paras 29 ff, and Weiß, 'Der Europäische Regulierungsverbund im Energierecht' ch 32 para 22, in Baur and others (eds), *Regulierung in der Energiewirtschaft* (2nd edn, Carl Heymanns 2016).

[81] See section F1(d)(iv) below.

[82] See section J2 below. See also Commission Regulation (EU) 838/2010 on laying down guidelines relating to the inter-transmission system operator compensation mechanism and a common regulatory approach to transmission charging [2010] OJ L250/5, requiring under 3. the approval by the Commission based on an opinion by ACER of so-called multi-party agreements between EU-ETS and TSOs from third countries prepared by ENTSO-E.

[83] See Arts 15, 16 Regulation 714/2009 (Elec) (n 21); Art 16 Regulation 715/2009 (Gas) (n 22).

[84] Commission Regulation (EU) 2015/1222 of 24 July 2015 establishing a guideline on capacity allocation and congestion management [2015] OJ L197/24, based on Art 18(4), (5) sentence 2 Regulation 714/2009 (Elec) (n 21); Vedder and others (n 3) para 4.284.

implementation by the competent national regulatory authorities[85] under the effective supervision of ACER and the Commission, in order to ensure compliance with the guidelines.[86]

(d) Planning, authorizing, and regulating cross-border infrastructure

(i) National procedures for sector-specific spatial planning, environmental permits, and economic cost regulation

A much more complex structure, with various composite procedures, is established with regard to the planning, authorization, and regulation of network infrastructures. This concerns infrastructure needed either directly for the cross-border exchange of energy (such as inter-connectors), or that which is indirectly relevant for the functioning of the internal energy market by avoiding congestions within a national grid (with potential to cause external effects to other Member States).[87] Planning and authorization procedures for such infrastructure projects have to coordinate the economic needs of complex energy networks with other societal interests (e.g., environmental impacts), or with other non-energy related projects in a particular region. In addition, network investments need to be regulated, in order to guarantee economic efficiency of such monopolized essential facilities. Planning procedures in Member States such as Germany may, though, have a different scope. Some procedures– like those under the Union's TEN-E guidelines—focus on sector-specific objectives, particularly on the provision of sufficient transmission capacities as a specific dimension of energy security. Safeguarding adequate transmission capacity is a complex task in itself, made more so, however, under the dynamic and multipolar interests emerging in liberalized and environmentally transformed energy markets, especially those subject to requirements for unbundling.

Sector-specific planning procedures—in other words, planning related directly to energy supply and infrastructure—must be coordinated with other, more general, spatial planning procedures, which have much broader scope and regulate more comprehensively a wide range of societal interests related to land use. Strictly, spatial planning procedures fall completely within national competence, but have nevertheless to be in accordance with EU environmental law (e.g., requirements of the Habitats Directive[88] or the Environmental Impact Assessment Directive),[89] while also being

---

[85] See Art 37(6)(c); (9) and Art 38(2)(a), (c) Directive 2009/72 (Elec) (n 25); Art 41(6)(c); (9) and Art 42(2) (a), (c) Directive 2009/73 (Gas) (n 25).

[86] See section J2 below; see also Pritzsche and Reimers (n 80) ch 17, paras 15 ff. Strobel, 'Der Ausbau grenzüberschreitender Verbindungsleitungen im Elektrizitätsbereich' (2016) *Deutsches Verwaltungsblatt* 543, 544 ff, 546 ff; König, *Engpassmanagement in der deutschen und europäischen Elektrizitätsversorgung* (Nomos 2013).

[87] On the following see Droste-Franke and others, *Balancing Renewable Electricity* (Springer 2012) 196 ff; Vedder and others (n 3) paras 4.317 ff; see also Strobel (n 86) 545 ff; Weiß (n 80) ch 32 paras 39 ff; Haller (n 43) 216 ff.

[88] Council Directive 92/43/EEC on the conservation of natural habitats and of wild fauna and flora [1992] OJ L206/7.

[89] Directive 2011/92/EU of the European Parliament and the Council on the assessment of the effects of certain public and private projects on the environment [2011] OJ L26/1.

influenced by other areas of Union policy (e.g., transport, regional policy, as well as energy policy). These sector-specific or spatial planning procedures have a regulatory effect on energy networks only on a rather high or abstract level, leaving considerable range for the detailed localization of transmission lines, pipelines, etc. Project authorizations in the last stage of this composite procedural framework do embody detailed regulation for energy networks in specified locations. In contrast to such planning and authorising procedures, procedures concerning network access charges focus on the economic efficiency of such projects with the aim of minimising the financial burdens for network users.

The multi-faceted interdependencies between sector-specific planning, spatial planning, environmental authorization procedures, and cost regulation are obvious and intensive. It is also obvious that cross-border project planning must be coordinated between the neighbouring Member States concerned, in order to avoid incoherent results of what might be otherwise disconnected planning procedures relating to the national components of cross-border inter-connection.

(ii) TEN-E guidelines for certain projects of common interest

Articles 170–172 TFEU provide a framework for Trans-European Networks,[90] but do not provide comprehensive legislative competences. Important planning and licensing competences remain on the Member State level. Article 171 TFEU authorizes the EU only:

- to establish guidelines which may especially identify projects of common interest
- to implement any measures that may prove necessary to ensure the interoperability of the networks, in particular in the field of technical standardization or
- to support mainly financial projects of common interest supported by Member States.

The most recent TEN-E-guidelines identify a number of projects of common interest. To this end, Article 3 of Regulation 347/2013 (TEN-E) establishes a bottom-up process, with twelve regional groups composed of representatives of the respective Member States, national regulatory authorities, TSOs, as well as of the Commission, ACER, and ENTSO-E. Decision-making powers in the groups are restricted to the Member States and the Commission which are to adopt a regional list of proposed projects of common interest. It is for the Commission to establish a Union list, on the basis of the regional lists, embodied in a delegated act. Most projects of common interest in the most recent Union list are interconnectors between national electrical networks, projects which have proved to be a major obstacle to the integration of European national electricity markets. In addition, TEN-E guidelines identify network expansions within Member States that are needed for trans-European transits or the cross-border exchange of electricity.

Article 7 of Regulation 347/2013 (TEN-E) provides for granting priority status to projects of common interest in a national authorization processes, by establishing

---

[90] Johnston and Block (n 2) paras 6.01 ff; Vedder and others (n 3) paras 4.317 ff.

their necessity from an energy policy perspective, without prejudice to their exact location, routing, or technology employed. Under Article 8 a Member State should designate one national competent authority—or, under certain conditions, additional authorities—to be responsible for facilitating and coordinating the authorization process for projects of common interest. An important instrument for such coordination is the so-called 'comprehensive decision'. This new approach—a 'one-stop-shop' together with the comprehensive decision—may be helpful in order to speed up processes. However, it does conflict with the complex procedural and organizational structure of traditional planning law, even that partly required by EU environmental law itself (for example, environmental impact assessment). Therefore, this approach is restricted to the coordination of several actors, but will not substitute for the exercise of decision-making powers by national authorities.

Furthermore, Article 6 of Regulation 347/2013 (TEN-E) authorizes the Commission to designate, in agreement with the Member States concerned, a European coordinator for projects of common interest that (may) encounter significant delays or difficulties in implementation. The European coordinator lacks formal legal powers, but may assist the competent national authorities by reinforcing the European dimension of the project and enhancing cross-border dialogue between the project promoters and persons affected. This official may also contribute by the coordination of national procedures for consulting affected persons. However, this role is to be seen not only as providing assistance to the Member States concerned, but also as a means of facilitating Commission 'oversight' of Member States with regard to network expansion. Therefore, the European coordinator submits an annual report to the Commission on the progress of the project(s) for which they been designated, and on any difficulties and obstacles likely to result from—or in—significant delay. Moreover, the Commission may request the coordinator's opinion when considering applications for Union funding of projects to which they have been appointed.

Another relevant instrument is supplementary funding under the TEN-E programme for projects of European interest.[91] However, EU funds are, of course, limited, compared with the financial resources needed for such undertakings. Nevertheless, the updated TEN-E project list serves at least as an influential means of steering national decision-makers by informing them of European priorities.

(iii) Regional and Union-wide planning responsibilities of TSOs and Union monitoring

Union energy law establishes—or at least assumes—some overall responsibility of transmission system operators (TSOs).[92] Under the Third Energy Package, this responsibility is highlighted in new planning instruments with regional or even EU-wide scope.[93] These measures are implemented by the respective ENTSO, complementing corporate investment plans on the national level.[94] All TSOs are to cooperate on Union

---

[91] See Art 14 ff Regulation 347/2013 (TEN-E) (n 13).
[92] See Art 12 Directive 2009/72 (Elec) (n 25); Art 13 Directive 2009/73 (Gas) (n 25).
[93] See Art 8(10), 12 Regulation 714/2009 (Elec) (n 21); Art 8(10), 12 Regulation 715/2009 (Gas) (n 22).
[94] For further details: Droste-Franke and others (n 87) 203 ff; Vedder and others (n 3) paras 4.243 ff; Gundel (n 1) paras 54, 62; Strobel (n 86) 545 ff.

level through the respective ENTSO, in order to promote inter alia the sound technical evolution of the European electricity transmission network.[95] The measures of ENTSO-E should include a non-binding Union-wide ten-year network development plan, including a two-yearly outlook on European generation adequacy,[96] covering the overall adequacy of the electricity system to supply current and projected demand for the subsequent five-year period and for a period five to fifteen years from the date of that outlook. The European outlook is to build on comparable national prospects prepared by each TSO.

The ten-year Union-wide development plan shall, in particular:

- build on national investment plans, taking into account regional investment plans, and, if appropriate, Union-relevant aspects of network planning, including guidelines for trans-European energy networks
- build on the reasonable needs of different system users regarding cross-border interconnections, integrating long-term commitments from investors and
- identify investment gaps, notably with respect to cross-border capacities.

While preparing the draft plan, the relevant ENTSO must undertake extensive consultations at an early stage, in an open and transparent manner, involving all relevant market participants, and, in particular, all stakeholder organizations.[97] Such consultation aims to identify the views and proposals of all relevant parties during the decision-making process. The pertinent regulations also establish a monitoring procedure for such planning by setting up the Agency for the Cooperation of Energy Regulators (ACER).[98] Therefore, ENTSO shall submit its draft plan, including information regarding the consultation process, for the opinion of ACER. This, duly reasoned, is to be provided within two months, together with recommendations to ENTSO-E, as well as recommendations to the Commission where ACER considers that the draft plan does not avoid discrimination, or enhance effective competition, market efficiency or sufficient cross-border interconnection open to third-party access.

In line with a general approach of fostering liberalization through regional co-operation, the regulations also provide that TSOs establish regional cooperation within ENTSO.[99] In particular, they are to publish a two-yearly regional investment plan, and may take investment decisions based on it. This last provision illustrates the general characteristic of EU investment regulation: highlighting self-regulation and cooperation in combination with complex arrangements for inter-organizational and multi-level consultation and consolidation. In doing so, EU energy law acknowledges (1) that network expansions can hardly be ordered by public authorities without relying on the knowledge of market participants, and (2) that the EU itself has only limited competence and resources in relation to the regulation of network expansion.

---

[95] See Art 4 Regulation 714/2009 (Elec) (n 21); Art 4 Regulation 715/2009 (Gas) (n 22).
[96] See Art 8(10) Regulation 714/2009 (Elec) (n 21); Art 8(10) Regulation 715/2009 (Gas) (n 22).
[97] See Art 10 Regulation 714/2009 (Elec) (n 21); Art 10 Regulation 715/2009 (Gas) (n 22).
[98] See Art 9 Regulation 714/2009 (Elec) (n 21); Art 9 Regulation 715/2009 (Gas) (n 22).
[99] See Art 12 Regulation 714/2009 (Elec) (n 21); Art 12 Regulation 715/2009 (Gas) (n 22).

(iv) The Union framework for the regulation of cross-border investments

In principle, national competences for the regulation of network charges also apply to cross-border facilities on the respective national territory. As already noted, general principles of network access tariffs regulation are set out in the Third Energy Package and the respective Commission guidelines.[100] In addition, Article 12 of Regulation 347/2013 (TEN-E) provides, in relation to projects of common interest, certain efficiency standards and, more especially, rules on the allocation of costs between the two affected TSOs proportionate to the net positive impact, and not simply according to the cost of facilities on their respective territory.[101] The need for coordinated regulatory decisions of the respective national authorities is obvious, so that the provision also sets out a framework of procedural coordination, involving both the support and the supervision of ACER.[102]

In order to provide investment incentives for new cross-border interconnectors, the regulations allow that these may, upon request, be exempted from obligations concerning congestion management or from price regulation.[103] Competent to grant such exemptions are the national regulatory authorities of the Member States affected. In order to highlight Union interests, ACER may submit an advisory opinion to those authorities. Moreover, national decisions must be notified to the Commission, which may then require the notifying authorities to amend or withdraw their decision to grant an exemption. In addition, Article 13 Regulation 347/2013 allows, within the national cost regulation frameworks, appropriate incentives to be offered for projects of common interest with higher risks.[104]

(e) Other composite procedures and information exchange

Additional composite procedures are provided for decision-making under Regulation 1227/2011 (REMIT) and under Regulation 994/2010 concerning security of supply with natural gas, as well as for decisions concerning the denial of gas network access in order inter alia to meet long-standing obligations (as provided for in Article 48(3) Directive 2009/73 (Gas)).[105] Also relevant are supervisory procedures in case of non-compliance with guidelines.[106] Another interesting feature are various provisions establishing duties—or even the requirement for networks—of information exchange, for instance, in order to ensure effective cooperation of national regulatory authorities, to safeguard the security of the networks in the context of congestion management, and to facilitate effective use of available transfer capacity.[107]

---

[100] See section F1(b) above.   [101] Strobel (n 86) 547.   [102] ibid 547 ff.

[103] See Art 17 Regulation 714/2009 (Elec) (n 21); Art 30 Regulation 715/2009 (Gas) (n 22) with Art 36 Directive 2009/73 (Gas) (n 25); Johnston and Block (n 2) paras 4.98 ff; Talus (n 1) 96 ff; Wegner, *Regulierungsfreistellungen* (Mohr 2010); Haller (n 43) 216 ff; Gundel (n 1) paras 43, 58; Weiß (n 80) ch 32 paras 39 ff. Up to now, this instrument has been used quite rarely: https://ec.europa.eu/energy/sites/ener/files/documents/exemption_decisions_15.pdf.

[104] Strobel (n 86) 549 f.   [105] Haller (n 43) 134 ff; Weiß (n 80) ch 32 para 38.

[106] See section J2 below.

[107] See Art 38(1) Dir. 2009/72 (Elec) (n 25); Art 15 Regulation 714/2009 (Elec) (n 21); see also Weiß (n 80) ch 32 paras 43 ff.

2 Energy Environmental Law

As mentioned earlier the Emissions Trading System, related to Union climate change policy, has a multi-level structure and has developed into a more centralized structure, with important decision-making competences of the Commission. This development is reflected in the procedures for allocation of emission permits and for the supervision of the system.[108]

G Abstract-general Administrative Acts and Measures within the Energy Sector

Abstract-general acts are an important characteristic of EU internal energy-market law, complementing the often rather vague legislative framework. The most important examples are Commission guidelines (1)[109] and network codes resulting significantly from contributions by ENTSO (2).[110] Thus, administrative rulemaking, as well as rulemaking by private parties, plays a major role in the administration of European energy regulation.

1 Commission guidelines

Guidelines issued by the European Commission are by no means a feature specific just to EU energy law. Instead, they are used widely in Union administrative law, with important examples in competition, state aid, or telecommunications law.[111] Unfortunately, the term 'guideline' does not refer to a legal instrument with settled characteristics. Instead, it is an umbrella term used in EU administrative law for a broad variety of measures. The most important distinction concerns whether guidelines are legally binding or some kind of non-binding, soft law. Guidelines qualify as binding if the relevant legislative act declares them to be so, or if the legislative framework establishes a qualified administrative procedure for their adoption.

Both types can be found in Union energy law. The most important examples for non-binding guidelines are those on state aids for environmental protection and energy 2014–2020.[112] The Commission can make guidelines on state aid, qualifying as soft law, in effect evading the framework established by Article 109 TFE (which provides a specific competence and strict procedure for the adoption of Council regulations on the topic). Such guidelines may give rise to legitimate expectations of Member States that the Commission will apply primary state aid law in accordance with its guidelines, but this does not bind the interpretation of Treaty provisions or secondary law by the Court.[113] Guidelines on state aid for measures of environmental protection and energy supply in the period 2014–2020 are a matter of discussion in this regard: their rather rigid requirements concerning certain national schemes promoting

---

[108] See section E2 above.   [109] ibid E.1(b)(i).   [110] ibid E1(b)(iii).
[111] See Haller (n 43) 174 ff.   [112] [2014] OJ C200/1.
[113] Gundel (n 1) para 31; see also on similar guidelines in state aid law: Case C-189/02 P *Dansk Rørindustri and Others v Kommission* [2005] ECLI:EU:C:2005:408, para 209 ff; Case C-310/99 *Italien v Kommission* [2002] ECLI:EU:C:2002:143, para 52.

renewable energy may conflict with the broad room for manoeuvre of the Member States established by Article 3(3) Directive 2009/28 (Renewables).[114]

In contrast to such guidelines which are formally non-binding, the Third Energy Package explicitly empowers the Commission variously to adopt guidelines[115] through a formal comitology process.[116] It establishes formal supervisory powers for both ACER and the Commission in case of non-compliance with them by a national regulatory authority.[117] Consequently, such guidelines directed to the internal energy market must qualify as legally binding on both the Commission and Member States or market actors.[118] Commentators have noted the power shift towards the Commission by the significantly extended competences to adopt guidelines in the third package, raising issues in relation both to subsidiarity and democratic legitimacy.[119]

2 Network codes as an example of co-regulation

The second important example for abstract-general measures in the energy sector is provided by the European network codes, adopted in a variation of composite procedures with major input from ENTSO (see above E.1(b)(iii)), but also from ACER, the Member States and the Commission.[120] Thus, the network codes are a significant example of co-regulation strategies in internal energy market law. Such codes are restricted to issues of cross-border networks and market integration, and are introduced without prejudice to Member States' rights to establish national network codes not affecting cross-border trade.[121]

The importance of ENTSO's network codes is obvious from their areas of coverage. These include rules on:

- transmission reserve capacity for operational network security
- network connection
- third-party access
- data exchange and settlement
- interoperability
- operational procedures in an emergency

---

[114] See Martin Burgi and Daniel Wolff, 'Der Beihilfebegriff als fortbestehende Grenze einer EU-Energieumweltpolitik durch Exekutivhandeln' (2014) *Europäische Zeitschrift für Wirtschaftsrecht* 647, 650, 653. This conflict would be eliminated by Art 4 of the proposal for a new directive on the promotion of the use of energy from renewable sources: COM(2016) 767 final, at 12–13.

[115] See esp. Art 18 Regulation 714/2009 (Elec) (n 21); these powers shall be enlarged according to the recent 'winter package': COM(2016) 861, p. 20; Art 23 Regulation 715/2009 (Gas) (n 22).

[116] See Art 46 Directive 2009/72 (Elec) (n 25); Art 23 Regulation 714/2009 (Elec) (n 21); Art 51 Directive 2009/73 (Gas) (n 25); Art 28 Regulation 715/2009 (Gas) (n 22).

[117] See Art 39 Directive 2009/72 (Elec) (n 25), Art 43 Directive 2009/73 (Gas) (n 25); for more details see section J2 below.

[118] Haller (n 43) 167 ff; Gundel (n 1) paras 30, 41; Pritzsche and Reimers (n 80) ch 17 para 13; Weiß (n 80) ch 32 paras 20 ff, 48.

[119] Haller (n 43) 183 ff.

[120] See Arts 6, 7, 8(1), (2), and (6)–(8) Regulation 714/2009 (Elec) (n 21); Arts 6, 7, 8(1), (2), and (6)–(8) Regulation 715/2009 (Gas) (n 22).

[121] See Art 8(7) Regulation 714/2009 (Elec) (n 21); Art 8(7) Regulation 715/2009 (Gas) (n 22).

- capacity-allocation and congestion-management
- trading related to technical and operational provision of network access services and system balancing
- transparency
- balancing, including network-related reserve power
- rules regarding harmonized transmission tariff structures, including locational signals and inter-transmission system operator compensation, and
- energy efficiency regarding electricity networks.[122]

As this shows, network codes thus developed by industry within the framework of self-regulation address not just technical issues, but also economically—even politically—sensitive matters of fair network access for competitors, energy security and tariffs. Consequently, the legislator does not rely simply on self-regulation, but rather has provided powers to the Commission, ACER and national regulatory authorities to frame and control ENTSO's industry self-regulation. First, the Commission, after consulting the Agency, ENTSO-E, and other relevant stakeholders, establishes an annual priority list identifying matters for coverage in the next round of ENTSO network codes.[123] Secondly, at the Commission's request, and after consulting ENTSO and other stakeholders, ACER submits a non-binding framework guideline, setting out clear and objective principles for the development of network codes relating to the areas identified in the priority list. Each such guideline is to contribute to the non-discriminatory, competitive and efficient functioning of the market.[124] The guidelines are scrutinized by the Commission, which may request modifications or, under certain conditions, even create a guideline of its own.[125] The guidelines then serve as the framework for ENTSO codes.[126] Thirdly, those codes become binding on market actors only through formal adoption by the Commission, after consulting with stakeholders and following a positive evaluation by ACER and passage through a comitology procedure involving Member States.[127] Fourthly, where ENTSO fails to present a draft network code punctually, the Commission may adopt one drafted by ACER or even by itself.[128]

---

[122] See Art 8(6) Regulation 714/2009 (Elec) (n 21); the recent 'winter package' will enlarge their possible content even further: COM(2016) 861, at 20; Art 8(6) Regulation 715/2009 (Gas) (n 22).

[123] See Art 6(1) Regulation 714/2009 (Elec) (n 21); the recent 'winter package' shall streamline the recent procedures, but will also include additional stakeholders, namely a new European entity of distribution system operators, in the procedure: COM(2016) 861, at 20; Art 6(1) Regulation 715/2009 (Gas) (n 22).

[124] See Art 6(2)–(3) Regulation 714/2009 (Elec) (n 21); Art 6(2)–(3) Regulation 715/2009 (Gas) (n 22).

[125] See Art 6(4)–(5) Regulation 714/2009 (Elec) (n 21); Art 6(4)–(5) Regulation 715/2009 (Gas) (n 22).

[126] See Art 6(6) Regulation 714/2009 (Elec) (n 21); Art 6(6) Regulation 715/2009 (Gas) (n 22).

[127] See Art 6(7)–(9) Regulation 714/2009 (Elec) (n 21); Art 6(7)–(9) Regulation 715/2009 (Gas) (n 22); in contrast to the Commission's adoption of amendments to existing network codes drafted by ENTSO (see Art 7(3) Regulation 714/2009 (Elec) (n 21); Art 7(3) Regulation 715/2009 (Gas) (n 22)) a comitology procedure is not explicitly required for the original adoption of new ENTSO network codes by the Commission. However, the Commission practice implies the comitology procedure in order to cast no doubt on the binding force of these codes: Haller (n 43) 93; see also Gundel (n 1) para 60 with fn 3; Markus Ludwigs, 'Regulative Teilkompetenzen der EU-Kommission' in Baur and others (n 80) ch 31 para 41.

[128] See Art 6(10)–(11) Regulation 714/2009 (Elec) (n 21); Art 6(10)–(11) Regulation 715/2009 (Gas) (n 22).

H Single-case Administrative Acts and Measures within the Energy Sector

As mentioned a number of times above, national as well as Union authorities are empowered to adopt single-case administrative acts. Most single-case decisions have to be taken by national regulatory authorities.[129] However, internal energy market law also provides for some important competencies of either ACER or the Commission for such decision-making. These include binding individual decisions by ACER, in specific cases and under certain conditions, on cross-border infrastructure issues and in the field of projects of common interest under the TEN-E framework.[130] Usually, ACER decides only where national authorities concerned fail to reach an agreement, or where requested jointly by them. The Commission may take single-case decisions, especially ones involving a non-compliance by a national regulatory authority with Commission guidelines.[131]

I Administrative Enforcement of EU Energy Law

The enforcement of EU energy law is mainly the task of national regulatory authorities. The internal energy market directives provide that Member States shall ensure that their authorities are granted the powers to impose effective, proportionate, and dissuasive penalties on electricity undertakings not complying with their obligations, or to initiate proceedings for a competent court to impose them.[132] These should encompass penalties of up to 10% of the annual turnover of TSOs or vertically integrated undertakings. The national regulatory body may act *ex officio*, or react to a private party complaint. Any party may refer such a complaint against a transmission or distribution system operator to the regulatory body which, acting as dispute settlement authority, shall issue a legally binding decision.[133] Additional enforcement powers for national authorities emerge from the Regulation 1227/2011 (REMIT).[134]

In contrast, sector-specific enforcement powers for Union authorities vis-à-vis private undertakings or their representatives are rather limited. One example is provided by the adoption of a European network code prepared by the Commission where ENTSO fails to draft a lawful code in time.[135] However, such limited sector-specific enforcement powers are complemented by the significant enforcement powers under general EU competition law.[136]

J Supervisory Arrangements in EU Energy Law

As highlighted, EU energy law is mainly implemented by national regulatory authorities. Therefore, it is their actions which are the main object of supervisory

---

[129] See above E.1(a).   [130] See above E.1(b)(ii); F.1(d)(ii)–(iv).   [131] See section J2 below.
[132] See Art 37(4)(d) Directive 2009/72 (Elec) (n 25); Art 41(4)d) Directive 2009/73 (Gas) (n 25).
[133] See Art 37(11) Directive 2009/72 (Elec) (n 25); Art 41(11) Directive 2009/73 (Gas) (n 25).
[134] See Art 13, 18 Regulation 1227/2011 (REMIT) (n 15).   [135] See above G.2.
[136] See also Talus (n 1) 110 ff; Vedder and others (n 3) paras 4.90 ff; Gundel (n 1) para 33.

arrangements, including administrative appeals and judicial review on national level (1), and control by EU authorities (2). However, in some cases Union authorities are empowered to implement EU energy law and they might then themselves be subject to administrative or judicial supervision (3). In addition, EU energy law provides special arrangements to effectuate political supervision by the EU legislative organs (4).

1 Complaints, administrative appeal and judicial review on national level

As mentioned earlier, private parties are entitled by the internal energy-- market directives to lodge complaints against a transmission or distribution system operator to the competent national regulatory authority.[137] Moreover, the directives provide rights for private parties, who are affected by a national regulatory decision, to lodge a complaint or an appeal against that decision to a body independent of the parties involved and of any government.[138] Additionally, decisions taken by national regulatory authorities shall be fully reasoned and justified in order to allow for judicial review by national courts.[139]

2 Supervision over national regulatory authorities by EU authorities

As already mentioned, the Commission is empowered to adopt legally binding guidelines on a wide range of regulatory issues.[140] Such guidelines are central to important supervisory competences of ACER and the Commission over national authorities. According to the energy market directives, a national authority or the Commission may request ACER's opinion on the compliance of a national regulatory decision with these guidelines.[141] Where the national authority which took the decision does not adhere to the ACER opinion, the Agency is to inform the Commission accordingly.[142] In addition, a national authority may inform the Commission where it considers that a decision, relevant to cross-border trade, by another Member State regulatory authority does not comply with Commission guidelines.[143] The final determination lies with the Commission, after hearing the responsible national authority and the parties to the original national proceedings.[144] The hearing requirement is a significant example of existing EU law relating to adequate hearing arrangements with regard to composite procedures.[145] The Commission's determination may require the national authority to withdraw its original decision. While the directives oblige the national authorities to comply with such a Commission determination, and to inform the Commission accordingly,[146] they provide no enforcement power if

---

[137] See section I above.
[138] See Art 37(12), (17) Directive 2009/72 (Elec) (n 25); Art 41(12), (17) Directive 2009/73 (Gas) (n 25).
[139] See Art 37(16) Directive 2009/72 (Elec) (n 25); Art 41(16) Directive 2009/73 (Gas) (n 25).
[140] See sections E1(b)(i); G.2.
[141] See Art 39(1) Directive 2009/72 (Elec) (n 25); Art 43(1) Directive 2009/73 (Gas) (n 25).
[142] See Art 39(3) Directive 2009/72 (Elec) (n 25); Art 43(3) Directive 2009/73 (Gas) (n 25).
[143] See Art 39(4) Directive 2009/72 (Elec) (n 25); Art 43(4) Directive 2009/73 (Gas) (n 25).
[144] See Art 39(5)–(7) Directive 2009/72 (Elec) (n 25); Art 43(5)–(7) Directive 2009/73 (Gas) (n 25).
[145] See also Gundel (n 1) para 57.
[146] See Art 39(8) Directive 2009/72 (Elec) (n 25); Art 43(8) Directive 2009/73 (Gas) (n 25).

a national regulatory authority fails to comply in time. Thus, the Commission would have to initiate an infringement procedure under Article 258 TFEU.[147] For ACER, less effective supervisory powers are provided in Article 16(4)–(5) Regulation 1227/2011 (REMIT).

3 Complaints, administrative appeal and judicial review on Union level

ACER is one of few Union agencies with competences to adopt legally binding acts, as distinct from more conventional procedure of submitting drafts to the Commission.[148] In the latter case the Commission's evaluation before the final adoption of an ACER draft can be regarded as a form of *ex ante* control by the Commission.

With regard to legally binding single-case decisions of ACER, these are not subject to an appeal to the Commission, unlike such matters in some other EU agencies. Instead, the relevant regulation establishes an agency-internal appeal procedure to the ACER Board of Appeal.[149] The regulation also provides for judicial review by the Union courts.[150]

4 Political supervision

European Union energy law establishes some instruments of political supervision. As ACER's Board of Regulators consists of national regulators, their actions are quite protected from political intervention as the internal energy market directives prohibit governmental incursion into the work of independent regulatory authorities.[151] In line with this general principle, Article 14(5) Regulation 713/2009 (ACER) provides that the Board of Regulators is to act independently and should not seek or follow instructions from any Member State government, from the Commission, or from another public or private entity. Some limited competences of political oversight are provided at least for the Council and the European Parliament in regard to the appointment of members of ACER's Administrative Board,[152] as well as concerning the appointment of the ACER director and the extension of his or her term of office.[153]

In addition, internal energy market law imposes duties on national and Union authorities to report to the legislative bodies about their regulatory practice.[154] Such obligations provide the informational basis for the legislator to adapt the legal framework to current developments.

---

[147] The Commission might also use its powers under EU competition law; see section E1(b)(i) above.
[148] ibid section E1(b)(ii).   [149] See Arts 18, 19 Regulation 713/2009 (ACER) (n 20).
[150] See Art 20 Regulation 713/2009 (ACER) (n 20).   [151] See section E1(b) above.
[152] See Art 13(1) Regulation 713/2009 (ACER) (n 20).
[153] See Art 16(2), (5) Regulation 713/2009 (ACER) (n 20).
[154] See for example Art 47 Directive 2009/72 (Elec) (n 25); Art 52 Directive 2009/73 (Gas) (n 25); Art 11(3) Regulation 713/2009 (ACER) (n 20); Art 24 Regulation 714/2009 (Elec) (n 21); Art 7(3)[3] Regulation 1227/2011 (REMIT) (n 15).

K Conclusion

Until now EU energy law has consisted of two rather distinct elements, one establishing the internal energy market and the other reducing the environmental impact of the energy sector. The challenge for the future is to integrate these two elements into a coherent and comprehensive framework. Concerning internal energy market law, two periods can be distinguished. In a first period the main objective was to liberalize national markets. Since the Third Energy Package of 2009 the legislator has tried to overcome barriers between the various liberalized national markets and to establish a genuinely integrated common energy market with significant cross-border competition. In addition, environmental concerns and the objective of energy security have been highlighted.

From the more abstract perspective of European administrative law EU energy law is a significant regulatory laboratory, having many features typical of modern administrative law generally: co-regulation; complex governance structures including a rather powerful EU agency, i.e., ACER; a broad range of legally binding Commission guidelines combined with effective enforcement instruments; and a variety of composite administrative procedures. Union energy law has been consolidated during the last five years. Nevertheless, a fourth energy package was proposed by the Commission in November 2016. In responding to this, the Union's legislative organs have to cope with the above-mentioned challenges of balancing and accommodating internal market law with the objectives of an environmentally friendly, decarbonized energy system. In accordance with such an integrated perspective, one cornerstone of the Commission's proposals is a Regulation on the Governance of the Energy Union. This proposal is aimed at establishing a more coherent framework by integrating and streamlining various planning and Union-wide reporting duties, as well as monitoring powers. Its overall objective is to implement in an integrated and coordinated way all five dimensions of the Energy Union: energy security; integration of energy markets; energy efficiency; decarbonization, including the support of renewable energy; and research, innovation and competitiveness.[155]

---

[155] COM(2016) 759 final.

15

Public Health Policy

Marcus Klamert

A Introduction

The field of EU health law is difficult to define.[1] One strand began with negative integration under the freedom to receive health-care services, as developed by the European Court of Justice in the 1990s.[2] This case law on patient mobility has recently been codified and expanded in the Cross-Border Health Care (CBHC) Directive 2011/24/EU.[3] Union health law concerns also the mobility of health-care professionals, by establishing a regime on the mutual recognition of their qualifications.[4] Another strand of European health law has always displayed positive integration for certain specific products. The first Tobacco Products Directive was adopted in 1989,[5] the first pharmaceuticals directive as early as the year 1965.[6]

Health considerations pervade all Union activities. This is a consequence of the so called mainstreaming provision of Article 9 TFEU, ordering the EU, in defining and implementing all its policies and activities, to take into account requirements linked among others to the protection of human health. Similar mandates are provided in the context of the harmonization of the internal market (Article 114(3) TFEU), and of the competence of the Union to regulate in the field of 'public health' itself (Article 168(1) TFEU).

What the Union must consider in its measures is something else from that for which it has a competence to regulate. While health considerations permeate all areas of activities, the Union nominally only has narrow powers for adopting directives and regulations in the field of public health as such. This explains the variety of forms EU health policy takes, and explains the diversity of regulatory and non-regulatory means

---

[1] For an overview see T Hervey, 'EU Health Law' in C Barnard and S Peers (eds), *European Union Law* (Oxford University Press 2014) 621–50. For a discussion, see T Hervey and J McHale, *European Union Health Law: Themes and Implications* (Cambridge University Press 2015) 53–55; and S Garben, 'Article 168 TFEU' in M Kellerbauer, M Klamert, and J Tomkin (eds), The EU Treaties and the Charter of Fundamental Rights (Oxford University Press 2019). On recent developments, see F Schmidt and S Sule, 'Von Patenten und Patienten: Die Entwicklung des EU-Gesundheitsrechts seit Lissabon' (2012) *European Journal of Business Law* 369.

[2] See eg ECJ, Case C-158/96 *Kohll* ECLI:EU:C:1998:171; Case C-372/04 *Watts* ECLI:EU:C:2006:325.

[3] Directive 2011/24/EU of the European Parliament and of the Council of 9 March 2011 on the application of patients' rights in cross-border healthcare [2011] OJ L88/45.

[4] Directive 2005/36/EC of the European Parliament and of the Council of 7 September 2005 on the recognition of professional qualifications [2005] OJ L255/22.

[5] Council Directive 89/622/EEC of 13 November 1989 on the approximation of the laws, regulations and administrative provisions of the Member States concerning the labeling of tobacco products [1989] OJ L359/1.

[6] Council Directive 65/65/EEC of 26 January 1965 on the approximation of provisions laid down by Law, Regulation or Administrative Action relating to proprietary medicinal products [1965] OJ 22/369.

chosen for this. The focus here is on those areas of EU health policy that are governed by administrative rules of some sort. For this reason, the health-related case law of the Court of Justice will not be dealt with, except when apposite to this focus.

B Tasks in the EU Public Health Sector

The main objectives of EU health policy can be broadly defined as: the prevention of disease; the promotion of healthier lifestyles and well-being; health information and education; protection from serious cross-border threats to health; improvement of access to healthcare and of patient safety; support of dynamic health systems and new technologies; the setting of high quality and safety standards for organs and other substances of human origin; and ensuring high quality, safety, and efficacy for medicinal products and for devices for medical use (see Article 168 TFEU).

The objective of the CBHC Directive 2011/24/EU (based on Article 114 TFEU) is to facilitate the access to safe and high-quality cross-border healthcare and to promote cooperation on healthcare between the Member States, by setting down requirements for the Member States concerned and on reimbursements, among other matters.[7] The objective of the Medicinal Products Directive (also based on what is now Article 114 TFEU) is the free movement of medicinal products, by providing rules on their market authorization, either centrally through the Commission or by a procedure for mutual recognition.[8]

C Sources of EU Public Health Law

The question of the competence of the Union in the area of public health is especially intricate. According to the TFEU, harmonization is ruled out except for narrow areas, the focus being on a decentralized and cooperative form of regulation of health matters. Article 6 TFEU lists the protection and improvement of human health under competences that support, coordinate, or supplement the actions of the Member States. Technically, therefore, public health is not a shared competence that would allow for centralized and hierarchical forms of regulation, such as directives and regulations. The area is even one that is subject to a 'sovereignty clause', whereby Union action 'shall respect the responsibilities of the Member States for the definition of their health policy and for the organization and delivery of health services and medical care' (Article 168(7) TFEU).

One must, moreover, distinguish between the competence of the Union within the field of 'public health', set out in Article 168 TFEU, and the competence of the EU to adopt measures related to 'health' in a broader sense, in the framework of other powers conferred by the Treaties. While the former is confined to a more societal understanding of (public) health and has an emphasis on preventive measures, the

---

[7] See Art 1 Directive 2011/24/EU (n 3).
[8] Directive 2001/83/EC of the European Parliament and of the Council of 6 November 2001 on the Community code relating to medicinal products for human use [2001] OJ L311/67.

latter can and does have a broader reach.[9] Article 168(1) mandates Union action complementing national policies for improving public health, preventing physical and mental illness and diseases, and obviating sources of danger to physical and mental health. Such action is to cover the fight against the major health scourges, by promoting research into their causes, their transmission, and their prevention, as well as health information and education, and monitoring, early warning of, and combating serious cross-border threats to health. The Union should also complement Member States' action in reducing drugs-related health damage, including information and prevention. A detailed duty of cooperation on health policy, addressed to both the Union and the Member States, emerges from Article 168(2). According to this provision, the Union should encourage cooperation between the Member States, in particular to improve the complementarity of their health services in cross-border areas. Moreover, Member States are also to coordinate among themselves, 'in liaison with the Commission'. Article 168(3) gives the EU a mandate to conclude international agreements with third countries and international organizations in the area of public health.[10]

The pockets of competence allowing for harmonization following the ordinary legislative procedure in Article 168 TFEU concern specific 'common safety concerns'. Thus, there is a specific mandate to adopt measures setting high standards of quality and safety for organs and substances of human origin, blood and blood derivatives, measures in the veterinary and phytosanitary fields which have as their direct objective the protection of public health, and measures setting high standards of quality and safety for medicinal products and devices for medical use.[11] As regards the first category, substances of human origin, Article 168(4)(a) provides for 'constitutional minimum harmonisation', by allowing Member States to maintain or introduce more stringent protective measures.[12] While the Treaty prescribes a high standard of protection, it therefore does not require EU law to be the source of the highest possible standard.[13] In addition, Article 168(5) allows the the European Parliament and the Council to adopt 'incentive measures' under the ordinary legislative procedure, in order to protect and improve human health, including with regard to cross-border health scourges, cross-border threats to health, and tobacco and the abuse of alcohol.

---

[9] See, for this distinction, B Schmidt am Busch, 'Artikel 186 AEUV' in E Grabitz, M Hilf, and M Nettesheim (eds), *Das Recht der Europäischen Union* (Beck August 2015) paras 8–9.

[10] On cooperation especially with the Council of Europe, see Hervey and McHale (n 1) 445–71.

[11] Directive 2002/98/EC of the European Parliament and of the Council of 27 January 2003 setting standards of quality and safety for the collection, testing, processing, storage and distribution of human blood and blood components [2003] OJ L33/30; Directive 2010/45/EU of the European Parliament and of the Council of 7 July 2010 on standards of quality and safety of human organs intended for transplantation [2010] OJ L207/14; Directive 2004/23/EC of the European Parliament and of the Council of 31 March 2004 on setting standards of quality and safety for the donation, procurement, testing, processing, preservation, storage and distribution of human tissues and cells [2004] OJ L102/48.

[12] See M Klamert, 'What We Talk About When We Talk About Harmonisation' (2015) *Cambridge Yearbook of European Legal Studies* 360.

[13] See M Dougan, 'Minimum Harmonization and the Internal Market' (2000) *Common Market Law Review* 853, 864.

Based on Article 168, harmonization would, therefore, be ruled out for tobacco re-lated measures. The most important incentive measures are the so-called Health Programmes (see H below). Article 168(6) allows the Council, on a proposal from the Commission, to adopt recommendations.[14]

So, according to the Treaty, harmonization is ruled out except for 'common safety concerns' in narrow areas of public health, the focus instead being on a decentral-ized and cooperative form of regulation. Technically, therefore, public health is not a shared competence that would allow for centralized and hierarchical forms of regula-tion, and Member State responsibilities for the definition of their health policy and for the organization and delivery of health services and medical care are protected under Article 168(7).

In practice, however, there is a lot of harmonization in the field. This has relied on, and is still relying on, Article 114 TFEU, comprising highly technical and detailed prescriptions for the Member States.[15] This is made possible because measures based on Article 114, while aiming at furthering the functioning of the internal market, can also pursue (public) health objectives. The limits of this competence have been clarified by the Court in the judgments on the legality of the Tobacco Advertising Directive 98/43/EC, the ('old') Tobacco Products Directive 2001/37/EC, and the new Tobacco Products Directive 2014/40/EU.[16] The complex and fully harmonizing CBHC Directive 2011/24/EU has been adopted based on Article 114 in conjunction with Article 168 TFEU.[17] The directives on medicinal products and medical devices dis-cussed below have also been based solely on what is now Article 114. The new med-ical devices regulation, in contrast, has been based on both Articles 114 and 168(4)(c), because it would pursue both corresponding objectives simultaneously, and they would be inseparably linked whilst one not being secondary to the other.[18] Only with regard to organs and with certain (non-industrialized) blood and tissues and cells can Article 114 TFEU not serve as a legal basis, as these 'substances of human origin' are not 'products' (see below G3).

---

[14] See, among others, Council Recommendation of 30 November 2009 on smoke-free environments [2009] OJ C296/4. See Garben (n 1) para 12.

[15] E Mossialos and others, 'Health Systems Governance in Europe: the role of European Union Law and Policy' in Mossialos and others (eds), *Health Systems Governance in Europe: The Role of European Union Law and Policy* (Cambridge University Press 2010) 1–81, at 4, who speak of a 'fundamental contra-diction' at the core of EU health law.

[16] See ECJ, Case C-376/98 *Tobacco Advertising I* ECLI:EU:C:2000:544; Case C-380/03 *Tobacco Advertising II* ECLI:EU:C:2006:772. Directive 2014/40/EU of the European Parliament and of the Council of 3 April 2014 on the approximation of the laws, regulations and administrative provisions of the Member States concerning the manufacture, presentation and sale of tobacco and related prod-ucts [2014] OJ L127/1. See on this new regime ECJ Case C-358/14 *Poland v Parliament and Council* ECLI:EU:C:2016:323; Case C-477/14 *Pillbox 38(UK)* ECLI:EU:C:2016:324; Case C-547/14 *Philip Morris Brands* ECLI:EU:C:2016:325.

[17] Directive 2011/24/EU (n 3) of the European Parliament and of the Council of 9 March 2011 on the application of patients' rights in cross-border healthcare [2011] OJ L88/45 (n 3).

[18] See Recital (2) Regulation (EU) 2017/745 of the European Parliament and of the Council of 5 April 2017 on medical devices, amending Directive 2001/83/EC, Regulation (EC) No 178/2002 and Regulation (EC) No 1223/2009 and repealing Council Directives 90/385/EEC and 93/42/EEC [2017] OJ L117/1.

D Legal Principles Specific to the Public Health Sector

1 Introduction

A principle that is *not* specific to the field, but which arguably underpins many developments in it (especially in case law) is that of solidarity.[19] It has a reduced relevance, however, for the administrative side of EU health law. For this reason, the focus here will be on the three principles of precaution, mutual recognition, and transparency. All three principles are, though, not specific only to the field of public health. The precautionary principle is a concept rooted in the field of environmental policy.[20] Mutual recognition is a general principle that made its official entry into EU law with the *Cassis de Dijon* judgment of the European Court of Justice (ECJ) in 1979, followed by the Commission Communication in 1980, and then by the introduction of the so-called New Approach in 1985.[21] In the framework of negative integration, such as with the freedom to provide services, mutual recognition is concerned with the setting and administration of regulatory standards by one Member State, that must be recognized by other Member States (provided they are equivalent to a substantial degree).[22] Transparency has its central application in the Union in the particular sense of 'institutional transparency', such as with regard to the access to documents.[23] However, all three principles, despite their application more broadly, play particularly important and specific roles within the field of public health addressed here.[24]

2 Precautionary principle and proportionality

The precautionary principle is a risk management approach that favours not pursuing a measure when it might cause harm to the public, and when there is no sufficient scientific basis of information. In other words, where there is preliminary objective scientific evidence indicating that there are reasonable grounds for concern about possible negative effects of a activity or product on public health, this would argue against their conduct or use.[25] The precautionary principle is thus 'a mechanism for determining risk management measures or other actions in order to ensure the high level

---

[19] See U Neergaard, 'EU Health Care Law in a Constitutional Light: Distribution of Competences, Notions of "Solidarity", and Social Europe' in J van de Gronden and others (eds), *Health Care and EU Law* (Springer 2011) 19–58.

[20] See Art 191. See H C H Hofmann, G C Rowe, and A H Türk, *Administrative Law and Policy of the European Union* (Oxford University Press 2011) 170–72, 453–57, with further references. Critical, and discussing the principle as a pretext for protectionism, see Hervey and McHale (n 1) 300.

[21] ECJ, Case 120/78 *Rewe-Zentral* [1979] ECR 649. See Hatzopoulos, 'Forms of mutual recognition in the field of services' in I Lianos and O Odudu (eds), *Regulating Trade in Services: Trust, Distrust and Economic Integration* (Cambridge University Press 2012) 59–98, 59.

[22] ECJ, Case C-76/90 *Säger* [1991] ECR I-4221, para 15. See M Klamert, 'Of Empty Glasses and Double Burdens: Approaches to Regulating the Services Market à propos the Implementation of the Services Directive' (2010) *Legal Issues of Economic Integration* 111.

[23] See Hofmann, Rowe, and Türk (n 20) 170–72; see also P Craig, *EU Administrative Law* (Oxford University Press 2012) 357–66.

[24] For precaution see GC, Joined Cases T-74/00, T-76/00, T-83/00, T-84/00, T-85/00, T-132/00, T-137/00, and T-141/00 *Artegodan* ECLI:EU:T:2002:283, para 184. See Craig, *EU Administrative Law* (n 23) 645.

[25] ECJ Case C-333/08 *Commission v France* ECLI:EU:C:2010:44, paras 91–96.

of health protection chosen in the Community ... where a risk to life or health exists but scientific uncertainty persists'.[26]

The precautionary principle is applied in at least three different yet related ways in the present context. While these concern above all food safety (not the focus of this piece), they arguably apply more broadly within public health. First, the precautionary principle is at the basis of any ex ante approval regime that requires marketing authorization for products. Above all, this is the case with some categories of medicinal products (pharmaceuticals), for which EU law provides an elaborate, centralized authorization regime (discussed further below). Precaution in this case manifests itself mainly in a reversal of the burden of proof as to the safety of the product concerned, placing the burden on the producer.[27] Secondly, the precautionary principle has been applied as a standard of review for secondary law in the field of food safety. Thus, in a judgment on the validity of a Commission decision banning the exportation of beef from the United Kingdom to reduce the risk of BSE transmission, the Court held as follows: 'Where there is uncertainty as to the existence or extent of risks to human health, the institutions may take protective measures without having to wait until the reality and seriousness of those risks become fully apparent.'[28] The protection of public health was held to take precedence over economic considerations.[29] Thirdly, the precautionary principle is invoked by the Union legislator as a justification for proposing harmonization measures in the first place. Regulation (EC) No 178/2002 on food safety states that, since the precautionary principle has been invoked to ensure health protection in the Union, thereby giving rise to barriers to the free movement of food or feed, it would be necessary to adopt a uniform basis throughout the EU for its use.[30]

In a similar vein, the precautionary principle flows into the *proportionality* assessment when proposing a certain level of protection. Thus, the level of protection applied in relation to a certain perceived risk will be the higher, the greater the scientific uncertainty with regard to such risk from the product or service concerned. This assessment may even lead to a total ban.[31] Arguably, precaution has underpinned the decision of the Commission to propose a strict regulation for 'novel tobacco products' and for electronic cigarettes, thus anticipating possible—but as yet unknown or unidentified—risks caused by categories of products not yet on the market.[32]

---

[26] Recital 21 of Regulation (EC) No 178/2002 of the European Parliament and of the Council of 28 January 2002 laying down the general principles and requirements of food law, establishing the European Food Safety Authority and laying down procedures in matters of food safety [2002] OJ L31/1.

[27] See Craig, *EU Administrative Law* (n 23) 650.

[28] ECJ Case C-157/96 *The Queen and Ministry of Agriculture, Fisheries and Food, Commissioners of Customs & Excise, ex parte: National Farmers' Union* ECLI:EU:C:1998:191, paras 63–65.

[29] ECJ, Case T-70/99 *Alpharma* ECLI:EU:T:2002:210, para 356.

[30] Recital (20) of Regulation (EC) No 178/2002 [2002] OJ L31/1. See also Art 5 of Regulation (EU) 609/2013 of the European Parliament and of the Council of 12 June 2013 on food intended for infants and young children, food for special medical purposes, and total diet replacement for weight control [2013] OJ L181/35.

[31] Communication from the Commission on the precautionary principle, COM(2000) 1 final.

[32] Novel tobacco products are products that do not fall into any of the categories mentioned in Art 2 No 14 of Directive 2014/40/EU (n 16) and are placed on the market after 19 May 2014. See also Recital (34) Directive 2014/40/EU.

In considering proportionality, the Court has relied heavily on WHO Guidelines attachted to the binding Framework Convention on Tobacco Control as having a 'particularly high evidential value', for both suitability and necessity.[33] Thus, the necessity of the prohibition of tobacco products with a characterizing flavour has been assessed (affirmatively) by the Court, against, for example, the options of raising the age limit for consumption, prohibiting the cross-border sale, and affixing a health warning.

3 Mutual recognition

Mutual recognition applies in three distinct constellations. In respect of medicinal products it underpins the obligation to recognize decisions of national regulatory authorities on marketing authorizations. For professional titles of health professionals, it underpins the obligation to recognize certain educational standards. Lastly, under the CBHC Directive 2011/24/EU, it applies to decisions by doctors in the case of patient mobility.

(a) Mutual recognition of administrative decisions

For medicinal products, the quintessentially centralized regulatory model of harmonization on standards is combined with the decentralized approach of mutual recognition. The Medicinal Products Directive fully harmonizes the reasons for refusing the marketing of pharmaceuticals, stipulating that authorization shall not be refused, suspended, or revoked, except on the grounds set out in the Directive.[34] No decision concerning suspension of manufacture or of importation of medicinal products coming from third countries, prohibition of supply, or withdrawal of a medicinal product from the market, may be taken except on the grounds set out in Articles 117 and 118 Directive 2001/83/EC. This full harmonization approach on standards is coupled with Chapter 4 of the Directive on mutual recognition procedure and decentralized procedure in decision-making (see G1 below).

(b) Mutual recognition of qualifications

Directive 2005/36/EC grants the right of a service provider to retain his professional title as proof of professional standards and quality when providing services in another Member State.[35] It applies to 'regulated professions', defined broadly as any 'professional activity' requiring specific professional qualifications, such as a professional title.[36] The facilitation of service provision must be ensured in the context of strict respect for public health and safety, and for consumer protection. There are, then,

---

[33] ECJ Case C-358/14 *Poland v EP and Council* (n 16), paras 85 and 90.
[34] See Art 126 Directive 2001/83/EC (n 8).
[35] [2005] OJ L255/22. Even in its parts on 'automatic recognition' it refers the host state to the amount of time the applicant has spent in a certain profession in the home state. See Arts 16–20 in conjunction with Annex IV of Directive 2005/36/EC. See further Klamert, Of Empty Glasses and Double Burdens (n 22).
[36] See Art 3(1)(a) Directive 2005/36/EC. The definition of 'regulated profession' is a matter of EU law. See Case C-586/08 *Rubino* [2009] ECR I-12013, para 23 and the case law cited.

specific provisions for regulated professions having public health or safety implications, which provide cross-frontier services on a temporary or occasional basis.[37] Mutual recognition is employed either to compensate for the lack of approximation of national rules for some professions, or to complement the minimum harmonization of Member State laws and regulations on some other professions. For professions in the health sector, mutual recognition is paired with the minimum harmonization of training requirements. According to the 'principle of automatic recognition', Member States must recognize evidence of formal qualifications as doctors, nurses, dental practitioners, and veterinary surgeons, as pharmacist, and as architect, where these satisfy minimum training conditions.[38] Evidence of such formal qualifications must be issued by the competent national bodies, and must be accompanied by certificates.

(c) Mutual recognition of prescriptions

The CBHC Directive 2011/24/EU provides that, in regard to authorized medicinal products, Member States must ensure that prescriptions issued in another Member State for a named patient can be dispensed on their territory in compliance with their national legislation in force. Any restrictions on the recognition of individual prescriptions are prohibited, unless these are limited to what is necessary and proportionate to safeguard human health, and are non-discriminatory, or relate to legitimate and justified doubts about the authenticity, content, or comprehensibility of an individual prescription.[39]

4 Transparency

Transparency guides national authorization regimes with regard to cases of patient mobility. In its case law on the freedom to provide and to receive services, the Court, as a matter of principle, does not distinguish between care provided in a hospital environment (*intra mural*) and care provided outside such an environment (*extra mural*) to a service recipient from another Member State.[40] However, the Court has found that treatment in the former situation may be subject to a requirement of prior authorization in the home state of the services recipient, based on the public interest in maintaining a balanced medical and hospital service for the entire population.[41] The authorization procedure must comply with requirements of transparency, timeliness, and legal protection. In contrast, an authorization requirement does not apply to non-hospital treatment in another Member State. Directive 2011/24/EU has recently codified this complex case law, making authorization the rule and providing an exhaustive list of the possible reasons for its refusal.[42]

---

[37] See Recital (6) Directive 2005/36/EC.
[38] See Arts 21, 24, 25, 31, 34, 35, 38, 44, and 46 Directive 2005/36/EC.
[39] See Art 11 Directive 2011/24/EU (n 3).
[40] See M Klamert, *Services Liberalization in the EU and WTO: Concepts, Standards and Regulatory Approaches* (Cambridge University Press 2014) 87.
[41] ECJ Case C-158/96 *Kohll* (n 2) para 50; Case C-56/01 *Inizan* ECLI:EU:C:2003:578, para 56.
[42] See Art 8(6) Directive 2011/24/EU (n 3), which lists unacceptable patient-safety risks, a substantial safety hazard for the general public, serious and specific concerns relating to the respect of standards and

The so-called Transparency Directive 89/105/EEC aims to ensure the transparency of national measures for controlling the pricing and reimbursement of medicinal products.[43] It defines a series of procedural requirements designed to verify that national pricing and reimbursement decisions do not create obstacles to the pharmaceutical trade within the internal market. A proposal for revision of this law, submitted by the Commission in 2013, was formally withdrawn in 2015, as it had no chance of adoption, nor would have delivered the expected results.[44]

Finally, transparency is also imposed with regard to measures of the Union itself. Thus, the Clinical Trial Regulation aims at providing more transparency on clinical trials data.[45] The EMA is responsible for establishing an EU Portal and Database for a streamlined application procedure, via a single entry point.[46] All information on this database submitted in a clinical trials application and during the assessment procedure is publically accessible, unless the confidentiality of the information can be justified.

E Sectoral Organization

Within the European Commission, DG Health and Food Safety (DG SANTE, the former and downsized DG SANCO, which had also included the consumer protection portfolio) has around 960 staff, of which about 660 work in Brussels, about 120 in Luxembourg, and 180 in Grange (near Dublin).[47] The pharmaceuticals portfolio has always been a matter of contestation between the health and the enterprise DGs of the Commission.[48] It was only during José Manuel Barroso's second Commission term that DG SANCO took over the portfolio from DG Enterprise (now DG GROW), and there were plans under Jean-Claude Juncker to reverse this decision.[49] Medical devices have always fallen within the purview of DG GROW.

Key agencies in EU public health law are the European Medicines Agency (EMA) and the European Center for Communicable Disease Control (ECDC).[50] The EMA

---

guidelines on quality of care and patient safety by the healthcare provider, and that healthcare can be provided domestically within a time limit which is medically justifiable.

[43] Council Directive 89/105/EEC of 21 December 1988 relating to the transparency of measures regulating the prices of medicinal products for human use and their inclusion in the scope of national health insurance systems [1989] OJ L40/8.

[44] See https://ec.europa.eu/growth/sectors/healthcare/competitiveness/products-pricing-reimburse ment/transparency-directive_en.

[45] Regulation (EU) 536/2014 of the European Parliament and of the Council of 16 April 2014 on clinical trials on medicinal products for human use [2014] OJ L158/1.

[46] ibid Arts 80 and 81.

[47] http://ec.europa.eu/dgs/health_food-safety/about_us/index_en.htm.

[48] For a discussion see M McKee, T Hervey, and A Gilmore, 'Public health policies' in Mossialos and others (n 15) 231–81, 233–34.

[49] See http://www.euractiv.com/section/health-consumers/news/pharma-industry-denies-it-lobbied-for-medicines-to-move-to-dg-enterprise/.

[50] Hervey and McHale (n 1) 66. See also G Permanand and E Vos, 'EU regulatory agencies and health protection' in Mossialos and others (n 15) 134–85. See in general on agencies, Hofmann, Rowe, and Türk (n 20) 241–44, and 285–307. The European Chemical Agency and the European Food Safety Agency cannot be covered within the remits of this contribution.

was established by Regulation (EC) No 726/2004,[51] and is responsible for coordinating the existing scientific resources put at its disposal by Member States for the evaluation, supervision, and pharmacovigilance of medicinal products. It comprises several committees: the Committee for Medicinal Products for Human Use (CMPHU), the Committee for Medicinal Products for Veterinary Use (CMPVU), the Committee on Orphan Medicinal Products (COMP), and the Committee on Herbal Medicinal Products (HMPC). Currently, the EMA is located in London, but will be relocated to Amsterdam following Brexit.

The European Centre for Disease Prevention and Control (ECDC) was established in 2005.[52] It is an EU agency aimed at strengthening Europe's defences against infectious diseases. Its mission is to identify, assess, and communicate current and emerging threats to human health posed by infectious diseases.[53]

The Consumers, Health and Food Executive Agency (CHAFEA) is a successor to the Executive Agency for Health and Consumers (EAHC), set up by the European Commission in 2006 to run among others the Public Health Programme. The Scientific Committee on Emerging and Newly Identified Health Risks (SCENIHR) provides the Commission with scientific advice on emerging or newly-identified health risks for preparing policy and proposals, and is made up of external experts. Research subjects include antimicrobial resistance, new technologies (e.g. nanotechnologies), medical devices, and methodologies for assessing new risks. SCENIHR can also be invited to address risks related to public health determinants and non-transmissible diseases. Thus, it was asked by the Commission to identify those additives, amongst the most commonly used additives by weight or number, that have certain harmful attributes such as contribution to the toxicity or addictiveness, or resulting in a characterizing flavour within the framework of the Tobacco Products Directive 2014/40/EU.[54]

F Administrative Procedures within the EU Public Health Sector

1 Direct and indirect administration

The so-called centralized procedure for pharmaceuticals under Regulation (EC) No 726/2004 is in fact an example for a 'composite decision-making procedure'.[55] The procedure is divided in an evaluation procedure before the EMA and a decision-making procedure before the European Commission, which is assisted by the Standing Committee on Medicinal Products for Human Use and by the Standing

---

[51] See Art 55 of Regulation (EC) No 726/2004 of the European Parliament and of the Council of 31 March 2004 laying down Community procedures for the authorisation and supervision of medicinal products for human and veterinary use and establishing a European Medicines Agency [2004] OJ L136/1.

[52] Regulation (EC) No 851/2004 of the European Parliament and of the Council of 21 April 2004 establishing a European Centre for disease prevention and control [2004] OJ L142/1.

[53] ibid Art 3. It issues rapid risk assessments, policy briefings, scientific advice, technical reports, surveillance reports, and guidance.

[54] Final Opinion on Additives used in tobacco products (Opinion 1) Tobacco Additives I of 25 January 2016. See Art 6 Directive 2014/40/EU (n 16).

[55] See Hofmann, Rowe, and Türk (n 20) 405–10.

Committee on Veterinary Medicinal Products.[56] While applications are made directly to the EMA, they eventually lead to the granting of a marketing authorization by the Commission, which is valid and binding in all Member States (see G1(b) below). Thus, it is formally the Commission which takes the final and binding decision on marketing authorizations. However, the EMA can equally take binding decisions that affect third parties, such as waivers from the obligation to produce certain information for paediatric medicines.[57] Moreover, its opinions have been said to not only being scientific in nature, but also to contain rule-making elements. Accusations that the Commission may then merely rubber-stamp these opinions have raised problems of legitimacy.[58] Other procedures for obtaining a marketing authorization for pharmaceuticals (discussed below) are examples of the indirect implementation of directives.

Under the new Tobacco Products Directive 2014/40/EU, a Member State may prohibit a certain category of tobacco or related products. Such a prohibition must be notified to the Commission, together with the grounds for introducing it. The Commission must then, within six months of the date of receiving the notification, approve or reject the national rule. Where the Commission does not adopt a decision within this period, the 'national provisions shall be deemed to be approved'.[59] Also, the decison on whether a tobacco product has a characterising flavour is taken by the Commission.[60]

Regarding indirect implementation, Article 9 CBHC Directive 2011/24/EU provides rules for administrative procedures regarding cross-border healthcare.[61] Thus, a so called 'Member States of affiliation' (i.e. a Member State competent to grant to a person a prior authorization to receive appropriate medical treatment) must ensure that administrative procedures regarding the use of cross-border healthcare, and the reimbursement of costs of healthcare incurred in another Member State are based on objective, non-discriminatory criteria which are necessary and proportionate to the objective to be achieved. Such a procedure must be easily accessible, and requests must be dealt with objectively and impartially. Moreover, Member States must set out reasonable periods within which requests for cross-border healthcare must be processed. They are also to ensure that individual decisions regarding the use of cross-border healthcare and reimbursement of costs of healthcare incurred in another Member State are properly reasoned and open to judicial review.

---

[56] See Art 87 Regulation (EC) No 726/2004 (n 51); Art 121 of Directive 2001/83/EC (n 8); Art 89 of Directive 2001/82/EC.

[57] See Art 57(1) Regulation (EC) No 726/2004 (n 51). Hervey and McHale (n 1) 67.

[58] See Hofmann, Rowe, and Türk (n 20) 243–44, with further references.

[59] See Art 24(3) Directive 2014/40/EU (n 16).

[60] Commission Implementing Regulation (EU) 2016/779 of 18 May 2016 laying down uniform rules as regards the procedures for determining whether a tobacco product has a characterising flavour [2016] OJ L131/48; Commission Implementing Decision (EU) 2016/786 of 18 May 2016 laying down the procedure for the establishment and operation of an independent advisory panel assisting Member States and the Commission in determining whether tobacco products have a characterising flavour [2016] OJ L131/79.

[61] See, critically, as a mere codification of case law without added value, S de la Rosa, 'The Directive on Cross-border Healthcare or the Art of Codifying Complex Case Law' (2012) *Common Market Law Review* 15, 34.

2 Cooperation through networks and alert systems

According to Article 168(2) TFEU, the Commission can take initiatives to promote coordination, 'in particular initiatives aiming at the establishment of guidelines and indicators, the organization of exchange of best practice, and the preparation of the necessary elements for periodic monitoring and evaluation.' The Commission has developed the EU Health Policy Platform as a communication and collaboration channel between DG SANTE and its stakeholders.[62] This should, among other things, contribute to building knowledge and expertise on public health issues, identify, share, and encourage the replication of good practices related to health policy, gather and circulate research outcomes, and improve the availability of results and outcomes to interested stakeholders.[63]

The CBHC Directive 2011/24/EU contains various mechanisms of cooperation in its Chapter IV. This has been claimed to 'give expression, in specific terms, to the complementary competence for which the Union has received recognition in the area of health'.[64] One form of co-operation in healthcare between Member States established by the CBHC Directive are European Reference Networks (ERNs). Some of these are supported through the Union's public health and research programmes, in particular in the area of rare diseases, paediatric cancer, and neurological complex diseases. The Commission is required to support the development of ERNs by adopting a list of criteria and conditions that they, and healthcare providers wishing to become a Member of an ERN, must fulfil, and by installing the procedure for the establishment and evaluation of the Networks.[65] In March 2017, twenty-four thematic ERNs began to operate, gathering over 900 highly specialized healthcare units from twenty-six countries.[66]

Based on Article 15 of the CBHC Directive, the Union must, moreover, support and facilitate cooperation between national authorities or bodies responsible for health technology assessment (HTA).[67] From this has emerged the HTA Network, supported by scientific and technical cooperation currently performed by 'EUnetHTA', within the framework of a Joint Action.[68]

Another instrument of cooperation are systems set up and administered by the Commission so as to foster the speedy exchange of specific, critical information between the Member States.[69] Actions within these systems can lead to products being recalled from the market. The oldest system in the sector is the Rapid Alert System for Food and Feed (RASFF).[70] Created in 1979, it facilitates the sharing of information

---

[62] See on the relation to Open Method of Coordination, S Greer and B Vanhercke, 'The Hard Politics of Soft Law: The Case of Health' in Mossialos and others (n 15) 186–30, 229.

[63] See http://ec.europa.eu/health/interest_groups/policy_platform/index_en.htm.

[64] De la Rosa (n 61) 42.   [65] Art 12 Directive 2011/24/EU (n 3).

[66] See http://europa.eu/rapid/press-release_IP-17-323_en.htm.

[67] See https://ec.europa.eu/health/technology_assessment/policy/network_en.

[68] Commission Implementing Decision of 26 June 2013 providing the rules for the establishment, management and transparent functioning of the Network of national authorities or bodies responsible for health technology assessment [2013] OJ LL175/71.

[69] See for an overview McKee, Hervey, and Gilmore (n 48) 251–56.

[70] See Commission Regulation (EU) No 16/2011 of 10 January 2011 laying down implementing measures for the Rapid alert system for food and feed [2011] OJ L6/7, laying down the implementing measures,

on food safety risks between the national food safety authorities, the Commission, and the European Food Safety Authority. The Early Warning and Response System (EWRS) for communicable diseases aims at ensuring a rapid and effective response by the EU to events (including emergencies) related to communicable diseases.[71] It is a web-based system, linking DG SANTE, national public health bodies, and the ECDC. In 2013, an EU Rapid Alert platform for human Tissues and Cells (RATC) was established, also as a web-based alert platform, to improve the safety of patients undergoing transplantation and medical procedures involving human tissues and cells (eg. bone marrow, cornea, skin, oocytes, sperm).[72] In addition to quality and safety information, it can also alert to illegal and fraudulent activities in the field as well as to epidemiological situations, such as disease outbreaks with cross-border implications. Since 2014, there is a web-based Rapid Alert system for Blood and Blood Components (RAB) for preventing cross-border incidents, operating in parallel with existing national vigilance systems.

G Legal Rules Governing the Substance of Public Health-specific Decision-making

Three areas, (1) medicinal products, (2) medical devices, and (3) substances of human origin, receive attention here.[73] It will be seen that each of these matters, although closely related and partly overlapping in their scope of application, are subject to markedly different rules. The fundamental difference among them is that pharmaceuticals must obtain a market authorization prior to being marketed within the EU, whereas there is no such requirement for medical devices. While both medicinal products and medical devices are extensively regulated on the legal basis of Article 114 TFEU, rules concerning substances of human origin are harmonized only within the confines of the much narrower mandate of Article 168(4) TFEU.

---

stipulating the duties of the RASFF network members and defining the different types of notifications. There are standard operating procedures drawn up by the RASFF network members.

[71] Commission Decision of 22 December 1999 on the early warning and response system for the prevention and control of communicable diseases under Decision No 2119/98/EC of the European Parliament and of the Council [2000] OJ L21/32.

[72] See Art 8 of Commission Directive 2006/86/EC of 24 October 2006 implementing Directive 2004/23/EC of the European Parliament and of the Council as regards traceability requirements, notification of serious adverse reactions and events and certain technical requirements for the coding, processing, preservation, storage and distribution of human tissues and cells [2006] OJ L294/32, requires Member State competent authorities to 'communicate to each other and to the Commission, such information as is appropriate with regard to serious adverse reactions and events in order to guarantee that adequate actions are taken'.

[73] Focus will be on the regime on the authorization of medicinal products and not on important recent measures regarding pharmacovigilance or falsified medicinal products. The safety of medicinal products is monitored throughout their entire lifespan through the EU system of pharmacovigilance. A Pharmacovigilance Risk Assessment Committee (PRAC) has come into function in 2012 with the implementation of the new EU pharmacovigilance legislation. See Directive 2010/84/EU of the European Parliament and of the Council of 15 December 2010 amending, as regards pharmacovigilance, Directive 2001/83/EC on the Community code relating to medicinal products for human use [2010] OJ L348/74; Directive 2011/62/EU of the European Parliament and of the Council of 8 June 2011 amending Directive 2001/83/EC on the Community code relating to medicinal products for human use, as regards the prevention of the entry into the legal supply chain of falsified medicinal products [2011] OJ L174/74.

1 Medicinal products (pharmaceuticals)

(a) Introduction

No medicinal product can be placed on the market of a Member State unless a marketing authorization has been issued.[74] The authorization regime for pharmaceuticals is divided up between, on the one hand, the national regulatory bodies, which are mainly responsible under the mutual recognition and the decentralized procedures, and, on the other hand, the EMA together with the European Commission, which are responsible under the centralized procedure. While the mutual recognition procedure and the decentralized procedure are governed by Directive 2001/83/EC, the centralized procedure falls under Regulation (EC) No 726/2004.

(b) Centralized procedures

As mentioned above, applications for the centralized procedure are made directly to the EMA and lead to a marketing authorization issued by the Commission that is valid and binding in all Member States.[75] The procedure is divided into an evaluation procedure before the EMA and a decision-making procedure before the Commission. Applications can be submitted either as full applications under Article 8(3) Directive 2001/83/EC or under one of the simplified procedures under Article 10(2)(i)–(iii) of that Directive. Thus, an applicant will not be required to provide the results of pre-clinical tests or clinical trials if they can demonstrate that the active substances of the medicinal product have been in well-established medicinal use within the EU for at least ten years (see the *Orphacol* case below under section I).

The centralized procedure is mandatory for a number of medicinal products, such as those using biotechnological processes, orphan medicinal products, human products containing a new active substance not authorized in the Community before 20 May 2004 and those which are intended for the treatment of AIDS, cancer, neurodegenerative disorder, or diabetes.[76] Orphan medicinal products are products intended for diagnosis, prevention, or treatment of life-threatening or very serious conditions that affect not more than five in 10,000 persons in the European Union.[77] The centralized procedure is optional for any other products containing new active substances not authorized in the Community before 20 May 2004, or for products which constitute a significant therapeutic, scientific or technical innovation, or for which a Union authorization is in the interests of patients.[78]

An application is assessed by one of the committees of the EMA (CMPHU, CMPVU, COMP, HMPC). A rapporteur and a co-rapporteur coordinate the EMA's assessment and prepare draft reports which, in the case of medicinal products for human use, are sent to the CMPHU, whose comments or objections are communicated to the applicant.

---

[74] See Art 6 Directive 2001/83/EC (n 8).   [75] See Art 4 of Regulation (EC) No 726/2004 (n 51).
[76] ibid Art 3 and the Annex.
[77] See Regulation (EC) No 141/2000 of the European Parliament and of the Council of 16 December 1999 on orphan medicinal products [2000] OJ L18/1 (n 71).
[78] See Art 3(2)–(3) Regulation (EC) No 726/2004 (n 51). See Hervey (n 1) 641.

The rapporteur and co-rapporteur assess the applicant's replies, submit them for dis-cussion to the CMPHU and prepare a final assessment report. Once the evaluation is completed, the CMPHU gives a favourable or unfavourable opinion as to whether to grant the authorization.[79] When the opinion is favourable, it includes the draft sum-mary of the product's characteristics, the package leaflet and the texts proposed for the various packaging materials. The time limit for the evaluation procedure is 210 days.[80] The EMA then has fifteen days to send the CMPHU's opinion and assessment report to the Commission.[81] This starts the decision-making process, where the Commission it-self has fifteen days to prepare a draft decision.[82] This draft decision is then forwarded to the Standing Committee on Medicinal Products for Human Use (or the Standing Committee on Veterinary Medicinal Product) as part of the comitology procedure.[83] Fifteen days after this procedure, the Commission takes the final decision on granting marketing authorization.[84] Marketing authorizations under the centralized procedure are valid for five years, and applications for renewal must be submitted at least six months before expiry of this period.[85]

A specific substantive rule of importance in the framework of marketing authoriza-tions is the precautionary principle, already discussed above more generally. As a rule in this area, products are considered dangerous, unless and until it is demonstrated by the producer that they are safe. Protective measures may be taken without having to wait until the reality and seriousness of those risks become fully apparent, where there is uncertainty as to the existence or extent of risks to human health.[86] While the risk assessment cannot be based on purely hypothetical considerations, where it proves to be impossible to determine with certainty the existence or extent of the alleged risk (because of the insufficiency, inconclusiveness or imprecision of the results of studies conducted), but the likelihood of real harm to public health persists should the risk materialize, the precautionary principle has been held to justify the adoption of re-strictive measures.[87] In a similar vein, the precautionary principle requires

> the suspension or withdrawal of a marketing authorisation where new data give rise to serious doubts as to either the safety or the efficacy of the medicinal product in question and those doubts lead to an unfavourable assessment of the benefit/risk balance of that medicinal product.[88]

Competent authorities must merely provide 'solid and convincing evidence which, while not resolving the scientific uncertainty, may reasonably raise doubts as to the safety and/or efficacy of the medicinal product'.[89] However, 'the withdrawal of a marketing authorization must in principle be regarded as justified only where a new

---

[79] See Art 9(1) of Regulation (EC) No 726/2004 (n 51).   [80] ibid Art 6(3).
[81] ibid Art 9(3).   [82] ibid Art 10(1).   [83] ibid Art 87.   [84] ibid Art 10(2).
[85] ibid Art 14(1)–(2).
[86] ECJ Case C-269/13 P *Acino* ECLI:EU:C:2014:25557, para 57; Case C-236/01 *Monsanto* ECLI:EU:C:2003:431, para 111.
[87] ECJ Case C-269/13 P *Acino* (n 86) para 58; Case C-192/01 *Commission v Denmark* ECLI:EU:C:2003:492, paras 49–52; Case C-333/08 *Commission v France* (n 25) para 93.
[88] GC, Joined Cases T-74/00, T-76/00, T-83/00, T-84/00, T-85/00, T-132/00, T-137/00, and T-141/00 *Artegodan* (n 24), para 192.
[89] ibid para 192.

potential risk or the lack of efficacy is substantiated by new, objective, scientific and/or medical data or information'.[90]

In this context, the principle of proportionality is equally important. The Commission is entitled to consider that varying the marketing authorizations (in accordance with Article 116 Directive 2001/83/EC) only with respect to the future is not a sufficiently appropriate measure, as this would not address the risk associated with the actual presence of the medicinal products concerned on the market.[91] Withdrawals from the market would, however, have to be restricted geographically.[92]

(c) Mutual recognition and decentralized procedure

The mutual recognition procedure, applicable to the majority of conventional medicinal products, is based on the principle of recognition of an already existing national marketing authorization by one or more Member States. An application for authorization can be addressed to one or more Member States.[93] As soon as one national authority decides to evaluate the medicinal product (the 'Reference Member State'), it notifies this decision to the other Member States (the 'Concerned Member States'), which will then suspend their evaluations.[94] The procedure for granting a marketing authorization must take no longer than 210 days.[95] In submitting the application for recognition of an authorization to other Member States, the Reference Member State must update any existing assessment report within ninety days.[96] Copies of this report, together with the approved summary of product characteristics (SPC), labelling, and package leaflet are then sent to all the other Member States.[97] These Concerned Member States then have ninety days to recognize the authorization decision, including the SPC, and labelling and package leaflet.[98]

Where a Concerned Member State considers that the marketing authorization of the medicinal product may present a risk to public health, and when there is no agreement between the Concerned Member States within ninety days, the matter is submitted to either the CHMP or the CVMP for arbitration.[99] The opinion of the Committee is then forwarded to the Commission, for the start of a decision-making process which (unsurprisingly) follows the rules laid down above for the centralized procedure.[100] The procedure is a decentralized one if an identical application is submitted simultaneously in several Member States, one of which being the Reference Member State.[101]

2 Medical devices

Medical devices comprise all kinds of medical products, including in-vitro diagnostic medical devices, from home-use items like sticking plasters, pregnancy tests and contact lenses, to professional employed equipment and devices such as X-ray machines, pacemakers, breast implants, hip replacements, and HIV blood tests. The

---

[90] ibid para 194. [91] GC, Case T-539/10 *Acino* ECLI:EU:T:2013:110, para 88.
[92] ibid para 89. [93] See Arts 8 and 17 Directive 2001/83/EC (n 8). [94] ibid Art 17(2).
[95] ibid Art 17(1). [96] ibid Art 28(1). [97] ibid Art 28(2). [98] ibid Art 28(4).
[99] ibid Art 29. [100] ibid Art 32. [101] ibid Art 28(2).

Medical Devices Directive 93/42/EEC has created a special, sector-specific version of the system of 'CE' product safety certification, which for other products is governed by the General Products Safety Directive 2001/95/EC.[102] Certification is provided by private certification bodies established in all Member States. The 'CE marking' confirms that a product has met all criteria of Directive 93/42/EEC, especially in the areas of safety and performance, and is allowed on the EU internal market.

Whether a product falls under the Medical Devices regime is a purely national decision, which need not be acknowledged by other Member States.[103] The Court has recognized that, so long as harmonization of the measures necessary to ensure the protection of health is not more complete, differences in the classification of products as between Member States continue to exist with medical devices.[104] Member States can, however, withdraw devices that, when correctly installed, maintained, and used for their intended purpose, compromise the health and/or safety of patients, users or other persons.[105] Member States must, though, presume that medical devices comply with essential requirements set out in Annex I of Directive 93/42/EEC.[106] The Commission becomes active only if the harmonized standards do not meet these essential requirements. In this case, that Directive provides for a comitology procedure involving the Committee on Standards and Technical Regulations.[107] The weaknesses of this regime have been laid bare recently by the Poly Implant Prothèse breast implants, which were manufactured in France but approved by a German certification body.[108]

In 2012, the Commission adopted a package of measures on innovation in health. The aim of those revisions was to extend the scope for legislation, better supervision of independent assessment bodies, clear rights for manufacturers/distributors, and stronger requirements for medical evidence.[109] Thus, Directive 93/42/EEC has been replaced by a regulation, Regulation (EU) No 2017/745, which will however apply only after a transitional period of three years after its entry into force (i.e., 2020).[110] It will reinforce both ex ante control and ex post control. For high-risk devices, there will be a new pre-market scrutiny mechanism. Criteria for the designation of products and the processes for the oversight of notified bodies will be improved, as well as increased transparency through the establishment of a comprehensive EU database on medical devices and of a device-traceability system based on 'Unique Device Identification'.

---

[102] Council Directive 93/42/EEC of 14 June 1993 concerning medical devices [1993] OJ L169/1. See Hervey (n 1) 640. See Chapter XIII on Product Regulation.

[103] ECJ Case C-109/12 *Laboratoires Lyocentre* ECLI:EU:C:2013:626.

[104] ECJ Case C-201/96 *Laboratoires de thérapeutique moderne (LTM)* ECLI:EU:C:1997:523, para 24. Medical devices are classified in Art 9 Directive 93/42/EEC. The classification rules, which are set out in Annex IX, can be adapted in accordance with the procedure referred to in Art 7(2) of the Directive.

[105] See Art 8 of Directive 93/42/EEC (safeguard clause).   [106] See ibid Arts 3 and 5.

[107] ibid Arts 6–7.

[108] See http://www.euractiv.com/section/health-consumers/news/eu-evaluates-danger-number-of-faulty-breast-implants/.

[109] See http://ec.europa.eu/growth/sectors/medical-devices/regulatory-framework/revision/index_en.htm.

[110] Regulation (EU) 2017/745. See also Regulation (EU) 2017/746 of the European Parliament and of the Council of 5 April 2017 on in vitro diagnostic medical devices and repealing Directive 98/79/EC and Commission Decision 2010/227/EU [2017] OJ L117/176. This Regulation will only apply five years after entry into force (ie in 2022).

Post market surveillance will be improved by the introduction of an 'implant card', containing information about implanted medical devices for patients, stricter surveillance requirements for manufacturers, as well as better coordination between the Member States.[111]

3 Substances of human origin

Under Article 168(4)(a) TFEU on measures setting high standards of quality and safety for organs and substances of human origin, Member States can maintain or introduce more stringent protective measures (constitutional minimum harmonization, see C above).[112] The difference in the approach chosen for regulating substances of human origin based on Article 168 on the one hand and pharmaceuticals based on Article 114 TFEU on the other hand has been illustrated with so-called blood products.

Blood products are industrially produced derivates of whole blood, such as certain kinds of plasma products. Plasma falls under the Blood Directive 2002/98/EC or under the Medicinal Products Directive 2001/83/EC, depending on the state of its processing. France defended its national monopoly for the marketing of plasma in the *Octapharma* case, arguing before the ECJ that stricter national measures allowed under constitutional minimum harmonization in the field of substances of human origin would prevail over legislative full harmonization (i.e., via secondary law) in the field of medicinal products).[113] The Court did not have to decide this issue, as both Directives quite clearly regulate their relationship to each other regarding the relevant plasma. Thus, the plasma concerned was held to fall under the Blood Directive 'solely with respect to its collection and testing'.[114] When blood in contrast is substantially manipulated in an industrial process, it falls under the Medicinal Products regime, and '[i]n cases of doubt, where, taking into account all its characteristics, a product may fall within the definition of a "medicinal product" and within the definition of a product covered by other Community legislation the provisions of this Directive shall apply'.[115] This meant that France could not prevent the marketing of the plasma product concerned on its territory. Thus, only a part of the lifespan of blood products and tissues and cells is harmonized, without the Member States being allowed to pass stricter rules. Depending on the stage of processing, blood therefore falls either under a fully harmonized regime (pharmaceuticals) or under a merely minimally harmonized regime (blood products).

H Forms of Acts and Measures for the Public Health Sector

It has been shown above that the Union competence for public health mandates or permits a number of different legal acts ranging from soft law recommendations,

---

[111] See http://ec.europa.eu/growth/sectors/medical-devices/regulatory-framework/revision_de.

[112] See Art 4(2) of Directive 2002/98/EC of the European Parliament and of the Council of 27 January 2003 setting standards of quality and safety for the collection, testing, processing, storage and distribution of human blood and blood components [2003] OJ L33/30.

[113] ECJ Case C-512/12 *Octapharma* ECLI:EU:C:2014:149.   [114] ibid para 46.

[115] Art 2(2) Directive 2001/83/EC (n 8).

incentive measures without harmonization, international agreements (all based on Article 168 TFEU), as well as harmonization measures (based either on Article 168 or 114 TFEU). There is, thus, an array of secondary law, on which level administrative tasks are particularly defined (see section B above), of international agreements, and of non-binding EU measures. Especially important for EU action in the field are incentive measures, which can take the form of regulations, yet these must not be of a harmonising nature.[116] Thus, the EU provides formal mechanisms for comparison of national systems against benchmarks, and thus for the dissemination of good practice, and provides resources to support certain types of behaviour, makes recommendations, or adopts codes of conduct.[117]

The Third Health Programme (2014–2020) is the main instrument the Commission uses for implementing the Union's health strategy.[118] The Health Programme is implemented by annual work plans setting priorities and providing the criteria for funding under the programme, which has a total budget of €449.4 million. The Programme aims, among other things, at contributing to the exchange of information on good practices between the Member States, the support of networks for knowledge-sharing or mutual learning, and to addressing cross-border health threats. Interventions can in particular take the form of grants by the Union or through public procurement.[119] In close cooperation with the Member States, the Commission monitors the implementation of actions under the Programme, and reports to a committee.[120] Measures that are more specific are adopted on the EU level in the form of action plans of the Commission (issued in the form of Communications from the Commission directed to other institutions). Action plans have, among others things, aimed at strengthening cooperation between Member States in relation to organ donation and transplantation, and on eHealth.[121]

International agreements concluded by the EU are by no means a form of measure restricted to the health sector, but are certainly employed here. The WHO Framework Convention on Tobacco Control (FCTC) is the first treaty negotiated under the auspices of the World Health Organization and the first international treaty on public health that makes binding prescriptions. European signatories are both the European Union and the Member States individually, which makes the FCTC a mixed agreement. The 'core demand reduction' provisions in the FCTC are price and tax measures aimed at reducing the demand for tobacco, and non-price measures aimed at reducing harms due to the product, such as the protection from exposure

---

[116] See Art 168(5) TFEU.   [117] Hervey and McHale (n 1) 59–60.

[118] Regulation (EU) No 282/2014 of the European Parliament and of the Council of 11 March 2014 on the establishment of a third Programme for the Union's action in the field of health [2014] OJ L86/1. For previous public health programmes see McKee, Hervey and Gilmore (n 48) 240–47.

[119] See Art 7 of Regulation (EU) No 282/2014. Grants must not exceed 60% or, in exceptional cases, 80% of eligible costs.

[120] ibid Arts 13 and 17(1).

[121] Communication from the Commission of 8 December 2008, Action plan on Organ Donation and Transplantation (2009–2015): Strengthened Cooperation between Member States, COM(2008) 819/3; Communication from the Commission to the European Parliament, the Council, the European Economic and Social Committee and the Committee of the Regions on eHealth Action Plan 2012–2020— Innovative healthcare for the 21st century. On such acts, see Hofmann, Rowe, and Türk (n 20) 511–14.

to tobacco smoke and the regulation of the contents of tobacco products. The 'core supply reduction' provisions are those on the illicit trade in tobacco products, sales to and by minors and provision of support for economically viable alternative activities. While the FCTC itself is binding, and an integral part of EU law as far as it falls within the competence of the EU, just as important are guidelines and recommendations developed through a consultative and intergovernmental process established by the Conference of the Parties to the FCTC. These guidelines are themselves an important factor in the justification of the level of protection sought be the Union legislator through tobacco regulation, as well as for associated recommendations.[122] So, the Council Recommendation on smoke-free environments refers to Article 8 FCTC and to guidelines adopted by the Second Conference of the Parties to the FCTC.[123] This recommendation aims at providing effective protection from exposure to tobacco smoke in indoor workplaces, indoor public places, public transport and, as appropriate, other public places. Member States must, among other things, monitor and evaluate the effectiveness of policy measures using certain indicators.

Important in the sector are also principles and guidelines of good manufacturing practice, which have been adopted based on Directive 2001/83/EC.[124] Despite their seemingly non-binding nature, products that do not comply with them will not obtain marketing authorization.

Secondary law also foresees a large number of delegating and implementing acts.[125] Single-case administrative decisions are especially foreseen under the centralized procedure under the medicinal products regime (see above and below).

I Administrative Enforcement and Supervision

Supervision under the medicinal products and the medical devices regimes involve the comitology procedure for ex ante control, as noted above. It is only in respect of medicinal products under Directive 2001/83/EC, however, that the Commission takes binding decisions based on expert committee recommendations. Such Commission decisions can be subject to *ex post* supervision by the ECJ. These two mechanisms of supervision, in the frame of the centralized procedure for medicinal product authorization, can be illustrated by the *Orphacol* case. There, a French company (Laboratoires CTRS, Cell Therapies Research & Services) had developed the medicinal product Orphacol to treat rare but very serious liver disorders. On 30 October

---

[122] See Recitals (7), (15), and (24) Directive 2014/40/EU (n 16). See ECJ Case C-358/14 *Poland v EP and Council* (n 16), paras 85 and 90. See also M Klamert, 'Review of di Fabio, Pitschas and Schroeder, Die Novellierung der europäischen Tabakproduktrichtlinie: Grundfragen der Vereinbarkeit mit EU- und WTO-Recht (ZLR-Schriftenreihe, 2014)' (2014) *European Journal of Risk Regulation* 562.

[123] Council Recommendation of 30 November 2009 on smoke-free environments (n 14).

[124] Commission Directive 2003/94/EC of 8 October 2003 laying down the principles and guidelines of good manufacturing practice in respect of medicinal products for human use and investigational medicinal products for human use [2003] OJ L262/22; Commission Directive 91/412/EEC of 23 July 1991 laying down the principles and guidelines of good manufacturing practice for veterinary medicinal products [1991] OJ L228/70.

[125] See eg Art 11(5) Cross-Border Health Care Directive 2011/24/EU (n 3); Art 27 Tobacco Products Directive 2014/40/EU (n 16); and Arts 24 and 29 Organs Directive 2010/45/EU (n 11).

2009, CTRS applied to the EMA under the simplified procedure which required proving a 'well-established use'. The CMPHU issued a positive opinion, followed by a revised opinion, which was also positive. In July 2011, the Commission submitted to the Standing Committee on Medicinal Products for Human Use a draft decision refusing to grant marketing authorization for Orphacol. In October 2011, the Standing Committee issued an opinion, not supporting the Commission's draft decision refusing to grant marketing authorization. In the same month, the Commission submitted the draft decision refusing to grant marketing authorization to the Appeal Committee. In November 2011, the Appeal Committee also issued a negative opinion on the Commission's draft decision, i.e. supporting the authorization. On 12 January 2012, CTRS brought an action before the General Court seeking a declaration that the Commission had unlawfully failed to act by not adopting a final decision.

While this case was pending, and thus mooting the claim regarding a failure to act, the Commission replaced the draft decision refusing the marketing authorization by adopting a (final) decision of 25 May 2012, also refusing to grant the marketing authorization, the Member States not reaching a qualified majority needed to block the draft. On 10 July 2012, CTRS brought another action before the General Court seeking annulment of the decision of 25 May 2012, alleging a violation of the post-Lisbon comitology procedures. In its judgment, the General Court found that the Commission was wrong to conclude in its decision that the data submitted by CTRS should have been comprehensive, and that it could not invoke the existence of exceptional circumstances in its application, based on well-established medicinal use.[126] The Commission eventually submitted a positive draft opinion on the authorization to the Standing Committee, which was then adopted unanimously.[127]

J Conclusion

It has been shown that the European Union has a wide variety of tasks in the field of public health, oscillating between a high degree of centralization (with pharmaceuticals) and a largely decentralized, heterogeneous regime (with medical devices). Because of the varied approaches to regulating medicinal products, medical devices, and substances of human origin, delimiting their scope becomes a vital exercise.

There is a strong connection between health issues and the common internal market, due to the fact that medical, medicinal, and blood products are tradable, just as patients are mobile and come within—or more particularly, may wish to enjoy—the free movement of services. This explains the prevalence of mutual recognition, a principle that applies in an especially wide array of permutations in the sector. Another important principle here is precaution, applicable to all stages of Union action, starting with the legislative initiative, the level of regulatory intensity, administrative-regulatory decisions and procedures, and finally the judicial review of measures.

---

[126] GC, Case T-301/12 *Laboratoires CTRS* ECLI:EU:T:2013:346.
[127] See, critically, https://guests.blogactiv.eu/2013/11/22/orphacol-an-incredible-comitology-case-explained-from-a-to-z/.

Secondary law in the field provides for complex administrative procedures, especially with respect to pharmaceuticals. Comitology is widely applied, and medicinal products are a showcase for composite decision-making, with the EMA (and its committees) and the Commission interacting closely to adopt finely tuned decisions. New legislation on cross-border health-care provides for administrative rules for Member States to consider, when enforcing their national implementing laws. Public health is also a sector where incentive measures and soft law are prevalent, compensating for the fact that the competence of the Union for harmonization under Article 168 TFEU is narrow. At the same time, health objectives pervade many measures taken under Article 114 TFEU, such as, most famously, those for tobacco regulation.

16

Labour Law and Social Policy

Nicola Kountouris and Alexandros Tsadiras

A Introduction

Labour law and social policy are sometimes perceived as somewhat peripheral areas of the European integration project, areas that do 'not enjoy the same status as the economic strand of internal market law'.[1] Armstrong, elaborating on the scholarship of Scharpf, and Joerges and Rödl, recalls that the original constitutional 'social deficit' 'was not ... a design flaw as such but rather an understanding of the relative roles of the EU and nation states'.[2] As argued by Giubboni, in the eyes of its founders, the EU/EEC was to have been primarily tasked with the (liberal) economic and market integration of the participating states, so as to increase their overall economic prosperity and endow the national welfare states with the resources necessary to perform their key redistributive tasks.[3] Almost without fail, specialist textbooks recall the paucity and lack of enforceability of the social policy provisions contained in the Treaty of Rome,[4] often noting that 'the first steps to European Labour' occurred 'in spite of the Treaty',[5] that is to say in the absence of clear law-making powers, that only started emerging with the Treaty of Maastricht and, more markedly, with the Treaty of Amsterdam.[6] To this day, political scientists add to this, overall, diminutive description of EU social policy by classifying it as 'social regulation', essentially formed to address 'market failures rather than redistribute resources between employers and workers',[7] as domestic labour law and social policy systems typically do. To the eye of most labour lawyers, EU labour and social law remain at best the poor relatives of other EU policy areas, especially of those areas that are more directly relevant to the establishment and functioning of the internal market, at worst the victims of, an increasingly dominant and pervasive, internal market itself.[8]

---

[1] A Rosas and L Armati, *EU Constitutional Law—An Introduction* (2nd edn Hart Publishing 2012) 210.

[2] K A Armstrong, *Governing Social Inclusion—Europeanization through Policy Coordination* (OUP 2010) 27.

[3] S Giubboni, *Social Rights and Market Freedoms in the European Constitution: A Labour Law Perspective* (CUP 2007) ch 1, 18: 'Keynes at home and Smith abroad'.

[4] Cf for instance R Nielsen and E Szyszczak, *The Social Dimension of the European Union* (Handelshøjskolens Forlag 1991) ch 1; C Barnard, *EU Employment Law* (4th edn OUP 2012) 4.

[5] M Weiss, 'Introduction' in M Schlachter (ed), *EU Labour Law—A Commentary* (Wolters Kluwer 2015) 5.

[6] For a more detailed historical account of the development of the EU social policy legal bases see J Kenner, *EU Employment Law: From Rome to Amsterdam and Beyond* (Hart Publishing 2003).

[7] S Hix and B Høyland, *The Political System of the European Union* (3rd edn, Palgrave 2011) 208.

[8] For a compelling and powerful exposition of these arguments cf S Giubboni (n 3). See also K D Ewing, 'The Death of Social Europe' (2015) 26 *King's Law Journal* 76.

The natural consequence of this approach could only be a relatively under-whelming and tenuous administrative account of supranational sources, institu-tions, and processes committed to, and charged with, the design, administration, and delivery of 'Social Europe'. There is little doubt that, in the eyes of the founding fathers of the EEC/EU, national administrations were destined to retain the pri-mary, if not exclusive, role in the design of labour regulation and in the delivery of welfare policies.

The analytical framework depicted above is far from inaccurate and continues, in many ways, to shape our understanding of European labour law and social policy. However, it somewhat underplays the fact that, in spite of this apparent 'social def-icit', EU labour law and social policy are, in fact, extremely dynamic, original, and discerning areas of the EU legal and regulatory edifice. Characterized as they are by ad hoc regulatory principles, *sui generis* sources of regulation, and the presence of dedi-cated administrative procedures and agencies, it could be argued that these policy areas have managed to thrive in the constitutional and administrative penumbra of other far more integrated and centralized areas of law making competence and regulation.

For instance, already in 1957 the Treaty of Rome contemplated the creation of an 'Economic and Social Committee acting in an advisory capacity',[9] and assisting the Council and the Commission, in a number of regulatory areas pertaining, dir-ectly and indirectly, to Europe's social affairs. This committee, which predates other analogous institutions such as the Committee of the Regions, sought to give voice to a range of national social and economic interest groups, including trade unions and employers. It may be worth recalling that the Treaty of Rome also envisaged the creation of a dedicated, if relatively underfunded,[10] mechanism of social redistribu-tion, the European Social Fund, 'in order to improve employment opportunities for workers and to contribute to the raising of their standard of living'[11] that '[i]n its early stages ... was used as a means to "compensate" for job losses'[12] arising from market integration, and eventually provided the blueprint for the establishment of the many other structural and investment funds that the EU relies upon in order to support its regional economic development policies, including the more recently introduced European Globalisation Adjustment Fund.[13] 'The first European regulatory agencies, CEDEFOP (Vocational training) and EUROFOUND (Improvement of living and working conditions), were set up in 1975'.[14] They played a key role in the implementa-tion of the 1974 Social Action Programme,[15] and acted as a precursor for that process

---

[9] Art 4(2) of the Treaty of Rome.

[10] According to the Commission the ESF absorbed '1% of the total Community budget in 1970'; European Commission, 'European Social Fund: 50 years investing in people' (2007) 3.

[11] Art 3(i) of the Treaty of Rome.

[12] European Commission, 'European Social Fund: 50 years investing in people' (n 10) 9.

[13] Regulation (EU) No 1309/2013 of the European Parliament and of the Council of 17 December 2013 on the European Globalisation Adjustment Fund (2014-2020) and repealing Regulation (EC) No 1927/2006.

[14] Commission of the EC, 'European agencies: The way forward' COM(2008) 135 final, 4.

[15] See Regulation (EEC) No 337/75 of the Council of 10 February 1975 establishing a European Centre for the Development of Vocational Training and Regulation (EEC) No 1365/75 of the Council of 26 May 1975 on the creation of a European Foundation for the Improvement of Living and Working Conditions.

of 'agencification' of the EU that intensified from the 1990s onward.[16] Perhaps most importantly, and quite uniquely, the making of labour law and social policy at the Union level is heavily informed, when not directly shaped, by the input provided by the so called 'European Social Partners', that is, by the various umbrella and sectoral organizations representing the interests of management and labour in Europe. Their input is mostly felt in the context of the process known as 'European Social Dialogue', but is also present in other contexts, including the highly contested OMC, or Open Method of Coordination,[17] which can be rightly described as both a mechanism of 'governance' and a system of 'accountability'[18] and is thus laden with often complex administrative structures.

Against this background, the present chapter seeks to explore the key administrative procedures, guiding principles, sources, and institutional actors that, jointly and severally, shape the administrative law profile of Social Europe, mainly by reference to the more discrete areas of labour law broadly understood (that is, as also including EU action in the employment policy field) and social policy, narrowly understood (that is, to the exclusion of the rules underpinning the operation of the ESF and of Union action in the fields of education, vocational training, consumer protection, and public health). In essence, the focus of the chapter is on the main forms and principles of administration through which policies under Titles IX and X of Part Three TFEU are produced and delivered.

As a preliminary observation, it would not be inaccurate to suggest that the political difficulties and the innate limitations of the EU's law-making capacity in the social field[19] have resulted in a rather rich, if relatively underexplored, web of administrative processes and, sometimes, fully fledged procedures, with highly relevant regulatory outcomes for the social and economic 'governance' of the EU and the social/labour law and industrial relations systems of its Member States.[20] By and large, the two Titles examined here depict labour law and social policy as two areas premised on a *sui generis* model of shared administration, with important administrative tasks being performed by various EU institutions, together with a network of committees acting in a technical and advisory capacity, various agencies, the 'social partners', national bureaucracies, and administrative bodies, as well as a prominent role reserved to the *modus operandi* of the OMC. The following sections explore these facets in further detail.

---

[16] C Harlow and R Rawlings, *Process and Procedure in EU Administration* (Hart Publishing 2014) 31–34.

[17] For an overview of the Social Partners involvement in the making of EU social policy cf P Craig, *EU Administrative Law* (2nd edn, OUP 2012) ch 8.

[18] Armstrong (n 2) 49.

[19] Cf the link that Mosher and Trubek establish between the limits of EU's law-making competence in the employment policy sphere and the development of the European Employment Strategy in the 1990s in J S Mosher and D M Trubek, 'Alternative Approaches to Governance in the EU: EU Social Policy and the European Employment Strategy' (2003) 41 *Journal of Common Market Studies* 63, 66.

[20] For an assessment of the impact of the EES and OMC on the Member States national systems of labour law and industrial relations, cf D Ashiagbor, *The European Employment Strategy* (OUP 2005); M Freedland and others, *Public Employment Services and European Law* (OUP 2007); S Velluti, *New Governance and the European Employment Strategy* (Routledge 2010).

B Definition of Tasks in the Administration of 'Social Europe'

The key employment and social policy provisions in the TFEU require the EU, its institutions, and the Member States, to pursue and achieve a very broad range of objectives and administrative tasks. In respect of the activities falling within Title IX, Part 3 TFEU, 'Employment', the Union and its Member States are charged with 'developing a coordinated strategy for employment and particularly for promoting a skilled, trained and adaptable workforce and labour markets responsive to economic change with a view to achieving the objectives defined in Article 3 of the Treaty on European Union'. The latter provision, better known for its reference to the concept of 'social market economy',[21] refers to a number of policy objectives, including 'full employment and social progress' and 'social justice and protection, equality between women and men, [and] solidarity between generations'.[22] By and large, especially when read in conjunction with Article 5(2) TFEU, the scheme of the Treaties would appear to suggest that, in the employment field, EU institutions are merely vested with a power to coordinate Member States' action by means of policy guidelines.

By contrast, the opening provision of the Title X Social Policy, speaks of

> The Union and the Member States, having … as their objectives the promotion of employment, improved living and working conditions, so as to make possible their *harmonisation* while the improvement is being maintained, proper social protection, dialogue between management and labour, the development of human resources with a view to lasting high employment and the combating of exclusion.[23]

This provision, especially if read in conjunction with Articles 4(2)(b) and 153(2)(b) TFEU, would thus appear to suggest that 'social policy' is mainly an area of 'shared competence', where the EU, in respect of the majority of the principal fields listed in the Title, 'may adopt … by means of directives, minimum requirements for gradual implementation'.[24]

Tempting as it may be to draw a swift and clear demarcation between these two policy areas by reference to the distinctions of 'soft law' versus 'hard law', and 'coordination' versus 'shared competence to harmonize',[25] it is important to warn against any hard and fast 'demarcation and delimitation' rules. As noted by Craig,[26] the Title IX Employment does not quite sit comfortably within any of the three main categories of competence recognized by the Lisbon Treaty. Technically Article 2(3) does speak of Member States' coordinating their 'employment policies as determined by the Treaties', a point broadly reflected in Article 5(2), but 'the fit between Article 2(3) and Article 5 TFEU is not perfect, insofar as the former refers to economic and employment policy,

---

[21] On which see the insightful analysis in C Joerges, 'A Renaissance of the European Economic Constitution?' in U Neergaard, R Nielsen, and L M Roseberry (eds), *Integrating Welfare Functions into EU Law—From Rome to Lisbon* (DJØF Publishing 2009) 29.

[22] Art 3(3) TEU.   [23] Art 151 TFEU (emphasis added).   [24] ibid Art 153(2)(b).

[25] See the useful and nuanced analysis in Barnard (n 4) 49.

[26] Art 2(3) and 5 TFEU; see P Craig, *The Lisbon Treaty: Law, Politics, and Treaty Reform* (OUP 2010) 179–80.

while the latter also covers social policy', in Article 5(3).[27] In respect of Article 5(3), and its relationship with the more detailed Title X Social Policy provisions, Craig rightly notes that 'the most natural 'linkage' would seem to be Article 156 TFEU', but even so,

> the wording of the respective provisions does not fit since Article 5(3) is framed in discretionary terms, "the Union may take initiative", while Article 156 TFEU is drafted in mandatory language, to the effect that the 'Commission shall' encourage the relevant cooperation and coordination.[28]

No less problematically, although it is clearly the case that 'certain aspects of social policy fall within shared competence, it is not clear which'.[29] Article 153(2) TFEU is couched in 'shared competence' terms but, whereas for the majority of fields the EU seems to have a clear competence to harmonize,[30] Article 153(2)(a) also refers to an unspecified competence to 'encourage cooperation' between Member States 'excluding any harmonization'. Again, the wording of this latter provision is couched in exhortatory terms, in contrast with the seemingly more mandatory language of Article 156 (the 'Commission shall'). It should be noted at this stage that, in the past, the Court of Justice has clearly claimed exclusive competence on behalf of the Union in respect of those social policy areas where the Union has adopted rules 'with a view to achieving an ever greater degree of harmonization'.[31] In these areas, according to the Court, any commitments undertaken by Member States, including those arising—for instance— from ILO Conventions of which they may be signatories, cannot be undertaken 'outside the framework of the Community institutions'.[32]

Both titles are replete with additional requirements and functions to be performed by the EU institutions tasked with the policy objectives set out in the Treaties. As far as the Title IX Employment is concerned, Article 148 spells out the key provisions and tasks, on the basis of which the entire OMC process in the employment policy context is formulated and operates. This is a far-reaching provision, involving, at various different stages, all the main EU institutions and other bodies, including the Economic and Social Committee and the Committee of Regions, and the Member States (discussed further below in section C). Article 149 confers powers on the Council and the Parliament to adopt further incentives and measures, as long as they do 'not include harmonisation' measures, for Member State cooperation in the field of employment. Article 150 provides the basis for Council and Parliament to establish an advisory 'Employment Committee'.[33] As far as the Social Policy Title is concerned, it is worth mentioning the standing obligation of the Commission to promote 'the consultation of management and labour at Union level',[34] in particular when considering 'proposals' or 'action' in the field,[35] and its duty to report on 'progress in achieving the objectives in Article 151'.[36] We can add here the Council's duty to establish a 'Social

---

[27] ibid 179.   [28] ibid 180.   [29] ibid.

[30] See Art 153(2)(b) TFEU referring to the fields in Art 153(1)(a)–(i), thus seemingly excluding 'social exclusion' and 'the modernisation of social protection systems without prejudice to point (c)'.

[31] Opinion 2/91 [1993] ECR I-1061.   [32] ibid para 26.

[33] Currently operating under Council Decision (EU) 2015/772 of 11 May 2015 establishing the Employment Committee and repealing Decision 2000/98/EC.

[34] ibid Art 154(1).   [35] ibid Art 154(2)–(3).   [36] Arts 159 and 161 TFEU.

Protection Committee' under Article 160.[37] Finally, Article 155 sustains the activities and procedures that are typically described as falling within the 'Social Dialogue' process, a *sui generis* regulatory activity that will be further explored below in section C.

Before concluding this section, it is appropriate to outline the key administrative tasks that are specifically assigned to the Economic and Social Committee, the Employment Committee, and the Social Protection Committee, the three bodies that, jointly and severally, are involved in the exercise of the majority of the administrative functions pertaining to the regulation of Social Europe.

The Economic and Social Committee (ESC) is one of the main EU advisory bodies, expressly referred to by the TFEU, and already contemplated in the Treaty of Rome. It is composed of 'representatives of organisations of employers, of the employed, and of other parties representative of civil society, notably in socioeconomic, civic, professional and cultural areas',[38] the number of representatives from each Member State varying according to the population of each country.[39] One of its six specialized sections, the Employment, Social Affairs, and Citizenship section, is more explicitly responsible for the main policy areas falling within the two Titles covered by this chapter. Article 304 TFEU provides that it 'shall be consulted by the European Parliament, by the Council or by the Commission where the Treaties so provide'. The two Titles explored here consider its consultative functions essential:

- when the 'European Council, the Council, on a proposal from the Commission ... each year draw up guidelines which the Member States shall take into account in their employment policies' (Article 148(2) TFEU);

- when the 'European Parliament and the Council ... adopt incentive measures designed to encourage cooperation between Member States and to support their action in the field of employment' (Article 149 TFEU);

- when the 'European Parliament and the Council' seek to take action, including by means of directives, in the social policy fields covered by Article 153 TFEU;[40]

- when the Commission seeks to 'encourage cooperation between the Member States and facilitate the coordination of their action in all social policy fields' included in Title X;[41]

- when the Parliament and Council 'adopt measures to ensure the application of the principle of equal opportunities and equal treatment of men and women' in the context of Article 157 TFEU; and

- when Parliament and Council 'adopt implementing regulations relating to the European Social Fund'.[42]

---

[37] In existence since 2000 and currently set up under Council Decision (EU) 2015/773 of 11 May 2015 establishing the Social Protection Committee and repealing Decision 2004/689/EC.

[38] Art 300(2) TFEU.   [39] Art 7 of Protocol on Transitional Provisions [2007] OJ C306/159.

[40] Art 153(2) TFEU.

[41] ibid 156 TFEU. The Article actually refers to 'all social policy fields under this Chapter', but this would appear to be a vestigial reference to the pre-Lisbon denomination of Title X of Part III TFEU as Chapter 1 of Title XI of Part Three of the then EC Treaty.

[42] ibid Art 164 TFEU.

Unlike the ESC, the Employment Committee and the Social Protection Committee are not directly regulated by the TFEU, but rather operate under two separate decisions adopted on the basis of Articles 150 and 160, respectively.[43] Article 2 of the Employment Committee Decision sets out the various tasks of this body, which include monitoring the employment situation in the EU Member States, formulating opinions upon the Council or the Commission's request or autonomously, and contributing to the Council's proceedings in the context of the OMC activities under Article 148. In essence, its role is that of an advisory expert body in the context of the European Employment Strategy. As for the Social Protection Committee, Article 2 of Decision 2015/773, outlines a similar set of coordinating, monitoring, and advisory tasks, but in respect of the wider 'social protection policy' area.

C Sources of Administrative Law in the Regulation of EU Labour Law and Social Policy

As outlined in the previous section, the TFEU contains a rich and complex network of primary general sources of law with fundamental implications for the conduct of, and the administrative tasks of, a number of key institutional actors in the social policy field.

Arguably, the most significant provisions are contained in Articles 148 and 153–155 TFEU. Article 148 sets out the main administrative tasks for the key EU institutions, the Economic and Social Committee, the Committee of the Regions, the Employment Committee, and the Member States in the context of the so called European Employment Strategy, a key dimension of the EU's OMC (which now constitutes part of the Europe 2020 growth strategy,[44] implemented through the European Semester,[45] an annual process promoting close policy coordination among Member States and Union institutions). Within this framework, the main actors specified in Article 148 TFEU are entrusted with the performance of four key tasks: the adoption of employment guidelines by the Council,[46] setting common priorities and targets for employment policies and agreed by national governments; the drafting by national governments of national reform programmes, setting out to the Commission 'the principal measures taken to implement its employment policy in the light of the guidelines for employment as referred to in' the Employment Guidelines;[47] the adoption by the Council of

---

[43] Council Decision (EU) 2015/772 of 11 May 2015 establishing the Employment Committee and repealing Decision 2000/98/EC; and Council Decision (EU) 2015/773 of 11 May 2015 establishing the Social Protection Committee and repealing Decision 2004/689/EC.

[44] European Council, Conclusions, EUCO 13/10 (17 June 2010).

[45] Art 2-a of Regulation (EU) No 1175/2011 of the European Parliament and of the Council of 16 November 2011 amending Council Regulation (EC) No 1466/97 on the strengthening of the surveillance of budgetary positions and the surveillance and coordination of economic policies. See European Parliament, 'An Assessment of the European Semester' (2010), IP/A/ECON/ST/2010-24. See also C Barnard, 'The Financial Crisis and the Euro Plus Pact: A Labour Lawyer's Perspective' (2012) 41 *Industrial Law Journal* 98.

[46] Art 148(2) TFEU. See Council Decision (EU) 2015/1848 of 5 October 2015 on guidelines for the employment policies of the Member States.

[47] ibid Art 148(3) TFEU.

an annual report examining the implementation of the employment policies of the Member States in the light of the guidelines and, if necessary, on recommendation from the Commission, the adoption of country specific recommendations;[48] and the drafting by the Commission of an annual Joint Employment Report, to be adopted by the Council and presented to the European Council, detailing the employment situation in the Union.[49] As will be noted below in section E, the Employment Committee is heavily involved throughout this process, including by means of consultation with the representatives of management and labour.

Articles 153–155 TFEU contain the main provisions detailing the role and involvement of EU institutions, of Member States, and of the Social Partners in pursuing the social policy objectives contained in Article 151 (see B above). Article 153 mainly sets out the key procedures and tasks that structure the functioning of the more 'Traditional Union Method',[50] the rule setting process typically associated with the adoption of hard law instruments such as regulations and directives. Article 154 attributes a number of consultative prerogatives to the Social Partners in the social policy context. Article 155 articulates the key role and involvement of the European social partners in the actual shaping and promulgation of Union level regulation in the social policy field, a process typically described as 'European Social Dialogue'.

As far as Articles 153 and 154 are concerned, it is worth noting the substantial degree of discretion enjoyed by the EU institutions in terms of agenda-setting powers, exercise of the regulatory competence, choice over the form of legal instrument to be adopted, and choice over the most appropriate implementing method. Under Article 153(2)(b), 'The European Parliament and Council can in most of the areas listed adopt directives that set minimum requirements for gradual implementation'. In doing so, the Treaty appears to place two main specific limits on the scope of Union actions, namely to 'avoid imposing administrative, financial and legal constraints in a way which would hold back the creation and development of small and medium-sized undertakings',[51] and adopt 'minimum requirements' for gradual implementation', having due 'regard to the conditions and technical rules obtaining in each of the Member States'. Both these limits on the exercise of the social policy competence, and indeed the more general limits placed by the Treaty in Articles 5(3)–(4) TEU, have, however, been interpreted fairly loosely by the ECJ in the 'Working Time Directive' Case,[52] noting that those provisions do 'not prevent [small and medium-sized] undertakings from being subject to binding measures',[53] nor do they limit 'action to the lowest common denominator, or even to the lowest level of protection established by the various Member States'.[54] As for the application of the subsidiarity and proportionality principles, the Court affirmed that

---

[48] ibid Art 148(4) TFEU.
[49] ibid Art 148(5) TFEU. See EU Council, Draft Joint Employment Report—Adoption (6149/16, 18 February 2016).
[50] See Craig, *EU Administrative Law* (n 17) 197.
[51] For a recognition of this limit in practice see Case C-189/91 *Kirsammer-Hack v Sidal* [1993] ECR I-6185.
[52] Case C-84/94 *UK v Council (Working Time)* [1996] ECR I-5755.   [53] ibid para 44.
[54] ibid para 56.

the Council must be allowed a wide discretion in an area which, as here, involves the legislature in making social policy choices and requires it to carry out complex assessments. Judicial review of the exercise of that discretion must therefore be limited to examining whether it has been vitiated by manifest error or misuse of powers, or whether the institution concerned has manifestly exceeded the limits of its discretion.[55]

Article 154(2), while assigning a general agenda setting power to the Commission, states that 'before submitting proposals in the social policy field, the Commission shall consult management and labour on the possible direction of Union action'. The criteria for choosing the appropriate social partners for the purposes of this consultation are outlined in the 1998 Communication from the Commission 'adapting and promoting the social dialogue at Community level'.[56] The purpose and wording of Article 154(4) and Article 155 TFEU would suggest that when the social partners decide that the dialogue between them 'may lead to contractual relations, including agreements', then the powers and administrative discretion enjoyed by the Commission are considerably diminished. According to the 1998 Communication, the social partners merely 'inform the Commission of their desire to embark upon a process of negotiation' and 'The opening of negotiations is totally in the hands of the social partners and the negotiation process is based upon principles of autonomy'.[57] Similarly, if the social partners choose to make a 'joint request' to the Commission for an agreement falling under matters covered by Article 153 TFEU to be incorporate in a Council decision, then the powers vested with the Commission ought to be seen as merely notarial in character and limited to 'assess[ing] ... the representativeness (sufficient representativeness taking into account the scope of the subject for negotiation) of the signatory parties, the legality of the clauses in the agreements in relation to Community law, and in particular, the provisions regarding small and medium-sized undertakings'.[58] However, in recent years, 'this scrutiny seems to have intensified',[59] leading in some cases to the rejection of 'joint requests'.[60] It is questionable whether this less deferential approach is in line with the letter and the spirit of Article 155 TFEU, and in particular with the principle of autonomy enshrined in the 1998 Communication.

D Underlying, Sector-specific Legal Principles in Regard to Social Policy

As already noted in Section B, regulatory action in the area of labour and social law is conducted on both Union and national level. It practically involves, on the one hand, the vertical symbiosis between a number of competent Union authorities, national

---

[55] ibid para 58.   [56] COM(98) 322 final, 20 May 1998.   [57] ibid 17.
[58] ibid 19. Cf also Communication from the Commission, 'The European social dialogue, a force for innovation and change' COM(2002) 0341 final, para 2.4.2.
[59] A A H van Hoek, 'The Social Dialogue as a Source of EU Legal Acts—Past Performance and Future Perspectives' in M Cremona and C Kilpatrick (eds), *EU Legal Acts: Challenges and Transformations* (OUP 2018) 154.
[60] European Commission, '"REFIT—Fit for growth": Examples how EU law is becoming lighter, simpler and cheaper' (MEMO, Brussels, 2 October 2013).

bodies, and social partners and, on the other hand, the horizontal cooperation amongst a multitude of Union institutions, agencies, and advisory committees. Naturally, general principles of EU law apply to both dimensions. On the vertical plane, principles such as the limited attribution of competences, subsidiarity, proportionality, and sincere cooperation retain their relevance. On the horizontal plane, principles such as transparency and respect for fundamental rights continue to inform the EU authorities' institutional life. Within this context, the principles of independence, participatory democracy, representativeness, and respect for fundamental rights deserve a more detailed analysis given the peculiar characteristics of the area of regulation and administrative action covered by this chapter.

Independence is a concept of cardinal significance within the EU institutional fabric, as it seeks to shield the decision-making process from external influences that could derail its activities to the detriment of Union interests. That notion is normally contemplated, either explicitly or implicitly, in a provision of EU primary law (such as the TFEU) or EU derivative law (such as the measure establishing the relevant authority or its statute). The importance of independence in the context of employment and social policy can hardly be overstated. It is emphasized that this field is traditionally characterized by differing political agendas and strong ideological divides not only between, but also within, Member States. Detachment from national preferences, which give domestic interests precedence over the Union's social agenda, is instrumental for the autonomy and proper functioning of the administrative machinery sustaining Social Europe. It is not, therefore, fortuitous that independence makes its presence felt in the field under review by the present chapter. It is enshrined for example in Article 245 TFEU. That provision endows the European Commission, an active participant in employment and social policy, with independence in order to ensure that the good of the Union retains its prominence in their judgement. More precisely, under Article 245(1), the 'Members of the Commission shall refrain from any action incompatible with their duties. Member States shall respect their independence and shall not seek to influence them in the performance of their tasks'.

Within this context, the provision with chief pertinence to our analysis is Article 300 TFEU, as it concerns two advisory committees, the expertise of which in employment and social issues is considerable and the input of which into the whole decision-making process by no means negligible. That provision shrouds the members of the Economic and Social Committee and of the Committee of the Regions with the cloak of independence. To be more specific, Article 300(4) stipulates that

> The members of the Economic and Social Committee and of the Committee of the Regions shall not be bound by any mandatory instructions. They shall be completely independent in the performance of their duties, in the Union's general interest.

This Treaty provision is further amplified in EU secondary law. The Statute of the Members of the European Economic and Social Committee (EESC) contains a separate chapter (IV) dedicated to independence and immunity.[61] Article 8 of the Statute refers to Article 300(4) TFEU, and reiterates the members' right and obligation to be

---

[61] See http://www.eesc.europa.eu/?i=portal.en.rules.29363.

completely independent in the execution of their tasks, in the general interests of the Union and the European public. The Rules of Procedure of the European Economic and Social Committee also underline the centrality of independence in the institutional life of that authority.[62] Rule 2 (Chapter I, Title I) on the organization of the Committee stresses that the members may not be bound by any mandatory instructions and, during the performance of their duties, they shall enjoy freedom of movement, personal inviolability and immunity. Finally, the EESC Code of Good Administrative Behaviour makes clear that EESC officials are impartial and independent in the performance of their duties. Their conduct should not be guided by political pressures, nor by personal, family, or national interest, and they should not be involved in decisions in which they, or any close member of their family, have a financial stake.[63] The above provisions are further complemented by the Rules of Procedure of the Committee of the Regions. Rule 2 (Chapter 2, Title 1) on the membership and constituent bodies of the Committee echoes Article 300(4) TFEU, emphasizing that the members and alternates of the Committee are not bound by any mandatory instructions and shall be completely independent in the performance of their duties, in the general interest of the Union.[64]

The general principles of *participatory democracy* and *representativeness* arguably acquire particular relevance in the context of the regulation and administration of Social Europe.[65] Articles 11(1) and (3) TEU require Union institutions to hear views and opinions on EU measures, and especially to enter into consultation procedures. The principle has proved to be elusive, and possibly even as not going beyond what was already required by specific Treaty provisions introducing distinct consultation duties.[66] In the social and labour context, however, this general requirement receives very specific and significant attention, in particular by reference to the role that the so called Social Partners are granted in the making of social policy in the EU. As noted by Craig, 'the most striking is of course the Article 155 TFEU procedure, allowing agreements concluded between the social partners to be transformed into formal law through a Commission proposal that is voted on by the Council'[67] (and without the involvement of the European Parliament). But social partners are also relevant and involved in the making and operationalizing of other key EU processes in the social sphere. From the adoption of relevant EU law directives, where under Article 154 TFEU they enjoy a right to be consulted, through their involvement in some thirty sectoral social dialogue committees,[68] to their (often diminutive)[69] role in various aspects

---

[62] See http://www.eesc.europa.eu/?i=portal.en.rules.8053.

[63] See Art 8 of the Code http://www.eesc.europa.eu/?i=portal.en.rules.8056.

[64] See http://cor.europa.eu/en/documentation/Pages/rules-of-procedure.aspx.

[65] See Art 10(3) TEU. European Parliament, 'The General Principles of EU Administrative Procedural Law' PE 519.224 (2015).

[66] Cf Case C-104/97 P *Atlanta AG v Commission* [1999] ECR I-6983.

[67] Craig, *EU Administrative Law* (n 17) 241.

[68] Commission Decision 98/5000/EC of 20 May 1998 on the establishment of Sectoral Dialogue Committees promoting the Dialogue between the social partners at European level (notified under document number [1998] OJ L225/27).

[69] Cf Eurofound, *Role of the social partners in the European Semester* (Publications Office of the European Union 2016).

of policy development under the various procedures falling under the general rubric of the Open Method of Coordination (OMC), it is arguable that EU law recognizes a special role, though not necessarily an unqualified one, for the social partners as beneficiaries of the principle of participatory democracy. This role, and the requirements that social partners ought to meet in order to qualify as participants in the shaping and management of Social Europe, was at the basis of the *UEAPME* judgment, where the Court helpfully commented on the legitimizing effect of the social partner's involvement in what is now Article 155 TFEU, by noting that

> the principle of democracy on which the Union is founded requires—in the absence of the participation of the European Parliament in the legislative process—that the participation of the people be otherwise assured, in this instance through the parties representative of management and labour.[70]

Academic authors have, however, criticized the lack of a trickle-down dynamic facilitating the spread of the principle beyond the more formal confines of Article 155, into some areas of Europe's economic and social governance. Sciarra, for instance, has aptly noted that in 'the attempt to facilitate coordination of policies and set targets within specific deadlines, the European Semester has progressively ignored the involvement of social partners'.[71]

The respect for *fundamental rights* is a far more established, though no less controversial, general principle. A certain degree of controversy has emerged, in particular, in respect of the involvement of EU institutions and of Member States in emergency financial assistance programmes vis-à-vis certain Member States affected by economic and financial difficulties and by the 'sovereign debt' crises. A number of academic authors have argued that some of the measures taken as a consequence of these financial assistance programmes may have resulted in several breaches of various fundamental rights, including fundamentals social rights, in a number of domestic legal orders,[72] and that redress ought to be possible at a supranational level, including within the EU system of remedies.[73] However, most of the attempts to challenge the legality of these programmes, or of specific measures adopted in the context of their implementation, have hitherto failed.[74] A particularly problematic decision has been that of the CJEU in *Pringle*, where the Court stated that Member States were not implementing Union law, within the meaning of Article 51(1) of the Charter (CFR), when they established the European Stability Mechanism, and were therefore not within the scope of application of the CFR and their actions were not reviewable by reference to its provisions.[75] However, in the more recent judgment in *Ledra*

---

[70] Case T-135/96 *UEAPME v Council* [1998] ECR II-2335, para 89.

[71] S Sciarra, 'Social Law in the Wake of the Crisis', WP CSDLE 'Massimo D'Antona'.INT: 108/2014 10.

[72] Cf for instance C Kilpatrick, 'On the Rule of Law and Economic Emergency: The Degradation of Basic Legal Values in Europe's Bailouts (2015) 35 *Oxford Journal of Legal Studies* 325. More generally see also Ewing (n 8) 76–98.

[73] A Koukiadaki, *Can the Austerity Measures Be Challenged in Supranational Courts? The cases of Greece and Portugal* (ETUC 2014).

[74] C Kilpatrick, 'On the Rule of Law and Economic Emergency: The Degradation of Basic Legal Values in Europe's Bailouts' (2015) 35 *Oxford Journal of Legal Studies* 325. See also the comprehensive monographic work by A Hinarejos, *The Euro Area Crisis in Constitutional Perspective* (OUP 2015).

[75] Cf in particular para 180 of Case C-370/12 *Pringle*.

Advertising,[76] the Court noted that

> the Commission, as it itself acknowledged in reply to a question asked at the hearing, retains, within the framework of the ESM Treaty, its role of guardian of the Treaties as resulting from Article 17(1) TEU, so that it should refrain from signing a memorandum of understanding whose consistency with EU law it doubts.[77]

This is an important reminder that the general principle of respect to fundamental rights continues to apply to EU institutions, even when they operate outside the strict confines of the Union legal framework. This could potentially require of the EU institutions a more cautious approach in the context of the policy recommendations expressed in the context of both the OMC and of the Memoranda of Understanding addressed to 'bailed-out' Member States.

E Administrative Procedures within the Social Policy Sector

In the field of employment and social policy, procedural rules are primarily established within the framework of the OMC and the social dialogue.

As regards the OMC, Article 148 TFEU sets out a seemingly neat process through which employment policy is formulated. There exists an abundance of academic commentary on the nature, form, and structure of the OMC in the Union space.[78] It is recalled that the OMC is a method of intergovernmental policy-making which aims at directing national policies towards certain common objectives in areas which fall partially or fully under national competence. In the context of employment, the OMC is in summary conducted in the following manner: The Council and the Commission act jointly to produce an annual report on the employment situation in the Union, which is then submitted to the European Council. On the basis of that report, the European Council reaches certain conclusions, which set the background against which the Commission consults the European Parliament, the Economic and Social Committee, the Committee of the Regions, and the Employment Committee. The outcome of that consultation informs the Commission's proposal to the Council, which in turn issues guidelines for the Member States to consider in the formulation of their employment policies. Member States are then required to provide each year a report to the Council and the Commission on the main measures adopted in the light of those guidelines.

A number of interesting points can be made in relation to the above process and its participants. With respect to the European Commission, the department responsible for issues falling within the area of interest under investigation is the DG Employment,

---

[76] Case C-8/15 P *Ledra Advertising v Commission and ECB* (20 September 2016).

[77] ibid para 59.

[78] Contributions in the form of books include F Snyder (ed), *The EU and Governance—L'UE et la Gouvernance* (Bruylant 2003); R Dehousse (ed), *L'Europe sans Bruxelles? Une analyse de la Methode Ouverte de Coordination* (L'Harmattan 2004); P Pochet (ed), *The Open Method of Coordination in Action: The European Employment and Social Inclusion Strategies* (PIE Peter Lang 2005); G de Búrca and J Scott, *Law and New Governance in the EU and the US* (Hart Publishing 2006); K A Armstrong (n 2). See also 'A Renewed Commitment to Social Europe: Reinforcing the Open Method of Coordination for Social Protection and Social Inclusion' COM(2008) 418 final http://eur-lex.europa.eu/legal-content/EN/TXT/?uri=URISERV%3Aem0011.

Social Affairs and Inclusion (DG EMPL). Its work is assisted by a number of comitology committees: the Committee for the technical adaptation of legislation on the minimum safety and health requirements for improved medical treatment on board vessels; the Committee for the technical adaptation of legislation on the introduction of measures to encourage improvements in the safety and health of workers at work; the Committee for the Fund for European Aid to the Most Deprived; and the Committee on Employment and Social Innovation.

As to the Economic and Social Committee, two particular findings are of pertinence to our discussion. First, in relation to voting, in principle its decisions are adopted by a simple majority of the votes cast (the chairman of the meeting having a casting vote). Voting is by open ballot, but with a recorded vote where one-quarter of the members so request. Secondly, in relation to composition, the Committee consists of six sections, our focus being on that for Employment, Social Affairs and Citizenship (SOC), which deals inter alia with employment, working conditions, education and social policy. It is composed of 135 members and its work is coordinated by a bureau of twelve of its members. In addition to responding to requests by the European Parliament, the Council and the Commission for opinions, the SOC may issue opinions on its own initiative, which normally contain proposals for improvement in areas under its competence.

Finally, the Employment Committee (EMCO) enjoys an advisory status within the policy framework of the European Employment Strategy, as the principal advisor to the Ministers of Employment and Social Affairs in the Employment and Social Affairs Council in the area of employment. This body was established in 2000 by a Council Decision issued under Article 150 TFEU.[79] It is composed of two members of each Member State and the Commission who are senior officials or experts showing exceptional competence in the area of employment and labour market policy. Its main tasks are to monitor employment policies and advice the Commission and the Council on the employment guidelines under Article 148 TFEU. Within that context, EMCO meets regularly with the European social partners (employers and trade unions).[80]

Moving on to the context of social dialogue, Article 151 TFEU acknowledges the negotiations conducted by the social partners in the field of social policy as an EU objective. Prior to submitting proposals in the social field, the European Commission is required to consult representatives of management and labour. Pursuant to Article 155, that consultation may evolve into negotiation and eventually lead to the conclusion of agreements, to be implemented according to national procedures and practices or by means of a Council decision following a relevant proposal from the Commission. The European Parliament is simply informed of these steps. For the adoption of the decision by the Council, a qualified majority suffices, unless unanimity is required due to the special nature of the subject matter of the agreement. The European social

---

[79] Council Decision 2000/98/EC of 24 January 2000 establishing the Employment Committee [2000] OJ L29/21), which has been repealed by Council Decision (EU) 2015/772 of 11 May 2015 [2015] OJ L121/12–15.

[80] For a criticism of the role played by EMCO thus far see M Rhodes, 'Employment Policy Between Efficacy and Experimentation' in H Wallace, M A Pollack, and A R Young (eds), *Policy-Making in the European Union* (OUP 2005) 298.

dialogue may be conducted either in a bipartite context, involving employer and employee organizations, or in a tripartite context, engaging also EU bodies.[81] The key bipartite structure through which social dialogue takes place is the Social Dialogue Committee. Established in 1992, it usually meets three or four times a year to discuss employer/worker views on various topics, to adopt texts negotiated by both parties, and to plan future initiatives. It brings together the European cross-industry social partners and representatives of national member organizations, up to a maximum of sixty-six representatives, equally divided between the employers' and the workers' representative organizations.[82] Social dialogue can also take place in a sectoral basis,[83] where forty-three committees have produced in excess of 500 documents ranging from process-oriented texts, such as guidelines and codes of conduct, and joint opinions and tools, such as declarations and handbooks, with the aim of improving conditions and practices in a range of specific industrial sectors.[84]

F Legal Rules Governing Sector-specific Decision-making on Employment and Social Policy

A close look at the legal framework regulating activity in the fields of employment and social policy by the institutional actors, be they national or Union entities, reveals that decision-making is premised on discretionary choices. These, however, need to be made within a specific policy environment with predetermined and stated priorities.

In the area of employment, for instance, national and Union authorities are free to develop a coordinated strategy jointly for promoting a skilled workforce and creating labour markets which are responsive to economic change. Such initiatives must, however, be in line with, and contribute to, the achievement of the objectives set out in Article 3 TEU, including price stability, balanced economic growth, and the achievement of a competitive social market economy fostering full employment and social progress. Furthermore, national authorities are called upon to formulate their employment policies in line with the above coordinated strategy, while however respecting the general guidelines of the economic policies adopted through the procedure contemplated in Article 121(2) TFEU.[85] In addition, while employment remains within the competence of the Member States, they are expected to treat its promotion as a matter of Union concern, and to coordinate their action in accordance

---

[81] Agreements concluded after negotiations had been carried out within the framework of the social dialogue include those on harassment and violence at work of April 2007 and on inclusive labour markets of 25 March 2010 https://www.etuc.org/sites/www.etuc.org/files/20100325155413125_1.pdf. See also Communication from the Commission, 'The European Social Dialogue: A Force for Innovation and Change' (COM(2002) 341 final of 26 June 2002) http://eur-lex.europa.eu/legal-content/EN/TXT/?uri=celex:52002DC0341.

[82] EU Commission, 'Vademecum: Commission Support to EU Social Dialogue A Practical Guide for European Social Partner Organisations and their National Affiliate' (May 2014) 11.

[83] See EU Commission, 'On the Functioning and Potential of European Sectoral Social Dialogues' SEC(2010) 964 final.

[84] ibid.

[85] See Council Recommendation (EU) 2015/1184 of 14 July 2015 on broad guidelines for the economic policies of the Member States and of the European Union [2015] OJ L192/27) http://eur-lex.europa.eu/legal-content/EN/TXT/?uri=OJ:L:2015:192:TOC.

with the employment guidelines issued through the OMC under Article 148 TFEU. Limitations are also placed upon Union authorities. The Union is welcome to take action with a view to encouraging cooperation between Member States in order to achieve a high level of employment, but in doing so it is expected to respect the vertical allocation of competence between the national and Union levels. The European Parliament and the Council in particular, which are empowered to adopt incentive measures to foster cooperation between Member States through, inter alia, exchanges of information and best practices, may not proceed to the harmonization of the national laws and regulations in the field of employment.

In the area of social policy, national and Union authorities shall aim at the improvement of living and working conditions, the development of human resources and proper social protection; however, they must also pay due regard to social rights such as those enshrined in the 1961 European Social Charter and in the 1989 Community Charter of the Fundamental Social Rights of Workers. Additionally, the Union should promote the role of the social partners in a way which guarantees that their autonomy is respected. Furthermore, Union authorities are empowered to support and complement national activities, but only within clearly stated fields.[86] Even within those fields, the European Parliament and the Council may adopt measures with a view to encouraging cooperation between national authorities, while any harmonization of domestic law is, at least in theory, excluded. Directives may be enacted in specific fields, which, however, may only lay down minimum requirements for gradual implementation, while refraining from introducing obstacles to small and medium-sized enterprises.

From the preceding brief analysis, it becomes evident that employment and social policy are regulatory terrains where the national and Union authorities involved need to tread carefully in order to exercise their powers while remaining within the realm of discretionary action allocated to them. Any disrespect, be it wilful or not, of those demarcation lines could lead to *ex post* judicial or non-judicial action, an issue to be dealt with below (Section H).

G Sector-specific Forms of Acts and Measures

The forms of action within employment and social policy are adapted to the peculiarities of the field. They can be usefully divided into three categories. First, there exists hard law, i.e., legally binding instruments in the form, mainly, of Union directives. Secondly, the EU has introduced 'soft law' measures, which, in theory, produce no legally binding effect, and only seek to provide some policy guidance. Thirdly, contractual forms of act may also come into play. Those types of measure are assessed in turn.

As regards 'hard law', the EU is granted a law-making competence—and is sometimes subject to an obligation—to issue directives inter alia within a number of social policy fields, including social security and social protection of workers, protection of workers where the employment is terminated, working conditions, protection

---

[86] See in that respect Art 153 TFEU.

of workers' health and safety, equality between men and women, etc.[87] That power is, however, limited in a variety of ways: it does not extend to pay, the combating of social exclusion, the modernization of social protection systems, the right of association, the right to strike, and the right to impose lock-outs. The Union functions by way of 'shared competence' and it can introduce minimum requirements only for the gradual implementation by the Member States. Also, any Union legislative measures should not discourage the creation and development of small and medium-sized undertakings.

It is noted that directives in the above fields are in principle adopted by the European Parliament and the Council acting in accordance with the ordinary legislative procedure after consulting the Economic and Social Committee and the Committee of the Regions. By way of exception, the enactment of directives concerning social security and social protection of workers, protection of workers in cases where their employment contract is terminated, representation and collective defence of workers and employers, and conditions of employment for third-country nationals legally residing in EU territory, requires unanimity within the Council with consultation of the European Parliament and the aforementioned Committees. The Council is empowered to decide unanimously to apply the ordinary legislative procedure under certain conditions.

In addition to Union directives, the TFEU contemplates 'soft law' options mainly in the form of policy coordination and recommendations.[88] On the one hand, *policy coordination* in employment is contemplated in Article 145 TFEU and forms part of the Europe 2020 strategy, implemented and monitored annually in the context of the European Semester. It is worth noting that two of the five main targets set to itself as part of 2020 objectives are the reduction by at least 20 million of the number of people in, or at risk of, poverty and social exclusion, and an employment rate of 75 per cent for people between 20 and 64 years of age. Policy coordination is further strengthened through the adoption of employment guidelines under Article 148 TFEU. Those

---

[87] See eg Council Directive 91/533/EEC of 14 October 1991 on an employer's obligation to inform employees of the conditions applicable to the contract or employment relationship [1991] OJ L288/32–35; Council Directive 94/33/EC of 22 June 1994 on the protection of young people at work [1994] OJ L216/12–20; Directive 2008/104/EC of the European Parliament and of the Council of 19 November 2008 on temporary agency work [2008] OJ L327/9–14; Council Directive 97/81/EC of 15 December 1997 concerning the Framework Agreement on part-time work concluded by UNICE, CEEP and the ETUC—Annex: Framework agreement on part-time work [1998] OJ L014/9–14); Council Directive 2000/43/EC of 29 June 2000 implementing the principle of equal treatment between persons irrespective of racial or ethnic origin [2000] OJ L180/22–26; Council Directive 2000/78/EC of 27 November 2000 establishing a general framework for equal treatment in employment and occupation [2000] OJ L303/16–22); Directive 2003/88/EC of the European Parliament and of the Council of 4 November 2003 concerning certain aspects of the organisation of working time [2003] OJ L299/9–19; Directive 2002/14/EC of the European Parliament and of the Council of 11 March 2002 establishing a general framework for informing and consulting employees in the European Community—Joint declaration of the European Parliament, the Council and the Commission on employee representation [2002] OJ L80/29–34; and Directive 2008/94/EC of the European Parliament and of the Council of 22 October 2008 on the protection of employees in the event of the insolvency of their employer [2008] OJ L283/36–42.

[88] Other forms of soft regulation also exist, such as codes of conduct and declarations, which are not however dealt here, as preference is given to the most widely used tools. For an extensive coverage of the soft law options, see the Commission's database of social dialogue texts http://ec.europa.eu/social/main.jsp?catId=521&langId=en.

guidelines put forward common priorities and targets for the national authorities to implement in their domestic employment policies. The current guidelines were issued in October 2015 and focus on four principal areas:[89] boosting demand for labour, mainly through job creation, less labour taxation and wage-setting mechanisms; enhancing labour supply, skills, and competences, through investment in all education and training systems and reduction of youth unemployment; improved functioning of labour markets, through the provision of tailored services to support jobseekers and the promotion of workers' mobility to exploit the potential of the European labour market; and fostering social inclusion, combatting poverty, and promoting equal opportunity, through the modernization of the national social protection systems, investment in human capital, and the design of domestic pension systems in a manner that ensures their sustainability and adequacy.

Together with other measures, *recommendations* are also a useful tool in the domain under review. It can be recalled that pursuant to Article 288 TFEU they lack binding force, they can however affect policy formulation and can be used by the Union judiciary as interpretative aids for legally binding instruments.[90] Article 153 TFEU specifies the exact fields where recommendations may be issued. Thus far, the Union has made generous use of that instrument, as is evident in the area of social protection, and the work environment and access to work. As regards social protection, examples include: Council recommendation of 31 March 1992 on child care; Council Recommendation of 24 June 1992 on common criteria concerning sufficient resources and social assistance in social protection systems; Council Recommendation of 27 July 1992 on the convergence of social protection objectives and policies; Commission Recommendation of 20 February 2013 Investing in children: breaking the cycle of disadvantage; and Council Recommendation of 9 December 2013 on effective Roma integration measures in the Member States.[91] As concerns the work environment and access to work, the Union has also been active through the adoption of, for example: Commission Recommendation of 3 October 2008 on the active inclusion of people excluded from the labour market; Council Recommendation of 22 April 2013 on establishing a Youth Guarantee; and Council recommendation of 15 February 2016 on the integration of the long-term unemployed into the labour market.[92] The contribution of those initiatives should not be disregarded simply because of their 'soft law'

---

[89] Council Decision (EU) 2015/1848 of 5 October 2015 on guidelines for the employment policies of the Member States for 2015 [2015] OJ L268/28–32 http://eur-lex.europa.eu/legal-content/EN/TXT/?uri=OJ%3AJOL_2015_268_R_0005.

[90] See eg Case C-322/88 *Salvatore Grimaldi v Fonds des maladies professionnelles* ECLI:EU:C:1989:646, where the effects of a recommendation in the context of occupational diseases are discussed.

[91] 92/241/EEC: Council recommendation of 31 March 1992 on child care [1992] OJ L12316–18; 92/441/EEC: Council Recommendation of 24 June 1992 on common criteria concerning sufficient resources and social assistance in social protection systems [1992] OJ L245/46–48; 92/442/EEC: Council Recommendation of 27 July 1992 on the convergence of social protection objectives and policies [1992] OJ L245/49–52; 2013/112/EU: Commission Recommendation of 20 February 2013 Investing in children: breaking the cycle of disadvantage [2013] OJ L59/5–16); Council Recommendation of 9 December 2013 on effective Roma integration measures in the Member States [2013] OJ C378/1–7.

[92] Commission Recommendation of 3 October 2008 on the active inclusion of people excluded from the labour market [2008] OJ L307/11–14; Council Recommendation of 22 April 2013 on establishing a Youth Guarantee [2013] OJ C120/1–6; and Council recommendation of 15 February 2016 on the integration of the long-term unemployed into the labour market [2016] OJ C67/1–5).

nature. They set the policy tone within the Union space, pave the way for further consensus, and gradually render national authorities more receptive to enactment of legally binding texts.

A particularly vivid example of how seemingly soft instruments can result in forceful and often radical policy and regulatory changes at a national level is provided by the numerous successive attempts by the Commission and the Council to promote the processes of decentralization of collective bargaining mechanisms at a national level, especially in the wake of the 2009/2010 economic crisis.[93] The Commission itself has recently acknowledged that: 'A number of country-specific recommendations addressed certain aspects of national wage-setting systems and therefore … Decentralisation of collective bargaining was seen as a measure to better align wages with productivity at local and firm level'.[94] It also acknowledged that, for Member States in receipt of financial assistance programmes, 'there was external pressure leading governments to act in response to recommendations from the Commission, the European Council and other international organisations'.[95] Such pressure were, apparently, by and large successful as '[c]ollective bargaining structures were further decentralized and collective bargaining coverage fell in many countries—in some southern European countries to unprecedented levels'.[96] It is worth noting that these pressures are ongoing, as best exemplified by the 2015 Council Recommendations to France, lamenting the fact that '[r]ecent reforms have created only limited scope for employers to depart from branch level agreements through company-level agreements. This limits companies' ability to modulate the workforce according to their needs'.[97]

In addition to the above types of action, the Social Dialogue acts as a source of *contractual* regulation. As previously noted, under Article 155 TFEU the social partners may enter into labour agreements, which normally regulate the symbiosis between the signatories and the employment relationships in the domains they cover. Customarily an implementation report follows, which seeks to establish whether the agreement was actually implemented in the national context. The implementation can be made either according to the national industrial specificities or by a Council decision. Agreements reached in the context of the Social Dialogue include: the framework agreement on telework of July 2002; the agreement on the European licence for drivers carrying out a cross-border interoperability service of January 2004; the European agreement on the implementation of the European hairdressing certificates of June 2009; and the agreement regarding the minimum requirements for standard player contracts in the professional football sector in the European Union and in the rest of the UEFA territory of April 2012.[98] An example of an Article 155 agreement turned into Union

---

[93] See I Schömann and S Clauwaert, *The Crisis and National Labour Law Reforms: A Mapping Exercise* (ETUI 2012); Ewing (n 8) 76.

[94] European Commission, 'Industrial Relations in Europe 2014' (2015) 9.   [95] ibid 11.

[96] ibid 10–11.

[97] Council Recommendation of 14 July 2015 on the 2015 National Reform Programme of France and delivering a Council opinion on the 2015 Stability Programme of France (2015/C 272/14).

[98] The relevant texts can be found at the Commission's database at http://ec.europa.eu/social/main.jsp?catId=521&langId=en. For an overview of sectoral activities see European Commission, 'European Sectoral Social Dialogue Recent developments 2010 edition' (2010).

legislation is Council Directive 1999/63 of 21 June 1999 concerning the organisation of working time of seafarers.[99]

H Supervision and Control of, and within, the Employment and Social Policy Sector

The activity within the realm of employment and social policy is predominately reviewed in an *ex post* manner by means of 'hard law' litigation (judicial review) and 'soft law' remedies (extra-judicial review). The role of the European Parliament as a means of political supervision is also briefly considered.

The judicial option involves scrutiny by the CJEU, triggered normally by a direct action for annulment against the problematic measure under Article 263 TFEU. The *UEAPME* case provides a fitting example in that context.[100] The factual setting of the case is simple. UEAPME (see Section E) complained that Council Directive 96/34/EC of 3 June 1996 on the framework agreement on parental leave had turned into hard law the relevant framework agreement, which has been however negotiated without their participation. The action was eventually declared inadmissible, but the discussion on the representativeness of the signatories to the agreement is of particular interest. The Union judiciary held that, while it is for the management and labour concerned, alone, to initiate and take charge of the negotiations, once the Commission takes control of the procedure and decides whether it is appropriate to submit a legislative proposal to the Council, the Union principles governing action in the field of social policy must be respected. One of the basic principles in that domain is adequate representativeness of the signatory parties, which ensures balanced consideration of the various interests involved. With that given, it is incumbent upon both the Commission and the Council to ascertain whether, having regard to the content of the agreement at issue, the signatories, taken together, are sufficiently representative. In a case where the requisite degree of representativeness is absent, the Commission and the Council must refuse to endow the signed agreement with legal force at Union level. That safeguard is particularly important in the context of agreements arrived at under Article 155 TFEU as, pursuant to that provision, the European Parliament is simply informed and therefore popular participation and/or representation must be ensured by other means.

The extra-judicial option (in effect a form of political supervision) involves investigation by the European Ombudsman under Articles 20(2) and 228 TFEU, and Article 43 of the EU Charter of Fundamental Rights into an instance of maladministration in the Union activity within the domain of employment and social policy.[101] Complaints

---

[99] Council Directive 1999/63 of 21 June 1999 concerning the Agreement on the organisation of working time of seafarers concluded by the European Community Shipowners' Association (ECSA) and the Federation of Transport Workers' Unions in the European Union (FST) [1999] OJ L167/33–37.

[100] Case T-135/96 *Union Européenne de l'artisanat et des petites et moyennes entreprises (UEAPME) v Council of the European Union* ECLI:EU:T:1998:128. The judgment retains its significance and relevance to that day, as it is the only one discussing a challenge of the application of Art 155 TFEU.

[101] The academic literature on the European Ombudsman is growing. See inter alia Craig, *EU Administrative Law* (n 17) ch 24, and T Hervey, J Kenner, S Peers, and A Ward (eds), *The EU Charter of Fundamental Rights: A Commentary* (Nomos 2014) comment on Art 43.

can therefore be launched with the Ombudsman challenging directly the administrative behaviour of Union authorities under Titles IX and X, Part Three TFEU. However, an even more interesting aspect of the extra-judicial tool is its utility as an indirect path to challenge national administrative activity and exert pressure on national administrations to implement employment and social policy measures fully and promptly. It is recalled that European Commission is empowered, acting as the 'guardian of the Treaties', to commence infringement proceedings against Member States allegedly in infringement of their EU commitment.[102] The European Ombudsman is in turn institutionally designed to assess the legality and propriety of the administrative behaviour of the Union institutions, bodies, offices, or agencies. The combined reading of the above findings yields an important conclusion: while the European Ombudsman is institutionally barred from directly examining national measures falling with the field of employment and social policy, this official can indirectly assess their compatibility with the Union *acquis* by virtue of their jurisdiction over the Commission.[103] Case 53/97/JMA is instructive in that regard.[104] The complainant had contacted the European Commission claiming that the Italian authorities had failed to transpose Council Directive 80/987/EEC on the protection of employees in the event of the insolvency of their employer[105] correctly, and requesting that infringement proceedings be commenced before the Union court. The Commission considered that no infringement of then EC law had occurred and therefore refused further involvement in the case. The complainant then turned to the European Ombudsman alleging that the Commission had failed to discharge its duties as 'guardian'. The Ombudsman's inquiry revealed that the Commission had been right to absolve the Italian authorities of any blame, as the temporal scope of application of the Union measure in question did not cover the case of the complainant.

In addition to the Luxembourg court and the European Ombudsman, the European Parliament could potentially provide an additional channel of political supervision over the OMC process. However, the role of the European Parliament therein is marginal, with the consequential implication being that its supervisory powers are inherently limited. It should be recalled that under Article 148 TFEU the European Parliament is simply consulted on the relevant report by the Commission along with the Economic and Social Committee, the Committee of the Regions, and the Employment Committee. In broader terms, it should be acknowledged that the OMC is a textbook example of cooperative federalism and, as such, relies heavily on, and

---

[102] Art 258 TFEU.

[103] For a detailed coverage of the Ombudsman's record in the field of Art 258 TFEU complaints see A Tsadiras, 'Guarding the Guardian: Article 258 TFEU complaints' before the European Ombudsman' (2015) 81 *International Review of Administrative Sciences* 621.

[104] Decision of the European Ombudsman on complaint 53/97/JMA against the European Commission, 16 April 1999 http://www.ombudsman.europa.eu/cases/decision.faces/en/812/html.bookmark. See also Decision of the European Ombudsman on complaint 3453/2005/GG against the European Commission, 14 September 2007, concerning Germany's alleged failure to comply with Directive 93/104/EC (Working Time Directive) http://www.ombudsman.europa.eu/cases/summary.faces/en/3619/html.bookmark.

[105] Council Directive 80/987/EEC of 20 October 1980 on the approximation of the laws of the Member States relating to the protection of employees in the event of the insolvency of their employer [1980] OJ L283/23.

empowers, the executive branches on both national and supranational levels, at the expense of their legislative counterparts. That has been pointed out by the European Parliament itself in a number of resolutions. For instance, in its 2003 resolution on the application of the Open Method of Coordination, the European Parliament considered that, while the OMC should be extended to cover additional fields, such as culture and sport, the role of Members of the European Parliament in the procedure must be clarified and enhanced so that the process gains democratic legitimacy.[106] Since the OMC does not result in binding EU legislation in which the European Parliament could participates or which could be reviewed by the CJEU, that inadequate parliamentary participation in, and judicial review of, the OMC process were subsequently lamented in the 2007 resolution on the use of soft law, where the OMC was even termed 'legally dubious'.[107] In their 2010 resolution on economic governance, the European parliamentarians went even further, suggesting that the reliance on OMC in the field of economic policy should be replaced by a broader use of binding measures.[108]

I Conclusion

Employment and social policy are thematic fields where intense interaction exists amongst a variety of institutional players, both public and private, at national and Union level. This naturally gives rise to a multitude of doctrinal and empirical questions pertaining to the manner in which the smooth and productive institutional coexistence of numerous players will be ensured in an area of policy and law necessitating delicate balancing of divergent, and often conflicting, interests. One aspect of that institutional cohabitation, as evidenced by the preceding analysis, is the presence of social partners and the duality of their role as stakeholders under Article 154 TFEU and co-legislators under Article 155. Challenges persist in relation to both of those capacities. As regards consultation, it is not entirely settled whether the social partners' involvement has made thus far any real and noticeable contribution when tested against the totality of the political and legislative progress in the field under investigation. This is particularly so in respect of their role in the context of the OMC, and more markedly in the context of economic governance. As concerns European level agreements, it is evident from a case like *UEAPME*, adumbrated above, that the Union's decision to convert an Article 155 agreement into a binding Union legal instrument can be challenged before the Union court by means of an action for annulment under Article 263. What remains to be seen is how the Union judiciary would react to an action brought by the social partners challenging the Commission's refusal to propose to the Council the embodiment of a collective agreement in an instrument with the force of a legal act, specifically a directive. In case such an action were admissible, it would be interesting to see not only the standard of judicial review, but also its intensity. Similar concerns do arise, at least in principle, in respect of the, otherwise extremely vital, social dialogue on this sectoral level.

[106] See http://www.europarl.europa.eu/sides/getDoc.do?type=TA&language=EN&reference=P5-TA-2003-268.
[107] See http://www.europarl.europa.eu/sides/getDoc.do?type=TA&language=EN&reference=P6-TA-2007-366.
[108] See http://www.europarl.europa.eu/sides/getDoc.do?type=TA&language=EN&reference=P7-TA-2010-224.

One of the most interesting and challenging testing grounds for the good administration of Social Europe has arguably emerged in the context of those OMC processes that accompany the Europe 2020 growth strategy,[109] as implemented through the European Semester,[110] and, perhaps more vividly, in the context of the economic adjustment programmes assisting a number of Member States that have signed specific Memoranda of Understanding (MoUs) with the Commission, the European Central Bank, and the IMF. In these contexts, it has been lamented by several academic authors that a number of the sector-specific legal principles applying to the regulation of Social Europe, and in particular the principles seeking to guarantee the participation of social partners in decision-making processes pertaining to Europe's economic and social governance, have been side-lined, or kept out altogether. As noted by Sciarra: '[t]here is enough evidence to prove that the European Semester does not interact in a constructive way with social dialogue and in some cases puts severe limits to it'.[111] It is in the same context, and in particular by reference to actions taken by EU institutions and Member States on the basis of MoUs, that even more troubling concerns have been raised about the applicability of fundamental rights and principles. As noted by Hinarejos, '[w]hile it is clear, then, that MoUs have to comply with EU measures on economic policy coordination, it is less clear whether they have to comply with the rest of EU law and, in particular, the Charter of Fundamental Rights'.[112] These concerns have been corroborated by several decisions of the CJEU, most notably by the Court's decision in *Pringle*. The more recent judgment in *Ledra Advertising*,[113] suggests that EU institutions participating in these processes may not be as immune to these important principles of EU constitutional and administrative law as previously thought, with the Commission, in particular, being 'required to observe compliance with commitments across EU law, not simply economic policy coordination, in its MoU roles'.[114] Undoubtedly, interesting developments lie ahead in this context, as in others.

---

[109] European Council, Conclusions, EUCO 13/10 (17 June 2010). Cf European Commission, 'Results of the public consultation on the Europe 2020 strategy for smart, sustainable and inclusive growth', COM(2015) 100 final.

[110] Art 2-a of Regulation (EU) No 1175/2011 of the European Parliament and of the Council of 16 November 2011 amending Council Regulation (EC) No 1466/97 on the strengthening of the surveillance of budgetary positions and the surveillance and coordination of economic policies. See European Parliament, 'An Assessment of the European Semester' (2010), IP/A/ECON/ST/2010-24. See also C Barnard, 'The Financial Crisis and the Euro Plus Pact' (n 45) 98.

[111] S Sciarra, 'Social law in the wake of the crisis', WP CSDLE 'Massimo D'Antona'.INT: 108/2014 11.

[112] A Hinarejos, *The Euro Area Crisis in Constitutional Perspective* (OUP 2015) 133.

[113] Case C-8/15 P *Ledra Advertising v Commission and ECB* (n 76).

[114] For a painstakingly comprehensive and insightful analysis of the 'liminal legality' of the Memoranda of Understanding see C Kilpatrick, 'The EU and its sovereign debt programmes: the challenges of liminal legality' (2018) 70 *Current Legal Problems* (forthcoming).

PART VI

COMPETITION AND REGULATION

17

Control of State Aid: A policy specific area of EU administrative law

Claire Micheau

A Introduction

The regulatory framework of State aid is central to the review of the use of public resources in the European Union. Article 107 of the Treaty on the Functioning of the European Union (TFEU) defines State aid as any aid which may distort competition and affect trade between Member States, by favouring some undertakings or the production of certain goods. The Treaty provisions entrust the Commission with the prevention of aid granted by Member States which could unduly distort competition in the internal market. When applying the Treaty provisions, the Commission not only ensures that the Member States do not provide aid limiting competition and tilting a level playing field, but also defines growth-oriented approaches and shapes policy instruments within the context of subsidization.

It is against this economic and legal backdrop that the administrative law of control over national aid has been conceived. At this preliminary point of the chapter, it is important to stress two main characteristic features of the administrative governance of State aid. The first one is the central role played by the European Commission. As will be addressed here, the Commission plays a key role in the review of State aid, enforcement proceedings, policy rule-making, and the adoption of the administrative decisions. The second feature is mirrored in the interplay between the Commission and the Member States: State aid rules govern the relationship between the Commission and the Member States, with private entities confined to the margins of the procedure. In contrast with the other areas of competition law regulating the economic activities between such private entities, State aid law focuses on the interventions by the Member States. In this regard, State aid law constitutes a specific area of EU administrative law since it does not directly govern the relationship between the administration of the Union (e.g., the Commission or national administrations implementing EU law) and its constituents citizens and businesses (i.e., the private entities) within the context of subsidization; rather, it relates virtually wholly to the relationship between the EU administration and the Member States, while leaving the onus on the Member States to enforce the associated decisions measures on the private entities affected, essentially within the national legal and administrative framework.

It is in the light of these considerations that the chapter presents the main aspects of State aid law from an administrative point of view. By doing so, this chapter outlines the administrative powers entrusted to the Commission, the role played by the Member States, the underlying principle of sincere cooperation which governs the entire State aid review procedure, the nature and legal effects of the administrative acts, and the judicial supervision of the national aid field.

B Administrative Tasks within the National Aid Sector

The administrative tasks which fall to the Commission can be divided into three major phases: the notification, the preliminary examination, and the formal investigation. These tasks incumbent upon the Commission find their source in the TFEU, amply expanded by the Court's case law. At the end of the 1990s, the Commission proposed the Procedural Regulation which incorporated and developed the rules which had thus far emerged from the Court's jurisprudence. It is further noteworthy that on the top of those key tasks, the Commission also handles others, including monitoring, recovery of illegal and incompatible national aid—this task being shared with the Member States— and policy-setting.

The first phase in the administration of State aid law consists in meeting the obligation of the notification of the aid. EU State aid law starts from the principle that any new aid has to be notified to the Commission. It is 'therefore' a system of ex ante authorization which prevails under EU law: as expressly provided for in Article 108 TFEU, 'the Commission shall be informed, in sufficient time to enable it to submit its comments, of any plans to grant or alter aid'; the Member State cannot grant the aid until the Commission has adopted a decision.

During the second phase, which encompasses the preliminary examination, the Commission forms a prima facie opinion on the compatibility of the aid with the internal market. At the end of that preliminary examination, three types of decisions can be adopted by the Commission: the measure does not constitute an aid; it is an aid which is compatible with the internal market; or it is an aid which raises doubts.[1]

If the Commission has doubts, it then initiates the formal investigation procedure, inviting the Member State and the interested parties involved to present their comments. At the end of the formal investigation, the Commission takes a position on the compatibility of the intended aid with the goals of the internal market.[2] In this context, the Commission can opt for three types of decisions to close the formal investigation: (i) the aid is compatible (i.e., a positive decision);[3] (ii) the aid may be regarded as compatible subject to obligations to enable compliance with the decision (i.e., conditional decision);[4] or (iii) the aid is not compatible, and should, therefore, not be put into effect (i.e., negative decision).[5]

---

[1] Art 4 of Council Regulation (EU) 2015/1589 of 13 July 2015 laying down detailed rules for the application of Article 108 of the Treaty on the Functioning of the European Union [2015] OJ L248/9 (former Council Regulation No 659/1999 of 22 March 1999 laying down of the EC Treaty [1999] OJ L83/1 amended by Council Regulation (EU) No 734/2013 of 22 July 2013 [2013] OJ L204/15) (Procedural Regulation).

[2] With regard to the time line of the procedure, the Commission is expected to adopt a decision within a period of 18 months from the opening of the procedure. This period can be extended, based on a common agreement between the Member State and the Commission (Art 7(6) Procedural Regulation (n 1)).

[3] Art 9(3) Procedural Regulation (n 1).   [4] ibid Art 9(4).   [5] ibid Art 9(5).

Alongside the notification procedure and its associated tasks, there are further administrative tasks for which the onus is on the Commission when the aid is unlawful, that is, when the aid has been granted without being notified.[6] The Commission must examine complaints submitted by interested parties on alleged unlawful aid. It can also examine on its own initiative any information, from whatever source.[7] These so-called *ex officio* investigations can be triggered by a large set of different sources, such as press releases, reports from a national court of auditors, or parliamentary questions.[8] According to Article 15 Procedural Regulation, at the end of the procedure the Commission can adopt three different types of decisions: (i) the measure is not an aid; (ii) the measure is an aid compatible with the internal market; or (iii) the measure is an aid that may be incompatible. In the last case, the Commission then launches the formal investigation procedure, which gives rise to a final decision.[9]

State aid proceedings are based on cooperation between the Commission and the Member State involved. This requires that the Member State provide the information requested by the Commission within the period prescribed. Since the 2013 amendment of the Procedural Regulation,[10] the powers of the Commission have been extended. The Commission can launch investigations into sectors of the economy or into aid instruments. To this end, it can require information from other sources, such as another Member State, an undertaking, or an association of undertakings in order to obtain all market information necessary to complete the examination of the measure.[11] Failure to provide information may lead to fines and periodic penalty payments imposed on such undertakings or associations.

In addition to notified aid and unlawful aid, the Commission also has administrative powers with regard to existing aid schemes. Existing aid schemes encompass mainly all aid in existence prior to the entry into force of the Treaty, and aid which has already been authorized by the Commission.[12] Existing aid schemes are subject to an *a posteriori* review. The onus is on the Commission to keep these schemes under observation. To this end, the Commission works in cooperation with the Member States, and can suggest recommendations to ensure that the existing aid schemes remain compatible with the internal market. If the Member State fails to take all appropriate measures to comply with the recommendations, the Commission initiates the preliminary examination procedure.[13]

Furthermore, the Commission has powers with regard to the recovery of aid. EU law subscribes to the principle that any aid which is unlawful and incompatible with

---

[6] ibid Art 1(f) defines unlawful aid as 'new aid put into effect in contravention of Art 108(3) (ex-Art 93(3)) of the Treaty)'.

[7] ibid Art 12(1).

[8] See eg Commission Decision of 12 July 2000 on the state aid granted by France to Scott Paper SA Kimberly-Clark, C38/1998 [2002] OJ L12/1.

[9] Before adopting a final decision, the Commission can take a decision of injunction to suspend or to recover the unlawful aid provisionally (Art 13 Procedural Regulation (n 1)).

[10] Council Regulation No 733/2013 of 22 July 2013 amending Regulation (EC) No 994/98 on the application of Articles 92 and 93 of the Treaty establishing the European Community to certain categories of horizontal state aid [2013] OJ L204/11.

[11] Art 7a Procedural Regulation (n 1).   [12] ibid Art 1(b).

[13] For further details on this procedure see Arts 21, 22, and 23 Procedural Regulation (n 1).

the internal market should be recovered in order to restore the previously existing situation and, thereby, to avoid distortion of competition.[14] The recovery of the aid is ordered by the Commission. There are, however, three major exceptions. First, the powers of the Commission to recover aid are subject to a limitation period of ten years.[15] This exception is justified for reasons of legal certainty. Secondly, the recovery is not contrary to a general principle of law.[16] Thirdly, the Court has consistently recognized, as a justification for not enforcing the decision, the existence of exceptional circumstances that would make it absolutely impossible for the Member State to execute the decision properly.[17] Apart from situations where these three exceptions apply, the Commission's decision needs to be implemented. Under Article 288 TFEU, decisions are binding in their entirety upon those to whom they are addressed. Therefore, whilst the Commission orders the recovery of the unlawful aid in its decision, it is the Member State which in fact implements the recovery decision. As pointed out in the Court's case law and restated in the 2007 Recovery Notice, the 'Commission's recovery decision imposes a recovery obligation upon the Member State concerned'.[18] The recovery should take place with no delay in compliance with national procedures,[19] provided the national procedures ensure the effective enforcement of the decision adopted by the Commission.[20] In that respect, the measures taken by the Member State must have a real effect on the recovery of the aid.[21] Should the Member State, however, fail to comply with its recovery obligation within the prescribed time limit, the Commission initiates infringement proceedings by referring the matter directly to the Court according to Article 108(2). It is also noteworthy that the Commission has further powers with regard to setting off illegal aid with approved aid: according to the *Deggendorf* principle,[22] the Commission can request the Member State to suspend the payment of any new aid until the recipient has reimbursed the unlawful and incompatible aid subject to a recovery decision.[23]

Alongside the administrative tasks of the Commission, it is important to note that the Council can also play a role in national aid review. Pursuant to Article 108(2), the Council can decide on the compatibility of the aid. Accordingly, at the request on the

---

[14] Case 70/72 *Commission of the European Communities v Federal Republic of Germany* [1973] ECR 813, paras 12–13; Case 310/85 *Deufil GmbH & Co KG v Commission of the European Communities* [1987] ECR 901, para 24; Case C-305/89 *Italian Republic v Commission of the European Communities* [1991] ECR I-1603, para 41; Case C-183/91 *Commission of the European Communities v Hellenic Republic* [1993] ECR I-3131, para 16.

[15] Art 17 Procedural Regulation (n 1).   [16] ibid Art 16(1).

[17] Commission Notice, 'Towards an effective implementation of Commission decisions ordering Member States to recover unlawful and incompatible state aid' [2007] OJ C272/5, paras 18–20 (Recovery Notice). See also for jurisprudential examples Case 52/84 *Commission of the European Communities v Kingdom of Belgium* [1986] ECR 89, para 14; Case C-499/99 *Commission of the European Communities v Kingdom of Spain* [2002] ECR I-6031, para 21; Case C-404/00 *Commission of the European Communities v Kingdom of Spain* [2003] ECR I-6695, para 45.

[18] Recovery Notice (n 17) para 31.

[19] For further development on the national administrative procedures see section J.

[20] Art 16(3) Procedural Regulation (n 1).

[21] Case C-415/03 *Commission of the European Communities v Hellenic Republic* [2005] ECR I-3875, para 35.

[22] Joined Cases T-244/93 and T-486/93 *TWD Textilwerke Deggendorf GmbH v Commission of the European Communities* [1995] ECR II-2265.

[23] For further development see Recovery Notice (n 17), paras 75–78.

Member State, the decision can be made by unanimous vote. Should the Commission have already initiated the procedure, this procedure remains pending until the Council adopts a decision. The Commission, however, can make its determination if the Council has failed to take a position within three months. Such a procedure, which is subject to political considerations, remains derogatory and, as such, it can be used only under 'exceptional circumstances'.[24] In practice, it has been initiated in a very limited number of cases.[25]

C Sources of Law in State Aid Administration

The Union legal framework for controlling national aid has its roots in the TFEU. Article 107 TFEU lays down the substantial rules applicable to State aid, including its definition and provisions on the compatibility with the internal market. In addition, Article 108 deals with the procedural framework, sketching the broad outlines of the administrative procedure by setting out the role of the Commission and that of the Council with regard to notified aid, unlawful aid, and existing aid schemes. Article 109, furthermore, focuses on the regulatory process of the application of Articles 107 and 108 TFEU.[26]

It is important to keep in mind that the TFEU does not provide further details on the substantial or procedural details on the State aid regime. In that respect, the Treaty provisions should be regarded just as the legal backdrop for national aid review since it provides only the major elements with no further precision, thereby leaving considerable discretion as to the exact formulation of State aid rules and their application. Interestingly, the wording of Articles 107–109 has not been substantially amended over the last sixty years, despite the ever-growing role of national aid issues in the Union and, as a corollary, the significant development of the applicable secondary law. It is in this context that the role played by the Court of Justice should be noted. While interpreting and developing the Treaty provisions, the Court's case law has played such a fundamental role that indeed this institution can be regarded as the architect of the current legal framework governing national aid.[27]

Alongside the driving force of the Court's jurisprudence as a source of State aid law, the field has been significantly developed by the Commission. In this regard, the Procedural Regulation[28] can be regarded as the most important source of secondary EU law. This regulation constitutes the key legal source of the administrative law

---

[24] Art 108(2) TFEU.

[25] See eg the *Belgian Coordination Centres* case, Council Decision of 16 July 2003 on the granting of aid by the Belgian Government to certain coordination centres established in Belgium, 2003/531/EC [2003] OJ L184/1. This case is of particular interest since it provides further interpretation on the notion of 'exceptional circumstances'; see Case C-110/02 *Commission of the European Communities v Council of the European Union* [2004] ECR I-6333; Case C-399/03 *Commission of the European Communities v Council of the European Union* [2006] ECR II-2265.

[26] Alongside these main provisions, it should be noted that the Treaty also provides state aid rules within the context of transport (Art 93 TFEU) and services of general economic interests (Art 106(2) TFEU).

[27] For further development on the prevalent role of the Court in State aid judicial review see section K.

[28] Council Regulation No 659/1999 of 22 March 1999 laying down detailed rules for the application of Article 93 (now Article 88) of the EC Treaty [1999] OJ L83/1, amended by Council Regulation (EU) No 734/2013 of 22 July 2013 [2013] OJ L204/15.

governing national aid.[29] It sets out the definition of the most significant notions (e.g. existing aid, new aid, aid scheme, individual aid, and unlawful aid) and provides clear guidance on the four major procedures applicable to notified aid, unlawful aid, misuse of aid, and existing aid schemes. It also deals with the rights of interested parties and the monitoring powers of the Commission (including the submission of the annual report and the rights to carried out on-site inspections). Interestingly, the Procedural Regulation has been recently amended[30] within a vast reform of the regime on national aid—the State Aid Modernisation initiative—to adapt the rules to the evolution of the market in the aftermath of the economic and financial crisis.[31] In this context, the amendments of the Procedural Regulation focus, among other things, on complaint-handling, and introduce market information tools and sector inquiries.

Another noteworthy instrument of secondary legislation in State aid law is the General Block Exemption Regulation,[32] adopted on the basis of Article 109 TFEU. This allows Member States to grant aid in certain areas, without having to notify them to the Commission for prior authorization, provided that certain predetermined conditions are satisfied. The underlying approach is that certain categories of aid are less likely to result in undue distortions of competition. This regulation directly—positively—impacts on the administrative burden of the Member States and the Commission, which thereby focus on the review of aid measures which are most likely to affect competition.

In addition, the legal framework applicable to national aid relies on a large range of instruments which aim to clarify and develop the rules, the vast majority being soft law.[33] To a certain extent, these instruments represent the codification of the Commission's practice and the Court's case law. They can be sector-based, such as coal,[34] steel,[35] postal services,[36] shipbuilding,[37] electricity,[38] or public service broadcasting.[39] They can also be horizontal, such as aid for research and development,[40]

---

[29] For further development on the contribution of the Procedural Regulation to State aid rules see A Sinnaeve, P J Slot, 'The New Regulation on State Aid Procedures' (1999) 36 *Common Market Law Review* 1153.

[30] Council Regulation (EU) No 734/2013 of 22 July 2013 amending Regulation (EC) No 659/1999 laying down detailed rules for the application of Article 93 EC [2013] OJ L204/15.

[31] Communication from the Commission to the European Parliament, the Council, the European Economic and Social Committee and the Committee of the Regions, *EU State Aid Modernisation* (SAM), COM/2012/0209 final.

[32] Commission Regulation (EU) No 651/2014 of 17 June 2014 declaring certain categories of aid compatible with the internal market in application of Articles 107 and 108 of the Treaty (Text with EEA relevance) [2014] OJ L187/1.

[33] For further development on the use of soft law within the context of State aid see section H.

[34] Council Regulation (EC) No 1407/2002 of 23 July 2002 on State aid to the coal industry [2002] OJ L205/1.

[35] Commission Communication, Rescue and restructuring aid and closure aid for the steel sector [2002] OJ C70/21.

[36] Commission Notice on the application of the competition rules to the postal sector and on the assessment of certain State measures relating to postal services [1998] OJ C39/2.

[37] Framework on State aid to shipbuilding [2203] OJ C317/11.

[38] Commission Communication relating to the methodology for analysing State aid linked to stranded costs, adopted on 26 July 2001, Commission letter SG (2001) D/290869.

[39] Commission Communication on the application of State aid rules to public service broadcasting [2001] OJ C320/5.

[40] Community Framework for State aid for research and development and innovation [2006] OJ C323/1.

environment,[41] or restructuring plans for undertakings and risk capital.[42] In addition, they can focus on the procedure, such as the Implementing Regulation,[43] the afore-mentioned Recovery Notice,[44] the Commission Notice on a Simplified Procedure,[45] or Code of Best Practice of State Aid.[46] It follows that there is an intense regulatory framework which plays a key role to provide guidance to the Member States and the economic stakeholders in the market. This framework is frequently reviewed and up-dated, in particular in the context of the earlier reform in the 2005–2009 State Aid Action Plan, and the most recent one of the 2012 State Aid Modernisation initiative, in order to rationalize the rules and ensure that rules on national aid remains tools adapted to meet the contemporary risks of market failure.

D Underlying Sector-specific Principles in State Aid Administration

In contrast with other areas of EU administrative law, State aid law does not rely on ex-clusive, sector-specific legal principles. This does not mean, however, that the general principles of Union law do not come into play in the administrative law and procedure governing national aid. For instance, the principle of good administration remains key during the proceedings. Another example is the compliance with the principle of transparency and legal certainty during the regulatory and decision-making pro-cess.[47] The discussion here does not aim, however, to provide an exhaustive catalogue of the application of the general principles to State aid law. Rather, it focuses on just three of these which are of particular relevance for State aid purposes: the principles of sincere cooperation, that of legitimate expectations during the recovery procedure, and that of the right of defence.

The most important principle that governs the State aid administrative procedure is the principle of sincere cooperation pursuant to Article 4(3) of the Treaty on European Union (TEU). This principle obliges the Member States to facilitate the achievement of Union tasks and it imposes joint duties of cooperation on EU institutions and the Member States. State aid proceedings rely on this principle, since they are based on a virtually permanent dialogue between the Commission and the Member State in-volved. For instance, the exchange of all necessary information to assess proposed aid reflects the cooperation between the Commission and the Member State during the en-tire decision-making process, i.e., the notification phase, the preliminary examination,

---

[41] Community Guidelines on State aid for environmental protection [2008] OJ C82/1.

[42] Community Guidelines on State aid to promote risk capital investments in small and medium-sized enterprises [2006] OJ C194/2.

[43] Commission Regulation (EC) No 794/2004 of 21 April 2004 implementing Council Regulation (EC) No 659/1999 laying down detailed rules for the application of Article 93 of the EC Treaty [2004] OJ L140/45.

[44] Recovery Notice (n 17).

[45] Commission Notice on a simplified procedure for the treatment of certain types of State aid [2009] OJ C136/3.

[46] Code of Best Practices for the conduct of State aid control procedures, [2018] OJ C 253/14.

[47] See eg Recital 21 Procedural Regulation (n 1); Community Framework for State aid for Research and Development and Innovation, para 1.1.

and the formal examination. With regard to existing aid schemes, Article 107 TFEU refers expressly to this principle when stating that the 'Commission shall, in cooperation with Member States, keep under constant review all systems of aid existing in those States'. Compliance with the principle of sincere cooperation is also directly relevant during the recovery procedure. In the context of the enforcement of the recovery decision, the Commission and the Member State must cooperate to restore the situation to that previously existing before the unlawful aid was granted. In practice, this principle applies in such a way that, if a Member State encounters unforeseeable difficulties in implementing the recovery decision within the required time limit, it must submit these problems for consideration to the Commission in order to overcome such difficulties.[48]

Along with the principle of sincere cooperation, there are some areas of State aid law where the compliance with EU general principles has gained importance. In that respect, the recovery procedure expressly takes into consideration the compliance with such principles. More precisely, as mentioned in the above, when unlawful and incompatible aid has been granted, it should be recovered to restore the situation existing previously. EU law provides, however, for an exception, according to which the Commission should not require the recovery of the aid if it is contrary to a general principle of law.[49] In this regard, the most common principles invoked by the parties are legitimate expectations, legal certainty, proportionality, and rights of defence. The Court has generally given a restrictive application of these principles in the context of recovery. The principle of legitimate expectations is the most important principle, regularly raised before the Court, and it has in fact been successfully applied in a limited number of cases.[50] With regard to the application of this principle, the Court held that

> the principle of the protection of legitimate expectations is part of the legal order of the Community, the fact that national legislation provides for the principles of the protection of legitimate expectations and assurance of legal certainty to be observed in a matter such as the recovery of unduly paid Community aid cannot be considered contrary to that same legal order.[51]

Moreover, the respect of the right of defence is key in State aid litigation. As has been mentioned, State aid provisions are designed in such a way that they focus on the Member States and the Commission as the main actors in the proceedings, thus leaving the interested private parties aside. In other words, the legal framework governing national aid is directed at the Member States, and not at undertakings. As

---

[48] In this regard, it is worth noting that the Commission Notice on recovery expressly refers to the principle of sincere cooperation as laid down in the Treaty (Recovery Notice (n 17) para 10).

[49] Art 16(1) Procedural Regulation (n 1).

[50] See eg Case 223/85 *Rijn-Schelde-Verolme (RSV) Machinefabrieken en Scheepswerven NV v Commission of the European Communities* [1987] ECR 4617; Commission Decision of 30 June 2004 on the aid scheme implemented by Sweden for an exemption from the tax on energy from 1 January 2002 to 30 June 2004 [2005] OJ L165/21, at 59–63. As pointed out by the Commission, the principle of legal certainty is also frequently invoked by the parties; see Recovery Notice (n 17) para 17.

[51] Case C-5/89 *Commission of the European Communities v Federal Republic of Germany* [1990] ECR I-3437, para 13.

such, the rights of interested private parties remain very limited during the primary administrative phases. However, the rights of defence become more relevant during recovery proceedings—most obviously when these are judicial—when such a party seeks to challenge a Commission's decision. To bring an action for annulment, a party must have standing. One of most difficult conditions is to prove that the interested party is 'individually concerned' according to Article 263 TFEU. In this regard, the Court's case law has developed a subtle and complex case law which draws a distinction between the different phases of the procedure. During judicial proceedings, when an interested party challenges a Commission decision adopted at the end of the preliminary examination, the respect of the right of defence is at the core of the reasoning held by the Court. In the well-known *Cook*[52] and *Matra*[53] cases, the Court stated that Article 108(2) TFEU provides procedural guarantees. However, if the Commission takes a decision at the end of the preliminary examination according to Article 108(3), the procedural safeguards provided for in Article 108(2) cannot apply. Therefore, the Court came to the conclusion that the interested party, which can demonstrate that it is in competition with the beneficiaries of the aid, is regarded as individually concerned, and therefore has standing since the decision has been adopted during the preliminary phase of the administrative procedure, without initiating the procedure under Article 108(2). Hence, 'the persons intended to benefit from those *procedural guarantees* may secure compliance therewith only if they are able to challenge that decision by the Commission before the Court'.[54] In other words, there would be a breach of the rights of defence, since an interested party would be deprived of procedural guarantees if it were not to have standing for bringing an action for annulment.

In outline, legal principles governing State aid administration do play a significant role during State aid proceedings, but they apply at different levels. The principle of sincere cooperation is omnipresent all through the proceedings and, as such, appears to be fundamental. It is a far-reaching underlying principle which applies at distinct stages, such as the exchange of information during the investigation or the implementation of the single administrative decision. In contrast, other general principles of EU law, such as the principle of legitimate expectation, apply largely the enforcement phase, but they remain subject to a restrictive interpretation. From a procedural point of view, the right of defence plays also a relevant role during the litigation phase, being regarded as the counterbalance of the absence of rights during the administrative procedure. Their application, however, has led to an excessively intricate case law, described by Jacobs AG as 'plainly unsatisfactory, being complex, apparently illogical, and inconsistent'.[55] This is all the more regrettable, since they should be enforced in 'an area in which, more than in any other, the law must be clear and consistent'.[56]

---

[52] Case C-198/91 *William Cook plc v Commission of the European Communities* [1993] ECR I-2487.

[53] Case C-225/91 *Matra SA v Commission of the European Communities* [1993] ECR I-3203.

[54] Case C-198/91 *William Cook plc v Commission of the European Communities* (n 52) para 23 (emphasis added by the author).

[55] Opinion of Jacobs AG delivered on 24 February 2005, Case C-78/03 P *Commission of the European Communities v Aktionsgemeinschaft Recht und Eigentum eV (ARE)* [2005] ECR I-10737, para 138.

[56] Opinion of Advocate General Bot delivered on 6 March 2008, Joined Cases C-75/05 P and C-80/05 P *Federal Republic of Germany v Kronofrance SA and Others* [2008] ECR I-6619, para 105.

E Organization, Institutions, and Structures in State Aid Administration

The administrative law governing national aid is based on a bilateral dialog between the Commission and the Member State concerned, the latter being the main addressee the Commission's decisions.[57] As has been discussed,[58] their relationship is governed by the underlying principle of sincere cooperation under Article 4(3) TUE. This involves, among others, exchange of all necessary information for assessing the aid and the sound national enforcement of a decision for recovery of unlawful aid vis-à-vis a private recipient.

In addition to the role played by the Commission, the Council can be part of the administrative procedure. The adoption of a derogation measure, overriding the determination of the Commission, laid down in Article 108(2) TFEU, allows the Council to take position on the compatibility of the aid. The Council needs to act unanimously to adopt such a decision at the request of the Member State, and only inasmuch as the decision is justified by exceptional circumstances. If the Commission has already initiated its review procedure, the case is suspended until the Council has made its position known within a time-period of three months. Such decisions, which are politically charged, remain, however, exceptional.[59]

As regards the interested parties,[60] it is noteworthy that their role, albeit important, remains limited. One should keep in mind that State aid law has a significant impact on certain private economic stakeholders with a possibly strong economic interest. State aid law affects stakeholders; however, the latter tend to be set aside since the EU administrative legal framework for scrutiny of national aid focuses on the measures adopted by a Member State as such. Despite their interests' being affected as beneficiaries of the aid, or as competitors of the aid beneficiaries, such stakeholders have only restricted rights during the administrative procedure. It is interesting to note, however, that, since the 2013 reform of the Procedural Regulation, the addressees of some specific national aid decisions of the Commission—such as decisions to provide information,[61] decisions to impose fines and periodic penalty payments,[62] and decisions of non-protected information[63]—can be undertakings or associations of undertakings.

According to the Procedural Regulation, the involvement of interested parties in the procedure is limited to the possibility of submitting a complaint—inasmuch as it is admissible—submitting comments, and receiving a copy of a pertinent decision adopted by the Commission. Also noteworthy is the fact that the 2013 reform has limited the rights of individuals even more than before. Under the former Procedural Regulation, the Commission was obliged to examine information on alleged unlawful

---

[57] Art 31 Procedural Regulation (n 1).   [58] See section D.

[59] For a concrete example on the Council's intervention see section B.

[60] The Procedural Regulation defines 'interested party' as 'any Member State and any person, undertaking or association of undertakings whose interests might be affected by the granting of aid, in particular the beneficiary of the aid, competing undertakings and trade associations' (Art 1(h) Procedural Regulation (n 1)).

[61] Art 7(7) Procedural Regulation (n 1).   [62] ibid Art 8(1) and (2).   [63] ibid Art 9(9).

aid from whatever source. However, given the ever-growing number of complaints that the Commission has faced over recent years, an amendment has been introduced in the Procedural Regulation on complaint-handling. Accordingly, the Commission may on its own initiative examine information regarding alleged unlawful aid from whatever source.[64] Article 24 limits, however, the right of third parties to lodge a complaint before the Commission. A complainant must now prove that its complaint is admissible, meaning that it can be regarded as an interested party under restricted criteria.[65] Should the party not fulfil these criteria, the complaint is treated as withdrawn according to Article 24(2) Procedural Regulation. Information provided is considered to be market information and it remains at the discretion of the Commission to initiate an *ex officio* investigation.[66] To a certain extent, the role of the interested third parties can be regarded as being confined to being merely an information source. With regard to such limited rights, the Court acknowledges that, although certain procedural rights are given to the aid recipient, 'those rights are designed to enable the beneficiary to provide information to the Commission and to put forward its arguments, but do not confer on it the status of a party to the procedure'.[67]

The role of both Union and national courts should be noted. The EU Courts occupy a central position in ensuring that the rules on State aid have been respected during the administrative procedure. Various actions can be taken before the Union courts with regard to State aid decisions, such as the actions for annulment, failure to fulfil an obligation, failure to act, and, to a certain extent, damages.[68]

Alongside this judicial review on the EU level, the law governing national aid is also marked by the role played by the national jurisdictions. According to well-established case law,[69] Article 108(3) TFEU has direct effect, that is, it provides rights enforceable through national courts.[70] In that respect, the Court of Justice affirms the principle of institutional and procedural autonomy for the application of the direct effect of Article 108(3).[71] It is therefore at the discretion of the Member States to define and apply the procedure which guarantees the direct effect of Article 108(3) procedurally.

---

[64] ibid Art 12 Procedural Regulation (n 1).

[65] Specifically, natural and legal persons submitting a complaint pursuant to Arts 12(1) and 24(2) Procedural Regulation (n 1) have to demonstrate that they are interested parties within the meaning of Art 1 (h) Procedural Regulation, meaning that they have to establish that their interests might be affected by the granting of aid. To that end, Art 24(2 Procedural Regulation has made the use of a complaints form compulsory. According to the Implementing Regulation, interested parties are obliged duly to complete the form provided for in Annex IV and give all the mandatory information requested.

[66] Art 12 Procedural Regulation (n 1).

[67] Case C-276/03 P *Scott SA v Commission of the European Communities* [2005] ECR 2005 I-8437, para 34.

[68] For further development on the judicial review see section K.

[69] Case 120/73 *Gebrüder Lorenz GmbH v Federal Republic of Germany et Land de Rhénanie-Palatinat* [1973] ECR 1471.

[70] The Court of Justice states as follows: 'the prohibition of the last sentence of [Article 108(3)] has a direct effect and gives rise to rights in favour of individuals, which national courts are bound to safeguard ... Thus the direct effect of the prohibition extends to all aid which has been implemented without being notified and, in the event of a notification, operates during the preliminary period, and where the Commission sets in motion the contentious procedure, up to the final decision' in ECJ, Judgment of 11 December 1973 in Case 120/73 *Gebrüder Lorenz GmbH v Federal Republic of Germany et Land de Rhénanie-Palatinat* (n 69) para 8.

[71] ibid para 9.

It follows that the national courts should ensure that the standstill obligation of the Member States (i.e., not implementing State aid measures without the approval of the Commission) is respected.[72] Further, in order to apply Article 108(3) on the domestic level, national courts have the power to interpret the notion of State aid as provided for in Article 107(1) TFEU.[73] National courts also have jurisdiction in the enforcement of recovery decisions. This includes preventing the payment of unlawful aid, ensuring the recovery of unlawful aid and illegal interests, and assessing damages for competitors and other interested parties.

It is important to point out that, if the Commission and national courts are essential during the proceedings, their roles remain different. This distinct allocation of competency has been amply stressed by EU case law.[74] Only the Commission is entitled to assess the compatibility of the aid with the internal market on the basis of Article 107(2) and (3) TFEU. As the Court of Justice has held,

> [w]hilst the Commission must examine the compatibility of the proposed aid with the common market, even where the Member State has acted in breach of the prohibition on giving effect to aid, national courts do no more than preserve, until the final decision of the Commission, the rights of individuals faced with a possible breach by State authorities of the prohibition laid down by Article 108(3) of the TFEU [ex. 88(3) EC].[75]

The role of the national courts, which has grown in importance, has been largely supported at EU level with the declared objective of establishing a sound balance of between them and the Commission. In this regard, in 2009 the Commission adopted the Notice on the Enforcement of State Aid Law by National Courts (Enforcement Notice),[76] aiming to shed light on the national remedies and private enforcement actions. As pointed out in that measure, the role of the national judiciary should be strengthened since it gives 'third parties the opportunity to address and resolve many State aid related concerns directly at national level ... [and] 'national courts can offer claimants very effective remedies in the event of a breach of the State aid rules'.[77]

Finally, amendments to the Procedural Regulation in 2013 have introduced, under Article 29, the possibility for national courts to ask the Commission for information or opinion. In addition, the Commission is empowered to submit on its own initiative written *amicus curiae* briefs to the national courts and it can make oral observations. Interestingly, this Commission competence—already provided for in the Enforcement

---

[72] There are, however, some exceptions, for instance where the measure falls within the remit of the General Block Exemption Regulation (Commission Regulation (EU) No 651/2014 of 17 June 2014 declaring certain categories of aid compatible with the internal market in application of Articles 107 and 108 of the Treaty (n 32)) or it is existing aid.

[73] Case 78/76 *Steinike & Weinlig* [1977] ECR 595, para 14; Case C-39/94 *SFEI and Others* [1996] ECR I-3547, para 49; Case C-368/04 *Transalpine Ölleitung in Österreich* [2006] ECR I-9957, para 39.

[74] See eg Case C-368/04 *Transalpine Ölleitung in Österreich* [2006] ECR I-9957, para 37; Joined Cases C-261/01 and C-262/01 *Van Calster and Cleeren* [2003] ECR I-12249, para 74.

[75] Case C-199/06 *CELF and Ministre de la Culture et de la Communication* [2008] ECR I-469, para 38.

[76] Commission Notice on the enforcement of state aid law by national courts [2009] OJ C85/1. This Notice replaced the Notice on Cooperation between National Courts and the Commission in the State Aid Field [1995] OJ C312/8.

[77] ibid para 5.

Notice[78]—draws inspiration from the Antitrust Cooperation Notice.[79] The new rules, then, strengthening the information channel between the Commission and national courts, should not be regarded as an excessive intervention of the Commission in domestic curial proceedings, risking a breach of the principle of independence of national courts. To the contrary, the rules can be seen as reflecting the importance that the EU institution attaches to the role of national courts. To this end, the Commission aims to assist national courts in pending cases by transmitting relevant information in its possession or providing opinions. In one respect, this new legal framework, which reinforces the relationship between the EU level and the national level, should be regarded as an application of the ever-present principle of the duty of sincere cooperation: while the Commission must assist national courts when applying State aid law, national courts should, conversely, assist the Commission to carry out its tasks.[80]

F Administrative Procedure within the State Aid Sector

Administrative procedure governing national aid control has been designed to regulate incentives often perceived as policy steering tools by national authorities. Therefore, it focuses on the relationship between the Member States and the Commission, the latter being regarded as the executive administrative body. As has been noted, the procedure is based on an ex ante control. Union law subscribes to the principle that any new aid should be notified to the Commission and not be put into effect until the Commission has adopted a decision of compatibility. However, with regard to existing aid schemes (which encompass, among others, national aid which was existing prior the entry into force of the Treaty or which had already been authorized by the Commission), EU law sets out an a posteriori control. Accordingly, the Commission is required to keep existing aid schemes under constant review, in cooperation with the Member State involved. Should an existing scheme no longer be compatible with Union policy, the Commission can propose appropriate measures. In outline, the administrative law of State aid relies on four distinct procedures which are laid down in the Procedural Regulation: (i) the procedure regarding notified aid (i.e., where the national authority has made a notification to the Commission), (ii) the procedure on unlawful aid where the Member State has failed to notify the aid, (iii) the procedure on existing aid, and (iv) the procedure on misuse of aid. These proceedings have already been explained throughout this chapter and will not be further discussed in this section.

It should be noted that *comitology* procedures are also applicable to a certain extent with the State aid control regime. An Advisory Committee on State Aid is established when the Commission adopts implementing measures (as always, chaired by the Commission and composed of representatives of the Member States).[81] Outside of

---

[78] ibid paras 77 ff.

[79] Commission Notice on the cooperation between the Commission and the courts of the EU Member States in the application of Articles 81 and 82 EC [2004] OJ C101, paras 15–30.

[80] See Case C-94/00 *Roquette Frères* [2002] ECR I-9011, para 31. For further details see the aforementioned Commission Notice on the enforcement of state aid law by national courts (n 76). This notice describes the cooperation between national courts and the Commission.

[81] On the Advisory Committee on State Aid see Art 34 Procedural Regulation (n 1).

the spectrum of this Committee, the Commission also conducts ad hoc meetings with the Member States within the framework of the *State Aid Network* in order to facilitate new approaches on some policies, increase transparency, and strengthen cooperation on State aid control. This network was created under the impulse of the 2005 reform in the State Aid Action Plan[82] which aimed, among other things, to generate 'more transparency in the general principles of State aid control and consider establishing a network of State aid authorities or contact points in order to facilitate the flow of information and exchange of best practices'.[83] Nonetheless, the involvement of comitology or network structures, regardless of their continuing or ad hoc nature, remain rare since the implementation of State aid discipline is conducted almost exclusively by the Commission, which concentrates essentially on administrative rule-making and individual decisions.

G Sector-specific Decision-making and the Margin of Discretion in State Aid Regulation

The exercise of discretion constitutes a significant element of State aid scrutiny and plays a more important role than in any other area of competition law. The implementation of State aid control policies needs to be adapted to policy strategies, to contribute to remedying market failures, and to be used as instruments for furthering economic development. It is, therefore, fundamental to design national aid and its control as flexible tools. This, however, must take place in compliance with Treaty provisions and the general principles of Union law, including the principles of equal treatment and transparency. It is against this backdrop that the discretion conferred upon the Commission is key to assessing the measures at stake and applying the rules within the sphere of State aid regulatory law.

In doing so, it is important to draw a distinction between the assessment of the notion of State aid on the one hand and the examination of its compatibility on the other hand. With regard to the very notion of State aid, the Commission does not have any leeway. Since State aid is a concept legally defined by the Treaty in Article 107(1) on the basis on four major criteria,[84] the Commission is subject to this definition and its interpretation by the Court. In other words, it is an objective notion[85] which the Commission must apply to measures subject to its review. As the Court has held,

---

[82] On the creation of this network see M Negenman, 'A State Aid Network?' (2011) 10(4) *European State Aid Law Quarterly* 621.

[83] Commission Document, 'State Aid Action Plan: A Roadmap for State Aid Reform 2005–2009', COM(2005) 107 final, para 53.

[84] As mentioned in the introduction, Art 107(1) TFEU defines state aid on the basis of criteria which are commonly assessed as follows: (i) the aid should be granted by a Member State or through state resources; (ii) it should provide for an advantage; (iii) it should be selective inasmuch as it favours certain undertakings or the production of certain goods; and (iv) it should distort or threaten to distort competition and affect trade between Member States.

[85] See Commission Notice on the notion of state aid as referred to in Article 107(1) of the Treaty on the Functioning of the European Union, C/2016/2946 [2016] OJ C262, paras 3 and 4.

the *concept of aid is objective*, the test being whether a State measure confers an advantage on one or more particular undertakings. The characterisation of a measure as State aid, which, according to the Treaty, is the responsibility of both the Commission and the national courts, *cannot in principle justify the attribution of a broad discretion to the Commission*, save for particular circumstances owing to the complex nature of the State intervention in question.[86]

In contrast, the Commission enjoys wide discretion with regard to the assessment of the compatibility of the national aid with the internal market. Article 107(2) TFEU does not confer leeway as such on the Commission, setting out, as it does, measures which are systematically regarded *de jure* as being compatible. Article 107(3), however, then confers a broad margin of discretion by averring to national aid which *may* be compatible with the internal market. To this end, the Commission has to carry out a case-by-case analysis, considering all relevant elements, including 'the circumstances already considered in a prior decision and the obligations which that decision may have imposed on a Member State'.[87] The Commission is also to take into account economic and social elements which are relevant on the EU level: Article 107(3) implies that the Commission has 'a discretion the exercise of which involves economic and social assessments which must be made in a Community context'.[88]

The application of this wide margin of discretion by the Commission is strictly controlled by the need to act in compliance with the principles of transparency and of equality of treatment. The Commission aims to strike a balance between the potentially positive impact of the aid (i.e., the objective of common interest) and the negative effects which could result in distortion of competition and trade.[89] Interestingly, in the wake of the State Aid Modernisation reform, the Commission has devised common principles relevant to the assessment of compatibility.[90] The stated objective of that reform was to adopt a common approach by revising guidelines and frameworks with the view to applying compatibility conditions based on common assessment principles.[91] More precisely, the Commission considers a national aid to be compatible

---

[86] Case T-67/94 *Ladbroke Racing Ltd v Commission of the European Communities* [1998] ECR 1998 II-1 para 52 (emphasis added). As pointed out by the Court, if the Commission is bound by the objective notion of State aid, it still has some assessment margin in situations involving complex economic assessments (see for instance Case C-290/07 P *Commission v Scott* [2010] ECR I-7763, para 66).

[87] Case C-261/89 *Italian Republic v Commission of the European Communities* [1991] ECR I-4437, para 20.

[88] Case 730/79 *Philip Morris Holland BV v Commission of the European Communities* [19801] ECR 2671.

[89] In this regard see Commission Document, 'State Aid Action Plan: A Roadmap for State Aid reform 2005–2009', COM(2005) 107 final, para 26.

[90] Communication from the Commission to the European Parliament, the Council, the European Economic and Social Committee and the Committee of the Regions, EU State Aid Modernisation (SAM), COM/2012/0209 final. With regard to the common principles, the objective consists in the 'identification and definition of common principles applicable to the assessment of compatibility of all the aid measures carried out by the Commission; such horizontal principles would clarify how the Commission would assess common features that are presently not treated in the same manner across the different guidelines and frameworks; those principles would have to be as operational as possible and could deal with the definition and assessment of genuine market failures, the incentive effect and the negative effects of public interventions, including, potentially, considerations on the overall impact of the aid' (para 18).

[91] For examples of the implementation of the common assessment principles see Guidelines on regional state aid for 2014–2020 [2013] OJ C209, paras 25 ff; Communication from the Commission— Guidelines on State aid to airports and airlines [2014] OJ C99, paras 83 ff.

with the internal market inasmuch as it fulfils the criteria of: (i) contribution to a well-defined objective of common interest; (ii) need for State intervention; (iii) appropriateness of the aid measure; (iv) incentive effect; (v) proportionality of the aid; and (vi) avoidance of undue negative effects on competition and trade between Member States. In addition, while applying its margin of discretion, the Commission takes into account whether the aid complies with the transparency criteria as provided for in the Transparency Communication of 27 June 2014. It follows that the Commission, while exercising its broad margin of discretion, takes into consideration the necessary adaptation of the economic and social assessment to the evolution of the (internal) market. This approach is mirrored in a recent review of the large range of guidelines and frameworks, in order to the greatest extent possible to treat all measures in the same manner on the basis of these common principles. In that respect, State aid appears nowadays, more than ever, as an adjustable, even flexible, tool regulating public interventions based on the overall impact of their effects.

A related consideration is the control of the Commission's exercise of discretion. Such control, albeit observable, remains limited. In that respect, the Court of Justice is confined to reviewing only manifest errors or misuse of powers.[92] Accordingly, 'it is not for the Court to substitute its own economic assessment for that of the author of the decision'.[93] Therefore, the Court should

> confine its review to determining whether the Commission complied with the rules governing procedure and the provision of the statement of reasons, whether the facts on which the contested finding was based are accurately stated and whether there has been any manifest error of assessment or any misuse of powers.[94]

In this regard, administrative law governing national aid is specific in the sense that it confers on the Commission a broad margin of discretion to conduct administrative rule-making and to issue individual decisions under a restricted supervision of the Court, the latter exercising 'judicial self-restraint'.[95]

H Abstract-general Administrative Acts in the State Aid Sector Concerned and the Use of Soft Law

A specific feature of the State aid control framework is the recurrent use of soft law as form of regulatory act. Since the 1970s, the Commission has issued a wide-ranging set of measures under various nomenclatures, such as guidelines, communications,

---

[92] See eg Case 57/72 *Westzucker GmbH v Einfuhr- und Vorratsstelle für Zucker* [1973] ECR 321, para 14; Case T-171/02 *Regione autonoma della Sardegna v Commission of the European Communities* [2005] ECR II-2123, para 97.

[93] Case T-126/99 *Graphischer Maschinenbau GmbH v Commission of the European Communities* [2002] ECR 2002 II-242, para 32; Case T-137/02 *Pollmeier Malchow GmbH & Co KG v Commission of the European Communities* [2004] ECR 2004 II-3541, para 52.

[94] Case T-126/99 *Graphischer Maschinenbau GmbH v Commission of the European Communities* [2002] ECR II-242, para 32.

[95] M Schweda, 'General Principles' in M Heidenhain (ed), *European State Aid Law* (C H Beck, Hart Publishing 2010) 154.

notices, disciplines, frameworks, codes, or even handbooks and vademecums.[96] These measures fall within the scope of soft law, commonly defined as 'rules of conduct which, in principle, have no legally binding force but which nevertheless may have practical effects'.[97] These measures set out 'indications as to the direction to be followed'[98] by the Commission and should not 'depart from the Treaty rules'.[99]

The question arises as to whether these instruments of soft law have a binding effect within the context of the State regulatory framework. In principle, such instruments should not be regarded as binding for national authorities or individuals. For instance, in the *Expedia* case, the Court stressed the non-binding nature of the *de minimis* notice for the courts of the Member States and competition authorities.[100] Similarly, the Court pointed out the non-binding nature of the Commission Communication on services of general interest in the *ASM Brescia* case.[101] This line of reasoning, however, does not mean that soft law instruments would invariably be deprived of binding effects. It is common ground that soft law instruments can be binding for the institution which has issued the instrument. As pointed out by the Court, rules applicable in a given sector, 'as set out by the Commission in a communication on its policy in that area ("discipline") and accepted by the Member States, *have a binding effect*'.[102] A deviation from such an instrument in administrative decisions could otherwise result in a breach of the principle of equal treatment.[103] In that respect, the well-known *Dansk Rørindustri* case coins the stance of the Court:

> In adopting such rules of conduct and announcing by publishing them that they will hence forth apply to the cases to which they relate, the institution in question imposes a limit on the exercise of its discretion and cannot depart from those rules under pain of being found, where appropriate, to be in breach of the general principles of law, such as equal treatment or the protection of legitimate expectations. It cannot therefore be excluded that, on certain conditions and depending on their conduct, such rules of conduct, which are of general application, may produce legal effects.[104]

---

[96] For examples of documents of soft law on state aid see section C.

[97] F Snyder, 'Soft Law and Institutional Practice in the European Community Law: Institutions, Processes, Tools and Techniques' (1993) 56 *Modern Law Review* 32. This definition has been consistently repeated by legal literature. For an overview of the quotations of this definition see S Onana, 'European Union Soft Law: New Developments Concerning the Divide between a Legally Binding Force and Legal Effect' (2012) 75 *Modern Law Review* 879, n 3.

[98] Case C-310/99 *Italian Republic v Commission* [2002] ECR I-2289, para 52.

[99] Case T-35/99 *Keller v Commission* [2002] ECR II-261, para 77.

[100] The Court came therefore to the conclusion that 'a Commission notice, such as the *de minimis* notice, is not binding in relation to the Member States' (Case C-226/11 *Expedia Inc v Autorité de la Concurrence and Others* [2012] ECLI:EU:C:2012:795, paras 24 and 29).

[101] Case T-189/03 *ASM Brescia v European Commission* [2009] ECR II-1831, para 128.

[102] Case C-313/90 *CIRFS and Others v European Commission* [1993] ECR I-1125, Sum 4 (emphasis added).

[103] See eg Case T-214/95 *Vlaamse Gewest v Commission* [1998] ECR II-717, para 89.

[104] In Joined Cases C-189/02 P, C-202/02 P, C-205/02 P to C-208/02 P, and C-213/02 P *Dansk Rørindustri and Others v Commission* [2005] ECR I-5425, para 210. See also Joined Cases C-182/03 and C-217/03 *Belgium and Forum 187 v Commission* [2006] ECR I-5479, para 70. For an exhaustive summary of the limits of Commission's power to adopt and apply informative acts see Opinion of AG Bot of 6 March 2008 in Joined Cases C-75/05 P and C-80/05 P *Germany v Kronofrance* [2008] ECR I-6619, paras 137–48.

It follows from this consideration that the Commission can issue measures in State aid law with self-binding effects.[105] The question is, then, why the Commission would opt to limit its own margin of discretion, instead of relying on a law-making process (formally) binding for the Member States and the economic stakeholders. Some reasons can be offered. First, the use of soft law—instead of hard law—presents certain practical advantages. It constitutes indeed a relevant tool to provide guidance and, thereby, to increase transparency and legal certainty. It is also a flexible instrument which can be adopted much faster than hard law and can therefore accelerate the decision-making process. Moreover, given the political dimension of State aid framework, it allows a consensus to be reached among the Member States and institutions, where hard law would probably have failed.[106] Secondly, historic reasons play a role. Within the regulatory context of national aid, the Commission unsuccessfully relied in the past on the legislative process (e.g., the 1966 failure of the proposal by the Commission for a Council regulation on State aid procedure, and the 1972 failure in regard to a regulation on regional aid). Against this backdrop, the Commission appears to be reluctant to use hard law, and is opting for soft law as a regular alternative.

Within any consideration of soft law, the Code of Best Practice on State Aid[107] commands attention. This was adopted for the reform of State aid control, issued as the final part of a simplification package comprising the Commission Notice on the enforcement of State aid law by national courts[108] and the Notice from the Commission on a simplified procedure for treatment of certain types of national aid.[109] It drew inspiration from the experience acquired in the application of Procedural Regulation and from internal Commission studies on the State aid procedure. The Code of Best Practice aims to provide guidance on the daily conduct of proceedings. This involves encouraging the use of prenotification contacts, streamlining information exchanges, enhancing the quality of Member State notifications, and, more generally, improving the transparency, the duration and the predictability about the timing of decisions. To this end, the Code of Best Practice relies on co-operation and mutual understanding : 'to ensure the correct and efficient application of the State aid rules, Member States and the Commission should closely cooperate as partners'.[110] It is interesting to note that this Code, contrary to soft law instruments which are self-binding on the Commission, expressly does not intend to create or alter rights or obligations incumbent on the Commission or the Member States.[111] In that respect, the Code of Best Practice serves as a pertinent example of a guidance document which relies the underlying discipline of the Commission and the Member States and which is based on mutual commitment, without introducing any self-restraining obligations on any side.

---

[105] In this sense see Case C-313/90 *CIRFS and Others v European Commission* (n 102).

[106] For a review of the pros and cons related to the use of soft law see F Beveridge and S Nott, 'A Hard Look at Soft Law' in P Craig and C Harlow (eds), *Law-making in the European Union* (Kluwer Law International 1998) 285–309.

[107] Code of Best Practices for the conduct of State aid control procedures [2018] OJ C 253/14.

[108] Commission Notice on the enforcement of state aid law by national courts (n 76). This notice replaced the Notice on Cooperation between National Courts and the Commission in the State Aid Field (n 76).

[109] Commission Notice on a simplified procedure for the treatment of certain types of State aid (n 45).

[110] Code of Best Practice in State Aid (n 107) para 5.   [111] ibid para 8.

In outline, the Union administrative decision-making process for national aid finds its source mainly in a large range of soft law documents, which have been amply designed, developed, and regularly reviewed. This proliferation of such instruments, which strike a balance between mere information and binding administrative rules, sets the Commission as the most important rule-maker in State aid law. Relying on soft law in an area which is politically charged appears to be a subtle choice: as pointed out by one commentator: 'yet while goals could have been achieved by means of legislation, it was the balance sought between policy flexibility on the one hand, and policy stability and credibility, on the other, that ultimately made soft law the instrument of choice within the State aid directorate'.[112]

I Single-case Administrative Acts and Measures within the Sector Concerned

Under the administrative law of national aid control regime, Commission decisions are the main single-case administrative acts, and these are at the core of the field. As has been explained, during the procedure the Commission adopts distinct decisions which are directed at the Member State involved. At the end of the preliminary examination, the Commission can take either a decision finding that the measure is not an aid, a decision not to raise objections, or a decision to initiate the formal investigation procedure.[113] At the end of the formal investigation, the Commission can adopt a positive decision (i.e., the aid is compatible with the internal market), a negative decision (i.e., the aid is not compatible and should therefore not be put into effect), or a conditional decision (i.e., the aid may be compatible provided that certain obligations are complied with).[114] Moreover, the Commission is empowered to adopt an information injunction (i.e., decision regarding the information to be provided),[115] as well as a suspension or recovery injunction (i.e., decision requesting to suspend the aid or to recover the aid provisionally until the Commission has adopted a decision).[116] Furthermore, since the amendment of the Procedural Regulation, the Commission can also adopt decisions whose addressees are private undertakings or associations of undertakings. These decisions relate to providing information,[117] imposition of fines, and periodic penalty payments,[118] and findings that information regarded as confidential is not protected.[119]

Along with these various types of decisions, consideration should be given to other administrative acts adopted by the Commission having a bearing on the procedure, such as measures relating to information or preparatory acts, the legal force of which may be open to question. Under Article 263 TFEU, the European Court can review the

---

[112] M Cini, 'The Soft Law Approach: Commission Rule-making in the EU's State Aid Regime' (2011) 8(2) *Journal of European Public Policy* 199.

[113] Art 4 Procedural Regulation (n 1).   [114] ibid Art 9.

[115] ibid Art 12. For an application of an injunction challenged before the Court see eg Joined Cases C-463/10 P and C-475/10 P *Deutsche Post AG and Federal Republic of Germany v European Commission* [2011] ECR I-9639.

[116] Art 13 Procedural Regulation (n 1).   [117] ibid Art 7(7).   [118] ibid Art 8(1) and (2).

[119] ibid Art 9(9).

legality of acts adopted by the institutions. According to well-established case law, the Court holds that measures 'which produce binding legal effects such as to affect the interests of an applicant by bringing about a distinct change in his legal position may be the subject of an action for annulment'.[120] In this regard, informative acts fail to satisfy the criteria of Article 263 TFEU. For example, a letter of the Commission informing the applicant of its decision is considered to be purely informal and not to produce binding effects.[121] Similarly, a letter sent by the Commission which replies to an information request for an individual is not actionable before the Court.[122] With regard to intermediate measures in State aid review, only measures stating the definitive position of the European institution involved can be challenged before the Court. Acts which are only at a stage prior to the final decision and whose objective is to prepare the final decision[123] are not challengeable.[124]

It follows, then, that the institutional decision as such constitutes the most prevalent single-case act of an administrative nature during the State aid procedures. Interestingly, this single-case act is not systematically unilateral. With regard to the review of existing aid schemes, agreements concluded between the Commission and the Member State can be regarded as being of bilateral nature. As pointed out in the Court's case law, 'the fact that the discipline is the outcome of *an agreement* between the Member States and the Commission cannot alter the objective significance of its terms or its binding effect'.[125] The Court thereby refers to the acceptance by the Member State of the appropriate recommendations[126] made by the Commission as an agreement.[127] But beyond this subtle distinction, the key feature which is relevant to

---

[120] Case T-212/00 *Nuove Industrie Molisane Srl v Commission of the European Communities* [2002] ECR II-347, para 36.

[121] Case T-82/96 *ARAP and Others v Commission of the European Communities* [1999] ECR II-1889, paras 29–30; upheld by Case C-321/99 P *ARAP and Others v Commission of the European Communities* [2002] ECR I-4287.

[122] Case T-154/94 *Comité des salines de France and Compagnie des salins du Midi et des salines de l'Est SA v Commission of the European Communities* [1996] ECR II-1377, paras 30 ff.

[123] Joined Cases C-463/10 P and C-475/10 P *Deutsche Post and Deutschland v Commission* [2011] ECR I-9639, paras 50–54; Case C-477/11 P *Sepracor Pharmaceuticals v Commission* ECLI:EU:C:2012:292, paras 52–58.

[124] The Court makes the following reasoning: '[a]n application for a declaration that the initiation of a procedure and a statement of objections are void might make it necessary for the court to arrive at a decision on questions on which the Commission has not yet had an opportunity to state its position and would as a result anticipate the arguments on the substance of the case, confusing different procedural stages both administrative and judicial. It would thus be incompatible with the system of the division of powers between the Commission and the Court and of the remedies laid down by the Treaty, as well as the requirements of the sound administration of justice and the proper course of the administrative procedure to be followed in the Commission' (Case 60/81 *IBM* [1981] ECR 2639, para 20). See also Case T-426/04 *Tramarin Snc di Tramarin Andrea e Sergio v Commission of the European Communities* [2005] ECR II-4765, para 25; Case C-521/06 P *Athinaïki Techniki AE v Commission of the European Communities* [2008] ECR I-5829, para 46.

[125] Case C-313/90 *CIRFS and Others v Commission of the European Communities* (n 102) para 36 (emphasis added).

[126] Once the Member State has accepted the recommendations, the latter are legally binding. If the Member State rejects the recommendations, the Commission can initiate the preliminary examination (see Art 23 Procedural Regulation (n 1)).

[127] This difference of nature can be relevant for the possible amendments of the act. As outlined in legal literature: '[a] unilateral guideline can be amended by the Commission -albeit not implicitly in a single case decision. An agreement under Article 108(2) TFEU (ex-Art 88(1)) can only be amended by agreement of those parties, which have concluded it'. See H C H Hofmann, 'Administrative Governance

assessing a single-case act in the State aid discipline remains whether it produces legal effects.

J Administrative Enforcement of EU Sectoral Law

The enforcement of a Commission decision is a significant aspect of State aid law with the national authorities and the Commission at the core. As the aforementioned 2007 Recovery Notice summarizes, '[b]oth the Commission and the Member States have an essential role to play in the implementation of recovery decisions and may contribute to a [sic] effective enforcement of recovery policy'.[128] A sound implementation of single administrative decisions is based on the principle of sincere cooperation as provided for in Article 4(3) TEU. This principle applied to State aid regulatory framework implies that the Member States and the Commission should cooperate to ensure the restoration of the competitive conditions in the internal market.

The allocation of powers between the Commission and the Member States is well defined. The Commission should order the recovery of the aid. This involves that it should provide clear indications regarding the amount of aid to be recovered, the beneficiaries liable to the obligation of repayment, and the time period to complete the recovery. Whereas the Commission adopts a decision *ordering* the recovery of the aid, it is the Member State which is in charge of *effectively enforcing* the recovery. In this regard, the Member State should take all necessary measures to recover the aid from the beneficiary, including interest at an appropriate rate fixed by the Commission.[129] As mentioned above, the Union has adopted a strict position towards the recovery, which can be ruled out only under three exceptions: (i) the aid been conferred outside a limitation period exceeding ten years; (ii) the recovery is contrary to a general principle of law; or (iii) there is an absolute impossibility for the Member State to enforce the decision properly.[130] Notwithstanding these exceptions, the national measures should result in an immediate and effective execution of the Commission's decision.[131] In this regard, the Court has consistently maintained that the Commission's decision addressed to the Member State is binding on all state organs, including the national courts.[132] Furthermore, as contemplated in the case law, the Member State involved should ensure that national procedures allow the immediate re-establishment of the previously existing situation and do not prolong the unfair competitive advantage.[133]

With regard to the applicable recovery procedure, of great interest is the study ordered by the Commission on the enforcement of State aid policy in the Member States in 2004,[134] showing the extent to which recovery procedures differ significantly among

---

in State Aid Policy' in H C H Hofmann and A H Türk (eds), *EU Administrative Governance* (Edward Elgar Publishing 2006) 197 (footnotes omitted).

[128] Recovery Notice (n 17) para 30.   [129] See Art 16(1) and (2) Procedural Regulation (n 1).
[130] See section B.   [131] Art 16(3) Procedural Regulation (n 1).
[132] See eg Case 249/85 *Albako Margarinefabrik Maria von der Linde GmbH & Co KG v Bundesanstalt für landwirtschaftliche Marktordnung* [1987] ECR 2345, para 17.
[133] Case C-232/05 *Commission v France ('Scott')* [2006] ECR I-10071, para 52.
[134] T Jestaedt, J Jones Day, J Derenne, and T Ottervanger, 'Study on the Enforcement of State Aid Law at National Level' (March 2006) *Competition Studies* 6, (Office for Official Publications of the European Communities) 522.

the Member States. Interestingly, the study points out that administrative procedures are more efficient than civil ones; this can be explained 'because the State is generally able to obtain immediate enforcement of its payment claim on the basis of an administrative procedure'.[135] Also noteworthy is the issue of which Member State organ is in charge of enforcing the Commission's decision. As explained, EU law does not require a specific organ to ensure the effective implementation of the recovery decision. Each Member State should, however, in compliance with its domestic legal system, designate the competent organ. The study observes, however, that, despite this margin of discretion, a principle common to all the Member States has emerged according to which recovery is conducted by the authority which granted the aid, involving thereby typically a large range of central, regional, and local bodies.[136]

In outline, the Commission and the Member States share the joint responsibility to ensure the enforcement of the State aid decisions. The Commission, in addition to being the administrative organ which adopts the decision, takes part in the enforcement procedure alongside the Member State. Moreover, the enforcement is carried out under the supervision of the Commission, the latter having discretion to refer the matter directly to the Court under Article 108(2) TFEU if the Member State fails to enforce the recovery decision within the prescribed time limit. The Commission appears, therefore, as the omnipresent body in the implementation of a State aid decision (from the initiation to the supervision) and the Member State as the administrative enforcer.

K Supervision and Control within the Sector of State Aid Regulation

With regard to the political control in the area of national aid, one can observe that such a control remains limited. If written parliamentary questions and queries from the EU ombudsman can be raised, they are non-specific to the area of State aid and, in practice, they play a minor role. In addition, the law-making process in Article 109 TFEU, which involves the Council and the Parliament—by way of consultation—has been used in relatively few instances.[137] Moreover, it is important to keep in mind that the powers entrusted to the Council under Article 108(2) are *not* to be considered as political supervision of the Commission. These powers, which have been described above,[138] allow the Council to adopt by unanimity a State aid decision at the request of a Member State. If the Commission has already initiated the procedure, the case remains pending within a time period of three months. It appears therefore that the Council does *not* control the Commission, but rather it takes over the role of the Commission. In other words, the powers entrusted to the Council are not for control purposes, but for decision-making purposes.

Concerning the possible role played by the Court of Auditors, this remains limited. As a preliminary comment, one should keep in mind that reports issued by the

---

[135] ibid 523.   [136] ibid 521.   [137] See eg the above-mentioned General Block Exemption.
[138] See section C.

Court of Auditors are not legally binding in State aid matters. That being said, the Court of Auditors has already investigated the State aid disciplines as conducted by the Commission. For instance, in a 2016 report the focus was on State aid rules in Union cohesion policy. In that respect, the Court of Auditors identified—perhaps unsurprisingly—a higher rate of infringements of State aid rules by the Member States than that mentioned by the national authorities themselves. It recommended, therefore, more awareness and strengthened support by the Commission. In response, the Commission committed itself to take actions to streamline the State aid rules and to promote the administrative capacity of the Member States.[139] It is in this context that the annual monitoring exercises carried out by the Commission on aid approved have gained importance.

As regards supervision of the Commission's actions, judicial review by the Court of Justice of the European Union (CJEU) is, as elsewhere, significant in EU law. More precisely, with regard to the possible actions before the Court related to State aid, the action for annulment is the most prevalent one, allowing challenges to the validity of the centrally important Commission decisions. In addition, the action for failure to fulfil an obligation, compelling a Member State to comply with the Commission decision, can be relevant, in particular with regard to recovery issues. In comparison with the action for annulment, the action for failure to act has only been occasionally successful in State aid review. Likewise, the action for damages, related to non-contractual liability, can be possible in State aid law, but its use remains limited in practice. That being said, one should bear in mind that State aid litigation is a major and ever-growing field of the courts' activities. In 2014, forty-one State aid cases have been completed by the Court of Justice and 148 by the General Court with judgments, opinions, or orders involving a judicial determination.[140] As the Court observed: '[t]he number of new cases brought also increased significantly (owing, in particular, to large sets of related cases *concerning State aid* and restrictive measures)'.[141] This increasing litigation reflects the central and far-reaching role of the CJEU in the judicial review of State aid.

The role of the CJEU should not be circumscribed merely to mechanical supervision and control of the administrative procedure in State aid matters. The European courts can, indeed, be regarded as a pioneering and fundamental contributor to devising and developing the rules on State aid. As has been pointed out,[142] the Treaty provisions are terse and require further interpretation. To fill the gaps, the case law has significantly developed the legal framework in interpreting the very notion of State aid and substantially evolving procedural rules. For example, the Court has

---

[139] See European Court of Auditors, *More efforts needed to raise awareness of and enforce compliance with State aid rules in cohesion policy*, Special Report No 24/2016. Another example of the role played by the Court of Auditors' state aid area can be found in the 2011 Report on State Aid Control, where the Court of Auditors focused on the management of state aid control by the Commission. Different aspects were reviewed and recommendations were issued, including with regard to the extensive time period for handling complaints or the prompt reaction of the Commission to face the financial crisis (see European Court of Auditors, *Report on whether the Commission's procedures ensure effective management of state aid control*, Report No 15/2011).

[140] Court of Justice of the European Union, Annual Report 2014, 104.

[141] ibid 123 (emphasis added).   [142] See section C.

recognized the direct effect of the last sentence of Article 108(3) TFEU, which restrains the Member State from giving effect to an aid measure until the Commission has adopted a final decision.[143] Another landmark example can be found in the *Kohlgesetz* case in which the Court established the principle of recovery of unlawful and incompatible aid.[144] In the same vein, the well-known *Altmark* case illustrates the importance of the case law in designing new rules. There, the Court laid down four criteria to assess the notion of 'advantage', establishing thereby a significant framework for undertakings entrusted with services of general economic interest.[145] In one respect, the State aid field, more than any other area of EU administrative law, is marked by the fundamental role of the Court which is so far-reaching that it is reflected in the entire design of State aid rules.

L Conclusion

This chapter on the administration of State aid policy has emphasized the roles of the main actors, namely the Commission and the Member States, stressing the key principle of sincere cooperation which is impressed upon the entire field. The strong powers of the CJEU when supervising the enforcement of State aid administrative rules and the contribution of the Court of Justice to the evolution of substantive State aid law have been noted.

With regard to the structure of administrative governance, two points deserve emphasis. First, in the review of State aid the role of the Commission is more specific and determining than in other fields of EU administrative law. The Commission is at the core of the administrative proceedings by exercising investigative and adjudicating powers. As aptly pointed out by legal literature: '[t]he policy field of State aid control has made a considerable contribution of the development of general EU administrative law - not least because of its nature as one of the few areas in which the Commission directly implements EC law'.[146] It is interesting to note that this approach, which consists in placing the Commission at the centre of the State aid regime, has been strengthened with the amendment of the Procedural Regulation, which increases the Commission's regulatory arsenal.

Secondly, the Commission, in which the administrative rule-making and enforcement powers are concentrated, relies mainly on soft law instruments to regulate State aid. One has observed the considerable margin of discretion available to the Commission, which, however, exercises self-restraint by regularly employing such soft law regulatory instruments. These instruments, which steer policies and frame public interventions in the market, limit the margin of discretion of the Commission by producing binding legal effects. They mirror the long-standing efforts aimed at balancing steering policies, controlling the Member States' subsidization process at

---

[143] Case 120/73 *Gebrüder Lorenz GmbH v Federal Republic of Germany et Land de Rhénanie-Palatinat* (n 69).

[144] Case 70/72 *Commission of the European Communities v Federal Republic of Germany* (n 14).

[145] Case C-280/00 *Altmark Trans GmbH* [2003] ECR I-7747.

[146] H C H Hofmann, 'Administrative Governance in State Aid Policy' in Hofmann and Türk (eds), *EU Administrative Governance* (n 127) 200–01.

the level of the internal market, and respecting the principles of legal certainty and equality of treatment. As such, they should not be regarded as piecemeal frameworks, but as the response to the long-standing issue of regulating the use of public resources in a field of high sensibility within the political process of the Member States and the European institutions.

18

Public Procurement Regulation

Christopher H Bovis

A Introduction

In the European Union, public procurement refers to all contractual relations for supplies, works, and services between public-sector authorities of Member States as well as entities operating as utilities in Member States and the private sector. Public procurement by EU Member States accounts for €1 trillion, representing 20 per cent of the EU gross domestic product (GDP).

EU public procurement regulation emerged as a result of its necessity for completing the Union's internal market. Its intellectual origins rest on a neo-liberal approach to European integration which identified purchasing practices and policies of Member States as considerable non-tariff barriers and as factors hindering the functioning of a genuinely competitive internal market.[1] The economic rationale for regulating public procurement has pointed towards the need to introduce competitiveness into the relevant markets, in order to increase cross-border trade of products and services destined for the public sector and to achieve price transparency and price convergence across the internal market of the European Union, thus achieving significant savings.[2] The need for competitiveness and transparency in public procurement markets is also considered as an imperative safeguard of fundamental treaty principles, such as the free movement of goods and services, the right of establishment, and the prohibition of discrimination on grounds of nationality.

The commonly accepted assumption by both European Union institutions and Member States is that public procurement is not subject to the same commercial pressures or organizational incentives as private sector procurement. As a result, public procurement regulation has prompted the establishment of a legal discipline for encouraging effective use of public financial resources, introducing greater efficiency and competition, and reducing the risk of favouritism and corruption. Public procurement regulation has reflected the need for integrated public markets in the European Union, where sufficient levels of competition induce optimal resource allocation patterns for contracting with the public and utilities sectors.

---

[1] See Commission of the European Communities, *White Paper for the Completion of the Internal Market*, COM(85) 310 final, 1985; see also Green Paper on Public Procurement in the European Union: *Exploring the way forward*, European Commission 1996; see also European Commission, Communication on Public Procurement in the European Union, COM(98) 143.

[2] See Commission of the European Communities, *The Cost of Non-Europe, Basic Findings, Vol 5, Part A; The Cost of Non-Europe in Public Sector Procurement* (Official Publications of the European Communities 1988). See also the Cecchini Report *1992 The European Challenge* (Wildwood House 1988).

Administrative competence in public procurement regulation reflects on three jurisdictional facets, an international one, an EU/centralized one and a national/decentralized one. First, public procurement regulation has extraterritorial effects, in as much as it is subject to the WTO Agreement on Government Procurement, which requires reciprocity in market access for public contracts from its signatories. Secondly, Union competence relates to procurement in dimensions triggered by the monetary thresholds of relevant public contracts. The EU legislator has opted for secondary legislation in the form of directives which, as the key legal instruments of the EU integration process, are addressed to Member States and are legally binding frameworks requiring further implementation through incorporating of their provisions into national legal orders. Thirdly, national competence covers sub-dimensional procurement, that is, procurement below thresholds which trigger Union control. Such procurement below the relevant monetary thresholds is excluded from the application of EU public procurement directives, although it is still subject to the fundamental principles of EU law (reflecting the procurement policy basis outlined above). National competence in procurement regulation embraces also judicial review of administrative acts and the awarding of contracts in public procurement.

B Administrative Tasks and Sources of Law in Public Procurement Regulation

The EU public procurement *acquis* derives from two main sets of sources: primary EU law, specifically the Treaty on the Functioning of the European Union (TFEU), in particular its provisions on free movement of goods, freedom of establishment, and the freedom to provide services, and secondary EU law, specifically a series of directives which give tangible shape to the principles enshrined in primary EU law, in particular the principles of equal treatment, non-discrimination, mutual recognition, proportionality, and transparency. The application of the public procurement directives is triggered by the concepts of *contracting authority* and *public contract*, as well as by reference to specified monetary thresholds in relation to the affected public contracts. If the contract amount is below such a threshold, the contact falls outside the scope of the directives. Despite this, it is still subject to the fundamental principles of EU law, and Member States are under an obligation to draw up coordinating national procurement rules and procedures so as to ensure that the principles enshrined in primary EU law are given practical effect, and that procurement below the relevant thresholds (so-called 'sub-dimensional' procurement) is still opened up to competition.

Member States may provide a common national legal framework which regulates sub-dimensional procurement, as well as contracts covered by the pertinent EU directives. Alternatively, Member States may maintain a less stringent regime for sub-dimensional contracts, taking the form of administrative guidance rather than formal legislation and allowing for shorter time limits for the submission of applications and tenders and less demanding rules for the publication and selection of tenders.

A significant source of the Union's public procurement *acquis* is the case law of the CJEU. The evolution of public procurement law has been shaped by the instrumental role of the Union courts.[3] The jurisprudence has influenced the interpretation of the relevant legal concepts, such as that of contracting authorities,[4] the scope of selection and qualification criteria,[5] and the potential for contracting authorities to use environmental and social considerations[6] as award criteria.

The procurement *acquis* also draws on the influence of foundation instruments. The 1986 Single European Act signified the importance of liberalized and integrated public procurement as an essential component of the Single Market.[7] The strategic importance of procurement for European integration was recognized by the 2011 Single Market Act, which itself prompted a series of reforms to the public procurement *acquis*.[8] These reforms aim at linking public procurement directly with the Europe 2020 Strategy, focused on the goals of growth and competitiveness.[9] The enactment of the 2011 measure[10] identified public procurement reforms as essential components for the achievement of those goals,[11] and as indispensable instruments of delivering public services.[12]

[3] See C Bovis, *Public Procurement in the EU: Jurisprudence and Conceptual Directions* (2012) 49 *Common Market Law Review* 1.

[4] See Case C-237/99 *Commission v France* [2001] ECR I-939; Case C-470/99 *Universale-Bau and Others* [2002] ECR I-11617; Case C-373/00 *Adolf Truley* [2003] ECR-193; Case C-84/03 *Commission v Spain* [2005] ECRI-139; Case C-44/96 *Mannesmann Anlagenbau Austria v Strohal Rotationsdurck GesmbH* [1998] ECR I-73; Case C-31/87 *Gebroeders Beentjes BV v Netherlands* [1988] ECR 4635; Case C-360/96 *BFI Holding* [1998] ECR I-6821; Joined Cases C-223/99 *Agora Srl v Ente Autonomo Fiera Internazionale di Milano* and C-260/99 *Excelsior Snc di Pedrotti runa & C v Ente Autonomo Fiera Internazionale di Milano* [2001] ECR 3605; Case C-343/95 *Diego Cali et Figli* [1997] ECR I-1547; Case C-380/98 *The Queen and HM Treasury, ex parte University of Cambridge* [2000] ECR I-8035; Case C-26/03 *Stadt Halle, RPL Recyclingpark Lochau GmbH v Arbeitsgemeinschaft Thermische Restabfall- und Energieverwertungsanlage TREA Leuna* [2005] ECR I-1; Case C-107/98 *Teckal Slr v Comune di Viano* [1999] ECR I-8121; Case C-18/01 *Korhonen and Others* [2003] ECR I-5321.

[5] See Case C-315/01 *GAT and Österreichische Autobahnen und Schnellstraßen AG (ÖSAG)* [2003] ECR I-6351; Joined Cases C-21/03 and C-34/03 *Fabricom SA v État Belge* [2005] ECR I-1559 [26]; Joined Cases C-285/99 and C-286/99 *Lombardini and Mantovani* [2001] ECR I-9233; Case C-324/98 *Telaustria and Telefonadress* [2000] ECR I-10745; Case C-126/03, *Commission v Germany* [2004] ECR I-11197; Case C-176/98 *Holst Italia* [1999] ECR I-8607, para 29; Case C-399/98 *Ordine degli Architetti and Others* [2001] ECR I-5409, para 92; Case C-314/01 *Siemens and ARGE Telekom & Partner* [2004] ECR I-2549, para 44; Case C-57/01 *Makedoniko Metro and Mikhaniki* [2003] ECR I-1091.

[6] See Case C-31/87 *Gebroeders Beentjes BV v Netherlands* (n 4); Case C-225/98 *Commission v French Republic (Nord-Pas-de-Calais)* [2000] ECR 7445; Case C-513/99 *Concordia Bus Filandia Oy Ab v Helsingin Kaupunki et HKL-Bussiliikenne* [2002] ECR 7213.

[7] See European Commission, *White Paper for the Completion of the Internal Market*, COM(85) 310 final; see also Green Paper on Public Procurement in the European Union: *Exploring the way forward* (n 1); see also European Commission, Communication on Public Procurement in the European Union (n 1).

[8] See Green Paper on the modernization of EU public procurement policy: *Towards a more efficient European Procurement Market*, COM(2011) 15/47.

[9] See European Commission, Communication to the European Parliament, the Council, the Economic and Social Committee and the Committee of the Regions, *Towards a Single Market Act*, COM(2010) 608 final.

[10] See European Commission, Communication to the European Parliament, the Council, the Economic and Social Committee and the Committee of the Regions, *Towards a Single Market Act* (n 9).

[11] See European Commission, Communication, Europe 2020, *A strategy for smart, sustainable and inclusive growth*, 3 March 2010, COM(2010) final.

[12] See European Commission, Guide to the application of the European Union rules on state aid, public procurement and the internal market to services of general economic interest, and in particular to social services of general interest, 7 December 2010, SEC(2010) 1545 final. See European Commission, *Buying Social: A Guide to Taking Account of Social Considerations in Public Procurement*, SEC(2010) 1258, final.

With regard to *secondary EU legal measures*, the early stages of the public procurement *acquis* had envisaged separate regimes for works, supplies, and services, with different sets of rules applicable to their respective regulation. The public supplies regime[13] was the first EU legal instrument introduced to regulate public procurement contracts and sought to introduce the principle of free movement of goods in trade between public authorities and the private undertakings. The Public Supplies Directive applied to all products, of whatever description, admitted to free circulation within the then European Community. These were products originating in a Member State together with third-country products admitted to the Community through a Member State. It indicated two types of barriers that states, territorial authorities, and other public corporations could impose upon the procuring of public supplies: (i) those preventing or inhibiting the supply of imported products; and (ii) those favouring the supply of domestic products or granting preferential treatment (other than state aids, which must be assessed under the state aid framework and taxation) to domestic suppliers. The directive listed a number of forms of discrimination against foreign goods. Among those were technical specifications which, although applicable to both domestic and imported products, had restrictive effects on trade.

The public works regime,[14] the second set of EU legal instruments regulating public procurement contracts, was enacted in order to abolish restrictions on the participation of non-nationals in public construction contracts, on the basis of the fundamental EU principles on the right of establishment and the freedom to provide services, and on the prohibition of discriminatory technical specifications, the adequate and prompt advertising of contracts, and the establishment of objective selection and award criteria. The Public Works Directive's major objective was the establishment and enhancement of a regime of transparency in the public works sector, where conditions of undistorted competition would ensure that contracts were allocated to contractors under the most favourable terms for the contracting authorities.

Thirdly, the utilities regime[15] addressed public procurement in supplies and works contracts in the transport, water, energy, and telecommunications sectors, previously excluded from the relevant supplies and works directives. The exclusion of the above-mentioned sectors from the framework of those prior directives was attributed to the fact that the authorities entrusted with the operation of public utilities had been subject to highly varied legal regimes in the Member States, ranging from completely state-controlled enterprises to privately controlled ones. Another reason for the belated regulation of utilities procurement can be attributed to the fact that, due to their purchasing volume and relative magnitude, public utilities procurement constituted an important domestic industrial policy instrument. As a result, Member States

---

[13] Public supplies: Directive 77/62/EEC, [1977] OJ, L13/1; Directive 88/295, [1988] OJ, L127/1; Directive 93/36/EC, [1993] OJ L199, as amended by Directive 97/52/EC, [1997] OJ L328 and Directive 2001/78/EC, [2001] OJ L285.

[14] Public works: Directive 71/304/EEC, [1971] OJ L185/1; Directive 71/305, [1971] OJ L185/5; Directive 89/440, [1989] OJ L234/2; Directive 93/37/EC, [1993] OJ L199, amended by Directive 97/52/EC, [1997] OJ L328 and Directive 2001/78/EC, [2001] OJ L285.

[15] Utilities: Directive 90/531, [1990] OJ L297; Directive 93/38/EC, [1993] OJ L199, amended by Directive 98/4/EC, [1998] OJ L101.

appeared reluctant in subjecting the establishment of their utilities to the rigorously transparent and competitive regimes of public works and supplies purchasing, as they had relied upon preferential and closed utilities procurement in order to sustain strategic industries. Another reason for the introduction of a distinctive legal regime for utilities procurement reflects the interface of the state with utilities companies, and specifically the manner in which national authorities can influence the purchasing behaviour of such entities, including participation in their capital structure and representation on their administrative, managerial, or supervisory bodies. Finally, the closed markets in which utilities operate, as a result of special or exclusive rights granted by the Member States, appeared as a compelling reason for the enactment of a distinctive regime for utilities procurement, ensuring, on the one hand, alignment with the public supplies and public works regimes, and, on the other hand, compliance with the fundamental principles of the Union treaties.

The Public Services Directive[16] was the final legal element in the Union package of instruments on public procurement contracts, enacted to close the gap in the liberalization of trade in services as envisaged by the EU Treaty and by international agreements such as the GATT. The directive was the first attempt to liberalize services in public markets, following the same principles as the other legislation on public procurement, such as compulsory EU-wide advertising of public contracts, prohibition of technical specifications capable of discriminating against potential bidders, and uniform application of objective criteria of participation in tendering and award procedures.

The Remedies Directives, specifically the Public Sector Remedies Directive[17] and the Utilities Remedies Directive,[18] were introduced in order to focus on the obligation of Member States to ensure effective and rapid review of decisions taken by contracting authorities which potentially breach public procurement rules. The Remedies Directives have been based on three principles: those of procedural autonomy, of effectiveness, and of procedural equality. The first principle affords discretion to Member States to organize public procurement review procedures the way which they deem appropriate for their respective legal order. The principle of the effectiveness of review procedures addresses the ability of aggrieved tenderers to set aside decisions of contracting authorities taken unlawfully, or to remove discriminatory technical, economic, or financial specifications in the invitation to tender, the contract documents, or in any other document relating to the contract award procedure. Set-aside procedures were deemed as a legitimate conditional remedy for the award of damages. Thirdly, the principle of procedural equality compels Member States to instigate

---

[16] Public services: Directive 92/50/EEC, [1992] OJ L209, amended by Directive 97/52/EC, [1997] OJ L328 and Directive 2001/78/EC, [2001] OJ L285.

[17] Directive 89/665/EEC of 21 December 1989 on the coordination of the laws, regulations and administrative provisions relating to the application of review procedures to the award of public supply and public works contracts [1989] OJ L395/33.

[18] Directive 92/13/EEC of 25 February 1992 coordinating the laws, regulations and administrative provisions relating to the application of Community rules on the procurement procedures of entities operating in the water, energy, transport and telecommunications sectors [1992] OJ L76/7.

public procurement review procedures in alignment with other national procedures for the review of administrative acts.

The constant evolution of the public procurement *acquis* resulted in an administrative legal framework which codified public sector procurement and maintained the separate regulation of utilities procurement through different instruments.[19] Codification which covers supplies, works, and services procurement in a single legal instrument,[20] has been justified by reference to the need to achieve the opening-up of closed and segmented public sector procurement markets, as well as to achieve legal efficiency, simplification, and compliance.[21] The dichotomy maintained between public sector and utilities procurement regulation can be justified by reference to the positive effects of liberalization of network industries, which has stimulated sectoral competitiveness. The separate regulation for utilities procurement, irrespective of whether in public or privatized ownership, has resulted in a less stringent regime there compared with the regime for public sector procurement.

Three later legal amendments have modified the initial public procurement directives. In particular, Directive 2014/24/EU replaces Public Sector Directive 2004/18 and Directive 2014/25/EU amends the Utilities Directive 2004/17, plus the new Directive 2014/23/EU adds provision on the award of concessions. The last of these represents the most significant recent development in the reform agenda of the EU in public procurement regulation. The main principles envisaged in the Concessions Directive are legal certainty and better access to the concession markets. Concessions are usually long term, complex arrangements, where the concessionaire assumes both responsibilities and risks traditionally borne by the contracting authorities and normally falling within their remit. Contracting authorities and entities should thus be allowed considerable flexibility in defining and organizing the procedure leading to the choice of concessionaire. The duration of a concession should be limited in order to avoid market foreclosure and restriction of competition.

EU public procurement regulation has been influenced by soft law. Three policy categories, the economy, public services, and the environment, have been the basis for soft law development in public procurement regulation. Soft law has impacted on economic aspects of public procurement regulation,[22] identifying national purchasing practices as a considerable non-tariff barrier, and as a hindrance to the functioning of a genuinely competitive internal market.

Such soft law has introduced regulatory and legal interventions with a view to supporting competitiveness in the relevant markets so as to increase cross-border

---

[19] See Directive 2004/18, [2004] OJ L134 of 30 April 2004 on the coordination of procedures for the award of public works contracts, public supply contracts and public service contracts (Public Sector Directive) and Directive 2004/17, [2004] OJ L134 of 30 April 2004 coordinating the procurement procedures of entities operating in the water, energy, transport and postal services sectors (Utilities Directive).

[20] See Public Sector Directive (n 19).

[21] See C Bovis, 'Developing Public Procurement Regulation: Jurisprudence and Its Influence on Lawmaking' (2006) 43 *Common Market Law Review* 461.

[22] *White Paper for the Completion of the Internal Market*, COM(85) 310 final; *The Cost of Non-Europe, Basic Findings, Vol 5, Part A; The Cost of Non-Europe in Public Sector Procurement* (n 2); Green Paper on Public Procurement in the European Union: *Exploring the way forward* (n 1); Communication on Public Procurement in the European Union, (n 1).

penetration of products and services destined for the public sector and to achieve price transparency and convergence across the European Union, thus resulting in significant savings. It has considerably influenced the demarcation of public procurement regulation and public services in the European Union. Although the term 'public services' does not feature in the Union *acquis* under Article 106 TFEU, surrogate concepts have contributed to constructing a notion where the state is expected, or even obliged, to enter the market place in order itself to deliver, or to organize the delivery of, public services. These surrogate concepts are reflected in formulations such *public service obligations* and *universal service obligations*, which have emerged in the sectoral liberalization processes of the European Union. The term *universal service obligations* denotes contractual or regulatory requirements imposed by public authorities upon undertakings with a view to maintaining regularity and affordability in the provision of the relevant services.[23]

Alongside both of those above-mentioned concepts, Article 106(2) TFEU has introduced the further concept of *services of general economic interest* (SGEI), the significance of which has been augmented by virtue of Article 16 TFEU,[24] although not defined further in the treaty or in secondary legislation. It refers, however, to services of an economic nature which the Member States or the Union subject to specific public or universal service obligations by virtue of a general interest criterion. Thus, SGEIs cover those provided by utilities or network industries such as transport, water, postal services, energy, and communications, as well as any other economic activities which may be subject to public service obligations. Public authorities in Member States, whether on the national, regional, or local level, have (depending on the allocation of powers under national law) considerable discretion in defining what they may regard as services of general economic interest.[25] The scope and organization of SGEIs vary considerably amongst the Member States, depending on the history and culture of public intervention in each of them. SGEIs are, therefore, very diverse, and disparities may exist in relation to users' needs and preferences, as a result of different geographical, social, and cultural situations. Accordingly, it is essentially the responsibility of the public authorities at national, regional, or local level to decide on the nature and scope of a service of general interest. In accordance with the principles of subsidiarity and proportionality, the Union acts only where necessary, and within the limits of the powers conferred on it by the TFEU. Its action respects the diversity of the situations in the Member States, and in the roles devolved to national, regional, and local authorities for ensuring the well-being of citizens and promoting social cohesion, while guaranteeing democratic choices in relation

---

[23] In the context of the Universal Services Directive EC No 2002/22, universal service obligations are services made available to the public at the quality specified to all end-users in their territory, independently of geographical location, and, in the light of specific national conditions, at an affordable price.

[24] Article 16 EC reads: 'Without prejudice to Articles 77, 90 and 92 [now Articles 73, 106, and 87 EC], and given the place occupied by services of general economic interest in the shared values of the Union as well as their role in promoting social and territorial cohesion, the Community and the Member States, each within their respective powers and within the scope of application of this Treaty, shall take care that such services operate on the basis of principles and conditions which enable them to fulfil their missions'.

[25] See Case T-17/02 *Fred Olsen* [2005] ECR II-2031, para 216; Case T-289/03 *BUPA and Others v Commission* [2008] ECR II-81, paras 166–69; Case T-309/04 *TV2* [2008] ECR II-2935, paras 113 ff.

to the level and quality of services. It is entirely up to the public authorities to decide whether to provide a service themselves, or to entrust it to a third party (external-ization). The public procurement rules apply only if the public authority decides to externalize such service provision by entrusting it to a third party against remuner-ation from the public sector.

Soft law also impacted on the relation of public procurement regulation to envir-onmental protection.[26] A comprehensive framework has been developed and imple-mented in conjunction with, and by reference to, existing EU legislation in areas such as standardization, eco-labelling, taxation, environmental agreements, state aid, and industry and product policy, and with a view of identifying the standards for awarding public contracts based on environmental criteria.

C Underlying Legal Principles in Public Procurement Regulation

The procurement directives seek to serve the following five principles:

 (i) transparency, through the mandatory publicity and monitoring requirements of public contracts

 (ii) non-discrimination, through the application of standardized selection and qualification procedures, and uniform award procedures

 (iii) objectivity, through the application of standardization and of award criteria for public contracts which do not permit preferential treatment

 (iv) accountability, through the obligation of reasoning and the monitoring of public contract awards and

 (v) justiciability, through redress and access to justice.

1 The principle of transparency in public procurement

The principle of transparency, embedded in the public procurement directives, sup-ports three main objectives: first, of establishing a system of openness in the public purchasing of the Member States, for greater degree of accountability and elimination of potential direct discrimination on grounds of nationality; secondly, of ensuring that transparency in public procurement represents a substantial basis for a system of best practice for both public and private sectors; and finally, of recognizing that it is imperative to the procedural integrity for redress and access to justice.

The principle of transparency has imprinted a significant effect on the regime, namely that of price competitiveness, an obvious trade effect. The fact that interested suppliers are aware of a contracting authority's determination to procure, and that

---

[26] Commission Interpretative Communication on the Community law applicable to public procurement and the possibilities for integrating environmental considerations into public procurement, COM(2001) 274, 4 July 2001; EU, *Internal Market Integration Strategy* 2001; EU Green Public Procurement emanates from Internal Market Priorities; *Buying Green!—A Handbook on green public procurement*, adopted in 2004 and revised in 2011, 2016; *Public Procurement for a Better Environment*, 2008.

other competitors are informed, indicates two distinct parameters relevant to price competitiveness and value for money. The first of these focuses on price comparison, revealing the possibility for contracting authorities to make informed assessments of both the prices and the quality of products and services. The second parameter has an effect on the pricing behaviour on the supply side of public procurement (the private sector), which can, amongst other things, no longer rely on the lack of price comparisons when dealing with the public sector. Transparency in public procurement ultimately results in price convergence for products and services destined for the public sector and in market integration.

2 The principle of non-discrimination

The principle of non-discrimination on grounds of nationality epitomizes the administrative law interface of public procurement regulation through standardization in selection and qualification criteria and through uniformity in the award procedures.

(a) The doctrine of equivalence in criteria

During the selection and qualification process of tenderers, contracting authorities vet all candidates according to objectively defined criteria aimed at eliminating arbitrariness and discrimination. The selection criteria are related to two major categories of qualifications: (i) legal, and (ii) technical/economic. Contracting authorities must strictly follow the homogeneously specified selection *criteria* for enterprises participating in the contract award procedures in order to avoid potential discrimination on the ground of nationality (including that of the seat or place of registration of corporations) and to exclude *technical specifications* capable of favouring national undertakings.

Standardization and specifications can act as a non-tariff barrier in public procurement contracts in two ways. First, contracting authorities may use divergent systems of standards and specifications as an excuse for disqualifying particular tenderers. It should be maintained here that the description of the intended supplies, works, or services to be procured is supposed to be made by reference to the common products classification (CPA),[27] the Statistical Classification of Economic Activities in the European Community (NACE),[28] and the Common Procurement Vocabulary (CPV).[29] However, this type of description is of generic nature and does not cover industrial specifications and standardization requirements. Secondly, standardization and specification requirements can be restrictively defined in order to exclude products or services of a particular origin, or to narrow the field of competition amongst tenderers.

---

[27] 'Classification of Products by Activity' (CPA version 2.1) was adopted in October 2014, entering into force 1 January 2015. Some sections of the CPA have been aligned with the UN Central Product Classification and its new version 2.1 (CPC Ver February 1) but overall the CPA has remained unchanged.
[28] 'Nomenclature statistique des activités économiques dans la Communauté européenne' (NACE Rev 2) has been in use from 1 January 2008 onwards.
[29] Adopted by Regulation (EC) 213/2008, in use since 17 September 2008.

National standards are not only the result of domestic legislation (which, of course, needs to be harmonized and mutually recognized across the common market); one of the most significant aspects of standardization and specification appears to be the operation of voluntary standards, mainly adopted on the industry level. The latter presents difficulties in any attempt at harmonization, as approximation and mutual recognition of standards relies on the willingness of the industry in question. Such voluntary standards and specifications are used often in the utilities sector, where the relevant procurement requirements are complex and cannot be specified solely by reference to 'statutory' standards, thus leaving a considerable margin of discretion in the hands of the contracting authorities, which may then be abused during the selection and qualification stages of procurement.

National technical standards, industrial product, and service specifications and their harmonization have been considered priority areas for the realization of the internal market. The 'equivalent standard' doctrine has been established,[30] where contracting authorities are prohibited from introducing technical specifications or trademarks which mention products of a certain make or source, or a particular process which favour or eliminate certain undertakings, unless these specifications are justified by the subject and nature of the contract, and on condition that they are only permitted if they are accompanied by the words 'or equivalent'. The rules on technical standards and specifications have been brought in line with the new policy which is based on the mutual recognition of national requirements, where the objectives of national legislation are essentially equivalent, and on the process of legislative harmonization of technical standards through non-governmental standardization organizations (CEPT, CEN, CENELEC).[31]

The relevant provisions of the procurement directives relating to the criteria of a tenderer's good standing and qualification are directly effective.[32] These criteria include grounds for exclusion from participation in the award of public contracts, such as bankruptcy, professional misconduct, failure to fulfil social security obligations, and obligations relating to taxes. They also refer to the technical ability and knowledge of the contractor, where proof of them may be furnished by educational or professional qualifications, previous experience in performing public contracts, and statements on the contractor's expertise. In principle, there are automatic grounds for exclusion, when a contractor, supplier, or service provider: (i) is bankrupt or is being wound up; (ii) is the subject of proceedings for a declaration of bankruptcy or for an order for compulsory winding up; (iii) has been convicted of an offence concerning his professional conduct; (iv) has been guilty of grave professional misconduct; (v) has not fulfilled obligations relating to social security contributions; and (vi) has not fulfilled obligations relating to the payment of taxes.

---

[30] See Case C-45/87 *Commission v Ireland* [1988] ECR 4929; see also Case C-359/93 *Commission v Netherlands* [1995] ECR I-157.

[31] See Art 7 Directive 88/295. See the White Paper on Completing the Internal Market, paras 61–79; see also Council Resolution of 7 May 1985, [1985] OJ C136 on a new approach in the field of technical harmonization and standards.

[32] See Case C-76/81 *SA Transporoute et Travaux v Minister of Public Works* [1982] ECR 457.

However, for the purposes of assessing the financial and economic standing of contractors, an exception to the exhaustive list covering the contractors' eligibility and technical capacity is provided for, where, in particular, contracting entities may request references other than those expressly mentioned therein. Evidence of financial and economic standing may be provided by means of references including: (i) appropriate statements from banks; (ii) the presentation of the firm's balance sheets or extracts where these are published under company law provisions; and (iii) a statement of the firm's annual turnover and the turnover on construction works for the three previous financial years. The non-exhaustive character of the list of references in relation to the contractors' economic and financial standing has been recognized,[33] so that the value of the works which may be carried out at one time may constitute proof of the contractors' economic and financial standing. The contracting authorities may fix such a limit, as the provisions of the directives do not aim at limiting the powers of Member States, but rather at determining the references or evidence which may be furnished in order to establish the contractors' financial and economic standing. It has been maintained that the examination of a contractor's suitability based on its good standing and qualifications, and on its financial and economic standing,[34] may take place simultaneously with the procedures for the awarding of a contract.[35] However, it must be noted that the two procedures (suitability evaluation and bid evaluation) are totally distinct processes which should not be confused with one another.[36]

(b) Uniformity in procedures

The principle of non-discrimination is extended to the award procedures for public contracts, where these may lead to discriminatory practices and decisions. Negotiation procedures are treated narrowly. According to the procurement directives, negotiated procedures without prior advertisement or notification shall be used restrictively, inter alia when, for technical or artistic reasons or reasons connected with the protection of exclusive rights, the services could only be procured from a particular provider and in cases of extreme urgency brought about by events unforeseeable by the contracting authority.[37] The existence of such reasons which then point to a particular contractor or service provider with which a contracting authority is to negotiate, without prior advertisement, has received a restrictive interpretation.[38] Abuse of exclusive rights is contrary to the right of establishment and freedom to provide services, and contradicts the principle of equal treatment which prohibits not only overt discrimination on grounds of nationality, but also all covert and/or indirect forms of discrimination.

---

[33] See Joined Cases C-27/86, 28/86, and 29/86: C-27/86 *Constructions et Enterprises Industrielles SA (CEI) v Association Intercommunale pour les Autoroutes des Ardennes*; Case 28/86 *Ing.A Bellini & Co SpA v Regie de Betiments*; Case 29/86 *Ing.A Bellini & Co SpA v Belgian State* [1987] ECR 3347.

[34] See Case C-31/87 *Gebroeders Beentjes BV v Netherlands* (n 4).

[35] See Case C-28/86 *Bellini* [1987] ECR 3347.

[36] See Case C-71/92 *Commission v Spain* [1993] ECR I-5923.

[37] See eg Art 32 of Directive 2014/24/EU of the European Parliament and of the Council of 26 February 2014 on public procurement [2014] OJ L94 of 28 March 2014, at 65–242.

[38] See Case C-199/85 *Commission v Italy* [1987] ECR 1039; see also Case C-3/88 *Commission v Italy* [1989] ECR 4035.

It should be noted that exclusive rights might include contractual arrangements such as know-how and intellectual property rights.

Urgency reasons, brought about by events unforeseen by contracting authorities, have received similarly restrictive interpretation.[39] There is need of a justification test based on the proportionality principle, as well as the existence of a causal link between the alleged urgency and the unforeseen events.[40]

3 The principle of objectivity in award criteria

The principle of objectivity in procurement regulation reflects the need for good governance and sound administration, and is depicted in the efforts to eliminate preferential treatment in the award criteria for public contracts. Throughout the evolution of the public procurement *acquis*, the procedural phase in the procurement process culminated in the application of objectively determined criteria demonstrating the logic behind the behaviour of contracting authorities. The criteria on which the contracting authorities must base the award of public contracts are essentially two:[41] (a) the criteria of the *most economically advantageous tender*, but allowing for (b) criteria of a not strictly economic kind; or (c) the *lowest price*, but taking into account the problem of (d) abnormally low tenders.

(a) The most economically advantageous tender

When the award is made to the tender most economically advantageous from the point of view of the contracting authority, various criteria linked to the subject-matter of the public contract in question can be taken into consideration, for example: quality, price, technical merit, aesthetic and functional characteristics, environmental characteristics, running costs, cost-effectiveness, after-sales service and technical assistance, and delivery date/period, or period of completion. The above listed criteria constituting the key parameters of the most economically advantageous offer are, however, not exhaustive.[42]

A wide interpretation of the criteria of most economically advantageous award has been accepted.[43] This has allowed contracting authorities to select the factors which they want to apply in evaluating tenders,[44] provided these factors are mentioned, in hierarchical order of priority, or descending sequence, in the invitation to tender or the contract documents,[45] so that tenderers and interested parties can clearly ascertain

---

[39] See Case C-199/85 *Commission v Italy* (n 38); Case C-3/88, *Commission v Italy* (n 38); Case C-24/91 *Commission v Spain* [1994] CMLR 621; Case C-107/92 *Commission v Italy* [1993] ECR I-4655; Case C-57/94 *Commission v Italy* [1995] ECR I-1249; Case C-296/92 *Commission v Italy* [1994] ECR I-1.

[40] See Case C-107/92 *Commission v Italy* (n 39) judgment of 2 August 1993.

[41] Art 53 Public Sector Directive (n 19).   [42] ibid Art 53(1)(a).

[43] Case 31/87 *Gebroeders Beentjes v Netherlands* (n 4) para 19.

[44] Case C-324/93 *R v The Secretary of State for the Home Department, ex parte Evans Medical Ltd and Macfarlan Smith Ltd* [1995] ECR I-563, where the national court asked whether factors concerning continuity and reliability as well as security of supplies fall under the framework of the most economically advantageous offer, when the latter is being evaluated.

[45] Case 31/87 *Gebroeders Beentjes v Netherlands* (n 4) para 22.

the relative weight of factors, other than price, for the evaluation process. However, factors, which have no strict relevance in determining the most economically advantageous offer by reference to objective criteria are seen as involving an element of arbitrary choice and therefore as incompatible with the directives.[46]

(b) Criteria related to the subject matter of the contract

The assessment of the most economically advantageous tender for a contract must contain factors which are related to the subject matter of the contract but could also include criteria that pursue advantages which cannot be objectively assigned a direct economic value. Not all of the award criteria used by the contracting authority to identify the most economically advantageous tender must, then, necessarily be of a purely economic nature.[47] Where the contracting authority decides to award a contract to the tenderer who submits the most economically advantageous tender, it may take into consideration different criteria, provided that they are linked to the subject matter of the contract, do not confer an unrestricted freedom of choice on the authority, are expressly mentioned in the contract documents or the tender notice, and comply with all the fundamental principles of Union law, in particular the principle of non-discrimination.[48]

(c) The lowest price

When the lowest price has been selected as the award criterion, contracting authorities must not refer to any qualitative consideration when deliberating upon the award of a contract. The lowest price is then the sole quantitative benchmark intended for differentiating the offers made.[49] However, contracting authorities can reject a tender where they regard the price attached to it as abnormally low, as discussed below.

(d) Abnormally low tenders

In cases that tenders appear to be abnormally low in relation to the goods, works or services, the contracting authority must request in writing details of the constituent elements of the tender which it considers relevant, before it rejects such tenders.[50] The clarification details[51] may relate in particular to:

(a) the economics of the construction method, the manufacturing process, or the services provided

(b) the technical solutions chosen and/or any exceptionally favourable conditions available to the tenderer for the execution of the work, or for the supply of the goods or services

(c) the originality of the work, supplies, or services proposed by the tenderer

---

[46] ibid para 37. [47] See Case C-513/99 *Concordia Bus Finland* (n 6) para 55.
[48] ibid para 69. [49] See Art 53(1)(b) Public Sector Directive (n 19). [50] ibid Art 55.
[51] ibid Art 55(1).

(d) compliance with the provisions relating to employment protection and working conditions in force at the place where the work, service, or supply is to be performed and

(e) the possibility that the tenderer has obtained or will obtain state aid.

Where a contracting authority establishes that a tender is abnormally low because of the last of these factors (state aid), the tender can be rejected on that ground alone only after consultation with the tenderer where the latter is unable to prove, within a reasonable time limit, that the aid in question was granted legally.[52] The fact that tenders are directly or indirectly subsidized by the state or other contracting authorities (or even by the contracting authority itself) can be legitimately part of the evaluation process.[53] Where the contracting authority rejects a tender in these circumstances, it must inform the Commission of its decision.

4 The principle of accountability

The effects of the principle of accountability on public procurement regulation have been felt in two main ways: the probity of procurement practices and the availability of judicial redress.

(a) The effect of probity in public procurement

The award of public contracts to economic operators who have participated in a criminal organization, or who have been found guilty of corruption or of fraud to the detriment of the financial interests of the European Union or of money laundering, should be avoided. Where appropriate, the contracting authorities should ask candidates or tenderers to supply relevant documents and, where they have doubts concerning the personal situation of a candidate or tenderer, they may seek the cooperation of the competent authorities of the Member State concerned. The exclusion of such economic operators is to occur as soon as the contracting authority has knowledge of a judgment concerning such offences, rendered in accordance with national law and having the force of *res judicata*. Where national law contains provisions to this effect, noncompliance with environmental legislation, or engaging in unlawful agreements in public contracts, either of which has been the subject of a final judgment (or a decision having equivalent effect) may be considered an offence bearing on the professional conduct of the economic operator concerned, or grave misconduct. Non-observance of national provisions implementing Directives 2000/78/EC[54]

---

[52] ibid Art 55(3).

[53] See Case C-94/99 *ARGE Gewässerschutz* [2000] ECR I-11037, where the Court adopted a literal interpretation of the directives and concluded that, if the legislature wanted to preclude subsidized entities from participating in tendering procedures for public contracts, it should have said so explicitly in the relevant directives. The Court did not elaborate on the possibility of rejection of an offer, which is appreciably lower than those of unsubsidized tenderers by reference to the abnormally low disqualification ground. See in particular paras 26 ff of the Court's judgment.

[54] See Council Directive 2000/78/EC of 27 November 2000 establishing a general framework for equal treatment in employment and occupation ([2000] OJ L303 of 2 December 2000, at 16).

and Directive 2006/54/EC,[55] concerning equal treatment of workers, where this has been the subject of a final court judgment (or equivalent) may be similarly regarded.

Article 45 Public Sector Directive deals with the personal situation of the candidate or tenderer. It provides that any candidate or tenderer who has been the subject of a conviction by final judgment, of which the contracting authority is aware, for one or more of the reasons listed below must be excluded from participation in a public contract:

(a) participation in a criminal organization, as defined in Article 2(1) of Council Joint Action 98/733/JHA[56]

(b) corruption, as defined in Article 3 of the Council Act of 26 May 1997[57] and Article 3(1) of Council Joint Action 98/742/JHA[58] respectively

(c) fraud within the meaning of Article 1 of the Convention relating to the protection of the financial interests of the European Communities[59]

(d) money laundering, as defined in Article 1 of Council Directive 91/308 on prevention of the use of the financial system for the purpose of money laundering.[60]

In cases of EU funded programmes in the Member States, or of co-financing contracts between Member States and EU Institutions, Member States bear the responsibility for investigating irregularities, and for making financial corrections required and for pursuing the recovery of European funds or of the co-financing portions of public contracts. Irregularity means any breach of Union law, or of national law relating to its application, resulting from an act or omission by an economic operator involved in the implementation of the European Structural and Investment Funds (ESIF), which has, or would have, the effect of prejudicing the budget of the Union by charging an unjustified item of expenditure to the budget of

---

[55] Directive 2006/54/EC of the European Parliament and of the Council of 5 July 2006 on the implementation of the principle of equal opportunities and equal treatment of men and women in matters of employment and occupation [2006] OJ L204 of 26 July 2006, at 23–36; replacing Council Directive 76/207/EEC of 9 February 1976 on the implementation of the principle of equal treatment for men and women as regards access to employment, vocational training and promotion, and working conditions ([1976] OJ L39 of 14 February 1976, at 40).

[56] See [1998] OJ L351 of 29 December 1998, at 1, repealed by Council Framework Decision 2008/841/JHA of 24 October 2008 on the fight against organised crime [2008] OJ L300 of 11 November 2008, at 42–45.

[57] See [1997] OJ C195 of 25 June 1997, at 1.

[58] See [1998] OJ L358 of 31 December 1998, at 2, repealed by Council Framework Decision 2003/568/JHA of 22 July 2003 on combating corruption in the private sector [2003] OJ L192 of 31 July 2003, at 54–56.

[59] See [1995] OJ C316 of 27 November 1995, at 48.

[60] See [1991] OJ L166 of 28 June 1991, at 77, now governed by Directive (EU) 2015/849 of the European Parliament and of the Council of 20 May 2015 on the prevention of the use of the financial system for the purposes of money laundering or terrorist financing, amending Regulation (EU) No 648/2012 of the European Parliament and of the Council, and repealing Directive 2005/60/EC of the European Parliament and of the Council and Commission Directive 2006/70/EC, [2015] OJ L141 of 5 June 2015, at 73–117.

the Union. Suspected fraud means an irregularity giving rise to the initiation of administrative and/or judicial proceedings at national level in order to establish the presence of intentional behaviour, in particular fraud. The distinction between irregularities and fraud is that fraud is a criminal act that can be determined only as the outcome of judicial proceedings. As such, it is only when the judicial procedure has come to an end that the actual amount of fraud can be determined. The purpose of financial corrections is to restore a situation where all of the expenditure declared for co-financing from the Structural Funds has been applied in line with the applicable national and EU rules. When it is not possible or practicable to quantify the amount of irregular expenditure precisely, or when it would be disproportionate to cancel the expenditure in question entirely, the Commission will base its financial corrections on extrapolation or a flat rate. The amounts and rates of such flat rate corrections are set out in EC Decision C(2013) 9527 of 19 December 2013 and are applied to individual cases of irregularities due to non-compliance with the rules on public procurement.

(b) Redress in public procurement

The spectrum of redress in public procurement contracts reflects on three pivotal concepts for remedies available to aggrieved parties before national courts: first, interim protection; secondly, set-aside and annulment of decisions of contracting authorities; and, finally, actions for damages. Three fundamental principles underlie redress in public procurement: those of effectiveness, of non-discrimination, and of procedural autonomy. Effective review of decisions or acts of contracting authorities is the essential requirement to ensure compliance with the substantive public procurement rules. The principle of effectiveness includes two individual features; first, the swift resolution of disputes, and secondly, enforceability of decisions. In particular, the Remedies Directives stipulate that Member States must take any measures necessary to ensure that decisions taken by the contracting authorities may be reviewed effectively, as rapidly as possible, and can be effectively enforced,[61] for the reason that such decisions have infringed EU law in the field of public procurement or national implementing law. There is an explicit obligation imposed on Member States to avoid introducing review procedures for decisions of contracting authorities and utilities, as well as procedures for the recovery of damages which differ, in a discriminatory manner, from review procedures for other administrative acts and from procedures for the recovery of damages under national law.[62] Finally, the Remedies Directives leave Member States with wide discretion as to the creation of the appropriate forum to receive complaints and to conduct legal actions against decisions of contracting authorities and utilities, as well as actions for damages in public procurement cases.[63]

---

[61] See Art 2(7) Directive 89/665 (n 17) and Art 2(8) Directive 92/13 (n 18).
[62] See Art 1(2) Directive 89/665 (n 17) and Art 1(2) Directive 92/13 (n 18).
[63] See Art 2(2) Public Sector Remedies Directive (n 17) and Art 2(2) Utilities Remedies Directive (n 18).

D Legal Rules Governing the Substance of Public Procurement Regulation

Two concepts are fundamental to the traction of public procurement law: the concept of contracting authorities (or contracting 'entities' in utilities procurement) and the concept of public contracts.

1 The concept of contracting authorities under public procurement law

(a) Generally

In both the Public Sector Directive and the Utilities Directive, the term contracting authorities or entities embrace national (state), regional, or local authorities (i.e., public authorities), bodies governed by public law, associations formed by one or several of such authorities, or other bodies governed by public law.[64] A 'body governed by public law' means any organization which satisfies the following conditions cumulatively: first, the organization must be established for the specific purpose of meeting needs in the general interest, but without having an industrial or commercial character; secondly, it must have legal personality; thirdly, it must be financed, for the most part, by a public authority (in the sense mentioned above), or other bodies governed by public law. Alternatively, and as part of the third criterion, a body governed by public law is one subject to management supervision by, or has an administrative, managerial, or supervisory board, of which more than half of the members are appointed by a public authority.

In the Utilities Procurement Directive, the term contracting entities also include public undertakings, over which the contracting authorities may exercise, directly or indirectly, a dominant influence by virtue of ownership, financial participation, or the rules which govern them.[65] The Utilities Directive includes as contracting entities also undertakings which, although they themselves are not contracting authorities or public undertakings, operate on the basis of special or exclusive rights granted by a competent authority of a Member State by virtue of legislative, regulatory, or administrative provisions.[66] The conferral of such special or exclusive rights substantially affects the ability of other entities to carry out such activities in the market place.[67]

---

[64] See Art 1(9) Public Sector Directive (n 19) and Art 2(1)(a) Utilities Directive (n 19). Non-exhaustive lists of bodies and categories of bodies governed by public law which fulfil the three cumulative criteria for a body governed by public law are set out in Annex III of the directive. Member States must periodically notify the Commission of any changes to their lists of bodies and categories of bodies.

[65] See Art 2(1)(b) Utilities Directive (n 19). Contracting authorities exercise dominant influence upon public undertakings when directly or indirectly, in relation to an undertaking, hold the majority of the undertaking's subscribed capital, or control the majority of the votes attaching to shares issued by the undertaking, or can appoint more than half of the undertaking's administrative, management, or supervisory body.

[66] ibid Art 2(3).

[67] See C Bovis, 'Public Procurement and Public Services in the EU' in I Lianos and O Odudu (eds), *Regulating Trade in Services in the EU and the WTO: Trust, Distrust and Economic Integration* (CUP 2012).

In addition to contracting authorities and contracting entities, a central purchasing body[68] is a contracting entity within the meaning of that directive.[69] A contracting authority within the meaning of the Public Sector Directive[70] also includes a body which acquires supplies or services intended for contracting entities, or awards public contracts, or concludes framework agreements for works, supplies, or services intended for contracting authorities. Contracts between public purchasing bodies and contracting authorities are excluded from the application of the public procurement directives, provided that the central purchasing body has complied with the relevant procurement rules laid down in the Utilities Directive or in the Public Sector Directive.[71]

The development of the concept of contracting authority is linked with the flexibility inherent in the regulatory regime, demonstrated through certain doctrines established by the jurisprudence of the Union courts. These include the doctrines of functionality and dependency in order to define the notion of contracting authorities, as well as the doctrines of dualism, commercialism, and competitiveness in order to determine the scope and thrust of public procurement rules.

(b) The doctrine of functionality

Functionality depicts a flexible and pragmatic approach in the applicability of the procurement directives. Entities and bodies which have been set up by the state to carry out tasks entrusted by legislation, but are not formally part of a state's administrative structure, could not fall within the term contracting authorities, since they are not formally part of the state, nor could they be classified as a body governed by public law.[72] The functional understanding of the concept of contracting authorities has marked the departure from a formalistic test, which had rigidly positioned an entity under state control via traditional public law analysis *stricto sensu*.[73] Functionality, as an ingredient of assessing the relationship between an entity and the state demonstrates, in addition to the elements of management or financial control, the importance of constituent factors such as the intention and purpose of the establishment of the entity in question.[74] The doctrine of functionality supports the principle of transparency, as its application enhances the coverage of public procurement regulation.

---

[68] See Art 1(8) Utilities Directive (n 19). [69] ibid Art 2(1)(a).
[70] See Art 1(9) Public Sector Directive (n 19).
[71] See Art 1(10) Public Sector Directive (n 19) and Art 29(1) and (2) Utilities Directive (n 19).
[72] This is particularly the case of non-governmental organizations (NGOs) which operate under the auspices of the central or local government and are responsible for public interest functions.
[73] The formality test and the relation between the state and entities under its control was established in Case C-249/81 *Commission v Ireland* [1982] ECR 4005; Case C-36/74 *Walrave and Koch v Association Union Cycliste International and Others* [1974] ECR 1423.
[74] See Case 31/87 *Gebroeders Beentjes BV v Netherlands* (n 4); Case C-353/96 *Commission v Ireland* [1998] ECR I-8565 and Case C-306/97 *Connemara Machine Turf Co Ltd v Coillte Teoranta* [1998] ECR I-8761; Case C-323/96 *Commission v Kingdom of Belgium* [1998] ECR I-5063.

(c) The doctrine of dependency

The doctrine of dependency brings entities which are dependent on public authorities within the scope of public procurement regulation, but excludes situations where such dependency amounts to an in-house relationship.

In this regard, bodies 'governed by public law' raise particular questions. The third criterion (above) in relation to such bodies—that they must be primarily *financed* by, be subject to supervision by, or have an administrative or supervisory board with a majority of members appointed by one or more public authorities—implies that they would have a close dependency on a public sector authority, in terms of *corporate governance, supervision*, and *financing*.[75] Even one such feature of dependency satisfies that third criterion, rendering public procurement rules applicable.

Supervision by the state, or other contracting authority, entails not only administrative verification of legality or of the appropriate use of funds, or other exceptional control measures, but also the conferring of a significant influence over management policy, such as the circumscribing of the scope of activities, the supervision of compliance, in addition to overall administrative supervision.[76] Dependency presupposes a control similar to that which a public authority exercises over its own departments. However, such a 'similarity' of control also suggests a lack of independence with regard to decision-making, so that an agreement between a contracting authority and an entity over which the former exercises such a high degree of control, and where that entity carries out an essential part of its activities for and on behalf of the contracting authority, is not a public contract (irrespective of that entity's being abstractly capable of being a contracting authority in its own right or not).[77] Such a level of control, as a reflection of dependency, reveals another facet of the concept of contracting authorities: the non-applicability of the public procurement rules for in-house relationships.

Financing by the state or a contracting authority is an indication that an entity could be a 'body governed by public law'. However, this indication is not absolute.[78] Only certain kinds of payment made to a body by a state or other public authority have the effect of creating or reinforcing a specific relationship of subordination and dependency. The funding of an entity within a general, non-specific framework indicates that the entity has close dependency links with the public authority concerned. If, however, there is a specific financing nexus, such as a contractual one, the dependency tie is not sufficiently close to allow the entity to be categorized as a body governed by public law on the third criterion. Such a relationship is analogous to the dependency that exists in normal commercial relations formed by reciprocal contracts, which

---

[75] This type of dependency resembles the Court's definition in its ruling on state controlled enterprises in Case 152/84 *Marshall v Southampton and South West Hampshire Area Health Authority* [1986] ECR 723.

[76] See Case C-237/99 *Commission v France* (n 4) judgment of 1 February 2001.

[77] See Case C-107/98 *Teckal Slr v Comune di Viano* (n 4).

[78] See Case C-380/98 *The Queen and HM Treasury, ex parte University of Cambridge* (n 4) judgment of 3 October 2000. The Court stipulated that the proportion of public finances received by an entity, as one of the alternative features of the third criterion of the term bodies governed by public law must exceed 50% to enable it meeting that criterion. For assessment purposes of this feature, there must be an annual evaluation of the (financial) status of an entity for the purposes of being regarded as a contracting authority.

have been negotiated freely between the parties. The existence of a contract between the parties, apart from the specific considerations of funding, is a strong indicator of supply substitutability, in the sense that the entity receiving the funding may well face competition in the relevant markets.

(d) The doctrine of dualism

The understanding of the concept of bodies governed by public law is problematic in a further sense. The dual capacity of an entity as a public service provider and a commercial undertaking respectively, and the weighting of the relevant (potentially regulated) activity in relation to the overall proportion of its output or activity, could be regarded as the decisive factor in determining whether an entity is a 'body governed by public law'. That argument appeared for the first time when it was suggested that, only where activities of an entity in pursuit of the 'public services obligations' supersede its overall commercial scope, would the entity be considered as one covered by public law, and therefore a contracting authority for the purpose of procurement regulation.[79] The doctrine of dualism specifically implies that contracting authorities may pursue dual activities: the procurement of goods, works, and services destined for public use, and participation in commercial undertakings. In other words, it is possible for them also to pursue activities other than those which meet needs of the general interest (of the public) not having an industrial and commercial character. The proportion of the one to the other is, however, irrelevant for the characterization of that entity as a body governed by public law. Rather, what is relevant is the intention in establishing the entity in question. It is this which reflects on the 'specificity' requirement, noting however that specificity does not mean exclusivity of purpose. Rather, it points to the intention of the establishment in order to meet general needs. Along these lines, mere ownership or financing of an entity by a contracting authority is not in itself a guarantee that the entity was established to meet general (public) need.

(e) The doctrines of commercialism and competitiveness

Commercial activity, and its relationship to needs in the general interest, represents the most important link between profit-making and public interest, as features underpinning the activities of bodies governed by public law. The criterion of the 'specific establishment of an entity to meet needs in the general interest having non-commercial or industrial character' has been clarified by the Court.[80] The absence of commercial or industrial character is viewed as an integral criterion intended to clarify the term 'needs in the general interest'. There may well be needs of general interest which have an industrial and commercial character. It is also possible that private undertakings can meet needs of general interest which lack industrial and commercial character.

---

[79] See Case C-44/96 *Mannesmann Anlangenbau Austria v Strohal Rotationsdurck GesmbH* (n 4).

[80] See Joined Cases C-223/99 *Agora Srl v Ente Autonomo Fiera Internazionale di Milano* and C-260/99 *Excelsior Snc di Pedrotti runa & C v Ente Autonomo Fiera Internazionale di Milano* (n 4) judgment of 10 May 2001; Case C-360/96 *BFI Holding BV* (n 4) judgment of 10 November 1998; Case C-44/96 *Mannesmann Anlangenbau Austria v Strohal Rotationsdurck GesmbH* (n 4) judgment of 15 January 1998.

The acid test for 'needs in the general interest not having an industrial or commercial character' as such is that the state or other contracting authorities choose themselves to meet these needs or that they have a decisive influence over their provision.

If an activity which meets general needs is pursued in a competitive environment, there is a strong indication that the entity, which pursues it is not a body governed by public law.[81] The reason for this conclusion can be found in the relationship between competitiveness and commerciality. Market forces reveal the commercial or industrial character of an activity, irrespective of the latter's meeting the needs of general interest or not. However, market competitiveness as well as profitability cannot be absolute, determining factors for the commerciality or the industrial nature of an activity. They are in themselves not sufficient to exclude the possibility that a body governed by public law may choose to be guided by considerations other than economic ones. The absence of competition is, then, not a condition necessarily to be taken into account in order to define a body governed by public law. The existence, however, of significant competition in the market place may be indicative of the absence of a need in the general interest lacking commercial or industrial elements.

2 The concept of public contracts

A precondition to the application of the public procurement directives is the existence of a 'public contract'. Public contracts[82] are contracts for pecuniary interest concluded in writing between one or more economic operators and one or more contracting authorities, having as their object the execution of works,[83] the supply of products,[84] or the provision of services.[85] Public procurement law has an exclusive legal basis for determining the meaning of a public contract. The determining factor of its nature is not what is described as a public contract—or how—in national law, nor is the legal regime (public or private) which governs its terms and conditions, nor are the intentions of the parties.[86] The crucial determinants of a public contract, apart from the obvious

---

[81] See Joined Cases C-223/99 *Agora Srl v Ente Autonomo Fiera Internazionale di Milano* and C-260/99 *Excelsior Snc di Pedrotti runa & C v Ente Autonomo Fiera Internazionale di Milano* (n 4).

[82] Art 1(2)(a) Public Sector Directive (n 19).

[83] ibid Art 1(2)(b) specifies as public works contracts, contracts which have as their object either the execution or both the design and execution, of works, or the completion, by whatever means, of a work corresponding to the requirements specified by the contracting authority. A work means the outcome of building or civil engineering works taken as a whole which is sufficient of itself to fulfil an economic or technical function.

[84] ibid Art 1(2)(c) specifies as public supply contracts, contracts having as their object the purchase, lease, rental or hire purchase, with or without option to buy, of products. A public contract having as its object the supply of products and which also covers, as an incidental matter, placement and installation operations must be considered as a public supply contract.

[85] ibid Art 1(2)(d) specifies as public service contracts, contracts other than public works or supply contracts having as their object the provision of services referred to in Annex II of the directive. A public contract having as its object both products and services within the meaning of Annex II must be considered as a 'public service contract' if the value of the services in question exceeds that of the products covered by the contract.

[86] See Case C-536/07 *Commission v Germany* ECR I-10355. The case (*Köln Messe*) considered the conclusion of a contract between the City of Cologne and Grundstücksgesellschaft Köln Messe for the construction and use for 30 years of four exhibition halls including ancillary buildings and relevant infrastructure through complex lease-back arrangements without a prior call for tender.

formal requirement of writing, are: (i) pecuniary consideration given by a contracting authority, in return for (ii) a work, product, or service of direct economic benefit to the contracting authority.

'Pecuniary consideration', as an essential ingredient of public contracts, could include a variety of payments, such as direct or deferred payment by the contracting authority to the economic operator, commitment to the lease-back of an asset after its construction, asset swaps between the contracting authority and the economic operator, or conferral on the economic operator of an exclusive right to collect third-party payments. A functional application of the concept brings leasing and sub-leasing arrangements into the category of pecuniary interest. The pecuniary element also is indissolubly linked with the ability of the contracting authority to specify the object of the contract and its requirements. Such specifications include the definition of the type of works or action on the part of contracting authorities with a decisive influence over the design of a project or the executions of works. The means of execution are irrelevant to the characterization as a public contract, in the sense that primary contracting or sub-contracting could be utilized for the fulfilment of the contract's object, with no effect on the nature of the contractual obligations or issues of liability issues arising from the contract.

Interestingly, the satisfaction of urban planning conditions is not considered as a specification by a contracting authority capable of constituting an immediate economic benefit, even if the public interest is served by such conditions. However, planning gain contracts (i.e., contracts which, for example, allocate to the contractor a gain from the increase in the value of land resulting from the execution of works) are covered by the public procurement directives, irrespective of the identity of the entity responsible for their execution. Conditions attached to planning permission requiring the provision of certain infrastructure (as specified by a contracting authority) by a landowner/developer are capable of generating contractual obligations which resemble public contracts.[87] Nevertheless, the relationship between the contracting authority and the landowner is not to be regarded as a public contract, since the contracting authority does not have any choice over who will be responsible for the execution of works generating the planning gain, since it is only the landowner (the recipient of the approval) who could be responsible. That relationship is regarded, however, as a *mandate* emanating from the contracting authority and obliges the landowner to treat planning gain requirements as elements of a public contract.

Agency (or representation) relations aimed at delegating project management to entities separate from contracting authorities (or their internal departments) can also be deemed public contracts. This requires, though, a written agreement between the contracting authority and the agent for pecuniary consideration in return for agency services, and that the agent is responsible for signature, project authorization, or payments to third parties on behalf of the contracting authority, that it does not have autonomy in executive decisions, and that it cannot be considered a beneficiary of the contract's objects.[88]

---

[87] See Case C-399/98 *Ordine degli Architetti and Others* (n 5).
[88] See Case C-264/03 *Commission v France* [2005] ECR I-8831.

Public contracts denote a demonstrable element of economic benefit, or of risk, directly accruing to the contracting authority. Features of a direct economic benefit include ownership of the asset(s) concerned by a contracting authority, a legal right to its use and future economic advantages, or the assumption of risk by the contracting authority in relation to the realization of the project. An agreement by which a contracting authority entrusts another contracting authority with the execution of a work constitutes a public works contract, regardless of whether or not it is anticipated that the former authority is, or will become, the owner of all or part of that work.[89] Ownership of an asset is crucial only in determining work-concession contracts, as that will be necessary as the basis of granting an exclusive exploitation right to the concessionaire.

National law may sometimes oblige the conclusion of a contract with undertakings which are themselves contracting authorities bound to apply the provisions of the public procurement directives to the award of any related sub-contract. Contracting authorities must regard the initial contract as a public contract, applying the procurement directives to its award, in order to preserve legal certainty and eliminate the potential evasion of public procurement rules by the division of sub-contracts into sums below the relevant monetary thresholds. In such situations, the contractual relation between two, *ipso facto*, contracting authorities is to be regarded as a prime public contact, capable of demonstrating a clear element of economic benefit or of risk attributable to the contracting authority, irrespective of any obligation imposed upon the second contracting authority to apply the public procurement rules for the award of relevant sub-contracts. In order to determine the value of a public contract, account must be taken of the total value of the works contract, including not only the total amounts to be paid by the contracting authority but also all the revenue received from third parties.

Sales of assets or land do not represent public contracts, unless that asset or land is immanent to the procurement transaction such that its sale and the consecutive public works should be viewed in their entirety as a public contract.[90] Sales of assets by contracting authorities to economic operators or other contracting authorities are not deemed public contracts, as a public contract is based on a 'purchasing' capacity of contracting authorities and on the imperative of a contracting authority in being able to determine standards and specifications suitable to meet the conditions of immediate economic benefit. The concept of public works contracts does not require that

---

[89] See Case C-220/05 *Jean Auroux and Others v Commune de Roanne* [2007] ECR I-385. In *Auroux*, a dispute arose relating to a leisure centre in the French town of Roanne, the design and execution of which was entrusted to a semi-public urban development company without the prior issue of a call for tenders. The project had some specific features in as much as only certain parts of the proposed leisure centre, once constructed, were intended for the town itself, while other parts were to be disposed of by the urban development company directly to third parties, although the town was to contribute towards their financing, take over those parts not disposed of at the end of the project, and bear the full risk of any losses incurred.

[90] See Case C-451/08 *Helmut Müller v Bundesanstalt für Immobilienaufgaben* [2010] ECR I-2673. The case was concerned with whether the rules on public contracts and, more specifically, the rules on public works concessions applied when a public authority sold assets and land to the prospective buyer who, in the opinion of the local authority responsible for town planning, presented the best and most interesting plans for the use of the land and the construction of buildings.

the works which are the subject of the contract be materially or physically carried out for the contracting authority, provided that they are carried out for that authority's *immediate* economic benefit.

E Enforcement in EU Public Procurement Law

The enactment of the Remedies Directives has brought a different dimension into the application of public procurement rules. Such a dimension relies on the decentralized enforcement and compliance of the substantive regime. Enforcement of procurement rules is, of its nature, often a matter for other potential recipients of contract awards, where the view is taken that a failure to adhere to such rules has disadvantaged them, rather than for a branch of the administration itself. Such 'private' enforcement may involve review procedures of an administrative kind and/or recourse to the courts. Three principles address the application of the Remedies Directives and the judicial review of public contracts: the principles of procedural autonomy, effectiveness, and procedural equality.

1 The principle of procedural autonomy

The principle of procedural autonomy affords discretion to Member States to organize public procurement review procedures in alignment with review procedures otherwise applicable under national administrative law. Procedural autonomy is reflected in *locus standi* requirements, time limitations for review, interim relief requirements, and actions for damages.

(a) Locus standi

Member States are not obliged to make review procedures available to any person wishing to obtain a public contract, but instead, require that the person concerned has been, or risks being harmed, by the alleged infringement.[91] In that sense, participation in a contract award procedure may validly constitute a condition which must be fulfilled before the person concerned can show an interest in attempting to obtaining the award of the contract at issue, or that he or she risks suffering harm as a result of the allegedly unlawful nature of the decision to award that contract to another.

(b) Time limits to enact review proceedings

Member States have wide discretion to establish the procedural framework for review procedures and the logistics for their operation. The existence of national legislation which provides that any application for review of decisions of contracting authorities must be commenced within a specific time-limit, and that any irregularity in the award procedure relied upon in support of such an application, must be raised within

---

[91] See Case C-249/01 *Hackermüller* [2003] ECR I-6319, para 18.

the same period, is compatible with the public procurement *acquis*,[92] provided that, in pursuit of the fundamental principle of legal certainty, such specific time limits are reasonable.[93]

(c) Requirements of interim measures

Member States have considerable discretion in determining requirements for interim relief in public procurement processes. Interim measures represent an autonomous legal remedy which is separate from any other judicial review process. Their objective is to correct the alleged infringement or prevent further damage to the interests concerned, to suspend the procedure for awarding of a public contract, and prevent the implementation of any decision taken by a contracting authority. Interim measures are granted with reference to a balance test which takes into consideration the likely consequences of such measures for all parties concerned, and for the public interest. The conditionality of an application for interim measures to set aside or annul an act (or a contracting authority's decision) is assessed[94] against the possible consequence that doing so might restricts interim judicial protection (where the suspension of an administrative act is procedurally conditional on initiated action in the courts for the annulment).[95] Not only actions against definitive acts but also against procedural acts, should be capable of suspension by the application of interim measures, where they might lead to the direct or indirect determination of the substance of the case, bring an end to the procedures for the awarding of a contract, or cause irreparable harm to legitimate rights of interested parties. The Remedies Directives do not provide for any derogation regarding the possibility of appeal against procedural acts, or administrative measures which do not bring administrative proceedings to an end.[96]

(d) Damages

Award of damages in the public procurement context is limited to persons economically harmed by an infringement on the part of the contracting authority. After the conclusion of a contract, damages represent the only remedy available. The Remedies Directives contain no further requirements, for example, as to the burden of proof and method of calculation of the damage. The national legislator is free to decide on such matters, but must, however, comply with the principle of procedural equality and the

---

[92] See Case C-470/99 *Universale-Bau and Others* (n 4).
[93] See Case C-261/95 *Palmisani* [1997] ECR I-4025, para 28, and Case C-78/98 *Preston and Others* [2000] ECR I-3201, para 33.
[94] See Case C-214/00 *Commission of the European Communities v Kingdom of Spain* ECR [2003] I-4667; Case C-236/95 *Commission v Greece* [1996] ECR I-4459.
[95] See Case C-236/95 *Commission v Greece* [1996] ECR I-4459.
[96] See Case C-81/98 *Alcatel Austria and Others* [1999] ECR I-7671. The conception of precluding the review of procedural acts is embedded in Community case law. See Case C-282/95 P *Guérin automobiles v Commission* [1997] ECR I-1503. The Court also held that the preparatory nature of the act against which the action is brought is one of the grounds of inadmissibility of an action for annulment, and that that is a ground which the Court may examine of its own motion; see Case 346/87 *Bossi v Commission* [1989] ECR 303.

principle of effectiveness. The level of damages awarded for breach of public procurement law varies enormously across the legal orders of the Member States. Effectiveness of the remedy varies according to whether courts can grant punitive damages, or award damages according to the principle of likelihood of harm, as distinct from, for example, legal systems which require proof that, but for the legal breach, the contract would have in fact been awarded to a particular tenderer.

2 The principle of effectiveness

The principle of effectiveness of review procedures under the Remedies Directives covers the ability of aggrieved tenderers to set aside decisions of contracting authorities taken unlawfully or to remove discriminatory technical, economic, or financial specifications in the invitation to tender, or in the contract and related documents. Set-aside procedures are deemed to be a legitimate conditional remedy for the award of damages.

3 Admissibility in review procedures

Persons for whom effective review must be available must include, at least, any person having or having had an interest in obtaining a public contract[97] who has been, or risks being, harmed by an alleged infringement.[98] An assessment of an aggrieved tenderer's interest in reviewing a decision or an act of a contracting authority should be examined on the basis that they did not participate in the contract award procedure, as well as that they did not appeal against the invitation to tender before the award of the contract. Thus, effectiveness of review does not require the prior designation of the applicant as a tenderer or candidate in procurement procedures.[99] The existence of an interest in obtaining a contract, where no bid had been submitted, has been confirmed for cases where it would have been possible for an undertaking to seek review of discriminatory specifications prior to submitting a bid and without waiting for the procedure for awarding the contract to be finalized.[100] A refusal to acknowledge such an interest of a person who had not participated in the award procedure, or who did not seek review in relation to the terms of the invitation to tender does not impair the effectiveness of the Remedies Directives.

The existence of both a collective and an individual interest in achieving the award of a contract in cases of consortia participation in procurement procedures has been recognized.[101] Not only may all the members of a consortium without legal personality, which participated and did not obtain the contract, acting together, bring an

---

[97] See Case C-26/03 *Stadt Halle, RPL Recyclingpark Lochau GmbH v Arbeitsgemeinschaft Thermische Restabfall- und Energieverwertungsanlage TREA Leuna* (n 4) judgment of 11 January 2005.

[98] See Case C-212/02 *Commission v Austria,* unpublished.

[99] See Case C-230/02 *Grossmann Air Service, Bedarfsluftfahrtunternehmen GmbH & Co KG and Republik Österreich* [2004] ECR I-1829.

[100] ibid.

[101] See Case C-129/04 *Espace Trianon SA and Société wallonne de location-financement SA (Sofibail) v Office communautaire et régional de la formation professionnelle et de l'emploi (FOREM)* [2005] ECR I-07805.

action against the decision awarding the contract, but *locus standi* is also recognized even where only one member of such a consortium seeks review. Interestingly, if the application of one of the consortium members is held inadmissible, *locus standi* of the other members of the consortium is not per se affected.[102]

Any remedies available to interested parties against decisions of contracting authorities extends also to decisions taken outside the formal award procedure and includes those prior to a formal call for tenders[103] (such as whether a particular contract falls within the personal and material scope of the public procurement directives), as well as a decision to withdraw invitations to tender and to abort procurement procedures already in train.[104] The Remedies Directives preclude national legislation from limiting review of the legality of the withdrawal of an invitation to tender to the mere examination of whether this decision was arbitrary. However, the scope of the obligation to notify reasons for abandoning the award of a contract[105] must take into account exceptional cases, and such action must necessarily be based on serious grounds.[106] Although a contracting authority is required to notify candidates and tenderers of the grounds for its decision where it decides to withdraw the invitation to tender for a public contract, there is no implied obligation on that authority to carry the award procedure to its conclusion.

Making *locus standi* conditional upon prior participation of aggrieved tenderers in conciliation procedures is seen as incompatible with the effectiveness principle,[107] thus recognizing the autonomous and unconditional character of judicial review procedures in public procurement. Even though Member States are free to determine the detailed rules for the review procedures required by the Remedies Directives,[108] they cannot place a strict interpretation on the term 'interest in obtaining a public contract' so as to exclude the full range of possible review applicants foreseen by Union law.[109] Thus, a participant unsuccessful in a contract award procedure who subsequently failed to initiate *pre*-judicial (in effect: administrative) proceedings, such as conciliation or mediation for the review the contracting authority's act or decision, cannot be regarded as having lost their interest in obtaining the contract, and therefore as being precluded from lodging an action to contest the legality of the contract award decision or any other sufficiently related decision of the contracting authority.[110]

---

[102] See Case C-492/06 *Consorzio Elisoccorso San Raffaele v Elilombarda Srl and Azienda Ospedaliera Ospedale Niguarda Ca' Granda di Milano* [2007] ECR I-08189.

[103] See Case C-26/03 *Stadt Halle, RPL Recyclingpark Lochau GmbH v Arbeitsgemeinschaft Thermische Restabfall und Energieverwertungsanlage TREA Leuna* (n 4).

[104] See Case C-92/00 *Hospital Ingenieure Krankenhaustechnik Planungs- GmbH (HI) and Stadt Wien* [2002] ECR I-5553, para 55.

[105] See [1993] OJ L199 at 54.

[106] See Case C-27/98 *Fracasso and Leitschutz v Salzburger Landesregierung* [1999] ECR I-5697, paras 23 and 25.

[107] See Case C-410/01 *Fritsch, Chiari & Partner, Ziviltechniker GmbH and Others and Autobahnen- und Schnellstraßen-Finanzierungs-AG. (Asfinag)* ECR [2003] I-11547.

[108] See Case C-327/00 *Santex* [2003] ECR I-1877, para 47.

[109] See Case C-410/01 *Fritsch, Chiari & Partner, and Others* (n 107) paras 31 and 34.

[110] See Case C-230/02 *Grossmann Air Service, Bedarfsluftfahrtunternehmen GmbH & Co KG and Republik Österreich* (n 99).

4 Sufficient time between contract award and contract completion

Member States are required to provide for effective review procedures, so that in an appropriate case the decision to award a contract can still be set aside prior to the formal conclusion of the contract.[111] In order to be effective, such procedures should be independent of those where damages are sought after the contract has been formally concluded.[112] A national legal system that makes it impossible to contest the award decision because both decision and formal contract conclusion occur simultaneously deprives interested parties of any possibility of having an unlawful award decision set aside or of preventing the contract from being formally concluded in fact. Effective legal protection requires, therefore, that a reasonable period must elapse between the two events, and that a duty be imposed on contracting authorities to inform all interested parties of the decision to award the contract.

The establishment of a reasonable intervening period is viewed as the answer to prevent the so-called 'race to sign' a public contract, and as the opportunity to allow interested parties to launch review procedures.[113] The threat that a contract will be declared ineffective is a deterrent against the breach of the relevant directives. It places, however, considerable discretion in the hands of a national authority.[114] A declaration of ineffectiveness may result in retrospective cancellation or reduction of contractual obligations, or the imposition of appropriate penalties (in the sense of fines levied on contracting authorities), or the shortening of formally concluded public contracts. Avoidance of the contract can be prevented for overriding reasons relating to a general interest and must be subject to alternative penalties. Such overriding reasons can be economic interests, in exceptional circumstances, which lead to a presumed conclusion of the contract, due to the disproportionate adverse consequences which would arise from its ineffectiveness. Economic interests directly linked to the contract, such as costs resulting from the delay in the execution of the contract, those resulting from the launching of a new procurement procedure or from the change of the contractor, and costs of legal obligations resulting from the avoidance of the contract are not deemed overriding reasons.

5 The principle of procedural equality

The principle of procedural equality obliges Member States to treat public procurement review procedures in the same way as domestic review procedures. The time allowed for assessing the legality of acts or decisions of contracting authorities remains

---

[111] See Case C-212/02 *Commission v Austria* (n 98) judgment of 24 June 2004.

[112] See Case C-81/98 *Alcatel Austria and Others* (n 96) para 43.

[113] See Art 2(a) Directive 2007/66 which stipulates a standstill requirement for 10 calendar days from the day following day of award decision if fax or electronic means are used, or 15 calendar days from the day following day of award decision if other means of communication are used, or 10 calendar days from the day following the date of the receipt of the contract award decision.

[114] See Art 2(d) Directive 2007/66 which lays down that Member States may provide that application for review regarding ineffectiveness of contracts must be made before 30 calendar days after publication of the contract award notice, provided that decisions of the contracting authority to award the contract without prior publication of the contract notice was justified or in any case before expiry of period of at least six months after the conclusion of the contract.

within the discretion of Member States,[115] subject to the requirement that the relevant national rules are not less favourable than those governing similar domestic actions.[116] The Remedies Directives do not provide for any specific limitation periods and, in the absence of Union rules, Member States are free to provide procedural rules if they conform with fundamental principles of the EC Treaty.[117]

National provisions concerning the possibility of seeking interim measures against acts or decisions of contracting authorities may not be specific to the award of public contracts, but must apply equally to all types of domestic administrative review procedures.[118] National legislation which restricts judicial protection in public procurement disputes by subjecting interim measures to special conditions, for example, that interested parties must bring an action for the annulment of the contested act of a contracting authority first, is in contradiction with the principle of procedural equality. In addition, domestic law which makes the award of damages conditional on proof of fault or fraud on the part of contracting authorities, reduces substantially the likelihood for aggrieved (potential) tenderers to obtain damages.[119] Any such conditionality contravenes the principle of effectiveness.

Bodies which are not contracting authorities, but whose decisions are capable of having certain effects on the outcome of a procurement procedure, are also covered by the Remedies Directives.[120] If national law renders it impossible to seek annulment of a decision and to obtain compensation for any damage incurred, even involving such authorities, this contravenes the principle of effectiveness.

F Remedies and Enforcement under the WTO Government Procurement Agreement

The legal regime regulating the public procurement of the Member States of the Union can have extra-territorial effect. This has been achieved by virtue of special intergovernmental agreements concluded between the then European Community and member states of the GATT. It was initially the Agreement on Government Procurement (AGP) within the GATT framework, concluded during the Tokyo Round of negotiations, which provided third-country contractors access to European public markets. The AGP was later amended by virtue of the WTO Government Procurement Agreement (GPA) during the Uruguay Round. In principle, access to the public sector markets of the EU Member States has been guaranteed, as far as the framework for the procedural and substantive stages of public procurement is concerned. However, even

---

[115] See Case C-92/00 *Hospital Ingenieure Krankenhaustechnik Planungs- GmbH (HI) and Stadt Wien* (n 104).

[116] See Case C-390/98 *Banks v Coal Authority and Secretary of State for Trade and Industry* [2001] ECR I-6117, para 121; Case C-453/99 *Courage and Crehan* [2001] ECR I-6297, para 29.

[117] See Case C-470/99 *Universale-Bau and Others* (n 4).

[118] See Case C-236/95 *Commission v Greece* [1996] ECR I-4459.

[119] See Case C-275/03 *Commission v Portugal* ECLI:EU:C:2004:632 and Case C-70/06 *Commission v Portugal* [2004] ECR I-0000.

[120] See Joined Cases C-145/08 *Club Hotel Loutraki AE and Others v Ethnico Symvoulio Radiotileorasis and Ypourgos Epikrateias* and C-149/08 *Aktor Anonymi Techniki Etaireia (Aktor ATE) v Ethnico Symvoulio Radiotileorasis* [2010] ECR I-4165.

the most comprehensive set of rules would be ineffective if its enforcement were inadequate. Access to justice for third-country providers as a result of the GATT/WTO agreements is thus as important as it is in regard to internal access to the public markets wholly within the European Union.

Both the GPA and its predecessor (AGP) are considered intergovernmental instruments which are addressed to states, and not intended to confer rights or duties upon individuals as such. Irrespective of the presence (or absence) of clarity and precision, conditionality in their rules, and discretion reserved to member states in the implementation, international agreements are not deemed to produce direct effect,[121] thus preventing individuals from taking advantage of treaty provisions in litigation before national courts. The Council, in its decision incorporating the GPA into Union law, specifically stipulate that the provisions of that agreement do not have direct effect.[122] However, there is an apparent contradiction between denying direct effect to the GPA provisions and the spirit and wording of the agreement itself. For example, express provision for remedies for aggrieved providers is made under Article XX GPA, where theses should be as favourable as those conferred upon contractors within the Union. Also, Article III GPA stipulates that signatories to the agreement should not be treated in a manner less favourable than are national providers or indeed providers from elsewhere. How in practice these provisions concerning access to justice on the national level of EU Member States for third-country providers will operate still remains to be seen.

As with its predecessor, the GPA has created an inter-governmental mechanism for settling disputes arising from its application. The mechanism, the Understanding on Rules and Procedures Governing the Settlement of Disputes (DSU) (in Annex II GPA), provides for a dispute settlement procedure between the parties, that is, states, and not individuals. The DSU appears, then, to elevate pre-contractual or contractual disputes between a third-country provider and a contracting authority to a grievance of an intergovernmental dimension. In order to invoke DSU, a state must first exhaust all means of settling the dispute in an amicable manner (direct consultation and negotiations) with the state allegedly in breach. If settlement cannot be reached, the state then may request the WTO Dispute Settlement Body to establish a panel in order to hear the case, appointed in consultation with the parties and comprised of persons with experience in the area of government procurement. The Panel has as its task of reporting to parties concerned, and the report is adopted by the Dispute Settlement Body. The latter would then request the state in breach to annul all steps taken which contravene the rules contained in the GPA. On failing to do so, the Dispute Settlement Body may authorize *unilateral suspension* of the GPA or any other WTO agreement in the territory of the state affected by the violation.

---

[121] See Joined Cases 21–24/72 *International Fruit Co NV v Produktschap voor Groenten en Fruit* [1972] ECR 1236. See also Case C-280/93 *Germany v Council* [1994] ECR 1-4973.

[122] See Art 3 of Council Decision 2014/115/EU of 2 December 2013 on the conclusion of the Protocol Amending the Agreement on Government Procurement [2014] OJ L68 of 7 March 2014, at 1-1.

G Supervision and Control of Public Procurement

On the administrative level, the European Commission has introduced a voluntary ex ante assessment mechanism of the procurement aspects of large scale infrastructure projects in an attempt to enhance legal certainty and to reduce speculative litigation which might delay or frustrate the delivery of critical infrastructure and large scale trans-European networks.

Relying on the courts, the European Commission may bring actions against Member States before the CJEU by virtue of Article 258 TFEU. These actions seek to ensure compliance by Member States and their contracting authorities with the substantive provisions of public procurement directives. The Commission may initiate proceedings, on its own initiative or in response to a complaint, against a defaulting Member State for failure to fulfil its treaty obligations. No specific legal interest is required as a condition of the admissibility, since it is the general responsibility of the Commission to observe, supervise, and ensure the correct application of Union law. Despite their high profile, the rulings in proceedings under Article 258 TFEU have limited effectiveness, being mainly declaratory in character in relation to Member State's failure to comply with EU law.

Supervision through the courts is also effected under Article 267 TFEU, which regulates the judicial co-operation between national judiciaries and the ECJ. More than 120 preliminary rulings over the last thirty years have shed light on the correct interpretation of the public procurement directives. These decisions have pronounced on the direct effect of those provisions, declared the incompatibility of national law with the letter and spirit of the directives, as well as with underlying principles of EU law, and offered to national judiciaries the necessary inferences for comprehending the concepts and doctrines of the Union's public procurement regulation.

According to Article 287 TFEU, the European Court of Auditors (ECA) is mandated to examine the accounts of all revenue and expenditure of the Union, to audit the legality and regularity of the underlying transactions and the soundness of financial management, and to provide the European Parliament and the Council with a statement of assurance (*déclaration d'assurance*). The supervisory areas of the ECA cover three major fields: (i) financial audit, where reliability of the accounts is checked and evidence obtained on the extent to which transactions, assets, and liabilities have been completely, correctly, and accurately entered in the accounting records and presented in the financial statements; (ii) compliance audit, where the legality and regularity of underlying transactions is checked, and evidence obtained to assess whether the revenue and spending operations underlying the EU budget have been carried out in accordance with contractual and legal requirements, and are correctly and accurately calculated; and (iii) performance audit, where soundness of financial management and demonstration of value-for-money is verified and where evidence is obtained to show that EU funds have been used economically, efficiently, and effectively, either by maximizing output for a given input or through minimizing costs for a defined objective.

H Conclusions

The evolution of public procurement regulation in the European Union points towards a strategy for eliminating discriminatory procurement practices across the Member States which have posed significant obstacles to the realization of the fundamental principles of free movement of goods, the right of establishment, and the freedom to provide services. That strategy has been based on two principal assumptions: the first assumption acknowledged the fact that, in order to eliminate preferential and discriminatory purchasing practices in European public markets, a great deal of *transparency* and *openness* was needed; the second assumption rested on the premise that the only way to regulate public procurement in the Member States effectively was through the process of *harmonization* of their existing laws and administrative practice, and not by attempting to make them all *uniform* throughout the Union. Harmonization comes with a decentralized regulatory system for public procurement, based on the principle of *subsidiarity*.

The most pronounced deficiency of the public procurement directives is their porosity of coverage, attributable to an attempt to achieve exhaustive harmonization. This porosity undermines their effectiveness by preventing their applicability to precisely specified contractual situations, as a result restricting an extension of their provisions *de lege ferenda*. Exhaustive harmonization excludes *de lege lata* from the regulatory scope public contracts below certain thresholds. It also excludes contracts involving certain agreements reflecting inter-administrative (and particularly infra-administrative) interfaces within the public sector, relations displaying a dominant influence of a utility on affiliated undertakings (in particular, service concessions), public contracts based on exclusive rights, public contracts in pursuit of services of general economic interest, in-house contracts, and contracts for non-priority services. The search for exhaustive harmonization also reflects the mutual exclusivity of the Public Sector Directive and the Utilities Directive, as well as their non-applicability to contracts awarded pursuant to international rules, or to secret contracts and contracts requiring special security measures or those related to the protection of Member States' essential interests. In addition, the Public Sector Directive also does not cover: contracts the object of which is to provide or exploit public telecommunications networks; contracts for the acquisition or rental of land; contracts related to broadcasting services; contracts related to financial securities, capital raising activities, and central bank services; employment contracts; and research and development contracts which do not benefit the relevant contacting authority. The Utilities Directive does not apply to: contracts awarded in a third country; contracts awarded by contracting entities engaged in the provision or operation of fixed networks for the purchase of water and for the supply of energy or of fuels for the production of energy; contracts subject to special arrangements for the exploitation and exploration of oil, gas, coal, or other solid fuels; contracts and framework agreements awarded by central purchasing bodies; contracts the subject of which is directly exposed to competition in markets to which access is not restricted; and contracts related to works and service concessions.

Exhaustive harmonization through *lex specialis* such as the public procurement directives cannot impose limits on the application of primary EU law to supplement their legal scope. The *lacunae* resulting from to the limitations of the directives, and particularly in areas which *de lege ferenda* cannot be conducive to regulatory control together with the need for conformity with general principles of EU law, have been acknowledged. Although the application of Union primary law is not precluded by the exhaustiveness of secondary law, the latter's *lex specialis* character in procurement regulation aims at complementing fundamental freedoms of EU law. Recognizing the porosity of the procurement directives draws attention to the necessity of supplementing their coverage with *acquis* deriving from fundamental principles of EU law. The need to increase compliance by contracting authorities by promoting the objectivity of the scope of the directives and by enhancing their justiciability, whilst in parallel limiting their inherent flexibility, is a further response to their porosity.

The evolution of the public procurement *acquis* has in part focused on regulatory standardization which has had recourse to both hard law and soft law. Hard law has utilized legislative measures with administrative law character in order to impose safeguards for certain key principles: transparency, through the mandatory publicity and monitoring requirements of public contracts; non-discrimination, through the application of standardized selection and qualification procedures and uniform award procedures; objectivity, through the application of award criteria for public contracts which do not permit preferential treatment; accountability, through the obligation of reasoning and monitoring of public contract awards; and justiciability, through redress and access to justice. EU public procurement regulation displays strong administrative law characteristics and has evolved as an essential component of the Single Market based upon these. The evolution of the regulatory framework for public procurement has been shaped by the instrumental role of the CJEU through the *rule of reason*, where jurisprudence has influenced the interpretation of the pertinent legal concepts. As well, soft law, in the form of guidelines, guidance notes, communications, white papers, etc. has created an appropriate environment for the procurement stakeholders that has augmented basic legal certainty and contributed significantly to best practice in accountability, transparency, and consistency in public service delivery.[123]

---

[123] See amongst other instruments of soft law, Commission of the European Communities, *The Cost of Non-Europe, Basic Findings, Vol 5, Part A; The Cost of Non-Europe in Public Sector Procurement* (n 2). See also the Cecchini Report *1992 The European Challenge* (n 2); Commission of the European Communities, *White Paper for the Completion of the Internal Market*, COM(85) 310 final; see also Green Paper on Public Procurement in the European Union: *Exploring the way forward* (n 1); European Commission, Communication on Public Procurement in the European Union, (n 1); European Commission, *Report to the Laeken European Council: Services of General Interest*, COM(2001) 598; European Commission, *Communication from the Commission to the Council, the European Parliament, the Economic and Social Committee and the Committee of the regions on the Status of Work on the Examination of a Proposal for a Framework Directive on Services of General Interest*, COM(2002) 689; European Commission, *Green Paper on Services of General Interest*, COM(2003) 270; European Commission, *Communication from the Commission to the European Parliament, the Council, the European Economic and Social Committee and the Committee of the Regions: White Paper on services of general interest*, COM(2004) 374; European Commission, Communication to the European Parliament, the Council, the Economic and Social Committee and the Committee of the Regions, *Towards a Single Market Act*, COM(2010) 608 final; European Commission, Communication, Europe 2020, *A strategy for smart, sustainable and inclusive growth* (n 11).

PART VII

DISTRIBUTIVE POLICY

19

The Common Agricultural Policy

Joseph A McMahon

A Introduction

'While the Common Agricultural Policy may be well known for the political and financial problems to which it gives rise, the legal issues underlying it have not been so widely discussed'.[1] Usher went on to note that the Common Agricultural Policy (CAP) lay behind many institutional developments, that agriculture was the first single market, and it was in the context of agricultural disputes that the Court of Justice of the European Union developed many of the general principles of Community (now European Union) law. So, whilst many will be familiar with the broad contribution that the CAP has made over the last sixty years, there are few who are more familiar with the legal intricacies of the policy. Part of the reason for this may be that close engagement with the administration of the CAP is not an easy exercise. Whilst the European institutions are responsible for setting not only the broad framework of the policy but also, in certain cases, the details of various aspects of the policy, implementation has been devolved to the Member States.

For a policy that has been so central to the process of European integration, it is surprising to note that the Treaty provisions dealing with agriculture have emerged largely unscathed from the process of Treaty reform which has fundamentally changed EU competences. Indeed, the latest set of reforms have returned the numbering of the provisions on agriculture to the original Treaty of Rome numbering, the main provisions being Articles 38–44 TFEU.[2] The limited nature of the changes to the provisions on agriculture since 1957 suggests that the Member States have never seriously questioned the provision of special treatment for the agricultural sector.

B Administrative Tasks in Implementing the Common Agricultural Policy

The nature of that special treatment begins with Article 38(1) which provides that, '[t]he Union shall define and implement a common agriculture and fisheries policy'. This should not be taken to suggest that there is one policy covering both agriculture and fisheries—there is both a Common Agricultural Policy and a Common

---

[1] J A Usher, *Legal Aspects of Agriculture in the European Community* (Clarendon Press 1988) vii.
[2] Arts 44–47 of the original Treaty contain transitional provisions of which Art 46 is still of relevance. There have been some minor changes to the provisions, for example Art 43(1) no longer calls for the convening of a conference to determine the broad outlines of the CAP.

Fisheries Policy.[3] The CAP emerges from the requirement in Article 38(4) that: 'The operation and development of the internal market for agricultural products must be accompanied by the establishment of a common agricultural policy'. Products subject to the CAP were laid down in Annex II of the Treaty and Article 38(3) empowered the Council to add to this list of products within two years of the entry into force of the Treaty. The Council exercised this power through Regulation 7a on 18 December 1959, just within the two-year period,[4] although it was not published until January 1961. It was argued in *König* that this delay invalidated the Regulation but the argument was rejected by the Court, which pointed out that belated publication of the Regulation had no effect other than the date on which it could be applied and take effect.[5]

The CAP has evolved significantly over its life-time. Originally, the policy was heavily reliant on control of the market in various agricultural products through a system of price support, backed up by an intervention system and control of trade. For the original Member States the mechanisms worked well, but problems were emerging by the time of the first enlargement, as production had increased leading to increasing intervention stocks of various products, deteriorating trade relationships with third countries, and increased pressure on the EU budget. Attempts to resolve these issues in the 1980s and 1990s by tinkering with the mechanisms of the original policy were unsuccessful, and a new direction was set for the CAP through the introduction of the Single Farm Payment, cutting the link between financial support and production. The policy has continued to evolve: the Single Farm Payment has become the 'Basic Payment', and the degree of discretion accorded to the Member States to support their farmers has grown. Whilst falling short of a renationalization of the policy, it accords with Article 39, which recognizes that the challenges facing agriculture in the EU are both common across the Member States and specific within the Member States; the development of the EU policy on rural development, after a slow start, also recognizes this diversity.

C Sources of Law in Administration of the Common Agricultural Policy

Article 39 TFEU, which lists the objectives of the CAP, reveals a contradiction between an economically oriented policy and one that would support the structural nature of agriculture in the original Member States. This article, which has remained unchanged since 1957, provides:

---

[3] It should be noted however that fisheries products are included within the definition of agricultural products subject to the CAP see eg Case 61/77 *Commission v Ireland* [1978] ECR 417 and Case 141/78 *Commission v France* [1979] ECR 2923. Such products are excluded from the scope of the WTO Agreement on Agriculture (Annex 1).

[4] [1961] OJ 7/71. In Joined Cases 2 & 3/62 *Commission v Luxembourg and Belgium* [1962] ECR 425 the Court noted that the list contained in Annex II should be regarded as exhaustive. Through Treaty amendment, Annex II has become Annex I but it has been amended to include cotton by the Greek Act of Accession; see Case 77/83 *CILFIT* [1984] ECR 1257.

[5] Case 185/73 *König* [1974] ECR 607, 616–17.

1. The objectives of the common agricultural policy shall be:
   (a) to increase agricultural productivity by promoting technical progress and by ensuring the rational development of agricultural production and the optimum utilisation of the factors of production, in particular labour;
   (b) thus to ensure a fair standard of living for the agricultural community, in particular by increasing the individual earnings of persons engaged in agriculture;
   (c) to stabilise markets;
   (d) to assure the availability of supplies;
   (e) to ensure that supplies reach consumers at reasonable prices.
2. In working out the common agricultural policy and the special methods for its application, account shall be taken of:
   (a) the particular nature of agricultural activity, which results from the social structure of agriculture and from structural and natural disparities between the various agricultural regions;
   (b) the need to effect the appropriate adjustments by degrees;
   (c) the fact that in the Member States agriculture constitutes a sector closely linked with the economy as a whole.

No hierarchy of objectives is indicated in Article 39(1). As early as 1968, the Court recognized that the Community institutions would have to balance the competing demands of Article 39(1) as they could not 'all be realised simultaneously and in full'.[6] In that case, *Beus,* the Court rejected a challenge to the legal basis of the Regulation at issue which alleged, inter alia, that it interfered with the realization of all the objectives in Article 39 (save guaranteeing the standard of living of producers) and the objectives of the Common Commercial Policy as expressed in Article 110 of the Treaty of Rome.

The classic formulation of the balancing act to be performed by the institutions occurred in *Balkan Import Export GmbH v Hauptzollamt Berlin Packhof,* a case involving Regulation 974/71, which provided for the application of a system of compensatory amounts in trade with other Member States and third countries, the legal basis for which was Article 103 of the Treaty of Rome on conjunctural policy.[7] As the system was limited to agricultural markets, the plaintiff argued that Article 103 was an inappropriate legal base and that Articles 40, 43, and 235 of the Treaty of Rome should have been used instead. It was also argued that the system infringed Articles 39 and 110 of the same Treaty. In their observations both the Council and the Commission defended the use of Article 103. The Court concluded that, as there was 'no adequate provision' in the CAP allowing for urgent measures to deal with the monetary situation arising from floating exchange rates, the Council was justified in making interim use of Article 103.[8] The Court also dismissed the argument based on the objectives of the CAP, stating:

In pursuing these objectives the Community institutions must secure the permanent harmonisation made necessary by any conflict between these aims taken

---

[6] Case 5/67 *Beus v Hauptzollamt Muenchen* [1968] ECR 83, 98.
[7] Case 5/73 *Balkan Import Export GmbH v Hauptzollamt Berlin Packhof* [1973] ECR 1091.
[8] ibid 1109.

individually and, where necessary, allow one of them temporary priority in order
to satisfy the demands of the economic factors or conditions in view of which their
decisions are made.[9]

This formulation (usually referred to as the *Balkan* formula) has been constantly repeated, with the Court limiting itself to an examination of whether the measure in
question contains a manifest error, constitutes a misuse of power, or whether the discretion enjoyed by the Community institutions has been exceeded.[10]

The *Balkan* formula conflicts with the Court's approach to the interpretation of
Article 2 of Regulation 26/62, whereby an agreement hoping for exemption from
the competition provisions must satisfy all the objectives of the CAP. This was
demonstrated by the decision in *Frubo*, in which the Court was asked to annul the
Commission Decision that Frubo's agreement infringed the competition provisions
of the Treaty, arguing that the Decision infringed not only Article 2 Regulation 26 but
also Articles 39, 40, and 85 of the Treaty of Rome.[11] Frubo argued that their agreement
met three of the objectives set out in Article 39(1), i.e., (c) to stabilize markets, (d) to
assure the availability of supplies, and (e) to ensure that supplies reach consumers at
reasonable prices. In response, the Court noted that the applicants had not shown how
their agreement was necessary to realize the objectives in Article 39(1)(a) and (b), so
the Commission was correct in deciding that Article 2 Regulation 26 was inapplicable.
The Court followed the approach taken by Warner AG, whose opinion noted the fal-
lacy underlying Frubo's argument:[12]

> The fallacy is that Article 2 confers on the parties to an agreement the right to claim
> exemption for any restriction it contains if only they can show that, in relation to the
> market in any agricultural product, the restriction conduces to the attainment of one
> or some of the objectives set out in Article 39 of the Treaty. The argument overlooks
> that the objectives set out in Article 39 are those of the common agricultural policy
> and that, as such, they relate to Community agriculture and are inseparable from
> each other.

So, for both the Advocate-General and the Court, an agreement could be exempted
from the competition provisions if it is designed and necessary to secure all the objectives listed in Article 39(1). The Court would later go on to accord precedence to the
objectives of the CAP over the objectives of competition policy.[13]

The *Balkan* formula also suggests that, at some stage, the Court may overrule an
institutional measure if the situation of 'temporary priority' is continued for a substantial period of time, thus jeopardizing the achievement of the other CAP objectives. This possibility was highlighted in *Behla-Mühle*, in which the Court used the
objectives in Article 39(1), the principle of non-discrimination in Article 40(2), and
the principle of proportionality, to rule that the obligations imposed by the contested

---

[9] ibid 1112.
[10] See eg Case 203/86 *Spain v Council* [1988] ECR 4563; Case C-280/93 *Germany v Commission* [1994]
ECR I-4973; and the repetition of the Balkan formula by the then Court of First Instance (now the
General Court) in Case T-489/93 *Unifruit Hellas* [1994] ECR II-1201.
[11] Case 71/74 *FRUBO v Commission* [1975] ECR 563.   [12] ibid 594.
[13] See eg Case C-137/00 *Milk Marque and National Farmers' Union* [2003] ECR I-7975.

Regulation were not necessary to attain the objectives of the CAP.[14] The Regulation, which was a temporary measure to correct imbalances in the common organization of the market in milk and milk products, imposed a financial burden not only on producers of milk and milk products, but also on producers in other agricultural sectors, requiring them to purchase certain quantities of an animal feed product at such a disproportionate price such as to constitute a discriminatory distribution of the burden of costs between the various agricultural sectors. *Behla-Mühle* hints at the limits to the latitude afforded the institutions by the *Balkan* formula. In the subsequent case of *Ludwigshafener Walzmühle*, the Court noted:[15]

> It should be remembered that, in determining their policy in this area, the competent Community institutions enjoy wide discretionary powers regarding not only establishment of the factual basis of their action but also definition of the objectives to be pursued, within the framework of the provisions of the Treaty, and the choice of the appropriate means of action.

The Court went on to note that the institutions must reconcile the various objectives laid down in Article 39, 'a fact which precludes the isolation of any one of those objectives ... in such a way as to render impossible the realization of other objectives'. After repeating the *Balkan* formula in *Crispoltoni II* the Court continued: 'That harmonisation must preclude the isolation of any one of those objectives in such a way as to render impossible the realisation of other objectives'.[16] At issue in this case was the system of maximum guaranteed quantities in the common organization of the market in tobacco which, it was argued, was not appropriate to the objective being pursued as it did not allow individual quotas to be set. The Court went on to reject allegations that the Regulation breached the principles of proportionality, non-discrimination, and protection of legitimate expectations. This case is noteworthy, as reform of the tobacco sector would introduce individual quotas.[17]

Whilst the Court is open to the possibility of its interfering with decisions made by the institutions surrounding the CAP's objectives, instances in which it has done so have been rare. This may be a consequence of the fact that the balancing, demanded by the *Balkan* formula, emerges not from Article 39(1), but rather from the nature of agricultural policy which requires the assessment of complex economic situations. This complexity is recognized in Article 39(2), which acknowledges the particular nature of agricultural activity, and that this activity varies between Member States, suggesting that legislation will be both general (covering all of the Union) and specific (reflecting the diversity of conditions among Member States). It should also be noted Article 39(2)(c), with its acknowledgement that 'agriculture constitutes a sector closely linked with the economy as a whole', demands that the wider treaty objectives must also be taken into account.[18] Despite this, it is considered that agriculture cannot be subjected to the same market instruments that characterize industrial

---

[14] Case 114/76 *Bela-Mühle* [1977] ECR 1211, 1221.
[15] Joined Cases 197–200, 243, 245, and 247/80 *Ludwigshafener Walzmühle* [1981] ECR 3211, 3251.
[16] Joined Cases C-133/93, C-300/93, and C-362/93 *Crispoltoni II* [1994] ECR I-4863, 4903.
[17] Regulation 2075/92, [1992] OJ L215/70.
[18] See also Case 68/86 *UK v Council* [1988] ECR 855, 895.

production, given that the former is less flexible, as it takes time to reflect changes in supply and demand and it is dependent on climatic conditions. Moreover, food is an essential product—it is needed for survival. Perhaps it is not surprising that the Court has been reluctant to interfere with the discretion of the institutions in the design and implementation of the CAP.

Whilst Article 39 has remained unchanged since 1957, over the same period the vast majority of that treaty has been subject to change, and the CAP has also evolved to reflect wider changes in the Union's competences. For example, it is now expected to be active in protecting the environment, the consumer, and animal welfare. Taking animal welfare as an example, the increased importance of this area was recognized in the Protocol, attached to the Treaty of Amsterdam, on the Protection and Welfare of Animals.[19] Article 13 TFEU now requires the EU and the Member States to 'pay full regard to the welfare requirements of animals, while respecting the legislative or administrative provisions and customs of the Member States relating in particular to religious rites, cultural traditions and regional heritage'. As for the impact of this objective of promoting animal welfare, reference can be made to the interpretation of the Treaty of Amsterdam's Protocol in *Jippes*, in which the Court pointed out that 'it is apparent from its very wording that it does not lay down any well-defined general principle of Community law which is binding on the Community institutions'.[20] That decision of the Court has been criticized, but the point remains that, although animal welfare (and consumer protection and protection of the environment) are now part and parcel of the CAP, Article 39 remains set in stone.[21]

D Underlying Principles Specific to the Common Agricultural Policy

Under Article 40(1) TFEU, a common organization of agricultural markets is to be established to attain the objectives set out in Article 39, with a choice being given between (a) common rules on competition, (b) compulsory co-ordination of the various national market organizations, or (c) a European market organization. The choice would be for the institutions to make in the exercise of their discretionary powers but a choice had to be made, its scope, though, being constrained by the need to realize the objectives in Article 39. The compass of the pertinent legislative power of the institutions is hinted at in this provision, which provides that the common organizational elements may include measures regulating prices, production aids, marketing aids, storage and carry-over arrangements, and measures to stabilize imports or exports.

---

[19] See also the introduction of animal welfare criteria into the cross-compliance criteria needed for the Single Farm Payment. Council Directive 98/58/EC of 20 July 1998 concerning the protection of animals kept for farming purposes [1998] OJ L221/23; Council Directive 91/629/EEC of 19 November 1991 laying down minimum standards for the protection of calves [1991] OJ L340/28, and Council Directive 91/630/EEC of 19 November 1991 laying down minimum standards for the protection of pigs [1991] OJ L340/33.

[20] Case C-189/01 *Jippes and Others* [2001] ECR I-5689, 5718.

[21] See R Ludwig and R O'Gorman, 'A Cock and Bull Story: Problems with the Protection of Animal Welfare in EU Law and Some Proposed Solutions' (2008) 20 *Journal of Environmental Law* 363. See also Case C-428/07 *Horvath* [2009] ECR I-6355 on environmental protection.

Such legislation, according to Article 40(2) TFEU, would exclude discrimination be-tween producers or consumers—recognition of the principle of non-discrimination.

In the application of the principle, the Court has indicated that in particular cir-cumstances differences in treatment do not amount to discrimination, or may be ob-jectively justified. One such case is *Royal Scholten Honig* in which a regulation freezing and eliminating production refunds for various starches used in the manufacture of isoglucose, and introducing production levies on the manufacture of isoglucose, was challenged by a number of isoglucose manufacturers.[22] The Court pointed out that Article 40(2) was 'merely a specific enunciation of the general principle of equality' which was one of the fundamental principles of Community law. Interestingly, the Court did not go on to examine the situation of producers, but rather products, i.e., the situation of isoglucose compared with other products of the starch industry, and found no discrimination. However, it did find that isoglucose and sugar were in a comparable position, and went on to conclude that the provisions of the Regulation on the production levy were contrary to Article 40(3). The approach of the Court in this instance—i.e., establishing whether the products (or producers) between which there is alleged discrimination are in a comparable (competing) situation, if so, moving on to establish whether there is a difference in treatment and, if so, whether this can be objectively justified (placing the burden of proof not on the producers but on the institutions)—has been followed on numerous occasions.[23] Although the principle mentions only producers and consumers, it has been extended to all operators (e.g., importers and exporters).[24]

Article 40(2) also provides that 'the common organisation shall be limited to pur-suit of the objectives set out in Article 39', usually read as importing the principle of proportionality. This legal principle, along with a number of others, was raised in *R v Minister of Agriculture, Fisheries and Food and Secretary of State for Health, ex parte Fedesa*, concerning the validity of Directive 88/146 prohibiting the use of certain hor-mones in livestock farming.[25] The Court defined the principle of proportionality as follows:[26]

> the lawfulness of the prohibition of an economic activity is subject to the condition that the prohibitory measures are appropriate and necessary in order to achieve the objectives legitimately pursued by the legislation in question; when there is a choice between several appropriate measures recourse must be had to the least onerous, and the disadvantages caused must not be disproportionate to the aims pursued.

---

[22] Joined Cases 103 and 145/77 *Royal Scholten-Honig v Intervention Board for Agricultural Products* [1978] ECR 2037.

[23] See eg Case 8/82 *Wagner* [1983] ECR 371; Case 58/86 *Coopérative agricole d'approvisionnement des Avirons* [1987] ECR 1423; and Case C-309/89 *Codorniu* [1994] ECR I-1853.

[24] See eg Case 165/84 *Krohn* [1985] ECR 3997 and Case C-280/93 *Germany v Council* [1994] ECR I-4973.

[25] Case C-331/88 *The Queen v Minister of Agriculture, Fisheries and Food and Secretary of State for Health, ex parte: Fedesa and Others* [1990] ECR I-4203. As the Court noted in Case C-155/89 *Belgian State v Philipp Brothers* [1990] ECR I-330</IBT, para 34: 'in order to establish whether a provision of Community law complies with the principle of proportionality, it is necessary to ascertain whether the means which that provision applies to achieve its aim correspond to the importance of that aim and whether they are necessary in order to achieve it'.

[26] ibid *ex parte Fedesa*, para 13.

In this case, that principle had not been infringed. As to whether the Directive breached the principle of legal certainty, the Court noted that this principle requires 'any measure adopted by the Community institutions to be founded on a rational and objective basis', with judicial review being limited to 'examining whether the measure in question is vitiated by a manifest error or misuse of powers, or whether the authority in question has manifestly exceeded the limits of its discretion'.[27]

The Court has consistently noted that, in matters concerning the CAP, the institutions have a discretionary power which corresponds to the political responsibilities given them by Articles 40 and 43 TFEU. So, a measure will be overruled only if it is manifestly inappropriate, having regard to the objective which the Institutions are seeking to pursue.[28] This is well-illustrated by the case-law on compensatory amounts which were introduced in the aftermath of the currency crisis of 1971 and of the floating of the exchange rates of all the Member States. The system of monetary compensatory amounts was incorporated into the CAP by Regulation 2746/72, which rendered their application compulsory in certain cases.[29] In the aftermath of the first enlargement, and of the decision of the United States government to float the dollar, further changes were made to the system, with the introduction of green currency rates.[30] The system generated considerable litigation before the Court, which recognized that the system of monetary compensatory amounts was a breach of the principle of market unity, but also acknowledged that such unity would result not only from the operation of the CAP but also the coordination of the economic and monetary policy of the Member States.[31] In *Schlüter,* the Court noted that '[d]iversion of trade caused solely by the monetary situation can be considered more damaging to the common interest bearing in mind the aims of the Common Agricultural Policy, than the disadvantage of the measures in dispute'.[32] It also noted that the system was designed to protect the European market—rather than national markets or the individual interests of traders—and concluded that the institutions could be held liable for damage to the legitimate expectations of traders only if they were to abolish, or modify, the monetary compensatory system immediately, without adopting transitional measures, and if a prudent trader could not reasonably foresee such abolition or modification.[33] Given the nature of the complex monetary difficulties faced by the

---

[27] ibid para 8. See also Case 1/73 *Westzucker* [1973] ECR 723 involving an overlap of the principle of legal certainty with the principle of protection of legitimate expectations.

[28] See eg Case 265/87 *Schraeder* [1989] ECR 2237.

[29] [1972] OJ L291/48. The legal basis of this measure included Art 43.

[30] See eg Regulation 222/73, [1973] OJ L27/4 (on the creation of representative rates for the UK and Ireland), Regulation 112/73, [1973] OJ L114/4 (on the introduction of an agreement by some Member States (the snake) to limit currency fluctuations within fixed margins) and Regulation 475/75, [1975] OJ L52/28 (on the introduction of green currencies).

[31] See eg Case 10/73 *Rewe-Zentral v Bundesmonopolverwaltung für Branntwein* [1973] ECR 1175; Case 43/72 Merkur [1973] ECR 1055; and Joined Cases 70 & 81/77 *Ramel* [1978] ECR 927. For comments on some of this jurisprudence see J Usher, 'Agricultural Markets: Their Price Systems and Financial Mechanism' (1979) 4 *European Law Review* 147 and P Gilsdorf, 'The System of Monetary Compensatory Amounts from a Legal Standpoint' (1980) 5 *European Law Review* 341, 433.

[32] Case 9/73 *Schlüter* [1973] ECR 1135, 1159.

[33] See eg Case 97/76 *Merkur* [1977] ECR 1063 and Case 146/77 *British Beef* [1978] ECR 1347. See also Case 74/74 *CNTA* [1975] ECR 533.

institutions during that period, it was rare for the Court to overrule the exercise of the discretion by the institutions in their responses to these.[34]

E Organization of the Common Agricultural Policy

Article 43(2) of the Treaty of Rome provided legislative power to the Council to define and implement the CAP by making regulations, issuing directives, or taking decisions, on a proposal from the Commission having consulted the European Parliament.[35] Failure to consult the European Parliament was declared by the Court in *Roquette* to be a breach of an essential procedural requirement, noting that the requirement was not satisfied by asking simply for the European Parliament's opinion, but that it was satisfied when it had expressed its opinion.[36] This issue is of historical interest only as, consistent with the increased legislative power accorded to the European Parliament in the various Treaty amendments, Article 43(2) TFEU provides now that, after consulting the Economic and Social Committee, using the ordinary legislative procedure the European Parliament and the Council will establish the common organization of agricultural markets, provided for inter alia in Article 40(1) TFEU, necessary in pursuit of the CAP's objectives.[37] It is worth noting here that Article 43(3) TFEU goes on to provide that the Council, acting on a proposal of the Commission, is to adopt measures on fixing prices, levies, aid, and quantitative limitations; this represents a considerable amount of legislation, raising the question of the demarcation between paragraphs (2) and (3).

Under Article 289 TFEU, there are two types of legislative procedure—the ordinary legislative procedure and the special legislative procedure—both of which involve the European Parliament. As Article 43(3) does not involve the European Parliament, this would suggest that that acts adopted under that provision are not legislative acts; Article 289(3) TFEU provides that only measures adopted under procedures outlined in it are such. So, what is the nature of those acts? Article 288 TFEU outlines the various legislative acts that can be adopted, so measures adopted by the Council under Article 43(3) TFEU would in fact be legally binding, the procedure specified there coming in addition to the ordinary and special legislative procedures. It could also be argued that the ordinary legislative procedure in paragraph (2) is to be the dominant means

---

[34] See eg Case 108/77 *Wagner* [1978] ECR 1187; Case 131/77 *Milac* [1978] ECR 1041; and Case 4/79 *Providence Agricole* [1980] ECR 2823.

[35] Article 43 also includes the power to conclude international agreements; see eg Joined Cases 3, 4, and 6/76 *Kramer* [1976] ECR 1279.

[36] Case 138/79 *Roquette v Council* [1980] ECR 3333, 3360–61. See also Case C-45/93 *European Parliament v Council* [1995] ECR I-643 on the European Parliament's duty of loyal cooperation, suggesting that it may not delay giving an opinion on proposals which are a matter of urgency.

[37] For discussion see eg C Roederer-Rynning and F Schimmelfennig, 'Bringing Co-decision to Agriculture: A Hard Case of Parliamentarization' (2012) 19 *Journal of European Public Policy* 951. It is worth noting here that, in contrast to other meetings of the Council (whose meetings are prepared by the Committee of Permanent Representatives), meetings of the Council composed of ministers of agriculture are prepared by the Special Committee on Agriculture (SCA), which was created by a decision of the representatives of the governments of the Member States in 1960. The SCA is composed of senior officials who are responsible for agricultural policy either in the Member States' permanent representations or in their ministries; the Commission also participates in these meetings.

of legislating, paragraph (3) being an exception. The latter provision does not suggest that the Council may adopt measures only if it has been explicitly given power to do so by legislation adopted under Article 43(2) TFEU. However, it would be difficult to imagine legislation adopted by the Council being contrary to the general policy decisions taken in the acts adopted under that Treaty provision. Equally, it is possible that legislation adopted under Article 43(2) TFEU could cover measures on fixing prices, levies, aids, and quantitative limitations, thus depriving the Council of its exclusive power under Article 43(3) TFEU. Such an approach would be more consistent with the broad thrust of the changes to the legislative procedure of having the European Parliament as co-legislator, but it is not demanded by the Treaty. Indeed, the latest legislative measure on the common organization of agricultural markets, Regulation 1308/2013, recognizes in its preamble that the Council has power under Article 43(3) TFEU, noting that, where that Treaty provision does apply, the Regulation would, in the interest of clarity, explicitly refer to it as the legal basis.[38]

Article 40 TFEU makes clear that 'the common organisation shall be limited to pursuit of the objectives set out in Article 39'. The ordinary legislative procedure, as set out in Article 43, was to be used to establish the common organizations of the market. This procedure has, however, also been used as a legal basis, either singly or together with some other Treaty provision, for legislation covering measures with objectives not found in Article 39. An early example cited by Usher is Community health legislation, more particularly Directive 69/464 on the control of potato wart disease, and Directive 69/465 on the control of the potato cyst eelworm.[39] Although these measures had joint legal bases, subsequent legislation would be adopted on the basis of Article 43 alone, leading to challenge before the Court, for example, by the United Kingdom in regard to the legal basis of Directive 85/649 on the use of hormones in beef.[40] There, the UK, supported by Denmark, argued that Article 43 did not constitute a sufficient legal basis for the Directive as, although it had agricultural policy objectives, it was also directed at harmonizing the laws of the Member States safeguarding the interests and health of consumers, not an objective of the CAP. In response, the Court noted that Article 43 has to be interpreted in the light of both Articles 39 and 40, and that from Article 39(2) it follows that 'agricultural policy objectives must be conceived in such a manner as to enable the Community institutions to carry out their duties in the light of developments in agriculture and in the economy as a whole'.[41] It continued:[42]

> Efforts to achieve objectives of the common agricultural policy, in particular under common organizations of the markets, cannot disregard requirements relating to the public interest such as the protection of consumers or the protection of the health and

---

[38] [2013] OJ L347/671. See eg Art 14 on the buying in price for intervention; Art 15(2) on fixing the level of the public intervention price; Art 18(3) on fixing the amount of aid for private storage; Arts 23(5) and (6) on EU aid for the School fruit and vegetable scheme; Art 27(7) on EU aid for the School milk scheme; Art 131(1) on fixing a surplus levy in temporary market management mechanisms; and, Art 198(2) on the fixing of export refunds.

[39] A J Usher, EC Agricultural Law (2nd edn, OUP 2001) 24. The Directives were published in OJ [1969] OJ L323/1 and 3.

[40] Council Directive 85/649/EEC, [1985] OJ L382/228.

[41] Case 68/86 *UK v Council* (n 18) 894.   [42] ibid 895.

life of humans and animals, requirements which the Community institutions must take into account in exercising their powers.

For the Court, there was thus no need to have recourse to another provision of the Treaty as a joint legal basis, as Article 43 contributed to the achievement of one or more of the objectives listed in Article 39. The Court went on to point out that, by virtue of Article 38(2) (which accords precedence to the specific provisions on agriculture over the more general provisions on the internal market), and in the absence of specific provisions outlining other objectives, the general provision on harmonization cannot restrict the scope of Article 43.[43] This approach has been followed in subsequent cases, but the judgment suggests that, in those instances in which there is a specific legal basis elsewhere in the Treaty, that provision should be joined to Article 43.[44] Although the Court chose to ignore the introduction of Article 152 EC Treaty (now Article 168 TFEU) (requiring that health protection measures should form a constituent part of other EU policies), in the challenge to Regulation 820/97, which introduced a new system for the registration of bovine animals and for the labelling of beef products, the immediate successor to this Regulation was based on Article 152(4) (b) EC Treaty (now Article 168(4)(b) TFEU).[45]

Article 43(1) TFEU provides that *common* organizations of the market to implement the CAP will replace *national* organizations, and for most agricultural products these had been established by the end of the transitional period. There were some notable exceptions—alcohol, potatoes, sheep meat, and bananas—some of which are, however, now subject to a common organization. The Court confirmed in *Charmasson*, a dispute concerning the imposition of a quota system for imports of bananas into France, that a national market organization should have objectives equivalent to those of the CAP—a simple quota system would, therefore, not suffice.[46] The decision in that case was restated in *Commission v Ireland*, in which the Court also recognized that the Treaty's rules on the free movement of goods applied for those agricultural products in respect of which a common organization of the market had not been established.[47] At this point it is worth recalling that, under Article 4(2)(d), agriculture is an area of competence shared between Union and Member States. It is clear that Member States' powers are in fact residual, acting only if such action is excluded neither explicitly nor

---

[43] ibid 896.

[44] See also eg Case 131/86 *UK v Council* [1988] ECR 905, Case 131/87 *Commission v Council (Glands)* [1989] ECR 3743; and Case 11/88 *Commission v Council (Pesticides)* [1989] ECR 3799.

[45] Council Regulation No 820/97 of 21 April 1997 establishing a system for the identification and registration of bovine animals and regarding the labelling of beef and beef products [1997] OJ L117/1. See Case C-269/97 Commission and European Parliament v Council [2000] ECR I-2257 and Council Regulation (EC) 999/2001 of 22 May 2001 laying down rules for the prevention, control and eradication of certain transmissible spongiform encephalopathies [2001] OJ L147/1. According to the third recital of the Preamble to this Regulation, it 'directly concerns public health and is relevant to the functioning of the internal market. It covers products which are included in Annex I to the Treaty as well as products which are not. Consequently, it is appropriate to choose Art 152(4)(b) of the Treaty as the legal basis.'

[46] Case 48/74 [1974] ECR 1383. See also Cases 90 and 91/63 *Commission v Luxembourg and Belgium* [1964] ECR 625 in which the court offered a similar definition and Case 237/82 *Kaas* [1984] ECR 483.

[47] Case 288/83 [1985] ECR 1761. See Case 232/78 *Commission v France* [1979] ECR 2729 in which the Court recognized that problems could arise with respect to competition policy and Case 114/83 *SICA* [1984] ECR 2589.

implicitly by EU law.[48] The major role for the Member States appears to be one of ensuring the effective supervision and enforcement of the CAP in accordance with EU implementing legislation and, in the absence of such legislation, implementation is to be on the basis of national law.[49] The Court noted in *Wachauf* that the requirements flowing from the protection of fundamental rights in the EU legal order are binding on Member States when they implement its rules, and that the Member States must, as far as possible, apply those rules in accordance with those requirements.[50]

F Administrative Procedures within the Common Agricultural Policy

In *Roquette*, the Court noted:[51]

> When the implementation by the Council of the agricultural policy of the Community involves the need to evaluate a complex economic situation, the discretion which it has does not apply exclusively to the nature and scope of the measures to be taken but also to some extent to the finding of the basic facts inasmuch as, in particular, it is open to the Council to rely if necessary on general findings. In reviewing the exercise of such a power the Court must confine itself to examining whether it contains a manifest error or constitutes a misuse of power or whether the authority in question did not clearly exceed the bounds of its discretion.

In other formulations of the scope of the Council's legislative powers, the Court has indicated that 'political responsibilities' are imposed on the Council by Articles 40 and 43.[52] Similar characterizations have been made of the power of Commission in those cases in which the Council has delegated its power to it in order to implement legislation.[53] Although the Court has given a wide interpretation of the concept of 'implementation', there are limits which must be respected.[54] In this regard, the Court has noted:

> Since only the Commission is in a position to keep track of agricultural market trends and to act quickly when necessary, the Council may confer on it wide powers in that sphere. Consequently, the limits of those powers must be determined by reference to the essential general aims of the market organization. However, it must be pointed out that such a wide interpretation of the Commission's powers can be accepted only in the specific framework of the rules on agricultural markets. It cannot

---

[48] See eg Case 48/85 *Commission v Germany* [1986] ECR 2549. Art 2(2) TFEU provides, in part: 'The Member States shall exercise their competence to the extent that the Union has not exercised its competence. The Member States shall again exercise their competence to the extent that the Union has decided to cease exercising its competence.'

[49] See eg Case 94/72 *Schlüter* [1972] ECR 307.

[50] Case 5/88 *Wachauf* [1989] ECR 2689. See also in Case C-260/89 *ERT* [1991] ECR I-2925 and Case C-2/92 *Bostock* [1994] ECR I-955.

[51] Case 138/79 *Roquette v Council* (n 36) 3358–59.

[52] See eg Case 138/78 *Stölting* [1979] ECR 713, Cases C-267-285 *Wuidart* [1990] ECR I-435 and Case C-343/07 *Bavaria and Bavaria Italia* [2009] ECR I-5491.

[53] See eg Case 78/74 *Deuka* [1975] ECR 421, 432.

[54] See eg Case 57/72 *Westzücker* [1973] ECR 231.

be relied upon in support of provisions adopted by the Commission on the basis of its implementing powers in agricultural matters where the purpose of the provision in question lies outside that sphere but within a sector subject to an exhaustive set of rules laid down by the Council which, moreover, do not confer any implementing powers on the Commission.[55]

In this particular case, the legislation at issue dealt with customs law, rather than agricultural law, so the Commission did not have the necessary powers.

In respect of the procedure for the making of implementing acts, the question arose in *Köster* whether a Commission consultation with a committee representing national interests (i.e., following the Management Committee procedure) was compatible with various provisions of the Treaty of Rome, including Article 43(2). In response, the Court noted that:[56]

> Both the legislative scheme of the Treaty, reflected in particular by the last indent of Article 155, and the consistent practice of the Community institutions establish a distinction, according to the legal concepts recognized in all the Member States, between the measures directly based on the Treaty itself and derived law intended to ensure their implementation. It cannot therefore be a requirement that all the details of the regulations concerning the common agricultural policy be drawn up by the Council according to the procedure in Article 43. It is sufficient for the purposes of that provision that the basic elements of the matter to be dealt with have been adopted in accordance with the procedure laid down by that provision. On the other hand, the provisions implementing the basic regulations may be adopted according to a procedure different from that in Article 43, either by the Council itself or by the Commission by virtue of an authorization complying with Article 155.

The implementing legislation was regarded by the Court as not going beyond the limits of the implementation of the principles of the basic regulation and as not interfering with the Commission's right of decision or jeopardising its independence since the Management Committee acted as a permanent mechanism of consultation between the Council and the Commission.[57] The ECJ also dismissed the objection to the procedure on the grounds that it deprived the Court of certain of its functions.

The Treaty of Lisbon has now formalized the rules on both delegated and implementing acts. Article 290 TFEU provides that the Commission may adopt *delegated* acts i.e., 'non-legislative acts of general application to supplement or amend certain non-essential elements of the legislative act'. The delegating legislative measure will explicitly define the objectives, content, scope, and duration of the delegation, the European Parliament and the Council having the power to revoke the delegation. The essential elements of a policy area are reserved for coverage in the delegating

---

[55] Case 22/88 *Vreugdenhil* [1989] ECR 2049, 2080.

[56] Case 25/70 *Macchiorlati Dalmas v High Authority* [1970] ECR 1161, 1170.

[57] See also Case 46/86 *Romkes* [1987] ECR 2671, 2686, in which it was pointed out that an implementing regulation adopted without consultation of the European Parliament must respect the basic elements laid down in the basic regulation after consultation of the European Parliament. For a history in this area see C Bergström, *Comitology: Delegation of Powers in the European Union and the Committee System* (OUP 2005).

legislative measure and are, accordingly, themselves not to be the subject of a delegation, in keeping with the longstanding jurisprudence of the Court.[58] Delegated acts
are to enter into force if no objection is expressed by the European Parliament or
the Council within a period set by the legislative act. Article 291 TFEU allows for
implementing acts by the Commission when 'uniform conditions for implementing
legally binding Union acts are needed', where the rules and general principles for the
Commission's exercise of implementing powers have been laid down in a regulation
of the Parliament and the Council adopted using the ordinary legislative procedure.[59]
It appears that the distinction between these two types of act rests with the question
of whether an act amends or supplements a legislative act: if it does so, it is a delegated
act; if it does not, it is an implementing act.[60]

Regulation 1308/2013, which establishes a common organization of the markets
in agricultural products, defines the scope of the Commission's power to adopt both
delegated and implementing acts across an extensive range of areas, including:[61]

- common provision on public intervention and aid for private storage in
  Articles 19–21
- school fruit and vegetable scheme in Articles 24 and 25
- school milk scheme in Articles 27 and 28
- aid in the olive oil and table olives sector in Articles 30 and 31
- aid in the fruit and vegetable sector in Articles 37 and 38
- support programmes in the wine sector in Article 53 and 54
- aid in the apiculture sector in Articles 56 and 57
- aid in the hops sector in Articles 59 and 60
- management of the authorisation scheme for vine plantings in Articles 69 and 70
- designations of origin and geographical indications in the wine sector in Articles
  109–111
- traditional terms in the wine sector in Articles 114–116
- labelling and presentation in the wine sector in Articles 122 and 123
- specific measures in the sugar sector in Articles 132 and 133
- system of production regulation in the sugar sector in Articles 143 and 144
- producer organizations and inter-branch organizations in Articles 173–175
- trade with third countries in Articles 177–179
- tariff quota management and special treatment of imports by third countries in
  Articles 186–188 and
- export refunds in Articles 202–204.

Article 227 of this Regulation confers the power to adopt delegated acts for a period of
seven years beginning on 20 December 2013—the Regulation itself did not enter into
force until 1 January 2014—the Commission being required to present a report on the

---

[58] See eg Case 23/75 *Rey Soda* [1975] ECR 1279; Joined Cases 103-109/78 *Société des Usines de Beauport*
[1979] ECR 17; and Case C-240/90 *Germany v Commission* [1992] ECR I-5383.
[59] For a discussion of Art 291 see Case C-65/13 *European Parliament v Commission* [2014] ECR I-2289
and its earlier jurisprudence in Case 16/88 *Commission v Council* [1989] ECR 3457.
[60] See COM(2009) 673 Implementation of Art 290 of the Treaty on the Functioning of the European
Union. See also Case C-427/12 *Commission v European Parliament and the Council* [2014] ECR I-170.
[61] [2013] OJ L347/671.

use of the delegation no later than nine months before the end of that period. Unless opposed by either the Council or the European Parliament, the delegation is tacitly extended for recurring seven-year periods. Paragraph 3 provides that the European Parliament or the Council may revoke the delegation at any time, without any retroactive effect on its prior exercise. As soon as it adopts a delegated act, the Commission shall notify the European Parliament and the Council (paragraph 4) both of which have two months to object to its entry in to force (paragraph 5).[62] Article 228 provides for an urgency procedure through which delegated legislation may enter into force without delay, so long as no objection is raised by the European Parliament and the Council, having been informed of the reasons for proceeding in this way. In case of objection, the Commission is to repeal the act.

The Regulation, in Article 229, provides, as the final provision of this Chapter, that the Commission is to be assisted the Committee for the Common Organisation of the Agricultural Markets. This body had its origins in Regulation 1234/2007 that established a single common organization of agricultural markets under which a single committee replaced a number of previous, highly specific committees.[63] This committee is one of a number assisting the Commission in agricultural policy, including the:[64]

- Rural Development Committee[65]
- Committee on the Agricultural Funds[66]
- Committee for Direct Payments[67]
- Agricultural Product Quality Policy Committee[68]
- Regulatory Committee on Organic Production[69]
- Committee on Agricultural Structures and Rural Development[70]
- Community Committee for the Farm Accountancy Data Network[71]

---

[62] That period shall be extended by two months at the initiative of the European Parliament or of the Council.

[63] Regulation 1234/2007, [2007] OJ L299/1 Art 195(1) established the Management Committee for the Common Organisation of Agricultural Markets and Art 195(3) established a Regulatory Committee.

[64] List available at http://ec.europa.eu/agriculture/committees/index_en.htm (last accessed 31 July 2016).

[65] See Art 84 of Regulation 1305/2013 on support for rural development by the European Agricultural Fund for Rural Development (EAFRD, [2013] OJ L347/487.

[66] See Art 116 of Regulation 1306/2013 on the financing, management and monitoring of the common agricultural policy, [2013] OJ L347/549. See also Art 41 of Regulation 1290/2005 on the financing of the CAP, [2005] OJ L209/1.

[67] See Art 71 of Regulation 1307/2013 establishing rules for direct payments to farmers under support schemes within the framework of the common agricultural policy [2013] OJ L347/608.

[68] See Art 57 of Regulation 1151/2012 on quality schemes for agricultural products and foodstuffs, [2012] OJ L303/1. This Committee replaced the Standing Committee on Protected Geographical Indications and Protected Designations of Origin and the Standing Committee on Traditional Specialities Guaranteed.

[69] See Art 37 of Regulation 834/2007 on organic production and labelling of organic products [2007] OJ L189/1.

[70] See Art 47(6) of Regulation 1260/1999 laying down general provisions on the Structural Funds [1999] OJ L161/1.

[71] See Art 18 of Regulation 1217/2009 setting up a network for the collection of accountancy data on the incomes and business operation of agricultural holdings in the European Community [2009] OJ L328/27.

- Implementation Committee on Aromatised Wine-based Drinks[72]
- Committee for Spirit Drinks[73]
- Committee on the Conservation, Characterisation, Collection and Utilisation of Genetic Resources in Agriculture[74] and
- Standing Forestry Committee.[75]

Each of these is a committee within the meaning of the Comitology Regulation (182/2011). That Regulation lays down rules and general principles in regard to the control by Member States of the Commission's exercise of implementing powers.[76] That Regulation notes that the basic (enabling) act may provide for the application of either an advisory or an examination procedure, the latter applicable to implementing acts of general scope and implementing acts relating to the CAP (Article 2(2)). Article 2(3) Comitology Regulation provides further that, even if the examination procedure is mandated, the advisory procedure may be used in 'duly justified' cases, but limited guidance is offered as to when this threshold is met (so that perhaps even the Council itself can to adopt implementing acts).[77] Unlike the advisory procedure, in which voting is by simple majority, Article 5 on the examination procedure indicates that a weighted voting system applies. In the event of a negative opinion is delivered by a committee, the Commission may resubmit an amended draft of the implementing act within two months, or within one month submit the proposal to the Appeal Committee established under Article 6. If the negative opinion relates to an implementing act needed without undue delay (e.g., to avoid creating a significant disruption of agricultural markets), Article 7 provides that the Commission may exceptionally adopt a draft implementing act, to be submitted immediately to the Appeal Committee. Where the latter delivers a negative opinion, the act is to be repealed immediately. The Commission may, in cases of urgency, adopt an implementing act immediately applicable, but remaining in force for only six months (unless the basic act provides otherwise) (Article 8). Here too, though, the Commission must submit the measure to the relevant committee within fourteen days and, in the event of a negative opinion, repeal it immediately.

The Comitology Regulation applies to implementing acts (Article 291 TFEU), as Article 290 TFEU sets out a distinct procedure for the adoption of delegated acts, and the provisions are mutually exclusive. This bifurcation of procedure

---

[72] See Art 12 of Regulation 1601/91 laying down general rules on the definition, description and presentation of aromatized wines, aromatized wine-based drinks and aromatized wine-product cocktails [1991] OJ L149/1.

[73] See Art 9(1) of Regulation 110/2008 on the definition, description, presentation, labelling and the protection of geographical indications of spirit drinks [2008] OJ L39/16.

[74] See Art 15 of Regulation 870/2004 establishing a Community programme on the conservation, characterisation, collection and utilisation of genetic resources in agriculture [2004] OJ L162/18.

[75] See Art 3 of Decision 89/367 setting up a Standing Forestry Committee [1989] OJ L165/14.

[76] [2011] OJ L55/13. For an excellent discussion of the Regulation see P Craig, 'Delegated Acts, Implementing Acts and the New Comitology Regulation' (2011) 36 *European Law Review* 671. See also R Schütze, '"Delegated" Legislation in the (New) European Union: A Constitutional Analysis' (2011) 74 *Modern Law Review* 661.

[77] See S Peers and M Costa, 'Accountability for Delegated and Implementing Acts after the Treaty of Lisbon' (2012) 18 *European Law Journal* 427, who argue that this would subvert Arts 290 and 291 TFEU.

makes it essential that the Commission abide by the distinction between these types of act, and that the European Parliament exercise oversight over the distinction, especially as it is given a greater role with respect to delegated acts. However, Article 11 Comitology Regulation allows the Parliament or the Council to declare that an implementing act exceeds the enabling power of the basic regulation adopted under the ordinary legislative procedure. Whilst the Commission is not obliged to withdraw the measure, it must take into account the view of these institutions in a review of the draft act, after which it must inform the Parliament and the Council as to whether it intends to maintain, amend, or withdraw the draft implementing act.

On 11 March 2014, the Commission adopted ten delegated acts supplementing:[78]

- Regulation 1307/2013 on Direct Payment with further rules on the definition of an 'active farmer', the Basic Payment, crop diversification, on the ecological focus area, young farmers, and voluntary coupled support[79]
- Regulation 1308/2013 on a common organisation of the markets in agricultural products, acts were adopted on wine, the School Fruit and Vegetable Scheme, fruit and vegetables, olive oil and private storage aid[80]
- Regulation 1305/2013 on support for rural development in order to ensure consistency across the Member States, out detailed rules were set out on young farmers, methods to avoid double funding and detailed rule on a number of other EAFRD measures[81] and
- Regulation 1306/2013 on financing, management and monitoring of the CAP acts were adopted dealing with rules on paying agencies and other bodies, financial management, clearance of accounts, securities and use of the Euro.[82]

The European Parliament and the Council were given a period of time to object to the delegated acts. Only one objection, to Delegated Regulation 639/2014, was raised, and only as regards the provisions on ecological focus areas, the subject of debate in the original legislation (being viewed as significant for safeguarding and improving biodiversity on farms). Members States would have had to ensure that only areas with nitrogen-fixing crops, sufficiently contributing to improving biodiversity, were

---

[78] Various implementing regulations were also adopted in each of these areas. There was also a delegated act on public intervention expenditure, which essentially continued the existing rules on expenditure financed by the EU budget in relation to public intervention, Commission Delegated Regulation 906/2014, [2014] OJ L255/1.

[79] See Commission Delegated Regulation 639/2014, [2014] OJ L181/1. See also Commission Implementing Regulation 640/2014, [2014] OJ L181/74.

[80] See Commission Delegated Regulation 612/2014, [2014] OJ L168/62 (Wine); Commission Delegated Regulation 500/2014, [2014] OJ L145/12 (School Fruit and Vegetable Scheme); Commission Delegated Regulation 499/2014, [2014] OJ L145/5 (fruit and vegetables); and Commission Delegated Regulation 612/2014, [2014] OJ L145/14 (private storage aid). Two Commission Implementing Regulations were also passed for wine (Regulation 614/2014, [2014] OJ L168/73) and for Olive Oil (Regulation 615/2014, [2014] OJ L168/95).

[81] See Commission Delegated Regulation 807/2014, [2014] OJ L227/1. See also Commission Implementing Regulation 808/2014, [2014] OJ L227/18.

[82] See Commission Delegated Regulation 640/2014, [2014] OJ L181/48 and Commission Delegated Regulation 907/2014, [2014] OJ L255/18. See also the Commission Implementing Regulations, respectively Regulation 809/2014 ([2014] OJ L227/69) and Regulation 908/2014 ([2014] OJ L255/59).

recognized as an ecological focus area.[83] The Delegated Regulation, as foreseen in the basic legislation, had set a weighting factor reflecting differences in terms of the bio-diversity significance of various types of ecological focus areas. The Parliament and the Council considered that this weighting factor should be increased above the level set in the original Delegated Regulation, a change duly made by Commission's substi-tute Delegated Regulation 1001/2014.[84]

G Supervising Implementation of the Common Agricultural Policy

Whilst legislative power resides in the EU institutions, much of the day-to-day ad-ministration of the CAP falls to national authorities, which are required to collect money on behalf of the EU and to make the payments required under, for example, the single common organization of the market.[85] Whereas the former accrues to the Union budget, the latter comes from a specific fund—originally the European Agricultural Guidance and Guarantee Fund (EAGGF), but now the European Agricultural Guarantee Fund (EAGF) and the European Agricultural Fund for Rural Development (EAFRD).[86] Article 4(1) of Regulation 1306/2013 on the finan-cing, management, and monitoring of the CAP provides that the EAGF will finance expenditure on:[87]

(a) measures regulating or supporting agricultural markets
(b) direct payments to farmers under the CAP
(c) the Union's financial contribution to information and promotion measures for agricultural products on the internal market of the Union and in third countries, undertaken by Member States on the basis of programmes other than those re-ferred to in Article 5 and selected by the Commission
(d) the Union's financial contribution to the Union School Fruit and Vegetables Scheme as referred to in Article 23 of Regulation (EU) No 1308/2013 and to the

---

[83] The General Court has dismissed an action brought by Hungary against Delegated Regulation 639/2014 alleging a misuse of power by the Commission and a breach of principles of legal certainty, non-discrimination and legitimate expectations as well as an interference with the right to property. See Case T-662/14 *Hungary v Commission* (not yet reported) Decision of 1 June 2016 http://eur-lex.europa.eu/legal-content/EN/TXT/HTML/?uri=CELEX:62014TJ0662&rid=2 (last accessed 21 July 2016).

[84] [2014] OJ L281/1.

[85] See eg Joined Cases 178–180/73 *Belgium and Luxembourg v Mertens* [1974] ECR 33 in which it was noted that it is for the Member States to take the necessary proceedings, either criminal or civil, to en-force of recover agricultural levies. See also Case 110/76 *Pretore de Cento v X* [1977] ECR 851 and Case 267/78 *Commission v Italy* [1980] ECR 31 for further developments in this area. There is no discretion for Member States as to whether they should recover such resources; see eg Joined Cases 205–215/82 *Deutsche Milchkontor* [1983] ECR 2633.

[86] In order to enable the common organizations to attain their objectives, Art 40(4) TFEU provides that one or more Agricultural Guidance and Guarantee Funds may be set up.

[87] [2013] OJ L347/549. Paragraph 2 goes on to provide that the Fund will also finance '(a) promotion of agricultural products, undertaken either directly by the Commission or through international organisa-tions; (b) measures, taken in accordance with Union law, to ensure the conservation, characterisation, collection and utilisation of genetic resources in agriculture; (c) the establishment and maintenance of agricultural accounting information systems; (d) agricultural survey systems, including surveys on the structure of agricultural holdings'.

measures related to animal diseases and loss of consumer confidence as referred to in Article 155 of that Regulation.

Article 5 of Regulation 1306/2013 covers EAFRD expenditure, i.e., the EU's financial contribution to rural development programmes implemented in accordance with the rural development legislation.[88] Both provisions note that expenditure is to be implemented in shared management between the Member States and the EU, and that such expenditure must be in accordance with European law. This latter requirement forms the legal basis of the Union's financial liability as indicated by a trilogy of early cases in which the Netherlands and Germany sought the annulment of Commission decisions relating for agricultural expenditure in 1971 and 1972.[89]

One of the issues in these cases was the interpretation of Article 8(2) of Regulation 729/70, which governed EAGFF expenditure at the time, providing that '[i]n the absence of total recovery, the financial consequences of irregularities or negligence shall be borne by the Community, with the exception of the consequence of irregularities or negligence attributable to administrative authorities or other bodies of the Member States'. It was argued that this provision should be interpreted to mean that the financial consequences of an incorrect application of the relevant law should be borne by the Union, if the error(s) made by the national authority rested on an interpretation made in good faith. After examining the different language versions of Article 8, the Court noted that the provision contained too many contradictory and ambiguous elements to provide an answer to the questions at issue. It decided that it needed to examine the context and the objectives of the rules in question.[90] The Court made reference to Articles 2 and 3 of the Regulation which provided, for example, that the EU would finance export refunds and intervention measures, provided that these were undertaken in accordance with the relevant rules. The Court concluded:[91]

> Those provisions permit the Commission to charge to the EAGGF only sums paid in accordance with the rules laid down in the various sectors of agricultural production while leaving the Member States to bear the burden of any other sum paid, and in particular any amounts which the national authorities wrongly believed themselves authorized to pay in the context of the common organization of the markets.

This strict interpretation of the conditions under which the EU is required to meet expenditure was necessary, not only considering the objectives of the Regulation, but also to implement the principle of equality between Member States, i.e., to prevent the authorities of one Member State giving a wide interpretation to a particular provision, thus favouring traders in that Member State to the detriment of traders in other Member States, where authorities had adopted a stricter interpretation.[92] Expenditure in these instances would have to be borne by the Member State concerned.

---

[88] See Regulation 1305/2013, [2013] OJ L347/487.

[89] Respectively Case 11/76 *Netherlands v Commission* [1979] ECR 245; Joined Cases 15 and 16/76 *France v Commission* [1979] ECR 321; and Case 18/76 *Germany v Commission* [1979] ECR 343. Under Regulation 729/70 ([1970] OJ L94/13) the EAGFF was to be part of the budget.

[90] Case 11/76 *Netherlands v Commission* (n 89), with equivalent paragraph in the other decision.

[91] ibid 279.

[92] See also Case 347/85 *UK v Commission* [1988] ECR 1749; and Case C-48/91 *Netherlands v Commission* [1993] ECR I-5611.

In each of these cases, the Court went on to examine whether the relevant expenditure had been in accordance with the relevant legislation. In the Netherlands case, the Court considered that expenditure by the Netherlands on the sale, at reduced prices, of butter from public stocks for export, and on export refunds for lactalbumin, had indeed not been incurred in accordance with the legislation, so that the Commission's decision denying reimbursement had been justified. In a second case, the Court considered that expenditure by Germany on aids for skimmed milk powder used in animal feed, on the sale at reduced prices of butter from public stocks for export, on the repurchase of butter sold at reduced prices and intended for processing into concentrated butter, and on costs of crushing and reconditioning sugar, were not justified as they did not comply with the relevant legislation. However, expenditure on aid for the purchase of butter by persons in receipt of social assistance had been in accordance with the relevant legislation, so the refusal by the Commission to meet this expenditure was annulled.

France had also requested the annulment of Commission decisions refusing to meet expenditure in 1971 and 1972 on aid for skimmed-milk powder used for animal feeding-stuffs and on aids for wine distillation. The Court confirmed that in reaching its decision it had to assess here too whether the expenditure had been incurred in accordance with the legislation. The Court rejected both requests. On the aids for wine distillation, France had considered the aids established by the Regulation insufficient and awarded additional national aid. The Commission had initially taken proceedings for breach of Treaty obligations under Article 169 (now Article 258 TFEU), but had later abandoned these. France had then argued that the Commission's decision to refuse to cover France's expenditure on aids for wine distillation was an abuse of procedure, given that the Commission had discontinued Article 169 proceedings. The Court rejected that argument, observing that the Article 169 procedure and that for the discharge of accounts served different aims, and were subject to different rules, noting in particular that, with respect to the latter, the Commission has no discretionary power to derogate from the legislative rules.[93]

The decisions in these cases were not surprising given the Court's previous decision in *Grand Moulin des Antilles* in which it had decided that the liability of Member States to make payments required under a common organization existed, even when the EAGGF refused, or was unable to reimburse, such payments.[94] In that case, the plaintiff had requested payments due to them under the common organization of the market in cereals, and had initiated an action for non-contractual liability against the EU for these payments, having been unsuccessful in such an application to the French national authorities. For the Court, the relevant legislation made it clear that payment, or refusal to pay, were decisions for the national authorities, and it was for the national court to give a ruling, opening the way for a preliminary reference to the Court. Thus, the plaintiff should have brought its action

---

[93] See Joined Cases 15 and 16/76 *France v Commission* (n 89) 339–40. See also Case 49/83 *Luxembourg v Commission* [1984] ECR 2931 in which the Court noted that a Member State may obtain reimbursement for national aid if it can prove that the aid was properly paid for in good faith.

[94] Case 99/74 *Grands Moulins des Antilles v Commission* [1975] ECR 1531.

against the national authorities, subject to national rules and in pursuit of national remedies.[95] As the Court noted in *Salumi*:[96]

> [I]n so far as no provisions of Community law are relevant, it is for the national legal system of each Member State to lay down the detailed rules and conditions for the collection of Community revenues in general and agricultural levies in particular and to determine the authorities responsible for collection and the courts having jurisdiction to decide disputes to which that collection may give rise but such procedures and conditions may not make the system for collecting Community charges and dues less effective than that for collecting national charges and dues of the same kind.

So, whilst the Commission may bring proceedings against Member States for failure to implement their obligations under the Treaty, and may have recourse to the competition provisions of the Treaty, it falls to the national courts to provide remedies for individuals adversely affected by the implementation of the CAP. Such national courts would then have the option of using the preliminary reference procedure to obtain a determination by the Court of Justice and the General Court on the interpretation and validity of legislation implementing the CAP. In the result, as already noted, it is the Member States which are responsible for any errors, delays, or wrongful interpretation of the legislation.

H Conclusions

The CAP has evolved considerably since its introduction, but ECJ case law in this area has been remarkably consistent. The institutions have enjoyed a wide margin of discretion in balancing the competing demands emerging from Union agricultural policy, thus it is not surprising that associated legislation has been upheld by the courts. Nevertheless, the many judicial decisions involving the CAP have had a significant impact on Union law, with many of the general principles of European law, and particularly aspects of European administrative law, finding their origins in this jurisprudence.

---

[95] On this point see previous decision by the Court in Case 96/71 *Haegeman* [1972] ECR 1005 and the later decision in Joined Cases 89 and 91/86 *Société l'Etoile Commerciale* [1987] ECR 3005. See also case 175/84 *Krohn* [1976] ECR 753; Case 238/78 *Ireks-Arkady* [1979] ECR 2955; and Joined Cases C-104/89 and C-37/90 *Mulder* [1992] ECR I-3061 for different decisions.

[96] Joined Cases 66, 127, and 128/79 *Salumi and Others* [1980] ECR 1237, 1263.

20

European Union Funds

Katerina Pantazatou

A Introduction

The European Union funds constitute the main budgetary instrument for the Union to promote its policy goals. The European Union Funds or European Structural and Investment Funds (generally, either EU funds or ESI funds) finance projects that pertain to a large array of areas, including regional and urban development, employment and social inclusion, maritime and fisheries policies, research and innovation, and humanitarian aid. Part of such funding is directed towards the Member States, whereas another part is intended for third countries.

More than half of the total Union funding is carried out through the five EU funds, the Cohesion Fund (CF), the European Regional Development Fund (ERDF), the European Social Fund (ESF), the European Agricultural Fund for Rural Development (EAFRD), and the European Maritime and Fisheries Fund (EMFF). Economic, social, and territorial cohesion, together with agriculture and fisheries, the policy areas that underpin the EU funds, fall within the competences shared between Union and Member States.[1] The involvement of several supranational, national, and sub-national actors in the many actions and procedures that constitute the management of the EU funds poses several questions of an administrative law nature explored in this chapter.

B Sources of Law

The underlying source of law for the programming period 2014–2020 is the Overarching or Common Provisions Regulation 1303/2013, which lays down the common legal framework for the ESI Funds. Each of the funds is, further, governed by a 'fund-specific' regulation.[2] The disbursement of monies from the EU budget and the (current) allocations for each fund, and, in a broader context, for each objective, are set out in the Multi-Annual Financial Framework (MFF) for the period 2014–2020.[3] The priorities and limits laid out in the MFF are reflected in the EU budget.

---

[1] Art 4(c) and (d) TFEU.

[2] For the Cohesion Fund (CF), Regulation No 1300/2013; for the European Regional and Development Fund (ERDF), Regulation No 1301/2013; for the European Social Fund (ESF), Regulation 1304/2013; for the European Maritime and Fisheries Fund (EMFF), Regulation 508/2014; for the European Agricultural Fund for Rural Development (EAFRD); and for the support from the European Regional Development Fund to the European territorial cooperation goal, Regulation 1299/2013.

[3] Council Regulation (EU, Euratom) No 1311/2013 of 2 December 2013 laying down the multiannual financial framework for the years 2014–2020.

Compliance with EU law is, as expected, a prerequisite throughout all the stages of funding actions and procedure, from the selection of projects through to preventive and/or corrective action, where this is deemed necessary.[4] The management of the Union funds by the European Commission and the Member States in accordance with 'the principles of sound financial management, transparency and non-discrimination', while ensuring the visibility of Union action when managing them, is required by the EU Financial Regulation 966/2012.[5]

C Sectoral Organization and Administrative Tasks for Union Funds

The EU funds constitute a typical example of integrated European administration. Regulation 1303/2013, together with the fund-specific regulations, allocates the administrative tasks with regard to the programming, implementation, reporting, monitoring, evaluation, and financial management of the ESI Funds among the Commission, the Member States, regional and local authorities, and other stakeholders. Decision-making powers are, thus, diffused not only from the supranational to the national level, but also from the national level on to the governmental (executive/administrative), regional, and local levels, and to private actors on the different territorial levels. The composite procedures that underpin such a scheme provide for the 'top down' allocation of the aforementioned tasks and responsibilities between national (including regional and local level) and supranational authorities which, in turn, engenders a very complex legal framework.

In principle, it is the European Commission which is entrusted with the design of the general framework for funds administration, by setting out the general objectives and programming, strategic guidelines, the main priorities, and the indicative allocations for each Member State.[6] In the agenda-setting and programming stage, the Common Strategic Framework lays out the general guiding principles, objectives, and key actions to be undertaken by the Member States. The latter, being the recipients of the EU funds, have to prove at this stage, through the partnership agreements and the operational programmes, that they comply with the principles and

---

[4] Art 6 of Regulation 1303/2013 and European Commission implementing Decision 2014/99/EU of 18 February 2014 setting out the list of regions eligible for funding from the European Regional Development Fund and the European Social Fund and of Member States eligible for funding from the Cohesion Fund for the period 2014–2020 [2014] OJ L50/22 of 20 February 2014 provides that: 'Operations supported by the ESI Funds shall comply with applicable Union law and the national law relating to its application (applicable law)'. More specific references are made throughout both the overarching Regulation as well as the fund-specific Regulations and include the need for compliance with the non-discrimination principle, public procurement rules, and state aid rules.

[5] Financial Regulation 966/2012 Art 59(1), and by reference to sound financial management see Art 4(8) Regulation 1303/2013 (n 4).

[6] Regulation 1303/2013 (n 4): Art 9 on the thematic objectives, Art 10 and Annex I on the Common Strategic Framework, and Annex VII for the allocation methodology. It is noteworthy that, although the partnership agreement, as drafted by the relevant Member State with the participation of all regional, local, and socio-economic partners, figures as the major programming document for cohesion policy, it is prepared in dialogue with the Commission and needs to be approved by it. Consequently, even at this level one can observe the composite administrative procedures underpinning the EU Funds.

objectives set out there, as well as with country-specific recommendations issued by the Commission or the Council, the European Semester requirements, and the ex ante conditionalities laid out in relevant regulations. At the same time, in carrying out planning and programming tasks, the Commission has very broad responsibilities regarding the administration of the budget, in particular as to regional policy and the ERDF. Accordingly, in respect of EU regional assistance, the Commission is responsible for laying down the criteria for identifying the eligible regions according to category (less developed regions, transition regions, most developed regions), and the priorities to be targeted with the funding. It enjoys broad discretion in dealing with the indicative allocations for each Member State. Conversely, the Member States are responsible for drafting their regional aid maps (in accordance with the Commission's Regional Aid Guidelines (RAG)).[7]

Once the Commission has ensured that the partnership agreements comply with its priorities, the Member States have a wide margin of independence for the implementation of EU Fund goals. They are responsible for designating different national and sub-national authorities to carry out specific tasks. In brief, Regulation 1303/2013 provides for the establishment of certain authorities by the Member States, in accordance with their own national institutional, legal, and financial framework: the managing authority and the regional authority (for the implementation of ERDF funding), the Monitoring Committee,[8] the Steering Committee, the certifying authority,[9] and a functionally independent audit authority. In addition to these authorities, the Member States can entrust intermediate bodies with carrying out certain (pre-agreed) tasks of the managing authority or the certifying authority, while the cooperation of national agencies is often sought with regard to enforcement and transparency.

Each of the above-mentioned bodies is assigned different administrative tasks, in particular with regard to the implementation, management, and monitoring of the Union's funds. The overarching responsibility 'for the effective and efficient implementation of the funds', which includes a substantial number of functions related to programme management and monitoring, financial management and control, as well as *project selection*, lies with the managing authorities.[10] The pertinent managing authority will be designated by each Member State for one or more operational programmes, and can be a national, regional, or local public authority or body, or a private

---

[7] Art 90 of Regulation 1303/2013 (n 4). Under the new Regulation the eligible regions for ESI aid are distinguished between the less developed regions (the former 'convergence regions') representing the poorest regions with less than 75% of EU average gross domestic product (GDP), the transition regions (a new category replacing the phasing in and phasing out categories) comprising areas with 75%–90% of EU average GDP, and the most developed regions, which include all other areas and which will have more than 90% of EU average GDP. See also Regulation 1303/2013 Annex VII: 'Allocation Methodology'.

[8] It is noteworthy that according to Art 48(1) of Regulation 1303/2013 (n 4), representatives of the partners referred to in Art 5, notably competent urban and other public authorities; economic and social partners; and relevant bodies representing civil society, including environmental partners, NGOs, and bodies responsible for promoting social inclusion, gender equality and non-discrimination, should be part of the monitoring committees.

[9] According to Recital (106) of Regulation 1303/2013 (n 4): 'to provide flexibility for Member States in setting up control systems, it is appropriate to provide for the option for the functions of the certifying authority to be carried out by the managing authority'.

[10] ibid Art 125: 'The managing authority shall be responsible for managing the operational programme in accordance with the principle of sound financial management'.

body.[11] Monitoring committees are responsible for the monitoring of the programme at issue, and for reviewing its implementation and progress towards achieving its objectives.[12] Steering committees, which are usually set up by the managing authorities, are entrusted with reviewing progress towards achieving the milestones, outputs, and results of the joint action plan,[13] whereas the audit authorities are assigned the job of auditing the operational programmes.[14]

In these administrative processes, the Commission has a more supervisory, yet vaguely defined, role, which consists of ensuring that the Member States have established management and control systems complying with the EU legal framework.[15] This general monitoring task of the Commission often blurs the lines of responsibility within the decision-making process, and hampers the attribution of accountability in cases of mismanagement of funds.[16] The Commission has, moreover, a dominant role in evaluation, performance review, enforcement, and auditing. It can impose sanctions where it detects a breach of EU rules or non-compliance with a partnership agreement and an operational programme, by suspending or cancelling the Union funding.[17]

The structural organization and the sequencing of administrative tasks can be represented in Figure 20.1.

D Underlying Sector-specific Legal Principles in Funds Management

In addition to standard EU legal principles, such as those of subsidiarity and proportionality, the Union funds are governed by a number of sector-specific principles aimed at better management and implementation of the funds. The most notable one among them, and perhaps a source of multiple problems, is the principle of *shared management*. Within the practice of shared management of EU funds, the Member States and the Commission 'shall be responsible for the management and control of programmes in accordance with their respective responsibilities laid down in ... Regulation [1303/2013] and in the fund-specific rules'.[18] The management and control of the funded programmes is, thus, shared among various supranational, national, and sub-national actors. The overarching Regulation lays out a very complicated and nebulous designation of competences across these actors.

Among the various competences and tasks shared between the Member States and the Commission, one has to distinguish among the following: *preparatory* action including setting of objectives, programming, and agenda-setting; *implementation* action comprising several, related sub-categories; *control* action, including reporting, monitoring, and evaluation of programmes, and *financial management* action. In principle, preparatory action is located on the (central) EU level, whereas the other activities are shared between the Union and the Member States administrations, with variations.[19]

---

[11] ibid Art 123.   [12] ibid Arts 47–49 and Art 110.   [13] ibid Art 128.   [14] ibid Art 127.
[15] ibid Art 75.   [16] See section I below.   [17] See section H below.
[18] Art 73 and preamble Recital (66) Regulation 1303/2013 (n 4).
[19] For more details see the previous section.

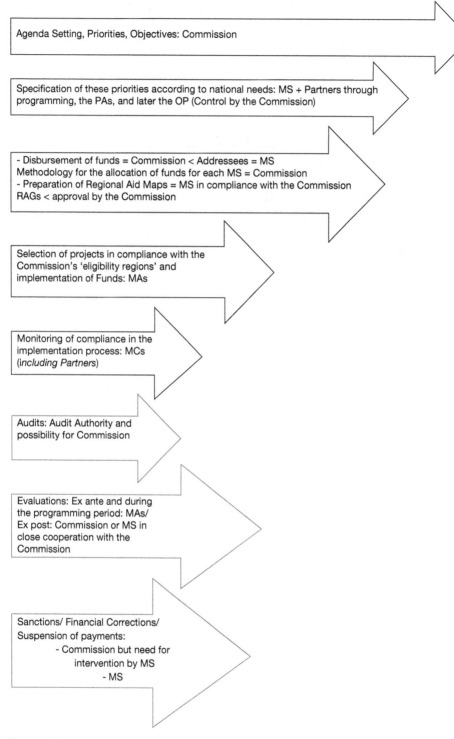

Agenda Setting, Priorities, Objectives: Commission

Specification of these priorities according to national needs: MS + Partners through programming, the PAs, and later the OP (Control by the Commission)

- Disbursement of funds = Commission < Addressees = MS
Methodology for the allocation of funds for each MS = Commission
- Preparation of Regional Aid Maps = MS in compliance with the Commission
RAGs < approval by the Commission

Selection of projects in compliance with the Commission's 'eligibility regions' and implementation of Funds: MAs

Monitoring of compliance in the implementation process: MCs (*including Partners*)

Audits: Audit Authority and possibility for Commission

Evaluations: Ex ante and during the programming period: MAs/ Ex post: Commission or MS in close cooperation with the Commission

Sanctions/ Financial Corrections/ Suspension of payments:
- Commission but need for intervention by MS
- MS

Figure 20.1

The *partnership principle* is another distinctive principle of EU cohesion policy, being complementary to the shared management principle. Its main goal is to involve, throughout all stages (implementation, monitoring, and evaluation of partnership agreements), different actors at both supranational and national level in order to

> ensure respect for the principles of multi-level governance, and also of subsidiarity and proportionality and the specificities of the Member States' different institutional and legal frameworks as well as to ensure the ownership of planned interventions by stakeholders and build on the experience and the know-how of relevant actors.[20]

The partnership principle finds expression through the partnership agreements, which are a vital component—and form of action—for the implementation of the EU funds. Each Member State prepares one partnership agreement for the whole programming period. The agreements' main role is the transposition of the Common Strategic Framework—in other words, the strategic guiding principles for the EU funds established by the Commission—into the national context.[21] Partnership agreements are, thus, drafted by the Member States in accordance with their own institutional and legal framework, and in cooperation with: competent regional and local authorities, including appropriate urban and other public authorities; economic and social partners; and other relevant bodies representing civil society, including environmental partners, non-governmental organizations (NGOs), and others responsible for promoting social inclusion, gender equality, and non-discrimination.[22] As the partnership agreement has, by way of an ex ante control, to be approved by the European Commission, one might question, however, whether any celebration of the partnership principle and of the engagement of actors from all across the national ladder might not be in vain.

Although the content of each partnership agreement is per se rather general, the preliminary assessments of them by the Commission for the programming period 2014–2020 highlights a number of challenges in meeting the expectations of the reform of Union funds management.[23] According to the Commission, Member States and regions have found it difficult to formulate well-defined, specific goals, to focus on objectives suggested by the Commission, and to set-up the requisite administrative network in order to comply with the ex ante conditionalities laid out in Regulation 1303/2013.[24] In an effort to connect the Member States' budgetary performance to the disbursement of EU funds, the Commission's assessment of partnership agreements will, therefore, also take into account national reform programmes and country-specific recommendations (under the European Semester) adopted in accordance

---

[20] Recital (11) Regulation 1303/2013 (n 4).   [21] ibid Arts 14 and15.   [22] ibid Art 5(1).

[23] These challenges differ from Member State to Member State as the observations of the Commission on the partnership agreements with the different Member States show. See Observations of the Commission on Partnership Agreements with Various Member States eg for Estonia: https://ec.europa.eu/info/sites/info/files/partnership-agreement-estonia-observations-april2014_en.pdf, eg for Finland: https://ec.europa.eu/info/sites/info/files/partnership-agreement-finland-observations-may2014_en.pdf.

[24] See Carlos Mendez and John Bachtler, 'Prospects for Cohesion Policy in 2014-20 and Beyond: Progress with Programming and Reflections on the Future' European Policy Research Paper No 88 (January 2015) 37.

with Article 121(2) TFEU, and relevant Council recommendations adopted in accordance with Article 148(4) TFEU, as well as ex ante evaluations of the programmes.[25] In case a particular Member State has not complied with the excessive deficit requirements, or with the relevant imbalance procedures and/or adjustment programmes, the Commission can propose to the Council the suspension of part, or all, of the commitments or payments to that Member State.[26] Similarly, a close link is established between the EU funds and the country specific recommendations of the Commission (provided pursuant to the European Semester), as they have to be taken into account in the preparation of the Member States' programmes.

Despite its purpose of integrating the representation of interested parties in the prioritization of goals, and in the negotiation process, in order to increase transparency and achieve better results, it often happens that potential partners who were not selected for participation are satisfied neither with the selection criteria and nor with the discretion left to the Member State with regard to partner involvement. In principle, at this stage, the Member States are bound only by the *principle of representativeness*, but that entails, in itself, a large degree of discretion.[27] This selectivity issue has an impact not only at the early stages of the drafting of the partnership agreement, but also on the later stages of the implementation and monitoring of the operational programmes.[28] It is almost certain, thus, that the selection—or non-selection—of partners at this early stage might prove to be catalytic throughout the whole programming period.

A precursor of multi-level governance, the partnership principle incorporated all the elements that make up this administrative structure—in Marks' words, 'supranational, national, regional, and local governments are enmeshed in territorially overarching policy networks'.[29] However, evidence from empirical research that was undertaken in three Member States (Austria, Hungary, and Slovakia) during the programming period 2000–2006 has shown that 'in each country NGO participation in the Monitoring Committees remained contentious, the working of the committees was rather formalistic, and the bodies' purpose and role conceptions were ambiguous'.[30] In contrast, the *Van den Brande Report* found that 'in general it seems that no fundamental problems exist with the respect of the multi-level governance and partnership principles during the drafting of partnership agreements'.[31] However, in

---

[25] Art 23 Regulation 1303/2013 (n 4).   [26] ibid Art 23(9).   [27] ibid Art 5(3)(a).

[28] ibid Art 5(2): 'the partners referred to in paragraph 1 shall be involved by Member States in the preparation of Partnership Agreements and progress reports and throughout the preparation and implementation of programmes, including through participation in the monitoring committees for programmes in accordance with Art 48'.

[29] Gary Marks, 'Structural Policy and Multilevel Governance in the EC' in A Cafruny and G Rosenthal (eds), *The State of the European Community Vol 2: The Maastricht Debates and Beyond* (Lynne Rienner and Longman 1993) 402–403. According to Marks, one of the 'founders' of the concept, the 'multi-level' part referred to the increased interdependence of governments operating at different territorial levels, while the 'governance' limb indicated the growing interdependence between governments and non-governmental actors at various territorial levels.

[30] Agnes Batory and Andrew Cartwright, 'Re-visiting the Partnership Principle in Cohesion Policy: The Role of Civil Society Organizations in Structural Funds Monitoring' (2011) 49 *Journal of Common Market Studies* 697, 697.

[31] Luc Van den Brande, *Multilevel Governance and Partnership* [*The Van den Brande Report*] October 2014.

agreement with earlier reports,[32] that report noted that the implementation and application of the principles of multi-level governance and partnership differed widely across the Member States.

The involvement of diverse actors depends on the institutional background and administrative system of the Member States, notably as regards the participation of local and regional authorities, and the different Member State cultures with respect to representation and participation of various socio-economic interest groups in decision-making procedures.[33] Such differentiation and adjustability ensures a certain degree of flexibility in adapting European cohesion policy management to national institutional arrangements. At the same time, however, it may result in a fragmentation of the implementation of that policy, undermining its normative objectives.[34] This problem becomes all the more evident not only at the programming stage, but also at the monitoring stage, as the partners selected to participate in the former phase also comprise part of the Monitoring Committees entrusted with monitoring the fund implementation.

Right from the EU cohesion policy's first emergence, the *principle of additionality* has been fundamental to the EU funds. This principle aims to ensure that assistance should not lead to Member States' reducing their own cohesion efforts, but should be additional to them.[35] The principle is complemented by the further *principle of co-financing* (or the *principle of complementarity*), which provides that, for the furnishing of Union financial assistance, national co-financing is presupposed. The co-financing rates are fixed and adjusted by the Commission in accordance with the priority axes, and the maximum rates of co-financing are set by the Commission according to the category of the region concerned, 'in order to ensure that the principle of co-financing is respected through an appropriate level of public or private national support'.

The recent financial crisis and fiscal commitments of all Member States are likely to have an impact on the absorption of the EU special funds, notably because of the application of these two principles of additionality and co-financing. The more the public finances of the Member States decline—or are to be used for very specific purposes—the less likely it is that they will wish to meet these demands to complement the Union's own investment in economic, social, and territorial cohesion. Although this may pose problems for the distribution and absorption of EU funds, in particular by the poorer or financially assisted Member States, the Commission has, by reason of the financial crises, shown flexibility with regard to these requirements,

---

[32] European Commission, 'The Partnership Principle in the implementation of the Common Strategic Framework Funds: elements for a European Code of Conduct on Partnership' SWD(2012) 106 final 3.

[33] See European Parliament, 'The Partnership Contracts: How to implement multilevel governance and to guarantee the flexibility' Note (2012) 25; and Luc Van den Brande, *The Van den Brande Report* (n 31) 16.

[34] European Parliament, 'An Assessment of Multilevel Governance in Cohesion Policy 2007-2013' Directorate-General for Internal Policies: Policy Department B: Structural and Cohesion Policies: Regional Development (2014) 15; and *The Van den Brande Report* (n 31) 16.

[35] Art 95, Recital (87) and Annex X of Regulation 1303/2013 (n 4) laying down the specific rules on additionality; 'support from the Funds should not replace public or equivalent structural expenditure by Member States', so that for each 'programming period' the Member State receiving EU aid should at least maintain its expenditure at the level of the previous programming period.

and has repeatedly waived or reduced the fixed co-financing rates, in order to facilitate the disbursement of the EU's own funds.[36] The lack of Member State public (co-) funding is not the only impediment to the distribution of the EU funds. Evidence from the Commission, for the previous programming period 2007–2013, highlight a series of other factors that affect the low absorption rates by some Member States. These include the challenges of preparing major infrastructure projects and obtaining the Commission's approval of these, the changes to EU legislation, and alterations within the national political arrangements (including changes in national and regional governments).[37] To these one could add the need for compliance with the often demanding ex ante conditionalities, and the related administrative infrastructure this entails.

The *concentration principle* constitutes another core principle of the EU funds. The concentration referred to is of two kinds. One is the *geographical* concentration, associated with the spatial coverage of EU funds (more precisely, the concentration of funds specifically in less developed geographical areas of the Union). The other is a *thematic* concentration, linked to the EU-wide objectives which are or can be pursued through funds policy. These are to be reflected in the operational programmes adopted by the Member States. The two variations of concentration are connected with one another: EU assistance has to be concentrated in the geographical areas of greatest need, as defined by the established objectives of different Union policy sectors. Currently, EU cohesion policy concentrates on eleven thematic objectives linked to the Europe 2020 agenda, the underlying rationale being the promotion of smart, sustainable, and inclusive growth, together with European territorial cooperation.[38] Under Regulation 1303/2013 the (geographically) eligible regions for ESI aid are distinguished between: the *less developed regions* (the former 'convergence regions'), representing the poorest regions with less than 75 per cent of EU average GDP; the *transition regions* (a new category replacing the phasing-in and phasing-out categories), comprising areas with 75–90 per cent of EU average GDP; and the *most developed regions*, which include all other areas, having more than 90 per cent of EU average GDP.[39] With regard

---

[36] For an overview of the Commission's response to the crisis with regard to the EU Cohesion policy see Wade Jacoby, 'The EU Factor in Fat Times and in Lean: Did the EU Amplify the Boom and Soften the Bust?' (2014) 52(1) *Journal of Common Market Studies* 52, 65–66. See also Art 24 Regulation 1303/2013 (n 4).

[37] European Commission, 'Cohesion policy: Strategic report 2013 on programme implementation 2007-2013' COM(2013) 210 final.

[38] Art 18 Regulation 1303/2013 (n 4). For the list of the 11 thematic objectives see Art 9: (1) strengthening research, technological development and innovation; (2) enhancing access to, and use and quality of, ICT; (3) enhancing the competitiveness of SMEs, of the agricultural sector (for the EAFRD) and of the fishery and aquaculture sector (for the EMFF); (4) supporting the shift towards a low-carbon economy in all sectors; (5) promoting climate change adaptation, risk prevention and management; (6) preserving and protecting the environment and promoting resource efficiency; (7) promoting sustainable transport and removing bottlenecks in key network infrastructures; (8) promoting sustainable and quality employment and supporting labour mobility; (9) promoting social inclusion, combating poverty and any discrimination; (10) investing in education, training and vocational training for skills and lifelong learning; (11) enhancing institutional capacity of public authorities and stakeholders and efficient public administration.

[39] Art 90 Regulation 1303/2013 (n 4).

to the thematic concentration, each of the funds pursues specific thematic objectives, allocated in different amounts accordingly.[40]

E Legal Rules Governing the Decision-making Process in the ESI Funds

The participation of various administrative actors, and unclear boundaries between the tasks of the participants in this multi-step procedure, make the decision-making process—and the subsequent allocation of responsibility in case of irregularities—a difficult undertaking. If one adds to this the complexities arising from the various conditionalities, as well as the burdensome and lengthy administrative proceedings, it comes as no surprise that the administration of EU funds policy is governed in effect by the use of broad discretionary powers on all levels in both implementation and monitoring.

On the implementation level, as has already been discussed, it is the Member States which are the recipients of the Union funds assistance to be subsequently managed and administered through the (national) managing authorities. In most cases of the ESI Funds, it is the managing authorities that enjoy some *discretion* in the implementation process, in particular as regards the selection of the specific beneficiaries, the amounts to be invested, and the purposes for which they will be used.[41] This discretion is, however, reduced not only by the omnipresent demands of compliance with Union law, and the ex ante and ex post conditionalities, but also through the extensive role of the Commission in ex ante appraisal of major projects.[42] In the same vein, one should not overlook the fact that the broad design framework, as this is expressed through the partnership agreements and the operational programmes implementing the ESI Funds, is prepared by the Member States in cooperation with their partners, but both types of instrument has to have *Commission approval*. Similarly, in the example of EU regional aid, it is the Commission which is responsible for laying down the criteria for identifying the regions eligible according to the categories noted above (less developed regions, transition regions, most developed regions), and for setting the priorities the funding is to target, thus limiting the margin of discretion left to each managing authority.

Further, a broad discretion is enjoyed by the Commission on the monitoring and enforcement level. As already stated, the Commission monitors whether the conditionality requirements are fulfilled and, if it observes any deficiencies with regard to the fulfilment of the ex ante conditionalities or the management or any other irregularities, it '*may decide* by means of implementing acts, to suspend all or part of interim

---

[40] The largest allocation is foreseen for transport and energy infrastructure accounting for just under a quarter of allocations form all Funds (€59.1 billion or 18.2% of the total). For the breakdown of financial allocations according to Member State, Fund, and objective see https://cohesiondata.ec.europa.eu/ (last accessed 17 November 2015).

[41] See eg Annex I to the Common Strategic Framework point 3.2: 'Member States and managing authorities responsible for the implementation of the ESI Funds shall work closely together in the preparation, implementation, monitoring and evaluation of the Partnership Agreement and programmes …'.

[42] See Arts 100–102 and recitals (92)–(94) Regulation 1303/2013 (n 4).

payments, after having given the Member State the opportunity to present its obser-vations'.[43] This broad discretion has the potential to lead not only to legal uncertainty and to fragmentary Commission enforcement, but also to a discriminatory treatment among the Member States.

F Administrative Acts in Funds Administration

1 Delegated acts

The Commission has broad powers to adopt delegated and implementing acts. The specific conditions for the adoption of delegated acts are laid out in Article 149 of the Common Provisions Regulation. The material scope of the delegated acts is, as ex-pected, limited, concerning in principle just matters that pertain mostly to supple-menting the overarching Regulation in regard to technicalities such as the calculation of costs and the determination of financial corrections. The Commission may, thus, adopt delegated acts that lay down rules concerning, inter alia: the management and control of financial instruments; the criteria for determining the level of financial cor-rection to be applied; the role, liabilities, and responsibility of the bodies implementing financial instruments; the criteria for determining the cases of irregularity to be re-ported; the methodology to be used in carrying out the quality review of a major pro-ject; the criteria for determining serious deficiencies in the effective functioning of management and control systems, including the main types of such deficiencies; the criteria for establishing the level of financial correction to be applied; and the criteria for applying flat rates or extrapolated financial corrections.[44]

So far, the Commission has, under the new legal framework, adopted seven delegated acts, most prominently the Delegated Regulation 240/2014 on the European code of conduct on partnership in the framework of the EU funds, the Delegated Regulation 480/2014 supplementing the overarching Regulation (in particular concerning the im-plementation and management of financial instruments and financial corrections),[45] and the Delegated Regulation 2015/1970 supplementing the overarching Regulation in laying down specific provisions on the reporting of irregularities.[46] The European Code of Conduct on Partnership itself sets out minimum requirements to ensure that the partnership principle is respected in the area of the EU funds. It does so by pro-viding specific criteria and guidelines with regard to the identification, participation, and involvement of the partners in almost all steps of the process (programming, im-plementation, monitoring, and evaluation).

---

[43] ibid Art 142(2). See also Art 19(5) with regard to the monitoring of the ex ante conditionalities: 'The Commission *may decide*, when adopting a programme, to suspend all or part of interim payments to the relevant priority of that programme pending the completion of actions referred to in paragraph 2 where necessary to avoid significant prejudice to the effectiveness and efficiency of the achievement of the spe-cific objectives of the priority concerned' *(emphasis added)*.

[44] For the list of applicable cases see ibid Art 149.

[45] Delegated Regulation 480/2014 was amended by Delegated Regulation 2015/616.

[46] For a list of the delegated acts adopted by the Commission prior to 17 November 2015 see http:// ec.europa.eu/regional_policy/en/information/legislation/delegated-acts/.

2 Implementing acts

As opposed to the delegated acts, the implementing powers of the Commission are only sparsely provided for in the overarching Regulation. In general, the Commission should adopt by means of implementing acts:[47]

- all decisions relating to the approval of partnership agreements, operational programmes, and annual plans
- decisions identifying the regions and Member States fulfilling the investment for growth and jobs criteria (ERDF)
- as regards the ERDF, the ESF, and the Cohesion Fund, decisions setting out the annual breakdown of commitment appropriations to the Member State
- decisions setting out the amount to be transferred from each Member State's Cohesion Fund allocation to the CEF
- decisions setting out the amount to be transferred from each Member State's Structural Funds allocation as aid for the most deprived
- decisions accepting transfers of parts of appropriations for the European territorial cooperation goal towards investment in growth and jobs and
- decisions whether or not to carry out a financial correction in the case of non-compliance.[48]

In order to set out an appropriate financial framework for the funds, the Commission is to establish, by means of implementing acts, the annual breakdown of available commitment appropriations, using an objective and transparent method with a view to targeting the regions whose development is lagging, including those receiving transitional support.

3 Individual acts

As the EU funding is effectively channelled to individual projects, it is evident that the administrative decisions taken in the context of the Union's funds will affect individuals, most commonly the applicants for funding and the associated beneficiaries. Upon the approval of the partnership agreements, in most cases it will be the managing authorities that will select the beneficiary and grant them financial assistance. In this case, the funds will be disbursed under a 'grant agreement' or 'subsidy contract' between the managing authorities and the selected 'lead partner'. The subsidy contract will be legally based on the overarching Regulation 1303/2013 and, in many cases, the

---

[47] See eg the Commission Implementing Regulation 2015/207 laying down detailed and technical rules implementing the Common Provisions Regulation with regard to the models for the progress report, the submission of the information on a major project, the joint action plan, the implementation reports for the Investment for growth and jobs goal and other issues requiring technical clarification. The legal basis of the adopted implementing act differs according to the subject matter. Depending on the issues the implementing act addresses, it can be legally based on many different provisions of the Common Provisions Regulation, such as; Art 41(4), Art 52(4), Art 101(2), Art 102(1), and many more.

[48] The legal basis of the adopted implementing act differs according to the subject matter, depending on the issues involved.

relevant fund-specific Regulation. It will include, inter alia, provisions specifying the amount to be disbursed, the reporting requirements, and its duration. It is the managing authorities which must verify that all relevant pre-conditions are met, and that the projects have been performed without any financial irregularities. For cases where irregularities are detected in project implementation, special provision is made in the relevant agreement between the lead partner and the managing authority.[49] Then, the managing authorities must claim the repayment of the amount concerned by way of an individual act. Examples from national law provide that

> [t]he administrative contract is the main form for grant provision; financial corrections, on the other hand, are determined, in terms of grounds and amounts, by means of an individual administrative act. As opposed to the individual administrative act, the administrative contract is not defined as a legal concept within the codification of the administrative process, except as a variant to the agreement under Article 20 of [Administrative Procedure Code].[50]

G Administrative Enforcement in Funds Administration

Once again, in regard to administrative enforcement, the powers are shared between the Commission and the Member States. It is primarily for the Member States to ensure that irregularities are prevented, detected, and corrected, by establishing a national, regional, or local public authority or body, as a managing, certifying authority, together with audit authorities,[51] and under certain circumstances by notifying the Commission of such irregularities.[52] The definition of 'irregularity' has been clarified under Regulation 1303/2013,[53] enabling the Member States to have a better understanding of when notification to the Commission is actually necessary.[54] Under the previous Regulation, the Member States were responsible for verifying that 'management and control arrangements have been set up and are being implemented in such a way as to ensure that European Union funds are being used efficiently and correctly'.[55]

The principal route for protecting the Union budget from incurring erroneous or irregular expenditure is by ensuring, already at the time of selection and implementation, that the EU legal framework has been respected. This can be achieved primarily via the introduction, under the new legal framework, of the ex ante conditionalities. Under Article 19 Regulation 1303/2013, it is the Member States which are to assess whether the general, fund-specific, and thematic ex ante conditionalities are fulfilled

---

[49] See eg the Subsidy Contract in the framework of the Danube Transnational Programme Art 12(1): 'In case of irregularities identified during the project implementation the [Managing Authority] is entitled to claim the repayment of contribution from the EU Funds in full or in part from the [Lead Partner] based on the irregularity report sent to the [Managing authority]'.

[50] S Mihaylova-Goleminova, 'Challenges and Opportunities Facing the Legal and Institutional Framework for the Management of ESI Funds in Bulgaria' (2015) 4 *European Structural and Investment Funds Journal* 239, 242.

[51] Art 122 Regulation 1303/2013 (n 4).   [52] ibid Art 122(2).   [53] ibid Art 2(36) and (38).

[54] The obligation to report to the Commission any 'irregularities' in the context of Regulation No 1260/1999 was one of the issues raised in Case C-410/13 'Baltlanta' UAB v Lietuvos valstybė ECLI:EU:C:2014:2134.

[55] Case C-410/13 'Baltlanta' (n 54).

in their programmes.[56] The summary of this assessment is included in the partnership agreement and, in case of non-fulfilment, the Member States should specify what actions are to be taken for the implementation of such conditionalities. If the relevant criteria for their fulfilment are not met by the programme submission, the Member States had to provide an action plan to ensure implementation by the end of 2016. The Commission was given the final word with regard to the appropriateness and adequacy of the framework for their satisfaction, having the power to suspend interim payments where this was not demonstrated.[57]

The problem with the fulfilment of the ex ante conditionalities relates to the need for increased administrative capacities in those Member States requiring assistance through the EU funds. Such capacity pertains not only to the requirement of the preparation of action plans where relevant criteria are not fulfilled within the given deadlines, but also to establishing a pre-existing network of mechanisms and measures to guarantee an appropriate regulatory framework and adequate institutional capacity in each Member State so as to ensure that the funding assistance would be used in the most efficient and effective way.[58]

Where this pre-emptive mechanism fails, then the Member States and/or the Commission can impose financial corrections, in other words, they may recover payments that should not have been made. For expenditure subject to shared management, this task is primarily reserved to the Member States, which can claim the money back either from its expenditure declarations or directly from the beneficiaries.[59] Consequently, it is the Member States that are responsible, on the first level, to investigate any irregularities, and for recovering, where needed, the amounts improperly paid.[60] Financial corrections should consist of cancelling all or part of the public contribution to an operation or operational programme, in accordance with the proportionality principle.[61] In such a case, however, the aforementioned cancelled contribution may be reused by the Member State within the operational programme concerned, under certain conditions.[62]

In some cases, the Commission can proceed itself to the suspension of payments, usually for reasons relating to deficiencies in the management, control, or the monitoring system of the operational programme, or serious irregularities and/or failure to meet priorities and ex ante conditionalities.[63] Accordingly, the Commission may proceed, by means of implementing acts, to cancel all or part of the Union contribution to an operational programme, and by effecting recovery from the Member State, in order to exclude from Union financing any expenditure which is in breach of applicable law.[64] In such a case, the revocation of the payment is primarily reserved to the Member States, which can claim the money back in the ways mentioned above.

---

[56] See also Annex XI Regulation 1303/2013 (n 4).   [57] ibid Art 19(5)–(8).
[58] See eg ibid Annex XI concerning the thematic objective of promoting climate change adaptation, risk prevention. and management, which requires, inter alia, the fulfilment of the following ex ante conditionalities: the existence of national or regional risk assessments for disaster management, taking into account climate change adaptation and the existence and development of waste management plans consistent with Directive 2008/98/EC, and with the waste hierarchy.
[59] For more details see section F in this chapter.
[60] Most commonly through the managing authorities, which are assisted by the monitoring committees.
[61] Art 143(2) Regulation 1303/2013 (n 4).   [62] ibid Art 143(3) and (4).   [63] ibid Art 142(1).
[64] ibid Arts 85, 144, 145.

When amounts unduly paid to a beneficiary cannot be recovered, and this is as a result of fault or negligence on the part of a Member State, the latter shall be responsible for reimbursing such amounts to the Union.[65] The Commission exercises a quasi-monitoring or auditing role, by having the opportunity to review the audit trail of any auditing authority, or take part in on-the-spot audits of such authority, or to carry out a re- performance of the audit activity in accordance with internationally accepted audit standards.[66] The detailed rules with regard to the Commission's powers and responsibilities in verifying the effective functioning of the Member States' management and control systems are adopted by the Commission by way of delegated acts.[67]

H Supervision, Monitoring, and Control in Funds Management

1 Administrative supervision within the funds sector

The supervisory role in the administration of the ESI Funds is, in principle, assigned to the Member States. Hence, oversight of the correct implementation of the programmes is entrusted to the monitoring committees, set up by the Member States in accordance with their institutional, legal, and financial framework.[68] The monitoring committees play a consultative role for the managing authorities. In addition, in order to ensure better monitoring of the implementation of the programmes, Member States are obliged to submit to the Commission progress reports on the implementation of the partnership agreements[69] and annual reports on the implementation of the programmes for each preceding financial year.[70] Further, annual review meetings between the Commission and each Member State examine the performance of each programme.[71]

While the biggest part of supervision and monitoring is done at Member State level, the Commission also maintains a supervisory role.[72] In this, it is assisted by the Coordination Committee, which oversees the implementation of the regulations governing the ESI Funds in accordance with the comitology procedure.[73] The Commission is, furthermore, obliged to keep the Council and the European Parliament informed, and to submit progress reports to them.[74] Those institutions, though, have a rather limited oversight role and can, effectively, object only to certain delegated acts adopted by the Commission as provided in Article 149(5) of Regulation 1303/2013, or revoke the delegation of power in certain cases.[75]

---

[65] ibid Art 122(2).   [66] ibid recital (122).
[67] ibid Arts 144(6) and 149. For the suspension of payments by the Commission see section F(iv) below.
[68] Arts 47–49Regulation 1303/2013 (n 4).   [69] ibid Art 52.   [70] ibid Art 50.
[71] ibid Art 51.
[72] For more details on the supervisory and monitoring role of the Commission see section G below.
[73] Art 150 Regulation 1303/2013 (n 4).
[74] On the several different reports the Commission needs to submit to the Council and the European Parliament, see eg Arts 5(6), 16(3), 23(15), and 53 of Regulation 1303/2013 (n 4).
[75] See eg Art 14(3) the European Regional Development Fund Regulation (Regulation 1301/2013) and Art 7(3) of the Cohesion Fund Regulation (Regulation 1300/2013).

2 European Court of Auditors and OLAF

The European Court of Auditors (ECA) is entrusted with overseeing the management of the EU budget. Thus, by necessary implication, it has the function of ensuring that the financial management of the EU funds has been sound. To that end it conducts audits both on Member State and Union level, reviewing the legality and regularity of the transactions underlying the consolidated accounts of the Union (Article 287 TFEU).

During the 2013 annual audit the ECA found, with regard to the regularity of the transactions underlying the EU accounts, that while both revenue and financial commitments for 2013 were regular, the estimated error rate for payments was 4.7 per cent, remaining persistently higher than the 'materiality threshold' of 2 per cent.[76] Errors arise when payments from the EU budget 'are neither legal nor regular, for example when claimed by ineligible beneficiaries, for expenditure that should not be financed by the EU, or when the conditions for receiving the aid are not followed'.[77] Thus, for a payment to be classified as 'error' it has to be contrary to the law and have a potentially harmful impact on the European Union's financial interests.[78] Typical sources of error, besides failed compliance with eligibility criteria, include serious breaches of public procurement rules. Such breaches may be deliberate, especially in order to favour certain applicants over others. However, they may also be inadvertent, for example, because of the complexity of the rules,[79] because of inadequate checks and controls by both the Commission and the Member States, because of a focus by the Member States merely on absorbing the Union assistance funds rather than on their wise application, or because of incorrect declarations of agricultural areas.[80]

Suspected fraud cases, that is, deliberate 'irregularities', are referred to the European Anti-fraud Office (OLAF).[81] It can issue administrative, financial, disciplinary, or judicial recommendations addressed to EU or national authorities. With regard to financial recommendations relating to EU funds management, following significant investigations OLAF recommended financial recovery of €476.5 million for 2014, almost triple those recommended for the second most problematic area, external aid

---

[76] Vitor Caldeira, 'Presentation of the Annual Reports 2013' Speech given to the Committee on Budgetary Control of the European Parliament Brussels, 5 November 2014.

[77] ECA, 'Making the best use of EU money: a landscape review of the risks to the financial management of the EU budget' (2014) 22.

[78] See Art 2(36) Regulation 1303/2013 (n 4): 'irregularity' means any breach of Union law, or of national law relating to its application, resulting from an act or omission by an economic operator involved in the implementation of the ESI Funds, which has, or would have, the effect of prejudicing the budget of the Union by charging an unjustified item of expenditure to the budget of the Union'. If an irregularity is committed deliberately it is classed as fraud.

[79] See ECA, 'Efforts to address problems with public procurement in EU cohesion expenditure should be intensified' Special Report (2015).

[80] It is noteworthy that errors detected and corrected before and independently of the checks carried out by the Court are excluded from the calculation and frequency of error, since they demonstrate that the control systems work effectively see Court of Auditors, *Annual Report concerning the financial year 2013* (4 September 2014) Annex 1.1 Pt (9).

[81] Fraud cases are defined by OLAF as the 'Use or presentation of incorrect or incomplete statements or documents leading to wrongful payment of funds from the EU budget or budgets managed by, or on behalf of, the EU nondisclosure of required information with the same effect misuse of funds for purposes other than those for which they were originally granted'.

(€174.0 million).[82] However, for the recovery of such amounts the competent authorities need to act. Articles 85 and 122 of Regulation 1303/2013 allow either the Commission 'to make financial corrections by cancelling all or part of the Union contribution to a programme and effecting recovery from the Member State, in order to exclude from Union financing expenditure which is in breach of applicable law'.[83] Alternatively, the Member States, in accordance with the principle of shared management in the implementation and control of the programmes, 'shall prevent, detect and correct irregularities and shall recover amounts unduly paid, together with any interest on late payments'.[84]

It is remarkable, however, that, of the €476.5 million that OLAF recommended for recovery in the area of EU funds for 2014, only €22.7 million was actually retrieved.[85] Besides the obvious difficulty that OLAF is not a prosecuting authority and cannot, thus, take disciplinary or legal action based on its investigations and recommendations, the limited recovery of the unduly paid EU funds can be attributed to other factors too. A first factor is the information that reaches OLAF. In 2014, as reported by OLAF, most incoming information related to the structural funds sector. However, while Member States have a duty to inform OLAF of possible cases of fraud, corruption, or other illegal activity affecting the financial interests of the Union, often such information never reaches the EU fraud office, because of the associated negative effect on national reputation and the suspicion of corruption, or because of the expectation that such action is futile.[86] A second factor pertains to the necessary involvement of the authority making the relevant disbursement, usually the managing authority. It is this authority which needs to demand the repayment from the beneficiary, and usually the competent minister who must authorize, and sign for, the recovery. Even where the national authorities' reluctance is overcome, and all responsible authorities act swiftly, it is likely, for two reasons, that the procedure will be frustrated: first, the beneficiary might appeal against the recovery procedure in national courts, inducing long judicial processes and delay; secondly, recovery may well lead to the beneficiary's bankruptcy.[87]

3 Judicial protection

Most cases on economic, social, and territorial cohesion that reach the Union courts are brought by the Member States under Article 263 TFEU, challenging a Commission decisions to reduce financial assistance for certain projects.[88] Initiating, provisional,

---

[82] OLAF Report, 'Fifteenth report of the European Anti-Fraud Office, 1 January to 31 December 2014' (2014) 21.

[83] Art 85 Regulation 1303/2013 (n 4).   [84] ibid Art 122.

[85] OLAF Report (n 82) 22, fig 25.

[86] According to a report of the Bureau of Investigative Journalism (7 July 2012) 'only 5% (54) of 1046 leaks relating to corruption in 2011 came from Member State authorities. More than half came from companies, lawyers, and anonymous individuals'. See https://www.thebureauinvestigates.com/2012/07/07/eu-member-states-fail-to-report-corruption-but-bureau-investigation-hits-home/ (last accessed 4 November 2015).

[87] For more details see section II.

[88] The Commission's decisions for reduction of financial assistance relate, usually, to the finding of irregularities in the application of European Union *rules on public procurement*. See eg Case C-192/

or preparatory actions and measures are, *in principle*, not subject to judicial review (on either national or EU level),[89] unless they affect the applicant independently of the final decision.[90] In the realm of the EU funds the most questionable decisions relate either to decision of the (national) competent administrative authority (usually the managing authority) not to grant funding to a candidate, or to the Commission's decision demanding repayment, or reducing the financial assistance provided to the Member States, because of the irregularities found in implementation.

The most difficult tasks for the judges are the identification of the actual decision-maker and the pursuant allocation of responsibility in the multi-step implementation process.[91] In this context, the sequence of the decision-making processes, and the degree of each administrative actor's discretion and participation in it, will define not only which court is competent to rule in the case, but also the reviewability of the act and the standing of the applicant.

In *Liivimaa Lihaveis*, the Court of Justice recently had to rule on the composite procedures in the EU funds and the need for effective judicial protection,[92] in a matter concerning an operational programme between Estonia and Latvia, governed by Regulations 1083/2006 and 1080/2006. The programme had been approved by the Commission and had received EU aid from the ERDF. As under the current overarching Regulation, the tasks of each of the committees involved in the management of the EU aid were enumerated in the pertinent regulation. Similar to the current legal framework, the managing authority was responsible, inter alia, for administering and implementing the operational programme in accordance with the principle of sound financial management (Article 60 of Regulation 1083/2006), whereas the monitoring committee had to ensure the effectiveness and quality of the operational programme-implementation by considering and approving the criteria for selecting the operations financed, reviewing their implementation and progress (Article 65), and by selecting the operations to be funded in accordance with the criteria set (Article 19(3) of Regulation 1080/2006). Despite the monitoring committee's pivotal role in the operations' selection, the final step in the award of ERDF funding consisted of the conclusion of a subsidy contract between the managing authority and the lead partner of the approved project.

While the Estonian Ministry of Interior performed the tasks of the managing, certifying, and audit authorities, the monitoring committee consisted of seven members

---

13 P *Spain v Commission* EU:C:2014:2156; Case C-115/12 P *French Republic v European Commission* ECLI:EU:C:2013:596.

[89] Case 60/81 *IBM v Commission* [1981] ECR 2639; Case C-521/04 P(R) *Tillack v Commission* [2005] ECR I-3103.

[90] Case 53/85 *AKZO Chemie and AKZO Chemie UK v Commission* [1986] ECR 1965.

[91] For a discussion of the many problems of judicial supervision in composite procedures see Herwig Hofmann and Alexander Türk, 'The Development of Integrated Administration in the EU and its Consequences' (2007) 13 *European Law Journal* 253, 268; Herwig Hofmann, 'Composite decision-making procedures in EU administrative law' in H C H Hofmann and A Türk (eds), *Legal Challenges in EU Administrative Law: Towards an Integrated Administration* (Edward Elgar Publishing 2009) 137, 152; Mariolina Eliantonio, 'Judicial Review in an Integrated Administration: The Case of "Composite" Procedures' (2014) 7 *Review of European Administrative Law* 65, 77.

[92] Case C-562/12 *Liivimaa Lihaveis* EU:C:2014:2229.

from both Member States, set up in accordance with the common agreement concluded between Latvia and Estonia. The monitoring committee had adopted a 'programme manual' in order to provide guidelines for applicants on the preparation of aid applications, and on implementing, monitoring, and reporting on the project. The manual provided, inter alia, for an *absolute ban on judicial review of a decision refusing funding for a project*, making decisions of the monitoring committee non-reviewable. Upon being rejected by the monitoring committee on qualitative criteria, the applicant initiated proceedings before the national administrative court, seeking the annulment of the monitoring committee's decision. The Estonian court dismissed the action on the ground that the decision was not an administrative act which could be challenged before an administrative court. In the court's view national provisions on administrative procedure were inapplicable to the monitoring committee, viewing the monitoring committee not as an administrative organ but as an international committee. The court held that, even if the monitoring committee's decision were to be considered as an administrative act, it was only an internal, as it had not terminated or altered any rights or obligations for persons outside the administration.

Upon appeal by the applicant to the higher-level national court, the latter asked the Court of Justice of the European Union (CJEU) for a preliminary ruling. In determining whether the review of the monitoring committee decision fell under the jurisdiction of the national court or the General Court of the CJEU, the Court of Justice began its reasoning by reviewing whether Article 263 TFEU applied. As a monitoring committee, set up for each operational programme by the Member State, is not endowed with legal personality by an EU measure, and is competent to draw up its own rules of procedure, it cannot be considered as an institution, body, office, or agency of the Union. Thus, the review of its funding decisions did not fall within the jurisdiction of the General Court. On the same reasoning, the Court pointed out that, as the contested decision does not constitute an act of a Union body, it cannot be reviewed under Article 267 TFEU. It would, indeed, be very difficult to impute the monitoring committee's decision to an EU institution, or to consider it, for instance, as the outcome of the Commission's decision-making.

The Court in *Liivimaa Lihaveis* also reviewed whether Article 47 of the Charter applied in the contested decision, considering first whether the programme manual implemented EU law within the sense of Article 51(1) CFR. The Court noted that an 'implementation of Union law' was to be found in the *EU legal requirement to implement the operational programme*. That, in turn, required the two Member States to establish the monitoring committee (Article 63(1) and (2) of Regulation 1083/2006) and to implement the operational programme in compliance with both overarching and fund-specific regulations. Having established that the Article 51(1) CFR proviso was satisfied, the Court examined whether the right to an effective remedy, as provided in Article 47 CFR, had been respected. In view of the fact that the monitoring committee's decision to reject a project for funding could, under the terms of the manual, not be appealed or contested, the Court ruled that the applicant remained without any effective remedy against the rejection decision, contrary to Article 47 CFR. Jaaskinen AG went one step further, seeking to establish whether the monitoring committee decision was 'a reviewable act in its own right' or only 'an internal procedural step before the final decision is taken by the managing authority'.[93] In view of the fact that, for the earmarking of ERDF funding, a subsidy contract had to be signed between the managing authority (and not the monitoring committee) and the successful candidate, the monitoring committee decision could be considered only *an internal procedural step*, not subject to review.[94] Whether the monitoring committee decision was, therefore, an intermediate act and hence, in principle, not subject to judicial review, would depend then on whether the managing authority was bound by the decision of the monitoring committee.[95] Alternatively, even if the monitoring committee act was seen as a decision adopted in the course of a preparatory procedure (the final decision being made by the managing authority), as long as it marked 'the culmination of a distinct stage in the main procedure and produce legal effects', it would attract judicial review.[96] In the appreciation, thus, of whether the decision of the monitoring committee is a reviewable act, the national court must consider, in accordance with the principle of effectiveness, whether there are alternative remedies providing legal protection in order to ensure effective judicial protection.

Liivimaa Lihaveis is reminiscent of *Borelli*, although there the composite procedure concerned a preparatory act on national level, concluding, however, with a decision of the Commission.[97] Having, in *Liivimaa Lihaveis*, excluded the application of Article 263 TFEU on grounds of a lack of jurisdiction of EU courts to rule on the lawfulness of a measure adopted by a national authority, the question of the legal standing of the applicant before Union courts did not then arise. Yet, once an (EU) act is found to be reviewable, the requirements of Article 263(4) TFEU could pose problems for individuals who do wish to go before the EU courts. The interpretation of the criterion of 'direct concern' by the Court of Justice requires a contested EU measure to affect the legal situation of the plaintiff directly, and to leaving no discretion to the originating authority in implementing it, the adoption of the implementing measure being automatic, resulting from EU legal rules without the intervening application of any other rules.[98] According to settled case law, the condition required by the second criterion can also be satisfied even where it may be theoretically possible for the authority not to give effect to the Union measure but their intention to act in conformity with it is not in doubt.[99]

The 'direct concern' requirement as understood by the Court begs the question as to whether a beneficiary, asked to repay the funds 'irregularly' used, or to experience

---

[93] Opinion of AG Jaaskinen in Case C-562/12 *Liivimaa Lihaveis* ECLI:EU:C:2014:155, para 58.

[94] ibid.

[95] Rule 5, point 8 of the Rules of Procedure of the Monitoring Committee stated that in: 'case the Managing Authority has profound objections concerning the compliance of a decision taken by the Monitoring Committee with the legal basis of the Programme, the decision shall not be taken until the Managing Authority by communicating with the relevant authorities and organisations will have clarified the matter ... A new decision by the Monitoring Committee must take the report into consideration'.

[96] ibid para 60 and references listed therein.

[97] Case C-97/91 *Oleificio Borelli v Commission* [1992] ECR I-6313.

[98] See Case C-404/96 P *Glencore Grain v Commission* [1998] ECR I-2435, para 41; Case C-386/96 P *Dreyfus v Commission* [1998] ECR I-2309, para 43; Case C-486/01 P *Front national v Parliament* [2004] ECR I-6289, para 34; Case C-125/06 P *Commission v Infront WM* [2008] ECR I-1451, para 47.

[99] Case 11/82 *Piraiki-Patraiki and Others v Commission* [1985] ECR 207, paras 8–10; Case C-386/96 P *Dreyfus v Commission* (n 98) para 44.

a reduction in those funds, meets the standing requirement of Article 263(4) TFEU. The main complexity in such a case lies in the essentially four-sided relationship: that among the original 'funders' (the EU, specifically the Commission), the (intermediate) addressees of the funding (the Member States), the granters of the (destination) funding (the authorities of the beneficiary's Member State), and the final recipient (the beneficiary). In this relationship it is the national authorities of the (potential) beneficiaries, mostly the managing authorities, that select the contractual partner to carry out a particular project. In earlier funds' cases, both the Court of Justice and the General Court have held that

> a Commission decision reducing or cancelling financial assistance granted by the ESF is capable of directly and individually concerning the beneficiaries of such assistance and of adversely affecting them, even though the Member State concerned is the sole interlocutor of the ESF in the relevant administrative procedure. It is the beneficiaries of the aid who are adversely affected by the economic consequences of the decision to reduce or cancel the assistance since they have primary liability for repayment of the sums paid without warrant.[100]

This line of case law, developed by the courts as a guarantee of the right of the beneficiaries to be heard, has been considered as the Courts' effort to 'go beyond the formality of the decisional procedure and to decide on the basis of the effective links that the acts of the EU institutions create with the persons affected by them'.[101] In the early *Lisrestal* cases the Courts went beyond the strict formality of procedures established in the area of the EU funds.[102] Thus, although according to the regulation then in force for that programming period (Regulation 2950/83) the sole interlocutor of the ESF was the recipient Member State (also responsible for the accuracy of the facts and accounts in claims for final payment and even guarantor of the proper implementation of the measures at issue), the Commission's decision to reduce the EU funding aid was found to concern the applicants directly and to affect them adversely.[103]

In later cases the courts seem to vacillate with regard to the applicants' legal position upon receipt of EU funds. The *Regione Siciliana* sagas are indicative of the courts' uncertainty in this area.[104] Both cases concerned EU funding from the ERDF to the

---

[100] Case T-102/00 *Vlaams Fonds voor de Sociale Integratie van Personen met een Handicap v Commission (Vlaams Fonds)* [2003] ECR II-2433, paras 60–61. See also Case T-450/93 *Lisrestal and Others v Commission* [1994] ECR II-1177, paras 43–48 and, upon appeal, Case C-32/95 P *Commission v Lisrestal and Others* [1996] ECR I-5373.

[101] Joana Mendes, *Participation in EU Rule-Making: A Rights Based Approach* (Oxford University Press 2011) 182. See also Joana Mendes, 'Participation and Participation Rights in EU Law and Governance' in H C H Hofmann and A Türk (eds), *Legal Challenges in EU Administrative Law—Towards an Integrated Administration* (Edward Elgar Publishing 2009) 257, 267.

[102] Case T-450/93 *Lisrestal and Others v Commission* (n 100) paras 43–48 and, upon appeal, Case C-32/95 P *Commission v Lisrestal and Others* (n 100).

[103] Case T-450/93 *Lisrestal and Others v Commission* (n 100) paras 42–48 and, upon appeal, Case C-32/95 P *Commission v Lisrestal and Others* (n 100) paras 26–34.

[104] Case T-341/02 *Regione Siciliana v Commission* [2004] ECR II-2877 and appeal dismissed before the CJEU; Case C-417/04 P *Regione Siciliana v Commission* [2006] ECR I-3881; and Case T-60/03 *Regione Siciliana v Commission* [2005] ECR II-4139, set aside before the CJEU; Case C-15/06 P *Regione Siciliana v Commission* [2007] ECR I-2591.

region of Sicily, for the construction of, in the first case, a motorway[105] and, in the second, a dam.[106] In both cases the Commission, having found irregularities in the use of funds, by decisions addressed to the Italian Republic, withdrew part of the financial assistance and ordered repayment of amounts considered to be paid unduly. The (ultimate beneficiary) applicants' legal standing was contested by the Commission on grounds that they lacked direct concern.[107] The Commission relied on the distinct relationships between the EU represented by the Commission, the Member States and the final beneficiaries. Relying on earlier case law,[108] it suggested, further, that the recovery of sums unduly paid was in fact left to the discretion of Italy.[109] The General Court agreed that the applicant was not directly concerned by the contested decision, and hence could not have brought an action for annulment (later upheld by the European Court of Justice (ECJ)). To support this, the General Court relied, first, on the fact that the withdrawal and the recovery of the sums unduly paid did not necessarily jeopardize the applicant's project, as Italy could have covered the needed funds from its own budget. Further, the court noted that, in contrast with the general practice in the area of unlawful aids, the contested decision did not require the Italian Republic to recover the sums unduly paid from the beneficiaries, Instead, recovery on the part of the Union needed to take place only vis-à-vis the Member State which had been granted the financial assistance. Thus, the demand for reimbursement of EU funds paid to the applicant would not result from the contested decision as such, but rather from steps taken that purpose by the competent national authority under its own legislation. In addition, according to the Court, Italy had its own decision-making powers with regard to the demand for reimbursement; in accordance with the Regulation in force at the time (Regulation No 4253/88) the Member States were responsible for exercising financial control and for recovering any amounts lost as a result of irregularity or negligence. It followed that Italy's discretion relied on the fact that it could decide not to claim reimbursement and to bear itself the burden of reimbursing to the ERDF the amounts it wrongly considered itself authorized to pay.[110]

In contrast to *Regione Siciliana I*, in the judgment in *Regione Siciliana II* the General Court found that the applicant was directly concerned by the Commission's decision and, hence, could bring an action for annulment.[111] To reach that conclusion the Court applied a more functional approach, which looked more to the substance, rather than to the formalities, of the decision's effects on the applicant concerned.[112]

---

[105] Case T-341/02 *Regione Siciliana v Commission* (n 104) and CJEU; Case C-417/04 P *Regione Siciliana v Commission* (n 104) (*Regione Siciliana I*).

[106] Case T-60/03 *Regione Siciliana v Commission* (n 104) and Case C-15/06 P *Regione Siciliana v Commission* (n 104) (*Regione Siciliana II*).

[107] The existence of individual concern in these cases is very rarely disputed by the Commission in these cases.

[108] Case T-244/00 *Coillte Teoranta v Commission* [2001] ECR II-1275, para 59–61.

[109] *Regione Siciliana I* (n 105) paras 36–41.

[110] Case T-341/02 *Regione Siciliana I* (n 104) paras 64–80.

[111] Case T-60/03 *Regione Siciliana v Commission* (n 104).

[112] Following its settled case law (Case 60/81 *IBM v Commission* (n 89) para 9; Case T-3/93 *Air France v Commission* [1994] ECR II-121, para 43; and Case T-87/96 *Assicurazioni Generali and Unicredito v Commission* [1999] ECR II-203, para 37), the Court reiterated that 'in order to ascertain whether the act of a Community institution is of direct concern to a person within the meaning of Art 230 EC *it is necessary to look to its substance in order to establish whether, regardless of its form, it has an immediate effect*

It first established the material change in the applicant's situation: it took the view that, while the applicant had believed that the amount disbursed had been entirely at its disposal—and had planned accordingly—the Commission's decision had led to the applicant's being deprived of the 'promised' amount, seeking alternative funding, and being obliged to repay the sums paid by way of advances to the national authorities, changing thus, the applicant's legal situation vis-à-vis the national authorities.[113] Contrary to what was accepted in *Regione Siciliana I* (i.e., that the national authorities could reimburse the requested amount from their own funds) the General Court in Regione Siciliana II maintained that

> the Italian authorities were bound by the ERDF rules and the conditions in the granting decisions. Hence, they were left no discretion, in demanding repayment as long as these rules were respected, and as a result the applicant was directly concerned.[114]

The General Court's judgment was set aside by the Court of Justice in a cross-appeal. The Court applied *mutatis mutandis* the same reasoning it had applied in *Regione Siciliana I*. It held that, as the authority responsible for project implementation, enjoying extensive competences in the dam construction (by comparison to its competences concerning the motorway network in *Regione Siciliana I*), the applicant (the regional government) had not itself been entitled to assistance. Although the applicant had been formally listed in the grant decision as the 'authority responsible for the application', this had not put it into a direct relationship with the (then) Community assistance, as the applicant and the addressee of the assistance was in fact the Italian Republic.[115] The Region of Sicily had argued that holding its action to be inadmissible would entail a denial of justice because, as an infra-state entity, it could not bring an action before the national courts against the Italian Republic.[116] The ECJ rejected this argument, holding that natural or legal persons who are unable directly, by reason of the conditions for admissibility laid down in the Article 263(4) TFEU, to challenge Community measures of the kind in that case, must be guaranteed an effective right of action before national courts, pursuant to the principle of sincere cooperation.[117]

The Court's recent restrictive interpretation with regard to the 'direct concern' issue raises serious questions, not only about an applicant's right to effective judicial protection, but also about the criteria the Court employs to recognize such a concern. In the face of the lack of a clear legislative rule, Lenaerts and others have suggested that the distinctive criterion is to be found in the 'circumstances in which the Commission

---

on that person's interests, so bringing about a distinct change in that person's legal situation' (emphasis added); Case T-60/03 *Regione Siciliana v Commission* (n 104) para 65.

[113] *Regione Siciliana II*, paras 48–55.   [114] *Regione Siciliana II* (n 104) paras 56–68.

[115] A similar pattern could also be discerned in the *Ente* case; Case T-189/02 *Ente per le Ville vesuviane v Commission*, not published in the ECR, information at [2007] ECR II-89 and, upon appeal, Joined Cases C-445/07 P and C-455/07 P *Commission v Ente per le Ville vesuviane* [2009] ECR I-7993. In this case, the CJEU argued, upon appeal, that even if Ente was designated by name as beneficiary of the EU financial assistance, this did not render Ente the beneficiary of the financial assistance. Instead, Italy was found to be the addressee of the financial assistance, which was also the addressee of the decision in question.

[116] Case C-15/06 P *Regione Siciliana II* (n 104) paras 28 and 39.   [117] ibid para 39.

decision was adopted'.[118] Underlying this theory, which draws upon earlier case law relating to the disbursement (and recapture) of EU funds to third countries,[119] is a factual appraisal of the applicant's ability to perform the transaction entered into with the beneficiary Member State, or to obtain payment for goods supplied on the agreed terms. If the applicant at issue is—despite the Commission's decision—able to meet such commitments, then it is to be regarded as not directly concerned.[120]

I Conclusion

In describing the complex legal framework that underpins the EU funds, this chapter has shown that the biggest advantage of the composite procedures that underlie EU funds administration seems to be also its biggest weakness. On the one hand, the implementation of the ESI Funds by national and sub-national authorities ensures that the funds are used by the Member States in the way most tailored to meet their needs. At the same time, however, these composite procedures have resulted in often defective judicial protection, high levels of financial irregularity, and a reluctance on behalf of the potential beneficiaries to apply for funds assistance. This, in conjunction with the many ex ante conditionalities and the high administrative costs these entail, have often led to a result opposite to that pursued by the ESI Funds in their underlying concept and purpose.

---

[118] Koen Lenaerts, Ignace Maselis, and Kathleen Gutman, *EU Procedural Law* (OUP 2014) 323 and case law listed therein.

[119] Case C-404/96 P *Glencore Grain v Commission* (n 98) paras 38–54; Case C-386/96 P *Dreyfus v Commission* (n 98) paras 40–56; Case C-391/96 P *Compagnie Continentale v Commission* [1998] ECR I-2377, paras 38–54; and Case C-403/96 P *Glencore Grain v Commission* [1998] ECR I-2405, paras 40–56.

[120] According to Lenaerts and others (n 118): 'This will be the case where the contract with the beneficiary State was concluded on account of the commitments which the Commission would enter into in its capacity as financing authority once it found that the contract was in conformity with the Union rules'.

PART VIII

INTERNAL ADMINISTRATION

21

European Union Civil Service Law

Kieran Bradley

A Introduction

The civil service law of the European Union governs the legal relationships between Union institutions and agencies,[1] on the one hand, and their staff and a number of categories of persons who may have rights under the EU Staff Regulations or equivalent instruments, on the other hand. These latter include in particular former staff in receipt of pensions or other benefits, family members of (former) staff who have a claim on the Union as a result of their links with the staff member, and candidates for competitions and contractual posts.[2] It is EU law in a relatively pure form, in that neither national law nor the Member State authorities (administrative or political) play any significant part in its application, except Member State governments in their role as Union legislators within the Council, and occasionally national courts called upon to apply EU staff law in national disputes, for example in tax or family law matters.[3] Despite its material content, European Union civil service law is also relatively impervious to the influence of EU social protection law adopted in favour of workers generally under Title X of Part Three TFEU (Social policy), subject to a small number of exceptions, such as minimum requirements in respect of health and safety standards, and social rights included in the European Union Charter of Fundamental Rights.[4]

B Administrative Tasks within the EU Civil Service Sector

While in content European Union civil service law is in effect employment and, increasingly, contract law, it takes the form of administrative law. Particularly since the 2004 accessions, the proportion of staff members of the institutions and agencies employed under contract, especially those with a fixed term contract, has increased steadily compared to the number of permanent officials. The 2014 reforms

---

[1] For convenience, the term 'institutions' will be used in this chapter to cover indistinctly institutions and other Union bodies, offices, and agencies (in line with Art 1(2)(a) of the Rules of Procedure of the Court of Justice); similarly, unless otherwise indicated, 'official' is used to include other staff members and persons who may have rights under the Staff Regulations and similar instruments.

[2] On the personal and material scope of EU staff law see Case C-417/14 RX-II *Missir Mamachi di Lusignano v Commission* EU:C:2015:588, paras 29–42.

[3] Respectively, Case C-263/91 *Kristoffersen* EU:C:1993:207 and Case C-430/97 *Johannes* EU:C:1999:293; the planned withdrawal of the United Kingdom from the European Union may also have a direct impact on Union staff but little or none on civil service law in general.

[4] Art 1e(2) Staff Regulations and Case C-597/12 RX-II *Commission v Strack* EU:C:2013:570, respectively.

will over time also lead to the replacement of posts as officials in some of the lower grades by those for contractual agents. The employment relationship between the staff, including contractual agents, and the Union's institutions is governed by public law and a series of standard EU regulations which are 'binding in [their] entirety and directly applicable in all Member States'. The staff of both the European Central Bank and the European Investment Bank is employed under contracts rather than under the EU Staff Regulations.

In their capacity as employers, the institutions take a vast number of decisions regulating the administrative position of each individual employee throughout his or her[5] career. Some of these decisions are taken once (e.g., appointment, non-renewal of contract, dismissal, retirement); some are taken at more or less regular intervals (e.g., granting of annual leave, promotion, transfer to a different post); while some are taken only in very particular circumstances, if at all (e.g., secondment in the interests of the service, attribution of unpaid leave, imposition of a disciplinary sanction). What these acts have in common is that they are all individual administrative decisions, subject to the general principles of EU administrative law. Where they adversely affect the legal position of the official concerned, they are open to challenge, firstly through an administrative complaints procedure,[6] and ultimately before the Court of Justice of the European Union.

C Sources of Civil Service Law

1 The Staff Regulations and conditions of employment of other servants

Article 336 TFEU provides a legal basis for the adoption of the basic instrument in this field. The Staff Regulations were originally adopted by the Council, then the sole legislature, as Regulation No 31 (EEC), 11 (EAEC), of 1962, which has been amended on over 140 occasions since.[7] Until the entry into force of the Lisbon Treaty, such measures were adopted by the Council in consultation with the European Parliament, whereas they are now subject to the ordinary legislative procedure. The most important recent reforms of the Staff Regulations were those of 2004, in preparation for the accession of ten new Member States, and those of 2014.[8]

The basic instrument is divided into two sections: the 'Staff Regulations' properly so called, which govern the relations between the institutions and permanent officials, and the Conditions of Employment of Other Servants (CEOS), which regulate those between the institutions and non-permanent staff. The CEOS apply many of the substantive provisions of the Staff Regulations by analogy to the non-permanent staff.

---

[5] Art 1c Staff Regulations provides that '[a]ny reference to a person of the male sex shall be deemed to constitute a reference to a person of the female sex ... unless the context clearly indicates otherwise'. This convention is applied for convenience in the present chapter.

[6] See section F2(i) below.

[7] [1962] OJ 45/1385 of 14 June 1962; see now http://eur-lex.europa.eu/legal-content/EN/TXT/?qid=15 37201689335&uri=CELEX:01962R0031-20180101.

[8] Respectively Council Regulation (EC, Euratom) No 723/2004, [2004] OJ L124/1, and Parliament and Council Regulation (EU, Euratom) No 1023/2013 [2013] OJ L287/15.

The Annexes to the Staff Regulations lay down provisions on a number of specific matters, such as entry competitions, entitlement to leave, the pension scheme, and the disciplinary procedure. Other regulations govern, for example, the conditions and procedure for applying EU income tax to the emoluments of officials and other staff.[9] Article 12 of the Protocol on the Privileges and Immunities of the European Union lays down provisions exempting the staff of the institutions from the application of national income tax, which is paid instead to the Union.[10]

According to Article 298 TFEU, in carrying out their missions, the institutions must 'have the support of an open, efficient and independent European administration', and the Union legislature must 'establish provisions to that end' in compliance with the Staff Regulations. It is not entirely clear whether the 'administration' in question is broader than the Union civil service, and whether such legislative provisions are intended to complement the Staff Regulations, or the Staff Regulations are themselves supposed to ensure the openness, efficiency and independence of the 'European administration'. In any case, no such provisions have yet been adopted.

2 Other relevant provisions

The Staff Regulations are applied in all the Union institutions with the exception of the European Central Bank and the European Investment Bank, each of which adopts its own staff regulations and ancillary instruments,[11] to which the employment contracts of their staff are subject.[12] In the case of certain agencies, the procedure for the appointment of the executive director and other agents occupying particular posts of responsibility is defined in the agency's foundational instrument; this does not, however, absolve the agency from its duties to respect Union civil service law generally.[13] As noted above, the Staff Regulations themselves provide an opening for the application, if need be, of the minimum health and safety requirements applicable to Union workers generally.[14]

3 Delegated acts

The Staff Regulations applicable to the institutions are supplemented by a small number of delegated acts on specific matters, such as the definition of the categories of officials entitled to allowances for carrying out shift work or standby duty, or compensation for the 'particularly arduous' character of their working conditions, or withdrawing the correction coefficient fixed for a particular city where the cost of living

---

[9] Regulation (EEC, Euratom, ECSC) No 260/1968 [1968] OJ L56/8, as amended (see now http://eur-lex.europa.eu/legal-content/EN/TXT/?qid=1537201783755&uri=CELEX:01968R0260-20021003).

[10] Protocol No 7 to the Treaties; see also Case C-263/91 *Kristoffersen* (n 3).

[11] For the ECB see Art 34.1, Protocol (No 4) on the Statute of the European System of Central Banks and of the ECB; the legal basis for the staff regulations of the EIB is the Bank's Rules of Procedure of 4 December 1958 (see Case F-115/11 *CG v EIB*, EU:F:2014:185, paras 2–4).

[12] For the ECB see eg Case T-129/14 P *Andres and Others v ECB* EU:T:2016:267; for the EIB see eg Case T-241/14 P *Bodson v BEI*, EU:T:2016:103.

[13] See eg Case T-27/15 P *European Medicines Agency v Hristov* EU:T:2016:388.

[14] Art 1e(2) Staff Regulations.

there no longer diverges from that in the capital of the Member State concerned sufficiently to justify its continuance (or where no official is stationed there).[15]

The exercise of such delegated powers is subject to both a right of revocation and a right of objection on the part of the European Parliament or the Council. These delegated acts are supplemented by general implementing provisions on a wide variety of matters which the institutions may, or in some cases must, adopt, as specified in the relevant provisions of the Staff Regulations.[16] All such supplementary rules, including general implementing provisions, must be brought to the attention of the staff, failing which the institution would be foreclosed from relying on the particular rule in a particular case.[17]

4 General principles of Union law

The general principles of Union law, such as the prohibition on discrimination of Article 10 TFEU and of a number of provisions of the CFR, apply in an unqualified manner to the institutions in the area of the management of their staff. Unsurprisingly, the most widely-cited provision of the Charter in this context is Article 41, the right to good administration, although the rights to an effective remedy and to a fair trial (Article 47) are also frequently relied upon in civil service litigation. Among the other Charter rights and obligations which the institutions have—with more or less plausibility according to the circumstances—occasionally been accused of violating, are those concerning respect for private and family life, protection of personal data, the rights of the child, the right to fair and unjust working conditions, and the presumption of innocence.

D Underlying Legal Principles Specific to the Civil Service

1 Development of EU administrative principles in civil service law

Many of the principles of the Union's administrative law were in fact first developed by the Court in its case law in this area, before being applied more generally, for example, to competition law. While there are few sector-specific principles per se, certain of the more general principles, such as that of good administration or the protection of acquired rights,[18] are obviously of more immediate relevance in this context than other such principles. The Staff Regulations themselves implement a number of the general principles, for example, by providing rules on the form of administrative decisions concerning individual officials. Such decisions must be communicated to the official in writing; where they adversely affect his legal position, the individual reasons must be given. Moreover, individual decisions which may directly affect the interests of other staff members (such as those on appointments, promotions, transfers,

---

[15] ibid Art 112(1), Arts 56a–56c (working conditions), and Annex XI Art 9(2) (correction coefficient) Staff Regulations, respectively.

[16] ibid Art 110(1) Staff Regulations.   [17] ibid Art 110(4) Staff Regulations.

[18] Respectively Case F-131/15 *Stips v Commission* EU:F:2016: 154 and Case C-443/07 P *Centeno Mediavilla* EU:C:2008:767.

termination of service, etc) must be published in a way that is 'accessible to all staff for an appropriate period of time'.[19]

It is, however, possible to discern a handful of sector-specific principles from the Staff Regulations and/or the extensive case law of the Court of Justice of the European Union (CJEU) in this area.

2 Reliance on the 'interest of the service'

The institution's duty to act in the interest of the service is only explicitly mentioned in a small number of provisions of the Staff Regulations. Thus, for example, it is the sole criterion on which the appointing authority decides to assign an official to a particular post in his function group.[20] By contrast, it is only one of a number of criteria on which the appointing authority decides whether or not an official may stand for public office and, if so, under what conditions.[21] The interests of the service may also prevent the institution from adopting a particular course of action it might otherwise take. This may work in the official's favour, for example, by restricting the possibility for the institution to refuse a part-time work regime, or to his disadvantage, for example, by precluding the institution from maintaining an official in service beyond his retirement age where he has requested to benefit from this facility.[22]

The term is interpreted as meaning the interest of the institution as a whole, rather than that of the particular service to which the staff member has been posted. In practice, the interest of the service may be considered the touchstone of legality in the exercise of the institution's discretion. That said, given the wide margin of discretion that the institution enjoys in its administrative capacity, it is in practice rather difficult for a disgruntled staff member to demonstrate that the institution has failed to act in accordance with the interest of the service. For some purposes, the 'interest of the service' is replaced by the 'legitimate interests of the [Union]', notably in decisions on a former official's request for authorization to work in an area related to his previous functions in an institution within three years of leaving the service; at such a point in time, the official is no longer a staff member of an institution (or 'the service') as such, the interests of which could be adversely affected.[23]

3 Duty to take account of the interests of the official

The interest of the service must, in most cases, be applied in conjunction with the duty of the institution, when taking an individual decision, to have regard to the welfare of the official concerned; this is often referred to as the institution's *devoir de sollicitude*,[24] or, occasionally and slightly misleadingly, in English as its 'duty of

---

[19] Art 25 Staff Regulations.   [20] ibid Art 7(1) 1st sub-para Staff Regulations.
[21] ibid Art 15(2) Staff Regulations.
[22] ibid Arts 55a(2) 2nd para, and 52 1st para, (a) Staff Regulations, respectively.
[23] ibid Art 16(2).
[24] Much of the case law of the CJEU in civil service matters in the last 25 years or so is only available in French (and the language of the case if this is not French), with the exception of judgments of the Court of Justice and a selection of 'landmark judgments' of the General Court and CST translated into all the official languages of the Union.

care'.[25] This duty, which is exclusively a creature of the case law of the CJEU, is predicated on the eminently sensible notion that the Staff Regulations 'reflect ... the balance of reciprocal rights and obligations' in the relationship between the institution and the staff.[26] However, the *devoir de sollicitude* cannot be relied upon in order to argue that the institution should take a course of action which would itself contravene the Staff Regulations. Moreover, some decisions do not require the institution to proceed to a separate evaluation of the interests of the official, for example, where the official's interest in obtaining a particular decision is already established at the outset. Thus, the institution may only decide to allow an official to remain in service beyond his retiring age if this is 'justified in the interest of the service'. However, the procedure for taking such a decision may only be launched at the request of the official concerned, and in these circumstances the decision 'depends entirely on the interest of the service, without the appointing authority being required to take into account the interests of the official making the request'.[27]

4 Duty to comply with self-imposed rules of conduct

Another principle which plays an essential role in the administrative practice of staff relations is the duty of the institution to comply with rules of conduct it has laid down for itself, such as decisions of general scope, guidelines, administrative procedures, internal directives, and so forth. While these unilateral measures do not create rules of law as do delegated acts or implementing provisions, the Court has held that the institution may depart from them only where it can provide a plausible statement of reasons for so acting, as otherwise the principle of the equality of treatment of officials would be infringed.[28] In *LIFE IV*, the Court of Justice extended this principle, by analogy, to the legislature when it was selecting the committee procedure to apply for supervising Commission's exercise of its implementing powers in an area of environmental policy under the old comitology regime, after acknowledging that the criteria for such a selection indicated in the relevant legislative act were not legally binding.[29] Although the transfer of administrative law principles first developed in staff law to the general administrative law of the Union is usually hailed as quite positive, it is not immediately obvious how a failure to provide reasons in such a case would infringe the principle of equality of treatment, or that the situation of those whose legal position was affected by the selection of the supervisory procedure (Member States and the Union's political institutions) was in any way analogous to that of officials.[30]

---

[25] 'Duty of care' is a term of art in the common law on civil liability, which is some way removed from the *devoir de sollicitude.*

[26] See eg Case F-36/14 *Bischoff v Commission* EU:F:2015:48, para 53.   [27] ibid para 54.

[28] Case 343/82 *Michael v Commission* EU:C:1983:360, para 14; the Court also admonished the institutions that such internal measures may 'under no circumstances ... establish rules which derogate from the provisions of the Staff Regulations (ibid para 16).

[29] Case C-378/00 *Commission v Parliament and Council* EU:C:2003:42.

[30] K Bradley, 'Comitology and the Courts: Tales of the Unexpected' in H Hofmann and A Türk (eds), *EU Administrative Governance* (Edward Elgar Publishing 2006) 417, 421–24.

5 Rule of correspondence

In the area of judicial review of the institutions' actions in civil service administration, the rule of correspondence should be mentioned. As noted below in more detail,[31] the vast majority of actions before the Union courts in this area must be preceded by an administrative complaint under Article 90(2) Staff Regulations. The Court has derived from this a requirement of admissibility, that all and any arguments raised in the legal proceedings must be raised previously in the administrative complaint. The rule is said to be justified by the very purpose of the complaint procedure, that is, to allow the administration to review its decision and, possibly, to obtain a non-judicial resolution of the dispute with the official; the administration would not be able to do so if it were not fully aware of the official's grounds for complaint.[32] In one of its more adventurous judgments, the Civil Service Tribunal loosened the strictures of this rule, primarily in view of the fact that the official is normally not represented by counsel at this stage of the procedure (and that his legal expenses in respect of the complaint would not be reimbursed even if he were successful), and that the official does not enjoy equality of arms with the institution.[33] The General Court reverted to a strict reading of the rule, although subsequently admitting a derogation to allow an official to raise a plea of illegality for the first time in his application to the Court.[34]

E Organization, Institutions, and Structures of the EU Civil Service

1 Key administrative actors

The key administrative actors in this area are the Union institutions and agencies, *qua* employers and, in the case of Parliament, the Council, and the Commission, in their capacities as the legislative and executive branches of the Union government. Thus, for example, prior to 1 January 2014, the Council was charged with deciding on the annual adjustment of the remuneration of officials, or refusing to so decide as the case may be;[35] from that date, any adjustment is effected automatically by the institutions concerned, in accordance with a number of economic indicators and the procedure set out in the Staff Regulations.[36] As noted above, the Commission may adopt delegated acts on certain matters.[37]

2 Adoption of implementing provisions

In their capacity as employers, the institutions adopt a wide variety of general implementing provisions.[38] For the most part, these are adopted by each institution

---

[31] See section F2(i), below.   [32] Case T-476/11 P *Commission v Moschonaki* EU:T:2013:557.
[33] Case F-45/07 *Mandt v Parliament* EU:F:2010:72.
[34] Respectively, Case T-476/11 P *Commission v Moschonaki* (n 32) and Case T-787/14 P *ECB v Cerafogli* EU:T:2016:633.
[35] See in particular Case C-63/12 *Commission v Council* EU:C:2013:752.
[36] Art 65(1) and Annex XI Arts 1–3.   [37] See section C3 above.
[38] Art 110(1) Staff Regulations.

separately, according to whatever procedure it determines. As with individual decisions, the institution may delegate the power to adopt such provisions to an 'appointing authority', which may be anything from the principal political or administrative authority within the institution (e.g. Bureau or Secretary General of the European Parliament, College of Commissioners) to a Director-General, or to an official further down the hierarchy.

Any implementing provisions adopted by the Commission apply automatically by analogy to the Union's agencies, although only after a nine-month lead-time. An agency may, however, also seek the Commission's authorization to apply different implementing rules, or not to apply certain of the Commission's implementing rules.[39]

3 Individual decisions

Individual decisions are taken by an even larger variety of appointing authorities within the institutions, from the institution per se (for example, for appointments at the level of Director-General) right down to officials in the various departments. In practice, some acts are generated automatically without the individual exercise of discretion, such as the determination of an official's net remuneration every month, set out in his pay slip and to be verified in good time in order to be able to challenge the amounts paid in fact.[40]

The institutions may also entrust the exercise of some or all of their powers, except as regards appointments, promotions, and the transfer of officials, either to a single institution or to an inter-institutional body.[41] Thus the Commission administers the pension scheme on behalf of all the institutions, although each institution decides for itself on the rules applicable to transfers into the Union pension scheme of pension rights acquired previously by officials in a national (or other international) scheme, or to transfers into another pension scheme of rights acquired by officials in the course of their career in the Union institutions. Responsibility for the selection of suitable candidates for appointment as officials in the institutions which apply the Staff Regulations, through competitions and other selection procedures, has been vested since 2002 in the European Personnel Selection Office (EPSO).[42] Judicial challenges to EPSO decisions must be directed against the Commission.[43]

The European Anti-fraud Office (OLAF) is an independent body within the European Commission whose remit is not limited to the sphere of activity of the Union institutions. It is charged under its founding instrument with investigating 'fraud, corruption and any other illegal activity affecting the financial interests of the European Union' committed within the institutions, or in the Member States or even

---

[39] ibid Art 110(2) Staff Regulations.
[40] Case F-77/15 *Zink v Commission* EU:F:2016:74; see also appeal judgment Case T-338/16 P, EU:T:2018:98.
[41] Art 2(2) Staff Regulations.
[42] Decisions 2002/620 and 2002/621 (as amended) [2002] OJ 2002 L197/53 and 56 (and [2010] OJ L26/24).
[43] See eg Case F-127/11 *Mendoza Asensi v Commission* EU:F:2014:14, where the Civil Service Tribunal was invited to modify, in the light of a radical change in the method for organising tests, the principle that the composition of the selection board must remain stable.

in third countries or other international organizations.[44] It may also investigate possible breaches by officials of their obligations under the Staff Regulations, although, of course, such breaches may equally be investigated by the institution itself.[45]

F Administrative Procedures within the Civil Service Sector

1 Acts of general application—adoption procedures

Not surprisingly, there is a wide variety of administrative procedures to cover the very large range of decisions of general scope the institution is called upon to take in the normal course of its activities as employer. Most of the more important such decisions may be taken only in consultation with the relevant committee which must be set up by each institution: a staff committee, one or more joint committees (comprising representatives of the staff committee and the administration of the institution in equal numbers), a disciplinary board, joint advisory committees, and a reports committee. A single invalidity committee is set up by agreement between the institutions, as may other joint committees if the institutions so chose.[46]

Of the statutory committees, the most important is the staff committee, charged with 'represent[ing] the interests of the staff vis-à-vis their institution and maintain[ing] continuous contact between the institution and the staff'. To this end, the staff committee may draw to the attention of the appointing authority any recurrent or systemic difficulties in the interpretation and application of the Staff Regulations, suggest improvements in the organization and operation of the service and in the working conditions of officials, and participate in the provision of, or provide, social welfare services.[47] Both the institution and the staff committee may consult the relevant joint committee on 'questions of a general nature'.[48] While each institution determines the composition and procedure of its own staff committee, as a gauge of its independence the members of the staff committee are elected for a three-year term by secret ballot, rather than being appointed by the institution itself.[49] Moreover, the electoral procedure itself is adopted by the general meeting of officials at the relevant place of employment or, for the larger institutions with more than one working place (in particular, Parliament and the Commission), their local section. The fact that the institution does not participate in any way in the definition of the conditions under which these elections are organized does not shelter it from litigation, including, on occasion, bitter internecine disputes between staff associations or even between members and former members of the same staff association.[50]

Joint committees tend to have more specific consultative functions; the Joint Advisory Committee on professional incompetence, for example, acts only where the institution proposes to dismiss or downgrade a sitting official whose professional performance has proven unsatisfactory.[51] The inter-institutional Staff Regulations

---

[44] Articles 1(1), 3, and 4 of Regulation (EU, Euratom) No 883/2013 [2013] OJ L248/1.
[45] Art 86(2) Staff Regulations; see also section F2 below.   [46] Art 9 Staff Regulations.
[47] ibid Art 9(3).   [48] ibid Art 9(4).   [49] ibid Annex II Art 1.
[50] See section F1 above; see eg Case F-87/13 and Case F-31/14, both *Colart v Parliament*, respectively EU:F:2014:53 and EU:F:2014:264.
[51] Art 51 Staff Regulations.

Committee, comprising equal numbers of representatives of the institutions and their respective Staff Committees, is consulted by the Commission on all proposals to amend the Staff Regulations; that Committee may also propose such revisions on its own initiative.[52]

Mention should also be made of a shadowy body known as the College of Heads of Administration of the institutions. Though not established by the Staff Regulations, it provides a forum for the administrations of the institutions to discuss common problems in the interpretation and application of their provisions, and to adopt, where appropriate, a common approach to such problems. Its conclusions have no legal value, although they tend in practice, unless and until challenged in legal proceedings, to be applied by the administrations of the institutions as if they had. The Court does not, however, give the conclusions of the College any particular weight.

2 Adoption of individual decisions: administrative complaints and disciplinary procedures

By way of illustration, it is useful to examine the complaints procedure and the disciplinary procedure, as examples of single-case decision-making.

(a) The administrative complaint procedure

Any act which affects an official adversely may be challenged by means of an administrative complaint submitted in accordance with Article 90(2) Staff Regulations. With very limited exceptions, the submission—and explicit or implicit rejection— of such a complaint is a necessary precondition for the initiation of proceedings before the CJEU; this requirement is waived only where the appointing authority responsible for handling the complaint is unable to modify the decision challenged (for example, the decision of an independent selection board excluding a candidate from a competition or on staff reports, regarding which the appointing authority has no discretion in the context of such a complaint).[53] In such circumstances, the applicant may by-pass the administrative complaint procedure, proceeding straight to judicial review. For the challenge to be admissible, the act contested must bring about a distinct change in the official's personal legal situation; an act, whether individual or of general scope, may not be challenged solely in pursuit of some general interest.[54]

The omission by the appointing authority to take a decision relating to the official may also be challenged. The official must first submit a request under Article 90(1) Staff Regulations that the decision be taken, and may initiate the complaint procedure

[52] ibid Art 10.
[53] For example, the decision of a selection board not to admit a candidate: see Case F-66/11 *Cristina v Commission* EU:F:2012:88.
[54] See eg in relation to the bringing of a complaint for psychological harassment Case F-95/09 *Skareby v Commission* EU:F:2011:9, para 26.

of Article 90(2) against the decision taken or refusal to take such a decision, as the case may be. The request procedure also applies where the official is claiming damages for harm putatively caused by an institution's behaviour, rather than by an adverse decision as such.[55]

The entire procedure is subject to fixed time limits. The official must submit a complaint within three months of the act's being publicized or notified to him, or the point in time at which the official had knowledge of the act, or, in the case of an implicit refusal to take a decision, within three months of the expiry of the time limit for replying to a request. The institution is subject to a time limit of four months for replying to the complaint; the official may then initiate legal proceedings against a complete or partial rejection of his complaint under Article 90(2) Staff Regulations within three months (plus ten days on account of distance under the Court's rules). The deadlines are strictly enforced against the complaining official, although less so as against the institution, in that the failure of the institution to respond in time merely reopens the time limits, without rendering the complaint automatically admissible. Thus, for example, where the institution does not reply within the four month deadline, an official might initiate proceedings before the Court on the basis of an implicit rejection, only for the institution to move the goalposts by adopting an explicit rejection of his complaint.[56] Respect of the time limits for both the submission of the administrative complaint, and the filing of legal proceedings, are matters which the Court is obliged to examine of its own motion if need be. The same is true of the other conditions of admissibility, such as the requirements that the act complained of adversely affect the official within the meaning of Article 90(2) Staff Regulations, and that the application to the Court not contain grounds of invalidity which were not raised in the complaint.[57]

Where the relevant provisions concerning the presentation of an annulment action do not lay down a precise time limit, as is the case for the staff regulations of the European Investment Bank, the applicants are entitled to expect the Court to allow them a 'reasonable period' after receipt of the contested act to initiate legal proceedings.[58] In line with the general administrative law of the Union, the reasonableness of the period 'is to be appraised in the light of all the circumstances specific to each case and, in particular, the importance of the case for the person concerned, its complexity and the conduct of the parties to the case'.[59] The Court may not apply by analogy the strict time limits of the Staff Regulations of the Union institutions to such a case.

---

[55] See eg Case F-23/15 *Kerstens v Commission* EU:F:2016:65, para 135.

[56] Art 91(3) 2nd indent Staff Regulations. In this case, the explicit rejection would have to be adopted before the period for initiating the proceedings before the Court has expired.

[57] On the existence of an act adversely affecting the complainant see eg Case F-77/15 *Zink v Commission* (n 40) para 3; on the necessity for correspondence between the complaint and the application to the Court see section D5 above.

[58] Case C-334/12 RX-II *Arango Jaramillo and Others v EIB* EU:C:2013:134, para 44.

[59] ibid para 28, citing Joined Cases C-238/99 P, C-244/99 P, C-245/99 P, C-247/99 P, C-250/99 P to C-252/99 P, and C-254/99 P *Limburgse Vinyl Maaschappij and Others v Commission* EU:C:2002:582, para 187.

(b) *The disciplinary procedure*

Article 86(1) Staff Regulations sternly admonishes each official that '[a]ny failure ... to comply with ... obligations under the[] Staff Regulations' renders him 'liable to disciplinary action'.[60] Though activated relatively rarely, given its potentially drastic consequences for the official concerned, the disciplinary procedure is set out in some detail in Annex IX to the Staff Regulations, which was radically revised and updated at the time of the 2004 reforms.[61] The procedure may be divided into four phases: initiation, preliminary decision on the existence of a violation of the Staff Regulations, examination and conclusions of the disciplinary board, and decision on the imposition of a penalty, although, as we shall see, not all of these phases need be operated in every disciplinary procedure. Each institution may, 'if it sees fit', adopt measures to implement Annex IX generally, but must adopt measures to implement Article 2 of Annex IX governing the investigation of a suspected disciplinary offence.[62] For convenience, the Commission's implementing provisions, which are more complete than those of most of the other institutions, will be cited by way of illustration.[63]

(i) Initiation of the procedure

The disciplinary procedure may be triggered by an administrative investigation conducted either by the appointing authority of the institution or by OLAF, where one or other of them 'becomes aware of evidence' that an official has failed to comply with his obligations under the Staff Regulations.[64] In practice, where OLAF launches such an investigation, the Commission suspends its own investigation until OLAF has concluded;[65] moreover the Commission has a special unit, the Investigation and Disciplinary Office (IDOC), which is responsible for investigating possible disciplinary offences, including psychological or sexual harassment.[66] Whichever authority is carrying out the administrative investigation, the official must 'rapidly be informed, provided this is not harmful to the investigation'.[67] Except where 'absolute secrecy' is required, no conclusions referring to the official by name may be drawn until he has had the opportunity to comment on the facts being investigated, and the conclusions must refer to the official's comments, unless he has made none. Where 'for objective reasons', the official is unable to attend a hearing, he may submit observations in writing, although a simple assertion of incapacity is not sufficient to justify non-attendance.[68]

The first phase is closed by the adoption of an investigation report. While at one point the Civil Service Tribunal held that these provisions did not require the

---

[60] Art 86(1) Staff Regulations.   [61] Council Regulation No 723/2004 (n 8).
[62] Respectively, Annex IX Arts 30 and 2(3) Staff Regulations.
[63] Commission decision of 28 April 2004 adopting general implementing provisions on the conduct of administrative enquiries and disciplinary proceedings (Commission GIPs).
[64] Art 86(2) Staff Regulations; OLAF is an independent office attached administratively to the Commission.
[65] Art 4(2) Commission GIPs (n 63).
[66] These notions are defined in Art 12a(3) and (4) Staff Regulations respectively.
[67] ibid Annex IX Arts 1(1) and 2(1).
[68] ibid Annex IX arts 1(2), 2(1), and 4; Case T-493/15 P *Commission v CX* EU:T:2016:636, para 49.

institution to carry out a full investigation where the facts may be established on the basis of documentary evidence alone, or to examine exculpatory evidence as well as incriminating evidence, the General Court has affirmed in no uncertain terms the institution's duty to carry out such an inquiry and to examine both exculpatory and incriminating evidence.[69] In any case, the Commission's general implementing provisions (GIPs) clearly do require an administrative inquiry; the Commission has argued that its GIPs are not limited to reproducing the relevant provisions of the Staff Regulations, but confer on the person concerned supplementary rights not expressly foreseen in the Staff Regulations.[70]

Following the closing of the investigation, the official is notified of 'all the evidence in the file' and must be allowed a second hearing by the appointing authority.[71]

(ii) Preliminary decision of the appointing authority

On the basis of the investigation, the appointing authority may take one of four decisions:

- no case can be made against the official, who is so informed
- notwithstanding a probable or established violation of the Staff Regulations, no disciplinary measure should be taken, although the official may receive a warning (which is not therefore considered a disciplinary sanction)
- disciplinary proceedings should be conducted without the participation of the Disciplinary Board or
- disciplinary proceeding should be conducted with the participation of the Disciplinary Board.

The first two of these possible decisions are self-explanatory. Where, in case of the third possibility, the appointing authority proceeds without the disciplinary board, it may at most impose one of the two lightest penalties provided (see (iv) below), a written warning or a reprimand, neither of which has financial consequences or a direct impact on the official's future career.

(iii) Proceedings before the Disciplinary Board

As noted, the fourth possible outcome of the preliminary decision is the initiation of proceedings before the Disciplinary Board. The rules which Annex IX lays down, in some detail, on the composition and functioning of the Disciplinary Board are intended to constitute guarantees of fair procedure for the official concerned, equivalent to those which apply in criminal proceedings. Thus, Board members must be 'completely independent in the performance of their duties'; at the end of the procedure, each member may attach a dissenting opinion to the Board's reasoned opinion. Members are appointed in principle for a three-year term, at least one member (who may be the chairman) must be chosen from outside the institution, and two of the four

---

[69] Joined Cases F-88/09 and F-48/10 *Z v Court of Justice* EU:F:2012:171, paras 269 and 270, overturned *pro tanto* by Case T-270/16 P *Kerstens v Commission* EU:T:2017:74, paras 62 and 76.
[70] Case F-23/15 *Kerstens v Commission* (n 55) paras 64–82 and 52.
[71] Annex IX Art 3(1) Staff Regulations.

voting members are appointed by the staff committee, rather than the administration of the institution concerned. Moreover, Disciplinary Board members must be of at least the same grade and function group as the official being investigated. The official may recuse one of the members of the Board within five days of its establishment, the institution may do so at any time, and members must recuse themselves in case of a conflict of interests, and may do so for other legitimate reasons. The deliberations and proceedings of the Board are secret.[72]

In initiating the proceedings, the appointing authority is obliged to 'stat[e] clearly the facts complained of and ... the circumstances in which they arose, including any aggravating or extenuating circumstances'; this report, presumably based essentially on the investigation report on which the appointing authority decided to initiate the Board proceedings, must be sent to the official. At this point the official is entitled to obtain and take copies from his entire personal file; he must be accorded a minimum of fifteen days to prepare his defence, either on his own, or assisted by a person of his choice (usually a lawyer where he is facing serious disciplinary charges).[73] Where a disciplinary sanction is ultimately imposed, the official must bear his own legal and other costs, although the appointing authority may decide otherwise 'where the burden on the official concerned would be unfair'.[74]

One of the Disciplinary Board members prepares a report on the charges, after hearing the official concerned. The official may make submissions orally and/or in writing, and may call witnesses, as may the institution's representative. Where OLAF has initiated the investigation, the Board may also hear its investigating officials. If need be, the Board may carry out its own investigations, and require the official and the institution to supply documents. Where the official 'acknowledges misconduct on his part and accepts unreservedly the [appointing authority's] report', the appointing authority may withdraw the case from the Board, and impose one of the four least serious sanctions, unless the offence is too serious.[75]

On the basis of the file, including any statement made to the Board and the results of its investigations, the Board adopts a 'reasoned opinion', on 'whether the facts complained of are established' and on a suitable penalty, if any. The opinion is signed by the members individually and sent to the appointing authority and, generally within two months, to the official concerned.[76]

(iv) Decision on the possible imposition of a disciplinary sanction

Within two months of receipt of the board's opinion, the appointing authority is to take a decision on whether or not to impose a sanction on the official. It is not obliged to follow the board's findings, whether as to the facts or the sanction proposed.[77] However, it may not enlarge the scope of the facts found against the official, and must in any case provide reasons for its decision. Where it decides not to impose a penalty,

---

[72] ibid Annex IX Arts 5–8.   [73] ibid Annex IX Art 13.
[74] ibid Annex IX Art 21 Staff Regulations.   [75] ibid Annex IX Art 14.
[76] ibid Annex IX Art 18; the time limit is extended to four months where the board has carried out an investigation.
[77] See eg Case F-149/15 *HG v Commission* EU:F:2016:155, para 78.

the official must be informed 'without delay' and may request that the decision be included in his personal file.[78] The possible sanctions are listed exhaustively in Article 9 of Annex IX, and range from a reprimand to dismissal with a reduction *pro tempore* of the official's pension entitlement. In line with the principle of *ne bis in idem* (double jeopardy), a single case of misconduct will not give rise to more than one penalty. The penalty must be 'commensurate with the seriousness of the misconduct'; in its assessment, the appointing authority must take account of a number of listed factors, such as the nature of the misconduct and the official's motives.[79] Unlike, for example, in the field of competition law, the Union courts are not entitled to increase a disciplinary penalty, even when this is manifestly inadequate in the circumstances. The institution is, however, obliged to take action to protect its officials.[80]

In accordance with a principle of certain legal systems that '*le pénal tient le disciplinaire en l'état*', the disciplinary procedure may not be closed as long as any criminal prosecution in respect of the same acts is still pending.[81] This is a matter over which the appointing authority has no control, and, given the duration of criminal proceedings in some Member States, it may lead to the rather perverse result that an official who is guilty of a very serious breach of his obligations under the Staff Regulations justifying his dismissal may be kept on the payroll for several years after the facts, while one who is guilty of a somewhat lesser breach, and who has not been prosecuted, may be dismissed in a much shorter timeframe.

G Legal Rules Governing the Substance of Decision-making in Civil Service Administration

The Staff Regulations lay down a variety of different procedures for the adoption of both individual measures and acts of general scope. In general, the appointing authority enjoys a wide discretion in adopting such legal acts within the confines, procedural and substantive, of the Staff Regulations, which in turn may restrict the scope of judicial review to which these acts are subject. By way of illustration, in relation to the promotion of officials, Article 45 Staff Regulations lays down a number of ground rules:

- promotion may be only to the next higher grade in the official's function group;
- only officials who have been in their current grade for two years are eligible for promotion;
- the appointing authority must make its choice on the basis of an examination of the comparative merits of all the officials eligible for promotion; and
- in the comparison of merits, the appointing authority must take account of the candidates' periodic evaluation reports, their use of foreign languages in the

---

[78] Annex IX Art 22 Staff Regulations.   [79] ibid Annex IX Art 10.
[80] Case F-23/15 *Kerstens v Commission* (n 55) para 105 and the case law cited.
[81] Annex IX Art 25 Staff Regulations; see eg Case F-54/11 *BG v European Ombudsman* EU:F:2012:114, paras 60–78; the appeal judgment did not examine this question on its merits (Case T-406/12 P, EU:T:2014:273).

exercise of their functions, and 'where appropriate, the level of responsibilities exercised by them'.[82]

Within this framework, the appointing authority

> possesses a wide discretion, and in that connection the [Union] Court's review must be confined to the question whether, having regard to the various considerations which have influenced the administration in making its assessment, the latter has remained within reasonable bounds and has not used its power in a manifestly incorrect way. The [Union] Court cannot therefore substitute its assessment of the qualifications and merits of the candidates for that of the appointing authority.[83]

As a result, it is rather difficult for an applicant staff member to overturn a promotion decision on substantive grounds, and it is often the procedure by which the institution applies Article 45 Staff Regulations, rather than the resulting decision per se, which is challenged.[84] Similarly, as regards the renewal of temporary contracts; the General Court has consistently rejected the attempts of the Civil Service Tribunal to impose even modest constraints on the margin of discretion of the appointing authority in this area, where these do not derive expressly from the text of the CEOS.[85]

H Abstract General Administrative Acts and Measures within the Civil Service Sector

The entire area of relations between the Union and its staff is covered by the Staff Regulations of the institutions (and the equivalent instruments of the two European Union banks), as well as the various delegated and implementing measures, including general implementing provisions adopted under Article 110 Staff Regulations. As mentioned above, the institutions are under a duty to comply with rules of conduct they adopt for the application of their staff regulations.[86]

I Civil Service Single-case Administrative Acts and Measures

On the basis of the Staff Regulations and their implementing provisions each institution adopts dozens, if not hundreds, of individual acts every year in respect of each staff member: a single monthly pay slip, for example, as well as indicating the amount of the salary the official actually receives and the income tax paid, also reflects what are formally decisions on his entitlement (or not) to a variety of social security and other allocations and benefits. Where the decision adversely affects the staff member,

---

[82] Art 45(1) Staff Regulations.
[83] Case C-277/01 P *Samper v Parliament* EU:C:2003:196, para 35.
[84] See eg Case F-51/14 *Ribeiro Sinde Monteiro v EEAS* EU:F:2015:11; and Case F-83/14 *Silvan v Commission* EU:F:2015:106. While the promotion procedures in these cases were similar in many respects, the results of the cases were different; both judgments were upheld on appeal (respectively Case T-278/15 P EU:T:2017:132 and Case T-698/15 P EU:T:2017:131).
[85] Cf Case F-63/11 *Macchia v Commission* EU:F:2012:83 and the appeal judgment, Case T-368/10 *Commission v Macchia* EU:T:2014:266.
[86] Section D4 above.

it must state the grounds on which it is based.[87] In practice, however, the pay slip is generated by a computer and is not accompanied by any explanation other than the codes which indicate somewhat laconically the types of payment or deduction made. It is also subject to the occurrence of technical glitches.[88] On one view, in order to safeguard his financial rights, the official would be obliged to examine every item indicated on the pay slip every month, and indeed verify if every payment to which he is entitled has in fact been made, and, if not, react within the time limit for submitting a staff complaint.

Obviously the more significant decisions in the career of an official, such as a change in functions, a promotion, or a disciplinary decision, for example, will be communicated to him individually in writing. As well as decisions addressed to the official, both decisions addressed to the staff in general (such as a list of persons promoted in a given year) and those addressed to one staff member, but of direct interest to another official, may be considered to affect the interests of the latter adversely; thus, for example, a decision not to proceed against an official accused of harassment affects the interests of the purported victim.[89] In line with other acts adopted by the Union institutions, individual acts and acts of general scope adopted in the area of staff relations enjoy a presumption of validity.

Given the public law character of staff relations, there is little room in practice for the conclusion of *collective agreements* between the administration of the institutions and their staff. That said, the institutions may conclude such agreements with representative trade unions and staff associations. While such agreements may neither amend the Staff Regulations or budgetary commitments, nor affect the functioning of the institution, the Staff Regulations do not otherwise restrict their material content.[90] The institution must also, for example, cooperate closely with the Staff Committee in implementing measures of a social nature and social welfare services.[91]

J Administrative Enforcement in the Civil Service Sector

The Member States play essentially no part in the administration of the Union civil service. However, Member State policies and decisions can have an impact on the rights of staff members, particularly in relation to their financial status.[92] The Commission has, therefore, occasionally had to defend the exemption from national income tax which officials enjoy, in respect of their emoluments from the Union from encroachment by national authorities, particularly Belgian, if need be by means of an administrative procedure and infringement proceedings before the Court of Justice.[93] Otherwise, the administrative 'enforcement' in relation to the Civil Service, because of its essentially

---

[87] Art 25, 2nd para Staff Regulations.
[88] See eg the facts of Case F-77/15 *Zink v Commission* (n 40).
[89] See Case F-95/09 *Skareby v Commission* (n 54).   [90] Art 10c Staff Regulations.
[91] ibid Art 1e.
[92] See eg Case C-263/91 *Kristoffersen* (n 3) and Case C-430/97 *Johannes* (n 3), not to mention Brexit as regards the rights of former officials resident in the United Kingdom.
[93] See eg Cases 85/85, 186/85, and 206/86, all *Commission v Belgium*, respectively EU:C:1986:129, EU:C:1987:208, and EU:C:1988:91.

wholly 'internal' character, is almost non-existent, although there is some form of supervision, as indicated in the next section.

K Supervision and Control within the Administration of the Civil Service

1 Internal supervision

To a large extent, the internal supervision of the application of the Staff Regulations is left to the parties concerned. The administrative authorities of each of the institutions ensures staff members carry out their duties correctly, while the individual staff member may submit an official complaint should other less formal channels not lead to a satisfactory resolution of his situation. The Staff Committee and the staff associations of the institutions may also play a role in this regard. Article 24b Staff Regulations expressly recognizes the right of association of officials, also classified as a fundamental right under Article 12(1) CFR.[94]

For the Commission, IDOC has a dual role: 'to conduct impartial administrative inquiries to determine whether there has been a failure to comply with the obligations incumbent on Commission officials and to carry out disciplinary procedures on behalf of the Appointing Authority'.[95] While it appears to carry out the latter role more or less correctly, doubt has been cast on the impartial character of its activities in relation to the investigation of instances of alleged workplace harassment. Thus, in investigating the circumstances of the *Tzirani* case, the Civil Service Tribunal elicited the surprising fact that, in a four-year period, IDOC had not established the existence of a single instance of psychological harassment, despite examining between five and ten complaints per year.[96] Commission officials may also turn to a staff Ombudsman, who may mediate a solution to the situation complained of; however, the utility of such a course of action is limited by the fact that submitting such a complaint does not absolve the official from complying with the time limits imposed by Articles 90 and 91 Staff Regulations.[97]

The other institutions do not appear to have an equivalent of either IDOC or the staff ombudsman. However, in the European Parliament, for example, administrative complaints are handled by its Legal Service, rather than the administrative department which adopted the decision or perpetrated the behaviour complained of. The general independence of this service from the rest of the Parliament's secretariat allows the appointing authority to benefit from a genuine second opinion, before taking its position on the administrative complaint.[98]

The Staff Regulations also provide a degree of protection to whistle-blowers. An official who finds evidence of a possibly illegal activity is obliged to inform his

---

[94] On the role of the Staff Committee see section F1 above.
[95] IDOC Activity Report 2012 para 1.
[96] Case F-46/11 *Tzirani v Commission* EU:F:2013:115, para 143.   [97] See section F2(i) above.
[98] On Parliament's Legal Service see generally K Bradley, 'The European Parliament and the European Court: Litigation and Other Interactions' in M-P Granger and C Guinchard, *The New EU Judiciary: An Analysis of Current Judicial Reforms* (Kluwer 2018) 233.

hierarchical superiors or OLAF, and may so inform the Presidents respectively of the Commission, of the Court of Auditors, or of the European Parliament, or the European Ombudsman.[99] If he chooses the latter course, he will be protected from 'prejudicial effects on the part of the institution' to which he belongs, if he reasonably believes his allegations are true and has previously disclosed the same information to the OLAF *in tempore non suspecto*. A suspiciously high proportion of officials who stand accused of disciplinary offences activate these provisions immediately after facts which trigger a disciplinary procedure have taken place, or at least claim the benefit of the protection of these rules in the course of such procedures.[100]

2 External supervision

There is very little external supervision of either the performance of the Union's staff, or of how the institutions carry out their duties in regard to their staff. As regards the former, the role of OLAF in investigating possible serious misconduct of staff members liable to result in disciplinary or criminal proceedings, has already been adumbrated above.[101] In carrying out its functions under the Treaty, the Court of Auditors may also comment incidentally on the way staff members have applied Union rules, although that would not normally be that Court's central concern.[102] Concerning the latter, while the Parliament's Committee on Legal Affairs has a general remit to ensure that the Treaty and the legal acts of the Union are respected,[103] it has shown almost no interest in staff matters, except in the context of legislative procedures regarding the amendment of the Staff Regulations.

The European Ombudsman (as distinct from the Commission's Staff Ombudsman noted above) may also investigate complaints of maladministration in staff matters, both individual and systemic in character. As regards individual complaints, however, the Ombudsman may only do so where the official has made a staff complaint and the appointing authority has not replied within the relevant deadline.[104] The launching of a complaint to the European Ombudsman does not, however, waive the requirement to respect the time limits applicable to any legal proceedings the complainant may wish to initiate (see above).

In fact, disputes between the institutions and their staff are in practice highly judicialized, in the sense that, in most cases, recourse to the Courts provides by far the most, or in some cases the only, effective remedy. In this context, it is noteworthy that the Union staff enjoyed the benefit of a specialized court, the Civil Service Tribunal, until this was abolished in September 2016 in the framework of a wider reform of the Union's judicial architecture.[105]

---

[99] Arts 22a and 22b(1) Staff Regulations.
[100] See eg Case F-23/15 *Kerstens v Commission* (n 55) para 87.
[101] Articles 1(4) and 4 of Regulation 883/2013 [2013] OJ L248/1.
[102] See by analogy Case F-30/08 *Nanopoulos v Commission* EU:F:2010:43, upheld on appeal in Case T-308/10 *Commission v Nanopoulos* EU:T:2012:370.
[103] Annex V s XVI(1) European Parliament Rules of Procedure.
[104] Art 2(8) Ombudsman's Statute.
[105] Regulations 2015/2422 and 2016/1192, respectively [2015] OJ L341/14 and [2016] OJ L200/137.

L Conclusion

By way of conclusion, there is little to add to what has been noted at the outset, namely that the administration of the Civil Service is a Union function which is largely *sui generis*. The law regulating the Union's Civil Service, which is essentially administrative in form even if it contains elements of employment law, therefore displays characteristics which are rather different from those applying to other branches of the Union administration both in the narrower and the wider sense. Nevertheless, as has also been noted, aspects of civil service administration and law have, in earlier periods at least, often given the lead for legal and organizational evolution in other, substantive policy sectors of the Union.

22

The Union Budget

Richard Crowe

A Introduction

The budget of the European Union is, in many respects, an innovative transnational public finance experiment. The transition to a system of own resources in the 1970s marked an attempt to push beyond the traditional model for financing international organizations (through 'national contributions' from the budgets of the participating states) to establish an autonomous European budgetary order that would complement the 'new legal order' of Community law.[1] Expectations may not have been fully realized in that regard, but today's Union does enjoy a level of budgetary autonomy far exceeding that accorded to other treaty-based organizations.[2] On the expenditure side, over 94 per cent of the budget is invested in common European policies,[3] and it performs transnational redistributive functions in certain policy sectors. Moreover, the institutional framework for the establishment and control of the budget includes particular features, such as a strong parliamentary dimension to decision-making on expenditure and an independent Court of Auditors, that are more characteristic of the budgetary system of a state.

In this context, a body of budgetary administrative law has developed that is particular to the Union. It is a complex body of law, the evolution of which impacts quite broadly on the design of the general administrative law of the Union. For example, the development of rules and procedures governing the disbursement, supervision, and control of Union funds under shared management on the territories of the Member States has been central to the emergence of an integrated European administration, or *Verwaltungsverbund*.[4] Moreover, the major overhaul of the Union's financial rules

---

[1] On the early history of the system of own resources see David Coombes, *The Power of the Purse in the European Communities* (Chatham House, 1972); The European Communities' own resources and the budgetary powers of the European Parliament: Selected documents (Secretariat of the European Parliament, October 1972). See also Report of the Study Group on the role of public finance in European integration (MacDougall Report) (European Commission: Brussels, April 1977).

[2] On the deficiencies of the current own resources system compared to the early ambitions see *First Assessment Report of the High-level Group on Own Resources* (Monti Group), Brussels, 17 December 2014 http://ec.europa.eu/budget/mff/hlgor. On the notion of Union budgetary autonomy see Aymeric Potteau, *Recherches sur l'autonomie financière de l'Union européenne* (Dalloz 2004); Claus-Dieter Ehlermann, 'The Financing of the Community: The Distinction Between Financial Contributions and Own Resources' (1982) 19 *Common Market Law Review* 571. For a comparison with the budgetary systems of traditional international organizations, such as the UN and IMF see Corinne Delon Desmoulin, *Droit budgétaire de l'Union européenne* (LGDJ, 2011) 14–17; see also Morgan Larhant, *Les finances de l'ONU ou la crise permanente* (Presses de Sciences Po 2016).

[3] Under 6% is spent on the Union's administration; see http://ec.europa.eu/budget/figures/interactive.

[4] Jens Peter Schneider, 'Europäisches Haushaltsverwaltungsrecht' in Jörg Philipp Terhechte (ed), *Verwaltungsrecht in der Europäischen Union* (Nomos Verlag 2011) 959–80 at 959. See also Herwig

that followed the resignation of the Santer Commission in 1999, and that culminated in the adoption of a new Financial Regulation in 2002,[5] impacted across all sectors where Union funds are administered, to such an extent that Craig wrote of a new 'constitutional framework for Community administration of the kind that has not existed hitherto'.[6]

Against that background, this chapter explores the distinctive features of the Union's administrative law in the budgetary domain, and draws attention to current trends in its ongoing evolution, with a particular focus on those developments that may have a broader relevance for the functioning of the Union's administration as a whole.

B Administrative Tasks in Relation to the Budget

The budgetary cycle in a parliamentary system is traditionally understood to consist of four phases, namely preparation, adoption, implementation, and control.[7] In the Union context, the annual budgetary cycle must be viewed in conjunction with a second, multiannual, cycle that comprises the preparation, adoption, implementation, and review of the Multiannual Financial Framework (MFF) legislative package, which fixes upper limits on expenditure, and allocates spending envelopes among both policies and Member States for a period of several years.[8] The administrative tasks that fall to be performed in the budgetary domain are determined, to a large extent, by the requirements of these annual and multiannual cycles. Moreover, the Union's administration will find itself performing tasks in relation to all four phases of the cycles simultaneously, but with reference to different financial years.[9]

Administrative tasks that fall to be performed during the preparatory phase of the annual cycle include budgetary forecasting, and the compilation of estimates of revenue and expenditure for the next financial year. As with many of the recurring tasks that are performed over the course of the budgetary cycle, the performance of these tasks relies upon the generation, gathering, maintenance, exchange, distribution, and analysis of accurate and up-to-date financial information, across the institutions, bodies, offices, and agencies of the Union, and between the different levels of implementation, notably between the Commission and the national administrations of the Member States. Other tasks performed during the financial year that rely heavily on information exchange include monitoring the rates of implementation, treasury

---

Hofmann and Alexander Türk (eds), *Legal Challenges in EU Administrative Law: Towards an Integrated Administration* (Edward Elgar Publishing 2009); Eberhard Schmidt-Aßmann and Bettina Schöndorf-Haubold (eds), *Der Europäische Verwaltungsverbund* (Mohr Siebeck 2005).

[5] Council Regulation (EC, Euratom) No 1605/2002 of 25 June 2002 on the Financial Regulation applicable to the general budget of the European Communities [2002] OJ L248/1.

[6] Paul Craig, *EU Administrative Law* (Oxford University Press 2006) 26.

[7] As set out by Louis XVIII's Minister of Finance, Baron Louis, when presenting the French budget to the *Chambre des députés* in 1814. See Gil Desmoulin, 'La loi organique relative aux lois de finances ou le renouveau de la règle des quatre temps alternés' (2004) (8–9) *La Révue du Trésor* 503, 503.

[8] Art 312(1) TFEU provides that the MFF shall be established for a period of at least five years, but since 1993 the practice has been to lay down the MFF for a period of seven years.

[9] On the significance of policy cycles and phasing in Union administrative law see Herwig C H Hofmann, Gerard C Rowe, and Alexander H Türk, *Administrative Law and Policy of the European Union* (Oxford University Press 2011) 26–36 and 57.

management, supervision, reporting, and budgetary control. In the budgetary domain, information is very much 'the raw material of public decision-making'.[10]

The preparatory phase also entails agenda-setting tasks, since drawing up proposals for the allocation of budgetary resources necessarily entails consideration of the policy priorities that should be implemented over the subsequent financial year. Similarly, agenda-setting tasks are performed in the multiannual context when proposals are drawn up for the MFF Regulation, the Own Resources Decision, and the accompanying regulations establishing multiannual funding programmes in different policy sectors.

Administrative tasks also fall to be performed during the adoption phase, when the administrations of the Commission, the European Parliament, and the Council provide administrative support to facilitate an agreement on the budget at political level, and then work together to prepare the final text for formal adoption.

The implementation phase lies at the heart of the budgetary cycle. Implementation of the budget is a notion whose precise scope has been subject to legal debate over the years, especially following the ruling of the Court of Justice in the case of *Commission v Council* in 1988.[11] That case concerned a Council regulation establishing a funding programme to support research in the fisheries sector. The regulation in question provided that the adoption by the Commission of single-case administrative decisions on the allocation of funds under the programme should be subject to a 'management committee' procedure. The Commission, supported by the European Parliament, argued that the adoption of single-case decisions on the allocation of budgetary resources fell within the scope of its exclusive power to implement the budget, in accordance with the first paragraph of Article 205 EC (now Article 317(1) TFEU), and could not be made subject to comitology procedures. The Council, on the other hand, argued that the adoption of such externally binding administrative decisions entailed the exercise of conferred powers of legislative implementation, and could therefore be made subject to a management committee procedure.

Darmon AG examined the then applicable Financial Regulation and found that the articles governing the commitment of expenditure employed terminology identical to that used in French legislation.[12] In French law, 'the power to enter into a [budgetary] commitment includes the power to adopt substantive individual decisions involving expenditure and is not limited to formal operations enabling expenditure to be recorded and effected'.[13] The Advocate-General observed that this approach prevailed in the laws of almost all the then Member States[14] and could see no reason to interpret the Financial Regulation any differently. He concluded that the adoption of single-case administrative decisions on the allocation of funds was a matter of implementation of

---

[10] ibid 411.
[11] Case 16/88 *Commission v Council*, EU:C:1989:397. For discussion of the case see Schneider (n 4) 959–80 at 964–67; J Inghelram, 'Finances of EU' in P J G Kapteyn, A M McDonnell, K J M Mortelmans, and C W A Timmermans, *The Law of the European Union and the European Communities* (4th edn Kluwer Law International 2008) 389–93; Gabriele Cipriani, 'The Responsibility for Implementing the Budget', *CEPS Working Document* 247, June 2006.
[12] Opinion of Darmon AG in Case 16/88 *Commission v Council*, EU:C:1989:280, para 28.
[13] ibid para 31.   [14] ibid paras 36–37.

the budget, an exclusive power of the Commission, not subject to comitology procedures.[15] The Court disagreed, ruling that, in Union law, budgetary commitments may not 'in themselves and irrespective of any substantive decision impose legally binding obligations on the Community *vis-à-vis* third parties'.[16] Conversely, the notion of implementation of legislation 'comprises both the drawing up of implementing rules and the application of rules to specific cases by means of acts of individual application'.[17] Thus, the adoption by the Commission of single-case administrative decisions allocating Union funds entailed the exercise of conferred powers of legislative implementation and was not (merely) a matter of budgetary implementation. Therefore, comitology procedures could be applied.

In light of this ruling, it might be concluded that the notion of implementation of the budget concerns only those internal, non-discretionary, administrative tasks, of a technical and accounting nature, necessary to mobilize appropriations corresponding to the externally binding legal commitments undertaken in the implementation of Union legal acts. In practice, however, the twin strands of legal and budgetary implementation are not so easily separated. In a related line of case law, the essence of which is now codified in Article 310(3) TFEU, the Court established that the engagement of any significant Union expenditure requires both a legal basis in a legally binding Union act and the availability of appropriations on a corresponding line of the budget.[18] At the level of implementation, the external legal commitment that engages the obligation to pay, and the internal budgetary commitment that reserves the necessary funds in the budget, are intricately linked in what Mancini AG called a scheme of 'dual implementation' of expenditure.[19] Indeed, a principal objective of the administrative reform programme, adopted following the resignation of the Santer Commission in 1999, was precisely to introduce a single line of administrative accountability, covering both the externally binding legal commitment of expenditure and the internally binding budgetary commitment, so that, as a general rule, the same Commission official who assumes a legal commitment vis-à-vis third parties should also be responsible, in his or her capacity as authorizing officer via a delegation, for assuming the internally binding budgetary commitment.[20] In this light, it is appropriate, for the purposes of this chapter, to adopt a broad interpretation of the notion of implementation of the budget as covering both the externally binding legal commitments giving rise to an obligation to pay and the corresponding internal financial and accounting operations.

---

[15] ibid para 44.   [16] Case 16/88 *Commission v Council* (n 11) para 19.   [17] ibid para 11.

[18] See eg Joined Cases 87 and 130/77, 22/83, 9 and 10/84 *Vittorio Salerno v Commission* EU:C:1985:318, paras 54–56; Case 242/87 *Commission v Council (Erasmus)* EU:C:1989:217, para 18; Case C-106/96 *UK v Commission* EU:C:1998:218, paras 26–28. Before being incorporated into the Treaties by the Treaty of Lisbon, this rule was first enshrined in Point 36 of the Interinstitutional Agreement on budgetary discipline and improvement of the budgetary procedure of 6 May 1999 ([1999] OJ C172/1), and then in Art 49 Financial Regulation 1605/2002.

[19] Case 85/86 *Opinion of Mancini AG in Commission v Board of Governors of the EIB* EU:C:1987:504, para 6. See further on the distinction between the two strands of implementation Wolfgang Schenk, 'Strukturen und Rechtsfragen der gemeinschaftlichen Leistungsverwaltung' (Mohr Siebeck 2006) 144.

[20] See Commission White Paper, 'Reforming the Commission: Part II: Action Plan', Brussels, 1 March 2000, COM(2000) 200, section XXIV(1).

After the close of the financial year, the control phase gives rise to a range of administrative tasks for European, national, and regional authorities, as well as for final beneficiaries. In particular, it is necessary to compile and verify accounts, and to draft, submit, and examine implementation reports. Auditing tasks also fall to be performed at various levels, including those of the European Court of Auditors. The resulting reports feed into the discharge procedure under Article 319 TFEU, which closes the annual cycle. That procedure entails the processing of large volumes of budgetary documentation, and the representatives in the European Parliament and the Council will frequently request additional explanations and clarifications from the pertinent administration before discharge is finally granted.

In addition to the recurring tasks performed over the course of the annual and multiannual cycles, the Commission's administration also prepares proposals for periodic revisions of the Financial Regulation. Delegated acts may also need to be drawn up and adopted, as foreseen in various acts of financial legislation, and the central administration prepares and regularly updates a plethora of guidelines, standards, and templates for use within the Union's institutions and other authorities to whom tasks of budget implementation are entrusted.

C Sources of Administrative Law

The Union's administrative law in the budgetary domain is drawn from a multiplicity of interrelated sources. At the level of primary law, Title II of Part Six TFEU (Articles 310–325) contains the fundamental provisions on the establishment and implementation of the budget.[21] The case law of the Court of Justice and general principles of Union law also play an important role. The most important legislative sources framing the administration of the budget are the Own Resources Decision, adopted on the basis of Article 311 TFEU, the MFF Regulation, adopted on the basis of Article 312(2) TFEU, and the Financial Regulation, adopted on the basis of Article 322(1) TFEU. Each of these three instruments is accompanied, in turn, by supplementary acts that regulate in greater detail the administration of Union revenue and expenditure.

The currently applicable Own Resources Decision No 2014/335[22] governs the functioning of the Union's system of revenue for the period 2014–2020.[23] It sets out the categories of own resources, fixes the own resources ceiling, and provides for correction or compensation mechanisms for certain Member States. In line with the second paragraph of Article 311 TFEU and Article 9 of the Own Resources Decision, an

---

[21] The Treaties also contain provisions on the financing of enhanced cooperations (Art 332 TFEU) and operations under the CFSP (Art 41 TEU). Protocols attached to the Treaties determine the financial consequences of the non-participation of the UK, Ireland, and Denmark in certain Union actions.

[22] Council Decision (EU, Euratom) No 2014/335 of 26 May 2014 on the system of own resources of the European Union [2014] OJ L168/105 (Own Resources Decision).

[23] The Own Resources Decision (ibid) is not adopted for a fixed time-period, but in practice a new Own Resources Decision is adopted for each MFF programming period and certain special arrangements for individual Member States laid down in Arts 2(4) and (5) Decision 2014/335 were agreed only for the period 2014–2020.

Implementing Measures Regulation No 608/2014[24] lays down the procedure for calculating and budgeting the annual budgetary balance, and sets out arrangements for controlling and supervising revenue. The detailed administrative rules and procedures, in accordance with which the Member States must make own resources available to the Commission, are laid down in what is known as the 'Making Available' Regulation No 609/2014, which is adopted on the basis of Article 322(2) TFEU.[25]

On the expenditure side, the currently applicable MFF Regulation No 1311/2013[26] sets out binding annual and overall ceilings on commitment appropriations by category of expenditure, and annual ceilings on payment appropriations for 2014–2020. It is accompanied by an inter-institutional agreement (IIA) on budgetary discipline, on cooperation in budgetary matters, and on sound financial management (the budgetary IIA).[27] IIAs have long played an important role in Union budgetary matters and, prior to the Treaty of Lisbon, the MFF was laid down in an IIA concluded between the Parliament, the Council, and the Commission.[28]

The most comprehensive source of administrative law in the budgetary sector is the Financial Regulation, which, in accordance with Article 322(1) TFEU, lays down rules on establishing and implementing the budget, presenting and auditing the accounts, and ensuring checks on the responsibility of financial actors. The Financial Regulation applies to all Union revenue and expenditure, and its Article 3 stipulates that any deviations from its terms in other acts of secondary legislation must be duly justified, thereby purporting to give it the status of a higher norm with regard to budgetary matters. The Financial Regulation has undergone several comprehensive reforms over the decades, most notably in 2002, when a new Financial Regulation incorporated many of the recommendations of the Committee of Independent Experts and of the Task Force for Administrative Reform, both of which were set up following the 1999 resignation of the Santer Commission.[29]

---

[24] Council Regulation (EU, Euratom) No 608/2014 of 26 May 2014 laying down implementing measures for the system of own resources of the European Union [2014] OJ L168/29.

[25] Council Regulation (EU, Euratom) No 609/2014 of 26 May 2014 on the methods and procedure for making available the traditional, VAT and GNI-based own resources and on the measures to meet cash requirements [2014] OJ L168/39, as amended by Council Regulation (EU, Euratom) 2016/804 of 17 May 2016 [2016] OJ L132/85 (Making Available Regulation).

[26] Council Regulation (EU, Euratom) No 1311/2013 of 2 December 2013 laying down the MFF for the years 2014–2020 [2013] OJ L347/884. On the contents of the MFF Regulation see Franck Dintilhac, 'Le nouveau cadre financier pluriannuel des dépenses de l'Union pour la période 2014–2020' (2014) 2 *Revue du droit de l'Union européenne* 315; Aymeric Potteau, 'Le cadre financier pluriannuel 2014–2020 ou l'austérité mâtinée de flexibilité' (2014) *Revue trimestrielle de droit européen* 795.

[27] Interinstitutional Agreement of 2 December 2013 between the European Parliament, the Council and the Commission on budgetary discipline, on cooperation in budgetary matters and on sound financial management [2013] OJ C373/1.

[28] See Auke Baas, '1982–2007: 25 ans d'accords interinstitutionnels budgétaires' (2007) 18 *European Business Law Review* 1283.

[29] See the Commission White Paper, 'Reforming the Commission', COM(2000) 200. For analyses of the reforms see Hofmann, Rowe, and Türk (n 9) 335–37; Schneider (n 4) 959–80 at 961–62; Paul Craig, 'A New Framework for EU Administration: The Financial Regulation 2002' (2004) *Law & Contemporary Politics* 102; Félix Craeyenest and Ilkka Saarilahti, 'Le nouveau règlement financier applicable au budget général de l'Union européenne: un maillon essential de la réforme de la Commission' (2004) 474 *Revue du Marché commun et de l'Union européenne* 30; Vincent Dussart, 'La réforme du Règlement financier communautaire: un exemple de la modernisation du droit budgétaire' (2002) 79 *Revue française de finances publiques* 141.

The currently applicable Financial Regulation No 966/2012[30] was the first to be enacted by the Parliament and Council acting jointly, pursuant to the ordinary legislative procedure, and it has already been subject to a number of targeted revisions.[31] More detailed implementing rules of a technical nature are laid down in the Financial Regulation's Rules of Application (RAP), which now take the form of a delegated act, adopted by the Commission under Article 290(1) TFEU.[32] However, in late-2016, the Commission presented a legislative proposal for a new Financial Regulation which, if adopted, would entail the abolition of the RAP. Many provisions of the current RAP would then be incorporated into a new Financial Regulation, which would henceforth function as a 'single rulebook' for the administration of the budget.[33]

In addition to these horizontally applicable financial rules, the sectoral legislative acts establishing Union funding programmes in individual policy areas—which function as the legal bases for sectoral programme expenditure for the purposes of Article 310(3) TFEU—lay down specific rules for the implementation of expenditure through those programmes. Common financial rules are applied across several funding programmes in the sectors of research,[34] structural and investment funds,[35] and external financing instruments.[36]

---

[30] Regulation (EU, Euratom) No 966/2012 of the European Parliament and of the Council of 25 October 2012 on the financial rules applicable to the general budget of the Union and repealing Council Regulation (EC, Euratom) No 1605/2002 [2012] OJ L298/1.

[31] See Regulation (EU, Euratom) No 547/2014 of the European Parliament and of the Council of 15 May 2014 amending Regulation (EU, Euratom) No 966/2012 on the financial rules applicable to the general budget of the Union [2014] OJ L163/18; Regulation (EU, Euratom) No 1142/2014 of the European Parliament and of the Council of 22 October 2014 amending Regulation (EU, Euratom) No 966/2012 as regards the financing of European political parties [2014] OJ L317/28; and Regulation (EU, Euratom) 2015/1929 of the European Parliament and of the Council of 28 October 2015 amending Regulation (EU, Euratom) No 966/2012 on the financial rules applicable to the general budget of the Union [2015] OJ L286/1.

[32] Delegated Regulation (EU) No 1268/2012 of 29 October 2012 on the rules of application of Regulation (EU, Euratom) No 966/2012 of the European Parliament and of the Council on the financial rules applicable to the general budget of the Union [2012] OJ L362/1.

[33] Proposal for a Regulation of the European Parliament and of the Council on the financial rules applicable to the general budget of the Union and amending a series of regulations, COM(2016) 605, Brussels, 14 September 2016.

[34] Regulation (EU) No 1290/2013 of the European Parliament and of the Council of 11 December 2013 laying down the rules for participation and dissemination in Horizon 2020: the Framework Programme for Research and Innovation (2014–20) and repealing Regulation (EC) No 1906/2006 [2013] OJ L347/81.

[35] Regulation (EU) No 1303/2013 of the European Parliament and of the Council of 17 December 2013 laying down common provisions on the European Regional Development Fund, the European Social Fund, the Cohesion Fund, the European Agricultural Fund for Rural Development and the European Maritime and Fisheries Fund and laying down general provisions on the European Regional Development Fund, the European Social Fund, the Cohesion Fund and the European Maritime and Fisheries Fund and repealing Council Regulation (EC) No 1083/2006 [2013] OJ L347/320. See, further, the chapter by Katerina Pantazatou in this book.

[36] Regulation (EU) No 236/2014 of the European Parliament and of the Council of 11 March 2014 laying down common rules and procedures for the implementation of the Union's instruments for financing external action [2014] OJ L77/95. See, further, the chapter by Phillip Dann in this book.

D Underlying Legal Principles

Several classical principles of budgetary law, inspired by the laws of the Member States, have been incorporated into Union law, either through the Treaties or the Financial Regulation, as have certain principles more commonly found in the rules of traditional international organizations, such as the principle of equilibrium. Article 6 Financial Regulation on 'Respect for budgetary principles' provides that '[t]he budget shall be established and implemented in accordance with the principles of unity, budgetary accuracy, annuality, equilibrium, unit of account, universality, specification, sound financial management ... and transparency'. Certain general principles of Union law, such as legal certainty, proportionality, and equal treatment, also play an important role in the law governing the disbursement of Union funds. An examination of all the budgetary principles is beyond the scope of this chapter,[37] but a limited number of particular relevance for the administration of the budget do merit closer consideration.

In the first instance, the principle of budgetary *annuality* was one of the fundamental principles of the systems of public finance developed in England and France from the 17th century onwards, and is common to the modern Member States of the Union. In Union law, the appropriations in the budget are authorized for an annual period running from 1 January to 31 December.[38] The choice of the calendar year as the Union's financial year had a spillover effect at national level, with several Member States deciding to shift to the calendar year for domestic budgetary purposes after acceding to the Union, thus facilitating a more coherent administration of funds under shared management.[39] An important derogation from the principle of annuality in the Union context lies in the distinction between commitment and payment appropriations. In accordance with the Union's financial rules, legal commitments for multiannual actions assumed in one financial year may remain valid until the corresponding payments are made in a later financial year,[40] thus facilitating the implementation of large-scale projects over several years.

The principle of *specification* finds its basis in Union law in Article 316 TFEU, which provides that appropriations in the budget are to be 'classified under different chapters which group items of expenditure according to their nature or purpose'.[41] Appropriations must be assigned to specified objectives and the officials responsible

---

[37] For detailed presentations of the budgetary principles see Desmoulin, *Droit budgétaire de l'Union européenne* (n 2) ch 5; European Commission, *European Union Public Finance* (5th edn Office for Official Publications 2014) ch 11; Inghelram, 'Finances of EU' (n 11) 369–77; Stéphane Saurel, *Le budget de l'Union européenne* (La documentation française 2010) ch 1; Daniel Strasser, *The Finances of Europe* (Office for Official Publications 1992) ch 3.

[38] See Arts 310(2) and 313 TFEU and Art 9 Financial Regulation 966/2012 (n 30).

[39] See Desmoulin, *Droit budgétaire de l'Union européenne* (n 2) 20–21. Today, only the UK retains a different financial year, running from 1 April to 31 March. As far as the Eurozone is concerned, Art 4 of Regulation (EU) No 473/2013 of the European Parliament and of the Council of 21 May 2013 on common provisions for monitoring and assessing draft budgetary plans and ensuring the correction of excessive deficit of the Member States in the euro area ([2013] OJ L140/11) now lays down a 'Common budgetary timeline' to be applied within the Member States for the purposes of the European Semester process.

[40] Art 10 Financial Regulation 966/2012 (n 30).

[41] See also Arts 24–29 Financial Regulation 966/2012 (n 30).

for implementing expenditure may use appropriations only for the objectives corresponding to the budget line in which they are entered. Since the turn of the millennium, the Union's budget has been structured according to an activity-based nomenclature, so that appropriations are organized according to policy activities.[42] This facilitates an alignment of the budgetary and policy implementation cycles, with the budget intended to present a clear overview of what policy activities are being pursued, and of the budgetary resources and personnel allocated to them. The adoption of an activity-based budget nomenclature was one element of a broader shift to activity-based management within the Commission, as initially foreseen in the 2000 White Paper on Reforming the Commission.[43]

The principle of *budgetary transparency* was introduced as part of the major overhaul of the Financial Regulation in 2002, with Article 34(1) Financial Regulation now requiring that the budget 'shall be established and implemented and the accounts presented in accordance with the principle of transparency'. This principle may be understood as a specific application, within the budgetary domain, of the general principle of transparency.[44] In accordance with this principle, the Commission is obliged to publish the Union's accounts and various reports concerning its management of the budget.[45] Since 2016, the Commission has adopted the practice of publishing a single annual 'Integrated Financial Reporting Package', consisting of the Annual Management and Performance Report[46] (which incorporates in one text both the Evaluation Report required under Article 318 TFEU and the Synthesis Report required by Article 66(9) Financial Regulation), the Financial Report,[47] a Communication on the Protection of the EU budget,[48] and the Annual Accounts.[49]

The principle of transparency also underpins the requirement for authorities entrusted with the management of Union funds to *publish information* on the recipients of those funds. The Court of Justice has taken the view that 'in a democratic society, taxpayers and public opinion generally have the right to be kept informed of the use of public revenues'.[50] Moreover, according to the Court, such publication 'reinforces public control of the use to which that money is put and contributes to the best use of public funds'.[51] However, the Court has also stressed that the principle of proportionality and the data protection rights of the recipients of public funding must

---

[42] For a detailed assessment of activity-based budgeting in the Union see Guillaume Caveroc, *Budgetierungsmethode der EU* (VDM Verlag Dr Müller 2007).

[43] See 'White Paper on Reforming the Commission: Part II: Action Plan' (n 20) ch III.

[44] On the general principle see Hofmann, Rowe, and Türk (n 9) 170–72.

[45] Art 34(2) Financial Regulation 966/2012 (n 30).

[46] Report from the Commission to the European Parliament, the Council and the Court of Auditors, '2015 Annual Management and Performance Report for the EU Budget', Strasbourg, 5 July 2016, COM(2016) 446.

[47] See http://ec.europa.eu/budget/financialreport/2015/.

[48] Communication from the Commission to the European Parliament, the Council and the Court of Auditors, 'Protection of the EU budget to end 2015', Brussels, 18 July 2016, COM(2016) 486.

[49] Communication from the Commission to the European Parliament, the Council and the Court of Auditors, 'Consolidated annual accounts of the European Union: Financial Year 2015', Brussels, 11 July 2016, COM(2016) 475.

[50] Joined Cases C-465, C-138/01, and C-139/01 *Österreichischer Rundfunk* EU:C:2003:294, para 85.

[51] Joined Cases C-92/09 and C-93/09 *Volker und Markus Schecke GbR and Hartmut Eifert v Land Hessen* EU:C:2009:284, para 75.

be respected when determining the extent of the information (required) to be published.[52] For its part, the Commission makes information on recipients of directly managed funds available through its Financial Transparency System.[53]

Finally, *sound financial management* is a core principle of the Union's budgetary administrative law. Article 310(5) TFEU requires the Union institutions and the Member States to ensure that the budget is implemented in accordance with this principle,[54] and the Financial Regulation expressly extends its application to situations of indirect management.[55] The principle also has a particular significance for the work of the Court of Auditors, whose task under Article 287(2) TFEU is not only to examine whether revenue and expenditure is lawful and regular, but also 'whether the financial management has been sound'. Article 30(1) Financial Regulation explains that sound financial management implies the use of appropriations 'in accordance with the principles of economy, efficiency and effectiveness'. These *three principles* of sound financial management are commonly referred to as the '3Es'. The principle of economy requires 'that the resources used by the institution in the pursuit of its activities shall be made available in due time, in appropriate quantity and quality and at the best price', the principle of efficiency 'concerns the best relationship between resources employed and results achieved', and the principle of effectiveness 'concerns the attainment of the specific objectives set and the achievement of the intended results'.[56] Article 30(3) Financial Regulation goes on to require that '[s]pecific, measurable, achievable, relevant and timed objectives shall be set for all sectors of activity covered by the budget' and the attainment of those objectives 'shall be monitored by performance indicators for each activity'. The principle of sound financial management thus serves as an essential conceptual link between the implementation of the Union's budget and the implementation of Union policies. It requires that the human and financial resources allocated to a policy objective are best used to achieve the desired policy outcome and that, in turn, policies are implemented having due regard to the economical, efficient, and effective use of the allocated resources.

E Organization, Institutions, and Structures

Article 317(1) TFEU provides that the Commission shall implement the budget on its own responsibility, and in cooperation with the Member States. The words 'in cooperation with the Member States' were added by the Treaty of Lisbon and might be considered to introduce an element of ambiguity with regard to the traditional view that the Commission is solely responsible for implementing the budget.[57] However,

---

[52] Regarding the publication of information on beneficiaries of Union funds see Joined Cases C-92/09 and C-93/09 *Volker und Markus Schecke GbR and Hartmut Eifert v Land Hessen* EU:C:2009:284. The need to respect data protection requirements is now expressly recalled in Art 35 Financial Regulation 966/2012 (n 30). See also Arts 21 and 22 Delegated Regulation 1268/2012 (n 32).

[53] See http://ec.europa.eu/budget/fts.

[54] This obligation on the Commission and the Member States is repeated in the first paragraph of Art 317 TFEU. See also Part III of the budgetary IIA of 2 December 2013.

[55] Art 60 Financial Regulation 966/2012 (n 30).   [56] ibid Art 30(2).

[57] On the historical evolution and meaning of this article see Cipriani, 'The Responsibility for Implementing the Budget' (n 11). See also Schneider (n 4) 959–80 at 964–67. Prior to Lisbon, the General Court stated clearly that the Commission remains responsible for the implementation of the entire

the corresponding provisions of the Financial Regulation continue to be based on the understanding that the Commission retains sole responsibility for implementation of the budget, although it may delegate pertinent tasks to other entities.[58] Moreover, Article 319(1) TFEU continues to make reference to a grant of discharge to the Commission alone. In this light, the words 'in cooperation with the Member States' may be understood as providing for a specific application, within the budgetary domain, of the general duty of mutual sincere cooperation.[59]

In practice, the Union's relatively small central administration relies to a great extent on the cooperation of national authorities and other entities entrusted with budget implementation tasks, both for the collection of Union revenue and for the incurring of expenditure. On the revenue side, responsibility for collecting the traditional own resources (TOR), consisting mainly of customs duties and sugar levies,[60] lies with the authorities of the Member States, acting under the supervision of the Commission.[61] Each Member State is required to inform the Commission of the national authorities responsible for establishing, collecting, making available, and controlling own resources, as well as the applicable national legal rules.[62] The treasury or other competent body of each Member State must also create a separate account in the name of the Commission, broken down by type of resources, to which the own resources due to the Union will be credited.[63]

On the expenditure side, the budget may be implemented through three different management modes, namely direct, shared, and indirect management.[64] Funds may be disbursed under direct management by Commission Directorates-General, staff of Union Delegations to whom powers of implementation have been delegated, or through the executive agencies.[65] The possibility of establishing executive agencies to implement specific Union programmes or projects, on behalf of the Commission and under its responsibility, was introduced by the 2002 Financial Regulation in

---

budget, regardless of the management mode employed. See Case T-308/05 *Italian Republic v Commission* EU:T:2007:382, para 109.

[58] Arts 58–63 Financial Regulation 966/2012 (n 30).

[59] With reference to the corresponding wording of the Treaty establishing a Constitution for Europe see Cipriani, 'The Responsibility for Implementing the Budget' (n 11) 2.

[60] Art 2(1)(a) Own Resources Decision 2014/335(n 22).   [61] ibid Art 8.

[62] Art 4 Making Available Regulation 609/2014 (n 25).

[63] ibid Arts 6(1) and 9(1). For a detailed explanation of the organizational and administrative adaptations that new Member States must make in the domain of own resources see 'Updated check-list of administrative conditions in the area of the European Union's own resources', European Commission DG BUDG, Brussels, 21 January 2011.

[64] The Commission's Financial Regulation proposal of 2016 suggests to rename the three modes as direct, shared and indirect 'implementation'. See Proposal for a Regulation of the European Parliament and of the Council on the financial rules applicable to the general budget of the Union and amending a series of regulations, COM(2016) 605, Brussels, 14 September 2016, draft Art 121. The old Financial Regulation 1605/2002 provided for five management modes. Under the Financial Regulation 966/2012 (n 30), decentralized management with third countries and joint management with international organizations now fall under indirect management. On the evolution and meaning of these various concepts see Jacques Ziller, 'Le concepts d'administration directe, d'administration indirecte et de coadministration et les fondements du droit administratif européen' and Claudio Franchini, 'Les notions d'administration indirecte et de coadministration' in Jean-Bernard Auby and Jacqueline Dutheil de la Rochère (eds), *Traité de droit administratif européen* (2nd edn, Éditions Bruylant 2014) 326–55.

[65] Art 58(1)(a) Financial Regulation 966/2012 (n 30).

response to the criticisms made by the Committee of Independent Experts of the previous system for outsourcing implementation of centrally managed programmes to technical assistance offices.[66] Executive agencies are established by a decision of the Commission for a limited timeframe, their operation being governed by a Council Regulation laying down the Statute for executive agencies.[67]

When the budget is implemented under shared management, payments to final beneficiaries are made by the designated national authorities, the Commission later reimbursing the eligible costs incurred. The sectoral legislation establishing Union funding programmes sets out the organizational requirements to be satisfied by the Member States, such as the need to designate management and certifying authorities for the implementation of European Structural and Investment Funds, or paying agencies and certification bodies under the Common Agricultural Policy.[68] Similarly, payments made by designated entrusted entities to final beneficiaries under indirect management are reimbursed in accordance with the terms of the delegation agreement. Entities commonly entrusted with the management of Union funds under indirect management include third countries, international organizations, the European Investment Bank (EIB), and the decentralized agencies.[69] Budget implementation tasks may be entrusted to private law entities only in very limited circumstances, and subject to strict conditions.[70]

The central hub in the system for administering Union revenue and expenditure is the Commission's Directorate General for Budgets (DG BUDG), which describes itself as 'the central service driving the execution of the full budgetary cycle, from the preparation of the draft budget to its implementation and the discharge by the European Parliament'.[71] Within the Juncker Commission, DG BUDG has around five hundred staff members, divided into five directorates. Directorates A and B are responsible, respectively, for expenditure and for own resources and financial planning. Directorate C is responsible for budget execution and includes units responsible for central treasury management, central accounting, and the recovery of debts. Directorate D is the Central Financial Service, playing a key role in advising all Commission services on matters relating to financial rules, procedures, and control systems. Finally, Directorate R is responsible for resources, including information and communication, and the implementation of financial information systems.

---

[66] See Hofmann, Rowe, and Türk (n 9) 339–44.

[67] Council Regulation (EC) No 58/2003 of 19 December 2002 laying down the statute for executive agencies to be entrusted with certain tasks in the management of Community programmes [2003] OJ L11/1. Currently, six executive agencies are entrusted with tasks relating to the implementation of MFF funding programmes for the period 2014–2020.

[68] For more comprehensive analyses of shared management see Hofmann, Rowe, and Türk (n 9) 347–59; Craig, *EU Administrative Law* (n 6) ch 4.

[69] Art 58(1)(c) Financial Regulation 966/2012 (n 30). On indirect management through agencies see Edoardo Chiti, 'Les agences, l'administration indirecte et la coadministration' in Auby and Dutheil de la Rochère (eds), *Traité de droit administratif européen* (n 64) 357–69.

[70] The delegation of tasks to private entities is governed by Art 63(2) Financial Regulation 966/2012 (n 30). See further Hofmann, Rowe, and Türk (n 9) 250–51.

[71] See presentation of the DG at http://ec.europa.eu/dgs/budget/mission/index_en.htm. On the evolving role of DG BUDG as central manager of the budget see K H Goetz and R Patz, 'Pressurised Budgets and the European Commission: Towards a More Centralized EU Budget Administration? (2016) *Journal of European Public Policy* 1038.

The Commission confers on other Union 'institutions' the requisite powers for the implementation of their sections of the budget.[72] In order to ensure a clear line of accountability in the management of the budget, the 2002 Financial Regulation introduced new provisions that impact upon the internal organization of those institutions.[73] In accordance with Article 65 Financial Regulation, each institution performs the role and duties of authorizing officer in respect of its own section of the budget, but delegates such duties internally to staff at an appropriate level. The authorizing officer is responsible for implementing revenue and expenditure in accordance with the principle of sound financial management, and for ensuring compliance with the requirements of legality and regularity.[74] Within the Commission, authorizing officer powers are delegated to Directors-General and certain other officials specified in the internal rules, who may then sub-delegate further, to the extent that such internal rules so allow.[75]

Each institution must also appoint an accounting officer, responsible for properly implementing payments, collecting revenue, recovering amounts established as being receivable, preparing and presenting the accounts, laying down the accounting procedures, validating the accounting systems, and treasury management.[76] The duties of the authorizing officer (under delegation) and the accounting officer must be segregated, and are mutually exclusive.[77] Furthermore, each institution must also establish an internal auditing function, to be performed in compliance with the relevant international standards.[78] The internal auditor may be neither authorizing officer by delegation nor accounting officer,[79] and must be 'totally independent in the performance of his or her duties'.[80] Within the Commission, the Internal Auditor is the Director-General of the Internal Audit Service.[81]

Budgetary control and the fight against fraud affecting the Union's finances have been fertile grounds for institutional innovation over the years, with a clear trend towards strengthening the central institutional framework. Most notably, the Court of Auditors was established by the Treaty of Brussels in 1975, at the time of the transition to the system of own resources, and it is now one of the Union institutions listed

---

[72] Art 55 Financial Regulation 966/2012 (n 30). It should be noted that the notion of 'institution' has a different meaning for the purposes Financial Regulation than it does under Art 13(1) TEU, with Art 2(b) of Financial Regulation 966/2012 (n 30) specifying that the Economic and Social Committee, the Committee of the Regions, the Ombudsman, the Data Protection Supervisor and the External Action Service are all 'institutions' for the purposes Financial Regulation, while the European Central Bank is not to be considered an institution.

[73] See Hofmann, Rowe, and Türk (n 9) ch 13.

[74] Art 66(1) Financial Regulation 966/2012 (n 30).

[75] For the scheme of internal delegations in the Commission see the Commission's 2016 Internal Rules, laid down by Commission Decision C(2016) 769 on the Internal Rules on the implementation of the general budget of the European Union (European Commission section) for the attention of the Commission departments, Brussels, 12 February 2016, as amended.

[76] Art 68(1) Financial Regulation 966/2012 (n 30).   [77] ibid Art 64(1).   [78] ibid Art 98(1).

[79] ibid.

[80] ibid Art 100(1). The Court of Justice has ruled that the notion of functional independence of financial actors does not require that the official holds any particular grade, but merely that 'he is not subordinate to any superior in the actual performance of his duties'. See Case 8/69 *Theodorus Mulders v Commission* EU:C:1969:69, para 15.

[81] See http://ec.europa.eu/dgs/internal_audit/index_en.htm.

in Article 13 TEU. Just as the Court of Auditors developed out of the earlier Audit Board of the European Communities,[82] so the European Anti-fraud Office (OLAF) was established in 1999 as a more functionally autonomous successor to the earlier Anti-Fraud Coordination Unit (UCLAF) within the Commission.[83] More recently, the Commission presented a proposal for the establishment of a European Public Prosecutor's Office (EPPO), as foreseen in Article 86(1) TFEU, which would build on the existing structures of OLAF and Eurojust.[84]

F Administrative Procedures

1 Preparation of the budget

The draft general budget is prepared within the broader framework of the Commission's Strategic Planning and Programming (SPP) cycle, thereby facilitating the allocation of resources in alignment with the Union's policy priorities.[85] At administrative level, the preparation of the draft budget for the year *n* begins around December of the year *n-2*, when the Director-General of DG BUDG sends a 'Budgetary Circular' to the Directors-General of the other DGs. This circular describes the overall economic and budgetary context and invites the DGs to submit their estimates of staff needs, and any proposed changes to the existing multiannual programming for their sector, by a specified date.[86] Once it has gathered together the requests of all the DGs, DG BUDG organizes inter-departmental hearings on the overall allocation of resources in the early part of the year *n-1*. A final round of negotiations takes place at the level of Directors-General in March or April and, where necessary, any particularly contentious matters may be referred to the College of Commissioners. As far as revenue is concerned, the Commission's forecasts will be based on its own estimates of TOR, and estimates of the Value Added Tax (VAT) and Gross National Income (GNI) bases supplied by the competent authorities of the Member States. These estimates are examined at a spring meeting of the Advisory Committee on Own Resources.[87]

During the same period, the Commission receives the budgetary estimates of the other Union institutions, as foreseen in Article 314(1) TFEU. When finalizing its draft budget, the Commission takes account of the budgetary 'Guidelines' resolutions

---

[82] On the functioning of this precursor to the Court of Auditors see Jean-Charles Leygues, 'La Commission de contrôle des Communautés européennes' (1974) 172 *Revue du Marché commun* 59.

[83] Art 2(1) of Commission Decision 1999/352/EC, ECSC, Euratom of 28 April 1999 establishing the European Anti-Fraud Office (OLAF) [1999] OJ L136/20. The Decision establishing OLAF was subsequently amended by Commission Decision 2013/478/EU of 27 September 2013 [2015] OJ L257/19, and by Commission Decision (EU) 2015/512 of 25 March 2015 [2015] OJ L81/4. On OLAF see Hofmann, Rowe, and Türk (n 9) 734–39.

[84] Proposal for a Council Regulation on the establishment of the European Public Prosecutor's Office of 17 July 2013, COM(2013) 534 final. See also Jan Inghelram, *Legal and institutional aspects of the European Anti-Fraud Office (OLAF): an analysis with a look forward to a European Public Prosecutor's Office* (Europa Law 2011).

[85] See Hofmann, Rowe, and Türk (n 9) 31–32.

[86] See European Commission, *European Union Public Finance* (n 37) 180.

[87] Established on the basis of Art 7(1) Own Resources Implementing Regulation 608/2014.

adopted by the European Parliament[88] and the Council,[89] as well as the views expressed by the representatives of those institutions in the Spring Budgetary Trilogue, as provided for in Point 2 of the Annex to the budgetary IIA. The Commission usually presents its Statement of Estimates, together with the Programme Statements and all the supporting documents required under Article 38 of the Financial Regulation, in April or May, with the formal adoption of the draft budget in all official languages following later in May or June.[90] The Commission may subsequently amend its draft budget and, in practice, it always adopts a Letter of Amendment in the Autumn to incorporate updated forecasts for own resources and for the agricultural sector.[91]

The Commission takes part in the budgetary Conciliation Committee (composed of equal representation of the Council and the Parliament), as foreseen in the second paragraph of Article 314(5) TFEU, and takes 'all necessary initiatives' to facilitate an agreement at political level between the European Parliament and the Council. Once an agreement has been reached on the annual budget on the political level, the services of all three institutions work together, in accordance with points 23–25 of the annex to the budgetary IIA, to translate the outcome of the negotiations into the formal text to be adopted as the general budget of the Union.

2 Collection of revenue

The procedures for making revenue available to the Union differ in respect of the TOR, on the one hand, and the GNI and VAT-based own resources, on the other. The Own Resources Decision provides that the TOR 'shall be collected by the Member States in accordance with the national provisions imposed by law, regulation or administrative action, which shall, where appropriate, be adapted to meet the requirements of Union rules'.[92] The Union's entitlement to TOR is established as soon as the conditions provided for by the relevant regulations have been met.[93] Entitlements established are entered in the Commission's account by the competent national authorities at the latest on the first working day after the nineteenth day of the second month following the month during which the entitlement was established.[94] The Member States are entitled to retain 20 per cent of the revenue to cover collection costs.[95]

With regard to the GNI and VAT-based resources, the Member States are required to credit to the Commission's account one-twelfth of the annual amount entered in the budget on the first working day of each month.[96] The Commission specifies the

---

[88] See eg European Parliament resolution of 15 March 2017 on general guidelines for the preparation of the 2018 budget, section III: Commission, P8_TA(2017)0085.

[89] See eg Council Budget Guidelines for 2018, Brussels, 7 February 2017, Council Document No 5877/17.

[90] See eg Draft General Budget of the European Union for the financial year 2017, Brussels, 18 July 2016, COM(2016) 300.

[91] See eg Letter of amendment No 1 to the draft general budget for the financial year 2017 (COM(2016) 679).

[92] Art 8(1) Own Resources Decision 2014/335 (n 22).

[93] Art 2(1) Making Available Regulation 609/2014 (n 25).　　[94] ibid Art 6(3).

[95] Art 2(3) Own Resources Decision 2014/335 (n 22).

[96] Art 10a(1) Making Available Regulation 609/2014 (n 25).

precise amounts due in a monthly 'call for resources' that it addresses to the Member States. The annual amounts of GNI and VAT-based resources due are calculated on the basis of estimates of the national GNI and VAT-own-resources bases supplied by the national statistical agencies of the Member States.[97] These estimates are verified by Eurostat and, in the case of GNI, a committee of Member State representatives, known as the GNI Committee.[98]

After the close of the financial year, the definitive statistics underlying the calculation of the national GNI and VAT-resources bases will become known, and the balance between what each Member State actually paid in the previous year (on the basis of the estimates), and what it should have paid (on the basis of the definitive statistics), will be calculated. A corresponding adjustment of the amounts due from each Member State is then applied. Corrections to, or adjustments of, the national GNI statistics for previous financial years may also give rise to adjustments in the own-resources contributions of individual Member States. Traditionally, such adjustments and corrections were applied in the call for resources for the month of December of the subsequent financial year. Following a controversy surrounding a particularly large GNI adjustment for the UK in December 2014, however, the rules were amended to allow for greater flexibility in the timing of payments.[99]

Within the Commission, it is the role of the authorizing officer to establish the precise amounts receivable, by verifying that a debt exists, and the condition under which it is due. The authorizing officer issues a recovery order,[100] instructing the accounting officer to recover the amount established,[101] and a debit note is drawn up.[102] The establishment of the amount receivable must be based on supporting documents certifying the Union's entitlement.[103] The national authorities are obliged to comply with the Commission's payment orders within three working days of receipt;[104] any delay in making payments will give rise to late payment interest.[105] Upon the recovery of the amounts receivable, the accounting officer makes an entry in the Union's accounts,

---

[97] The VAT resources base is calculated in conformity with Council Regulation (EEC, Euratom) No 1553/89 of 29 May 1989 on the definitive uniform arrangements for the collection of own resources accruing from value added tax [1989] OJ L155/9. Calculation of the GNI base is governed by Council Directive 89/130/EEC, Euratom of 13 February 1989 on the harmonisation of the compilation of gross national product at market prices [1989] OJ L49/26 and Council Regulation (EC, Euratom) No 1287/2003 of 15 July 2003 on the harmonisation of gross national income at market prices (GNI Regulation) [2003] OJ L181/1.

[98] Provided for in Art 4 of Council Regulation (EC, Euratom) No 1287/2003 of 15 July 2003 on the harmonisation of gross national income at market prices (GNI Regulation) [2003] OJ L181/1.

[99] See the new Arts 10, 10a, and 10b introduced by Council Regulation (EU, Euratom) 2016/804 of 17 May 2016 of 17 May 2016 amending Regulation (EU, Euratom) No 609/2014 on the methods and procedure for making available the traditional, VAT and GNI-based own resources and on the measures to meet cash requirements [2016] OJ L132/85.

[100] Arts 77 and 78 Financial Regulation 966/2012 (n 30) and Art 79 Delegated Regulation 1268/2012 (n 32).

[101] Art 80(2) Delegated Regulation 1268/2012 (n 32).

[102] Art 78(2) Financial Regulation 966/2012 (n 30).

[103] Art 82(1) Delegated Regulation 1268/2012 (n 32).

[104] Art 15(1) Making Available Regulation 609/2014 (n 25).

[105] ibid Art 12. Failure to make own resources available on time may also give rise to an infringement action against the Member State concerned. See eg Case C-423/08 *Commission v Italy* EU:C:2010:347; Case C-442/08 *Commission v Germany* EU:C:2010:390.

and informs the authorizing officer responsible.[106] The Commission is entitled to draw on the sums credited to its own resources accounts to the extent necessary to cover the cash resource requirements arising out of its implementation of the budget.[107]

3 Expenditure operations

The incurring of Union expenditure follows the four classical phases of commitment, validation, authorization, and payment.[108] Before operational expenditure may be committed, however, Article 84 Financial Regulation requires the competent institution to adopt a 'financing decision' including a number of elements of information: the policy objective of the expenditure; a description of the actions to be financed; an indication of the amount allocated to each action; the expected results; the method of implementation; and an indicative implementation timetable.[109]

In practice, Commission implementing decisions laying down annual work programmes in individual policy sectors will often contain all the information necessary for performing the dual function both of laying down a framework for the administrative implementation of a programme, in conformity with the relevant basic act, and of establishing a financing decision, for the purposes of Article 84 Financial Regulation.[110] Under shared management, the applicable sectoral legislation will frequently indicate the instruments which may perform the function of a financing decision in the sector concerned. For example, the second paragraph of Article 76 Common Provisions Regulation[111] stipulates that the decision of the Commission adopting an operational programme shall constitute the financing decision for the purposes of Article 84 Financial Regulation. Under indirect management, a financing decision may, for example, take the form of a Commission Action Plan in external relations.[112] The Commission's 2016 proposal for a new Financial Regulation proposes to generalize this practice of adopting a single instrument to serve a dual implementation purpose.[113]

Once a financing decision has been adopted, the competent authorizing officer (under delegation) may then proceed to launch calls for proposals, or calls for tender, with a view to adopting single-case administrative decisions on the allocation of funds. In line with the case law of the Court of Justice,[114] the Financial Regulation now expressly provides that the *commitment of expenditure* entails two distinct operations, namely the engagement of a budgetary commitment and a legal commitment.[115] Following the 2002 reform of the Financial Regulation, the budgetary commitment and the legal commitment must, as a general rule, be adopted by the same authorizing

---

[106] Art 86 Delegated Regulation 1268/2012 (n 32).
[107] Art 14 Making Available Regulation 609/2014 (n 25).
[108] Art 84(1) Financial Regulation 966/2012 (n 30).   [109] ibid Art 84(3).
[110] Art 94(3) Delegated Regulation 1268/2012 (n 32).
[111] Regulation (EU) No 1303/2013 (n 35).
[112] See eg Recitals 4 and 5 of Regulation (EU) No 236/2014 (n 36).
[113] See Proposal for a Regulation of the European Parliament and of the Council on the financial rules applicable to the general budget of the Union and amending a series of regulations, COM(2016) 605, Brussels, 14 September 2016, draft Art 108(2).
[114] See section B above.   [115] Art 85 Financial Regulation 966/2012 (n 30).

officer,[116] thus ensuring that a single official is held accountable for both the externally binding legal act that gives rise to an obligation to pay, and the internally binding reservation of appropriations in the budget. With the exception of crisis situations, the authorizing officer must make a budgetary commitment *before* entering into a legal commitment with third parties.[117]

The *validation of expenditure* is the act by which the authorizing officer verifies the existence of the creditor's entitlement, determines or verifies the reality and the amount of the claim, and verifies the conditions according to which the payment is due.[118] The validation is based on supporting documents justifying the payment.[119] The authorizing officer expresses his validation decision by signing a 'passed for payment' voucher (which would be replaced by an electronic signature under the Commission's 2016 proposal for a new Financial Regulation).[120] Validation is followed by the *authorization stage*, in which the authorizing officer instructs the accounting officer to pay the amount that has been validated.[121] The instruction is given by means of a 'payment order'. Responsibility for *executing the payment* then lies with the accounting officer. Payments may be made in full, or through pre-financing, interim, or final instalments.[122] Payment must be made within ninety, sixty or thirty calendar days, depending on the nature of the agreement, contract, or decision concerned.[123] In the event of late payment, creditors—other than Member States—are entitled to default interest.[124]

4 Budgetary control

The procedures for presentation of the accounts, financial reporting, auditing, and the grant of discharge again follow recurring annual cycles. These procedures are discussed in more detail in the section on budgetary control and supervision (section I, below).

5 Information management

Sectoral legislative acts governing the administration of Union funds may lay down sector-specific rules on the management of financial information, including on the retention of documents. However, the RAP also lays down generally applicable rules binding on the financial actors responsible for implementing the budget. For example, the authorizing officer by delegation is required to 'set up paper based or electronic systems for the keeping of original supporting documents relating to and subsequent to budget implementation and budget implementation measures'.[125] As a general rule,

---

[116] ibid Art 85(1), third paragraph. The limited derogations from the rule are set out in Art 97 of the Delegated Regulation 1268/2012 (n 32).

[117] Art 86(1) Financial Regulation 966/2012 (n 30).   [118] ibid Art 88.

[119] Art 100(1) Delegated Regulation 1268/2012 (n 32).

[120] Proposal for a Regulation of the European Parliament and of the Council on the financial rules applicable to the general budget of the Union and amending a series of regulations, COM(2016) 605, Brussels, 14 September 2016, draft Art 109(3).

[121] Art 89(1) Financial Regulation 966/2012 (n 30).   [122] ibid Art 90(1).

[123] ibid Art 92(1).   [124] ibid Art 92(5).

[125] Art 48 1st para Delegated Regulation 1268/2012 (n 32).

such documents must be kept for at least five years from the date of budgetary discharge.[126] Personal data contained in supporting documents should be deleted where those data are not necessary for budgetary discharge, control, and audit purposes.[127] The accounting officer is subject to similar obligations.[128] The own resources rules impose obligations on Member States with regard to the retention of documents concerning own resources.[129] The Commission is also charged with maintaining and managing certain databases, notably for the purposes of information exchange aimed at protecting the financial interests of the Union.[130]

G Administrative Acts and Measures

1 Agenda-setting/preparatory measures

The Commission exercises considerable agenda-setting influence, in the multiannual context through its proposals for the MFF legislative package, and in the annual context through its draft annual budget. The annual budget is the instrument which, for each financial year, both forecasts and authorizes all revenue and expenditure considered necessary for the Union.[131] Article 314(1) TFEU provides that the budget is adopted in accordance with a special legislative procedure, but the budget is not, in itself, a legislative act. In the *Budget Signature* case,[132] the Court of Justice ruled that the budget 'is essentially an accounting document' which 'is annexed to the act by which the President *[of the Parliament]* declares, on the basis of Article 314(9) TFEU, that the budget has been definitively adopted'.[133]

However, the figures indicated in this accounting document must be aligned with the Union's policy priorities for the financial year in question. In that respect, the Financial Regulation requires that the Commission's draft budget be accompanied by financial programming that provides 'forecasts of the budgetary implications of legislation in force and pending legislative proposals'.[134] The draft budget must also be accompanied by a whole plethora of working documents, intended to allow the elected representatives in the European Parliament and the Council to make informed choices regarding the final allocation of resources.[135]

2 Subordinate legislation

The Financial Regulation grants extensive powers to the Commission to set out more detailed rules on the administration of the budget in the delegated act laying down the RAP.[136] In total, more than one hundred articles of the currently applicable Financial Regulation empower the Commission to lay down more detailed rules. Across some

---

[126] ibid Art 48(d) Delegated Regulation 1268/2012 (n 32).   [127] ibid Art 48 3rd para.
[128] ibid Art 64 Delegated Regulation 1268/2012 (n 32).
[129] See Art 3 Making Available Regulation 609/2014 (n 25) on 'Conservation of supporting documents'.
[130] Art 108(1) Financial Regulation 966/2012 (n 30). See section H below.
[131] Art 2(c) Financial Regulation 966/2012 (n 30).
[132] Case C-77/11 *Council v Parliament* EU:C:2013:559.   [133] ibid para 59.
[134] Art 38(2) Financial Regulation 966/2012 (n 30).
[135] ibid the list of documents at Art 38(3).   [136] Delegated Regulation 1268/2012 (n 32).

290 articles, the RAP regulates matters ranging from the budget nomenclature[137] and the rights and obligations of financial actors,[138] to the procedures for opening procurement tenders[139] and the contents of grant applications.[140] In its 2016 proposal for a new Financial Regulation, the Commission has proposed to abolish the RAP in the interests of simplification and flexibility, with a number of its articles to be incorporated into the Financial Regulation, and other matters to be dealt with in the future through more extensive administrative rulemaking within the Commission.[141]

3 Administrative rule-making

Article 47 RAP requires that 'each institution shall lay down in its internal rules such measures for the management of appropriations as it considers necessary for proper implementation of its section of the budget'. The RAP also requires each institution to draw up a code of professional standards on matters of internal control.[142] The services of the Commission frequently adopt standards, models, and guidelines for use by other Union institutions, bodies, offices, and agencies, and by the authorities of the Member States and delegated entities entrusted with tasks of budget implementation. For example, the accounting officer of the Commission is responsible for laying down accounting rules and harmonized charts of accounts that are employed by all Union accounting officers.[143]

4 Single-case administrative acts and measures

Competence for adopting single-case administrative acts and measures vis-à-vis final beneficiaries of Union funding varies, depending on the management mode employed. Under direct management, the legal commitment will often take the form of an agreement concluded with the beneficiary of Union funding, following a call for proposals, as in the case of grants and public contracts, but it may also take the form of a unilateral decision of the Commission, as in the case of a decision awarding a prize.[144] Under shared and indirect management, the national authorities or delegated entities adopt single-case decisions, with the Commission reimbursing the eligible costs. In recent years, there has been an increased use, across all management modes, of financial instruments, which may take the form of 'equity or quasi-equity investments, loans or guarantees, or other risk-sharing instruments'[145] and may involve the conclusion of agreements directly with beneficiaries, or with financial intermediaries.[146]

---

[137] ibid Art 25.   [138] ibid Art 45.   [139] ibid Art 157.   [140] ibid Art 196.

[141] Proposal for a Regulation of the European Parliament and of the Council on the financial rules applicable to the general budget of the Union and amending a series of regulations, COM(2016) 605, Brussels, 14 September 2016.

[142] Art 50 Delegated Regulation 1268/2012 (n 32).

[143] Arts 68(2) and 143(1) Financial Regulation 966/2012 (n 30).

[144] However, it is also possible that the award of a prize may be based on an agreement between the Commission and the prize winner. See ibid Art 138(5).

[145] ibid Art 2(p). On legal issues relating to the provision of loans and guarantees from the budget see Michail Vitsentzatos, 'Loans and Guarantees in the European Union Budget' (2014) 15 *ERA Forum* 131.

[146] See Arts 139–140 Financial Regulation 966/2012 (n 30) and Arts 216–226 Delegated Regulation 1268/2012 (n 32).

H Administrative Enforcement

The procedures for administrative enforcement in budgetary matters differ depending on the management mode employed. Under direct management, the Commission's agreements or contracts with beneficiaries invariably contain standard clauses allowing the Commission to withhold payments, or to seek recovery if the beneficiary does not comply with the terms of the award. Direct recourse to judicial redress is also possible in such cases. In situations of shared and indirect management, however, the Commission must rely on the national authorities or entrusted entities for frontline enforcement vis-à-vis final beneficiaries.

On the central level, the provisions of the Financial Regulation concerning the protection of the Union's financial interests against unreliable economic operators were substantially revised in 2015 in order to establish a new early detection and exclusion system (EDES), which replaced the previous Early Warning System (EWS) as from 1 January 2016.[147] Information on risks threatening the Union's financial interests may be transmitted to the Commission by authorizing officers, OLAF, national authorities implementing the budget under shared management, and entrusted entities under indirect management.[148] The information is centralized in a Commission database.[149] Economic operators must be notified of the entry of information relating to them in the central database, and may, where appropriate, seek its rectification, erasure, or amendment.[150]

The new Article 106(1) Financial Regulation further sets out a number of 'situations of exclusion', such as bankruptcy, fraud, corruption, serious breach of contract, or grave professional misconduct, on the basis of which an economic operator may be excluded from Union procedures leading to the award of procurement contracts, grants, and prizes, or to the benefits of Union funding provided through financial intermediaries.[151] Financial penalties may also be imposed on economic operators who attempt to obtain access to Union funds while being in one of the situations of exclusion.[152] In severe cases, information relating to the exclusion and/or financial penalty may be published on the Commission's website, with a view to reinforcing the deterrent effect.[153]

The decision to exclude an undertaking from Union funding procedures and/or to impose a financial penalty will usually be based on a final court judgment or administrative decision establishing that the economic operator is in one of the situations of exclusion.[154] However, an economic operator may also be excluded on the basis of a preliminary classification in law, where no final judgment or administrative

---

[147] Regulation (EU, Euratom) 2015/1929 of the European Parliament and of the Council of 28 October 2015 amending Regulation (EU, Euratom) 966/2012 on the financial rules applicable to the general budget of the Union [2015] OJ L286/1. This was accompanied by a revision of the RAP through Commission Delegated Regulation (EU) 2015/2462 of 30 October 2015 amending Delegated Regulation (EU) No 1268/2012 on the rules of application of Regulation (EU, EURATOM) No 966/2012 of the European Parliament and of the Council on the financial rules applicable to the general budget of the Union [2015] OJ L342/7.
[148] Art 108(2) Financial Regulation 966/2012 (n 30).   [149] ibid Art 108(1).   [150] ibid.
[151] ibid Art 105a(1)(b).   [152] ibid Art 106(13).   [153] ibid Arts 106(16) and (17).
[154] ibid Art 105a(2).

decision has yet been adopted. The facts and findings that may form the basis for an exclusion or penalty, in the absence of a final judgment or administrative decision, include 'facts established in the context of audits or investigations carried out by the Court of Auditors, OLAF or internal audit, or any other check, audit or control performed under the responsibility of the authorising officer',[155] non-final administrative decisions, including disciplinary measures taken by supervisory bodies,[156] and decisions of the European Central Bank (ECB), EIB, or international organizations.[157]

Before excluding an undertaking or imposing a penalty on the basis of a preliminary classification in law, the competent authorizing officer must refer the dossier to a Central Exclusion Panel,[158] chaired by a high-level independent expert.[159] The panel examines the dossier and issues a recommendation. The competent authorizing officer is not bound by the recommendation, but must provide justifications if he or she decides to deviate from it.[160] In any event, the decision to exclude or to impose a penalty will be reviewed, following notification of the final judgment or administrative decision.[161]

The Court of Justice has long held that the duty of mutual sincere cooperation obliges the Member States to take all effective measures to penalize conduct harmful to the financial interests of the Union,[162] but that obligation is now more explicitly expressed in the Treaties, notably in Article 325(2) TFEU, and in the Financial Regulation, which obliges Member States to 'take all necessary measures, including legislative, regulatory and administrative measures, to protect the Union's financial interests'.[163] This includes carrying out '*ex ante* and *ex post* controls including, where appropriate, on-the-spot checks on representative and/or risk-based samples of transactions'.[164] National authorities 'shall also recover funds unduly paid and bring legal proceedings where necessary in this regard'.[165] This is consistent with the legal framework governing the protection of the Union's financial interests in the Member States, including by means of criminal law.[166] Similar obligations to recover unduly paid funds are placed on entrusted entities under indirect management.[167]

---

[155] ibid Art 106(2)(a).   [156] ibid Art 106(2)(b).   [157] ibid Art 106(2)(c).
[158] ibid Art 108(5).   [159] ibid Art 108(7).   [160] ibid Art 105a(2), 3rd para.
[161] ibid Art 106(2), 2nd para.
[162] Case 68/88 *Commission v Greece* EU:C:1989:339, para 23; Case C-186/98 *Criminal proceedings against Nunes and de Matos* EU:C:1999:376, paras 9–11.
[163] Art 59(2) Financial Regulation 966/2012 (n 30).   [164] ibid.
[165] ibid. The Court of Justice has ruled that this provision provides a legal basis for a decision of the national authorities to recover amounts from a beneficiary of Union funding, without a need for any further legal basis in national law. See Case C-599/13 *Somalische Vereniging Amsterdam en Omgeving (Somvao) v Staatssecretaris van Veiligheid en Justitie* EU:C:2014:2462.
[166] See Council Act of 26 July 1995 drawing up the Convention on the protection of the European Communities' financial interests (the PIF Convention), OJ 1995 C 316/48 and its protocols; Council Regulation (EC, Euratom) No 2988/95 of 18 December 1995 on the protection of the European Communities' financial interests [1995] OJ L312/1; Proposal for a Directive of the European Parliament and of the Council on the fight against fraud to the Union's financial interests by means of criminal law COM(2012) 363.
[167] Art 60(3) Financial Regulation 966/2012 (n 30).

I Budgetary Control, Supervision, and Judicial Review

1 Control and supervision

(a) Internal control

Article 32(1) Financial Regulation requires that the budget must be implemented 'in compliance with effective and efficient internal control as appropriate in each method of implementation, and in accordance with the relevant sector-specific rules'. Internal control is defined as 'a process applicable at all levels of management and designed to provide reasonable assurance of achieving' the objectives of the effectiveness, efficiency, and economy of operations, the reliability of reporting, the safeguarding of assets and information, the prevention, detection, correction, and follow-up of fraud and irregularities, and the adequate management of risks.[168]

Following the 2002 reform of the Financial Regulation, the main responsibility for ensuring effective internal control now lies with the authorizing officer by delegation, who must 'put in place the organizational structure and the internal control systems suited to the performance of his or her duties'.[169] The Commission has established Internal Control Standards to assist its authorizing officers in the performance of this task.[170] The activities of the authorizing officer are also subject to control by the accounting officer, who is empowered to carry out any checks he or she deems necessary in order to sign off the accounts.[171] At the end of the financial year, the authorizing officer must present an Annual Activity Report that includes a 'management declaration', by which the official declares, *inter alia*, that the control procedures put in place give the necessary guarantees concerning the legality and regularity of the underlying transactions covered by the report.[172]

The internal auditor contributes to internal control by advising on risks, issuing independent opinions on the quality of management and control systems, and issuing recommendations for improvements.[173] The College of Commissioners is also assisted by an Audit Progress Committee. Each institution must also set up a specialized financial irregularities panel,[174] to which suspected irregularities may be referred by authorizing officers,[175] or by any member of staff who considers that they are required to

---

[168] ibid Art 32(2).   [169] ibid Art 66(2).

[170] See, in particular, 'Communication to the Commission from Commissioner Oettinger: Revision of the Internal Control Framework', SEC(2017) 2373, Brussels, 19 April 2017; 'Revision of the Internal Control Standards and Underlying Framework: Strengthening control effectiveness', SEC(2007) 1341, Brussels, 16 October 2007; 'Clarification of the responsibilities of the key actors in the domain of internal audit and internal control in the Commission', SEC(2003) 59, Brussels, 21 January 2003; 'Supporting the reform of financial management: A new framework for authorising officers', SEC(2000) 2203/5, Brussels, 13 December 2000.

[171] Art 68(5) Financial Regulation 966/2012 (n 30).

[172] ibid Art 66(9). See also Commission Communication on Activity-based Management including the Guidelines on the Declaration of the Authorising Officer by Delegation of 21 January 2003, COM(2003) 28.

[173] Art 99(1) Financial Regulation 966/2012 (n 30). On the role of the Commission's Internal Audit Service see Communication to the Commission on the Mission Charter of the Internal Audit Service, C(2015) 2451, 20 April 2015.

[174] Art 73(6) Financial Regulation 966/2012 (n 30).

[175] Art 76(1) Delegated Regulation 1268/2012 (n 32).

apply an irregular decision.[176] In its 2016 proposal for the new Financial Regulation, the Commission proposes that all institutions should use a central panel.[177] On the basis of the opinion of its panel, an institution may decide to initiate proceedings for disciplinary action against its officials, or to seek the payment of compensation.[178] Suspected cases of illegal activity, fraud, or corruption are referred to OLAF.[179] If systemic problems are detected, the panel should send a report with recommendations to the authorizing officer and to the internal auditor.[180]

When Union funds are implemented under shared management, the designated national managing authorities must set up and ensure the functioning of effective and efficient internal control systems.[181] As part of its risk assessment for implementation under shared management, the Commission must monitor the management and control systems established in the Member States.[182] The Commission carries out on-the-spot audits and checks in the Member States,[183] also in relation to the collection of Union revenue.[184] The Commission may apply 'financial corrections', in the form of exclusions from financing, interruptions of payment deadlines, or suspension of payments, when it finds that funds are not being managed in conformity with the applicable rules.[185] In some sectors, such financial corrections will be applied in the context of the clearance of account procedures, as provided for in the applicable sectoral legislation.[186]

Under the current administrative architecture for the implementation of the budget, the Commission may delegate tasks of budget implementation, but it remains ultimately responsible for all weakness in internal control, even if they arise at national and regional levels. As Cipriani wrote in 2006, 'within the framework of 'shared management' the Community authorizing officer commits and validates the appropriations without normally having any genuine control of the way the management and control systems on the ground work'.[187] Several initiatives over the intervening decade have sought to address this issue, including the Action Plan towards an Integrated Internal

---

[176] Art 66(8) Financial Regulation 966/2012 (n 30).

[177] Proposal for a Regulation of the European Parliament and of the Council on the financial rules applicable to the general budget of the Union and amending a series of regulations, COM(2016) 605, Brussels, 14 September 2016.

[178] Art 73(6) 2nd para Financial Regulation 966/2012 (n 30).   [179] ibid Art 72(2).

[180] ibid Art 73(6) 2nd para.   [181] ibid Art 59(4)(a).

[182] ibid Art 59(2), 4th para. See Commission Communication, 'Impact of the action plan to strengthen the Commission's supervisory role under shared management of structural actions', COM(2010) 52, Brussels, 18 February 2010. On the obligations of Member States to prevent, detect and correct irregularities and fraud see Paul Craig, 'Accountability' in Anthony Arnull and Damian Chalmers (eds), *The Oxford Handbook of European Union Law* (Oxford University Press) ch 17.

[183] The exercise of the Commission's powers in this regard is regulated by Council Regulation (Euratom, EC) No 2185/96 of 11 November 1996 concerning on-the-spot checks and inspections carried out by the Commission in order to protect the European Communities' financial interests against fraud and other irregularities [1996] OJ L292/2.

[184] Art 2(3)(d) Making Available Regulation 609/2014 (n 25).

[185] Art 59(6) Financial Regulation 966/2012 (n 30).

[186] On financial corrections in the CAP, see eg Carine Roussel, 'Le coût caché de la PAC: les corrections financières infligées aux États membres en cas de mauvais contrôles des dépenses agricoles' (2011) 544 *Revue du Maché commun et de l'Union européenne* 36.

[187] Cipriani, 'The Responsibility for Implementing the Budget' (n 11) 9.

Control Framework,[188] the 'single audit' in cohesion policy,[189] and the requirement for designated national bodies to present an annual management declaration.[190] Nevertheless, areas of shared management remain the main source of irregularities identified by the Court of Auditors in its annual reports.[191]

Entities entrusted with budget implementation tasks under indirect management are also required to set up and ensure the functioning of an effective and efficient internal control system, with a view to guaranteeing a level of protection of the financial interests of the Union equivalent to that required under the Financial Regulation.[192] Their internal control systems are subject to assessment *ex ante* by the Commission,[193] and the Commission may suspend payments at any stage if systemic errors are detected.[194] Entrusted entities are also required to present a management declaration to the Commission together with their accounts.[195] The Commission's 2016 initiative for a new Financial Regulation proposes greater reliance in future on the internal control and audit mechanisms of trusted, long-term implementation partners, such as the EIB, with a view to lightening the administrative burden on those entrusted entities, and avoiding excessive duplication of internal control efforts.[196]

(b) External control

The external audit of Union revenue and expenditure is carried out by the Court of Auditors. The Court of Auditors is competent to audit the legality and regularity of all revenue and expenditure of the Union, including Union funds managed by entrusted entities,[197] and to assess whether the financial management has been sound. It may conduct on-the-spot audits in the Member States, as well as on the premises of any natural or legal person in receipt of payments from the budget.[198] In the Member

---

[188] See Communication from the Commission to the European Parliament, the Council and the Court of Auditors Impact Report on the Commission Action Plan towards an Integrated Internal Control Framework, COM(2009) 43, Brussels, 4 February 2009. For an analysis of this concept see Christoph Thäsler, *Finanzkontrolle im europäischen Mehrebensystem* (Universitätsverlag Osnabrück/ V&R unipress 2012).

[189] Art 73 of Council Regulation (EC) No 1083/2006 of 11 July 2006 laying down general provisions on the ERDF, the ESF and the Cohesion Fund and repealing Regulation (EC) No 1260/1999, OJ 2006 L 210/25 introduced a possibility for the Commission to rely on the audits of national authorities and thus avoid duplication of efforts. For an assessment of the results see Court of Auditors Special Report No 16/2013, 'Taking stock of 'single audit' and the Commission's reliance on the work of national audit authorities in cohesion' [2014] OJ 8/6. See also Vitor Caldeira, 'The coordination of internal controls: the single audit: towards a European Union internal control framework' (2005) *Public Expenditure Control in Europe* 184.

[190] Art 59(5)(a) Financial Regulation 966/2012 (n 30).

[191] For the year 2015, the Court of Auditors found the highest levels of error, at 5.7% in spending under 'economic, social and territorial cohesion'. See Annual report of the Court of Auditors on the implementation of the budget concerning the financial year 2015, together with the institutions' replies [2016] OJ C375/1.

[192] Art 60(2) Financial Regulation 966/2012 (n 30).   [193] ibid Art 61.

[194] ibid Art 60(4).   [195] ibid Art 60(5).

[196] Proposal for a Regulation of the European Parliament and of the Council on the financial rules applicable to the general budget of the Union and amending a series of regulations, COM(2016) 605, Brussels, 14 September 2016.

[197] Art 40(g) RAP requires that delegation agreements must include clauses facilitating the exercise by the Court of Auditors of its audit powers in respect of Union funds managed by entrusted entities.

[198] Art 287(3) TFEU.

States, the audit is carried out in liaison with the national supreme audit institutions.[199] Any information necessary to allow the Court of Auditors to perform its task must be forwarded to it upon request.[200] In addition to the Union budget proper, the Court of Auditors is also competent to audit the European Development Funds[201] and the satellite budgets of all bodies, offices, or agencies of the Union, in so far as the basic act setting them up does not provide otherwise.[202]

The Court of Auditors assesses the legality of revenue and expenditure having regard to the criteria for the legality of acts set out in Article 263 TFEU.[203] Unlike certain national supreme audit institutions, the Court of Auditors does not exercise judicial powers and its assessments of legality perform a function different from those of the Court of Justice.[204] The Court of Auditors also assesses regularity, a notion defined very broadly as covering any infringement of a provision of Union law 'which has, or would have, the effect of prejudicing the general budget of the Union' either 'by reducing or losing revenue accruing from own resources collected directly on behalf of the Union, or by an unjustified item of expenditure'.[205] In practice, the notions of legality and regularity can be difficult to distinguish and, since the auditing consequences of non-compliance are the same in both cases, the Court of Auditors applies the two notions together, and verifies that transactions are both 'legal and regular'.[206] It is not the role of the Court of Auditors to determine if an irregularity it uncovers constitutes fraud;[207] instances of suspected fraud are referred instead to OLAF.[208]

Since the Treaty of Maastricht, the Court of Auditors is required to provide the Parliament and the Council with an annual statement of assurance (DAS)[209] as to the reliability of the Union's accounts, and as to the legality and regularity of the underlying transactions.[210] The Court applies a demanding materiality threshold of 2 per

---

[199] ibid.

[200] ibid. For an example of a refusal by a Member State to cooperate in an audit of the Court of Auditors see Case C-539/09 *Commission v Germany* EU:C:2011:733.

[201] See Art 49 of Council Regulation (EU) No 2015/323 of 2 March 2015 on the financial regulation applicable to the 11th European Development Fund ([2015] OJ L58/17) requires the Court of Auditors to provide the Parliament and Council with a statement of assurance with regard to the EDF, as it does for the Union's budget.

[202] Art 287(1) TFEU.

[203] See the European Court of Auditors 'Financial and Compliance Audit Manual' (2012 edn) 211.

[204] See Case 294/83 *Parti écologiste 'Les Verts' v European Parliament* EU:C:1986:166, para 28; and Opinion of Mancini AG in Case 204/86 *Greece v Council* EU:C:1988:259, para 5. On the scope of the legality audit see Jan Inghelram, 'The European Court of Auditors: Current legal issues' (2000) 37 *Common Market Law Review* 129, 133–34.

[205] The Court of Auditors cites approvingly this definition of 'irregularity', which is laid down in Art 1(2) of Council Regulation (EC, Euratom) No 2988/95 of 18 December 1995 on the protection of the European Communities financial interests [1995] OJ L312/1. See the European Court of Auditors 'Financial and Compliance Audit Manual' (n 203) 211.

[206] See the European Court of Auditors 'Financial and Compliance Audit Manual' (n 203) 211.

[207] Case T-277/97 *Ismeri Europa v Court of Auditors* EU:T:1999:124, para 123.

[208] See Decision of the Court of Auditors No 35-2014 laying down internal procedures for cooperation between the European Anti-Fraud Office and the European Court of Auditors (the Court) concerning audit related matters and information received from third parties (denunciations) forwarded by the Court, Luxembourg, 20 November 2014.

[209] The annual statement of assurance is more commonly known by its French acronym, DAS ('déclaration d'assurance').

[210] Art 287(1) TFEU.

cent for errors, representing monies not used or administered in accordance with applicable rules and regulations. Although the Court of Auditors now routinely issues positive opinions on the reliability of the Union's accounts and the legality and regularity of *revenue*, is has persistently delivered adverse opinions on the legality and regularity of Union *payments*, with the error level for the financial year 2015 estimated at 3.8 per cent.[211] Frequently identified irregularities include declarations of ineligible costs in payments claims, serious errors in public procurement, and incorrect declarations of agricultural support area by farmers. In addition to strengthening internal control, especially under shared management, the Court of Auditors has suggested that the error rate could be reduced by seeking 'to simplify and avoid unnecessarily complex and/or burdensome rules that do not add value with respect to the results to be achieved by the policy'.[212]

In addition to legality and regularity audits, the Court of Auditors is also competent to audit whether there has been sound financial management. Increasing importance is attributed in this regard to the conduct of performance audits, which lead to the adoption of Special Reports under the third paragraph of Article 287(4) TFEU.[213] The Court of Justice has observed that the reports of the Court of Auditors 'are intended to give guidance to the budgetary authority required to discharge the accounts and, more generally, to all public bodies capable of contributing to the filling or correction of any lacunae or dysfunction observed by the Court of Auditors in those areas'.[214] An increased emphasis by the Court of Auditors on auditing the performance and effectiveness of Union revenue and expenditure may be seen as complementing a broader shift towards performance-based budgeting in the Union, as advocated by the Commission when it launched its 'EU budget focused on results' initiative in 2015.[215]

2 Political supervision

Political supervision of the Commission's management of the budget is exercised by the European Parliament and the Council. The most prominent instance of political supervision is the ex post budgetary discharge procedure, pursuant to Article 319 TFEU.[216] That article provides for the Parliament, acting on a recommendation from the Council, to grant a discharge to the Commission in respect of its implementation

---

[211] Annual report of the Court of Auditors on the implementation of the budget concerning the financial year 2015, together with the institutions' replies [2016] OJ C375/1, 11.

[212] ibid 196.

[213] The Court of Auditors adopted 24 special reports in 2014, 22 in 2015, and 28 in 2016.

[214] Case C-539/09 *Commission v Germany* EU:C:2011:733, para 62.

[215] See Paul Stephenson, 'Reconciling Audit and Evaluation? The Shift to Performance and Effectiveness at the European Court of Auditors' (2015) *European Journal of Risk Regulation* 79. On the meaning of performance-based budgeting see 'Performance-based budgeting', European Parliament, DG IPOL, July 2015. See also the proceedings of the Commission's 'EU Budget Focused on Results' conference of 22 September 2015: http://ec.europa.eu/budget/budget4results/index_en.cfm.

[216] On the discharge procedure see 'Parliamentary Control of Budget Implementation', European Parliament, Directorate-General for Internal Policies, Policy Department D: Budgetary Affairs, 2012; Yves Petit, 'La procédure de décharge sur l'exécution du budget général de l'Union européenne et ses enjeux' *Mélanges en hommage à Guy Isaac: 50 ans de droit communautaire* (LGDJ 2004) 949–72; Laurent Beurdeley, 'Les motifs du refus de décharge relatif au budget général de l'Union européenne' (2000) 443 *Revue du Marché common et de l'Union européenne* 696.

of the budget. Discharge is normally granted before 15 May of the year $n + 2$ in respect of the year n,[217] although the final vote may be postponed if, for example, relevant information is lacking.[218]

The Council and the Parliament carry out their political assessments having regard to the annual accounts and the various reporting packages submitted to them by the Commission, as well as to the annual report of the Court of Auditors, the DAS, and any Special Reports relating to the year in question.[219] The European Parliament's Committee on Budgetary Control organizes public hearings with authorizing officers by delegation of the Union institutions and agencies. As far as shared management is concerned, the Commission transmits relevant observations made by the Court of Auditors in its annual report to the competent national authorities and their replies are summarized in a Commission report that is submitted to the Parliament and the Council by 28 February of the year $n + 2$, so that the information may be taken into account in the discharge process.[220] The Council has persistently resisted efforts aimed at obliging Member State governments to provide national declarations of assurance signed at political level in respect of Union funds disbursed on their territories. Nevertheless, the possibility of adopting such declarations is now mentioned in the Financial Regulation, and a small number of Member States do adopt them on a voluntary basis.[221]

Although Article 319(1) TFEU refers to the grant of discharge to the Commission alone, the Parliament, acting pursuant to its Rules of Procedure, grants a separate discharge to each Union institution with respect to the implementation of its section of the general budget. This practice has not gone uncontested, with the Council refusing to cooperate in the Parliament's adoption of a separate discharge decision concerning it. A stand-off has developed between the Parliament and the Council on this issue, with the Parliament persistently refusing to grant discharge to the Council on grounds of lack of cooperation,[222] and the Council, for its part, largely ignoring the Parliament's decision.[223]

The final decision of the Parliament granting or refusing discharge is accompanied by decisions closing the accounts for the year $n-2$ and resolutions setting out observations intended to guide the future conduct of authorizing officers. The responsible authorizing officers may be held to account by the Parliament's Committee on Budgetary Control for any failures to respect those observations during the course of subsequent financial years. In that regard, Article 319(3) TFEU provides that the Commission

---

[217] Art 164(1) Financial Regulation 966/2012 (n 30).   [218] ibid Arts 164(2) and (3).

[219] ibid Art 165(2).   [220] ibid Art 162(5).

[221] See the final paragraph of ibid Art 59(5). See also Stéphane Saurel, *Le budget de l'Union européenne* (La documentation française 2010) 68–69.

[222] See eg European Parliament decision of 27 October 2016 on discharge in respect of the implementation of the general budget of the European Union for the financial year 2014, Section II: European Council and Council, P8_TA(2016)418; and European Parliament decision of 27 April 2017 on discharge in respect of the implementation of the general budget of the European Union for the financial year 2015, Section II: European Council and Council, P8_TA(2017)147.

[223] For a discussion of the legal issues at stake see 'The European Parliament's Right to Grant Discharge to the Council: Documentation of a Workshop held on 27 September 2012', European Parliament, DG IPOL, March 2013.

'shall take all appropriate steps to act on the observations in the decisions giving dis-charge', and on the comments accompanying the Council's recommendation.[224] The Parliament, in its Rules of Procedure, reserves the right to initiate legal action against the Commission if it fails do so.[225]

Discharge has been refused to the Commission on two occasions: in 1984 with regard to the implementation of the 1982 budget, and in 1998 with regard to the implementation of the budget for 1996. In itself, a refusal of discharge produces no legal effects,[226] but, as Inghelram has suggested, 'if a refusal of discharge is seen to imply the view that the Commission has failed to fulfil its tasks of budget manage-ment as a whole, then logically it should be followed by a motion of censure of the Commission as a whole'.[227] Indeed, the Santer Commission resigned in anticipa-tion of a motion of censure following the Parliament's refusal of discharge for the year 1996, and the publication of the first report of the Committee of Independent Experts.[228]

3 Judicial review

The vast majority of cases that come before the Union courts concerning the admin-istration of the budget involve challenges to administrative decisions by which a re-covery of funds is sought or expenditure is committed. Actions for judicial review of grant or procurement awards brought by disappointed applicants or tenderers are also common. Disputes concerning the implementation of grant agreements or public contracts will take the form of contractual disputes, with the Commission's standard contract clauses usually stipulating that the Union courts will have juris-diction to adjudicate, as foreseen in Article 272 TFEU.[229] The General Court some-times even reclassifies actions for annulment as contractual disputes where it finds that the substance of the dispute relates to the application of a grant agreement. In *Technische Universität Dresden*, for example, an action for annulment brought by a beneficiary of Union funding against a Commission measure intended to enforce a grant agreement, which would otherwise have been declared inadmissible, was re-classified by the General Court as a contractual action, which was admissible.[230]

It is common for Member States to seek judicial review of recovery and finan-cial corrections adopted by the Commission in relation to the implementation of funds under shared management. As Cipriani observes, financial corrections very often give rise to court actions that can endure for many years, and this possibility

---

[224] See also Art 166 Financial Regulation 966/2012 (n 30).

[225] See Art 6(3) of Annex IV to the Parliament's Rules of Procedure (8th parliamentary term, January 2017).

[226] Jean-Paul Jacqué, *Droit institutionnel de l'Union européenne* (8th edn, Dalloz 2015) 678.

[227] Inghelram, 'Finances of EU' (n 11) 397.

[228] See Paul Craig, 'The Fall and Renewal of the Commission: Accountability, Contract and Administrative Organisation' (2000) *European Law Journal* 98.

[229] See eg Art 57.2 of the Horizon 2020 Model Grant Agreement of 1 July 2016. http://ec.europa.eu/research/participants/data/ref/h2020/grants_manual/amga/h2020-amga_en.pdf.

[230] Case T-29/11 *Technische Universität Dresden v Commission* EU:T:2014:912. See also Joined Cases T-428/07 and T-455/07 *CEVA v Commission* EU:T:2010:240.

to prolong the procedure through litigation may undermine the dissuasive effect of such corrections.[231] In 2015, for example, the Court of Justice annulled five financial correction decisions, valued at €457 million, relating to the closure of European Regional Development Fund operational programmes in Spain and German, dating right back to the 1993–1999 MFF programming period.[232] Having annulled the decisions, the Court ruled that the Commission should proceed with the full reimbursements to the Member States, with important consequences for the implementation of the 2015 budget.

Cases have also arisen where individual beneficiaries of Union funding under shared management have sought judicial review of financial correction or recovery decisions, addressed by the Commission to a Member State, but allegedly producing adverse effects for the applicant undertaking. In some cases, the Court of Justice has ruled that actions brought by legal persons against financial corrections applied by the Commission to Member States were inadmissible, since the undertaking was not directly concerned by the correction for the purposes of Article 263 TFEU.[233] However, there have been other cases where the Court has found that decisions of the Commission suspending, reducing, or withdrawing Union assistance under shared management were of direct concern to the final beneficiaries.[234] Indeed, cases brought by natural or legal persons regarding the disbursement of Union funds under shared management provide prime illustrations of the problems of effective judicial protection that may arise in the context of top-down composite administrative procedures.[235]

The application of budgetary control and anti-fraud procedures has also given rise to a good deal of litigation in actions brought by natural or legal persons. In *Ismeri v Court of Auditors*, for example, the Court of Justice recognized that critical remarks relating to an undertaking in a report of the Court of Auditors could give rise to an action for damages, and the undertaking concerned should be given an opportunity to be heard before such a report is concluded.[236] Similar concerns for fair procedures and the protection of rights of defence are evident in rulings of the Union courts concerning the entry of names in databases,[237] and in actions brought by natural or legal persons in the context of OLAF investigations.[238]

---

[231] Cipriani, 'The Responsibility for Implementing the Budget' (n 11) 14–15.

[232] Case C-263/13 P *Spain v Commission*, EU:C:2015:415, and Joined Cases C-549/12 P and C-54/13 P *Germany v Commission*, EU:C:2015:412. In late 2014, the Court also annulled four correction decisions related to the closure of Spanish Cohesion Fund projects from the 1993–1999 and 2000–2006 programming periods in Case C-513/13 P *Spain v Commission* EU:C:2014:2412; see also Case C-192/13 P *Spain v Commission* EU:C:2014:2156; Case C-197/13 P *Spain v Commission* EU:C:2014:2157; and Case C-429/13 P *Spain v Commission* EU:C:2014:2310.

[233] See eg Joined Cases C-89 and 91/86 *Étoile commerciale et CNTA v Commission* EU:C:1987:337.

[234] See eg Case C-32/95 P *Commission v Lisrestal* EU:C:1996:402.

[235] See, further, the chapter of this book by Katerina Pantazatou. See also Giacinto della Cananea, 'The European Union's Mixed Administrative Proceedings' (2004) 68 *Law and Contemporary Problems* 197.

[236] Case C-315/99 P *Ismeri Europa Srl v Court of Auditors* EU:C:2001:391.

[237] See eg Case C-564/13 P *Planet AE v Commission* EU:C:2015:124; Case T-298/16 *East West Consulting v Commission* (pending).

[238] See eg Case T-193/04 *Hans-Martin Tillack v Commission* EU:T:2006:292; see also Case T-47/16 *Sigma Orionis SA V European Research Agency* (pending).

J Conclusion

The Union's budgetary administrative law has played a central role in the evolution of the general administrative law of the Union. The debates surrounding the periodical revisions of the Union's budgetary rules and procedures have often served to illustrate broader concerns regarding the structure and functioning of the Union's administration as a whole. Reflecting a wider debate about excessive administrative burdens resulting from Union rules, the Commission's 2016 proposal for a revision of the Financial Regulation is just the latest in a series of efforts to strike an appropriate balance in the budgetary domain between considerations of control, supervision, and accountability—all considerations which tend to demand more detailed, complex and onerous administrative rules and procedures—and the desire to improve efficiency and user-friendliness through simplification and enhanced administrative flexibility.

Debates about the appropriate administrative architecture for the implementation and control of the budget, meanwhile, point to more fundamental tensions of a general nature regarding the appropriate division of competences and responsibilities between the Union and its Member States, with the central administration in Brussels being held responsible for weaknesses in budgetary implementation and control that, in practice, can often be remedied only through greater efforts on the national and regional levels. In recent times, a renewed emphasis on performance-based budgeting, in the context of the Commission's 'EU budget focused on results' initiative, suggests that achieving a closer alignment of the Union's budgetary and policy implementation cycles will also remain a focus of administrative reforms over the years to come.[239] In this regard, evolutions in the Union's administrative law in the budgetary domain are likely to continue to impact more broadly across the Union's administration as a whole.

---

[239] See the proceedings of the first annual 'EU Budget Focused on Results' conference of 22 September 2015. http://ec.europa.eu/budget/budget4results/index_en.cfm.

PART IX

CONCLUSION

23

Synthesis and Assessment

Herwig C H Hofmann, Gerard C Rowe, and Alexander H Türk

As set out in our introductory chapter, this work has been designed as an examination of the diverse forms and structures of administrative law applicable within various, specific areas of European Union policies. Its intention is to allow insight into the administrative implementation of Union policies in parallel with one another, reviewing and reflecting on both the differences and commonalities of approach in the varied policy sectors. The administrative differences between sectors may, in fact, lie simply in the policy-specific search for answers to problems already solved in another context, be the consequence of pure 'path dependency', or reflect a carefully designed approach which takes into account existing general legal principles, but does so in applying them to a discrete policy field. The starting assumption of this work was that some elements of Union administrative law are applicable cross-sectorally, but much is particular to individual policy settings. In fact, only relatively little existing EU law of a cross-sectoral kind can serve as an—even nascent—body of coherent, general Union administrative law. Most of the law applicable to the practical implementation of EU policy and its legal embodiment—broadly, the administrative law of the Union—has arisen in policy-specific settings. Perhaps the most widely applicable basis of administrative structure, organization, procedure, information management, and supervision is the Comitology Regulation 182/2011, applied to administrative rule-making by the Commission for implementing acts under Article 291 TFEU. However, even a regulation such as this, and its actual application, covers only a small part of overall administrative activity. Comparable examples of relatively widely applicable administrative legislation relate to access to information, data protection, and financial management, and certain others as well. Even taking all such instruments and frameworks together, however, can account for only a small proportion of the totality of administrative law measures relating to implementation across the whole gamut of Union policy.

It is, of course, not the case that the body of general administrative law as such is only very slight. There is in fact a significant corpus of such law.[1] The point we wish to emphasize here is that that administrative-law corpus does not sufficiently encompass all the administrative activities and practices found within the Union. At least, there are innumerable additional legal rules and frameworks which supplement (or just duplicate) that ample body of general administrative law. Given, then,

---

[1] See for that eg H C H Hofmann, G C Rowe, and A H Türk, *Administrative Law and Policy of the European Union* (OUP 2011); P Craig, *EU Administrative Law* (3rd edn, OUP 2018) and several other works in various languages.

an insufficiency of general administrative EU law (or perhaps a superfluity of variation), we are attempting to deduce and distil from the policy-specific diversity what might be called the 'common core' of EU administrative law, and in so doing also to identify those elements which are inherently unique to the sector(s) in which they have emerged.

Article 298 TFEU requires that the Union establish 'by means of regulations [enacted] in accordance with the ordinary legislative procedure' (paragraph 2) provisions creating an 'open, efficient and independent European administration' (paragraph 1). The European Parliament (EP) has repeatedly passed resolutions asking the European Commission to submit proposals for such legislation.[2] In fact, the EP in 2016 took the unprecedented step of adding, to its resolution requesting the Commission to present a legislative proposal on a regulation covering certain basic administrative procedures, a draft text of a regulation with explanations and recitals. Never before, except perhaps for the Spinelli draft Constitutional Treaty of 1984 had the Parliament itself drafted a legal text. This comes to show the great importance of the issue to democratic control of the executive, but also the great frustration of the parliamentarians with the Commission. The Commission has subsequently confirmed that it had no intention to propose such regulation or regulations.[3] Instead, it has insisted that each sector should have its own specific administrative law. It is the situation which results from that approach with which this book is confronted, and upon which the contributions offer reflections, not only regarding the diversity of solutions found to problems common to all policy areas, but also—at least indirectly—through a comparative review allowing hints at the possibilities available for a convergent and unifying evolution of European administrative law and regulation.

There are, then, two aspects to be highlighted: first, the diversity in administrative law and practice across the Union; and secondly, the degree to which a convergence or unification of this law and practice might be desirable and achievable. As to the first aspect, the contributions to the present work testify to this diversity, setting out the heterogeneity of administrative tasks, for the achievement of which the administrative law must provide a framework. The studies also point to the degree to which sector-specific principles have emerged either as emanations of sectoral particularity, or perhaps rather as sectoral expressions of general principles of EU law. Concerning the second aspect, the contributions point very clearly—despite the range, multiplicity, and variability—to recurring figures such as administrative rule-making functions and procedures, single-case decision-making, the use of administrative contracts, information-management rules and practices, and accountability and supervisory mechanisms, for which standardization across all or most sectors would be quite imaginable.

---

[2] European Parliament, Resolution of 9 June 2016 for an open, efficient and independent European Union administration, 2016/2610(RSP) and European Parliament, Texts adopted—Thursday, 9 June 2016—A regulation for an open, efficient and independent European Union administration, P8_TA-PROV(2016)0279; see also: European Parliament, Resolution of 26 October 2017 on monitoring the application of EU law 2015, 2017/2011(INI).

[3] Answer given by First Vice-President Timmermans on behalf of the Commission to a Parliamentary question on the Law of Administrative Procedure of the European Union, E-001249/2016, 11 May 2016.

This final chapter synthesizes the most significant conclusions emerging from the individual sectoral surveys, noting both similarities and differences. In doing so, we also broadly follow the (more-or-less) standardized chapter structure which most of the contributions have followed (set out in our introduction in Chapter 1): tasks, sources of law, sector-specific principles, sectoral organization, sectoral procedures, decision-making rules, abstract-general administrative acts, single case administrative acts, administrative enforcement, and supervision of administrative actors. At the end we undertake an overall assessment of EU administrative law, in the light of both the individual sectoral studies and of the synthesis which we provide here.

A Administrative Tasks, Phases, and Actors

The spread and multiplicity of administrative tasks pursued across the policy sectors of the European Union is broad, perhaps even vast. As administrative action is 'undertaken within the framework of, and for the purpose of achieving, the overall policies and goals of the Union',[4] it is not surprising that administrative functions vary according to the sectors concerned, depending on the specific policy objectives set in each and on the competences allocated to each. In the face of such variance in sectoral tasks, of which the chapters in this book provide an indicative picture, it is useful to establish a set of typologies, as follows.

1 The phase-related dimension of the disbursement of tasks

A possible taxonomy of tasks—especially from a sectoral-comparative perspective—emerges from their possible alignment with the phases of implementational and administrative action, or with policy-cycle models. Indeed, in some sectors, multi-annual and annual cycles clearly dominate the administrative activities undertaken in respect of planning, adoption of budgets and programmes, implementation, monitoring, and review.[5] In other sectors, mainly those concerned with market regulation,[6] highly elaborated functional phases typically encompass the full gamut of administrative activities from agenda-setting, through preparatory involvement in policy articulation and selection, implementation, and monitoring, to evaluation, with feedback loops from various later phases to earlier ones. There are, however, also areas in which administrative action takes place at irregular, and less or more frequent, intervals, such as in the management of the Union Civil Service.[7]

Preparatory activities, which include planning and agenda-setting, are particularly important functions in certain sectors, in relation to the phasing of bureaucratic action.[8] Planning involves in itself a wide scope of administrative (sub-)tasks, not least of which are information gathering and management, or the conduct of consultation

---

[4] Hofmann, Rowe, and Türk, *Administrative Law and Policy of the European Union* (n 1) 57.
[5] See the chapters on budgetary matters (22), structural funds (20), development and humanitarian aid (6), and economic governance (10).
[6] See the chapters on energy (14), transport (12), and agriculture (19).   [7] Chapter 21.
[8] See the chapters on budget (22), the ENP (3), enlargement (2), environmental law (13), and structural funds (20).

processes. The responsibility for drafting proposals is pervasive to all policy fields, but can be highly disparate, being not limited to proposals for Union legislation as such, but also encompassing budgetary acts, financing programmes, international agreements, accession treaties, guidelines for negotiations with a departing Member State under Article 50 TEU, and more. As the chapters on the budget,[9] and economic and monetary union[10] show, the collection and evaluation of information is of crucial importance in respect of many such steps. A similarly wide array of tasks emerges in respect of formal implementational measures, such as subordinate legal acts and administrative rules of a general nature,[11] the disbursement of funds,[12] the management of the Union budget,[13] and the adoption of programming instruments.[14]

Information management, mostly in the context of information networks, is virtually a constant element in the taxonomy of tasks. Several contributions in this survey confirm that the administrative functions of the collection, generation, management, distribution, and regulation of information have become important facets of Union administration and the law surrounding it, with key examples in relation to asylum, monetary union, health, energy, environmental protection, or agriculture.[15] Information management pervades virtually every aspect of Union administrative law, and can increasingly be seen as the backbone of the achievement of administrative tasks across all sectors. This factor permeates all phases of administrative activities, from preparatory activities such as agenda-setting, through the drafting and adoption of both general and specific acts (e.g., the declaration of protected habitats within the Natura 2000 framework)[16] and their enforcement (e.g. through reporting obligations as to the application of Union subsidies), and in the supervision of the administration itself (e.g., in information gathering by OLAF). The management of information in the EU often occurs through networks. These are regulated in motley ways, but normally so as to reflect the integrative, multi-level administrative nature of the Union, where administrative execution is only rarely concentrated centrally in EU bodies.[17] In most areas, central bodies merely coordinate information networks, or provide for their infrastructure. Otherwise, centralized functions are limited to the supervision of, and control over, the decentralized enforcement of Union policy by national authorities. Such control itself involves a number of different information-management tasks for such EU actors, such as on-the-spot inspections,[18] verification of accounts and auditing,[19] enforcing reporting obligations,[20] and monitoring.[21]

---

[9] Chapter 22.   [10] Chapter 10.

[11] See the chapters on transport (12), energy (14), neighbourhood (3), EMU (10), state aid (17), budget (22) and the Union's civil service (21).

[12] See the chapters on development aid (6), enlargement (2), the Union's neighbourhood policy (3), and agriculture (19).

[13] Chapter 22.

[14] See in particular the chapters on structural funds (20), EMU (10), enlargement (2), the Union's neighbourhood policy (3), and health (15).

[15] See chapters 8, 10, 15, 14, 13, and 19 respectively.   [16] Chapter 13.

[17] See the chapters on the Union's civil service (21) and state aid (17).

[18] See the chapter on structural funds (20).

[19] See the chapters on budget (22), agriculture (19), development aid (6), and structural funds (20).

[20] See the chapter on environment (13).

[21] See the chapters on neighbourhood (3), enlargement (2), EMU (10), health (15), procurement (18), state aid (17), and transport (12).

2 The plurality of actors involved in administrative tasks

The present sectoral studies not only demonstrate the *multi-faceted* nature of administrative tasks and their institutional implications. It also makes clear what is perhaps even more characteristic of EU administration and the associated administrative law, its *polycentric* nature.[22] The administrative implementation of Union objectives is effected mainly through the decentralized actions of Member State administrations. In fact, there is a profusion of actors within the Union's multi-level administrative space, bringing with it the need for a high degree of coordination and cooperation in the performance of those multi-faceted tasks. Such cooperation takes place *horizontally*, on the Union level, within the framework of a Union executive which is at its core collegial, but nevertheless somewhat fragmented in the allocation of administrative functions across Commission services, special units, increasingly powerful agencies, networks, and private actors. *Vertically*, cooperation occurs between Union administrative actors on the one hand and national authorities on the other. Such vertical cooperation characterizes virtually all fields of European Union administration (except the Union Civil Service),[23] involving the Member States continually and closely within bodies and entities—severally stamped with the Union title and flag—, such as committees or agencies, often with a high degree of external social and expert participation (e.g., in the expert committees in the field of Union nature conservation,[24] or in social policy, or product safety). This is a distinguishing characteristic of EU administration and administrative law, perhaps unique if considered comparatively with other systems. An important characteristic which one in fact observes across all policy areas is the general openness, often coupled with an obligation, for the involvement not only of private, societal forces, but also of international actors from outside of the EU.

That the European Union entertains relationships with states and administrative and other actors external to the Union, that is, outside EU territory, comes as no surprise. As some of the sectoral studies here make clear, this may even be a dominant element in Union administrative implementation.[25] Such relationships with territorially external actors—whether public and private—has assumed increased importance across many sectors. This is not just the case in sectors specifically tasked with external relations, and touches even those areas which, on their face, do not have a primarily non-EU international focus.[26] Indeed, with very few exceptions (such as the Union Civil Service), administrative tasks within the differing sectors of Union law require engagement with a range of actors internationally external to the Union. The management of such relations adds another layer of complexity to the coordination of, and cooperation between, administrative actors in the realization of Union policies.

The intricate forms of cooperative interaction and coordination identified here are almost invariably supported by some form(s) of information network. Indeed, the sophistication in administrative cooperation via information networks can, as the

---

[22] Hofmann, Rowe, and Türk, *Administrative Law and Policy of the European Union* (n 1) 57–59.
[23] Chapter 21.   [24] Chapter 13.
[25] Noting particularly the chapters on enlargement (2), neighbourhood (3), external trade (4), and development.[26] See eg the involvement of bodies 'foreign' to the EU, at least in an advisory capacity in Union nature conservation (ch 13).

sectoral studies here show, be understood as a hallmark of the distinctive nature of EU administrative law. Information networks and cooperation constitute a *topos* of the regulatory-administrative landscape across virtually all fields of policy.

Added to these distinctive structural and organizational elements of cooperation and coordination, the mainly decentralized pursuit of EU policy objectives through administrative actors within Member States, calls for involvement of the Union executive in shaping, guiding, coercing, monitoring, supervising, and controlling national administrative action to ensure conformity and sufficiency. This itself heightens the demands for a high level of cooperation and coordination between Union and national actors. In some policy areas, the guidance powers of the Commission or of an EU agency, in relation to competent national authorities, may lead to the adoption of binding acts.[27] As a matter of terminology, even the word 'guideline' (or whatever comparable term may be used in the different policy sectors) does not necessarily imply non-binding character. Clarification and precision is needed here, since there may be direct impacts on individuals where, for example, so-called guidelines are binding on national authorities.

B Sources of EU Administrative Law

Unsurprisingly, the contributions to this book show that primary Union law as well as the general principles of EU law, as developed in the caselaw of the CJEU, are key legal sources underlying administrative activity across all policy areas. It is equally unsurprising that secondary legislative measures of the Union must be added to these, but almost invariably in each case with a sector-specific focus. That latter qualification is applicable also to a further important, if only relatively sporadic, source, namely international agreements, where the external trade sector offers a key example.[28]

1 The Treaties and the Charter

EU Treaty provisions relevant for administrative implementation of Union law, limited though they may be in their *direct* implications, offer a framework for manifold administrative activities and responsibilities. One might say that all Treaty provisions are indeed relevant in some sense, simply because it is their implementation—or observance—which generate the impetus for the public administrative activity of the Union in all its emanations. More particularly, however, certain generally applicable Treaty provisions, such as those on the basic values of the Union (notably Articles 2 and 9–12 TEU) can be identified. In addition to this, all our policy area studies note the importance of issues emerging from the Treaties, such as the principles of conferral, proportionality, and subsidiarity, which all bear on administrative tasks and their performance. Next to these, the Treaties contain provisions on administrative cooperation which includes the practically relevant matter of information exchange (Article 197 TFEU) and a provision requiring the Union to adopt legislation in the

---

[27] See the chapters on energy (14) and EMU (10).
[28] Chapter 4.

form of regulations to ensure that the Union has an 'open, efficient and independent European administration' as referred to in Article 298 TFEU, already noted above. The latter provision thus, after the entry into force of the Treaty of Lisbon, arguably provides the legal basis for some form of general regulation of Union administrative practice. Next to these few, but important, Treaty provisions generally applicable across all policy sectors, there is a host of policy-specific primary law, out of which emerges much of the associated administrative law, but without detailed Treaty specification to that effect. The monetary union, for all that, could well qualify as the policy area with the most detailed Treaty provisions on related administrative activities,[29] in particular in providing the European Central Bank with a vast array of powers.

Union Treaty law regularly has a specific importance for executive-administrative organization and procedure. Amongst the Union institutions, the Commission has typically the most far reaching administrative powers under the Treaties. In addition to its responsibility for budget implementation, the Commission has been directly granted broad decision-making powers in primary law, for example, in the fields of state aid and competition law.[30] Treaty provisions have also granted it more narrowly defined powers in respect of non-discrimination in the transport sector,[31] and for undertaking initiatives concerning trans-European networks.[32] In the context of state aid, the Treaty also provides a framework within which the Commission acts, supplemented by rules of the Council. In contrast, in the competition field, the Council is entrusted with considerable powers to lay down procedural arrangements. In the field of employment policy[33] and economic governance,[34] the Commission shares broad governance powers with the Council, within the structural and procedural framework of the Open Method of Coordination. A few Treaty provisions, for example in the area of freedom, security and justice (AFSJ),[35] require the involvement of the European Council, mainly in the form of providing strategic guidance. Yet other Treaty provisions provide the constitutional framework for individual EU agencies, such as Eurojust and Europol.[36] In the field of social policy,[37] the Treaty expressly empowers private actors to implement Union policy, by agreements adopted between and among social partners.

Alongside Treaty provisions, the Charter of Fundamental Rights constitutes an important source of administrative law, by setting limits on the exercise of administrative powers. Such limits may be of a substantive kind, as we see from the chapter on data protection which notes that Article 8(2) CFR requires a specific standard of administrative control. Limits emerging from the Charter also relate, for example, to procedural or supervisory requirements, such as those set out in Article 41 CFR on good administration,[38] or in Article 47 CFR as regards judicial review.[39]

---

[29] Chapter 10.   [30] Chapters 17 and 18.
[31] See Arts 93, 95, 96, and 97 TFEU. For further details see Chapter 12.
[32] See Art 171(2) TFEU.   [33] Chapter 16.   [34] Chapter 10.   [35] See Art 68 TFEU.
[36] ibid Arts 85 and 88.   [37] Chapter 16.
[38] See A H Türk, 'Administrative Law and Fundamental Rights' in S Douglas-Scott and N Hatzis (eds), *Research Handbook on EU Law and Human Rights* (Edward Elgar Publishing 2017).
[39] See H C H Hofmann, 'General principles of EU Law and EU Administrative Law' in S Peers and C Barnard (eds), *European Union Law* (2nd edn, Oxford University Press 2017).

Equally important in the context of a fair and impartial public administration are provisions on equality and non-discrimination (most notably Articles 20, 21, and 23 CFR). Further, information-related rights are essential in relation to administrative steps: rights to access information (Article 42 CFR), or privacy and data protection (Articles 7 and 8 CFR).

2 Union secondary legislation

The Treaties and the Charter (EU primary law) provide the general constitutional framework, with occasional—perhaps unsystematic—detail in some respects, within which the Union legislator adopts legislative acts (EU secondary law) on policy substance and administrative implementation, in the pursuit of objectives or aspirations often only vaguely defined or specified in Union treaty law. Yet, it is sectoral EU secondary law which constitutes the main source of law for administrative action in the Union, by all relevant administrative actors. Disputes concerning the legal (primary law) bases for the adoption of secondary Union legal measures are often, therefore, also of consequence for administrative action, whether this concerns structures, powers, procedures, acts, or supervision. Issues of, and controversies about, the competence of institutions responsible for the adoption of secondary legislative acts, or the procedures by which they were adopted, may both have an impact on the administrative activities undertaken on the basis of such acts, and derive in part from administrative actions which contributed to the emergence of such secondary legislative measures in the first place. The sectoral survey here, not unexpectedly, demonstrates that Union secondary legislation is very diversified across policy sectors, whether in regard to its specificity concerning the organizational form of administrative implementation, the administrative competences available, or the level of procedural detail laid down. The intensity and specificity of the secondary legislative regulation of such matters differ across sectors, from those which have been intensely covered for some time,[40] through others showing a more recent trend towards more intensive coverage,[41] to yet others moving more slowly in this direction.[42]

3 Principles emerging from decisions of the CJEU

All the present contributions underscore the significance that caselaw of the CJEU has as a source of law, both of a constitutional nature and as regards the reading of secondary law, for the Union's administrative action. This can be seen expressed in a number of ways. First, given the often rather general terms of Treaty provisions, the Court's rulings have provided necessary details, as regards both policy substance and implementational process, for the exercise of Commission powers, for example in state aid and competition law. Secondly, principles which have been, at least initially,

---

[40] See the chapters on development aid (6), transport policy (12), agriculture (19), budgetary matters (22), and the Union's civil service (21).
[41] See the chapters on economic governance (10) and energy law (14).
[42] See the chapter on asylum (8).

developed judicially have often come to form the backbone of Union secondary legislation. This is so in respect of State aid,[43] procedural legislation, and both substantive and procedural obligations in the field of public procurement[44] imposed by Union legislation on national authorities. Thirdly, unwritten general principles of Union law have provided a constitutional framework within which the administration is bound to exercise its powers, even absent express legislative provisions.

4 International agreements

International agreements and practice form an important source of law not only in policy areas with an explicitly external dimension.[45] Such agreements may be ones concluded between or among Member States, to function alongside—in parallel with, or supplementary to—applicable Union law, for example in the area of economic union,[46] where agreements between Member States complement EU-internal arrangements. Such agreements can also be ones concluded between the Union with non-EU states or with international organizations. An example comes from the transport field,[47] where the Union actively participates in international organizations. Finally, international agreements can be a preparatory step towards EU substantive and administrative law, for example in the field of data protection where adequacy decisions on the standard of foreign data protection provisions constitutes a particularly sensitive area,[48] aiming to ensure that data transfers to states outside the EU are subject to sufficient safeguards and review.[49] Other examples of such kinds of agreements are well illustrated in the policy fields of Union enlargement, neighbourhood, and external trade (and, one assumes, in the context of the departure of a Member State from the Union).

C Underlying Sector-specific Principles

Each sectoral policy area typically—perhaps invariably—makes recourse to, and adheres to, legal principles (usually emerging from secondary legislation) specific to the sector concerned and/or to general principles of law developed by the CJEU as these have been adapted to the discrete needs of the sector. The origins of the latter general principles (and sometimes the sector-specific ones) can often be found in national or international law, but have been given specific expression and application by the Union courts or legislation.

In contrast to sector-specific principles, general principles of EU law play an important role in all EU policy fields, not least because of their role as part of Union primary law. Some of these are codified in the Treaties, others are spelt out in the caselaw, and they address substantive and procedural matters. Such principles include

---

[43] Chapter 17.   [44] Chapter 18.
[45] See the chapters on development co-operation and humanitarian aid (6), neighbourhood policy (3), and enlargement (2).
[46] Chapter 10.   [47] Chapter 12.   [48] Chapter 9.
[49] See Case C-363/14 *European Parliament v Council* EU:C:2015:579.

the rule of law, democracy, the protection of fundamental rights, equality and non-discrimination, the right to an effective judicial remedy, proportionality, subsidiarity, impartiality, sincere cooperation, good administration, legality, transparency, and assorted sub-principles arising from these main themes, such as the principles of equivalence and effectiveness of EU law, the protection of legitimate interests, rights of defence, all of which pervade the policy areas under discussion. The sectoral chapters demonstrate that such principles have mostly undergone some further specification in order to meet the particular needs of a sector, in which they may often have been applied already for a considerable time. The general duty of sincere cooperation falling upon Member States, for example, finds its discrete expression in the (not always observed) obligation of burden-sharing in the area of asylum policy.[50] Similarly, in public procurement, the principles of transparency, non-discrimination, objectivity (good governance), and accountability have acquired specific meanings there.[51]

On the other hand, our survey shows not unexpectedly a wide diversity of principles apparently specific only to individual sectors. In budget law[52] we find the principles of annuality, specification, and sound financial management affecting administrative practice. The principle that the first state of arrival has the responsibility of processing an asylum claim has been the cornerstone of EU asylum law,[53] with obvious implications for administrative organizational arrangements and procedures. In development aid we encounter the principles of development orientation, and collective and individual autonomy;[54] in Union Civil Service law the principles of the interests of the service, *devoir de solicitude*, and the rules of correspondence;[55] in data protection we find a wealth of principles that guide administrative action, such as fair and lawful processing, purpose limitation, data minimization, adequacy and relevance, accuracy, limited storage period, data security, consistency;[56] in enlargement policy we see conditionality, compliance, coherence and complementarity as principles underlying implementation actions;[57] in the field of the European Neighbourhood Policy (ENP), we can note the principle of joint ownership;[58] the principles of partnership, conditionality, concentration, and programming underpin structural funds;[59] and in environmental protection, principles such as those of ecological sustainability, integrated pollution prevention, and polluter-pays influence numerous elements within the administration of the sector.[60] Some such discrete principles can in fact be encountered in more than one field, even if not in all or many, for example, independence,[61] differentiation,[62] and conditionality.[63] It could, however, be argued that even many principles (but not all) which appear at first glance as specific to one or more sectors can ultimately be traced back to a core of general principles. For example, the specific principles in data protection law could be seen as discrete emanations of the principles of

---

[50] Chapter 8. See also E Thielemann, 'Burden-Sharing' in E Jonwa, A Menon, and S Weatherill (eds), *The Oxford Handbook of the European Union* (OUP 2012); E Kucuk, 'Solidarity in EU Law: An Elusive Political Statement or a Legal Principle with Substance?' (2016) 23 *Maastricht Journal of European and Comparative Law* 6.

[51] Chapter 18.   [52] Chapter 22.   [53] Chapter 8.   [54] Chapter 6.   [55] Chapter 21.

[56] Chapter 9.   [57] Chapter 2.   [58] Chapter 3.   [59] Chapter 20.   [60] Chapter 13.

[61] See the chapters on energy law (14), social policy (16), monetary union (10), data protection (9).

[62] See the chapters on data protection (9), enlargement (2), and ENP (3).

[63] See the chapters on enlargement (3), and EMU (10).

legality, proportionality and equality. The specific demands of environmental impact assessment might be said to have their roots in the general principle of good administration, as a reflection of the obligation on public decision-makers properly to inform themselves. The principles applicable to the structural funds could be seen as specific expressions of the principles of sincere cooperation, efficiency, and legality.

The status, role, and function of such principles in each of the sectors is not always clear. Union law could arguably benefit, therefore, from explicit articulation and clarification of the general principles of EU law which have application to the administration of Union policy, and especially of how their legal content forms administrative decision-making. A clear articulation of where general principles find concrete application or specification in particular policy areas might, for example, be achieved in a policy-specific body of rules—or in the jurisprudence of the CJEU—which deliberately and expressly distinguishes between them and additional *lex specialis* elements of the individual policy area. Put slightly differently, there would appear to be benefit in express recognition of where and when recourse is had to general principles, if only to ensure their consistent and coherent employment across the full gamut of Union activity. In doing so, express attention to different categories of principles and rights becomes possible. Famously, EU law has developed many different categories of principles: general principles of EU law; principles demanding to be complied with, but which do not have the status of primary law; and policy-specific principles such as those just exemplified above.[64] Especially in connection with procedural rights within the administrative setting, individual citizens would certainly benefit if there were a clear enunciation of default protections, rights, and claims, set out in a generally applicable legislative act of the Union.

D Sectoral Organization, Institutions, and Structures

We have argued elsewhere that the Union's organizational arrangements and structures of implementation have the characteristics of an *integrated* administration, in which Union and national administrations, while remaining organizationally and bureaucratically distinct, are functionally—and almost inseparably—intertwined in the pursuit of Union objectives resulting in a high level of procedural cooperation.[65] The sectoral policy studies presented here by and large confirm this proposition. All the same, they point to a multiplicity of ways in which national and Union administrations, together with other actors, interact to realize such an integrative administration in the different sectors.

The Union's structural organization consists of a scope of arrangements that facilitate this functional integration of national and Union administrations. As the chapter on the EMU demonstrates, such structural arrangements can be established even (but rather rarely) by primary Union law.[66] The European System of Central

---

[64] Additionally, the distinction between rights and principles introduced by the Charter in Art 52(5) has added to the general confusion surrounding this matter.
[65] Hofmann, Rowe, and Türk, *Administrative Law and Policy of the European Union* (n 1) ch 1.
[66] Chapter 10.

Banks is a particularly prominent example of an institutionalized arrangement of functional integration, in the field of monetary policy. Perhaps somewhat less prominently, but extremely pervasively indeed, comitology committees can be found in virtually all areas of Union administration, a consequence of the detailed framework established by secondary law (Comitology Regulation 182/2011) in conjunction with primary law requirements (Article 291 TFEU). As a forum enabling Member State influence and control upon the implementation of Union law by the Commission, comitology committees constitute one important example of the system of integrated administration.[67] Again, notwithstanding that, in some sectors[68] comitology plays a particularly strong role, while in others[69] it is less pronounced. In our view, this reflects, at least to some extent, the regulatory intensity of the sector in issue, as well as the typical approaches to delegation. Where there are strong agencies or less need for implementing acts on the EU-level, comitology appears to be a less prominent feature of the landscape.

In all policy areas, then, there are shades and forms of administrative integration—an organizational, procedural, informational intertwining—, facilitated by a medley of institutional arrangements and of discrete bodies tasked with ensuring that 'open, efficient and independent European administration' of Article 298(1) TFEU, which bears yet a further mention here. In what follows, we suggest a taxonomy of the variations on the basic integrative model, and the elements which contribute multifariously to the emergence of such variation.

1 Sectors inclined to centralized implementation

In a limited number of policy fields we find relatively centralized arrangements, typically where the Commission plays the central role in implementation, for example, in the field of state aid policy.[70] The Commission also logically plays a predominant role in administering the Union Civil Service and the Union budget.[71] It is, however, important to note that we can find, even within such centripetal administrative formations, the presence of a large assortment of actors. For example, in the budget field,[72] the reforms ensuing upon the Santer Commission disruptions have led to a number of key administrative (supervisory and controlling) actors, such as the authorizing and accounting officer, internal auditing, and executive agencies. The Commission, in this and related contexts, such as staffing, is supported by executive agencies (so, as regards the Civil Service, EPSO), or specialized committees (again, for the Civil Service, the Staff Committee).[73] One should also note here that in many areas it is the Commission which makes subordinate legislation for implementation purposes. This may appear to be a fully centralized administrative function, and indeed in formal terms it is. Nevertheless, here also the Commission is 'supported'—actually, controlled—

---

[67] A H Türk, 'Comitology' in A Arnull and D Chalmers (eds), *The Oxford Handbook of European Law* (OUP 2015).

[68] See the chapters on agriculture (19), development cooperation (6), environment (13), transport (12), neighbourhood (3), and health (15).

[69] See the chapters on budget (22), humanitarian aid (6), and social policy (16).   [70] Chapter 17.

[71] Chapters 21 and 22.   [72] Chapter 22.   [73] Chapter 21.

by actors from the Member States, through the comitology committees. In that sense, then, one needs to be very cautious in drawing conclusions about the actual degree of centralization of decision-making competences for the purposes of administrative implementation.

2 Specific arrangements of coordination and cooperation

An increasingly important structural arrangement, which draws in national authorities so as to create an integrated system, is the establishment, on the supranational level, of agencies (and comparable bodies), which are, by now, pillars of the Union's executive construction.[74] Increases in the regulatory intensity in any given sector will often be accompanied by an evolution of such bodies from initially informal networks to formalized agency structures, encompassing not just relevant national administrative authorities, but also (other) national and even international (i.e., non-EU) actors. For example, in asylum policy,[75] the evolution of the European Asylum Support Office into an agency was a result of increased harmonization in that sector. In the energy sector,[76] we see the integration of national regulators into a Union agency in the form of ACER, the task of which is to coordinate on the EU level the work of national energy regulators. In some policy areas, agencies have a quasi-regulatory role, including involvement in administrative rule-making and decision-making with external effect.[77] The most prominent examples of this are the three financial agencies, the EIOPA, the ESMA, and the EBA in charge respectively of insurance, securities, and banking regulation.

Next to agencies, however, there is a host of other bodies charged with dispersed administrative functions, often supervisory in nature. The chapter on data protection,[78] for example, illustrates this through individual data protection mechanisms (in areas where the EDPS has no powers), such as Europol's Cooperation Board and Eurojust's Joint Supervisory Body. Whether the dispersal of legal competences for data protection across the EDPS, national data protection authorities, and such separate data protection bodies as those just mentioned for Europol and Eurojust actually makes a positive contribution to the achievement of the European administration envisaged by Article 298(1) TFEU remains to be seen.

Integrated organizational arrangements can also be found in the shape of formally established committees that bring together a wide array of other actors. The strictest form in which this takes place is within the comitology process, under Regulation 182/2011 and Article 291 TFEU (noted already at the start of this section). It suffices to note here that the comitology system is, in its overall structure,

---

[74] S Griller and A Orator, 'Everything under control? The "way forward" for European agencies in the footsteps of the Meroni doctrine' (2010) 35 *European Law Review* 3; H C H Hofmann, A Morini, Pluralisation of EU Executive: Constitutional Aspects of Agencification (2012) 37 *European Law Review* 419; M Busuioc, *European Agencies: Law and Practices of Accountability* (Oxford University Press 2013).
[75] Chapter 8.   [76] Chapter 14.
[77] See the discussion in ch 10 on financial regulation, and in ch 15 in relation to the European Medicines Agency. See also the chapter on transport (12).
[78] Chapter 9.

a generally applicable one, but, in the detail of the hundreds of committees which operate within it, in practice always sector-specific. To that system must be added the scientific committees assisting the Commission or agencies on the Union level, found in most policy fields (and for example, particularly prominent in fields such as public health or environmental protection).[79] Such expert committees are established outside of the format of comitology.

The Open Method of Coordination, employed in the fields of employment policy[80] and economic cooperation,[81] constitutes a further set of discrete structural arrangements, subjecting Member States to a Union-oriented discipline. This, at least in its original form, relies less on hierarchically imposed formal legal rules, and more on soft law instruments such as guidelines and benchmarks.[82] While this rather more relaxed approach still applies in the area of employment policy, the recent financial and sovereign debt crisis in the Union and its Member States has seen a hardening of the formerly soft, non-binding modes of integration in the direction of more concerted, formally binding rules, in order to ensure budgetary discipline amongst the member countries of the eurozone.

Among the wide diversity of integrative structural forms in Union administration we also find the involvement of private parties in numerous policy fields. One example is the role for societal actors outside bureaucratic circles—'social partners'—in the field of social policy,[83] through social dialogue committees designed to bring together employer and employee representatives from across the Member States on the Union level. This integration of private parties in that field is both a form of co-regulation (in that workplace agreements can be declared to be generally applicable) and a form of self-regulation (in that diverse private parties themselves are the rule-makers, in principle acting without input from the institutional actors). The involvement of private parties is also of considerable importance in the fields of goods standardization,[84] energy,[85] and to some extent environment.[86] The energy field in particular shows innovative forms of co-regulation, integrating transmission systems operators into a European network structure, which itself is subject to regulatory control by ACER and the Commission.

Finally, the arrangements in the European External Action Service (EEAS) offer an example of special arrangements for cooperation between Member States and EU institutions. The special nature of these arrangements arises not only from the role of EU institutions as such, but also because activities which involve very high levels of integration are mixed together with activities of a less integrated kind, where the Member States have a rather bigger say and greater competencies. Arrangements in the EEAS are complex, not least due to the fact that they have keen relevance to the Union's CFSP, development aid, and European neighbourhood policy,[87] involving a convergence of EU institutional and Member State resources.

---

[79] Chapters 15 and 13.   [80] Chapter 16.   [81] Chapter 10.
[82] See generally K Armstrong, 'The Open Method of Coordination' in R Schütze and T Tridimas (eds), *Oxford Principles of European Union Law* (OUP 2018) ch 24.
[83] Chapter 16.   [84] Chapter 11.   [85] Chapter 14.   [86] Chapter 13.
[87] Chapters 6 and 3.

3 Sectors inclined toward Member State implementation

At the end of the spectrum away from centralized EU administration, we find policy areas where national authorities are entrusted with the administration of Union law. The purely centralized model is, as was discussed above, in fact rarely used, and essentially only for subject matters which can genuinely be regarded as internal to the Union administration in the narrow sense, specifically staffing and budget (regarding spending directly undertaken by EU bodies and agencies). Despite the fact that important budgetary elements are present in fields such as agriculture or the administration of structural funds, the Commission exercises there mainly an oversight function in a setting of shared administration with Member States.[88] In other areas as well, we see that it falls to the national authorities to implement and apply Union law under the supervision of the Commission.[89]

In respect of structural funds EU law makes, however, specific demands for certain institutional arrangements, under which Member States must designate certain discrete authorities to fulfil the roles of management authority, monitoring committee, steering committee, certifying authority and audit authority respectively.[90] Union law is thus, to a certain extent, dictating specific organizational arrangements in the Member States. The requirement of establishing independent national regulatory authorities is another typical tool of EU law which in effect imposes certain organizational arrangements on national administrations. Two of the most striking examples of this can be found in the field of the EMU, in which national central banks and banking supervisors are required by Union law to be independent.[91] This model has also been pursued in the fields of energy, transport,[92] and data protection, where Member States must establish independent supervisory authorities.[93] In the last of those fields, the Court has also established especially stringent standards with respect to the nature of the independence of the national authorities. Often such demands for discrete organizational structures at national level go hand in hand with requirements for cooperation within a network of regulatory bodies, as requirements in the field of energy regulation for certain forms of cooperation within ACER demonstrate.

Where implementation takes place essentially in, and through, national administrations, EU law limits Member State autonomy by reference usually to requirements of equivalence and effectiveness, arising from the general principle of sincere cooperation (Article 4(3) TEU). Where these standards are satisfied, the national administration can, in effect, operate independently. Sometimes the standards are stricter: in the field of asylum policy[94] Union law imposes requirements with the objective of ensuring efficient, but also fair and balanced decision-making by national authorities; and in respect of public procurement,[95] EU law prescribes the remedies which need to be made available to parties which have been unlawfully disadvantaged in a procurement process.

---

[88] Chapters 19 and 20.
[89] See the chapters on asylum (8), public procurement (18), and environment (13).
[90] Chapter 20.   [91] Chapter 10.   [92] See the chapters on energy (14) and transport (12).
[93] Chapter 9.   [94] Chapter 8.   [95] Chapter 18.

Finally, a notable feature of the structural arrangements in many of the policy fields covered in this book is the often intense interaction with third countries and international bodies. This is most obvious in the Union's external policy fields,[96] but can be observed even in essentially internal fields, where we can find strong international cooperative arrangements, for example the mixed committees in the field of transport.[97] In the field of the EMU, public international law arrangements have been used to structure the relations between the Union and its Member States on the one hand with non-EU states and international organizations on the other. In this field, next to agreements under public international law, Member States have created certain bodies under private law in order to pursue some of the Treaty objectives.[98] Thus, we encounter Union institutions (such as the Commission and the ECB) participating in private law arrangements (such as the EFSF) or subsequently in international agreements (such as the ESM), concluded by eurozone member countries outside the sphere of Union law. Similarly, the Stability Pact, although concluded as an international agreement outside Union law, includes the Commission and the Court as actors from the European Union. This latter type of agreement often requires EU institutions (particularly the Commission) to perform duties and take on responsibilities within the framework of international law agreements in the interests of the Union.

4 A propensity for experimentation and its risks

Overall, European Union law displays a propensity for experimentation in its design of organizational arrangements for the implementation of EU law. Within the broad compass of possible approaches and models, several trends stand out. One is the increasing tendency towards 'agencification', that is, either the creation of agencies on the European level, or the requirement on Member States to create independent agencies for the implementation of EU law. The second observable trend is that all levels of administration of Member States and the Union are increasingly linked through networks of information exchange and of enforcement. Thirdly, there appear to be multiple and varied configurations of administrative actors, including EU agencies, international bodies, Member State actors, private parties and others, which might be involved in the discharge of administrative tasks across the full ambit of EU policy. This can be described as a 'disaggregation of states', in that there is, for example, no longer just a single central point within a state responsible for external relations (e.g., the foreign office, or similar entity). Rather, interaction now takes place horizontally between, for example, Member States and EU bodies, or between the EU and international organizations and bodies, policy-by-policy, through specialist actors, or on the expert level. Despite the possible value of an experimental approach of combining sundry actors in such deconcentrated ways, certain basic building-blocks for interaction and the establishment of mutual obligations should be relied upon. For reasons of transparency, predictability, and consistency in compliance with the rule of law,

---

[96] See the chapters on development cooperation and humanitarian aid (6), enlargement (2), and the ENP (3).
[97] Chapter 12.   [98] Chapter 10.

such standard elements should, in our view, become part of the generally applicable regime governing EU administrative practice (to which we return explicitly in the final section of this chapter). We would argue that, a combination of (evolutionary) experimentation coupled with standardized—and well-articulated and understood—administrative structures would ultimately be more productive than recourse to essentially untried mechanisms with the concomitant risks of legal uncertainty, inadequate levels of transparency, insufficient oversight, and inadequate protection of individual rights.

E Administrative Procedures and Acts

The administrative procedures through which national and European administrations, private parties, and third countries interact with varying levels of intensity, are revealed by the contributors to this work as being both diverse and complex. As regards other sub-topics, we offer here suggestions for categorizing such procedural elements. At this point one should perhaps offer an explanatory comment. In earlier sections we have addressed matters such as tasks, actors, sources, and structures. These—essentially static—elements might loosely be regarded as diverse forms of 'hardware', whereas procedures, that is, a course of action or sequence of steps, and their associated forms of administrative acts—dynamic elements—might in contrast be considered the 'software' of public administrative activity. Whether one finds this analogy informative or not, the point should be made that the 'dynamic' elements are capable of existing, and operating, only within a setting provided by the 'static' elements. This distinction underlies the types of matters falling within this section of the chapter, and within the corresponding parts of the sectoral contributions presented in this book. A further preliminary note may also be useful: in addressing the typical functions of the administration, we made some reference to the 'phases' of administrative activity; such phases can in themselves perhaps be conceived as (coherent and periodic) clusters of particular procedural steps, and we make some further reference to phases of activity in what follows.

1 Agenda-setting and planning

In the phase of agenda-setting and planning, steps often assimilated into a wider strategic and programming cycle, the Commission occupies a central role in all policy areas considered in this volume. Despite that, in that phase the Commission interacts variously, but always intensively, with other Union bodies, national authorities, private parties, and third countries. The nature of the planning phases and of the activities associated with them differs across the sectors and administrative fields, depending on the intensity and character of the regulation found in each one. For example, in the preparation of the Union's annual budget,[99] the Commission is part of a highly formalized planning process of interaction with other Union institutions. On

---

[99] Chapter 22.

the other hand, in its external actions,[100] the Commission enjoys considerable latitude, with few process-constraints being imposed in its interaction with third countries (noting, for all that, in the field of external trade a growing role for the European Parliament and for comitology, despite a dominance by the Commission).[101] In some areas, there is a need for the Commission to consult particular EU agencies, such as in the field of banking[102] (as well as in insurance and securities regulation).[103] In others, the Commission is accorded a leading role in the agenda-setting and programming stage, such as in the structural funds sector.[104]

Our sectoral survey here shows that preparatory measures come in widely assorted forms. While the Commission exercises its Union-internal agenda-setting role mainly through proposals, communications, and white papers, in the international-external sphere it might more commonly resort to 'action plans' and progress reports as preparatory measures, for example in the Union's neighbourhood policy.[105] In addition, as the contribution on transport policy[106] shows, other bodies can exercise an influence on the setting of the Union's agenda. For example, legislation may mandate that the Commission take particular steps here, including the submission of legislative proposals. For its part, the Council may resort to resolutions and conclusions to set out its position on policy development. Similarly, as the chapter on data protection notes,[107] the Council by way of resolutions, and the European Council in its adoption of strategic guidelines in the AFSJ, will materially influence policy programming in this field.

Overall, the agenda-setting and policy-formulation phase is shaped predominantly by the requirements of work programmes, sometimes coupled with an obligation to publish such programmes and, with respect to some agencies, to have them approved in advance. In this phase, and in the later phase of the preparation of specific executive rule-making, not only of delegated and implementing acts but arguably also of plans, guidelines and other tools intended to influence implementation, there is a need to generate, gather, provide, and exchange information. This is so in order to ensure that the value choices of Article 11 TEU—transparency, coherence, and the capacity of expression and exchange of citizens' views as a foundation for the active participation of a well-informed public—can be realized. Such central values need to be furthered by the *active* provision of information, concerning both policy, and regulatory intentions and goals, and responding to reasonable needs and expectations articulated by the public. Obligations pointing to this arise from the principles of good administration and of the exercise of diligence (the administrative 'duty of care'), reinforced by the requirement of reasoned and proportional decision-making. Deliberate, systematic procedures are necessary to support the capturing of key data—facts, expertise, political social and cultural values, economic and other interests: impact assessment studies, cost-benefit analyses, and agency-guided expertise have all become commonplace in many policy areas, sometimes a necessity in the face of intensified proportionality

---

[100] See the chapters on development co-operation and humanitarian aid planning (6), ENP (3), enlargement (2), and external trade (4).

[101] Chapter 4.   [102] Chapter 10.

[103] For the EBA, see Arts 8(2)(g) and 34(1) of Regulation 1093/2010, as amended [2010] OJ L331/12.

[104] Chapter 20.   [105] Chapter 3.   [106] Chapter 12.   [107] Chapter 9.

review of administrative action. However, their ad hoc nature in motley fields, and the lack of a consistent approach, result in unnecessary variance and a lack of coordination and coherence, often making it difficult for those not experts in a specific sector to grasp how, and why, things are done. Through more standard approaches there is much potential for strengthening the expression of the values just noted, upon which the Union's policy-making and legal system are based.

2 Administrative rule-making

(a) Procedures

In relation to the adoption of subordinate legislative rules on the Union level, the studies here point only to a limited number of procedural circumstances in which EU institutions exercise implementing powers centrally, and effectively alone. Concerning the Union Civil Service,[108] interaction for the purpose of rule-making occurs within a relatively restricted circle of Union institutions and a limited number of committees. Also, in the field of monetary policy,[109] we encounter a relatively centralized procedural regime for subordinate rule-making. In the field of transport,[110] we also observe a limited number of acts adopted just by the Commission or of de facto binding administrative rules adopted by a Union agency (such as the European Aviation Safety Agency).

Implementation through rule-making has, nevertheless, traditionally been characterized by heterogeneous procedures involving considerable interaction between assorted actors on both European and national levels. The adoption of subordinate rules is, in most areas, characterized by highly interactive and complex procedural arrangements. We have already noted above the key role of comitology committees in the subordinate legislative process. In most areas, comitology procedures in fact dominate the process for the making of *implementing* acts on the Union level, by the Commission or exceptionally by the Council (Article 291 TFEU). The rather formalized nature of comitology committees provides both the Commission and national authorities with a stable, predictable, and standardized procedural framework for their interaction in the adoption of subordinate rules. Such rules can include traditional (tertiary) legislative measures (Commission regulations) and general programming and planning measures. The CAP[111] provides examples of the former, development and humanitarian aid policy[112] provides examples of the latter. Legislative acts, which may determine the comitology procedure(s) applicable, often also lay down the procedural arrangements for the adoption by the Commission of *delegated* acts (Article 290 TFEU). While the procedures for the adoption of delegated acts may be less formalistic, they are often characterized by politically sensitive interactions among the Commission, the Council, and the European Parliament.

In many areas, Union rule-making is dominated by a range of composite procedures. As the chapter on public health[113] shows, such procedures may be initiated on

---

[108] Chapter 21.   [109] Chapter 10.   [110] Chapter 12.   [111] Chapter 19.
[112] Chapter 6.   [113] Chapter 15.

the national level, as in the case of the decentralized procedure for the approval of pharmaceutical products (and as in environmental protection, regarding the admission of chemicals to the European market, or the transboundary transport of waste),[114] or on the European level where essentially centralized procedures are employed (see above). Increasingly Union agencies form an integral part of such composite procedures.[115] These may also include interaction with third countries, as in the field of Union enlargement, with private parties, as in the energy field,[116] or with Member States, as in the case of structural funds.[117]

The Commission has in its 2015 Better Regulation package (in the form of soft law) promised a series of far reaching reforms in the phase of administrative rule-making. However, these have been directed to only a limited scope of initiatives, and have not been given binding nature. Instead, they remain within the small print of convoluted, non-binding policy documents.[118]

(b) Forms of acts

Delegated and implementing acts in the form of regulations, directives, and decisions adopted by the Commission, in accordance with Articles 290 and 291 TFEU respectively, are the main forms of subordinate legislation and occur in all policy areas. Implementing decisions are common forms of acts as a legal basis of Union financing actions. In development and humanitarian aid,[119] for example, multi-annual indicative programmes, annual action programmes, and humanitarian aid operational priorities take the form of implementing decisions. Similarly, the Union's neighbourhood policy[120] uses such measures to adopt multi-annual single-support frameworks, and strategy and multi-annual indicative programmes for single or multiple countries, as do also the annual work programmes in the field of public health.[121] In other areas, such as energy,[122] Union legislation provides for the adoption of guidelines or network codes, which are adopted in the form of Commission regulations. In the field of public health[123] the Commission adopts principles and guidelines of good manufacturing practice by way of (Commission) directives, often referred to also as 'specific directives'[124] (a term used albeit also for certain directives of the Council).[125]

---

[114] Chapter 13.
[115] See the chapters on public health (EMA) (15), transport (EASA, ERA) (14), and energy (ACER) (12).
[116] Chapter 16.   [117] Chapter 20.
[118] European Commission, 2015 Better Regulation guidelines and toolbox, Chapter IV Guidelines on preparing proposals, implementation, and transposition, 38 https://ec.europa.eu/info/law/law-making-process/planning-and-proposing-law/better-regulation-why-and-how/better-regulation-guidelines-and-toolbox_en.
[119] Chapter 6.   [120] Chapter 3.   [121] Chapter 15.   [122] Chapter 14.
[123] Chapter 15.
[124] See eg Art 4(1) Commission Directive 2006/141/EC of 22 December 2006 on infant formulae and follow-on formulae [2006] OJ L401/1–33, as provided for in Council Directive 89/398/EEC of 3 May 1989 on the approximation of the laws of the Member States relating to foodstuffs intended for particular nutritional uses [1989] OJ L186/27.
[125] Council Directive 78/142/EEC of 30 January 1978 on the approximation of the laws of the Member States relating to materials and articles which contain vinyl chloride monomer and are intended to come into contact with foodstuffs [1978] OJ L044/15.

A mixture of administrative instruments can also be observed in the field of monetary union,[126] including guidelines (which then are binding directly only on national central banks (NCBs)).

There exists an even greater spread of administrative rules. A recurring form is that of (non-binding) guidelines, which are, however, used in different policy fields with different purposes. In the field of labour law,[127] employment guidelines adopted on the basis of Article 148 TFEU set common priorities and targets for national authorities to implement within their national employment policies, as part of the OMC. Such guidelines are different from those that the Commission lays down to guide its discretion, as in the field of state aid,[128] which are binding only on the Commission and on those Member States which accept them. In the field of budget implementation the Commission draws up standards and guidelines that are intended for use by other Union institutions, national authorities, and delegated bodies.[129] The intention there is to achieve a common approach to budget implementation. Similarly, Commission guidelines in the transport sector[130] are intended to promote harmonized application of Union law, in the form of recommendations, or to facilitate Member State cooperation. For this purpose, the Commission is also asked to draw up annual guidelines for humanitarian operations. In that external sphere, a large variety of non-binding instruments, such as Commission country action plans, strategy papers and progress reports, or Council and European Council conclusions are employed.[131]

Finally, contractual arrangements between the social partners form an important outcome of the Union's social dialogue procedures. These can lead to generally applicable rules, if declared so by Member States or EU bodies.[132] Specific examples of agreements between social partners can also be found in the area of transport policy.[133] Major issues with regard to negotiated rule-making (as well as in fact individual decisions) which, as a matter of legal policy, still need close attention include questions of participation, representation and representativeness, the possibilities of influence by particular interests (lobbying), transparency, and enforcement. These are important matters of a systemic nature, and EU administrative law still needs to provide explicit legal frameworks, beyond and across individual sectoral policy areas.

3 Open method of coordination

Outside the confines of more traditional procedural arrangements, the studies here also reveal the reliance on a number of sector-specific procedures. In particular, in the areas of employment policy,[134] and economic policy,[135] the Open Method of Coordination has come to occupy a central role in the decision-making process. This procedure relies on a close interaction between Union and national executive authorities to the exclusion of the European Parliament. As a form of *executive* governance, the procedure was intended to follow a reiterative process, initially of the issue of Union guidelines, then the formation of national implementation plans, followed by a

---

[126] Chapter 10.   [127] Chapter 16.   [128] Chapter 17.
[129] Chapter 22.   [130] Chapter 14.
[131] See the chapters on neighbourhood (2), external trade (3), and development (6).
[132] Chapter 16.   [133] Chapter 14.   [134] Chapter 16.   [135] Chapter 10.

Commission evaluation, as a whole intended to encourage participation, deliberation, and learning based on 'benchmarks' rather than relying on fixing standards in hard (or formal) law. While this approach is still followed in the field of employment,[136] the OMC process in the field of the economic union[137] has been now largely supplemented with hard law elements, involving accelerated procedures and sanctions for eurozone members. International agreements, as in the case of the Fiscal Compact, have given rise to more hybrid forms of Union law.

4 Co-regulation

Our studies also show the increasing use of co-regulation involving Union institutions and private parties, not only in the traditional areas of product standardization[138] and labour law,[139] but also within the energy sector.[140] For example, in the latter, Transmission System Operators (TSOs), within the framework of the European Network of TSOs (ENTSO), play an important role in the process leading to the adoption of network codes. The sectoral examination also hints at how the extent of involvement and impact of private actors can vary in such procedures. While, on one side of the spectrum social partners[141] may enjoy considerable, perhaps even decisive, influence within the process of adoption of autonomous agreements, on the other side of the spectrum, the ENTSO is closely integrated into a composite procedure involving the ACER, the Commission and comitology committees, so that its impact is somewhat relativized.[142] Whether, how, and under which conditions, private parties are involved in rule-making, even negotiated rule-making, requires in fact much further scrutiny.

5 Single-case decision-making

The wide scope of decisions taken by EU institutions, agencies and other bodies is brought out by the present contributions. While such decision-making activity is fully to be expected in the Union Civil Service,[143] in budget management,[144] and in state aid,[145] single-case decisions also occur in the field of data protection[146] (by the Commission), energy policy[147] (by ACER or the Commission), public health[148] (by the EMA or the Commission), and transport[149] (by the Commission in its supervisory capacity, based directly on the relevant Treaty provisions, or by the Commission, EASA, and ERA in the implementation of Union legislation), and in environmental protection and customs (typically by Member State authorities).[150] In addition to single-case decisions which are legally binding, the studies here also reveal a wide use of non-binding measures, such as the provision of information or of preparatory measures in state aid cases.[151]

---

[136] Chapter 16.   [137] Chapter 10.   [138] Chapter 11.   [139] Chapter 16.
[140] Chapter 14.   [141] Chapter 16.   [142] Chapter 14.   [143] Chapter 21.
[144] Chapter 22.   [145] Chapter 17.   [146] Chapter 9.   [147] Chapter 14.
[148] Chapter 15.   [149] Chapter 12.   [150] Chapters 13 and 5.   [151] Chapter 17.

The steps leading to the adoption of single-case decisions by Union bodies are usually tightly regulated by Treaty provisions, EU secondary legislation, and the requirements established in CJEU caselaw. Highly formalized procedures apply in particular where Union institutions are entrusted with the adoption of administrative acts that have negative consequences for their addressees. This includes disciplinary action in Civil Service proceedings,[152] sanctions against private parties in the field of monetary union,[153] decisions concerning data protection,[154] state aid decisions,[155] and supervisory decisions in transport matters.[156] Similarly tightly regulated are procedures that involve revenue and expenditure operations in the field of budget management,[157] with some variability consequent upon the particular management mode employed (direct, indirect, and shared management).

At the other end of the spectrum, where national authorities are entrusted with the implementation of Union law, the studies here show that they are often integrated into a procedural framework which is also more or less tightly regulated. In the field of asylum policy,[158] national discretion has increasingly been reduced in favour of procedural standards set by Union law. Similar procedural restrictions apply where national regulators exercise their powers in the field of energy law, data protection law, environmental law, and public procurement law.[159] In the structural funds sector,[160] however, the Member States enjoy a wide margin of discretion in the application of EU funds to national and regional projects. The Commission's role is, in that context, more limited to a monitoring function which relies on a number of procedures to ensure compliance with Union financial rules.

Given that the decentralized implementation of Union law by national authorities is the default position (Article 291(1) TFEU), it is not surprising that the contributions here highlight the important role of binding measures adopted in the Member States, be it, for example, procurement decisions,[161] or authorizations in public health matters.[162] All the same, it is noteworthy to observe that many such single-case decisions are taken by national authorities which, in accordance with the requirements of EU law, must act independently of Member State influence as such. Whether it concerns decisions by a controller or national supervisory authority in the field of data protection,[163] by national regulatory authorities in the field of energy policy,[164] or by the national management authority in structural fund cases,[165] the independence of such national bodies in adopting their decisions, although strictly within a Member State and acting on the national level, is striking.

6 Agreements

In contrast to the unilateral measures addressed in the preceding sub-sections, the present survey shows recourse to quite a number of bilateral arrangements. In certain areas these take the form of contractual arrangements, such as those between

[152] Chapter 21. [153] Chapter 10. [154] Chapter 8. [155] Chapter 17.
[156] Chapter 12. [157] Chapter 22. [158] Chapter 8. [159] Chapters 14, 9, 13, and 18.
[160] Chapter 20. [161] Chapter 18. [162] Chapter 15. [163] Chapter 9.
[164] Chapter 14. [165] Chapter 20.

controller and processor in the field of data protection,[166] or a grant agreement or subsidy contract in structural fund cases.[167] The contributions here also provide examples of agreements between public authorities, such as those between the Commission and Member States as part of the review of existing aid,[168] or administrative agreements in the transport sector[169] with the aim of furthering administrative cooperation via networks of national regulators *inter se,* and of national regulators together with Union agencies and other actors.

The contributions also highlight the proliferation of international arrangements between Union bodies and third countries. Such arrangements can be binding international agreements, and it is not surprising to find a considerable number of such agreements in the areas touching the Union's external relations. In the enlargement field[170] we encounter (general) Association Agreements, as well as (sector-specific) agreements in relation to migration, air transport, CFSP, visa facilitation, external trade, and financial framework agreements. Some are multilateral, illustrated by (again) Association Agreements, by the Energy Community Treaty and the Treaty on the Common European Aviation Area, by the General Agreement on Trade in Services (GATS)), the Agreement on Trade-Related Aspects of Intellectual Property Rights (TRIPs) and the GATT/WTO all in the context of external trade,[171] and by agreements in relation to river basin management within Union water protection policy (although these, even though under the aegis of the Union's water framework, may be just between certain Member States and third countries, without EU membership).[172] Some international agreements may be bilateral, for example, the EU-Japan free trade agreement and the EU-China bilateral investment treaty.[173] Similarly, agreements are also relied upon for the implementation of the Union's neighbourhood policy,[174] such as the EU Association Agreement with Ukraine, or for financing agreements in the field of development aid. In addition, outside the fields of external policy, we can encounter bilateral agreements, for example in the fields of economic and monetary union,[175] and of public health.[176] Finally, a novel form of international arrangement can be found in the field of economic and monetary union,[177] where the relevant study highlights a special emanation of what we would identify as 'intergovernmental private law'.

Our contributions emphasize the importance of non-binding tools in the management of international relations, going hand-in-hand with formal arrangements. In the field of enlargement[178] we encounter cooperative arrangements between EU agencies and accession candidates, or action plans and association agendas, adopted by joint bodies towards the implementation of agreements. In the public health sector[179] we see the importance of guidelines and recommendations, as in the case of the Conference of Parties to the FCTC.[180]

Some of our contributions highlight certain procedural deficits in the engagement of Union institutions with third countries. As the contribution on the Union's neighbourhood policy shows, it is not clear that the comitology procedure is legally

---

[166] Chapter 9.　　[167] Chapter 20.　　[168] Chapter 6.　　[169] Chapter 12.
[170] Chapter 2.　　[171] Chapter 4.　　[172] Chapter 13.　　[173] Chapter 4.
[174] Chapter 3.　　[175] Chapter 10.　　[176] Chapter 15.　　[177] Chapter 10.
[178] Chapter 2.　　[179] Chapter 15.
[180] See Case C-358/14 *Poland v European Parliament and Council* EU:C:2016:323, para 45.

appropriate for the adoption of Memoranda of Understanding (MoUs) with neigh-bouring countries.[181] Similarly, the engagement of Union agencies with third country authorities in the enlargement process is pursued through a multitude of *sui generis* procedures, employing sundry types of *sui generis* instruments.[182] In contrast, as regards the financial support of third countries, procedures are more tightly controlled by the provisions of the Financial Regulation and comparable sector-specific instruments. Anomalies emerge, as the chapter on development and humanitarian aid[183] testifies, in the arrangements with ACP countries. International administrative ar-rangements require—and would indeed be amenable to—a stricter degree of scrutiny apropos their application and impact.

7 Procedures within information networks

Our studies show the increasing importance of procedures within cooperative in-formation networks. These can include national, European, and international actors of a public sector kind, as well as private parties, in diverse combinations. The sys-tems of, and procedures for, information exchange within and through such net-works vary considerably. In the area of budget control, there are especially detailed rules on reporting and on budget-implementing measures. The Commission is spe-cifically charged with maintaining certain databases for the purposes of informa-tion exchange, with law enforcement bodies responsible for protecting the financial interests of the Union.[184] Other examples of information networks for law enforce-ment purposes are more elaborate, especially in the Area of Freedom, Security and Justice (AFSJ), involving the linkage of databases of independent EU agencies, such as Europol and Frontex, and large police and immigration databases, most notably the Schengen and the Visa Information System (VIS), and EURODAC (for the collection of biometric details of asylum seekers and individuals crossing an EU border). The in-formation 'nodes' of such networks provide access for European and Member State authorities, as well as certain other actors.[185]

Some information exchange is geared towards risk regulation in the internal market. Here we encounter examples such as the rapid alert system in the field of public health,[186] networks for information exchange in the energy field,[187] and the mutual as-sistance mechanism in the field of data protection.[188] The last of these also provides an example of notification obligations (so-called 'push' requirements). Other fields such as taxation involve, on the other hand, certain rights to request information (so-called 'pull' requirements). Reliance on cooperative information networks also characterizes other regulatory contexts, such as the environment protection sector.[189]

Legal requirements or empowerments for the establishment of information net-works are typically derived from the relevant policy-specific legislation. Legislation creating an agency is also generally where the obligation or the mandate to estab-lish and maintain databases and information exchange systems is to be found. In

---

[181] Chapter 3.   [182] Chapter 2.   [183] Chapter 6.   [184] See the chapter on budget (22).
[185] See the chapters on criminal law (7) and asylum (8).
[186] Chapter 15.   [187] Chapter 16.   [188] Chapter 9.   [189] Chapter 13.

some policy areas, information networks are established as a result of agreements between the actors involved in a field, for example, the 2010 agreement between Eurojust and Europol on exchange of 'strategic and technical information, including personal data'.[190]

In recent years the trend in a number of policy areas has been towards greater interoperability of information systems, intended to facilitate the efficient use of information once collected. In fields where no, or only limited, discretion exists in decision-making, such interoperability is often directed towards algorithmic data searching, enabling, in the medium term, also the use of automated decision-making systems, with or without final human input. These developments in a number of fields raise complex questions about the adequacy of procedural arrangements to safeguard the transfer and use of personal or business data, to control access by third parties, to ensure appropriate access by affected third parties, and to guarantee the judicial protection of the rights of all such potentially affected actors. Information exchange systems lie at the heart of composite administrative structures, mentioned above, and such procedures invariably cross several regulatory levels and spaces, involving steps and measures available to copious authorities. The classic administrative law challenges of controlling executive bodies and their activities, and ensuring rights of review, rights of information, and access to documents, coupled with ensuring responsibility and liability for wrongdoing by officials, and guaranteeing access to competent judicial fora, are all compounded in settings of networked information exchange. Increased interoperability, while arguably desirable to attain certain policy goals, exacerbates these issues, and demands a concomitant strengthening of rules and practices ensuring transparency and accountability, ideally of a general, cross-sectoral nature rather than being particular to individual policy fields.

F Legal Rules Governing the Substance of Decision-making

The studies here show that the executive implementation of European Union policy across the different sectors typically relies on the bestowing of administrative competences which generally involve the exercise of some kind of discretion. Often such discretion is broadly framed, leaving administrative officials with wide powers, subject to few limitations. This is so not only where, for example, the Commission is entrusted with agenda-setting powers in external relations.[191] That institution is generally accorded a broad discretion where it adopts administrative rules for policy implementation, whether these are legally binding or eventually just non-binding guidance.[192] The contributions to this book reveal a wide discretion (or margin of appreciation) in the application of Treaty or legislative provisions in certain situations, such as the assessment of compatibility of state aid with Article 107(3) TFEU,[193] or applying the criterion of adequacy in data protection cases.[194] This is also the case concerning

---

[190] See the chapter on data protection in police and justice cooperation (9).
[191] See the chapters on enlargement (2), neighbourhood policy (3), development cooperation and humanitarian aid (6).
[192] See the chapters on transport (12), budget (22), or agriculture (19).   [193] Chapter 17.
[194] Chapter 9.

the Commission's monitoring and enforcement of rules in structural funds cases.[195] Discretionary powers are entrusted not just to the Commission, but also to other actors, such as to the ECB in the area of monetary union,[196] or to social partners in the field of social policy.[197]

Constraints on such discretionary powers vary, as authors in this collection show. Agenda-setting powers and, to a lesser extent, funding allocation in the context of the Union's external aid relations seem the least regulated.[198] Limitations arise there mainly as a result of executive self-limitation. Similarly, the Commission's broad discretion in assessing the compatibility of state aid with Article 107(3) TFEU, mentioned above, is mainly constrained by its own self-imposed guidelines, but also under general principles of law.[199] In monetary policy matters, the ECB's discretion is mainly circumscribed by open-textured Treaty provisions, but also against the backdrop of the increasingly assertive use of proportionality as a general principle by the Court.[200] Where broadly worded Treaty provisions in the field of economic policy have recently been supplemented by more tightly expressed secondary legislation, the OMC still operates in the area of employment policy under a broader, less constraining, Treaty framework.[201]

In the light of rather limited substantive constraints on widely framed administrative discretion, the sectoral studies highlight the importance of procedural rules and principles, as well as firm standards for the transparency of decision-making, as a counterweight. Such procedurally embodied limits are particularly well developed in state aid cases,[202] for the transfer of funds in external relations,[203] and for the administration of the structural funds.[204] Additional to these, though, the Union legislator could limit the discretion of administrative officials through more narrowly expressed enabling provisions. Union courts could also be more restrictive in their application of Treaty provisions, secondary legislation, and general principles of law, when subjecting administrative decisions to judicial review.

The contributions show a clear trend in favour of a higher degree of Union-level constraint on the exercise of discretion by national administrative officials who, as already noted, still constitute the main locus for the implementation of Union law in many areas. Such decision-making constraints can be seen in the Common European Asylum System,[205] where EU legislation has progressively narrowed the vast discretion of national authorities in applying European law. Similarly, the organizational and structural demands on the implementation of the Union's transport,[206] energy,[207] and environment policy,[208] data protection,[209] and the administration of structural funds[210] on the national level, have seen an increased functional integration of national administrations within the Union's administrative space. In areas such as public procurement,[211] where national authorities have traditionally enjoyed considerable autonomy, Union legislation and caselaw now impose ever greater demands for

---

[195] Chapter 20.   [196] Chapter 10.   [197] Chapter 16.
[198] See the chapters on enlargement (2), neighbourhood (3), and development (6).
[199] Chapter 17.   [200] Chapter 10.   [201] Chapter 16.   [202] Chapter 17.
[203] See the chapters on enlargement (2), neighbourhood (3), and development (6).
[204] Chapter 20.   [205] Chapter 8.   [206] Chapter 12.   [207] Chapter 14.
[208] Chapter 13.   [209] Chapter 9.   [210] Chapter 20.   [211] Chapter 18.

remedial action and procedural compliance, thus also placing a brake on the breadth and liberty of discretionary decision-making.

G Administrative Enforcement

Our contributions show that the traditional, decentralized enforcement model, whereby Member State authorities enforce Union law wholly according to national standards and within national procedures, has given way in many areas to a more complex interaction between EU and national law, often considerably restricting national autonomy, or indeed removing it entirely. So, in the areas of public procurement and asylum,[212] national autonomy in the enforcement of EU rules has become increasingly restricted. For example, there has been a move from minimum procedural rules in respect of asylum, to a more comprehensive set of European procedural provisions.[213] The adoption of an EU Remedies Directive, requiring national authorities to provide a particular set of remedies in case of a breach of public procurement rules by national authorities, is a further such example.[214] We can add to these the significant requirement that national administrative authorities, in the energy and transport sectors, are to have the power to impose sanctions, including criminal sanctions, in cases of breach of Union law in those fields.[215] Further, we observe that EU law increasingly strives to insist on the independence of national administrative authorities in pursuit of effective enforcement in fields such as data protection,[216] energy,[217] and transport law.[218]

In many instances, the Union exercises enforcement powers in parallel with those exercised by national authorities. While in some instances, as in the fields of energy and transport policy,[219] the enforcement competences of Union officials may be subject to limits (or even non-existent), in other areas, such as data protection, they are more extensive.[220] A distinct, but related, factor can be seen in the increasing use of shared enforcement, namely that EU and national authorities together may undertake measures for the enforcement of Union law. We can note here too the comparable claim, made by other scholars, that there has been a shift in direct enforcement of EU law from being primarily the responsibility of Member States to being a shared responsibility of national and Union actors.[221] This can be observed in state aid law,[222] where a Commission decision orders the recovery of aid, but it is for the Member

---

[212] See chapters 18 and 8.   [213] Chapter 8.
[214] Chapter 18.   [215] Chapters 12 and 14.   [216] Chapter 9.   [217] Chapter 14.
[218] Chapter 12.
[219] Chapters 12 and 14. In the field of transport, Regulation 11 concerning the abolition of discrimination in transport rates and conditions ((1960) 1121, as amended by Regulation 569/2008 [2008] OJ L161/1, provides for enforcement by the Member States, and empowers the Commission to conduct inspections to check compliance with such obligations imposed on undertakings (Art 14), and it may in cases of discrimination within Art 95(1) TFEU, impose a penalty on a responsible carrier (Art 18).
[220] Chapter 9.
[221] See M Scholten, M Maggetti, and E Versluis, 'Political and Judicial Accountability in Shared Enforcement in the EU' in M Scholten and M Luchtman (eds), *Law Enforcement by EU Authorities* (Edward Elgar Publishing 2017) 353.
[222] Chapter 17.

State to enforce such a recovery decision. Similarly, complex mechanisms for shared enforcement also exist where Union funds are administered in the shared management mode, as in the case of structural funds,[223] and agriculture.[224] In those areas we encounter a tendency for the development of enforcement networks. Such networks are often the logical response to the adoption of national and Union acts by way of composite procedures. While increasing the effectiveness of EU law enforcement, such networks raise difficult questions regarding the sharing of information, accountability, and the appropriate forum for judicial review.

Finally, in those areas where the Union itself exercises direct powers of enforcement, we encounter a diversity of Union actors charged with that task. This might be the Commission, the Council, agencies, and other Union bodies, depending on the sector and the issue. The enforcement of Union law without any involvement of Member States is, notably, rather the exception (e.g., the field of Union Civil Service law).[225] Nevertheless, we need to remind ourselves that there are areas, such as customs and external trade, where very significant aspects of enforcement are in the hands of national authorities (even though even there legislation and other measures seek to ensure uniformity in the application of Union law).[226] A number of the chapters on the Union's external relations demonstrate a strong role for the Commission and, to a more limited extent, the Council, in the enforcement of EU law vis-à-vis third countries. In the absence of traditional enforcement mechanisms for ensuring compliance through judicially enforceable measures, Union legislation often provides for *ex ante* provisions in agreements concluded with third countries, thus allowing it to impose sanctions on them and, where necessary and/or effective, their citizens, for example in the form of suspension of financial instruments, or regarding access to the Union market.[227] It is of interest that, in the latest rounds of accession negotiations, new Member States were subjected to a spread of post-accession enforcement mechanisms, even after joining the Union, thus prolonging the opportunity for the Union to exert effective political, legal and economic influence.[228]

At this point, for purposes of clarity, we should once again make clear the distinction between enforcement and supervision. The classic sense of 'enforcement' is that of measures against (mainly) private subjects in connection with the fulfilment of their legal obligations (whether under environmental law, competition law, agricultural law, customs law, or the legal regimes on consumer protection, banking, transport, telecommunications, foodstuffs or energy). 'Supervision', on the other hand, should be understood as an element of the (full) achievement of the administrative responsibilities in the field concerned, that is, specifically related to ensuring that the responsible administrative officials of the sector concerned (on whatever level) do their job, and do so correctly (including, strictly speaking, the supervision of their carrying out their enforcement responsibilities).

---

[223] Chapter 20.   [224] Chapter 19.
[225] Chapter 21. See generally M Scholten and M Luchtman (eds), *Law Enforcement by EU Authorities: Implications for Political and Judicial Accountability* (Edward Elgar Publishing 2017).
[226] Chapters 4 and 5.   [227] See the chapters on free movement of goods (11) and customs (5).
[228] Chapter 2.

Admittedly, in some sectors, including some addressed in this work, these two categories might be confused. Enforcement in the public procurement sector could, for example, possibly be confused with supervision, but that is because the conduct of (correct) procurement procedures is the task of the (national) public administration. The 'contracting authorities' of procurement law—national public authorities—are here, then, themselves the addressees of Union regulation.[229] By way of contrast, in competition law or the agriculture sector it is (almost invariably) only private actors which are the focus of regulatory strictures, and against whom enforcement, as such, occurs. In certain sectors (external relations, enlargement, neighbourhood policy, foreign aid) we should add that enforcement, in the classic sense of sanctions against private subjects (or possibly elements of the (national) administrations) will hardly be present at all (except perhaps for misuse of Union finances). In the data protection sector there is also room for confusion: there can be enforcement of data protection standards *by and through* administrative data protection authorities against other bodies and persons (e.g., in the PJC sector, essentially against *other* public authorities). On the other hand, there can be the insistent application (which might misleadingly be called 'enforcement') of data protection requirements against (lower level) data protection authorities themselves. The former actions should better be regarded as genuine *enforcement*, the latter, however, rather as *supervision and control*. In this particular policy field, it may appear difficult to maintain this distinction, even be considered hair-splitting; nevertheless, it is still possible both conceptually and practically, and to do so aids analytical clarity.

H Supervision

The supervisory arrangements within the Union are varied, and frequently operate across different governance levels. This is not surprising given the involvement of different actors and procedures on national and supranational level in the administration of EU law. What is surprising, as our contributions show, is the diversity of arrangements in the several policy fields concerning the three different—classic—modes of supervision and control (administrative, political and judicial, as noted already in Chapter 1).

1 Administrative Supervision

Arrangements for administrative supervision are often oriented towards supervision by Union administrative officials of the application of Union law by national authorities, but control by Union administrators over other Union administrative actors

---

[229] Enforcement against national public officials (as distinct from the supervision of them) can occur in other sectors as well, eg in the environmental sphere (ch 13), data protection (ch 9), European funds (ch 20), or abuse of Union finances (ch 22). Some enforcement may also direct essentially central EU officials in the contest of budgetary law (eg involving OLAF investigations against EU-internal actors including agencies, services, and individuals) or in civil service law (noting also the possible corollary: that 'private' actions may be brought by civil servants against the administration, as civil service law has partly a 'bilateral' character).

cannot be overlooked. The contributions here show, as with other elements of public administration, a wide scope in the mechanisms employed. These extend from special internal investigatory bodies in the field of the EU Civil Service law, such as the Investigation and Disciplinary Office (IDOC) and a staff Ombudsman,[230] to more complex arrangements, as in the case of budget management, where authorizing and accounting officers, internal auditors, and the Audit Progress Committee, together with specialized irregularity committees, ensure the proper application of EU law by Union officials.[231] In some policy fields, such as transport and energy, supervisory control, here by the Commission over Union agencies, is more limited.[232] A special arrangement for agency control can be found in the case of Europol, where national supervisory authorities and the European Data Protection Supervisor (EDPS) exercise joint supervisory powers.[233]

Of particular note within the realm of administrative supervision are examples of independent supervision, that is, supervisory control in effect outside the normal hierarchy of administrative organization, in particular by the Court of Auditors and OLAF. Both of these are especially important where the Union disburses funds, but they have a *pervasive* horizontal function across different policy fields, so that one needs in fact to identify them as part of the general regime of administrative law, rather than of the specialized (sectoral) regimes. Similarly, in the field of data protection, the supervisory role of the EDPS over data controllers on the Union level is similarly a general element.[234] In areas where European agencies are entrusted with the adoption of binding acts, Boards of Appeal[235] in each pertinent sector perform an important function of administrative control, as is the case of energy policy, where an appeal lies to a Board of Appeal for decisions taken by ACER.[236]

The often decentralized application of Union law on the national level mandates administrative supervisory arrangements on the Union level, in particular to ensure a consistent application of EU law across the Member States. As the contributions on the budget[237] in general, and on structural funds[238] and agriculture[239] in particular, show, the Commission's role in supervising Member States in the shared management of Union funds, or the indirect management by third parties, is in fact often rather limited. The Commission can monitor the management and control systems of Member States, can conduct on-the-spot audits and checks, and can even impose financial corrections. It is, however, doubtful that such arrangements are sufficient to allow the Commission adequately to discharge its responsibility for the safeguarding, and proper disbursement, of EU funds. Increasingly, therefore, Union law requires Member States to set up national supervisory bodies with independent powers. Such arrangements can also be found in other policy fields, where Commission supervision of national authorities is similarly limited.[240]

---

[230] Chapter 21. [231] Chapter 22. [232] Chapters 12 and 14. [233] Chapter 9.
[234] Chapter 9.
[235] See B Marchetti (ed), *Administrative Remedies in the European Union: The Emergence of a Quasi-Judicial Administration* (G Giappichelli Editore 2017).
[236] Chapter 14. [237] Chapter 22. [238] Chapter 20. [239] Chapter 19.
[240] See the chapters on energy (16), transport (14), and data protection (9).

2 Political Supervision

Our contributors also reveal a wealth of arrangements for the political supervision of EU administrative activities. The most common of these is the use of comitology committees as ex ante control mechanisms of the Member States over the making of implementing acts by the Commission under Article 291 TFEU, and the veto powers for the Council and the European Parliament in relation to the adoption of delegated acts under Article 290 TFEU. Other mechanisms of ex ante control include the involvement of Union institutions in the appointment process of the EDPS[241] or of the directors of Union agencies, as in the case of ACER.[242] The increasing role of the European Parliament in relation to the conclusion of external trade agreements is a further example of such control.[243]

Union legislation in a number of policy fields also provides for ongoing obligations on the Commission to report to the Council and the Parliament.[244] Mechanisms for regular or ex post monitoring also exist through questions in the European Parliament, parliamentary committees of inquiry, or the budgetary discharge of the Commission by the Parliament. Scrutiny by committees of the EP is well illustrated by the example of environmental protection.[245] Parliamentary questions are mainly directed at the Commission, but can also concern directors of agencies or the President of the ECB. An interesting supervisory mechanism is the Joint Parliamentary Scrutiny group, consisting of members of national parliaments and the European Parliament, entrusted with the (political) monitoring of Europol activities.[246] An important supervisory function is also exercised by the European Ombudsman (who reports to the Parliament), as a number of contributions make clear.

As the study of the European neighbourhood policy demonstrates, supervisory functions can also be exercised by NGOs, which frequently review progress reports and action plans adopted by the Commission in this field. This can also be regarded as a form of political supervision.[247] A further, very distinctive, mechanism—which can be said to have at least some supervisory character, although perhaps only indirectly—is provided in the context of external trade under the Trade Barriers Regulation which essentially provides for EU industries to request Union action in dispute settlement proceedings before the WTO (where the industries themselves have no standing).[248]

3 Judicial Supervision

Judicial supervision, in its most concentrated form, occurs through the Union courts, not only in their ex post control of the Union's administration, but also in the ex ante setting of procedural and substantive standards for administrative action. At the same time, one must recall that, in many circumstances, supervision effected by the Union courts can come into play only because legal actions have begun in national courts and then, in requests for preliminary rulings, have moved to the level of the Union

---

[241] Chapter 9.   [242] Chapter 14.   [243] Chapter 4.
[244] See the chapters on data protection (9), energy (16), structural funds (20), and transport (14).
[245] Chapter 13.   [246] Chapter 7.   [247] Chapter 3.   [248] Chapter 4.

judiciary. That in itself, as some contributions have noted, is coupled with often complicated questions of standing and judicial competence. In certain areas, as in the field of state aid law,[249] sparse Treaty provisions have been developed into a reliable legal framework for judicial review, which has then been incorporated into Union legislation. All the same, our contributions highlight certain difficulties in relation to the role of the courts in control over the administration, mainly relating to matters of access to justice:

First, the use of soft law by Union institutions, agencies, and bodies often has the effect of evading direct judicial review. This is the case in external relations areas,[250] where soft law is a prevalent instrumental approach, but also in other areas such as structural funds,[251] monetary union,[252] and state aid,[253] where such instruments are also of considerable importance. Secondly, in many areas, direct access to Union courts is impeded by strict rules of standing. Such difficulties arise not only in respect of the requirement of *individual* concern, which often precludes challenges to administrative acts of general application, but also that of *direct* concern, as our chapters on development aid,[254] Union budget law,[255] and structural funds[256] illustrate. Such issues also arise in relation to anti-dumping or countervailing measures, and trade defence measures in the external trade sector.[257] An important innovation exists, therefore, in the field of data protection,[258] where the EDPS can bring actions before the Union courts, thus introducing a form of collective interest representation.[259] In the third place, the discretion exercised by the Commission in many policy fields, such as agriculture,[260] monetary union,[261] and external relations,[262] often precludes substantive review by the Union courts, and restricts their purview to procedural legality and manifest errors of assessment. Fourthly, difficulties also arise in the many areas of Union law, where administrative acts are adopted following composite procedures, involving administrative actors on national and Union levels.[263]

Identifying the appropriate forum for judicial review in all such situations, and providing robust review of the disparate input of multiple actors, in order to ensure effective judicial protection of individuals, remains the holy grail of judicial review in Union administrative law.

I Overall Assessment

The findings of the sectoral studies of EU administrative law in this book provide a rich and diverse basis for informing and supplementing any discussion of EU administrative law as a whole. These findings together provide a substantial corpus of material which, in turn, also enriches our understanding of the general part of Union administrative law. For that purpose, much of it is, in fact too dense to be presented here in this concluding chapter, but will ultimately make a significant contribution

---

[249] Chapter 17.
[250] See the chapters on development aid (6), neighbourhood policy (3), and enlargement (2).
[251] Chapter 20.   [252] Chapter 10.   [253] Chapter 17.   [254] Chapter 6.
[255] Chapter 22.   [256] Chapter 20.   [257] Chapter 4.   [258] Chapter 9.
[259] Art 79 GDPR.   [260] Chapter 19.   [261] Chapter 10.   [262] Chapters 2, 3, 4, and 6.
[263] See eg the chapters on transport (12), energy (14), and environment (13).

to the detailed treatment of general EU administrative law in the imminent second edition of *Administrative Law and Policy in the European Union.*[264] This last section of the final chapter of the present work offers, however, an overall assessment of Union administration and administrative law from the sectoral perspective, in particular in order to suggest certain broad conclusions which can be drawn from the diverse and interesting contributions here.

What emerges from the present study is the picture, on the one hand, of an increasingly centralized and often dense legislative framework, within which administrative tasks are, on the other hand, allocated across a wide range of Union and national administrative authorities, or intersections of these. This is a characteristic of the European Union which, when considered from a federalist standpoint, demands caution in respect of the lessons to be drawn from comparisons with systems such as those of Belgium, Germany, and even Spain, as well as those of the United States, Australia, or Canada. The special, indeed remarkable, nature of the shared and cooperative processes of Union administration—reflecting in many ways the essential character of the operation of the Union as a whole—are, without qualification, distinctive and valuable.

As we have seen, the administrative functions of the European Union are carried out mainly within highly integrated organizational and procedural arrangements,[265] using a complex mix of general and specific measures having legal effects over a wide spectrum. We have also noted that the exercise of administrative powers is very substantially discretionary, with the consequence of restricting judicial review to the enforcement of fundamental and common legal principles which have the aim or effect of ensuring procedural standards but, concomitantly, leaving room for only marginal substantive review. One can further note that, within the organizational framework of the Union's integrated administration,[266] national authorities still play a preponderant role, but with increasingly strong supranational mechanisms for achieving uniformity and supervisory control.

Given the nature of such an integrated administrative scheme, information sharing and systems of information exchange take on an increasing importance in maintaining a single, or at least coherent, legal space which is distinguished by cooperative interaction of participants from different levels and along different vectors. Against this background, it is important to conclude that the often complex nature of the EU administrative space,[267] the diversity of actors, and the complexity—and not infrequently, the opaque nature—of information management systems, can mask the lines of responsibility and accountability, and limit judicial redress, accordingly blunting both political and judicial control.

Needless to say, such a summary, generalized, image of EU administration and its administrative law obscures some important distinctions among the many separate sectors. The Union administrative system does, at one end of the spectrum, certainly

---

[264] Hofmann, Rowe, and Türk, *Administrative Law and Policy of the European Union* (n 1).
[265] ibid ch 1.   [266] ibid 8.
[267] See H C H Hofmann, 'Mapping the European Administrative Space' (2008) 31(4) *West European Politics* 662.

provide examples of exclusively supranational administrative competence, such as in the application of Union Civil Service law.[268] Equally, at the other end of the spectrum, only very limited—and purely supplementary—supranational administrative action can be observed in, say, certain public health matters.[269] Nevertheless, such entirely divergent examples of centralized and decentralized administration within the Union setting are increasingly rare. Almost unfailingly, some variant of cooperative, shared, participatory, multi-level, and interactive avenues for administrative implementation are followed, in reflection of the essential nature of the European Union itself. The Union can be seen as a system of multi-directional, multi-vectoral, multi-layered, co-operative arrangements and structures, which are interdependent, concerted, coord-inated, and indeed symbiotic. In that sense, it is a union of states willing to cooperate, in order to address common global, international, supranational and transterritorial problems and challenges, and to take advantage of coordinated measures. The system of administrative implementation considered here should be understood against this background.

This portrait of an integrated but varied EU administrative system has emerged as a result of decades of political and economic activity in pursuit of European inte-gration. The techniques and legal frameworks for administrative action have devel-oped in the respective policy areas at different speeds, and with different intensities. Overall, one can detect a general trend towards greater regulatory intensity on the European level. That said, this feature does not set the European Union apart from many national systems: it is a commonplace (although often challenged by particular interests) that pluralistic, post-industrial, globalized societies demand complex, so-phisticated, and typically intense forms of economic and social regulation. Some fa-cets of the multi-national compact, which is the European Union, may in themselves indeed heighten such needs. Here, increased regulatory intensity can be driven by a multitude of impulses, be it the need for more centralized crisis management (such as in the economic and monetary union,[270] or in migration matters),[271] the need for le-gislative consolidation of years of administrative and judicial practice (such as in state aid law[272] and procurement law[273]), the collective desire for the improved realization of the benefits of the internal market (as in the energy[274] and transport[275] sectors), or the need to respond to shared risks (as in the environmental protection sector).[276] These trends and impulses have been supplemented both by an increased hierarchical differentiation and by a heightened parliamentarization of the law-making process, which itself has occurred within, and as a result of the evolution of, a more mature constitutional legal order.[277] An expansion of EU legislation as such has, at least in some part, also been driven by a need to provide a systematic legal framework for the burgeoning ambit of organizational patterns and structures across the numerous fields of Union policy.

---

[268] Chapter 21.   [269] Chapter 15.   [270] Chapter 10.   [271] Chapter 8.
[272] Chapter 17.   [273] Chapter 18.   [274] Chapter 14.   [275] Chapter 12.
[276] Chapter 13.
[277] A H Türk, 'Primary Legislation and Legislative Procedures' in R. Schütze and T Tridimas (eds), *Oxford Principles of EU Law* (OUP 2018).

Procedural interactions between the different administrative bodies that make up the Union's fragmented executive[278] have become increasingly complex.[279] Horizontal interactions have taken on additional vertical and transverse structural and procedural elements, some of which themselves involve the participation of national authorities, with different degrees of intensity. The long-established use of comitology has been supplemented over time by the development of other forms of committee activity and of networks, and these have often acted as precursors for agency structures. In particular, the agencification in Union administrative law[280] has become a pervasive and increasingly powerful tool of administrative integration. Coupled with such developments has been the expansion of supranational mechanisms for the collection, management, and dissemination of information.

All such developments—in their particular emanations within the EU—can be said, on the one hand, to reflect ways of ensuring Member State input (and compromise), and of maximizing the expertise feeding into policy implementation. The latter, on the other hand, being essentially technocratic in nature, poses important challenges for the (pan-European) democratic legitimacy of policy and regulatory outcomes. Article 11 TEU, imposes an obligation to enhance the role of civil society. In particular, it demands more and better crafted mechanisms for maximizing the diversity of input, while at the same time minimizing the risk of disproportionate lobbying opportunities for particular interests and the concomitant reduction in import of the broader public good. This call stands in tension with the composite, multi-layered, and multi-directional administrative arrangements identified here. These are arrangements which make it increasingly difficult for individuals and groups, potentially affected but outside the executive and bureaucratic frame (including that of the professional lobbying industry), to represent their position effectively.[281] Although some amelioration has occurred in certain sectors through a greater involvement of private actors—seen as offering more flexible, efficient, and effective means of attaining policy outcomes[282]—this does not necessarily increase the general democratic accessibility of EU administrative action. In addition, the characteristics of Union administration we have identified also hamper both the insistence on accountability and the allocation of responsibility within structures of judicial and political supervision.[283]

As regards the instruments and measures available to the assorted administrative actors, the present studies show that there is a wide scope. Traditional hard-law instruments, as set out in Article 288 TFEU, are complemented by a vast array of soft law instruments with a diversity of legal effects.[284] These latter instruments (in

---

[278] D Curtin, *Executive Power of the European Union* (OUP,2009) 8.

[279] C Harlow and R Rawlings, *Process and Procedure in EU Administration* (Hart Publishing 2014).

[280] M Chamon, *EU Agencies—Legal and Political Limits to the Transformation of the EU Administration* (OUP 2016).

[281] See J Mendes, *Participation in European Union Rulemaking: A Rights-based Approach* (OUP 2011).

[282] See H Schepel, *The Constitution of Private Governance—Product Standards in the Regulation of Integrating Markets* (Hart Publishing 2005).

[283] See Curtin (n 278) ch 9; G J Brandsma, *Controlling Comitology: Accountability in a Multi-level System* (Palgrave Macmillan 2013); V A Schmidt, 'Democracy and Legitimacy in the European Union Revisited: Input, Output and "Throughput"'(2013) 61 *Political Studies* 2.

[284] See O Stefan, 'Helping Loose Ends Meet? The Judicial Acknowledgement of Soft Law as a Tool of Multi-Level Governance', (2014) 21 *Maastricht Journal of European and Comparative Law* 359.

particular differing forms of interpretive guidance) can assume considerable importance for those affected, as they provide the detail on how the administration will exercise its often considerable discretion. At the same time, by operating in the shadow
of hard law, these common administrative tools of choice obscure the power exercised by public administrators. In some sectors, such as economic union, other, hybrid arrangements can be found, where internal legal instruments are complemented
by international agreements between Member States, together with what has been
termed 'intergovernmental private law' outside the Union's constitutional framework.[285] In other areas, such as social policy, private party agreements substitute for
formal legislative or soft-law instruments adopted by Union bodies.[286]

While enforcement is, by and large, still mainly entrusted to national authorities,
the procedural autonomy of the latter, while traditionally limited by the principles of
equivalence and effectiveness enunciated by the Court, has become increasingly restricted in other ways by EU legislation,[287] and increasingly been accompanied by a
shift of enforcement responsibilities to central Union authorities.[288] First, Union law
may demand that certain remedial action be made available, whether in the form of
concrete remedies (as in the procurement sector),[289] or more generally through an
effective sanctions regime. Secondly, Union legislation, in particular in the fields of
regulated networks,[290] has progressively required that national law give to national
authorities entrusted with the enforcement of Union law both greater operational independence and a wider array of powers. Thirdly, where Union supervision is rather
limited, as in the case of structural funds, EU legislation requires resource-intensive
organizational and procedural arrangements for the enforcement of European law by
national authorities.[291] On the other hand, mechanisms for private enforcement are
still limited.

On the level of the European Union, we see an increased focus on internal administrative supervision mechanisms within the Commission. This, however, is complemented by the still important role of comitology as a control mechanism of the
Member States over the Commission,[292] as well as by political supervision through
both the European Parliament and the Council, mainly in the form of increased reporting obligations ex post on the part of the Commission, the ECB and European
agencies. The sectoral studies raise, however, concerns about the availability of effective judicial supervision. While all chapters acknowledge the pivotal role of the
Court in providing legal principles ex ante that bind and guide the exercise of administrative action by the Commission (or, more recently, agencies), judicial control in
strict form ex post is regarded as being much weaker. This is seen to lie mainly in the
strict rules on *locus standi* for the admissibility of actions against the Commission, as

---

[285] Chapter 10. See also K Armstrong, 'The New Governance of EU Fiscal Discipline' (2013) 38(5)
European Law Review 601.
[286] Chapter 16.
[287] See M Scholten, 'Mind the Trend! Enforcement of EU Law Has Been Moving to "Brussels"' (2017)
24 *Journal of European Public Policy* 1348.
[288] See generally Scholten and Luchtman (eds), *Law Enforcement by EU Authorities* (n 221).
[289] Chapter 18.   [290] See the chapters on energy (16) and transport (14).   [291] Chapter 20.
[292] Türk, 'Comitology' (n 67).

well as in the reduction of substantive judicial scrutiny in the light of the considerable discretion accorded to the Commission in certain areas.

In summary, a growing and intensifying body of EU administrative law has now reached a level of complexity which demands simplification, rationalization, harmonization, and standardization. Notwithstanding that, this does not require a complete jettisoning of existing rules, structures, procedure and practices. Its effective achievement lies rather in taking those elements of Union administrative activity which can be regulated in a cross-sectoral manner within a general legislative measure on Union administrative law and practice. For all the variability across policy areas, there are possibilities for distilling the basic elements of EU public administration—and of constructing a 'rule-book' recognizing their essential characteristics and functions in association with the typical phases and sequences of activities carried out by administrative actors. Such a framework would indeed potentially provide an outside observer with a type of road-map for the implementational decision-making and activity in the European Union. Further, one can easily imagine that the typical organization and procedural steps involved in such activity would, for example, be able consistently to be linked with, and made subject to, over-arching legal principles applicable to them. That would provide a setting in which the constitutional system of rights and values established for the Union generally could be predictably linked to the day-to-day conduct of its administrative functions. Such a measure might then, in meeting the call of Article 298 TFEU, take the form of an EU regulation on administrative procedure (to take the common, but slightly misleading, nomenclature, but better characterized simply as an 'administrative code').

This conclusion does not deny that there are policy-specific matters which demand discrete treatment; there is indeed no shortage of such matters. Nevertheless, comprehensive legislation on the 'general part' of Union administrative law is entirely possible. Not only would such a measure be highly beneficial in its own right: the very process of its development and emergence, the discourse about its shape and content, would all provide a highly desirable opportunity for discussion and debate about the kinds of concerns we have mentioned here (democratic legitimacy, accountability, supervision, and many others). Such a general legislative framework of administrative action would allow a more appropriate balance between those subjects amenable to standardized treatment and those demanding their own particular resolution. This step would provide more clarity and transparency, more effective application of the rule of law, keener acknowledgment of the demands of democratic governance, better protection of individual rights, and a sharper focus on the principles of good administration. In addition, it would likely lead quite simply to a reduction in the volume and density of sector-specific legislation and related instruments, a further benefit to all parties involved in the administrative system of the European Union.

Index

Figures are indicated by an italic *f* following the page number